Telecommunications
Law and Policy

Carolina Academic Press
Law Advisory Board

Gary J. Simson, Chairman
Mercer University School of Law

Raj Bhala
University of Kansas School of Law

Davison M. Douglas
Dean, William and Mary Law School

Paul Finkelman
Albany Law School

Robert M. Jarvis
Shepard Broad Law Center
Nova Southeastern University

Vincent R. Johnson
St. Mary's University School of Law

Peter Nicolas
University of Washington School of Law

Michael A. Olivas
University of Houston Law Center

Kenneth L. Port
William Mitchell College of Law

H. Jefferson Powell
Duke University School of Law

Michael P. Scharf
Case Western Reserve University School of Law

Michael Hunter Schwartz
Dean, William H. Bowen School of Law
University of Arkansas at Little Rock

Peter M. Shane
Michael E. Moritz College of Law
The Ohio State University

Introductory Materials

The topics addressed in this book are not only related in terms of basic technologies, but also they share common economic and institutional characteristics. On the economic front, the range of technologies we discuss raises the question of whether competition is either unworkable or undesirable. To give but one example, policymakers have long worried that the economics of local wireline telephone service are such that either only one firm can survive in the long run ("competition is unworkable") or a single firm can provide a given quality of phone service at lower total cost than can multiple competitors ("competition is undesirable"). Policymakers in this area therefore struggled with the question of whether regulation should displace competition as the principal mechanism for ensuring good performance. Similar arguments that regulation might have advantages over competition arise in every telecommunications market. This is therefore another reason to consider all of these topics in a single conversation. On the institutional side, the Federal Communications Commission has extensive regulatory authority over traditional telephony, broadcast, cable television, and satellite services, and at least some residual authority over all other telecommunications technologies. Thus, before we discuss the substantive telecommunications policy issues, Chapters One and Two begin with the basic economic and institutional issues that will be discussed throughout the book.

Now, some acknowledgments. This book grew out of an earlier book written by Tom Krattenmaker, and so first and foremost our thanks to Tom for getting us started back in 2001. Howard Shelanski and Phil Weiser were on previous editions, and their ideas and analyses remain in these pages, for which we are deeply indebted. We also thank Doug Lichtman who was on the first two editions. Jack Balkin, Dale Hatfield, Karl Mannheim, Preston Padden, John Roberts, Peter Shane, and Doug Sicker also have contributed significantly to this project over the years. We owe each sincere thanks for helping us think through issues. Our thanks go to Stanley Besen and Lucas Powe as well. While their contributions came to us through Krattenmaker, those suggestions nevertheless benefit the book still today. Sincere thanks, too, to the family at Carolina Academic Press. Linda, you especially have been supportive of our work on this project; we genuinely appreciate everything you do for us and our readers. For this edition we owe a particular debt to a few people whose careful reading of the text helped it immeasurably: Julie Moushon and Balfour Smith from Duke Law School and Duke Law students Ben Chalfin, Matthew Craig, Daniel Stockton, and Bill Warren.

One final word before we step aside: the materials included in this book have been ruthlessly edited for style, length, and clarity. To avoid clutter, we have left almost all of those changes unmarked. While we are confident that none of our edits altered the meaning of the relevant passages, we do want to warn readers that the materials have been edited so as to maximize their value in the educational setting and, thus, attorneys looking to cite materials in court documents are advised to look to the original sources before quoting any of the materials excerpted here.

With that, we welcome you to the text. We hope you find your study of telecommunications law to be a rewarding one.

Stuart Benjamin and Jim Speta

Preface

The theme of almost any law school casebook is apparent from the outset. An administrative law casebook, for example, pulls together materials about governmental administration. An antitrust law book evaluates the basic laws and judicial decisions that protect competition by limiting how and when firms can cooperate, engage in potentially anticompetitive behavior, and merge with one another. Thus, even though an administrative law book will consider agencies as diverse as the Environmental Protection Agency and the Federal Aviation Administration, and even though an antitrust law book will apply to industries ranging from real estate to computer software to supermarkets, it is not difficult to describe the overarching themes that structure the set of materials covered by the text.

The implicit logic of a telecommunications book, at least on first blush, may be harder to understand. Why should statutes and regulations related to broadcast television, cable, satellite, wireline telephony, cellular telephony, and the Internet all be considered in a single volume? Do these communication mechanisms really have that much in common?

The challenge of capturing the story of telecommunications law is particularly interesting and important today because of technological convergence. This means that once-distinct technologies—for example, the traditional telephone infrastructure and the traditional cable infrastructure—can provide very similar and substitutable services, including telephone service, cable television, and broadband Internet access. The question of how to treat different technologies, be they telephone networks, cable networks, or wireless providers, can no longer be answered by reference to the service that those networks titularly support. Given that this answer was often the way such policies developed in the past, this book can be read on two levels: (1) what is the best policy for telecommunications networks of all kinds; and (2) in light of the legacy of policies long in place (and a statute first written in 1934), how can the administering agency (in almost all cases, the Federal Communications Commission) move towards the best policy (or find a second best one) if practical, legal, or political constraints limit its ability to get there?

Given the nature of technological convergence, it is hard to consider any one branch of telecommunications in isolation. It is the combination of broadcast, cable, telephone, and Internet regulation that together determine how wire, air, and other telecommunications resources are allocated between all their myriad competing uses. Because almost any telecommunications resource can be put to more than one telecommunications use, telecommunications topics are necessarily interconnected. And, as noted above, today's decisionmakers are not writing on a clean slate, creating challenges insofar as decisions of yesterday, such as how much wireless spectrum to dedicate to over-the-air television broadcasts, are not easily reversed to address the needs of today—say, more spectrum for wireless broadband services.

Copyright Permissions

Our sincere thanks go to the following copyright holders, who have granted permission for us to reprint or excerpt copyrighted materials in this book:

Aspen Publishers, Inc., for permission to excerpt Federal Telecommunications Law by Peter W. Huber, Michael K. Kellogg, and John Thorne. Copyright 1992 by Peter W. Huber, Michael K. Kellogg, and John Thorne. All rights reserved.

Aspen Publishers, Inc., for permission to excerpt Federal Telecommunications Law, Second Edition, by Peter W. Huber, Michael K. Kellogg, and John Thorne. Copyright 1999 by Peter W. Huber, Michael K. Kellogg, and John Thorne. All rights reserved.

Yochai Benkler and the Harvard Journal of Law and Technology for permission to excerpt Yochai Benkler, Some Economics of Wireless Communications, 16 Harv. J.L. & Tech. 25 (2002).

Ronald Coase for permission to excerpt Why Not Use the Pricing System in the Broadcast Industry? Testimony before the FCC (December 1959), reprinted in 4 Study of Radio & T.V. Broadcasting (No. 12,782) (1959).

The Duke University School of Law, Law and Contemporary Problems, Stanley Besen, and Robert Crandall, for permission to reprint The Deregulation of Cable Television, 44 Law & Contemp. Probs. 77 (1981).

Thomas Krattenmaker and Lucas Powe, for permission to adapt various sections of their text, Regulating Broadcast Programming (1994). All rights reserved.

Lawrence Lessig for permission to reprint It's Time to Demolish the FCC, Newsweek (December 22, 2008, updated March 13, 2010).

Oxford University Press and Peter Huber for permission to excerpt Law and Disorder in Cyberspace: Abolish the FCC and Let Common Law Rule the Telecosm. Copyright 1997 by Oxford University Press, Inc. All rights reserved.

Richard Posner, for permission to excerpt Bad News, The New York Times Book Review (July 31, 2005).

The University of Chicago, the Journal of Legal Studies, and Thomas W. Hazlett for permission to reprint a figure from Thomas W. Hazlett & David W. Sosa, Was the Fairness Doctrine a "Chilling Effect"? Evidence from the Postderegulation Radio Market, 26 J. Legal Stud. 294 (1997). Copyright 1997 by the University of Chicago.

The Yale Law Journal Company and William S. Hein Company for permission to excerpt Cass Sunstein, The First Amendment in Cyberspace, 104 Yale L. J. 1757–1804 (1995).

Justice Antitrust Division on Its Decision to Close Its Investigation of (2008), 505

XM Satellite Radio, *see also* Sirius Satellite Radio

Nuvio Corp. v. FCC (2006), 660
Posner, Bad News (2005), 474
President's Council of Advisors on Science and Technology, Realizing the Full Potential of Government-Held Spectrum to Spur Economic Growth (2012), 107
Program Access Rules and Examination of Programming Tying Arrangements, Review of the Commission's (2010), 433
Prometheus Radio Project v. FCC [*Prometheus I*] (2004), 383
Promoting Efficient Use of Spectrum Through Elimination of Barriers to the Development of Secondary Markets (2004), 119
Red Lion Broadcasting Co. v. FCC (1969), 678
Redevelopment of Spectrum to Encourage Innovation in the Use of New Telecommunications Technologies (1992), 81
Reno v. ACLU (1997), 818
Request of ABC, Inc. for Declaratory Ruling (1999), 700
Retransmission Consent, Amendment of the Commission's Rules Related to (2011), 322
Retransmission Consent, Amendment of the Commission's Rules Related to (2014), 328
Sable Communications of California, Inc. v. FCC (1989), 809
Schurz Communications, Inc. v. FCC (1992), 372
SBC Communications, Inc., *see* Applications of Ameritech Corp.
Service Rules for the 698–746, 747–762 & 777–792 MHz Bands (2007), 622
Simon Geller for Renewal of License of WVCA-FM and Grandbanke Corporation for Construction Permit, Applications of (1985), 146
Sirius Satellite Radio Holdings Inc. and XM Satellite Radio Holdings, Inc. Subject to Conditions, Commission Approves Transaction Between (2008), 508
Sirius Satellite Radio Inc., *see also* XM Satellite Radio Holdings Inc.
Spectrum Policy Task Force Report (2002), 72
Sunstein, The First Amendment in Cyberspace (1995), 468
Technology Transitions (2014), 578
Time Warner Entertainment Co. v. FCC (1996), 710
Time Warner Entertainment Co. v. FCC (1997), 712
Time Warner Entertainment Co. v. FCC [*Time Warner II*] (2001), 407
Turner Broadcasting System, Inc. v. FCC [*Turner I*] (1994), 332
Turner Broadcasting System, Inc. v. FCC [*Turner II*] (1997), 345
Unbundled Access to Network Elements: Review of the Section 251 Unbundling Obligations of Incumbent Local Exchange Carriers (2005), 248
United States Telecom Ass'n v. FCC [*USTA II*] (2004), 233, 242
United States v. American Telephone & Telegraph Co. (1982), 204
United States v. Playboy Entertainment Group, Inc. (2000), 798
United States v. Southwestern Cable Co. (1968), 589
Unlicensed Operation in the TV Broadcast Bands and Additional Spectrum for Unlicensed Devices Below 900 MHz and in the 3 GHz Band (2008), 98
Verizon Communications Inc. v. FCC (2002), 254
Verizon Communications Inc. v. Law Offices of Curtis V. Trinko, LLP (2004), 522
Verizon v. FCC (2014), 632
Violent Television Programming and Its Impact on Children (2007), 843
Waldman et al., The Information Needs of Communities: The Changing Media Landscape in a Broadband Age (2011), 482
XM Satellite Radio Holdings Inc.'s Merger with Sirius Satellite Radio Inc., Statement of the Department of

Comcast Corp. v. FCC (2009), 414
Comcast Corp. v. FCC (2010), 628
Comcast Corp., *see also* Applications of Comcast Corp.
Commercial Operations in the 3550–3650 MHz Band, Amendment of the Commission's Rules with Regard to (2012), 111
Communiqué on Principles for Internet Policy-Making: OECD High Level Meeting on the Internet Economy (2011), 540
Comparative Broadcast Hearings, Policy Statement on (1965), 142
Competitive Bidding for Commercial Broadcast and Instructional Television Fixed Service Licenses, Implementation of Section 309(j) of the Communications Act—(1998), 174
Denver Area Educational Telecommunications Consortium, Inc. v. FCC (1996), 782
Digital Audio Radio Satellite Service in the 2310-2360 MHz Frequency Band, Establishment of Rules and Policies for the (1997), 285
FCC v. Fox Television Stations, Inc. (2009), 768
FCC v. Fox Television Stations, Inc. (2012), 777
FCC v. Midwest Video Corp. [*Midwest Video II*] (1979), 591
FCC v. Pacifica Foundation (1978), 740
FCC v. WNCN Listeners Guild (1981), 138
Federal-State Joint Board on Universal Service (1997), 562
Framework for Global Electronic Commerce, A (1997), 539
General Fairness Doctrine Obligations of Broadcast Licensees, Inquiry into the Commission's Rules and Regulations Concerning the (1985), 685
General Electric Co., *see* Applications of Comcast Corp.
General Motors Corp. and Hughes Electronics Corp., Transferors, and the News Corp. Ltd., Transferee, for Authority to Transfer Control (2004), 423
"Golden Globe Awards" Program, Complaints Against Various Broadcast Licensees Regarding Their Airing of the (2004), 764
Huber, Law and Disorder in Cyberspace: Abolish the FCC and Let Common Law Rule the Telecosm (1997), 859
Huber, Kellogg, and Thorne, Federal Telecommunications Law, 198
In re FCC 11-161 (2014), 553, 567
Indecent Communications by Telephone, Regulations Concerning (1990), 814
Key Internet Domain Name Functions, NTIA Announces Intent to Transition (2014), 543
Kwerel and Felker, Using Auctions to Select FCC Licensees (1985), 168
Lessig, It's Time to Demolish the FCC, (2008), 864
Local Competition Provisions in the Telecommunications Act of 1996, Implementation of the (1996), 225
Lutheran Church–Missouri Synod v. FCC (1998), 160
Metro Broadcasting, Inc. v. FCC (1990), 151
Miami Herald Publishing Co. v. Tornillo (1974), 676
Minnesota Public Utilities Commission v. FCC (2007), 655
Mobile Spectrum Holdings: Expanding the Economic and Innovation Opportunities of Spectrum through Incentive Auctions, Policies Regarding (2014), 453
National Broadband Plan: Connecting America (2010), 565, 615
National Cable & Telecommunications Ass'n v. Brand X Internet Services (2005), 600
National Cable & Telecommunications Ass'n v. FCC (2009), 428
NBC Universal, Inc., *see* Applications of Comcast Corp.
New Federal Communications Commission for the 21st Century, A (1999), 856

Table of Materials

ACLU v. Mukasey (2008), 832
Action for Children's Television v. FCC [*ACT III*] (1995), 750
Alliance for Community Media v. FCC (2008), 295
American Broadcasting Companies, Inc. v. Aereo, Inc. (2014), 310
American Council on Education v. FCC (2006), 664
Applications of Ameritech Corp., Transferor, and SBC Communications, Inc., Transferee, for Consent to Transfer Control of Corporations Holding Commission Licenses and Lines Pursuant to Sections 214 and 310(D) of the Communications Act and Parts 5, 22, 24, 25, 63, 90, 95 and 101 of the Commission's Rules (1999), 492
    Separate Statement of Commissioner Harold Furchtgott-Roth Concurring in Part, Dissenting in Part (1999), 496
Applications of Comcast Corp., General Electric Co. and NBC Universal, Inc. for Consent to Assign Licenses and Transfer Control of Licenses (2011), 490, 510
Appropriate Framework for Broadband Access to the Internet over Wireline Facilities (2005), 620
Ashcroft v. ACLU [*Ashcroft II*] (2004), 825
AT&T Corp. v. City of Portland (2000), 596
AT&T Corp. v. Iowa Utilities Board (1999), 235

Benkler, Some Economics of Wireless Communications (2002), 90
Besen and Crandall, The Deregulation of Cable Television (1981), 278
Broadcast Ownership Rules and Other Rules Adopted Pursuant to Section 202 of the Telecommunications Act of 1996, 2006 Quadrennial Regulatory Review—Review of the Commission's (2008), 397
Broadcast Renewal Applicants, Competing Applicants, and Other Participants to the Comparative Renewal Process and to the Prevention of Abuses of the Renewal Process, Formulation of Policies and Rules Relating to (1989), 165
Cablevision Systems Corp. v. FCC (2011), 441
Changes in the Entertainment Formats of Broadcast Stations (1976), 136
Children's Television Programming and Advertising Practices (1983), 716
Children's Television Programming, Policies and Rules Concerning (1991), 721
Children's Television Programming, Policies and Rules Concerning (1996), 723
Children's Television Programming, *see also* Violent Television Programming
Coase, Why Not Use the Pricing System in the Broadcast Industry? (1959), 59, 273
Comcast Cable Communications, LLC, v. FCC (2013), 447

§ 16.A.2. Regulation of Cable Indecency	780
§ 16.A.2.a. *Denver Area*	781
Denver Area Educational Telecommunications Consortium, Inc. v. FCC	782
§ 16.A.2.b. *Playboy Entertainment*	797
United States v. Playboy Entertainment Group, Inc.	798
§ 16.A.3. Regulation of Indecency via Telephone	809
Sable Communications of California, Inc. v. FCC	809
Regulations Concerning Indecent Communications by Telephone	814
§ 16.A.4. Regulation of Internet Indecency	817
Reno v. ACLU	818
Ashcroft v. ACLU [*Ashcroft II*]	825
ACLU v. Mukasey	832
§ 16.B. Violent Programming	839
Violent Television Programming and Its Impact on Children	843

Epilogue

Chapter Seventeen · Why an FCC?	855
Introduction	855
A New Federal Communications Commission for the 21st Century	856
Huber, Abolish the FCC and Let Common Law Rule the Telecosm	859
Lessig, It's Time to Demolish the FCC	864
Statutory Appendix	869
Conceptual Index and Telecommunications Glossary	943

National Broadband Plan: Connecting America	615
§ 14.C.2. Net Neutrality Policy (and Jurisdiction, Again)	619
Appropriate Framework for Broadband Access to the Internet Over Wireline Facilities	620
Service Rules for the 698–746, 747–762 & 777–792 MHz Bands	622
Comcast Corp. v. FCC	628
Verizon v. FCC	632
§ 14.D. Voice over Internet Protocol	653
Minnesota Public Utilities Commission v. FCC	655
Nuvio Corp. v. FCC	660
American Council on Education v. FCC	664
§ 14.E. "Over the Top" Online Video Competition	668

PART SIX

DIRECT REGULATION OF CONTENT

Chapter Fifteen · Direct Regulation of Content Deemed Valuable	675
Introduction	675
§ 15.A. The Fairness Doctrine and Related Obligations	676
§ 15.A.1. *Tornillo* and *Red Lion*	676
Miami Herald Publishing Co. v. Tornillo	676
Red Lion Broadcasting Co. v. FCC	678
§ 15.A.2. The FCC Abandons the Fairness Doctrine	685
§ 15.A.2.a. The Fairness Doctrine Report	685
Inquiry into the Commission's Rules and Regulations Concerning the General Fairness Doctrine Obligations of Broadcast Licensees	685
§ 15.A.2.b. *Syracuse Peace Council*	693
§ 15.A.3. The Personal Attack and Political Editorial Rules	696
§ 15.A.4. Political Broadcasting	699
Request of ABC, Inc. for Declaratory Ruling	700
§ 15.A.5. The Scarcity Rationale in Other Media	710
Time Warner Entertainment Co. v. FCC	710
Time Warner Entertainment Co. v. FCC	712
§ 15.B. Children's Television	715
Children's Television Programming and Advertising Practices	716
Policies and Rules Concerning Children's Television Programming	721
Policies and Rules Concerning Children's Television Programming	723
Chapter Sixteen · Direct Regulation of Content Deemed Harmful	739
Introduction	739
§ 16.A. Indecency	740
§ 16.A.1. Regulation of Broadcast Indecency	740
FCC v. Pacifica Foundation	740
Action for Children's Television v. FCC [*ACT III*]	750
Complaints Against Various Broadcast Licensees Regarding Their Airing of the "Golden Globe Awards" Program	764
FCC v. Fox Television Stations, Inc.	768
FCC v. Fox Television Stations, Inc.	777

Applications of Comcast Corp., General Electric Co. and NBC
Universal, Inc. for Consent to Assign Licenses and Transfer Control
of Licensees — 510
§ 11.B. Antitrust in a Regulatory Thicket — 522
Verizon Communications Inc. v. Law Offices of Curtis V. Trinko, LLP — 522

PART FIVE
THE INTERNET

Chapter Twelve · Introduction and Evolution — 529
§ 12.A. The History and Architecture of the Internet — 529
  § 12.A.1. Basic Characteristics — 531
  § 12.A.2. Network Elements — 533
  § 12.A.3. Packet Switching and Addressing — 534
  § 12.A.4. Services — 535
  § 12.A.5. Layers — 536
§ 12.B. Initial Principles of Internet Policy — 537
A Framework for Global Electronic Commerce — 539
Communiqué on Principles for Internet Policy-Making: OECD High Level
  Meeting on the Internet Economy — 540
NTIA Announces Intent to Transition Key Internet Domain Name Functions — 543

Chapter Thirteen · Universal Service: From Telephony to Broadband — 545
§ 13.A. Origins of Universal Service Policy — 545
§ 13.B. Equity and Efficiency in Subsidizing Universal Service: Ramsey
  Pricing versus Distributional Policy — 547
§ 13.C. Universal Service After Divestiture — 549
§ 13.D. Universal Service After the 1996 Act — 551
  § 13.D.1. Access Charge Reform — 552
  § 13.D.2. Intercarrier Compensation Reform — 553
  In re FCC 11-161 — 553
§ 13.E. Broadband Universal Service — 561
Federal-State Joint Board on Universal Service — 562
National Broadband Plan: Connecting America — 565
In re FCC 11-161 — 567
§ 13.F. A New Blank Slate: The IP Transition — 578
Technology Transitions — 578

Chapter Fourteen · Broadband Jurisdiction and Structural Regulation — 587
Introduction — 587
§ 14.A. The Ancillary Jurisdiction Doctrine and the Past as Prologue? — 588
United States v. Southwestern Cable Co. — 589
FCC v. Midwest Video Corp. [*Midwest Video II*] — 591
§ 14.B. Regulatory Characterization of Broadband Services — 595
AT&T Corp. v. City of Portland — 596
National Cable & Telecommunications Ass'n v. Brand X Internet Services — 600
§ 14.C. Net Neutrality — 614
  § 14.C.1. The Broadband Internet Access Marketplace — 614

§ 10.C.3.a. Extension of the Program Access Rules to DirecTV 422
   General Motors Corp. and Hughes Electronics Corp., Transferors, and
      the News Corp. Ltd, Transferee, for Authority to Transfer Control 423
§ 10.C.3.b. MVPD Access to Buildings 428
   National Cable & Telecommunications Ass'n v. FCC 428
§ 10.C.3.c. Extension of the Program Access Rules to Terrestrially
   Distributed Programming 433
   Review of the Commission's Program Access Rules and Examination of
      Programming Tying Arrangements 433
   Cablevision Systems Corp. v. FCC 441
§ 10.D. MVPD Non-Discrimination Obligations 446
   Comcast Cable Communications, LLC v. FCC 447
§ 10.E. Spectrum Caps 453
   Policies Regarding Mobile Spectrum Holdings: Expanding the Economic
      and Innovation Opportunities of Spectrum through Incentive Auctions 453
§ 10.F. Choice 468
   § 10.F.1. Is More Always Better? 468
   Sunstein, The First Amendment in Cyberspace 468
   Posner, Bad News 474
   § 10.F.2. What Could the FCC Do About It? 482
   Waldman et al., The Information Needs of Communities:
      The Changing Media Landscape in a Broadband Age 482

Chapter Eleven · Antitrust and Merger Review 487
Introduction 487
§ 11.A. Merger Enforcement and Telecommunications Regulation 488
   § 11.A.1. Background on Merger Policy 488
   Applications of Comcast Corp., General Electric Co., and
      NBC Universal, Inc. for Consent To Assign Licenses and Transfer
      Control of Licensees 490
   § 11.A.2. The SBC/Ameritech Proceeding 491
   Applications of Ameritech Corp., Transferor, and SBC Communications, Inc.,
      Transferee, for Consent to Transfer Control of Corporations Holding
      Commission Licenses and Lines Pursuant to Sections 214 and 310(d) of
      the Communications Act and Parts 5, 22, 24, 25, 63, 90, 95 and 101 of
      the Commission's Rules 492
   Separate Statement of Commissioner Harold Furchtgott-Roth
      Concurring in Part, Dissenting in Part 496
   § 11.A.3. Reconsidering the FCC's Merger Review Process 501
   § 11.A.4. The FCC's Own Institutional Reforms 501
   § 11.A.5. The Elusive Effort to Restrict the Scope of FCC Merger Review 503
   Statement of the Department of Justice Antitrust Division on Its Decision
      to Close Its Investigation of XM Satellite Radio Holdings Inc.'s Merger
      with Sirius Satellite Radio Inc. 505
   Commission Approves Transaction between Sirius Satellite
      Radio Holdings Inc. and XM Satellite Radio Holdings, Inc.
      Subject to Conditions 508
   § 11.A.6. The Comcast/NBCU Proceeding 510

Establishment of Rules and Policies for the Digital Audio Radio Satellite Service in the 2310–2360 MHz Frequency Band	285
§ 8.D. Who Regulates Cable Television?	289
§ 8.E. Promoting Competition in MVPD Markets	294
Alliance for Community Media v. FCC	295

Chapter Nine · Shared Content 303

Introduction	303
§ 9.A. Individual Programs	303
§ 9.A.1. Compulsory Copyright Licenses	303
§ 9.A.1.a. Cable Television	303
§ 9.A.1.b. Direct Broadcast Satellite	306
§ 9.A.2. What Constitutes a Performance under Copyright Law?	310
American Broadcasting Companies, Inc. v. Aereo, Inc.	310
§ 9.A.3. Syndicated Exclusivity and Network Nonduplication	318
§ 9.B. Programs Grouped into Signals	320
§ 9.B.1. Retransmission Consent	321
Amendment of the Commission's Rules Related to Retransmission Consent	322
Amendment of the Commission's Rules Related to Retransmission Consent	328
§ 9.B.2. Must-Carry	331
§ 9.B.2.a. First Amendment Challenges to Cable Must-Carry	332
Turner Broadcasting System, Inc. v. FCC [*Turner I*]	332
Turner Broadcasting System, Inc. v. FCC [*Turner II*]	345
§ 9.B.2.b. DBS Carry One, Carry All	358
§ 9.C. Programming Delivered à la Carte	362
§ 9.D. The FCC's Role in Digital Copyright Policy	364

PART FOUR
ANTITRUST AND STRUCTURAL REGULATION OF MEDIA

Chapter Ten · Structural Regulation of Media 369

Introduction	369
§ 10.A. Structural Regulation of Broadcasting	369
§ 10.A.1. Television Networks and Vertical Integration	370
Schurz Communications, Inc. v. FCC	372
§ 10.A.2. Ownership Restrictions	379
Prometheus Radio Project v. FCC [*Prometheus I*]	383
2006 Quadrennial Regulatory Review — Review of the Commission's Broadcast Ownership Rules and Other Rules Adopted Pursuant to Section 202 of the Telecommunications Act of 1996	397
§ 10.B. Structural Regulation of Cable Providers	405
§ 10.B.1. Judicial Review of the FCC's Cable Ownership Rules	406
Time Warner Entertainment Co. v. FCC [*Time Warner II*]	407
Comcast Corp. v. FCC	414
§ 10.C. Regulation of Vertical Foreclosure by MVPDs	418
§ 10.C.1. The Initial Program Access Rules	419
§ 10.C.2. Extensions of the Program Access Rules	420
§ 10.C.3. Expansion of the Program Access Theory	422

§6.D.1. Competition in CPE	198
Huber, Kellogg & Thorne, Federal Telecommunications Law	198
§6.D.2. Competition in Long Distance Telephony	201
§6.D.3. Communications and Computer Convergence	202
§6.E. Breaking Up Bell: The 1984 Divestiture	203
§6.E.1. The MFJ	204
United States v. American Telephone & Telegraph Co.	204
§6.E.2 Discussion of the Government's Theory	210

Chapter Seven · Control of Telephone Monopolies — 217

Introduction	217
§7.A. Rate Regulation	217
§7.A.1. Rate of Return Regulation	218
§7.A.2. Price Cap Regulation	220
§7.A.3. Rate Regulation as Markets Become Competitive	220
§7.B. The Telecommunications Act of 1996	222
§7.B.1. Introduction	222
§7.B.2. The Local Competition Provisions	224
Implementation of the Local Competition Provisions in the Telecommunications Act of 1996	225
§7.B.3. Jurisdiction to Implement the 1996 Act: Local Competition, National Regulation	230
United States Telecom Ass'n v. FCC [*USTA II*]	233
§7.C. Unbundling, Interconnection, and Line-of-Business Regulation Under the 1996 Act	235
§7.C.1. Identifying UNEs	235
§7.C.1.a. *Iowa Utilities Board*	235
AT&T Corp. v. Iowa Utilities Board	235
§7.C.1.b. After *Iowa Utilities Board*	239
United States Telecom Ass'n v. FCC [*USTA II*]	242
§7.C.1.c. FCC Response to *USTA II*	248
Unbundled Access to Network Elements: Review of the Section 251 Unbundling Obligations of Incumbent Local Exchange Carriers	248
§7.C.2. Pricing Network Elements	252
Verizon Communications Inc. v. FCC	254
§7.C.3. Interconnection	262
§7.C.4. BOC Line of Business Restrictions	266

PART THREE

MULTICHANNEL VIDEO AND BROADCASTING

Chapter Eight · Multichannel Video Foundations — 271

Introduction	271
§8.A. Paying for Television	271
Coase, Why Not Use the Pricing System in the Broadcast Industry?	273
§8.B. Why Regulate? Are There Natural Monopolies?	276
§8.C. Why Regulate? Implications for Broadcast	277
Besen & Crandall, The Deregulation of Cable Television	278

§ 5.A.1.a.1. The *Shuler* Case   128
§ 5.A.1.a.2. The *Brinkley* Case   129
§ 5.A.1.a.3. The Judicial Response   130
§ 5.A.1.b. More Recent Developments   130
§ 5.A.2. License Transfer   134
§ 5.A.2.a. Format Changes   136
Changes in the Entertainment Formats of Broadcast Stations   136
§ 5.A.2.b. A Reversal, and a Reversal of That Reversal   137
FCC v. WNCN Listeners Guild   138
§ 5.B. License Assignment via Merit-Based Hearings   140
§ 5.B.1. Comparative Hearings   141
§ 5.B.1.a. Basic Comparative Hearing Criteria   142
Policy Statement on Comparative Broadcast Hearings   142
§ 5.B.2. Licensing Case Study   146
Applications of Simon Geller for Renewal of License of WVCA-FM and
  Grandbanke Corporation for Construction Permit   146
§ 5.B.3. Special Considerations for Racial Minorities and Women   151
§ 5.B.3.a. Minority Preferences before *Adarand*   151
Metro Broadcasting, Inc. v. FCC   151
§ 5.B.3.b. Preferences for Women   157
§ 5.B.3.c. *Adarand* (*Metro Broadcasting* Overruled)   158
§ 5.B.3.d. Equal Employment Opportunity Regulations   160
Lutheran Church–Missouri Synod v. FCC   160
§ 5.C. Transition to Assignment via Auctions   164
§ 5.C.1. Reform of the Licensing Process   165
Formulation of Policies and Rules Relating to Broadcast Renewal Applicants,
  Competing Applicants, and Other Participants to the Comparative
  Renewal Process and to the Prevention of Abuses of the Renewal Process 165
§ 5.C.2. Lotteries and Auctions   167
Using Auctions to Select FCC Licensees   168
§ 5.C.3. Initial Assignment by Auction   174
Implementation of Section 309(j) of the Communications Act —
  Competitive Bidding for Commercial Broadcast and Instructional
  Television Fixed Service Licenses   174

PART TWO

Regulating Monopoly — The Case of Telephony

Chapter Six · Early Telephone Regulation through Divestiture   187
Introduction   187
§ 6.A. Telephone History   188
§ 6.B. Infrastructure   193
§ 6.B.1. Telephone System Vocabulary   193
§ 6.B.2. Telephone Economics   194
§ 6.C. Telephone Regulation   195
§ 6.C.1. Categories of Regulation   195
§ 6.C.2. Who Regulates   196
§ 6.D. Precursors to Divestiture   198

PART ONE

SPECTRUM

Chapter Three · Regulating the Spectrum — 41
Introduction — 41
§ 3.A. Defining Spectrum — 42
   § 3.A.1. Characteristics of Radio Waves — 42
   § 3.A.2. Transmitting Through the Air — 44
   § 3.A.3. Transmitting Using Wires — 44
   § 3.A.4. Signal Modulation — 45
   § 3.A.5. Newer Wireless Technologies — 47
   § 3.A.6. The Spectrum as a Resource — 49
§ 3.B. A Brief History of Early Spectrum Regulation — 50
§ 3.C. Rationales for Regulation — 55
   § 3.C.1. Scarcity/Interference — 55
   Coase, Why Not Use the Pricing System in the Broadcast Industry? — 59
   § 3.C.2. Consumer Preferences — 63
§ 3.D. An Overview of Spectrum Management — 65
§ 3.E. Regulatory Tradeoffs and Allotment — 66

Chapter Four · Zoning the Spectrum — 69
Introduction — 69
§ 4.A. Models of Spectrum Control — 69
   Spectrum Policy Task Force Report — 72
§ 4.B. Implementing Flexibility — 79
   Redevelopment of Spectrum to Encourage Innovation in the Use of New Telecommunications Technologies — 81
§ 4.C. Dedicating Spectrum to Unlicensed Uses — 90
   Benkler, Some Economics of Wireless Communications — 90
§ 4.D. Approaches to Unlicensed Access — 97
   § 4.D.1. White Spaces — 97
   Unlicensed Operation in the TV Broadcast Bands and Additional Spectrum for Unlicensed Devices Below 900 MHz and in the 3 GHz Band — 98
   § 4.D.2. Spectrum Sharing — 106
   President's Council of Advisors on Science and Technology, Realizing the Full Potential of Government-Held Spectrum to Spur Economic Growth: Executive Summary — 107
   Amendment of the Commission's Rules with Regard to Commercial Operations in the 3550–3650 MHz Band — 111
§ 4.E. Spectrum Leasing and Private Commons — 117
   Promoting Efficient Use of Spectrum Through Elimination of Barriers to the Development of Secondary Markets — 119

Chapter Five · Structuring and Assigning Licenses — 125
Introduction — 125
§ 5.A. License Renewal and Transfer — 126
   § 5.A.1. License Renewal — 126
      § 5.A.1.a. Early History — 127

Contents

Table of Materials	xvii
Copyright Permissions	xxi
Preface	xxiii

INTRODUCTORY MATERIALS

Chapter One · Introduction to Telecommunications Regulation	3
§ 1.A. Communications as a "Regulated Industry"	4
§ 1.A.1. Justifications for Regulation	5
§ 1.A.1.a. Market Failure Justifications	6
§ 1.A.1.b. Additional Justifications	10
§ 1.A.2. Basic Regulatory Tools	11
§ 1.A.3. The Challenges of Regulation	14
§ 1.B. A Policy Analysis Framework	16
Chapter Two · Telecommunications Policy in Institutional Perspective	17
Introduction	17
§ 2.A. The Institutional Dimensions of Telecommunications Policy	17
§ 2.B. The Federal Communications Commission	20
§ 2.C. Regulatory Integration Under the 1934 Act	21
§ 2.D. Institutional Structure and the FCC	23
§ 2.E. The FCC in a Functional Perspective	25
§ 2.E.1. Command and Control	25
§ 2.E.2. Rulemaking versus Adjudication	26
§ 2.E.3. Licensing	29
§ 2.E.4. Norm Entrepreneur	29
§ 2.E.5. Standard Setting	30
§ 2.F. The Statutory and Broader Institutional Context	31
§ 2.F.1. The Structure of the 1934 Act	32
§ 2.F.2. Other Relevant Statutes and Agencies	34
§ 2.F.3. FCC Discretion and Its Constraints	35

For Arti and Denise

Copyright © 2015
Carolina Academic Press
All Rights Reserved

ISBN 978-1-61163-691-8
LCCN 2014953062

Carolina Academic Press
700 Kent Street
Durham, NC 27701
Telephone (919) 489-7486
Fax (919) 493-5668
www.cap-press.com

Printed in the United States of America

Telecommunications Law and Policy

FOURTH EDITION

Stuart Minor Benjamin
Duke University

James B. Speta
Northwestern University

Carolina Academic Press
Durham, North Carolina

Chapter One

Introduction to Telecommunications Regulation

The fundamental problem of contemporary communications law is also the fundamental problem facing a contemporary casebook on "telecommunications law and policy." The problem facing the law is that we have been experiencing technological convergence: communications services—whether the delivery of voice, video, or data—can be accomplished over multiple platforms using different technologies. The current student or practitioner thus finds it unsurprising that an increasing number of people have no landline telephone service, relying instead on cell phones or Internet voice services or both. Video is available via over-the-air broadcasting (though few now watch it that way), cable television wires, satellite signals, or any device with an Internet connection.

By contrast, communications law—at least in its basic statutory dimension—is largely unconverged. The Communications Act still has separate titles governing telephone service, broadcasting, and cable services, reflecting the time in which these platforms provided relatively distinct types of services. When Congress last enacted major revisions to the Communications Act (in 1996), it did not focus on the Internet. As a result, the Act lacks any comprehensive treatment of the Internet. The Internet's significance became clear only later, and Congress has not revised the Act since then. Of course, to speak of the Internet as a single platform is itself an egregious error, as almost every communications platform now provides Internet access, and one of the important questions is what meaningful differences exist among the various forms of Internet access

Layered on top of the problem of the law lagging behind technological convergence is the ascendancy of a set of policy tools, principally competition economics, that are used to address communications law across the traditional legal boundaries. These tools assess the need for and effectiveness of regulation quite apart from the historical paths that led to the different statutory regimes.

This is the policy context into which this casebook steps. The reality is that the practitioner of telecommunications policy—whether a representative of the Federal Communications Commission (FCC) or a regulated company or a member of the public seeking to influence policy—must make arguments at multiple levels. Notably, effective arguments must account for the underlying technology and economics (and other policy dimensions) as well as place those arguments within an existing statutory, regulatory, and institutional structure that is very much attached to history and its own internal precedents. Although this sounds daunting, it is also what makes this particular field so

3

intellectually rich and challenging—in addition, of course, to the fact that communications is one of the most important sectors in the modern economy.

To respond to this challenge, the first two chapters of this casebook provide an overview that frames the policy debates that recur throughout the more particularized regulatory disputes that arise in subsequent chapters. This chapter marshals the arguments for specialized communications regulation and the tools that have most frequently been deployed to try to meet the justifications on which that regulation has been built. In particular, this chapter seeks to answer two fundamental questions: (1) why might one pay special regulatory attention to communications, and (2) what are the principal instruments of that regulatory toolbox? The next chapter turns to institutional questions. It provides a brief overview of the Communications Act as it now stands, discusses a little bit of its history, and then focuses on issues related to institutional design and governance structures.

The remainder of the book follows a more traditional organization, framing issues largely within the context in which they arose. We begin with these two overview chapters because we believe that they will help establish connections between the materials that follow. Indeed, while the law remains segregated, the FCC, aided by others, has addressed each communication service in some part based on a set of common principles. In the final chapter, we come full circle and return to an institutional focus, asking whether the history and future of telecommunications regulation argue for a very different regulator.

§ 1.A. Communications as a "Regulated Industry"

Communications has long been considered a "regulated industry." Telephony has been subject to special federal regulation since 1910, and broadcasting since 1927. But the fundamentals of communications regulation were established long before those dates. In fact, the key sections of Title II of the Communications Act of 1934 were lifted almost word for word from the Interstate Commerce Act of 1887, which subjected railroads to the specialized regulation of the Interstate Commerce Commission (substituting, of course, telephony for railroads). The Interstate Commerce Act also served as the model for numerous other instances of regulation—including air service (the Civil Aeronautics Act), trucking (the Motor Carriers Act), electricity (the Federal Power Act), and stockyards (the Packers and Stockyards Act). Indeed, one could focus on regulated industries generally: the schemes of regulation governing railroads, electricity, communications, and many other industries have much in common. Communications regulation is thus a case study of a particular kind of regulation, shared at times by substantial portions of the economy.

Regulation more generically speaking is, of course, all around us. Despite the meaningful senses in which the United States is a free-market economy, few enterprises are not subject to substantial regulation, be it health and safety, wage and hour, or environmental regulation. Even bakeries (which economists sometimes use as examples of highly competitive markets) face controls on what they must pay their workers and the purity of their products.

Describing an industry as a "regulated industry" has a particular meaning. At an institutional level, a regulated industry is typically supervised by a specialized administrative agency, which implements sector-specific legislation. Thus, a regulated industry is one that is subject to more than the general regulation to which every economic actor is subject and one that is subject to more than a specific instantiation of health and safety regulation. For example, the manufacture of automobiles is not considered to be a regulated industry, notwithstanding that automobile factories are subject to environmental regulation, occupational safety and health regulation, labor law, and employment law, and notwithstanding that automobiles may not be sold until they are certified as meeting highly detailed Motor Vehicle Safety Standards, emissions controls, and other specific requirements.

What are the central features of regulated industries? While these have changed over time, the classic model—the model of the Interstate Commerce Act and the original Communications Act—had three essential characteristics. First, the government (through a sector-specific, expert agency) limited entry into and exit from the market. The Communications Act of 1934 prohibits anyone from providing interstate telephone service or transmitting using the airwaves without an appropriate license from the FCC. Second, the government regulated the key economic terms under which companies provided service. Under the 1934 Act, for example, telephone companies were required to file, in advance of providing service, tariffs that set forth their rates and terms for all services. The FCC was empowered to suspend, investigate, and reject those tariffs if it found them improper. This economic regulation is perhaps the hallmark of what was known as a regulated industry and became its most controversial feature. Third, government officials often set rates to address the social policy goal of ensuring "universal service"—i.e., requiring some customers (e.g., businesses) to pay rates well above cost to enable others (e.g., residential consumers) to pay rates well below cost.

In this chapter, we survey both the economic and noneconomic justifications for applying a special body of law—sector-specific regulation—to communications services; their theoretical and factual bases, how well they have been translated into regulatory policy, and whether they remain valid as communications markets continually change. Many of these justifications are not unique to communications: they can apply to many individual industries, just as the regulated industries model has governed many industries over time, and they can provide justification for the application of certain non-sector-specific legal regimes, such as general antitrust law.

§1.A.1. Justifications for Regulation

One could argue that regulation does not need a justification, or, perhaps more precisely, that regulation needs no more justification than those with the ultimate power to regulate—generally Congress—deem adequate. At least since the New Deal and the overruling of the *Lochner* decision,[1] courts have not considered themselves in the business of determining whether Congress had an *adequate* justification for regulating. Indeed, even during the so-called *Lochner* era, courts provided considerable leeway to regulators in industries "affected with a public interest."[2]

Recognizing that all regulation is essentially a political act does not make an inquiry into the justifications for regulation fruitless. And, indeed, in the regulated industries field, one can identify a more or less coherent set of justifications that have been offered for specialized regulation. Because political actors make arguments, they appeal to history, and they operate within a defined set of institutions. They also operate within a wider intellectual discourse, in which academics and other commentators assess both the arguments made for and the effectiveness of the regulation offered.

---

1. *See* W. Coast Hotel Co. v. Parrish, 300 U.S. 379 (1937) (effectively overruling Lochner v. New York, 198 U.S. 45 (1905)).
2. *See* German Alliance Ins. Co. v. Lewis, 233 U.S. 389 (1914) (holding that regulation of fire insurance rates is constitutional because fire insurance is "affected with a public interest").

At a more practical level, regulated industries law operates within the constraints of administrative law, which means that courts determine whether the agency has violated the Administrative Procedure Act (APA). This role requires the courts to decide whether an agency action is consistent with its statutory authority and the agency acted in a manner that is not "arbitrary [and] capricious."[3]

In communications policy, the justifications for regulation can be broadly (and coarsely) divided into market-failure justifications and other justifications. Put more simply, some justifications for regulation are based on the notion that communications markets do not work. Other justifications are based on the notion that, even if these markets function reasonably well, they nevertheless do not provide the socially optimal level or mix of communications services.

§ 1.A.1.a. Market Failure Justifications

Historically, most regulation of wireline communications rested on concerns over monopoly. Monopoly is a market failure because monopolists choose to produce a lower quantity of goods or services and charge higher prices than would prevail in competitive markets. Communications markets present particularly challenging monopoly problems, because the monopoly power may exist for multiple reasons.

The first, most traditional, monopoly story was that of natural monopoly. What is a natural monopoly? Consider the following excerpt from Judge Richard Posner, taken from a case in which a would-be cable franchisee accused the City of Indianapolis of violating antitrust law by discouraging competition in the local cable market:

> The cost of the cable grid appears to be the biggest cost of a cable television system and to be largely invariant to the number of subscribers the system has. [O]nce the grid is in place—once every major street has a cable running above or below it that can be hooked up to the individual residences along the street—the cost of adding another subscriber probably is small. If so, the average cost of cable television would be minimized by having a single company in any given geographical area; for if there is more than one company and therefore more than one grid, the cost of each grid will be spread over a smaller number of subscribers, and the average cost per subscriber, and hence price, will be higher.
>
> If the foregoing accurately describes conditions in Indianapolis it describes what economists call a "natural monopoly," wherein the benefits, and indeed the very possibility, of competition are limited. You can start with a competitive free-for-all—different cable television systems frantically building out their grids and signing up subscribers in an effort to bring down their average costs faster than their rivals—but eventually there will be only a single company, because until a company serves the whole market it will have an incentive to keep expanding in order to lower its average costs. In the interim, there may be wasteful duplication of facilities. This duplication may lead not only to higher prices to cable television subscribers, at least in the short run, but also to higher costs to other users of the public ways, who must compete with the cable television companies for access to them. An alternative procedure is to pick the most efficient competitor at the outset, give him a monopoly, and extract from him in exchange a commitment to provide reasonable service at reasonable rates. In essence [the] antitrust allegations [in this case] accuse the City of Indianapolis of hav-

---

3. 5 U.S.C. § 706(2)(A).

ing taken this alternative route to the monopoly that may be the inevitable destination to which all routes converge.⁴

In the United States, the preferred method of regulating markets for goods and services is usually to rely on competition, with many firms offering substitutable goods and services and thus trying to sell to the same customers. This competition among firms for consumers' patronage tends to force firms to move prices toward the marginal cost—the cost of producing each additional unit—of the relevant good or service. As a firm raises its prices above its marginal cost, it will find its customers shifting their purchases to competitors that charge lower prices. For the same reason, competition tends to reward firms that produce goods and services efficiently; because their costs are lower, these firms can underprice less efficient rivals. Ideally, then, competition forces firms both to put their resources to their most productive uses (what economists sometimes call "productive efficiency") and to sell their products to anyone willing to pay a price equal to the firm's marginal costs of producing them (what economists sometimes call "allocative efficiency"). When a firm does not face pressure from competition, it can stay in business even when it does not use the most efficient production technology, and it can raise its profits by charging prices above marginal cost. The firm may win, but society loses, because some consumers who are willing to pay a price equal to marginal cost, but not the higher price that a firm with market power charges, will not obtain the firm's product. This is the inefficiency that results from monopoly: higher prices and lower outputs than if prices were closer to marginal cost. The difference between the higher social surplus generated by competition and the lower social surplus that results when a firm or group of firms has market power is called in economics the deadweight loss from monopoly.

As Judge Posner points out, however, natural monopoly, in the rare cases where it occurs, turns the comparative efficiency of competition over monopoly on its head. A natural monopoly is said to exist in any market where the costs of production are such that it is less expensive for demand to be met by one firm than it would be for that same demand to be met by more than one firm. This occurs when, over a sufficiently large range of output, the addition of each new customer lowers the average cost of serving every other customer. *Total* costs for the natural monopoly firm increase as demand increases; the important feature is that the firm's average cost *per unit* of output declines with increasing demand.

Declining per-unit average cost can occur for three principal reasons. One possibility is that the good or service at issue requires a very large fixed expense that must be incurred no matter how many units are sold. As the firm increases production, those fixed costs can be spread over an ever larger number of units of output, reducing the per-unit average cost. Local telephone networks were long considered to fit this pattern. A telephone company must build its network of wires, purchase switching machinery, create databases, and hire personnel before it can transmit its first call. The company recovers that investment by factoring a share of these fixed costs into the retail price of telephone service. With each new subscriber, the phone company can further spread its fixed costs and thereby allocate a lower proportion of those costs to each customer. The cost of each individual's phone service thus declines as the number of callers on the network increases.

A second reason that a firm may have declining per-unit costs—and may be a natural monopoly—does not depend at all on fixed costs. A firm that has already recovered its fixed costs, or that has few fixed costs to begin with, might still have *incremental* costs of pro-

---

4. Omega Satellite Prods. Co. v. Indianapolis, 694 F.2d 119, 126 (7th Cir. 1982).

duction that decline as output increases. In this case, the firm is gaining a cost advantage not by spreading its fixed costs ever more thinly, but instead by experiencing reduced marginal costs for each successive unit of output. This kind of increasing returns to scale could arise for a number of reasons. Machinery might become more fuel- and labor-efficient when operated at higher capacities, or a workforce may become more efficient as it becomes more experienced. Such increasing returns will not often occur over very broad ranges of output and will therefore rarely be sufficient to lead to a natural monopoly, but in theory a natural monopoly could arise even if fixed costs are not substantial.

The third common reason for declining per-unit costs is demand variability. In order to provide satisfactory electric service, your local electric company must be ready to supply you with a great deal of power at any instant, even when you are not currently consuming it. Having all that idle capacity is expensive, however, since your electricity needs are likely modest outside peak times. The same is true for your neighbor, and her neighbor, too, of course. Consequently, if each of you were being served by separate firms, those firms would have significant resources invested in idle equipment. By having a single firm serve all of you, however, the costs of providing electricity can be lowered dramatically. You three can share a given amount of excess capacity, putting the equipment to better use since the variance in each of your demands will cancel out that of the others to some degree, and thus you three can share some of that excess capacity without any of you experiencing a noticeable degradation in service.

For a natural monopoly to exist, it is very important that per-unit costs not only be declining, but also that they be declining over *most of the range of output that the market will demand*. To see why, think about the automobile industry. The fixed costs of automobile production are very high. An automobile maker must build a manufacturing plant, purchase machinery, and install a management system before it can produce its first car. The firm recovers those fixed costs by including a share of them in the price of each car it makes. So the average cost per car decreases as the number of cars produced at the plant increases. Should automobile manufacturing be considered a natural monopoly, then? Probably not. First, if a single plant cannot meet the market's entire demand for cars, then the decline in per-unit costs will stop before all consumers are served. At that point, the firm would have to build a new plant and incur a new set of fixed costs to serve the remaining consumer demand. In such a case, it is no more efficient to have the same firm build the new plant to serve the market rather than a new firm. Preventing the entry of other firms would needlessly sacrifice all the familiar benefits of competition—like lower prices, higher output, better quality, and product innovation. Second, even if a single plant could produce enough cars to satisfy consumer demand, it might still not be the case that per-unit costs are declining over a large enough range of output to make the producer a natural monopoly. Fixed costs might be spread so thinly as to be almost zero on a per-unit basis well before the market's demand has been satisfied. In that case, it might be possible for multiple firms to be in the market without affecting each other's ability to reach the most efficient scale of production.

In the following chapters, we will assess whether communications markets are, in fact, naturally monopolistic and whether the regulatory responses have been appropriate.

Another reason that communications markets have tended towards monopoly is the phenomenon of network effects. Such effects arise when the value a consumer places on a good increases along with the number of other consumers simultaneously consuming the good. The basic intuition is this: telephone service is not worth much to me if I am the only one with a telephone (or fax machine, or email account, or any number of other connectivity-based goods), and the value of having a telephone increases based on the number of people that I can call. If more than one network exists and the networks are not interconnected, then consumers will be drawn (all other things being equal) to the network with the greatest number of customers (or, more precisely, the network that consumers expect to have the greatest number of customers). And, eventually, smaller networks will either fail, be absorbed, or focus narrowly on niche services that are more highly valued by a small number of customers.

The telephone network, of course, provides the paradigmatic example of network effects: the more subscribers the network has, the more desirable it is to be on the network. Network effects can also arise in virtual networks and, in the Internet age, have become increasingly common. For example, the FCC, in considering the merger of AOL and Time Warner, found that AOL enjoyed powerful network effects in its instant messaging service. Moreover, based on its view that AOL's installed base of users—and the attendant network effect—would impede competition, the agency ordered AOL to make any broadband instant messaging service interoperable with rival systems.[5]

The AOL instant messaging case study is instructive on two levels. First, it underscores that interoperability mandates—or interconnection requirements, as they are referred to in the case of the physical telephone network—are core competition policy tools to address concerns of monopoly based on network effects. Second, the AOL case raised questions about the merits of interoperability mandates, given that the concern related to AOL's monopoly in instant messaging never materialized (and the FCC later lifted the mandate). Indeed, in a number of important communications markets—such as the Internet backbone networks that hand off Internet communications and are owned by firms like AT&T—no such requirements are currently in place.

Network effects and interoperability (or interconnection) mandates have also played an important role in antitrust litigation. In the case against Microsoft at the turn of the century, for example, the district court adverted to a different kind of network effect, one that is sometimes called an indirect network effect.[6] Such network effects arise where there is a platform good (such as a computer operating system) and a variety of applications that can be run on the platform. Consumers may value a platform good partially based on the number of applications that are available for it. Generally speaking, applications providers will choose to produce their products for the platform that has the greatest number of customers, thereby creating a positive feedback loop, potentially creating an entrenched monopoly platform.

In the *Microsoft* case, the district court called the positive feedback loop enjoyed by Microsoft an "applications barrier to entry." By that, the court meant that new operating systems could not easily enter the market to compete with Microsoft Windows, because, without access to an existing base of applications, consumers would not adopt those new operating systems platforms. One can easily think of similar examples, such as the availability of videos in the high definition optical disc format war between Blu-ray and HD DVD. To be sure, as suggested by the AOL instant message example, network effects will not always be strong enough to cause a tipping effect and enable one firm to monopolize the market. Nonetheless, it is incontrovertible that strong network effects can bolster monopoly power and make it more difficult to displace.

---

5. See Applications for Consent to the Transfer of Control of Licenses and Section 214 Authorizations by Time Warner Inc. and America Online, Inc., Transferors, to AOL Time Warner Inc., Transferee, Memorandum Opinion and Order, 16 FCC Rcd. 6547, 6627–29 (2001).

6. United States v. Microsoft Corp., 87 F. Supp. 2d 30, 38–39 (D.D.C. 2000).

7. *Id.* at 36.

It is important, as an analytical matter, to distinguish between network effects and economies of scale. Both can occur at the same time, and, when they do, the push towards monopoly market structure will be strong. But they are different phenomena: network effects operate on the demand side, making the good more valuable to consumers; economies of scale, by contrast, arise on the supply side, making the good cheaper through decreasing marginal costs of production.

Natural monopolies and network effects are the two main ways in which monopolies can arise because of the nature of the service involved. Monopolies can arise in other ways as well. A firm could, for example, merge with another firm such that the combined entity controls one or more markets.[8] Monopolies can also arise as a result of government policies. Indeed, in some circumstances, governments have granted monopolies to particular firms. In the early years of cable television, for instance, local governments often granted cable television providers local monopolies, a practice that continued until Congress prohibited it.

A third market failure justification on which much communications regulation—particularly of broadcasting—has been (at least historically) based is the "public goods" problem. A public good is any product or service for which demand is nonrivalrous—which means that one consumer's consumption of a good does not affect any other person's ability to consume that same good. One person's watching a television broadcast, for example, does not affect any other person's ability to watch that same broadcast signal, unlike the manner in which, say, one person's consumption of a banana makes it impossible for anyone else to consume that same banana. Classic examples of public goods include lighthouses and national defense. The implication of nonrivalry is that the marginal cost of serving an additional customer is zero, which, in classic economics, suggests that the price for the good should be zero as well. That cannot be the case, of course, for television service has initial fixed costs, such as the costs of producing the programs, of erecting the antennae, and of operating the station—and those costs need to be recovered. But a competitive market may underproduce public goods because of the difficulty of setting a price that recovers costs.

The problem of nonrivalry can be compounded by the problem of nonexcludability. For instance, under the original broadcast technology the owner of video programming had no technological means to exclude nonpaying customers. If a seller can exclude nonpaying buyers (and prevent resale), then the seller may be able to set a price above marginal cost. Still, in competitive markets, the public goods effect can result in underprovision, even if excludability is possible.

§ 1.A.1.b. Additional Justifications

Market failures are, of course, not the only bases for communications regulation and, in many regards, not the most important. Many aspects of communications regulation respond to concerns that even a well-functioning market might not provide what we want from our communications services.

The most salient of these other considerations is the idea of universal service. The term universal service was actually coined by the Bell System and its visionary leader Theodore Vail, who operated the company under the motto "One Policy, One System, Universal Service." From a regulatory perspective, no efficient market will provide service to every-

---

8. This is a classic antitrust issue. Chapter Eleven considers FCC merger review, which often looks beyond the issues that traditional antitrust regulators focus on.

one, for there will be some set of customers unable (or unwilling) to pay the price of the service—even if the price is nonmonopolistic. When the service is monopolistic or characterized by network effects, the possibility that some people will be priced out of the market is even greater.

Regulation arises to meet this issue in markets in which the good is considered to be a basic good that, for reasons of equality, free speech, or other values, members of the citizenry should be provided even if they cannot themselves afford it. Communications service is hardly the only, or most obvious, possible basic good, as various government programs provide some level of food, housing, medical treatment, education, and certain other goods. One can create economic arguments for universal service of these—that providing them increases total social productivity, at least over the long run—and, as we will see, those arguments have also been deployed for universal service of basic communications. But whatever the economic justifications, equity and equality have usually been the driving factors. Government regulation to further the provision of both basic telephone service and free, over-the-air television has rested on universal service values.

In addition to the concern that a market may not provide service to everyone (at a cost that everyone can afford), telecommunications regulation has sometimes reflected the view that the mix of goods being offered is not acceptable. Communications regulation is often based on the notion that certain services or content have low social value and other services or content have high social value (apart from the values assigned by the market). The law has thus limited indecent communications services, even if the market demands them. Similarly, the law has required communications providers to affirmatively offer certain services—ranging from 911 services to public and government cable channels to educational or children's television programming.

Similarly, to take another modern example that we will discuss extensively in Chapter Fourteen, the debate over network neutrality regulation implicates a number of these dimensions. Advocates of network neutrality regulation argue that broadband access markets are quite concentrated and that this concentration gives broadband carriers the incentive and opportunity to foreclose access to some content and applications. The argument has also been made that network access rules drive deployment of broadband services at lower prices, increasing the percentage of the public that subscribes to broadband. Finally (although this summary is far from exhaustive), network neutrality advocates have said that regulation would further the creation of a participatory speech culture by ensuring the widest possible use of content and tools that allow individual citizens to participate. On the other side, carriers and others opposing network neutrality regulation argue that market competition is adequate and that such rules will interfere with the incentives to deploy broadband networks and offer new and innovative services; they also argue that network neutrality rules will weaken the ability of providers to stop illegal activity and protect consumers (say, from malware).

§ 1.A.2. Basic Regulatory Tools

Just as many of the arguments for regulation have a few recurring forms, the laws and regulations affecting communications industries also come in a number of identifiable varieties. A historical and intellectual inquiry can focus on a basic set of regulatory strategies and tools that are consistently applied in communications and related markets.

The first set of regulatory tools covers the natural monopoly ground. If monopoly is natural, then competition should not be permitted (because it is wasteful). And so common carrier regulation began with a premise of licensing: companies would operate in defined service territories and not be permitted to offer service without a license. Then, because monopolies would otherwise charge high prices, the law required that service be provided at "just and reasonable" rates. In principle, rate regulation could be designed to mimic a competitive market—to allow the regulated company to earn revenues just sufficient to cover its costs and therefore to keep the price for the public as low as possible. Common carriers, including telecommunications companies, were also required to provide their service on a nondiscriminatory basis.

To support these obligations, common carrier law usually required companies to file tariffs, which were schedules of all of their services and the rates that would be charged for those services. In the case of telephone companies, these tariffs could run to the hundreds of pages. The regulator required the company to submit cost information that would support any rates proposed in the tariffs, and the law would give the regulator the power to investigate, suspend, or refuse any tariff that failed to be "just and reasonable" or nondiscriminatory. This tariff-filing regime has been largely dismantled (for a variety of reasons we will explore). At one time, however, it governed the vast majority of utility and transportation industries, including, of course, telecommunications.

The final common carrier duty—in addition to providing just, reasonable, and nondiscriminatory service—was to serve all who wanted service. At first, the duty simply required that the carrier provide service to anyone in its territory (or line of business) that requested service and was prepared to pay. Later, the government added explicit universal service policies, which have since evolved. In telecommunications, universal service policies began through permitted or mandated internal cross-subsidies—telephone systems were required to offer some services below cost and were permitted to charge above-cost prices for other services in order to cover their total revenue requirements. As we discuss in Chapter Thirteen, the universal service system has evolved over time.

Although broadcasting and cable television have never been regulated as common carriers, both of those services had somewhat equivalent regulations. Broadcasters were forbidden to offer subscription-based broadcast service: they had to broadcast "in the clear"—signals that were unscrambled and could be seen by anyone who bought a standard receiver. Cable television companies, in exchange for a municipal franchise, were generally required to wire all parts of a city, not just those parts where the income of the residents made offering such service more profitable. Municipal franchises also contained other requirements for cable companies, such as mandates to carry and support public, educational, and governmental channels.

Common carrier regulation responded to the carrier's ability to charge monopoly prices (or only offer monopoly quantities) in its primary markets. But one of the related problems is the tendency of monopoly to expand into related markets, some of which might be competitive or potentially competitive. This, in fact, was one of the central stories of the integrated Bell System. It was probably never the case that telephone handsets were a natural monopoly, and yet the Bell System monopolized that adjunct market. The premise of the U.S. government's 1974 antitrust case against Bell[9] was that, while local telephone service might remain a natural monopoly, at least three related markets—consumer telephone equipment, telephone network equipment, and long-distance telephony—had become at least potentially competitive and that Bell was using its monopoly over

---

9. United States v. American Tel. & Tel. Co., 552 F. Supp. 131 (D.D.C. 1982), *aff'd sub nom.* Maryland v. United States, 460 U.S. 1001 (1983).

the local system to maintain monopolies in these other markets. We discuss this case at length in Chapter Six.

The first impulse of regulators is often to control the monopolist in all related markets, even if those markets are potentially competitive—and to subject any competitors to the same regulatory structures. Thus, water carriers and motor carriers (i.e., ships and barges and trucks) were brought into the same highly regulated structure as the railroads: licensed, required to file tariffs, and rate regulated. Regulation's second response (manifested through antitrust law, at least in the Bell case) is to segregate the monopolist and to forbid it to operate in the potentially competitive market. The government's first antitrust case against Bell[10] resulted in a consent decree that restricted Bell to common carrier communications markets (ruling out, for example, its entry into computer markets). The government's second antitrust case resulted in a 1982 decree breaking up the company based largely on monopoly versus competitive lines of business. Thus, the decree included a line-of-business restriction that forbade the local Bell Operating Companies (BOCs) from offering long-distance service, consumer premises equipment, or network equipment. The theory was that, if the BOCs were restricted to their monopoly markets, they would deal equally with all companies in the competitive markets (although the decree also included an "equal access" provision for good measure). Finally, when the costs of structural separation requirements were considered to be too great, regulation moved to open-access rules or other rules designed to provide some assurance to companies in competitive markets needing access to the monopolized service that they could purchase network access (or network elements) at nondiscriminatory prices. This progression, while dominant, was neither uniform, uncontested, nor inevitable, as we will see in later chapters.

Some of the same impulses of government management of market forces also manifest themselves in spectrum regulation. Although the need to control interference was a basic justification for licensing, licensing also allowed the FCC to exert economic control over the industry. In issuing licenses, the FCC went far beyond policing against interference. Rather, the FCC identified particular communications services that were in the public interest and issued licenses that were restricted to particular services. Thus, a company that won a license to offer a paging service could not, on the same spectrum in the same location, decide instead to offer video services, even if it concluded that video service is what the market preferred. This allowed the FCC to consider market structure issues in establishing licenses. That is, the FCC expressly took into account industry viability in determining how many licenses to issue in a particular service, and sometimes limited the number of licenses in order to protect licensee profits (which might overcome "destructive competition" or public goods effects).

On the content side, fewer generalizations are possible. Congress and the FCC both instituted mandatory service requirements and prohibitions. Telecommunications carriers were required to provide emergency services and to engineer their networks in ways that assisted law enforcement; they were also required to protect consumer privacy. Broadcasters were, at times, required to cover issues of public interest, to allow rights of reply, to sell cheap advertising to political candidates, to provide educational programming, and to avoid indecency. Indeed, the regulation of content and market activity need not be logically joined, and some countries, such as Canada, have different agencies licensing spectrum and content.

---

10. United States v. Western Elec. Co., 1956 Trade Cas. ¶ 68,246 (D.N.J.).

§ 1.A.3. The Challenges of Regulation

So far, we have discussed the benefits of regulation and its use as a set of legal tools designed to correct problems (real or perceived). But what of its costs? Part of the movement towards deregulation since the late 1970s reflects an increased appreciation for (or at least an increased focus on) the costs of regulation and the potential negatives of a regulatory system. In other words, modern regulatory analysis consists of a cost/benefit analysis not just of the industry that regulation seeks to address but also of regulation itself.

The most obvious cost of regulation is the cost of the regulatory structure itself. The FCC's budget is over $300 million, covering about 2000 Commission employees. One can add to this the cost of parallel state regulators, judicial costs created by litigation under communications regulation, and, from the perspective of industry at least, attorneys' fees required by the existence of regulation.

Beyond these direct costs is the potential that regulation itself creates market distortions. When companies must ask regulatory permission in order to enter new businesses or offer new services, they must incur the expense of regulatory applications. But the process also creates the opportunity for others to gain through the regulatory system. At a minimum, the disclosure required by the application process can eliminate an advantage of being first to market with an innovation. More problematically, the process can allow incumbents to oppose new applications that threaten their entrenched market positions. Thus, to return to one earlier example, if the hypothetical paging operator filed an application to begin to offer broadcasting services because it perceived additional market demand for such services, one could expect existing broadcasters to oppose the application. The incumbents might contend that the applicant was wrong on the facts about the market, or they might contend that, if there were unmet market demand, FCC action allowing them (the incumbents) to serve it would best promote the public interest.

Such a scenario highlights two further problems. The first is the informational problems of regulation. If the FCC is to make the licensing decision based on whether or not unmet demand exists, then the FCC must have the ability to investigate such demand or at least to assess the conflicting evidence and expert testimony presented by the parties. This example pales in comparison to the informational demands of rate regulation. In such a system, the regulator must be able to penetrate the cost information provided by the regulated company to determine whether claimed expenditures actually occurred and whether those expenditures were reasonable. In the opinion in which it approved the Bell breakup, the district court considered the alternative of a regulatory injunction—essentially an order forbidding anticompetitive behavior that the court itself would supervise. In dismissing that option, the court commented on testimony that it had received on the effectiveness of FCC regulation:

> Two former chiefs of the FCC's Common Carrier Bureau, the agency charged with regulating AT&T, testified that the Commission is not and never has been capable of effective enforcement of the laws governing AT&T's behavior. In their view, this inability was due to structural, budgetary, and financial deficiencies within the FCC as well as to the difficulty in obtaining information from AT&T. Whatever the true cause, it seems clear that the problems of supervision by a relatively poorly-financed, poorly-staffed government agency over a gigantic corporation with almost unlimited resources in funds and gifted personnel are no more likely to be overcome in the future than they were in the past.[11]

---

11. *American Tel. & Tel. Co.*, 552 F. Supp. at 168.

This is obviously not a sanguine perspective on the effectiveness of telecommunications regulation.

The second problem may require a fundamental reconception of the regulatory system. So far, we have essentially told what is sometimes called the normative story of regulation: the government perceives a problem, and then it acts in the (perceived) public interest to solve that problem. The alternative view of regulation is sometimes called the positive view of regulation—that is, that regulation is itself a system and that all interested parties seek to further their own interests by acting within the system. It requires little imagination to realize that, when regulation exists, the regulated companies themselves will make arguments that serve their own narrow economic interests instead of the broader public interest.

But broaden this perspective from the regulated entities to encompass the legislators, regulators, judges, and others in a regulatory system, and assume that each of these types of entities has its own interests, and one can generate a much different criticism. "Public choice" economics began to evaluate regulatory systems from this perspective in the 1960s and 1970s and became part of the intellectual movement supporting deregulation. Public choice theory assumes that all government actors maximize, at least in part, their own private goals, so that the key question regarding public actors is what they want to maximize. Consider, first, legislators. The basic premise is that those who desire to become legislators (for whatever personal reasons) desire principally to remain legislators. In some cases, they may adopt policies that are broadly popular, even if they are not economically efficient. For example, legislators may demand from telephone service providers reduced prices for residential consumers—a service that most voters care very much about, even if cross-subsidization would cause inefficiently high prices for business services. Businesses don't vote; individual households do. In other cases, legislators may maximize their chances of being reelected by adopting policies that respond to industry desires, because industry is in a position to offer greater campaign contributions, and such contributions are necessary to reelection campaigns. Alternatively, rational legislators may threaten regulation against incumbents but, after raising campaign contributions, then take no action at all.

Regulators may have similar personal interests. If one values being a regulator, then one may value even more being an "important" regulator, which means seeking to expand the regulatory scope of one's office or agency. Relatedly, an agency that regulates more or that charges higher industry fees may fund higher salaries or more nonsalary perks, such as cars and drivers for busy commissioners. Alternatively, a rational regulator may recognize that most regulators serve limited terms and, in considering future employment options, may realize that employment within the regulated industry (or as a lawyer or lobbyist representing the industry) is the most likely and most remunerative path. This may constrain a regulator's desire to take actions adverse to industry. Even apart from narrow self-interest, industry may be more present in a regulator's life, due to better funding, better advocacy, and more frequent appearances. For all of these reasons, a regulatory body may become captured by the industry it regulates.

For their part, members of the industry should be expected to make arguments that are in their own economic interest. But the public choice perspective on the regulatory system takes this insight a step further. Regulation can give companies a competitive advantage just as surely as can a new technology or good advertising or any other business feature. In the context of traditional regulation, where companies are not permitted to provide service without a government license, legal barriers to entry are absolute and can be much more permanent than any economic barrier. As dominant as the Bell System was when long distance was provided by copper-wire cable, the invention of microwave transmission technology radically changed the economics of long distance and made competition (more) possible. And yet new entrants into this field needed the FCC's permission to offer each new kind of service, which gave AT&T the opportunity to fight.

When viewed as yet another competitive tool, regulation therefore becomes just another place in which companies may invest—and they should rationally invest in regulation that benefits them (and injures their competitors) to the point where the returns from such investment are balanced by the costs. In other words, companies will not simply live within pre-existing regulation and manage it in the best way possible. Companies will sometimes affirmatively seek legislation and regulation that is solely in their economic interest (and, often, adverse to their competitors' interests).

To be sure, public choice theory does not necessarily explain everything, and some notable legislative and regulatory acts (such as airline deregulation) defy public choice explanations. Moreover, we believe that legislators and regulators usually act in what they perceive to be the public's best interests, all things considered. Nonetheless, we also believe that the public choice lens is an important perspective to consider when evaluating any given policy.

§ 1.B. A Policy Analysis Framework

This chapter is not meant to be exhaustive, but rather to provide an introduction to some of the major issues that cut across all of telecommunications policy. In the next chapter, we turn to some of the history of the sector-specific regulation that covers communications and to the specific institutions that administer communications law. Then, in the main corpus of the casebook, we will turn to the specific legal and policy controversies. As we do so, however, we hope that the foregoing text provides something of a structure for considering specific areas of communications law and policy. The list below provides a checklist of sorts for considering particular issues using the framework set out above:

- What, if any, are the market failures said to justify the proposed government intervention? Do the asserted failures match up with a well understood economic theory? How do they match up with the historical bases for regulation?
- What are the other asserted justifications for the regulation? Who in particular is the regulation supposed to help?
- What will the government need to know in order to administer the proposed regulation effectively? Where will it gather this information, and how will it know whether it is reliable?
- Other than the intended consequences of the regulation (i.e., meeting the asserted needs), what are the likely market and nonmarket effects of the regulation? Is it possible that the regulation will entrench existing players and provide a barrier to entry to innovative upstarts?
- How will the government assess whether its regulation is working?
- Can the regulation be explained as a product of public choice theory—in the interests of the regulators and/or the regulated, narrowly conceived, rather than in the interests of the public generally?

Chapter Two

Telecommunications Policy in Institutional Perspective

Introduction

Having summarized the reasons for telecommunications regulation, we now turn to the basic institutional choices that must be confronted in telecommunications policymaking. In doing so, we start from a set of basic questions—why establish a Federal Communications Commission to regulate telecommunications markets? How does such a regulatory agency operate—i.e., what functions does it serve? Why would regulators opt for one particular institutional strategy over another one?

All too often, students and practitioners of telecommunications policy take basic institutional questions for granted, focusing instead on legal or policy issues such as whether the Commission has authority to act in a particular area or whether such actions are prudent. Before evaluating such questions, we will first emphasize the often overlooked issue that *how* the Commission acts can sometimes make or break its ability to deliver on a particular policy goal. We will begin our examination of the institutional perspective at the beginning—how and why the FCC was established in the first place. In reading the story, keep in mind that an "independent" regulatory agency (a point to which we shall turn shortly) was not the only way in which the economic and noneconomic telecommunications policy issues could have been addressed.

We start with an overview of the various institutional choices that Congress confronts in designing a regulatory regime. With those in mind, we drill down into the choice that Congress did make, creating an expert administrative agency, to highlight some of the institutional choices that must be made about (or within) the agency itself. In so doing, we identify the discrete set of functions performed by the FCC as well as how its legacy structure affects its performance in those areas.

§ 2.A. The Institutional Dimensions of Telecommunications Policy

Government regulation can take a variety of different forms. A core reason why institutional structure and strategies are overlooked by practitioners—as well as scholars—

of telecommunications policy is that the critical "constitutive choices"[1] are taken as a given. It was not a given in the 1920s and 1930s, for example, that the radio spectrum would be regulated by a commission. To be sure, there are powerful virtues that inhere in the capabilities of an expert commission and that commended the Federal Radio Commission (FRC) and then the FCC as the appropriate body to oversee the uses of the radio spectrum.[2] Nonetheless, government regulation of the spectrum could have been achieved through a number of different mechanisms—utilizing courts, legislatures, and/or agencies, on the federal and/or state level. Admittedly, some approaches would have been more complicated than others. For example, leaving spectrum regulation to state entities might have introduced significant coordination, compliance, and enforcement costs because, whether intentionally or not, telecommunication broadcasts frequently cross state lines.[3] That said, the case could be made (and still can) that common law courts—with a tradition of enabling intangible or fluid property rights (e.g., water law)—could best ensure the effective use of the radio spectrum.[4]

For a period in the 1920s, common law courts were in the business of regulating the use of the wireless spectrum.[5] Pointing to such history, Professor Thomas Hazlett has suggested that, had the model of common law adjudication of wireless spectrum been allowed to develop, it would have led to more efficient uses of the wireless spectrum than under the oversight of the FCC.[6] Although often regarded as background law rather than regulation, common law evolution, where the courts come to address a problem that had not previously arisen, is a form of government intervention. Indeed, the same evolution from common law to administrative law can be seen in telephony as well: the English law of common carriage was a feature of the common law long before it was imposed by statute.[7]

Even assuming a preference for regulators with a national purview, there were still a number of options on the federal level. Spectrum regulation could have been left, for example, to a specialized federal court with national jurisdiction (like the Court of Appeals for the Federal Circuit, which hears all patent appeals). Or regulatory authority could have been vested in an agency directly controlled by the President rather than the more independent FCC that eventually was created.[8]

---

1. Paul Starr, The Creation of the Media 4 (2004).
2. *See* Philip J. Weiser & Dale Hatfield, Spectrum Policy Reform and the Next Frontier of Property Rights, 15 Geo. Mason L. Rev. 549 (2008).
3. Spectrum does not respect national boundaries either, and yet we are governed by a federal commission and not a global one. Thus, while countries engage in bilateral coordination (say, between the U.S. and Mexico) as well as multilateral coordination through the International Telecommunications Union, the basic authority over spectrum rests at the national level.
4. Some commentators argue just this. *See* Peter Huber, Law and Disorder in Cyberspace (1997), excerpted in Chapter Seventeen.
5. *See* Chapter Three.
6. Thomas W. Hazlett, The Rationality of U.S. Regulation of the Broadcast Spectrum, 33 J.L. & Econ. 133 (1990).
7. *See generally* James B. Speta, A Common Carrier Approach to Internet Interconnection, 54 Fed. Comm. L.J. 225 (2002) (reviewing the history of common carrier law).
8. Interestingly, in 1927 the House of Representatives wanted to leave licensing power with the Secretary of Commerce. The Senate did not, instead preferring an independent regulatory commission. The 1927 Radio Act reflected a compromise between the two. For one year, a geographically balanced five-member commission was to exercise the government's licensing function; then that function would revert to the Secretary of Commerce. Senator Clarence Dill of Washington, the Senate's expert on radio and a key figure in drafting the Act, liked the compromise because, understanding both Congress and bureaucracy, he believed "if we ever got a commission, we would never get rid of it." Erik Barnouw, A Tower in Babel 199 (1966). He was right. Congress ultimately abandoned the

There is no ready answer to this basic question of institutional design. The main arguments that carried the day in 1927 were twofold. First, it was widely believed that an independent administrative agency could develop relevant expertise. The argument was that judges are generalists with too few resources at hand, and, though Congress and the executive branch have greater resources at their disposal, they too lack the narrow focus that was thought to enhance the development of sound regulation in this complicated area.⁹ Second, it was similarly believed that using an independent agency was the only way to sufficiently insulate spectrum decisions from the political process. During the period when the FRC and, later, the FCC were created, there was widespread belief that politically insulated expert administrators would do a better job of managing complex regulatory undertakings than would their masters in Congress and the White House.[10]

At the other end of the spectrum, Congress could have given commissioners life tenure and the further accouterments of even greater independence. But that likely would have seemed to be too much insulation. One person's insulation, after all, is another's unaccountability. So Congress settled upon a multimember commission, currently with five commissioners each serving a five-year term of office. Replacements for commissioners who leave during their term serve only for the unexpired portion, and there can be no more than a bare majority (three, currently) of commissioners from any one political party. The President nominates commissioners, who are confirmed by the Senate, and designates one commissioner to serve as Chair, which means that the Chair is almost always from the President's party. These structural details are codified at 47 U.S.C. § 154.

When evaluating matters of institutional design, the first question is whether FCC oversight is appropriate at all. In the world of telecommunications policy, most policy practitioners jump from the premise that there is a policy concern to the conclusion that the FCC should be involved in solving it. But such a step is hardly self-evident. In the case of network neutrality, for example, the Federal Trade Commission (FTC) conducted a study and suggested that the consumer protection side of the issue (i.e., transparency as to how providers are operating) and the competition policy side of the issue (i.e., whether broadband providers are abusing their market position) are well handled by the FTC.[11]

The FTC's optimistic rhetoric about its potential role in the network neutrality debate did not ultimately lead that agency to play a larger role in resolving such issues. The reasons for the FTC's lack of action in the network neutrality arena are varied. For present purposes, it suffices to note that conventional wisdom and prevailing practice hold that industry-specific regulatory authorities possess valuable expertise and should take the lead on issues arising within their purview.

The institutional side of the network neutrality debate still begs the normative question of why the FCC is uniquely capable of resolving certain types of disputes. To sum-

---

provision to return powers to the Commerce Department, and the successor to the "one year agency," the Federal Communications Commission, remains with us.

9. It is, of course, debatable whether a narrow focus is preferable. After all, what looks like admirable focus to one person may look like blinders to another. And note that, precisely because a narrowly focused agency deals with a smaller number of regulated entities than would an agency with a broader purview, the potential for industry capture may be greater.

10. Although the Federal Radio Commission was created before the New Deal and the FCC was created during it, one commonality between the periods was a belief in the wisdom of governance via independent regulatory commissions. *See* Joseph B. Eastman, The Place of the Independent Commission, 12 Const. Rev. 95 (1928); James M. Landis, The Administrative Process (1938).

11. FTC, Broadband Connectivity Competition Policy (2007), *available at* http://www.ftc.gov/sites/default/files/documents/reports/broadband-connectivity-competition-policy/v070000report.pdf.

marize the arguments on both sides of this issue, advocates of authorizing courts to decide matters such as property rights in spectrum or network interoperability issues like those raised in the network neutrality debate emphasize the greater analytical rigor employed by courts and their relative insulation from political pressures.[12] By contrast, those defending the FCC underscore the importance of technical expertise and, in some cases, the importance of making predictive judgments to prevent the relevant harm—say, interference in the use of radio communications or blocking of Internet traffic—from taking place. As a normative matter, this debate goes on. As a matter of practice, however, the primacy of the expert agency in such matters remains intact.

§ 2.B. The Federal Communications Commission

Since the early part of the 20th century, the United States has largely empowered the FCC as the appropriate institution for communications regulation.[13] Before 1934, telegraph, telephone, and radio communications were governed by separate laws and separate governmental bodies. Radio, for example, was first regulated by the Radio Act of 1912, which required all users of the radio spectrum to obtain a license and placed licensing authority with the U.S. Secretary of Commerce.[14]

The thrust of the 1912 Act was to allocate different blocks of spectrum to different users—such as the military, commercial interests, and amateur radio operators—and to prioritize their access to the airwaves. Emergency signals such as marine distress calls had first priority for transmission, military signals came next, followed by commercial uses, and, finally, amateur signals. Fifteen years later, Congress passed the Radio Act of 1927, which repealed the 1912 Act. Like its predecessor, the 1927 Act stipulated that spectrum could be used only upon grant of license. And, for the first time, it formally declared the electromagnetic spectrum to be government property and moved the authority for issuing such licenses from the Secretary of Commerce to a new Federal Radio Commission.[15]

The 1927 Act broadly defined radio communications as "any intelligence, message, signal, power, pictures, or communication of any nature transferred by electrical energy from one point to another without the aid of any wire connecting the points."[16] Importantly, this legislation formally introduced the requirement that licensees serve the "public interest, convenience, or necessity"[17]—of which there will be considerably more discussion later in the book. The Act did not in any way address wireline communications such as telegraphy or telephony.

---

12. We return to this argument in Chapter Seventeen, in particular with an excerpt from Peter Huber.

13. In many other countries, communications were (and are) provided by government itself. Telephony was often part of a national postal system (under the so-called "PTT"—Post, Telephone, and Telegraph—model) until it became large enough to become its own government agency. On the broadcast side, many governments ran all or many of their nation's broadcast channels (e.g., the BBC). In the mid-20th century, in fact, the United States was fairly unique in that most broadcasters and telephone networks were privately owned. For a comparative discussion of these different models, see Starr, *supra* note 1.

14. Ch. 287, 37 Stat. 302 (1912) (repealed 1927). Congress had previously passed the Wireless Ship Act, ch. 379, 36 Stat. 629 (1910) (repealed 1954), which required all passenger ships to carry wireless sets.

15. Ch. 169, 44 Stat. 1162 (1927) (repealed 1934).

16. *Id.* at 1173.

17. *Id.* at 1167.

Regulation of telephone and telegraph services developed separately from regulation of radio in the early 1900s. For a time, no federal regulation of telephone service existed. The first statute to regulate telephone service was the Mann-Elkins Act of 1910,[18] passed more than 15 years after the original Bell telephone patents had expired and well after numerous independent telephone carriers had entered into competition with the Bell system. The Mann-Elkins Act assigned regulatory jurisdiction over telephony to the Interstate Commerce Commission, which already had authority over the railroads as well as other network services.

The mandate of the Mann-Elkins Act was fairly narrow by current standards. The Act categorized telephone service providers as "common carriers"—i.e., carriers that were "obligated to provide service on request at just and reasonable rates, without unjust discrimination or undue preference."[19] The ICC's charge was to enforce these common carrier requirements. The Mann-Elkins Act, however, neither required that telephone carriers file tariffs (rate plans) nor authorized the ICC to implement such a requirement. The Act thus gave the agency very limited authority, and the ICC, in turn, largely adopted a strategy of benign neglect towards telephone service, holding only four proceedings to investigate telephone rates between 1910 and 1934.[20] To be sure, the ICC did try actively to regulate merger and acquisition behavior in the telephone industry. Nonetheless, the ICC was far more concerned with regulating railroads than with regulating telephones and did little to oversee the performance of the telecommunications industry.

The ICC was not the only regulatory authority concerned with telecommunications, however. Unlike radio, telephony was subject not just to federal oversight, but to state regulation as well. State regulators reviewed rates, established accounting rules, and implemented service requirements related to local telephone service. As we will discuss in greater detail in Chapter Six, the states' regulatory sphere was strictly limited to intrastate telephone service and its related facilities. But given that the vast bulk of telephone calls were typically "local," this limitation did not mean that state commissions were weak or insignificant regulatory forces. Even today, the boundary between state and federal regulatory jurisdiction over telephone carriers continues to be an area of important and vigorous dispute.[21]

§ 2.C. Regulatory Integration Under the 1934 Act

The Communications Act of 1934[22] undertook an important organizational task. It extended jurisdiction over telecommunications to an expert agency rather than assigning such jurisdiction to entities that had other concerns, such as the ICC or the Department of Commerce. But instead of creating separate experts for each telecommunications field, the 1934 Act provided for a single expert agency with broad purview.[23] The Radio Act of

---

18. Mann-Elkins Act of 1910, ch. 309, 36 Stat. 539.
19. *Id.* §§ 7, 12.
20. Peter W. Huber, Michael K. Kellogg & John Thorne, Federal Telecommunications Law 215 (2d ed. 1999).
21. We address jurisdictional issues primarily in Chapters Six and Seven.
22. Communications Act of 1934, 48 Pub. L. No. 73-416, ch. 652, 48 Stat. 1064 (codified as amended at 47 U.S.C. §§ 151–609).
23. This was an open question in certain settings. For example, we will see in Chapter Fourteen that there was considerable doubt over whether the FCC had authority to regulate cable television under the 1934 Act. The Supreme Court ultimately held that it (for the most part) did, and Congress later amended the 1934 Act to make that authority explicit.

1927 created a focused agency for spectrum management (the Federal Radio Commission); the 1934 Act, by contrast, created a regulatory agency for telephony and charged that same agency with the duty to regulate the airwaves. In establishing the Federal Communications Commission, the Act abolished the Federal Radio Commission, repealed the Mann-Elkins Act, and put an end to the fragmented jurisdiction that had existed until 1934. As the statute itself explains,

> For the purpose of regulating interstate and foreign commerce in communication by wire and radio so as to make available, so far as possible, to all people of the United States, a rapid, efficient, Nation-wide, and world-wide wire and radio communication service with adequate facilities at reasonable charges, for the purpose of the national defense, and for the purpose of securing a more effective execution of this policy by centralizing authority heretofore granted by law to several agencies and by granting additional authority with respect to interstate and foreign commerce in wire and radio communication, there is created a commission to be known as the "Federal Communications Commission," which shall be constituted as hereinafter provided, and which shall execute and enforce the provisions of this chapter.[24]

Under the Communications Act, the FCC was charged with promulgating regulations to implement its provisions and interpret the many gaps and ambiguities that appeared throughout the lengthy statute. This implementing role was of immediate and substantial importance. For while the Act incorporated many aspects of preexisting regulation (like the licensing requirements for broadcasters and common carriage obligations for telephone companies), it also markedly increased the scope of federal communications regulation. It was in the exercise of that new authority that the FCC would ultimately find its most significant powers.

The institutional question, of course, overlaps with the broader substantive question, and the interaction of the two helps to produce policy outcomes. As an original matter, either a commission or a court (whether a specialized court or a court of general jurisdiction) could oversee the use of spectrum and ask, as the Communications Act provides, whether one user creates "harmful interference"[25] to other users. Viewed in this light, the comparative institutional competence question can turn on whether a commission or courts possess the necessary expertise to make this judgment.[26] But, in this country, the question of spectrum use has historically gone far beyond the question of interference to also include what types of service would be provided over the spectrum. Indeed, in 1943, the Supreme Court made clear that the Communications Act did not limit the FCC to the supervision of interference but also tasked it with overseeing how spectrum was used. In particular, Justice Frankfurter wrote in the landmark case of *NBC v. United States* that because "the radio spectrum is not large enough to accommodate everybody,"[27] the FCC

---

24. Communications Act of 1934 §1 (codified as amended at 47 U.S.C. §151). The section has been amended twice: in 1937, when the words "for the purpose of promoting safety of life and property through the use of wire and radio communication" were added, and in 1996, when the words "without discrimination on the bases of color, religion, national origin or sex" were added.

25. *See, e.g.*, 47 U.S.C. §302a(a); 47 U.S.C. §303(y)(2)(C).

26. We will not delve into the issue here, but it merits note that this question is similarly debated in an array of technology policy contexts. In the related context of the ability of antitrust courts to evaluate technical cooperation, Judge Posner has suggested that courts (and agencies) are wanting because "the enforcement agencies and the courts do not have adequate technical resources, and do not move fast enough, to cope effectively with a very complex business sector that changes very rapidly." Richard A. Posner, Antitrust in the New Economy, 68 Antitrust L.J. 925, 925 (2001).

27. NBC v. United States, 319 U.S. 190, 212 (1943).

is authorized to oversee not merely whether different users are creating undue interference but also whether their use of the spectrum is in the "public interest."

The Congressional mandate that the FCC exercise its "public interest" authority to make judgments about who is worthy to hold a license to use spectrum gave the agency wide discretion. In the wake of the New Deal, there was still considerable confidence that administrative agencies could possess and exercise broad discretion effectively, reflecting what is often called the "wise man" theory of regulation.[28] As Alfred Kahn (a pioneer of airline deregulation and author of the influential book, The Economics of Regulation) later put it, however, such a theory overlooks that "the dispensation of favors to a selected few is a political act, not a judicial one."[29] After all, what legal or technical criteria can make clear which uses—say, livestock breeding versus dairy inspection, as the FCC decided in a particular case[30]—have a stronger claim on wireless spectrum?

§ 2.D. Institutional Structure and the FCC

Choosing an independent agency does not end the process of making institutional choices. The agency must itself be organized, and the agency must determine the manner in which it will do business. In particular, the agency must decide (self-consciously or not) the manner in which it will make and enforce its policy judgments.

The wise man theory of regulation that governed spectrum regulation for much of the agency's history directly translated into how the FCC was organized to oversee the use of spectrum. In particular, the FCC identified different possible uses of the spectrum and then assigned different units within the Commission to regulate particular uses. Most notably, the Media Bureau oversees licenses to operate TV and radio stations. The International Bureau oversees licenses to operate satellite transmission systems (as such licenses are often related to international treaty obligations). The Office of Engineering and Technology oversees those uses of the wireless spectrum that are authorized without the need to hold a license at all—the so-called "unlicensed uses" of the spectrum, such as Wi-Fi.[31] On the carrier side of the agency, the Wireline Competition Bureau covers wireline telephony while cellular telephony is under the Wireless Telecommunications Bureau.

As a case study in how the internal organization of the agency makes an important difference, consider the operation of the four bureaus involved with overseeing the use of wireless spectrum. As an initial matter, authorizing four different bureaus to oversee spectrum use makes it harder to develop a consistent philosophy and set of practices to manage interference in different contexts. Indeed, the FCC has largely resisted the calls to establish a comprehensive framework to govern what constitutes "harmful interference," instead leaving the individual bureaus with substantial leeway to fight out and establish rules that protect users against interference within their respective spectrum

---

28. Douglas W. Webbink, Frequency Spectrum Deregulation Alternatives 10 (FCC, Working Paper No. 2, 1980), *available at* http:/www.fcc.gov/Bureaus/OPP/working_papers/oppwp2.pdf. The "wise man" is, of course, the regulator, who "is capable of deciding what is *best* for the public." *Id.*

29. Thomas K. McCraw, Prophets of Regulation 286 (1984).

30. *See* Petition of Lehigh Coop. Farmers, Inc., Memorandum Opinion and Order, 10 F.C.C. 2d 315 (1967) (selecting the best applicant for a radio license based indirectly on the value of occupations catered to).

31. "Wi-Fi" refers to wireless local area networks that use a particular set of specifications (known as 802.11) developed by the Institute of Electrical and Electronics Engineers, or IEEE.

uses.³² By contrast, if a single bureau were authorized and required to develop and oversee all uses of spectrum, there would be a natural incentive to develop a more consistent approach to spectrum management. With four different bureaus having a stake in the outcome, however, the internal bureaucratic battles result in a détente that leaves the guiding approach toward spectrum management undefined and leaves each bureau with leeway in managing interference as it sees fit.³³

The difference between the model of defining and adjudicating a standard such as harmful interference and developing rules specific to each industry may not be immediately apparent. One critical difference is that a firm developing new wireless technologies must—unless it gains access to the category of "flexible use" spectrum authorized for cellular services—ask the FCC to modify the heavily prescribed limitations set forth in the relevant service rules.³⁴ To appreciate the impact of this system, consider Qualcomm's early attempt to bring TV programming to mobile phones called MediaFLO.³⁵ When Qualcomm evaluated its plans for rolling out this service, it determined that MediaFLO might create interference with adjacent services.³⁶ Given the case-by-case spectrum management process, however, Qualcomm had no clear guidance as to what principles would govern such interference so it petitioned the FCC for guidance.³⁷ Qualcomm, a company with substantial resources and sophisticated knowledge about how the FCC operates, was able to submit a petition and receive an answer within twenty months—a relatively fast turnaround for the FCC. For upstarts, however, this sort of entry barrier is enough to destroy a new business concept in its infancy, particularly because competitors can use the process to delay the new offering, hinder its effectiveness (by advocating overly strict limitations), and learn more about it before it hits the market.

The outcome of the Qualcomm matter reveals a core limitation of the FCC's current system of spectrum regulation. In that matter, the FCC considered establishing a more systematic (and less ad hoc) standard for interference management that would be im-

---

32. *See, e.g.*, R. Paul Margie, Can You Hear Me Now?: Getting Better Reception from the FCC's Spectrum Policy, 2003 Stan. Tech. L. Rev. 5.

33. The notable exception was the Spectrum Policy Task Force chartered by Chairman Michael Powell. That effort took an interdisciplinary and systematic look at how spectrum was managed and how interference was treated. Its recommendations, however, were not acted upon. *See* Establishment of an Interference Temperature Metric to Quantify and Manage Interference and to Expand Available Unlicensed Operation in Certain Fixed, Mobile, and Satellite Frequency Bands, Order, 22 FCC Rcd. 8938 (2007) (abandoning effort launched in Establishment of an Interference Temperature Metric to Quantify and Manage Interference and to Expand Available Unlicensed Operation in Certain Fixed, Mobile, and Satellite Frequency Bands, Notice of Inquiry and Notice of Proposed Rulemaking, 18 FCC Rcd. 25,309 (2003)).

34. As the U.S. Government Accountability Office reported:

> [F]or most frequency bands FCC allocates, the agency issues service rules to define the terms and conditions for spectrum use within the given bands. These rules typically specify eligibility standards as well as limitations on the services that relevant entities may offer and the technologies and power levels they may use. These decisions can constrain users' ability to offer services and equipment of their choosing.

JayEtta Z. Hecker, U.S. Gov't Accountability Office, GAO-06-526T, Telecommunications: Options for and Barriers to Spectrum Reform 7 (2006), *available at* http://www.gao.gov/new.items/d06526t.pdf.

35. Qualcomm Incorporated Petition for Declaratory Ruling, Order, 21 FCC Rcd. 11,683 (2006). Qualcomm said it would offer between 50 and 100 local and national channels either in real time or in clip-casting for later viewing. *Id.* at 11,684.

36. *See id.* at 11,685.

37. *See id.* at 11,683.

plemented through a new, streamlined procedure.[38] The FCC declined to do so, however, instead adhering to its traditional public interest, case-by-case determination system.[39] Unfortunately, the FCC's current system invites rent-seeking (i.e., delay-inducing) behavior by competitors and creates, as Thomas Hazlett put it, "a moral hazard for incumbents who are rewarded for raising interference complaints simply to block competition."[40] In arguing for a new approach to spectrum management, FCC Chairman Michael Powell cited this very dynamic, condemning how the current system created "interference rules that are barriers to entry, that assume a particular proponent's business model or technology, and that take the place of marketplace or technical solutions."[41]

§ 2.E. The FCC in a Functional Perspective

When Congress enacted the Communications Act and amendments, it specified a set of titles that regulate particular technologies (e.g., telephone service, radio communications, cable television). As noted above, the FCC has followed this silo-based approach and has established a set of different bureaus to oversee different industry segments (e.g., Wireless, Media, Wireline). From a functional perspective, however, there are certain responsibilities that are handled across and within each bureau. One can thus imagine, and different officials and commentators have suggested, that the agency could be reorganized along functional lines. Tracing out the discussion above, we discuss in this section key functions that the FCC historically and currently performs.

§ 2.E.1. Command and Control

The FCC was established with a mandate to regulate in the public interest using a model of "command and control" regulation. In the case of how spectrum was used and how the monopoly telephone company (AT&T) operated, the FCC instituted rules that limited how regulated companies could operate. Those rules came to be known as "ex ante" regulation, as they required the FCC to authorize ahead of time what actions the regulated firms could take. If a regulated broadcaster or telephone company wanted to offer a new service (e.g., voicemail) or use its spectrum license differently, it needed to first ask permission. When a firm requests permission, competitors can oppose the application on any ground, drag out the proceeding, and seek more information about the new service. For an environment in which such events (i.e., the development of a new service) were rare, ex ante regulation constituted a reasonable system for preserving stability and safeguarding against unwanted behavior. For a more dynamic marketplace, however, the limitations of this model become increasingly problematic and costly to society.

The underpinnings of the command and control model of regulation for telecommunications policy began to break down in the 1990s as the industry confronted technological convergence. Stated simply, technological convergence is the coming together of different services on account of technological change.

---

38. *Id.* at 11,696–97, 11,699.
39. *Id.* at 11,696, 11,700–01.
40. Thomas W. Hazlett, Liberalizing US Spectrum Allocation, 27 Telecomm. Pol'y 485, 486 (2003).
41. Michael K. Powell, Chairman, FCC, Broadband Migration III: New Directions in Wireless Policy, Remarks at the Silicon Flatirons Telecommunications Program 8 (Oct. 30, 2002), *available at* http://hraunfoss.fcc.gov/edocs_public/attachmatch/DOC-227944A1.pdf.

In recent decades, the telecommunications world moved from one in which ex ante rules were the norm to one in which more dynamic business models made it difficult to justify the delays that inhere in such a regime. But, as we noted above, the institutional limitations of this change are sometimes overlooked. For instance, in the face of more diverse uses of wireless spectrum, many commentators have called on the FCC to treat spectrum more like traditional property and judge the equivalent of trespass through adjudicative processes.

§ 2.E.2. Rulemaking versus Adjudication

As the discussion above illustrates, institutional structure directly constrains and influences substantive policy decisions. The links between institutional structure and ultimate policy determinations are complex insofar as regulatory agencies can, at least as a theoretical matter, change their institutional strategy to address particular policies. In *SEC v. Chenery Corp.*, the Supreme Court made clear that, absent specific statutory language requiring adjudication or rulemaking, the choice is largely up to the agency.[42] In principle, as in *Chenery* itself, agencies can select adjudication over rulemaking so that they can address statutory problems as they arise.[43]

Adjudications are a significant part of the FCC's docket, as they include actions on possible rule violations, licensing disputes, and other proceedings focused on specific acts or actors. An example would be a hearing to determine whether the broadcast of a particular television program violated the Commission's rules barring indecency. When the FCC implements a statute, however, it usually does so via rulemaking. Congress enacts the statute and leaves some aspect of the statute's administration to the FCC, and the Commission assumes that responsibility by launching a rulemaking process.

The rulemaking process formally begins with the Commission issuing a Notice of Proposed Rulemaking (NPRM). An NPRM lays out the issues it is considering, discusses them, and proposes a response to them (sometimes accompanied by a set of proposed rules). The NPRM requests comments from interested parties on the proposed course of action. Of course, parties often communicate with the Commission before it issues an NPRM in the hope of influencing these proposals; after an NPRM is issued, however, there is a statutorily mandated comment period to ensure that all interested parties have an opportunity to comment before any regulation is adopted.

In some cases, the Commission takes a prior step by issuing a Notice of Inquiry (NOI). The Administrative Procedure Act does not require, or even mention, NOIs (whereas it requires NPRMs), but agencies sometimes use them when they are not ready to issue an NPRM. An NOI raises the issue to be addressed and invites comments but usually does not propose any particular rules. An NOI generally functions to help the agency gather information on a particular topic.

Sometimes an agency takes no further action on a subject after an NOI, and sometimes it takes no further action after an NPRM. And, of course, most of the ideas suggested to an agency are never the subject of any formal action. But if an agency wants to promulgate a substantive rule, then after issuing an NPRM (whether or not preceded by

---

42. SEC v. Chenery Corp., 332 U.S. 194, 203 (1947) ("[T]he choice made between proceeding by general rule or by individual, ad hoc litigation is one that lies primarily in the informed discretion of the administrative agency.").

43. *Id.* at 201, 203. The Court noted, however, that whether the decision produced by the adjudication should be given retroactive effect was another matter. *Id.*

an NOI), the agency generally must respond to comments, formulate final rules, and write a statement of basis and purpose for those rules. The Commission often calls its documents containing the final rules, responses to comments, and explanation a "Report and Order."

The rulemaking procedure outlined above may sound reasonably streamlined. In practice, however, it often is not. Frequently, the FCC will issue an NPRM or NOI and later (in response to comments, on its own initiative, or in response to external events) decide to issue a further NPRM or NOI, calling for a new round of comments and responses on a defined set of issues. On the back end, a final order might not resolve all outstanding issues and might instead request comment on some additional matters. The result is that many orders are final orders as to some matters and an NPRM or NOI as to others. The possibility of multiple NPRMs and multiple orders, combined with the opportunities for communications to the Commission not only during the official comment period but also before a rulemaking formally commences, makes for a more fluid rulemaking process than one might imagine from merely reading the statutory provisions that govern how the FCC operates.

When a final Report and Order is issued, even that is not the end of the process. A party can petition the FCC for reconsideration, but the Commission rarely grants such requests. This is not surprising. After all, the whole point of soliciting comments after the issuance of proposed rules is to allow parties to present their arguments before final rules are issued. Other avenues for reconsideration are more promising, however. First, Congress can (but rarely does) overturn an FCC decision by legislation. A second and far more common path is for an aggrieved party to file suit challenging the agency action as inconsistent with federal law.

It is not the openings of FCC NPRMs that generally raise concerns, but their conclusions. Rather than reopen proceedings for further comment once the agency identifies a set of model rules, the FCC has historically used the so-called ex parte process to focus on the questions in controversy. For students of the judicial system, the concept of an ex parte process may sound strange; after all, the judicial system bans such contacts. At the FCC, however, such contacts are allowed, pursuant to a filing submitted by the interested party. That filing is generally far from a full discussion of the relevant issues. Rather, it tends more toward a brief statement that there was a discussion about issues raised in a pending NPRM. As such, only those parties who are quite adept at following the debate at the FCC are able to participate in such a process.

To appreciate the FCC's attachment to proceeding by rulemaking, consider the FCC's conduct of the high-profile and self-styled adjudication in 2008 responding to Comcast's secret degradation of some peer-to-peer services. In that case, the Commission evaluated whether Comcast complied with the Commission's theretofore nonbinding Internet policy principles.[44] In reaching its conclusion that Comcast had violated these principles, the FCC did not follow any of the traditional elements of a formal adjudication process— i.e., it did not admit evidence under oath; it did not provide for cross-examinations; it did not evaluate whether expert opinions should be credited as grounded in technical expertise; and it did not find facts. Instead, it used the same process that the agency uses for notice and comment rulemakings. Courts and commentators have long criticized that process. Judge Posner observed that "[t]he nature of the record compiled in a notice and

---

44. *See* Formal Complaint of Free Press and Public Knowledge Against Comcast Corporation for Secretly Degrading Peer-to-Peer Applications, Memorandum Opinion and Order, 23 FCC Rcd. 13,028 (2008), *vacated*, Comcast Corp. v. FCC, 600 F.3d 642 (D.C. Cir. 2010).

comment rulemaking proceeding—voluminous, largely self-serving commentary uncabined by any principles of reliability, let alone by the rules of evidence—further enlarges the Commission's discretion and further diminishes the capacity of the reviewing court to question the Commission's judgment."[45] With respect to the Comcast matter, FCC Commissioner McDowell dissented from the FCC's order along these very lines, noting, among other things, that "[t]he evidence in the record is thin and conflicting."[46]

A core institutional challenge for the FCC is to learn from the limitations highlighted by cases like *Comcast* and develop greater adjudicative capabilities. Unfortunately, the FCC's limits in holding adjudications exhibited in the *Comcast* case reflect an apparent institutional weakness in how the agency operates. To appreciate this point, consider its treatment of XM and Sirius after years of flagrant violations of the terms of their licenses. In the words of Commissioner Deborah Taylor Tate, Sirius Satellite Radio "failed to comply—knowingly and repeatedly—with the specifications for its FM modulators and the terms of its Special Temporary Authorizations ... for more than five years."[47] These years of lawless behavior did not, however, result in any formal enforcement proceeding, adjudication, or contested proceeding. Rather, the FCC took action and entered into a consent decree with the two companies only as part of a merger review process, with Sirius agreeing to a "voluntary contribution" of $2,200,000[48] and XM agreeing to $17,394,375.[49]

The absence of an effective ex post adjudication process for penalizing legal violations has a number of consequences. First, it can lead the Commission to accommodate parties who previously violated rules that were not enforced.[50] Second, because enforcement does not proceed in a clear and predictable fashion, many efforts to conduct enforcement processes follow the FCC's traditional model of negotiated solutions (rather than adjudicated results).[51]

---

45. Schurz Communications, Inc. v. FCC, 982 F.2d 1043, 1048 (7th Cir. 1992).
46. Formal Complaint of Free Press and Public Knowledge Against Comcast Corp., 23 FCC Rcd. at 13,092 (dissenting statement of Comm'r Robert M. McDowell). Commissioner McDowell elaborated on this point, explaining that:
> All we have to rely on are the apparently unsigned declarations of three individuals representing the complainant's view, some press reports, and the conflicting declaration of a Comcast employee. The rest of the record consists purely of differing opinions and conjecture.

Id. (footnote omitted).
47. Sirius Satellite Radio Inc., Order, 23 FCC Rcd. 12,301, 12,324 (2008) (statement of Comm'r Deborah Taylor Tate).
48. *Id.* (describing the consent decree the FCC entered into with Sirius).
49. XM Radio, Inc., Order, 23 FCC Rcd. 12,325, 12,347 (2008) (statement of Comm'r Deborah Taylor Tate) (describing the consent decree the FCC entered into with XM).
50. *See, e.g.*, Unlicensed Operation in the TV Broadcast Bands, Second Report and Order and Memorandum Opinion and Order, 23 FCC Rcd. 16,807 (2008) (adopting new rules legalizing the unlicensed use of TV spectrum locations that are unused by licensed services); *see also* Harold Feld, We File Wireless Microphone Complaint: Shure Says Breaking Law Should Be OK if You Sound Good, Wetmachine (July 16, 2008), www.wetmachine.com/tales-of-the-sausage-factory/we-file-wireless-microphone-complaint-shure-says-breaking-law-should-be-ok-if-you-sound-good (complaining that the FCC should not "reward" users of illegal wireless microphones by offering them priority over authorized users).
51. The practice of treating enforcement actions as a political negotiation is discussed and criticized in a House Commerce Committee majority report. *See* Majority Staff of H. Comm. on Energy and Commerce, 110th Cong., Deception and Distrust: The Federal Communications Commission Under Chairman Kevin J. Martin 18–19, 23–24 (2008).

§ 2.E.3. Licensing

In the wake of the enactment of the Communications Act, the decision of whether to license a party to use the radio spectrum was invariably an important decision. The grant of a license to use scarce spectrum entitled a firm to a privileged position in the market. In theory, the license came with public interest obligations (see Chapter Fifteen), but enforcement of those obligations was, to put it mildly, uneven. Similarly, licensing decisions were not permanent. A licensee traditionally faced a renewal process whereby it would need to justify its continued merit to hold a license. The renewal process, with rare exceptions, involved more theoretical than real scrutiny of the behavior of the license holders. In most cases, the incentives for the agency were clear: if the license renewal was denied, the agency faced a legal and/or political battle. If the agency renewed the license, by contrast, it would find little outcry in all but the most exceptional cases. In 1996, as discussed in Chapter Five, Congress curtailed even the theoretical role for license renewals, enacting into law a presumption that licenses would automatically be renewed.[52]

In one situation, however, licenses are often subject to serious scrutiny: a merger or acquisition in which a license changes hands. In such cases, the FCC enjoys a parallel role to that of the antitrust authorities (i.e., the Department of Justice and FTC). For both wireless spectrum licenses and licenses to operate wireline facilities, the FCC's oversight over any license transfers has enabled it to conduct its own merger review. This redundancy has generated significant criticism, with former FCC Commissioner Harold Furchtgott-Roth calling for an end to the FCC's role in merger review.[53] We will return to this issue in Chapter Eleven.

§ 2.E.4. Norm Entrepreneur

One of the least publicly appreciated roles played by the FCC (and other government agencies) is that of norm entrepreneur. This role, first suggested by Cass Sunstein,[54] is both significant and controversial. Consider, for example, the network neutrality issue discussed above. For several years, the principal governmental response was a speech by Chairman Powell setting forth a series of norms for how broadband providers were expected to behave.[55] That effort was significant because it filled a policy vacuum. It was

---

52. *See* Telecommunications Act of 1996 § 204, 47 U.S.C. § 309.
53. *See* Harold W. Furchtgott-Roth, Testimony Before the Antitrust Modernization Commission 93–94 (Dec. 5, 2005) (transcript *available at* http://govinfo.library.unt.edu/amc/commission_hearings/pdf/051205_Regulated_Industries_Transcript_reform.pdf). For other views, *see* Rachel E. Barkow & Peter W. Huber, A Tale of Two Agencies: A Comparative Analysis of FCC and DOJ Review of Telecommunications Mergers, 2000 U. Chi. Legal F. 29; Donald J. Russell & Sherri Lynn Wolson, Dual Antitrust Review of Telecommunications Mergers by the Department of Justice and the Federal Communications Commission, 11 Geo. Mason L. Rev. 143 (2002); Bryan N. Tramont, Too Much Power, Too Little Restraint: How the FCC Expands Its Reach Through Unenforceable and Unwieldy "Voluntary" Agreements, 53 Fed. Comm. L.J. 49 (2000).
54. The term appears to stem from Cass R. Sunstein, On the Expressive Function of Law, 144 U. Pa. L. Rev. 2021 (1996). For a notable use of the term in connection with a government agency, see Steven Hetcher, The FTC as Internet Privacy Norm Entrepreneur, 53 Vand. L. Rev. 2041 (2000).
55. Michael K. Powell, Chairman, FCC, Preserving Internet Freedom: Guiding Principles for the Industry, Remarks at the Silicon Flatirons Symposium: The Digital Broadband Migration: Toward a Regulatory Regime for the Internet Age (Feb. 8, 2004), *available at* http://hraunfoss.fcc.gov/edocs_public/attachmatch/DOC-243556A1.pdf.

controversial because it neither reflected the pedigree of official agency action nor could bind parties who deviated from the norms.

Whether or not the FCC should act as a norm entrepreneur will continue to be debated. Insofar as the agency uses this authority, it will often do so to catalyze self-regulation by the industry. While the "bully pulpit" or "regulation by raised eyebrow" can catalyze self-regulation,[56] it provides no official oversight. By contrast, a system of "co-regulation" involves the intermingling of official authority and unofficial authority.[57] Notably, by standing with "the shotgun behind the door,"[58] a government agency can enable the private system of dispute resolution to operate more effectively insofar as official accountability will ensure that private regulatory efforts will be genuine and not merely a veneer to mask noncompliance.

§ 2.E.5. Standard Setting

The FCC's role in setting standards for telecommunications technologies remains, like its norm entrepreneurship role, a controversial one.[59] Government standard setting is a notoriously difficult act, as it requires government officials to act based on limited expertise (relative to private sector counterparts), susceptibility to political pressures, and less flexibility to respond to market changes. Nonetheless, throughout the history of the telecommunications industry, the FCC has taken this role very seriously, producing what many regard as mixed results.

The least controversial role for government standard setting is in addressing collective action problems to respond to key social policy concerns, thereby preventing market failure. Consider, for example, hearing aid compatibility with the telephone network. The FCC acted under congressional direction to embrace and enforce compliance with an industry standard.[60] In so doing, the FCC addressed a coordination challenge that the carriers themselves had failed to overcome insofar as they did not take the necessary steps to provide a crucial service to an important segment of the population.

A second type of standard setting occurs when an incumbent firm possesses significant market power and interconnection to its platform is necessary to promote competition. We will save for Chapter Seven a discussion of when such a conclusion is warranted. For now, consider the uncontroversial case, at least historically, of the regulation of AT&T and its unwillingness to provide access to the telephone network for what it called "foreign devices." After years of litigation and regulatory proceedings, the FCC finally succeeded in establishing what it called its Part 68 rules, which required that AT&T (and other incumbent providers) allow such attachments, provided the attachment produc-

---

56. These concepts are hardly new ones. *See* H. Thomas Austern, Expertise in Vivo, 15 Admin. L. Rev. 46 (1963) (discussing "jaw-bone enforcement" and "the lifted eyebrow"); Lars Noah, Administrative Arm-Twisting in the Shadow of Congressional Delegations of Authority, 1997 Wis. L. Rev. 873.

57. *See* Philip J. Weiser, The Future of Internet Regulation, 43 U.C. Davis L. Rev 529 (2009).

58. This concept comes from securities regulation, where official oversight over self-regulatory organizations is a common practice. *See id.* at 552–53, 574.

59. For two discussions, see Kathleen M.H. Wallman, The Role of Government in Telecommunications Standard-Setting, 8 CommLaw Conspectus 235 (2000); Dale N. Hatfield, Challenges of Network Design in an Increasingly Deregulated, Competitive Market, Remarks at the IEEE International Symposium on Integrated Network Management (Mar. 27, 2003), *available at* http://www.ieee-im.org/2003/presentation%20files/RemarksDH_IM2003.doc.

60. Hearing Aid Compatibility Act of 1988, Pub. L. No. 100-394, 102 Stat. 976 (codified as amended at 47 U.S.C. §§ 609–610).

ers followed the necessary steps to avoid harm to the network.[61] Indeed, such rules continue to remain in place, which is why many devices have an FCC label verifying that they will not harm a network if connected. The FCC no longer performs the process of certifying compliance with these rules, as it delegated this role in 2000 to a set of authorized private sector bodies.[62]

Government standard-setting compliance efforts can take different forms. Most notably, the government can focus on compliance with a standard as opposed to focusing on the means of such compliance. For example, the FCC's Part 15 rules discussed in Chapter Four allow for equipment to use any number of technologies to achieve a specified functional requirement—i.e., that frequency emissions fall within the prescribed power limit and do not interfere with licensed users. The manufacturers of such devices can continually reevaluate the best means for making such devices compliant with the Part 15 rules. By contrast, the government departed from this approach when it adopted a specific technological standard for the transmission of digital television. *See* Advanced Television Systems and Their Impact upon the Existing Television Broadcast Service, Fourth Report and Order, 11 FCC Rcd. 17,771 (1996).

Finally, it bears noting that the FCC generally seeks to follow the modern practice of relying on private sector, voluntary, and consensus-based standards bodies wherever possible.[63] Some scholars have criticized this practice, suggesting that government agencies should be more active in standard setting insofar as delegating authority or relying on private actors lacks democratic legitimacy (a criticism also leveled at norm entrepreneurship).[64] Nonetheless, the FCC has concluded, as it explained in delegating compliance with its Part 68 rules to private bodies, that public management of this function undermines the "goals of reduced governmental involvement in the standards process and expedited development of technical criteria for new technology."[65] As such, when the FCC considered imposing an interconnection mandate on the AOL instant messaging product (an effort it later abandoned), it chose to rely on a private standard-setting body to establish the necessary specifications.[66]

§ 2.F. The Statutory and Broader Institutional Context

The Communications Act of 1934 has been amended numerous times, and several of those amendments have been sufficiently extensive that they are often referred to as Acts

---

61. Proposals for New or Revised Classes of Interstate and Foreign Message Toll Telephone Service (MTS) and Wide Area Telephone Service (WATS), First Report and Order, 56 F.C.C. 2d 593, 594–96 (1975), *modified*, 58 F.C.C. 2d 716 (1976), *modified*, 58 F.C.C. 2d 736 (1976), *aff'd sub nom.*, N.C. Utils. Comm'n v. FCC, 552 F.2d 1036 (4th Cir. 1977).
62. 2000 Biennial Regulatory Review of Part 68 of the Commission's Rules and Regulations, Report and Order, 15 FCC Rcd. 24,944 (2000).
63. *See* Office of Mgmt. & Budget, Exec. Office of the President, Circular No. A-119 Revised, Federal Participation in the Development and Use of Voluntary Consensus Standards and in Conformity Assessment Activities (1998), *available at* http://www.whitehouse.gov/omb/circulars/a119/a119.html.
64. *See* Jody Freeman, Private Parties, Public Functions and the New Administrative Law, 52 Admin. L. Rev. 813, 816–19 (2000); Jody Freeman, The Private Role in Public Governance, 75 N.Y.U. L. Rev. 543, 556–64 (2000).
65. 2000 Biennial Regulatory Review of Part 68, 15 FCC Rcd. at 24,957.
66. For a discussion of this decision, see Philip J. Weiser, Internet Governance, Standard Setting, and Self-Regulation, 28 N. Ky. L. Rev. 822 (2001).

in and of themselves, despite being incorporated into the 1934 Act. Principal examples of such amendments are the Cable Communications Policy Act of 1984,[67] the Cable Television Consumer Protection and Competition Act of 1992,[68] and the Telecommunications Act of 1996,[69] all of which amended (among other things) scattered sections of 47 U.S.C.—the location of the 1934 Act. In this book, we will often refer to those laws by their own names, but readers should understand that, as a technical matter, they are statutory amendments to the 1934 Act.

§ 2.F.1. The Structure of the 1934 Act

The 1934 Act is codified at Title 47 of the United States Code and, in turn, divided into seven subchapters or "Titles" of its own. Titles I, IV, V, and VII set forth general provisions that relate either to the FCC itself or to issues that transcend any particular industry sector or category of service. Title I,[70] for example, sets forth general provisions pertaining to the structure, jurisdiction, and operation of the Federal Communications Commission. That title, as we discuss below, plays a special role as it provides the FCC with ancillary jurisdiction authority to act in a "common law-like" fashion to regulate new technologies. Titles IV[71] and V,[72] by contrast, address solely procedural matters, with the former focusing on enforcement jurisdiction and requirements for administrative proceedings and the latter focusing on penalties and forfeitures for violation of regulations under the Act. Title VII of the Act,[73] which is entitled "Miscellaneous Provisions," covers issues ranging from the President's emergency powers in this area to closed captioning of video programming. Titles II, III, and VI—the subchapters with which this book will be primarily concerned—differ in that they prescribe distinct sets of regulation for ostensibly distinct categories of services, service providers, and technologies.

Overall, the structure of the Act follows the deceptively simple outlines of the telecommunications industry as Congress found it in 1934. Under Title II of the Act were the "natural monopolies"—the telephone and telegraph companies that transmitted information by wire, operated as common carriers, and should therefore, it was assumed, be subject to classic public utility regulation. As such, Title II envisioned a role for the FCC in regulating the entry, rates, and services of common carriers of telephonic communications (especially Bell); auditing their books; and assuring that they provided nondiscriminatory access to all.

The provisions of Title II cover a vast number of topics in the regulation of telecommunications—from rates, competition, and network interconnection to harassing phone calls, services for the disabled, and the regulation of payphones. Although neither Title II nor any other subchapter of the Communications Act explicitly regulates the Internet, Title II contains provisions that affect network infrastructure essential to the Internet. (The FCC has also regulated aspects of the Internet under its Title I authority.) We will

---

67. Cable Communications Policy Act of 1984, Pub. L. No. 98-549, 98 Stat. 2779 (codified as amended in scattered sections of 15, 18, 46, 47, and 50 U.S.C.).
68. Cable Television Consumer Protection and Competition Act of 1992, Pub. L. No. 102-385, 106 Stat. 1460 (codified as amended in scattered sections of 47 U.S.C.).
69. Telecommunications Act of 1996, Pub. L. No. 104-104, 110 Stat. 56 (codified as amended at 47 U.S.C. § 151 *et seq.*).
70. 47 U.S.C. §§ 151–161.
71. *Id.* §§ 401–416.
72. *Id.* §§ 501–510.
73. *Id.* §§ 601–621.

examine many aspects of regulation under Title II (especially Title II as it was amended by the Telecommunications Act of 1996) in Chapters Six and Seven of this book. The relation of Title II to the Internet will be discussed in Chapter Fourteen.

Title III of the Act[74] establishes the regulatory regime for radio spectrum and broadcast services. In 1934, this principally involved overseeing the AM radio stations that were gaining popularity throughout the country and just beginning to link up into networks. A notable role for the FCC was to ensure that these stations did not interfere with each other. However, it was not long before the FCC began to adopt other regulations related to broadcasting, including ones addressing the content of the transmissions themselves. Title III, too, covers substantial ground, ranging from the licensing of spectrum and construction of radio facilities to more particular regulation of the content of broadcast communications. The most important aspects of Title III for our purposes are those that involve the allocation of spectrum and those that impose restrictions and conditions on the use of that spectrum. We address the many interesting issues arising under Title III in Chapters Three through Five and Fifteen.

Under the Communications Act, broadcasters were not to be regulated as (and indeed did not behave as) common carriers. Rather, broadcasters offered selected programs to appeal to listeners and then sold commercial time to advertisers who thereby gained access to those listeners. Title III focused on this commercial radio phenomenon, and thus it portrays a Commission particularly concerned with the licensing process—deciding who should be licensed to broadcast, on what frequencies, and in which communities. Notably, in contrast to Title II, Title III says nothing about controlling rates or providing equal access to broadcast stations.

Finally, Title VI[75] addresses "cable services" and, obviously, governs the regulation of cable television as well as many other services provided over the cable infrastructure. Some of the provisions here also extend either implicitly or explicitly to other multi-channel video programming distribution (MVPD) systems such as direct broadcast satellite service and video services delivered over the telephone network. The current Title VI was not, of course, part of the original 1934 Act because cable service did not then exist. It was added over time through amendments to the Act, notably in the 1984 and 1992 Cable Acts mentioned above.[76] (Before that time, the FCC relied on its Title I authority to regulate cable television.) We examine the regulation of cable television and related MVPD services in Chapters Eight through Ten.

Today, of course, some firms act like broadcasters but transmit by wire (e.g., cable television), while other firms act like common carriers but transmit through the airwaves (e.g., mobile telephone). As noted above, the phenomenon of providing similar services based on different technologies—say, providing telephone service both by wire and by air—is known as "technological convergence." In the wake of technological convergence, different titles of the Act may thus apply to a single service, as in the case for mobile telephony where, for example, spectrum licensing provisions from Title III and network

---

74. *Id.* §§ 301–399B.
75. *Id.* §§ 521–573.
76. For most of the provisions of the 1934 Act, a reference to a section "of the Communications Act" corresponds to its location in 47 U.S.C. So, for example, § 201 of the Communications Act is codified at 47 U.S.C. § 201. This is not true of Title I (too old) or Title VI (too new). For Title I, § 1 of the Communications Act is codified at 47 U.S.C. § 151, § 2 is codified at 47 U.S.C. § 152, and so on. For Title VI, § 601 of the Communications Act is codified at 47 U.S.C. § 521, § 602 of the Communications Act is codified at 47 U.S.C. § 522, and so on.

interconnection provisions from Title II are both relevant. And a single title of the Act may apply to multiple and very different services, as is plainly the case for Title III which, as we just pointed out, applies both to broadcast television and to cellular telephony. Moreover, in a classic case of technological convergence, networks that were originally used for one kind of service (e.g., video) are now increasingly capable of delivering multiple kinds of services (e.g., video and high-speed data transmission). In short, technological changes—and the Internet in particular, which is a powerful force driving technological convergence—have ensured that the concepts of "broadcaster" and "common carrier" no longer have the unambiguous, objective implications assumed by Congress in 1934.

§ 2.F.2. Other Relevant Statutes and Agencies

To be sure, the Communications Act of 1934 (including its amendments) is not the only statute relevant to the regulation of U.S. telecommunications. As we will see, antitrust and copyright laws have also been very important. The Copyright Act of 1976[77] specifically created compulsory licenses that allow cable operators to retransmit copyrighted content at regulated rates. And the Satellite Home Viewer Improvement Act of 1999[78] amended the Copyright Act to recognize a similar, but not quite identical, compulsory license for providers of direct broadcast satellite service. These provisions of the Copyright Act are considered in Chapter Nine. Similarly, one of the most important events in the history of American telecommunications—the breakup of the Bell Telephone System in 1984—resulted not from anything in the 1934 Act, but from an antitrust suit under the Sherman Act.[79] That suit is considered in significant detail in Chapter Six.

Just as the Communications Act is not the only law relevant for telecommunications in the United States, the FCC is not the only relevant federal agency or authority. The case that broke up Bell was brought by the Antitrust Division of the U.S. Department of Justice (although the FCC was involved). Since 1996, the Department of Justice also has had primary responsibility for reviewing mergers and acquisitions in all sectors of the communications industry. The respective roles of the antitrust agencies and the FCC in telecom mergers will be discussed in Chapter Eleven.

In addition, another executive branch entity, the National Telecommunications and Information Administration (NTIA), located within the Department of Commerce, plays two important roles. First, NTIA and the FCC together determine what parts of the electromagnetic spectrum will be reserved for federal government use;[80] NTIA then manages all the spectrum assigned to the government. In discharging these responsibilities, NTIA relies heavily on advice from the Interdepartment Radio Advisory Committee, which is composed of representatives from the various federal agencies that use the spectrum extensively. Second, NTIA bears principal responsibility for determining presidential policy on telecommunication issues. To this end, NTIA has a substantial research staff and frequently submits comments on major FCC policymaking proceedings.

The above agencies operate within the United States, but one international entity bears mention. Radio waves do not respect geopolitical boundaries, so it is necessary for spec-

---

77. Copyright Act of 1976, Pub. L. No. 94-553, 90 Stat. 2541 (codified as amended in scattered sections of 2, 15, 17, 18, 26, 28, 39, and 44 U.S.C.).
78. Satellite Home Viewer Improvement Act of 1999, Pub. L. 106-113, 113 Stat. 1501 (codified as amended in scattered sections of 17 and 47 U.S.C.).
79. Sherman Act of 1890, ch. 647, 26 Stat. 209 (codified at 15 U.S.C. §§ 1–7).
80. *See* 47 U.S.C. § 902.

trum allocation in the United States to conform to rules established by the International Telecommunications Union (ITU), an organization established by treaty. Particularly for terrestrial transmission of radio waves, ITU regulations are typically not very confining. Usually, within any range of the spectrum, international standards permit a wide variety of uses. Further, international law does not restrict any spectrum usage within a country so long as that use does not radiate into other countries.

While it is important to note the role of other governmental agencies and departments in regulating telecommunications, the FCC has the overwhelming share of authority in this domain. So, while other regulatory or enforcement entities will enter into the discussions in this book, our principal focus will be on the FCC and its activities.

§ 2.F.3. FCC Discretion and Its Constraints

The Commission enjoys considerable discretion when it comes to guiding spectrum policy. Indeed, section 303 of the Communications Act of 1934 broadly states:

Except as otherwise provided in this chapter, the Commission from time to time, as public convenience, interest, or necessity requires, shall—

(a) Classify radio stations;

(b) Prescribe the nature of the services to be rendered by each class of licensed stations and each station within any class;

(c) Assign bands of frequencies to the various classes of stations, and assign frequencies for each individual station and determine the power which each station shall use and the time during which it may operate;

(f) Make such regulations not inconsistent with law as it may deem necessary to prevent interference between stations; [and]

(r) Make such rules and regulations and prescribe such restrictions and conditions, not inconsistent with law, as may be necessary to carry out the provisions of this chapter, or any international radio or wire communications treaty or convention.

This might sound like an enormous degree of discretion—and it is—but, in practice, there are constraints. First, courts have interpreted the "public interest, convenience, or necessity"[81] as itself imposing some limitations on the FCC; indeed, they had to in order to find the agency constitutional, as otherwise this would have been an unconstitutional delegation of the legislative power to an entity outside the legislative branch.[82]

Second, Congress can, and often does, give the FCC more specific mandates in particular contexts, such as legislation enacted in the 1990s requiring that spectrum be assigned via auction (which we discuss in Chapter Five). Third, other statutes—most

---

81. Note that this formulation, from 47 U.S.C. § 307(c)(1), differs from the one quoted above and refers particularly to broadcasting license renewals.
82. This issue was directly addressed in NBC v. United States, 319 U.S. 190 (1943), in which the Supreme Court rejected the argument that "public interest, convenience, or necessity" was unconstitutionally broad. The Court concluded that "the public interest, convenience, or necessity [is] a criterion which is as concrete as the complicated factors for judgment in such a field of delegated authority permit" and that the terms do not convey unlimited powers to the FCC, as they indicate that the FCC should be guided by, for example, "the ability of the licensee to render the best practicable service to the community reached by his broadcasts." *Id.* at 216 (citations omitted) (internal quotation marks omitted).

notably the Administrative Procedure Act[83]—impose additional constraints on agency actions and give individuals the right to sue the agency if it runs afoul of these requirements. So, for example, the FCC is required to follow certain rulemaking procedures that, among other things, give the public ample opportunity to comment on proposed regulations. The Government in the Sunshine Act similarly prohibits three or more Commissioners from deliberating on Commission business unless they announce the meeting seven days in advance and hold the meeting in public.[84] Fourth and finally, the political branches can exercise control over the agency via ad hoc levers, such as reducing the FCC's budget, refusing to confirm newly appointed commissioners, or subjecting FCC actions to intensive public hearings and debate.

The rules governing suits against the FCC are, by and large, the same as those employed more generally in administrative law. This means that most agency final actions (whether rulemakings or adjudications), and some decisions not to act, can be appealed to a federal court. By statute, the United States Court of Appeals for the District of Columbia Circuit has exclusive jurisdiction to hear challenges to most licensing decisions made by the FCC.[85] Almost all other final FCC actions (including, notably, rulemaking proceedings) can be challenged in any United States Court of Appeals,[86] though a disproportionate share are heard by the appeals court in the District of Columbia, where the FCC is located.

Most agency findings of fact, exercises of discretion, and policy judgments are subject to "arbitrary and capricious" review, under the catchall provision of the Administrative Procedure Act that empowers courts to "set aside agency action, findings, and conclusions found to be ... arbitrary, capricious, an abuse of discretion, or otherwise not in accordance with law."[87] This is fairly lenient review, in which the court will inquire whether the agency based its decision on substantial evidence, considered arguments on the opposite side, and explained the basis of its decision. The courts do not (or at least are not supposed to) substitute their judgments on the merits for those of the agency; such decisions would defeat the purpose of having an expert agency in the first place.

Legal interpretations made by the agency are subject to a slightly different form of review. When, as is usually the case, the Commission makes such interpretations in a rulemaking, they are subject to *Chevron* analysis. Chevron U.S.A. Inc. v. Natural Resources Defense Council, Inc., 467 U.S. 837 (1984). Under *Chevron*, the court first determines "whether Congress has directly spoken to the precise question at issue. If the intent of Congress is clear, that is the end of the matter," and there will be no deference to the agency's determination. *Id.* at 842–43. But "if the statute is silent or ambiguous with respect to the specific issue, the question for the court is whether the agency's answer is based on a permissible construction of the statute," *id.* at 843, which entails quite considerable deference to the agency. If the Commission makes a legal interpretation in a more informal context (such as an informal adjudication), then the deference accorded by a federal court will "'depend upon the thoroughness evident in its consideration, the

---

83. Administrative Procedure Act, Pub. L. No. 79-404, 60 Stat. 237 (1946) (codified as amended in scattered sections of 5 U.S.C.) (establishing processes and standards for agency decisionmaking as well as standards for judicial review of agency decisions).

84. Government in the Sunshine Act, Pub. L. No. 94-409, 90 Stat. 1241 (1976) (codified as amended at 5 U.S.C. §552b).

85. *See* 47 U.S.C. §402(b).

86. *See id.* §402(a); 28 U.S.C. §2342(1).

87. 5 U.S.C. §706(2).

validity of its reasoning, its consistency with earlier and later pronouncements, and all those factors which give it power to persuade, if lacking power to control.'"[88]

Suits challenging major FCC actions are frequently filed, and sometimes they meet with success. A sizable percentage of the judicial opinions excerpted in this book, in fact, were brought as challenges to FCC rulemakings.

---

88. United States v. Mead Corp., 533 U.S. 218, 228 (2001) (quoting Skidmore v. Swift & Co., 323 U.S. 134, 140 (1944)).

PART ONE
SPECTRUM

Chapter Three

Regulating the Spectrum

Introduction

Section 301 of the Communications Act of 1934 announces that the federal government controls the spectrum and that the government will permit "the use of such channels, but not the ownership thereof, by persons for limited periods of time, under licenses granted by Federal authority." For most readers, the fact that the federal government regulates the "airwaves" is at once familiar and alien.[1] It is familiar in the sense that we have heard it many times. News articles regularly refer to the Federal Communications Commission and its decisions about whether a new cell phone service will be offered in a given geographic region or whether a television broadcaster will be fined for airing a naughty word. It is alien, however, in that we rarely pause in our daily lives to think about what we mean when we say that information is traveling over the airwaves, let alone to puzzle about why government regulation of the spectrum is arguably appropriate.

Thus, in this chapter, we attempt to lay this groundwork. We begin with a quick primer on the concept of spectrum. As we have already hinted, many technologies transmit information over the airwaves. It turns out that these technologies distinguish themselves by transmitting information at different frequencies (or wavelengths), and the radio spectrum (often simply called "the spectrum") is the term for the full range of frequencies at which information can be transmitted through the air.[2] The purpose of this primer is not to simulate a master class for engineers or physicists. Rather, the idea is to explain the technological context for the regulatory and policy materials that follow.

Next, we briefly survey the early history of spectrum regulation. This history provides an important backdrop, introducing readers to the events that first focused public attention on the various regulatory issues that are the concern of this book. We then consider several possible rationales for spectrum regulation. We focus primarily on the classic argument that spectrum must be regulated because it is a scarce resource. We also introduce the hypothesis that broadcast regulation is necessary to counteract the influence of advertisers. After that, we provide a brief overview of the steps entailed in the FCC's regulation of the spectrum. Finally, we discuss the regulatory tradeoffs entailed in allotting licenses.

---

1. Technically speaking, radio waves can travel in free space where there is no air. Most popular accounts, however, refer to radio waves as using "airwaves," and we will use this convention as well.
2. The "radio spectrum" is a subset of the larger electromagnetic spectrum, which includes gamma rays, ultraviolet waves, and other forms of electromagnetic radiation.

§ 3.A. Defining Spectrum

There are many ways to communicate at a distance. Young children coordinate from afar by shouting back and forth. Drivers on the road exchange information by using turn signals and other visual cues. Ships once communicated through semaphore flags.

Broadcast technologies like radio and television allow individuals to communicate at a distance using radio waves that travel unfettered through the air. This is no small trick. The telegraph used wires to connect people in one city to people in another. The postal service originally carried notes by horseback and wagon. But the information transmitted through broadcast technology requires no carrying case, no dedicated path, and no container.

For the purposes of understanding telecommunications regulation, readers do not need detailed knowledge of exactly how radio-based communication works. Nonetheless, it is helpful to know a few details about how radio waves carry information from place to place.

§ 3.A.1. Characteristics of Radio Waves

Modern communications technologies seem infinitely more advanced than smoke signals, but they have much in common: each transmits information to a receiver that processes the information. In this way, each can very quickly send information over a reasonably long distance. Employing telecommunications technologies rather than smoke signals means that more information can be packed into a second's worth of transmission and that the information can be transmitted over a longer distance. But, in essence, cellular telephony and satellite television are just the latest in an evolving technology for extending the speed and reach of information transmission.

One important characteristic of a radio wave is its frequency. In normal usage, the word "frequency" refers to the number of times a given event repeats during a specific period. In telecommunications, the word has a similar meaning. Radio waves typically look a lot like any other wave—they start at zero, then move up and down in the pattern of a sine wave before returning to zero. Each movement from zero up to the crest, back through zero and down to the trough, and back up to zero again is a cycle. The unit of measurement of frequency is called the "hertz." A one-hertz (Hz) wave completes one cycle every second, and a one-kilohertz (kHz) wave accomplishes one thousand cycles in that same amount of time. The physical distance between the crests of each wave constitutes the wavelength, and this distance decreases as the frequency increases. Very long waves thus have very low frequencies because they repeat infrequently. Short waves have high frequencies because they recur more often.

For our purposes, we will use the term "spectrum" to refer to the range of radio wavelengths (i.e., frequencies) currently suitable for wireless transmission. Unsurprisingly, the usable spectrum—like chemistry's periodic table—has expanded substantially during the past 100 years. For example, when the FCC was first established in 1934, spectrum capacity was less than 300 megahertz (MHz), which is to say less than 300 million hertz. That increased by more than a factor of 100 by the end of World War II, to 40 gigahertz (GHz), or 40 billion hertz, and by a factor of 1000 by the early 21st century (to above 300 GHz).

Different frequencies of radio waves have somewhat different characteristics. Broadcasts at the very lowest frequencies require very large antennas because exceedingly long waves must be propagated. Radio waves in the medium frequency (300–3000 kHz), which include AM radio broadcasts, are reflected back to earth by the ionosphere. This effect occurs particularly at night, because during the day incoming solar radiation has the effect of lowering the ionosphere, limiting the distance to which radio waves can be reflected. At night, the lack of sunlight results in a higher ionosphere, thus considerably extending the reach of many of these signals.[3] Transmissions in the very high frequency (VHF) and ultra high frequency (UHF) ranges (30–300 MHz and 300–3000 MHz, respectively) are not reflected back to earth and so can usually be captured clearly only by a receiver that is within the transmitting antenna's line of sight. Above UHF, which includes the super high and extremely high frequencies (3–30 GHz and 30–300 GHz, respectively), the wavelengths are so small that they can be packed into narrow focused beams of electromagnetic radiation, like those employed in microwave and radar.

The different characteristics of the various frequencies are important to note, but there is no invariable requirement that a particular service use only an exact set of frequencies. Every service can operate on more than one set of frequencies, and every frequency is suitable for more than one service. Radio broadcasting, for example, takes place all the way from 535 kHz to 108 MHz. And cordless landline telephones have operated at Commission-approved frequencies ranging from 1.7 MHz to 5.8 GHz (which is 5800 MHz).

That said, to generate a good quality signal for a given service, some bands are likely to be more desirable than others. Radio propagation characteristics, for instance, make certain frequency ranges more suitable for particular purposes than others. The presence of other services on nearby (or the same) frequencies also might matter. For example, a service within one set of frequencies can create spillover effects that would render neighboring frequencies unsuitable for some services (say, broadcast television) but satisfactory for another service (say, satellite television)

Separate from its location in the spectrum (frequency), the extent of the spectrum that a signal occupies (bandwidth) is also often very important. More bandwidth means more capacity for data transmission. The preferred amount of bandwidth for a particular use depends on the amount and types of information that must be impressed on the radio waves. For example, much more bandwidth is required to carry a television signal than to carry the human voice. Indeed, because television signals contain an audio component, the point is axiomatic. The preferred amount of bandwidth also depends on the type of technology being employed. The same information subjected to traditional analog transmission methods will require more bandwidth than if transmitted using digital technology, which allows for the compression of the information as a means of economizing on bandwidth. Digital compression works by eliminating either redundant information (lossless) or a small amount of relevant information (lossy). Information that is compressed in a lossy manner (for instance, songs encoded in MP3 format) may therefore have a lower quality than the original. However, the amount of information removed is usually small enough to leave an adequate representation.

In discussing signal propagation thus far, we have held constant one critical part of the equation: the sophistication of the receiver. In reality, however, the capability of receivers (and "filtering" technology) makes a huge difference. In a world of unsophisticated receivers, signals in the same frequency band at the same time are very likely to cancel each other out because the receiver cannot focus on particular types of signals. The typical receiver for broadcast TV, for example, does not differentiate between dif-

---

3. This also means that, for signals at these frequencies, the problem of interference is greater at night than during the day.

ferent types of transmissions within a particular channel (i.e., set of frequencies). But this limited receiver technology is not innate. Indeed, in certain cases, receiver systems are becoming more and more sophisticated and thus more able to distinguish the signal from the noise. Consequently, the use of spectrum, including for "guard bands" that constitute a form of interference protection, is often traded off against more sophisticated receiver systems that can limit the degree of interference from rival transmissions.

§ 3.A.2. Transmitting Through the Air

When transmitting through the air, the radio waves can be radiated in all directions or to only a single point. Conventional broadcast television stations radiate in all directions. A series of microwave transmitters linked together into a 2000-mile hookup, by contrast, each radiate only to a given area. The direction and characteristic of the radiated signal is determined by the size, shape, and direction of the transmitting antenna. For example, television stations allow their signals to travel in all directions because their viewers are typically scattered throughout a geographic region. Cell phone transmissions similarly radiate, this time in order to make it possible for communication to occur between a moving caller and a stationary cellular tower. Omnidirectional antennas similarly allow dispatchers and taxi drivers to converse via radio waves, even though the taxi drivers are constantly changing their geographic positions.

Whether transmitted through wire or air, a signal can be sent or radiated at varying degrees of power. Compare the transmitter in a mobile phone to the broadcast transmitter for a major metropolitan TV station. The amount of transmission power affects both the distance over which the signal can be transmitted and the signal's clarity at its reception point.

A telecommunications system can be designed so that recipients are also transmitters. Where this two-way communication occurs, the system is usually termed interactive. Cell phone systems are interactive because one can both receive and transmit voice information through the handset. By contrast, conventional television broadcast systems are not interactive.

§ 3.A.3. Transmitting Using Wires

Just as radio waves can propagate through the air, they also can propagate down a wire. Wire is just a means of guiding electromagnetic signals. With excellent shielding (as with coaxial cable), a wire can convey over a distance a very large range of frequencies. For telecommunications, then, the medium of transmission can be a wire or the airwaves—and in this text we ultimately will think about both wireline technologies, like landline telephony and cable television, and wireless ones, like broadcast and satellite television, cellular telephony, and Wi-Fi internet.

Historically, the wire used most often by consumers was the unshielded twisted pair copper wires conventionally used by local telephone companies. The advantage of such wires is that they are cheap and easy to splice. One disadvantage is that, because they are unshielded, they are subject to interference from nearby wires. This is because every device that generates radio frequency energy during the course of its operation (e.g., light switches, DVRs, garage door openers) emits radio frequency energy that can interact with other nearby electric devices. The effect can be mitigated with shielding from insulators. However, as the name implies, unshielded wires have little to no insulation and are thus more susceptible to interference from nearby devices. Their bigger disadvantage, though, flows from the fact that different kinds of wires have different propagation characteristics—which means that some wires can carry higher frequencies than can others, resulting in greater capacity or bandwidth. Copper wires—at least without the aid of electronics equipment used to create DSL connections—cannot transmit at high frequencies and thus have fairly low bandwidth.

Today, transmitting information by wire at higher bandwidth usually employs one of two technologies. Coaxial cable is a braided metallic cylinder surrounding a wire. The wire carries the radio waves while the cylinder prevents signals from other wires, or outside radiation, from interfering with the signals on the wire. The genius of coaxial cable is that the outside cylinder offers superior noise suppression while the braiding allows the cable to remain flexible. Moreover, the wire inside has greater capacity than do conventional unshielded twisted pair copper wires. Fiber optic cable, a technology that entered widespread use in the 1980s, uses light traveling through optical fiber made of very thin glass to transmit information. It has even greater bandwidth than coaxial cable. Fiber optic cable forms the bulk of the long distance telephone network and the Internet backbone. It is particularly well suited for information transmitted at high bandwidth, for transmission over very long distances, and for carrying many signals within one cable. With the increasing demand for bandwidth, fiber optic connections have increasingly been deployed closer to consumers and small organizations. (Large organizations routinely are connected directly to fiber optic cables.)

When information is being transmitted by wire, the system may be designed so that many streams of information are in the wire and the recipient chooses one stream (an example here is cable television) or so that the wire leading directly to the recipient carries less information (landline telephone for many years carried only one conversation at a time). In the latter case, decisions as to what information is sent to the recipient are made further up the wire by specialized computers called switches and routers.

All else equal, the more bandwidth available for a given transmission, the more data can be transmitted. A broader range of frequencies for a given service (say, broadcasting or cell phone service), or for a given signal within that service (say, 6 MHz for a television channel as opposed to 2 MHz), allows for more data to be sent. This is true for wireless and wired communications. Using the same technology, a wire with greater capacity (e.g., optical fiber) can transmit many more video streams than can a wire with less capacity (e.g., copper wire). And a 20 MHz swath of frequency can carry more data than a 5 MHz swath can carry.

§ 3.A.4. Signal Modulation

Earlier we drew the analogy to smoke signals and pointed out that modern telecommunications technologies are not so different from this sort of more primitive communication mechanism. Nonetheless, to progress from smoke signals to wireless radio transmissions required that people learn to use electromagnetic radiation to carry information. Radio waves—waves that today carry sound, pictures, numbers, and other information through the air—are basically sine waves that are generated and modulated by a power source and then transmitted by that power source to a device (the receiver, radio, or TV set) that detects the sine wave and demodulates the signal to extract the information.[4] Today, a perception exists that there are almost countless telecommunications prod-

---

4. To "invent" broadcast radio, then, one had to discover how to modulate the human voice onto radio waves and then to demodulate that information at a receiver. Similarly, television requires the ability to break a picture down into bits of data (millions of points of light).

ucts, markets, and technologies available. Yet virtually all of them are defined simply by the modulation technique and the transmission process they employ. That is, telecommunications technologies, and thus telecommunications markets, are usually defined by the manner in which information is modulated and the means by which that information is later demodulated.

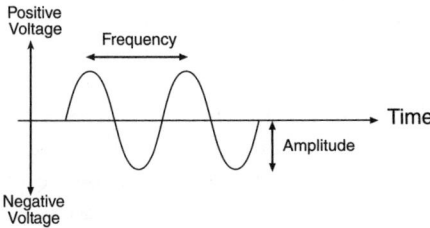

Radio Waves. Radio waves are typically transmitted as sine waves. Two important attributes of the wave are its frequency and its amplitude.

Information can be modulated onto sine waves in one of two principal ways: (1) by varying the waves' strength (called amplitude modulation, or AM) or (2) by varying their frequency (termed frequency modulation, or FM). Amplitude modulation is attractive because it requires less of the available spectrum than does FM; amplitudes can be modulated while keeping frequency constant. The charm of FM, by contrast, is that in FM transmissions all of the electrical power necessary to generate the FM signal can also be employed to transmit it. AM "wastes" some power by investing it in varying amplitude.

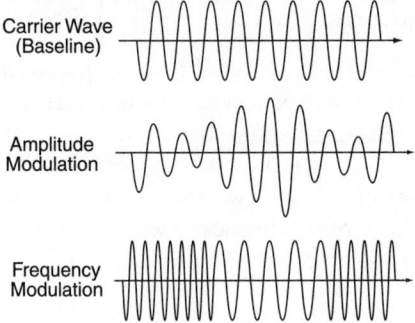

Amplitude and Frequency Modulation. Information can be encoded on sine waves by means of amplitude modulation and also by means of frequency modulation. Compare the AM signal pictured here to the unmodified carrier baseline. Can you see how the amplitude of the AM signal could be used to communicate information? Similarly, compare the FM signal to the carrier baseline. Again, can you see how information might be contained in these patterns?

It admittedly simplifies matters somewhat to describe telecommunication as we have simply as modulating and electronically transmitting information, but most telecommunications technologies and markets are defined by these two characteristics. In analog television, the visual pieces of information (pictures) are amplitude modulated while the audio pieces of information are frequency modulated. Communications satellites are essentially very tall transmitting and receiving antennas. Landline telephone communication is like AM radio in that it requires little spectrum because it transmits only voice information, but it is unlike radio in that it transmits locally by wire, and so it is somewhat easier to exclude people from listening in on the communication and there is less of a problem with congestion.

"Analog" and "digital" are terms frequently employed to describe two ways of transmitting information. Analog transmission employs a continuous signal varying the amplitude or frequency of a sine wave. To transmit a picture by analog signal requires that the carrier wave replicate the information contained in the picture. A digital system encodes and transmits the information in a binary digit — a "bit," for short. The digital transmission of a series of pictures requires only that one send the information that differs from one frame to the next. Digital systems, as noted above, can compress information and be more efficient than analog systems.

Radio transmissions are subject to interference. Consequently, if a device is communicating information by varying its amplitude, other sources of electromagnetic radiation (say, a microwave oven or lightning) might result in the receiver misinterpreting relatively small changes in amplitude. In general, all background sources of interference are referred to as "noise" and any radio system must take into account the possibility that different sources of interference may exist at any given time. Digital systems are more resistant to such distortions creeping into the signal because they need only distinguish between two digital possibilities (a "1" or "0") as opposed to many possible analog signal levels. Relatedly, because digital technology — that is, the use of bits — is the essence of how computers operate, computer processing power can more easily be used in conjunction with digital transmission systems. Indeed, computers can facilitate digital communication by engaging in error checking and other forms of digital processing that improve transmission reliability and quality.

To retrieve information that has been modulated, of course, one needs a receiver that can decode the signal. This can create substantial problems, particularly where different firms or individuals own the modulator and demodulator. For example, the benefits of owning an FM radio transmitter are slight if no one owns an FM radio receiver, and, of course, vice versa. Similarly, an FM radio station cannot take many steps — other than increasing the power level of its transmission — to address interference issues because the receivers used to access its broadcasts are controlled by third parties (i.e., consumer electronics firms, and ultimately consumers).

Similarly, altering the technology employed in a telecommunications system can change the effects it produces. For example, the extent to which a radio signal creates potential interference with other signals is reduced if the signal is not radiated in all directions, but is transmitted only from one point to another or is radiated at less power. The amount of information that can be transmitted through a cable of a certain size can be increased by switching from coaxial to fiber optic cable. The amount of spectrum necessary to transmit a television signal can be reduced if a digital, rather than an analog, signal can be employed. By increasing the power at which a satellite transmits television signals, one can reduce the size of the antenna necessary to receive those signals (and vice versa).

§ 3.A.5. Newer Wireless Technologies

This book will spend a considerable amount of time discussing broadcasting as a quintessential use of the airwaves. This focus reflects the historical significance of broadcasting, which set many of the basic premises of the current regulatory regime for spectrum. It does not, however, reflect either the current technological or economic landscape. As we discuss in Chapter Eight, broadcasting is of decreasing relevance for most television viewers in that they receive TV programming via either cable or satellite connections. And, while broadcast is obviously still an important spectrum use, modern conversations about spectrum policy by necessity focus just as heavily on newer technologies like broadband cellular telephony and Wi-Fi.

The decline of broadcasting as a medium for transmitting television signals reflects an observation made by MIT Media Lab pioneer Nicholas Negroponte. As Negroponte noted, a generation of Americans who grew up watching TV delivered over the airwaves and talking on telephones connected by wires has given way to a generation who watches TV delivered by wire and talks on telephones linked through the air.[5] As Negroponte appreciated, the airwaves are, relatively speaking, not well suited to delivering high bandwidth video signals but are excellent for delivering voice conversations. Moreover, mobility in TV sets has not been a crucial feature (though many people watch video on other mobile devices); by contrast, Americans have learned to love mobile phones, which became more popular than their landline counterparts in the early twenty-first century.

The technology that gave rise to cell phones was invented at Bell Labs in the middle of the twentieth century. The basic technological insight behind the invention was that wireless communications did not need to be broadcast at high power, but rather could be delivered to limited areas at lower power through a "cellular" architecture. The service thus became known as cellular telephony.[6] Cellular telephony services can be narrowband or broadband (that is, they can operate in a narrow swath of frequencies or a broad swath of frequencies). Either way, mobile phone service uses cells and towers, so we will stick to the term that reflects the network's design and thus refer to all forms of mobile narrowband and broadband service as cell phone service.

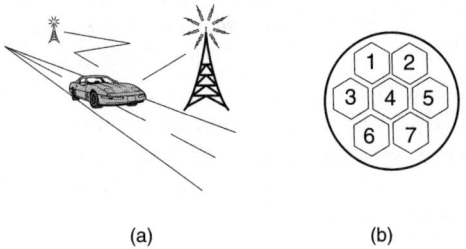

(a) (b)

Cellular Telephony. The panel to the left shows the basic concept: as the portable communications equipment moves away from one receiver, it moves toward another, and thus service is maintained. The panel on the right shows how cells are used to divide a service area into smaller geographic cells. The more cells, the lower the necessary transmission power, and the greater the maximum number of simultaneous users.

As the diagram above indicates, the relevant geographic area ("service area") for cell phone systems is broken into discrete "cells," each of which is served by its own receiving and transmitting equipment. Cell phones, then, can transmit signals at relatively low power, but, because so many cells are established, the transmissions can usually nevertheless be picked up by some nearby cell tower. As the cell phone moves, its signals are picked up by the (new) nearest cell site, and so the cell phone can move from site to site

---

5. Nicholas Negroponte, Wireless Revisited, Wired (Aug. 1997), http://www.global-media.org/neome/docs/PDF's/02%20-%20other/alle%20artikelen%20van%20Negroponte.pdf

6. The FCC classifies all commercially available mobile services in the category of "commercial mobile radio services," or CMRS. *See* 47 C.F.R. § 20.3.

while remaining in constant contact with the telephone network. Indeed, so long as there is a cell tower in the vicinity, that tower will pick up the cell phone's transmission and relay it to its destination.

The modern architecture of cell phone technology took hold in the 1980s and launched what continues to be a revolution in wireless technology. The original systems relied on the basic technology developed in Bell Labs, known as the Advanced Mobile Phone System, or AMPS. The FCC mandated that each licensed provider—and there were two in each geographic area and scores throughout the country—adopt this technology, ensuring that there was one compatible technology throughout the country. Consequently, customers of different systems could use their handset to operate anywhere by "roaming" on systems operated by a firm other than their provider.

In Europe, the European Telecommunications Standards Institute mandated that all providers adopt the same digital second generation system (Global System for Mobile Communications, or GSM). In the United States, by contrast, cellular providers were free to adopt any technology they chose (provided they allowed the system to revert to the analog AMPS standard) and a number of different alternatives emerged. The principal rival to GSM was code division multiple access, or CDMA. This technology takes advantage of a concept known as "spread spectrum," which uses several frequencies at once, managing them by algorithms that can flexibly allocate bandwidth. By contrast, rival systems like GSM divide up transmissions by time (time division multiple access, or TDMA) or by frequency (frequency division multiple access, or FDMA) and are generally not as efficient in terms of the bandwidth they consume. The fourth generation (4G) standard for cellular systems builds on the two technologies and is termed Long Term Evolution, or LTE. In the United States and around the world, carriers have deployed LTE technology to support greater levels of bandwidth for mobile Internet use. LTE uses a variant of FDMA called OFDMA (orthogonal frequency division multiple access) whereby a cell phone makes multiple connections to a cell tower on different frequencies, allowing for data to be transferred at a much faster rate.

The concept of spread spectrum is hardly unique to CDMA. Many wireless local area networks (for example, Wi-Fi systems) similarly rely on this concept to enable wireless modems to operate effectively and, up to a point, dynamically avoid interference with one another. Similarly, the technique of frequency hopping (rapid changing of frequencies during transmission) is often used in spread-spectrum systems, such as the Bluetooth standard that enables data exchanges over short distances.

Another emerging technology is the use of cognitive radio systems. Such systems, which often rely on software-defined radios, continuously monitor which channels are in use and which are not, and switch to unused channels in order to avoid interference. This technology promises to facilitate greater levels of spectrum efficiency. Traditionally, even for CDMA-based networks, radio transmissions operated using a limited number of frequencies. Cognitive radio systems, by contrast, can be engineered to operate over a broad range of frequencies and to opportunistically use available spectrum otherwise left unused.

§ 3.A.6. The Spectrum as a Resource

In almost every case, more than one telecommunications technology can accomplish a given end. Transoceanic cables can substitute for geostationary orbiting satellites. Telephone calls and television signals can be transmitted by wire or over the air. A weak signal can be strengthened by boosting the power at which it is radiated, by using a relay station to capture and retransmit the signal, or by installing more capable receivers that can identify the signal more effectively. In much the same way, coaxial or fiber optic cables will periodically have repeaters that strengthen the signal over long distances. Multichannel packages of television signals can be sent to the home by cable or satellite.

Choosing a telecommunications technology is therefore like choosing virtually any other good. One compares price and quality. For a specific task, some are cheaper, some are faster, and some are more reliable. The distinct advantage of spectrum, for instance, is mobility and the absence of the large infrastructure investment associated with wired systems. Wireline communication, in turn, offers enhanced privacy. Should one write, call, email, or text? Presumably, the choice is made by comparing the costs and benefits of each. Further, as new desires arise, new configurations of telecommunications technology will be developed to create cost-effective ways of satisfying these desires. Cable television wedded the use of wires and radio technology to serve the desires of viewers for more signals of greater clarity. Cellular telephony combined the same technologies to increase accessibility at some cost in clarity and in the ability to exclude unwanted listeners.

The government treats spectrum as if it were a natural resource, one to be allocated for specific uses and assigned to specific users. This is a helpful way to look at spectrum in that it reminds us that spectrum shares many basic properties with other natural resources:

Spectrum can help to create both wealth and value. People are often willing to pay substantial sums for the ability to send or receive large quantities of data quickly and from far away.

Spectrum can be used in varying amounts for the same purpose. To get a television signal from a New York stage to a Los Angeles nightclub, one could use no spectrum (send it via wire, door to door), some spectrum (wire from New York to Los Angeles, but broadcast to the nightclub), or nothing but spectrum (transmit directly from stage to satellite, which transmits, in turn, directly to the nightclub).

Spectrum use is costly in that any spectrum committed to one use can no longer be employed toward a different valuable end. If one person is broadcasting a television signal on channel two in New York, that means someone else cannot use those frequencies for cellular telephony, FM radio, or dispatching ambulances.

Lastly, while the absolute amount of available spectrum is finite, the amount of usable spectrum can be increased with appropriate investments in technology. Not only do improvements in technology add to the range of usable spectrum, but also within any existing range of usable frequencies spectrum capacity can be increased by advances in technology. To pick one notable example, digital compression allows a broadcaster to send much more information over the same amount of spectrum that would otherwise be occupied by an uncompressed analog signal. In short, "[w]ith airwaves, as with other media, the more you spend, the more you can send; it all comes down to engineering and smart management."[7]

§ 3.B. A Brief History of Early Spectrum Regulation[8]

The event that first triggered substantial government interest in regulating the radio spectrum was the sinking of the *Titanic* in 1912. At the time the *Titanic* went down, the only

---

7. Peter Huber, Law and Disorder in Cyberspace 75 (1995).
8. Some of the material below is adopted, with permission, from Thomas Krattenmaker & Lucas A. Powe, Jr., Regulating Broadcast Programming (1994).

significant spectrum regulation in effect was a law passed in 1910 that required passenger ships above a certain size to carry wireless sets.[9] The *Titanic* tragedy suggested, however, that this sort of light-handed regulation was insufficient. Most importantly for our purposes, the law as it stood in 1912 said nothing about the airwaves the equipment used, which led to significant misreporting of information in the days following the accident. For example, congested airwaves caused a message from the ship that picked up *Titanic* survivors to be combined with an unrelated message about a failed oil tanker, the result being an errant report that the *Titanic* was being safely towed to Halifax.[10] Such confusion and misinformation contributed to a sense that it was time to regulate spectrum more significantly.

The sinking of the *Titanic* provided a focal point for action, and so a few months after that tragedy Congress passed the Radio Act of 1912.[11] As Thomas Krattenmaker and Lucas Powe explain in the excerpt below, this would turn out to be a key piece of legislation in that it established several concepts that continue to influence spectrum policy through the present day:

> First, the federal government would control broadcasting. No one could broadcast without a license. Second, the spectrum would be allocated among uses and users. Thus the military obtained excellent wavelengths. Ships were given their own block. And amateurs, those unrecognized stations, were relegated to oblivion. They could listen anywhere along the spectrum, but could transmit only on [what at that time were] technologically unusable short waves. Third, some communication was more important than others, and the government would determine which was which. Distress calls took precedence. Then came the Navy; operators near a military installation had to reduce transmitting power to just one kilowatt. If war came, there was no doubt about military paramountcy. After the military, commercial [use] was next; amateur was last.[12]

A few years later, World War I would reaffirm these priorities and principles. Wireless communication was a military tool during wartime, with the Navy using wireless both to coordinate the fleet in battle and to pass timely information to the troops. Wireless played a significant propaganda role as well. German authorities used friendly wireless operators in the United States to disseminate information from the German perspective, at least until April 1917 when federal authorities seized the handful of wireless stations then in operation (approximately eighty in total) and stopped the German transmissions. Perhaps the war's most significant effect on spectrum policy, however, was the fact that many American soldiers were trained in the use of the wireless. When the war ended, those soldiers returned to civilian life and brought with them an enthusiasm for, and understanding of, wireless broadcast.

One important reason for the early growth of commercial radio broadcasting was that it found a sympathetic champion in its licensor, Secretary of Commerce Herbert Hoover. Hoover remolded the Radio Act of 1912 from its original emphasis on wireless point-to-point telegraphy to one that fostered a wider use of the newly emerging technology of broadcast radio. The Radio Act had created a division among military, commercial (meaning for-profit, such as telegraphy), and amateur uses. Hoover subdivided the commercial category, creating a separate grouping called "broadcasting" to satisfy the needs of the

---

9. Wireless Ship Act, Pub. L. No. 61-262, 36 Stat. 629 (1910).
10. Susan Douglas, Inventing American Broadcasting 1899–1922 at 227 (1987).
11. Pub. L. No. 62-264, 37 Stat. 302 (1912).
12. Krattenmaker & Powe, *supra* note 8, at 6.

thousands of Americans purchasing receiving sets.[13] True amateurs were forced to use undesirable wavelengths under 200 meters, but the "more powerful and sophisticated amateur stations" were relicensed under this new "commercial" category and authorized to use 360 meters (833.3 kHz).[14] "Broadcasting" (propagating a signal for all to receive) thus became a permissible commercial venture, just as telegraphy (transmitting personal messages from point to point) had been for some time.

As both champion of the new industry and the official in charge of licensing in the 1920s, Hoover now faced a problem that would plague him and the industry throughout the early years: signal interference. The periodical Radio Broadcast editorialized in both October and November of 1921 about the crowding of the air and its "resulting interference of signals between the several stations, which made listening no pleasure."[15]

In 1922 Hoover convened the first of four National Radio Conferences. He said that broadcasting used "a great national asset" (the spectrum) and believed "it becomes of primary public interest to say who is to do the broadcasting, under what circumstances, and with what type of material."[16] At its end, the conferees—broadcasters, manufacturers, and a handful of other important players—unanimously resolved: "It is the sense of the conference that radio communication is a public utility and as such should be regulated and controlled by the federal government in the public interest."[17]

When Congress did not act, Hoover took action on his own. In December 1922, Hoover expanded the frequencies available for commercial broadcasting from enough to support two stations per city to three and reassigned broadcasters to these frequencies.[18] To prevent further congestion resulting from added applications in the expanding industry, he would either deny applications or require some form of time sharing between broadcasters. Hoover's policies, however, were undermined two months after they were announced. In Hoover v. Intercity Radio Co., 286 F. 1003 (D.C. Cir. 1923), the court held that Hoover had the discretion under the Radio Act to select a frequency and set the hours of use in order to minimize interference but that he lacked discretion to deny any application for a license.

Despite *Intercity Radio*, Hoover reallocated broadcasters' frequencies, this time squarely contrary to the express language of the Radio Act. He moved commercial users into spectrum reserved for government. The Navy was also moved from its statutory spectrum space but voiced no objections because the move necessitated purchasing new and better equipment.[19] Broadcasters were placed between 550 and 1365 kHz. In an article entitled "Secretary Hoover Acts," Radio Broadcast noted that the broadcast interference problem had been "suddenly remedied" without passage of any legislation.[20]

By the end of 1925, 578 stations were broadcasting.[21] And, as the industry matured, stations began to broadcast for longer hours and with increased power, resulting in wide-

---

13. Erik Barnouw, A Tower in Babel 91 (1966).
14. Douglas, *supra* note 10, at 301.
15. Lucas A. Powe, Jr., American Broadcasting and the First Amendment 55 (1987).
16. Radio Regulation Conference Opens in Washington, 79 Electrical World 446, 447 (March 4, 1922) (quoting Hoover's February 27, 1922, speech to the first National Radio Conference).
17. Urges Federal Rule of Radiophones, 82 Telephony 23, 23 (March 18, 1922) (quoting resolution from the first National Radio Conference).
18. Philip T. Rosen, The Modern Stentors: Radio Broadcasting and the Federal Government 1920–1934, at 54 (1980).
19. *Id.* at 58.
20. Quoted in *id.* at 57.
21. Powe, *supra* note 15, at 58.

spread interference. Hoover first addressed this problem by urging stations to work out time-sharing agreements or to agree to have one station buy the other's license. Often these measures worked; in some cases, however, they did not. In Cincinnati, two stations on the same frequency could not find a satisfactory solution and simply broadcasted simultaneously for weeks.[22] When private parties could not agree, Hoover stepped in. Sometimes, he ordered time sharing. Other times, he demonstrated how excruciatingly slow the application process for new licenses could be.[23] Eventually, after the fourth National Radio Conference in November 1925, Hoover announced that no more applications (including those for increased power) would be granted.[24]

Hoover's approach came under pressure in December 1925 when the Chicago-based Zenith Corporation jumped from 930 kHz to 910 kHz for its Chicago broadcasts. Hoover had assigned Zenith 930 kHz. But, because this was the same frequency that General Electric had previously obtained in Denver, Hoover had limited Zenith to Thursdays between 10 p.m. and midnight, and only if GE chose not to broadcast then. Finding the limitations unacceptable, Zenith bolted for clearer air at 910 kHz, a Canadian frequency, ceded by treaty.[25] When Hoover, now without options, moved against Zenith, his whole regulatory house of cards collapsed. The federal district judge read the Radio Act even more narrowly than the D.C. Circuit had in *Intercity Radio*;[26] Hoover's duty was to license, not to impose restrictions on a station's frequency, power, or hours of operation.[27] He could encourage time sharing, but imposing it was beyond his power.

Hoover did not appeal; instead he arranged for the acting attorney general to state that the *Zenith* opinion was correct.[28] The next day Hoover issued a statement abandoning his efforts to regulate radio and urging that the stations undertake self-regulation.[29] The result of this capitulation, which Hoover knew was inevitable, was chaos.

Louis Caldwell, the first general counsel of the Federal Radio Commission, described the six months following *Zenith*: "Nearly 200 new broadcasting stations crowded into channels already congested with about 550 stations. Existing stations 'jumped' their waves and increased their power at will; reception was practically ruined for the listening public, and anarchy reigned in the realm of radio."[30] As the Supreme Court subsequently noted, "[t]he result was confusion and chaos. With everybody on the air, nobody could be heard."[31]

As we noted in Chapter Two, the Radio Act of 1927 responded to the perceived chaos by declaring that there could be no private ownership of the airwaves; they were public and use could only occur with the government's permission. That permission, in the form of a license, would be granted without charge, but for no more than three years.

Congress knew that these licenses could not be granted to all comers. Thus, unlike the old Radio Act, the 1927 Act gave the licensor guidance as to which applications should prevail. Any number of standards was possible: for example, first come, first served; a lottery; or an auction. Congress, however, had determined that the license should be free,

---

22. *Id.* at 59.
23. Thomas W. Hazlett, The Rationality of Broadcast Regulation, 33 J.L. & Econ. 133, 146 (1990).
24. Rosen, *supra* note 18, at 79–80.
25. Powe, *supra* note 15, at 59–60.
26. United States v. Zenith Radio Corp., 12 F.2d 614 (N.D. Ill. 1926).
27. NBC v. United States, 319 U.S. 190, 212 (1943).
28. Fed. Reg. of Radio Broad., 35 Op. Att'y Gen. 126 (1926).
29. NBC v. United States, 319 U.S. at 212.
30. Louis Caldwell, Clearing the Ether's Traffic Jam, Nation's Business, Nov. 1929, at 34–35.
31. NBC v. United States, 319 U.S. at 212.

so the idea of an auction was out. Adopting the idea that Hoover had articulated at the first National Radio Conference, Congress instead required licensees to render public service in exchange for the privilege of using the now federally owned spectrum. Licenses would be granted according to the needs of the "public interest, convenience, or necessity"—a standard already in use in the public utilities and transportation areas.[32]

This background reveals that a central feature of the 1927 Radio Act was its deliberate choice to preclude private ownership of spectrum rights while licensing those rights for brief periods to private users free of charge. Nothing in the nature of broadcasting or the electromagnetic spectrum made that choice inevitable. However, no other alternatives were seriously considered. Senator Clarence Dill stated that "the one principle regarding radio that must always be adhered to, as basic and fundamental, is that government must always retain complete and absolute control of the right to use the air."[33] A contemporaneous analysis in the Yale Law Journal stated that the idea "that the government 'owns the ether'... was an *idée fixe* in the debates of Congress."[34] Enacting this idea meant that administrators would parcel out, among competing technologies, permitted uses of the spectrum. Administrators also would select, from among competing applicants, which subset would become spectrum licensees. In short, government ownership meant government control—a point probably not lost on lawmakers of the time.

Congress deferred most issues to the future, of course, choosing the relatively amorphous public interest standard as a codification of whatever standards would ultimately be applied. This was probably a welcome result from Hoover's perspective. Hoover had always understood that there would be some sort of amorphous quid pro quo for licensing: "It becomes of primary public interest to say who is to do the broadcasting, under what circumstances, and with what type of material."[35] And in broadcast—as distinct from comparable regulations applicable to transportation or public utilities—that public interest quid pro quo would determine not only the issues of the need for service and who would provide it, but also the somewhat novel issue of what the service itself would be.

The broadcast establishment, which accurately assumed that regulation would prefer its interests to those of the marginal stations and potential entrants, fully concurred in a public interest regulatory scheme. Each National Radio Conference endorsed Hoover's program. When Hoover, in 1925, stated that "we can surely agree that no one can raise a cry of deprivation of free speech if he is compelled to prove that there is something more than naked commercial selfishness in his purpose,"[36] the National Association of Broadcasters agreed: "The test of the broadcasting privilege [must] be based on the needs of the public."[37]

House sponsor Wallace White of Maine echoed the point after House passage of the Act. Under the Radio Act of 1912, an individual could "demand a license whether he will render service to the public thereunder or not." No longer. One of the "great advantages" of the 1927 Act is the requirement of service to the public.[38] As his Senate counterpart,

---

32. Ch. 169, 44 Stat. 1167 (1927) (repealed 1934).
33. Clarence Dill, A Traffic Cop for the Air, 75 Review of Reviews 181, 184 (1927).
34. Note, Federal Control of Radio Broadcasting, 39 Yale L.J. 245, 250 (1929).
35. Speech to first National Radio Conference, quoted in Daniel E. Garvey, Secretary Hoover and the Quest for Broadcast Regulation, 3 Journalism History No. 3 at 67 (1976).
36. Opening address to the fourth National Radio Conference, reprinted in Radio Control, Hearings Before the Senate Interstate Commerce Committee, 69th Cong. 1st Sess. 56 (1926).
37. Resolution of the National Association of Broadcasters (NAB), presented at the fourth National Radio Conference, quoted in *id.* at 59.
38. Wallace White, Unscrambling the Ether, The Literary Digest, March 5, 1927, at 7.

Senator Dill, so vigorously put it, "Of one thing I am absolutely certain. Uncle Sam should not only police this 'new beat'; he should see to it that no one uses it who does not promise to be good and well behaved."[39]

§ 3.C. Rationales for Regulation

Thus far we have discussed the history of spectrum regulation and the nature of spectrum. As to the latter, section 3.A.6 of this chapter pointed out that wireless frequencies are just a resource employed in assembling telecommunications services, much as wood pulp is a resource used in the production of newspapers. What remains to be explained is why the federal government is so involved in the allocation of frequencies given that—beyond establishing some basic property rules—it is not very involved at all with wood pulp or other resources.

It may seem tempting to say that the federal government controls the spectrum because it "owns" the airwaves but does not own other resources.[40] But that just begs the question why the government asserts ownership over all the spectrum. The government once owned huge chunks of land that it sold (or gave) to settlers. Why shouldn't it have done the same thing with spectrum? The government can assume ownership of any property for public use via eminent domain (so long as it pays just compensation). Why does it make sense for the government to own the airwaves but not assume ownership of other resources?

Aside from the more general justifications for regulation discussed in Chapter One, an additional argument has traditionally been made in favor of government regulation of spectrum: that the spectrum is scarce. Note that this argument arose principally in the broadcast context—as that was the main use of spectrum for much of the 20th century—but it applies to spectrum regulation more generally. As you consider this argument, see if it helps you to answer the following questions: Why did the federal government decide to seize the spectrum and give an administrative agency, rather than producers, ultimate control over how producers would deliver information products over the air to consumers? Why did the government likewise give that same federal agency influence over the content of the information transmitted instead of simply allowing consumers to determine content through their viewing and purchasing decisions? Are there good reasons that we allocate spectrum to broadcasters through an administrative agency but leave the distribution of their other equipment—say, antennas—to conventional markets?

§ 3.C.1. Scarcity/Interference

Two parties cannot broadcast on the same frequency, at the same time, in the same place, in the same direction without causing one another at least some interference. If two parents simultaneously call for their respective children from the same porch, on the same street, at the same time, the two messages will likely become incomprehensively garbled. Similarly, if one person starts tapping his finger in a pond, the ripples will travel cleanly until someone else starts tapping in that same water, at which time both patterns will

---

39. Dill, *supra* note 33, at 181.
40. The relevant federal statute, 47 U.S.C. § 301, does not explicitly claim government ownership of the spectrum, but instead asserts government control. That, however, is not central to the problem with this argument.

likely be lost. One goal of telecommunications policy is to ensure that broadcasters do not interfere with one another in comparable ways, rendering each other's communications incomprehensible.

Low levels of interference are ubiquitous. As noted earlier in the chapter, every transmitter creates an electromagnetic field, so even turning on a light creates a tiny amount of interference for nearby users of adjacent frequencies. In some cases, the emitted radio frequency energy is so small that it does not create a noticeable loss of signal quality. The real fear is of more significant interference—"harmful interference," as it were—such that one set of radio waves overlap with another set to a sufficient degree that a receiver can hear neither clearly. This concept, however, is to some extent in the eye of the beholder, because interference is a function of what the receiver can hear. More sophisticated receivers are better able to find the intended signal and thus avoid interference.

Significant interference can arise in a number of ways. For instance, interference can be caused not merely by other intentional transmitters, but also by natural phenomena like thunderstorms. Lightning, after all, is an energy wave that propagates through the air, and to date the government has had no luck convincing lightning to confine itself to particular frequencies at particular times. Electric devices created by humans (from neon signs to garage door openers and Wi-Fi modems) similarly put out electromagnetic waves that can interfere with licensed broadcast technology. This means that any regulation designed to avoid interference between radio waves has to consider much more than just the obvious telecommunications sources.

Another complicating factor is that patterns of interference can arise in unexpected ways. For instance, radio station A might not interfere with radio station B at a time when those are the only two stations using the airwaves, but radio station A might interfere with station B when a new station C joins the spectrum. This problem is known as intermodulation. This effect occurs because two (or more) radio waves of different frequencies can combine to make waves at a third frequency, which could then interfere with other waves being broadcast at that frequency. Similarly, stations A and B might not interfere during the day, but they might interfere at night, because (as we noted above) radio waves travel differently depending on whether the sun is out or not.

When someone or something trespasses on your land, you can usually identify the trespasser. With spectrum, the matter is much more complex. Even if there is a stable set of transmitters using a particular set of frequencies, the level of interference that each transmitter produces vis-à-vis the other transmitters may change as conditions change. It thus may be difficult, if not impossible, to identify a particular transmitter that is creating the repeated interference that another is experiencing. Indeed, the question of causation might be a theoretical one in situations in which the presence of multiple transmitters produces interference. If the combination of multiple transmitters creates interference, how should we apportion blame among them? By the happenstance of which arrived last? And the situation becomes all the more complex when we add mobility to the picture. When transmitters (e.g., cell phones) are in motion, interference is constantly changing.

The case of managing interference disputes, and the analogy to disputes over land, lends itself to an application of the Coase Theorem. This theorem, unbeknownst to most law students (or professors), emerged from eventual Nobel Laureate Ronald Coase's study of spectrum.[41] What Coase realized about the spectrum is that a dispute about interfer-

---

41. The first footnote of Coase's The Problem of Social Cost states: "This article, although concerned with a technical problem of economic analysis, arose out of the study of the Political Economy of Broadcasting which I am now conducting. The argument of the present article was implicit

ence did not lend itself to a judgment that one user created a nuisance for the other—say, a TV station next to a dispatch system. Rather, the relevant benefit (freedom from interference) and harm (harmful interference) were reciprocal. As such, neither the party creating the interference (the high-powered TV station) nor the party experiencing the interference (the low-powered dispatch system) could claim an a priori right against the other. In Coase's view, then, the critical role of government was not to determine who had a prevailing moral right against another—which is exactly how the FCC traditionally thought of spectrum management—but rather who had what property right.

With property rights well defined and enforced, Coase explained, parties to a dispute could bargain as to how to allocate the right. In our TV station–dispatch system hypothetical, Coase would suggest that the FCC needed merely to specify the nature of the property rights of each party and, assuming no transaction costs, the two parties should reach an efficient outcome. The genius of this insight is that this efficient outcome can include a maze of possibilities that command-and-control regulation might overlook, including the higher power system paying for the lower power system to upgrade its receivers to protect that system against interference.

Even if the FCC were to define property rights along the lines discussed above, the FCC would need to adopt both a before-the-fact and after-the-fact oversight of interference management. Most users value certainty of transmission very highly. Identifying the source of interference so that it does not recur in the future will provide little solace to the user whose very important message was not successfully transmitted. As a result, a system that relies solely on ex post solutions is not one that most service providers would favor. And the points previously noted highlight the complexities of reaching private agreements among all the parties who could contribute to interference. Most commentators thus conclude that the most efficient response to the possibilities of interference includes some role for the government—a regulatory regime that has some ex ante rules that the government can impose on everyone. But that does not necessarily justify any role for the government beyond policing interference.

A bigger government role in spectrum regulation has often been justified based on a concern related to interference: scarcity. If two radio stations cannot both broadcast on the same frequency at the same time, and if there are a limited number of frequencies at which radio communication can take place, then at some point demand might exceed supply. How soon that constraint is reached depends heavily on government policy. If the government sets a low price for spectrum use, demand will quickly reach unsustainable levels. If price for access to spectrum rises, private parties will search for alternative communications technologies wherever possible as well as means for using their spectrum more efficiently (e.g., upgraded receivers).

This idea—that spectrum is subject to interference and thus scarce—has long been the most common argument put forward in favor of government regulation of spectrum. The Supreme Court itself adopted this rationale in its earliest case addressing the government's control over the spectrum, NBC v. United States, 319 U.S. 190 (1943). The Court stated that

[There are] certain basic facts about radio as a means of communication— its facilities are limited; they are not available to all who may wish to use them;

---

in a previous article dealing with the problem of allocating radio and television frequencies (The Federal Communications Commission, 2 J.L. & Econ. (1959))...." Ronald H. Coase, The Problem of Social Cost, 3 J.L. & Econ. 1, 1 n.1 (1960).

the radio spectrum simply is not large enough to accommodate everybody. There is a fixed natural limitation upon the number of stations that can operate without interfering with one another. Regulation of radio was therefore as vital to its development as traffic control was to the development of the automobile. In enacting the Radio Act of 1927, the first comprehensive scheme of control over radio communication, Congress acted upon the knowledge that if the potentialities of radio were not to be wasted, regulation was essential.

Id. at 213. As we will see in Chapter Fifteen, the Supreme Court adopted similar reasoning in Red Lion Broadcasting Co. v. FCC, 395 U.S. 367, 399 (1969).

The Court was understandably concerned that interference would destroy the utility of the spectrum as a resource. As we have stressed, if two transmitters broadcast at the same time, on the same frequency, from the same location, in the same direction, and at the same power, neither of them is likely to be heard. But every rivalrous resource is subject to interference. If two people try to sit in the same desk chair at the same time, they will interfere with each other. That's why we call such goods "rivalrous." Saying that wireless frequencies are scarce because of interference does not distinguish them from virtually every other good.

The Supreme Court in *NBC* and *Red Lion* emphasized that there was excess demand for the free broadcasting licenses provided by the government, and suggested that this highlighted the scarcity of spectrum. But, again, every productive resource—labor, steel, land, investment capital—is scarce in that (a) if given away at no charge people would request more of it than is available and (b) if we could create more of it, that additional increment also could be put to productive use. To say that spectrum is scarce in this way is quite true, then, but the statement fails to distinguish spectrum from virtually every other resource, most of which are not regulated.

One might want to argue that wireless frequencies are different from other resources in that the frequencies are finite, and most other resources are not. But, as we noted previously, the throughput of spectrum has increased dramatically over the years. Improvements in technology have greatly increased the range of usable spectrum, as higher and higher frequencies can be used to send data. And technology has also enabled us to send more and more data over the same swath of frequencies (through, for example, digital compression). Besides, at any given point there are only so many trees in the world, so many pounds of steel, and so on. Just as we could expend more resources to get more newsprint, we could expend more resources to increase the communications capacity of the spectrum.

The foregoing addresses the question whether spectrum is unusually scarce. The argument does not stop there, of course; the key assertion is that scarcity justifies government control. But to say that spectrum is "scarce" is only to say that the use of spectrum must be allocated among those who desire it. Use of any scarce resource must be allocated. In the U.S. economy, this allocation usually is accomplished by prices set in open markets. It is unsatisfying, then, to say that administrative allocation of spectrum is necessary because of spectrum scarcity. The real issue seems to be whether spectrum is "scarce" in some special way (unlike, say, land or iron ore) that peculiarly requires a nonmarket allocation mechanism.

To return to the chair example above, two people cannot comfortably sit at the same time in the same desk chair, yet that fact has not led government to regulate chair use. Rather, ownership of the chair is taken to confer the authority to exclude others from sitting in it, and, with that property right in place, government regulation is deemed unnecessary. Thomas Hazlett puts the point this way: "The interference problem is [rightly understood to be] one of defining separate frequency 'properties,' but it is logically unconnected to the issue of who is to harvest those frequencies. To confuse the *definition* of spectrum rights with the *assignment* of spectrum rights is to believe that, to keep intruders out of (private) backyards, the government must own (or allocate) all the houses. It is a public policy non sequitur."[42]

A property rights approach was in fact taken early in the history of spectrum regulation. In *Tribune Co. v. Oak Leaves Broadcasting*,4[43] the Chicago Tribune Company alleged that WGN (a radio station it owned) had been broadcasting daily for two years, had expended substantial money on equipment, and had a large and regular audience; and that the defendant, Oak Leaves, after jumping frequencies twice, had landed within 40 kHz of WGN's frequency. WGN asserted that Oak Leaves had moved in so close because it was an unpopular station. According to WGN, Oak Leaves' hope was that some of WGN's listeners would tune to the wrong station by accident. Oak Leaves essentially responded that the separation was ample, and therefore it had not harmed WGN.

It is obvious from the opinion that the "thousands of affidavits"[44] filed by the parties allowed the trial judge to learn a considerable amount about a new and complex industry. His opinion notes the local mores whereby all the Chicago stations went silent on a specific night so that their listeners could tune in to distant stations. It also notes that the public had become educated in the use of radio and knew how to obtain the type of programming it desired. This would prove difficult, the judge concluded, unless at least a 50 kHz separation was maintained within a 100-mile radius.

The trial judge thus resolved the issue by defining property rights. Drawing analogies to the law of unfair competition and also the law of water rights, the judge concluded that, by reason of use and expenditure of money and effort, the plaintiff had under the common law acquired something "generally recognized" as property.[45] According to the judge, 40 kHz was not a sufficient separation to respect that property, and so judgment came down in favor of the plaintiff.

The property rights approach did not carry the day. The federal government today regulates the spectrum, and the main justification put forth in support of that regulation is scarcity/interference. Thus, the question of whether something about telecommunications makes scarcity and interference unique deserves a closer look. It is to that endeavor we now turn, beginning with remarks given in 1959 before the FCC by Coase.

WHY NOT USE THE PRICING SYSTEM IN THE BROADCAST INDUSTRY?

Ronald Coase, Testimony before the FCC, December 1959
Reprinted in 4 Study of Radio & T.V. Broadcasting (No. 12,782) (1959)

I appear before you with a strong conviction and a bold proposal. My conviction is that the principles under which the American economic system generally operates are fundamentally sound. My proposal is that the American broadcasting industry adopt those principles.

---

42. Hazlett, *supra* note 23, at 138.
43. Tribune Co. v. Oak Leaves Broadcasting Station (Ill. Cir. Ct. 1926), reprinted in 68 Cong. Rec. 215, 215–19 (1926).
44. *Id.* at 218.
45. *Id.* at 219.

In presenting my case, I suffer from the disadvantage that, at the outset, I must attack a position which, although I am convinced it is erroneous, is nonetheless firmly held by many of those most knowledgeable about the broadcasting industry. Most authorities argue that the administrative assignment of radio and television frequencies by the Commission is called for by the technology of the industry. The number of frequencies, we are told, is limited, and people want to use more of them than are available.

But the situation so described is in no sense peculiar to the broadcasting industry. All resources used in the economic system are limited in amount and are scarce in that people want to use more of them than exists. This is so whether we think of labor, land, or capital. However, we do not ordinarily consider that this situation calls for government regulation. It is true that some mechanism has to be employed to decide who, out of the many claimants, should be allowed to use the scarce resources. But the usual way of handling this problem in the American economic system is to employ the pricing mechanism, and this allocates resources to users without the need for government regulation.

This is the system under which broadcasting concerns obtain the labor, land, and capital equipment they require. There is no reason why the same system could not be adopted for radio and television frequencies. If these were disposed of by selling or leasing them to the highest bidder, there would be no need to use such criteria as proposed or past programming as a basis for the selection of broadcast station operators. Such a system would require a delimitation of the property rights acquired, and there would almost certainly also have to be some general regulation of a technical character. But such regulation would not preclude the existence of private rights in frequencies, just as zoning and other regulations do not preclude the existence of private property in houses.

Such a use of the pricing mechanisms would bring the same advantages to the radio and television industry as its use confers on the rest of the American economy. It would avoid the need for much of the costly and time-consuming procedures involved in the assignment of frequencies by the Commission. It would rule out inefficient use of frequencies by bringing any proposal for the use of such frequencies up against the test of the market, with its precise monetary measure of cost and benefit. It would avoid the threat to freedom of the press in its widest sense which is inherent in present procedures, weak though that threat may be at the moment. And it would avoid that arbitrary enrichment of private operators of radio and television stations which inevitably follows from the present system. A station operator who is granted a license to use a particular frequency in a particular place may be granted a very valuable right, one for which he would be willing to pay millions of dollars and which he would be forced to pay if others could bid for the frequency. We sometimes hear denunciations of giveaways and their corrupting influence. You, gentlemen, are administering what must be one of the biggest giveaways of all.

It has been my experience that such a suggestion as I have made horrifies my listeners. I am told that it is necessary to choose those who should operate radio and television stations to make sure that the public interest is served and that programs of the right kind are transmitted. But, put this way, the case for governmental selection of broadcast station operators represents a significant shift of position from that which justifies it on technological grounds. It is, of course, a tenable position. But if the object of the selection is, in part, directly or indirectly, to influence programming, we have to face squarely the issue of freedom of the press so far as broadcasting is concerned.

But in any case it may be doubted whether an indirect attempt to influence programming through the selection of broadcast station operators could ever be very effective.

For over 30 years, the federal government has been selecting broadcast station operators on the basis, among other things, of their good character and their devotion to the public interest. By now one would expect the broadcasting industry to be a beacon of virtue, shining out in a wicked world. Such, I am afraid, is not the case.

Notes and Questions

1. Defining Property Rights. In order for a market system to work, the government would need to delimit specific bundles of rights that could then be recognized in particular users. Just as land ownership includes, among other things, the right to exclude others under certain circumstances and rights with respect to the use of natural resources above and below ground level, spectrum ownership, too, would have to be articulated in terms of specific rights to use and exclude. How difficult would that articulation be? More difficult than it is in other settings? Enough to explain why we regulate spectrum but not wood pulp? (Does the current system suffer from the same difficulties, or does government involvement mean that there is less of a need for clearly delimited rights?)

Think specifically about how you would define property rights in spectrum. Perhaps in terms of inputs, with the government recognizing in a particular party the (transferable?) right to build a tower of a certain height, at a particular location, transmitting a signal at a particular frequency and power level, during particular times, and in a particular direction? Indeed, a group of scholars in 1969 proposed just such a definition of spectrum property rights based on parameters of time, geographic area, power, and wave frequency.[46] As noted in Chapter Two, the FCC has shied away from a more precise effort to define interference rights. Ofcom, the UK's telecom regulator, has attempted to do just that.[47]

2. The Coase Theorem. Coase is perhaps most famous for his work on the importance of transaction costs. Yet, might it be argued that, in his remarks before the FCC, Coase neglects the important role transaction costs play in the market for telecommunications services? Think about how many parties use spectrum on both the national and international level, both as suppliers of telecommunications services and as consumers of those services, or how even a single radio signal at a relatively low energy level can still interfere with dozens of signals hundreds of miles away. Does Coase jump over this point too quickly? Are transaction costs a good reason for government regulation of the spectrum? Does Coase's argument apply more strongly to some services, such as those with a limited number of spectrum licensees (e.g., cellular telephony), than to others (e.g., radio broadcasting)?

3. Zoning. Thus far, the theme of this section has been to point out that scarcity/interference is a common problem to which the typical response is not to regulate but instead to define property rights and then defer to market interactions. With respect to land ownership, however, government does regulate — in the form of zoning laws, tort suits for

---

46. Arthur S. De Vany et al., A Property System for Market Allocation of the Electromagnetic Spectrum: A Legal-Economic-Engineering Study, 21 Stan. L. Rev. 1499 (1969).

47. *See* Spectrum Usage Rights: A Guide Describing SURs, Ofcom, 4 June 2008, *available at* http://stakeholders.ofcom.org.uk/binaries/spectrum/spectrum-policy-area/spectrum-management/spectrum-usage-rights/sursguide.pdf. Other U.S. commenters have suggested the FCC undertake a similar effort. *See* Philip J. Weiser & Dale N. Hatfield, Spectrum Policy Reform and the Next Frontier of Property Rights, 15 Geo. Mason L. Rev. 549 (2008); Robert Matheson & Adele Morris, The Technical Basis for Spectrum Rights: Policies to Enhance Market Efficiency, Brookings, Mar. 3, 2011, *available at* http://www.brookings.edu/research/papers/2011/03/03-spectrum-rights-matheson-morris.

nuisance, and so on. Does Coase's attack call all these "regulations" into question? Or is Coase's argument consistent with a methodological framework that would call for a "zoning" of the spectrum? How would such a system work?

Looked at another way, is there something special about both land and spectrum that distinguishes them from other goods? For example, the government uses land for public purposes (say, government buildings and public parks) and the government also has significant demand for spectrum (for example, military use and police radio). Does this fact help to explain why, in telecommunications and land use, scarcity/interference has led to government regulation whereas elsewhere it has led to more market-based solutions?

4. Reactions to Coase. Private spectrum rights came to be politically unimaginable by the middle of the 20th century. Perhaps the most striking evidence is that, right after Coase delivered the talk excerpted above, the floor was opened for questions, and then-FCC Commissioner Philip Cross began the question period by asking Coase, in all seriousness, "Are you spoofing us? Is this all a big joke?"[48] When Coase expressed those same ideas in a paper for the Rand Corporation, one referee who reviewed the document advised Rand to kill the project entirely, and another "stated that, by definition, the spectrum was a public good and consequently a market solution was not appropriate and that the project represented a waste of Rand's resources."[49] Consider the following statement from the memorandum rejecting Coase's paper for Rand: "I am afraid that to issue [Coase's paper] ... is asking for trouble in the Washington/Big Business maelstrom because we haven't in the first place measured up to the intellectual requirements of the problem selected for study."[50] Were those in power unable to imagine private spectrum rights, or merely unwilling to part with the power that government control of the spectrum created?

5. Interference as Opportunity. Thomas Hazlett argues that the 1927 policy debate in Congress over the creation of the Federal Radio Commission was "led by men who clearly understood—and articulated—that interference was not the problem, interference was the opportunity."[51] That is, according to Hazlett, those leading the debate saw concerns about interference as enabling them to justify government control of the airwaves. Is that the reason that members of Congress coalesced so firmly around government control? What groups might have effectively resisted such control, and why didn't that happen?

6. For Further Consideration. What is lost by the use of an administrative agency instead of market forces? Are there corresponding gains? Are traditional worries about markets— say, the fear of monopoly or concerns about wealth effects—somehow more salient in the telecommunications context? Can a market work in telecommunications given that, for services like broadcasting, the equipment that transmits signals is typically owned by one group (broadcasters), whereas the equipment that receives those signals is typically owned by another, independent group (consumers)? Is this why we regulate? If we ask advertising-based broadcasters to bid for spectrum, would they bid less than subscription services would, on the theory that the revenues from commercial advertisements are likely less than what viewers would directly pay for content? (If that is the case, is it an argument against free broadcast and in favor of subscription television instead?) Does regulation perhaps preserve for the government more flexibility than a market regime would?

---

48. Ronald Coase, Comment on Thomas W. Hazlett: Assigning Property Rights to Radio Spectrum Users: Why Did FCC License Auctions Take 67 Years?, 41 J.L. & Econ. 577, 579 (1998).
49. *Id.* at 580.
50. *Id.*
51. Hazlett, *supra* note 23, at 162.

Given the newness of the technology, was that a good justification for at least the early pattern of regulation?

---

§ 3.C.2. Consumer Preferences

In most markets, we assume that consumer preferences should be respected. That is, if consumers want to binge on reality TV, they should be able to—even if that means fewer viewers are watching the nightly news or listening to congressional debates on C-SPAN. There is reason to wonder, however, whether the broadcast marketplace should, in fact, so completely respect consumer preferences, or whether instead regulation ought to constrain and mold consumer choice.

There are two principal arguments to consider here. First, there is what might be thought of as the paternalistic argument that, when it comes to information consumption, consumers don't know what is in their own long-term best interests. Cass Sunstein has made this argument, although he seems to object to the "paternalism" label:

> What people now prefer and believe may be a product of insufficient information, limited opportunities, legal constraints, or unjust background conditions. People may think as they do simply because they have not been provided with sufficient information and opportunities. It is not paternalistic, or an illegitimate interference with competing conceptions of the good, for a democracy to promote scrutiny and testing of preferences and beliefs through deliberative processes.
>
> It may seem controversial or strange to say that there is a problem for the Madisonian system if people do not seek serious coverage of serious issues. Perhaps this suggestion is unacceptably paternalistic; perhaps we should take people however we find them. But the system of deliberative democracy is not supposed simply to implement existing desires. Its far more ambitious goal is to create the preconditions for a well-functioning democratic process.[52]

Second, there is an externality argument that similarly might cause us to question consumer sovereignty in broadcast markets, to wit: one person's consumption of broadcast content may affect another person's well-being. For example, some people believe that repeated exposure to television violence causes viewers to become more violent.[53] If that is true, then this is a negative externality, and because of this externality it might not be wise to allow viewers to determine for themselves how many hours of violent television they watch each week. Each viewer's choice, after all, neglects the harm that decision imposes on others.

A similar point can be made with respect to the decision to watch (and, in a subscription system, pay for) children's educational television. Educational television arguably creates a positive externality in that these programs help young viewers become more informed, and hence more productive, citizens. Because of this externality, if left to make their own decisions, children might not watch as much educational television as would be optimal from a societal perspective.[54]

---

52. Cass R. Sunstein, Democracy and the Problem of Free Speech, 19, 21 (1993).
53. We consider televised violence in Chapter Sixteen.
54. We also consider children's television in Chapter Fifteen.

Notes and Questions

1. Distinctions. Are the "paternalistic" and "externality" arguments different, or does one simply recast the other in new words? Similarly, is there really a distinction between a "positive" and a "negative" externality in this setting, or does that distinction also collapse, depending on your political perspective?

2. Remedies. To whatever extent we find the paternalistic and externality arguments convincing, what types of responses might they justify? Consider, for example, educational television. If the FCC believes that it would benefit society to have more children watching educational television, is it a sufficient response for the government to increase the amount of educational television available—perhaps by, say, offering more funding to PBS? Must the government do more, perhaps both funding PBS and restricting the simultaneous broadcast of programs that children prefer? After all, merely having virtuous programming available will not change anything if nobody watches. Consider in this light news analyst Jeff Greenfield's remark that, "when you no longer need the skills of a safecracker to find PBS in most markets, you have to realize that the reason people aren't watching is that they don't want to."[55]

3. Implications for Other Media. Neither the paternalistic argument nor the externality argument is specific to broadcast, or even to telecommunication more generally. Any form of communication (movies, magazines, street theater, even good old-fashioned conversation) can affect participants in ways they themselves might fail to account for and can also affect other people, even those not directly involved in the communication. As you read the remaining materials in this book, consider on what basis we might distinguish among different forms of telecommunication, and between telecommunication and communication more generally, and what sort of regulations those various distinctions might justify. Is broadcasting uniquely powerful? If so, is that an argument in favor of greater regulation, or greater freedom from regulation? Assuming that scarcity and interference do distinguish broadcasting, does that justify limiting nonmeritorious programming, subsidizing meritorious programming, or both?

4. Federal Support of Noncommercial Broadcasting. The federal government supports noncommercial programming in a variety of ways. First, since 1939 for radio and 1952 for broadcast television, the FCC has reserved frequencies explicitly for noncommercial educational uses.

Second, and as alluded to above, in addition to the spectrum licenses that all broadcasters received at no charge until 1997, noncommercial broadcasters receive direct government funding—most prominently through the Corporation for Public Broadcasting, a federally chartered nonprofit corporation that receives money from Congress and in turn funds various radio and television stations, including stations that are affiliated with the Public Broadcasting Service (PBS). This funding has been a source of periodic controversy, with some members of Congress suggesting that the federal government could better spend its money in other ways, and private parties at times challenging the government's relationship with noncommercial broadcasters on First Amendment grounds. One particularly notable controversy involved a statutory provision that forbade any noncommercial educational broadcasting station that received a grant from the Corporation for Public Broadcasting from "engag[ing] in editorializing."[56] A sharply divided Supreme

---

55. Quoted in Krattenmaker & Powe, *supra* note 8, at 314.
56. Section 399 of the Public Broadcasting Act of 1967, Pub. L. No. 90-129, 81 Stat. 365.

Court found that the provision violated the First Amendment in FCC v. League of Women Voters, 468 U.S. 364 (1984). More recently, after a state-owned public television broadcaster included only those candidates with substantial popular support in a congressional debate, a candidate who had little popular support filed suit alleging that the station had violated his First Amendment rights by excluding him from the debate. The Supreme Court ruled that the debate was a nonpublic forum from which the public broadcaster could exclude the candidate because it had engaged in a viewpoint-neutral exercise of its journalistic discretion. Arkansas Educational Television Comm'n v. Forbes, 523 U.S. 666 (1998).

Third, several federal statutes give special treatment to noncommercial programming. For instance, the statute requiring cable operators to carry local broadcasters has a separate provision requiring cable operators to carry "noncommercial educational television stations," 47 U.S.C. §535; similarly, a statute governing direct broadcast satellite (DBS) providers requires that they devote a portion of their channel capacity "exclusively for noncommercial programming of an educational or informational nature," 47 U.S.C. §335.

§3.D. An Overview of Spectrum Management

For the reasons—based on history, politics, and policy—discussed above, the FCC is indeed in charge of regulating the private use of spectrum. But what exactly does it mean to regulate spectrum use?

The Commission's first step is to determine which services it will allow on which frequencies, and how many users it will allow to provide those services. This process (called allocation) entails the FCC deciding what services it is going to permit and the quantity and wavelengths of frequencies at which it will allow those services. As an example, the Commission might decide to authorize FM radio broadcasting on the 20 megahertz between 88 MHz and 108 MHz. In any given allocation, the FCC can permit one type of service, several types of services, or any type of service, and can make its rules accordingly. And it can choose to grant licenses to one entity, a number of designated entities, or to leave a set of frequencies completely open for unlicensed use.

Once the Commission has determined the quantity and particular set of frequencies to allocate for a given service or services, it determines how (if at all) to allot licenses for the service, and what sort of service rules it will impose. That is, the Commission decides how big a range of frequencies each license will cover (e.g., 100 licenses covering 20 kilohertz each, which totals 2 megahertz, or 20 licenses covering 100 kilohertz each, also totaling 2 megahertz); how much area each license is authorized to cover (e.g., Indiana alone, Indiana plus Ohio, or the entire United States); what the limits are on the power levels of the transmitters; and whether and how it will create buffers between users or between services to avoid interference. Taken together, these decisions are sometimes called the band plan.

The Commission's next step is to create rules for the assignment, transfer, renewal, and termination of licenses to use spectrum in ways consistent with the band plan. Over time, the Commission has varied its approach tremendously with respect to this task. In the beginning, licensees were chosen in merit-based hearings where each licensee was evaluated in terms of its ability to provide the service in question. Licenses lasted for a few years, after which time a licensee had to petition the Commission for renewal. Transfer was cumbersome and termination was a real threat. More recently, by contrast, the Commission typically assigns licenses using an auction mechanism where the license goes to the highest bidder. Renewals are almost never questioned, licensees are for the most part free to transfer their licenses during the license term, and there is no significant danger of termination.

The next two chapters focus on allocation (Chapter Four) and assignment (Chapter Five). We do not offer a separate chapter on allotment and service rules. Instead, we introduce those concepts more fully below, and then we further develop them as appropriate in the context of the other discussions.

Notes and Questions

1. The Land Analogy. In the chapters that follow, we will obviously say much more about each of these Commission tasks. For now, however, can you articulate comparable tasks that must be accomplished with respect to the allocation and use of land? Are zoning regulations the equivalent of the band plan? What are the rules that govern the initial assignment, transfer, and renewal of rights to land? Are there any public interest obligations imposed on land owners, akin to the public interest obligations imposed on spectrum licensees?

2. Left Hands and Right. What relationships do you see between the various tasks that the Commission performs? For example, if transfer is relatively easy to accomplish and not at all subject to Commission review, does it matter how the Commission initially assigns licenses? Whoever receives the licenses at first will simply turn around and sell it to the highest bidder, right? Similarly, if initial assignment is done by auction, is there any reason to impose public interest obligations? After all, under an auction the government garners the full value of the license; why not use that money to fund educational television, subsidize telephone service, or accomplish any other public interest goal?

3. Neither Fish nor Fowl. FCC commissioners sometimes view their job as akin to a federal judge. Other times, FCC commissioners believe they are extensions of the legislative branch. Yet other times, FCC commissioners believe they work for the President and are, in effect, an extension of the administration. What role do you think is appropriate? What are the advantages and disadvantages of each? Given the tasks before the Commission, can an FCC commissioner be too political or not political enough in her orientation?

§ 3.E. Regulatory Tradeoffs and Allotment

The FCC has often articulated the goals of broadcast regulation to be competition and diversity. *See, e.g.*, 1998 Biennial Regulatory Review, Notice of Inquiry, 13 FCC Rcd. 11,276, 11,277 ¶ 4 (1998) ("For more than a half century, the Commission's regulation of broadcast service has been guided by the goals of promoting competition and diversity."). A third goal that the Commission sometimes includes with competition and diversity is localism. *See, e.g.*, Broadcast Localism, Notice of Inquiry, 19 FCC Rcd. 12,425 ¶ 1 (2004) ("As with competition and diversity, localism has been a cornerstone of broadcast regulation for decades.").

These three goals are in tension with one another. Treating diversity as a goal separate and distinct from competition must mean that, in some cases, (small amounts of) competition should be sacrificed to achieve (larger amounts of) diversity. Otherwise, the goal of diversity is doing no work. Such a focus on diversity might be justified either because of the perceived failure of competition to work adequately or because of a view that diversity may be more important than efficient competition.

The conflict between localism and the other goals, meanwhile, has been significant and foundational. The best example arises out of the allotment of broadcast television stations. The FCC chose to place at least one television station in as many communities as possible.[57] The FCC could have designated single nationwide licenses as opposed to ones based in local communities. By so doing, a single firm could broadcast on channel 2 in a more effective fashion and without the need for as many empty stations that ensue when one firm broadcasts on channel 2 from, say, New York City and another firm broadcasts on channel 3 from Philadelphia. Because of interference concerns where these channels might overlap (say, in Princeton, New Jersey), the result of this policy is that large swaths of territory will not be within range of a channel 2 signal (New York City) or a channel 3 signal (Philadelphia). Creating nationwide licenses would have given individuals access to more stations (by avoiding interference problems created through assigning stations to each city).

The FCC's decision not to maximize the number of stations but instead to focus on ensuring local stations in each community thus meant that individuals would be able to see local news and weather, but it also reduced the number of national broadcast networks that could be created—helping ensure that, for decades, there would be only three commercial broadcast television networks. Even as of 1980, an FCC study found that although 92% of U.S. households could receive at least three commercial television channels (ABC, CBS, and NBC), only 64% could receive a fourth channel, making it hard for a fourth network to compete.[58] The irony is that the existence of only three national broadcast networks led the Commission to regulate the networks' behavior. The FCC, concerned that the existence of only three networks did not ensure adequate competition, imposed a series of restraints on the networks' relationships with their affiliates and their program suppliers (discussed in Chapter Ten).

This is not to suggest that the Commission necessarily made a mistake in focusing on localism, but rather that the goals of competition, diversity, and localism are in tension with one another.[59] With this as with every other decision that the FCC (or anyone else) makes, there are tradeoffs.

That said, some decisions on how to design the scope of spectrum licenses are widely recognized, in retrospect, to have been mistakes. There is broad agreement, for example, that regulators erred when they followed a local model for cellular providers. In that

---

57. Sometimes Congress made the allotment choices itself. Notably, a 1928 amendment to the Radio Act mandated an equalization of radio stations across five geographical zones. 45 Stat. 373 (1928). Offered by Congressman E.L. Davis of Tennessee, it sought to replace stations in the more populous East with newcomers in the South and West.

58. *See* FCC Network Inquiry Special Staff, New Television Networks: Entry, Jurisdiction, Ownership, and Regulation 68 (1980); Christopher S. Yoo, The Rise and Demise of the Technology-Specific Approach to the First Amendment, 91 Geo. L.J. 245, 275–79, 279 n.155 (2003).

59. For a more negative view of the FCC's allotment decisions, see Thomas G. Krattenmaker & L.A. Powe, Jr., Converging First Amendment Principles for Converging Communications Media, 104 Yale L.J. 1719, 1736 (1995) (noting that the FCC's allocation plan "gave great weight to factors such as placing at least one transmitter in as many communities (and, therefore, congressional districts) as possible..., and for almost forty years guaranteed that there would be but three national networks. The allocation plan sacrificed viewer interests in access and diversity to narrow political concerns and entrenched industry goals.").

case, the decision to create a large number of locally based licenses proved highly inefficient because users wanted national service. The FCC's initial emphasis on localism for cell phone service was eventually overcome through market consolidation, but that emphasis resulted in early network infrastructure that was less advanced and efficient.

Notes and Questions

1. Broader Applications. The Commission has not emphasized localism or diversity in its regulation of telephony. Is that a mistake? How might they apply in the context of telephone regulation? In the context of Internet regulation?

2. Principles. Is there any metric for the FCC to use in trading off among competition, diversity, and localism? Should it add other goals to those three, or subtract one or two? On what basis should it decide whether to do so?

Chapter Four

Zoning the Spectrum

Introduction

We know from the previous chapter that the government decided to control the spectrum but to allow private uses of much of it.[1] The next question is what sort of spectrum usage rights the FCC confers on private users. Should the Commission grant licenses requiring particular services and technologies, with no ability on the part of the licensee to change services or subdivide its spectrum rights? Should it grant licenses providing the licensee with complete flexibility? Should it allow unlicensed uses, either in addition to or instead of licensed uses? Over time, the Commission's answer has changed. In the early days, the Commission was heavy-handed: through its band plan, the Commission would decide not only exactly what services would be offered at what frequencies, but also how many licensees would be allowed to offer those services. Today, by contrast, the Commission has moved toward allowing spectrum flexibility. In an increasing range of frequencies, the Commission allows market forces to determine both what services are available and how many service providers will offer them. Meanwhile, the Commission has also allowed for some unlicensed usage, though far less than some unlicensed advocates have sought.

This chapter addresses these issues. We begin in § 4.A. by considering different models of spectrum control, looking at the Commission's own study of the tradeoffs. In § 4.B. we turn to the Commission's implementation of its zoning rules, using as a case study a key order moving toward greater flexibility. Sections 4.C. and 4.D. examine dedicating spectrum for unlicensed uses and allowing unlicensed uses on a more opportunistic basis. Section 4.E. concludes by considering spectrum leasing and private commons.

§ 4.A. Models of Spectrum Control

Traditionally, the FCC would identify one or two services as permissible on a swath of frequencies and choose a licensee who would then be allowed to operate one or both services on the relevant frequencies. The Commission would make clear that its licensees were under no circumstances allowed to use their frequencies for unapproved services, even if those other uses would not cause interference problems. Relatedly, although licensees

---

1. As we noted in Chapter Two, many frequencies are dedicated to government use and managed by the National Telecommunications and Information Administration.

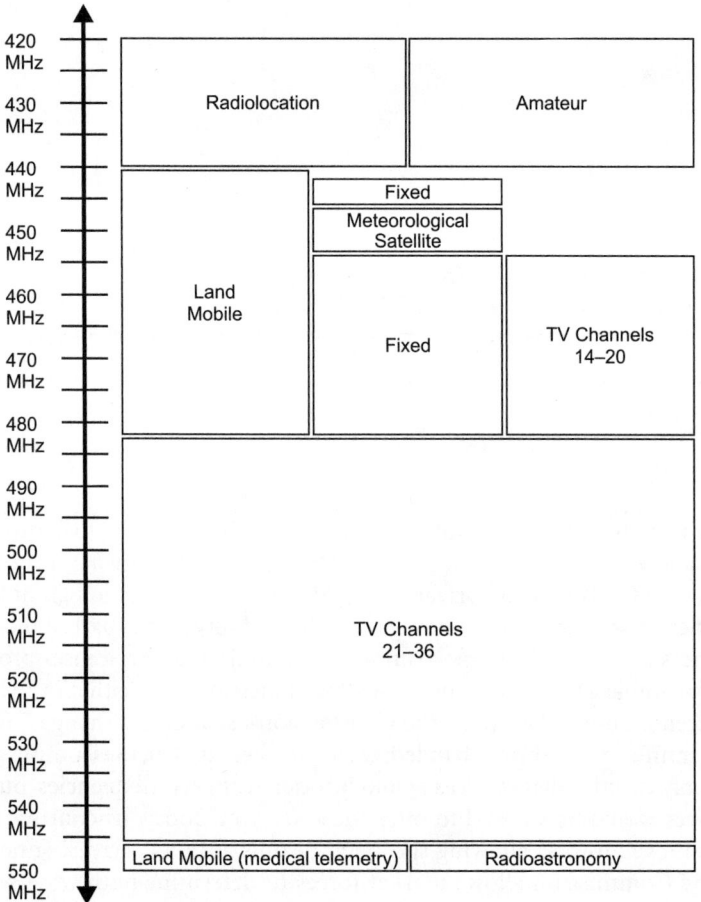

Spectrum Management. This chart shows the main current allocations on a small slice of frequencies in the spectrum — from 420 MHz to 550 MHz. As we noted in Chapter Three, a given frequency will usually be suitable for several competing uses (e.g., land mobile and television broadcasting in the chart above), and a given use can usually be assigned to a variety of places on the spectrum (e.g., television broadcasting occupies many different frequencies, starting at 54 MHz). The FCC's website has a spectrum dashboard with much more detail (http://reboot.fcc.gov/reform/systems/spectrum-dashboard).

could transfer their licenses to third parties, they could not subdivide their spectrum usage rights and transfer some of them to a third party (say, the right for a third party to engage in a low-power noninterfering use) while keeping the rest. As a matter of engineering, usage rights are readily divisible across frequency, space, and time, but under FCC rules for many years licensees' only option was to transfer all their rights en masse. Thus legal rules limited what science would otherwise have allowed and market forces might otherwise have demanded.

This traditional command-and-control approach has some obvious drawbacks. First, it produces underused, and in some cases unused, spectrum. Spectrum is underused because, even if a service does not utilize its spectrum efficiently (e.g., is relying on antiquated equipment), the licensee cannot do anything with the spectrum if it made better use of it. Because licensees will not benefit from using less spectrum (via, for example, digital compression), they have no incentive under command-and-control regulation to expend any resources to economize on spectrum. Not only does command-and-control regulation fail to encourage efficient use of spectrum, it actively discourages it. In particular, if a spectrum licensee opts for more effective technology and frees up spectrum as a result, that spectrum might well give the government the opportunity to increase competition by letting someone else use the newly free spectrum to compete against that licensee.

Command-and-control regulation produces unused spectrum, moreover, in cases where there is a single authorized service but that service is not profitable in a given area. That has long been the case, for instance, with UHF (ultra high frequency) television outside of the biggest cities; in many places, UHF television has not been sufficiently attractive to entice any broadcasters, and thus UHF spectrum has been idle in those communities.[2]

Second, allowing only one service on a given swath of spectrum prevents licensees from introducing new services. Innovative services will not have the opportunity to prove their value if they are not allowed on the spectrum in the first place. Flexibility would both give licensees the incentive to optimize their use of spectrum and provide the FCC with new information about how spectrum can be used and how valuable particular services are.

The FCC has recognized the benefits of moving away from command and control toward more flexibility and market forces. The 2010 National Broadband Plan said:

> The current spectrum policy framework sometimes impedes the free flow of spectrum to its most highly valued uses. The federal government, on behalf of the American people and under the auspices of the FCC and NTIA, retains all property rights to spectrum. In several instances, both agencies assign large quantities of spectrum to specific uses, sometimes tied to specific technologies. In some cases, this approach is appropriate to serve particular public interests that flexible use licenses and market-based allocations alone would not otherwise support. However, because mission needs and technologies evolve, there must be a public review process to ensure that decisions about federal and non-federal use that may have worked in the past can be revisited over time. In general, where there is no overriding public interest in maintaining a specific use, flexibility should be the norm.
>
> In the case of commercial spectrum, the failure to revisit historical allocations can leave spectrum handcuffed to particular use cases and outmoded services, and less valuable and less transferable to innovators who seek to use it for new services. The market for commercial, licensed spectrum does not always behave like a typical commodities market. Commercially licensed spectrum does not always move efficiently to the use valued most highly by markets and consumers. For example, a megahertz-pop may be worth a penny in one industry context and a dollar in another.[3] Legacy "command and control" rules, high transaction costs and highly fragmented license regimes sometimes preserve outmoded band plans and prevent the aggregation (or disaggregation) of spectrum into more valuable license configurations.

---

2. *See* Stuart Minor Benjamin, The Logic of Scarcity: Idle Spectrum as a First Amendment Violation, 52 Duke L.J. 1, 18 (2002).

3. Dollars per megahertz of spectrum, per person reached ($ per megahertz-pop) is the convention used to estimate the market value of spectrum. In the [2007 auction of spectrum that had been devoted to broadcasting], $ per megahertz-pop values ranged from $0.03 in Paducah, Ken., Cape Girardeau, Mo., and Harrisburg-Mt. Vernon, Ill., to $3.86 in Philadelphia. [Footnote relocated.]

FCC, National Broadband Plan, § 5.1 (2010), *available at* http://www.fcc.gov/national-broadband-plan.

The FCC's most sustained discussion of different possible models of spectrum regulation was an FCC task force whose mission was to "[p]rovide specific recommendations to the Commission for ways in which to evolve the current 'command and control' approach to spectrum policy into a more integrated, market-oriented approach that provides greater regulatory certainty while minimizing regulatory intervention" and also protecting against interference. Spectrum Policy Task Force Report, FCC, ET Docket No. 02-135 at 1 (Nov. 2002). That task force issued a report in 2002 that reviewed spectrum policy and recommended significant changes designed to meet these stated goals.

Spectrum Policy Task Force Report
FCC, ET Docket No. 02-135 (Nov. 2002),
available at https://apps.fcc.gov/edocs_public/attachmatch/DOC-228542A1.pdf

V. Key Elements of New Spectrum Policy

A. Maximizing Flexibility of Spectrum Use

As a general proposition, flexibility in spectrum regulation is critical to improving access to spectrum. In this context, "flexibility" means granting both licensed users and unlicensed device operators the maximum possible autonomy to determine the highest valued use of their spectrum, subject only to those rules that are necessary to afford reasonable opportunities for access by other spectrum users and to prevent or limit interference among multiple spectrum uses. Flexibility enables spectrum users to make fundamental choices about how they will use spectrum (including whether to use it or transfer their usage rights to others), taking into account market factors such as consumer demand, availability of technology, and competition. By leaving these choices to the spectrum user, this approach tends to lead to efficient and highly-valued spectrum uses. In most instances, a flexible use approach is preferable to the Commission's traditional "command-and-control" approach to spectrum regulation, in which allowable spectrum uses are limited based on regulatory judgments.

The Commission should seek to avoid rules that restrict spectrum use to particular services or applications, so long as the user operates within the technical parameters applicable to the particular band in question. Furthermore, these technical parameters should themselves be limited to those that are necessary to define the user's RF [radio frequency] environment in terms of maximum allowable output and required tolerance of interference.

Such flexibility can be implemented under more than one regulatory model for defining spectrum usage rights. As discussed further below, the Task Force advocates expanding the future use of two alternative regulatory models—one based on awarding exclusive spectrum usage rights and the other on creating unlicensed spectrum "commons"—both of which are premised on the concept of flexible use. Under either model, the Commission should give spectrum users maximum possible autonomy in the following areas:

> *Choice of uses or services that are provided on spectrum.* Spectrum users should have the maximum possible flexibility to decide how spectrum will be used, e.g., whether to provide commercial services or to use spectrum for private, internal needs, so long as they comply with the general parameters applicable to the band (including any applicable power limits or interference limits).

Choice of technology that is most appropriate to the spectrum environment. Spectrum users should be allowed to choose the technology that is best-suited to their proposed use or service. They should be allowed to adapt their technology to their particular spectrum environment, e.g., to use lower power in spectrum-congested areas and higher power in less-congested (e.g., rural) areas.

Right to transfer, lease, or subdivide spectrum rights. An efficient secondary markets regime should be in place to facilitate the negotiated movement of spectrum rights from one party to another. In more narrowly-defined services (e.g., public safety), spectrum users should have the ability to lease excess capacity for other uses through time sharing of spectrum or other mechanisms.

B. Clear and Exhaustive Definition of Spectrum Rights and Responsibilities

While commenters and workshop participants were vocal about their desire for more flexible rights, they were equally interested in firmness and clarity in the rules they are required to follow. Most commenters and workshop participants also agreed with the proposition that spectrum users' rights and obligations are often not defined with sufficient clarity under the FCC's current rules. An overarching principle eventually emerged: all spectrum users require clear rules governing their interactions with the Commission and other spectrum users. Regardless of how or to whom particular rights are assigned, ensuring that all rights are clearly delineated is important to avoiding disputes, and provides a clear common framework from which spectrum users can negotiate alternative arrangements.

VII. Spectrum Usage Models

A. Comparison of Alternative Spectrum Usage Models

The Task Force examined the Commission's spectrum policies and rules in relation to three general models for assigning spectrum usage rights:

"Command-and-control" model. The traditional process of spectrum management in the United States, currently used for most spectrum within the Commission's jurisdiction, allocates and assigns frequencies to limited categories of spectrum users for specific government-defined uses. Service rules for the band specify eligibility and service restrictions, power limits, build-out requirements, and other rules.

"Exclusive use" model. A licensing model in which a licensee has exclusive and transferable rights to the use of specified spectrum within a defined geographic area, with flexible use rights that are governed primarily by technical rules to protect spectrum users against interference. Under this model, exclusive rights resemble property rights in spectrum, but this model does not imply or require creation of "full" private property rights in spectrum.

"Commons" or "open access" model. Allows unlimited numbers of unlicensed users to share frequencies, with usage rights that are governed by technical standards or etiquettes but with no right to protection from interference. Spectrum is available to all users that comply with established technical "etiquettes" or standards that set power limits and other criteria for operation of unlicensed devices to mitigate potential interference.

There is, of course, some overlap among these models as well as variations that combine elements of each. For example, spectrum users that are regulated on a command-and-control basis may have some of the same rights as spectrum users who are subject to the exclusive use model (e.g., exclusive and transferable rights, interference protection). Moreover, spectrum that is subject to the exclusive use or commons model may nonetheless be subject to some degree of command-and-control restriction (e.g., limiting usage based on international allocation restrictions). Nonetheless, the key distinction between the command-and-control approach and the other two models is that the former typically imposes significantly greater usage restrictions on spectrum (and sometimes on the eligibility of spectrum users), thereby restricting flexibility of spectrum use to a far greater degree than either of the other two models.

The Task Force recommends that the Commission base its spectrum policy on a balance of the three basic spectrum rights models outlined above: an exclusive use approach, a commons approach, and (to a more limited degree) a command-and-control approach. It is further recommended that the Commission fundamentally alter the existing balance among these models—which is dominated by legacy command-and-control regulation—by expanding the use of both the exclusive use and commons models throughout the radio spectrum, and limiting the use of the command-and-control model to those instances where there are compelling public policy reasons. Thus, to the extent feasible, the Commission should identify more spectrum for both licensed and unlicensed uses under flexible rules, and should transition existing spectrum that is subject to more restrictive command-and-control regulation to these models to the greatest extent possible.

In proposing to reshape the balance among the three models, the Task Force recognizes that the models themselves are not pure and mutually exclusive approaches to spectrum management, but rather are representative approaches on a broader continuum that may be subject to variation in particular instances. Thus, for any given spectrum band or proposed use, the Commission may find it beneficial to incorporate elements from more than one model. For example, as discussed further below, spectrum that is licensed under an exclusive use approach could also be subject to an "underlay" easement that is available to low-power unlicensed devices using a commons approach. Similarly, services that require some dedication of spectrum on a command-and-control basis (e.g., public safety) may benefit from partial application of the exclusive-use model to enable them to lease spectrum capacity to others when it is not otherwise needed. As a general matter, however, the Task Force believes that there is considerable room to move from the largely ad hoc regulation of particular bands that has evolved historically to a more consistent and comprehensive application of these models across the radio spectrum as a whole. If these models are consistently applied in all Commission spectrum policy decisions, it has the potential to significantly reduce the artificial scarcity of spectrum that currently exists as a result of barriers to access. This approach will have the beneficial effect of reducing the cost of obtaining exclusive spectrum rights in the market and will also help to alleviate congestion of spectrum that is made available on a commons basis, thus mitigating the risk of the "tragedy of the commons"—oversaturation resulting in inefficient use.

B. Application of Exclusive Use and Commons Models

The recommendation to move towards greater reliance on exclusive use and commons models requires that the Commission determine the appropriate balance between these two models. Ultimately, wherever there are competing uses for a resource—that is, wherever there is scarcity—some mechanism must exist for allocating that resource. A mechanism based on markets, such as an exclusive use model, will be most efficient in most cases. However, government may also wish to promote the important efficiency and innovation benefits of a spectrum commons by allocating spectrum bands for shared use, much as it allocates land to public parks.

There are a number of variables that may be relevant to this determination with respect to any particular band, but the Task Force believes that the key factors to be considered are (1) spectrum scarcity, and (2) transaction costs associated with moving spectrum from less efficient to more efficient use. In this context, "spectrum scarcity" means the degree to which particular spectrum is subject to competing demands for use so that the demand exceeds the current supply; and "transaction costs" means the expenditure of time and resources required for a potential spectrum user to obtain the spectrum access rights from one or many parties necessary to its proposed spectrum use.

1. Factors Favoring Exclusive Use Model

The exclusive use model should be applied to most spectrum, particularly in bands where scarcity is relatively high and transaction costs associated with market-based negotiation of access rights are relatively low. The exclusive use model is appropriate because where spectrum is subject to competing demands, and therefore more likely to have a high market value, this approach creates the strongest incentives for parties to put spectrum to its highest valued use. In addition, where rights and responsibilities are clearly defined and effectively enforced, the characteristics of this model—e.g., exclusivity, flexibility, and transferability—generally provide a clear framework for market-based assignment and negotiation of access rights among spectrum users, thereby limiting transaction costs.

These variables suggest that in the lower portion of the radio spectrum, particularly bands below 5 GHz, the Commission should focus primarily, though not exclusively, on using the exclusive use model. The propagation characteristics in this portion of the spectrum (which can support a wide variety of high- and low-power, fixed and mobile uses), combined with the high level of incumbent use (including government as well as nongovernment uses), result in a large number of competing demands for a relatively small amount of available spectrum. These factors tend to weigh in favor of an exclusive use approach with flexible rules because it provides a mechanism for spectrum users to choose among the full range of technically feasible spectrum use options based on market forces. Moreover, the typical transaction costs associated with negotiation of access rights tend to be relatively low in relation to the value of this spectrum.

Even in situations where usable spectrum is scarce but transaction costs are potentially high, the exclusive use model still may be most appropriate, though other variables may also come into play. The presence of high transaction costs means that some transfers of spectrum will not occur, and some valuable uses therefore will not appear in the market. However, wherever scarcity exists, there will be competing claims to the resource, and the exclusive use model is most effective at balancing these competing claims. Moreover, the greater the scarcity, the greater will be the incentive for parties to find ways to overcome these high transaction costs. In contrast, as discussed below, a commons approach may be less effective in cases of high scarcity, despite its advantages in addressing high transaction costs.

Finally, while these factors weigh in favor of applying the exclusive use model under the above-described circumstances, it should be emphasized that they do not preclude the introduction of unlicensed "underlays" into exclusive use bands. As discussed below, the criteria that favor use of the commons model apply to potential underlay uses of spectrum below the interference temperature threshold, and may apply in some cases to opportunistic uses above the threshold, depending on the nature of the proposed use.

2. Factors Favoring Commons Model

The commons model should be applied to significant portions of the spectrum, particularly in bands where scarcity is low and transaction costs associated with market mechanisms are high. The commons approach makes increased access possible by replacing the negotiation of spectrum access rights among rights holders and prospective users with a commons model governed by user protocols and etiquette. These protocols promote efficiency through spectrum sharing, typically by requiring commons to operate at low power for a short time in limited areas, which allows multiple users to operate on the same spectrum. This approach also promotes technological innovation by providing a spectrum environment in which to develop new technologies. Users do not pay for access to the spectrum, so they will channel their investment exclusively into developing robust technology that can function in this environment and continue to function as the environment grows more congested.

Where both spectrum scarcity and transaction costs are low, the commons model again may be the most appropriate, though this situation is less clear. Under these circumstances, the presence of low transaction costs would add to the efficiency-creating characteristics of the commons. On the other hand, it also is possible that the exclusive use model would provide comparable benefits, as the price will be close to zero if spectrum is abundant. With low transaction costs as well as low price, interested users should have unrestricted access to the spectrum they need.

The variables described above tend to tilt in favor of expanded use of the commons model in higher spectrum bands, particularly above 50 GHz, based on the physical characteristics of the spectrum itself. In these bands, the propagation characteristics of spectrum preclude many of the applications that are possible in lower bands (e.g., mobile service, broadcasting), and instead favor short-distance line-of-sight operation using narrow transmission beams. Thus, these bands are well-suited to accommodate multiple devices operating within a small area without interference. Moreover, administering these uses on an individualized licensed basis would involve very high transaction costs.

The Task Force does not advocate the wholesale conversion of all spectrum to a commons approach as some commenters appear to advocate. Although the commons model is in many ways a highly deregulatory "Darwinian" approach, as its proponents point out, productive use of spectrum commons by unlicensed devices, particularly in lower spectrum bands, typically requires significant regulatory limitations on device transmitter power that preclude many other technically and economically feasible spectrum uses that rely on higher-power signal propagation over longer distances, or that require greater protection from interference. In addition, some commons proponents themselves state that setting aside additional spectrum for use on a commons basis is not essential to the continued success of unlicensed technology because the technological capability exists to prevent congestion from occurring in existing unlicensed bands.

This does not, however, mean that only higher band spectrum should be subject to a commons approach. The record shows that the Commission's dedication of some lower band spectrum to unlicensed uses, e.g., 2.4 GHz, is yielding significant technological and economic benefits in the form of low-power short-distance communications and emerging mesh network technologies that should be further encouraged. The Task Force therefore recommends that the commons model continue to be applied selectively to other lower spectrum bands.

In addition, the commons approach has potential applicability in the creation of underlay rights across the entire range of spectrum for low-power, low-impact devices. To the extent that the Commission establishes "interference temperature" rules for particular bands,[4] the spectrum environment that is created below the temperature threshold

---

4. [An omitted section of the report explains that "The interference temperature metric would establish maximum permissible levels of interference, thus characterizing the 'worst case' environment in which a receiver would be expected to operate. Different threshold levels could be set for each band, geographic region or service." Eds.]

has the characteristics that weigh most heavily in favor of the commons approach: low scarcity due to technical restrictions on the power and operating range of devices and high transaction costs associated with negotiating access. Therefore, the commons approach should presumptively be used for operations below the interference temperature threshold. In addition, the commons model may be appropriate for some opportunistic, non-interfering uses of exclusively licensed spectrum above the interference temperature threshold, although this approach raises more significant challenges.

An important caveat must accompany any recommendation for a commons model: although there are indications that technology can go a long way to forestall scarcity concerns, if scarcity eventually does arise in particular spectrum bands in the future, then the commons model may need to evolve to address the problem. Because there is no price mechanism in the commons model to use as a tool for allocating scarce resources among competing users, there is always the risk that free access will eventually lead to interference and over-saturation, i.e., the "tragedy of the commons." These problems can be overcome to some extent through regulatory guidance, requirements such as power and emission limits, and sharing etiquettes. But if actual spectrum scarcity still occurs, rights may need to be redefined and market mechanisms (e.g., band managers) introduced because without them there are insufficient incentives to avoid overuse.

C. Limited Use of Command and Control

The command-and-control model should be applied only in situations where prescribing spectrum use by regulation is necessary to accomplish important public interest objectives or to conform to treaty obligations. With respect to the command-and-control model, as noted above, the Task Force recognizes that continued use of this approach may be required in situations where prescribing spectrum use by regulation is necessary to accomplish compelling public interest objectives. However, such objectives should be carefully defined, and the amount of spectrum subject to a command-and-control regime should be limited to that which ensures that those objectives are achieved. Many spectrum users will claim that they warrant special consideration and thus deserve exemption from any reform of their service allocation rules. It is therefore critical to distinguish between special interest and the public interest, establishing a high bar for any service to clear prior to receiving an exemption.

In general, command-and-control regulation should be reserved only for spectrum uses that provide clear, non-market public interest benefits or that require regulatory prescription to avoid market failure. For example, radioastronomy may need to have dedicated, protected spectrum bands for the foreseeable future, due to its highly sensitive applications and the fact that its benefits accrue to society as a whole and only over the long run. Public safety and critical infrastructure may also require dedicated spectrum at particular times to ensure priority access for emergency communications. Other areas where limited use of command-and-control may be justified include international/satellite, public safety, and broadcasting.

Subject to these exceptions, the Commission should eschew command-and-control regulation, and legacy command-and-control bands should be transitioned to more flexible rules and uses to the maximum extent possible (whether under the exclusive rights or the commons model).

3. Broadcasting

The Commission has traditionally allocated spectrum specifically for broadcast use, based on statutory public interest considerations and the free over-the-air nature of broadcast service. Many commenters argue that these characteristics distinguish broadcasting from other market-based uses of spectrum, and that the Commission should therefore continue to dedicate some spectrum specifically for broadcast use on a command-and-control basis. Other commenters contend that the continued dedication of spectrum for broadcasting, and particularly for commercial broadcasting, is increasingly anachronistic as the public gains access to alternative sources of programming and information from cable television, satellite services, the Internet, and other outlets.

The Task Force concludes that for the time being, there are valid reasons to continue applying the "command-and-control" model to existing broadcast spectrum. Broadcast service is traditionally not subscriber-based; rather, it provides "universal" news, information, and entertainment services to the general public. As such, broadcasting has consistently been a central focus of Congress and the Communications Act, which regulates broadcast content and behavior by placing certain public interest obligations on broadcast licensees. In addition, localism and diversity of ownership are two important public interest objectives that have been associated with broadcasting to a greater degree than other spectrum uses. Finally, the broadcaster's relative lack of control over receiver equipment affects the rapidity with which technological advances can be introduced into the marketplace and assimilated by consumers—a factor that has complicated the DTV transition.

The transition of broadcast to a digital world, which is already under way, should help to increase the efficiency and flexibility in use of broadcast spectrum. As broadcasters convert to digital, some broadcast spectrum can be recovered for reallocation and reassignment to more flexible uses, as in the case of the 700 MHz band. The Commission has also allowed for some flexible use of broadcast spectrum,[5] and should consider additional ways to allow greater flexibility consistent with broadcasters continuing to meet their core public interest responsibilities. In addition, the Commission can take steps to make "white space" in the broadcast bands available for other uses.

Over the longer term, the Commission should periodically reevaluate its broadcast spectrum policies to determine whether they remain necessary to accomplish the public interest objectives they are intended to promote. In particular, such reevaluation should consider the extent to which the public interest benefits provided by dedication of spectrum to broadcasting under a command-and-control regime can be provided through the application of more flexible, market-oriented spectrum policies. It is likely that there will be a continued need to set aside some spectrum for non-market based broadcast uses, such as noncommercial and educational broadcasting. Assuming that technological advances continue to occur and that scarcity of access to spectrum resources decreases, however, it is equally likely that the continued application of command-and-control policies to commercial broadcasting spectrum could be substantially relaxed, or may not be needed at all, to ensure the public availability from multiple sources, including alternative technologies, of the types of information and programming that commercial broadcasters provide.

---

5. Broadcast spectrum can be used for ancillary or supplementary services that do not interfere with the primary broadcast signal, e.g., through use or leasing of the vertical blanking interval to provide telecommunications services. *See* 47 C.F.R. § 73.646. In the digital context, broadcasters may provide ancillary and supplementary services such as subscription television programming, computer software distribution, data transmission, teletext, interactive services, and audio signals so long as such services do not interfere with the required provision of free over-the-air programming. *See* Advanced Television Systems and Their Impact upon the Existing Television Broadcast Service, Fifth Report and Order, 12 FCC Rcd. 12,809 ¶ 29 (1997); *see also* 47 U.S.C. § 336.

Notes and Questions

1. How Much Flexibility? At the time this report was written, the FCC had a long history of command-and-control regulation. Yet, here, the report makes it seem almost obvious that flexible approaches are better. Is it possible that the FCC was simply being short-sighted all these years? Is the report slighting the reasons why the FCC has for so many years limited licensees' choice of services?

2. Models of Spectrum Control. The report lists two main alternatives to "command and control": exclusive use and commons. Are there other models that might be worth considering? The report states that exclusive use "does not imply or require creation of 'full' private property rights in spectrum." Should the report have advocated the creation of such property rights? Is the explanation that 47 U.S.C. § 301 prohibits any private party from obtaining such rights, so that the Commission cannot, on its own, grant them? Or is there some other reason to want "exclusive use" that does not encompass full private property rights?

3. Subtle Constraints. The report casts the commons approach as a flexible approach, but then concedes that "productive use of spectrum commons ... typically requires significant regulatory limitations on device transmitter power that preclude many other technically and economically feasible spectrum uses that rely on higher-power signal propagation over longer distances, or that require greater protection from interference." What does this sentence mean? Is the point here that even the seemingly uber-flexible commons necessarily excludes certain uses and users?

4. The Exception for Broadcasting. Is the report persuasive in suggesting that command and control may still be appropriate for broadcasting? The report justifies mandatory allocation of spectrum for broadcasting in part based on the fact that control of broadcasting has been a central focus of policymakers, who have imposed public interest obligations. Is that an appropriate consideration? Is it problematic for an agency to use regulation (public interest obligations) to justify further regulation (requiring that spectrum be used for broadcasting)? Note that the final sentence of this section suggests that further developments may render command-and-control regulation unnecessary. What sort of developments, beyond those that have already occurred, would justify abandonment of command and control? Might the spectrum policy announced in this report have that effect, by opening up spectrum and therefore reducing scarcity problems?

5. Scarcity. One factor emphasized throughout the report is the relative scarcity of the spectrum under consideration. What claim is made about scarcity under a commons approach? Will scarcity disappear, such that an unlimited number of users can step forward to use the commons without any shortage of supply? If so, how exactly would that work? If not, then what is the claim? That scarcity is less likely to occur? That scarcity can be more equitably addressed? Something else?

§ 4.B. Implementing Flexibility

A major drawback of command-and-control regulation is the underutilization of spectrum: people might be able to add new services and/or increase the utilization of existing services, but government restrictions prevent that from happening. This concern about the wasting of spectrum is a major impetus for changes in spectrum policies. One response is to reallocate spectrum from one specified use to another, on the theory that the latter will have a higher value. This is a longstanding practice on the part of the FCC, and it does not conflict with the command-and-control model: the Commission replaces one specified service with another.

As the report reflects, the FCC has clearly endorsed spectrum flexibility. How should the Commission transition to greater flexibility? The Commission is not operating on a clean slate—virtually all the frequencies suitable for new, flexible licenses are already licensed (or is utilized by the federal government for its own activities). So a big question is how the Commission should deal with existing licensees.

One possibility is for the Commission simply to allow existing licensees to provide the new services.[6] Such an approach has the virtue of simplicity, but it also has some potential drawbacks. It would entail an enormous windfall for most licensees, who either received their licenses gratis (as is the case for broadcasting licenses that have not been sold by the original licensee) or paid relatively small sums for their licenses—prices that were low precisely because the licenses narrowly constrained the services that could be offered. Instead of the government receiving revenues from auctioning licenses, all the value from the newly broadened rights would go to existing licensees. Giving rights to existing licensees also could create significant transaction costs, especially if licenses for the existing service were allotted in small geographic regions (as most were) and new services would be most valuable on a broader geographic basis. Finally, giving new flexible rights to existing licensees could create holdout costs: a licensee whose license was necessary for the creation of a nationwide band in a certain frequency would seek to extract huge sums from the entity that had gathered all the other frequencies in that band.

At the other extreme, a quite different approach also has the virtue of simplicity: the Commission could simply revoke all the existing licenses for a given set of frequencies. Recall that, under 47 U.S.C. § 301, licenses do not confer any property rights on licensees, and the FCC has the legal authority to revoke licenses and repurpose spectrum. This would likely reduce investment and upset investment-backed expectations due to the abruptness of the revocation. Avoiding abrupt changes allows for greater investment— more expected years of operation should translate into more investment.

Middle ground approaches also exist. The FCC proposed, and Congress adopted, one such possibility—"incentive auctions" under which auction revenue would be shared with incumbent licensees who agreed to relinquish some of their spectrum usage rights. These auctions are discussed below, and in Chapter Five.

A different possible middle ground is to authorize new services to be provided by new licensees who operate alongside the existing incumbents providing their original service. Note that this leaves the original licensee with no incentive to economize on its use of spectrum. Allowing a new licensee to offer the new service introduces another wrinkle as

---

6. In the 1980s, for instance, the FCC authorized FM, AM, and television licensees to use part of their spectrum for secondary uses. *See* Amendment of Parts 2 and 73 of the Commission's AM Broadcast Rules Concerning the Use of the AM Carrier, Report and Order, 100 F.C.C. 2d 5 (1984); FM Licensees: Amendment of the Commission's Rules Concerning Use of Subsidiary Communications Authorizations, Final Rule, 48 Fed. Reg. 28,445 (1983); The Use of Subcarrier Frequencies in the Aural Baseband of Television Transmitters, Final Rule, 49 Fed. Reg. 18,100 (1984). These licensees still had to use their spectrum primarily to provide their primary service; but to the extent that there was any spectrum remaining under these licenses, they could also provide nonbroadcast services such as private paging, data transmission, and dispatch services.

well: if two or more licensees are licensed to use the same frequency but as part of different services, the Commission will have to articulate and enforce rules that determine which service has priority in the event that there turns out to be interference.

As it happens, the Commission has never simply decided to end a service—it has always given licensees time and some opportunity to recoup their costs. Beyond that, the FCC usually presumes the status quo, putting the burden on a new service to justify changing the existing arrangement. And it often treats as a relevant consideration the preservation of the existing service, even if that service has not proven valuable to users.

This may reflect not only concerns about investment but also a basic rule of political economy: incumbents standing to lose their licenses face a certain loss, and will organize effectively to keep that license; potential entrants lose an opportunity to buy a license, which is less certain (because they may not win the auction) and less beneficial (because they will pay market prices at auction) than keeping the license is for the incumbent. The result is that incumbents who fear losing their licenses usually lobby more effectively than potential entrants.

An early example of an attempt to move toward flexibility while offering something to incumbents was the Commission's decision to open up spectrum for broadband personal communications services, as reflected in the excerpt below. This proceeding presents an important step in the movement towards greater flexibility and a very important allocation in its own right. But note that the Commission is still deciding how much spectrum to allocate to these new services, exactly which frequencies will be allocated for the new uses, how the transition from the existing services and licensees to the new services and licensees will occur, etc. That is, it is still making many of the decisions that are the hallmark of command-and-control regulation. As you read it, consider what choices the Commission is making, and why it is making them.

REDEVELOPMENT OF SPECTRUM TO ENCOURAGE INNOVATION IN THE USE OF NEW TELECOMMUNICATIONS TECHNOLOGIES

Notice of Proposed Rulemaking, 7 FCC Rcd. 1542 (1992)

1. By this Notice [of Proposed Rulemaking or NPRM], the Commission proposes to establish new areas of the spectrum to be used for emerging telecommunications technologies. These new frequency bands would be designated from 220 MHz of the spectrum between 1.85 and 2.20 GHz. We further propose to provide a regulatory framework that will enable the existing fixed microwave users in these bands to relocate to other fixed microwave bands or alternative media with minimum disruption to their operations. We believe this can best be accomplished through the use of a flexible negotiations approach that permits financial arrangements between incumbents and new service providers during an extended transition period. We also propose to permit state and local government facilities, including public safety, to continue their current operations on a fully protected basis by exempting such facilities from any mandatory transition period.

NEED FOR EMERGING TECHNOLOGIES BANDS

4. In recent years, technological advancements in digital and signal processing systems have opened possibilities for the development of a broad range of new radio communication services. These technological advances have increased the need for spectrum to foster the growth and development of new services, primarily for mobile applications. However, this has created an environment in which new services are vying with each other and with existing users for relatively small slivers of spectrum that are incapable

of supporting full implementation of new service. The Commission currently has pending before it a number of requests for new services and technologies for which sufficient spectrum is unavailable. These requests include: 200 MHz for new personal communications services (PCS); 40 MHz for data PCS; 33 MHz for a generic mobile satellite service; 70 MHz for a digital audio broadcasting service; and 33 MHz for low Earth orbit satellites.

6. [W]e need to develop a plan that includes specific provisions for minimizing impact on existing services. Nevertheless, we believe that establishing these emerging technologies bands is desirable and will again prove advantageous for facilitating the continuing development of new communications technologies and the growth and expansion of existing services.

7. The current lack of available spectrum tends to have a chilling effect on the incentives for manufacturers and financial institutions to develop and fund new communications research. The emerging technologies bands would help provide some of the structure, in terms of frequency of operation and operating plan, that is needed to facilitate the development of equipment. At the same time, this new concept would provide considerable flexibility with regard to the types of technologies and services that can be authorized.

SPECTRUM ISSUES

9. [I]n the early 1970s [when the Commission foresaw emerging technologies and set aside space for them], spectrum was available in the lower frequency bands that was only lightly used and the licensees on those frequencies could be relocated relatively easily. [T]oday [t]here are substantial operations on virtually all of the lower frequency bands, so that establishment of emerging technologies bands will unavoidably necessitate relocation of significant numbers of existing users. The task, then, is to identify a relatively wide band of frequencies that can be made available with a minimum of impact on existing users and that also can provide suitable operating characteristics for new, primarily mobile, services.

10. The spectrum selected must meet the requirements of a broad range of possible services, including land mobile and satellite. The factors that must be considered include:

Cost of equipment—If the spectrum chosen is in a range for which state-of-the-art equipment is not available, then high costs would delay the introduction of new services.

Amount of spectrum—There must be enough spectrum available to allow substantial development and economies of scale.

Feasibility of relocation—The existing licensees must be able to relocate with a minimum of cost and disruption of service to consumers.

Nongovernment spectrum—In order to avoid the need for coordination and to speed the process of transition, the new bands should come entirely from spectrum regulated by the FCC.

International developments—It is desirable for the spectrum chosen to be compatible with similar international developments.

11. *Spectrum Study.* With the above considerations in mind, the Commission's staff conducted a study to examine the possibility of creating emerging technologies bands. This study identified the most suitable region of the spectrum, determined the existing users of that spectrum, explored alternatives for relocating those users to higher bands or other media with a minimum disruption of service, and examined the cost of such re-

location. The study concluded that 220 MHz in the 1.85–2.20 GHz region could be designated for innovative technologies and services.

12. The study limited the consideration of candidate frequency bands to those in which mobile operations are practicable with current state-of-the-art electronic components and manufacturing capabilities. It found that while experimental mobile use is taking place at higher bands, the state-of-the-art technology for the compact, lightweight, portable electronic components expected to be used in new services generally will limit operations in those services to frequencies under 3 GHz. Thus, the study concluded that frequencies above 3 GHz would not be acceptable. It next found that the spectrum below 1 GHz generally does not appear to offer any possibilities for spectrum availability. Most of this spectrum is used for broadcasting and land mobile services that would be very difficult to relocate. These services have very large numbers of users, particularly in the major urban areas, and there are no bands with similar technical characteristics to which the existing users could be relocated. The remaining frequencies below 1 GHz are narrow, scattered bands that would not provide sufficient spectrum. [For the above reasons, the study concentrated on the spectrum between 1 and 3 GHz.]

14. The study identified three non-Government bands from this spectrum for consideration: 1.85–2.20, 2.45–2.50, and 2.50–2.65 GHz. The study found the 2.45–2.50 GHz band, which is allocated for use by Industrial, Scientific, and Medical (ISM) equipment, less desirable because it has a limited amount of spectrum (50 MHz) and because there is no replacement band that offers the same physical characteristics for the existing ISM operations in that band. The 2.50–2.60 GHz band, which is used for multipoint distribution service (MDS) and instructional television fixed service (ITFS), also was eliminated because there are no other frequency allocations currently available to which existing MDS operations could be relocated.

15. The remaining 1.85–2.20 GHz band is used for fixed private and common carrier microwave services, public land mobile service, broadcast auxiliary operations, and multipoint distribution service. Specifically, the 1.85–1.99, 2.11–2.15, and 2.16–2.20 GHz bands are used for private operational fixed and common carrier microwave operations. The private operational fixed licensees are local governments (including public safety), petroleum producers, utilities, railroads, and other business users such as the manufacturing, banking, and service industries. Systems range from a few links to very large systems that use hundreds of links. They are used as part of communications systems for local government and public safety organizations. These facilities are also used to control electric power, oil and gas pipeline and railroad systems, and to provide routine business voice, data, and video communications. The common carrier licensees are telephone, cellular telephone, and paging providers. Telephone companies use this band to provide telephone service to remote areas, cellular companies to interconnect cell sites with mobile telephone switching offices, and paging companies for control and repeater stations.

16. The 1.99–2.11 GHz band is used for broadcast auxiliary services. The licensees in this service are television broadcasters and cable television operators. Broadcast auxiliary services include studio-to-transmitter links, inner city relays, and electronic news gathering (ENG) mobile operations. These services are used to transmit video programming from remote sites to the studio and from the studio to the transmitter sites. The 2.15–2.16 GHz band is used for multipoint distribution service (MDS) and its licensees are, for the most part, wireless cable television operators. MDS is used to supply video programming to subscribers over city-wide areas and to rural areas where it is not economical to install cable service.

17. The study finds that the private and common carrier fixed microwave operations using this spectrum can be relocated to higher frequency bands that provide for similar type services and can support propagation over similar path lengths. Further, it observes that there are other reasonable alternatives for fixed microwave such as fiber, cable and satellite communications, which can utilize off-the-shelf equipment to provide these services.

18. The study also concludes that it is not practicable at this time to relocate the broadcast auxiliary and the multipoint distribution services that use spectrum in the 1.85–2.20 GHz range. It finds that currently there is heavy use of the ENG bands and that the forthcoming introduction of broadcast advanced television service may result in more congestion in these bands. Since there currently are a large number of MDS applications before the Commission and the MDS service is a developing industry, the study further finds that it would not be desirable to relocate the MDS channels at 2 GHz.

19. *Proposed Reallocations.* Based on the findings of our staff study, we propose to reallocate 220 MHz of the 1.85 to 2.20 GHz band that is currently used for private and common carrier fixed microwave services. The specific frequencies proposed to be reallocated are the 1.85–1.99, 2.11–2.15, and 2.16–2.20 GHz bands. We believe that this spectrum will meet the requirements of a significant number of new services and technologies. The private and common carrier fixed microwave services operating in these bands provide important and essential services. Accordingly, we intend to pursue this reallocation in a manner that will minimize disruption of the existing 2 GHz fixed operations.

20. In this regard, we propose to make available all fixed microwave bands above 3 GHz, both the common carrier and the private bands, for recommendation of fixed microwave operations currently licensed in the 1.85–2.20 GHz spectrum.[7]

22. *Transition Plan.* Our proposed transition plan would consist of three basic elements, discussed below.

23. First, we wish to ensure the availability of the existing vacant 2 GHz spectrum for the initial development of new services and to discourage possible speculative fixed service applications for this spectrum. We therefore will continue to grant applications for fixed operations in the proposed new technologies bands; however, applications for new facilities submitted after the adoption date of this Notice will be granted on a secondary basis only, conditioned upon the outcome of this proceeding. [For the meaning of "secondary basis," see ¶ 24.]

---

7. We also will encourage fixed microwave operators to consider other non-radio alternative media to meet their telecommunication needs, particularly fiber optic circuits. In allocating spectrum, one of the primary considerations is whether there is a technological dependence of the service on radio rather than wire lines. Mobile communications necessarily will always require use of radio spectrum, and in the past the Commission provided large amounts of spectrum for fixed microwave because wireline alternatives often were economically prohibitive. However, in the last five years technological advancements in optical communications have resulted in fiber being very competitive with fixed microwave. Further, the capacities of fiber optic circuits greatly exceed those of fixed microwave. For these reasons, many common carrier and private communication requirements, which in the past were met by fixed microwave, are now met with fiber optic circuits. In connection with encouraging migration to other, non-radio alternative media, we ask for comment on whether we should award tax certificates to fixed microwave licensees who receive financial compensation from an entity seeking to use the spectrum for new technology as part of an agreement to surrender their license and use other, non-radio alternative media. Grant of tax certificates in such circumstances would appear to be similar to our recent decision to award tax certificates to AM broadcast licensees receiving financial compensation for surrendering their licenses for cancellation. *See* Review of the Technical Assignment Criteria for the AM Broadcast Service, Report and Order, 6 FCC Rcd. 6273, 6472 (1991). [Footnote relocated.]

24. Second, except for state and local licensees, we propose to allow currently licensed 2 GHz fixed licensees to continue to occupy 2 GHz frequencies on a co-primary basis with new services for a fixed period of time, for example ten or fifteen years. Ten years could generally be expected to provide for a complete amortization of existing 2 GHz equipment. A fifteen year period would extend the relocation period through the useful life of that equipment. At the end of this transition period, these facilities could continue to operate in the band on a secondary basis. This means that if, after the transition period, new services were not able to use the spectrum because of interference from fixed microwave systems, those fixed microwave systems would be required to eliminate the interference, negotiate an arrangement for continued operation with the new service operator, or cease operation. This would allow some fixed microwave systems to continue operations indefinitely, particularly in rural areas where less spectrum may be required for new services.

25. We recognize that state and local government agencies would face special economic and operational considerations in relocating their 2 GHz fixed microwave operations to higher frequencies or alternative media. We are particularly sensitive to the need to avoid any disruption of police, fire, and other public safety communications. To address these concerns, we propose to exempt state and local government 2 GHz fixed microwave facilities from any mandatory transition periods. Rather, these facilities would be allowed to continue to operate at 2 GHz on a co-primary basis indefinitely, at the discretion of the state and local government licensees. These agencies would be permitted to negotiate the use of their frequencies with other parties. In this manner, transfer of state and local government operations could be arranged so as to accommodate fully any special economic or operational considerations with regard to the institutions affected.

26. To provide maximum flexibility in the relocation process, we believe it is desirable to permit parties seeking to operate new services to negotiate with the existing users for access to the 2 GHz frequencies and, conversely, to permit incumbents to negotiate with the new service providers for continued use of the spectrum. Therefore, we propose to allow providers of new services assigned spectrum allocated to the new emerging technologies bands to negotiate financial arrangements with existing licensees. This would encourage reaccommodation and underwriting of the costs of transition for the 2 GHz users. In return, the new licensees would receive earlier access to the frequencies used by the existing fixed microwave operators. Such arrangements would allow market forces to achieve a balance between the need to minimize the reaccommodation cost to existing operators and the immediate need for the spectrum to permit provision of these new services. It would also provide incumbents with a way to assure that the new licensees would not interfere with their expanded facilities or current facilities at the end of a mandatory transition period.[8]

Notes and Questions

1. Broadband PCS. The FCC ultimately adopted the reallocation plan laid out in this NPRM. *See* Redevelopment of Spectrum to Encourage Innovation in the Use of New Telecommunications Technologies, First Report and Order and Third Notice of Proposed Rulemaking, 7 FCC Rcd. 6886 (1992). That plan came to be known as the "broadband"

---

8. Our principal desire is to compensate existing 2 GHz users for the costs of relocation. We recognize, however, that such market-based negotiations could possibly result in windfalls for the incumbent 2 GHz licensees. [Footnote relocated.]

PCS plan (as opposed to "narrowband" PCS) because it provided sufficient spectrum for bandwidth-intensive data transmission and thus paved the way for the mobile phones with enhanced capacity that we now take for granted.

2. Valuing PCS. Why did the Commission decide to allocate any spectrum to PCS? That is, how did the FCC know that spectrum would be more valuable if used for PCS than if used for other services? Conversely, why allocate only 220 MHz to PCS? If PCS is so valuable, how did the Commission know that it didn't warrant an even larger chunk of frequency?

3. Finding Frequencies. To find spectrum for PCS, the Commission first studied the physical properties of the technology and determined, within a very wide margin, which areas of the spectrum seemed best suited for PCS transmission and reception. It concluded that some frequencies (those above 3 GHz) were technologically unsuited to PCS and thus those ranges were no longer considered. Next, the Commission identified other ranges (specifically, frequencies below 1 GHz) and determined that they were already so crowded that they, too, would not be made available for PCS. That left the range between approximately 1 GHz and 3 GHz. The FCC identified services already in that range that, in the Commission's view, should be relocated to make room for PCS, and then announced a transition plan that would move those services out.

But how did the FCC make each of these determinations? Consider each step in isolation. First, the unusable frequencies. The Commission states in ¶ 12 that it limited its consideration of "candidate frequency bands to those in which mobile operations are practicable with current state-of-the-art electronic components and manufacturing capabilities." How confident are you that the Commission can make this sort of technical determination accurately? Besides, even if then-current PCS designs did not work in certain frequency bands, why couldn't the Commission tell PCS innovators to develop variants of the technology that would? The Commission itself reports that "experimental mobile use" was already taking place in these unusable bands. Why not encourage that innovation? In fact, if higher frequencies tend to be particularly uncrowded—something the Commission hints at early in the document—shouldn't the Commission shunt PCS to those higher frequencies, in essence encouraging new technologies to make use of underused spectrum resources?

Now, let's turn to the frequencies below 1 GHz, also discussed in ¶ 12, that were ruled out because they were already being used by broadcasters and land mobile services. How did the Commission know that these services should be left in place whereas services in the 1 GHz to 3 GHz range would ultimately be moved? Did the FCC determine, in each of these instances, that PCS was not a more valuable use for the spectrum at issue? Or was the Commission instead making a prediction about transaction costs? On what basis exactly?

Finally, consider the frequencies between 1 GHz and 3 GHz that the Commission deemed acceptable for PCS. How did the agency determine that PCS was a more valuable use of this spectrum than the private operational fixed services and the common carrier microwave operations that were already there? If PCS is a more valuable use, why did the Commission structure a complicated transition period? Won't the more valuable use simply buy out the less valued uses? Indeed, why did the Commission not simply announce that, henceforth, any license (including those already outstanding) for the 1.85–1.99, 2.11–2.15 and 2.16–2.20 GHz bands would be interpreted so as to permit the licensee to offer PCS service, and, further, that those licenses were now freely transferable?

4. A Windfall? How would you respond to footnote 8 if you were an incumbent licensee? What if you were a potential PCS provider? In fact, the FCC modified the transition plan in later orders to mitigate potential windfalls and provider greater structure, via three "negotiation periods." The first, called the "voluntary negotiation period," had no requirement for negotiation or negotiation parameters. That was followed by a "mandatory negotiation period" in which the PCS operator and the microwave operator were required to negotiate in good faith. If those negotiations failed, the "involuntary relocation" period commenced, in which the PCS operator could require the incumbent microwave licensee to relocate if it offered the microwave licensee comparable facilities and paid the cost of relocating (and the FCC capped the relocation costs, to avoid microwave incumbents padding them). The first two periods were longer for public safety licensees (up to five years) than for other licensees (two years). *See* Amendment to the Commission's Rules Regarding a Plan for Sharing the Costs of Microwave Relocation, Second Report and Order, 12 FCC Rcd. 2705 (1997). The Commission also provided an inducement for successful negotiations in the form of the tax certificates mentioned in footnote 7 (offering favorable tax treatment). Those certificates were issued only to microwave licensees who reached agreements before the end of the mandatory negotiation period. *See* Clarification of Procedures for Issuance of Tax Certificates Regarding Relocation of Microwave Incumbent Licensees, Public Notice, 13 FCC Rcd. 6661 (1998).

5. Treating Incumbents. Should the FCC have given the incumbents less time to stay in their existing allocations and/or no promise of substitute spectrum? Should it have given them more time? On what should this decision be based?

6. Necessary Conditions. Allocating spectrum for new technologies seems to create a paradox. Firms are reluctant to invest research dollars creating new equipment until they are sure that the Commission will license the new service in the designed-for band. The Commission, meanwhile, is reluctant to allocate spectrum to a technology that is unproven both as a technical matter and in terms of its desirability to consumers. How did the Commission address this problem in this spectrum decision?

7. Metrics. How should telecommunications policy respond to the spectrum requirements of new technologies? Can the FCC estimate and compare the likely value of competing uses? Given the large coordination problems that need to be resolved, would it be folly to just leave these issues to the marketplace? Are there intermediate steps? How would you respond if Congress were to put forward legislation conferring perpetual spectrum property rights on current licensees and then permitting those licensees to sell their rights to whomever they chose for use in whatever service the market deemed most valuable?

8. PCS Explosion. The FCC's 2010 National Broadband Plan summarized the impact of the PCS allocation as follows:

> From 1994 to 2000, the FCC auctioned the Personal Communications Service (PCS) spectrum, which made mobile voice communications a mass-market reality and unleashed a tidal wave of innovation and investment. These auctions more than tripled the stock of spectrum for commercial mobile radio services. With spectrum as the catalyst, the mobile industry profoundly changed during this period:
> - The number of wireless providers increased significantly in most markets.
> - The per-minute price of cell phone service dropped by 50%.
> - The number of mobile subscribers more than tripled.
> - Cumulative investment in the industry more than tripled from $19 billion to over $70 billion.
> - The number of cell sites more than quadrupled, from 18,000 to over 80,000.
> - Industry employment tripled from 54,000 to over 155,000.

FCC, National Broadband Plan § 5.1 (2010), *available at* http://transition.fcc.gov/national-broadband-plan/national-broadband-plan.pdf.

What, if anything, should we learn from these later developments? That is, what does this tell us about how the FCC should act the next time there is a new proposed use of the spectrum? Is it possible to abstract from this experience, and, if so, exactly what should we abstract?

9. Flexible Licenses. The licenses granted to the winners of the PCS auction provided a considerable degree of flexibility. In particular, the FCC specified that the licenses could be used to provide "any mobile communications service" as well as "fixed services" provided in combination with mobile ones—as long as the license is not used to provide a broadcasting service. 47 C.F.R. § 24.3. The Commission has taken similar actions in other frequencies. For instance, in Service Rules for the 746–764 and 776–794 MHz Bands, and Revisions of Part 27 of the Commission's Rules, First Report and Order, 15 FCC Rcd. 476 (2000), the Commission issued an order reallocating spectrum that had been dedicated to broadcasting. Instead of picking a particular service that licensees could offer, the Commission authorized licensees to choose among a wide range of wireless services. Similarly, in Service Rules for Advanced Wireless Services in the 1.7 GHz and 2.1 GHz Bands, Report and Order, 18 FCC Rcd. 25,162 ¶ 13 (2003), the FCC issued an order announcing that "[i]n order to promote innovative services and encourage the flexible and efficient use of the 1710–1755 and 2110–2155 MHz bands, we permit licensees to use this spectrum for any use permitted by the United States Table of Frequency Allocations contained in Part 2 of our rules (i.e., fixed or mobile services)."

It bears mentioning, though, that neither in these nor in any other orders has the FCC given licensees the freedom to choose any service they desired. For instance, in the 2003 order noted immediately above, the FCC stated that the bands could not be used for broadcasting, *id.* ¶ 58, and in the 2000 order noted above it disallowed conventional television service. 15 FCC Rcd. 476 ¶ 15. Why impose any restrictions? The main reason, according to the FCC, was that the danger of interference is too great. The 2000 order explained that

> Establishing regulatory flexibility sufficient to accommodate conventional television broadcasting would impose disproportionate, offsetting burdens on wireless services, constraining their technical effectiveness and, consequently, their economic practicability.
>
> The interference problem arises from the disparity between the two services' characteristic power levels, and between their transmitter tower heights. Any substantial disproportion between the power levels of services sharing a spectrum band creates much greater interference difficulties for the lower-power service than when sharing or adjacent-band services operate at comparable power levels. The disparity between television transmitter tower heights and those used by typical wireless providers adds to the difficulty by accentuating the power of the more powerful service.

Id. ¶¶ 16–17.

10. Flexibility via Another Route. In ¶ 14 of the 1992 NPRM excerpted above, the FCC chose not to reallocate the spectrum dedicated to instructional television fixed service, and therein lies a story. In 1963, the FCC allocated the 2500–2690 MHz band to ITFS, and decided that the licensees would be accredited schools seeking to augment their educational mission.[9] There were two problems, however: in some areas there were no ap-

---

9. Amendment of Parts 2 and 4 of the Commission Rules and Regulations to Establish a New Class of Educational Television Service, Report and Order, 39 F.C.C. 846, ¶¶ 15–29 (1963).

plicants for those frequencies, and those who did apply for this spectrum were given much more spectrum than they wanted to use for their ITFS transmissions.[10] Both problems arose from the fact that the FCC had allocated this bandwidth for ITFS, and nothing else. Instead, the FCC responded to this problem by allowing ITFS licensees to lease "excess capacity" to operators of a service known as multichannel multipoint distribution service (MMDS).[11] Even with both uses, however, the demand was not sufficient to fully occupy the entire range of frequencies allotted for these purposes.[12] Later, the FCC broadened the category of services that can occupy this spectrum (renaming MMDS as Broadband Radio Service and ITFS as Educational Broadband Service).[13] The FCC still does not allow complete choice, but it has broadened the choice available to contain a range of broadband services (though still not any noninterfering service).

11. Incentive Auctions. As noted above, in 2010 the FCC's National Broadband Plan proposed what it termed "incentive auctions," and in 2012 Congress enacted legislation implementing such auctions. FCC, National Broadband Plan, § 5.3 (2010), *available at* http://transition.fcc.gov/national-broadband-plan/national-broadband-plan.pdf; Middle Class Tax Relief and Job Creation Act of 2012, Pub. L. No. 112-96, 126 Stat. 156. Title VI of that legislation, sometimes called the Spectrum Act, provides for incentive auctions. As we discuss more fully in Chapter Five, the incentive auctions seek to implement flexibility by giving incumbent licensees (in this case, broadcasters) an incentive to relinquish their spectrum usage rights, and allowing the winning bidders to provide a wide range of services.

Why not simply give flexibility to existing licensees to offer new services? Part of the reason was that this would create a very large windfall for the licensees, most of which bought their licenses on the secondary market at low prices that reflected the authorized uses of the spectrum. And part of the reason involved efficiency. Notably, converting individual, local 6 MHz broadcast licenses into regional or national licenses suitable for wireless broadband would require a very large number of transactions, and thus high transaction costs. No channel is licensed in every community (to avoid interference), so buying all the broadcast television licenses on a particular channel in a region or nationwide would still leave large geographic areas not covered by those licenses. And once any entity started buying television licenses on a given channel with the intent of converting them into a regional or national wireless system, other television licensees on that channel would know that they could hold out for a supracompetitive price because they would be needed in order for the channel to be cleared in the target area.

---

10. *See* Amendment of Parts 2, 21, 74 and 94 of the Commission's Rules and Regulations in Regard to Frequency Allocation to the Instructional Television Fixed Service and the Multipoint Distribution Service, Report and Order, 94 F.C.C. 2d 1203, ¶ 25 (1983) (noting the lack of interest in some of the frequencies devoted to ITFS, and the surplus bandwidth for those who did have the licenses).

11. Amendment of Parts 21 and 74 of the Commission's Rules With Regard to Filing Procedures in the Multipoint Distribution Service and in the Instructional Television Fixed Service, Report and Order, 10 FCC Rcd. 9589, ¶ 1 (1995); Amendment of Parts 2, 21, 74 and 94 of the Commission's Rules, 94 F.C.C. 2d at ¶ 85.

12. *See, e.g.*, Amendment of Parts 1, 21 and 74 to Enable Multipoint Distribution Service and Instructional Television Fixed Service Licensees to Engage in Fixed Two-Way Transmissions, Report and Order on Reconsideration, 14 FCC Rcd. 12,764, ¶ 56 (1999) (stating that "most [ITFS channels] have lain fallow").

13. Amendment of Parts 1, 21, 73, 74 and 101 of the Commission's Rules to Facilitate the Provision of Fixed and Mobile Broadband Access, Educational and Other Advanced Services in the 2150–2162 and 2500–2690 MHz Bands, Report and Order and Further Notice of Proposed Rulemaking, 19 FCC Rcd. 14,165 (2004).

In any event, the legislation achieved the FCC's goal of giving it the ability to shift some very valuable frequencies from legacy uses like broadcasting to newer uses that people apparently value much more highly (that is what the much higher valuations for new wireless services indicate). And the legislation envisioned a very complex auction design — much more complex than any previous FCC auction scheme, and perhaps the most complex government auction ever.

As to the degree of flexibility, the Spectrum Act grants the FCC incentive auction authority "to permit the assignment of new initial licenses subject to flexible-use service rules." Spectrum Act § 6402. Accordingly, the Commission's order implementing the Spectrum Act provides that the new licenses may be used for any fixed or mobile service that is consistent with the allocation of the band. Expanding the Economic and Innovation Opportunities of Spectrum through Incentive Auctions, Report and Order, 29 FCC Rcd. 6567, 6870 ¶ 741 (2014).

§ 4.C. Dedicating Spectrum to Unlicensed Uses

Spectrum flexibility was one prominent theme of the Spectrum Policy Task Force Report. Another was the question of the model of individual usage that might be desirable on any given set of frequencies. The report suggested that in some circumstances a spectrum commons might be preferable to exclusive use. More recently, the 2010 National Broadband Plan recommended the following with respect to unlicensed devices:

> As the FCC seeks to free up additional spectrum for broadband, it should make a sufficient portion available for use exclusively or predominantly by unlicensed devices. This would enable innovators to try new ideas to increase spectrum access and efficiency through unlicensed means, and should enable new unlicensed providers to serve rural and unserved communities. Such an approach would represent a departure from the way the FCC has treated most unlicensed operations in the past. Unlicensed operations are typically overlays to licensed bands, with intensive unlicensed use emerging in some bands (e.g., the 2.4 GHz band) over a long period of time. However, targeting bands for unlicensed use could yield important benefits.

FCC, National Broadband Plan, Recommendation § 5.11 (2010), *available at* http://transition.fcc.gov/national-broadband-plan/national-broadband-plan.pdf.

Both the Spectrum Policy Task Force Report and the National Broadband Plan offer limited support for commons in the lower band spectrum — sometimes called "beachfront property" because it can be used for so many services and thus is the most desirable spectrum. By contrast, some commentators have advocated dedicating large swaths of lower band frequencies exclusively to unlicensed uses. One of the most prominent is Yochai Benkler. Below, we excerpt Benkler's most complete articulation of how, in his view, an unlicensed commons should be implemented.

Some Economics of Wireless Communications
Yochai Benkler, 16 Harv. J.L. & Tech. 25 (2002)

In the first half of the 20th century there was roughly universal agreement that "spectrum" was scarce, and that if it was to be used efficiently, it had to be regulated by an expert agency. A little over forty years ago, Coase wrote a seminal critique of this system, explaining why spectrum scarcity was no more reason for regulation than is wheat scarcity. "Scarcity" was the normal condition of all economic goods, and markets, not regulation, were the preferred mode of allocating scarce resources. In the 1960s and 1970s, a number of academic studies of property rights in spectrum elaborated on Coase's work, but these remained largely outside the pale of actual likely policy options. It was only in the 1980s that a chairman of the Federal Communications Commission voiced support for a system of market-based allocation, and only in the 1990s did Congress permit the FCC to use auctions instead of comparative hearings to assign spectrum. But auctions in and of themselves, without flexible use rights, are but a pale shadow of real market-based allocation. Indeed, they might better be understood as a type of fee for government licenses than as a species of market allocation. Since the mid-1980s, and with increasing acceptance into the 1990s, arguments emerged within the FCC in favor of introducing a much more serious implementation of market-based allocation. This would call for the definition and auctioning of perpetual, exclusive property rights akin to those we have in real estate, which could be divided, aggregated, resold, and reallocated in any form their owners chose to use.

Just as this call for more perfect markets in spectrum allocations began to emerge as a real policy option, a very different kind of voice began to be heard on spectrum policy. This position was every bit as radically different from the traditional approach as the perfected property rights approach, but in a radically different way. The argument was that technology had rendered the old dichotomy between government licensing of frequencies and property rights in frequencies obsolete. It was now possible to change our approach, and instead of creating and enforcing a market in property rights in spectrum blocks, we could rely on a market in smart radio equipment that would allow people to communicate without *anyone* having to control "the spectrum." Just as no one "owns the Internet," but intelligent computers communicate with each other using widely accepted sharing protocols, so too could computationally intensive radios. In the computer hardware and software markets and the Internet communications market, competition in the *equipment market*, not competition in the infrastructure market (say, between Verizon and AOL Time Warner), was the driving engine of innovation, growth, and welfare. This approach has been called a "spectrum commons" approach, because it regards bandwidth as a common resource that all equipment can call on, subject to sharing protocols, rather than as a controlled resource that is always under the control of someone, be it a property owner, a government agency, or both. It is important to understand, however, that this metaphor has its limitations. Like its predecessor positions on spectrum management, it uses the term "spectrum" as though it describes a discrete resource whose utilization is the object of analysis. In fact, as this Article explains, "spectrum" is not a discrete resource whose optimal utilization is the correct object of policy. The correct object of optimization is wireless network communications capacity. Like trade with India, which is only one parameter of welfare in Britain, bandwidth is only one parameter in determining the capacity of a wireless network. Focusing *solely* on it usually distorts the analysis. I will therefore mostly refer in this Article to "open wireless networks" rather than to spectrum commons. Like "the open road" or the "open architecture" of the Internet, it describes a network that treats some resources as open to all equipment to use, leaving it to the equipment manufacturers—cars or computers, respectively, in those open networks—to optimize the functionality they provide using that resource.

Most of the initial responses to this critique were largely similar to the responses that greeted the economists' critique forty years ago—incomprehension, disbelief, and mockery, leading Noam to call the standard economists' view "the new orthodoxy." *See* Eli Noam, Spectrum Auction: Yesterday's Heresy, Today's Orthodoxy, Tomorrow's Anachronism. Taking the Next Step to Open Spectrum Access, 41 J.L. & Econ. 765, 768 (1998). But reality has a way of forcing debates. The most immediate debate-forcing fact is the breathtaking growth of the equipment market in high-speed wireless communications devices, in particular the rapidly proliferating 802.11x family of standards (best known for the 802.11b or "Wi-Fi" standard), all of which rely on utilizing frequencies that no one controls. Particularly when compared to the anemic performance of licensed wireless services in delivering high-speed wireless data services, and the poor performance of other sectors of the telecommunications and computer markets, the success of Wi-Fi forces a more serious debate. It now appears that serious conversation between the two radical critiques of the licensing regime is indeed beginning to emerge, most directly joined now in a new paper authored by former chief economist of the FCC, Gerald Faulhaber, and Internet pioneer and former chief technologist of the FCC, Dave Farber. Gerald Faulhaber & David Farber, Spectrum Management: Property Rights, Markets, and the Commons, *available at* http://assets.wharton.upenn.edu/~faulhabe/SPECTRUM_MANAGEMENTv51.pdf.

What I hope to do in this Article is (a) provide a concise description of the baseline technological developments that have changed the wireless policy debate; (b) explain how these changes provide a critique of a spectrum property rights approach and suggest that open wireless networks will be more efficient at optimizing wireless communications capacity; and (c) outline a transition plan that will allow us to facilitate an experiment in both approaches so as to inform ourselves as we make longer-term and larger-scale policy choices in the coming decade.

To provide the economic analysis, I offer a general, though informal, model for describing the social cost of wireless communications, aggregating the equipment and servicing costs involved, the displacement of communications not cleared, and the institutional and organizational overhead in the form of transaction costs and administrative costs. In comparing these, I suggest that while investment patterns in equipment will likely differ greatly, it is not clear that we can say, a priori, whether equipment costs involved in open wireless networks will be higher or lower than equipment costs involved in spectrum property-based networks. Investment in the former will be widely decentralized, and much of it will be embedded in end-user owned equipment that will capitalize ex ante the cost and value of free communications over the lifetime of the equipment. Investment in the latter will be more centrally capitalized because consumers will not both invest ex ante in capitalization of the value of free communication and pay usage fees ex post. Since the value added by spectrum property is in pricing usage to improve the efficiency of allocation over time, it will need lower ex ante investment levels at the end user terminal and higher investment levels at the core of the network. Which of the two will have higher total costs over the lifetime of the network is not clear.

The most complicated problem is defining the relative advantages and disadvantages of spectrum property-based networks and open wireless networks insofar as they displace some communications in order to clear others. Backing out of contemporary multi-user information theory, I propose a general description of the displacement effect of wireless communications. Then, I suggest reasons to think that open wireless networks will systematically have higher capacity, that is, that each communication cleared through an open network will displace fewer communications in total. This, in turn, leaves the range in which spectrum property-based systems can improve on open wireless systems in terms of efficiency as those cases where the discriminating power of pricing is sufficiently valuable to overcome the fact that open wireless systems have cleared more communications but without regard to the willingness and ability of the displaced communications to pay. As a spectrum property-based network diverges from locally and dynamically efficient pricing, the likelihood that it will improve efficiency declines.

As for overhead, or transaction and administrative costs, I suggest reasons to think that both direct transaction costs associated with negotiating transactions for spectrum and clearing transmission rights, and administrative costs associated with a property-type regime rather than with an administrative framework for recognizing and generalizing privately set equipment standards, will be lower for open wireless networks. In particular, I emphasize how the transaction costs of a property system will systematically prevent efficient pricing, and therefore systematically undermine the one potential advantage of a spectrum property-based system.

My conclusion is that the present state of our technological knowledge, and the relevant empirical experience we have with the precursors of open wireless networks and with pricing in wired networks, lean toward a prediction that open wireless networks will be more efficient in the foreseeable future. This qualitative prediction, however, is not sufficiently robust to permit us to make a decisive policy choice between the two approaches given our present limited practical experience with either. We can, however, quite confidently state the following propositions:

1. Creating and exhaustively auctioning perfect property rights to all spectrum frequencies is an unfounded policy. None of our technical, theoretical, or empirical data provides sufficient basis for believing that an exhaustive system that assigns property rights to all bands of frequencies will be systematically better than a system that largely relies on equipment-embedded communications protocols that are permitted to use bandwidth on a dynamic, unregulated basis.

2. Creating such a property system will burden the development of computationally intensive, user equipment-based approaches to wireless communications, potentially locking us into a lower development trajectory for wireless communications systems. This is particularly so for the dominant position that advocates creating perfect property rights in spectrum blocks, but is true even with modified systems, such as the Faulhaber-Farber proposal to include an easement for non-interfering transmissions or the Noam proposal of dynamic market clearance on the basis of spot-market transactions and forward contracts.

3. It is theoretically possible that pricing will sometimes improve the performance of wireless communications networks. The geographically local nature of wireless communications network capacity, the high variability in the pattern of human communications, and the experience of wired networks suggest, however, that if pricing will prove to be useful at all:

3a. It will be useful only occasionally, at peak utilization moments, and the cost-benefit analysis of setting up a system to provide for pricing must consider the value of occasional allocation efficiency versus the cost of the drag on communications capacity at all other times.

3b. It will be more useful if there are no property rights to specific bands, but rather all bandwidth will be available for dynamic contracting through an exchange system on the Noam model.

3c. At most, the possibility of implementing pricing models suggests the creation of some spectrum for a real-time exchange alongside a commons. It does not support the proposal of a Big Bang auction of perfect property rights in all usable frequencies.

As a policy recommendation, it is too early to adopt a Big Bang approach to spectrum policy—either in favor of property or in favor of a commons. From a purely economic perspective, it would be sensible for current policy to experiment with both. What follows is a proposal that offers a series of steps that could embody such an experiment.

1. Increase and improve the design of the available spaces of free utilization of spectrum by intelligent wireless devices, so as to allow equipment manufacturers to make a credible investment in devices that rely on commons-based strategies:

1a. Dedicating space below the 2 GHz range that would be modeled on one of two models: (a) [FCC] equipment certification, with streamlined FCC certification processes, or (b) Privatization to a public trust that serves as a non-governmental standards clearance organization.

1b. Improving the U-NII Band regulations for the 5 GHz range by designing the regulatory framework solely on the basis of the needs of open wireless networking, rather than, as now, primarily in consideration of protecting incumbent services. This would require: (a) Clearing those bands from incumbent services, and (b) Shifting that band to one of the models suggested for the 2 GHz range.

1c. Permitting "underlay" and "interweaving" in all bands by implementing a general privilege to transmit wireless communications as long as the transmission does not interfere with incumbent licensed devices. "Underlay" relates to what is most commonly discussed today in the name of one implementation—ultrawideband—communications perceived as "below the noise floor" by the incumbent licensed devices, given their desired signal-to-interference ratios. "Interweaving" relates to the capability of "software defined" or "agile" radios to sense and transmit in frequencies only for so long as no one is using them, and to shift frequencies as soon as their licensed user wishes to use them.

1d. Opening higher frequency bands currently dedicated to amateur experimentation to permit unregulated commercial experimentation and use alongside the amateur uses. This will allow a market test of the plausible hypothesis that complete lack of regulation would enable manufacturers to develop networks, and would lead them to adopt cooperative strategies.

2. Increase the flexibility of current spectrum licensees to experiment with market-based allocation of their spectrum. This would include adoption of the modified property right proposed by Faulhaber and Farber for some incumbent licensees and implementation of a scaled-down auction of spectrum rights with structurally similar characteristics to the proposed Big Bang auction.

3. Subject both property rights sold and commons declared to a preset public redesignation option, exercisable no fewer than, say, ten years after the auction or public dedication, to allow Congress to redesignate the spectrum from open to proprietary, or vice versa, depending on the experience garnered.

3a. Congress could, from time to time, extend the ten-year period, if it believes that the experiment is not yet decisively concluded, so as to preserve a long investment horizon for the firms that rely on either the proprietary or the open resource set.

3b. The exercise date of the option would reflect the discount rate used by spectrum buyers for the property system and by equipment manufacturers for the commons, and would be set so as to minimize the effect of the redesignation right on present valuation of investments in buying spectrum or designing equipment for ownerless networks.

Experience built over time with these systems will teach us what mix of strategies our general long-term approach should use: expanding commons-based techniques, expanding property rights in spectrum, or neither.

Notes and Questions

1. Dedicated Spectrum versus Underlay Rights. Benkler lists a number of possible forms of spectrum rights. Most notably, he refers to dedicated spectrum as well as underlay rights. The latter is what Faulhaber and Farber propose as an easement creating an underlay commons, and what the Spectrum Policy Task Force Report conceptualizes as an underlay commons below an interference temperature. This is not inconsistent with having property rights in spectrum.[14] Dedicating spectrum to a commons, however, is inconsistent with property rights. The whole point is that no one would have the right to exclude; the sole use of the spectrum would be as a commons. Benkler's disagreement with Faulhaber and Farber is that he advocates such a devotion of spectrum to commons, and his article focuses on that proposal.

2. Open Access? One can imagine a regime of truly open access to the spectrum, a regime in which anyone could transmit over a given set of frequencies however she sees fit. The concern about such freedom is interference: any given user has an interest in ensuring that her message gets through, even if that means increasing power and/or the number of messages sent (to create redundancy) such that others' messages cannot be heard. Recognizing this danger, the FCC has never allowed truly open access. For unlicensed uses, the FCC sets out the protocols that acceptable devices must use and then certifies equipment that meets that standard.

Benkler does not deny that interference can occur with truly open access. Rather, in the remainder of the paper he argues that new network designs can eliminate the dangers posed by interference, with the result that a commons is an efficient—indeed, possibly the most efficient—option. Specifically, he envisions abundant networks comprising devices that operate at low-power, send computationally complex transmissions, and not only send the owner's messages but also repeat others' messages, so that each additional user also represented additional capacity. Benkler's proposal would have the FCC or a private entity certify that user devices meet these standards. The envisioned networks will thus have some controls. In order to avoid the interference that would arise from truly open access, some entity—whether public or private—will determine what sort of devices can operate.

3. Policing the Spectrum Commons. Advocates of a "spectrum commons" approach sometimes downplay the considerable challenges of ensuring that users of unlicensed spectrum cooperate with one another. In the worst of all worlds, users of unlicensed spectrum will interfere with one another and continually adjust their equipment to overpower one another. To avoid such a "tragedy of the commons" scenario, government regulation, market forces, or self-regulatory efforts need to facilitate cooperation (say, by enforcing a limit on power levels or enforcing the use of cooperative protocols that require users to "listen before talking"). Some combination of such efforts may well be critical to enabling unli-

---

14. As one of us put it, "This is purely a question of how the rights in the license are constructed and construed. If a license to broadcast television were construed as giving the licensee complete control over a given range of frequencies, then any potential user would have to obtain the existing licensee's agreement before it could offer a new service. If, on the other hand, a license to broadcast were construed as conferring only the right to broadcast on that range of frequencies without interference, and as not including a broader property right in that range of frequencies, then a potential new user would not have to gain the agreement of the licensee." Stuart Minor Benjamin, The Logic of Scarcity: Idle Spectrum as a First Amendment Violation, 52 Duke L.J. 1, 85 n.259 (2002).

censed spectrum to achieve the hopes that policymakers have for it. *See* Philip J. Weiser & Dale N. Hatfield, Policing the Spectrum Commons, 74 Fordham L. Rev. 663 (2005).

4. Why Won't a Private Entity Create These Networks? Just as the FCC could design transmission standards and certify devices, so too could an owner of spectrum in fee simple. If the envisioned abundant networks are so capacious, why wouldn't private owners with full property rights create them? Benkler responds to this question in another paper, arguing that the transaction costs of privately creating these networks are high, because the FCC usually allocates spectrum in small slices (e.g., six megahertz for each broadcaster), but an abundant network might occupy 50 or 100 megahertz. *See* Yochai Benkler, Overcoming Agoraphobia: Building the Commons of the Digitally Networked Environment, 11 Harv. J.L. & Tech. 287, 364–65 (1998). A response, of course, would be to have the FCC start licensing spectrum in larger chunks and thus eliminate these costs.

A very different argument is that owners won't create these networks even if the spectrum is allotted in big swaths, because abundant networks will be less remunerative for the owners. But why would that be? Owners would have lots of pricing options—for example, per message, per minute, per month, and/or bundled in the price of the user device. Is the problem that owners would not be able to capture the value of these networks? The question, though, is a comparative one—whether it is more difficult to capture the value of these networks than of other kinds of wireless services—and it is not at all clear that capturing the value of the envisioned networks is any more difficult. Finally, maybe the problem is that these abundant networks will not be as remunerative because people will simply pay more money for other services. But if that is so, isn't the entire case for those networks undermined?

5. Should We Prefer Government-Created Networks? Assuming that private owners would create these networks, that still does not mean that private ownership is preferable. What are the tradeoffs? To oversimplify dramatically, the main advantage of private ownership is flexibility. The profit motive gives private owners a greater incentive to choose the best system and to make changes as new possibilities arise. And private companies' decisions are not subject to the exhaustive procedures that are imposed on government actors. The main disadvantage of private ownership is the danger of monopoly. But can't the danger of monopoly be minimized by the FCC auctioning off enough spectrum to support five or ten of these envisioned networks (just the sort of "big bang" that Faulhaber and Farber advocate)? More generally, are there other ways the government could avoid monopolization (spectrum caps; requiring that bidders act only as band managers; mandating interoperability)?

Does the foregoing miss the real advantage of government-created networks, namely that the government would let users access the spectrum free of charge? But why is that desirable? Everyone who creates a network (whether cellular telephony, broadcast television, or car dealerships) wants the government to contribute, free of charge, some otherwise expensive element of that network. Why subsidize these networks? Is it because government control will in fact be more responsive to users' desires than private control will be? Does that position understate the government's incentives and/or the possibility that the market will provide citizens with the networks that they want?

6. Uncertainty. One obvious difference between the government creating these abundant networks and leaving it to the private market is that the latter option does not guarantee that they will be created. But is that a bug or a feature? These networks may not develop as hoped, either because they do not work as planned, or they do work but people do not flock to them. Is it better for the risk of failure to fall on private owners rather than on taxpayers?

7. Further Reading. Many of the issues raised here are covered in greater detail in Stuart Minor Benjamin, Spectrum Abundance and the Choice Between Private and Public Control, 78 N.Y.U. L. Rev. 2007 (2003).

---

§ 4.D. Approaches to Unlicensed Access

§ 4.D.1. White Spaces

Dedicating spectrum to a commons is one way to provide for unlicensed uses, but the FCC can permit unlicensed uses without dedicating frequencies to them. That is, the Commission can allow unlicensed services to operate on frequencies that are not fully utilized by the primary, authorized service.

One way of doing this is to allow unlicensed uses in unutilized frequencies. That is the idea behind allowing unlicensed uses in broadcast television frequencies that are not used by television stations or other authorized services, often called white spaces. These white spaces are generally vacant frequency bands between occupied (licensed) broadcast channels.

The possibility of white space devices produced debate on two questions. First, should such devices be permitted? Broadcasters said no, contending that the risk of interference is too great and highlighting that such spaces serve to protect them against the possibility of interference. Google, Intel, Microsoft and others argued in favor, saying that the devices can avoid interference and provide for the possibility of wireless broadband networks with considerable download speeds (because of the favorable propagation characteristics of the spectrum devoted to broadcasting). The second question is whether the spectrum white spaces should be licensed or unlicensed (with most of the companies supporting white space devices arguing for unlicensed).

The FCC addressed both questions. In 2004 the Commission issued a Notice of Proposed Rulemaking proposing to allow unlicensed devices to utilize the white spaces, and to require that such devices use "smart radio" technology to avoid interference. Unlicensed Operation in the TV Broadcast Bands, Notice of Proposed Rulemaking, 19 FCC Rcd. 10,018 (2004). In 2006, the FCC issued a First Report and Order that approved the use of vacant TV channels for fixed low-power devices, but called for further study on the question whether "personal/portable" low-power devices (such as laptops and PDAs) could also use these empty airwaves without causing harmful interference to over-the-air broadcasting. Unlicensed Operation in the TV Broadcast Bands, First Report and Order and Further Notice of Proposed Rulemaking, 21 FCC Rcd. 12,266 (2006). This led to a series of engineering studies to determine the level of interference that portable white space devices would present. The FCC issued its Second Report and Order, granting conditional, unlicensed use of white spaces in 2008. The following excerpt of that order focuses on the key threshold decision regarding unlicensed uses.

Unlicensed Operation in the TV Broadcast Bands and Additional Spectrum for Unlicensed Devices Below 900 MHz and in the 3 GHz Band

Second Report and Order and Memorandum Opinion and Order, 23 FCC Rcd. 16,807 (2008)

I. Executive Summary

1. In this Second Report and Order, we adopt rules to allow unlicensed radio transmitters to operate in the broadcast television spectrum at locations where that spectrum is not being used by licensed services (this unused TV spectrum is often termed "white spaces"). This action will make a significant amount of spectrum available for new and innovative products and services, including broadband data and other services for businesses and consumers. The actions we take here are a conservative first step that includes many safeguards to prevent harmful interference to incumbent communications services. Moreover, the Commission will closely oversee the development and introduction of these devices to the market and will take whatever actions may be necessary to avoid, and if necessary correct, any interference that may occur. Further, we will consider in the future any changes to the rules that may be appropriate to provide greater flexibility for development of this technology and better protect against harmful interference to incumbent communications services. Briefly, the rules we are adopting provide for the following capabilities and safeguards:

• We are providing for both fixed and personal/portable devices to operate in the TV white spaces on an unlicensed basis.

• All devices, except personal/portable devices operating in client mode, must include a geolocation capability and provisions to access over the Internet a database of protected radio services and the locations and channels that may be used by the unlicensed devices at each location. The unlicensed devices must first access the database to obtain a list of the permitted channels before operating.

• The database will be established and administered by a third party, or parties, to be selected through a public notice process to solicit interested parties.

• Fixed devices may operate on any channel between 2 and 51, except channels 3, 4 and 37, and subject to a number of other conditions such as a restriction against co-channel operation or operation adjacent TV channels pending consideration of further information that may be submitted into the record in this proceeding. Fixed devices may operate at up to 4 Watts EIRP (effective isotropic radiated power).

• Personal portable devices may operate on any unoccupied channel between 21 and 51, except channel 37. Personal portable devices may operate at up to 100 milliwatts of power, except that operation on adjacent channels will be limited to 40 milliwatts.

• Fixed and personal/portable devices must also have a capability to sense TV broadcasting and wireless microphone signals as a further means to minimize potential interference. However, for TV broadcasting the database will be the controlling mechanism.

• Wireless microphones will be protected in a variety of ways. The locations where wireless microphones are used, such as entertainment venues and for sporting events, can be registered in the database and will be protected as for other services. In addition, channels from 2 through 20 will be restricted to fixed devices, and we anticipate that many of these channels will remain available for wireless microphones that operate on an itinerant basis. In addition, in 13 major markets where certain channels between 14 and 20 are used for land mobile operations, we will leave 2 channels between 21 and 51 free of new unlicensed devices and therefore available for wireless microphones. Finally, as noted above, we have required that devices also include the ability to listen to the airwaves to sense wireless microphones as an additional measure of protection for these devices.

• Devices must adhere to certain rules to further mitigate the potential interference and to help remedy potential interference should it occur. For example, all fixed devices must register their locations in the database. In addition, fixed devices must transmit identifying information to make it easier to identify them if they are found to interfere. Furthermore, fixed and personal/portable devices operating independently must provide identifying information to the TV bands database. All devices must include adaptable power control so that they use the minimum power necessary to accomplish communications.

• All white space devices are subject to equipment certification by the FCC Laboratory. The Laboratory will request samples of the devices for testing to ensure that they meet all the pertinent requirements.

• We will permit applications for certification of devices that do not include the geolocation and database access capabilities, and instead rely on spectrum sensing to avoid causing harmful interference, subject to a much more rigorous set of tests by our Laboratory in a process that will be open to the public. These tests will include both laboratory and field tests to fully ensure that such devices meet a "Proof of Performance" standard that they will not cause harmful interference. Under this procedure the Commission will issue a Public Notice seeking comment on the application, as well as test procedures and methodologies. The Commission will also issue a Public Notice seeking comment on its recommendations. The decision to grant such an application will then be made at the Commission level.

• The Commission will act promptly to remove any equipment found to be causing harmful interference from the market and will require the responsible parties to take appropriate actions to remedy any interference that may occur.

II. Introduction

2. This action will open for use a significant amount of spectrum with very desirable propagation characteristics that has heretofore lain fallow. These new rules will allow the development of new and innovative types of unlicensed devices that provide broadband data and other services for businesses and consumers without disrupting the incumbent television and other authorized services that operate in the TV bands. In addition, because transmissions on frequencies in the TV bands are less subject to propagation losses than transmissions in the spectrum bands where existing low power broadband unlicensed operations are permitted, i.e., the 2.4 GHz and 5 GHz bands, we anticipate that allowing unlicensed operation in the TV bands will benefit wireless internet service providers (WISPs) by extending the service range of their operations. This will allow wireless broadband providers that use unlicensed devices to reach new customers and to extend and improve their services in rural areas. We anticipate that allowing use of the TV white spaces by unlicensed devices will have significant benefits for both businesses and consumers and thereby promote more efficient and effective use of the TV spectrum.

3. The plan we are adopting will allow both fixed and personal/portable unlicensed devices to operate on unused television channels in locations where such operations will not result in harmful interference to TV services (including reception by cable headends and low power TV stations, i.e., TV translator, low power TV, TV booster, and Class A TV stations) and other services that use the TV bands. We recognize the importance of protecting licensed services from harmful interference and the novel challenges involved in reliably

identifying unused TV channels. We therefore are taking a cautious and conservative approach in this plan, balancing the need to provide sufficient opportunities for proponents to develop viable unlicensed TV band devices (TVBDs) with measures to ensure that such devices fully protect the important licensed services that operate in the TV bands.

4. We anticipate that the capabilities of products for operating in this spectrum will develop and evolve over time and that much will be learned about the potential for unlicensed TVBDs to cause interference to licensed services and how to avoid that interference. We may therefore need to revisit these rules to make adjustments both to provide more flexibility for unlicensed devices and to refine the protections for licensed services.

III. Background

11. The Commission provides for the operation of unlicensed radio transmitters in Part 15 of its rules. Under these rules, unlicensed devices generally operate on frequencies shared with authorized services and at relatively low power, i.e., at power levels 1 Watt or less. Operation under Part 15 is subject to the condition that a device does not cause harmful interference to authorized services, and that it must accept any interference received. The current Part 15 rules provide substantial flexibility in the types of unlicensed devices that can be operated, but prohibit the operation of unlicensed devices on certain frequencies, including the bands used for broadcast television service.

12. The broadcast television service operates under Part 73 of the rules. TV stations operate on six-megahertz channels designated channels 2 to 69 in four bands of frequencies in the VHF and UHF regions of the radio spectrum (54–72 MHz, 76–88 MHz, 174–216 MHz and 470–806 MHz). As noted above, television stations are now in the process of converting from analog to digital transmissions. During the transition to digital transmissions, each full service television station that was authorized before 1997 is required to broadcast on two channels, one digital and one analog. At the end of the transition on February 17, 2009 [later moved to June 12, 2009], each full service TV station must cease analog operation and operate on a single digital channel. Because the new digital TV transmission system is more spectrally efficient than the analog TV transmission system, the Commission has relaxed some of the current analog TV channel separation requirements for digital operation and has eliminated others. Consequently, it has been able to accommodate all existing television stations with channels for post-transition operation in less spectrum. The Commission has specified that digital television stations will operate only on channels 2–51 after the transition and has reallocated television channels 52–69 for other uses.

13. To avoid interference between TV stations, stations on the same and adjacent channels (and in the case of analog TV service certain other channel relationships) must comply with minimum separation distance requirements and other technical provisions. As a result of these provisions, there are geographic areas between the stations on any given channel in local areas where TV service is not available. There are typically a number of TV channels in a given geographic area that are not being used by full service digital TV stations because such stations would not be able to operate without causing interference to co-channel or adjacent channel stations. The minimum separation distances (spacings) between stations are based on the assumption that the stations will operate at the maximum permitted antenna height and power. However, a transmitter operating on a vacant TV channel, e.g., a channel not used by a high power TV station in a given geographic area due to interference concerns, at a lower antenna height and/or power level than a TV station operating at the maximum allowed facilities would not need as great a separation distance from co-channel and adjacent channel TV stations to avoid causing interference to

such stations. Also, in some areas channels that could be used by a full service television station simply are not being used. This situation will remain after the transition.

14. In addition to full service TV stations operating under Part 73 of the rules, certain other licensed services are permitted to operate on TV channels. Class A television stations operate under Subpart J of Part 73 of the rules. Low power TV, TV translator and TV booster stations are permitted to operate under Part 74 of the rules on a secondary basis to full service TV stations and on an equal basis with Class A TV stations, provided they meet technical rules to prevent interference to reception of such stations. Part 74 also permits certain broadcast auxiliary operations on TV channels 14–69 on a secondary basis. In addition, Part 74 permits certain entities to operate wireless microphones on vacant TV channels on a non-interference basis.

16. On May 13, 2004, the Commission adopted a Notice of Proposed Rulemaking in this proceeding in which it proposed to allow unlicensed operation in the TV bands at locations where frequencies are not in use by licensed services. To ensure that no harmful interference will occur to TV stations and other authorized users of the spectrum, the Commission proposed to define the conditions under which a TV channel is unused and to require unlicensed devices to incorporate "smart radio" features to identify the unused TV channels in the area where they are located. For the purpose of minimizing interference, the Commission proposed to classify unlicensed TVBDs in two general functional categories. The first category would consist of lower power "personal/portable" unlicensed devices, such as Wi-Fi-like cards in laptop computers or wireless in-home local area networks (LANs). The second category would consist of higher power "fixed" unlicensed devices that would operate from a fixed location and could be used to provide commercial services such as wireless broadband Internet access.

IV. Discussion

32. As supported by the record in this proceeding, we conclude that low power devices can and should be allowed to operate in the TV bands on frequencies that are not being used by authorized services. This decision will provide significant benefits for the public by enabling the development and operation of a wide range of new unlicensed wireless communications devices and systems in spectrum where signals are less subject to propagation losses than they are in the bands currently available for such devices. The propagation characteristics of these bands will allow the development of devices that can provide service at greater ranges than existing unlicensed devices. Proponents of broadband devices and services in particular indicate that there is need for new broadband devices that will take advantage of the more desirable propagation characteristics of the TV bands. As indicated above, we believe that the propagation advantages of this spectrum will make it possible for WISPs and others to improve or extend their reach to customers in rural and other less densely populated area. We also anticipate that these new devices will have economic benefits for consumers and businesses by facilitating the development of additional competition in the broadband market.

33. It is, of course, most important that we ensure that new unlicensed devices do not interfere with the incumbent licensed services in the TV bands. We now conclude that, with appropriate requirements and conditions on their operation, it is possible for both fixed and personal/portable low power devices to use the TV white spaces without disrupting the important television, public safety, and other services that use these frequencies. Because unlicensed broadband devices will share spectrum with broadcast TV and other licensed services, they will need the capability to avoid causing harmful interference to licensed services in the TV band. Specifically, an unlicensed device will need to be able to determine

whether a TV channel or portion of a TV channel is unused before it transmits. Additionally, an unlicensed device will need features that enable it to avoid occupying a frequency band or to cease operation on a frequency when a licensed user commences transmission on a channel that was previously unused by a television band licensed service. The rules we are adopting will require that unlicensed TVBDs include these capabilities.

A. Licensed vs. Unlicensed Operation

36. A number of commenters submit that vacant spectrum in the TV bands should be licensed and that this regimen is necessary in order to enable the use of that spectrum for providing wireless broadband and mobile data services. These parties argue that companies need the assurance that they will be entitled to protection from harmful interference before they will make the investments necessary to provide these services. They claim that licensing would encourage innovation because a licensee would receive all of the benefits of its innovation instead of having to share those benefits with others. Other parties continue to argue that this spectrum would be more effectively used on an unlicensed basis. For example, the New America Foundation responds that the existing unlicensed bands have been used for a large number of innovative products, that innovation is encouraged by the low barriers to entry in an unlicensed regime, and that the TV bands have better propagation properties than currently available unlicensed bands, which would cause innovation to flourish. It further states that many unlicensed uses such as community networks and rural service do not require a large infrastructure investment, so licensing is not needed to ensure the provision of service. Tropos Networks adds that the expense of acquiring licenses can make providing wireless broadband services prohibitive in rural and Native American tribal areas. Those supporting the licensed and unlicensed approaches argue a number of additional points and counter points as described below.

37. Charles Jackson and Dorothy Robyn argue that the TV bands are not well suited to the low-power uses planned by unlicensed advocates. They contend that under an unlicensed approach, devices would likely have to operate in 6 megahertz channels—which are far smaller than the available bandwidth in the 2.4 GHz or 5.0 GHz unlicensed bands— because the TV band white spaces occur in 6 megahertz increments. Jackson/Robyn further argue that the use of this spectrum for low-power unlicensed devices would fail to take advantage of the better propagation properties of the TV bands compared to those of higher frequencies and to exploit the capability that it is easier to manufacture equipment that generates significant power in the TV bands than at higher frequencies. The White Space Coalition disputes these views, arguing that Jackson/Robyn's claim that the TV band is not suited to unlicensed uses is premised on the assumption that future unlicensed uses will be identical to the current uses of those unlicensed bands. It contends that the better propagation properties of the TV bands would make it likely that new unlicensed applications would be developed in the future that would not be possible in other bands.

38. Supporters of a licensed approach also hold that there is no need for additional spectrum for unlicensed devices. In this regard, Qualcomm submits that there is no evidence that consumers have had to return unlicensed devices because the unlicensed spectrum is too crowded. The Association for Maximum Service Television and the National Association of Broadcasters, in joint comments (MSTV/NAB), add there is over 100 megahertz of unlicensed spectrum below 2 GHz and that 255 MHz of spectrum in the 5 GHz band was made available for unlicensed use in 2003 and so there is plenty of spectrum available for unlicensed use. The White Space Coalition counters these arguments, stating that the propagation characteristics of the TV band are superior to the other unlicensed bands for many applications and that none of the other unlicensed spectrum is below 900 MHz.

44. *Discussion*: [O]ur goal in this proceeding is to allow new uses of radio on unused television channels at locations where such operations will not result in harmful interference to, or disrupt, TV and other authorized services. For the reasons discussed below, we conclude that it is in the public interest to allow TV band devices to operate in these bands on an unlicensed basis pursuant to restrictions carefully designed to protect users of incumbent licensed services. This approach permits us to introduce new innovative uses while protecting the continued operation and growth of the TV broadcast and other authorized services in these bands. Because unlicensed operations are not allowed to cause interference to authorized services, the interference protection status of existing services operating in these bands will not be affected, consistent with the Commission's goals in this proceeding.

45. The record developed in response to the [2004 Notice of Proposed Rulemaking and the 2006 Report and Order] indicates that there is a need for additional spectrum for unlicensed broadband devices, particularly in the lower frequency bands. A number of WISPs have noted that the TV frequencies would provide improved signal coverage over other unlicensed bands, including improved in-building penetration properties which other unlicensed bands lack. We disagree with Jackson/Robyn that the 6 megahertz size of TV channels and propagation characteristics of these bands make them inappropriate for unlicensed use. Unlicensed devices will not be limited to 6 megahertz bandwidth, as they will be allowed to operate across multiple channels in locations where the bandwidth is available. The signal coverage afforded by the propagation characteristics of this spectrum is also desired by proponents of unlicensed devices in that it will facilitate the provision of improved and/or more economical wireless Internet service to consumers, particularly in rural areas where transaction costs may be higher than elsewhere. Further, as argued by comments filed by the White Space Coalition and other parties who have expressed interest in developing or operating low power devices in these bands, other innovative uses for this spectrum may emerge once it is made available for unlicensed use.

46. While we recognize the arguments in the record in support of a licensed approach for making the TV white space spectrum available for new uses, we conclude that such an approach is not practicable for many kinds of devices that could use these bands, and thus would reduce the benefits available. [A] licensed model tends to work best when spectrum rights are clearly defined, exclusive, flexible and transferable. When spectrum rights lack these attributes, potential licensees face uncertainty and may lack incentives to invest in a license or offer service. We conclude that attributes supporting the successful use of licensing would be difficult to accomplish here, particularly if we want to maintain our stated goal of not affecting the interference protection status of existing services. The frequencies and amount of unused TV band spectrum will vary from location to location and could change over time as additional television stations and other primary and secondary operations are licensed or as existing operations change frequency. For example, the assignment of channels for digital operation to low power television stations is not scheduled to be complete by the end of the DTV transition in 2009. Also, currently authorized DTV stations have recently been permitted to submit applications asking to modify their facilities and/or change channels. These changes could complicate licensing of the white spaces spectrum, particularly if the Commission were to license the spectrum pursuant to auction. Because we have decided to require that TV band devices protect other types of licensees in the bands, a licensed TV band device could potentially lose its ability to operate on some, or even all, of its authorized frequencies when new operations with higher allocation status are authorized to operate in the same area.

48. With regard to the argument that a licensing regime would encourage investment in the provision of services using wireless spectrum, we observe the stability normally pro-

vided by exclusive licensing would be difficult to achieve for TV band device operation. To avoid affecting the interference protection status of incumbent services, the licenses here would afford no right to interference-free operation. Instead, the licensee would merely have the right to operate on those television channels that are not currently in use by other higher-priority users. The specific channels and amount of available spectrum available at a given location could change over time as additional television channels are allocated, as low power auxiliary devices make use [of] the channels, and the other services that use these bands similarly initiate new or modify existing operations. Hence, we do not believe that the issuance of licenses would necessarily provide the benefits that the proponents of licensing claim because of the tenuous nature of the rights that would actually be granted by the license. Furthermore, there has been tremendous growth in the development of new technologies and the introduction of new services that rely on unlicensed devices, which belies the assertion that a licensing regime is needed to encourage investment in spectrum development.

49. We are also not persuaded by other arguments raised in support of a licensing regime for TV band devices. We note that a number of parties draw attention to the potential revenue that could be raised by auctioning the unused television bands under a licensing regime. We believe that these arguments are misplaced and do not address our goal in this proceeding, which is to allow new uses on unused television channels in locations where such operations will not result in harmful interference to or disrupt TV and other authorized services. Thus, the regulatory model used here must be appropriate to facilitate new uses while protecting the various types of incumbent uses, not chosen merely because it could provide revenue from auctioning licenses. We are also not persuaded by Jackson/Robyn's claim that licensing TV band devices would allow the television bands to be used more efficiently—i.e., licensed users could negotiate interference protection arrangements and thus increase the use of available spectrum for TV band devices, which in turn would allow the use of the bands to evolve over time to more efficient uses as market conditions and technology change dictate. As discussed above, licensing TV band devices is not practicable while also protecting the present and future use of the band for broadcasting and other incumbent uses. Allowing licensed TV band devices to negotiate interference requirements with licensed users as Jackson/Robyn suggest would signal a fundamental shift from our stated goal to avoid disruption of TV and other authorized services by TV band devices.

Notes and Questions

1. Sensing. In the order above the Commission said it would rely on spectrum sensing and geolocation combined with access to a database of existing spectrum use to determine if a channel was available. In 2010, the Commission finalized the rules for white spaces devices, eliminating the sensing requirement for devices that include geolocation/database functions, because it found that sensing technology was not sufficiently mature for consumer devices and would delay market entry. Unlicensed Operation in the TV Broadcast Bands, Second Memorandum Opinion and Order, 25 FCC Rcd. 18,661 (2010).

2. Idle Hands. Beyond the specifics of the services envisioned, or the choice between licensed and unlicensed, there is the simple fact that government restrictions—here preventing non-television users from this valuable spectrum—have left some transmission capacity idle. The idea with these new services is that they can be added even though there is no room for more of the previously authorized services. These new services use unutilized spectrum, in that way increasing the total capacity of information carried over the air. Is there an argument that the First Amendment obliges Congress and the FCC to allow such services? After all, the idea behind these services is that there is idle spectrum out there—spectrum that could be used to support communication but is currently unused because of the regulations in place. If that is right, is there any defense, or are regulations that bar white spaces or underlay service unlawful restrictions on speech? *See* Stuart Minor Benjamin, The Logic of Scarcity: Idle Spectrum as a First Amendment Violation, 52 Duke L.J. 1 (2002).

3. Finding Space after Incentive Auctions. The prospect of repurposing some of the frequencies devoted to broadcast had major implications for white spaces, since those spaces exist in unused frequencies. The order above permits unlicensed uses of white spaces, but some urban areas did not have white space channels. And a repacking of the broadcast spectrum as part of the incentive auctions, by using the broadcast spectrum more efficiently, would impact (and possibly shrink) the white spaces that did exist. One possible area for white spaces devices is guard bands — narrow bands of frequencies that separate two wider frequency ranges in order to minimize interference between them. Guard bands would be necessary between spectrum still devoted to broadcast television and spectrum newly devoted to new flexible uses, as well as between uplinks and downlinks for new broadband services, so they presented an obvious opportunity for unlicensed devices. In addition to guard bands, the government might choose to devote some of the former television broadcast spectrum to unlicensed uses. So two obvious possibilities for unlicensed devices were A) broadcast spectrum devoted to unlicensed uses, and B) large guard bands that would ensure the availability of white spaces in every community. In the Spectrum Act, Congress weighed in. Section 6403(c)(1) requires a forward auction in which "the Commission assigns licenses for the use of the spectrum that the Commission reallocates." In other words, the Commission must license the frequencies relinquished in the reverse auction, so it could not leave some of them unlicensed. As to guard bands, §6407(a) of the Spectrum Act provides that notwithstanding §6403(c), the Commission can create guard bands, and §6407(c) states that the Commission may permit the use of guard bands for unlicensed use. But §6407(b) provides that "guard bands shall be no larger than is technically reasonable to prevent harmful interference between licensed services outside the guard bands." This limited the ability of the Commission to create frequencies for unlicensed uses in the spectrum that broadcasters would relinquish. Was that a mistake? On what basis could one determine whether more spectrum formerly devoted to broadcasting should have been opened to unlicensed uses?

4. Substitutes. There are other frequencies on which unlicensed devices can operate, such as the 5 GHz band where they do operate. The appeal of the frequencies relinquished by broadcasters (which are in the 600 MHz range) for unlicensed devices is that these lower frequencies have different, and in many ways more attractive, propagation characteristics. As the Commission stated in its 2014 order implementing incentive auctions, "spectrum in the 600 MHz frequency range has excellent propagation characteristics that allow signals to reach farther and penetrate walls and other structures, thus making it well suited for a variety of unlicensed applications." Expanding the Economic and Innovation Opportunities of Spectrum Through Incentive Auctions, Report and Order, 29 FCC Rcd. 6567, 6685 ¶271 (2014). But, of course, that also makes them more valuable for licensed devices — and more valuable for the federal treasury, via the auction proceeds they generate. Which way do these points cut, in terms of the desirability of devoting more of this spectrum to unlicensed uses?

5. Competition. Broadway theaters, sports arenas, and movie studios, among others, rely on wireless microphones. Wireless microphones users (and manufacturers, of course) would like spectrum dedicated for wireless microphones (without buying it at auction, of course). Users and manufacturers of other unlicensed devices, meanwhile, would like to have the broadest range of frequencies for *their* devices. In its 2014 order implementing incentive auctions, the Commission concluded that "television channels that remain unused by broadcast television stations after the incentive auction should not be designated exclusively for wireless microphones, and instead should also be made available for potential use by unlicensed television white space devices." *Id.* ¶ 269. On what basis should the FCC evaluate the tradeoffs between allowing, on any given frequency, unlicensed devices versus wireless microphones?

---

§ 4.D.2. Spectrum Sharing

Another approach to unlicensed uses is to allow spectrum sharing. One possibility, as we noted above, is for the FCC to allow unlicensed uses operating under restrictions that minimize interference with existing uses. The idea is that those services create new communications capacity on spectrum that is unsuited to additional high-power uses.

Such sharing is usually dynamic. Dynamic spectrum use involves the ability to identify and use slices of spectrum that are available at a given location for a short period of time — perhaps days, hours, seconds, or fractions of seconds. White spaces devices are an example of dynamic spectrum use. The use of dynamic technologies underscores the point that licensed and unlicensed uses are not goals in themselves but means to an end: more efficient use of the valuable resource we call the spectrum.

The greatest opportunities for unlicensed uses arise under the Part 15 rules noted in the 2008 white spaces order excerpted above. These rules enabled widespread deployment of Wi-Fi and Bluetooth, among others. The Commission summarized Part 15 as follows:

> Part 15 of the Commission's rules permits the operation of radio frequency devices without issuing individual licenses to operators of these devices. The Commission's Part 15 rules are designed to ensure that there is a low probability that these devices will cause harmful interference to other users of the same or adjacent spectrum. Typically, unlicensed devices operate at very low power over relatively short distances, and often employ various techniques, such as dynamic spectrum access or listen-before-talk protocols, to reduce the interference risk to others as well as themselves. The primary operating condition for unlicensed devices is that the operator must accept whatever interference is received and must not cause harmful interference. Should harmful interference occur, the operator is required to immediately correct the interference problem or to cease operation.

Revision of Part 15 of the Commission's Rules to Permit Unlicensed National Information Infrastructure (U-NII) Devices in the 5 GHz Band, First Report and Order, 29 FCC Rcd. 4127 ¶ 3 (2014).

As the title of the order quoted above indicates, the Commission has implemented its Part 15 rules to encourage the deployment of unlicensed devices that it calls "Unlicensed National Information Infrastructure (U-NII) devices" (mentioned in Benkler's excerpt above). Notably, the Commission modified its Part 15 rules to allow for such devices on a wide swath of frequencies in the 5 GHz band. In 2003, the Commission issued an order revising its rules to open up 255 MHz of spectrum in the 5.470–5.725 GHz band for unlicensed devices. Revision of Parts 2 and 15 of the Commission's Rules to Permit Unlicensed National Information Infrastructure (U-NII) Devices in the 5 GHz Band, Report and Order, 18 FCC Rcd. 24,484 (2003). The spectrum involved in this order was not devoted exclusively to unlicensed uses. It has authorized users and any unlicensed users must avoid interference with them. *See id.* ¶¶ 13, 29. Specifically, the unlicensed devices operate based on dynamic frequency selection, which is designed to detect and avoid harmful interference to the military and weather radar systems that also operate on these frequencies. In 2014, the Commission modified its rules to make it easier for unlicensed devices to operate in the 5.15–5.35 and 5.47–5.85 GHz bands. 29 FCC Rcd. 4127 (2014). The order aligned some of its rules to increase the range of frequencies over which unlicensed wireless devices could easily operate.

The Commission took a somewhat different approach in dealing with the 3650–3700 MHz band. Once again, there were existing authorized users of that spectrum, and the FCC decided to add new uses to the band, but not to devote the spectrum exclusively to those new users. Wireless Operations in the 3650–3700 MHz Band, Report and Order and Memorandum Opinion and Order, 20 FCC Rcd. 6502 ¶¶ 15, 17, 25 (2005). What is interesting for our purposes is that the order provides that "new terrestrial operations in the band [will] be licensed on a nationwide, non-exclusive basis." *Id.* ¶ 16. This is not a purely unlicensed approach, as the Commission is requiring licenses; but it is not the ordinary exclusive use approach, as the licenses are non-exclusive. While these licensees "will not have interference protection rights of primary, exclusive use licensees, the licensing scheme imposes on all licensees the mutual obligation to cooperate and avoid harmful interference to one another." *Id.* How will the FCC effectuate such cooperation? It requires every licensee to register their fixed and base stations, and to utilize "contention-based" protocols. In the Commission's words: "Such systems allow multiple users to share the same spectrum by defining the events that must occur when two or more devices attempt to simultaneously access the same channel and establishing rules by which each device is provided a reasonable opportunity to operate." *Id.*

The Commission has taken yet a different approach to the sharing of some nearby frequencies with the federal government. The President's Council of Advisors on Science and Technology (PCAST) issued a report on this possibility in 2012, which is excerpted below:

President's Council of Advisors on Science and Technology, Realizing the Full Potential of Government-Held Spectrum to Spur Economic Growth: Executive Summary

available at
http://www.whitehouse.gov/sites/default/files/microsites/ostp/pcast_spectrum_report_final_july_20_2012.pdf

In 2011, global mobile data more than doubled for the fourth year in a row. The number of devices connected to mobile networks worldwide is around five billion today, and could rise to 50 billion by 2020. By that time, wireless technologies are expected to contribute $4.5 trillion to the global economy through the expansion of existing business and the creation of new opportunities. This growth has created unprecedented demand for commercial access to wireless spectrum. At the same time, U.S. Federal spectrum needs are also rising. For example, the number of unmanned aerial systems (UAS) operated by the Department of Defense (DOD) has drastically increased from 167 to nearly 7500 from 2002 to 2010, and the systems are carrying larger payloads and collecting increased volumes of intelligence, surveillance, and reconnaissance (ISR) data. This has resulted in a dramatic increase in the number of sorties flown and domestic training requirements, all of which require spectrum.

PCAST finds that clearing and reallocation of Federal spectrum is not a sustainable basis for spectrum policy due to the high cost, lengthy time to implement, and disruption to the Federal mission. Further, although some have proclaimed that clearing and reallocation will result in significant net revenue to the government, we do not anticipate that will be the case for Federal spectrum. In March of 2012, the National Telecommunications and Information Administration (NTIA) concluded that clearing just one 95 MHz band by relocating existing Federal users to other parts of the spectrum would take 10 years, cost some $18 billion, and cause significant disruption to incumbent users. NTIA, An Assessment of the Viability of Accommodating Wireless Broadband in the 1755–1780 MHz Band (2012), www.ntia.doc.gov/report/2012/assessment-viability-accommodating-wireless-broadband-1755-1850-mhz-band. The last successful auction that involved cleared Federal spectrum, in 2006, yielded a total of $13.7 billion for 90 MHz, but only half of the auctioned spectrum was Federal (the other half was already commercial), and the Federal agencies then required $1.5 billion over the next 6 years to relocate services out of the cleared bands. In the end, therefore, the Federal contribution of 45 MHz realized a net of just $5.35 billion. When this net revenue is annualized over 10 years or more, the typical duration of a license, the amount of revenue the Federal Government will receive is small. These modest sums should not be driving the direction of spectrum policy.

Historically, spectrum was managed by assigning exclusive rights to use a specific frequency in a specific location. Initially, these authorizations were granted to governmental and commercial users at no cost. Since the mid-1990s, long term commercial licenses have generally been assigned through competitive auctions. Winning bidders typically receive spectrum access in the form of exclusive assignments of frequencies to chosen services (i.e., licenses), ensuring that no other services infringe on that assignment (i.e., no interference). This study finds that today's apparent shortage of spectrum is in fact an illusion brought about because of the way spectrum is managed. If the Nation instead expands its options for managing Federal spectrum, we can transform the availability of a precious national resource—spectrum—from scarcity to abundance. This expansion can be done in such a way that it will not result in a loss of revenue to the Federal Government and may result in new revenue either from enhanced economic growth and innovation or from modest leasing fees. But in either case, the value to the Federal Government will be greater if the spectrum is available for reuse or relicensing more often than it is today. The new system for Federal spectrum management that this report calls for—a new spectrum architecture and a corresponding shift in the architecture of future radio systems that use it—can multiply the effective capacity of spectrum by a factor of 1,000.

The essential element of this new Federal spectrum architecture is that the norm for spectrum use should be sharing, not exclusivity. Technology innovations of recent years make this transformation eminently achievable. Two trends are especially important. First, instead of just the tall cell towers that provide coverage for very large geographic areas, many wireless services are already moving to "small cell" operations that provide services for very small geographic areas, reducing the potential for interference so that other services may operate much closer to them. The huge explosion of Wi-Fi services is one example of this evolution. Second, improvements in performance make it possible for devices to deliver services seamlessly even in the presence of signals from other systems, so that they do not need exclusive frequency assignments, only an assurance that potentially interfering signals will not rise above a certain level.

Taking these and other developments into account, this report argues that spectrum should be managed not by fragmenting it into ever more finely divided exclusive frequency assignments, but by specifying large frequency bands that can accommodate a wide variety of compatible uses and new technologies that are more efficient with larger blocks of spectrum.

The recommendations in this report are based on starting with low-risk existing technologies, early versions of which are already being deployed today. Enacting these recommendations will create market opportunity for newer technologies, enabling them to mature faster, accelerating the growth of spectrum sharing capacity, and leading to the development of an ongoing innovation cycle. However, the policies proposed are consistent with the later deployment of these non-commercial technologies, only when they are validated for their operational use in Federal spectrum.

To make an analogy, today's spectrum use resembles road transportation at the beginning of the automotive revolution when we created our highways and interconnection and commerce flowed. The mid-1980s innovation of "unlicensed" spectrum use, which makes spectrum available at no cost to any user willing to abide by technical conditions of use, has been essential to the rise of Wi-Fi and represents a wireless analogy to the early shared roadways. The rest of the spectrum system, however, still looks like a series of narrow roads. What PCAST proposes is creating the spectrum equivalent of wide multi-lane superhighways, where the lanes are continuously shared by many cars, trucks, and other vehicles. Spectrum superhighways would be large stretches of spectrum that can be shared by many different types of wireless services, just as vehicles share a superhighway by moving from one lane to another. In contrast to the way we have allocated spectrum, the road system has always let Federal and commercial vehicles share the same highways, with the proviso that government use was allowed to preempt commercial users' rights for reasons of public safety, emergency medical rescue, or national security. There is no reason that the same principles cannot apply to spectrum management. Users of spectrum can make use of the wireless equivalents of signals, sensors, and stop lights to avoid "collisions" with other users. Just as we created the initial transcontinental superhighways in the 20–30 years that followed the 1939 FDR-commissioned blueprint "Toll Roads and Free Roads," we have the chance to create spectrum superhighways today.

As a result, the most urgent recommendation in this report is that the President issue a new memorandum that states it is the policy of the U.S. government to share underutilized Federal spectrum to the maximum extent possible that is consistent with the Federal mission, and requires the Secretary of Commerce to immediately identify 1,000 MHz of Federal spectrum in which to implement the new architecture and thereby create the first shared-use spectrum superhighways.

As part of the process to reach this 1,000 MHz goal, PCAST recommends that the Federal Government, using industry partners, establish a new Federal Spectrum Access System (SAS) that will serve as an information and control clearinghouse for band-by-band spectrum registrations and conditions of use and allow non-Federal users to access underutilized spectrum in Federal bands. The SAS will put into practice the fundamental principle that underutilized spectrum capacity should be used or shared to the greatest possible extent. Another recommended change is that Federal spectrum, instead of being divided into small, dedicated frequency blocks as it is at present, should be divided into substantial frequency blocks spanning several hundred megahertz. Establishing these wide bands will make it easier for spectrum sharing to be the norm, a transformation in which all Federal agencies would be required to cooperate. Making spectrum access available to a wide range of services and applications will also require provision of a framework that establishes minimum technical standards for the coexistence of transmitters and receivers, in contrast to the present system that focuses on transmitters. Finally, simple measures that assess individual spectrum uses solely by their need for megahertz must be replaced by more sophisticated metrics that reveal how effectively a stretch of spectrum can accommodate a variety of complementary services within a given area.

We recognize that the new spectrum architecture proposed in this report represents a major evolution of existing spectrum management practices. Implementing it will not be easy and may take a long time. But just as the transcontinental highway system began with one road, we must act immediately to act on the initial 1,000 MHz. Before they will embrace the new system, incumbent Federal spectrum users will need to have confidence that sharing of the spectrum they have been allocated will not cause harmful interference to the technologies that they operate, and commercial operators with new technologies will need to be made sure of the reliability of the spectrum access needed for their business models. So, to get started, we are proposing three key elements of a significant pilot program that includes immediate actions toward implementing our recommendations:

1. The immediate sharing of new low-power civil devices in two existing Federal bands, of over 100 MHz combined.
2. The creation of a group of industry executives (e.g. CEOs), selected by the President and called the Spectrum Sharing Partnership Steering Committee, to recommend a policy framework, centered on a public private partnership for sharing Federally-held spectrum, and implementation milestones that lay the groundwork for the first spectrum superhighways.
3. The creation of an urban Test City in a major U.S. city along with a Mobile Test Service that can relocate to urban, rural, and Federal facilities as needed to support rapid experimentation in spectrum management technology and practice.

We estimate that the overall costs of implementing this program, over the next 3 years, will be in the range of about $80 million. We view the Federal Government as the initial funding source to cover costs, along with a public private partnership that will have the aim of transferring most costs to the private sector over the course of time.

Federal users currently have no incentives to improve the efficiency with which they use their own spectrum allocation, nor does the Federal system as a whole have incentives to improve its overall efficiency. This report therefore proposes an accounting, allocation, and incentive system (nominally called "Spectrum Currency") that would reward agencies that move quickly to promote more effective spectrum use by making some of their spectrum available for sharing with other Federal and non-Federal users.

One of the other important directions that spectrum policy must take is to create a marketplace that can accommodate the widest range of commercial users, from initial venture-funded startups to established service providers. Today's spectrum ecosystem offers only the choice between unlicensed and long term, renewable licensed spectrum. The number of business entities that can participate in auctions for nationwide, long term spectrum licenses, is limited. Experimenting with shorter-term, lower cost, spectrum license options for commercial users sharing Federal spectrum, will foster new innovative ideas, increase the number of participants in this market, contribute to economic growth, and also provide a way to collect an ongoing stream of revenue, if that is desired.

Notes and Questions

1. Focusing on Federal Spectrum. This report responds to a widespread belief that spectrum used by the federal government presents a particularly promising opportunity as a source of new spectrum capacity for new services. Those seeking frequencies focused on the federal government because much of the government's spectrum is fairly lightly used. To put the point differently, in terms of underutilized spectrum, some of the swaths of spectrum used by the federal government are particularly attractive candidates.

2. Sharing. The fact that spectrum is lightly used does not necessarily mean that clearing it of those uses will be easy, and in fact PCAST finds that it will not be easy. Thus PCAST suggests sharing. Is the case for sharing a compelling one? Should PCAST have pushed harder to have the government report simply vacate the spectrum? Or, by contrast, is imposing sharing a mistake, given the importance of the government uses?

3. Government Incentives. As the PCAST report acknowledges, federal users lack an incentive to vacate, or efficiently use, spectrum, because they cannot monetize it. This is analogous to the command-and-control approach to spectrum discussed in § 4.A. of the casebook. Indeed, in some ways the problem is worse than the command-and-control regime that applied to many commercial uses, because federal government users cannot confidently transfer their spectrum usage in return for something else they value. PCAST suggests overcoming this problem by creating a shadow currency that would value spectrum and that could be used by agencies insofar as they freed up spectrum capacity. The problem is that such a shadow currency has not been implemented, and agencies may fear that it will never actually materialize (e.g., even if they receive such currency, it will be used as a justification to reduce other spending, mitigating its value). Is there any credible commitment that the President, or Congress, could make that would come close to approximating the value of the spectrum and thus provide government users with a significant incentive to give up some of their spectrum?

4. FCC Response. The FCC responded to the PCAST report, and the possibility of spectrum sharing more generally, in the following notice of proposed rulemaking:

Amendment of the Commission's Rules with Regard to Commercial Operations in the 3550–3650 MHz Band

Notice of Proposed Rulemaking, 27 FCC Rcd. 15,594 (2012)

I. INTRODUCTION AND EXECUTIVE SUMMARY

1. With this Notice of Proposed Rulemaking, we propose to create a new Citizens Broadband Service in the 3550–3650 MHz band (3.5 GHz Band) currently utilized for military and satellite operations, which will promote two major advances that enable more efficient use of radio spectrum: *small cells* and *spectrum sharing*. We also seek comment on whether to include under these proposed new, flexible rules the neighboring 3650–3700 MHz band, which is already used for commercial broadband services. Together, these proposals would make up to 150 megahertz of contiguous spectrum available for innovative mobile and fixed wireless broadband services without displacing mission-critical incumbent systems.

3. The PCAST Report identifies two technological advances as holding great promise for increasing our nation's wireless broadband capabilities. First, increased use of small cell network deployments can multiply wireless capacity within existing spectrum resources. Second, increased spectrum sharing can make large swaths of otherwise "stovepiped" spectrum — nationwide bands set aside for important, but localized, government and non-government uses — newly available for broadband use. The proposed Citizens Broadband Service would foster the widespread utilization of both of these technological advances and promote the efficient use of the 3.5 GHz Band.

4. Small cells are low-powered wireless base stations intended to cover targeted indoor or localized outdoor areas ranging in size from homes and offices to stadiums, shopping malls, hospitals, and metropolitan outdoor spaces. Typically, they provide wireless con-

nectivity in areas that present capacity and coverage challenges to traditional wide-area macrocell networks. Small cells can be deployed relatively easily and inexpensively by consumers, enterprise users, and service providers. Networks that incorporate small cell technology can take advantage of greater "reuse" of scarce wireless frequencies, greatly increasing data capacity within the network footprint. For example, deploying ten small cells in a location in place of a single macro cell could result in a tenfold increase in capacity, using the same quantity of spectrum. Small cells can also be used to help fill in coverage gaps created by buildings, tower siting difficulties, and/or challenging terrain.

5. Spectrum sharing in this context refers to the use of automated techniques to facilitate the coexistence of disparate unaffiliated spectrum dependent systems that would conventionally require separate bands to avoid interference. Such coexistence may happen, for example, by authorizing targeted use of new commercial systems in specific geographical areas where interference into incumbent systems is not a problem. The need to minimize interference risks has caused, over time, much spectrum to be reserved for "high value" systems that protect national security, safety of life, etc. For example, the military may need spectrum for advanced radar systems or hospitals may deploy networks to enable real-time monitoring of patient vital signs. However, many of these uses are highly localized in nature. Therefore, more agile technologies and sharing mechanisms could potentially allow large quantities of special-purpose federal and non-federal spectrum to be used for more general purposes, such as commercial broadband services, on a shared basis.

6. The 3.5 GHz Band appears to be an ideal band in which to propose small cell deployments and shared spectrum use. The NTIA Fast Track Report identified the 3.5 GHz Band for potential shared federal and non-federal broadband use. NTIA, An Assessment of the Near-Term Viability of Accommodating Wireless Broadband Systems in the 1675–1710 MHz, 1755–1780 MHz, 3500–3650 MHz, 4200–4220 MHz, and 4380–4400 MHz Bands (October 2010) (Fast Track Report), available at http://www.ntia.doc.gov/files/ntia/publications/fasttrackevaluation_11152010.pdf. Incumbent uses in the band include high powered Department of Defense (DoD) radars as well as non-federal Fixed Satellite Service (FSS) earth stations for receive-only, space-to-earth operations and feeder links. In the adjacent band below 3550 MHz there are high-powered ground and airborne military radars. The Fast Track Report recommended, based on the commercial wireless broadband technology that was assessed, that new commercial uses of the band occur outside of large "exclusion zones," which we estimate to cover approximately 60 percent of the U.S. population, to protect government operations. For this reason, and because of limited signal propagation at 3.5 GHz, the commercial wireless industry has expressed a viewpoint that the 3.5 GHz Band would not be particularly well-suited for macrocell deployment, with some suggesting that it might be more appropriate for fixed wireless or unlicensed use. We agree with the PCAST Report that the perceived disadvantages of the 3.5 GHz Band might be turned into advantages from the standpoint of promoting spectrum sharing and small cell innovation. Such a paradigm could vastly increase the usability of the band for wireless broadband.

III. DISCUSSION

A. Licensing Framework

1. Proposed Multi-Tier Framework

53. We propose a three-tiered licensing and interference protection framework to manage access to and use of the 3.5 GHz Band, providing different levels of protection for

different levels of access in the 3.5 GHz Band. The three proposed tiers are Incumbent Access, Priority Access, and General Authorized Access. To govern the interaction between the three tiers, we propose to establish a spectrum access system (SAS), incorporating a geo-location enabled dynamic database and, potentially other appropriate mitigation techniques.

54. Under the proposed framework, Incumbent Access users would include authorized federal and grandfathered FSS users in the 3.5 GHz Band. Incumbent Access users would have protection from harmful interference from all other users in the 3.5 GHz Band, which would be achieved through appropriate interference mitigation techniques, including geographic restrictions on Citizens Broadband Service use in the SAS. In this way, our proposal would ensure that federal users and grandfathered FSS licensees would be able to continue to use the band without interference from new Citizens Broadband Service users.

55. In the Priority Access tier, the Commission would authorize certain users with critical quality-of-service needs to operate with a measure of interference protection in portions of the 3.5 GHz Band at specific locations. Priority Access users would be eligible to use authorized devices on an interference protected basis within their facilities as controlled by the SAS. The Priority Access tier would be available only in areas where Citizens Broadband Service devices would not cause interference to incumbent operations and would not be expected to receive interference from incumbents (Priority Access Zones). In addition, Priority Access users would be required to provide interference protection to and accept interference from Incumbent Access users (even though no such interference would be anticipated in Priority Access Zones), but would not be required to provide such protection to General Authorized Access (GAA) users.

56. In the GAA tier, licensees would be authorized to use the 3.5 GHz Band on an opportunistic basis within designated geographic areas. GAA users would be required to accept interference from Incumbent and Priority Access tier users and would be required to avoid causing harmful interference to any users in those tiers. GAA use would permit ready access to unused portions of the 3.5 GHz Band for a broad class of residential, commercial, enterprise, and government users. Uses could include fixed or mobile consumer level devices, similar to Wi-Fi or TV White Spaces devices. Use of GAA devices would be permitted in Priority Access Zones as well as areas where such devices would not cause harmful interference to incumbent operations but where signals from incumbent operations could be expected to interfere with GAA uses on occasion (GAA Zones). Additionally, a supplemental proposal would allow GAA use at higher power levels in non-congested areas where those power levels do not pose an interference risk to higher tier users.

57. In general, under this three-tiered licensing proposal we believe incumbent users would be able to operate on a fully protected basis, while the technical benefits of small cells could be leveraged to facilitate innovative and efficient uses in the 3.5 GHz Band. Figure 1, below, provides a conceptual illustration how the different tiers, and corresponding zones, might interrelate from a geographic perspective within the 3.5 GHz Band. We seek comment on these tentative conclusions. We also seek detailed comments on the proposed three-tiered licensing and interference protection model, including the proposed geographic restrictions on Citizens Broadband Service operations, and request comprehensive analyses of the costs and benefits of this approach.

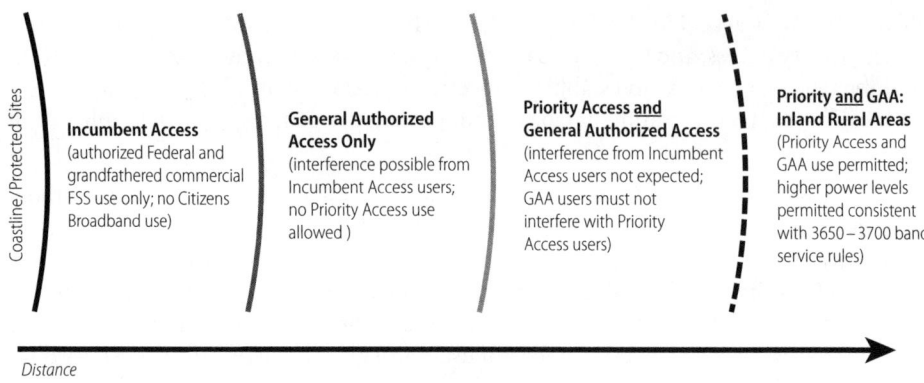

Figure 1

59. *Federal Radar Interference into Citizens Broadband Service Systems.* [T]he Fast Track Report proposed exclusion zones around DoD radars that were calculated to protect not only the DoD radar systems but also to prevent harmful interference from such systems into commercial devices. Under our proposal, GAA use would be allowed in areas where small cell devices would not cause harmful interference to incumbent operations but where signals from incumbent operations could possibly interfere with GAA uses on occasion (GAA Zones). In addition, we propose to allow "mission critical" operations in Priority Access Zones, where interference from radars into small cell use would not be expected. [In this NPRM], we inquire about possible technological approaches to designing resilient small cells that can avoid interference from high-powered radars. Nonetheless, given the Fast Track Report's concerns about incumbent interference into commercial systems, should GAA operations be permitted in areas where they can possibly receive interference from radars? Or should such use be restricted to areas where no harmful interference from Incumbent Access users would be expected. Similarly, should "mission critical" operations be permitted in the 3.5 GHz Band? Or does the threat of such interference render the band unusable for such sensitive operations, suggesting they be prohibited even in places where there is no expectation of harmful interference from DoD radars? How do the answers to these questions affect the value of the band? We seek comment on these important questions that go to the heart of the proposed Citizens Broadband Service.

60. *Federal Use of Citizen's Band Service.* We are cognizant that, much as federal agencies today make extensive use of commercial wireless technologies including cellular networks and Wi-Fi, so, too, they might find great value in small cell use. Therefore, we seek comment on the applicability of the Citizens Broadband service, including GAA and Priority Access tiers, to federal users. Federal agencies are permitted to operate various systems consistent with the FCC rules in various frequency bands. These federal systems are required by Section 2.103 of the Commission's rules, 47 C.F.R. § 2.103, and NTIA's Manual of Regulations and Procedures for Federal Radio Frequency Management (NTIA Manual) to operate in accordance with FCC rules and technical requirements, http://www.ntia.doc.gov/files/ntia/publications/redbook/2013/May_2013_Edition_of_the_NTIA_Manual.pdf. Non-federal services used by federal agencies span the various methods of authorization used by the FCC including license-by-rule, individual and blanket licenses, and unlicensed operation. We propose that federal end users be able to make use of our proposed three-tier access system provided that agencies follow the technical and regulatory requirements developed through our rulemaking process. We seek comment on this proposal, including the appropriate regulatory means to effectuate it.

2. Proposed Licensing Model

61. We propose to establish the Citizen's Broadband Service by rule under Section 307(e) of the Communications Act, 47 U.S.C. § 307(e). We believe that a license-by-rule licensing framework would allow for rapid deployment of small cells by a wide range of users, including consumers, enterprises, and service providers, at low cost and with minimal barriers to entry. Much wireless broadband use occurs indoors or in other enclosed facilities. Typically, the owners or users of such facilities already have access to the siting permissions, backhaul facilities, electrical power, and other key non-spectrum inputs for the provision of service. Moreover, our proposal for small cell operation at the relatively high frequency 3.5 GHz Band would generally tend to contain service within such facilities, allowing for a very high degree of spectrum reuse. Therefore, authorizing these end users—or their agents or assignees—to have direct access to the 3.5 GHz Band in the physical locations that they otherwise are able to access would seem to facilitate expeditious and low-cost provision of service. A license-by-rule framework is very compatible with and conducive toward these aims.[15]

62. Section 307(e) states in part that, "[n]otwithstanding any license requirement established in this Act, if the Commission determines that such authorization serves the public interest, convenience, and necessity, the Commission may by rule authorize the operation of radio stations without individual licenses in the following radio services: (A) citizens band radio service;...." *Id.* § 307(e)(1). Section 307(e) states further that, "[f]or purposes of this subsection, the terms 'citizens band radio service'... shall have the meanings given them by the Commission by rule." *Id.* § 307(e)(1). We believe that a license-by-rule framework is an appropriate methodology for authorizing users in the 3.5 GHz Band consistent with the tiers of service proposed herein. This proposed framework would facilitate the rapid deployment of compliant small cell devices in critical use facilities, while minimizing administrative costs and burdens on the public, licensees, and the Commission. Moreover, this proposed framework would allow the Commission a great deal of flexibility to establish appropriate service and allocation rules. It would also promote administrative efficiency by maintaining the rules governing the Citizens Broadband Service in a single rule part. Thus, we tentatively conclude that authorizing the operation of compliant devices in the 3.5 GHz Band by rule under Section 307(e) of the Act would further the public interest, convenience, and necessity. However, we also seek comment on alternative licensing and spectrum access models.

5. Alternative Licensing and Spectrum Access Models

83. While we believe that the three-tiered license-by-rule approach described above would provide a comprehensive framework for authorizing and managing access to the 3.5 GHz Band, we acknowledge that other approaches could be taken to manage non-federal access to the band. To that end, we seek detailed comment on alternative licensing and spectrum access models for the 3.5 GHz Band, taking into account: (1) the need for compatible operation with Incumbent Access users, including the acceptance of interference from these users and (2) our proposed technical rules to enable small cell use in this band. Com-

---

15. [The Commission explains elsewhere in this NPRM that "A license-by-rule approach would provide individuals, organizations, and service providers with 'automatic' authorization to deploy small cell systems, in much the same way that our Part 15 unlicensed rules have allowed widespread deployment of Wi-Fi access points." ¶ 11. Eds.]

menters should thoroughly compare and contrast their preferred alternative models to the proposals set forth herein.

84. *Two-Tier Variation.* We seek comment on whether a two-tiered model composed solely of Incumbent Access and Priority Access tiers would be more appropriate for the 3.5 GHz Band. Under this regulatory model, Incumbent Access users would continue to be protected from harmful interference and the remaining available spectrum would be licensed under criteria similar to those applicable to the proposed Priority Access tier. Similar database and technological coordination techniques described above would apply to this model as well and access would be permitted only within designated geographic areas. However, GAA use would not be permitted under this alternate proposal. We expect that this model would be compatible with the alternative licensing approaches described herein. We seek comment on this two-tier alternative, including the costs and benefits. What impact could this alternative have on spectrum efficiency in the 3.5 GHz Band relative to our three-tiered approach? Under this approach, should Priority Access users be allowed to operate in areas where interference could be expected from Incumbent Access users? Is there a specific licensing approach that is most compatible with this model? How would the use of a two-tiered framework affect the costs and benefits to wireless operators, enterprise users, consumers, or other potential users of the spectrum?

85. *Geographic Area Exclusive Licensing Alternative.* Rather than utilizing the license-by-rule approach described above, should the Commission entertain mutually exclusive applications for the Priority Access tier within defined geographic service areas? We note that Section 309(j) of the Communications Act provides that the Commission will resolve mutually exclusive applications accepted for spectrum licenses through competitive bidding, subject to specified exemptions. 47 U.S.C. § 309(j)(1). Nevertheless, the Commission, consistent with Section 309(j), has the "freedom to consider all available spectrum management tools and the discretion to evaluate which licensing mechanism is most appropriate for the services being offered." Implementation of Sections 309(j) and 337 of the Communications Act of 1934, as Amended, Report and Order and Further Notice of Proposed Rulemaking, 15 FCC Rcd. 22,709, 22,721 ¶ 25 (citing 47 U.S.C. § 309(j)(3)(D)) (2000). In licensing users of private radio spectrum, the Commission has traditionally limited the filing of mutually exclusive applications where "the frequencies are intensively shared, assigned on a first-come, first-served basis, and/or subject to frequency coordination." Implementation of Sections 309(j) and 337 of the Communications Act of 1934 as Amended, Notice of Proposed Rulemaking, 14 FCC Rcd. 5206, 5216 ¶ 13 (1999). Commenters that support exclusive geographic area licensing should assess the costs and benefits of this approach as opposed to a license-by-rule framework. Commenters should also consider whether the entire band should be licensed in this alternative way, or just a portion? Should the whole band be licensed on a nationwide basis, or should it be subdivided into discrete spectrum blocks and/or geographic license areas? Commenters are also encouraged to consider the feasibility of a hybrid model in which geographic area licenses would be issued for public property or outdoor areas, while a license-by-rule approach would be employed in private property or indoor areas. Would such an approach combine benefits of both licensing models? If so, how would our proposed low-power technical rules and the propagation characteristics of the 3.5 GHz Band effectively reduce harmful interference between different kinds of users?

86. *Other Authorization Alternatives.* Alternatively, should we adopt a "licensed light" approach akin to the licensing methodology used in the 3650–3700 MHz band? Or could our three-tiered framework be implemented on an unlicensed basis pursuant to Part 15 of the Commission's rules? *See, e.g.*, 47 C.F.R. §§ 15.707–717 (allowing the unlicensed use

of the TVWS coordinated through a database). We believe that our proposed licensing framework offers certain advantages over these alternative frameworks, including a unified licensing model for both tiers of licensed service, reduced administrative burden, and the potential for improved economies of scale in the equipment marketplace. Commenters that support an alternative regulatory framework should explain in detail how an alternative approach would be structured, its legal basis, its relative costs and benefits, and the advantages it would have over our license-by-rule proposal.

Notes and Questions

1. If You Can Share Here ... The NPRM suggests in ¶ 6 that the 3.5 GHz band is unusually well-suited to sharing (and, relatedly, small cell deployments), and that the commercial wireless industry had a similar view. What metrics should the Commission use to determine whether it should adopt sharing in other bands? Should the Commission propose benchmarks in advance that it will use to evaluate the success of sharing? Should it propose benchmarks for evaluating each of the different approaches in each band? What should those benchmarks be?

2. License-by-Rule. Note that the NPRM proposes a license-by-rule regime, though it also mentions other possibilities. Is that too permissive? Too restrictive? What would you need to know in order to determine whether that was the best approach?

3. Is This Really Permissible under § 307(e)? Look at the language of § 307(e). Does the term "citizens band radio service" encompass what the FCC is proposing here? How much extra leeway is provided by the language in § 307(e) stating that "'citizens band radio service'... shall have the meanings given [it] by the Commission by rule"? Is there any limit to what it can call "citizens band radio service"? How would you articulate that limit, and on what basis?

4. Tiers. On what grounds should the Commission choose between two tiers and three tiers (or four, for that matter)? Who would favor three tiers and who would favor two, and why?

5. Who Gets Priority? A key decision will be who gets priority access. How should that decision be made? What should be the key criteria? Elsewhere in the NPRM, the Commission suggests that Priority Access "could include hospitals, utilities, state and local governments, and/or other users with a distinct need for reliable, prioritized access to broadband spectrum at specific, localized facilities." ¶ 9. Does that make sense? If not, what does? If you are worried that the Commission will adopt a bad definition, is that an argument against having priority access in the first place?

§ 4.E. Spectrum Leasing and Private Commons

One way of achieving spectrum flexibility is by authorizing either existing or new licensees to offer new services. Another way is by authorizing users to offer services that dynamically avoid significant interference. Yet a third way is to allow licensees to offer a wide variety of services on their portion of the spectrum and then further allow them to subdivide and lease those spectrum rights to third parties.

Note that, if a licensee can divide its spectrum rights in any way that it chooses, and a lessee can utilize those rights in any way that it chooses, then effectively there is complete spectrum flexibility. Indeed, under such a regime the only limit would be that a licensee that wanted to offer a new service might have to create a new subsidiary to which it would lease some set of its spectrum rights. The FCC has not, in fact, allowed lessees to offer any service they please (or even any noninterfering service). But it has authorized licensees to lease part of their spectrum rights, thereby making those rights divisible commodities. *See* Promoting Efficient Use of Spectrum through Elimination of Barriers to the Development of Secondary Markets, Report and Order and Further Notice of Proposed Rulemaking, 18 FCC Rcd. 20,604 (2003).

Under 47 U.S.C. § 310(d), no "station license or any rights thereunder shall be transferred, assigned or disposed of in any manner... except upon application to the Commission and upon finding by the Commission that the public interest, convenience, and necessity will be served thereby." In 1963, the FCC construed § 310(d) to require that licensees exercise close working control over all of the facilities using their spectrum, which effectively precluded transferring meaningful authority to third parties other than through a sale of the entire license. *See* Intermountain Microwave, Public Notice, 12 F.C.C. 2d 559, 560 (1963). In its 2003 order, the Commission partially reversed course, concluding that § 310(d) does not require such close control, and that instead "effective working control" was sufficient. 18 FCC Rcd. 20,604, ¶ 3. The order then provided that licensees can lease spectrum usage rights, without the need for prior Commission approval, so long as the licensee exercises effective working control over the use of the spectrum it leases.

The FCC's news release summarizes the central provisions of the order:

> Under the leasing rules adopted in the Report and Order, licensees in the covered services may lease some or all of their spectrum-usage rights to third parties, for any amount of spectrum and in any geographic area encompassed by the license, and for any period of time within the term of the license.
>
> The Report and Order creates two different mechanisms for spectrum leasing depending on the scope of the rights and responsibilities to be assumed by the lessee. The first leasing option—"spectrum manager" leasing—enables parties to enter into spectrum leasing arrangements without obtaining prior Commission approval so long as the licensee retains both de jure control (i.e., legal control) of the license and de facto control (i.e., working control) over the leased spectrum pursuant to the updated de facto control standard for leasing.
>
> The second option—de facto transfer leasing—permits parties to enter into long-term or short-term leasing arrangements whereby the licensee retains de jure control of the license while de facto control is transferred to the lessee for the term of the lease. De facto transfer leases under this option will require prior Commission approval under a streamlined approval process. Under the de facto transfer leasing option, the Report and Order establishes different rules and procedures for long-term and short-term leases ("short-term" leases are defined as leases of 360 days or less in duration).

FCC News Release, FCC Adopts Spectrum Leasing Rules and Streamlined Processing for License Transfer and Assignment Applications, and Proposes Further Steps to Increase Access to Spectrum through Secondary Markets, 2003 WL 21088542 (May 15, 2003). This represented a significant increase in a licensee's ability to transfer a portion of its spectrum rights. It does not go as far as Coase might like (because it obviously falls short of full divisibility and transferability), but it enhanced the development of secondary markets in spectrum.[16]

---

16. The order implementing incentive auctions applies these rules to the licenses created under the Spectrum Act. Thus it allows for spectrum leasing as well as geographic partitioning and spectrum dis-

One matter the 2003 order on spectrum leasing left open was the question of how, if at all, it would provide for the creation of spectrum commons. The Commission addressed that issue in a 2004 order. The relevant excerpt follows.

Promoting Efficient Use of Spectrum Through Elimination of Barriers to the Development of Secondary Markets

Second Report and Order, Order on Reconsideration, and Second Further Notice of Proposed Rulemaking, 19 FCC Rcd. 17,503 (2004)

IV. Second Report and Order

B. Policies to Facilitate Advanced Technologies

86. Because we believe that smart or opportunistic technologies hold significant potential to promote access to and more efficient use of the spectrum, we clarify our existing spectrum leasing rules, and introduce an additional means, to help facilitate the development of arrangements involving the use of these new and evolving technologies in services for which spectrum leasing is permitted. Opportunistic use technologies facilitate many dynamic ways of sharing spectrum. For example, smart or cognitive radio devices can potentially sense and adapt to their spectrum environment, find and use spectrum in locations or during time intervals that will not cause interference to other users, and operate across multiple bands and using different protocols. Such devices may also have networking capability, either on a peer-to-peer (device-to-device) basis or by interacting with available wide-area or local-area networks. The spectrum access capabilities of these technologies can be achieved by a variety of potential cooperative approaches, such as secondary markets arrangements, in which users of licensed spectrum arrange access with licensees under mutually agreeable terms.[17] With smart or cognitive radios, for example, it is possible to reconfigure the performance parameters of the individual devices to allow more opportunistic uses of the spectrum. As these capabilities become available on a broader basis, the Commission can facilitate these additional forms of spectrum access by ensuring that our licensing and technical rules do not inadvertently impose barriers to the deployment of such capabilities if and when licensees (or spectrum lessees) seek to take advantage of such capabilities. These cooperative uses of these capabilities would also complement other approaches to promoting spectrum access, e.g., facilitating access for advanced technologies on an unlicensed basis. The approaches considered in this order are cooperative in nature—avoiding placing regulatory barriers on licensees (or spectrum lessees) that wish to provide for opportunistic uses of spectrum pursuant to the

---

aggregation. Expanding the Economic and Innovation Opportunities of Spectrum Through Incentive Auctions, Report and Order, 29 FCC Rcd. 6567 ¶¶ 801, 804 (2014).

17. While a secondary markets approach to promoting access to licensed spectrum is largely market-based and cooperative, other policy options to promoting such access are possible, including some that are not primarily based on cooperation among private actors and that may spring from Commission regulations. For example, in two proceedings currently before the Commission, we discuss a range of policy options, including cooperative approaches as well as the use of licensed spectrum without the licensee's consent. *See* Facilitating Opportunities for Flexible, Efficient, and Reliable Spectrum Use Employing Cognitive Radio Technologies, Notice of Proposed Rulemaking and Order, 2003 WL 23022050 (Dec. 30, 2003); Establishment of an Interference Temperature Metric to Quantify and Manage Interference and to Expand Available Unlicensed Operation in Certain Fixed, Mobile and Satellite Frequency Bands, Notice of Inquiry and Notice of Proposed Rulemaking, 18 FCC Rcd. 25,309 (2003).

terms and conditions that they set—so long as they fall within the licensee's spectrum usage rights and are not inconsistent with applicable technical and other regulations imposed by the Commission to prevent harmful interference to other licensees.

a. Facilitating advanced technologies within existing regulatory frameworks, including dynamic spectrum leasing arrangements

88. We clarify that our spectrum leasing policies and rules permit parties to enter into a variety of dynamic forms of spectrum leasing arrangements that take advantage of the capabilities associated with advanced technologies. [P]arties may enter into spectrum leasing arrangements in which licensees and spectrum lessees share use of the same spectrum, on a non-exclusive basis, during the term of the lease. For example, a licensee and spectrum lessee may enter into a spectrum manager or de facto transfer lease in which use of the same spectrum is shared with each other by employing opportunistic devices.[18] In another variation, a licensee could enter into a spectrum manager lease with one party that has access to the spectrum on a priority basis, while also leasing use of the same spectrum to another party on a lower-priority basis, with the requirement that the lower priority spectrum lessee employ opportunistic technology to avoid interfering with the priority lessee. Of course, the licensee may not lease spectrum usage rights that exceed the rights it currently holds and, as these examples illustrate, the licensee may choose to lease a more restricted bundle of usage rights.

89. Significantly, these arrangements could facilitate opportunistic use by parties operating at the same power level and under similar technical parameters as the licensee, or they could promote such use at lower power levels. We also emphasize that neither scenario would affect unlicensed operations to the extent they are permitted in that particular licensed band pursuant to Commission rules under Part 15. For example, Part 15 users can operate pursuant to applicable technical and operational rules whether or not opportunistic use or other advanced technologies are employed or authorized by the licensee. We would also expect that new and innovative radiofrequency devices would be agile enough to function on an unlicensed basis or as part of licensed operations. Moreover, the examples discussed here do not provide an exhaustive list of all the possible arrangements that could involve the use of opportunistic devices and be consistent with secondary markets and service rules already in place. Accordingly, we seek comment on the types of additional commercial or sharing arrangements that would further exploit the benefits of new and innovative technological advances.

90. We recognize that, in some cases, under the current framework for spectrum manager and de facto transfer lease arrangements, these options may not be economically or technically feasible due to the transaction costs associated with coordinating many users in a single band, or many users employing advanced technologies to access multiple bands by frequency-hopping. Nonetheless, we do not believe that these should be insurmountable barriers and we concur with the Spectrum Policy Task Force Report that "a secondary markets approach by opportunistic devices does not necessarily require the prospective opportunistic user to negotiate individually with each affected licensee," and that band managers, clearinghouses, and other intermediaries could facilitate these transactions.[19] We also agree with the Spectrum Policy Task Force Report finding that a "secondary market approach has significant potential to foster opportunistic technologies, such as agile frequency-hopping radios, software-defined radios, and adaptive antennas, at reasonable

---

18. An example of such an arrangement would be a cellular licensee that leases to a manufacturer of low-power opportunistic devices for use of the licensed spectrum on a noninterfering basis.

19. Spectrum Policy Task Force Report at 57.

transaction costs."[20] In short, while the existing spectrum leasing options may not meet all types of spectrum access needs, we have great confidence in the ability of market participants to find innovative means of enhancing spectrum access and lowering transaction costs, and we therefore expect the market for spectrum usage rights to become increasingly efficient. At the same time, licensees and spectrum lessees may wish to make spectrum available in ways not anticipated by the Commission's current rules, and such innovative efforts may be a driving force in promoting the development of advanced technologies and the efficient use of the spectrum. We therefore introduce a new concept under our current exclusive-use licensing models that may foster the experimentation and new uses of licensed spectrum without unnecessary regulatory intervention.

b. Private Commons

91. To facilitate the use of advanced technologies, and thus better promote access to and the efficient use of spectrum, we expand the spectrum licensing framework by identifying an additional option that may be utilized by current and future licensees and spectrum lessees. This concept, which we call a "private commons," will allow licensees and spectrum lessees to make spectrum available to individual users or groups of users that do not fit squarely within the current options for spectrum leasing or within the traditional end-user arrangements associated with the licensee's (or spectrum lessee's) subscriber-based services and network infrastructures. New technologies enable users, through use of advanced devices, to engage in a wide range of communications that do not require use of a licensee's (or lessee's) network infrastructure. To facilitate the use of these technologies, we adopt the private commons option, which will permit, and be restricted to, peer-to-peer communications between devices in a non-hierarchical network arrangement that does not utilize the network infrastructure of the licensee (or spectrum lessee).

92. The private commons option provides a cooperative mechanism for licensees (or lessees) to make licensed spectrum available to users employing these advanced technologies in a manner similar to that by which unlicensed users gain access to spectrum to suit their particular needs, and to do so without the necessity of entering into individual spectrum leasing arrangements under our existing rules. In the 2.4 GHz and 5 GHz bands, for instance, users gain access and use of the spectrum with specified types of low-power communications devices provided they comply with technical requirements established by the Commission and set forth in our Part 15 rules. In these bands, users then can create their own networks—such as those that are ad hoc or "mesh" in nature—using equipment that complies with Commission established requirements. The private commons option provides a potentially complementary access model,[21] in which licensees (or spectrum lessees) would determine to make access available to a similar class of users, and would do so under technical requirements for sharing use of the licensed band established and managed by the licensee (or lessee).[22] The nature of these types of users' access to

---

20. *Id.*
21. Consistent with our discussion of dynamic leasing arrangements, the general ability of a licensee to deploy a private commons model is not intended to, and does not, overturn rights under Part 15, as it exists or as amended, to operate in a band or limit the Commission's ability to implement new underlay approaches when considering particular bands. For instance, a licensee could not, as its own technical condition, restrict the emission limits of devices in a private commons to a level below the level authorized for that band under the Commission's Part 15 rules for unlicensed devices, such as UWB devices, and thereby eliminate the opportunity for such devices to use that spectrum.
22. Such technical requirements, of course, would have to be consistent with all of the Commission's technical rules applicable to the service or band at issue for preventing interference to other licensees.

spectrum under this private commons option thus differs qualitatively from the nature of access provided to spectrum lessees under the Commission's spectrum leasing policies and procedures. In the private commons, the licensee (or lessee) authorizes users of devices operating at particular technical parameters specified by the licensee (or lessee) to operate on the licensed frequencies, consistent with the applicable technical requirements and use restrictions under the license authorization, using peer-to-peer (device-to-device) technologies. In spectrum leasing arrangements, individually negotiated spectrum access rights are provided to entities that traditionally obtained licenses and that would then provide traditional network based services to end-users.

94. These private commons arrangements may take a variety of forms, but will share a number of defining characteristics, as described herein. The private commons option will allow for flexible uses of licensed spectrum rights in which the licensee or lessee does not necessarily offer services (in whole or part) over its own end-to-end physical network of base stations, mobile stations, and other elements. The licensee or spectrum lessee, as a manager of a private commons, will set terms and conditions for use in the private commons by users (consistent with the terms of the license and applicable service rules), and retain both de facto control of the use of the spectrum within the private commons and direct responsibility for compliance with the Commission's rules. And, while private commons arrangements will not be subject to the same notification requirements that are required by our spectrum leasing rules, licensees (or spectrum lessees) managing the commons will be required at this time to notify the Commission about any private commons they establish prior to users being permitted to operate within that private commons.

95. We anticipate at least two types of private commons that licensees (or spectrum lessees) could make available to individuals or groups of users. In the first example, a private commons could be created by a licensee (or spectrum lessee), which may or may not otherwise have a network infrastructure to provide services, by granting access for a fee (e.g., on a transaction, usage, fixed, or other basis) to users who employ smart or opportunistic wireless devices that conform to the terms and conditions established by the licensee (or lessee), such as a requirement that devices operating in the licensed band use a particular technology, hardware, or software. The users' devices may be used to engage in peer-to-peer (device-to-device) communications, such as by becoming part of compatible ad hoc or "mesh" wireless networks. Such users may need access to a particular licensed spectrum band in lieu of (or perhaps in addition to) gaining access to other bands that may be more heavily used or that do not allow for the quality of service necessary for a particular application. This type of private commons might be particularly valuable to users that find existing bands that provide for unlicensed operations to be crowded or otherwise less desirable.

96. Under a second potential type of private commons arrangement, the licensee (or spectrum lessee) would not charge an ongoing access fee or otherwise have any direct relationship with the users. For instance, manufacturers of smart or opportunistic devices, or the developers of software or hardware used within such devices, may wish, as licensees or spectrum lessees, to provide spectrum access to anyone who purchases their devices, or devices with their hardware or software. This type of arrangement might be particularly effective in promoting new technologies or new uses by providing an opportunity for equipment developers to capitalize on their investments and innovations without having to get a license directly from the Commission, but could arrange for users of the equipment to access the spectrum usage rights from an existing licensee. Because a licensee (or spectrum lessee) could offer to private commons users the interference protection rights of its license, this arrangement could provide some additional benefits as compared with possible lower-powered, unlicensed operation in the same or other bands.

98. We believe that a private commons will provide an important complement to the spectrum leasing policies we have already adopted to facilitate spectrum access, as well as to unlicensed access to spectrum. We expect the combination of spectrum leasing arrangements, private commons, and the various ways in which licensees currently may utilize advanced technology will further enhance this move towards greater spectrum access, and we are optimistic about the potential benefits that are likely to emerge as licensees and other users find more ways to promote access to and the efficient use of spectrum. We note that the flexibility afforded by a private commons may help make possible a number of new means to apply advanced radio technologies, including such concepts as "policy radio," an emerging approach that would allow use that is even more dynamic than that described above.

99. We also envision this approach as part of a balance between license-based access mechanisms, such as the spectrum leasing and private commons models that allow licensees and spectrum lessees to define access rights based on market forces, and unlicensed access mechanisms that allow free access by non-interfering devices pursuant to regulation. We recognize that there is an ongoing and important debate on spectrum policy, with some parties stressing the merits of unlicensed and shared uses, both within a free and open "spectrum commons" and in licensed bands under private control, and other parties arguing for the merits of "exclusive" licensed use of spectrum. We are not here taking sides in that debate. Rather, we expect that existing and new licensees and spectrum lessees in various services and spectrum bands will consider the market potential of a private commons and other arrangements and seek opportunities to lower transaction costs and provide multiple avenues of spectrum access and a range of devices to consumers, businesses and other entities. In addition, we anticipate that, as unlicensed use becomes more popular, users of unlicensed devices that operate under the Part 15 rules may have an incentive to seek access to a managed private commons in licensed bands that may be less susceptible to overcrowding and, because of the benefit of interference protection, may be a way to avoid the potential risks associated with the "tragedy of the commons." Licensees and spectrum lessees in turn will have an incentive to provide private commons through a variety of means, with terms and conditions that are most valued by users. We expect these users will choose the most efficient means of spectrum access for their particular needs, considering the costs and benefits of all options, including private commons and unlicensed use.

Notes and Questions

1. What's New? Does the language of the order suggest that its approach differs from what exclusive use would entail? If so, how? That is, does this proposal allow for any uses of spectrum that would not be permissible if all frequencies were privately owned, and freely transferable and divisible?

2. What Does Experience Reveal? No private commons were created in response to this order. What should that tell us? That not enough people would use a commons to make it economically attractive? That more than enough people would use a commons to make it economically attractive, but licensees are too short-sighted, intransigent, or ideologically opposed to commons to create them, despite the money they would make? That more than enough people would use a true commons to make it economically viable, but not enough would use a private commons because of differences between government-created commons and private commons? What differences would those be?

Chapter Five

Structuring and Assigning Licenses

Introduction

The previous chapter considers how the Commission determines the contours of the spectrum uses that it authorizes—determining how to divide up bandwidth, whether it will create licenses, and how much flexibility users will have. Assuming the Commission decides to create some spectrum licenses, it must figure out how it will distribute those licenses, and how easily licensees can keep or transfer those licenses. In this chapter, we focus on those questions. These categories have some malleability: one can, for example, conceptualize restrictions on license transferability as limits inherent in the license or as limits on their transfer. We place them in the latter category, and thus in this chapter. Specifically, this chapter addresses the restrictions on a spectrum licensee renewing or transferring its license and the question how the Commission chooses the private party to whom to assign the license in the first place.

We begin in § 5.A. with renewal and transfer. One of the basic questions for anyone seeking a license is what restrictions exist on its ability to retain or transfer its license. And note that restrictions on how a transferee can use a license reduce the value of the ability to transfer, and thus of the license. Section 301 of the Communications Act prohibits private ownership of spectrum rights, but guaranteed renewal and free transferability would constitute a major step toward a property regime for spectrum licenses. This section of the chapter studies how close the current rules are to emulating that sort of a property regime, and it discusses advantages and disadvantages of such an approach.

Section 5.B. begins our consideration of license assignment, focusing on merit-based hearings. The Commission once chose licensees based on their ability to serve the "public interest, convenience and necessity." As we will explain, there were several types of merit-based hearings along these lines, including uncontested hearings, in which a single license applicant would be evaluated in isolation; comparative hearings, in which two license applicants would go head-to-head; and renewal hearings, in which an existing licensee would be evaluated to determine whether it should keep its license. Merit-based hearings are no longer a part of spectrum regulation, and the purpose of this material is to show how difficult it was to empower an administrative agency to make these sorts of decisions while still maintaining some sense that the decisions were based on objective, verifiable, and constitutionally valid criteria.

Section 5.C. turns to the mechanisms that displaced merit-based hearings: first lotteries and ultimately auctions. As we will explain, assignment via auction has become the norm: most spectrum licenses today are auctioned to the highest bidder and from there treated much like any other commodity—sold, resold, and in other ways transferred without any further input from the government.

The materials in this chapter heavily involve broadcast licenses. This reflects the fact that, until the rise of cellular communications in the 1980s, broadcasting was the highest-valued use of spectrum, and the central decisions about spectrum licenses arose in the context of broadcasting. But the principles at issue apply to spectrum licenses generally, and that broader application has become more prominent as non-broadcast uses of the spectrum have become more valuable

§ 5.A. License Renewal and Transfer

As Chapter Four indicates, one important stick in the bundle of rights that a licensee would want is flexibility in choosing what service to offer. Another is the ability to exclude those who interfere (and the FCC does police interference). A third is the ability to keep the license indefinitely and to transfer it freely. A licensee with all these rights has moved reasonably close to fee-simple property rights in spectrum, even if they are not denominated as such because 47 U.S.C. § 301 prohibits private ownership of spectrum. Renewal and transfer thus loom very large for licensees. We begin with license renewal and then consider license transfer.

§ 5.A.1. License Renewal

Spectrum licenses are of limited duration. Commercial television and radio licenses, for example, are awarded under current law for eight-year periods. 47 U.S.C. § 307(c)(1). Licenses for flexible licenses in the 600 MHz Band have an initial term of twelve years, with subsequent license terms of ten years.[1] Every licensee must therefore periodically appear before the FCC and petition that its license be renewed. This gives the FCC extraordinary power to influence licensee behavior; every decision a licensee makes throughout its tenure is made in the shadow of an implicit threat of an FCC response come renewal time. This form of implicit regulation—regulation through the threat of license nonrenewal or some lesser ramification such as renewal for a shorter-than-normal period—is a prime example of what is often referred to as regulation by raised eyebrow.

Indeed, the threat of nonrenewal is the primary means that the Commission has used in attempting to influence licensees' behavior. When the government has wanted a licensee to offer more programming that the government deems valuable (such as children's television), or to offer less programming that the government deems unworthy (such as commercials), or to adopt certain business practices (such as an affirmative action program), the main lever that the government has used to influence licensees in the desired direction has been the specter of license nonrenewal. Licenses are sufficiently valuable to licensees that they generally fall into line and obey the government's directives in order to keep their licenses at renewal time.

---

1. Expanding the Economic and Innovation Opportunities of Spectrum Through Incentive Auctions, Report and Order, 29 FCC Rcd. 6567 ¶ 37 (2014). The FCC also imposes build-out benchmarks, and its rules provide that failure to meet the initial benchmark shortens the initial license term to ten years. *Id.* n.63.

§5.A.1.a. Early History

Section 29 of the 1927 Radio Act provided that the Federal Radio Commission's (FRC) licensing power did not include the power of censorship and licensing therefore could not "interfere with the right of free speech by means of radio communications."[2] Congress did not clarify how the mandate in §29 would mesh with the equally strong mandate to award licenses in the public interest. The FRC, in its First Annual Report, defined the task ahead in a manner that set the regulatory agenda for decades: §29 prohibits censorship, but "the physical facts of radio transmission compel what is, in effect, a censorship of the most extraordinary kind.... [T]here is a definite limit, and a very low one, to the number of broadcasting stations which can operate simultaneously." Consequently, some applicants must be told "there is no room for you."[3]

By the summer of 1928, the Commission believed that whatever §29 might say about censorship, the Commission had to evaluate programming:

> Since the number of channels is limited and the number of persons desiring to broadcast is far greater than can be accommodated, the commission must determine from among the applicants before it which of them will, if licensed, best serve the public. In a measure, perhaps, all of them give more or less service. Those who give the least, however, must be sacrificed for those who give the most. The emphasis must be first and foremost on the interest, the convenience, and the necessity of the listening public, and not on the interest, convenience, or necessity of the individual broadcaster or the advertiser.[4]

The Commission then admonished those stations playing phonograph records because such a station would not give the public anything it could not receive elsewhere in the community.[5]

Over the next year, the Commission turned on what it called "[p]ropaganda stations (a term which is here used for the sake of convenience and not in a derogatory sense)."[6] A year earlier it had warned New York socialist station WEVD (named for the socialist leader Eugene Victor Debs) to operate "with due regard for the opinions of others."[7] The Commission, relying on scarcity, asserted that stations should aim their programs at everyone. There was "not room in the broadcast band for every school of thought, religious, political, social, and economic, each to have its separate broadcasting station, its mouthpiece in the ether. If franchises are extended to some it gives them an unfair advantage over others, and results in a corresponding cutting down of general public-service stations."[8] Thus when the Chicago Federation of Labor applied for an increase in power and hours for its station WCFL, arguing that it broadcast programs of particular interest to organized labor and that its number of listeners was sufficient to justify the increase, the Commission responded "that there is no place for a station catering to any group [and] that

---

2. Radio Act of 1927, ch. 169, §29, 44 Stat. 1162, 1172–73.
3. Annual Report of the Federal Radio Commission for the Fiscal Year 1927, 1 FRC Ann. Rep. 1, 6 (1927) (quoting Henry A. Bellows, Comm'r, FRC, Address Before the League of Women Voters (Apr. 29, 1927)).
4. Statement Made by the Commission on August 23, 1928, Relative to Public Interest, Convenience, or Necessity, 2 FRC Ann. Rep. 166, 170 (1928).
5. *Id.* at 168.
6. Great Lakes Broad. Co., 3 FRC Ann. Rep. 32, 34 (1929).
7. Decisions of Aug. 22, 1928, 2 FRC Ann. Rep. 154, 155 (1928).
8. Great Lakes Broad. Co., 3 FRC Ann. Rep. at 34.

all stations should cater to the general public and serve public interest against group or class interest."[9]

The Commission campaigned against what it feared would be a balkanizing of the dial. "If, therefore, all the programs transmitted are intended for, and interesting or valuable to, only a small portion of that public, the rest of the listeners are being discriminated against." Broadcasters should strive for "a well-rounded program" that meets the needs of all potential listeners.[10] Whether there were several stations in the area was irrelevant; each station was required to serve all potential listeners.

Whether a station was popular was also irrelevant. If a station was not meeting the needs of its community, then it could be replaced even if it was highly popular. Commission actions against the Reverend Bob ("Fighting Bob") Shuler and the famous "goat gland doctor," John R. Brinkley, illustrate this principle. Further, each case generated appellate litigation that fully vindicated the FRC, setting a judicial pattern of deference that continued for decades.[11]

§ 5.A.1.a.1. The *Shuler* Case

In 1926 a wealthy widow from Berkeley, impressed by one of Reverend Bob Shuler's indignant sermons, gave him $25,000 to purchase KGEF Los Angeles, a one-kilowatt station broadcasting 23 hours per week on a shared frequency. Shuler broadcast his sermons each Sunday and took two additional weekday hours for himself. On Tuesdays he hosted the "Bob Shuler Question Hour" and on Thursdays he gave "Bob Shuler's Civic Talk."

As a rigid moralist with an intense dislike for prostitution and alcohol, Shuler found a wide array of targets in Prohibition-era Los Angeles. During his two weekday hours he railed against what he perceived to be widespread local corruption. Over the years Shuler built such a following that commercial stations were unable to sell advertising time opposite these two programs. "Question Hour" was the fourth most popular show in the market, and audience surveys showed that "Fighting Bob" reached an audience of about 600,000 as he lashed out at an imperfect world.

Shuler's application for renewal in 1930 stated that KGEF had "thrown the pitiless spotlight of publicity on corrupt public officials and on agencies of immorality, thereby gladly gaining their enmity and open threats to 'get' this station's license." The FRC hit Shuler with a hearing that aired charges that he had used his station irresponsibly in attacking virtually all aspects of Los Angeles city government. The hearing lasted sixteen days, with testimony from 90 witnesses. At its end the hearing examiner ruled for Shuler.[12]

Shuler's opponents then went to the full Commission, which reversed and ordered KGEF off the air immediately. The Commission issued "Grounds for Decision," among which were that "Station KGEF has been used to attack a religious organization and members thereof, thus serving to promote religious strife and antagonism," "[t]he programs

---

9. Chi. Fed'n of Labor v. FRC, 3 FRC Ann. Rep. 36, 36 (1929).
10. Great Lakes Broad. Co., 3 FRC Ann. Rep. at 34.
11. Many of the facts about Shuler and Brinkley are taken from Lucas A. Powe, Jr., American Broadcasting and the First Amendment, 13–18, 23–27 (1987). Much more detail on Dr. Brinkley is available in R. Alton Lee, The Bizarre Careers of John R. Brinkley (2002).
12. Application of Trinity Methodist Church, South (Station KGEF), Statement of Facts, Grounds for Decision, and Order of the Commission, FRC Docket No. 1043, at 1, 3 (Nov. 13, 1931) (available at Nat'l Archives, RG173).

of applicant station have featured broadcasts by Shuler which have been sensational in character rather than instructional or entertaining," and that a Los Angeles state court had convicted him of contempt of court for his broadcasting "remarks [that] amounted to an assault upon a juror."[13]

§ 5.A.1.a.2. The *Brinkley* Case

The FRC believed "Fighting Bob" Shuler had been operating KGEF as a personal outlet, a category that the Commission had ranked even lower than propaganda stations. That spelled nothing but trouble for Brinkley, the "goat gland doctor," whose KFKB was a personal outlet par excellence. Yet it was also the most popular station, not just in central Kansas, but in the entire United States, outpolling the runner-up by a four-to-one margin. KFKB blanketed the area between the Rockies and the Mississippi and beyond, and Brinkley held his audience with an astute combination of fundamentalist theology and medical information. Brinkley gained his notoriety with the latter.

Brinkley's initial fame had come from his efforts to rejuvenate the male sex drive by implanting the gonads of a young Ozark goat in the patient's scrotum. A public-spirited man, he even sponsored a Little League baseball team nicknamed the Brinkley Goats. Yet Brinkley understood that there was a limited future in goat-gland transplants, and by the late 1920s his medical business focused on the prostate. Using both mail and KFKB, Brinkley attempted to reach "the prostate man" and convince him that he had a problem that Brinkley could solve. "It certainly behooves a man who has an enlarged prostate to consider it, and we are indeed glad to hear from such men for we are convinced we can render [them] a real, genuine, and lasting service."

On a typical day Brinkley took to the air twice (after lunch and dinner) to speak on medical problems. The evening program would be a gland lecture, explaining the male change of life. "Our bodies are not holding up as well as those of our forefathers did. Enlargement of the prostate is on the increase." His other program was his "Medical Question Box," which grew out of his enormous daily mail. Typically he would pick up some letters on the way to the microphone, leaf through them, and choose which to read on the air. He would then quickly give his diagnosis and prescribe the medicine required—by number, e.g., "Brinkley's 2, 16, and 17. If his druggist hasn't got them, he should write and order them from the Milford Drug Company, Milford, Kansas." As this indicates, Brinkley had expanded into the pharmaceutical business.

Predictably, the "goat gland doctor" drew the ire of organized medicine, which challenged both his right to broadcast and his right to practice medicine. On a single unlucky Friday the thirteenth, in June 1930, he lost both. The FRC found that Brinkley's "Medical Question Box" diagnosis, based on "what symptoms may be recited by the patient in a letter addressed to him, is inimical to the public health and safety, and for that reason is not in the public interest"; furthermore, KFKB was a "mere" adjunct to his medical practice and insufficiently attuned to the needs of Kansas.[14]

---

13. *Id.* at 6, 11. The religious organization was the Catholic Church. *See, e.g., id.* at 7 ("Shuler has repeatedly attacked the Catholic Church in his broadcasts.").

14. KFKB Broad. Ass'n v. FRC, 47 F.2d 670, 671–72 (D.C. Cir. 1931). The FRC held that "the operation of Station KFKB is conducted only in the personal interest of Dr. John R. Brinkley. While it is to be expected that a licensee of a radio broadcasting station will receive some remuneration for serving the public with radio programs, at the same time the interest of the listening public is paramount, and may not be subordinated to the interests of the station licensee." *Id.* at 671.

§ 5.A.1.a.3. The Judicial Response

Both Shuler and Brinkley appealed to the D.C. Circuit. Both lost. The court reviewing Brinkley's appeal agreed fully with the Commission that broadcasts should have a "public character. Obviously, there is no room in the broadcast band for every business or school of thought."[15] Broadcasting is "impressed with a public interest," and therefore the Commission "is necessarily called upon to consider the character and quality of the service to be rendered." The court summarily dismissed Brinkley's argument that the Commission had engaged in forbidden censorship. Section 29 went exclusively to prior scrutiny. What the Commission did, by contrast, was exercise its "undoubted right" to look at past performance. The court stated that, "In considering an application for a renewal of the license, an important consideration is the past conduct of the applicant, for 'by their fruits ye shall know them.' Matt. VII:20."[16]

The court treated Shuler's appeal similarly. There was no censorship or denial of free speech "but merely the application of the regulatory power of Congress in a field within the scope of its legislative authority."[17] Shuler remained free to "inspire political distrust and civic discord"; he simply couldn't demand to use an instrumentality of interstate commerce "for such purposes."[18] The Commission was duty-bound to look at Shuler's past broadcasts, and its conclusion that the public interest would not be served by relicensing him was hardly arbitrary and capricious.[19]

§ 5.A.1.b. More Recent Developments

The big policy debate regarding license renewal has been over how much discretion the FCC should enjoy with respect to its renewal decisions. One possibility is to give the FCC broad discretion, the logic being that the FCC is supposed to select the most promising licensees and greater discretion to analyze an incumbent's record would maximize the FCC's ability to do just that. True, this might be a little unfair to incumbents: by its nature, the comparative hearing process requires that the FCC make comparisons between would-be licensees, and yet, in this setting, the FCC really would have nothing to compare the incumbent's record to, except perhaps a challenger's promises. But the FCC could surely account for this imbalance, for example by holding challengers to the promises they make. There are two possible advantages to empowering the FCC in this way: first, if subject to broad review, poor and even average incumbents could be identified and replaced as their licenses expire; and second, during their terms, licensees hoping ultimately to renew their licenses would be very responsive to regulation by raised eyebrow, thus empowering the FCC to adjust its policies from time to time to respond to changing conditions.

Another possibility would be to constrain the FCC via a strong presumption of renewal with perhaps some small, well-articulated, and relatively stable list of standards that must be met before that presumption would take hold. Such an approach would allow the agency to weed out certain types of poor or average licensees, but it would leave

---

15. *Id.* at 672. The Commission might have contrasted KFKB with a Gary, Indiana, station that prevailed over two Chicago stations because its programs were "musical, educational and instructive in their nature and [stressed] loyalty to the community and the Nation." FRC v. Nelson Bros. Bond & Mortg. Co., 289 U.S. 266, 271 (1933).
16. *KFKB*, 47 F.2d at 672.
17. Trinity Methodist Church, South v. FRC, 62 F.2d 850, 851 (D.C. Cir. 1932).
18. *Id.* at 853.
19. *Id.* at 852.

the agency with much less power to regulate implicitly. Regulation by raised eyebrow works, after all, only to the extent that the FCC has discretion in its renewal decisions. The prime advantage of this approach would be that licensees would likely have stronger incentives to make long-term investments related to their licenses. A broadcast licensee, for instance, would be more likely to invest in expensive equipment and marketing if it knew that, so long as it followed the various announced FCC rules and met any articulated renewal standards, it would be allowed to keep its license and thus reap long-term benefits from those investments. Indeed, a further possibility is that the government could go further and guarantee renewal for incumbents, which would, of course, render the time limits on licenses meaningless and deprive the Commission of any leverage flowing from renewal.

The government's policies on license duration and renewal expectancies have changed over the years. License duration has generally become longer (e.g., the 1996 Telecommunications Act extended the length of broadcast licenses from five years to eight years).[20] More importantly, renewal expectancies have become stronger. The story there, though, is a bit complicated—especially as it involved a back-and-forth between the Commission and the D.C. Circuit.

The government's shaping of broadcasting in the 1920s through denials of renewal gave way by the 1950s and 1960s to a presumption of renewal for broadcast licensees (the main licensees at the time) so strong that it "[gave] the incumbent a virtually insuperable advantage on the basis of his past broadcast record *per se.*"[21] In 1969, "the Commission for the first time in its history, in applying comparative criteria in a renewal proceeding, deposed the incumbent and awarded the frequency to a challenger."[22] This nonrenewal angered some powerful groups and prompted proposed legislation that would have strengthened the presumption of renewal. The FCC then issued a policy statement giving a renewal applicant a "controlling preference" if it could demonstrate substantial past performance without serious deficiencies.[23] This decision angered other groups—members of Congress, some citizens' groups, and, most importantly, the D.C. Circuit, which struck it down.[24] The FCC later provided that a licensee would be entitled to a renewal expectancy if its performance was "sound, favorable and substantially above a level of mediocre service which might just minimally warrant renewal," but that too was struck down by the D.C. Circuit.[25] The FCC then made the renewal expectancy simply one of several factors considered in a comparative hearing, with the weight of the expectancy varying with the quality of the licensee's broadcast record, and the D.C. Circuit found that formulation acceptable.[26]

The D.C. Circuit was interpreting the Communications Act, and in 1996 Congress resolved the debate by amending the Communications Act to increase the renewal expectancy

---

20. Telecommunications Act of 1996, Pub. L. No. 104-104, §203, 110 Stat. 56, 112 (codified at 47 U.S.C. §307(c)(1)).
21. Citizens Commc'ns Ctr. v. FCC, 447 F.2d 1201, 1208 (D.C. Cir. 1971).
22. *Id.* (citing WHDH, Inc., Bos., Mass., 16 F.C.C. 2d 1 (1969), *aff'd sub nom.* Greater Bos. Television Corp. v. FCC, 444 F.2d 841 (D.C. Cir. 1970)).
23. Policy Statement Concerning Comparative Hearings Involving Regular Renewal Applicants, Public Notice, 22 F.C.C. 2d 424, 425–26 (1970), *rev'd sub nom. Citizens Commc'ns Ctr.*, 447 F.2d 1201 (D.C. Cir. 1971).
24. *Citizens Commc'ns Ctr.*, 447 F.2d at 1204–05.
25. Cowles Fla. Broad., Inc. (WESH-TV), Daytona Beach, Fla., Memorandum Opinion and Order, 62 F.C.C. 2d 953, 955 (1977), *rev'd sub nom.* Cent. Fla. Enters. v. FCC, 598 F.2d 37 (D.C. Cir. 1978).
26. Cowles Broad., Inc. (WESH-TV), Daytona Beach, Fla., 86 F.C.C. 2d 993 (1981), *aff'd sub nom.* Cent. Fla. Enters. v. FCC, 683 F.2d 503 (D.C. Cir. 1982).

for broadcast licensees. Section 204 of the Telecommunications Act of 1996[27] amended the Communications Act to provide that, when an incumbent broadcaster seeks renewal of its license, the FCC must grant the application if the licensee has served the public interest, has committed no "serious violations" of the Communications Act or the FCC's rules, and has not committed any other violations "which, taken together, would constitute a pattern of abuse," 47 U.S.C. § 309(k). Even then, the FCC can impose a smaller sanction than nonrenewal, such as renewal for a shorter-than-normal duration, *see id.* § 309(k)(2), or renewal plus a fine under 47 U.S.C. § 503. If and only if the incumbent flunks one of the tests mentioned above and "no mitigating factors justify the imposition of lesser sanctions," the Commission must deny the incumbent's renewal application and consider other applicants for the license. *Id.* § 309(k)(3). Importantly, this renewal presumption precludes the FCC from considering other licensees. Section 309(k)(4) explicitly states that "the Commission shall not consider whether the public interest, convenience, and necessity might be served by the grant of a license to a person other than the renewal applicant." In response to the 1996 Act, and much to the delight of incumbents, the FCC abolished comparative hearings for broadcast-license-renewal applicants shortly thereafter.[28]

Nonbroadcast spectrum licensees have not received similar attention from the courts or Congress, but they, too, have a strong presumption of renewal. Build-out requirements sometimes obligate licensees for new services to deploy those new services within specific time limits,[29] but, beyond that, licensees can expect renewal if they have "substantially complied" with statutory and regulatory requirements and provided "service which is sound, favorable, and substantially above a level of mediocre service which just might minimally warrant renewal."[30] The language that the D.C. Circuit rejected in the context of broadcast license renewals has thus become the standard for nonbroadcast license renewals.

Notes and Questions

1. Empirical Evidence. Denials of license renewals have been few and far between. During the 1970s, for example, the Commission revoked or denied only 64 radio and television station licenses. Moreover, a study of those denials and revocations reveals that, even before deregulation, factors mentioned in the Policy Statement on Comparative Broadcast Hearings, Public Notice, 1 F.C.C. 2d 393 (1965) (excerpted below), rarely accounted for license revocations or refusals to renew. Instead, the most frequent reasons given by the agency were: misrepresentations to the Commission (18); abandonment of license or failure to prosecute renewal (16); departure from promised programming (11); fraudulent billing practices (11); and unauthorized transfer of control (10). In most cases, more than one reason was given. Over-commercialization was cited once, violation of the personal-attack rules twice, and fairness violations three times. Further, the study's authors note that, even when used, programming-related rationales "were usually part of

---

27. Telecommunications Act of 1996, Pub. L. No. 104-104, § 204(a)(1), 110 Stat. 56, 112–13 (codified as amended at 47 U.S.C. § 309(k)).

28. Implementation of Sections 204(a) and 204(c) of the Telecommunications Act of 1996 (Broadcast License Renewal Procedures), Order, 11 FCC Rcd. 6363 (1996).

29. *See* 47 C.F.R. § 25.144(b) (2010) (requiring that digital satellite radio licensees must have one space station in orbit within four years and full operation within six years).

30. *See* 47 C.F.R. § 22.940 (using this language with respect to renewal of licenses for cellular telephony services), § 24.16 (personal communications services), § 27.14 (miscellaneous wireless services), § 90.743 (private land mobile services), and § 101.1011 (local multipoint distribution services).

a longer litany of charges against the licensee." Frederic A. Weiss et al., Station License Revocations and Denials of Review, 1970–78, 24 J. Broad. 69, 77 (1980). The Commission, in short, was reluctant to rely on subjective factors alone when denying a renewal application.

In more recent years, denials of renewals have been even rarer, and even then have been based only on objective factors. For instance, among the handful of denials or revocations, one was a revocation of a direct broadcast satellite license because the licensee failed to commence operations within the specified time limit, see Advanced Communications Corp. v. FCC, 376 F.3d 1153 (D.C. Cir. 2004), and another was a denial of renewal of an amateur radio license to a licensee based on his fraud conviction and his misrepresentations about that conviction to the Commission, see Schoenbohm v. FCC, 204 F.3d 243 (D.C. Cir. 2000).

The most significant FCC denial of a renewal since the passage of the Telecommunications Act of 1996 was reversed by the D.C. Circuit. In 1999, by a 3–2 vote, the Commission denied the renewal application of Trinity Broadcasting of Florida, finding that Trinity had lied to the Commission in asserting that two of its stations were controlled by racial minorities. (The multiple ownership rules in effect at the time limited the number of stations in which a person could have an attributable interest to 12, but a person could have interest in additional stations that were "minority-controlled.") Applications of Trinity Broadcasting of Florida, Inc., and Glendale Broadcasting Company, Decision, 14 FCC Rcd. 13,570 (1999). The D.C. Circuit vacated the FCC's denial of Trinity's license renewal application, ruling that Trinity did not have fair warning of the FCC's interpretation of "minority-controlled" as requiring not only that a majority of an applicant's board of directors be minorities but also that an applicant demonstrate actual control by minorities. Trinity Broad. of Fla., Inc. v. FCC, 211 F.3d 618, 631–32 (D.C. Cir. 2000).

2. Odd Regulatory Strategy? Why did (and does) the FCC have a fairly extensive set of regulations that it enforces only through the threat of nonrenewal and yet weaken the force of that threat by very rarely denying a renewal application? Is the answer that the FCC wants to exercise significant control over licensees? If so, then it would presumably regularly reject incumbents who do the worst job (relative to the other incumbents) of following the agency's wishes. Is the answer, instead, that the FCC is captured by incumbents and wants to let them operate as they see fit? If so, then why have the regulations in the first place? Is the answer that the FCC wants to give the appearance of regulating behavior without actually exercising much influence? If so, whom is the FCC trying to fool? Or is the answer that even a very small chance of losing valuable licenses will cause licensees to follow the Commission's regulatory "suggestions"? On this, see Lutheran Church–Missouri Synod v. FCC, 141 F.3d 344 (D.C. Cir. 1998), excerpted later in this chapter.

3. Alternatives. Conventional wisdom has it that a renewal presumption increases a licensee's incentive to make long-term investments related to its license. But couldn't the incentive to make long-term investments be maintained by a system that denied incumbents any renewal expectancy but, instead, allowed rejected incumbents to auction off their licenses to the highest bidder? Their long-term investment would increase the value of the license in that auction, would it not? Relatedly, did Congress understand that it could grant a renewal expectancy and yet still have the FCC seriously review incumbents' records? For instance, is there any argument against requiring that an incumbent satisfy a set of stringent criteria in order to receive a strong renewal presumption? So long as those criteria are well articulated ex ante, the FCC's discretion would be minimized, and licensees would therefore still have a strong incentive to make long-term investments, right? Did Congress let incumbents off too easily, then?

§ 5.A.2. License Transfer

Through the years, the Commission has, with one main exception, refrained from placing restrictions on the transfer of licenses. As a result, licensees have always been free to transfer their licenses to other entities, and licenses have routinely changed hands from the earliest days of licensing to the present. The exception was that, in the days when the FCC assigned licenses via comparative hearings, there was a brief waiting period during which the party originally awarded a license was not allowed to sell it. Specifically, between 1962 and 1982 a broadcast licensee had to wait three years from the moment it was awarded the license before it could transfer that license to another entity.[31] In 1982 the FCC reduced the waiting period for transfers to one year, and, at that, only for licensees who won their licenses in comparative hearings.[32]

The reason for having any waiting period at all was that waiting periods gave the FCC's initial assignment hearings meaning. The FCC's assignment hearings took the agency, and the applicants, a significant amount of time (and money) and were designed to find the entity that would provide the best service. Allowing immediate transfer would render the FCC's careful weighing meaningless — or, more precisely, would simply determine which private party would obtain the right to turn around and auction that license to the highest bidder.

The FCC put forward the argument against having a waiting period in its notice proposing shortening the waiting period from three years to one:

> [T]he "three year rule" artificially restricts a station from going to its "higher valued use." A buyer ready and willing to utilize its resources to pay the required price for a given property is more likely to provide the service most desired in a community than an unwilling owner restricted from selling a property it no longer desires only by Commission fiat. Further, the rule's restrictions impose an undesirable cost upon both the present owner, who may be forced to suffer financial loss or forego more appropriate investment opportunities, and upon the public, which may suffer reduced service from a failing operation or lose the opportunity to receive better service which an influx of new capital or a more willing operator might provide.[33]

The argument for a waiting period became much weaker (if not nonexistent) when the FCC abandoned hearings and began to make initial assignments by auction. Today, then, licensees are free to transfer their licenses at will, subject only to the relatively limited hearings authorized by § 310(d) of the Communications Act, 47 U.S.C. § 310(d). That provision reads in relevant part:

> No construction permit or station license ... shall be transferred ... to any person except upon application to the Commission and upon finding by the

---

31. *See* Amendment of Part I of the Commission's Rules Adding Section 1.365 Concerning Applications for Voluntary Assignments or Transfers of Control, Report and Order, 32 F.C.C. 689 (1962).
32. Amendment of the Commission's Rules Regarding Applications for Voluntary Assignments or Transfers of Control, Final Rule, 47 Fed. Reg. 55,924 (Dec. 14, 1982).
33. Applications for Voluntary Assignments or Transfers of Control, Proposed Rule, 47 Fed. Reg. 985, 986 (Jan. 8, 1982).

Commission that the public interest, convenience, and necessity will be served thereby.... [B]ut in acting thereon the Commission may not consider whether the public interest, convenience, and necessity might be served by the transfer, assignment, or disposal of the permit or license to a person other than the proposed transferee or assignee.

Notes and Questions

1. How Much Further to Full Property Rights? If licensees can freely transfer their licenses to other entities and have a near-guaranteed renewal expectancy, how far are we from fee-simple property rights in spectrum? The answer is that this is necessary but not sufficient, because the flexibility discussed in Chapter Four is also necessary. Transfer of the whole license is valuable, but even more valuable is the ability to transfer (through sale or lease) portions of one's spectrum rights in addition to the entire right. That way, the licensee can subdivide its rights as it sees fit. Furthermore, the ability to transfer does not include the ability to provide an entirely different service; the transferee is still subject to the limitations in the original license. So unless the licensee has freedom to choose its services, transfer is not as valuable as it could be. Under these circumstances, the right to transfer with near-guaranteed renewal is akin to owning a building and having the right to transfer that ownership — but no right to subdivide the building or put any part of it to another purpose. However, once we combine free transfer and guaranteed renewal with the sort of flexibility discussed in Chapter Four, we have effectively granted fee-simple property rights.

2. If Transfers Are a Good Idea. Consider the FCC's reasoning for rejecting its three-year rule. What are the implications for spectrum rights more generally? Specifically, does this reasoning tell us anything about the desirability of having defined license terms, with some possibility of nonrenewal, rather than permanent licenses? Does it support the FCC's moves (discussed in Chapter Four) to allow licensees to subdivide their spectrum rights and transfer a portion of them?

3. Elephants in the Room. Under current law, the FCC is not allowed to consider whether transfer to some other party — someone other than the willing transferor and the willing transferee — would better serve the public interest. Why? Can you structure a rule that would allow the FCC to consider outsiders? What problems might arise under that approach?

4. Transfers and Renewals. The transferee of a license receives not only the license but also the same renewal expectancy that the original incumbent had. Does this make sense? The argument for including the renewal expectancy is similar to that for freer transfers more generally, except that it applies at the back end of a license period: if the government refused to give the buyer a renewal expectancy, then transfers toward the end of a license period would be more risky and thus less common. The incumbent would have a nontransferable right of great value, which would inhibit a transfer to an entity that had a higher-valued use (but no renewal expectancy). But the counterargument is similar to the argument against having a renewal expectancy in the first place: why should any entity have an indefinite lease on spectrum? Just as an applicant for an initial license would know that it had, say, eight years to operate (and no more, if there were a rule against renewal), a potential buyer of that license halfway into the license term would know that it had four years to operate.

§ 5.A.2.a. Format Changes

The materials that follow focus on one of the few significant issues to arise in the context of transfer hearings: the question of whether (and how) the FCC should analyze transfers that would likely lead to a change in the programming mix available in a given community. That is, the materials below consider how the FCC should react if, for example, the local classical music station petitions to sell its license to a new owner who proposes to use the license to air heavy metal 24 hours a day, seven days a week.

The D.C. Circuit, in a series of rulings in the early 1970s, held that if the transfer of a radio license would lead to a format change that would eliminate the only broadcast provider of an entertainment format and there was a significant amount of public protest over the change, the FCC was obliged to hold a hearing to determine whether that transfer comported with "the public interest, convenience, and necessity."[34] In 1976, the FCC responded with a policy statement concluding that review of format changes was not compelled by the language or history of the Communications Act, would not advance the welfare of the radio listening public, would pose substantial administrative problems, and would deter innovation in radio programming. We do not excerpt here the statutory discussion, but the following are the key elements on the last three points:

Changes in the Entertainment Formats of Broadcast Stations

Memorandum Opinion and Order, 60 F.C.C. 2d 858 (1976)

11. The Commission's long and continuing reluctance to define and enforce the "public interest" in entertainment format preservation is based both on practical considerations and on our understanding of the structure and meaning of the Communications Act. The practical problems are simple to comprehend. To determine, in the context of a prospective format change, whether the public interest would be served by allowing it, we must ascertain: (1) what the station's existing format is; (2) whether there are any reasonable substitutes for that format in the station's market; (3) if there are not, whether the benefits accruing to the public from the format change outweigh the public detriment which the format abandonment would entail.

14. In practical terms, "format" means program material. As Commissioner Robinson has put it: "What makes one format unique makes all formats unique.... Questions of pacing and style, the personalities of on the air talent (both individually and in combination with one another) all contribute to those fugitive values that radio people call a station's 'sound' and that citizens' groups (and alas, appellate judges) call format." Notice of Inquiry, 57 F.C.C. 2d 580, 594, 595 (1976) (concurring statement).

15. The Commission does not know, as a matter of indwelling administrative expertise, whether a particular format is "unique" or, indeed, assuming that it is, whether it has been deviated from by a licensee.

16. The evidence on this record supports the conclusion that the marketplace is the best way to allocate entertainment formats in radio, whether the hoped for result is expressed in First Amendment terms (i.e., promoting the greatest diversity of listening choices for the public) or in economic terms (i.e., maximizing the welfare of consumers of radio programs). We recognize that the market for radio advertisers is not a completely faith-

---

34. *See, e.g.*, Citizens Comm. to Save WEFM v. FCC, 506 F.2d 246 (D.C. Cir. 1974); Citizens Comm. to Preserve the Voice of the Arts in Atlanta v. FCC, 436 F.2d 263 (D.C. Cir. 1970).

ful mirror of the listening preferences of the public at large. But we are not required to measure any system of allocation against the standard of perfection; we find on the basis of the record before us that it is the best available means of producing the diversity to which the public is entitled.

17. Format allocation by market forces rather than by fiat has another advantage as well. It enables consumers to give a rough expression of whether their preference for diversity within a given format outweighs the desire for diversity among different formats. As Commissioner Robinson has observed, "with respect to formats which objectively seem identical, people—radio listeners—can and do make distinctions. For example, in most large markets there are a number of ... formats which seem identical on any objective or quantifiable basis; yet they are far from interchangeable to their respective audiences. Indeed, if people did not distinguish among these stations, there would be no reason for them to co-exist—and little economic likelihood that they would." 57 F.C.C. 2d at 594–595.

18. [A]udience ratings for major market radio stations tend to differ nearly as much for stations programming similar types of music (e.g., middle of the road) as they do for stations programming markedly different types (e.g., progressive rock as opposed to classical). This finding strongly indicates that audiences carefully discriminate in selecting stations. There is no way to determine the relative values of two different types of programming in the abstract. This is a practical, empirical question, whose answer turns on the intensity of demand for each format. In these circumstances, there is no reason to believe that government mandated restrictions on format changes would promote the welfare of the listening public. Indeed, in view of the administrative costs involved in such a program of regulation, and in view of the chilling effect such regulations would doubtlessly have on program innovation, there is every reason to believe that government supervision of formats would be injurious to the public interest.

19. Finally, allocating entertainment formats by market forces has a precious element of flexibility which no system of regulatory supervision could possibly approximate. In our society, public tastes are subject to rapid change. The people are entitled to expect that the broadcast industry will respond to these changing tastes—and the changing needs and aspirations which they mirror—without having to endure the delay and inconvenience that would be inevitable if permission to change had to be sought from a government agency.

20. These costs, and the uncertainties that impose them, have a constitutional dimension as well. Under the threat of a hearing that could cost tens or hundreds of thousands of dollars, many licensees might consider the risks of undertaking innovative or novel programming altogether unacceptable. The existence of the obligation to continue service, we find, inevitably deprives the public of the best efforts of the broadcast industry and results in an inhibition of constitutionally protected forms of communication with no off-setting justifications, either in terms of specific First Amendment or diversity related values or in broader public interest terms.

§ 5.A.2.b. A Reversal, and a Reversal of That Reversal

The D.C. Circuit was not amused, and it rejected the FCC's 1976 policy statement in WNCN Listeners Guild v. FCC, 610 F.2d 838 (D.C. Cir. 1979) (en banc).[35] The court reiterated:

---

35. In the court's words, "we hold the Policy Statement under review to be unavailing and of no force and effect." *WNCN Listeners Guild*, 610 F.2d at 858.

> The basic premise of our format cases is that the Communications Act's public interest, convenience, and necessity standard includes a concern for diverse entertainment programming. Congress set aside the radio spectrum as a public resource and acted to secure its benefits, not only to those in the cultural mainstream, but to all the people of our richly pluralistic society. It is surely in the public interest, therefore, as that was conceived of by a Congress representative of all the people, for all major aspects of contemporary culture to be accommodated by the commonly-owned public resources whenever that is technically and economically feasible.

Id. at 842 (internal quotation marks omitted). In the court's view, "when a significant sector of the populace is aggrieved by a planned programming change, this fact raises a legitimate question as to whether the proposed change is in the public interest." *Id.* at 853 n.47.

The Supreme Court had the last word, however. It reversed the D.C. Circuit and held that the 1976 policy statement was not inconsistent with the Communications Act. The relevant portion of the opinion is excerpted below.

FCC v. WNCN LISTENERS GUILD
450 U.S. 582 (1981)

WHITE, J., delivered the opinion of the Court. MARSHALL, J., filed a dissenting opinion, in which BRENNAN, J., joined.

JUSTICE WHITE delivered the opinion of the Court.

The Commission has provided a rational explanation for its conclusion that reliance on the market is the best method of promoting diversity in entertainment formats. The Court of Appeals and the Commission agree that in the vast majority of cases market forces provide sufficient diversity. The Court of Appeals favors Government intervention when there is evidence that market forces have deprived the public of a "unique" format, while the Commission is content to rely on the market, pointing out that in many cases when a station changes its format, other stations will change their formats to attract listeners who preferred the discontinued format. The Court of Appeals places great value on preserving diversity among formats, while the Commission emphasizes the value of intraformat as well as interformat diversity. Finally, the Court of Appeals is convinced that review of format changes would result in a broader range of formats, while the Commission believes that Government intervention is likely to deter innovative programming.

[The Commission's] decision was in major part based on predictions as to the probable conduct of licensees and the functioning of the broadcasting market and on the Commission's assessment of its capacity to make the determinations required by the format doctrine. It did not assert that reliance on the marketplace would achieve a perfect correlation between listener preferences and available entertainment programming. Rather, it recognized that a perfect correlation would never be achieved, and it concluded that the marketplace alone could best accommodate the varied and changing tastes of the listening public. These predictions are within the institutional competence of the Commission.

It is contended that rather than carrying out its duty to make a particularized public interest determination on every application that comes before it, the Commission, by invariably relying on market forces, merely assumes that the public interest will be served by changes in entertainment format. Surely, it is argued, there will be some format changes that will be so detrimental to the public interest that inflexible application of the Commission's [1976] Policy Statement would be inconsistent with the Commission's duties. But radio broadcasters are not required to seek permission to make format changes.

A major underpinning of its Policy Statement is the Commission's conviction, rooted in its experience, that renewal and transfer cases should not turn on the Commission's presuming to grasp, measure, and weigh the elusive and difficult factors involved in determining the acceptability of changes in entertainment format. To assess whether the elimination of a particular "unique" entertainment format would serve the public interest, the Commission would have to consider the benefit as well as the detriment that would result from the change. Necessarily, the Commission would take into consideration not only the number of listeners who favor the old and the new programming but also the intensity of their preferences. It would also consider the effect of the format change on diversity within formats as well as on diversity among formats. The Commission is convinced that its judgments in these respects would be subjective in large measure and would only approximately serve the public interest. It is also convinced that the market, although imperfect, would serve the public interest as well or better by responding quickly to changing preferences and by inviting experimentation with new types of programming. Those who would overturn the Commission's Policy Statement do not take adequate account of these considerations.

[Dissenting opinion of JUSTICE MARSHALL is omitted.]

Notes and Questions

1. **The Several Opinions.** What would the rule espoused by the D.C. Circuit have required the Commission to do in the event of a proposed format change? Why did the FCC reject this rule? Why was the D.C. Circuit not persuaded by the Commission's policy statement? Did the Supreme Court side with the FCC because it thought the FCC had provided the better analysis or because it thought this was a matter best left to the FCC's discretion? What should the FCC and the Supreme Court have done?

2. **The Dispute.** Is the dispute between the FCC and the D.C. Circuit a disagreement over what comports with the public interest or a dispute over whether it is possible, as a practical matter, to discern where the public interest lies in format cases?

3. **If You Can't Measure This.** Can the FCC's position that no one can measure the relative value of different formats be squared with its frequent claim that diversity in programming is a general goal of the Commission and the Communications Act? If the FCC cannot distinguish among formats, how can it measure whether its other regulations — e.g., limiting multiple ownership of broadcast facilities or encouraging minority ownership of broadcast licensees — promote diversity of programming?

4. **Long-Term Consistency?** Recall that, in the early years of broadcasting, the FRC denied licenses to stations that catered to a small minority of listeners; its interpretation of its public-interest mandate led it to require that all stations appeal to the general public. By the 1970s, the D.C. Circuit was interpreting the FCC's public-interest obligations as protecting the rights of small groups to have a station that responded to their particular interests. Are these two positions in conflict?

5. **Realistic Alternatives.** Would a requirement that a licensee adhere to a format that it wished to abandon be (a) administratively enforceable and (b) constitutional?

6. Reliance on the Market. Is the Commission's reliance on market forces consistent with the notion that a broadcast licensee must serve "the public interest"? In what sense is the Commission relying on market forces? Does the FCC simply conclude that, because the agency cannot compare the loss to some people when a service is discontinued versus the loss to other people who do not receive a new service, the Commission will always defer to the market's choice? Since, by this reasoning, the FCC cannot evaluate the market's choice either, what basis does the Commission have for deferring to markets?

7. Subsidies. Is a better answer to the problem of changing program formats simply to have government subsidize broadcast content targeted at those populations the market (arguably) underserves? Even the dissenters think that this will be a rare occurrence, so we are not talking about a great deal of money, are we?

8. The One Remaining Form of Transfer Review—Mergers. There is one remaining, and important, form of transfer review, arising out of concerns about the possible anticompetitive effect of transfers. When licensees seek to merge, the FCC must approve the licenses transfers as part of its merger review. Unlike the case above (arising out of rules that were specific to transfers), the transfer review is part of a much broader merger review by the Commission. Interestingly, sometimes the jurisdictional hook for the FCC's merger review is the fact that one of the companies needs FCC approval to transfer its various licenses to the other. We consider FCC merger review and the debate over this jurisdictional hook in Chapter Eleven.

---

§ 5.B. License Assignment via Merit-Based Hearings

When new spectrum becomes available under the band plan or when a new service is approved for use as part of the band plan, the Commission has to decide whether the service will be a licensed or unlicensed service. If unlicensed, the FCC must promulgate the various technical standards discussed in the previous chapter. If licensed, the FCC must not only define the details of those licenses—how much spectrum will be allocated per license, what uses will be permitted, and so on—but also how the licenses will be distributed.

In the early days, that latter question was answered simply: licenses were given out at no monetary charge, with licensees chosen by the Commission through merit-based hearings. The key statutory section on assigning licenses is 47 U.S.C. § 309. With respect to hearings, it provides in relevant part:

(a) [T]he Commission shall determine, in the case of each application filed with it..., whether the public interest, convenience, and necessity will be served by the granting of such application....

(d) ... (1) Any party in interest may file with the Commission a petition to deny any application [even if that party does not itself seek the license]....

(e) ... If ... a substantial and material question of fact is presented ... [the Commission] shall formally designate the application for hearing.... Any hearing subsequently held upon such application shall be a full hearing in which the applicant and all other parties in interest shall be permitted to participate....

Section 308(b) of the Act requires that applicants demonstrate "citizenship, character, and financial, technical, and other qualifications." *Id.* § 308(b). The FCC translated this into requirements that were fairly easily met: an applicant had to show citizenship, that it satisfied rudimentary character qualifications (which essentially meant not being a convicted felon, a past violator of FCC rules, or a past violator of federal antitrust law), that it had both the financial ability and the technical experience to construct and operate the applied-for broadcast station, that the relevant community needed the proposed broadcaster, and that the license applicant would be responsive to community needs.

The statutory scheme entails three main types of hearings: (1) hearings in which the FCC assigns a new license; (2) hearings in which the FCC either renews an incumbent's license or transfers that license to a competing applicant; and (3) hearings in which the FCC decides whether to approve a proposed license transfer from an incumbent to a new owner of the incumbent's choosing. Through these hearings the FCC directly determined who would own each broadcast license and indirectly exerted considerable influence over the content those broadcast licensees would air.

Contested hearings could arise in either of two ways. A party might contest a rival's application by filing a petition to deny, in that way opposing the application but not seeking the license for itself. Or a party might itself seek either the same or a mutually exclusive license (a license that would cause undue interference with the license at issue if both were granted), which would trigger a comparative hearing in which the two applicants would be judged relative to one another.

§ 5.B.1. Comparative Hearings

In 1944, a case arose in which the FCC had before it two mutually exclusive applications for broadcast licenses. Even though only one of the licenses could be granted, the Commission considered the applications separately. In fact, on the very same day, the FCC first granted one of the applications without a hearing and then set a hearing at which it offered to consider the other. That, this second applicant claimed, was a farce; his application was effectively precluded by the earlier grant, which took place before his application was even considered. This second applicant therefore brought suit alleging that the Communications Act of 1934 required the FCC to hold comparative hearings in cases involving mutually exclusive applications. The case ultimately reached the Supreme Court as Ashbacker Radio Corp. v. FCC, 326 U.S. 327 (1945).

The FCC's position was simple: the Commission was not precluded "at a later date from taking any action which it may find will serve the public interest" and, thus, the fact that the first application was granted even before the second application was considered was not particularly momentous. *Id.* at 331. The Supreme Court summarized the Commission's position:

> No licensee obtains any vested interest in any frequency. The Commission for specified reasons may revoke any station license ... and may suspend the license of any operator.... It may also modify a station license if in its judgment "such action will promote the public interest, convenience, and necessity, or the provisions of this chapter ... will be more fully complied with." And licenses for broadcasting stations are limited to three years,[36] the renewals being subject to the same considerations and practice which affect the granting of original applications.

---

36. [Under current law, broadcast licenses are limited to eight years. *See* 47 U.S.C. § 307(c). Eds.]

Id. at 331–32 (footnote and citations omitted). As the Court pointed out, however, all of these remedies were available against any licensee, whether or not that license had been granted in peculiar circumstances like those at issue here. Moreover, by granting the earlier application, the Commission had placed the later applicant "under a greater burden than if its hearing had been earlier." *Id.* at 332. As the Court put it, "Legal theory is one thing. But the practicalities are different." *Id.* As a practical matter, it was difficult for a newcomer to make the comparative showing necessary to displace an established licensee.

The Supreme Court thus held § 309 of the Communications Act to require that mutually exclusive applications be considered in a single hearing. "[W]here two bona fide applications are mutually exclusive the grant of one without a hearing to both deprives the loser of the opportunity which Congress chose to give him." *Id.* at 333. With that, comparative hearings became a staple Commission responsibility.

§ 5.B.1.a. Basic Comparative Hearing Criteria

The criteria used in uncontested hearings were usually useless in the comparative setting. Both applicants were almost always U.S. citizens, technically capable, and so on. Indeed, the D.C. Circuit acknowledged the absence of clear standards in Johnston Broadcasting Co. v. FCC, 175 F.2d 351 (D.C. Cir. 1949), flatly stating that, in comparative hearings, "there are no established criteria by which a choice between the applicants must be made." *Id.* at 357. To weigh the comparative merits of competing applications, then, the Commission had to make findings concerning "every difference, except those which were frivolous or wholly unsubstantial, between the applicants." *Id.* Comparative hearings therefore brought a potentially limitless range of issues into contention.

The Commission's broad discretion opened the door to other considerations—most notably political ones. Licenses given out in Franklin D. Roosevelt's and Harry Truman's administrations (mainly radio) tended to go to Democrats who supported the New Deal. In fact, one licensee was Lyndon Johnson's wife, Lady Bird, who received licenses despite no prior industry experience.[37] Licenses given out in Dwight Eisenhower's administration (mainly television) tended to go to Republican supporters.[38]

On several occasions, the Commission sought to add structure to the otherwise amorphous comparative hearing. The main such attempt was the Policy Statement on Comparative Broadcast Hearings, excerpted below. This document pulled together principles from a number of previous cases, and it ultimately turned out to be the FCC's most complete statement of the standards it applied when choosing among competing applicants.

POLICY STATEMENT ON COMPARATIVE BROADCAST HEARINGS
Public Notice, 1 F.C.C. 2d 393 (1965)

One of the Commission's primary responsibilities is to choose among qualified new applicants for the same broadcast facilities. This commonly requires extended hearings into a number of areas of comparison. The hearing and decision process is inherently complex, and the subject does not lend itself to precise categorization or to the clear making of precedent. The various factors cannot be assigned absolute values and the differences between applicants with respect to each factor are almost infinitely variable.

---

37. *See* Robert Caro, Means of Ascent 89–105 (1990).
38. *See* William B. Ray, FCC: The Ups and Downs of Radio-TV Regulation 45 (1990); Bernard Schwartz, Comparative Television and the Chancellor's Foot, 47 Geo. L.J. 655, 690–94 (1959).

Furthermore, membership on the Commission is not static and the views of individual Commissioners on the importance of particular factors may change. For these and other reasons, the Commission is not bound to deal with all cases at all times as it has dealt in the past with some that seem comparable; and changes of viewpoint, if reasonable, are recognized as both inescapable and proper.

We believe that there are two primary objectives toward which the process of comparison should be directed. They are, first, the best practicable service to the public, and, second, a maximum diffusion of control of the media of mass communications. The value of these objectives is clear. Diversification of control is a public good in a free society, and is additionally desirable where a government licensing system limits access by the public to the use of radio and television facilities. Equally basic is a broadcast service which meets the needs of the public in the area to be served, both in terms of those general interests which all areas have in common and those special interests which areas do not share. An important element of such a service is the flexibility to change as local needs and interests change. Since independence and individuality of approach are elements of rendering good program service, the primary goals of good service and diversification of control are also fully compatible.

Several factors are significant in the two areas of comparison mentioned above, and it is important to make clear the manner in which each will be treated.

1. Diversification of control of the media of mass communication.

Diversification is a factor of primary significance since, as set forth above, it constitutes a primary objective in the licensing scheme.

As in the past, we will consider both common control and less than controlling interests in other broadcast stations and other media of mass communications. The number of other mass communication outlets of the same type in the community proposed to be served will also affect to some extent the importance of this factor in the general comparative scale.

2. Full time participation in station operation by owners.

We consider this factor to be of substantial importance. It is inherently desirable that legal responsibility and day-to-day performance be closely associated. In addition, there is a likelihood of greater sensitivity to an area's changing needs, and of programming designed to serve these needs, to the extent that the station's proprietors actively participate in the day-to-day operation of the station. This factor is thus important in securing the best practicable service. It also frequently complements the objective of diversification, since concentrations of control are necessarily achieved at the expense of integrated ownership.

We are primarily interested in full-time participation. No credit will be given to the participation of any person who will not devote to the station substantial amounts of time on a daily basis. In assessing proposals, we will also look to the positions which the participating owners will occupy, in order to determine the extent of their policy functions and the likelihood of their playing important roles in management. Merely consultative positions will be given no weight.

While, for the reasons given above, integration of ownership and management is important per se, its value is increased if the participating owners are local residents and if they have experience in the field. Participation in station affairs by a local resident indicates a likelihood of continuing knowledge of changing local interests and needs. Previous broadcast experience, while not so significant as local residence, also has some value when put to use through integration of ownership and management.

Past participation in civic affairs will be considered as a part of a participating owner's local residence background, as will any other local activities indicating a knowledge of and interest in the welfare of the Community.

Since emphasis upon [previous broadcasting experience] could discourage qualified newcomers to broadcasting, and since experience generally confers only an initial advantage, it will be deemed of minor significance.

3. Proposed program service.

The importance of program service is obvious. The feasibility of making a comparative evaluation is not so obvious. Hearings take considerable time and precisely formulated program plans may have to be changed not only in details but in substance, to take account of new conditions obtaining at the time a successful applicant commences operation. Thus, minor differences among applicants are apt to prove to be of no significance.

[T]he applicant has the responsibility for a reasonable knowledge of the community and area, based on surveys or background, which will show that the program proposals are designed to meet the needs and interests of the public in that area. Failure to make contacts with local civic and other groups and individuals will be considered a serious deficiency.

In light of the considerations set forth above, and our experience with the similarity of the program plans of competing applicants, taken with the desirability of keeping hearing records free of immaterial clutter, no comparative issue will ordinarily be designated on program plans and policies, or on staffing plans or other program planning elements, and evidence on these matters will not be taken under the standard issues. The Commission will designate an issue where examination of the applications and other information before it makes such action appropriate.

No independent factor of likelihood of effectuation of proposals will be utilized. The Commission expects every licensee to carry out its proposals, subject to factors beyond its control, and subject to reasonable judgment that the public's needs and interests require a departure from original plans.

4. Past broadcast record.

This factor includes past ownership interest and significant participation in a broadcast station by one with an ownership interest in the applicant. It is a factor of substantial importance upon the terms set forth below.

A past record within the bounds of average performance will be disregarded, since average future performance is expected. We are interested in records which, because either unusually good or unusually poor, give some indication of unusual performance in the future. Thus, we shall consider past records to determine whether the record shows (i) unusual attention to the public's needs and interests, such as special sensitivity to an area's changing needs through flexibility of local programs designed to meet those needs, or (ii) either a failure to meet the public's needs and interests or a significant failure to carry out representations made to the Commission.

5. Efficient use of frequency.

In comparative cases where one of two or more competing applicants proposes an operation which, for one or more engineering reasons, would be more efficient, this fact can and should be considered in determining which of the applicants should be preferred.

6. Character.

Significant character deficiencies may warrant disqualification, and an issue will be designated where appropriate. In the absence of a designated issue, character evidence will not be taken. Our intention here is not only to avoid unduly prolonging the hearing process, but also to avoid those situations where an applicant converts the hearing into a search for his opponents' minor blemishes, no matter how remote in the past or how insignificant.

Notes and Questions

1. What Role for Precedent? Reread the second paragraph of the Policy Statement. Is it surprising? How would you respond if the Supreme Court were to include a paragraph like that at the start of the majority opinion in an important case? Is the FCC's inclusion of this paragraph different? If so, why?

2. Character. The Commission eliminated character as an issue in comparative hearings in 1986, at least so long as any character deficiencies do not rise to the level of questioning the applicant's basic qualifications (i.e., its ability to obtain an uncontested license). Policy Regarding Character Qualifications in Broadcast Licensing, Report, Order and Policy Statement, 102 F.C.C. 2d 1179 (1986); *see also* Policy Regarding Character Qualifications in Broadcast Licensing, Policy Statement and Order, 5 FCC Rcd. 3252 (1990). The main reason was that comparative hearings on character were costly, with large amounts of finger-pointing and name-calling but little payoff in terms of revealing valuable comparative information.

3. *Bechtel*. A significant dismantling of the comparative hearing process came in Bechtel v. FCC, 10 F.3d 875 (D.C. Cir. 1993), in which the D.C. Circuit ruled that the FCC's preference for integrating ownership and management—item number two in the Policy Statement—was arbitrary and capricious. Several applicants had submitted mutually exclusive applications to construct and operate an FM radio station, so the FCC had to choose among them. Bechtel said that she was going to invest in equipment that would allow the station to reach more listeners than her rivals would. But, as the D.C. Circuit noted, "Bechtel's application received little attention because, alone among the four applicants, she did not propose to integrate ownership and management of the new station." *Id.* at 877.

The FCC justified using integration as a factor on the theory that integrated owners would probably be more active and effective when it came to running the station, for example being more likely to learn about and react to local conditions. In response, Bechtel noted that after one year of ownership, "a licensee who had won his station through his integration proposal could turn around and sell it without regard to the buyer's integration or lack thereof." *Id.* at 879 (internal quotations omitted). So whatever benefits integration offered might be quite short-lived. Beyond that, Bechtel argued that there was no evidence that integration (when it did exist) actually produced the benefits that the Commission ascribed to it. The D.C. Circuit agreed with Bechtel, finding that the FCC's predictive judgment was no longer a sufficient ground for favoring integration. "Despite its twenty-eight years of experience with the policy, the Commission has accumulated no evidence to indicate that it achieves even one of the benefits that the Commission attributes to it." *Id.* at 880. Without evidence that integration mattered, the FCC's policy could not stand.

This put the Commission in a difficult position. Section 309 required it to engage in comparative hearings, but (as the FCC noted in its order embracing auctions, excerpted later in this chapter) integration of ownership and management was "our central comparative criterion." Implementation of Section 309(j) of the Communications Act—Competitive Bidding for Commercial Broadcast and Instructional Television Fixed Service Licenses, First Report and Order, 13 FCC Rcd. 15,920 ¶ 37. The Commission decided not to appeal the *Bechtel* ruling and instead to simply suspend all mutually exclusive applications for commercial broadcast stations in which integration was an issue. These applications were frozen for several years, with the Commission unable to reform or delete the integration criterion. The problem was solved by the switch to auctions, discussed later in this chapter.

§ 5.B.2. Licensing Case Study

APPLICATIONS OF SIMON GELLER FOR RENEWAL OF LICENSE OF WVCA-FM AND GRANDBANKE CORPORATION FOR CONSTRUCTION PERMIT

Memorandum Opinion and Order, 102 F.C.C. 2d 1443 (1985)

BACKGROUND

1. This proceeding involves the application of Simon Geller for renewal of his license to operate Station WVCA FM (WVCA), Gloucester, Massachusetts, and the mutually exclusive application of Grandbanke Corporation (Grandbanke) for a construction permit. On June 15, 1982, the Commission issued a Decision denying Geller's application and granting Grandbanke's. The Commission held that Geller's past performance as a broadcaster had been minimal and, thus, undeserving of a renewal expectancy. The Commission further held that this inadequate past record diminished the comparative credit that Geller would otherwise be due for his advantages with respect to diversification of media ownership and integration of ownership into management. In the Commission's view, Grandbanke was entitled to decisive preferences for its superior proposed programming and more efficient use of frequency. However, the District of Columbia Circuit Court of Appeals remanded this proceeding to the Commission for further consideration. The Court held that the Commission had failed to explain adequately the justification for diminishing Geller's advantages for diversification and integration and thereby had given unjustified weight to Geller's past record.[39]

GELLER'S BROADCAST RECORD—RENEWAL EXPECTANCY

9. During the 1972–75 license term at issue here, WVCA presented less than 1% nonentertainment programming and no programming in response to ascertained community needs. Virtually all of WVCA's programming was devoted to symphonic music. WVCA broadcast no news, no editorials, and no locally produced public affairs programs. The station did, however, broadcast 18 public service announcements a week.

10. In view of his failure to present substantial nonentertainment programming responsive to the needs and interests of the community, the Commission concluded that Geller's past performance was minimal and, hence, undeserving of a renewal expectancy.

---

39. Committee for Community Access v. F.C.C., 737 F.2d 74 (D.C. Cir. 1984). [The flavor of the 1984 D.C. Circuit opinion is captured by its opening sentence: "This case represents yet another meandering effort by the Federal Communications Commission ... to develop a paradigm for its license renewal hearings." Eds.]

The Commission noted that WVCA is the only broadcast facility licensed to Gloucester and that Geller's financial shortcomings did not mitigate the inadequacy of WVCA's programming. Under Commission precedent, a renewal applicant with a substantial past record, receives a renewal expectancy in the form of a preference taken into account along with all other preferences in the overall comparative analysis. Because Geller's performance was less than substantial, he received no such preference.

11. The Court of Appeals affirmed the Commission's denial of a renewal expectancy to Geller.

PROPOSED PROGRAMMING

12. Geller proposes to continue his present format, broadcasting 99.52% symphonic music, no news, 0.24% public affairs, and 0.24% other nonentertainment programming. Grandbanke proposes to devote 16.9% of its broadcast time to news, 5.9% to public affairs, and 5.9% to other nonentertainment programming, with 55% of its news to be local and regional. Unlike Geller, Grandbanke proposes that its informational programming will be directly related to ascertained community needs and interests. Whereas Geller proposed a 44 hour 27 minute a week program schedule, Grandbanke proposes to broadcast 136 hours of programming a week.

13. The Commission concluded that Grandbanke deserved a substantial preference for proposed programming for its demonstrated superior devotion to public service. This preference arose from Grandbanke's superior attention to presenting informational programming responsive to ascertained community needs and interests and was enhanced by the significant discrepancy between the applicants' proposed hours of operation and the relative restrictiveness of Geller's programming.

14. As it did with respect to the renewal expectancy, the court affirmed the award of a substantial preference to Grandbanke for its proposed programming.

EFFICIENT USE OF FREQUENCY

15. Because of differences between their engineering proposals, Grandbanke's facilities will have greater coverage than Geller's. Grandbanke's 1 mV/m contour will cover more than 300 square miles, providing a signal to nearly 360,000 people, as opposed to Geller's 73 square miles and 43,000 people.

16. The Commission awarded Grandbanke a slight preference based on the superiority of its coverage. Only a slight preference was warranted since the areas in question are already well served by at least five other aural signals.

17. The court did not specifically address this issue. Grandbanke will therefore continue to receive a slight preference.

INTEGRATION OF OWNERSHIP INTO MANAGEMENT

18. Geller is WVCA FM's sole owner and employee and will devote full time to the operation of the station. He has been a resident of Gloucester for 13 years. Grandbanke proposes that its 66% owner Edward Mattar will serve as the station's general manager. Mattar has had 3 years of broadcast experience and proposes to move to Gloucester in the event Grandbanke's application is granted.

19. The Commission previously held that despite Geller's technical advantages under the integration criterion, Geller merited only a slight preference over Grandbanke. The Commission reasoned that the rationale of the integration criterion was that an integrated owner would tend to be more sensitive to an area's changing needs and that Geller's poor past broadcast record detracted from these assurances.

20. The court criticized the Commission's conclusions in this regard. In the court's view, the Commission had failed to reconcile its integration analysis in this case with past precedent. The court noted that the Commission did not make, as it usually does, an explicit analysis of the quantitative and qualitative aspects of integration. Moreover, the court noted that the Commission does not customarily reduce the merit accorded for a quantitative integration advantage unless the applicant has committed misconduct. The court speculated that the Commission may have engaged in the type of "functional analysis" of the essentially structural characteristic of integration, which was previously disapproved by the court. Considering the Commission discussion too cursory and vague, the court remanded the matter for further analysis.

21. In his Comments, Geller maintains that his integration advantage is entitled to special weight because of his commitment to Gloucester and his long and unique relationship with that community. Geller claims that he has long served as the "voice of Cape Ann" despite receiving only a meager income. Grandbanke argues that reconsideration of the integration factor should not yield a different result. According to Grandbanke, the Commission normally accords no more than a moderate preference for a quantitative disparity in proposed integration such as that found here. Grandbanke contends that Geller's past deficiencies as a licensee fail to enhance his proposed integration and in fact detract from it.

22. Having reexamined the integration aspect of this case pursuant to the court's remand, we conclude that our prior treatment of this issue constituted the type of functional analysis previously criticized by the court. We will therefore reevaluate the integration criterion using our ordinary analytical approach. This approach encompasses a weighing of the customary quantitative and qualitative factors, without attempting to factor in other considerations, such as renewal expectancy and Geller's past broadcast record.

23. Turning first to the quantitative aspect of integration, we agree with Grandbanke that, consistent with precedent, an applicant proposing 100% integration deserves a moderate preference over an applicant proposing 66% integration. Qualitatively, Geller's integration is enhanced by his long term local residence, which outweighs Grandbanke's proposal that Mattar will move to Gloucester prospectively and Mattar's limited broadcast experience. Geller will therefore receive a qualitatively enhanced moderate integration preference to be taken into account in the overall comparative analysis.

DIVERSIFICATION OF MEDIA OWNERSHIP

24. Geller owns no media interests other than WVCA. On the other hand, Grandbanke's principals have interests in other broadcast stations. Edward Mattar, Grandbanke's 66% owner, has a 100% interest in Station WINQ FM, Winchendon, Massachusetts. Stockholders with a 34% interest in Grandbanke have a 100% interest in Station WNCS FM, Montpelier, Vermont.

25. The Commission awarded Geller a moderate preference for diversification. In the Commission's view, based on the degree of media ownership alone, Geller would have been entitled to a substantial preference. However, the Commission believed that Geller's preference should be diminished because of his failure to present substantial amounts of informational programming. The Commission reasoned that the rationale of diversification was to present the public with diverse and antagonistic points of view. Since Geller had virtually abandoned his role as an information source, the Commission concluded that he did not qualify as a diverse and antagonistic voice or deserve full credit for diversification.

26. The court rejected the Commission's analysis. The court held that the crux of the diversification issue is ownership, based on the probability that diverse ownership will lead to a diversity of views. Moreover, the court held that a direct evaluation of the content of a broadcaster's views would be questionable under the First Amendment. In this vein, the court indicated that there was no basis for inferring that the amount of informational programming presented necessarily represented the broadcaster's value as a diverse voice. On remand, the court required, at minimum, that the Commission adequately explain its apparent departure from established principles.

27. In his Comments Geller urges that his diversification advantage deserves special weight because he owns no other media interests whereas Grandbanke's principals have connections with several regional interests. Grandbanke maintains that Geller deserves no more than a moderate diversification advantage based on considerations of ownership alone. Grandbanke observes that its principals' outside media interests are relatively small and not located in the service area of the proposed station.

28. Having reexamined our diversification analysis pursuant to the court's mandate, we conclude that it must be revised. As in the case of integration, we believe that our prior discussion relied on an improper functional analysis. In accordance with the court's ruling, we will not look behind the presumption that underlies the diversification criterion. Our prior conclusion that, based on considerations of media ownership alone, Geller deserves a substantial preference stands unabridged. Accordingly, Geller will receive a substantial preference for diversification.

OVERALL COMPARATIVE ANALYSIS

29. The Commission ultimately concluded that Geller's license renewal application should be denied and Grandbanke's application for a construction permit should be granted. The Commission found that Grandbanke's substantial preference for proposed programming and slight preference for efficient use of frequency outweighed Geller's slight integration advantage and moderate diversification advantage. Because the court disagreed with the manner in which the Commission considered the integration and diversification criteria, it did not reach the overall comparison between Geller and Grandbanke.

30. In his Comments, Geller maintains that once his integration and diversification preferences are given their proper weights, undiminished by "multiple counting" of his past broadcast record, these advantages are decisive. Grandbanke, which considers Geller's integration and diversification advantages to be moderate, submits on the other hand that its advantages for proposed programming and efficient use of frequency are dispositive. Grandbanke continues to assert that Geller's failure to provide substantial amounts of informational programming responsive to local needs and interests should weigh heavily in the comparative balancing.

31. The framework for the comparative evaluation of broadcast applicants is provided by the Commission's 1965 Policy Statement on Comparative Broadcast Hearings. There, the Commission enunciated two primary objectives: (1) best practicable service to the public, and (2) diversification of control of the media of mass communications. The former objective encompasses several factors of which those relevant here are: (1) integration of ownership into management, (2) proposed programming, and (3) efficient use of frequency. Under the best practicable service to the public criterion, we have concluded that Grandbanke deserves a substantial preference for proposed programming and a slight preference for efficient use of frequency, while Geller deserves an enhanced moderate preference for integration. On balance, we believe Grandbanke should receive a moder-

ate preference for best practicable service. As to diversification, the other primary criterion, Geller receives a substantial preference. Thus, we are faced with a situation in which each applicant is superior to the other with respect to one of the primary objectives of the comparative process. However, the substantial preference awarded to Geller for diversification clearly outweighs the moderate preference awarded to Grandbanke for best practicable service. For this reason, we believe that Geller is ultimately the preferred applicant.

Notes and Questions

1. Geller's Renewal Expectancy. The key decision that hurt Geller—and led to the unusually detailed FCC comparative analysis of Geller and Grandbanke—was the FCC's refusal to grant Geller a preference for renewal expectancy. Did Geller fail to gain a renewal expectancy simply because he failed to program what the FCC thought people in Gloucester would (or should) want to hear? Is the FCC's reasoning consistent with the First Amendment? If so, then why is it "questionable under the First Amendment" (¶ 26) to measure the value of diverse ownership in part by whether the owner engages in informational programming?

2. Current Law. Under the current law regarding license renewals, the FCC would have to either renew Geller's license or deny his application before considering Grandbanke's—and the chances of renewal would be very high for Geller or most any other incumbent. Does this seem preferable to the approach taken in the *Geller* case by the Commission? Is it in tension with the logic of *Ashbacker*?

3. Commission Discretion. Suppose the Commissioners, for whatever reason, wanted to give Grandbanke the license. How hard would it have been to write an opinion doing so? Consider, for example: (a) Why does the FCC equate the importance of best practicable service and diversification (¶ 31)? If the Commission had announced that it considered service to be three times as important as diversification (perhaps, in part, because service encompasses at least three times as many factors as diversification, or because, in this case, Grandbanke would reach more than three times as many listeners as Geller) and so would award the license to Grandbanke, would the decision have been equally rational? (b) What is a "qualitatively enhanced moderate preference" (¶ 23)? Did the Commission give the term its precisely correct weight?

4. Back and Forth. The government's response to this renewal application went back and forth (in more than one sense) over many years: in 1975 Geller applied for renewal; in 1977 the FCC designated Geller's renewal application for a hearing; in 1978 an administrative law judge entered an initial decision (subject to FCC review) awarding the renewal (and thus the license) to Geller; in 1982 the FCC adopted virtually all of the administrative law judge's factual findings but concluded that Grandbanke should receive the license; in 1984 the D.C. Circuit remanded the case to the FCC for reconsideration; in 1985 the FCC issued the order excerpted above; then Grandbanke unsuccessfully petitioned the FCC for reconsideration and the D.C. Circuit for review of the FCC's decision, the latter of which was dismissed—thus ending the legal proceedings on this renewal—in 1988.[40]

---

40. *See* Simon Geller, Initial Decision of Administrative Law Judge John H. Conlin, 90 F.C.C. 2d 284 (1978); Simon Geller, Decision, 90 F.C.C. 2d 250 (1982) (FCC decision); Comm. for Cmty. Access v. FCC, 737 F.2d 74 (D.C. Cir. 1984) (remanding FCC decision); Simon Geller, Memorandum Opinion and Order, 102 F.C.C. 2d 1443 (1985) (FCC decision on remand); Simon Geller, Order, 1986 WL 292010 (FCC Mar. 17, 1986) (denying Grandbanke's petition for reconsideration); Grandbanke Corp. v. FCC, No. 86-1230 (D.C. Cir. Feb. 8, 1988) (dismissing Grandbanke's appeal).

What, if anything, does this lengthy set of proceedings tell us? That the hearing process takes too long? That the FCC's standards are too indeterminate? That the courts are creating confusion? That there are too many lawyers and too much procedure?

5. Coasian Bargains. In 1988—to no one's surprise—Geller, having received his renewal, sold his station for $1 million and moved to Las Vegas. *See* William Grimes, Simon Geller, 75; Ran Radio Station All by Himself, N.Y. Times, July 14, 1995, at A23. Why doesn't the Commission's analysis proceed from the premise that the matter to be decided is who is to be allowed to reap the value of programming WVCA, either by operating it or by selling it as the winner chooses?

---

§ 5.B.3. Special Considerations for Racial Minorities and Women

The 1965 Policy Statement contains no explicit reference to preferences for racial minorities or women, and the FCC's initial interpretation of both that document and the Communications Act was that no preference to minority ownership was appropriate unless the record indicated that the owner's race likely would affect the content of the broadcaster's service. The D.C. Circuit rejected the FCC's interpretation in TV 9, Inc. v. FCC, 495 F.2d 929 (D.C. Cir. 1973), and in 1978 the Commission created preferences for applicants who were women or members of racial minorities. The following cases address these programs.

§ 5.B.3.a. Minority Preferences before *Adarand*

METRO BROADCASTING, INC. v. FCC
497 U.S. 547 (1990)

BRENNAN, J., delivered the opinion of the Court, in which WHITE, MARSHALL, BLACKMUN, and STEVENS, JJ., joined. STEVENS, J., filed a concurring opinion. O'CONNOR, J., filed a dissenting opinion, in which REHNQUIST, C.J., and SCALIA and KENNEDY, JJ., joined. KENNEDY, J., filed a dissenting opinion, in which SCALIA, J., joined.

JUSTICE BRENNAN delivered the opinion of the Court.

The issue in these cases is whether certain minority preference policies of the Federal Communications Commission violate the equal protection component of the Fifth Amendment. The policies in question are (1) a program awarding an enhancement for minority ownership in comparative proceedings for new licenses, and (2) the minority "distress sale" program, which permits a limited category of radio and television broadcast stations to be transferred only to minority-controlled firms. We hold that these policies do not violate equal protection principles.

I

A

Although for the past two decades minorities have constituted at least one-fifth of the United States population,[41] in 1971, minorities owned only 10 of the approximately 7,500

---

41. The FCC has defined the term "minority" to include "those of Black, Hispanic Surnamed, American Eskimo, Aleut, American Indian and Asiatic American extraction." Statement of Policy on Minority Ownership of Broadcasting Facilities, Public Notice, 68 F.C.C. 2d 979, 980 n.8 (1978).

radio stations in the country and none of the more than 1,000 television stations; in 1978, minorities owned less than 1 percent of the Nation's radio and television stations, *see* FCC Minority Ownership Task Force, Report on Minority Ownership in Broadcasting 1 (1978) (hereinafter Task Force Report); and in 1986, they owned just 2.1 percent of the more than 11,000 radio and television stations in the United States. Moreover, these statistics fail to reflect the fact that, as late entrants who often have been able to obtain only the less valuable stations, many minority broadcasters serve geographically limited markets with relatively small audiences.

The Commission has recognized that the viewing and listening public suffers when minorities are underrepresented among owners of television and radio stations:

> "Acute underrepresentation of minorities among the owners of broadcast properties is troublesome because it is the licensee who is ultimately responsible for identifying and serving the needs and interests of his or her audience. Unless minorities are encouraged to enter the mainstream of the commercial broadcasting business, a substantial portion of our citizenry will remain underserved and the larger, non-minority audience will be deprived of the views of minorities."

Task Force Report, at 1.

[T]he FCC adopted in May 1978 its Statement of Policy on Minority Ownership of Broadcasting Facilities, 68 F.C.C. 2d 979. [T]he FCC concluded:

> "[T]he views of racial minorities continue to be inadequately represented in the broadcast media. This situation is detrimental not only to the minority audience but to all of the viewing and listening public. Adequate representation of minority viewpoints in programming serves not only the needs and interests of the minority community but also enriches and educates the non-minority audience. It enhances the diversified programming which is a key objective not only of the Communications Act of 1934 but also of the First Amendment."

Id., at 980–981.

Describing its actions as only "first steps," *id.*, at 984, the FCC outlined two elements of a minority ownership policy.

First, the Commission pledged to consider minority ownership as one factor in comparative proceedings for new licenses. When the Commission compares mutually exclusive applications for new radio or television broadcast stations, it looks principally at six factors: diversification of control of mass media communications, full-time participation in station operation by owners (commonly referred to as the "integration" of ownership and management), proposed program service, past broadcast record, efficient use of the frequency, and the character of the applicants. In the Policy Statement on Minority Ownership, the FCC announced that minority ownership and participation in management would be considered in a comparative hearing as a "plus" to be weighed together with all other relevant factors. The "plus" is awarded only to the extent that a minority owner actively participates in the day-to-day management of the station.

Second, the FCC outlined a plan to increase minority opportunities to receive reassigned and transferred licenses through the so called "distress sale" policy. As a general rule, a licensee whose qualifications to hold a broadcast license come into question may not assign or transfer that license until the FCC has resolved its doubts in a noncomparative hearing. The distress sale policy is an exception to that practice, allowing a broadcaster whose license has been designated for a revocation hearing, or whose renewal application has been designated for hearing, to assign the license to an FCC-approved minority enterprise. The assignee must meet the FCC's basic qualifications, and the minority ownership must exceed 50 percent or be controlling. The purchase price must not exceed 75 percent of fair market value.

II
A

Congress found that "the effects of past inequities stemming from racial and ethnic discrimination have resulted in a severe underrepresentation of minorities in the media of mass communications." H.R. Conf. Rep. No. 97-765, p. 43 (1982). Congress and the Commission do not justify the minority ownership policies strictly as remedies for victims of this discrimination, however. Rather, Congress and the FCC have selected the minority ownership policies primarily to promote programming diversity, and they urge that such diversity is an important governmental objective that can serve as a constitutional basis for the preference policies. We agree.

We have long recognized that "[b]ecause of the scarcity of [electromagnetic] frequencies, the Government is permitted to put restraints on licensees in favor of others whose views should be expressed on this unique medium." Red Lion Broadcasting Co. v. FCC, 395 U.S. 367, 390 (1969). The Government's role in distributing the limited number of broadcast licenses is not merely that of a "traffic officer," National Broadcasting Co. v. United States, 319 U.S. 190, 215 (1943); rather, it is axiomatic that broadcasting may be regulated in light of the rights of the viewing and listening audience and that "the widest possible dissemination of information from diverse and antagonistic sources is essential to the welfare of the public." Associated Press v. United States, 326 U.S. 1, 20 (1945). Safeguarding the public's right to receive a diversity of views and information over the airwaves is therefore an integral component of the FCC's mission. We have observed that the Communications Act has designated broadcasters as "fiduciaries for the public." FCC v. League of Women Voters of California, 468 U.S. 364, 377 (1984).

[T]he diversity of views and information on the airwaves serves important First Amendment values. The benefits of such diversity are not limited to the members of minority groups who gain access to the broadcasting industry by virtue of the ownership policies; rather, the benefits redound to all members of the viewing and listening audience.

B

We also find that the minority ownership policies are substantially related to the achievement of the Government's interest. One component of this inquiry concerns the relationship between expanded minority ownership and greater broadcast diversity; both the FCC and Congress have determined that such a relationship exists.

1

As the Commission observed in its 1978 Statement, "ownership of broadcasting facilities by minorities is [a] significant way of fostering the inclusion of minority views in the area of programming" and "[f]ull minority participation in the ownership and management of broadcast facilities results in a more diverse selection of programming." 68 F.C.C. 2d at 981. The FCC's conclusion that there is an empirical nexus between minority ownership and broadcasting diversity is a product of its expertise, and we accord its judgment deference.

Furthermore, the FCC's reasoning with respect to the minority ownership policies is consistent with longstanding practice under the Communications Act. From its inception, public regulation of broadcasting has been premised on the assumption that diversification of ownership will broaden the range of programming available to the broadcast audience.[42] The Commission has never relied on the market alone to ensure that the needs of the audience are met. Indeed, one of the FCC's elementary regulatory assumptions is that broadcast content is not purely market driven; if it were, there would be little need for consideration in licensing decisions of such factors as integration of ownership and management, local residence, and civic participation.

2

Congress also has made clear its view that the minority ownership policies advance the goal of diverse programming. In recent years, Congress has specifically required the Commission, through appropriations legislation, to maintain the minority ownership policies without alteration.

Section 115 of the Communications Amendments Act of 1982 directs that, "[t]o further diversify the ownership of the media of mass communications, [a] significant preference [is to be given] to any applicant controlled by a member or members of a minority group." 47 U.S.C. §309(i)(3)(A) (1982). Observing that the nexus between ownership and programming "has been repeatedly recognized by both the Commission and the courts," Congress explained that it sought "to promote the diversification of media ownership and consequent diversification of programming content," a principle that "is grounded in the First Amendment." H.R. Conf. Rep. No. 97-765, p. 40 (1982). With this new mandate from Congress, the Commission adopted rules to govern the use of a lottery system to award licenses for low power television stations.

As revealed by the historical evolution of current federal policy, both Congress and the Commission have concluded that the minority ownership programs are critical means of promoting broadcast diversity. We must give great weight to their joint determination.

C

The judgment that there is a link between expanded minority ownership and broadcast diversity does not rest on impermissible stereotyping. Although all station owners are guided to some extent by market demand in their programming decisions, Congress and the Commission have determined that there may be important differences between the broadcasting practices of minority owners and those of their nonminority counterparts. This judgment — and the conclusion that there is a nexus between minority ownership and broadcasting diversity — is corroborated by a host of empirical evidence.[43]

---

42. The Commission has always focused on ownership, on the theory that "ownership carries with it the power to select, to edit, and to choose the methods, manner and emphasis of presentation, all of which are a critical aspect of the Commission's concern with the public interest."

43. For example, the Congressional Research Service (CRS) analyzed data from some 8,720 FCC-licensed radio and TV stations and found a strong correlation between minority ownership and diversity of programming. See CRS, Minority Broadcast Station Ownership and Broadcast Programming: Is There a Nexus? (June 29, 1988). While only 20 percent of stations with no Afro-American ownership responded that they attempted to direct programming at Afro-American audiences, 65 percent of stations with Afro-American ownership reported that they did so. Only 10 percent of stations without Hispanic ownership stated that they targeted programming at Hispanic audiences, while 59 percent of stations with Hispanic owners said they did.

Evidence suggests that an owner's minority status influences the selection of topics for news coverage and the presentation of editorial viewpoint, especially on matters of particular concern to minorities. Minority-owned stations tend to devote more news time to topics of minority interest and to avoid racial and ethnic stereotypes in portraying minorities.[44] In addition, studies show that a minority owner is more likely to employ minorities in managerial and other important roles where they can have an impact on station policies.[45] While we are under no illusion that members of a particular minority group share some cohesive, collective viewpoint, we believe it a legitimate inference for Congress and the Commission to draw that, as more minorities gain ownership and policymaking roles in the media, varying perspectives will be more fairly represented on the airwaves.

III

The Commission's minority ownership policies bear the imprimatur of longstanding congressional support and direction and are substantially related to the achievement of the important governmental objective of broadcast diversity.

[Concurring opinion of JUSTICE STEVENS and dissenting opinion of JUSTICE KENNEDY are omitted.]

JUSTICE O'CONNOR, with whom CHIEF JUSTICE REHNQUIST, JUSTICE SCALIA, and JUSTICE KENNEDY join, dissenting.

II

[T]he policies challenged in these cases were not designed as remedial measures and are in no sense narrowly tailored to remedy identified discrimination. The FCC appropriately concedes that its policies embodied no remedial purpose, Tr. of Oral Arg. 40–42, and has disclaimed the possibility that discrimination infected the allocation of licenses.

III

The asserted interest in this case is certainly amorphous: the FCC and the majority of this Court understandably do not suggest how one would define or measure a particular viewpoint that might be associated with race, or even how one would assess the diversity of broadcast viewpoints.

Under the majority's holding, the FCC may also advance its asserted interest in viewpoint diversity by identifying what constitutes a "Black viewpoint," an "Asian viewpoint," an "Arab viewpoint," and so on; determining which viewpoints are underrepresented; and then using that determination to mandate particular programming or to deny licenses to those deemed by virtue of their race or ethnicity less likely to present the favored views. Indeed, the FCC has, if taken at its word, essentially pursued this course, albeit

---

44. For example, a University of Massachusetts at Boston survey of 3,000 local Boston news stories found a statistically significant difference in the treatment of events, depending on the race of ownership. *See* K. Johnson, Media Images of Boston's Black Community 16–29 (Jan. 28, 1987) (William Monroe Trotter Institute, University of Massachusetts at Boston).

45. Afro-American-owned radio stations, for example, have hired Afro-Americans in top management and other important job categories at far higher rates than have white-owned stations, even those with Afro-American-oriented formats. The same has been true of Hispanic hiring at Hispanic-owned stations, compared to Anglo-owned stations with Spanish-language formats.

without making express its reasons for choosing to favor particular groups or for concluding that the broadcasting spectrum is insufficiently diverse.

The FCC's extension of the asserted interest in diversity of views in this case presents, at the very least, an unsettled First Amendment issue. The FCC has concluded that the American broadcasting public receives the incorrect mix of ideas and claims to have adopted the challenged policies to supplement programming content with a particular set of views. Although we have approved limited measures designed to increase information and views generally, the Court has never upheld a broadcasting measure designed to amplify a distinct set of views or the views of a particular class of speakers.

IV
A.

The FCC's choice to employ a racial criterion embodies the related notions that a particular and distinct viewpoint inheres in certain racial groups, and that a particular applicant, by virtue of race or ethnicity alone, is more valued than other applicants because "likely to provide [that] distinct perspective." Brief for FCC in No. 89-453, p. 17. The policies directly equate race with belief and behavior, for they establish race as a necessary and sufficient condition of securing the preference. The policies impermissibly value individuals because they presume that persons think in a manner associated with their race.

B.

[R]ace-neutral and untried means of directly accomplishing the governmental interest are readily available. The FCC could directly advance its interest by requiring licensees to provide programming that the FCC believes would add to diversity. [Y]et in adopting the challenged policies, the FCC expressly disclaimed having attempted any direct efforts to achieve its asserted goal. The FCC and the Court suggest that First Amendment interests in some manner should exempt the FCC from employing this direct, race neutral means to achieve its asserted interest. They essentially argue that we may bend our equal protection principles to avoid more readily apparent harm to our First Amendment values. But the FCC cannot have it both ways: either the First Amendment bars the FCC from seeking to accomplish indirectly what it may not accomplish directly; or the FCC may pursue the goal, but must do so in a manner that comports with equal protection principles. And if the FCC can direct programming in any fashion, it must employ that direct means before resorting to indirect race-conscious means.

Other race-neutral means also exist, and all are at least as direct as the FCC's racial classifications. The FCC could evaluate applicants upon their ability to provide and commitment to offer whatever programming the FCC believes would reflect underrepresented viewpoints. If the FCC truly seeks diverse programming rather than allocation of goods to persons of particular racial backgrounds, it has little excuse to look to racial background rather than programming to further the programming interest. Also, race-neutral means exist to allow access to the broadcasting industry for those persons excluded for financial and related reasons. The Court reasons that various minority preferences, including those reflected in the distress sale, overcome barriers of information, experience, and financing that inhibit minority ownership. Race-neutral financial and informational measures most directly reduce financial and informational barriers.

C.

The FCC's policies assume and rely upon the existence of a tightly bound "nexus" between the owners' race and the resulting programming. [But] the market shapes programming to a tremendous extent. Members of minority groups who own licenses might be thought, like other owners, to seek to broadcast programs that will attract and retain audiences, rather than programs that reflect the owner's tastes and preferences.

Notes and Questions

1. The Commission's Goals. Precisely what are the constitutionally permissible and substantial goals that the FCC's policies are designed to achieve? Would the reasoning of *Metro Broadcasting* also permit the Commission (or Congress) to award a "plus" to people over 65? To religious minorities?

2. And Its Assumptions. Is the FCC's position that licensees tend to air programs aimed at people just like themselves? No television network is run by angst-ridden teenagers, yet many networks' program offerings often successfully target the teen audience. What is the argument behind the FCC's position?

3. Promoting Diversity. Could the FCC determine that an ethnic group's views or interests were overrepresented on radio or television and so assign demerits to applicants of that race? Can you logically distinguish this program from the programs the Commission endorses?

4. Testing the Results. If the FCC were to attempt to ascertain whether its minority-preference and distress-sale policies were working effectively, what questions should it seek to answer and what data would be relevant? If these policies cannot be adequately tested, what does that tell us about them? About the decision in *Bechtel*?

5. Race or Speech? Is this case about "race" or "speech"? Apparently, the majority and the dissenters in *Metro Broadcasting* differ in the latitude each would grant to the FCC and to Congress to employ race-specific standards. Do they not also differ in the latitude each would ascribe to the Commission in adopting regulations that are justified with reference to the content of broadcast programming? Doesn't the majority envision an FCC that is legally and practically empowered to control program content in ways that the dissenters would find legally objectionable and practically unrealistic?

6. More Direct Approaches. The dissent and majority seem to differ on the question of whether the FCC should be forced to accomplish program diversity directly (say, a regulation that explicitly requires licensees to air diverse programming) or whether, instead, the indirect approach of using ownership diversity as a proxy for program diversity is acceptable. But should the FCC be forced to develop a regulation that directly responds to its policy goal? If the FCC cannot promulgate such a regulation, does that support the dissent's position that the policy goals at issue here are too amorphous and that the regulation must be struck down on that ground?

§ 5.B.3.b. Preferences for Women

Preferences for women fared somewhat differently from the above-discussed minority preferences, both in their status as FCC policies and in their judicial reception. The Statement of Policy on Minority Ownership of Broadcasting Facilities, Public Notice, 68 F.C.C. 2d 979 (1978), contained three major programs for racial minorities: the comparative-hearing preference and the distress-sale policy, both discussed in *Metro Broadcasting*, and a tax-certificate program that gave companies preferential tax treatment on their capital gains if they sold broadcast facilities to minority-owned or minority-controlled entities. The FCC decided that women should benefit from some of these advantages as well, and so, in 1978, female ownership was also deemed a "plus" in the comparative hearing process, albeit a smaller plus than minority ownership would be.[46] Women who were not minorities were not, however, allowed to participate in the tax-certificate or distress-sale programs.

Two years after the Supreme Court issued its opinion in *Metro Broadcasting*, a panel of the D.C. Circuit decided Lamprecht v. FCC, 958 F.2d 382 (D.C. Cir. 1992). The panel, dividing 2–1, struck down the FCC's policy of awarding extra credit to female applicants in comparative hearing proceedings.

The majority in *Lamprecht* held that *Metro Broadcasting* required that any predictive judgments about the behavior of men and women as station owners must be sustained by meaningful evidence in order to avoid the risk that such judgments merely reflected stereotypical assumptions about men and women. The court concluded that the FCC offered no evidence that women and men were likely to program stations differently. The court also examined a study by the Congressional Research Service but concluded that the study had methodological flaws and, more importantly, failed to establish a substantial nexus between gender and the likelihood of offering women's programming.

Dissenting, Judge Mikva accused the *Lamprecht* majority of deliberately misreading *Metro Broadcasting*. Mikva argued that *Metro Broadcasting* dictated that courts should defer to Congress's conclusions about the link between ownership and programming so long as the conclusions reflect reasoned analysis rather than archaic stereotypes.

§ 5.B.3.c. *Adarand* (*Metro Broadcasting* Overruled)

In Adarand Constructors, Inc. v. Pena, 515 U.S. 200 (1995), the Supreme Court struck down a federal program that granted preferential treatment to racial minorities in bidding on public-works projects. The five justices in the *Adarand* majority were the four *Metro Broadcasting* dissenters plus the subsequently appointed Justice Thomas (the author of *Lamprecht*). With respect to *Metro Broadcasting*, the Court stated:

> [W]e hold today that all racial classifications, imposed by whatever federal, state, or local governmental actor, must be analyzed by a reviewing court under strict scrutiny. In other words, such classifications are constitutional only if they are narrowly tailored measures that further compelling governmental interests. To the extent that *Metro Broadcasting* is inconsistent with that holding, it is overruled.

Id. at 227.

The FCC did not respond to *Adarand* by jettisoning its programs for racial and ethnic minorities; nor is it clear that the FCC had to. The *Adarand* majority did not say that the programs at issue in *Metro Broadcasting* were unconstitutional, as those programs were not before the *Adarand* Court. The majority held only that *Metro Broadcasting* had employed too lenient a standard of review.

The tax-certificate program and the "plus" in comparative hearings have been abolished, but those changes were the result of statutory amendments rather than FCC actions. Spurred by Viacom's planned $2.3 billion sale of cable systems to a consortium led by an African-American businessman (creating a tax certificate that would reduce Viacom's tax liability by about $600 million), Congress in 1995 voted to repeal the tax certificate pro-

---

46. "We hold that merit for female ownership and participation is warranted upon essentially the same basis as the merit given for black ownership and participation, but that it is a merit of lesser significance." Mid-Florida Television Corp., Decision, 70 F.C.C. 2d 281, 326 (Rev. Bd. 1978).

gram.[47] The "plus" in the comparative hearing process was similarly eliminated by a 1997 enactment (codified as § 309(j) of the Communications Act) that for all intents and purposes ended the use of comparative hearings, replacing them with auctions as the assignment mechanism of choice. Section 309(j) does provide, however, that the FCC should "ensure that small businesses, rural telephone companies, and businesses owned by members of minority groups and women are given the opportunity to participate in the provision of spectrum-based services, and, for such purposes, consider the use of tax certificates, bidding preferences, and other procedures." 47 U.S.C. § 309(j)(4)(D).

The Commission later issued an order containing fairly modest provisions aimed at promoting diversity in media ownership. Promoting Diversification of Ownership in the Broadcasting Services, Report and Order and Third Further Notice of Proposed Rulemaking, 23 FCC Rcd. 5922 (2008). For instance, regarding distress sales, the Commission decided to "allow[] a licensee whose license has been designated for a revocation hearing or whose renewal application has been designated for a hearing on basic qualifications issues to sell its station prior to the commencement of the hearing to an 'eligible entity.'" *Id.* ¶ 39.

As this quotation highlights, the definition of "eligible entity" was of central importance. The 2008 order defined "eligible entity" as a small business under the Small Business Administration standards. Those standards are based on the revenue of a business and do not depend in any way on the ethnicity or gender of its owners. *See id.* ¶ 6. The order added:

> We recognize that some commenters have urged us to take action to increase the ownership of broadcast stations by minorities and women specifically. [W]e seek comment on whether we should adopt an alternative definition of 'eligible entity' that would specifically identify these groups. In the meantime, we have decided to employ a race- and gender-neutral definition in the rules we adopt today so as to avoid constitutional difficulties that might create impediments to the timely implementation of the steps we take today to diversify broadcast ownership. [W]e believe that the measures we adopt today will be effective in creating new opportunities for broadcast ownership by a variety of small businesses and new entrants, including those owned by women and minorities.

Id. ¶ 9. The definitional question was the main point of contention among the Commissioners. Commissioner Adelstein stated that "[t]he definition of the entities eligible is so broad ... that minority- and women-owned businesses are likely to be incidental beneficiaries at best." *Id.* at 5987 (Adelstein, Comm'r, concurring in part and dissenting in part). Commissioner Copps complained that "we are told to be content with baby steps to help women and minorities—but the fine print shows that the real beneficiaries will be small businesses owned by white men." *Id.* at 5979 (Copps, Comm'r, concurring in part and dissenting in part).

The 2008 order was challenged in federal court in the same litigation (excerpted in Chapter Ten) that addressed the FCC's ownership rules. Prometheus Radio Project v. FCC, 652 F.3d 431 (3d Cir. 2011) (*Prometheus II*). The Third Circuit rejected the definition of "eligible entity," stating:

> [T]he eligible entity definition adopted in the Diversity Order lacks a sufficient analytical connection to the primary issue that Order intended to address. The Commission has offered no data attempting to show a connection between the

---

47. Act of Apr. 11, 1995, Pub. L. No. 104-7, § 2, 109 Stat. 93, 93–94 (repealing 26 U.S.C. § 1071 (1994)); *see also* Senators Join Opposition to Tax Break, Broadcasting & Cable, Mar. 20, 1995.

definition chosen and the goal of the measures adopted—increasing ownership of minorities and women. As such, the eligible entity definition adopted is arbitrary and capricious, and we remand those portions of the [order] that rely on it. We conclude once more that the FCC did not provide a sufficiently reasoned basis for deferring consideration of the proposed SDB [socially and economically disadvantaged business] definitions and remand for it to do so.

Id. at 471.

§ 5.B.3.d. Equal Employment Opportunity Regulations

The policies at issue in *Metro Broadcasting* were relevant only during particular events, namely the initial assignment of broadcast licenses, renewal hearings, and any proposed transfer from one licensee to another. But, throughout the licensing period, licensees are subject to a related and ongoing obligation: equal employment opportunity regulations. Those regulations are considered in the case excerpted below.

LUTHERAN CHURCH–MISSOURI SYNOD V. FCC
141 F.3d 344 (D.C. Cir. 1998)

Opinion for the court filed by Circuit Judge SILBERMAN, in which Circuit Judges WILLIAMS and SENTELLE concur.

SILBERMAN, Circuit Judge:

Lutheran Church–Missouri Synod appeals the Federal Communication Commission's finding that it transgressed equal employment opportunity regulations through the use of religious hiring preferences and inadequate minority recruiting.

II

The Church contends that the affirmative action portion of the Commission's equal employment opportunity (EEO) regulations is a race-based employment program in violation of the equal protection component of the Fifth Amendment.

The Commission (but not the Department of Justice (DOJ)) asserts that the Church lacks Article III standing to raise an equal protection challenge since it—as opposed to a hypothetical non-minority employee—has not suffered an equal protection injury. It is undeniable, however, that the Church has been harmed by the Commission's order finding it in violation of the EEO regulations. The order is a black mark on the Church's previously spotless licensing record and could affect its chances of license renewal down the road. And the remedial reporting conditions, which require the Church to keep extremely detailed employment records, further aggrieve the Church by increasing an already significant regulatory burden.

Independent of the order, the regulations cause the Church economic harm by increasing the expense of maintaining a license. Every broadcast station must develop a fairly elaborate EEO program and document its compliance. 47 C.F.R. § 73.2080(b) & (c). Particularly for smaller stations like [the ones at issue here], this requirement can be burdensome. It involves paperwork, monitoring, and spending more money on advertisements. And if the rules do force a station to discriminate, they expose it to risk of liability under 42 U.S.C. § 1983.

To the extent the Commission suggests that the personal nature of the equal protection right precludes third party standing, the Supreme Court has explicitly rejected that view. When the law makes a litigant an involuntary participant in a discriminatory scheme, the litigant may attack that scheme by raising a third party's constitutional rights.

The Church argues that under Adarand Constructors, Inc. v. Pena, 515 U.S. 200 (1995), the Commission's use of racial classifications provokes strict scrutiny, a standard the EEO program cannot survive. The FCC has identified "diversity of programming" as the interest behind its EEO regulations. The Church protests that this is an insufficient interest and that furthermore, the regulations do not serve it. The Commission, applying its *King's Garden* policy [exempting religious broadcasters from the FCC's ban on religious discrimination, but only for employees reasonably connected to the espousal of religious philosophy over the air], decided that the Church could not prefer Lutheran to non-Lutheran secretaries because low-level employees would have little or no effect on the broadcast of religious views. At the same time, however, the Commission has defended its affirmative action recruiting policy by arguing that *all* employees affect programming diversity. How, the Church asks, can the FCC maintain that the religion of a secretary will not affect programming but the race of a secretary will? After all, religious affiliation, a matter of affirmative intellectual and spiritual decision, is far more likely to affect programming than skin color. Appellant contends that the FCC's convoluted reasoning undermines the suggestion that there is any kind of link between the Commission's means and end, much less a narrowly tailored one.

[T]he EEO regulations before us extend beyond outreach efforts and certainly influence ultimate hiring decisions. The crucial point is not, as the Commission and DOJ argue, whether they require hiring in accordance with fixed quotas; rather, it is whether they oblige stations to grant some degree of preference to minorities in hiring. We think the regulations do just that. The entire scheme is built on the notion that stations should aspire to a workforce that attains, or at least approaches, proportional representation. The EEO program guidelines instruct the broadcaster to:

> (3) Evaluate its employment profile and job turnover against the availability of minorities and women in its recruitment area. For example, this requirement may be met by:
>
> (i) Comparing the composition of the relevant labor area with the composition of the station's workforce;
>
> (ii) Where there is *underrepresentation* of either minorities and/or women, examining the company's personnel policies and practices to assure that they do not inadvertently screen out any group and take appropriate action where necessary. Data on representation of minorities and women in the available labor force are generally available on metropolitan statistical area (MSA) or county basis.

47 C.F.R. §73.2080(c) (emphasis added). The very term "underrepresentation" necessarily implies that if such a situation exists, the station is behaving in a manner that falls short of the desired outcome. The regulations pressure stations to maintain a workforce that mirrors the racial breakdown of their "metropolitan statistical area."

Nor can it be said that the Commission's parity goals do not pressure license holders to engage in race-conscious hiring. In 1980, the Commission issued processing guidelines disclosing the criteria it used to select stations for in depth EEO review when their licenses came up for renewal:

> (1) stations with less than five full-time employees will continue to be exempt from having a written EEO program;
>
> (2) stations with five to ten full-time employees will have their EEO program reviewed if minority groups and/or women are not employed on their full-time

staffs at a ratio of 50% of their workforce availability overall and 25% in the upper-four Form 395 job categories;

(3) stations with 11 or more full-time employees will have their EEO programs reviewed if minority groups and/or women are not employed full-time at a ratio of 50% of their availability in the workforce overall and 50% in the upper-four job categories; and

(4) all stations with 50 or more employees will have their EEO programs reviewed.

EEO Processing Guidelines for Broadcast Renewal Applicants, 46 Rad. Reg. 2d (P & F) 1693 (1980). It cannot seriously be argued that this screening device does not create a strong incentive to meet the numerical goals. No rational firm—particularly one holding a government-issued license—welcomes a government audit.

In 1987, the Commission changed its policy to de-emphasize statistics, but this new policy did not abandon the 1980 numerical processing guidelines. Amendment of Part 73, Report and Order, 2 FCC Rcd. 3967 (1987). But the fact that the FCC looks at more than "numbers" does not mean that numbers are insignificant. A station would be flatly imprudent to ignore any one of the factors it knows may trigger intense review—especially if that factor, like racial breakdown, is particularly influential. As a matter of common sense, a station can assume that a hard-edged factor like statistics is bound to be one of the more noticed screening criteria. The risk lies not only in attracting the Commission's attention, but also that of third parties. "Underrepresentation" is often the impetus (as it was in this case) for the filing of a petition to deny, which in turn triggers intense EEO review. Amendment of Part 73, ¶ 48. Further, and most significant in a station's calculus, the Commission itself has given every indication that the employment profile is a serious matter. In its proposed EEO forfeiture guidelines, for example, minority underrepresentation is grounds for an upward adjustment in forfeiture amount.

[W]e do not think it matters whether a government hiring program imposes hard quotas, soft quotas, or goals. Any one of these techniques induces an employer to hire with an eye toward meeting the numerical target. As such, they can and surely will result in individuals being granted a preference because of their race. Strict scrutiny applies and we turn to whether, in accordance with recognized doctrine, the regulations are narrowly tailored to serve a compelling state interest.

The Commission has unequivocally stated that its EEO regulations rest solely on its desire to foster "diverse" programming content. The only possible statutory justification for the Commission to regulate workplace discrimination would be its obligation to safeguard the "public interest," and the Supreme Court has held that an agency may pass anti-discrimination measures under its public interest authority only insofar as discrimination relates to the agency's specific statutory charge. Thus the FCC can probably only regulate discrimination that affects "communication service"—here, that means programming. 47 U.S.C. § 151.

The Commission never defines exactly what it means by "diverse programming."[48] (Any real content-based definition of the term may well give rise to enormous tensions with the First Amendment. Compare *Metro Broadcasting*, 497 U.S. at 567–68 (opinion of the Court) with *id.* at 616 (O'Connor, J., dissenting)). The government's formulation of the interest seems too abstract to be meaningful. The more appropriate articulation would seem the more particular: the fostering of programming that reflects minority viewpoints or appeals to minority tastes.

---

48. It is clear, though, that the Commission is not referring to format diversity—i.e., the FCC's interest in ensuring that not every station on the spectrum is devoted to news radio.

[*Metro Broadcasting*] held only that the diversity interest was "important." We do not think diversity can be elevated to the "compelling" level. We do not mean to suggest that race has no correlation with a person's tastes or opinions.[49] We doubt, however, that the Constitution permits the government to take account of racially based differences, much less encourage them. One might well think such an approach antithetical to our democracy.

[W]e note the sort of diversity at stake in this case has even less force than the "important" interest at stake in *Metro Broadcasting*. While the minority ownership preferences involved in *Metro Broadcasting* rested on an *interstation* diversity rationale, the EEO rules seek *intrastation* diversity. It is at least understandable why the Commission would seek station to station differences, but its purported goal of making a single station all things to all people makes no sense. It clashes with the reality of the radio market, where each station targets a particular segment: one pop, one country, one news radio, and so on.

Even assuming that the Commission's interest were compelling, its EEO regulations are quite obviously not narrowly tailored. The majority in *Metro Broadcasting* never suggested that low-level employees, as opposed to upper-level employees, would have any broadcast influence. Nor did the Commission introduce a single piece of evidence in this case linking low-level employees to programming content. Indeed, as appellant emphasizes, the FCC's *King's Garden* policy indicates that the Commission itself does not believe that there is any connection between low-level employees and programming substance. The Commission reprimanded the Church for preferring Lutheran secretaries, receptionists, business managers, and engineers precisely because it found these positions not "connected to the espousal of religious philosophy over the air." Yet it has defended its affirmative action rules on the ground that minority employees bring diversity to the airwaves. The FCC would thus have us believe that low-level employees manage to get their "racial viewpoint" on the air but lack the influence to convey their religious views. That contradiction makes a mockery out of the Commission's contention that its EEO program requirements are designed for broadcast diversity purposes. The regulations could not pass the substantial relation prong of intermediate scrutiny, let alone the narrow tailoring prong of strict scrutiny.

Notes and Questions

1. "Processing Guidelines" and License Renewal. The FCC implemented its EEO program via processing guidelines that affected the incumbent's license-renewal process. This possibility of nonrenewal for failure to comply with the processing guidelines helped the church establish standing. Can you see why the FCC might not have wanted to announce a formal policy that failure to comply with its processing guidelines could never be the deciding factor against renewal? Does this mean that the FCC had the worst of both worlds—in reality, it would not deny renewal, but it did not want to so aver and thus it created standing for a licensee to challenge its processing guidelines?

---

49. For example, BBDO's annual television survey consistently finds that blacks and whites prefer different television shows—during the 1996–97 season, the black "top twenty" list and the white "top twenty" list had only four programs in common. But it is not simply a question of race. Among teens aged 12 to 17, 8 out of 20 programs appeared on both lists; in the over 50 age group, there were 13 crossover programs. Latino and white viewing preferences, moreover, are very similar, with 13 of the top twenty programs in common. Race, by itself, seems a rather unreliable proxy for taste.

2. Intrastation and Interstation Diversity. Note that *Lutheran Church* distinguishes sharply between interstate and intrastation diversity. Why should we distinguish between these two kinds of diversity? Does the court overstate the difference between them? Are you persuaded that the "purported goal of making a single station all things to all people makes no sense"?

3. Subsequent Events. The government filed a petition for rehearing in the D.C. Circuit shortly after the above decision came down. When that court declined to grant a rehearing, the FCC decided not to seek Supreme Court review, leaving the opinion excerpted above as the last word on the case. In response to *Lutheran Church*, the Commission issued new rules in 2000 that it presented as race- and gender-neutral. Review of the Commission's Broadcast and Cable Equal Employment Opportunity Rules and Policies and Termination of the EEO Streamlining Proceeding, Report and Order, 15 FCC Rcd. 2329 ¶¶ 217–220 (2000). The rules required a licensee either to undertake FCC-approved recruitment initiatives (with no requirement of reporting the race and sex of job applicants) or to design its own outreach program and report the race and sex of each job applicant. The D.C. Circuit held that this second option "create[s] pressure to recruit women and minorities, which pressure ultimately does not withstand constitutional review," and so vacated the rules. MD/DC/DE Broadcasters Ass'n v. FCC, 236 F.3d 13, 18 (D.C. Cir. 2001). In 2002, the Commission issued a third set of rules containing more modest programs that the D.C. Circuit had not questioned, and those rules were not challenged.

Separately, individual commissioners have encouraged broadcasters to implement affirmative action programs even though they are no longer required to do so in light of *Lutheran Church*. Then-Chairman Kennard, for instance, offered to support broadcasters' efforts to relax limitations on the number of telecommunications properties a single party can own if broadcasters would in exchange help to increase the number of minority-owned stations. See Steven A. Holmes, Broadcasters Vow to Keep Affirmative Action, N.Y. Times, July 30, 1998, at A12.

4. Responding to Constraints. The Third Circuit, in the *Prometheus II* opinion noted just before the excerpt above, pushed the FCC to consider programs targeted towards women and racial minorities that would be strong candidates for invalidation under the reasoning of *Lutheran Church*. How should the FCC respond when one circuit court's instructions are in some tension with those of another? Should it try to guess what the Supreme Court would do? More generally, how should the FCC navigate between the goal of encouraging ownership by women- and minority-controlled businesses and the constitutional strictures articulated in *Lutheran Church* and *Adarand*? How much leeway does it have? How much leeway should it have, and why?

§ 5.C. Transition to Assignment via Auctions

In the preceding sections, we observed the FCC's attempts to exercise its statutory responsibility to select licensees on the basis of a "public interest" standard. Implicit in all those policy discussions was the assumption that the public-interest test meant that the Commission should select, from among the applicants in front of it, the one who, as operator of the station at issue, was most likely to serve what it regarded as the public interest.

Over time both the Commission and members of Congress came to question this assumption. Was the FCC using clear and useful metrics in its decisions?

Meanwhile, as we noted above, the transferability of licenses and the presumption of renewal meant that licenses, once assigned via hearing, were routinely sold by the initial licensee. The FCC would engage in an expensive and time-consuming hearing to select initial licensees, but those licensees could (and frequently did) turn around and sell their licenses off to the highest bidder. Licensing hearings did not necessarily determine who would be allowed to program a given station; rather, they often determined who would be allowed to auction off the license that the government would for some reason not sell itself. Policymakers came to realize that any method of assignment is an auction mechanism; all that changes is the identity of the auctioneer. Thus the decision was made to abandon merit-based hearings and move primarily toward explicit auctions.

Our discussion of auctions proceeds in three steps. First, we consider some of the final adjustments the FCC made to the licensing process in the late 1980s. These adjustments help us to begin to think about the hearing process in strategic context, a useful perspective for the discussions that follow. Second, we consider the relative merits of auctions, lotteries, and hearings as mechanisms for assigning spectrum licenses. Third, we examine the current statutory provision that authorizes spectrum auctions and look at some anecdotal evidence and commentary about how the auction process has worked thus far.

§ 5.C.1. Reform of the Licensing Process

FORMULATION OF POLICIES AND RULES RELATING TO BROADCAST RENEWAL APPLICANTS, COMPETING APPLICANTS, AND OTHER PARTICIPANTS TO THE COMPARATIVE RENEWAL PROCESS AND TO THE PREVENTION OF ABUSES OF THE RENEWAL PROCESS

First Report and Order, 4 FCC Rcd. 4780 (1989)

22. *Need for Limits.* Abuse of the renewal process hurts the public interest in several ways. Incumbent licensees are required to expend considerable amounts of money to defend against and pay off challengers, including those who are unfunded and have no real intention of owning or operating a station. Moreover, the staff and management of the incumbent are forced to spend considerable funds as well as time and effort opposing challenges to license renewals. The expenditure of such resources that otherwise might have been devoted to programming and other services, to defend against an abusive challenge is inefficient and wasteful.

24. Respondents to a National Association of Broadcasters survey variously reported, for example, that they have been threatened with license renewal challenges unless they contributed to the challenger's organization, that they regularly contribute to certain groups to avoid license renewal challenges, and that they have been subjected to costly competing applications by disgruntled former employees.

25. *Competing Applications.* We are adopting a policy prohibiting all payments to competing applicants (other than the incumbent licensee) for the withdrawal of an application prior to the Initial Decision stage of a comparative hearing.[50] Thereafter, we will

---

50. The Initial Decision is the determination by an Administrative Law Judge, after a full hearing on the merits, as to the applicant that should be awarded the broadcast license.

approve settlements that do not exceed the withdrawing party's legitimate and prudent expenses for filing and litigating the competing application.

26. This should virtually eliminate those applicants whose purpose in filing is to settle out for profit and generally assure that applications are being filed solely for their intended purpose—that of acquiring a broadcast license. An applicant that makes it through the Initial Decision stage has demonstrated that it is willing to develop a complete record on all pertinent hearing issues. For these reasons, we believe that an applicant's prosecution of its application through the Initial Decision stage is a persuasive indication of the bona fides of the application.

39. *Petitions to Deny.* A person has the statutory right to file a petition to deny to challenge an incumbent licensee's renewal application on the grounds that the licensee lacks qualifications or that the grant of renewal would be inconsistent with the public interest. Petitions to deny in the comparative renewal context are often filed to achieve nonfinancial goals such as to require a licensee to cure a deficiency in its performance, to provide certain types of programming, to continue to consider issues of concern to its community of license, or to improve its employment record regarding minorities and women. Petitions to deny can be dismissed in exchange for the payment of money and/or for promises to implement some type of nonfinancial reform. Where a petition to deny is dismissed in exchange for an agreement by a licensee to implement nonfinancial reforms, such settlements are often referred to as citizens' agreements. Our policy with regard to settlements of petitions to deny depends on whether the petition is dismissed in exchange for money or for a nonfinancial promise.

40. Where a petition to deny is settled in exchange for money, we will allow such payments provided they do not exceed the petitioner's legitimate and prudent expenses in prosecuting its petition. We must not discourage the use of petitions to deny in order to further our public interest goals. Petitions to deny play a critical role in our current regulatory scheme. Members of the public, through the use of petitions to deny, serve as private attorneys general informing us of deficiencies in the performance of licensees and helping us ensure that licensees serve the public interest.

41. By prohibiting payments in excess of legitimate and prudent expenses we are removing the profit motive for filing petitions to deny.

43. *Citizens' Agreements.* A citizens' agreement is a contract in which a petitioner to deny agrees to dismiss its petition in exchange for a promise by the licensee to implement a nonfinancial reform such as a programming or an employment initiative.

44. [M]any of the same concerns regarding potential abuse that motivated our restrictions on money payments in exchange for the withdrawal of petitions to deny appear to be equally applicable to citizens' agreements.

45. Ostensibly "nonfinancial" citizens' agreements often involve financial expenditures by the licensee to implement the reforms promised to the petitioner. Those expenditures may inure to the financial benefit of the petitioner, directly or indirectly. Consequently, these "nonfinancial" agreements can create the potential for abuse. Concessions extracted from the licensee under these agreements can merely be disguised private payoffs for dismissing a license renewal challenge where the petitioner itself, or an affiliated person or entity, is paid to implement the reform.

46. In light of this potential for abuse, we will review all citizens' agreements reached in exchange for dismissing a petition to deny on a case by case basis to determine whether the agreement furthers the public interest. In making this determination, we will presume that any agreement with a petitioner that calls for the petitioner, or any person or

organization related to the petitioner, to carry out, for a fee, any programming, employment or other "nonfinancial" initiative does not further the public interest and hence will likely be disapproved. In contrast, a licensee's agreement with a petitioner to make changes in operations or programming, either by itself or through disinterested third parties without further participation by the petitioner, will likely be approved.

Notes and Questions

1. **Broad Application.** The rules adopted in the above report and order applied only to license renewal proceedings. Subsequently, however, the Commission determined that it should apply these rules to petitions to deny in all proceedings, including those in which a firm sought a new license and those in which a firm sought to modify, assign, or transfer an existing license. The Commission therefore banned any individual or group from making or receiving monetary payments in excess of legitimate and prudent expenses in a wide array of instances, each of which had formerly been vulnerable to this same sort of strategic threat. *See* Amendment of Sections 1.420 and 73.3584 of the Commission's Rules Concerning Abuses of the Commission's Processes, Report and Order, 5 FCC Rcd. 3911 (1990).

2. **Surprise?** When the government (or any other entity) controls something valuable that it will give free of monetary charge, shouldn't we expect that many entities will seek to participate in the windfall? In the renewal context, the incumbent who expects to receive a renewal won't give up any of its bounty without a reason, so someone seeking some of the rents conferred by the government needs to devise a system to extract them from the eventual winner. And an obvious way of obtaining some of the renewal value is to present a credible threat to the renewal along with an offer to eliminate that threat in return for a side payment. Indeed, mounting a credible threat and gaining a side payment may provide a bigger payoff (relative to the challenger's costs) than would mounting a successful challenge to the incumbent. So why should we be surprised at any of the tactics to which the Commission is responding? The only surprise would be if the Commission could effectively stop these side payments, given the obvious incentives for them to arise.

3. **Abuses Defined.** More fundamentally, in what sense are the practices regulated here "abuses" of the licensing process? Do citizens' agreements or petitions to deny that are filed only to obtain cash settlements cause any "harm" beyond transferring money from one person to another? Is such a transfer a harm or a benefit to the interests of the listening and viewing public?

4. **Other Reforms.** Could the licensing process have been changed in ways more clearly and directly beneficial to listeners and viewers? Was the move to auctions necessary, or could the hearing process have been salvaged by more aggressive reforms? If auctions turn out to have significant drawbacks of their own, would you advise against returning to comparative hearings as an assignment mechanism? If so, what approach would you favor?

§ 5.C.2. Lotteries and Auctions

The FCC has used three primary mechanisms for the initial assignment of spectrum licenses: merit, as measured by the Commission (the comparative hearings studied in the previous section); random selection (lotteries); and willingness to pay (auctions). Random selection, as it turns out, was short-lived.

In 1982, Congress authorized the Commission to assign licenses by random selection. The provision, codified at 47 U.S.C. § 309(i)(1), provided that:

> [I]f there is more than one application for any initial license or construction permit, then the Commission shall have the authority to grant such license or permit to a qualified applicant through the use of a system of random selection.[51]

The FCC employed lotteries several times between 1982 and 1997 (the year Congress mandated the use of auctions for most license allocations and all but revoked the FCC's lottery authority). For example, lotteries were used to distribute certain licenses for low-power television service, *see, e.g.*, Amendment of the Commission's Rules to Allow the Selection from Among Certain Competing Applications Using Random Selection or Lotteries Instead of Comparative Hearings, Second Report and Order, 93 F.C.C. 2d 952 (1983), and again to distribute licenses for cellular telephony in markets other than the thirty largest, *see* Amendment of the Commission's Rules to Allow the Selection from Among Mutually Exclusive Competing Cellular Applications Using Random Selection or Lotteries Instead of Comparative Hearings, Report and Order, 98 F.C.C. 2d 175 (1984). In both cases, the FCC maintained its role in establishing the band plan—that is, defining exactly what the license allowed its holder to do. From there, however, the FCC simply accepted applications, screened them to make sure that applicants met basic qualification standards (like financial ability and certain technical capabilities), and then randomly awarded the licenses to some subset of the qualified applicants.

The FCC never used lotteries as a mechanism for allocating licenses for AM, FM, or conventional television stations, however. Said the Commission: "We are concerned that any potential gains in efficiency that may be achieved by use of a lottery would be outweighed by the possible reduction in quality of broadcasting licensees and service to the public. Therefore, we will terminate the lottery proceeding and seek instead to improve the efficiency and integrity of our current comparative hearing process for the grant of new broadcasting facilities." Amendment of the Commission's Rules to Allow the Selection from Among Competing Applicants for New AM, FM, and Television Stations by Random Selection (Lottery), Order, 5 FCC Rcd. 4002 ¶ 3 (1990).

To explore the relative advantages and disadvantages of auctions, lotteries, and comparative hearings, consider the following:

USING AUCTIONS TO SELECT FCC LICENSEES

Evan Kwerel & Alex D. Felker, FCC Office of Plans & Policy, Working Paper No. 16 (1985), *available at* http://transition.fcc.gov/Bureaus/OPP/working_papers/oppwp16.pdf

I. Introduction

As part of its duties under the Communications Act of 1934, the Federal Communications Commission is charged with managing the radio frequency spectrum. Traditionally, the Commission has performed this duty by first *allocating* a portion of spectrum in a given area to a particular purpose. Then the Commission *assigns* channels within an allocation to individual licensees. Both allocations and assignments have important impli-

---

51. The provision as passed in 1982 remains largely intact except for one important substantive change: section 309(i)(5) provides that, with the exception of licenses for noncommercial educational or public broadcast stations, "the Commission shall not issue any license or permit using a system of random selection under this subsection after July 1, 1997." 47 U.S.C. § 309(i)(5).

cations for consumer welfare and have been the subject of many public policy analyses. This paper examines only the assignment process and assumes no changes are made in either the current eligibility criteria for holding a license or the terms, conditions or rights of a license. We conclude that in most cases auctioning previously unassigned channels is likely to result in the same ultimate assignment as present mechanisms. But because they require winning bidders to make substantial payments in return for being licensed, auctions are an efficient way of reducing the number of applicants. Thus, auctions are likely to impose lower costs on the Commission and society than the other methods considered.

II. Description of Alternative Procedures for Selecting FCC Licensees

A radio channel that is assigned to only one party is said to be *exclusive*. If more than one party applies for a given exclusive channel, these applications are said to be *mutually exclusive*.

There are three methods that could be used to select among mutually exclusive applications: comparative hearings, lotteries, and a system of competitive bids (auctions).

A. Comparative Hearings

In practice, comparative hearings have proven to be a costly and generally ineffective means of selection. There are two main problems with this process. First, there is substantial disagreement about what the comparative criteria should be and how they should be weighted, and it is not unusual for disagreement to exist as to which applicant is, in fact, the most socially worthy. There is considerable doubt, therefore, as to how effective comparative hearings are in furthering social goals.

A second problem concerns the cost of these hearings (including delay). It is not uncommon for litigation to drag on for years, with participants incurring huge legal bills. These long litigation periods harm both the applicant ultimately selected and the public. The new licensee loses an income stream; the public is without an additional service. But because delay favors existing licensees, they have strong incentives to file petitions to deny or otherwise utilize the administrative process as a means of retarding competitors' entry.

B. Lotteries

In recognition of these and other problems, the Congress in 1982 gave the Commission permissive authority to award licenses by random selection. The FCC's initial experience with lotteries suggests that this method has its own significant difficulties. Once it became known that the lottery entry requirements were reasonably low, many individuals elected to participate. In the Low Power Television Service alone there are about 20,000 applications awaiting lottery.

The Commission has attempted to reduce its administrative burden by creating narrow filing "windows" and encouraging settlements among applicants. But applicants have, in turn, adjusted their filing strategies. Hence, with each new call for lottery applications, larger numbers of applications are received.

C. Auctions

A third possible selection method is a competitive bidding system where licenses are awarded to those users willing to pay the most for them. Although they have never been used to award radio licenses, federal government experience with auctions is longstanding and extensive.

The U.S. Department of the Interior (DOI), for example, has been successfully auctioning leases on tracts in the Outer Continental Shelf (OCS) for 31 years. The OCS is a major source of domestic oil and gas production, and between 1954 and 1983 total revenues from the auctions program were approximately $68 billion. Under the OCS Lands Act of 1953, private parties submit sealed bids for the right to explore and develop a specified tract on the OCS. The DOI has used a number of different systems for auctioning leases. Currently, a tract is leased to the party offering the highest up front "cash bonus" provided there are at least three bids. If there are fewer than three bids, the high bid is not accepted unless it exceeds the U.S. Geological Survey's estimate of the tract's value. In addition to paying a cash bonus for a tract, the lessee must also pay the government a fixed share of the revenues produced on the tract. The "royalty rate" is typically 16 ⅔ percent of the market price of the oil and gas at the wellhead. About 30 percent of the total government revenues from OCS leasing have come from royalty payments. The primary economic reason for relying on a royalty system in addition to cash bonus bids is that oil exploration is an extremely risky enterprise and royalties provide for a sharing of this risk between the government and private parties. Discussions with DOI officials indicate that the sealed bid auctions have been relatively simple to administer and free of any charges of corruption.

Other examples of federal auctions are: Treasury Bill auctions; leases of geothermal steam land; auctions of seized and unclaimed property; disposing of surplus equipment by the General Services Administration; and disposing of dead seamen's effects.

III. Comparison of Selection Procedures

In this section comparative hearings, lotteries, and auctions are compared with respect to their ownership effects, processing speeds, private costs, and government costs. Other considerations in choosing among selection methods are also discussed.

A. Effect on Ownership

The initial method of selecting a license may have little effect on who ultimately holds it because FCC licensees have considerable freedom[52] to trade their authorizations.[53] For example, in 1983 sixty-five percent of commercial television licenses [and seventy-five percent of commercial radio licenses] were held by someone other than the initial licensee. Thus, the qualifications of most present-day broadcasters were never considered in a comparative context.

---

52. It was obviously Congress' intent to allow licensees to trade authorizations when it is in their economic interest to do so. Even though the Act requires Commission approval prior to license transferral or assignment, it prohibits the Commission from considering the possible effects of transferring or assigning a license to any entity other than the one proposed. See, 47 U.S.C. § 310(d). Between 1962 and 1982 broadcasters were required to hold their station licenses at least three years. On the grounds that the competitive broadcast environment would prevent significant service deterioration in the absence of this restriction, the FCC relaxed the antitrafficking rules in 1982. At present, most broadcast authorizations may be reassigned at any time. However, licenses won in a comparative hearing or due to lottery preferences are still subject to a one-year holding period.

53. Two qualifications to this statement come to mind. First, if all applicants are equivalent, the initial selection method will determine the final user because by assumption no other party would be willing to offer to pay the initial licensee more than it is worth to him. Of course, in this case, it does not matter, from the viewpoint of economic efficiency, which applicant receives the license. Second, high transactions costs may prevent resale even if applicants differ in their valuations of the license. For example, suppose there are only two parties who put a positive value on the license and that party A values it $100 more than party B. If the government held an oral auction party A would bid the highest and receive the license. If, however, the government used a comparative hearing or lottery to assign the license, party B might receive it. If reselling the license cost more than $100, party B would be the ultimate holder of the license because the cost of reselling it would exceed the additional value party A placed on it. This just illustrates the inefficiency of not using an auction initially.

In the cellular [telephone] service many applicants have elected to reach settlements amongst themselves rather than face the uncertainties of either comparative hearings or lotteries. The Commission has generally honored these agreements and in those cases where all mutually exclusive applicants have settled, the agency has issued an authorization without utilizing any selection procedure.

Since the assignment method has little effect on who holds a license in the long run, we conclude that ownership distributions would not be significantly changed if initial authorizations were awarded by auction. But, as will be argued in the following section, auctions would reduce the delays and transactions costs involved in initial assignments and avoid the need for resale.

This conclusion about the ultimate ownership distribution should lay to rest any concerns that under an auction large firms would monopolize spectrum. We believe that this is unlikely for at least four reasons. If such firms were willing and able to monopolize spectrum under auctions, they could also do so under the current selection schemes by purchasing licenses from parties that won the initial assignment. Yet monopolization has not been observed in spectrum, nor has it been observed for other resources such as land that are also fixed in supply. Moreover, apparently no firm has sufficient wealth to buy up all the spectrum. Thirdly, since much of the usable radio spectrum has already been assigned, monopolizing the spectrum is unlikely to be a profitable strategy unless it could be accomplished without alerting the present holders of licenses. Otherwise existing licensees would hold out for high prices so as to reap much of the potential gains from monopolizing the market. Finally, any move to "corner the spectrum market" would presumably violate existing antitrust laws.

B. Delay in Making Assignments

Each assignment mechanism imposes a delay cost upon both the licensee and the public. The public's cost due to loss of service is difficult to estimate. But the cost imposed upon the successful applicant can be estimated by calculating the difference between the present value of the assignment under both delayed and non-delayed scenarios. With a nominal annual interest rate of 10%, a one year delay imposes a cost equal to 9% of the assignment's value, a two year delay imposes a 17% penalty, and a three year delay a 25% penalty.

Comparative hearings are generally lengthy proceedings. Broadcast cases often go on for two years or longer. Even the especially streamlined hearings used to grant cellular radio licenses in the top 30 markets averaged 18 months in length.

Lotteries have proven to be slower than expected. Most of the delay is created by huge numbers of applications, each of which must be logged, filed and prescreened prior to selection. Over 5000 applications were filed for cellular radio markets 91–120, and it is our best guess that the processing delay in these cases will average at least 12 months.

Auctioned assignments will probably attract far fewer applicants than lotteries because under an auction the winner must pay for the license. Thus, administrative delays will likewise be much shorter.

C. Private Application Costs

Comparative hearings and lotteries use up a great deal of real resources (primarily the time of legal, engineering, and economic consultants).[54] Auctions, however, involve pri-

---

54. Note that much of these resources are not "wasted" for successful applicants, because presumably the contribution of these consultants would be valuable in formulating a business. For un-

marily a transfer of resources (to the government in the form of the winning bid). Hence the use of auctions to award licenses could substantially reduce the total private and public resources expended in the process.

D. Cost of Administering Selections

There are two components to the cost incurred by the FCC in selecting among mutually exclusive applicants. One is "professional" cost. This includes the money spent on salary and support for professionals to review and analyze applicant documentation, and select a licensee. For example, professional costs are the major component of the FCC expenditures for a comparative hearing before an administrative law judge. We refer to the other cost category as "administrative." It includes money spent on space to house applications, as well as salary and support for the staff who records applicant information and maintains the documents. For lotteries and auctions, FCC costs are primarily administrative. Auctions would have lower administrative costs than lotteries because they would attract fewer applicants.

E. Other Considerations in Choosing Among Selection Methods

Auctions could prove attractive to taxpayers not just because they would reduce FCC costs but because they would provide a return for the valuable consideration granted licensees. The revenues raised through auctions would also help reduce the budget deficit.

Auctions could also provide the Commission with useful information on the value of spectrum in alternative uses. The amount bidders are willing to pay for a license reflects their estimates of the value customers place on the service they propose to provide. The Commission should consider reallocating spectrum to the higher valued use if it were to find that the bids on licenses for one use greatly exceeded the bids on licenses for similar spectrum allocated to another use.[55]

These findings of efficiency gains from auctions only apply in the case of selecting licensees for *unassigned* channels. Auctioning licenses at renewal appears to be analogous to having the government own all the land in a city and auction off parcels for five year terms. Licensees would tend to be discouraged from investing in equipment, training, and marketing that would have little value without a license.

Notes and Questions

1. Governmental Costs. Are you persuaded by Kwerel and Felker's discussion of the governmental costs of the different approaches? Hearings, of course, can be expensive to conduct, especially given the many possible layers of review. Auctions and lotteries seem likely to be less expensive, the main costs of each being paperwork-related—for example the costs of confirming that applicants meet some basic financial qualifications. Lotteries are likely to be more expensive on this score than auctions, however, since (assuming that lotteries are inexpensive for applicants to enter) there would likely be more applications to process in a lottery than in a comparable auction or hearing.

---

successful applicants, however, all these expenditures are truly wasted, and represent a waste to society as well.

55. It is important to understand the limited nature of the proposal discussed here. We are proposing that auctions be used only to choose among potential *users*. The *use* of the spectrum would continue to be determined by an administrative process. Even greater public benefits could be achieved, however, by allowing winning bidders increased flexibility in what they do with their assignments.

2. Private Costs. Similarly, which approach likely minimizes private costs for applicants? Hearings are expensive for applicants because they must pay for representation (perhaps at several formal interactions) and submit to a possibly expensive fact-finding process. Some of those expenses have value, of course; the ascertainment procedure, for example, is expensive for an applicant but also generates information that may be useful to the applicant should he be awarded the license at issue. Lotteries are probably the least expensive for applicants, the only real cost being the time to fill out a lottery application. And the primary expense involved in auctions would be the cost of developing a good bidding strategy, a cost that surely varies considerably party to party and auction to auction.

3. Rewards to the Government. Would one approach better inform the FCC as to how it should design the band plan? Does one approach give the government greater revenues? Does one approach give the government greater influence over licensee behavior? Auctions surely get a plus on the first two counts here. First, auctions help the government see how much a given slice of spectrum is worth, which might help the FCC in its spectrum-management duties. Note that this information is available under hearings and lotteries, too, but only some time after the initial assignment, when licensees start to sell their licenses on the open market. Second, auctions obviously fill the government's coffers rather effectively; it is hard to imagine those same revenues being generated by hearings or lotteries. As for the third factor—the extent of the government's influence over licensee behavior—it seems that hearings would earn the nod on this criterion because, while auctions largely defer to the marketplace and lotteries defer to chance, hearings (as we have seen) to some degree force licensees to defer to the FCC and its ever-powerful eyebrow. Whether that's good or bad as a policy matter, of course, depends on your perspective.

4. Empirical Data. The FCC's actual experience with hearings and lotteries confirmed many of Kwerel and Felker's hypotheses about their costs. For instance, when the FCC held hearings for cellular telephony licenses, there were more than ten applicants for each available license, and many of those applications contained more than 1000 pages of argument and documentation. The result was that the selection of licensees took almost two years on average. The FCC's switch to lotteries entailed its own complications, as the Commission itself noted:

> Initially, the Commission screened applicants and allowed only qualified providers to participate in the lottery. Even this minimal degree of screening proved to be extremely burdensome on the Commission's resources. For example, it took twenty months for the first set of cellular applications to be screened before the lottery.
>
> By 1987, the FCC was forced to abandon pre-lottery screening and open the process to all potential applicants. "Application mills" sprang up to assist almost 400,000 different firms claiming to be spectrum "providers" in their efforts to win a cellular license, and a broad range of spectrum speculators participated in and won lotteries in cellular and other services. Many license winners, with no intention of providing service to the public, were now eager to trade their license rights for windfall profits, and a secondary market in FCC licenses emerged. Even when lotteries themselves could be conducted quickly, it took years for secondary markets to reassign licenses to the parties that valued them the most and to aggregate these licenses efficiently.

FCC Report to Congress on Spectrum Auctions, 1997 WL 629251, at 6 (1997). The report noted that there were almost 400,000 cellular license lottery applications. *Id.* The sheer weight of the lottery applications was so great that the shelving collapsed in an FCC facility holding the applications. Nicholas W. Allard, The New Spectrum Auction Law, 18 Seton Hall Legis. J. 13, 26 n.46 (1993).

§ 5.C.3. Initial Assignment by Auction

In 1977, two FCC commissioners said that the odds of Congress abandoning comparative hearings "are about the same as those on the Easter Bunny in the Preakness." Formulation of Policies Relating to the Broadcast Renewal Applicant, Stemming from the Comparative Hearing Process, Report and Order, 66 F.C.C. 2d 419, 434 n.18 (1977) (separate statement of Hooks & Fogarty, Comm'rs). By 1985 the FCC Chairman called for auctions, and Congress authorized them in 1993 and mandated them in 1997. Whether that strikes you as a speedy or slow process of change, it was certainly a major transformation in the method of assignment approach. The idea that licenses should be auctioned went from unrealistic to conventional wisdom in the space of twenty years, and auctions became a settled aspect of telecommunications policy—as settled as the preference for hearings had once seemed to be.

The Commission was first given the authority to auction licenses in 1993,[56] but at that time auction authority extended only to common carrier and private radio licenses. Common carrier services are those (like telephone service) for which traffic is received on equal terms from all parties irrespective of its specific content. In 1997, however, Congress expanded the Commission's auction authority, requiring the use of auctions for nearly all initial licenses and construction permits. See 47 U.S.C. § 309(i)–(j). The statute contains a few exceptions to its auction mandate, notably excluding licenses for digital television service (which were given to existing broadcasters) and licenses for which the comparative hearing process had already commenced as of July 1997.[57] With respect to the latter category, the Commission was given the option to use auctions. The FCC exercised that option in the main order implementing the 1997 legislation, excerpted below.

IMPLEMENTATION OF SECTION 309(J) OF THE COMMUNICATIONS ACT—COMPETITIVE BIDDING FOR COMMERCIAL BROADCAST AND INSTRUCTIONAL TELEVISION FIXED SERVICE LICENSES

First Report and Order, 13 FCC Rcd. 15,920 (1998)

II. BACKGROUND AND SUMMARY

2. As fully described in the Notice of Proposed Rulemaking in this proceeding, 12 FCC Rcd. 22,363 (1997) (hereafter Notice), the Commission has traditionally used comparative hearings to decide among mutually exclusive applications to provide commercial broadcast service, and it has used a system of random selection to award certain types of broadcast licenses, such as low power television and television translator, pursuant to Section 309(i), 47 U.S.C. § 309(i). For purposes of comparative hearings, the Commis-

---

56. See Omnibus Budget Reconciliation Act of 1993, Pub. L. No. 103-66, § 6002, 107 Stat. 312, 387–97 (codified as amended at 47 U.S.C. § 309).

57. The other exceptions to the FCC's auction authority are licenses and construction permits for public-safety radio services and for noncommercial-educational and public-broadcast stations. 47 U.S.C. § 309(j)(2).

sion has developed a variety of comparative criteria, *see* Policy Statement on Comparative Broadcast Hearings, Public Notice, 1 F.C.C. 2d 393, 394 (1965), including the "integration" of ownership and management, which presumed that a station would offer better service to the extent that its owner(s) were involved in the station's day-to-day management. However, in Bechtel v. FCC, 10 F.3d 875, 878 (D.C. Cir. 1993), the United States Court of Appeals for the District of Columbia Circuit held that "continued application of the integration preference is arbitrary and capricious, and therefore unlawful." The Commission subsequently froze all ongoing comparative cases (including comparative renewal cases) pending resolution of the questions raised by *Bechtel*.

3. Subsequently, on August 5, 1997, Congress enacted the Balanced Budget Act of 1997, which expanded the Commission's auction authority under Section 309(j) of the Communications Act to include commercial broadcast applicants. Amended Section 309(j) provides that, except for licenses for certain public safety noncommercial services and for certain digital television services and noncommercial educational or public broadcast stations, "the Commission shall grant the license or permit to a qualified applicant through a system of competitive bidding ... [i]f ... mutually exclusive applications are accepted for any initial license or construction permit." Balanced Budget Act of 1997, § 3002(a)(1), codified as 47 U.S.C. § 309(j). In addition, Section 3002(a)(2), codified as 47 U.S.C. § 309(i), amends Section 309(i) to terminate the Commission's authority to issue any license through the use of a system of random selection after July 1, 1997, except for licenses or permits for stations defined by Section 397(6) of the Communications Act (i.e., noncommercial educational or public broadcast stations). Finally, Section 3002(a)(3) adopts Section 309(*l*), codified as 47 U.S.C. § 309(*l*), which governs the resolution of pending comparative broadcast licensing cases. Specifically, it says the Commission "shall have the authority" to resolve mutually exclusive applications for commercial radio or television stations filed before July 1, 1997 by competitive bidding procedures. It specifies further that any auction conducted under this provision must be restricted to persons filing competing applications before July 1, 1997.

4. As a result of the Budget Act, the Commission no longer has the option of resolving competing applications for commercial broadcast stations by comparative hearings except for certain applications filed before July 1, 1997, and it lacks the authority to resolve competing applications for commercial broadcast stations by a system of random selection. The Commission began this rulemaking proceeding to implement these provisions of the Budget Act.

III. DISCUSSION

B. Resolution of Comparative Initial Licensing Cases Involving Applications Filed Before July 1, 1997

1. Discretion to Use Auctions in Pending Cases

26. As noted above, Section 309(l) expressly governs the resolution of pending mutually exclusive applications for new commercial radio and television stations filed before July 1, 1997. [T]his provision accords us the discretion to decide such cases either by a competitive bidding proceeding or through the comparative hearing process.

2. Public Interest Considerations Favoring Resolution by Competitive Bidding

34. We believe that auctions will generally be fairer and more expeditious than deciding the pending mutually exclusive applications filed before July 1, 1997 through the comparative hearing process. We conclude that auctions will generally expedite service and better serve the public interest in these cases. Based upon our long experience with the comparative

process, we believe that once the competitive bidding procedures, as well as any special processing rules for these pending comparative cases are in place, auctions will result in a more expeditious resolution of each particular case, thereby expediting the initiation of new broadcast service to the public. In this regard, we note that, despite the 180-day period during which we waived our settlement rules as required by Section 309(l)(3), there are approximately 150 proceedings involving more than 600 pre-July 1, 1997 mutually exclusive applications that remain to be decided.

36. We have long noted the potential for delay inherent in the adjudicatory nature of the comparative process. In connection with a rulemaking initiated in 1989 to explore the possibility of using lotteries to award initial broadcast licenses, for example, we estimated that a routine comparative proceeding can take from three to five years or more to complete after designation of the mutually exclusive applications for hearing, and that complex cases may take much more time.[58] More recently in Orion Communications Limited v. FCC, 131 F.3d 176, 180 (D.C. Cir. 1997), the court recognized that repetitious appeals may prolong proceedings for years even after the Commission's decision.

37. Here, the potential for delay is also increased by the court's decision in *Bechtel* invalidating our central comparative criterion, integration of ownership and management, and the resulting freeze on the processing and adjudication of comparative proceedings in effect since February 1994. Moreover, we note many other relevant factors (e.g., local residence, civic participation, past broadcast experience) were "enhancements" of the integration criterion. Determining which of these criteria could best survive *Bechtel*-type scrutiny and determining how such criteria should now be weighted is a difficult process that no doubt would lead to serious challenges in the courts with the outcome unclear. Indeed, there is wide disparity in the record as to what the best approach would be. The value of developing a revised comparative system (and expending the associated administrative costs) is further attenuated by the fact that it would only be used for these pending cases (and potentially also a very small number of comparative renewal cases) and would have no future applicability. Thus, we conclude that using a system of competitive bidding rather than the comparative hearing process for competing pre-July 1, 1997, applications that are subject to Section 309(l) will avoid the difficulties and potential delays of developing and defending new or modified comparative criteria to apply in the cases that did not settle during the 180-day period that ended February 1, 1998.

38. Moreover, we are acutely aware of the delay already occasioned in all of the frozen *Bechtel* cases. Section 309(j)(3) provides that "[i]n identifying classes of licenses and permits to be issued by competitive bidding," the Commission shall seek to promote "(A) the development and *rapid* deployment of new technologies ... *for the benefit of the public ... without administrative or judicial delays.*" (Emphasis added.) As a more general matter, expedited service to the public is an important public interest consideration. We estimate that it would take many years for the Commission's administrative law judges to

---

58. *See* Amendment of the Commission's Rules to Allow the Selection from Among Competing Applicants for New AM, FM, and Television Stations by Random Selection, Notice of Proposed Rulemaking, 4 FCC Rcd. 2256, 2257 (1989), cataloguing various factors contributing to this delay, including the heavy use by comparative broadcast applicants of motions to enlarge issues; complex and intricate discovery procedures that materially add to the cost and length of comparative proceedings; lengthy hearings that may involve numerous witness and hearing exhibits; the 30–90 day time period for filing findings with the Administrative Law Judge; the approximately six-month period that it takes the Administrative Law Judge to issue his opinion; and the time for any administrative or judicial appeals.

adjudicate and decide well over 100 cases. Auctions can be carried out much more quickly. And, whatever the cause of past delay in resolving these cases, we believe that minimizing further delay and now providing new service to the public as quickly as possible best serves the public interest.

39. Some commenters favoring the use of comparative hearings for these pending cases express concern that the switch to auctions will detrimentally affect the quality of broadcast service. They focus particularly on the impact that auctions will allegedly have in terms of securing service that is narrowly tailored to the needs of the small, local community. As to these more general policy concerns, however, Congress itself has made the judgment that auctions are generally preferable to comparative hearings by requiring them for commercial broadcast applications filed on or after July 1, 1997. In giving us discretion to determine whether or not to use auctions in pending cases, we believe Congress intended us to focus on any special circumstances in these cases that would tip the policy balance in favor of comparative hearings, not to re-visit the general congressional determination that broadcast auctions serve the public interest. In any event, it is far from clear that a licensee that wins its license in an auction has less incentive to serve the needs and interests of the community than one who wins in a comparative hearing.

40. Moreover, auctions will have significant public interest benefits. In a 1997 report to Congress, we indicated that our experience with auctions shows that competitive bidding is a more efficient and cost-effective method of assigning spectrum in cases of mutual exclusivity than any previously employed method, including comparative hearings. And, as we stated in the Notice, we have relied on the relative advantages of auctions—which also include the public interest benefits of encouraging the efficient use of the frequency, assigning the frequency to the eligible party that values it the most and recovering for the public a portion of the value of spectrum made available for commercial use—in other contexts in which we have faced a choice of either using comparative hearings or a system of competitive bidding to resolve mutual exclusivity among license applicants. We believe many of these same benefits will apply in this context.

C. General Rules and Procedures for Competitive Bidding

4. Designated Entities

186. Section 309(j) of the Communications Act provides that the Commission "ensure that small businesses, rural telephone companies, and businesses owned by members of minority groups and women are given the opportunity to participate in the provision of spectrum-based services." 47 U.S.C. § 309(j)(4)(D). To achieve this congressional goal, the statute directs the Commission to "consider the use of tax certificates, bidding preferences, and other procedures."[59] *Id.* In addition, Section 309(j)(3)(B) instructs the Commission, in establishing eligibility criteria and bidding methodologies, to promote "economic opportunity and competition ... by avoiding excessive concentration of licenses and by disseminating licenses among a wide variety of applicants, including small businesses, rural telephone companies, and businesses owned by members of minority groups and women," which are collectively referred to as "designated entities." 47 U.S.C. § 309(j)(3)(B). Section 309(j)(4)(A) further provides that to promote these objectives, the Commission shall consider alternative payment schedules, including lump sums or guaranteed installment payments. 47 U.S.C. § 309(j)(4)(A). In addition to the statutory directive to "ensure"

---

59. Congress repealed, as of January 17, 1995, that portion of Section 1071 of the Internal Revenue Code, 26 U.S.C. § 1071, under which the Commission administered the tax certificate program.

opportunities for designated entities in spectrum auctions, the Commission has had a long-standing commitment to promoting the diversification of ownership of broadcast facilities. Indeed, "a maximum diffusion of control of the media of mass communications" was one of the two primary objectives of the traditional comparative broadcast licensing system. Policy Statement on Comparative Broadcast Hearings, Public Notice, 1 F.C.C. 2d 393, 394 (1965). Section 257 of the Telecommunications Act of 1996, moreover, directed the Commission to identify and eliminate market entry barriers for small and entrepreneurial telecommunications businesses.

187. To fulfill our obligations under Section 309(j), the Notice sought comment on whether bidding credits or other special measures were necessary to encourage participation by rural telephone companies, small businesses, and minority- and women-owned businesses in the provision of broadcast services, and, if so, how eligibility for any such special measures should be established. In particular, we requested comment on how special measures for minority- and women-owned entities could be developed consistent with applicable constitutional standards. The Notice also asked for comment on the advisability of adopting bidding credits or other measures to promote diversification of ownership, and on the appropriateness of adopting rules to prevent unjust enrichment in connection with the special measures approved for designated entities.

188. Many commenters argue that the present record is insufficient to support the adoption of bidding credits for women and minorities under the standards enunciated in United States v. Virginia, 518 U.S. 515 (1996) and Adarand Constructors, Inc. v. Pena, 515 U.S. 200 (1995). Some commenters urge that we delay the adoption of competitive bidding procedures for broadcast auctions until completion of studies already in progress that may shed light on these questions. And, although a number of commenters support the adoption of bidding credits for small businesses, they have supplied relatively little information regarding the capital requirements of, or the characteristics of the expected pool of bidders for, the various broadcast services. Determining the details of any small business credit is also complicated in the broadcast context by the fact that, at least traditionally, most applicants for new broadcast stations are in fact small businesses under almost any reasonable definition, particularly in the context of radio. Pursuant to our Section 257 proceeding, we have commenced a series of studies to examine the barriers encountered by small, minority- and women-owned businesses in the secondary markets and the auctions process. We believe it is important to complete these studies and provide for an opportunity for public comment before any ultimate determination of what rules we should have for designated entities. At the same time, we believe that it is important to move forward promptly with auctions. Particularly with regard to pending cases, considerations of fairness demand that no further delays occur and that we proceed expeditiously to licensing.

189. In proceeding with auctions before determining what rules we may ultimately adopt for small, minority- or women-owned businesses, we are, of course, sensitive to our statutory obligations regarding designated entities. As a preliminary matter, we note that, based on our experience in conducting comparative hearings under the 1965 Policy Statement on Comparative Broadcast Hearings, it is likely that the vast majority of the pending pre-July 1st applicants are small businesses, and indeed likely very small businesses. With respect to specific measures that may further assist designated entities, we note that all of the commenters who addressed the question supported a bidding credit or other special measure for applicants with no or few other media interests. We conclude that, based on the record to date, adopting such a "new entrant" bidding credit would be the most appropriate way to implement the statutory provisions regarding opportunities for small, minor-

ity- and women-owned businesses before the completion of the studies mentioned above and related public comment. Providing bidding credits to entities holding no or few mass media licenses will promote opportunities by minorities and women consistent with congressional intent without implicating prematurely the constitutional issues raised in ¶ 188.

Notes and Questions

1. The First Amendment. Should the fact that a license was auctioned, as opposed to being given out in some form of a merit-based hearing, matter at all to First Amendment analysis? For example, should a "purchaser" enjoy greater First Amendment protections than a "recipient"? And where does that leave a firm that purchased its license from another firm, the original firm having gotten the license from the government through a comparative hearing? Is this "purchaser" different in any meaningful way from the firm that purchased as part of a government-sponsored auction?

2. Strategic Behavior. One concern for any auctioneer is the possibility that bidders will collude or otherwise act strategically to depress the purchase price of the auctioned good. Such concerns have arisen in the FCC auction context. One notable example involved a 1997 auction in which a Texas firm seems to have successfully "warned off" potential auction rivals by, in early auction rounds, using the last three numbers of its bid to signal other bidders. Thus, in an auction with 493 different license areas (each denominated by a number), the firm bid $1,375,013 in the auction for license number 264, and $1,615,264 in the auction for license number 013, in what the FCC concluded was an effort to indicate to a rival bidder that it would stop bidding for license 264 if the rival would stop bidding for license 013. The strategy could have backfired, of course, by attracting rivals' attention to the desired licenses and in that way pushing bids up. But the FCC apparently believed otherwise since it not only sanctioned the Texas firm but also rounded bid amounts in subsequent auctions. *See* Application of Mercury PCS II, LLC for Facilities in the Broadband Personal Communications Systems in the D, E, and F Blocks, Memorandum Opinion and Order, 13 FCC Rcd. 23,755 (1998); Applications of Mercury PCS II, LLC for Facilities in the Broadband Personal Communications Systems in the D, E, and F Blocks, Notice of Apparent Liability for Forfeiture, 12 FCC Rcd. 17,970 (1997).

More generally, economists observed that the FCC's policy of revealing bidders' license selections and the identity of the bidders in each round could lead to anticompetitive behavior in the multiple-round auctions that the FCC conducts—bidders might use the information to signal to each other and divide the licenses at below-market prices and to retaliate against competing bidders. This concern was particularly great in auctions for multiple, substitutable blocks of licenses in which the number of bidders was relatively low compared to the number of licenses offered. The FCC responded to this concern with an order providing that it will withhold the identity of the bidders, their selected licenses, and the amounts of winning bids unless the Commission finds that the auction will likely be sufficiently competitive to make anticompetitive behavior unlikely. It makes this determination of likelihood by looking at bidders' eligibility. "Specifically, if all the bidders' bidding eligibility, measured in bidding units (subject to a cap on the amount of any one bidder's eligibility) divided by all licenses in the auction, measured in bidding units is equal to or greater than three, we believe the auction will be sufficiently competitive." Auction of Advanced Wireless Services Licenses Scheduled for June 29, 2006, Public Notice, 21 FCC Rcd. 4562 ¶ 4 (2006).

Preventing anticompetitive behavior is important not just because the government might be shortchanged but also because the government would not be getting an important quid pro quo from bidders: information on how valuable particular bands of spectrum are in particular areas and for particular uses. Auctions, after all, were in part designed to help the government better understand spectrum value and in that way better manage the band plan. Low bids undermine this goal by keeping true market valuations hidden, although the possibility of license resale in part mitigates this problem.[60]

3. Unintended Consequences. Crafting auction rules is difficult for another reason: government auction policies might have unintended consequences. Consider the minority preferences alluded to at the end of the above order. Ian Ayres and Peter Cramton argue that, whatever the intended effect, minority auction preferences might increase the net revenues earned by the government. *See* Ian Ayres & Peter Cramton, Deficit Reduction Through Diversity: How Affirmative Action at the FCC Increased Auction Competition, 48 Stan. L. Rev. 761 (1996). Ayres and Cramton studied an auction in which designated bidders were, first, allowed to pay for licenses in installments over a ten-year period at a favorable interest rate and, second, granted a 40 percent bidding credit (or discount, i.e., paying only $6 million for a winning bid of $10 million) applicable to ten of the thirty licenses up for auction. The combined effect of both policies, according to the authors, was that "favored bidders had to pay the government only 50 percent of a winning bid." *Id.* at 763. The authors argue that bidding preferences nevertheless increased government auction revenue. Their logic: the existence of preferences caused unsubsidized bidders to bid more, "both because they had fewer licenses for which to compete (once the substantial designated preferences effectively set aside ten of the thirty licenses) and because they had to compete against the subsidized designated bidders crossing over to bid on non-set-aside licenses." *Id.* Ayres and Cramton thus conclude that bidding preferences might not be as costly to the government as one might at first suspect, a result that might not help these preferences satisfy *Adarand* requirements but surely would make these preferences more politically acceptable. As the following note reveals, the FCC's special rules for small businesses had other unintended consequences.

4. Bidding Preferences and NextWave. As ¶ 186 notes, 47 U.S.C. § 309(j)(4)(D) authorizes the FCC to consider bidding preferences for "small businesses, rural telephone companies, and businesses owned by members of minority groups and women." With respect to two major broadband-PCS auctions scheduled for summer 1995, the Commission announced a number of measures to implement § 309(j)(4)(D): it would limit the bidders to entities with annual gross revenues of less than $125 million and total assets of less than $500 million; give a 10 percent bidding credit to "small businesses" (defined as having less than $40 million in gross revenues), a 15 percent credit to businesses owned by minorities or women, and a 25 percent credit to businesses that met both these criteria; allow large bidders to invest heavily in small business bidders; and reduce the upfront payment for winning bidders and allow them to pay in installments. *See* Implementation of Section 309(j) of the Communications Act—Competitive Bidding, Fifth Report and Order, 9 FCC Rcd. 5532 ¶¶ 12–18 (1994). The Commission said these measures would "encourag[e] large companies to invest in designated entities, promot[e] economic opportunity by assisting designated entities in overcoming the additional hurdle presented by auctions, and ensur[e] that licenses are disseminated widely." *Id.* ¶ 16.

Two months before the auction was to occur, the Supreme Court decided *Adarand*. In response, the FCC eliminated its race and gender distinctions, making all small businesses eligible for the 25 percent bidding credit. Implementation of Section 309(j) of the

---

60. Resale helps, of course, only if it actually happens. If the top-valuer buys the license in an auction at an artificially low price, there might be no market transaction since the top-valuer would already have possession of the license.

Communications Act—Competitive Bidding, Sixth Report and Order, 11 FCC Rcd. 136 (1995).

The auction produced more than $10 billion in net winning bids, and many initially considered it a great success. Two problems arose, however. First, there were accusations that some ineligible bidders had created small businesses as front organizations to bid for them, violating FCC rules. *See, e.g.*, United States *ex rel.* Taylor v. Gabelli, 345 F. Supp. 2d 313 (S.D.N.Y. 2004). Second and more importantly, many of the winning small businesses had difficulty raising the funds to pay for their winning bids and thus failed to make their payments on the licenses. They sought relief from the FCC, which responded by suspending installment payments and allowing winning bidders to return all their licenses and receive amnesty in the form of debt forgiveness or to surrender half of their spectrum for re-auction and pay for the other half. Amendment of the Commission's Rules Regarding Installment Payment Financing for Personal Communications Services (PCS) Licensees, Second Report and Order and Further Notice of Proposed Rulemaking, 12 FCC Rcd. 16,436 ¶ 6 (1997). But one firm, NextWave Personal Communications, refused to renegotiate and instead filed a petition for bankruptcy. The dispute went all the way to the Supreme Court. In that case, FCC v. NextWave Personal Communications Inc., 537 U.S. 293 (2003), the Court held that the revocation of NextWave's licenses was not in accordance with bankruptcy law. In 2004, the FCC and NextWave finally settled their dispute. Under the terms of the deal, NextWave returned roughly three-quarters of the disputed licenses to the Commission but kept licenses in lucrative markets like Boston, Los Angeles, Philadelphia, and Washington, DC. *See* Stephan Labaton, NextWave Pact with FCC Ends Airwave Dispute, N.Y. Times, Apr. 21, 2004, at C1. And the FCC has avoided a recurrence of this problem by never again allowing winning bidders to pay in installments after they received their licenses. Auction winners receive licenses only after they have fulfilled their bids. *See* Amendment of Part 1 of the Commission's Rules—Competitive Bidding Procedures, Third Report and Order and Second Further Notice of Proposed Rulemaking, 13 FCC Rcd. 374, 398–400 (1997).

5. Revising the Commission's Auction Authority. Since 1997 Congress has not always embraced auctions. Notably, § 647 of the 2000 ORBIT Act states that, "[n]otwithstanding any other provision of law, the Commission shall not have the authority to assign by competitive bidding orbital locations or spectrum used for the provision of international or global satellite communications services." ORBIT Act, Pub. L. No. 106-180, § 647, 114 Stat. 48, 57 (2000) (codified at 47 U.S.C. § 765(f)). So spectrum for international satellite-based services cannot be auctioned. After this provision was enacted, the FCC issued an order providing for auctioning of spectrum for direct broadcast satellite (DBS) that would be "predominantly domestic" with only "incidental provision of transborder service." Auction of Direct Broadcast Satellite Licenses, Order, 19 FCC Rcd. 820, 826 ¶¶ 14, 16 (2005). A company that had applied for DBS licenses and wanted to avoid auctions challenged the FCC's order. The D.C. Circuit found that the statutory language was ambiguous, but that the FCC's characterization of DBS as predominantly domestic was inconsistent with its treatment of other services. On that basis, the court rejected the Commission's order rejecting auctions as arbitrary. Northpoint Technology, Ltd. v. FCC, 412 F.3d 145 (D.C. Cir. 2005). The FCC responded by freezing all new DBS applications. Direct Broadcast Satellite (DBS) Service Auction Nullified, Public Notice, 20 FCC Rcd. 20,618 (2005).

6. Auction Revenues. Auctions have been a financial windfall for the government. The FCC has conducted dozens of auctions for spectrum licenses, producing tens of billions of dollars in net winning bids. The prices paid for different kinds of licenses have varied greatly, depending on such factors as the frequencies involved, the amount of bandwidth allotted to each license, and the services authorized. For instance, the January 2001 auction of 422 broadband PCS licenses yielded $16,857,046,150 in net winning bids whereas the October 2001 auction of 317 narrowband PCS licenses yielded $8,285,036 in net winning bids and the December 2005 auction of 22 Multichannel Video Distribution & Data Service (MVDDS) licenses yielded $133,160 in net winning bids. *See* Auctions Summary, FCC, http://wireless.fcc.gov/auctions/default.htm?job=auctions_all.

7. The Logic of Auction Revenues. The positive political dynamic engendered by the adoption of auctions is that the government has an incentive to ensure that unused or vastly underused spectrum is vacated so that it can be auctioned to a buyer that will put it to a more socially valuable use. The negative political dynamic of spectrum auctions is that politicians sometimes view spectrum policy as a subset of budgetary policy—i.e., asking how spectrum policy can be engineered to deliver the most revenue to the government. This mindset might lead the government to withhold spectrum in order to create more demand and, consequently, higher prices. This mindset might also lead the government to be more skeptical of leaving spectrum unlicensed because, regardless of the merits of that policy, it will not produce auction revenue. Is the logic of auction revenues, on balance, a positive or negative force in spectrum policy?

8. Incentive Auctions. The order excerpted above reflects the FCC's embrace of auctions. And § 647 of the 2000 ORBIT Act is an outlier: Congress has embraced auctions as well. The embrace of auctions is reflected in the incentive auctions proposed by the FCC's National Broadband Plan and legislated by Congress. The Plan proposed that

> Congress should grant the FCC authority to conduct incentive auctions to accelerate productive use of encumbered spectrum. Incentive auctions can provide a practical, market-based way to reassign spectrum, shifting a contentious process to a cooperative one. In an incentive auction, incumbents receive a portion of the proceeds realized by the auction of their spectrum licenses. This sharing of proceeds creates appropriate incentives for incumbents to cooperate with the FCC in reallocating their licensed spectrum to services that the market values more highly. A market-based mechanism—an auction—determines the value of the spectrum; market-based incentives, such as a share of the revenue received, encourage existing licensees to participate, accelerating the repurposing of spectrum and reducing the cost. Incentive auctions can be especially useful where fragmentation of spectrum licenses makes it difficult for private parties to aggregate spectrum in marketable quantities.

FCC, National Broadband Plan, § 5.3 (2010), *available at* http://www.fcc.gov/national-broadband-plan.

In 2012, Congress passed legislation that implements these auctions. Middle Class Tax Relief and Job Creation Act of 2012, Pub. L. No. 112-96, 126 Stat. 156. Title VI of that legislation creates a new statutory section entitled "Incentive Auctions" that authorizes the FCC to share auction revenue with a licensee that "relinquish[es] voluntarily some or all of its licensed spectrum usage rights in order to permit the assignment of new initial licenses subject to flexible-use service rules." *Id.* § 6402 (creating a new provision, 47 U.S.C. § 309(j)(8)(G)). The FCC has always had the ability to reclaim spectrum from existing licensees, authorize new services for that spectrum, and assign it to licensees for those new services. What the Commission lacked was the ability to share auction revenues with those who relinquished spectrum usage rights. This legislation permitted such sharing.

There was no debate over the assignment mechanism that would be used: auctions were the clear choice. The debate over the legislation, and the legislation itself, focused particularly on spectrum devoted to broadcasting, as data indicated that the gap between the value of spectrum to broadcasters (particularly those with low viewership) and the value to providers of services like wireless broadband was extremely large. Indeed, the size of that gap helps to explain why incentive auctions were included in a broader budget-related bill: Incentive auctions offset the cost of other measures in the legislation because they were projected to raise billions of dollars for the federal government, in light of the difference in value between the old and new uses. As the title of the legislation indicates, incentive auctions were part of a legislative package designed to fund programs and reduce taxes. Inclusion of incentive auctions helped make the legislation revenue-neutral.

But how could the government gain those revenues? Why wouldn't existing licensees hold out for valuations that captured for themselves all the difference in value between the old and new uses? The answer, in particular with respect to broadcasters, turns in significant part on the fact that the revenue projections, and a successful auction, did not depend on all broadcast licensees giving up all their spectrum usage rights. If a significant portion of licensees agreed to relinquish all their spectrum usage, or a portion of those rights (in which case they would share channels with another broadcaster, something that digital compression allows), the government could have a successful auction. And that, in turn, meant that the government could ask existing licensees to submit their reservation price (the price at which they would be willing to sell their license), knowing that it did not need to pay the reservation price for a broadcaster who submitted an exorbitant one.

The incentive auctions for broadcast television spectrum entail two auctions—a "reverse auction" in which broadcasters submit their prices to relinquish spectrum, and a "forward auction" of flexible-use licenses for the newly available spectrum in which new users would submit their prices to license spectrum. *See id.* §§ 6403(a) & (c). This arrangement allows the Commission to construct supply and demand curves and then determine the optimal amount of spectrum to shift from existing to new users and uses. A third major element of the incentive auction process involves the Commission reorganizing the broadcast television spectrum, by reassigning some licensees to different frequencies and setting up channel-sharing for those who give up some but not all of their frequencies. Such moves are essential to creating blocks of spectrum for new licensees. The legislation provided for such consolidation (often called repacking), with some limitations—notably that broadcast licensees cannot be involuntarily relocated from UHF to VHF channels. *See id.* § 6403(b)(3).[61] As the FCC noted in its 2012 notice of proposed rulemaking on incentive auctions in discussing reverse auctions, forward auctions, and repacking,

> [e]ach of the three pieces presents distinct policy, auction design, implementation and other issues, and the statute in a number of cases imposes specific requirements for each piece. At the same time, all three pieces are interdependent: the amount of spectrum available in the forward auction will depend on reverse auction bids and repacking, winning reverse auction bidders will be paid from the forward auction proceeds, and our repacking methodology will help to de-

---

61. There is some irony here, as in the early decades of television broadcasting VHF (channels 2 to 13) were the prime channels, and UHF (channels 14 and above) were less desirable and less valuable. Indeed, as Chapter Eight highlights, early FCC policy regarding cable television was heavily influenced by the Commission's desire to help UHF gain a foothold in its competition against the dominant VHF broadcasters. UHF is now more valuable because VHF's advantage of being lower on the television dial is overwhelmed by UHF frequencies' better propagation characteristics for new wireless services.

termine which reverse auction bids we accept and what channels we assign the broadcast stations that remain on the air. For the incentive auction to succeed, all three pieces must work together.

Expanding the Economic and Innovation Opportunities of Spectrum Through Incentive Auctions, Notice of Proposed Rulemaking, 27 FCC Rcd. 12,357 ¶ 5 (2012).

The result was perhaps the most complex auction plan in human history. The FCC brought in economists who specialize in auctions and created an incentive auctions task force, and the resulting order implementing auctions (promulgated two years after the notice of proposed rulemaking quoted above) contained more than 800 paragraphs plus a technical appendix. Expanding the Economic and Innovation Opportunities of Spectrum Through Incentive Auctions, Report and Order, 29 FCC Rcd. 6567 (2014). As we noted in Chapter Four, this complexity could have been avoided by simply allowing existing licensees to provide new services, but at a cost in efficiency (and in revenue for the government). Another way of simplifying would have been for the government simply to have reclaimed the relevant spectrum and then auctioned it, but that would have raised fairness concerns for the licensees removed from the spectrum and would have been politically impossible.

PART TWO

REGULATING MONOPOLY— THE CASE OF TELEPHONY

Chapter Six

Early Telephone Regulation through Divestiture

Introduction

In this chapter, we introduce the fundamentals of telephone regulation and trace several key features up to and through the Bell System's Divestiture. We start with some history, focusing in particular on the rise of the Bell Telephone Company and the important role played by Bell's refusal to interconnect with rival firms. Then, we turn to vocabulary and economics—the idea being to arm readers with both the words they will need to talk about telephone infrastructure and the associated intuitions about how that infrastructure affects market behavior. This discussion has two purposes: first, to explore telephone regulation itself; and, second, for the more general and important purpose of discussing these regulatory tools for addressing the problem of monopoly in communications networks (a project which continues into the next chapter). These regulatory techniques were best developed and were most extensively applied in telephony, but one can consider them for any communications market in which monopoly is a concern—as it was in cable television for a time and still is in the debate over broadband regulation.

We then turn to the regulation preceding the breakup of the Bell System and the breakup itself. After Bell succeeded in securing monopoly franchises over local telephone service from state regulators across the United States, the company set about building an enterprise that controlled not only local phone service but also long-distance service, customer premises equipment, and network equipment like switches. A good way to think of Bell's scope is that the company controlled every service and piece of equipment involved in any telephone call in the United States.[1] We consider three important areas in which regulators and courts limited Bell's monopoly scope prior to the 1974 antitrust case. We first look at the process by which competition crept into the market for consumer premises equipment. We then examine the more important case of competition for interstate toll service. Finally, we discuss Bell's entry into computing and data processing. With those precursors under our belt, we move on to the most important event in the changing boundaries between competitive and monopoly telecommunications services: the 1984 divestiture of Bell and implementation of its governing consent decree.

---

1. This statement is not literally true. Many independent telephone companies existed alongside Bell even at its peak, but Bell did manufacture almost all network equipment, provide almost all long distance service, and provide monopoly local service in the vast majority of the country.

Bell faced three major antitrust suits designed to scale back its monopoly. The first was a 1912 suit that resulted in the "Kingsbury Commitment" that purported to limit Bell's ability to acquire independent telephone companies but that ultimately did little to impede Bell's march. The second, filed in 1949 and aimed at Bell's control over the network equipment market, culminated in a 1956 consent decree under which Bell by and large agreed to refrain from manufacturing equipment other than for its own network and agreed to license its patents to other manufacturers upon payment of royalties. As the consent decree neither set prices for those royalties nor required Bell to buy any equipment from the third-party manufacturers, that decree, too, accomplished little in the telephone market (though it did prevent Bell from offering computer services, which seemed much less important at the time).

The third antitrust prosecution of the Bell Telephone Company began in 1974. That suit, unlike the previous two, proved enormously effective; indeed, it would culminate a decade later in the breakup decree (divestiture) that split up the Bell System and significantly narrowed the scope of monopoly in the telephone industry. But the events that set the stage for the eventual breakup began well before 1974. By the time the decree was accepted by District Court Judge Harold Greene in 1982, "most of the events that would transform the shape of the industry" were already "well under way." Glen O. Robinson, The Titanic Remembered: AT&T and the Changing World of Telecommunications, 5 Yale J. on Reg. 517, 520 (1988).

§ 6.A. Telephone History

On March 10, 1876, Alexander Graham Bell declared, "Mr. Watson, come here, I want you," and with those words began what would be a technological revolution of extraordinary import. Bell knew it from early on, confidently predicting what must have sounded unthinkable at the time—that "a telephone in every house [would someday] be considered indispensable." Robert W. Garnet, The Telephone Enterprise: The Evolution of Bell System's Horizontal Structure 1876–1909, at 12 (1985).

Of course, even Bell did not get all the details quite right. For example, Bell assumed that phones would be linked one-to-one instead of being linked together into web-like networks. From a legal standpoint, this is much more than a technical detail:

> Initially, telephones were linked one to one. It took until 1878, two years after the invention of the telephone itself, for the budding new telephone companies to grasp the necessity of a telephone "exchange." The telephone exchange—a simple switchboard at first—radically increased a telephone's utility by enabling each phone to reach any other phone connected to the same exchange. Demand for service increased dramatically.
>
> The advent of the telephone exchange gave rise to the first rumblings about the need for—or inevitability of—monopoly provision of telephone service. A central switchboard and the wires leading to it represented a large, fixed capital investment; the costs of an exchange seemed to decline rapidly as more subscribers were added. By fragmenting the market, competition appeared to drive up costs and nullify the key advantage of a central exchange, which was to connect everyone to everyone else.

Peter W. Huber et al., Federal Telecommunications Law 8 (2d ed. 1999).

But was monopoly provision really inevitable? Certainly not at the start: when the original Bell patents expired in 1893–94, only about one in 250 Americans had a telephone. Bureau of the Census, Historical Statistics of the United States: Colonial Times to 1970, Part 2, at 784 (1975). Free of patent limits, numerous independent companies entered the telephone business and the spread of telephony grew rapidly. Indeed, the proportion of Americans with telephones more than doubled in the next five years and, by 1920, more than one third of all households had service. *Id.* New, independent carriers unaffiliated with Bell carried much of that expanding telephone traffic.

Part of the entrants' success came from serving markets ignored by Bell. Bell had been pursuing high-volume, business-generated traffic by connecting first the largest cities and then branching out to smaller ones. Milton Mueller, Universal Service in Telephone History, 17 Telecomm. Pol'y 352, 357 (1993). Bell's President, Theodore Vail, modeled his strategy on Western Union's 19th century linking of offices in commercial centers and envisioned that his company would control a nationwide network interconnecting all nodes of business activity.[2] As a result, in 1894 only 3% of Bell's subscribers were in rural areas, even though 62% of Americans lived in communities defined as rural. Mueller at 357. Small independent phone companies, farming organizations, and rural cooperatives established thousands of local exchanges in areas not reached by Bell. *Id.* at 360.

In time, however, the Bell System was unable to avoid extending its operations into less dense regions. The independents—many of whom had joined in coalition—had accumulated enough customers in the urban periphery to make access to their systems valuable to the urban customers targeted by Bell. The dense population centers that Bell sought to monopolize became contested ground. To retain those markets, Bell had to satisfy urban customers who valued access to people served by the independents. Bell's management had discovered that "whenever you have the farmers tied to your exchange you have got the merchants where you want them."[3]

In the first two decades of the twentieth century, Bell and the independents invaded each others' territories to the point that over half of the U.S. population could choose between rival local telephone carriers. *Id.* at 359. Available data show that traffic was about equally divided between Bell and the independent carriers by 1908, when the Bell System carried an average of 16,029,000 conversations per day while independents together carried 15,956,000. Historical Statistics of the United States 783. At least by this measure, the collective market share of competitive carriers had gone from zero to 50% in only fifteen years.

There was, however, an inherent instability in the way local telephone competition had developed. In general, customers of independent carriers and customers of Bell could not call each other because the competing networks did not interconnect to exchange customers' local calls. When phones were relatively rare and the bulk of one's calls went to one or a few parties whose service decisions could be coordinated, it may have been only a modest inconvenience that customers could only call other people served by the same carrier. But as the telephone became a more basic and ubiquitous tool for business and personal communication, people came increasingly to value not just connections between parties in regular contact who could coordinate to be on the same network, but also, in the words of Bell President Vail, "communication with some other one, who, until the particular necessity arose, might have been unknown and unthought of." Mueller at 364 (*quoting* Annual Report, AT&T 39 (1910)). In Vail's view, giving customers the ability to

---

2. Mueller at 357. For a different take on Vail's model, *see* Paul Starr, The Creation of the Media 207 (2004) (arguing that Vail modeled Bell on the Post Office).

3. Cumberland Telephone Journal, Vol. 10, Jan. 15, 1904, at 12, AT&T-Bell Labs Archives, *quoted in* Mueller at 361.

contact parties unknown to them when subscribing to a telephone network was justification for monopoly: "this necessity, impossible to predetermine, [makes] universal service the only perfect service." *Id.* By "universal service," Vail arguably meant one provider, not the term's modern connotation of telephone service that is available to everyone at affordable rates.[4]

Implicit in Vail's observation was the idea of network effects, which we discussed in Chapter One—that, as more people can be reached through a given communications system, the more valuable that system is to any individual consumer. Competition that pulled subscribers to different, noninterconnected systems undermined this customer-side economy of scale.

Vail's basic argument, while grounds for increasing the number of telephones any given subscriber could reach, did not necessarily support a commitment to a government-protected monopoly. Mandatory interconnection of competing networks could have accomplished the same goal. The precedent for such a mandate was mixed, however. The Post Roads Act of 1866, ch. 230, 14 Stat. 221, *repealed by* Act of July 16, 1947, ch. 256, 61 Stat. 327, had required interconnection among competing or nonoverlapping telegraph systems,[5] but neither the statute nor its underlying principle extended to common carriers (companies that carry goods, people, or information for all comers at set rates) generally. Indeed, the Supreme Court made clear in 1886 that common carriage did not generally encompass the traffic of other carriers—in the Court's words, there was no obligation to be a "common carrier of common carriers." St. Louis I.M. & S. Ry Co. v. S. Express, 117 U.S. 1, 21 (1886). When the Mann-Elkins Act of 1910 deemed telephone companies to be common carriers, it did not specifically impose on them any interconnection obligations towards other phone companies, and state courts provided similarly little help to competitors seeking to interconnect with Bell.[6]

Of course, the Bell companies and independents could have chosen to interconnect, but they did not. Perhaps each side hoped that by standing its ground, it would eventually gain an edge that would make its network the most valuable to subscribers and push the competing network out of business. The data show such a stand to have been more plausible for Bell than for the independents. In 1910, Bell served about 4 million of the 7.6 million telephones in the United States. The remaining 3.6 million were served by the independents. Historical Statistics of the United States 783. But this figure to some extent overstates the independents' competitiveness against the Bell companies. Not all independents competed against a Bell company; many served areas Bell did not want to serve.

---

4. *Id.* Paul Starr, in contrast to Mueller's account, believes that Vail indeed envisioned the current, subsidized service model as part of his "universal service" concept. *See* Starr, *supra* note 1, at 446.

5. *See* Western Union Telegraph Co. v. Pub. Serv. Comm'n. of N.Y., 230 N.Y. 95, 101 (1920) ("each [telegraph carrier] represents the public when applying to the other for service and no discrimination can be made by either against the other, but each must render to the other the same services it renders to the rest of the community under the same conditions").

6. *See* Home Tel. Co. v. People's Tel. Co., 141 S.W. 845, 848 (1911). The distinction between a customer's access to a network under traditional common carrier law and a cocarrier's access to a network for interconnection purposes largely reflects (1) where interconnection may occur; (2) whether interconnection is comparable to what the carrier gives its own affiliates; and (3) what price the carrier may charge for interconnection. *See, e.g.,* Pacific Tel. & Tel. Co. v. Anderson, 196 F. 699, 703 (E.D. Wash. 1912) (holding that a cocarrier is not entitled to interconnection); *see also* James B. Speta, A Common Carrier Approach to Internet Interconnection, 54 Fed. Comm. L.J. 225, 258 (2002) (discussing the issue).

Perhaps sensing its advantages over the independents, Bell pursued dominance of the telephone market. It was greatly helped in this quest by its acquisition in 1913 of the patents for amplification technology that vastly improved long-distance service. Bell refused to allow independents to interconnect to its improved long-lines network and many independents were forced to either merge into the Bell System or go out of business. *See* Roger G. Noll & Bruce M. Owen, The Anticompetitive Uses of Regulation: *United States v. AT&T, in* The Antitrust Revolution 291 (John E. Kwoka Jr. & Lawrence J. White, eds., 1989). Indeed, Bell's market share climbed steadily from 1910 on, with particularly rapid gains starting in 1913. Historical Statistics of the United States 783.

As the Bell System acquired rivals, accumulated market share, and refused to interconnect either its local or long-distance networks with competitors, the enterprise not surprisingly attracted the trust-busting zeal of the times. On the heels of its victory over Rockefeller and Standard Oil in 1911, Standard Oil Co. v. U.S., 221 U.S. 1 (1911), the Justice Department filed an antitrust suit against Bell in 1913.

The government's suit alleged that Bell had improperly leveraged its dominance in the long-distance market to force competing local carriers into closing down or merging with the Bell System. Bell advanced two kinds of arguments in its defense: one favoring monopoly, the other denigrating the alternatives. The pro-monopoly argument was essentially Vail's claim that a "universal" provider would benefit customers more than a divided system. Interconnection would also, of course, have delivered the same benefits to consumers, and would furthermore have preserved the additional benefits of competition. Against that alternative, Bell contended that technical incompatibility and coordination difficulties rendered interconnection among competing systems inferior to integrated monopoly, and that mandatory interconnection was furthermore unfair to the larger system which had undertaken the bulk of the facilities investment upon which smaller systems would be able to free ride.

Ultimately, in what has come to be called the "Kingsbury Commitment," after the Bell vice president who negotiated with the government, the parties settled in 1914 on terms that proved enormously favorable for the Bell System. The government implicitly accepted Bell's arguments for a "universal service" monopoly and halted its pending antitrust action. In return, Bell promised to submit to a degree of regulatory oversight, to cease acquiring independent competitors, and to interconnect those competitors that remained to Bell's long-distance network. But the agreement also contained a great deal of built-in flexibility—"to conform to the development of telephony and to maintain the efficiency of the service"[7]—that ultimately undermined some of the settlement's central parts, such as the nonacquisition provision.

If the Kingsbury Commitment intended to preserve local competition from further erosion by prohibiting Bell from acquiring additional local companies, it was on the path to failure from the outset. Because the settlement required Bell to interconnect independents to its long-distance network, but not to its local system, subscribers to systems that competed with Bell still found themselves unable to call people on Bell's local networks, and vice versa. Ultimately, the continued existence of competition without interconnection proved untenable. Mueller recounts that "[a]s the nation became more urbanized and integrated, many telephone users, particularly small and medium sized businesses, found a divided service to be intolerable." Mueller at 365. With private incentives having failed to produce local interconnection, and with regulators having apparently abandoned the option, a transition began

---

7. United States v. AT&T, 1 Decrees & Judgments in Civil Federal Antitrust Cases 554, ¶ 14 (D. Or. 1914) (No. 6082).

to occur in which an antitrust settlement that purported to preserve competition gave way to state and federal policies that embraced a monopoly model for telephone service.

Bell's emerging dominance is revealed in the data from 1916 (the first date on which we have comparable data). The combined book value for the independent carriers was just over $250 million while Bell's was then just under $1 billion, their profits were just under $10 million compared to Bell's $52 million, and their networks contained roughly 4 million miles of wire as opposed to Bell's approximately 20 million miles. Historical Statistics of the United States 785, 787.

In all fairness to Bell's consolidation campaign, the inefficiency of separate, noninterconnecting telephone systems was burdensome to consumers. To reduce that burden, federal authorities allowed consolidation of competing carriers. The Department of Justice approved most of Bell's special applications to acquire local companies in the years the consent decree was in force. Huber et al., at 27 & n.113. And, in 1918, Congress and the President gave the Postmaster General emergency powers over the phone system which led to further consolidations. *Id.* Finally, in 1921, Congress suspended the nonacquisition provisions of the Kingsbury Commitment for good and gave the Interstate Commerce Commission authority to exempt telephone company mergers from the antitrust laws. Willis-Graham Act of 1921, Pub. L. No. 67-15, 42 Stat. 27 (codified as amended at 47 U.S.C. §221(a)), *repealed by* Telecommunications Act of 1996, §601(b)(2), Pub. L. No. 104-104, 110 Stat. 56, 143. The resulting statute, the Willis-Graham Act, was expressly aimed at eliminating the inefficient fragmentation of the phone system. *Id.*

On its face, the Willis-Graham Act did not create an open season for acquisitions. The Act only withheld antitrust enforcement for consolidations that were "of advantage to the persons to whom service is to be rendered and in the public interest." 47 U.S.C. §221(a). In practice, however, the hurdle proved a low one. In the years following the Willis-Graham Act, the traffic on independent companies declined precipitously in proportional terms and, for a long period, in absolute terms as well. Historical Statistics of the United States 783. More strikingly, the number of telephones connected to independent networks that did not interconnect with the Bell System—that is, those that likely overlapped with and competed against Bell—declined from over 1 million in 1917, to under 500,000 in 1921, to less than 100,000 by 1931. *Id.* Over that same period, the total number of telephones in the United States grew from under 12 million to nearly 20 million. *Id.*

An important effect of the Willis-Graham Act was to make the Bell System's conduct a matter for regulatory oversight as well as corporate strategy, leading in time to a system of regulated monopoly franchises. The "efficiency" from consolidation was the benefit to customers of being connected to the whole universe of other telephone subscribers. But other goals soon entered into consideration that further entrenched monopoly franchising in state and federal regulatory policy. The most prominent of those goals was making telephone service affordable to all Americans and thereby increasing the spread of telephony. As one lively commentary puts it, regulators aimed to put a "telephone within arm's reach of the chicken in every pot"[8]—and to do it, in large part, by cooperating with and regulating a national, unified Bell Telephone Company.

In summary, then, from the late 1800s until the breakup in 1982, basic economic arguments put Vail and his successors in an enviable position. They were able to establish and maintain Bell's domination of the telephone industry, all the while arguing that Bell domination was actually in the public interest.

---

8. Peter W. Huber et al., Federal Telecommunications Law 22 (2d ed. 1999).

§6.B. Infrastructure

§6.B.1. Telephone System Vocabulary

As the above discussions already make clear, one hurdle to studying telephone regulation is simply mastering the vocabulary of telephone service provision. To assist in that process, we pause here to survey the key terminology of a traditional telephone network.

Consumers have in their homes standard equipment (like telephones and routers) capable of encoding and receiving voice and data communications. Businesses have similar basic equipment. This equipment is what insiders call customer premises equipment, which is abbreviated CPE. The Telecommunications Act of 1996 defines CPE as "equipment employed on the premises of a person (other than a carrier) to originate, route, or terminate telecommunications." 47 U.S.C. §153(14).

Some CPE is used in the provision of basic telephone service. Basic telephone service, in turn, is termed POTS, which stands for plain old telephone service. This is in contrast to newer services that are not considered as fundamental as the basic ability to originate and terminate telephone communications.

CPE is connected by wire to a central hub, often located in the telephone company's central office. Originally, the key piece of equipment kept in this hub was a switchboard where an operator would connect one party to another by plugging the caller's and recipient's wires into a common jack. This was all done by voice; so a caller would first identify to the operator the person he wanted to ring, and the operator would then make the connection manually. Privacy issues were significant under this system and affected how telephones were used at this time.

Today, automatic equivalents to the switchboard (such as routers, switches, and exchanges) serve this same basic purpose. There are minor distinctions that can be drawn here, but the basic idea is the same for each of these devices: these are computers that direct telephone traffic from one part of the network to another. They are really just substitutes for wire: the modern telephone network could in theory be accomplished by having every telephone connected to every other telephone via billions of one-to-one wires. Given the expense associated with laying wires, we use fewer wires and allow switches, routers, exchanges and sometimes human operators to connect phones in a web-like pattern instead.

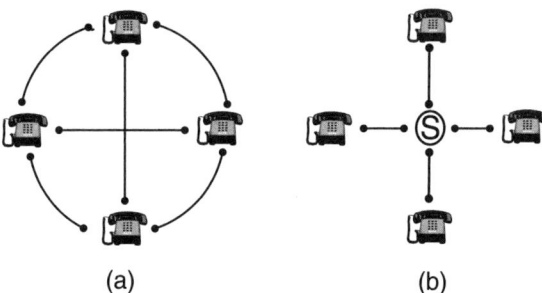

(a)   (b)

Switches. Switches substitute for wire, as these pictures make clear. The panel to the left shows how four telephones might be connected one-to-one by wire. The panel to the right replaces those wires with a switch. Note how significantly the switch reduces the complexity of the network.

Building on the word "exchange," insiders typically refer to the local phone company as the local exchange carrier (LEC) since there is typically one major switch that serves each large geographic area and the local phone company is the business entity that owns and operates that switch. Long distance phone companies, by contrast, are referred to as interexchange carriers (IXCs) since their job is to carry phone traffic from one local exchange to another.

Two other phrases often associated with the local phone company are "the local loop" and "the last mile." The local loop is the part of the network that connects individual subscribers to the main local switch. This is in a very literal sense the "last mile" of the phone system. This part of the phone network has always been the subject of considerable attention and concern since many people believe this part to be a natural monopoly. The belief is that the costs of operating two or more local switches—and then either connecting them to each other or connecting each telephone to each local switch—would greatly exceed the costs of simply operating one switch to which all local telephones were connected. Understanding this claim is of central importance to understanding the entire regulatory regime related to telephone service; and so it is to this claim, and its logical extensions, that we now turn our attention.

§ 6.B.2. Telephone Economics

Throughout his career, Theodore Vail argued that one firm—namely, his firm—should provide all telephone service nationwide. His argument was, of course, in part self-serving, but that does not necessarily mean that it was wrong.

First, the fact that the telephone system exhibits network properties is relatively uncontroversial; significantly more controversial are its implications. After all, while it might be true that, if left with the discretion to do so, a company like Bell would refuse to interconnect with competitors as a way of taking strategic advantage of any network externalities, it is also true (as hinted at above) that interconnection can be imposed even on unwilling firms. For one thing, subscribers can create de facto interconnection simply by purchasing access to multiple networks. If every family had both a Bell telephone with which to contact Bell customers and also, say, a Sprint telephone with which to contact all Sprint customers, there would be no need for interconnection between the Bell and Sprint networks. A more efficient and direct option might be to use legal rules to force Bell and Sprint to interconnect. The real question in both cases is whether the costs associated with interconnection are so great that competition/interconnection makes society worse off than would monopoly/no interconnection.

Second, a stronger argument in favor of Vail's monopoly vision was that, like the telegraph arguably had been in the past and as cable television would be considered in the future, the provision of telephone service was a natural monopoly. As we explained in Chapter One, this means that—due to the structure of costs in this market—the cheapest way to provide nationwide telephone service might be to have a single firm provide service to all interested customers: to provide telephone service, a firm must incur a significant fixed investment (this time to build the initial network of wires, switches, and so on); but, once that investment has been made, the marginal cost of adding an additional phone customer is almost zero. There is an economy of scale, then, in having a single firm build the local loop instead of having multiple firms each build possibly overlapping networks.

Demand variability also bolsters this claim. An individual's demand for phone service varies significantly from moment to moment and day to day; yet, in order to provide adequate phone service, the phone company has to be ready to serve a given user whenever that user happens to pick up the telephone. By having a single firm serve a large number of users, the costs of providing phone service can be lowered dramatically. Several users can share a given amount of capacity, putting the equipment to better use since the variance in each consumer's demand would to some degree cancel out, leaving less of the phone system's capacity to sit idle at a given time.

Vail's vision of a single telephone company was supported not just by network externality arguments and not just by conventional natural monopoly arguments, but also by the concept of economies of scope. An economy of scope is said to exist in settings where a single firm can produce a given quantity of each of two or more goods more cheaply than multiple firms can produce those same total quantities. Shoe production is an intuitive example; once a given firm is producing left shoes of a certain style, it is likely true that this same firm can produce the corresponding right shoes more cheaply than could any rival. The economy of scope argument is not a straightforward natural monopoly argument. We know, for example, that a great many shoe companies today compete in the shoe market, and we have no reason to believe that costs would be reduced were all shoes made by a single firm. The economy of scope argument suggests only that, if a company is in the business of selling one of two interrelated products, it likely makes sense for that same company to sell both.

In the telephone setting, this argument combined with the various natural monopoly arguments to make a strong case in favor of a large, integrated phone company. First, because the provision of local telephone service to some degree exhibited the properties of a natural monopoly, Vail could argue that there should be a single telephone company in each community. Second, because of economies of scope, it was likely that having the same firm provide telephone service in both local and long distance markets would minimize overall costs as telephone traffic moved from one part of the network to another. The economy of scope argument thus completed Vail's intuitive claim. Therefore, Vail's argument was that to realize the full efficiencies possible in this setting, not only should there be a single network in every community, but those networks should all be jointly operated by a single national firm. Naturally, in Vail's view, that company was Bell.

§ 6.C. Telephone Regulation

We have introduced some of the history, vocabulary, and economics of the telephone system. We turn now to the regulatory issues. Specifically, we build here on the generalities of Chapters One and Two and offer a brief overview of the types of telephone regulations that have been imposed over time. We will say much more about each of these categories in the chapters that follow. We also here consider the question of how federal and state authorities share regulatory power over telephone service.

§ 6.C.1. Categories of Regulation

The economics of the telephone system were for a long time interpreted to mean that the most efficient way to provide telephone service nationwide was to do so using a single monopoly provider. Thus early regulations focused on ensuring that Bell would be the only telephone company in a given region. That, however, was only the tip of the regulatory iceberg, because a firm protected from competition would ultimately behave as any monopolist would: maximizing profits by charging consumers higher-than-competitive prices. To avoid this outcome, state public utility commissions regulated the rates that the local exchange carriers charged to consumers in their franchise areas.

A second important area of telecommunications regulation was related to the scope of the monopoly franchise. The Bell System encompassed not just a state-by-state franchise over local service, but also nationwide long-distance telephone service, the manufacture and sale of customer premises equipment, and the manufacture and sale of network equipment like switches and routers. Over how many of these different markets should Bell's monopoly extend? Both antitrust law and regulation played a role in answering this question, and, certainly by the mid-1930s, policing the boundaries of monopoly was a second significant regulatory task on the agenda.

The third major category of regulation involved universal service policies and responded directly to concerns that some citizens would not share in the benefits of telephone service because no carrier could serve them profitably. In granting monopoly franchises to Bell, state regulators found an opportunity to demand certain things in return; and one of the key conditions of the monopoly grants was that Bell would provide quality service to all consumers in a territory and do so at fair and generally equal rates. In the jargon of telecommunications regulation, this obligation is often referred to as the responsibility to be the carrier of last resort. If, for example, an individual moves to the top of a mountain in a given service territory, that individual has the right to request service at a fair rate (which is usually a statewide averaged rate) even if, in a competitive market, no firm would bother to serve such an awkwardly located and expensive-to-reach customer. Implementing and enforcing these policies was thus the third important focus of telephone regulation during the 20th century.

§ 6.C.2. Who Regulates

From its creation in 1934, the FCC has always shared jurisdiction over telephony with state regulators. The 1934 Act's limitation of federal authority is clearly stated, if not always so easily implemented in practice: the Act is not to be construed "to give the Commission jurisdiction with respect to ... practices, services, facilities, or regulations for or in connection with *intra*state communication service by wire or radio of any carrier." 47 U.S.C. § 152(b) (emphasis added). Indeed, the 1934 Act on its face restricts FCC jurisdiction to "*inter*state and foreign communication by wire or radio." 47 U.S.C. § 152(a) (emphasis added). The Act thus appears to keep the Commission out of the business of regulating what, in 1934, accounted for the vast bulk of telephone usage: local telephony.

The 1934 Act in this way marked an important departure from earlier telephone regulation. Before the Act, telephone service had been regulated by the Interstate Commerce Commission (ICC), an agency charged with the task by the Mann-Elkins Act of 1910, Pub. L. No. 61-281, 36 Stat. 539. The ICC had enjoyed broad power to preempt any state regulation with which it disagreed. In fact, in *The Shreveport Rate Case* of 1914, the Supreme Court affirmed that the ICC had preemption authority whenever an intrastate rate would frustrate the achievement of a federal statutory goal. Houston & Tex. Ry. v. U.S., 234 U.S. 342 (1914) (*The Shreveport Rate Case* or *Shreveport*). Although that case involved railroad rates, not telephony, the Court was interpreting the ICC's authority under a statute that applied equally to both.

The scope of federal authority in telephony had received a further, though less direct, boost from the Supreme Court in 1930 as well. In Smith v. Illinois Bell Telephone Company, 282 U.S. 133 (1930), the Court ruled that state regulations must be strictly limited to intrastate facilities and services. Rates for local service could not incorporate the full costs of local network facilities so long as even a tiny fraction of the traffic on those facilities was interstate. The costs imposed on the local network by interstate calls had to be "separated" from the intrastate costs for the purposes of setting local rates. While this case did not directly broaden federal authority, it did narrow state authority.

The Communications Act of 1934 effectively nullified *The Shreveport Rate Case*'s applicability to telecommunications. The rule of construction contained in § 152(b) of the 1934 Act is sweeping: "*nothing* in this chapter shall be construed" to preempt state jurisdiction over intrastate services or facilities. The implication is that, even if state regulation of intrastate service might make implementation of some telephony provision of the 1934 Act more difficult, federal regulators cannot, as they could under *Shreveport*, preempt the inconvenient state law. Section 152(b) thus appears to give clear primacy to state regulators where intrastate telephony is involved. One limitation on that primary state role is that § 410(c) of the Act gives the FCC ultimate authority, after consultation with a joint board of state and federal regulators, to decide the respective degrees to which network facilities are used for interstate and intrastate service. Section 410 thus gives the Commission some discretion to decide where to draw the line between interstate and intrastate telecommunications and, within reason, to adjust its jurisdiction accordingly.

The practical complications of § 410 aside, the 1934 Act quite consciously tried to reserve substantial authority to the states. But the actual operation and judicial interpretation of § 152(b) turned out, for a time at least, to be somewhat different from what might have been expected given the text of the provision. After several decades during which there was little conflict between state and federal goals—and correspondingly few jurisdictional squabbles—some disagreement began to arise, notably as the FCC began to promote competition in certain areas of telecommunications. One particular set of conflicts resulted in a series of court decisions that greatly expanded federal regulatory power at the expense of the states. The first such decision was in N.C. Util. Comm'n v. FCC, 537 F.2d 787 (4th Cir. 1976) (*NCUC I*). There, the United States Court of Appeals for the Fourth Circuit ruled that the FCC could preempt a state law regulating certain types of basic telephone equipment so long as the equipment affected by the regulation would be used for interstate, as well as intrastate, telephone communication. The FCC had been trying to promote competition in the market for telephone equipment and found the state law at issue to be antithetical to that policy. Notable about the Fourth Circuit's decision was that it allowed preemption even though the telephone equipment at issue was used almost exclusively for local calling.

A second case arising one year later out of the same regulatory proceeding even more radically expanded federal jurisdiction. In N.C. Util. Comm'n v. FCC, 552 F.2d 1036 (4th Cir. 1977) (*NCUC II*), the Fourth Circuit decided that it was a practical impossibility to separate the interstate and intrastate uses of most telephone equipment and thus granted the FCC even broader authority to preempt state law. In short, while under *NCUC I* the FCC could preempt a state law only if it could be shown to affect interstate telephone service, under *NCUC II* the FCC could preempt a state law in any case where the effects on interstate and intrastate service were inseparable. This in some ways turned § 152(b) on its head by shifting the presumption in favor of federal rather than state regulation. Moreover, it seemed to reinstate the pro-preemption doctrine of *The Shreveport Rate Case*, a doctrine that was well known when Congress decided to adopt a contrary rule of construction in the 1934 Act.

The *NCUC* cases would not remain good law for long. A number of other federal courts had adopted the *NCUC* tests, *see, e.g.*, Cal. v. FCC, 567 F.2d 84 (D.C. Cir. 1977); N.Y. Tel. Co. v. FCC, 631 F.2d 1059 (2d Cir. 1980), when, in 1986, the question of federal authority in telecommunications finally reached the Supreme Court. The case was La. Pub. Serv. Comm'n v. FCC, 476 U.S. 355 (1986) (*Louisiana PSC*). At issue was the FCC's decision that its depreciation rules for the installation of wires on a customer's premises would preempt any state regulations prescribing different depreciation rates. The Supreme Court reversed the FCC's ruling, holding that, although 47 U.S.C. §220 gave the agency broad authority to prescribe depreciation rates, it did not unambiguously provide for preemption of contrary state depreciation rules. The Court further found that the rates at issue did not involve either costs that were incapable of separation between interstate and intrastate components or a conflict that would completely negate the federal rule. The Court therefore held that, where separation is not impossible and where application of a federal rule will not be nullified by contrary state provisions, preemption of state regulation of intrastate telecommunications can occur only where expressly and unambiguously provided for by statute. *Id.* at 375–76.

The principle for allocation of jurisdiction between state authorities and the FCC has not changed much since *Louisiana PSC*. As we will see in Chapter Seven, however, the Telecommunications Act of 1996 in some instances gives the Commission the kind of express authority that, under *Louisiana PSC*, is necessary for preemption of state regulations governing intrastate communications. But let us hold off on those issues and consider them later in the context of the events that made them important.

§ 6.D. Precursors to Divestiture

We now turn to the events preceding the Bell Divestiture: three regulatory episodes that attempted, and to various degrees succeeded, in controlling the scope and impact of Bell's monopoly. In particular, we look at FCC efforts to inject competition into consumer premises equipment (CPE), into long distance service, and into early versions of converged computer/communications services.

§ 6.D.1. Competition in CPE

FEDERAL TELECOMMUNICATIONS LAW
Peter W. Huber, Michael K. Kellogg & John Thorne,
663–70 (2d ed. 1999)

Bell did not sell equipment; it sold service. Its customers in turn bought service, and service alone. Thus, Bell supplied not only the wires and switches of the network, but also all CPE and inside wiring.[9] To freeze out alien CPE, Bell [prohibited subscribers from interconnecting any non-Bell product] with Bell's network. Such prohibitions appeared in private contracts with telephone subscribers as early as 1899, and they were incorporated in Bell company tariff schedules [public documents that described the services Bell offered and stipulated price and other conditions of service] by 1913. The ostensible purpose of these provisions was to protect the physical integrity of the network from dangers such as erratic voltage generation caused by defective equipment. Their practical effect was to eliminate all competitive suppliers of CPE.

It took some time before the FCC seriously questioned the equipment monopoly; the first suggestion that the link [between provision of equipment and provision of service]

---

9. [At this time, most phone system subscribers rented their CPE from Bell instead of owning their CPE outright. This made the CPE more analogous to other Bell components—wires, switches, and so on—than it might seem to modern audiences. Eds.]

might not be inextricable did not come until 1948. That year, the Commission struck down "foreign attachment" provisions that prohibited the use of recording devices in connection with interstate service. [The Commission found that] [r]ecording devices could in fact be used without causing "any perceptible effect on the functioning of the telephone apparatus or the quality of the telephone service," Use of Recording Devices in Connection with Telephone Services, 11 F.C.C. 1033, 1036 (1947); all federal tariffs purporting to bar the use of recording devices were therefore rejected.

[O]nly six years later, the Commission was in full retreat. That year it upheld Bell's refusal to permit the Jordaphone, [an early] answering machine, to be connected to the network. Unlike ordinary "recording devices," the Jordaphone "opens and closes the telephone circuit"; this was enough to justify different treatment. Jordaphone Corp. v. AT&T, 18 F.C.C. 644, 699 (1954). Bell had made no showing whatsoever that the network would suffer any substantial harm from Jordaphones. Nevertheless, the Commission decided that this kind of recording device would be used primarily with intrastate calls and should thus be left to the jurisdiction of individual state public utility commissions.

The following year the Commission issued perhaps its most comical order, revealing how a regulatory mind-set can sometimes overwhelm common sense. At issue was the "Hush-A-Phone," a metal device (packed with sound-muffling asbestos) that snapped onto the mouthpiece of the phone to provide some privacy and quiet in crowded office environments. Bell complained to the Commission that the Hush-A-Phone might muffle voices and lower the overall quality of telephone service; moreover, there was "no appreciable public demand" for the product. Hush-a-Phone Corp. v. AT&T, 20 F.C.C. 391, 397 (1955). The FCC agreed: "the unrestricted use of foreign attachments ... may result in impairment to the quality and efficiency of telephone service, damage to telephone plant and facilities, or injury to telephone company personnel." *Id.* at 419. Foreign attachments would have to be analyzed one case at a time. And, after lengthy analysis, the Commission concluded that this particular snap-on cup would "be deleterious to the telephone system and injure the service rendered by it." *Id.* at 420. As a general principle, "telephone equipment should be supplied by and under control of the carrier itself." *Id.*

The D.C. Circuit sensibly reversed in a brief per curiam. The court found no support for the Commission's suggestion "that the use of a Hush-A-Phone affects more than the conversation of the user—that its influence pervades, in some fashion, the whole telephone system." Hush-A-Phone Corp. v. United States, 238 F.2d 266, 268 (D.C. Cir. 1956). But the court went on to establish a principle of much wider significance: it affirmed "the telephone subscriber's right reasonably to use his telephone in ways which are privately beneficial without being publicly detrimental." *Id.* at 269. Moreover, the court explained, "the mere fact that the telephone companies can provide a rival device would seem to be a poor reason for disregarding Hush-A-Phone's value in assuring a quiet line." *Id.* at 268, n.9.

The full implications of the D.C. Circuit's decision in *Hush-A-Phone* were not realized for over a decade, when the Commission handed down its 1968 *Carterfone* decision. Use of the Carterfone Device in Message Toll Telephone Service, 13 F.C.C. 2d 420 (1968). At issue was a device permitting direct communication between a mobile radio and the landline network.[10] True to form, Bell objected to the device, but failed to demonstrate that

---

10. [The Commission described the Carterfone device as follows: "The Carterfone is designed to be connected to a two-way radio at the base station serving a mobile radio system. When callers on the radio and on the telephone are both in contact with the base station operator, the handset of the operator's telephone is placed on a cradle in the Carterfone device. A voice control circuit in the Carterfone automatically switches on the radio transmitter when the telephone caller is speaking;

it would harm the network. The Commission rejected Bell's argument. Instead, the Commission ruled that the basic principle of *Hush-A-Phone* applied: any form of CPE could be attached to the network "so long as the interconnection does not adversely affect the telephone company's operations or the telephone system's utility for others." *Id.* at 424. Unvarnished claims of threatened harm to the network would no longer suffice.

Even after *Carterfone*, competitive providers of CPE did not have unfettered access to the network. Bell responded to *Carterfone* by filing new tariffs, tariffs that permitted customers to connect to the telephone network, but only through interconnecting devices called "protective connecting arrangements" (PCAs) [that Bell itself would sell to interested parties]. Further, any "network control signaling" devices—devices, like the ordinary dial telephone, that actually put electronic signals onto the phone network—still had to be furnished, installed, and maintained by Bell. The Commission turned aside the immediate challenges to these tariffs. *Carterfone*, the Commission reasoned, permitted interconnections with—but not substitutions or replacements for—the "system," expansively defined. This substantially eviscerated *Carterfone*.

Notes and Questions

1. Subsequent Events. The FCC would ultimately reverse course. In 1972, the Commission began an inquiry into the issue of competitive CPE; that inquiry culminated in 1976 in a program of "technical registrations" for all CPE. Under this program, CPE suppliers had a choice: they could purchase a "protective connecting arrangement" (PCA) interface from Bell, or they could register their CPE with the Commission and show that the equipment would not harm the telephone network. Bell's stranglehold on the CPE market was thereby broken.

2. Ulterior Motives. In rejecting Bell's various technical justifications for its CPE tariff, the FCC apparently suspected Bell's ulterior motive was the desire to eliminate competition in the CPE market. But why would that be in Bell's interest? After all, Bell already controlled the phone network; why would it need two "stacked" monopolies—first the phone network, then the attached CPE? In fact, wouldn't Bell have been better off having competitive supply of CPE, since competitive supply would likely mean decreased costs and higher quality? Wouldn't those changes increase the profits Bell could make through its service monopoly? If telephone rates had been unregulated at the retail level, a good argument might be made that Bell could make up any profits lost due to CPE competition by raising the monopoly price of its services. But because telephone service itself was regulated, Bell not surprisingly looked to other, less regulated lines of business like CPE as places to earn additional profits.

3. Bell/Microsoft/Apple. How similar is the Bell CPE issue to the more recent claims that Microsoft or Apple has intentionally made it difficult for unaffiliated firms to develop software for the Windows operating system or for the iPhone and iPad, respectively? That is, as we ask immediately above, would not Microsoft be better off allowing competition in the software market, the argument being that high quality and low prices in the software market would drive demand for the operating system, and so it would

---

when he stops speaking, the radio returns to a receiving condition. A separate speaker is attached to the Carterfone to allow the base station operator to monitor the conversation, adjust the voice volume, and hang up when the conversation has ended." *Carterfone*, 13 F.C.C. 2d at 420–21. Eds.]

actually be in Microsoft's interest to allow competition in the software market so long as Microsoft could maintain its monopoly on the operating system? Or, in Apple's case, would it sell more products if it simply allowed all apps to be downloaded onto them? Note that Microsoft's and Apple's prices are not regulated. How, if at all, might that fact make a difference?

---

§ 6.D.2. Competition in Long Distance Telephony

At the same time that competition was emerging in the market for CPE, competition in the provision of interstate telephone service was also on the rise. This incipient competition resulted in part from the development of a new technology that eroded major barriers to entry in the long distance market: microwave transmission.

Why was the introduction of this technology so important? To be sure, Bell's monopoly over long distance telephony was supported by its control over local exchange service in most markets. But it was also supported by the high costs to an entrant of both obtaining the rights of way and digging the trenches needed to lay the transmission cable essential for providing telephone service. Microwave technology helped to reduce the entry barriers created by these two costs by greatly reducing the need to lay cable. A firm could transmit information by microwave, incurring only the more modest costs of constructing transmission and relay towers at sufficient intervals.

The FCC was at first resistant to new entry in the market for interstate communications. But in a 1959 decision, the Commission authorized the use of this new technology as part of a tailored form of interstate service called "private line service." Allocation of Frequencies in the Bands Above 890 MHz, Report and Order, 27 F.C.C. 359 (1959). Private line service allowed large corporations to customize transmission capacity to meet their specialized needs. Instead of using the traditional telephone system, these firms could use their own "private" service to, for example, transmit information from one branch office to another. Importantly, private line service was not generic long distance service. Private lines did not compete head-on with Bell long distance service because private lines served only particularly demanding users with peculiar transmission requirements.

Or so it was at first. Gradually, the FCC opened the door to more complete rival offerings. The coup de grace came in 1974 when the Commission required Bell to allow new private long distance networks to connect to Bell's local telephone grids, thereby making it possible for Bell's local customers to use the private, non-Bell alternatives for interexchange communication. Bell resisted this last change quite heavily, and that resistance was one of the behaviors emphasized in the antitrust case that followed.

Bell, of course, was resisting in part for anticompetitive reasons. No monopolist is happy to see competition begin to emerge. It should be emphasized, however, that Bell had a second reason to resist, and this one has much more policy allure. At the time, phone rates were heavily regulated, and those regulations intentionally pegged long distance rates at a level above the competitive rate. The idea was to allow Bell to earn extra profit in the long distance market such that local telephone rates could be kept artificially low. Given that, it is no surprise that private parties wanted to enter the long distance market; prices there were, by design, quite high. But that was the regulator's choice, not Bell's. If competition were allowed to drive down long-distance prices, prices for local phone service would have either had to rise correspondingly or be subsidized through some other mechanism.

§ 6.D.3. Communications and Computer Convergence

A third area in which the FCC tried to delimit the scope of Bell's monopoly and which can be seen as a precursor to the Bell breakup involved the technological convergence of computer and communications technology. In 1949, the government filed its second antitrust action against Bell, this time arguing that Bell had impermissibly used its patents on telecommunications equipment to monopolize "almost the entire telephone operating and manufacturing fields." Peter W. Huber et al., Federal Telecommunications Law 355 n.115 (2d ed. 1999) (quoting the government's complaint in United States v. Western Elec. Co., No. 17-49 (D.N.J. Jan. 14, 1949)). That case was settled in 1956, in large part because the Eisenhower administration was unsympathetic to the suit; the settlement at the time appeared to be a total victory for Bell. Under the settlement terms, Bell agreed that its manufacturing arm, Western Electric, would produce only equipment used in the provision of telecommunications services, and, further, that Bell itself would not engage "in any business other than the furnishing of common carrier communications services." United States v. Western Elec. Co., 1956 Trade Cas. (CCH) ¶ 68,246, ¶ 71,138 (D.N.J. 1956). These were seemingly token sacrifices; at the time, they represented Bell's approximate policies anyway.

As the market for computer services matured, however, the restrictions began to seem more binding. Bell scientists had invented the transistor—a key computer component—in 1947, and yet the 1956 decree seemed to bar Bell from participating in the industry that the transistor made possible. As Roger Noll and Bruce Owen put it, "with its leadership in semiconductor technology, Bell was positioned to be a very effective early competitor in computers; indeed, one can speculate that AT&T might well have been better off giving up the telephone but retaining its rights in transistors and computers." Roger Noll & Bruce Owen, The Anticompetitive Uses of Regulation: *United States v. AT&T*, *in* The Antitrust Revolution 294 (John E. Kwoka Jr. & Lawrence J. White, eds., 1989). Bell sought to offer services in new areas, and on several occasions, most notably 1980, the question arose whether that 1956 agreement really did prohibit Bell from providing so-called "advanced" services.

For example, in the early 1980s, large mainframe computers were very expensive both to build and to operate. Because of this, many firms wanted to pool their resources, building a single large computer and then sharing access to it. At the time, the easiest way to accomplish that sharing was to access the commonly owned computer over the telephone system, with each firm having a remote connection (a dummy terminal) that linked to the shared computer resource. But did the consent decree bar Bell from providing this sort of distributed computing service, or was this a permissible "common carrier communications service"? Questions like these did not admit easy answers, and as we will see later in Chapter Fourteen, they continued to vex the Commission as it tried to decide the extent to which Internet access should be considered a "telecommunications" service or something else for regulatory purposes.

With respect to the intersection of computing and telephone service in the 1970s and 1980s, the Commission recognized, on the one hand, that keeping Bell out of an unregulated market for data processing and computer services did not make sense. On the other hand, the Commission was concerned that Bell's control over the long-distance lines that connected users to mainframe computers, and those computers to each other, afforded Bell a potentially decisive advantage over other providers of computers and data processing services. The Commission tackled these thorny issues in its 1980 *Computer II* inquiry.

In *Computer II* the agency did two very important things: first, it deregulated all equipment used for "enhanced services" beyond basic telephone transmission and switching. Amendment of Section 64.702 of the Commission's Rules and Regulations (Second Computer Inquiry), Final Decision, 77 F.C.C. 2d 384 (1980) (*Computer II*). This was good for firms providing computers and data processing services because they would not be regulated in their connections with the Bell System. Second, however, *Computer II* freed Bell to enter into the provision of such enhanced services. *Id.* To address concerns that Bell's control over the underlying telephone network would allow it to handicap its advanced-services rivals, the Commission required Bell to set up a wholly separate corporate subsidiary to provide CPE and enhanced services. *Id.*

Notes and Questions

1. **Structural Separation.** Did the Commission adequately balance the benefits and harms when it chose to abandon attempts at line drawing and instead rely on structural separation? The benefit, of course, was that structural separation allowed the FCC to defer to market forces in the markets for both CPE and "enhanced" services. But the harm was a possibly significant loss of the efficiencies that would have been possible had Bell been allowed to integrate its telecommunications and computer arms.

2. **Regulatory Competence.** Beyond the issue of correct policy, does the FCC's change in course enhance or detract from your confidence in the regulatory process? Going into the next section, which discusses the use of antitrust to break up the Bell System, think about the oddity of one part of the federal government (the Justice Department) bringing a lawsuit that essentially says that another part of the government (the FCC) has not been able to effectively regulate the anticompetitive behavior of a company.

§ 6.E. Breaking Up Bell: The 1984 Divestiture

The most dramatic effort to limit the scope of the Bell System's monopoly took place in 1984 when, pursuant to a consent decree with the Department of Justice, Bell was broken up into several completely independent companies. The breakup followed from the government's filing of the aforementioned 1974 antitrust suit. The government was at that point dissatisfied with the state of competition and specifically complained that: (1) Bell was gaining an unfair advantage in the CPE, computer, and long distance markets because it could discriminate against rivals who needed access to Bell's local telephone exchanges in order to compete effectively; and (2) that Bell was manipulating the regulatory environment to gain unfair cost advantages, specifically by assigning some costs to its regulated/monopolistic markets even though those were in fact incurred in unregulated/competitive markets. Anticompetitive discrimination in interconnection and predatory cross-subsidization through cost misallocation were thus the cornerstones of what would become the lawsuit that brought down Bell.

The antitrust case itself took until 1981 to come to trial, ultimately before Judge Harold Greene of the United States District Court in Washington, D.C. Part way through the trial, Bell and the government submitted to Judge Greene a proposed consent decree to settle the case. Judge Greene thus never had an opportunity to rule on the merits of the government's antitrust claims, although he did reject Bell's motions to dismiss and for judgment at the close of the government's case. *See* United States v. AT&T, 524 F. Supp. 1336 (D.D.C. 1981); United States v. AT&T, 461 F. Supp. 1314 (D.D.C. 1978). Under the Tunney Act (codified at 15 U.S.C. §16), Greene could review the proposed consent decree only to determine whether its acceptance would be "in the public interest." Greene conducted that review, required several changes, and then accepted the decree as changed. That decree is known today as the "Modification of Final Judgment"—because it not only resolved the 1974 case but also modified the final judgment previously entered in 1956—and it is usually referred to simply as the MFJ.

The MFJ stripped Bell of its local exchange carriers but then freed the firm to provide long distance service, to manufacture equipment, and indeed to compete in virtually any market. Meanwhile, the agreement imposed strict limitations upon the now-separate local exchange carriers (LECs) in terms of their business ventures outside the provision of basic local telephone service. All of these results stemmed from a desire to keep the computer, telephone equipment, long distance, and enhanced services markets free of both discriminatory interconnection and predatory cross-subsidization.

The reading that follows is an excerpt from Judge Greene's opinion modifying, and then accepting as modified, the parties' proposed consent decree. On company names: Until now, we have referred to the pre-divestiture AT&T simply as "Bell." We used Bell only to make it easy for readers to distinguish the old monopolist from the post-divestiture AT&T that is still active today. Judge Greene, meanwhile, refers to the pre-divestiture monopolist as "the American Telegraph & Telephone Company" or simply "AT&T."

As you parse the consent decree, be careful to keep track of exactly which entity is under consideration. The post-divestiture AT&T was no longer the entire Bell System, but instead became a long-distance carrier (AT&T) and, through its Western Electric subsidiary, an equipment company. (That company ceased to exist, by stages, in the 1990s and 2000s.) The Bell Operating Companies (BOCs), meanwhile, are the subdivisions of Bell that provided local exchange service and, after divestiture, were separated from the long distance and equipment companies.

§6.E.1. The MFJ

UNITED STATES V. AMERICAN TELEPHONE & TELEGRAPH CO.
552 F. Supp. 131 (D.D.C. 1982),
aff'd sub nom., Maryland v. United States, 460 U.S. 1001 (1983)

GREENE, District Judge:

These actions are before the Court for a determination whether a consent decree proposed by the parties is in the "public interest" and should therefore be entered as the Court's judgment.

I. Preliminary Considerations

A. History of the Litigation

On January 14, 1949, the government filed an action in the District Court for the District of New Jersey against the Western Electric Company, Inc.[11] and the American Tele-

---

11. Western Electric is the wholly owned subsidiary of AT&T that manufactures telecommunications equipment for AT&T's Long Lines Department and the Operating Companies. In addition, Western Electric provides telecommunications equipment and services to government agencies and, to a limited extent, the independent telephone companies.

phone and Telegraph Company, Inc. The complaint alleged that the defendants had monopolized and conspired to restrain trade in the manufacture, distribution, sale, and installation of telephones, telephone apparatus, equipment, materials, and supplies, in violation of the Sherman Act. The relief sought included the divestiture by AT&T of its stock ownership in Western Electric; termination of exclusive relationships between AT&T and Western Electric; divestiture by Western Electric of its fifty percent interest in the Bell Telephone Laboratories research facility; separation of telephone manufacturing from the provision of telephone service; and the compulsory licensing of patents owned by AT&T on a non-discriminatory basis.

The [1956] consent decree which was the product of this process included neither the divestiture of Western Electric nor any of the other structural relief originally requested by the government. Instead, an injunction was issued which precluded AT&T from engaging in any business other than the provision of common carrier communications services; precluded Western Electric from manufacturing equipment other than that used by the Bell System; and required the defendants to license their patents to all applicants upon the payment of appropriate royalties.

This was the status of the Western Electric suit when the government filed a separate antitrust action on November 20, 1974, in this Court against AT&T, Western Electric, and Bell Telephone Laboratories, Inc. The complaint in the new action alleged monopolization by the defendants with respect to a broad variety of telecommunications services and equipment in violation of §2 of the Sherman Act. The government initially sought the divestiture from AT&T of the Bell Operating Companies (hereinafter generally referred to as Operating Companies or BOCs) as well as the divestiture and dissolution of Western Electric.

B. The Proposed Decree

Section I of the proposed decree would provide for significant structural changes in AT&T. In essence, it would remove from the Bell System the function of supplying local telephone service by requiring AT&T to divest itself of the portions of its twenty-two Operating Companies which perform that function.

Section II of the proposed decree would complement these structural changes by various restrictions which are said to be designed (1) to prevent the divested Operating Companies from discriminating against AT&T's competitors, and (2) to avoid a recurrence of the type of discrimination and cross-subsidization that were the basis of the AT&T lawsuit.

The first group of these provisions would require the divested Operating Companies to provide services to interexchange carriers equal in type, quality, and price to the services provided to AT&T and its affiliates. In addition, they would be prohibited from discriminating between AT&T and other companies in their procurement activities, the establishment of technical standards, the dissemination of technical information, their use of Operating Company facilities and charges for such use, and their network planning.

The second type of restriction imposed upon the Operating Companies is said to be intended to prevent them from engaging in any non-monopoly business so as to eliminate the possibility that they might use their control over exchange services to gain an improper advantage over competitors in such businesses. Thus, the Operating Companies would not be permitted (1) to manufacture or market telecommunications products and customer premises equipment; (2) to provide interexchange services; (3) to provide directory advertising such as the Yellow Pages; (4) to provide information services; and

(5) to provide any other product or service that is not a "natural monopoly actually regulated by tariff."

IV. The Divestiture

A. Conditions Necessitating Antitrust Relief

1. Evidence of Anticompetitive Actions by AT&T

The government asserted that AT&T monopolized the intercity telecommunications market and the telecommunications product market in a variety of ways in violation of the Sherman Act. The evidence that was produced during the AT&T trial indicates that, at least with respect to several of the government's claims, this charge may be well taken.

In its intercity case, the government alleged that AT&T used its control over its local monopoly to preclude competition in the intercity market. The government proved *inter alia* that after 1968 AT&T included a "customer premises" provision in its interconnection tariff which deterred potential competitors from entering that market; that it refused to provide FX and CCSA services to specialized common carriers and domestic satellite carriers until 1974 when the FCC specifically ordered it to do so;[12] and that it attempted to prevent competitors from offering metered long distance service that would compete with AT&T's own regular long distance service.

AT&T's basic rationale for these policies was that it was attempting to prevent competitors from "cream-skimming." As viewed by AT&T, it would have been able successfully to combat cream-skimming if it had priced each of its routes on the basis of the costs for operating that route. However, it concluded that the FCC had rejected this approach when it endorsed national rate averaging in the interest of promoting the goal of universal service. Accordingly, AT&T argued that, since rate averaging is inconsistent with competition, and since the basic rate averaging policy had been required by the FCC as being in the public interest, it was acting reasonably under the Communications Act in preventing competition as best and as long as it could.

What this line of reasoning fails to consider is that, at least by the mid-1970s, the FCC had clearly begun to promote competition in telecommunications. The government contended during the trial—correctly, in the Court's view—that AT&T had an obligation to follow the more recent FCC policy rather than previous policies which may have suited AT&T better, particularly since there was never a direct FCC rule against de-averaging.

What is significant about these events is that AT&T was able to adopt the policies described above in large part because of its control over the local exchange facilities. For example, it was because of its ownership and control of the local Operating Companies—whose facilities were and are needed for interconnection purposes by AT&T's competitors—that AT&T was able to prevent these competitors from offering FX and CCSA serv-

---

12. FX (foreign exchange) service permits a customer to make or receive local calls through a distant switching center by effectively providing a long extension cord in the form of a dedicated line between the customer's location and a telephone company switching system in the distant location (the foreign exchange). See United States v. AT&T, 524 F. Supp. 1336, 1355 n.77 (D.D.C. 1981). CCSA (common control switching arrangement) is essentially a miniature AT&T long distance network, except for the fact that it is used by only one customer, albeit a customer, such as the federal government, with large telecommunications needs.

ices. Similarly, AT&T was able to deter competition by manipulating prices for access to the Operating Company networks.

AT&T's control over the local Operating Companies was central also to the anticompetitive behavior alleged with respect to the second facet of the government's case, that involving customer-provided terminal equipment.

The government proved that AT&T prohibited the attachment of competitors' equipment to the network except through a protective connecting arrangement (PCA). There was evidence that some experts (including a panel of the National Academy of Sciences) believed that such a PCA was necessary if the nationwide telephone network was to be protected from a variety of harms. On the other hand, the government's evidence indicated that AT&T required PCAs for equipment that in all probability could not harm the network; that there were delays in providing PCAs; that the PCAs were over-designed and over-engineered, and, thus, over-priced; that PCAs were required for competitive equipment while identical equipment sold by AT&T did not require their use; and that PCAs could not guard against all of the harms to the network that AT&T professed to fear.

Additionally, the alternative option of certification was available but never seriously pursued by AT&T. Moreover, when ultimately certification was directly mandated by the FCC as a substitute for the protective connecting arrangement, the telephone network did not cease to function in its customary fashion. Indeed, AT&T was unable during the trial to prove any actual harm to the network from the elimination of the PCAs.

In its procurement part of the case, the government alleged, and there was proof, that AT&T used its control over the local Operating Companies to force them to buy products from Western Electric even though other equipment manufacturers produced better products or products of identical quality at lower prices. Here, too, AT&T's control of the Operating Companies was central to the allegedly anticompetitive behavior.[13]

B. Effect of the Divestiture

[T]he ability of AT&T to engage in anticompetitive conduct stems largely from its control of the local Operating Companies. Absent such control, AT&T will not have the ability to disadvantage competitors in the interexchange and equipment markets.

For example, with the divestiture of the Operating Companies, AT&T will not be able to discriminate against intercity competitors, either by subsidizing its own intercity services with revenues from the monopoly local exchange services, or by obstructing its competitors' access to the local exchange network. The local Operating Companies will not be providing interexchange services, and they will therefore have no incentive to discriminate. Moreover, AT&T's competitors will be guaranteed access that is equal to that provided to AT&T, and intercity carriers therefore will no longer be presented with the problems that confronted them in that area.

Abuses will also be unlikely in the equipment interconnection area, because the Operating Companies will not manufacture equipment and will therefore lack AT&T's incentive to favor the connection of one manufacturer's equipment over another's. Any pro-Western Electric bias on the part of these companies will be eliminated once the intra-enterprise relationship between the Operating Companies and Western Electric is broken.[14]

---

13. It should be noted, however, that the government's procurement case was not extremely strong.
14. Any cross subsidization of AT&T's intercity services and equipment manufacturing operations with revenue from its monopoly local exchange services will likewise be eliminated.

VII. Restrictions on the Divested Operating Companies

The proposed decree limits the Operating Companies, upon their divestiture, to the business of supplying local telephone service. In addition to a general prohibition against the provision of "any product or service that is not a natural monopoly service actually regulated by tariff," there are more specific restrictions that deny the Operating Companies the opportunity to engage in the following activities: (1) the provision of interexchange services; (2) the provision of information services; (3) the manufacture of telecommunications products and customer premises equipment; (4) the marketing of such equipment; and (5) directory advertising, including the production of the "Yellow Pages" directories.

A. Interexchange Services

To permit the Operating Companies to compete in this market would be to undermine the very purpose of the proposed decree—to create a truly competitive environment in the telecommunications industry. The key to interexchange competition is the full implementation of the decree's equal exchange access provisions. If the Operating Companies were free to provide interexchange service in competition with the other carriers, they would have substantial incentives to subvert these equal access requirements.

B. Information Services

The proposed decree prohibits the Operating Companies from providing information services, an umbrella description of a variety of services including electronic publishing and other enhanced uses of telecommunications.

All information services are provided directly via the telecommunications network. Here, too, the Operating Companies could discriminate by providing more favorable access to the local network for their own information services than to the information services provided by competitors, and here, too, they would be able to subsidize the prices of their services with revenues from the local exchange monopoly.

C. Manufacture of Equipment

There is a substantial likelihood that, should the Operating Companies be permitted to manufacture telecommunications equipment, nonaffiliated manufacturers would be disadvantaged in the sale of such equipment and the development of a competitive market would be frustrated. The Operating Companies would have an incentive to subsidize the prices of their equipment with the revenues from their monopoly services as well as to purchase their own equipment, even though it was more expensive and not of the highest quality. In that respect, the Operating Companies lack the competitive restraints that ordinarily prevent the typical vertically integrated company from engaging in such practices: the absence of competition in the end product market—exchange telecommunications—immunizes these purchasing decisions from competitive pressures. The Operating Companies therefore would be able to pay inflated prices for poor quality equipment and to reflect these costs in their rates without suffering a diminution in revenues.[15]

Moreover, if they were permitted to manufacture CPE, the Operating Companies would have substantial incentives to favor their own manufacturing arms by providing to

---

15. This rationale does not require the divestiture of Western Electric from the Bell System because AT&T's end products—interexchange services and information services—will be subject to competitive pressures. If AT&T paid a higher price for its equipment and that cost was reflected in higher rates, consumers would switch to a carrier with prices which reflected purchasing decisions based upon the principles of best quality and least cost.

them information regarding changes in network standards, thus permitting them to gain an advantage over non-affiliated manufacturers. In addition, they could subsidize the price of this equipment with revenues from the exchange monopoly.

F. Removal of the Restrictions

It is probable that, over time, the Operating Companies will lose the ability to leverage their monopoly power into the competitive markets from which they must now be barred. This change could occur as a result of technological developments which eliminate the Operating Companies' local exchange monopoly or from changes in the structures of the competitive markets. Thus, a restriction will be removed upon a showing that there is no substantial possibility that an Operating Company could use its monopoly power to impede competition in the relevant market.

XII. Conclusion

The American telecommunications industry is presently dominated by one company: AT&T. It provides local and long distance telephone service; it manufactures and markets the equipment used by telephone subscribers as well as that used in the telecommunications network; and it controls one of the leading communications research and development facilities in the world. According to credible evidence, this integrated structure has enabled AT&T for many years to undermine the efforts of competitors seeking to enter the telecommunications market.

The key to the Bell System's power to impede competition has been its control of local telephone service. The local telephone network functions as the gateway to individual telephone subscribers. It must be used by long distance carriers seeking to connect one caller to another. Customers will only purchase equipment which can readily be connected to the local network through the telephone outlets in their homes and offices. The enormous cost of the wires, cables, switches, and other transmission facilities which comprise that network has completely insulated it from competition. Thus, access to AT&T's local network is crucial if long distance carriers and equipment manufacturers are to be viable competitors.

AT&T has allegedly used its control of this local monopoly to disadvantage these competitors in two principal ways. First, it has attempted to prevent competing long distance carriers and competing equipment manufacturers from gaining access to the local network, or to delay that access, thus placing them in an inferior position vis-à-vis AT&T's own services. Second, it has supposedly used profits earned from the monopoly local telephone operations to subsidize its long distance and equipment businesses in which it was competing with others.

The divestiture of the local Operating Companies from the Bell System will sever the relationship between this local monopoly and the other, competitive segments of AT&T, and it will thus ensure—certainly better than could any other type of relief—that the practices which allegedly have lain heavy on the telecommunications industry will not recur.

With the loss of control over the local network, AT&T will be unable to disadvantage its competitors, and the restrictions imposed on AT&T after the government's earlier antitrust suit—which limited AT&T to the provision of telecommunications services—will no longer be necessary.

The decree will thus allow AT&T to become a vigorous competitor in the growing computer, computer-related, and information markets. Other large and experienced firms are presently operating in these markets, and there is therefore no reason to believe that AT&T will be able to achieve monopoly dominance in these industries as it did in telecommunications. At the same time, by use of its formidable scientific, engineering, and management resources, including particularly the capabilities of Bell Laboratories, AT&T should be able to make significant contributions to these fields, which are at the forefront of innovation and technology, to the benefit of American consumers, national defense, and the position of American industry vis-à-vis foreign competition.[16]

After the divestiture, however, the Operating Companies will possess a monopoly over local telephone service. Therefore, the Operating Companies should be prohibited from providing long distance services and information services, and from manufacturing equipment used in the telecommunications industry. Participation in these fields carries with it a substantial risk that the Operating Companies would use the same anticompetitive techniques used by AT&T in order to thwart the growth of their own competitors. Moreover, contrary to the assumptions made by some, Operating Company involvement in these areas could not legitimately generate subsidies for local rates. Such involvement could produce substantial profits only if the local companies used their monopoly position to dislodge competitors or to provide subsidies for their competitive services or products—the very behavior the decree seeks to prevent.

Different considerations apply, however, to the marketing of customer premises equipment—the telephone and other devices used in subscribers' homes and offices—and the production of the Yellow Pages advertising directories. For a variety of reasons, there is little likelihood that these companies will be able to use their monopoly position to disadvantage competitors in these areas. In addition, their marketing of equipment will provide needed competition for AT&T, and the elimination of the restriction on their production of the Yellow Pages will generate a substantial subsidy for local telephone rates.[17]

§ 6.E.2 Discussion of the Government's Theory

The two main charges leveled against Bell were predatory cross-subsidization and discriminatory interconnection. To better understand these charges, consider two possible competitors to Bell: a firm that manufactures and sells interactive data processing telephones (let's call them computer phones), and an ordinary hot dog stand.

(1) *Predatory cross-subsidization*. In Judge Greene's opinion, the cross-subsidization claim is framed as follows: because Bell was not effectively controlled by price regulation, it was able to earn monopoly profits from its ownership of local exchange carriers; Bell could use, or threaten to use, those monopoly profits to subsidize below-cost pricing in other markets. In the context of our simple example, the argument would be that Bell could sell its computer phones below cost due to its monopoly profits from local exchange service, driving out any would-be competitor not on the merits of its computer phone but simply because Bell had such large cash reserves that it could subsidize this form of anticompetitive behavior.

That characterization of the cross-subsidization argument is problematic, however, in that it implies that Bell could use the same tactic in *any* market. That is, with the kind of

---

16. [The court reiterated, however, its view that competitive and First Amendment concerns justified a seven-year ban on AT&T's entry into electronic publishing. Eds.]

17. The decree also provides for another method of subsidizing these rates. It permits the Operating Companies, under the supervision of state and federal regulators, to levy access charges upon long distance carriers and those companies that provide information services. These charges may, if the regulators desire, be set at levels which continue the present level of subsidy for local telephone rates.

cross-subsidization described above, why couldn't Bell use its monopoly profits to subsidize the costs not only of long distance telephony but also of hot dog production, selling Bell hot dogs at prices below cost and driving Oscar Mayer out of the hot dog business? That, in fact, was not the government's theory; and so it is important to understand how the government's actual argument distinguished computer phones from hot dogs.

The key insight for understanding the government's theory of the case is this: the government's claim is not that Bell could monopolize computer phones because it had a lot of money. It does not ordinarily make sense for a company to sell its products below cost. Even cash-rich firms do not like to waste money. Rather, the government's claim was that Bell could sell computer phones below cost but nevertheless not lose money. Bell could, as an accounting matter, shift costs from the competitive computer phone market to its regulated local exchange business. If additional costs in the regulated business were simply factored into the rate base and thereby produced additional revenue in the regulated market (as ordinarily would be the case with rate-of-return regulation), then Bell could both recover its costs incurred in the competitive market and enjoy a competitive advantage in that market.

Here's how the scheme would work. If some of the costs of manufacturing computer phones could show up on Bell's books as costs of running the local exchange service, then the firm could underprice computer phones but recoup the difference by raising local telephone rates. Bell's captive local telephone customers would in essence subsidize prices for Bell's not-at-all-captive computer phone customers. Bell could get away with this cost shifting because the phony costs would be so similar to costs legitimately incurred in the provision of local telephone service that, to some extent at least, Bell's regulators would not notice. Charges related to the production of hot dog buns would be obvious to even the least competent regulator; but costs related to computer phones might be hard to distinguish from costs legitimately incurred in developing and maintaining the local telephone system. That is the subterfuge that makes "cross-subsidization" possible. Bell was in a special situation because it could use a regulated market to subsidize costs from a competitive one—something General Motors, McDonald's, and Oscar Mayer cannot do.

This wrinkle in the cross-subsidy theory is also the theory's Achilles heel: if cross-subsidy is a realistic fear only in cases where it may be difficult to sort out improper from proper cost accounting, then there is always a risk that legitimate cost accounting might be condemned (inadvertently) as predatory. To return to computer phones, suppose that there are economies of scope in making computer phones such that it is cheaper for a firm to make computer phones if the firm also runs a local exchange service. Perhaps, for example, expenditures to design and configure the local telephone network also help a firm to design and configure computer phones. If Bell were to allocate some of these joint costs to local service, is that a predatory act against competing computer phone makers? If not, how will regulators or antitrust authorities know which acts are predatory and which are not? Has the regulated firm engaged in illegal predation every time it allocates costs in a manner that regulators subsequently deem inappropriate?

In any event, note that there are several preconditions that must be satisfied before a firm like Bell has an incentive to engage in predatory cross-subsidization. First, the firm has to have a dominant position in a market where demand is relatively inelastic. That is, the theory requires that the firm raise prices in its regulated market, something the firm would not want to do if those higher prices would cause its customers to leave in droves. Second, rate regulation has to be such that the regulator allows the regulated firm to increase its price only if the firm can show increased costs. Without that link between its asserted costs and the regulated price, the regulated firm would have had no reason to misallocate its costs because claiming higher costs in the regulated market would not accomplish anything for the firm. Third, there has to exist a competitive market with sufficiently overlapping costs such that the firm can incur costs in that competitive market but persuade regulators that those costs should be attributed to the regulated market instead. In Bell's case, for example, the market for hot dogs would not have sufficed. Arguably, however, the markets for computer equipment, CPE, and long distance service did.

(2) *Discriminatory interconnection.* The second major charge leveled against Bell was that Bell used its monopoly over local exchange services to deny competitors in other markets (for example, computer phones) necessary access to the local exchange. The claim, in short, is that Bell raised its rivals' costs; or, in other words, that Bell was able to sell computer phones more cheaply because its costs of interconnection were lower. While subsidization claims focus on cost allocation as an accounting matter, discrimination claims focus on engineering and technology issues related to local exchange service itself.

Discriminatory interconnection is relevant only in instances where access to the monopolized telecommunications service (here, the local loop) is crucial to success in some otherwise-competitive market. Thus, if Bell said that only Bell computer phones could be connected to Bell-owned local exchanges, Bell might well gain a monopoly over computer phone sales. People would not want to buy computer phones that could not be connected to the phone system. But Bell could not plausibly threaten to obtain a monopoly in selling hot dogs by refusing to provide phone service to non-Bell hot dog stands. One can operate a hot dog stand without connecting it to the phone system.

An important question to ask when considering the discrimination theory is the question we briefly mentioned in the context of the market for CPE, namely: why would Bell try to expand its monopoly in local phone service provision into some related competitive market? Think, for example, about computer phones. Would Bell have been better off allowing for competitive provision of computer phones, since more competition would lead to better computer phones and hence more demand for local service? The problem for Bell was that it would not have been able to extract the value of efficiency gains by raising the prices it charged for local phone service, because regulation constrained its ability to raise those prices.

Thus, again, it is the fact that Bell was regulated in one market that made anticompetitive behavior attractive in another. If Bell could have exercised its monopoly power unchecked in the local exchange market, it is very possible that Bell would not have engaged in discriminatory interconnection. Competition in computer phones would have led to increased demand for telephone service; and Bell would have adjusted its price and reaped rewards accordingly. Because Bell was constrained in the local exchange market, however, Bell had good reason to try to shift its market power from the regulated market to a competitive one where that power could be exercised more freely.

Notes and Questions

1. The Importance of Being Regulated. During all of its alleged bad acts, Bell was a regulated firm. Why was that not an absolute defense to the antitrust charge? That is, if Bell was doing something wrong, was it not the fault of the regulators for either not regulating correctly or not enforcing their regulations? Is it wrong to allow the government two bites at the apple: one through regulation and then a second through antitrust litigation?

2. New Entities. The divestiture gave rise to seven Regional Bell Operating Companies (RBOCs), also called Regional Holding Companies (RHCs) or simply Baby Bells. As the RBOC moniker suggests, these were regional combinations of BOCs. The Justice Department and AT&T discussed breaking Bell up into just two companies—one long-distance and manufacturing and one, nationwide local company. It was thought that having seven, separate regional companies would allow the companies to have appropriate scale but also allow regulators to begin to benchmark the companies against one another.

3. LATAs. The MFJ broke telephone service into small geographic regions called local access and transport areas (LATAs). Calls that originated and terminated within a single LATA were called intraLATA and were to be carried by the relevant local phone company—either a divested BOC or an unaffiliated competitor. IntraLATA calls could show up on customer bills as local calls, but they could also show up as "in-state long distance"; the precise rates and categories were determined by the local phone company subject to approval by the applicable state public utility commission. InterLATA calls, by contrast, were calls that crossed LATA boundaries. BOCs, and the RBOCs that owned them, were forbidden to carry interLATA traffic, and so these calls had to be handed off to interexchange carriers (IXCs) like MCI, Sprint, and the post-divestiture AT&T. One way to think about LATAs is to remember that the MFJ in essence quarantined the local telephone market, and LATAs were the boundary lines of that quarantine.

4. Equal Access. Part VIII of the MFJ is labeled "equal exchange access" and, in this section, Judge Greene considers the obligations to be imposed upon the BOCs with respect to their treatment of interexchange carriers. Judge Greene points out that, prior to divestiture, significant "bias [had] been designed into the integrated telecommunications network" and thus, in Judge Greene's view, it was "imperative that any disparities in interconnection be eliminated so that all interexchange and information service providers will be able to compete on an equal basis." 552 F. Supp. at 195. Equal-access rules were the decree's means for accomplishing just that, ensuring that AT&T would not enjoy an artificial advantage in the long-distance market after divestiture. As the Commission later explained the rule:

> Equal access not only ensured that IXCs would receive equal transmission quality, but also that callers would have the opportunity to pre-subscribe their telephones to an IXC other than AT&T. Before the advent of equal access, all interstate calls dialed on a 1+ basis were routed to AT&T. A caller could reach an [alternative carrier] only by dialing a seven-digit phone number, as well as an often-lengthy identification code, prior to dialing the called number. Equal access enabled callers to select a carrier other than AT&T to provide them long-distance phone service on a simple "1+" dialing basis. Moreover, the balloting process through which equal access was implemented educated customers as to the availability of alternative suppliers of telecommunications services and encouraged them to make a choice among IXCs.

Competition in the Interstate Interexchange Marketplace, Notice of Proposed Rulemaking, 5 FCC Rcd. 2627, ¶ 41 (1990).

The BOCs were not the only local exchange carriers required to grant equal access to long distance companies. In 1985, the FCC extended that obligation to all independent local exchange carriers, basing its decision in part on a 1983 consent decree between the government and a large independent LEC in which that LEC had agreed, like the BOCs in the MFJ, to provide equal access. MTS and WATS Market Structure Phase III, Report and Order, 100 F.C.C. 2d 860, ¶ 9 (1985). The Commission's 1985 decision thus evened the playing field, applying the same equal-access requirement to all LECs whether they were subject to a particular consent decree or not.

5. Other Solutions. Focus on the government's claim that Bell might be using its local phone service monopoly to subsidize its activities in the possibly competitive market for CPE. Instead of solving this problem by divestiture, could the government have solved it by changing the way it regulated prices in the local telephone market? For instance, why not set prices without regard to costs, in that way eliminating Bell's incentive to misallocate its costs from competitive to regulated markets? Alternatively, could the danger have been eliminated by somehow introducing competition into the market for local exchange service? What about by allowing new entry into the market for CPE?

6. Alternatives to the MFJ. Overall, were preferable alternatives to the breakup of the Bell System overlooked? How about:

(a) Confining the relief to divestiture of Western Electric and Bell Laboratories (to rid Bell of its incentive to monopolize CPE) and adoption of the equal-access rules in the decree (to level the playing field in the long distance market);

(b) Going through with divestiture, but refusing to shackle the new BOCs;

(c) Leaving all of these issues to the FCC. The Commission could continue its technical registration program for CPE; develop and implement equal-access rules for long-distance service providers; monitor Bell's prices and costs; and so on;

(d) Spending these energies on attacking the problem at its source—the absence of competition in the local exchange service. (Does the growth of cell phone and cable television services suggest that this might have been a fruitful strategy?); or

(e) Treating the phone system as we treat highways: have the government (or a private/public corporation) build and operate the network of wires and switches, and leave the provision of equipment and services to others.

7. Allocating Cellular. In its initial complaint, the Justice Department took the position that Bell was also using its control over the local exchange to injure the cellular telephony market. But when it came time to allocate cellular licenses, the Decree allocated them to the BOCs, defining such services as part of "exchange" communications and not allocating them to AT&T under the theory that they were potentially competitive services. *See* U.S. Department of Justice, Response to Public Comments on Proposed Modification of Final Judgment, 47 Fed. Reg. 23,320 (May 27, 1982). In 1982, cellular systems did use the local exchange significantly to complete calls and to provide internal connections between towers and switches in the cellular network. But allocating them to non-BOCs may have given a boost to the development of alternative infrastructures, and would have anticipated the current market in which cellular telephony and landline telephony are at least partial competitors.

8. Administering the Decree. The MFJ might sound as if it was a document designed to end the Bell antitrust litigation. In reality, all parties to the case knew that the MFJ would need to be adjusted over time. Experience would teach which restrictions were too broad or too onerous, and changes in market conditions would make some once-reasonable restrictions unnecessary in later years. To handle all this, Judge Greene maintained significant flexibility both to eliminate decree provisions and to grant specific waivers, either in response to a request by one of the parties or completely of his own accord. The Bell System divestiture thus remained on Judge Greene's docket from 1982, the year he first approved the consent decree, until 1996, when the Telecommunications Act of 1996 explicitly took Judge Greene out of the telecommunications business.

9. MFJ Waivers. Almost as soon as the MFJ was in effect, the RBOCs began to seek waivers of the decree's restriction; they sought literally hundreds of such waivers. From 1984 to 1996, when Congress repealed the MFJ in the Telecommunications Act of 1996, Judge Greene effectively sat as a one-person telephony regulator, granting nearly three hundred waivers over the life of the decree. Bell South Corp. v. FCC, 162 F.3d 678, 681 (D.C. Cir. 1998). But those waiver grants tell only a fraction of the story, for the judge denied far more petitions than he granted.[18] Not surprisingly, the waiver requests involved hundreds of detailed questions whose answers were unclear under the necessarily blunt decree: Did a 5% ownership stake by an RBOC in a small equipment manufacturer violate the equipment ban? (Judge Greene decided yes.) Did a BOC violate the long-distance ban by transporting information necessary for its own, internal operations across LATA boundaries over its own facilities? (No.) Could a BOC provide time-of-day or weather information without violating the information services restriction? (Yes.) Most often the questions at issue were very narrow and technical. Other times, however, the RBOCs sought more fundamental relief, such as relaxation of the long-distance restriction to permit out-of-region service. While the RBOCs were successful in getting relief on a number of peripheral matters, Judge Greene never willingly budged from the core restrictions and generally gave those fairly broad interpretations.

10. Removal or Modification of MFJ Restrictions. The MFJ's line-of-business limitations were not written in stone—there was a process by which the court could modify or lift them. The MFJ provided that the Department of Justice would report to the District Court every three years on the continuing need for the restrictions and that the District Court would then consider the report, hold hearings, and act as it believed the evidence warranted. In 1990 the U.S. Court of Appeals issued its decision reviewing Judge Green's first Triennial review decision. United States v. Western Elec. Co., 900 F.2d 283 (D.C. Cir. 1990).

The D.C. Circuit by and large affirmed Judge Greene's decisions in the first Triennial Review proceedings, with one very important exception. The appeals court ruled that Judge Greene had not justified his decision to keep the information services restriction in place. The district court had found "no significant, relevant change in" market conditions justifying removal of this restraint. The court of appeals remanded this issue to the district court for reconsideration on grounds that Judge Greene had used too stringent a standard of review for removal of the information services restrictions. It was important to the court of appeals that the lifting of that restriction had not only been uncontested by the DOJ, but indeed advocated. On remand, the district court determined that under the standard set out by the court of appeals it had no choice under the facts but to lift the information services restriction. The court of appeals, on review of the district court's remand decision, affirmed the result as justified by the applicable facts even while finding that the district court incorrectly interpreted the standard for lifting the line-of-business restrictions. United States v. Western Elec. Co., 993 F.2d 1572 (D.C. Cir. 1993). In clarifying the appropriate standard of review, the D.C. Circuit, per Judge Stephen Williams (who would strongly influence telecommunications policy under the 1996 Act), held that "[t]he district court may reject an uncontested modification only if it has exceptional confidence that adverse antitrust consequences will result—perhaps akin to the confidence that would justify a court in overturning the predictive judgments of an administrative agency." *Id.* at 1577. The appeals court thus affirmed elimination of the information services decree. The main restrictions of the MFJ remained in force, however, until the 1996 Act vacated the decree in its entirety.

---

18. For a discussion of the standards by which Judge Greene was to evaluate any proposed waivers or modifications, *see* Huber et al. at 386–91.

11. *Computer III* and FCC Line-of-Business Regulation. As we noted previously, in *Computer II* the FCC had imposed "structural separation" rules requiring Bell companies to provide "enhanced" services through separate subsidiaries. In a 1986 proceeding known as *Computer III*, the Commission returned to the issue post-divestiture and ruled that the divested BOCs should no longer be required to maintain corporate separation between their common carrier communications services and the unregulated provision of enhanced or data processing services over the telecommunications network. Amendment of Sections 64.702 of the Commission's Rules and Regulations (Third Computer Inquiry), Report and Order, 104 F.C.C. 2d 958 (1986) (*Computer III*). As the Ninth Circuit Court of Appeals described the Commission's rationale:

> The FCC decided that its structural separation regulations had imposed costs in terms of the unavailability of certain services, lost economies and efficiencies, and the inability of customers to obtain complete telecommunications and data processing solutions from a single vendor. The FCC also determined that the BOCs' ability to cross-subsidize had been restricted because of divestiture, the growth of competitive alternatives to the BOCs' ordinary telephone service, and political and regulatory pressures at the state level to keep local phone rates down. The BOCs' ability to discriminate by providing inferior network access had also diminished, according to the FCC, because of industry-wide coordination of network standards and the threat that enhanced services competitors could bypass the BOCs' local exchanges.

California v. FCC, 905 F.2d 1217 (9th Cir. 1990).

The Ninth Circuit reversed and remanded the decision to end structural separation as arbitrary and capricious on the record presented. The agency, in turn, reaffirmed its *Computer III* rules, albeit with further explanation specifically tailored to respond to the court's criticisms. *See* Computer III Remand Proceedings: Bell Operating Company Safeguards and Tier 1 Local Exchange Company Safeguards, Report and Order, 6 FCC Rcd. 7571 (1991). The Ninth Circuit again rejected as inadequate the FCC's cost-benefit analysis of ending structural separation requirements. California v. FCC, 39 F.3d 919 (9th Cir. 1994). The back-and-forth ended only in 1996, when the Telecommunications Act of 1996 established an entirely new set of restrictions and thus mooted these debates.

Chapter Seven

Control of Telephone Monopolies

Introduction

This chapter describes several phases in the regulatory control of telephone monopolies, which, as noted, can be applied more generally to other communications or utility monopolies. The chapter first discusses rate regulation: the attempt by government agencies to directly monitor the prices set by telephone carriers. Rate regulation may seem to be the most direct response to the phenomenon of natural monopoly, and for a significant period of time telecommunications regulators did rely heavily on reviewing and limiting carriers' rates. Here, we consider the techniques of rate regulation, which have varied, and their various costs and challenges. Rate regulation was intimately tied to ideas of universal service—the idea that telecommunications was a utility service that everyone should enjoy, but we defer discussion of universal service until Chapter Thirteen. Second, the chapter introduces the quite different regulatory scheme advanced by the Telecommunications Act of 1996, which not only sought to control local monopolies but introduced regulatory tools intended to break down any residual local monopoly.

§ 7.A. Rate Regulation

Although the precise scope of the Bell monopoly was always a matter of dispute, there was never any doubt that the provision of local telephone service and, for several decades at least, the provision of long distance service were both part of Bell's allowable monopoly franchise. The regulatory priority for these monopoly services, then, was simply to constrain their prices. But how?

Two primary strategies were used. The first, known as "cost of service" or "rate of return" regulation, is a regulatory approach under which rates are based on the costs incurred by the regulated party. If the regulated party can show higher costs, the regulator approves correspondingly higher rates. The second, "price cap" regulation, distances itself from cost estimates. This time, an initial maximum price is set with an eye toward likely costs, but after that the maximum price stays the same over a longer period than under rate of return regulation regardless of whether costs rise or fall.

Of these two kinds of price restraints, rate of return regulation is the older and more traditional method. In the past few decades, however, regulators have increasingly migrated to the price cap model, for reasons that will become apparent below.

§ 7.A.1. Rate of Return Regulation

Under rate of return regulation, prices in the regulated market are based on the costs incurred by the regulated party. Suppose, for instance, that the regulated party can prove that it spends $10 per customer on labor to provide the regulated service and that it had to invest another $5 million to build the relevant physical infrastructure. Under rate of return regulation, the regulator would allow a price that (a) let the regulated party recover in full its $10 marginal costs and (b) let the regulated party in addition earn a return on its $5 million investment. The rate of return would in theory be set so as to match comparable market investments. That is, if investments in unregulated but comparable industries would typically yield a yearly 8% return on investment, regulators would attempt to approve prices such that here, too, that $5 million would return at approximately the 8% rate.

Note that the above discussion keeps referring to regulators "approving" rates rather than setting them. That is because the typical process under rate of return regulation is to have the regulated party propose a price and then have the regulator approve or disapprove that price. More specifically, the regulated party submits a document known as a tariff, and in that document it puts forward information about the service, the costs of providing that service, and the proposed pricing. Tariffs are then made available to the public and evaluated by the relevant regulator—here, state public utilities commissions. Under the Communications Act and most state statutes, the carrier's proposed rates take effect a relatively short time after they are filed, unless the regulator affirmatively acts to suspend them, pending investigation, or rejects them.

The fact that rate of return regulation is based on the regulated firm's costs raises an obvious problem: the critical information—information about costs—is hard for the regulator to verify, and thus the regulated party has a significant ability to manipulate the numbers and in that way influence the regulatory result. This was a particularly serious problem in the days when Bell was the only national telephone service provider. In those days, there were no "rival" firms against whose numbers Bell's numbers could be compared.

Even in cases where regulators can obtain accurate cost data, rate regulation raises several additional perplexing problems. Start with the difficulty of allocating costs. Regulators must divide a firm's costs into three categories: costs that may be passed on to consumers and on which the firm is allowed to earn a return; costs that may be passed through to consumers but on which regulators do not allow a return; and costs that the firm may not pass through at all to consumers. Typically, regulators allow firms a return on things like expenditures on physical capital and the costs of financing the firm operations. Firms may pass through, but not earn a return on, expenditures like tax payments, labor wages, and energy costs. These are real costs but not capital costs. Firms may not pass through the costs of advertising, executive pay bonuses, or investments that regulators deem "imprudent."[1] Decisions to disallow "imprudent" costs often protect consumers from bearing costs that the monopoly could never pass through if it faced competition, but they also are vulnerable to hindsight bias. A regulator who knows that a given investment turned out poorly might punish the relevant firm even though, at the time, the decision to invest was honest, efficient, and well-reasoned.

---

1. For example, the California Public Utilities Commission excluded from the rate base nearly 80 percent of the costs Pacific Gas & Electric incurred in building the Diablo Canyon Nuclear Power Plant because it believed that "unreasonable management was to blame for a large part of [the] cost overrun." State of California, Public Utilities Commission Annual Report 1986–1987, at 13 (1987).

Another problem with rate of return regulation is that it leaves the regulated party with little incentive to economize on its expenditures. After all, so long as the firm appears to be incurring reasonable costs—and, realistically, how well can the regulator distinguish reasonable from unreasonable expenses?—under rate of return regulation the firm will be allowed to increase its prices and in that way recoup those investments. Firms regulated under rate of return regulation are thus often accused of "gold-plating"—figuratively, using expensive gold wire when simple copper would do.

As the FCC noted in an order moving away from rate of return regulation,

> In a competitive environment, where prices are dictated by the market, a company's unit costs and profits generally are related inversely. If one goes up, the other goes down. Rate of return regulation stands this relationship on its head. Although carriers subject to such regulation are limited to earning a particular percentage return on investment during a fixed period, a carrier seeking to increase its dollar earnings often can do so merely by increasing its aggregate investment. In other words, under a rate of return regime, profits (i.e., dollar earnings) can go up when investment goes up. This creates a powerful incentive for carriers to "pad" their costs, regardless of whether additional investment is necessary or efficient.

Policy and Rules Concerning Rates for Dominant Carriers, Report and Order and Second Further Notice of Proposed Rulemaking, 4 FCC Rcd. 2873 ¶ 30 (1989).

Gold-plating is not as bad a problem as it might at first appear, however, and the reason is that there is often time between a change in costs and the corresponding change in the regulated price. For instance, if costs are at a certain level in January and, at that time, the regulator approves particular local telephone prices effective January through October, the telephone provider has some incentive to economize on its expenses. Any cost savings accomplished during that time period translates into increased profits. Those profits will be lost once the government resets prices so as to reflect the new, presumably lower costs; but, during the time lag between changes in costs and changes in the approved schedule of prices, even a firm regulated under rate of return regulation can in theory have some incentive to spend wisely.

Firms regulated under rate of return principles not only have a dampened incentive to minimize costs; they also have strong incentives to pretend that costs incurred as part of other services were actually incurred as part of the regulated service. Suppose, for example, that a telephone provider has to incur a significant expense in order to upgrade its infrastructure to provide Internet service. If the firm can make the regulator think that this expense was incurred in order to provide a regulated service (say, local telephone service), the firm will be able to recoup this cost by raising local telephone prices and thus will have an unfair advantage when it comes to competing in the market for Internet service provision. Note that, unlike the gold-plating example, expenses incurred in this example are not necessarily wasteful or inefficient; the problem here is that the regulation is being used to gain an unearned advantage in a related, unregulated market.

A final limitation of rate of return regulation derives from the fact that regulators tend to require long depreciation periods for physical plant investments. From the perspective of a state regulator, for example, a decision to allow a switch to be depreciated over ten years as opposed to, say, five years means that the regulated company's cost structure will be lower (because it will have to wait longer before buying a new switch). If, as is often the case, regulators are primarily concerned with keeping rates low, there is a very strong temptation to adopt artificially long depreciation schedules. That might be fine, but it does mean that out-of-date equipment will often remain in use much longer than it would in a competitive industry. In competitive sectors, after all, firms are not given the luxury of living by depreciation schedules. (For example, when MCI and Sprint invested in new long haul facilities that used fiber optic technology—and advertised the ability to hear a pin drop when making calls on their networks—AT&T had no choice other than to write off its undepreciated investment in its antiquated microwave network.)

§ 7.A.2. Price Cap Regulation

Under price cap regulation, the government regulates by announcing the maximum price that will be allowed for a given service and, usually, by further specifying a formula under which that price will automatically adjust over time given, say, expected efficiency improvements and inflation. Price cap regulation can be accomplished in other ways as well. For instance, instead of specifying a cap for each regulated service, the government might announce a maximum average price for a group of services, in that way leaving the regulated party a little more flexibility in its price setting decisions.[2] The key intuition behind price cap regulation is that the government's maximum price does not vary closely with the regulated party's costs. If the regulated party can lower its costs, it can maintain its price and keep the extra profit for itself. The main allure of price cap regulation is thus that, like competition, price cap regulation creates a strong incentive for regulated firms to minimize their costs.

That said, note that price cap works only if the government genuinely commits not to change the cap in light of changed circumstances. That commitment turns out to be hard to maintain. If costs drop precipitously, there is typically political pressure to lower the price cap accordingly and shift some of those savings (which become firm profits under a price cap) to customers. If costs skyrocket, the pressure goes in the other direction, as service providers pressure the government for relief from the cap. The more the price cap responds to these sorts of cost-based factors, the more price cap begins to mimic rate of return regulation. Judicial review can potentially solve this problem, holding the regulator's feet to the fire despite these sorts of political pressures.

Another wrinkle to consider with respect to price caps is the worry that they might cause firms to skimp on quality—the opposite of gold-plating. After all, there are two ways to reduce costs: one is by identifying efficiency-enhancing improvements, but the other is by degrading the service. Strategic service degradation is a difficult strategy to thwart. Competition prevents this sort of thing in a normal market, but the markets at issue here are monopolies. The regulator can in theory stop this response by defining and requiring a specific level of service. Indeed, many states that migrated to price cap regulation later developed retail quality of service standards that specified levels of expected performance. That said, this sort of regulatory oversight is imperfect, and some regulated firms may well profit from the strategy of "starving the network" even in the face of retail quality of service regulation.

§ 7.A.3. Rate Regulation as Markets Become Competitive

One of the major challenges that regulators face is managing rate regulation as markets make the transition from regulated monopolies to more competitive structures. Given

---

2. A helpful analogy here might be to think of the salary cap in professional football. The teams are to a large degree free to set salaries for individual players, but the NFL constrains the maximum amount of money a team can pay its players in a given season. The league, in other words, sets a price cap on the group of salaries but not on any salary in particular.

that the lack of competition is generally the reason an industry is regulated to begin with, one might think that rate regulation should end with the arrival of competition. Generally, this presumption is correct; the problem for regulators, however, is that competition often is not immediately strong enough to discipline the dominant former monopolist. The FCC's approach therefore has been to conduct an ongoing examination to determine when a firm is no longer dominant before repealing or reducing rate regulation.

The effects of incorrectly regulated rates become particularly acute when a market is undergoing the transition to competition, especially in industries like telecommunications characterized by high fixed costs of production. Long-run prices for any good or service must be high enough for firms to recover their production costs. When firms must make large, fixed investments in infrastructure to provide service, prices must be above marginal cost if firms are to recover their initial capital outlays. No firm goes into business to lose money, although that is exactly what would happen if a high-fixed-cost industry had its prices driven down to the textbook competitive ideal of prices equal to marginal (or average variable) costs. *See, e.g.*, Hal R. Varian, Intermediate Microeconomics: A Modern Approach 410 (8th ed. 2009). Some margin above incremental, variable cost is necessary.[3] If regulators set prices so low that they do not provide an attractive rate of return on total costs, unregulated competitive entrants will not find the market attractive to enter. If regulators choose competitive pricing standards inappropriate to the economics of the industry and, in their efforts to restrain the dominant firm's perceived market power, force prices too close to marginal costs, regulators risk deterring the competitive entry that could obviate the need for regulation in the first place.

In a market moving toward competition, regulators walk a very fine line: regulated prices that are too high can act as focal points around which market prices cluster. That is, even if the regulated firm has downward pricing flexibility, prices may be higher than in an unregulated setting if the incumbent must file tariffs that give advance notice of its intention to lower prices. There is empirical evidence that AT&T acted as a price leader in the long distance telephony market when it was required to file tariffs as a dominant firm. The principal competitors, MCI and Sprint, knew in advance what AT&T's prices would be and had incentive to follow just under the "umbrella" of AT&T's prices rather than aggressively cutting prices themselves. Paul W. MacAvoy, Testing for Competitiveness of Markets for Long Distance Telephone Services: Competition Finally?, 13 Rev. Indus. Org. 295, 298–305 (1998). Regulated prices that are too high thus accomplish nothing, except possibly to raise consumer prices in a market that would otherwise be naturally moving toward competition.

Prices that are too low also do harm. Entrants move into markets where they expect to earn a profit, and thus they need to be able to charge a high enough price to justify the necessary entry investments. If regulators allow or require the incumbent to set rates below that level, the result will be to deter competition and impede the benefits it would provide to consumers. Regulators thus face a tall order in markets in which competition is emerging: set rates at exactly the level that will allow an efficient firm to attract the investment necessary to compete in the marketplace. Rates above that level will make consumers worse off than the unregulated market. Rates below that level will deter competition that would naturally lower prices and obviate the need for administratively costly regulation. Given the difficulties that regulators inevitably face in setting rates with such pre-

---

3. Economists sometimes refer to this idea as "workable" competition to distinguish it from the textbook ideal of "perfect" competition. *See* J.M. Clark, Toward a Concept of Workable Competition, 30 Am. Econ. Rev. 241 (1940).

cision, regulators must be extremely cautious about extending rate regulation schemes from a monopoly setting into an emerging competitive environment.

Notes and Questions

1. **Comparisons.** How different are price caps from rate of return regulation in practice? After all, as we point out above, rate of return regulation begins to resemble price cap in instances where the relevant regulators are slow to adjust prices in response to changes in costs. Similarly, price cap regulation begins to resemble rate of return in instances where regulators respond to changes in cost.

2. **Costs Shared by Multiple Products.** The general theory behind rate of return regulation does not tell us very much about how common costs should be allocated among various intertwined products. For example, how should a regulator assign the capital costs of installing, and the operating costs of maintaining, a local switch that will be used to provide local, long distance, and toll-free services? This is a particularly important question in instances where one of those services is subject to competition but the others are not. In such a case, after all, the regulated firm has an incentive to allocate the bulk of the common cost to the monopolized service, thereby enhancing its ability to underprice rivals in the competitive market while simultaneously tricking the regulator into thinking that higher prices in the regulated market would be appropriate. This is a variant of the now familiar predatory cross-subsidization argument.

The allure of price cap regulation in this setting is partly the standard attraction that price caps give firms an incentive to economize on costs, and partly a more tailored advantage: under price caps, a firm has less of an incentive to cross-subsidize by unfairly allocating common costs to monopolized markets. This is true because, in theory, price cap regulation is not tied to costs. That is not strictly true in practice, however, insofar as price caps do respond over time to changes in cost. Indeed, if a regulated firm thinks that there is some probability that the government will respond to cost changes, that firm will again have an incentive to allocate a disproportionate share of its common costs to the regulated market. In essence it will continue to behave as if rate of return regulation were still in place. In short, unless the FCC and Congress can credibly commit not to react to unexpected profits, this strategic interaction will be at play and price cap regulation will not completely eliminate the incentive to engage in predatory cross-subsidization.

3. **Regulating Bell.** In light of the discussion above, should the FCC have adopted price cap regulation for Bell back before divestiture? Would that have obviated the need for the 1974 antitrust case?

§ 7.B. The Telecommunications Act of 1996

§ 7.B.1. Introduction

A central premise of the Bell Divestiture was that the provision of local telephone service was a natural monopoly. This view took hold back in the 1920s and led to the system of state-sanctioned local monopolies that both predated and survived the Bell breakup. Indeed, while the MFJ (discussed in Chapter Six) rejected the notion that long distance service should be provided by a single monopolistic firm, even the MFJ took local exchange monopolies as a given. The consent decree thus did nothing to promote competition in the local loop. That meant that state public utilities commissions still had to regulate rates in the local market, and that the FCC (along with courts interpreting the MFJ) still had to design and enforce line of business restrictions so as to protect competitive markets from predatory behavior by the various local phone service monopolists.

By the 1990s, however, both policymakers and entrepreneurs were ready to question the underlying assumption that local service should be provided by state-sanctioned monopolists. New firms had by this time already begun to compete with the incumbent LECs in providing business customers with connections to the long distance networks. A few firms had even obtained the necessary authorizations to operate switches for the purpose of providing competing residential service, although little such service was actually being offered. Moreover, cable companies held out the promise that they could provide local telephone service that would compete with the incumbent providers. True, none of this necessarily meant that there weren't efficiencies to having a single provider of local telephone service; but all of this did suggest that perhaps those efficiencies were not as great as was once thought. The 1990s thus saw increasing political pressure to abandon the assumption of local telephone monopolies and instead to set free competitive forces. The result was the Telecommunications Act of 1996.[4]

The 1996 Act had three major themes. First, the Act was designed to facilitate local telephone competition, both by eliminating state-imposed barriers to competition and by requiring existing local exchange carriers to cooperate with potential competitive entrants. This was in many ways the heart of the new Act, in that these provisions implemented the modern belief that local exchange carriers should not be shielded from competition but should instead be subject to it.

Second, the Act set out to increase competition in telecommunications markets that were already open to competition, for example the long distance market. Under the MFJ, these markets were arguably not as competitive as they might otherwise have been because the Bell Operating Companies were still forbidden, by the decree's line of business restrictions, from entering many of these markets. The 1996 Act, however, specifies the conditions under which these restrictions will be removed. The key intuition behind all of these provisions is that, if the Act were successful at introducing competition into the local market, the BOCs would no longer enjoy monopoly power and thus would no longer be able to engage in discriminatory interconnection or predatory cross-subsidization. As soon as that happened, there would be no reason to keep these firms from entering competitive markets and going head-to-head with other long distance carriers.

Third and finally, and as discussed in Chapter Thirteen, the Act substantially reformed the funding and definition of universal service. Many of these changes were necessary adjustments motivated by the new competitive structure made possible by the Act. Implicit cross-subsidies, for example, are unworkable in a world in which competitors can enter the markets where prices are artificially high but avoid entirely the markets where prices are correspondingly low. Some, however, reflected a growing policy concern that universal service needed to be redefined so as to promote increased access not just to

---

4. Telecommunications Act of 1996, Pub. L. No. 104-104, 110 Stat. 56, *codified at* 47 U.S.C. §§ 151 *et. seq.* The 1996 Act is technically an amendment to the Communications Act of 1934, which remains the umbrella statute for U.S. telecommunications. The 1934 Act, with the 1996 Act and other past amendments, is contained in Title 47 of the United States Code. All statutory sections referred to here, unless otherwise noted, are therefore found in 47 U.S.C.

"plain old telephone service" but also to more advanced telecommunications services such as, for example, Internet service.

The next several sections are organized around these themes. We first introduce the local competition provisions and explore some thorny jurisdictional issues that were raised by the Act. We then consider local competition in further detail and also examine the details of long distance entry.

§ 7.B.2. The Local Competition Provisions

The Telecommunications Act of 1996 radically revised prior law by both eliminating state-imposed barriers to competition and forcing existing local exchange carriers to cooperate with potential competitive entrants. The goal of all these provisions was the same: to facilitate competition in the local loop to the extent possible given the economics of the industry.

The simplest provisions to understand are those designed to make it possible for new entrants—so-called competitive local exchange carriers or CLECs—to build their own competing local telephone infrastructure and to interconnect that infrastructure with the existing telephone network. Competitors who choose to build their own infrastructure are known as facilities-based competitors because they aim to provide local service either exclusively or predominantly over their own facilities. The provisions most relevant to their efforts are § 253(a), which preempts state and local laws that create barriers to entry into the local exchange markets, and §§ 251(a) and 251(c), which require rival local exchange carriers to exchange traffic with entrants such that customers on any one telephone network can communicate with customers on every other network. Note that all of these provisions do important work. The state law preemption provision stops local authorities from protecting favored local exchange carriers. The interconnection provisions, meanwhile, stop incumbent LECs from using the network externalities discussed in Chapter One to their strategic advantage. After all, refusal by the existing local exchange carrier to interconnect with a rival's system would mean that customers of the new firm would be unable to call, or receive calls from, anyone not on the new network—a result that would effectively eliminate the new firm's business prospects, even if it were to build a state-of-the-art rival telephone network.

A more complicated set of provisions attempted to facilitate entry by firms who might not find it in their interest to build their own entire local telephone network but who would be interested in providing some services or infrastructure on their own while purchasing other services or infrastructure from others (most notably, the relevant incumbent LEC). These provisions attempted to foster entry by forcing LECs to make their services and infrastructure available to competitors at regulated rates.

Two statutory options for entrants are relevant here: the resale provisions and the unbundling provisions. Let's consider the resale provisions first. Under §§ 251(b)(1) and 251(c)(4), a CLEC has the right to purchase (at regulated rates) telecommunications services from a rival and then resell those services directly to consumers under the CLEC's own name. Section 251(b)(1) applies to all local exchange carriers and requires that they neither prohibit, nor impose "unreasonable or discriminatory conditions or limitations on," this sort of resale. Section 251(c)(4), meanwhile, applies only to so-called incumbent local exchange carriers (ILECs), which the Act defines in § 251(h) to include any LEC that provided telephone exchange service as of the date of enactment of the 1996 Act. The provision reaffirms the resale requirement and further stipulates that ILECs must offer to resell relevant telecommunications services "at wholesale rates."

The second option available to a would-be competitor is to use §251(c)(3) to purchase, again at regulated rates, access to particular components that are part of an incumbent's existing telephone network, such as the incumbent's switches, transport lines, and customer loops. These components are referred to in the Act as "network elements." This provision is generally referred to as the Act's "unbundling" provision because it requires incumbent firms to separate (or unbundle) particular elements of their networks and to allow entrants to purchase access to any of those elements. The elements themselves are termed unbundled network elements or UNEs. Note that the unbundling provisions allow a CLEC to purchase shared access to the building blocks of a telephone network, whereas the resale provisions allow a CLEC to purchase complete telecommunications services. And, again in contrast to the resale provisions, the unbundling provision applies only to ILECs.[5]

Not surprisingly, the parts of the 1996 Act that imposed "interconnection" and "unbundling" duties on incumbent local exchange carriers, notably §§ 251 and 252, have been the source of substantial controversy. As you consider the material that follows, you may find it helpful to break the main points of controversy into three categories of disputes: (1) which government actors have jurisdiction to establish rules related to UNEs; (2) which elements must be unbundled; and (3) how UNE prices will be set.

We begin our study of those controversies with the first FCC order that explained and attempted to implement the 1996 Act's local competition provisions.

Implementation of the Local Competition Provisions in the Telecommunications Act of 1996
First Report and Order, 11 FCC Rcd. 15,499 (1996)

C. Economic Barriers

10. The removal of statutory and regulatory barriers to entry in the local exchange market, while a necessary precondition to competition, is not sufficient to ensure that competition will supplant monopolies. An incumbent LEC's existing infrastructure enables it to serve new customers at a much lower incremental cost than a facilities-based entrant that must install its own switches, trunking [interswitch wiring], and loops to serve its customers. Furthermore, absent inter-connection between the incumbent LEC and the entrant, the customer of the entrant would be unable to complete calls to subscribers served by the incumbent LEC's network. Because an incumbent LEC currently serves virtually all subscribers in its local serving area, an incumbent LEC has little economic incentive to assist new entrants in their efforts to secure a greater share of that market. An incumbent LEC also has the ability to act on its incentive to discourage entry and robust competition by not interconnecting its network with the new entrant's network or by insisting on supracompetitive prices or other unreasonable conditions for terminating calls from the entrant's customers to the incumbent LEC's subscribers.

11. Congress addressed these problems in the 1996 Act by mandating that the most significant economic impediments to efficient entry into the monopolized local market be removed. The incumbent LECs have economies of density, connectivity, and scale; traditionally, these have been viewed as creating a natural monopoly. The local competition provisions of the Act require that these economies be shared with entrants. We believe they

---

5. Standard pronunciations for the various terms here are as follows. The abbreviations LEC, ILEC, and CLEC are pronounced "lek," "aye-lek," and "see-lek," respectively. Meanwhile, the abbreviation UNE is pronounced "yoo-nee."

should be shared in a way that permits the incumbent LECs to maintain operating efficiency to further fair competition, and to enable the entrants to share the economic benefits of that efficiency in the form of cost-based prices.

12. The Act contemplates three paths of entry into the local market—the construction of new networks, the use of unbundled elements of the incumbent's network, and resale. The 1996 Act requires us to implement rules that eliminate statutory and regulatory barriers and remove economic impediments to each. We anticipate that some new entrants will follow multiple paths of entry as market conditions and access to capital permit. Some may enter by relying at first entirely on resale of the incumbent's services and then gradually deploying their own facilities. This strategy was employed successfully by MCI and Sprint in the interexchange market during the 1970s and 1980s. Others may use a combination of entry strategies simultaneously—whether in the same geographic market or in different ones. Some competitors may use unbundled network elements in combination with their own facilities to serve densely populated sections of an incumbent LEC's service territory, while using resold services to reach customers in less densely populated areas. Still other new entrants may pursue a single entry strategy that does not vary by geographic region or over time. Our obligation in this proceeding is to establish rules that will ensure that all pro-competitive entry strategies may be explored. As to success or failure, we look to the market, not to regulation, for the answer.

13. We note that an entrant, such as a cable company, that constructs its own network will not necessarily need the services or facilities of an incumbent LEC to enable its own subscribers to communicate with each other. A firm adopting this entry strategy, however, still will need an agreement with the incumbent LEC to enable the entrant's customers to place calls to and receive calls from the incumbent LEC's subscribers. Sections 251(b)(5) and (c)(2) require incumbent LECs to enter into such agreements on just, reasonable, and nondiscriminatory terms and to transport and terminate traffic originating on another carrier's network under reciprocal compensation arrangements. In this item, we adopt rules for states to apply in implementing these mandates of section 251 in their arbitration of interconnection disputes, as well as their review of such arbitrated arrangements, or a BOC's statement of generally available terms. We believe that our rules will assist the states in carrying out their responsibilities under the 1996 Act, thereby furthering the Act's goals of fostering prompt, efficient, competitive entry.

14. We also note that many new entrants will not have fully constructed their local networks when they begin to offer service. Although they may provide some of their own facilities, these new entrants will be unable to reach all of their customers without depending on the incumbent's facilities. Hence, in addition to an arrangement for terminating traffic on the incumbent LEC's network, entrants will likely need agreements that enable them to obtain wholesale prices for services they wish to sell at retail and to use at least some portions of the incumbents' facilities, such as local loops and end office switching facilities.

15. Congress recognized that, because of the incumbent LEC's incentives and superior bargaining power, its negotiations with new entrants over the terms of such agreements would be quite different from typical commercial negotiations. As distinct from bilateral commercial negotiation, the new entrant comes to the table with little or nothing the incumbent LEC needs or wants. The statute addresses this problem by creating an arbitration proceeding in which the new entrant may assert certain rights, including that the incumbent's prices for unbundled network elements must be "just, reasonable and nondiscriminatory." We adopt rules herein to implement these requirements of section 251(c)(3).

D. Operational Barriers

16. The statute also directs us to remove the existing operational barriers to entering the local market. Vigorous competition would be impeded by technical disadvantages and other handicaps that prevent a new entrant from offering services that consumers perceive to be equal in quality to the offerings of incumbent LECs. Our recently-issued number portability Report and Order addressed one of the most significant operational barriers to competition by permitting customers to retain their phone numbers when they change local carriers.[6]

17. Closely related to number portability is dialing parity. Dialing parity enables a customer of a new entrant to dial others with the convenience an incumbent provides, regardless of which carrier the customer has chosen as the local service provider. The history of competition in the interexchange market illustrates the critical importance of dialing parity to the successful introduction of competition in telecommunications markets. Equal access enabled customers of non-AT&T providers to enjoy the same convenience of dialing "1" plus the called party's number that AT&T customers had. Prior to equal access, subscribers to interexchange carriers (IXCs) other than AT&T often were required to dial more than 20 digits to place an interstate long distance call. Industry data show that, after equal access was deployed throughout the country, the number of customers using MCI and other long distance carriers increased significantly. Thus, we believe that equal access had a substantial pro-competitive impact. Dialing parity should have the same effect.

18. This Order addresses other operational barriers to competition, such as access to rights of way, collocation, and the expeditious provisioning of resale and unbundled elements to new entrants. The elimination of these obstacles is essential if there is to be a fair opportunity to compete in the local exchange and exchange access markets. As an example, customers can voluntarily switch from one interexchange carrier to another extremely rapidly, through automated systems. This has been a boon to competition in the interexchange market. We expect that moving customers from one local carrier to another rapidly will be essential to fair local competition.

E. Transition

21. We consider it vitally important to establish a pro-competitive, deregulatory national policy framework for local telephony competition, but we are acutely mindful of existing common carrier arrangements, relationships, and expectations, particularly those that affect incumbent LECs.

22. In this regard, this Order sets minimum, uniform, national rules, but also relies heavily on states to apply these rules and to exercise their own discretion in implementing a pro-competitive regime in their local telephone markets. On those issues where the need to create a factual record distinct to a state or to balance unique local considerations is material, we ask the states to develop their own rules that are consistent with general guidance contained herein. The states will do so in rulemakings and in arbitrating interconnection arrangements. On other issues, particularly those related to pricing, we facilitate the ability of states to adopt immediate, temporary decisions by permitting the states to set proxy prices within a defined range or subject to a ceiling. We believe that some states

---

6. Telephone Number Portability, First Report and Order and Further Notice of Proposed Rulemaking, 11 FCC Rcd. 8352 (1996). Consistent with the 1996 Act, 47 U.S.C. § 251(b)(2), we required LECs to implement interim and long-term measures to ensure that customers can change their local service providers without having to change their phone number. Number portability promotes competition by making it less expensive and less disruptive for a customer to switch providers, thus freeing the customer to choose the local provider that offers the best value.

will find these alternatives useful in light of the strict deadlines of the law. For example, section 252(b)(4)(C) requires a state commission to complete the arbitration of issues that have been referred to it, pursuant to section 252(b)(1), within nine months after the incumbent local exchange carrier received the request for negotiation. Selection of the actual prices within the range or subject to the ceiling will be for the state commission to determine. Some states may use proxies temporarily because they lack the resources necessary to review cost studies in rulemakings or arbitrations. Other states may lack adequate resources to complete such tasks before the expiration of the arbitration deadline. However, we encourage all states to complete the necessary work within the statutory deadline.

F. Executive Summary

1. Scope of Authority of the FCC and State Commissions

24. The Commission concludes that sections 251 and 252 address both interstate and intrastate aspects of interconnection, resale services, and access to unbundled elements. The 1996 Act moves beyond the distinction between interstate and intrastate matters that was established in the 1934 Act, and instead expands the applicability of national rules to historically intrastate issues, and state rules to historically interstate issues. In the Report and Order, the Commission concludes that the states and the FCC can craft a partnership that is built on mutual commitment to local telephone competition throughout the country, and that under this partnership, the FCC establishes uniform national rules for some issues, the states, and in some instances the FCC, administer these rules, and the states adopt additional rules that are critical to promoting local telephone competition. The rules that the FCC establishes in this Report and Order are minimum requirements upon which the states may build.

3. Interconnection

26. Section 251(c)(2) requires incumbent LECs to provide interconnection to any requesting telecommunications carrier at any technically feasible point. The interconnection must be at least equal in quality to that provided by the incumbent LEC to itself or its affiliates, and must be provided on rates, terms, and conditions that are just, reasonable, and nondiscriminatory. The Commission concludes that the term "interconnection" under section 251(c)(2) refers only to the physical linking of two networks for the mutual exchange of traffic.

4. Access to Unbundled Elements

27. Section 251(c)(3) requires incumbent LECs to provide requesting telecommunications carriers nondiscriminatory access to network elements on an unbundled basis at any technically feasible point on rates, terms, and conditions that are just, reasonable, and nondiscriminatory. In the Report and Order, the Commission identifies a minimum set of network elements that incumbent LECs must provide under this section. States may require incumbent LECs to provide additional network elements on an unbundled basis. The minimum set of network elements the Commission identifies are: local loops, local and tandem switches (including all vertical switching features provided by such switches), interoffice transmission facilities, network interface devices, signaling and call-related database facilities, operations support systems functions, and operator and directory assistance facilities.

5. Methods of Obtaining Interconnection and Access to Unbundled Elements

28. Section 251(c)(6) requires incumbent LECs to provide physical collocation of equipment necessary for interconnection or access to unbundled network elements at the

incumbent LEC's premises, except that the incumbent LEC may provide virtual collocation if it demonstrates to the state commission that physical collocation is not practical for technical reasons or because of space limitations. The Commission concludes that incumbent LECs are required to provide for any technically feasible method of interconnection or access requested by a telecommunications carrier, including physical collocation, virtual collocation, and interconnection at meet points.

6. Pricing Methodologies

29. The 1996 Act requires the states to set prices for interconnection and unbundled elements that are cost-based, nondiscriminatory, and may include a reasonable profit. To help the states accomplish this, the Commission concludes that the state commissions should set arbitrated rates for interconnection and access to unbundled elements pursuant a forward-looking economic cost pricing methodology. The Commission concludes that the prices that new entrants pay for interconnection and unbundled elements should be based on the local telephone companies' Total Service Long Run Incremental Cost of a particular network element, which the Commission calls "Total Element Long-Run Incremental Cost" (TELRIC), plus a reasonable share of forward-looking joint and common costs. States will determine, among other things, the appropriate risk-adjusted cost of capital and depreciation rates. For states that are unable to conduct a cost study and apply an economic costing methodology within the statutory time frame for arbitrating interconnection disputes, the Commission establishes default ceilings and ranges for the states to apply, on an interim basis, to interconnection arrangements.

8. Resale

32. The 1996 Act requires all incumbent LECs to offer for resale any telecommunications service that the carrier provides at retail to subscribers who are not telecommunications carriers. Resale will be an important entry strategy both in the short term for many new entrants as they build out their own facilities, and for small businesses that cannot afford to compete in the local exchange market by purchasing unbundled elements or by building their own networks. State commissions must identify marketing, billing, collection, and other costs that will be avoided or that are avoidable by incumbent LECs when they provide services wholesale, and calculate the portion of the retail rates for those services that is attributable to the avoided and avoidable costs. The Commission identifies certain avoided costs, and the application of this definition is left to the states. If a state elects not to implement the methodology, it may elect, on an interim basis, a discount rate from within a default range of discount rates established by the Commission. The Commission establishes a default discount range of 17–25% off retail prices, leaving the states to set the specific rate within that range, in the exercise of their discretion.

Notes and Questions

1. Judicial Challenge. Many of the rules adopted pursuant to the above proceeding were challenged in court. Several of the opinions that resulted from those challenges are excerpted in the materials that follow.

2. Test Your Understanding. Suppose a firm does not wish to offer full telephone service, but only one or more advanced features. For example, suppose a firm wants to market to businesses a teleconferencing service, whereby customers can pick up a phone in the office, dial a pre-determined number, and be directly connected to six predetermined recipients. How might the firm take advantage of the new local competition provisions to build such a service without having to build an entire local telephone plant as well?

3. Resale. Now suppose that the firm wants to be a pure reseller, buying local phone service from the incumbent LEC and reselling it to consumers under the firm's own brand. Can the firm resell a service without adding any value other than perhaps its own innovative approach to marketing and billing? If so, what policy goals are advanced by allowing this sort of "competition"? In what way does it challenge an incumbent LEC's monopoly in the local loop, or otherwise benefit consumers?

4. Evaluate the Act. Reviewing your answers to the previous two questions, what are the respective costs and benefits of the local competition rules? How much regulatory oversight is required to make this scheme work? Is the result something more than competition in billing for otherwise identical services? Is this a practical way to facilitate entry by full-service and/or niche-service providers?

5. Finding the Natural Monopoly. How do the resale and interconnection provisions relate to claims that the local loop is a natural monopoly? Is the intuition here that these regulations allow competitors to share the natural monopoly portions of the local network but compete in all other respects? If so, who defines which are the natural monopoly portions and which are, instead, the competitive segments? Do these regulations permit competitive forces to answer that question, the idea being that CLECs will exercise the resale and unbundling provisions with respect to portions that exhibit natural monopoly properties but choose to build other portions for themselves? (Think carefully about this; the answer is of critical importance to understanding the political dynamics that follow.)

6. Calling Judge Greene. If, in 1980, someone had conceived of the provisions that are now §§ 251 and 252 of the 1996 Act, would Judge Greene—the judge who oversaw the Bell Divestiture—have been well advised to reject the consent decree and instead adopt rules forcing mandatory interconnection, unbundling, and the like?

7. *Iowa Utilities Board*. As was noted above, several aspects of the Local Competition First Report and Order were challenged in court, and several of those cases have made multiple roundtrips between the FCC and the federal courts. Many of the most important issues, however, were raised in a case that early on went to the Supreme Court. AT&T Corp. v. Iowa Utils. Bd., 525 U.S. 366 (1999). The Court took the case on writ of certiorari to the Court of Appeals for the Eighth Circuit which had ruled, among other things, that the Telecommunications Act of 1996 did not grant the Federal Communications Commission rulemaking jurisdiction over intrastate matters. Accordingly, the Eighth Circuit's decision had invalidated many of the FCC's local competition regulations, including those governing the pricing of unbundled network elements. Before we turn to the Supreme Court's response and subsequent FCC and judicial actions on the substance of the Commission's regulations, we look more closely at this question of jurisdiction to regulate under the 1996 Act.

§ 7.B.3. Jurisdiction to Implement the 1996 Act: Local Competition, National Regulation

As we discussed in Chapters Two and Six, federal and state regulators traditionally operated under a model of dual federalism in which each regulator enjoyed its own distinct sphere of authority. The 1996 Act assailed that divide, instituting a model of cooperative federalism. In particular, under the 1996 Act, states were no longer free to regulate intrastate services on their own, but rather were asked to work in partnership to facilitate local competition.[7] Needless to say, the transition did not go smoothly and the new jurisdictional arrangement gave rise to litigation and legal uncertainty.

The jurisdictional battle began shortly after the enactment of the 1996 Act. After the incumbent local exchange carriers challenged the FCC's rules, the Eighth Circuit invalidated some of those rules on the ground that—under the preemption standard set forth in La. Pub. Serv. Comm'n v. FCC, 476 U.S. 355 (1986) (*Louisiana PSC*)—the FCC lacked jurisdiction to promulgate those rules. As we discussed in Chapter Six, *Louisiana PSC* stands for the proposition that, under § 152(b), the FCC can preempt state regulations governing intrastate telecommunications only if the Act expressly and unambiguously provides for such preemption. The Eighth Circuit found that §§ 251 and 252 of the 1996 Act expressly refer to state commissions as the bodies responsible for setting UNE rates, and, further, that neither provision provides the necessary unambiguous authority for preemption by the FCC. The Supreme Court reviewed the Eighth Circuit's decision, starting its opinion by explaining the jurisdictional dispute at the heart of the case:

> The basic attack was jurisdictional. The LECs and state commissions insisted that primary authority to implement the local-competition provisions belonged to the States rather than to the FCC. They thus argued that many of the local-competition rules were invalid, most notably the one requiring that prices for interconnection and unbundled access be based on "Total Element Long Run Incremental Cost" (TELRIC)—a forward-looking rather than historic measure. The Court of Appeals agreed and vacated the pricing rules, as well as several other aspects of the Order, as reaching beyond the Commission's jurisdiction. It held that the general rulemaking authority conferred upon the Commission by the Communications Act of 1934 extended only to interstate matters, and that the Commission therefore needed specific congressional authorization before implementing provisions of the 1996 Act addressing intrastate telecommunications. It found no such authorization for the Commission's rules regarding pricing, dialing parity, exemptions for rural LECs, the proper procedure for resolving local-competition disputes, and state review of pre-1996 interconnection agreements. Indeed, with respect to some of these matters, the Eighth Circuit said that the 1996 Act had affirmatively given exclusive authority to the state commissions.
>
> The Court of Appeals found support for its holdings in 47 U.S.C. § 152(b) (§ 2(b) of the Communications Act of 1934), which, it said, creates a presumption in favor of preserving state authority over intrastate communications. It found nothing in the 1996 Act clear enough to overcome this presumption.

AT&T Corp. v. Iowa Utils. Bd., 525 U.S. 366, 374–75 (1999).

The Supreme Court reversed the Eighth Circuit's holding with respect to jurisdiction:

---

7. As a technical matter, states were not required to implement the 1996 Act, as commandeering of this type is unconstitutional under the Tenth Amendment. *See* Printz v. United States, 521 U.S. 898 (1997). As a practical matter, and with very few exceptions, the states have opted to maintain some authority (within a federal framework) rather than yield the entire field of facilitating local competition to the FCC.

> Section 201(b), a 1938 amendment to the Communications Act of 1934, provides that "the Commission may prescribe such rules and regulations as may be necessary in the public interest to carry out the provisions of this Act." Since Congress expressly directed that the 1996 Act, along with its local-competition provisions, be inserted into the Communications Act of 1934, 1996 Act, § 1(b), the Commission's rulemaking authority would seem to extend to implementation of the local-competition provisions.
>
> The incumbent LECs and state commissions (hereinafter respondents) argue, however, that § 201(b) rulemaking authority is limited to those provisions dealing with purely interstate and foreign matters, because the first sentence of § 201(a) makes it "the duty of every common carrier engaged in interstate or foreign communication by wire or radio to furnish such communication service upon reasonable request therefor...." It is impossible to understand how this use of the qualifier "interstate or foreign" in § 201(a), which limits the class of common carriers with the duty of providing communication service, reaches forward into the last sentence of § 201(b) to limit the class of provisions that the Commission has authority to implement. We think that the grant in § 201(b) means what it says: The FCC has rulemaking authority to carry out the "provisions of this Act," which include §§ 251 and 252, added by the Telecommunications Act of 1996.

Id. at 377–78.

Moreover, the Court found that § 152(b) did not constitute a bar to the FCC's pricing rules because the 1996 Act expressly applies to intrastate telecommunications and thus expressly gives the Commission authority to make rules on those intrastate matters covered by the 1996 Act:

> Our view is unaffected by 47 U.S.C. § 152(b), which reads: "Except as provided in §§ 223 through 227..., inclusive, and § 332..., and subject to the provisions of § 301 of this title..., nothing in this chapter shall be construed to apply or to give the Commission jurisdiction with respect to ... charges, classifications, practices, services, facilities, or regulations for or in connection with intrastate communication service...." The local-competition provisions are not identified in § 152(b)'s "except" clause. Seizing on this omission, respondents argue that the 1996 Act does nothing to displace the presumption that the States retain their traditional authority over local phone service.
>
> The fallacy in this reasoning is that it ignores the fact that § 201(b) explicitly gives the FCC jurisdiction to make rules governing matters to which the 1996 Act applies.

Id. at 379–80.

In reaching this decision, the Supreme Court seems to have limited the scope of *Louisiana PSC*. The Court interpreted that case to require express and unambiguous preemption authority only in situations where the FCC has not otherwise been given explicit rulemaking authority. *Id.* at 381. In addition to its potential importance for the development of telecommunications markets, then, the Court's decision in *Iowa Utilities Board* marks an important further evolution in the division of regulatory authority between the FCC and state commissions.

The majority opinion on jurisdiction met with vigorous dissent. Justice Thomas's partially dissenting opinion, *id.* at 402, in which Justice Breyer and Chief Justice Rehnquist joined, found nothing in § 201(b) to trump the overarching rule of construction established in § 152(b). Justice Thomas found that, if anything, the local competition provisions of the 1996 Act were deliberately meant to "respect[] the States' historical role as the dominant authority with respect to intrastate communications." *Id.* at 411. In his own partial dissent, *id.* at 412, Justice Breyer further emphasized the role of state commissions in the statutory provisions at issue. He pointed to the express reference in § 252(c) to "State commission[s]" as the entities charged to set rates for unbundled network elements. Justice Breyer rejected both the argument that the 1996 Act in some way required the particular method prescribed by the Commission, *id.* at 424, as well as the alternative argument that the states retained sufficient discretion under the Commission rules to have meaningful independent jurisdiction over UNE rates, *id.* at 423.

Notes and Questions

1. Jurisdictional Policy. While the courtroom debate turns on technical detail, the policy issue underlying the 1996 Act's jurisdiction provisions is a simple one: are there convincing arguments as to why the federal commission should take the lead in implementing the resale and unbundling provisions? Are these issues of primarily local concern? Is the point here that these local regulations can be expected to have a significant effect on the national telecommunications market? Or is it simply that, as an expert agency, the FCC is more likely to set appropriate rules? Does the statute allow the Court to adequately consider these core issues? If so, is that an appropriate task for judges? If not, is that wise, on the theory that this should be Congress's responsibility, or foolish, because it relegates the Justices to arguing over strained readings of ambiguous phrases?

2. Choosing Not to Regulate. In the decision excerpted above, the Supreme Court held that the FCC had authority to exercise jurisdiction over UNE rates. Several years later, a jurisdictional dispute again arose but this time over the FCC's decision *not* to exercise its authority under the Act. In its 2003 Triennial Review Order on unbundled network elements (discussed in greater detail in the next sections), the FCC declined to decide whether ILECs should have to unbundle switching to residential and other "mass-market" customers. The FCC instead stated that "the Commission sets out specific criteria that states shall apply to determine, on a granular basis, whether economic and operational impairment exists in a particular market. State Commissions must complete such proceedings within 9 months." Press Release, FCC, FCC Adopts New Rules for Networking Unbundling Obligations of Incumbent Local Phone Carriers (Feb. 20, 2003). The ILECs again challenged the FCC on jurisdictional grounds. This time, the argument was not that the FCC improperly preempted the states, but that the Commission improperly delegated authority to the states. *See* United States Telecom. Ass'n v. FCC, 359 F.3d 554 (D.C. Cir. 2004). The U.S. Court of Appeals for the D.C. Circuit agreed and held that the FCC improperly handed off its responsibility to decide which network elements ILECS have to unbundle for the benefit of CLECs. The relevant excerpt from the D.C. Circuit's decision follows.

UNITED STATES TELECOM ASS'N v. FCC [*USTA II*]
359 F.3d 554 (D.C. Cir. 2004)

Opinion for the court filed by Senior Circuit Judge WILLIAMS, in which Circuit Judges EDWARDS and RANDOLPH concur.

WILLIAMS, Senior Circuit Judge:

The FCC acknowledges that § 251(d)(2) instructs "the Commission" to "determine[]" which network elements shall be made available to CLECs on an unbundled basis. But it claims that agencies have the presumptive power to subdelegate to state commissions, so long as the statute authorizing agency action refrains from foreclosing such a power. Given the absence of any express foreclosure, the Commission argues that its interpretation of the statute on the matter of subdelegation is entitled to deference under Chevron U.S.A. v. Natural Resources Defense Council, Inc., 467 U.S. 837 (1984). And it claims that its interpretation is reasonable given the state commissions' independent jurisdiction over the general subject matter, the magnitude of the regulatory task, and the need for close cooperation between state and federal regulators in this area.

The Commission's position is based on a fundamental misreading of the relevant case law. When a statute delegates authority to a federal officer or agency, subdelegation to a subordinate federal officer or agency is presumptively permissible absent affirmative evidence of a contrary congressional intent. But the cases recognize an important distinction between subdelegation to a *subordinate* and subdelegation to an *outside party*. The presumption that subdelegations are valid absent a showing of contrary congressional intent applies only to the former. There is no such presumption covering subdelegations to outside parties. Indeed, if anything, the case law strongly suggests that subdelegations to outside parties are assumed to be improper absent an affirmative showing of congressional authorization.

This distinction is entirely sensible. When an agency delegates authority to its subordinate, responsibility—and thus accountability—clearly remain with the federal agency. But when an agency delegates power to outside parties, lines of accountability may blur, undermining an important democratic check on government decision-making. Also, delegation to outside entities increases the risk that these parties will not share the agency's "national vision and perspective," Nat'l. Park and Conservation Ass'n v. Stanton, 54 F. Supp. 2d 7, 20 (D.D.C. 1999), and thus may pursue goals inconsistent with those of the agency and the underlying statutory scheme. In short, subdelegation to outside entities aggravates the risk of policy drift inherent in any principal-agent relationship.

The fact that the subdelegation in this case is to state commissions rather than private organizations does not alter the analysis. Although United States v. Mazurie, 419 U.S. 544 (1975), noted that "limits on the authority of *Congress* to delegate its legislative power ... are [] less stringent in cases where the entity exercising the delegated authority itself possesses independent authority over the subject matter," *id.* at 556–57 (emphasis added), that decision has no application here: it involved a constitutional challenge to an express *congressional* delegation, rather than an administrative subdelegation, and the point of the discussion was to distinguish the still somewhat suspect case of congressional delegation to purely private organizations.

We therefore hold that, while federal agency officials may subdelegate their decision-making authority to subordinates absent evidence of contrary congressional intent, they may not subdelegate to outside entities—private or sovereign—absent affirmative evidence of authority to do so.

The Commission's plea for *Chevron* deference is unavailing. A general delegation of decision-making authority to a federal administrative agency does *not*, in the ordinary course of things, include the power to subdelegate that authority beyond federal subordinates. It is clear here that Congress has not delegated to the FCC the authority to subdelegate to outside parties. The statutory "silence" simply leaves that lack of authority untouched. In other words, the failure of Congress to use "Thou Shalt Not" language doesn't create a statutory ambiguity of the sort that triggers *Chevron* deference.

We therefore vacate, as an unlawful subdelegation of the Commission's § 251(d)(2) responsibilities, those portions of the Order that delegate to state commissions the authority to determine whether CLECs are impaired without access to network elements, and in particular we vacate the Commission's scheme for subdelegating mass market switching determinations.

Notes and Questions

1. Separating Law and Policy. In the decision excerpt above, the court finds that the FCC could not, as a matter of law, delegate its rulemaking authority to the states. As a matter of policy, however, might such delegation sometimes be beneficial because of states' greater knowledge of their local market conditions? Are there reasons to give up these advantages and force the Commission to make the necessary decisions instead?

2. State Law, State Regulators, and the 1996 Act. In light of the two excerpts above, one might well wonder what states *could* do. The Supreme Court says they cannot have exclusive jurisdiction over UNE pricing, and the Court of Appeals says they cannot be given jurisdiction to establish which elements must be unbundled. What is left for the states to regulate? That is, under the 1996 Act as interpreted above, exactly how much authority do state regulators have left?

§ 7.C. Unbundling, Interconnection, and Line-of-Business Regulation Under the 1996 Act

§ 7.C.1. Identifying UNEs

§ 7.C.1.a. *Iowa Utilities Board*

In the last section, we included several short excerpts from the Supreme Court decision in *Iowa Utilities Board*, focusing there on the jurisdictional issues raised. Here, we begin with a longer excerpt where the Court considers a challenge to the FCC's preliminary list of the network elements that ILECs must unbundle for use by CLECs.

AT&T CORP. v. IOWA UTILITIES BOARD
525 U.S. 366 (1999)

SCALIA, J., delivered the opinion of the Court, Parts I, III-A, III-C, III-D, and IV of which were joined by REHNQUIST, C.J., and STEVENS, KENNEDY, SOUTER, THOMAS, GINSBURG, and BREYER, JJ., Part II of which was joined by STEVENS, KENNEDY, SOUTER, and GINSBURG, JJ., and Part III-B of which was joined by REHNQUIST, C.J., and STEVENS, KENNEDY, THOMAS, GINSBURG, and BREYER, JJ. SOUTER, J., filed an opinion concurring in part and dissenting in part. THOMAS, J., filed an opinion concurring in part and dissenting in part, in which REHNQUIST, C.J., and BREYER, J., joined. BREYER, J., filed an opinion concurring in part and dissenting in part. O'CONNOR, J., took no part in the consideration or decision of these cases.

JUSTICE SCALIA delivered the opinion of the Court.

Until the 1990s, local phone service was thought to be a natural monopoly. States typically granted an exclusive franchise in each local service area to a local exchange carrier (LEC), which owned, among other things, the local loops (wires connecting telephones to switches), the switches (equipment directing calls to their destinations), and the transport trunks (wires carrying calls between switches) that constitute a local exchange network. Technological advances, however, have made competition among multiple providers of local service seem possible, and Congress recently ended the longstanding regime of state-sanctioned monopolies.

The Telecommunications Act of 1996 (1996 Act or Act) fundamentally restructures local telephone markets. States may no longer enforce laws that impede competition, and incumbent LECs are subject to a host of duties intended to facilitate market entry. Foremost among these duties is the LEC's obligation under 47 U.S.C. § 251(c) to share its network with competitors. Under this provision, a requesting carrier can obtain access to an incumbent's network in three ways: It can purchase local telephone services at wholesale rates for resale to end users; it can lease elements of the incumbent's network "on an unbundled basis"; and it can interconnect its own facilities with the incumbent's network. When an entrant seeks access through any of these routes, the incumbent can negotiate an agreement without regard to the duties it would otherwise have under §§ 251(b) or (c). *See* § 252(a)(1). But if private negotiation fails, either party can petition the state commission that regulates local phone service to arbitrate open issues, which arbitration is subject to § 251 and the FCC regulations promulgated thereunder.

Six months after the 1996 Act was passed, the FCC issued its First Report and Order implementing the local-competition provisions. Implementation of the Local Competition Provisions in the Telecommunications Act of 1996, First Report and Order, 11 FCC Rcd. 15,499 (1996). The numerous challenges to this rulemaking, filed across the country by incumbent LECs and state utility commissions, were consolidated in the United States Court of Appeals for the Eighth Circuit.

Incumbent LECs also made several challenges, only some of which are relevant here, to the rules implementing the 1996 Act's requirement of unbundled access. *See* 47 U.S.C. § 251(c)(3). Rule 319, the primary unbundling rule, sets forth a minimum number of network elements that incumbents must make available to requesting carriers. The LECs complained that, in compiling this list, the FCC had virtually ignored the 1996 Act's requirement that it consider whether access to proprietary elements was "necessary" and whether lack of access to nonproprietary elements would "impair" an entrant's ability to provide local service. *See* § 251(d)(2). In addition, the LECs thought that the list included items (like directory assistance and caller I.D.) that did not meet the statutory definition of "network element." *See* § 153(29). The Eighth Circuit rebuffed both arguments, holding that the Commission's interpretations of the "necessary and impair" standard and the definition of "network element" were reasonable and hence lawful thanks to *Chevron* deference. Chevron U.S.A. Inc. v. Natural Res. Def. Council, Inc., 467 U.S. 837 (1984).

II

B

We are of the view that the FCC did not adequately consider the "necessary and impair" standards when it gave blanket access to these network elements, and others, in Rule 319. That rule requires an incumbent to provide requesting carriers with access to a minimum of seven network elements: the local loop, the network interface device, switching capability, interoffice transmission facilities, signaling networks and call-related databases, operations support systems functions, and operator services and directory assistance. 47 C.F.R. §51.319 (1997). If a requesting carrier wants access to additional elements, it may petition the state commission, which can make other elements available on a case-by-case basis.

Section 251(d)(2) of the Act provides:

"In determining what network elements should be made available for purposes of subsection (c)(3) of this section, the Commission shall consider, at a minimum, whether

"(A) access to such network elements as are proprietary in nature is necessary; and

"(B) the failure to provide access to such network elements would impair the ability of the telecommunications carrier seeking access to provide the services that it seeks to offer."

We agree with the incumbents that the Act requires the FCC to apply *some* limiting standard, rationally related to the goals of the Act, which it has simply failed to do. In the general statement of its methodology set forth in the First Report and Order, the Commission announced that it would regard the "necessary" standard as having been met regardless of whether "requesting carriers can obtain the requested proprietary element from a source other than the incumbent," since "requiring new entrants to duplicate unnecessarily even a part of the incumbent's network could generate delay and higher costs for new entrants, and thereby impede entry by competing local providers and delay competition, contrary to the goals of the 1996 Act." First Report and Order ¶ 283. And it announced that it would regard the "impairment" standard as having been met if "the failure of an incumbent to provide access to a network element would decrease the quality, or increase the financial or administrative cost of the service a requesting carrier seeks to offer, compared with providing that service *over other unbundled elements in the incumbent LEC's network*," Id. ¶ 285 (emphasis added)—which means that comparison with self-provision, or with purchasing from another provider, is excluded. Since any entrant will request the most efficient network element that the incumbent has to offer, it is hard to imagine when the incumbent's failure to give access to the element would not constitute an "impairment" under this standard.

The Commission asserts that it deliberately limited its inquiry to the incumbent's own network because no rational entrant would seek access to network elements from an incumbent if it could get better service or prices elsewhere. That may be. But that judgment allows entrants, rather than the Commission, to determine whether access to proprietary elements is necessary, and whether the failure to obtain access to nonproprietary elements would impair the ability to provide services. The Commission cannot, consistent with the statute, blind itself to the availability of elements outside the incumbent's network. That failing alone would require the Commission's rule to be set aside. In addition, however, the Commission's assumption that any increase in cost (or decrease in quality) imposed by denial of a network element renders access to that element "necessary," and causes the failure to provide that element to "impair" the entrant's ability to furnish its desired services is simply not in accord with the ordinary and fair meaning of those terms. An entrant whose anticipated annual profits from the proposed service are reduced from 100% of investment to 99% of investment has perhaps been "impaired" in its ability to amass earnings, but has not ipso facto been impaired "in its ability to provide the services it seeks to offer"; and it cannot realistically be said that the network element enabling it to raise its profits to 100% is "necessary."

The Commission began with the premise that an incumbent was obliged to turn over as much of its network as was "technically feasible," and viewed (d)(2) as merely permitting it to soften that obligation by regulatory grace:

> "To give effect to both §§ 251(c)(3) and 251(d)(2), we conclude that the proprietary and impairment standards in § 251(d)(2) grant us the authority to refrain from requiring incumbent LECs to provide all network elements for which it is technically feasible to provide access on an unbundled basis."

First Report and Order ¶ 279.

The Commission's premise was wrong. Section 251(d)(2) does not authorize the Commission to create isolated exemptions from some underlying duty to make all network elements available. It requires the Commission to determine on a rational basis which network elements must be made available, taking into account the objectives of the Act and giving some substance to the "necessary" and "impair" requirements. The latter is not achieved by disregarding entirely the availability of elements outside the network, and by regarding any "increased cost or decreased service quality" as establishing a "necessity" and an "impair[ment]" of the ability to provide services.

C

It would be gross understatement to say that the Telecommunications Act of 1996 is not a model of clarity. It is in many important respects a model of ambiguity or indeed even self-contradiction. But Congress is well aware that the ambiguities it chooses to produce in a statute will be resolved by the implementing agency, *see Chevron*. We can only enforce the clear limits that the 1996 Act contains, which in the present case invalidate only Rule 319.

For the reasons stated, the judgment of the Court of Appeals is reversed in part and affirmed in part and is remanded for proceedings consistent with this opinion.

[Opinions of Justices SOUTER, THOMAS, and BREYER concurring in part and dissenting in part are omitted.]

Notes and Questions

1. The Statutory Design. The majority opinion holds that the FCC erred in interpreting the 1996 Act's provisions on unbundled network elements. What were the Commission's errors and what does the Court's decision require the agency to do on remand? What factors should determine whether an incumbent local exchange carrier must make a particular network element available to competitors? According to the Court, what does the statute say? In your opinion, what *should* the statute say?

2. What Should Be Unbundled? The question of what should constitute an unbundled network element is one that we will further consider in the materials that follow. Even at this early stage, consider what touchstones you might suggest to the FCC as a way of determining which items should be unbundled. Why should the local switch be unbundled but not, say, access to the ILEC's fleet of service trucks? What about historical information about customer calling habits? Access to the ILEC's administrative staff? What policies are motivating your intuitive responses to these suggestions? Can you formulate those into a coherent set of principles for unbundling?

3. Resale versus Unbundling. One issue along these lines is the question of whether CLECs should have to own some of their own facilities before using the unbundling provision to get access to the ILEC's infrastructure. That is, can a CLEC build its network by buying *all* of the necessary components as UNEs, or are the unbundling provisions open only to CLECs who have built some, but not all, of their own network? What does the FCC say on this issue? The Court? Does the result even matter given that CLECs always have the option to purchase the service in question under the resale provisions? (Yes—but do you see why?)

4. New Infrastructure. Why aren't the unbundling and resale provisions limited to services and infrastructure that were deployed as of the enactment of the 1996 Act? Would not such a limitation level the playing field as of 1996 but also leave ILECs with substantial incentives to innovate? If the FCC had adopted such an interpretation, would the Court have allowed it to stand?

5. Facilities-Based Competition. Overall, what is the logic of having unbundling and resale as entry options? Don't these options discourage facilities-based competition? Isn't that contrary to the real goal of the 1996 Act? But wait: if facilities-based competition were the real goal of the 1996 Act, wouldn't the resale and unbundling provisions sunset after, say, ten years?

---

§ 7.C.1.b. After *Iowa Utilities Board*

In 1999, and in partial response to *Iowa Utilities Board*, the Commission issued its Third Report and Order on the local competition provisions. Implementation of the Local Competition Provisions of the Telecommunications Act of 1996, Third Report and Order and Fourth Further Notice of Proposed Rulemaking, 15 FCC Rcd. 3696 (1999) (1999 UNE Order). The order accomplished two objectives. First, and as required by the Court, the Commission offered more substantive definitions of the "necessary" and "impair" standards. Second, the Commission announced several additional factors that would receive consideration in the Commission's unbundling analysis above and beyond the statutory two.

With regard to the meanings of "necessary" and "impair," the FCC wrote:

Section 251(d)(2)(A)'s "necessary" standard is a stricter standard that applies to proprietary network elements. Section 251(d)(2)(B)'s "impair" standard applies to non-proprietary network elements. [The FCC elsewhere in the 1999 UNE Order defines a proprietary network element as follows: "if an incumbent LEC can demonstrate that it has invested resources (time, material, or personnel) to develop proprietary information or network elements that are protected by patent, copyright, or trade secret law, the product of such an investment is 'proprietary in nature' within the meaning of § 251(d)(2)(A)."] Applying a stricter standard to proprietary network elements is consistent with Congress' intention to spur innovation and investment by both incumbent and competitive LECs. In applying these standards, we look first to what is occurring in the marketplace today.

Necessary. A proprietary network element is "necessary" within the meaning of § 251(d)(2)(A) if, taking into consideration the availability of alternative elements outside the incumbent's network, including self-provisioning by a requesting carrier or acquiring an alternative from a third-party supplier, lack of access to that element would, as a practical, economic, and operational matter, preclude a requesting carrier from providing the services it seeks to offer.

Impair. The incumbent LECs' failure to provide access to a non-proprietary network element "impairs" a requesting carrier within the meaning of § 251(d)(2)(B)

> if, taking into consideration the availability of alternative elements outside the incumbent's network, including self-provisioning by a requesting carrier or acquiring an alternative from a third-party supplier, lack of access to that element materially diminishes a requesting carrier's ability to provide the services it seeks to offer. In order to evaluate whether there are alternatives actually available to the requesting carrier as a practical, economic, and operational matter, we look at the totality of the circumstances associated with using an alternative. In particular, our "impair" analysis considers the cost, timeliness, quality, ubiquity, and operational issues associated with use of the alternative.

1999 UNE Order at 3704–05. Meanwhile, with regard to other factors relevant to unbundling analysis, the FCC wrote:

> We also interpret the obligations imposed in § 251(d)(2) within the larger statutory framework of the 1996 Act. Congress apparently contemplated that we would consider additional factors by directing the Commission, in § 251(d)(2), to "consider at a minimum" the "necessary" and "impair" standards. The Supreme Court decision requires us to apply a limiting standard "rationally related to the goals of the Act." Accordingly, in addition to the factors set forth above, we may consider the following factors:
>
> Rapid Introduction of Competition in All Markets. We may consider whether the availability of an unbundled network element is likely to encourage requesting carriers to enter the local market in order to serve the greatest number of consumers as rapidly as possible.
>
> Promotion of Facilities-Based Competition, Investment, and Innovation. We may consider the extent to which the unbundling obligations we adopt will encourage the development of facilities-based competition by competitive LECs, and innovation and investment by both incumbent LECs and competitive LECs, especially for the provision of advanced services.
>
> Reduced Regulation. We may consider the extent to which we can encourage investment and innovation by reducing regulatory obligations to provide access to network elements, as alternatives to the incumbent LECs' network elements become available in the future.
>
> Certainty in the Market. We may consider how the unbundling obligations we adopt can provide the uniformity and predictability that new entrants and fledgling competitors need to develop national and regional business plans. We also consider whether the rules we adopt provide financial markets with reasonable certainty so that carriers can attract the capital they need to execute their business plans to serve the greatest number of consumers.
>
> Administrative Practicality. We may consider whether the unbundling obligations we adopt are administratively practical to apply.

1990 UNE Order at 3705.

The Commission concluded its 1999 UNE Order with a modified list of UNEs that was less elaborate and considerably narrower than the list that the Supreme Court overturned in *Iowa Utilities Board*. Alas, even that list was by no means final.

In December 2001, the FCC initiated a "triennial" review of its unbundling rules by issuing a notice of proposed rulemaking that examined whether the list of unbundled network elements should change in light of developments since 1999. Review of the Section 251 Unbundling Obligations of Incumbent Local Exchange Carriers, Notice of Proposed

Rulemaking, 16 FCC Rcd. 22,781 (2001). The 2001 NPRM raised a number of interesting questions, focusing mostly on how the Commission should apply the necessary and impair standards it had articulated in the 1999 UNE Order. While that notice of proposed rulemaking was pending, however, the U.S. Court of Appeals for the D.C. Circuit in May 2002 questioned significant portions of the 1999 UNE Order, including the Commission's revised standard itself, and remanded the rules to the Commission for further consideration. *See* United States Telecom Assoc. v. FCC, 290 F.3d 415 (D.C. Cir. 2002) (*USTA I*). Among other things, the court in *USTA I* held that "impairment" had to mean something more than the normal cost disadvantages faced "by virtually any new entrant in any sector of the economy"; that nationally uniform unbundling rules ignored the fact that impairment was not uniform across all markets; and that the FCC had to take "intermodal" competition (that is, competition from cable, wireless, and other technologies) into account in determining impairment.

In February 2003, the Commission announced both the results from the triennial review and its response to the D.C. Circuit remand. *See* Press Release, FCC, FCC Adopts New Rules for Network Unbundling Obligations of Incumbent Local Phone Carriers (Feb. 20, 2003). The 2003 UNE Triennial Review Order involved unusual political compromises and alliances, and contained several fundamental changes from previous UNE regulation. Review of the Section 251 Unbundling Obligations of Incumbent Local Exchange Carriers, Report and Order and Order on Remand and Further Notice of Proposed Rulemaking, 18 FCC Rcd. 16,978 (2003). For instance, the FCC revised its impairment standard to require evidence that lack of access to a UNE would pose "barriers to entry, including operational and economic barriers, which are likely to make entry into a market uneconomic." *Id.* ¶ 25. Additionally, the Commission made its analysis of impairment more "granular" by taking into account "market-specific variations ..., including considerations of customer class, geography, and service." *Id.* ¶ 118. And the FCC brought states into the UNE regulation process in a new way, setting forth criteria under which the states themselves were to decide whether circuit switching should be unbundled within their jurisdictions.

Three changes, however, attracted particular attention. First, the FCC made clear that new investments in fiber optic connections — notably, fiber to the home (FTTH) or hybrid-fiber loops — would be exempt from § 251's unbundling obligations. The FCC explained that, if such new investments were subject to the 1996 Act's forced leasing requirement, it would deter ILECs from building these facilities in the first instance.

Second, at the time of the 2003 order, there was a significant controversy underway over something known as UNE-P or "UNE Platform." UNE-P is a collection of network elements that, when bought together, allows the purchaser to provide basic telephone service. A CLEC that purchases UNE-P is thus in essence engaged in resale: the CLEC has bought access to all the necessary equipment from the ILEC, and it is now branding the service as its own. The trick is that, from a regulatory perspective, such a CLEC is providing service under the UNE provisions, rather than the resale provisions. This is an important distinction because these provisions embrace radically different pricing structures. Something bought through the UNE regime is priced at low TELRIC rates; whereas something bought through the resale regime is priced at higher wholesale rates. Thus, the question of whether ILECs should be required to offer UNE-P was a contentious one.

In the 2003 UNE Triennial Review Order, the Commission addressed UNE-P indirectly by calling into question whether one key element of the platform — circuit switching — would continue to be unbundled. The Commission adopted a presumption against unbundled switching for business customers and deferred to the states on the question of mass-market (i.e., residential and small business) switching. That put at risk UNE-P availability. Incumbents could offer it on a voluntary basis, albeit at unregulated rates, but under the 2003 order in many markets it would no longer be obligatory.

Third, the 2003 order removed from the list of mandatory UNEs the high-frequency portion of the local loop. At the time, a standard telephone line was frequently divided into two parts when the telephone subscriber desired high-speed Internet access — a high-frequency part that was useful for delivering broadband Internet to the home, and a low frequency part that was used primarily for traditional voice service. Under the "line sharing" rule, the FCC had required ILECs to unbundle the high-frequency portion of the local loop such that CLECs could provide DSL broadband service without also providing voice. In the 2003 UNE Triennial Review Order, the FCC repealed that obligation. As a result, it was harder for CLECs to offer DSL service. The only ways for a CLEC to do so were either (a) to offer DSL and voice together, thus using the entire local loop; or (b) to purchase the complete local loop but then find some other party willing to sublicense the low-frequency portion, a practice known as "line splitting" instead of line sharing.

In March 2004, the D.C. Circuit reviewed the 2003 UNE Triennial Review Order and — surprise, surprise — found elements of that newest set of rules lacking, vacating several and remanding them to the Commission for yet another round of analysis. We pick up the story there, with an excerpt from that decision (which we also excerpted in the previous section). We will then discuss the 2005 UNE Order the FCC issued in response to that decision.

United States Telecom Ass'n v. FCC [*USTA II*]

359 F.3d 554 (D.C. Cir. 2004)

Opinion for the court filed by Senior Circuit Judge WILLIAMS, in which Circuit Judges EDWARDS and RANDOLPH concur.

WILLIAMS, Senior Circuit Judge:

I. Legal Background

In its first effort to interpret the "impairment" standard of § 251(d)(2) of the Telecommunications Act of 1996, the Commission held that lack of unbundled access to an element would "impair" a CLEC's ability to provide telecommunications service "if the quality of the service the entrant can offer, absent access to the requested element, declines and/or the cost of providing the service rises." Implementation of the Local Competition Provisions in the Telecommunications Act of 1996, 11 FCC Rcd. 15,499, 15,643 ¶ 285 (1996) (First Report and Order).

The Supreme Court found this reading of "impair" unreasonable in two respects. First, the Commission had irrationally refused to consider whether a CLEC could self-provision or acquire the requested element from a third party. AT&T Corp. v. Iowa Utilities Bd., 525 U.S. 366, 389 (1999) (*AT&T*). Second, the Commission had considered *any* increase in cost or decrease in quality, no matter how small, sufficient to establish impairment — a result the Court concluded could not be squared with the "ordinary and fair meaning" of the word "impair." *Id.* at 389–90 & n.11. The Court admonished the FCC that in assessing which cost differentials would "impair" a new entrant's competition within the meaning of the statute, it must "apply *some* limiting standard, rationally related to the goals of the Act." *Id.* at 388.

Responding to the *AT&T* decision, the Commission adopted a new interpretation under which a would-be entrant is "impaired" if, "taking into consideration the availability of alternative elements outside the incumbent's network, including self-provisioning by a requesting carrier or acquiring an alternative from a third-party supplier, lack of access to that element *materially diminishes* a requesting carrier's ability to provide the services it seeks to offer." Implementation of the Local Competition Provisions of the Telecommunications Act of 1996, 15 FCC Rcd. 3696, 3725 ¶ 51 (1999) (Third Report and Order) (emphasis added). But in United States Telecom Association v. FCC, 290 F.3d 415 (D.C. Cir. 2002) (*USTA I*), we held that this new interpretation of "impairment," while an improvement, was still unreasonable in light of the Act's underlying purposes.

The fundamental problem, we held, was that the Commission did not differentiate between those cost disparities that a new entrant in *any* market would be likely to face and those that arise from market characteristics "linked (in some degree) to natural monopoly ... that would make genuinely competitive provision of an element's function wasteful." *USTA I*, 290 F.3d at 427. This distinction between different kinds of incumbent/entrant cost differentials is qualitative, not merely quantitative, which is why the Commission's addition of a requirement that the cost disparity be "material" was inadequate. *Id.* at 427–28.

We also made clear that the Commission's broad and analytically insubstantial concept of impairment failed to pursue the "balance" between the advantages of unbundling (in terms of fostering competition by different firms, even if they use the very same facilities) and its costs (in terms both of "spreading the disincentive to invest in innovation and creating complex issues of managing shared facilities," *id.* at 427), a balance that we found implicit in the *AT&T* Court's insistence on an unbundling standard "rationally related to the goals of the Act," *id.* at 428 (quoting *AT&T*).

We also objected to the Commission's decision to issue, with respect to most elements, broad unbundling requirements that would apply "in every geographic market and customer class, without regard to the state of competitive impairment in any particular market." *USTA I*, 290 F.3d at 422. Though the Act does not necessarily require the Commission to determine "on a localized state-by-state or market-by-market basis which unbundled elements are to be made available," *id.* at 425 (quoting Third Report and Order, 15 FCC Rcd. at 3753, ¶ 122), it does require "a more nuanced concept of impairment than is reflected in findings ... detached from any specific markets or market categories." *USTA I*, 290 F.3d at 426. Thus, the Commission is obligated to establish unbundling criteria that are at least aimed at tracking relevant market characteristics and capturing significant variation.

Finally, we vacated the Commission's decision to require ILECs to unbundle the high-frequency portion of their copper loops to requesting CLECs — a practice known as "line sharing" and used by CLECs to provide broadband DSL service — because the Commission had failed to consider adequately whether intermodal competition from cable providers tilted the balance against this form of unbundling in the broadband market.

In response to *USTA I* the Commission again revised its definition of impairment. This time around, the Commission determined that a CLEC would "be impaired when lack of access to an incumbent LEC network element poses a *barrier or barriers to entry*, including operational and economic barriers, that are *likely to make entry into a market uneconomic*. That is, we ask whether all potential revenues from entering a market exceed the costs of entry, taking into consideration any countervailing advantages that a new entrant may have." Review of the Section 251 Unbundling Obligations of Incumbent Local Exchange Carriers, 18 FCC Rcd. 16,978, ¶ 84 (2003) (Order) (emphasis added). The Commission clarified that the impairment assessment would take intermodal competition into account. *Id.* ¶¶ 97–98.

The Commission responded to our demand for a more "nuanced" application of the impairment standard by purporting to adopt a "granular" approach that would consider "such factors as specific services, specific geographic locations, the different types and capacities of facilities, and customer and business considerations." *Id.* ¶ 118. Where the Commission believed that the record could not support an absolute national impairment finding but at the same time contained too little information to make "granular" determinations, it adopted a provisional nationwide rule, subject to the possibility of specific exclusions, to be created by state regulatory commissions under a purported delegation of the Commission's own authority.

The Commission also resolved to use the "at a minimum" language in § 251(d)(2) to "inform [its] consideration of unbundling in contexts where some level of impairment may exist, but unbundling appeared likely to undermine important goals of the 1996 Act." *Id.* ¶ 173. Specifically, in connection with two broadband elements, "fiber-to-the-home" (FTTH) and hybrid loops (see below), it brought into the balance the risk that an unbundling order might deter investment in such facilities — contrary, as it saw the matter, to the statutory goal of encouraging prompt deployment of "advanced telecommunications capability." *Id.* ¶¶ 172–73 (quoting § 706 of the Act). Additional issues also emerged in the rulemaking and will be addressed below.

3. The Commission's definition of "impairment"

As a general matter the ILECs argue the Commission's impairment standard is so open-ended that it imposes no meaningful constraints on unbundling, and would be unlawful even if applied by the FCC itself. More specifically, the ILECs claim that the Commission's unbundling test unlawfully permits states to consider as a potential source of impairment retail rates that are held below cost by state regulation against the ILECs' will, and unlawfully precludes consideration of intermodal competition when determining whether a market is suitable for competitive supply.

On the general point about the open-endedness of the Commission's standard, we observe that the Order's interpretation of impairment is an improvement over the Commission's past efforts in that, for the most part, the Commission explicitly and plausibly connects factors to consider in the impairment inquiry to natural monopoly characteristics (declining average costs throughout the range of the relevant market), or at least connects them (in logic that the ILECs do not seem to contest) to other structural impediments to competitive supply. These barriers include sunk costs, ILEC absolute cost advantages, first-mover advantages, and operational barriers to entry within the sole or primary control of the ILEC. In contrast to the First Report and Order and the Third Report and Order, the Commission has clarified that only costs related to structural impediments to competition are relevant to the impairment analysis.

Relation of "impairment" to the "at a minimum" clause. We note that there are at least two ways in which the Commission could have accommodated our ruling in *USTA I* that its impairment rule take into account not only the benefits but also the costs of unbundling, in order that its standard be "rationally related to the goals of the Act." *See USTA I*, 290 F.3d at 428. One way would be to craft a standard of impairment that built in such a balance, as for example by hewing rather closely to natural monopoly features. The other is to use a looser concept of impairment, with the costs of unbundling brought into the analysis under § 251(d)(2)'s "at a minimum" language. The Commission has chosen the latter, and we cannot fault it for doing so. This is especially true as the statutory structure suggests that "impair" must reach a bit beyond natural monopoly. While for "proprietary" network elements the statute mandates a decision whether they are "necessary," §251(d)(1)(A), for nonproprietary ones it requires a decision whether their absence would "impair" the requester's provision of telecommunications service, §251(d)(1)(B). Thus, in principle, there is no statutory offense in the Commission's decision to adopt a standard that treats impairment as a continuous rather than as a dichotomous variable, and potentially reaches beyond natural monopoly, but then to examine the full context before ordering unbundling.

That said, we do note that in at least one important respect the Commission's definition of impairment is vague almost to the point of being empty. The touchstone of the Commission's impairment analysis is whether the enumerated operational and entry barriers "make entry into a market uneconomic." Order ¶84. Uneconomic by whom? By *any* CLEC, no matter how inefficient? By an "average" or "representative" CLEC? By the most efficient existing CLEC? By a hypothetical CLEC that used "the most efficient telecommunications technology currently available," the standard that is built into TELRIC? We need not resolve the significance of this uncertainty, but we highlight it because we suspect that the issue of whether the standard is too open-ended is likely to arise again.

Intermodal alternatives. As for the ILECs' claim that the Commission's impairment standard unlawfully excludes consideration of intermodal alternatives, we observe that the Commission expressly stated that such alternatives are to be considered when evaluating impairment. Order ¶¶97–98, 443. Whether the weight the FCC assigns to this factor is reasonable in a given context is a question that we need not decide, except insofar as we reaffirm *USTA I*'s holding that the Commission cannot ignore intermodal alternatives.

Impairment in markets where state regulation holds rates below historic costs. In the name of "universal service," state regulators have commonly employed cross-subsidies, tilting rate ceilings so that revenues from business and urban customers subsidize residential and rural ones. On remand from our decision in *USTA I*, the Commission decided to consider regulated below-cost retail rates as a factor that may "impair" CLECs in competing for mass market customers. *See* Order ¶518. The ILECs object strenuously, and it appears virtually certain that the issue will recur on remand.

The interesting case is the one where TELRIC rates are so low that unbundling *does* elicit CLEC entry, enabling CLECs to cut further into ILEC revenues in areas where the ILECs' service is mandated by state law—and mandated to be offered at artificially low rates funded by ILECs' supracompetitive profits in other areas. If the scheme of the Act is successful, of course, the very premise of these below-cost rate ceilings will be undermined, as those supracompetitive profits will be eroded by Act-induced competition. In competitive markets, an ILEC can't be used as a piñata. The Commission has said nothing to address these obvious implications, or otherwise to locate its treatment of the issue in any purposeful reading of the Act.

B. *Unbundling of High-Capacity Dedicated Transport Facilities*

2. *Remaining dedicated transport issues*

a. *Route-specific analysis of dedicated transport*

In *USTA I* we expressed skepticism regarding whether there could be impairment in markets "where the element in question—though not literally ubiquitous—is significantly deployed on a competitive basis," giving as a specific example interoffice dedicated transport. *USTA I*, 290 F.3d at 422. We do not see how the Commission can simply ignore facilities deployment along similar routes when assessing impairment. Suppose points A, B, and C are all in the same geographic market and are similarly situated with regard to the "barriers to entry" that the Commission says are controlling. Suppose further that multiple competitors supply DS1 transport between points A and B, but only the ILEC and one other CLEC have deployed DS1 transport between A and C. The Commission cannot ignore the A–B facilities deployment when deciding whether CLECs are impaired with respect to A–C deployment without a good reason. The Commission does explain why competition on the A–B route should not be *sufficient* to establish competition is possible on the A–C route, Order ¶ 401, but this cannot explain the Commission's implicit decision to treat competition on one route as *irrelevant* to the existence of impairment on the other.

b. Wireless providers' access to unbundled dedicated transport

[T]he ILEC petitioners also attack the Commission's conclusion that providers of wireless service (also known as commercial mobile radio services, or CMRS) qualify for unbundled access to these facilities. According to the ILECs, the Commission not only failed to conduct the requisite impairment analysis for wireless providers, but in fact found that wireless growth has been "remarkable": 90% of the U.S. population lives in areas served by at least three wireless providers, 40% of Americans and 61% of American households own a wireless phone, wireless prices have been steadily declining, and 3–5% of wireless customers use wireless as their only phone, treating it as a full substitute for traditional land line service. Order ¶ 53. Although the ILECs implicitly concede that wireless providers would be impaired if they were denied any access to ILEC dedicated interoffice transport facilities, they point out that wireless providers have traditionally purchased such access from ILECs at wholesale rates (a transaction classified, since adoption of the Act, under § 251(c)(4)). And the data above clearly show that wireless carriers' reliance on special access has not posed a barrier that makes entry uneconomic. Indeed, the multi-million dollar sums that the Commission regularly collects in its auctions of such spectrum, and that firms pay to buy already-issued licenses, seem to indicate that wireless firms currently expect that net revenues will, by a large margin, more than recover all their non-spectrum costs (including return on capital).

The FCC and the wireless intervenors do not challenge the assertion that the current regime has witnessed a rapidly expanding and prosperous market for wireless service. Rather, they rely on the principle that "evidence that requesting carriers are using incumbent LEC tariffed services" is not "relevant to [the] unbundling determination." Order ¶ 102.

[T]he purpose of the Act is not to provide the widest possible unbundling, or to guarantee competitors access to ILEC network elements at the lowest price that government may lawfully mandate. Rather, its purpose is to stimulate competition—preferably genuine, facilities-based competition. Where competitors have access to necessary inputs at rates that allow competition not only to survive but to flourish, it is hard to see any need for the Commission to impose the costs of mandatory unbundling.

We therefore hold that the Commission's impairment analysis must consider the availability of tariffed ILEC special access services when determining whether would-be entrants are impaired, and vacate paragraphs 102–03 of the Order. This of course still leaves the Commission free to take into account such factors as administrability, risk of ILEC abuse, and the like. What the Commission may not do is compare unbundling only to self-provisioning or third-party provisioning, arbitrarily excluding alternatives offered by the ILECs.

III. CLEC Objections

A. Unbundling of Broadband Loops

3. Line sharing

In *USTA I*, we vacated the Commission's decision to provide CLECs with unbundled access to the high frequency portion of copper loops, primarily because the Commission had failed to consider the relevance of intermodal competition in the broadband market. On remand, the Commission decided to reverse its earlier position and eliminated this unbundling mandate. [W]e find that even if the CLECs are right that there is some impairment with respect to the elimination of mandatory line sharing, the Commission reasonably found that other considerations outweighed any impairment. We therefore uphold the Commission's rules concerning line sharing on the grounds that the decision not to unbundle this element was reasonable, even in the face of some CLEC impairment, in light of evidence that unbundling would skew investment incentives in undesirable ways and that intermodal competition from cable ensures the persistence of substantial competition in broadband.

VI. Conclusion

To summarize: We vacate the Commission's subdelegation to state commissions of decision-making authority over impairment determinations, and we also vacate and remand the Commission's nationwide impairment determinations [that formerly relied on the safety valve of state subdelegation].

We vacate the Commission's decision not to take into account availability of tariffed special access services when conducting the impairment analysis, and we therefore vacate and remand the decision that wireless carriers are impaired without unbundled access to ILEC dedicated transport.

Notes and Questions

1. Impairment. What was the court's concern about the substance of the FCC's impairment determinations? Did the court object to the general formulation of the impairment test or to the application of that test to specific network elements?

2. Delegation to the States. On the procedural side, the court ruled that the FCC could not delegate the more "granular" impairment determination to the states. The court decided that such delegation is impermissible as a matter of law. But putting the law aside, did the FCC's attempt to involve the states make sense as a matter of policy? On one hand, multiple jurisdictions most likely would have led to inconsistent decisions and a patchwork of uneven obligations for the ILECs. On the other hand, states may be in a better position to know the details of their local markets. Was the FCC right as a policy matter or were there alternative options it could have chosen that would have led to more "granular" unbundling decisions while avoiding a patchwork of state-by-state rules?

3. Alternatives to Unbundling. Notice that the court rejected the FCC's attempt to extend ILEC unbundling obligations to wireless telephone carriers. What was the basis for the FCC's determination that these carriers suffered any impairment? What was the basis of the court's rejection of that determination—that there was no evidence of impairment, that there were alternatives to unbundling, or both? The case takes an important step in deciding that tariffed access to network elements could defeat a finding of impairment where the evidence shows that competitors are able to enter and prosper using tariffed access instead of TELRIC-priced UNEs. Does that make sense, or does it give too much power to the ILECs, who might now strategically start offering access at plausible, but above-TELRIC, prices?

4. An Unusual Vacation. In most of the cases we have seen thus far, when the D.C. Circuit finds the legal justification for a regulation wanting, it remands to the Commission for further proceedings. Vacatur is typically reserved for those rare situations where the court doubts that the agency will be able to justify retaining its rule and further believes that vacatur will cause only minimal disruption. In *USTA II*, however, the court ordered that the rejected rules be vacated within 60 days "in light of the Commission's failure, after eight years, to develop lawful unbundling rules, and its apparent unwillingness to adhere to prior judicial rulings." 359 F.3d at 595. Was it appropriate for the D.C. Circuit to give the FCC a mere sixty days to redo the regulations? Which way does the eight-year gestation of these rules cut? Does it indicate that the issue is too complex for resolution in sixty days, or that the FCC has been wasting time? What information would you need in order to answer that question? Do you think the D.C. Circuit had that information? Is perhaps the D.C. Circuit itself to blame for the long delays in implementing the 1996 Act, given its persistent unwillingness to accept the Commission's rules?

---

§ 7.C.1.c. **FCC Response to *USTA II***

The D.C. Circuit in *USTA II* sent the Commission back to the drawing board once more. The FCC responded by adopting the below-excerpted order from 2005.

UNBUNDLED ACCESS TO NETWORK ELEMENTS: REVIEW OF THE SECTION 251 UNBUNDLING OBLIGATIONS OF INCUMBENT LOCAL EXCHANGE CARRIERS

Order on Remand, 20 FCC Rcd. 2533 (2005)

I. Introduction

2. In this Order, the Commission takes additional steps to encourage the innovation and investment that come from facilities-based competition. By using our section 251 unbundling authority in a more targeted manner, this Order imposes unbundling obligations only in those situations where we find that carriers genuinely are impaired without access to particular network elements and where unbundling does not frustrate sustainable, facilities-based competition. This approach satisfies the guidance of courts to weigh the costs of unbundling, and ensures that our rules provide the right incentives for both incumbent and competitive LECs to invest rationally in the telecommunications market in the way that best allows for innovation and sustainable competition.

IV. Unbundling Framework

22. In this Order, we retain the unbundling framework we adopted in the [2003] Triennial Review Order, but clarify the impairment standard in one respect and modify our unbundling framework in three respects. First, we clarify that when evaluating whether lack of access to an incumbent LEC network element "poses a barrier or barriers to entry ... that are likely to make entry into a market uneconomic," we make that determination with regard to a reasonably efficient competitor. Second, in response to the *USTA II* court's directive, we modify our approach regarding carriers' unbundled access to in-

cumbent LECs' network elements for provision of certain services, setting aside the Triennial Review Order's "qualifying service" interpretation of section 251(d)(2), but nevertheless prohibiting the use of unbundled elements exclusively for the provision of telecommunications services in sufficiently competitive markets. Third, to the extent that we evaluate whether requesting carriers can compete without unbundled access to particular network elements, we endeavor, as instructed by the D.C. Circuit, to draw reasonable inferences regarding the prospects for competition in one geographic market from the state of competition in other, similar markets. Fourth, as directed by *USTA II*, we consider the appropriate role of tariffed incumbent LEC services in our unbundling framework. We determine that in the context of the local exchange markets, a rule prohibiting access to UNEs when a requesting carrier is able to compete using an incumbent's tariffed offering would be inappropriate.

A. Reasonably Efficient Competitor

24. We clarify that, in assessing impairment pursuant to the standard set forth in the Triennial Review Order, we presume a reasonably efficient competitor. In the Triennial Review Order, the Commission concluded that a requesting carrier was impaired "when lack of access to an incumbent LEC network element poses a barrier or barriers to entry, including operational and economic barriers, that are likely to make entry into a market uneconomic." The *USTA II* court found that the Commission had failed to answer the question, "Uneconomic by whom?"

26. To the extent that the Commission was unclear on this point in the Triennial Review Order, we take this opportunity to emphasize that when we consider whether "lack of access to an incumbent LEC network element poses a barrier or barriers to entry, including operational and economic barriers, that are likely to make entry into a market uneconomic," we refer to whether entry is economic by a hypothetical competitor acting reasonably efficiently. In analyzing entry from the perspective of the reasonably efficient competitor, we do not attach weight to the individualized circumstances of the actual requesting carrier.

B. Service Considerations

2. Prohibition on Unbundling for Exclusive Service to Competitive Markets

35. As the D.C. Circuit stressed in its *USTA I* and *USTA II* decisions, the Commission must take into account both the benefits and costs of unbundling before it may require an incumbent LEC to provide unbundled access to network elements pursuant to section 251(c)(3). Applying this requirement in the context of markets where competition has evolved without access to UNEs, the D.C. Circuit stated that it is "hard to see any need for the Commission to impose the costs of mandatory unbundling" in cases "where robust competition in the relevant markets belies any suggestion that the lack of unbundling makes entry uneconomic."

36. In response to the court, we consider the state of competition in the mobile wireless services market and long distance services market in determining whether a requesting carrier may obtain access to a UNE solely to provide those services. Based on the record, the court's guidance, and the Commission's previous findings, we find that the mobile wireless services market and long distance services market are markets where competition has evolved without access to UNEs. We further find that whatever incremental benefits could be achieved under the Act by requiring mandatory unbundling in these service markets would be outweighed by the costs of requiring such unbundling. As we found in the Triennial Review Order, unbundling can create disincentives for incumbent

LECs and competitive LECs to deploy innovative services and facilities, and is an especially intrusive form of economic regulation—one that is among the most difficult to administer. Therefore, as an exercise of our "at a minimum" authority, we decline to order unbundling of network elements to provide service in the mobile wireless services market and the long distance services market.

C. Reasonable Inferences

42. In addition to striking down the Commission's subdelegation of authority to state commissions, the D.C. Circuit also directed the Commission to treat competitive deployment in one market as probative of the prospects for competition in similar markets—that is, to draw inferences regarding the prospects for competitive entry in one market based on the state of competition in another market. Thus, for example, the court directed the Commission, when evaluating whether requesting carriers are impaired without unbundled access to incumbent LECs' dedicated transport facilities along a particular route, to consider evidence of deployment along similar routes.

44. We believe that, where warranted, our exercise of discretion to use reasonable inferences instead of fact-specific proceedings conducted by this Commission to determine impairment is reasonable and best serves the public interest. First, it would be impossible for this Commission to conduct the fact-intensive, market-specific inquiries that we previously asked the states to conduct to determine carriers' impairment with regard to various elements. Our choice below to draw inferences based on factors including the number of business lines and/or competitive fiber-based collocators in a given central office is a workable standard that permits us to adopt rules that provide for a substantial degree of geographic specificity without reliance on state decision-making. Accordingly, this approach allows the Commission to execute its statutory obligation to render unbundling determinations without "loftily abstract[ing] away all specific markets" while also avoiding individualized review of each discrete geographic market such as that which we previously asked the states to perform.

Notes and Questions

1. Fourth Time a Charm. "Because we conclude the Commission's fourth time is a charm," the D.C. Circuit wrote in reviewing the FCC order set out above, "we deny all petitions for review." The D.C. Circuit's decision thus ended—almost 10 years after it began—a game of litigation ping pong over the proper scope of the 1996 Act's unbundling obligations. In so doing, it turned away the incumbents' arguments that the FCC's triggers for deregulation were too low and that the availability of special access services (a retail offering) should be relevant to whether unbundled access is required. Similarly, the court turned away the arguments made by competitors that the limitations on high capacity circuits and unbundled switching were too stringent. *See* Covad Commc'n Co. v. FCC, 450 F.3d 528 (D.C. Cir. 2006).

2. Impairment. How does this new unbundling order alter the impairment test? What is the FCC's definition of "uneconomic" entry? Note that this order looks beyond local exchange service alone in judging the business case for entry. As ¶ 24 indicates, the FCC will examine whether, given all services the entrant could provide using the UNEs, entry would be economic.

3. Reasonably Efficient Entrant. In response to *USTA II*, the FCC says in this order that it will assess impairment to a "reasonably efficient" entrant. What does this mean? Does the standard differ if the entrant is a cable company with a network already in place instead of a new CLEC starting from scratch? Should impairment for the cable company be judged according to a "reasonably efficient" cable operator standard and impairment for the startup CLEC be judged according to a reasonably efficient "new firm" standard? How should successful entry by a cable company that can use its existing facilities to provide phone service affect the impairment analysis as to a CLEC starting from scratch?

4. A Real-World Test Case. In Anchorage, Alaska, a cable company called GCI has taken over half the local exchange market from the incumbent LEC, ACS. GCI can use its cable plant to serve its local telephone customers. Should ACS have to continue to provide UNEs in Anchorage? In a similar set of circumstances, the FCC concluded that Qwest was entitled to a limited degree of relief from unbundling obligations as to its Omaha operations. *See* Petition of Qwest Corp. for Forbearance Pursuant to 47 U.S.C. § 160(c) in the Omaha Metropolitan Statistical Area, Memorandum Opinion and Order, 20 FCC Rcd. 19,415 (2005). In particular, the FCC stated that it would grant relief from unbundling requirements—like the obligation to provide local loops and transport—"where a facilities-based competitor has substantially built out its network." *Id.*¶ 2.

More recently, the FCC has revised its approach to forbearance of ILEC unbundling requirements, adopting essentially an antitrust approach. The FCC will evaluate an ILEC's request to lift unbundling using "a market power analysis." "Under this approach, we separately evaluate competition for distinct services, for example differentiating among the various retail services purchased by residential and small, medium, and large business customers, and the various wholesale services purchased by other carriers." Petition of Qwest Corp. for Forbearance Pursuant to 47 U.S.C. § 160(c) in the Phoenix, Arizona, Metropolitan Statistical Area, Memorandum Opinion and Orders, 25 FCC Rcd. 8622, 8623 (2010).

5. Costs and Benefits of Unbundling. The Commission says it is refining its analysis to take better account of the costs of unbundling. Accordingly, the FCC says it will not order unbundling in markets that are already competitive, because in such cases there would be no benefit to unbundling to offset the costs. What are the costs and how does the FCC measure them? The order makes clear there will be no unbundling in markets that are already competitive. But what about markets that are in transition but perhaps not yet competitive? The hard cases are not wireless and long distance, but local markets in which unbundling may still have benefits but also entails costs. How, under this order, do you think the FCC will assess such tradeoffs?

6. Pick and Choose. One important debate that we have edited out of the above documents is a debate over an FCC rule known as the "pick-and-choose" rule. Under the pick-and-choose rule, the FCC had interpreted § 252(i) of the 1996 Act to require an ILEC to allow any CLEC to pick and choose terms from among any and all UNE interconnection agreements the ILEC had signed with any other CLEC. The result was that if an ILEC signed an agreement with CLEC 1 that gave very low loop rates in return for higher switching rates because that package was good for CLEC 1, but then signed an agreement with CLEC 2 that gave very low switching rates in return for higher loop rates because *that* package was good for CLEC 2, CLEC 3 could come along and demand the low loop rates from the first agreement and the low switching rates from the second. For better or worse, the pick-and-choose rule thus provided obvious disincentives for the ILEC to enter into agreements tailored to the particular needs of a given entrant. In July 2004, the FCC abandoned the pick-and-choose rule and replaced it with an "all-or-nothing" approach. Under that rule, a CLEC can either choose the entire agreement negotiated with any other entrant or negotiate its own agreement from scratch with the ILEC. Review of the Section

251 Unbundling Obligations of Incumbent Local Exchange Carriers, Second Report and Order, 19 FCC Rcd. 13,494 (2004).

---

§ 7.C.2. Pricing Network Elements

In its opinion in *Iowa Utilities Board*, the Supreme Court did not reach the validity of the Commission's pricing rules for unbundled network elements. It instead considered the jurisdictional and definitional issues discussed above and then remanded the challenge to the pricing rules for further consideration by the United States Court of Appeals for the Eighth Circuit. We excerpt the Supreme Court's subsequent decision below. Before turning to that document, however, it might be helpful to think through a simple example and in that way clarify exactly why this pricing issue has turned out to be such a difficult one. (Unfortunately, and significantly, the 1996 Act itself offers little guidance, with § 252 stipulating only that the prices for access to network elements must be based on "cost.")

Suppose that, in 1995, an ILEC invested $2 million to develop and install an advanced telecommunications device called the HyperSwitch. The HyperSwitch is a fictional component we invented just for this example, but, to be concrete, let us imagine that the HyperSwitch is a switch that is particularly efficient in networks where the amount of data traffic greatly exceeds the amount of voice traffic. Further suppose that, having built the HyperSwitch, the ILEC incurs an additional expense of two cents per call for each call routed through the switch. This marginal cost might represent any number of real-world costs, for example the cost of the electricity required to run the HyperSwitch, or the maintenance costs associated with switch use. The point is that, wholly apart from fixed costs (here, $2 million), there are marginal costs incurred on a per call basis, which is to say that it costs the ILEC something (two cents) every time anyone uses its switch.

Now, thinking about the HyperSwitch as a possible unbundled network element, our question is a deceptively simple one: what price should the ILEC be required to charge a CLEC for use of the HyperSwitch?

Let's state at the outset exactly what is at stake here. First, there is a distributional/fairness issue to keep in mind. The ILEC, at least, will argue that the regulated price must be high enough so as to allow the recovery of not just its marginal costs but also some fair proportion of its fixed costs. Set too low a price and the ILEC will complain that the regulation imposes an unfair burden — perhaps a burden so substantial as to amount to an unconstitutional "taking" of the ILEC's property. Note that this distributional issue affects other parties in addition to the ILECs. For example, if a potential new entrant were to determine that the government is treating ILECs unfairly, that new entrant might decide to enter instead an unregulated industry, not wanting to take the chance that the government will someday similarly mistreat it. ILEC distributional issues, then, are important to more than just the ILECs.

Second and relatedly, there is the question of the ILEC's future incentives to innovate. If the ILEC knows that its facilities will be offered to rivals at regulated rates and, worse, thinks that those rates will be too low, the ILEC might be reluctant in the future to invest in new technologies like the HyperSwitch. This is particularly troubling if we think that, thanks to their years of experience and considerable resources, incumbents are particularly well-suited to engage in innovation.

Third, there is a short-term efficiency worry to grapple with. Any price above marginal cost threatens to create a state of affairs where the HyperSwitch will be underused. After all, if the regulated price exceeds marginal cost, firms willing to pay more than marginal cost but less than the regulated price will not purchase access. Conversely, prices below marginal cost might lead to overuse.

Fourth and finally, we have to worry about the CLEC's incentive to invest in new technologies. If ILEC equipment is available at bargain basement prices, CLECs will be less likely to venture into the business of developing new equipment. This might not matter if we believe that ILECs will handle all necessary innovation; but, to whatever extent we want CLECs to innovate, this is a significant concern. Conversely, if ILEC equipment is priced at too high a level, CLECs might build their own infrastructure even in cases where society would prefer that the CLEC just share the existing equipment. CLECs would be building not because the new infrastructure was cost-justified, but instead because the regulated price was so artificially high that the CLEC would rather build than pay the regulated rate. (Of course, in this situation the ILEC might voluntarily lower its asking price and in that way avoid the inefficient build-around.)

As even this deeply oversimplified example suggests, the reason it is so difficult to price unbundled network elements is that it is difficult to write a rule that simultaneously responds to all of the relevant concerns. Allow the incumbent to recover some of its up-front investment by charging more than marginal cost, and not only will the network element be underused, but also the CLEC might end up building new infrastructure even when, from a societal perspective, that redundant infrastructure is unnecessary. Force the incumbent to charge marginal cost, by contrast, and not only must the incumbent absorb a significant loss, but in the future incumbent firms will hesitate to invest in new technologies. Efficiently pricing our hypothetical HyperSwitch, in short, is a Herculean task.

Faced with these competing considerations, the FCC chose TELRIC, which at first looks like a rule that sacrifices some degree of efficiency in order to treat the ILECs well. Under TELRIC, the price an entrant pays for access to an incumbent's network element reflects the ILEC's marginal costs plus (a) a proportional share of most other, nonmarginal costs associated with the relevant network element and (b) a reasonable profit. To be more specific, under TELRIC an incumbent is allowed to charge CLECs a price for access that includes (1) any costs directly attributable to the CLECs' use (marginal costs); (2) a proportional share of the depreciation in the element's value over time; (3) a proportional share of overhead costs associated with the element's use (personnel costs, billing costs, and so on); and (4) a share of the cost of the capital invested in the element (either interest paid or the foregone returns on alternative investments). TELRIC thus seems to establish prices that are above marginal cost—indeed, prices that allow ILECs to recover nearly all of the costs associated with any particular network element.

A wrinkle, however, undermined this simple logic. The FCC decided that, when calculating rates under TELRIC, it would not consider what insiders call the "embedded costs" of facilities put in place before the 1996 Act. These embedded costs include any portion of the fixed costs of building the network that the incumbent has not yet recovered through its service prices. Instead, the Commission decided that, at any point in time, "the total element long-run incremental cost of an element should be measured based on the use of the most efficient telecommunications technology currently available and the lowest cost network configuration, given the existing location of the incumbent LEC's wire centers." 47 C.F.R. § 51.505(b)(1). The Commission's policy has therefore been the rule explained above, except that the costs are based not on the costs associated with the incumbent LEC's actual network, but on the costs associated with a hypothetically efficient network.

Unsurprisingly, ILECs challenged the FCC rules. First, the incumbents argued that a rule barring them from recovering the embedded costs of their networks constituted a taking of their property in violation of the Fifth Amendment. Second, the incumbents contended that, even if TELRIC did not represent an unconstitutional taking, the rule violated the plain language and express purpose of the 1996 Act. Section 252 did not say much, but it did say that prices for access to network elements had to be based on "cost"—and the incumbents argued that "cost" meant real costs and could not reasonably be interpreted to mean costs associated with some hypothetical telephone network that might never even be built. The Eighth Circuit reviewed these claims and struck down the Commission's pricing rules in 2000. Iowa Utils. Bd. v. FCC, 219 F.3d 744 (8th Cir. 2000). Both sides of the case appealed to the U.S. Supreme Court. The Court issued its decision in 2002, upholding the Commission's TELRIC approach as a reasonable exercise of agency discretion and as not presenting a facial violation of the Takings Clause. Excerpts of the majority opinion and of Justice Breyer's dissenting opinion follow.

VERIZON COMMUNICATIONS INC. v. FCC
535 U.S. 467 (2002)

SOUTER, J., delivered the opinion of the Court, in which REHNQUIST, C.J., and STEVENS, KENNEDY, and GINSBURG, JJ., joined, in which SCALIA and THOMAS, JJ., joined as to Part III, and in which THOMAS, J., also joined as to Part IV. BREYER, J., filed an opinion concurring in part and dissenting in part, in which SCALIA, J., joined as to Part VI. O'CONNOR, J., took no part in the consideration or decision of the cases.

Justice SOUTER delivered the opinion of the Court.

I

Two sets of related provisions for opening local markets concern us here. First, Congress required incumbent local-exchange carriers to share their own facilities and services on terms to be agreed upon with new entrants in their markets. 47 U.S.C. § 251(c). Second, knowing that incumbents and prospective entrants would sometimes disagree on prices for facilities or services, Congress directed the FCC to prescribe methods for state commissions to use in setting rates that would subject both incumbents and entrants to the risks and incentives that a competitive market would produce. § 252(d).

A

Under the local-competition provisions of the Act, Congress called for ratemaking different from any historical practice, to achieve the entirely new objective of uprooting the monopolies that traditional rate-based methods had perpetuated.

II

As to pricing, the Act provides that when incumbent and requesting carriers fail to agree, state commissions will set a "just and reasonable" and "nondiscriminatory" rate for interconnection or the lease of network elements based on "the cost of providing the ... network element," which "may include a reasonable profit." § 252(d)(1). In setting these rates, the state commissions are, however, subject to that important limitation previously unknown to utility regulation: the rate must be "determined without reference to a rate-of-return or other rate-based proceeding." In AT&T Corp. v. Iowa Utilities Board,

525 U.S. 366 (1999), this Court upheld the FCC's jurisdiction to impose a new methodology on the States when setting these rates. The attack today is on the legality and logic of the particular methodology the Commission chose.

As for the method to derive a "nondiscriminatory," "just and reasonable rate for network elements," the Act requires the FCC to decide how to value "the cost ... of providing the ... network element [which] may include a reasonable profit," although the FCC is (as already seen) forbidden to allow any "reference to a rate-of-return or other rate-based proceeding," §252(d)(1). Within the discretion left to it after eliminating any dependence on a "rate-of-return or other rate-based proceeding," the Commission chose a way of treating "cost" as "forward-looking economic cost," 47 C.F.R. §51.505 (1997), something distinct from the kind of historically based cost generally relied upon in valuing a rate base. The FCC defined the "forward-looking economic cost of an element [as] the sum of (1) the total element long-run incremental cost of the element [TELRIC]; [and] (2) a reasonable allocation of forward-looking common costs," §51.505(a), common costs being "costs incurred in providing a group of elements that cannot be attributed directly to individual elements," §51.505(c)(1). Most important of all, the FCC decided that the TELRIC "should be measured based on the use of the most efficient telecommunications technology currently available and the lowest cost network configuration, given the existing location of the incumbent['s] wire centers." §51.505(b)(1).

"The TELRIC of an element has three components, the operating expenses, the depreciation cost, and the appropriate risk-adjusted cost of capital." Implementation of Local Competition in Telecommunications Act of 1996, First Report and Order, 11 FCC Rcd. 15,499, ¶703 (1996) (First Report and Order). *See also* 47 C.F.R. §§51.505(b)(2)–(3) (1997). A concrete example may help. Assume that it would cost $1 a year to operate a most-efficient loop element; that it would take $10 for interest payments on the capital a carrier would have to invest to build the lowest cost loop centered upon an incumbent carrier's existing wire centers (say $100, at 10 percent per annum); and that $9 would be reasonable for depreciation on that loop (an 11-year useful life); then the annual TELRIC for the loop element would be $20.

[T]he Eighth Circuit held that §252(d)(1) foreclosed the use of the TELRIC methodology. In other words, the court read the Act as plainly requiring rates based on the "actual" not "hypothetical" "cost ... of providing the ... network element," and reasoned that TELRIC was clearly the latter. Iowa Utils. Bd. v. FCC, 219 F.3d 744, 750–751 (8th Cir. 2000). The Eighth Circuit added, however, that if it were wrong and TELRIC were permitted, the claim that in prescribing TELRIC the FCC had effected an unconstitutional taking would not be "ripe" until "resulting rates have been determined and applied." *Id.* at 753–754.

Before us, the incumbent local-exchange carriers claim error in the Eighth Circuit's holding that a "forward-looking cost" methodology (as opposed to the use of "historical" cost) is consistent with §252(d)(1), and its conclusion that the use of the TELRIC forward-looking cost methodology presents no "ripe" takings claim. The FCC and the entrants, on the other side, seek review of the Eighth Circuit's invalidation of the TELRIC methodology and the additional combination rules. We granted certiorari, 531 U.S. 1124 (2001), and now affirm on the issues raised by the incumbents, and reverse on those raised by the FCC and the entrants.

III

A

The incumbent carriers' first attack charges the FCC with ignoring the plain meaning of the word "cost" as it occurs in the provision of §252(d)(1) that "the just and reasonable rate for network elements ... shall be ... based on the cost (determined without reference to a rate-of-return or other rate-based proceeding) of providing the ... network element...." The incumbents do not argue that in theory the statute precludes any forward-looking methodology, but they do claim that the cost of providing a competitor with a network element in the future must be calculated using the incumbent's past investment in the element and the means of providing it. They contend that "cost" in the statute refers to "historical" cost, which they define as "what was in fact paid" for a capital asset, as distinct from "value," or "the price that would be paid on the open market." The argument boils down to the proposition that "the cost of providing the network element" can only mean, in plain language and in this particular technical context, the past cost to an incumbent of furnishing the specific network element actually, physically, to be provided.

The incumbents have picked an uphill battle. At the most basic level of common usage, "cost" has no such clear implication. A merchant who is asked about "the cost of providing the goods" he sells may reasonably quote their current wholesale market price, not the cost of the particular items he happens to have on his shelves, which may have been bought at higher or lower prices.

When the reference shifts from common speech into the technical realm, the incumbents still have to attack uphill. To begin with, even when we have dealt with historical costs as a ratesetting basis, the cases have never assumed a sense of "cost" as generous as the incumbents seem to claim. "Cost" as used in calculating the rate base under the traditional cost-of-service method did not stand for all past capital expenditures, but at most for those that were prudent, while prudent investment itself could be denied recovery when unexpected events rendered investment useless. And even when investment was wholly includable in the rate base, ratemakers often rejected the utilities' "embedded costs," their own book-value estimates, which typically were geared to maximize the rate base with high statements of past expenditures and working capital, combined with unduly low rates of depreciation. *See, e.g.*, FPC v. Hope Natural Gas Co., 320 U.S. 591, 597–598 (1944). It would also be a mistake to forget that "cost" was a term in value-based ratemaking and has figured in contemporary state and federal ratemaking untethered to historical valuation.

What is equally important is that the incumbents' plain-meaning argument ignores the statutory setting in which the mandate to use "cost" in valuing network elements occurs. First, the Act uses "cost" as an intermediate term in the calculation of "just and reasonable rates," 47 U.S.C. § 252(d)(1), and it was the very point of *Hope Natural Gas* that regulatory bodies required to set rates expressed in these terms have ample discretion to choose methodology, 320 U.S. at 602. Second, it would have been passing strange to think Congress tied "cost" to historical cost without a more specific indication, when the very same sentence that requires "cost" pricing also prohibits any reference to a "rate-of-return or other rate-based proceeding," § 252(d)(1), each of which has been identified with historical cost ever since *Hope Natural Gas* was decided.

The fact is that without any better indication of meaning than the unadorned term, the word "cost" in § 252(d)(1), as in accounting generally, is "a chameleon," Strickland v. Comm'r, Maine Dept. of Human Servs., 96 F.3d 542, 546 (1st Cir. 1996), a "virtually meaningless" term, R. Estes, Dictionary of Accounting 32 (2d ed. 1985). As Justice Breyer put it in *Iowa Utilities Bd.*, words like "cost" "give ratesetting commissions broad methodological leeway; they say little about the 'method employed' to determine a particular rate." 525 U.S. at 423 (opinion concurring in part and dissenting in part). We accordingly reach the conclusion adopted by the Court of Appeals, that nothing in § 252(d)(1) plainly requires reference to historical investment when pegging rates to forward-looking "cost."

B

The incumbents' alternative argument is that even without a stern anchor in calculating "the cost ... of providing the ... network element," the particular forward-looking methodology the FCC chose is neither consistent with the plain language of § 252(d)(1) nor within the zone of reasonable interpretation subject to deference under Chevron U.S.A. Inc. v. Natural Resources Defense Council, Inc., 467 U.S. 837, 843–845 (1984). This is so, they say, because TELRIC calculates the forward-looking cost by reference to a hypothetical, most efficient element at existing wire-centers, not the actual network element being provided.

a. [Undermining Competition]

The incumbents' (and Justice Breyer's) basic critique of TELRIC is that by setting rates for leased network elements on the assumption of perfect competition, TELRIC perversely creates incentives against competition in fact. The incumbents say that in purporting to set incumbents' wholesale prices at the level that would exist in a perfectly competitive market (in order to make retail prices similarly competitive), TELRIC sets rates so low that entrants will always lease and never build network elements. And even if an entrant would otherwise consider building a network element more efficient than the best one then on the market (the one assumed in setting the TELRIC rate), it would likewise be deterred by the prospect that its lower cost in building and operating this new element would be immediately available to its competitors; under TELRIC, the incumbents assert, the lease rate for an incumbent's existing element would instantly drop to match the marginal cost of the entrant's new element once built. According to the incumbents, the result will be, not competition, but a sort of parasitic free-riding, leaving TELRIC incapable of stimulating the facilities-based competition intended by Congress.

At the end of the day, theory aside, the claim that TELRIC is unreasonable as a matter of law because it simulates but does not produce facilities-based competition founders on fact. The entrants have presented figures showing that they have invested in new facilities to the tune of $55 billion since the passage of the Act (through 2000). The FCC's statistics indicate substantial resort to pure and partial facilities-based competition among the three entry strategies: as of June 30, 2001, 33 percent of entrants were using their own facilities; 23 percent were reselling services; and 44 percent were leasing network elements (26 percent of entrants leasing loops with switching; 18 percent without switching). The incumbents do not contradict these figures, but merely speculate that the investment has not been as much as it could have been under other ratemaking approaches, and they note that investment has more recently shifted to nonfacilities entry options. We, of course, have no idea whether a different forward-looking pricing scheme would have generated even greater competitive investment than the $55 billion that the entrants claim, but it suffices to say that a regulatory scheme that can boast such substantial competitive capital spending over a 4-year period is not easily described as an unreasonable way to promote competitive investment in facilities.

C

The incumbents' claim of TELRIC's inherent inadequacy to deal with depreciation or capital costs has its counterpart in a further argument. They seek to apply the rule of constitutional avoidance in saying that "cost" ought to be construed by reference to historical investment in order to avoid a serious constitutional question, whether a methodology so divorced from investment actually made will lead to a taking of property in violation of the Fifth (or Fourteenth) Amendment. The Eighth Circuit did not think any such serious question was in the offing, 219 F.3d at 753–754, and neither do we.

At the outset, it is well to understand that the incumbent carriers do not present the portent of a constitutional taking claim in the way that is usual in ratemaking cases. They do not argue that any particular, actual TELRIC rate is "so unjust as to be confiscatory," that is, as threatening an incumbent's "financial integrity." Duquesne Light Co., 488 U.S. at 307, 312. Indeed, the incumbent carriers have not even presented us with an instance of TELRIC rates, which are to be set or approved by state commissions and reviewed in the first instance in the federal district courts, 47 U.S.C. §§ 252(e)(4) and (e)(6). And this, despite the fact that some States apparently have put rates in place already using TELRIC.

The 1996 Act sought to bring competition to local-exchange markets, in part by requiring incumbent local-exchange carriers to lease elements of their networks at rates that would attract new entrants when it would be more efficient to lease than to build or resell. Whether the FCC picked the best way to set these rates is the stuff of debate for economists and regulators versed in the technology of telecommunications and microeconomic pricing theory. The job of judges is to ask whether the Commission made choices reasonably within the pale of statutory possibility in deciding what and how items must be leased and the way to set rates for leasing them. The FCC's pricing and additional combination rules survive that scrutiny.

The judgment of the Court of Appeals is reversed in part and affirmed in part, and the cases are remanded for further proceedings consistent with this opinion.

Justice BREYER, concurring in part and dissenting in part.

I agree with the majority that the Telecommunications Act of 1996 does not require a historical cost pricing system. I also agree that, at the present time, no taking of the incumbent firms' property in violation of the Fifth Amendment has occurred. I disagree, however, with the Court's conclusion that the specific pricing and unbundling rules at issue here are authorized by the Act.

II

The Telecommunications Act is not a ratemaking statute seeking better regulation. It is a deregulatory statute seeking competition. It assumes that, given modern technology, local telecommunications markets may now prove large enough for several firms to compete in the provision of some services—but not necessarily all services—without serious economic waste. It finds the competitive process an indirect but more effective way to bring about the common objectives of competition and regulation alike, namely low prices, better products, and more efficient production methods. But it authorizes the Commission to promulgate rules that will help achieve that procedural goal—the substitution of competition for regulation in local markets—where that transformation is economically feasible. The Act does not authorize the Commission to promulgate rules that would hinder the transition from a regulated to a competitive marketplace—whether or not those rules directly mandate lower "element" prices along the way.

The statute, then, seeks new local market competition insofar as local markets can support that competition without serious waste. And we must read the relevant rate setting provision—including the critical word "cost"—with that goal in mind.

III

The Commission's critics—Verizon, other incumbents, and experts whose published articles Verizon has lodged with the Court—concede that the statute grants the Commission broad authority to define "costs." They also concede that every rate-setting system has flaws.

Nonetheless, the critics argue, the Commission cannot lawfully choose a system that thwarts a basic statutory purpose without offering any significant compensating advantage. They take the relevant purpose as furthering local competition where feasible. They add that rates will further that purpose (1) if they discourage new firms from using the incumbent's facilities or "elements" when it is significantly less expensive, economically speaking, for the entrant to build or to buy elsewhere, and (2) if they encourage new firms to use the incumbent's facilities when it is significantly less expensive, economically speaking, for the entrant to do so. They point out that prices that approximately reflect an actual incumbent's actual additional costs of supplying the services (or "element") demanded will come close to doing both these things. But prices like the Commission's, based on the costs that a hypothetical "most efficient" firm would incur if hypothetically building largely from scratch, would do neither. Indeed, they would do exactly the opposite, creating incentives that hinder rather than further the statute's basic objective.

First, the critics ask, why, given such a system, would a new entrant ever build or buy a new element? After all, the Commission's rate-setting system sets the incumbent's compulsory leasing rate at a level that would rarely exceed the price of building or buying elsewhere. Second, what incentive would the Commission's rules leave the incumbents either to innovate or to invest in a new "element?" The rules seem to say that the incumbent will share with competitors the cost-reducing benefits of a successful innovation, while leaving the incumbent to bear the costs of most unsuccessful investments on its own. Why would investment not then stagnate?

Nor, in the critics' view, do the regulations possess any offsetting advantages. The hypothetical nature of the Commission's system means that experts must estimate how imaginary firms would rebuild their systems from scratch—whether, for example, they (hypothetically) would receive permission to dig up streets, to maintain unsightly telephone poles, or to share their pole costs with other users, say, cable operators—and they must then estimate what would turn out to be most "efficient" in such (hypothetical) future circumstances.

IV

The criticisms described in Part III are serious, potentially severing any rational relation between the Commission's regulations and the statutory provision's basic purposes. Hence, the Commission's responses are important. Do those responses reduce the force of the criticisms, blunt their edges, or suggest offsetting virtues? I have found six major responses. But none of them is convincing.

First, the FCC points out that rates will include not only a charge reflecting hypothetical "most-efficient-firm" costs but also a depreciation charge—a charge that can reconcile a firm's initial historic investment, say, in equipment, and the equipment's current value, which diminishes over time. If, for example, an incumbent's reasonable investment, measured actually and historically, came to $50 million, but FCC experts predict a "most-efficient-firm-building-from-scratch" future replication cost of $30 million, a depreciation charge could permit the incumbent to recoup the otherwise missing $20 million. And, in theory, a state commission might structure a potentially complex depreciation charge so as both to permit recovery of historic investment and also to offset many of the improper investment incentives described in Part II.

This response, however, does not reflect what the Commission's regulations actually say. Those regulations say nothing about permitting recovery of reasonable historic investment nor about varying the charge to offset perverse investment incentives. Rather, they strongly indicate the opposite. They clearly require state commissions to use current depreciation rates right alongside the Commission's new and different "most-efficient-firm-building-from-scratch" charges. *See* First Report and Order ¶ 702. They do create an exception from "current" rates. But to take advantage of that exception "incumbent LECs" have to bear the "burden of demonstrating with specificity that the business risks that they face in providing unbundled network elements and interconnection services would justify a different ... depreciation rate." *Id.*

Second, the FCC points out that a state commission can adjust permissible profit rates. In theory, such an adjustment could offset many of the improper investment incentives described in Part II. But, like the depreciation regulations, the profit regulations say nothing about the matter. Indeed, like the depreciation regulations, they suggest the opposite. The relevant FCC regulations say that "the currently authorized rate of return at the federal or state level is a reasonable starting point." *Id.* They, too, add an exception, available to "incumbent LEC's" that successfully "bear the burden of demonstrating with specificity that the business risks that they face in providing unbundled network elements and interconnection services would justify a different risk-adjusted cost of capital." *Id.* But this exception, like the depreciation exception, cannot respond to the critics' claims in the ordinary case for similar reasons.

Third, the Commission supports the reasonableness and practicality of its system with the claim that "a number of states" have used it successfully, as have several European nations. As to domestic experience, I can find no evidence that, prior to the promulgation of the rules at issue here, any State had successfully implemented the FCC's version of TELRIC. It is hardly surprising that since then several States have tried to apply it. Nor is it surprising that their implementation has produced criticisms similar to those made here.

Fourth, the FCC adds that its system seeks to base rates on the costs a hypothetical "most efficient firm" hypothetically would incur were it "building from scratch." And such a system, in its view, will "simulate" or "best replicate, to the extent possible, the conditions of a competitive market." This response, however, does not do more than describe that very feature of the system upon which the critics focus their attack.

Fifth, the Commission says that its regulations are simply suggestive, leaving States free to depart. The short but conclusive answer to this response is that the Commission considered a "suggestive" approach and rejected it.

Sixth, the majority (but not the Commission) points out that local commissions are likely to leave any given set of rates in effect for some period of time. And this "regulatory lag" will solve the problem. I do not understand how it could solve the main problem—that of leading new entrants to lease a more costly incumbent "element" where building or buying independently could prove less costly. Nor, given any new entrant's legal right to obtain a regulator's decision, am I certain that lags will prove significant. But, in any event, lags will differ, depending upon regulator, time, and circumstance, thereby introducing a near random element that might, or might not, ameliorate the system's otherwise adverse effects.

In sum, neither the Commission's nor the majority's responses are convincing.

Notes and Questions

1. Basis for Majority Opinion. What is the basis for the majority's decision? Is it that TELRIC represents a reasonable interpretation of the text of the 1996 Act, as a matter of administrative law? Or is it that TELRIC in fact achieves the Act's goals, as an empirical matter? Is the majority opinion's discussion of empirical evidence of competitive entry necessary to its decision, or is it dicta?

2. Key Difference Between Majority and Dissent. Justice Breyer dissents on the ground that TELRIC does not, as a matter of accepted economic theory, foster the 1996 Act's goal of creating genuine local exchange competition. What is the essence of his argument? How does he respond to the majority's claim that, theory aside, facilities-based local competition is developing?

3. Relationship to Impairment Test. Recall that the Supreme Court rejected the FCC's initial list of unbundled network elements on grounds that the Commission had applied the wrong standard for unbundling. What does the empirical evidence cited by the majority in support of TELRIC tell us about impairment, and about the relationship between TELRIC pricing and impairment? On one hand, the fact that facilities-based entry is occurring simultaneously with unbundling could mean that there is no impairment, but that TELRIC prices are so low that some entrants use UNEs rather than building their own facilities. On the other hand, the data could mean that there is impairment, but that TELRIC prices are so high that firms nonetheless build their own facilities instead of always entering through unbundling. Which of these possibilities is more likely? Which opinion, the majority or the dissent, does that possibility support?

4. Takings. The Supreme Court was not particularly sympathetic to the incumbents' assertion that the Commission's pricing methodology, if deemed permissible under the statute, would result in regulated prices so low as to constitute a taking of the incumbents' property without just compensation in violation of the Fifth Amendment, which states "Nor shall private property be taken for public use, without just compensation." Sidak and Spulber explain the Takings issue in the TELRIC context as follows:

> The sweeping deregulation of public utilities being proposed and implemented at the state and federal levels promises to bring the benefits of competition to markets for electric power and telecommunications. Those benefits include improvements in operating efficiencies, competitive prices, efficient investment decisions, technological innovation, and product variety. The benefits of competition, however, do not include forced transfers of income from utility shareholders to their customers and competitors. As regulators dismantle barriers to entry and other regulatory restrictions, they must honor their past commitments and avoid actions that threaten to confiscate or destroy the property of utility investors on an unprecedented scale.

J. Gregory Sidak & Daniel F. Spulber, Deregulatory Takings and the Regulatory Contract 1–2 (1997). The crux of the Court's response was that the issue was not yet ripe; the incumbents should wait and raise their objection once they had specific TELRIC rates in hand. But is that a sensible response? Delay might bring a reviewing court the benefit of having real numbers to work with. But delay also comes at a cost: without the promise of an eventual takings claim, incumbents have no choice but to fight tooth and nail to recover their historic costs through TELRIC. Had the Court evaluated and embraced the takings logic, by contrast, incumbents would have had less incentive to resist TELRIC pricing. For further discussion along these lines, *see* Douglas Lichtman & Randy Picker, Entry Policy in Local Telecommunications: *Iowa Utilities* and *Verizon*, 2002 Sup. Ct. Rev. 41, 66–68.

5. The Devil Is in the Details. The discussion above, as befitting a casebook, suggests a critical role for the relevant legal standard. In practice, however, TELRIC as a methodology turns out not to significantly constrain state regulators in their pricing outcomes. In the wake of the 1996 Act's passage, for example, the price of local loops in Chicago was under $3 whereas in New York City local loops were priced around $10. Reflecting the considerable opportunity for state regulators to reach vastly different results in applying the TELRIC standard, Raymond Gifford (former Chairman of the Colorado Public Utilities Commission) called TELRIC just a malleable means of inviting entry into selected markets by "creating a margin between wholesale and retail rates." Raymond L. Gifford, Regulatory Impressionism: What State Regulators Can and Cannot Do, 4 Rev. Network Econ. 466, 474 (2003).

6. TELRIC in the Aftermath. The Supreme Court upheld the FCC's TELRIC approach. But that does not mean the pricing of network elements ceased to be an issue. Within TELRIC there were still many administrative details to be argued: What is the correct cost of capital? How flexible should depreciation rates be and who should set them? Which elements should be priced on a usage-sensitive basis and which at a flat rate? How often should TELRIC be readjusted? In September 2003, the FCC initiated an NPRM in which it proposed modifications to how it would measure forward-looking economic costs of unbundled network elements. Review of the Commission's Rules Regarding the Pricing of Unbundled Network Elements and the Resale of Service by Incumbent Local Exchange Carriers, Notice of Proposed Rulemaking, 18 FCC Rcd. 18,945 (2003). Most importantly, the FCC "tentatively conclude[d] that our TELRIC rules should more closely account for the real-world attributes of the routing and topography of an incumbent's network in the development of forward looking costs." *Id.* ¶ 52. Unfortunately, the FCC never actually concluded this rulemaking proceeding, leaving the matter to the state commissions as they implemented further agreements between incumbents and new entrants. As unbundling has become much less of an issue, so too has TELRIC. But the discussion in this section is important for understanding regulation of rates for telecommunications inputs, an issue that is likely to remain important as smaller wireless carriers continue to seek regulated special access and roaming from the large, nationwide wireless networks.

---

§ 7.C.3. Interconnection

Although we have surveyed many parts of the 1996 Act by this point, we have focused thus far only on the statutory provisions that promote local competition through unbundling and resale. As we noted earlier, however, the 1996 Act promotes local competition in another, even more fundamental way: it requires that rival LECs interconnect with one another to exchange network traffic. In other words, §§ 251 and 252 require that all telecommunications carriers accept telephone traffic bound for their customers even if that traffic originated on a rival firm's telephone network and, conversely, that they originate all of their customers' calls even when that traffic is bound for a customer of a rival network.

Why is this important? As we discussed in Chapter Six, back in the early days of the telephone system, Bell strategically refused to connect its telephone network to networks developed and owned by rivals. Denying interconnection was for Bell an effective tool; rivals could not realistically compete with the Bell network if their customers could not call Bell customers. This lesson was not lost on the architects of the 1996 Act, who worried that incumbent LECs would similarly deny interconnection to CLEC entrants and, in that way, undermine local competition. Without interconnection, it would be impossible for those new entrants to match the incumbent's established network benefit; thus, without interconnection, it would be impossible for those entrants to seriously challenge the incumbents' dominant positions in the various local exchange markets.

The FCC has defined interconnection as "the physical linking of two networks for the mutual exchange of traffic." 1996 Local Competition First Report and Order, ¶ 26. Unlike the Act's unbundling provisions, which apply only to ILECs, the basic interconnection provisions of §§ 251 and 252 apply to all telecommunications carriers, whether established incumbents or new entrants. Section 251(a) sets forth the basic interconnection mandate: carriers must (1) interconnect directly or indirectly with the facilities and equipment of other carriers, and (2) refrain from installing any network facilities or functions that interfere with such interconnection. Section 251(c)(2) imposes some further obligations on the ILECs. In the Commission's words, "§ 251(c)(2) requires incumbent LECs to provide interconnection to any requesting telecommunications carrier at any technically feasible point. The interconnection must be at least equal in quality to that provided by the incumbent LEC to itself or its affiliates, and must be provided on rates, terms, and conditions that are just, reasonable, and nondiscriminatory." *Id.*

The 1996 Act not only mandated interconnection, but also set out some general guidelines for the terms on which such "mutual exchange of traffic" should proceed. Most generally, § 251(b)(5) provides that all telecommunications carriers must "establish reciprocal compensation for the transport and termination of telecommunications." And § 252(d)(2) adds that, to qualify as "just and reasonable," reciprocal recovery by each carrier of the costs of transporting and terminating other carriers' traffic must be limited to "a reasonable approximation of the additional costs of terminating such calls." The Huber treatise usefully summarizes the Act's reciprocal compensation scheme as follows:

> When a customer of carrier A places a local call to a customer of carrier B, Carrier A must pay Carrier B for terminating the call. Conversely, when a customer of Carrier B places a call to a customer of Carrier A, Carrier B must pay. The Act provides that state commissions shall not consider reciprocal compensation arrangements to be just and reasonable unless they provide for the mutual and reciprocal recovery by each carrier of the costs associated with the transport and termination on each carrier's network of calls that originate on the other's network; such costs are to be determined on the basis of a reasonable approximation of the additional costs of terminating such calls. In other words, the Act looks to the marginal cost of carrying the additional traffic, not the fully distributed costs of the network.

Peter W. Huber et al., Federal Telecommunications Law 476 (2d ed. 1999). This standard is obviously different from the TELRIC standard. With interconnection, the focus is on the marginal costs imposed; with unbundling, the TELRIC standard in addition to marginal costs takes into account asset depreciation, capital costs, and other network costs.

While the 1996 Act requires reciprocal agreements for the transport and termination of traffic, note that it does leave open the possibility that carriers would elect not to charge each other for such services. § 252(d)(2)(B)(i) makes clear that nothing in the Act precludes "arrangements that waive mutual recovery (such as bill-and-keep arrangements)." Under bill-and-keep, Carriers A and B do not pay each other to terminate calls moving from the network of one to the network of the other. Instead, the carriers assume that these numbers will cancel out in the end and so each agrees to simply charge its own subscribers for local service and then originate and terminate whatever calls happen to pass through the system.

Interconnection in general, and reciprocal compensation in particular, raise a number of hard questions in practice. For one, exactly what telecommunications traffic is subject to reciprocal compensation agreements? Does § 251(b)(5) apply to any and all traffic, or to local calls only? The question is an important one. Elsewhere in the 1996 Act—and a topic we deal with more fully in Chapter Thirteen in the context of post-Divestiture universal service—long-distance carriers are obligated to pay local carriers something called an "access charge" which is a traditionally above-cost fee through which long-distance carriers subsidize local providers. If long distance traffic were interpreted to fall within the reciprocal compensation regime, what would happen to this form of subsidy? In ¶ 1034 of its 1996 Local Competition First Report and Order, the Commission resolved this issue by distinguishing access charges from reciprocal compensation, ruling that reciprocal compensation applies only "to traffic that originates and terminates within a local area." Traffic that originates in one local area but terminates in another is therefore long-distance traffic, and hence subject to the access charge regime.

A second interconnection issue involves the question of which local service providers are eligible for reciprocal compensation. The 1996 Act makes clear that the provisions apply to "telecommunications carriers," but the Act left it to the Commission to decide what kind of entity qualifies under that designation. For example, must conventional, wireline telephone companies enter into reciprocal compensation agreements with wireless communications providers? The FCC also addressed this issue in its 1996 Local Competition First Report and Order, ruling in ¶¶ 999–1015 that wireline carriers and Commercial Mobile Radio Service providers (a technical designation for all the firms that sell mobile telecommunications for profit directly to the public) did have to interconnect with each other and also were on the hook for reciprocal compensation.

Although the basic rules of interconnection and compensation for telephony are well settled (they continue to be a significant controversy in broadband, which we will discuss in Chapters Thirteen and Fourteen), specialized scraps continue—particularly when one party or another is perceived as taking advantage of the system. In the era of the dial-up Internet, some ISPs established affiliated CLECs and sought reciprocal compensation payments from the ILECs. Given the technology, all of the traffic, and hence all of the money, flowed in one direction (to the CLEC) because people only called the ISP connection number, and no traffic flowed out. After a series of proceedings, including several proceedings in the D.C. Circuit, the FCC eventually put an end to that practice. *See generally* Core Commc'ns, Inc. v. FCC, 592 F.3d 139 (D.C. Cir. 2010).

An even more pointed dispute came to light when, in April 2007, several large carriers, notably large wireless carriers like AT&T/Cingular, acknowledged that they were blocking calls to certain free (to end-user consumers) conference calling services. FCC Chair Kevin Martin responded to this admission by warning the blocking carriers that unless they stopped blocking the calls, the FCC "would end up taking action as we saw necessary." The carriers at issue quickly agreed to stop blocking calls to the services at issue, but they have continued to pursue actions against such services. Why? Because, according to the blocking carriers, such services make their money by taking improper advantage of the current intercarrier compensation regime. Some free conferencing services work by routing their calls through small, local telephone exchanges in Iowa, hence the 712 area codes for those calls. The local, rural carriers through which the conference call services work charge termination fees (which include a number of subsidies) to the networks carrying the incoming calls. The terminating rural carriers then share these fees with the conference-call service provider. In this way consumers pay nothing, but the networks that originate calls to the "free" services pay substantial fees (which they typically do not or cannot pass through to consumers) that generate profits both for the conference-call service provider and the rural network that terminates its incoming calls.

AT&T and other carriers, while apparently no longer blocking calls to the services at issue, filed lawsuits and complaints to the FCC against the rural carriers in Iowa alleging that their deals with the conference-call services were scams that violate FCC rules and other laws. The FCC made clear that while it would entertain those petitions, the allegedly injured carriers could not block consumers' ability to reach the conference-call services in the interim.

Another difficult issue that arose involved the extent to which providers of local exchange service had to interconnect with carriers that were not themselves providing retail telecommunications services, and therefore were not seeking interconnection for the purpose of connecting their customers to the customers of other networks. The question came up in the context of efforts by Time Warner Cable (TWC) to connect its VoIP subscribers to the public switched telephone network (PSTN). To do so, TWC contracted with MCI and Sprint for wholesale transport and connection to the PSTN. Certain state commissions (South Carolina and Nebraska) ruled that the 1996 Act did not require rural ILECs to interconnect with MCI and Sprint where the interconnection was for those carriers' wholesale customers rather than for those carriers' retail subscribers. The rationale for the distinction was ostensibly that wholesale services were not qualifying "telecommunications" for purposes of the 1996 Act's interconnection requirements. The FCC's Wireline Competition Bureau issued a declaratory ruling stating that the states' interpretations of §§ 251(a) and (b) were incorrect and that local exchange carriers must interconnect with providers of wholesale telecommunications carriers. Time Warner Cable Request for Declaratory Ruling that Competitive Local Exchange Carriers May Obtain Interconnection Under § 251 of the Communications Act of 1934, as Amended, to Provide Wholesale Telecommunications Services to VoIP Providers, Memorandum Opinion and Order, 22 FCC Rcd. 3513 (2007).

Notes and Questions

1. The Ghost of Intercarrier Compensation. The Time Warner decision and the call blocking issue discussed above both purport to be about interconnection. In fact, however, concerns about intercarrier compensation — or lack thereof — underpin the disputes in both cases. In the Time Warner case, the rural telephone companies were concerned that, to the extent calls were traveling to and from Voice over IP providers, those providers would not pay the same amount as traditional providers. In the call blocking case, the traditional providers resented delivering calls to rural carriers who were serving the conferencing service. In both cases, denial of interconnection was a self-help remedy. Should this remedy be permitted? If it were permitted, what would be the consequence?

2. Wholesale versus Retail. In most cases, VoIP providers contract with established firms to provide transport connectivity and interconnection. (In many cases, they also will contract for numbers, emergency 911 support, and other services.) From a legal perspective, VoIP providers take the position that they are not telecommunications carriers, but rather customers of telecommunications carriers. If VoIP providers are only customers and have no legal standing to request interconnection on their own right, should they be entitled to obtain interconnection derivatively through other telecommunications carriers? How about phone numbers?

3. Completing the Circle. Google Voice provides a range of services that build on a customer's existing wireless, VoIP, or wireless phone service. One of its services allows a subscriber to call the Google Voice platform to make an outgoing call. Google Voice then initiates a call to the outgoing number and calls the subscriber's number to (in effect) conference in the subscriber to the outgoing call. Google Voice provides for the transport of those calls and the termination of those calls to the called party, and in that context is subject to access charges. In fall 2009, it was reported that Google Voice was refusing to deliver calls to certain exchanges. A group of twenty members of Congress, as well as AT&T, sent letters to the FCC questioning whether Google's actions were consistent with the Commission's call blocking prohibitions and with Google's support for open Internet mandates. Google responded by reducing the number of blocked numbers, but not ending the practice entirely. It contended that a few rural carriers with high access charges were engaged in "traffic pumping," with the result that calls to a relatively small number of phone numbers accounted for 1.1% of calls and 26.2% of costs (because the underlying carriers would assess charges of up to 39 cents per minute to receive these calls). Beyond that, Google noted that Google Voice is a free service, and thus contended that it is not offered "for a fee" as required by the statutory definition of a "telecommunications service." Google also asserted that its service did not meet the definition of "interconnected VoIP service" under the Commission's rules, since it does not "require[] a broadband connection from the user's location." The FCC took no action against Google. Is this situation stable? Defensible?

§ 7.C.4. BOC Line of Business Restrictions

In addition to opening the local exchange to competition through interconnection obligations, unbundling, and resale, the 1996 Act also attempted to increase competition in telecommunications markets beyond the local loop, including the market for long distance telephone service.

As we pointed out, these two sets of provisions are logically related. To whatever extent the local competition provisions are successful, LECs will no longer enjoy monopoly power and thus will no longer be able to engage in discriminatory interconnection or predatory cross-subsidization. Given that, the old "line of business restrictions" lose their principal justification. So long as there is local exchange competition, there is no reason to keep the BOCs from entering competitive markets and going head-to-head with rival firms.

We will say very little about the statutory provisions that guide Bell entry into competitive markets, because these provisions are today largely only of historical interest. They were controversial at the time they came into effect, to be sure. But, by 2002, the controversies had mostly died down. The Bell companies worked their way through the requirements set out in 47 U.S.C. §§ 271–75, and as a result those companies were set free to compete in the various markets that had previously been off-limits. That said, for those interested in the history, the central provision was § 271, which provided that BOCs could immediately offer out-of-region long distance service—that is, long distance service to customers who live outside the relevant BOC's local market—but could not offer in-region long distance services or manufacture telecommunications equipment until they had first been certified to do so by the FCC. To be certified for these purposes, a BOC had to demonstrate to the Commission that it met the fourteen requirements specified in a "competitive checklist" established by § 271(c)(2)(B). Most of these conditions related to the local competition provisions discussed earlier in this chapter. For example, before being allowed to offer in-region long distance service, a BOC had to show that it was providing or had offered to provide unbundled network elements, number portability, and nondiscriminatory access to its poles. In short, a BOC's ability to offer in-region long distance services and to manufacture equipment was conditioned on its meeting the 1996 Act's local competition responsibilities.

Notes and Questions

1. Why Not Mandates? Overall, the statute set up the removal of the restriction on BOC provision of long distance service as a quid pro quo: BOCs that cooperated with respect to the local competition provisions were, in exchange, given as a reward the right to enter the long distance service market. Is there a reason why Congress adopted this sort of incentive approach instead of simply mandating particular cooperative behaviors by a date certain?

2. End of an Issue. At this point, § 271 applications have long ceased to be a major issue. Indeed, the reintegration of the telecommunications network is now complete: the BOCs not only provide local and long-distance service, but the two largest BOCs (Verizon and AT&T (which is really SBC, having adopted the AT&T name) have purchased their former long distance foes (MCI and AT&T). These purchases, of course, would have been illegal before the BOCs received the authority to provide long distance service.

PART THREE

MULTICHANNEL VIDEO AND BROADCASTING

Chapter Eight

Multichannel Video Foundations

Introduction

Because most communities have only a handful of television broadcasters, consumers originally enjoyed a limited number of programming options at any given time. This limited amount of choice gave rise to a "mass medium" where the major networks developed programming that appealed widely across varied tastes, political perspectives, and ethnic backgrounds. Consequently, shows like "I Love Lucy" became national obsessions and Americans regularly turned to Walter Cronkite for their news.

That dynamic changed in the 1980s and 1990s when the mass television audience turned to cable and direct broadcast satellite (DBS) services for their video delivery. Known in FCC parlance as "multichannel video programming distributors" (MVPDs), cable, satellite, and fiber optic services deliver, as the name suggests, multiple channels simultaneously. Thus, whereas broadcasters provide programming for the mainstream audience, MVPDs offer 24-hour news networks, sports-only networks, children's programming networks, and, with increasing channel capacity, ever more specific niche offerings.

In this chapter, we begin our study of MVPD services. We start with a brief look at the economics of paid television as compared to advertiser-supported television. We then review the history of cable television, discussing the series of regulatory initiatives launched during its existence and focusing on the issue of the division of regulatory authority between federal and local agencies. We conclude with a look at the emerging online video market.

§ 8.A. Paying for Television

An obvious difference between broadcast television and the MVPD outlets is that broadcast television is supported by advertisers and thus "free" to consumers, whereas cable television, DBS, and most other content platforms must be purchased on some combination of a per show, per channel, and/or per month schedule. Here, we want to consider that difference in isolation and understand the degree to which explicit prices are a virtue or a vice in this context.

Note at the outset that it is not the technology that drives this distinction. Broadcast television stations could, as a technological matter, charge viewers for their programs. For instance, broadcasters could scramble their signals and then sell set-top decoder boxes

Direct Broadcast Satellite. Direct broadcast satellite systems use satellites to transmit content to subscribers. Content is sent to the satellite from an uplink station and received by small antenna receptors situated near subscriber homes.

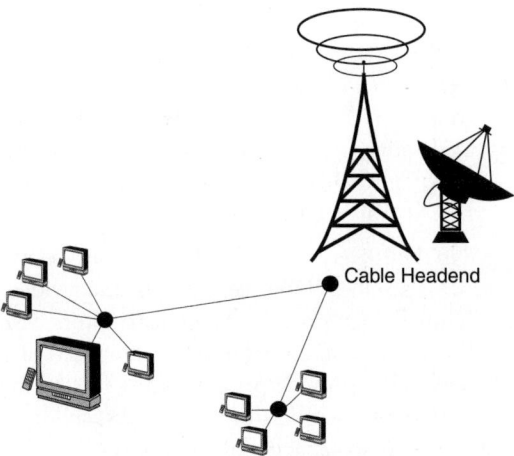

The Cable Network. Cable television is provided over a grid of coaxial or fiber optic cable that runs along city streets and ultimately connects individual residences to the cable network. In this illustration, we show that network and also the cable headend, which is where the cable network receives incoming signals by satellite, wire, air, or some other delivery mechanism.

that would decode only the paid-for content. (Indeed, at one point in time some stations did just that.) Cable similarly could be an advertiser-supported medium. Targeted ads for sporting equipment and memorabilia could, in theory at least, fund a channel like ESPN (though perhaps not at the level it currently enjoys, drawing on both advertising support and subscriber fees). Similarly, the same advertisers who today fund ABC when it is delivered over the airwaves could just as easily fund ABC were it delivered for free by wire, assuming the costs of deploying and maintaining the wire were equivalent to delivering TV programming over-the-air. A question for policymakers is whether they ought to favor subscription services over those funded by advertising revenues (or vice versa). Indeed, at one point in time, the concept of pay TV was viewed as antithetical to sound telecommunications policy.

Consider the context for the policies at issue. Once a television program is broadcast in a given community, it costs nothing to allow an additional listener or viewer to receive the signal. Broadcast content, in other words, is "nonrivalrous"—or what an economist would term a "public good." To some commentators, the nonrivalrous nature of broadcast content implies that this content should be made available free of charge, funded either through government subsidies (think PBS) or advertiser sponsorship. Charging consumers for content, these commentators argue, has the effect of denying certain consumers access to the content—and why should any family be denied access to television programming when there would be no additional cost to allowing them to listen or watch?

On the other side of the debate, however, charging consumers for TV programs serves two important functions in this setting: they can help content providers better measure the intensity of consumer preferences for particular programs, and they can give content providers a strong incentive to satisfy those preferences. To take a specific example, advertiser-supported television is not particularly responsive to consumer preferences because, while broadcasters care that viewers watch a given program (and see the commercials), so long as a viewer is willing to watch, broadcasters do not care how much the viewer enjoys the program. Intensity of preference, in other words, is neither very relevant to, nor very apparent in, the advertiser-supported system.

Subscription services, then, likely offer a different mix of programs than what would be offered were advertisers footing the bill. For example, under a pay-per-view model, there is a far greater incentive to air niche programs that attract fewer but more enthusiastic viewers. The downside to pay-per-view, of course, is that absent perfect price discrimination, there is inefficient exclusion: some consumers who value a given program above its marginal cost (zero) are nevertheless unwilling to pay the market price and thus are denied access.[1] We will return to the concept of "price discrimination"—which refers to the effort to charge different prices to different consumers based on their willingness to pay—later. For now, however, the basic point is that pay television might yield content that better matches viewer preferences, but free television distributes mainstream fare more widely and effectively.

Consider in this light the second half of the speech economist Ronald Coase gave before the FCC in 1959. The first half, excerpted in Chapter Three, argued that scarcity and interference were not good justifications for heavy-handed government broadcast regulation. This second half evaluates the case for a system of advertiser-supported television.

Why Not Use the Pricing System in the Broadcast Industry?

Ronald Coase, Testimony before the FCC, December 1959,
reprinted in 4 Study of Radio & T.V. Broadcasting (No. 12,782) (1959)

The essence of a commercial broadcasting system is that the operator of a radio or television station is paid for making broadcasts or allowing them to be made. But he is not paid by those who listen to or view the programs. He is paid by those who wish listeners to receive a particular message—the advertisement, or commercial. However, simply to broadcast the commercial will not usually lead people to listen or view. A program, therefore, has to be broadcast to induce people to listen or view. In a commercial broadcasting system, the object of the program is to attract an audience for the commercials.

With such a system, what programs will be broadcast? They are the programs which maximize the difference between the profits yielded by broadcast advertising and the costs

---

[1]. Readers interested in exploring these issues more rigorously should consult Jora Minasian, Television Pricing and the Theory of Public Goods, 7 J.L. & Econ. 71 (1964). Some empirical evidence is presented in Roger Noll et al., Economic Aspects of Television Regulation 129–50 (1973).

of the program. If programs were supplied in the way which is normal in the American economic system, the programs which would be broadcast would be those which maximize the difference between the amount people would pay to hear or see the programs and the cost of the programs. It is easy to see that these are completely different ways of determining what programs to transmit—and that a broadcasting system organized as other industries are (with revenue accruing directly from the consumers) would lead to a very different structure of programs. But how different and in what ways?

It is clear that some programs which people would be willing to pay for will have costs which are higher than the profits that would accrue from any commercials that might be associated with them and that therefore they would not be made available with the commercial system. Again, with commercial broadcasting, a program which attracts a larger audience may be chosen even though viewers or listeners in total would pay more for one which would attract a smaller audience. The result of all this is that commercial broadcasting leaves some sectors of the public with the feeling that they are not being catered for. And this is true.

I need not go into the rationale of the competitive system, which treats all money demands equally and operates in such a way as to maximize the value of output. But it will hardly come as a surprise to you that, holding these views, I urge you to do all you can to bring about the introduction of subscription television (and subscription radio, too, if possible). There may be practical difficulties standing in the way of subscription television. But I am convinced that there are no substantial objections to subscription television *in principle*.

Much is made of the fact that with commercial television the service is free. The argument is essentially the same as that for socialism and the Welfare State. What is being attacked is the price mechanism. The factors of production used in television are not made available for nothing. They will be paid for by someone: the government out of the proceeds of taxation, the advertiser, or the consumer. What is important is that factors of production should be used where their output is most valuable, and this is most likely to happen if the use of factors of production is determined by what consumers are willing to pay. The objection to a "free" system is that it is not really "free" and it is less efficient.

It has been pointed out that, with subscription television, programs will only be seen by those who have the money to pay for them. But if reliance on ability to pay is so unfortunate when applied to television programs, how much worse it must be when applied to food or clothing or housing—or even to television sets and phonograph records.

Notes and Questions

1. Nonrivalrous Goods. Our discussion above began by pointing out that broadcast content is nonrivalrous, a notion discussed more generally in Chapter One. Unlike, say, pizza, one person's consumption of broadcast does not diminish another person's ability to consume. Can you think of other examples of nonrivalrous goods? Are these goods provided by the government, provided by private parties through unregulated market mechanisms, or provided by private parties but in markets subject to significant government regulation? Does your answer help to explain why broadcast is regulated?

2. Excludability. Public goods are always nonrival, but they are sometimes nonexcludable as well. Nonexcludable goods are goods such that, if one person consumes the good, it is impossible to prevent others from consuming that same good simultaneously. A street light is a classic example. The inability to exclude poses a problem in that the threat of exclusion is often what motivates consumers to pay for goods they value. Thus, if an inventor cannot exclude others from using his innovative idea and offering a rival product (without having to incur the development costs or pay a license fee), or the owner of the park cannot deny access to those who refuse to pay for its maintenance, that inventor and that owner might well not be able to collect the revenues they need to stay in business. Coase does not say anything about excludability in the excerpt above, but can you apply this idea to the cable and broadcast setting? For instance, if ABC were to adopt technologies that made broadcast excludable, would that solve the problems about which Coase wrote?

3. **Food, Clothing, and Housing.** Coase concludes his remarks by noting that, if reliance on ability to pay is troubling in the broadcast setting, it should be all the more troubling when applied to food, clothing, or housing. Is that a fair analogy?

4. **Summing Valuations.** In an advertiser-supported regime, a television broadcaster might choose to air a program that 500,000 people each value at $1 instead of offering a program that 490,000 people each value at $10. No one who respects consumer preferences can regard that situation as maximizing consumer welfare, and subscription television would presumably air the latter program. But compare the program that 500,000 people each value at $1 with a program that 1000 people each value at $510. Again, we would expect an advertiser-supported regime to offer the former and subscription television to offer the latter. Should we prefer the advertiser-supported regime in that case?

5. **Advertising Distortions.** Do the distortions introduced by advertiser support go away as the number of broadcast channels increases? Do you see why they might? Do any distortions remain? Similarly, are there distortions of any sort inherent in pay systems? Under what conditions?

6. **The Costs of "Free" Television.** Advertiser support is not really free. For one thing, advertisers must recoup their costs, and presumably do so through increased prices on goods that viewers of the show are likely to purchase. Moreover, while there might be some informational and entertainment value in watching commercials, to some degree the time spent watching commercials is a cost to viewers as well. Some viewers, for example, would pay a modest sum if there were an option to purchase advertising-free TV (as when they buy DVDs of a TV show). Then again, advertising also benefits consumers. To that end, some studies suggest that advertising increases the degree of competition in a given market and that the resulting competition, in turn, leads to lower prices even though the firms all incur increased advertising expenses. One such study compared eyeglass prices in markets where advertising was permitted to eyeglass prices in markets where an advertising ban was in effect. The market with advertising averaged lower prices. *See* Lee Benham, The Effect of Advertising on the Price of Eyeglasses, 15 J.L. & Econ. 337 (1972).

7. **Are Advertiser Preferences Illegitimate?** An implicit assumption in the above is that advertiser preferences are somehow illegitimate. Is that true? Why shouldn't broadcast content in part be determined by advertiser preferences and in part by viewer preferences, exactly as the current advertiser-supported system operates today? Indeed, it seems that consumers prefer a mix of subscription fees and advertising. The law of diminishing returns suggests that consumers generally will prefer solutions that are neither wholly subscription nor wholly advertising. Some types of programs or consumers may be exceptions to this generality, to be sure, but almost all multichannel services both charge subscription fees and provide programs that contain advertising.

8. Hooray for Hollywood? Movie theaters sell tickets person by person. Is movie content, then, like subscription television in that we might expect it to better reflect viewer preferences than does advertiser-sponsored television?

---

§ 8.B. Why Regulate? Are There Natural Monopolies?

There are many possible reasons for regulating MVPD providers. One reason is that MVPD has implications for broadcast. So, if the federal government wants a vibrant broadcast television market because such a market furthers important political or educational goals, the federal government might want to regulate MVPDs in order to ensure broadcast's continued vitality. Another reason, however, is that the costs of providing MVPD service might mean that MVPD service is a natural monopoly. We introduced the concept of a natural monopoly in Chapter One. Recall that if a firm produces a good with no ready substitute and has declining per unit costs over the entire range of consumer demand, the market will be most efficiently served by a single provider (a monopoly). You should probably look back to Chapter One, and particularly to the excerpt from Judge Posner in which he discusses the possibility that cable television systems are natural monopolies.

Is conventional television broadcasting a natural monopoly service? Once a program is transmitted, the marginal cost to the broadcaster of serving an additional viewer is zero. So if the market at issue were that for distribution of a particular program, there might be a case for calling broadcast a natural monopoly. Having additional broadcasters distribute the same program would only raise costs. But that is much too narrow a market definition. Consumers don't watch some generic product called "broadcast"; they watch particular programs that in many cases are not substitutes for each other. So, at issue in broadcasting is not just the production and distribution of a single program at any point in time, but of multiple, simultaneous programs. Given that fact, the question becomes whether a single broadcaster can make and/or distribute programming more cheaply than can multiple, competing broadcasters.

On the program production side, there is little case to be made for the existence of a natural monopoly. Putting aside the important point that it is probably not beneficial to confine a creative enterprise to one or a few producers, the incremental costs of producing programming (actors, writers, and so on) are very large in comparison to the small fixed costs (e.g., studios and equipment) and there seems little reason that the incremental costs should decline as a studio produces more shows. On the distribution side, a single broadcaster does not have the capacity to deliver all programs that air at a given time. And once a new set of transmission facilities is needed to broadcast the programming that the market demands, the benefits of spreading fixed costs are truncated and the conditions for natural monopoly probably disappear. The arguments for natural monopoly in conventional broadcasting are thus very weak.

This brings us to cable television, long regulated as a natural monopoly. Does it meet the conditions discussed in Chapter One? There seems little question that the fixed costs of building a cable system are very high. Moreover, building a high-capacity system that can carry all the program channels needed to meet market demand probably doesn't cost much more than building a low-capacity system. Finally, the cost per customer of providing cable distribution declines as more households subscribe to the service. The incremental costs of connecting additional homes to the cable system are very modest and probably constant. Accordingly, spreading the fixed costs of cable distribution over an increasing number of households reduces the cost per subscriber—and, once a complete cable network is in place, there is good reason to think that the per unit distribution costs decline over the entire range of consumer demand. Entry by a second cable system would therefore raise the average per household costs of providing service. At least as far as program distribution (as distinguished from program production, packaging and marketing) is concerned, then, there is a plausible argument that cable systems exhibit natural monopoly properties.

Notes and Questions

1. New Technologies. The text above discusses cable television. Do the same natural monopoly arguments work for other MVPD providers, like direct broadcast satellite providers? Do these arguments apply to Netflix? And does anything in the analysis change in instances where, instead of having two entrants proposing to use the same delivery technology, one entrant proposes to use (say) cable, whereas the other proposes to deliver via satellite?

2. Periodic Competition. Suppose that a city were to announce that it was going to authorize only one firm to lay cable lines under city streets, but that every five years it would auction off the right to be that firm. Would this structured, periodic competition produce the same benefits as more open competition? Can you come up with a variant that would? *See* Harold Demsetz, Why Regulate Utilities?, 11 J.L. & Econ. 55 (1968); Oliver Williamson, Franchise Bidding for Natural Monopolies—In General and with Respect to CATV, 7 Bell J. Econ. 73 (1976).

3. Separate Content From Conduit? In the 1970s, the President's Office of Telecommunications suggested that cable providers be barred from entering the content business. In principle, the concern was that control over distribution and interests in programming would result in the use of monopoly power in one market to control the other (e.g., from distribution to content). This principle also underpinned the syndication and financial interest rules, which limited the ability of the major networks to enter into the content business and are discussed in the next chapter. A principal counterargument is that the owner of a platform has a powerful incentive to develop—through its own affiliates or nonaffiliated providers—valuable content for its platform. In the case of cable networks, it was thus not an accident that both vertically integrated offerings (such as HBO) as well as non-vertically integrated ones (such as MTV) were instrumental in spurring the increasing popularity of cable.

Of the two principles outlined above, which strikes you as more compelling? What information about technology, market structure, and the effectiveness of different possible regulatory strategies (e.g., mandated access to distribution or content) would influence your view on which principle should guide policymakers in this area?

§ 8.C. Why Regulate? Implications for Broadcast

Cable television began in the 1940s as "community antenna television" (CATV), with cable operators using towers and well-placed antennas to pick up broadcast signals that could then be transmitted through coaxial cable to nearby residents. This retransmission of local signals alarmed neither broadcasters nor the FCC. At worst it was redundant, with cable bringing signals to consumers who could already receive them over the air. And at best it benefited both consumers and broadcasters, with cable in these cases bringing broadcast signals to consumers who otherwise would have gone unserved.

As cable began to take on an expanded role, however, both broadcasters and the FCC became concerned. Should cable operators be allowed to "import" broadcast signals from distant communities, in essence bringing new broadcasters into the local marketplace? If so, should they have to compensate the foreign broadcasters who, perhaps unwittingly, supplied the content? What about the local broadcasters who would now face new competition in the local market? And should cable providers themselves be allowed to originate content, either charging subscribers a flat fee or offering programs on a pay-as-you-go basis? These were some of the issues that needed to be addressed early in cable's history.

The text that follows is an overview of early FCC policy with respect to cable television, and it provides a good snapshot of the FCC's original understanding of cable as both friend and foe to the broadcast-dominated media marketplace. As the authors indicate at the outset, they see these early battles as a cautionary tale for policymakers to consider when evaluating the imposition of regulation requirements on new entrants. Do you agree?

The Deregulation of Cable Television
Stanley M. Besen & Robert W. Crandall, 44 L. & Contemp. Probs. 77 (1981)

The cable television industry provides an interesting case study of regulation for several reasons. First, like trucking or intrastate natural gas, the cable television industry developed as a substitute for a regulated service. Television broadcasting had been regulated by the FCC for some time when cable television operators began to offer retransmissions of distant broadcast signals. It is not surprising that this new industry was soon viewed as a threat to the established, regulated television industry. Extension of regulation to the new challenger was a natural response for the regulators.

Second, cable television offers a classic example of how markets operate to thwart regulators' attempts to cross subsidize "meritorious" services. The FCC has limited the number of television outlets in each major market and required that part of the profits generated as a result be devoted to "public service" programming. [But] cable television [was] capable of adding immensely to the number of signals available in a market, increasing the competition broadcasters face [and] reduc[ing] local broadcasters' ability to offer these merit programs. Perceiving a threat to its policy of cross-subsidization, the Commission could be expected to attempt to limit competition.

Third, cable television provides an excellent example of how difficult it is to restrict entry when technology is changing rapidly. Just as the Interstate Commerce Commission [saw] its ability to regulate railroads compromised by the invention of the truck and then the airplane, the FCC has found it difficult to continue to protect its television broadcast licensees from the onslaught of technology. If technological change is sufficiently rapid, deregulation may be unavoidable in almost any sector.

Fourth, the case of cable television regulation demonstrates how difficult it is to make a sustainable and convincing case for protecting the public from competition. Virtually all of the premises upon which the Commission regulated cable television have been shown to be invalid. This is, and was, no surprise to students of the industry who argued that they were invalid from the outset. The rapid change of direction by the Commission must be attributed, at least in part, to the mounting evidence which demonstrates that the Commission's fears of the effects of cable growth were exaggerated.

The Regulatory History

The first cable television (CATV) system began operation in Astoria, Oregon in 1949; the first commercial system was initiated one year later in Lansford, Pennsylvania. By the end of the 1950s, there were approximately 640 systems serving about 650,000 subscribers, and the nascent industry had begun to receive the attention of the FCC. It is fair to say, however, that during this period the attitude of the Commission was essentially one of "benign neglect," of permitting cable to develop without government intervention absent a definitive showing that such growth was not in the public interest.

A. The "Auxiliary Service" Inquiry

The Commission's early views on cable television are provided extensively in its 1959 Report and Order in its inquiry into the effect of cable and other "auxiliary services" on the development of television broadcasting. Inquiry into the Impact of Community Antenna Systems, TV Translators, TV "Satellite" Stations, and TV "Repeaters" on the Orderly Development of Television Broadcasting, Report and Order, 26 F.C.C. 403 (1959). The Commission's basic concern, one that continued over the two decades of cable regulation, was stated at the outset of its Report and Order:

> [T]here is presented a problem of conflicting interests and objectives. On the one hand are the interests of the general public of the areas involved in the preservation of a local television outlet, with the attendant advantages which a community gains from having a local means of self-expression, and (in some cases but not in all) the preservation of the *only television service* to some of the public, such as rural residents who cannot be served by CATV. On the other hand is the interest of another group, such as city residents who want and can afford to pay for CATV service, in obtaining *multiple television service.*

Id. ¶ 5.

The conflict the Commission described was the basis of the claims of some broadcasters who argued that, where cable systems carry signals which viewers in their markets cannot receive over-the-air, local stations lose audiences and advertising revenues. This, in turn, leads to a reduction in local service and, in the extreme, to the local station being forced off the air. Thus, the broadcasters held, if cable were permitted to import distant signals, some viewers might lose their only television service. This claim influenced the next two decades of government regulatory policy toward cable.

In examining the "evidence" presented on the relation of station viability to the existence of cable and the other auxiliary services, the Commission first concluded that it believed the public would benefit substantially from essentially unfettered growth of auxiliary services, including cable: "... [W]e do not now envision where we could find that the public interest would be disserved by affording an opportunity for choice of service and the benefits of competition and diversity of expression." *Id.* ¶ 86. The only *possible* exception might be where it was the one and only local broadcast service whose existence was threatened: "... [T]here is some merit in the broadcasters' position [that the 'only service' must be maintained] ... especially ... where the number losing their only service is considerably greater than the number who would receive the multiple service." *Id.* ¶ 90.

The Commission did feel that regulation might be required in two areas. First, the Commission had been asked to rule that section [325(b)] of the Communications Act, which forbids the rebroadcast of the signal of a broadcast station without its permission, applied also to the retransmission by cable systems of broadcast signals. The Commission indicated that it did "not believe that ... section [325(b)] in its present form includes the requirement that CATVs get the consent of the stations whose signals they carry." *Id.* ¶ 67. But, the Commission went on, "... [W]e intend to recommend to Congress that an appropriate amendment to section [325(b)] be enacted, so as to extend the 'consent' requirement to CATVs." *Id.* This marks the first public-policy pronouncement in favor of "retransmission consent," an issue which has remained before the Commission for over two decades in one form or another.

The Commission also found favor with the suggestion that cable systems be required to carry the signals of local or nearby stations (if they so request) and indicated that it would recommend such an amendment to the Communications Act. However, it rejected a proposal that cable systems be forbidden to duplicate programs carried by local stations, even when those stations protest the duplication.

B. A Change in Policy: Carter Mountain

The first policy change occurred in connection with what appeared to be a routine authorization of microwave facilities to carry broadcast signals to cable systems. Carter Mountain Transmission Corporation had applied for FCC authorization and, nine days after the Commission's report on the impact of "auxiliary services" on television broadcasting, its application was granted without a hearing. Shortly thereafter, a protest was filed by a local broadcast station and the effective date of the authorization was suspended. In 1961, the Commission's Hearing Examiner, echoing the Commission's views in the auxiliary services inquiry, denied the protest:

> [W]hatever impact the operations of the CATV systems may have on protestant's operation of station KWRB-TV, these are matters of no legal significance to the ultimate determination made that a grant of the subject application of Carter, a bona fide communications common carrier, will serve the public interest. Even if considered, the record precludes any reliable approach to an accurate estimate of that impact.

Carter Mountain Transmission Corp., 32 F.C.C. 459, 486 n.31 (1962).

A year later, on appeal to the Commission, the authorization was denied. In what can only be regarded as a startling reversal of its earlier views, the Commission argued:

> A grant of common carrier radio facilities requires a finding that the public interest will be served thereby; certainly the well-being of existing television facilities is an aspect of this public interest. Thus it is not only appropriate, it is necessary that we determine whether the use of the facility applied for would directly or indirectly bring about the elimination of the only television transmission or reception service to the public.

Id. at 461.

Moreover, the Commission apparently no longer harbored doubts about its ability to determine whether cable would harm broadcasters: "If the CATV pattern is permitted to be altered ... the local station ... would find it more difficult to sell its advertising in the face of a split audience, and this situation ... results in our judgment that the demise of this local operation would result." *Id.* at 464.

Finally, where previously it could find no reason why it should not afford "an opportunity for choice of service and the benefits of competition and diversity of expression" it now found:

> True, a grant of the instant application would permit the rendition of better service by the CATV, but at the expense of destroying the local station and its rural coverage.... It must be concluded, ... [that] the need for the local outlet and the service which it would provide to outlying areas outweighs the need for the improved service which Carter would furnish....

Id. at 464–65. The Commission invited Carter to refile its application if it could show that the cable system would carry the signal of the local station and not carry the signals of other stations which duplicated its programming.

C. Rules Concerning Microwave-Served CATV

Three years later, the Commission moved to codify its policies respecting the authorization of microwave facilities which served cable systems. There were to be two kinds of regulations, both in the form of conditions imposed on the authorization of microwave facilities to serve cable systems. One requirement was that the cable system carry the signals of all local stations. The second rule was that a cable system not carry the programs of a distant station when they duplicated the programs of local stations during a period of fifteen days before or after the local broadcast.

Both requirements derived from the Commission's view that the competition provided by cable television systems to local broadcasters is different from the competition provided by additional broadcast stations. When a cable system did not carry the local signals, a viewer subscribing to the service could only receive a local station by disconnecting the cable and attaching an antenna. To the extent that this proved cumbersome, access to cable subscribers was denied to local broadcasters. The requirement that local signals be carried was designed to remedy this difficulty.

The nonduplication requirement was designed to deal with the fact that cable systems carried broadcast signals without obtaining the consent of either the originating station or the producers of its programs. The Commission held: "The CATV system that provides its subscribers with the signals of distant stations presently stands outside of the program distribution process...." Rules re Microwave-Served CATV, 38 F.C.C. 683, 704 (1965). Also: "... [I]n the absence of a market in which the question of competitive access to programming by stations and CATVs can be resolved, our aim is to preserve for stations the competitive exclusivity they have been able to obtain as against other stations, but nothing more." *Id.* at 720. The asserted rationale for the nonduplication rule was preservation of this exclusivity.

Although the Commission's stated purpose in adopting these rules was to make competition between broadcasting and cable "fair and reasonable," the Commission clearly was concerned as much with the outcome as with the fairness of the process: "The question at the heart of these proceedings is whether and to what extent rulemaking action is necessary or appropriate to integrate CATV service into our existing television system — to ensure that CATV performs its valuable supplementary role without unduly damaging or impeding the growth of television broadcast service." *Id.* at 701.

The Commission continued to be concerned with the impact of cable in the smallest markets, but its list of concerns had grown since 1959:

> We think it clear ... that the most serious effects will be felt by (1) stations in smaller one- and two-station markets, where the public does not receive the full

services of all three national networks off-the-air, (2) by marginal stations in larger markets, and (3) by new stations coming on the air.

Id. at 711. Since, by definition, there will always be marginal stations in larger markets so long as not all channel assignments are filled, the Commission was no longer limiting its purview to situations in which the only local broadcast service was threatened. Indeed, it was likely that every market would contain at least one station in one of the Commission's three areas of concern.

D. The Second Report and Order

The following year, 1966, was a watershed in the regulation of cable. Never before had the Commission's regulation of cable been more wide-ranging or restrictive. In adopting its Second Report and Order, 2 F.C.C. 2d 725 (1966), the Commission restated that its actions were designed to prevent "unfair" competition by cable systems and to foreclose any "adverse impact" on broadcasting that CATV growth might produce. The role of cable was to be that of a "supplement" to the over-the-air broadcast system.

The Second Report and Order marked three notable shifts in FCC policy. First, the Commission had progressed from 1959, when it claimed that it was unable to measure the harm caused by cable, to a point where, seven years later, it stated confidently that "the materials before us would appear to indicate substantial growth and substantial impact by CATV in the large markets." *Id.* at 744 n.30.

Second, the Commission's locus of concern had shifted from markets where the only local broadcast service is threatened by cable to the major markets which have many stations:

> We have selected the top 100 markets for special attention because it is in these markets that UHF stations or wire pay-TV based upon CATV operations are most likely to develop and therefore the problems raised are most acute.... The top 100 markets include roughly 90 percent of the television homes in this country. Our policy therefore focuses on the critically important areas.

Id. at 783.

Third, for the first time in its deliberations respecting cable, the Commission expressed concern for the impact that cable growth might have on the emergence of UHF television stations, especially in the major markets. The Commission's policy of placing many television allocations in the UHF band and intermixing VHF and UHF stations in the same markets, established in its Sixth Report and Order on Television Allocations, 41 F.C.C. 148 (1952), had encountered serious problems. Many of the UHF stations which had gone on the air in 1954 had failed. More than 40 percent of UHF stations reported operating at a loss compared to less than 15 percent of VHF stations.

With the passage of the All-Channel Receiver Act in 1962 and the subsequent enactment of Commission rules to implement its provisions, the Commission assumed responsibility for the healthy growth of UHF. In its Second Report and Order, the Commission determined that the expansion of cable would harm the prospects for UHF. Thus, the Commission concluded, cable development would have to be tightly circumscribed in those markets where it believed that UHF prospects were brightest, the top 100.

The Commission's new cable policy had two facets. First, it extended to all cable systems, not just those employing microwave, the requirement that all local stations be carried and that imported signals not duplicate local programming. Second, and more importantly, the Commission announced that it would not permit the carriage of a distant broadcast signal into one of the top 100 markets without a showing in an evidentiary hearing that such carriage "would be consistent with the public interest, and particularly the establishment and healthy maintenance of UHF television broadcast service." 2 F.C.C. 2d at 782. Thus, even cable systems which adhered to the local carriage and nonduplication rules would still be required to demonstrate that their carriage of distant signals would not threaten even marginal UHF stations.

In the only evidentiary hearing completed for a major market, the Commission reversed the decision of its Hearing Examiner and imposed restrictions on the ability of one of the San Diego cable systems to carry the signals of Los Angeles independent stations. This decision, combined with the administrative burden of the evidentiary hearing process, made it clear that the development of cable in the major markets would be stopped completely unless the rules were regularly evaded by staff action or were abandoned completely.

E. Affirmation of Jurisdiction

[T]he Commission's authority to adopt the rules contained in its Second Report and Order was upheld by the Supreme Court in United States v. Southwestern Cable Co., 392 U.S. 157 (1968). Relying on the Communications Act, which obligates the Commission to provide "a fair, efficient, and equitable distribution" of television service, and on the Commission's findings that achievement of this goal requires the use of the UHF band and that cable threatens UHF television, the Supreme Court upheld the Commission's authority to regulate cable. Without determining the limits of the Commission's regulatory authority, the Court found that the rules adopted in 1966 were "reasonably ancillary" to the fulfillment of the Commission's responsibilities in regulating broadcasting.[2]

G. Cablecasting: Prescriptive Rather than Proscriptive Regulation

In 1969, the Commission addressed the issue of origination by requiring all cable systems with 3,500 or more subscribers to originate programming. The Commission described the benefits which could be expected from origination and why it had refused to accede to broadcaster requests that origination be banned entirely because it would divert audience from "free" television:

> [W]e do not think that the public should be deprived of an opportunity for greater diversity merely because a broadening of selections may spread the audience and reduce the size of the audience for any particular selection. Such competition is not unfair, since broadcasters and CATV... originators stand on the same footing in acquiring the program material with which they compete.

Amendment of Part 74, Subpart K, of the Commission's Rules and Regulations Relative to Community Antenna Television Systems, First Report and Order, 20 F.C.C. 2d 201, 203 (1969).

In addition, the Commission saw benefits from the potential for cable networking of originated programming. But despite the Commission's words, some doubts remained about its sincerity. First, the Commission imposed a rule limiting advertising on originated programming to "natural breaks" which reduced the attractiveness of providing such programs on an advertiser-supported basis. Second, by leaving the question whether to permit advertising on cable network operation "open," it discouraged such networking. Finally, while it stated that it saw no need to place limits on originated programs supported by direct subscriber payments, in the following year it did just that.

---

2. [Ancillary jurisdiction is discussed at greater length in Chapter Fourteen. Eds.]

In extending the rules which had been applied to over-the-air pay television to pay-cable operations, the Commission stated that:

> [W]here cablecasting is accompanied by a per-program or per-channel fee, it is akin to subscription television and presents the same threat of siphoning programs away from free television in favor of a service limited to those ... to whom the cable is geographically available. Remedial action in this area should not wait upon the threat becoming actuality.

Amendment of Part 74, Subpart K, of the Commission's Rules and Regulations Relative to Community Antenna Television Systems, Memorandum Opinion and Order, 23 F.C.C. 2d 825, 828 (1970). The rules prevented cablecasting for which a per-program or per-channel charge was made of: "(i) movies which had been in theatrical release more than 2 years prior to the cablecast, (ii) sporting events which had been telecast in the community on a non-subscription basis during the previous two years, and (iii) series programming of any type." These regulations also limited feature films and sporting events to 90 percent or less of total programming hours and banned advertising on pay channels entirely.

K. Court Interpretations of the Commission's Rules

Two actions taken by the courts were especially important for the development of cable. The first, and more significant, came when, in Home Box Office v. FCC, 567 F.2d 9 (1977), the Court of Appeals for the District of Columbia vacated the Commission's pay cable rules. These rules had sharply limited the ability of cable systems to offer feature films and sports events on subscription channels in order to prevent the "siphoning" of programming from broadcasting to cable. In effect, the Commission was regulating a nonbroadcasting activity, pay cable, in order to provide protection to broadcasters. Although the court ruled that "... we think that the strategy the Commission has employed in implementing its interest in preventing siphoning creates a restriction 'greater than is essential to the furtherance of that interest,'" *Id.* at 50 (citing United States v. O'Brien, 391 U.S. 367, 377 (1968)), it also appeared to say that, in any event, it would not have affirmed any pay-cable rules because of doubts that the Commission had jurisdiction to impose them. In light of this chastisement by the court of appeals, the Commission has not tried to reimpose pay-cable rules.

A second significant ruling occurred in FCC v. Midwest Video Corp., 440 U.S. 689 (1979) (*Midwest Video II*). In United States v. Midwest Video Corp., 406 U.S. 649 (1972) (*Midwest Video I*), the Supreme Court had ruled, in a five-to-four decision, that the FCC had the authority to require cable systems to originate programming. A plurality of four found that there was no rational distinction between regulations designed to avoid adverse impact, such as those upheld in *Southwestern Cable*, and those whose purpose was to enhance the quality of television service, such as the Commission's origination rules.

In *Midwest Video II*, however, the Commission's rules requiring that channels be made available by cable operators for access by third parties on a non-discriminatory basis and that cable systems be required to have a minimum capacity of 20 channels were overturned by the Supreme Court. The majority argued that, while the origination rules required cable operators only to fulfill a role comparable to that played by broadcasters, the access rules required them to operate as common carriers. The Communications Act prohibits the imposition of common carrier regulation of broadcasters and the majority reasoned that this stricture applied to cable systems as well.[3]

---

3. [*Midwest Video I* and *Midwest Video II* are discussed at greater length in Chapter Fourteen. Eds.]

Notes and Questions

1. Why Protect Broadcast? In the early years of cable television, the FCC often regulated cable television with an eye toward protecting the preexisting broadcast industry. But is it clear to you why the FCC favored broadcast? Was this just politics, with the well-funded broadcast lobby championing its own interests over those of the public? Was it a simple reluctance to disturb the status quo? It should be noted that the FCC never seemed to consider the possibility of the opposite regulatory approach, namely regulating broadcast so as to promote the development of cable. This is not so ridiculous as it might at first sound; if the FCC's real concern was providing a wide variety of content diversity, that goal could in theory have been accomplished by a thriving cable industry.

2. The "Level Playing Field" or "Regulatory Parity" Principle. What merit is there to the claim that for regulation to be successful, similar regulations must apply to all similar services? When incumbents call for the regulation of new entrants to protect basic policies—say, a commitment to localism—or on fairness grounds, how should policymakers respond?

3. Responding to New, Possibly Disruptive, Technologies. A major theme in telecommunications law is how the FCC responds to new technologies that threaten incumbents (as most of them do). As the excerpt above reveals, broadcasters saw dangers to television broadcasting arising from cable television, and the FCC was often sympathetic to broadcasters' concerns. In the 1990s, radio broadcasters raised similar concerns about the advent of satellite radio. The capacity of satellite radio, and the possibility of it "siphoning" programming from broadcasters, were analogous to the earlier threats posed by cable television to television broadcasting. So radio broadcasters made arguments against satellite radio that resonated with earlier arguments against cable television. As the excerpt below reflects, those arguments met with less success in the 1990s than they had in an earlier era.

ESTABLISHMENT OF RULES AND POLICIES FOR THE DIGITAL AUDIO RADIO SATELLITE SERVICE IN THE 2310–2360 MHz FREQUENCY BAND

Report and Order, Memorandum Opinion and Order, and Further Notice of Proposed Rulemaking, 12 FCC Rcd. 5754 (1997)

I. INTRODUCTION

1. Digital Audio Radio Service by satellite promises to provide continuous nationwide radio programming with compact disc quality sound. Motorists on the highways of America may soon be able to tune in to one of many satellite DARS channels offering a particular format without interruption or fading as they travel across the United States. This new service also has the potential to increase the variety of programming available to the listening public. Providers may, for example, offer niche channels that would serve listeners with special interests. Satellite DARS has the technological potential to serve listeners in areas of the country that have been underserved. While, to some extent, DARS will compete with local radio, we anticipate that it will also complement terrestrial radio.

2. After carefully reviewing [all comments in this proceeding] we have concluded that it is in the public interest to license satellite DARS. Opponents of the new service have

not shown that its potential adverse impact on local radio service outweighs its potential benefits.

7. In the Notice and in prior Orders, we discussed the benefits of satellite DARS proffered by the proponents. These include introduction of a new radio service to the public, a national distribution of radio programming to all areas, including underserved and unserved areas and population groups, the creation of jobs and the promotion of technological development in the satellite and receiver industries, and the improvement of U.S. competitiveness in the international economy. We sought comment on our tentative conclusion that satellite DARS offers substantial public benefits.

8. We also invited detailed comment and information on the economic impact of satellite DARS on existing radio broadcasters. We acknowledge the high level of concern that terrestrial broadcasters have expressed about satellite DARS. In addition to three associations of broadcasters, more than one hundred terrestrial radio stations owners or operators have submitted individual letters opposing satellite DARS.

9. Recognizing the significant public value of terrestrial radio service, we must weigh the potential public interest benefits of satellite DARS against its potential adverse impact on terrestrial radio. This impact is relevant "to the extent that [it] would predictably lead to serious loss of important services to consumers, taking into account the potential for future enhancements of terrestrial broadcasting by the introduction of new technologies." Establishment of Rules and Policies for the Digital Audio Radio Satellite Service in the 2310–2360 MHz Frequency Band, Notice of Proposed Rulemaking, 11 FCC Rcd. 1 (1995). In the Notice we emphasized that, pursuant to section 7 of the Communications Act, opponents of a new technology, such as satellite DARS, bear the burden of demonstrating that it is inconsistent with the public interest. We have previously noted that, "The public interest in this regard is the provision of services of value to the listening public and includes the protection of competition, not competitors." Id. ¶ 11.

1. Public Interest Benefits

10. Satellite DARS can offer high quality radio signals to listeners who currently receive few terrestrial radio signals.

14. Satellite DARS may also be able to foster niche programming because it can aggregate small, nationally dispersed listener groups that local radio could not profitably serve. Commenters suggest that satellite DARS could fulfill a need for more educational programming, rural programming, ethnic programming, religious programming, and specialized musical programming. One nationally representative survey found that 10–27% of the respondents indicated a strong interest in accessing programming formats that are not widely available. Evidence from a survey by the National Endowment for the Arts suggests that niche marketing opportunities exist for some of the less popular radio formats.

15. We believe that licensees will have an incentive to diversify program formats and thereby provide valuable niche programming. We recognize that satellite DARS licensees are likely to provide the programming that is most profitable. Nonetheless, given that we anticipate each satellite DARS licensee will control more than 20 channels, each licensee will have an incentive to diversify programming so that one channel will not directly compete with another channel that the licensee itself controls.

17. We conclude that licensing operators to provide satellite DARS will yield substantial benefits to consumers. We now evaluate whether opponents have met their burden

of showing that these benefits are outweighed by the potential harm to listeners from potential loss of terrestrial service resulting from increased competition from satellite DARS.

2. Impact on Terrestrial Radio Listenership

18. In the Notice, we sought comment on the effect of satellite DARS on terrestrial radio listenership. Given the distinguishing features of satellite DARS—it is a national service, it will require new and relatively costly equipment, and it may be offered via paid subscription—we find that the effect of satellite DARS on terrestrial radio is likely to be significantly smaller than the effect of additional terrestrial radio stations.

21. Estimating listening time diversion depends on the share of listening time allocated to satellite DARS when the listener has a choice between satellite DARS and terrestrial radio. Drawing an analogy with the diffusion of cable services indicates that established programming loses audience share relatively slowly. In 1984, about a decade after the introduction of premium cable services and the development of 24 to 36 channel cable TV systems, cable channels attracted 14% of television viewing time. After another decade, the share of cable channels in television viewing time rose to 30%. An important weakness in this analogy is that the difference between cable programming and network programming during this period is probably significantly greater than will be the difference between satellite DARS programming and terrestrial radio programming. Nonetheless, we believe that owners of satellite DARS receivers will continue to allocate a significant share of their listening time to terrestrial radio in order to hear music or news of local interest. Even with rapid, further penetration of satellite DARS receivers, we expect that satellite DARS' share of radio listening time will grow relatively slowly over decades.

3. Impact on Terrestrial Radio Advertising Revenues

23. While we recognize that satellite DARS has significant competitive advantages in offering advertising to a national audience with satellite DARS receivers, several factors may limit the possible significance to terrestrial radio of such additional competition. First, at this time, only one out of the four satellite DARS applicants has indicated an intention to implement its system on a non-subscription, advertiser-supported basis. Second, a large share of the national radio audience is not likely to have satellite DARS receivers, at least for a significant period of time. Third, national advertising revenue amounts to only 18% of terrestrial radio advertising revenue and is on average less important for small-market stations than for large-market stations. Local advertising revenue is much more important than national advertising revenue for terrestrial radio's viability and prevalence, and, at this time, we have no evidence that satellite DARS would be able to compete for local advertising revenue.

24. More important to terrestrial radio is possible competition with satellite DARS for listener attention because this new offering could reduce the size of the local listening audience available for terrestrial radio stations to sell. We recognize that a decrease in the audience size could lead to some reduction in terrestrial station revenues. As discussed above, however, we believe the reduction would be modest, although the record leaves room for significant uncertainty.

4. Effects on Terrestrial Stations' Profitability and Viability

29. Our concern about licensing satellite DARS focuses on its impact on the provision of locally oriented radio service. Satellite DARS proponents argue that the ability to offer local content will give terrestrial broadcasters a competitive advantage. Terrestrial broadcasters argue that providing local content is a public service that depends, in effect, on cross-subsidization from more profitable programming.

30. We conclude that the record lacks systematically sampled, quantitative evidence about the listening time, revenue base, and profitability of local content. Nonetheless, if local content were relatively unprofitable for every station, one would expect competition among terrestrial stations to result in minimal local programming on most stations. Yet the record indicates that such analysis is not necessarily accurate; despite vigorous competition among stations, some stations provide much local programming, while others provide relatively little. Competition from satellite DARS may create incentives for at least some terrestrial stations to increase their emphasis on local programming in order to attempt to differentiate their service from satellite DARS. It is unclear the degree to which that might affect overall station profits.

31. In sum, although healthy satellite DARS systems are likely to have some adverse impact on terrestrial radio audience size, revenues, and profits, the record does not demonstrate that licensing satellite DARS would have such a strong adverse impact that it threatens the provision of local radio service.

32. We also note that revenue of terrestrial radio is projected to grow at a real (inflation adjusted) rate of about 4% per year. Such projected revenue should mitigate, at least to some extent, the eventual impact on terrestrial stations of satellite DARS. We reject as unnecessary a proposed phase-in and evaluation period for satellite DARS. We conclude that opponents of satellite DARS have not shown that its potentially adverse impact on local radio outweighs its potential benefits to the American radio listener.

33. There is uncertainty inherent in any attempt to predict the impact of satellite DARS on the terrestrial radio industry. The technologies, structure, and regulation of the communications industry are changing dramatically. Developments in the next decade may significantly change the market for both satellite DARS and terrestrial broadcasting. Although opponents of satellite DARS have not shown that it will have a sudden and dramatic adverse impact on terrestrial broadcasting, we cannot entirely rule out the possibility of a major adverse impact. We emphasize that we remain committed to supporting a vibrant and vital terrestrial radio service for the public. Accordingly, we will continue to monitor and evaluate the potential and actual impact of satellite DARS, particularly in small radio markets, so that we will be able to take any necessary action to safeguard the important service that terrestrial radio provides.

Notes and Questions

1. What Is Different? How do you explain the FCC's rejection of the broadcasters' arguments? The Commission acknowledges the likelihood of an adverse impact on terrestrial service, but says that the record "does not demonstrate that licensing satellite DARS would have such a strong adverse impact that it threatens the provision of local radio service." ¶ 31. Is that the right standard? Why?

To the extent that satellite radio was approved because it will serve new customers and create incentives to develop new technology, what new service will not be approved? Does not every service promise to serve a new need or an old need in a new way, and will not every service therefore also create incentives for the development of new technology?

2. How Local Stations Compete. The Commission in the above document tries to understand whether and how satellite radio will change the behavior of terrestrial local radio stations. One possibility is that satellite will force local stations to drop local programming and instead pick up arguably more profitable fare. Another possibility is that satellite will force local stations to become more local, in that way distinguishing their offerings even more sharply from those available (for a fee) from satellite. Which of these arguments seems more likely to hold? Does the Commission have before it adequate evidence to make this decision?

3. Is National Radio New? Reading the Commission's document, one might imagine that satellite is the first example of national radio programming. Of course, it is not, as many national talk radio hosts and listeners can attest. True, these programs are delivered over terrestrial equipment, but does that meaningfully distinguish syndication and other forms of radio consolidation from satellite?

---

§ 8.D. Who Regulates Cable Television?

As will be discussed more fully in Chapter Fourteen, the FCC initially found itself without a clear statutory mandate to address cable television. At the time of its initial growth, the FCC had Title II, which addressed common carrier telephony, and Title III, which addressed broadcasting. Cable—the delivery of video over wires—did not fit either scheme. At first, the FCC declined to regulate cable television, but it later decided that it could regulate because the exercise of such authority would be "ancillary" to its power over broadcasting.

Although the Supreme Court generally (but not uniformly) upheld the Commission's cable regulations, Congress finally stepped in. Almost twenty years after the FCC first began to regulate cable television under its Title I authority, Congress devised a statutory framework to govern the industry and provided the FCC with explicit jurisdiction over cable television. That framework, set out in the Cable Communications Policy Act of 1984, Pub. L. No. 98-549, 98 Stat. 2779, amended the 1934 Act by adding a Title VI that regulates cable television. It also amended § 152(a) of the Communications Act, 47 U.S.C. § 152, to clearly state that the "provisions of this [Act] shall apply with respect to cable service, to all persons engaged within the United States in providing such service, and to the facilities of cable operators which relate to such service."

The Commission is not the only regulatory authority that has shown interest in cable television over the years. Local government has also been quite active in the regulation of local cable providers. Indeed, local governments for a long time insisted that cable providers apply to them for permission to be a local "cable franchisee" and local governments would often extract costly concessions from cable providers in exchange for granting those franchise rights. At the same time that Congress stepped in to establish jurisdiction for the FCC, Congress stepped into this jurisdictional issue as well. Three statutes were passed between 1984 and 1996: the Cable Communications Policy Act of 1984; the Cable Television Consumer Protection and Competition Act of 1992, Pub. L. No. 102-385, 106 Stat. 1460; and the Telecommunications Act of 1996, Pub. L. No. 104-104, 110 Stat. 56. Taken together, the three significantly constrained local authority over cable service.

Four constraints turned out to be of practical importance. First, the 1984 Act limited local government's ability to use the threat of franchise nonrenewal as a means by which to discipline cable franchisees. The Act did so by creating a strong presumption that a cable franchisee will have its franchise renewed at the end of its term. Under the Act, local authorities can refuse to renew only by producing evidence of substantial noncompliance with franchise terms and, even then, the local authority must give the cable operator notice and an opportunity to cure any alleged failures. 47 U.S.C. § 546. Renewals cannot be denied on the basis of the mix or quality of the cable services provided by the system, at least if those services comply with franchise terms. Decisions not to renew are subject to judicial review.

Second, the 1984 Act capped the franchise fee that local government could charge, specifically prohibiting local authorities from charging a fee exceeding five percent of the cable system's gross revenues. 47 U.S.C. § 542(b).

Third, the 1992 Act prohibited local government from (1) granting exclusive franchises and (2) unreasonably refusing to award additional competitive franchises. 47 U.S.C. § 541. That is, local authorities could neither make a legally binding promise that a particular franchisee would be the exclusive cable provider nor credibly commit to accomplishing the same result de facto by refusing to award later franchises. This constrained local government's clout; after the 1992 Act, local governments were no longer in the business of granting lucrative, legally guaranteed monopolies. Instead, to whatever extent the market would bear, cable franchisees would be subject to competition.

Fourth, the three statutes together largely stripped local government of its power to regulate cable rates. The 1984 Act took the first step, forbidding local rate regulation in situations where the FCC determined that local cable providers faced "effective competition." The Commission interpreted that phrase quite broadly, announcing that a cable provider faces effective competition so long as its subscribers could receive three over-the-air television signals. Rate regulation thus largely disappeared. The 1992 Act called for the reinstitution of a stronger form of rate regulation. That Act required cable operators to (1) establish a "basic tier" of services consisting of all signals carried pursuant to must-carry obligations and retransmission consent and also all public, educational, or governmental channels; (2) price that basic tier separately; and (3) force subscribers to purchase the basic tier as a precondition to subscribing to other services. The statute then permitted local authorities to regulate rates for the basic tier, and again established an exception that would stop rate regulation in instances where the Commission determines that there is adequate competition. This time, the Commission's standards were more demanding. As a result, most providers were subject to rate regulation, at least until DBS providers rose to prominence and began to provide the competition contemplated by the statute. Meanwhile, the 1992 Act gave the Commission authority to entertain complaints regarding cable services that were outside the basic tier, but the Telecommunications Act of 1996 repealed that authority. The 1996 Act also set a series of tests that essentially eliminated all rate regulation when there is effective competition. Thus, as a result of these three Acts, there is limited rate regulation still in place—notably, only for the basic tier at the local level where other MVPD providers have not yet been deemed to provide adequate competition. In most of the country, then, the result is that cable prices are not subject to rate regulation.

Our commentary thus far focuses on the ways in which the 1984 and 1992 Cable Acts constrained local government. The Acts were not entirely bad news for local authorities, however. Indeed, even though the Acts constrained local government's ability to regulate price and limited the size of any franchise fee, the Acts did at the same time combine to authorize local government to impose three significant obligations on cable franchisees. First, the 1984 Act added § 611 to the Communications Act of 1934, which provides that local franchising authorities "may ... require as part of a [cable] franchise ... [or] franchise renewal ... that channel capacity be designated for public, educational, or governmental use." 47 U.S.C. § 531(b). As the name implies, these "PEG" channels carry governmental and educational information that might be of interest to local subscribers but be undersupplied by market forces. These channels constitute an implicit tax imposed on franchisees; instead of taking a higher fee and then purchasing channel capacity, the local government is allowed to take a fee of no more than five percent of revenues but can then require the franchisee to provide a certain number of PEG channels.

Second, the 1984 and 1992 Acts combined to add §612 to the Communications Act. This provision requires certain cable systems to lease some of their channel capacity to unaffiliated firms, and to do so at regulated rates. 47 U.S.C. §532. These channels are typically referred to as "leased access" channels. Whether channels must be set aside and, if so, how many, is determined by the statute based on the size of the cable system at issue. The statute further allows cable operators who are required to provide leased access capacity to instead devote up to one third of that capacity to "programming from a qualified minority programming source or from any qualified educational programming source, whether or not such source is affiliated with the cable operator." 47 U.S.C. §532(i).

Third, the Acts did leave local governments with the power to require that any would-be cable provider negotiate and sign a franchise agreement with local authorities. To be sure, the various constraints above limited the terms of that agreement; but still much was in play. For instance, under most franchise agreements, cable franchisees must commit to meet certain deployment goals ("build-out requirements") on specific deadlines. And franchise agreements can obligate would-be franchisees to provide cable infrastructure that the locality itself can use, such as through the PEG channels authorized (but not required) by federal law. Indeed, burdens along these lines can be so severe that there have been movements to strip local government of the franchising power entirely. The argument is that franchise agreements impose such burdens on entrants that they are chilling what would otherwise be significant MVPD entry— not only from traditional providers like cable companies, but also from newer entrants like telephone companies which are experimenting with the use of the telephone infrastructure as a delivery mechanism for video programming.

In terms of litigation, most of the changes we summarize here were put into place without triggering court review. The most notable exception: cable operators brought suit contending that the PEG and leased access provisions violate their First Amendment rights and therefore are unconstitutional on their face. The highest court to address those claims was the Court of Appeals for the D.C. Circuit, in Time Warner Entertainment Co. v. FCC, 93 F.3d 957 (D.C. Cir. 1996).[4] With respect to leased access, the court found that the regulation was not content based because "[programmers'] qualification to lease time on those channels depends not on the content of their speech, but on their lack of affiliation with the operator, a distinguishing characteristic stemming from considerations

---

4. The challenges to the PEG and leased access provisions were part of a larger facial challenge to many different portions of the 1984 and 1992 Cable Acts. All told, the plaintiff cable television system owners/operators and programmers argued that the following provisions infringed upon their First Amendment right to freedom of speech: §§611 (public, educational, and governmental programming) and 612 (leased access) of the 1984 Act, and §§3 (rate regulation), 10(d) (obscenity liability), 11(c) (subscriber limitation, channel occupancy, and program creation restrictions), 15 (premium channel preview notice), 19 (vertically integrated programming), 24 (municipal immunity), and 25 (direct broadcast satellite set-aside) of the 1992 Act. *See Time Warner*, 93 F.3d at 962. In addition, the suit originally included a constitutional challenge to the must-carry provisions (§§4 and 5) of the 1992 Cable Act. Pursuant to a special jurisdictional provision of the 1992 Cable Act that applied only to challenges to §§4 and 5, the must-carry challenge was severed, sent to a three-judge panel of the district court, and appealed directly to the Supreme Court, resulting in Turner Broadcasting Sys., Inc. v. FCC, 512 U.S. 622 (1994) (*Turner I*), and, after the *Time Warner* opinion was issued, Turner Broadcasting Sys., Inc. v. FCC, 520 U.S. 180 (1997) (*Turner II*). Both *Turner I* and *Turner II* are excerpted and discussed in Chapter Nine.

relating to the structure of cable television." *Id.* at 969. The court's application of the intermediate scrutiny applicable to content-neutral speech regulations is encapsulated in the following paragraph:

> Time Warner thinks it sufficient to allege in its brief that there is not now, nor will there be under new FCC regulations, any appreciable demand by unaffiliated programmers for access to cable systems because cable systems are already carrying a wide variety of programs from diverse sources and because leased access does not make economic sense in light of the costs of production. For the sake of argument, we shall accept this assertion as true. We will assume, in other words, that on remand Time Warner could prove the factual propositions contained in its brief. Would that render the leased access provisions unconstitutional? We think not. If unaffiliated programmers have not and will not lease time on the channels set aside for them—if, in other words, Time Warner made its best case—we fail to see how the company could establish that the provisions violate its First Amendment right to free speech. Under § 532(b)(4), a "cable operator may use any unused channel capacity" set aside for leased access "until the use of such channel capacity is obtained, pursuant to a written agreement, by a person unaffiliated with the operator." That is, if unaffiliated programmers have not and, as Time Warner predicts, will not exploit the leased access provisions, then the provisions will have no effect on the speech of the cable operators. None of their programming would have to be dropped. The channels set aside for leasing will either be vacant or they will be occupied according to the wishes of the cable operators. The operators' editorial control will remain unimpaired and so will their First Amendment right to determine what will appear on their cable systems.

Id. at 970–71. As to PEG channels, the court stated as follows:

> To prevail in its facial challenge, Time Warner must "establish that no set of circumstances exists under which the Act would be valid." United States v. Salerno, 481 U.S. 739, 745 (1987). Consideration of this standard is somewhat tricky here since rather than *requiring* PEG channel capacity, the statute merely *permits* local franchise authorities to require PEG programming as a franchise condition. In fact, prior to the passage of the 1984 Cable Act, and thus, in the absence of federal permission, many franchise agreements provided for PEG channels. In passing the PEG provision, Congress thus merely recognized and endorsed the preexisting practice of local franchise authorities conditioning their cable franchises on the granting of PEG channel access. All the statute does, then, is preempt states from prohibiting local PEG requirements (if any states were to choose to do so) and preclude federal preemption challenges to such requirements, challenges that cable operators might have brought in the absence of the provision. [A] statute that simply permits franchise authorities to regulate where they had previously done so raises no First Amendment problems unless the localities themselves infringe on cable operators' speech.
>
> Time Warner must therefore show that no franchise authority could ever exercise the statute's grant of authority in a constitutional manner. We can, of course, imagine PEG franchise conditions that would raise serious constitutional issues. For example, were a local authority to require as a franchise condition that a cable operator designate three-quarters of its channels for "educational" programming, defined in detail by the city council, such a requirement would certainly implicate First Amendment concerns. At the same time, we can just as

easily imagine a franchise authority exercising its power without violating the First Amendment. For example, a local franchise authority might seek to ensure public "access to a multiplicity of information sources," Turner Broad. Sys., Inc. v. FCC, 512 U.S. 622, 663 (1994), by conditioning its grant of a franchise on the cable operator's willingness to provide access to a single channel for "public" use, defining "public" broadly enough to permit access to everyone on a nondiscriminatory, first-come, first-serve basis. Under *Turner*, such a scheme would be content-neutral, would serve an "important purpose unrelated to the suppression of free expression," *id.* at 662, and would be narrowly tailored to its goal. Time Warner's facial challenge therefore fails.

93 F.3d at 972–73.

Notes and Questions

1. PEG and Leased Access. Note the differing rationales behind PEG and leased access channels. The idea behind PEG channels is to expand the information provided to the public on crucial issues. In this way, the goal of increasing valuable programming via PEG channels is similar to the theory of Red Lion Broadcasting Co. v. FCC, 395 U.S. 367 (1969), which is excerpted in Chapter Fifteen. Commercial leased access regulations, by contrast, are usually defended on the ground that they promote competition among program suppliers. The theory is that a cable network might seek to enter into a contract with a cable operator that effectively excludes other networks, but the leased access capacity will enable those other networks to get on the system nevertheless. Thus the rationale behind leased access is to make sure that cable companies do not freeze out potentially popular channels with which the cable companies are not affiliated.

2. Rationale for Regulation. What programs will be shown on cable under the present leased access regime that would not obtain carriage without leased access? Won't cable operators, seeking to satisfy a wide range of viewers' desires, carry any available programming that is expected to be profitable? If a hypothetical XYZ pay cable network offering movies and sports can make more money for the cable system than, say, HBO, won't the cable system carry XYZ?

3. Heads I Win, Tails You Lose? With regard to leased access, was Time Warner in a no-win position? If Time Warner argued (as it did) that it already carried a wide variety of programs from different sources so there was no demand (and thus no need) for leased access, the D.C. Circuit could respond (as it did) that the leased access regime did not harm Time Warner. If Time Warner argued instead that many unaffiliated programmers would be clamoring for leased access channels and filling up the leased access channels, then the court might well respond that this demonstrated the need for leased access, and thus showed that leased access was responding to a real, nonconjectural harm. Could Time Warner have made an argument that would have avoided both of these responses? If not, what does that tell us?

4. Compelled Access. The general problem of compelled access to media platforms is one that we have seen and will continue to see throughout this casebook. The question is always the same: should we impose on broadcasters, cable operators, newspaper publishers, and other owners of communication infrastructure "common carrier" obligations, in essence separating legal authority over the conduit from legal authority over the content? Despite the prevalence of the issue, courts have not settled on a single approach to the question of whether mandated access can be squared with the First Amendment principle of freedom of speech and the press. Meanwhile, we never question the imposition of common carrier duties on telephone companies, but—following the apparent lead of Miami Herald Publishing Co. v. Tornillo, 418 U.S. 241 (1974) (discussed in Chapter Fifteen)—seem to assume that it is flatly unconstitutional to impose common carrier obligations on the print media. Is a single, coherent principle available for resolving questions about compelled access to the mass media?

5. In Cash or in Kind? Is it surprising that local authorities are significantly constrained in their ability to extract cash from cable franchisees (in the form of franchise fees) but are given broad discretion to extract in-kind compensation in the form of PEG and leased access channels? Is there a logic here? Aren't we more likely to see an efficient use of resources if, instead, local authorities were allowed to take cash but then had to purchase channel space?

6. The Federal/Local Relationship. Does the federal government's imposition of limitations on local discretion raise concern? Has the federal government left local officials with sufficient discretion to allow them to vindicate genuine local interests? And why is the federal government the better arbiter of what are and are not beneficial policies with respect to cable television? Is there any reason to trust the judgment of federal officials more than local ones?

7. Regulators as Bottleneck. The 1984 Act, the 1992 Act, and the 1996 Act all suggest, in various ways, that local government is an obstacle to entry in the cable market. If that is true, why do these statutes leave the local government with franchising authority at all? That is, why should would-be entrants have to apply to the relevant local government and negotiate franchise terms within the constraints of federal law, rather than more simply entering upon compliance with some statewide or federally mandated list of requirements? Those requirements could include default provisions requiring that a franchise fee be paid to the local government and that a certain number of PEG channels are provided. The point is that the rules could be set up such that there were established requirements, rather than requirements that must be negotiated each time. In short, given how little discretion they legitimately have anyway, why not put local governments out of the business of cable regulation entirely?

---

§ 8.E. Promoting Competition in MVPD Markets

As telephone companies upgraded their infrastructures with more fiber optics to have the bandwidth to compete with cable companies' Internet and video services, the telephone companies pushed not only to enter video markets but also to do so via statewide franchises. Telephone companies feared that obtaining local franchises would be burdensome and that local cable companies might be powerful in some local jurisdictions. This led to some states, including major ones such as California, Texas, and New Jersey, to pass legislation providing for statewide franchising. In addition, the FCC adopted an order aimed at easing the path of telephone companies into video programming markets, by "adopt[ing] measures to address a variety of means by which local franchising authorities, i.e., county- or municipal-level franchising authorities, are unreasonably refusing to award competitive franchises." Implementation of Section 621(a)(1) of the Cable Communications Policy Act of 1984, Report and Order, 22 FCC Rcd. 5101 ¶ 1 (2007). Set forth below is an excerpted version of the Sixth Circuit opinion upholding the FCC's Order.

Alliance for Community Media v. FCC
529 F.3d 763 (6th Cir. 2008)

Opinion for the Court filed by Circuit Judge COLE, in which Circuit Judges SUHRHEINRICH and GIBBONS concur.

COLE, Circuit Judge:

I. BACKGROUND

A. Factual Background

[In the 1992 Cable Act,] Congress revised section 621(a)(1) of the Communications Act of 1934 (the Act) to codify restraints on the licensing activities of a local franchising authority (LFA) such that it may grant "1 or more franchises within its jurisdiction; except that a franchising authority may not grant an exclusive franchise and *may not unreasonably refuse to award an additional competitive franchise.*" 47 U.S.C. § 541(a)(1) (emphasis added). Through this amendment, Congress further endowed potential entrants with a judicial remedy by entitling them to commence an action in a federal or state court within 120 days after receiving a final, adverse decision from an LFA. It is the legitimacy and precise import of these restraints that give rise to the instant controversy.

According to the legislative history, Congress enacted this amendment in part because the local franchising requirements provided most cable subscribers with "no opportunity to select between competing cable systems." H.R. Rep. No. 102-862, at 55 (1992) (Conf. Rep.). Therefore, the purpose of these constraints was to foster heightened competition in the cable market:

> Based on the evidence in the record taken as a whole, it is clear that there are benefits from competition between two cable systems. Thus, the Committee believes that local franchising authorities should be encouraged to award second franchises. Accordingly, [the 1992 Cable Act,] as reported, prohibits local franchising authorities from unreasonably refusing to grant second franchises.

S. Rep. No. 102-92, at 13 (1991).

B. Procedural Background

Over a decade following the passage of the 1992 amendments to the Communications Act, the FCC compiled data suggesting that competition had yet to materialize as a reality for the cable market. To investigate the state of the cable market, the FCC adopted a Notice of Proposed Rulemaking invit[ing] comment on approaches to implementing section 621(a)(1) of the Communications Act of 1934. Responding to charges from potential entrants into the cable marketplace that "the current operation of the local franchising process serves as a barrier to entry[,]" the FCC solicited comment on "whether the franchising process unreasonably impedes the achievement of the interrelated federal goals of enhanced cable competition and accelerated broadband deployment and, if so, how the Commission should act to address that problem." Implementation of Section 621(a)(1) of the Cable Communications Policy Act of 1984, Notice of Proposed Rulemaking, 20 FCC Rcd. 18581 (2005).

After reviewing the "voluminous record" generated by the rulemaking proceeding, consisting of "comments filed by new entrants, incumbent cable operators, LFAs, consumer groups, and others[,]" the FCC ascertained the need for new rules to ensure that the local franchising process operated in a fully competitive fashion, free of barriers to entry. Implementation of Section 621(A)(1) of the Cable Communications Policy Act of 1984, Report and Order, 22 FCC Rcd. 5101, 5110 ¶ 18. Accordingly, on December 20, 2006, by a vote of three to two, the FCC adopted the Order at issue. Attached to the Order was the dissenting opinion of Commissioner Jonathan S. Adelstein. The thrust of Commissioner Adelstein's dissent was that the Order "substitutes [the FCC's] judgment as to what is reasonable—or unreasonable—for that of local officials—all in violation of the franchising framework established in the Communications Act." *Id.* at 5193.

II. DISCUSSION

A. The FCC's Authority to Issue the Order

At the outset, petitioners contest the FCC's underlying authority to promulgate rules implementing section 621(a)(1) of the Communications Act. Petitioners maintain that the FCC exceeded the bounds of its authority when it adopted the Order because Congress never explicitly or implicitly delegated power to the FCC to interpret section 621(a)(1). In contrast, the FCC insists that it undoubtedly possesses the requisite authority to implement the Order and that petitioners' argument "rest[s] on a fundamental misunderstanding of the statutory scheme." Respondent's Br. 21.

In support of its jurisdictional argument, petitioners emphasize that nowhere in the plain language of section 621(a)(1) does any reference to the Commission appear. Turning to the text, section 621(a)(1) reads as follows:

> (a) Authority to award franchises; public rights-of-way and easements; equal access to service; time for provision of service; assurances
>
> (1) A franchising authority may award, in accordance with the provisions of this subchapter, 1 or more franchises within its jurisdiction; except that a franchising authority may not grant an exclusive franchise and may not *unreasonably refuse to award an additional competitive franchise*. Any applicant whose application for a second franchise has been denied by a final decision of the franchising authority may appeal such final decision pursuant to the provisions of section 555 of this title for failure to comply with this subsection.

47 U.S.C. § 541(a)(1) (emphasis added).

Petitioners are thus correct in noting that, while the text expressly references franchising authorities, it is silent as to the agency's role in the process of awarding cable franchises. Where petitioners' argument falls short, however, is in equating the omission of the agency from section 621(a)(1) with an absence of rulemaking authority.

In AT&T Corp. v. Iowa Utilities Board, 525 U.S. 366 (1999), the Supreme Court considered a challenge by state utility commissions and local exchange carriers to local competition rules issued by the FCC pursuant to the Telecommunications Act of 1996. In considering whether the FCC possessed the regulatory authority to interpret the provisions of the Telecommunications Act of 1996 at issue, the Court hinged its analysis on section 201(b), a 1938 amendment to the Communications Act of 1934. Section 201(b) provides, in relevant part, that "[t]he Commission may prescribe such rules and regulations as may be necessary in the public interest to carry out the provisions of this Act." 47 U.S.C. § 201(b). The Court reasoned that "[s]ince Congress expressly directed that the 1996 Act, along with its local-competition provisions, be inserted into the Communications Act of 1934 ... the Commission's rulemaking authority would seem to extend to implementation of the local competition provisions." 525 U.S. at 377–78. In other words, *AT&T Corp.* espoused a plain reading of section 201(b): "We think that the grant in § 201(b) means what it says: The FCC has rulemaking authority to carry out the 'provisions of this Act,' which include §§ 251 and 252, added by the Telecommunications Act of 1996." *Id.* at 378.

We find that the logic of *AT&T Corp.* controls the disposition of the jurisdictional argument petitioners raise here. Just as Congress ratified the Telecommunications Act of 1996 as an amendment to be incorporated into the original Communications Act of 1934, Congress likewise passed the Cable Television Consumer Protection and Competition Act of 1992, Pub. L. No. 102-385, 106 Stat. 1460, which revised section 621(a)(1) to include the bar on unreasonable refusals to award additional franchises, as an amendment to the original Communications Act of 1934. Through this process of amendment, Congress incorporated section 621(a)(1) into the Communications Act of 1934, and the statutory language at issue here thus qualifies as a "provision[] of this Act" within the meaning of section 201(b). Thus, because "the grant in § 201(b) means what it says[,]" we are bound by this plain meaning and thereby conclude that, pursuant to section 201(b), the FCC possesses clear jurisdictional authority to formulate rules and regulations interpreting the contours of section 621(a)(1). *See AT&T Corp.*, 525 U.S. at 378.

B. Chevron *Analysis*

1. Chevron *Step 1: Statutory Ambiguity*

The initial question under step one of the *Chevron* framework is "whether Congress has directly spoken to the precise question at issue" by employing precise, unambiguous statutory language. Chevron USA v. Natural Resources Defense Council, 467 U.S. 837, 842 (1984).

In the case at bar, the statutory phrase within section 621(a)(1) which emerges as a candidate for ambiguity is "*unreasonably* refuse to award an additional competitive franchise." 47 U.S.C. § 541(a)(1) (emphasis added).

While we have not previously interpreted the phrase "unreasonably" under section 621(a)(1), in the context of other provisions of the Communications Act, courts called upon to ascertain the ambiguity of descriptors such as "reasonable" and "unreasonable" have found these words subject to multiple constructions.

Of course, the detection of inherent ambiguity in words such as "reasonable" and "unreasonable" by other courts in other sections of the Communications Act does not terminate the analysis here, because such observations are divorced from the specific context of Title VI. As petitioners argue, while "unreasonable" may generally engender ambiguity and multiplicity of meaning, it is not inconceivable that its particular usage within section 621(a)(1) is perfectly clear. Thus, we must probe the structure and history surrounding the enactment of section 621(a)(1) to establish whether the use of "unreasonable" in this case fosters ambiguity.

Immediately following section 621(a)(1)'s limitation on unreasonable refusals to award additional franchises, the provision cross-references section 635 and thereby charges the courts with the task of determining whether there has been a "failure to comply with this subsection." 47 U.S.C. § 541(a)(1). Congress's provision of judicial review as a means to monitor a given LFA's compliance with section 621(a)(1) suggests that it is not instantaneously apparent whether a refusal to grant a prospective franchisee's application is necessarily reasonable or not. The legislative decision to delegate to jurists the task of construing and enforcing section 621(a)(1)'s insistence on reasonableness suggests that the statutory phrase at issue is capable of multiple meanings. To choose between these several meanings, courts will have to engage in fact-finding and uncover the particularities of the case at hand. Thus, to give meaning to an "unreasonable denial" will depend upon "a specific factual scenario." Coupled with case law finding the term "reasonable" generally to engender ambiguity, the fact-sensitive nature of the reasonableness inquiry in the instant context indicates that section 621(a)(1)'s usage of "unreasonably" is ambiguous under *Chevron*'s first step. Accordingly, our next task is to determine whether the FCC's explication of this statutory ambiguity is reasonable.

2. Chevron *Step 2: Reasonableness of the Order*

At this juncture, we must decide whether the FCC's Order constitutes a permissible construction of the pivotal statutory phrase, "unreasonably refuse to award," within section 621(a)(1). In answering this question, we "need not conclude that the agency construction was the only one it permissibly could have adopted to uphold the construction, or even the reading [we] would have reached if the question initially had arisen in a judicial proceeding." Battle Creek Health Sys. v. Leavitt, 498 F.3d 401, 408–09 (6th Cir. 2007). A review of the legislative history as well the language of the provision at issue is the chief method by which we approach the second step of *Chevron*. Because the Order encompasses four different rules specifying the meaning of "unreasonably refuse" within section 621(a)(1), we proceed by assessing the reasonableness of each rule in its own right.

a. Rule 1: Timing Requirements for Awarding New Franchises

The first rule contained in the Order concerns the time period within which LFAs must address franchise applications to satisfy section 621(a)(1)'s requirement of reasonableness. The FCC selected 90 days and six months as the time frames within which LFAs must respectively rule on the proposals of applicants with existing access to rights-of-way and wholly new applicants. The FCC further prescribed temporary interim franchises as a remedy for an LFA's failure to comply with the applicable time frame.

Urging this Court to reject the timing requirement as an impermissible construction of the statute, petitioners characterize this portion of the Order as "creating an arbitrary shot-clock for new franchise applications" and "spawning unilaterally-imposed interim franchises permitting unauthorized access to public and private property and denying community needs and interests." Petitioner ACM's Br. 28–29. The FCC, on the other hand, insists that the time frames are a lawful and reasonable regulatory response to "unreasonable delays in the franchising process." Respondent's Br. 39–40.

[T]he reasons mobilizing the FCC to promulgate these time limits appear more than reasonable. Due to protracted franchise negotiations, the agency found that prospective entrants were abandoning attempts to join the cable market and acceding to otherwise unacceptable franchise terms simply to expedite the process. The Commission thus prescribed the time frames as a way to remedy the "excessive delays result[ing] in unreasonable refusals to award competitive franchises," and reverse the factors "depriv[ing] consumers of competitive video services" and "hamper[ing] broadband deployment." Covad Comm. Co. v. FCC, 450 F.3d 528, 541 (D.C. Cir. 2006). In furtherance of these ends, the FCC reasonably found that six months would provide LFAs with "a reasonable amount of time to negotiate with an entity that is not already authorized to occupy" rights-of-way. Order at 5137 ¶ 72. This determination was predicated on "substantial [record] evidence that six months provides LFAs sufficient time to review an applicant's proposal, negotiate acceptable terms, and award or deny a competitive franchise." *Id.*

Similarly, for companies with existing access to rights-of-way, the FCC reasonably found that their cable franchise applications should take less time to review and process because "an LFA need not devote substantial attention to issues of rights-of-way management." *Id.* at 5135 ¶ 70. Specifically, the agency explained that since incumbent cable operators already demonstrated their "legal, technical, and financial fitness" to use rights-of-way to provide service, "an LFA need not spend a significant amount of time considering the fitness of such applicants to access public rights-of-way." *Id.* at 5136 ¶ 70. That 90 days represents a reasonable time frame for incumbent providers is underscored by the fact that numerous state statutes require decisions on cable franchise applications in fewer than 90 days. Accordingly, we conclude that the first rule included in the Order represents a permissible construction of the statute.

b. Rule 2: Limitations on Build-Out Requirements

The second rule contained in the Order places limits on the use of build-out requirements as a franchise term. Specifically, the Commission explained that "an LFA's refusal to grant a competitive franchise because of an applicant's unwillingness to agree to unreasonable build-out mandates constitutes an unreasonable refusal to award a competitive franchise." *Id.* at 5103 ¶ 5. The Order further stipulates types of mandates that would qualify as unreasonable, such as requiring an operator to serve everyone in a given area as a precondition for providing service, requiring incumbent operators to "build out beyond the footprint of their existing facilities before they have even begun providing service," *Id.* at 5143 ¶ 89, and placing more stringent service requirements on new entrants than those facing incumbent operators. In contrast, the agency described as reasonable an LFA's consideration of "benchmarks requiring the new entrant to increase its build-out after a reasonable period of time had passed after initiating service and taking into account its market success." *Id.*

In arguing for the unreasonableness of this second rule, petitioners assert that the agency has effectively "amend[ed] the will of Congress by adding exceptions to a statute that do not otherwise exist." Petitioner ACM's Br. 33. That is, petitioners claim that "[s]everal of the scenarios identified by the FCC as examples of 'unreasonable build-out mandates' involve issues that have nothing to do with the one and only condition placed on an LFA by Congress—namely, that an LFA must allow a reasonable period of time for build-out." *Id.* at 34.

The agency, in turn, retorts that this second rule is both lawful and reasonable because it sensibly responds to the state of the record evidence. Based on its extensive fact-finding, the FCC discovered that commanding prospective cable entrants to expand rapidly their networks "greatly hinder[s] the deployment of new video and broadband services." Respondent's Br. 33. Beyond the entry-deterring effects of build-out requirements, the agency maintains that its limitations on build-out mandates are "in effect timing restrictions" that accordingly fall well within Congress's requirement that LFAs provide a reasonable period of time for build-out. *Id.* at 55.

At the most fundamental level, petitioners and respondent are enmeshed in a quarrel over whether section 621(a)(4)(A) confers on LFAs the *right* to impose build-out requirements (as petitioners would have it) or amounts to a *limitation* on the authority of LFAs to secure build-out requirements through franchise negotiations (as respondent would have it). In ascertaining the reasonableness of this second rule under *Chevron*, the legislative history of section 621(a)(4)(A) can help to illuminate whether the statutory text is better characterized as a rights-conferring or an authority-limiting provision.

When integrating section 621(a)(4)(A) into the Act through the 1984 Amendments, Congress enacted the current version of the statute from which the following language was excised: an LFA's "refusal to award a franchise shall not be unreasonable if, for example, such refusal is on the ground ... of inadequate assurance that the cable operator will, within a reasonable period of time, provide universal service throughout the entire franchise area." H.R. Rep. No. 102-628, at 9 (1992). That is, Congress explicitly considered and rejected the preceding language, which would have situated all build-out requirements as presumptively reasonable. Under this discarded version, the key phrase "shall not be unreasonable" indicates that LFAs would have exercised the affirmative right to impose build-out requirements on prospective entrants.

In contrast, under the existing version of section 621(a)(4)(A), the statutory language fixes a durational requirement on LFAs when attaching build-out mandates to the terms of a franchise. The language, however, does not establish a presumption of reasonableness underlying all build-out requirements. That is, it is quite possible for an LFA to furnish a cable entrant with "a reasonable period of time to become capable of providing cable service to all households in the franchise area" yet still act unreasonably overall in imposing the build-out requirement on the entrant in the first place. Thus, in light of Congress's patent consideration and rejection of statutory language that would have created a presumption of reasonableness surrounding build-out requirements, we find the FCC to have the better argument. Accordingly, section 621(a)(4)(A) is more aptly designated as a limitation on the authority of LFAs, rather than an affirmative bestowal of rights. The FCC's subsequent explication of this limitation on build-out requirements, in the context of section 621(a)(1)'s requirement of reasonableness, thus appears to us a permissible construction of the Act, which warrants judicial deference under *Chevron*.

c. Rule 3: Franchise Fees

[The court upheld the FCC's limits on franchise fees—requirements that LFAs count other costs and fees toward the 5% cap and that franchise fees are not due on non-cable services—as reasonable under *Chevron*.]

d. Rule 4: Limitations on PEG Capacity

[The court upheld a reasonableness limit on LFA demands for PEG channels from new entrants, as well as a requirement of pro-rata cost sharing with the incumbent, as reasonable under *Chevron*.]

C. Arbitrary and Capricious Analysis

As their final ground for relief, petitioners challenge the FCC's rule-making activity as arbitrary, capricious, an abuse of discretion, and otherwise not in accordance with the law. Specifically, petitioners insist that the Order is based on a record replete with "allegations against LFAs which are anonymous, hearsay-based, inaccurate, and outdated." Petitioner ACM's Br. 7. Notwithstanding petitioners' contention, we conclude that the FCC's rulemaking activity was rooted in a sufficient evidentiary basis.

Turning to the record, it appears that the FCC spearheaded its regulatory activity only after pursuing a more than adequate fact-finding endeavor. That is, there is ample record evidence supporting the Commission's finding that the operation of the franchising process had impeded competitive entry in multiple ways. Prior to promulgating the Order, the FCC obtained a massive record consisting of 465 comments. These 465 comments created a picture of excessive delay in the grant of new franchises. For example, Verizon's comments indicated that, of its 113 franchise negotiations pending as of March 2005, only ten resulted in franchise grants after one year. Likewise, comments from petitioner NTCA reflected that a "common complaint ... is that applications for franchising authority languish, unreasonably delaying the franchise process and the ability of competitors to offer service." Similar comments from BellSouth and other service providers make clear that the Order's attempt to remedy the problem of undue delay was consistent with the evidence before the Commission and represents a "rational connection between the facts found and the choice made." Motor Vehicle Mfrs. Ass'n of U.S. v. State Farm Mut. Auto. Ins. Co., 463 U.S. 29, 43 (1983) (quoting Burlington Truck Lines v. United States, 371 U.S. 156, 168 (1962)).

In a similar vein, the 465 comments presented to the Commission contained substantial evidence that build-out requirements were posing significant obstacles to new entrants in providing video and broadband services. For example, comments submitted by service provider Qwest indicated that it withdrew franchise applications in eight different regions due to economically burdensome build-out requirements. Likewise, the record demonstrated that LFAs were imposing various demands on service providers, including those unrelated to cable service, those involving excessive franchise fees, and those involving excessive PEG requirements, that were significantly escalating prospective entrants' costs and thereby deterring entry. Based on the foregoing, we conclude that the administrative record fully supported the agency's rulemaking and belies any claims of arbitrary or capricious regulatory activity.

For the reasons articulated above, we DENY the petitions for review.

Notes and Questions

1. Competition versus Rate Regulation. Until the Telecommunications Act of 1996 rejected the concept of rate regulation of cable services, regulation represented the primary strategy for protecting consumers against monopoly pricing. But Congress concluded that satellite TV firms, which had already begun to emerge as competitors to cable operators, as well as telephone companies, would protect consumers by offering a choice in the marketplace. Satellite TV firms did, in fact, pick up considerable market share, but telephone companies largely stayed on the sidelines. Over the decade between 1995 to 2005, according to the Commission, cable rates rose 93% while other telecommunications services declined in price. Does that mean that competition failed, that competition takes time, or that the statistics (which do not focus on improvements in the quantity or quality of cable programming) are flawed?

2. FCC Latitude in Statutory Interpretation. The Communications Act includes §201(b), which provides, in relevant part, that "[t]he Commission may prescribe such rules and regulations as may be necessary in the public interest to carry out the provisions of this Act." Does this clause provide the FCC with special latitude? With greater latitude than other agencies would have?

3. Federalism and Localism. Is the fact that the federal regulations here restricted localities relevant? To Commissioner Adelstein it is, and he suggested that the decision was "a clear rebuke of this storied relationship with local government ... [and] a one-size-fits-all approach is antithetical to clear congressional intent that cable systems be 'responsive to needs and interests of local community.'" Implementation of Section 621(a)(1) of the Cable Communications Policy Act of 1984, Report and Order, 22 FCC Rcd. 5101, 5193 (2007) (Adelstein, Comm'r, dissenting). Does it matter that the decision displaced local authority but not state authority? What justifies such a distinction?

4. Build-Out Requirements. One of the most controversial issues related to grants of local franchises to second entrants is whether a requirement to build out service to all consumers is a legitimate requirement. To new entrants, such a requirement presents a formidable barrier to entry. To incumbents, such a burden merely creates a level playing field. On what basis should the FCC choose whether such requirements are good policy?

5. Congressional Action versus Agency Action. Does it matter that Congress, at the time of the FCC's decision, had been considering franchise reform legislation? Why or why not?

6. The Shot Clock. A central part of the Commission's order is a 90-day shot clock. Is it reasonable to believe that delays in negotiation are caused by the municipality and not the applicant? How can this regime ensure a requirement to negotiate in good faith?

7. Regulatory Parity. In 2007, the Commission adopted a companion order that extended a number of the rules in the above order to incumbents. That is, the order above imposed restrictions on local franchising authorities that were designed to protect new entrants, and this second order extended many of those protections to incumbents as well. *See* Implementation of Section 621(a)(1) of the Cable Communications Policy Act of 1984, Second Report and Order, 22 FCC Rcd. 19,633 (2007). In the wake of the decision, Commissioner Adelstein remarked: "While I understand the need for regulatory parity, today's decision represents a 'race to bottom,' an unraveling of important local protections set in motion by the Commission's prior misguided decision-making in the First Report and Order [excerpted above]." *Id.* at 19,659. If the Commission finds itself with different rules for different players, under what circumstances is it better to keep asymmetric regulation and in what situations should it insist on regulatory parity between players?

Chapter Nine

Shared Content

Introduction

Whether or not the broadcasting of television programming over the air continues to make sense as a method of distributing programming is a topic of considerable debate. It is not debatable, however, that access to local broadcast content is critical to the success of any multichannel video programming distributor (MVPD). Consider, for example, if your local telephone company offered a package of video programming that did not include your local channels. For many consumers, this offering would be a nonstarter; not surprisingly, the satellite industry's initial inability (for both technological and legal reasons) to offer local broadcast programming hampered its development.

In this chapter, we therefore focus on the rules that govern MVPD access to broadcast content. We start with the rules that apply to television programs in isolation, in essence asking whose permission is necessary if a cable company or a direct broadcast satellite (DBS) provider wants to simulcast an episode of a show that is already being aired on a broadcast channel. Then we consider the somewhat overlapping rules that govern access to channels, by which we mean the stream of programs that a broadcaster strings together as part of an integrated offering.

§ 9.A. Individual Programs

§ 9.A.1. Compulsory Copyright Licenses

§ 9.A.1.a. Cable Television

As the first entrant into the video marketplace, cable television providers tested the waters as to whether local broadcast programming could be retransmitted without permission. As the previous chapter noted, the first regulatory issue was copyright. As a matter of copyright law, the relevant programs were obviously protected. But cable operators were simply retransmitting content that had already been made public. Once the copyright holders had agreed to put their programs out for all to see, the question became whether they had a claim to additional royalties when a cable operator retransmitted that same program. Stated differently, the question presented to the courts was whether the cable company was acting as a passive conduit—like a viewer—or engaging in a public performance of the work.

In Fortnightly Corp. v. United Artists, 392 U.S. 390 (1968), the Supreme Court confronted exactly this question. The facts were simple. A West Virginia cable operator had begun to retransmit five broadcast signals that were already available over the air in its local market. United Artists, which represented copyright holders that held rights in many of the programs being aired on those broadcast channels, sued the cable operator for infringement, arguing that the cable operator could not air copyrighted content without first obtaining licenses from the copyright holders. The Court ruled that there was no infringement. Just as a viewer was free to receive the broadcasts by antenna and then display the content on his home television, so cable operators, in the Court's view, were free to capture these signals by antenna and display them on the multiple television sets attached to the cable network.

In Teleprompter v. CBS, 415 U.S. 394 (1974), the Supreme Court reaffirmed and expanded on this logic. In this case, the cable provider was capturing broadcast signals in one community and then using microwave relays to transport those signals to its cable system hundreds of miles away. The issue, then, was not the local retransmission of broadcast signals (*Fortnightly*), but instead the importation of broadcast signals from distant communities. The Court recognized that a viewer might not be able to afford amplifying equipment that would provide access to those distant signals, but as in *Fortnightly* it held that that the cable provider was more like a viewer than a broadcaster. "The reception and rechanneling of [broadcast television signals] for simultaneous viewing is essentially a viewer function, irrespective of the distance between the broadcasting station and the ultimate viewer." *Id.*, at 408. There was no copyright liability for the cable provider displaying those distant signals, just as there was no copyright liability for normal viewers.

None of this would remain good law for very long. The Copyright Act of 1976, Pub. L. No. 94-533 (codified as amended at 17 U.S.C. § 101 *et seq.*), changed a good many details of copyright law, and one of those changes effectively reversed *Fortnightly* and *Teleprompter*. Under the new Act, the retransmission of copyrighted broadcast content by a cable operator was defined to be copyright infringement. See 17 U.S.C. §§ 101, 106(4), & 501(c). Home viewers were still implicitly licensed to capture broadcast signals off the air and display them privately, but cable operators could no longer borrow broadcast content with impunity.

Had the Copyright Act of 1976 stopped there—defining cable retransmission to be infringement but doing no more—then every time a cable operator wanted to retransmit a local signal, it would have had to acquire a license from every relevant content owner. If the local NBC affiliate was airing thirty copyrighted programs a day, that would mean that the cable operator would need thirty licenses to air the full day's content. This might have meant tracking down and negotiating with each and every copyright owner. Alternatively, some sort of clearinghouse organization (comparable to the role played by BMI and ASCAP in the music industry) might have emerged to handle these permissions en masse. Or, in what HBO ultimately managed to pull off (and became the norm for cable networks), TV stations could themselves obtain such permissions and offer cable distributors one-stop-shopping access to them.

Congress was unwilling to risk the possibility that the negotiated solution model would break down. Consequently, in addition to defining cable retransmission as infringement, Congress added to the Copyright Act what is today 17 U.S.C. § 111. That provision establishes a system of compulsory licenses in favor of "cable systems" (i.e., cable operators) who want to retransmit copyrighted broadcast content. These are *compulsory* licenses: copyright owners have no choice but to authorize retransmission so long as the cable operators satisfy the terms of the licenses as set out by Congress. Particularly important among those conditions is § 111(c)(3)'s stipulation that neither the content of the particular program at issue, nor any commercial advertising or station announcements transmitted by the primary transmitter immediately before or after the program's transmission, be "willfully altered by the cable system through changes, deletions, or additions." Under the royalty provision, cable operators enjoy a compulsory license for all retransmitted broadcast content and must pay royalties for their use of the programming. Cable operators, however, did win a crucial carve-out from the obligation to pay royalties; they need not pay royalties for either (1) network programming; or (2) local non-network programming.

The House Report on the Copyright Act of 1976, H.R. Rep. No. 94-1476, explains all of the above as follows:

> In general, the Committee believes that cable systems are commercial enterprises whose basic retransmission operations are based on the carriage of copyrighted program material and that copyright royalties should be paid by cable operators to the creators of such programs. The Committee recognizes, however, that it would be impractical and unduly burdensome to require every cable system to negotiate with every copyright owner whose work was retransmitted by a cable system. Accordingly, the Committee has [decided] to establish a compulsory copyright license for the retransmission of over-the-air broadcast signals.
>
> The Committee determined, however, that there was no evidence that the retransmission of "local" broadcast signals by a cable operator threatens the existing market for copyright program owners. Similarly, the retransmission of network programming, including network programming which is broadcast in "distant" markets, does not injure the copyright owner. The copyright owner contracts with the network on the basis of his programming reaching all markets served by the network and is compensated accordingly.
>
> By contrast, retransmission of distant non-network programming by cable systems causes damage to the copyright owner by distributing the program in an area beyond which it has been privately licensed. Such retransmission adversely affects the ability of the copyright owner to exploit the work in the distant market. It is also of direct benefit to the cable system by enhancing its ability to attract subscribers and increase revenues. For these reasons, the Committee has concluded that the copyright liability of cable television systems under the compulsory license should be limited to the retransmission of distant non-network programming.

Notes and Questions

1. The *Fortnightly* Approach. Who was being hurt under the Supreme Court's interpretation of copyright law in *Fortnightly*? Local broadcasters? The copyright holders? Was the real problem just that the legal rule was unclear? That is, had copyright owners known that cable operators could retransmit their programs with impunity, could they have been fully compensated by raising the prices they charged broadcasters in the first place?

2. Drawing Distinctions. Was the Supreme Court's interpretation of copyright law defensible? Was it really that difficult to distinguish television viewers from cable operators for copyright purposes? Doesn't copyright law draw those sorts of distinctions all the time?

3. Compulsory Licenses. Why did Congress choose a compulsory licensing scheme as opposed to defining secondary transmission to be copyright infringement and then allowing the market to establish the terms and royalties for retransmission? Is the House Report's claim that this would have been "impractical" and "unduly burdensome" convincing given that BMI and ASCAP have long successfully acted as copyright clearinghouses for the music industry, collecting royalties from radio stations, restaurants, and other entities that broadcast and otherwise perform musical compositions and then distributing those moneys to the appropriate copyright holders?

4. The Logic of the House Report. Are there any situations in which the logic of the House Report with respect to network programming, local programming, and non-network distant programming fails, or did Congress get things right when it established royalties only for a small subset of copyrighted programs?

5. The End of the Compulsory Copyright for Distant Signals? The Copyright Office has argued that the provision for compulsory licenses is no longer sound policy (assuming it ever was). In particular, the Office suggested that given the increased market power of cable companies, they should be able to negotiate with broadcasters without governmental assistance in the form of compulsory licenses, which are priced at below-market rates. *See* Satellite Home Viewer Extension and Reauthorization Act § 109 Report (2008), *available at* http://www.copyright.gov/reports/section109-final-report.pdf. What arguments can you make for either side? What do you predict would take place if the compulsory copyright requirement were lifted? Who would be in favor of (and against) following the Copyright Office's recommendation?

---

§ 9.A.1.b. Direct Broadcast Satellite

In the early years of DBS's development, DBS providers relied on the Satellite Home Viewer Act of 1988 (SHVA), Pub. L. No. 100-667, 102 Stat. 3949, for compulsory licenses. This legislation provided a limited copyright license to retransmit the programming of "distant" broadcast stations to households that would otherwise be "unserved" by a local network affiliate. 17 U.S.C. § 119(d)(10)(a). This exception allowed satellite carriers to deliver network programming to certain satellite dish owners without the copyright owners' permission. By enacting this provision, Congress sought to achieve two goals: (1) making network programming available to the small number of households that otherwise lack access to it; and (2) simultaneously preserving the existing national network/affiliate television distribution system by preventing satellite delivery of network programming to other households. In seeking to accommodate these goals, Congress limited the satellite compulsory license to "unserved households" for private home viewing. 17 U.S.C. § 119(a)(2)(B).

Under SHVA, the definition of an "unserved household" had two parts. First, it "cannot receive, through the use of a conventional outdoor rooftop receiving antenna, an over-the-air signal of grade B intensity (as defined by the [FCC])" from a local network station of the same network. 17 U.S.C. § 119(d)(10)(A). Second, to be "unserved," a household must not have recently received network stations via cable. 17 U.S.C. § 119(d)(10)(B).

DBS providers read this statutory authority broadly, and they used it to deliver network programming from ABC, CBS, Fox, and NBC to a large number of their customers. In particular, some providers offered the same network signal to all of their subscribers, rather than retransmit the signal of each local affiliate to the subscribers in that area. That is, a DBS provider would contract with a single television network affiliate (e.g., WRAL in Raleigh, North Carolina) and would then retransmit its signal nationwide. It would replace the local commercials with national advertisements and split the revenue with the local affiliate. (This differed from retransmission via cable, since cable operators must, under the must-carry provision, retransmit local stations.) The DBS provider would not have a license with the national broadcaster (CBS, in the case of WRAL). Instead, it would simply have an agreement with the local affiliate. The key was that such an agreement was limited to "unserved households" as defined by the SHVA.

The DBS providers, as noted above, adopted a broad definition of SHVA's "unserved households" requirement. Here is how a judge described it in the case that effectively ended the DBS providers' approach to the issue:

> PrimeTime [the DBS service provider] or its distributors ask potential subscribers three questions: 1) whether they intend to use the programming for residential use; 2) whether they have subscribed to cable in the last 90 days; and 3) whether the household receives an acceptable picture through the use of a conventional rooftop antenna.[1] PrimeTime has always made its initial eligibility determinations exclusively on what the subscriber tells the customer service representative in response to these three questions.

CBS Broadcasting Inc. v. PrimeTime 24 Joint Venture, 48 F. Supp. 2d 1342, 1349 (S.D. Fla. 1998).

The broadcast networks took the DBS provider to court to end this practice and ensure that the statutory requirements were adhered to appropriately. In the case quoted above, the court ruled for the broadcasters, concluding as follows:

> PrimeTime's efforts to comply with the SHVA [through] its use of questionnaires are insufficient to meet Congress' objective test. [A]sking potential subscribers about picture quality simply fails to provide evidence that such subscribers fit within Congress' definition of an "unserved household."
>
> PrimeTime's actions have affected the network/affiliate relationship because individuals who subscribe to its service do not watch local network programs provided by the affiliates. This is due to the fact that PrimeTime does not transmit local affiliate programming or advertising. Instead, as mentioned previously, PrimeTime transmits the network programs broadcast by the handful of affiliates with which it has a contractual agreement, and substitutes local advertising with national advertising. Accordingly, PrimeTime's violation of the SHVA is reducing the number of viewers for local affiliate programming and advertising, which in turn reduces an affiliate's revenue stream.
>
> The Court finds that PrimeTime's actions constitute a pattern or practice of violating the SHVA. PrimeTime has failed to establish that any of its three million subscribers meet SHVA's criteria for eligibility. Furthermore, the evidence shows that PrimeTime made a conscious decision to flout the law when it was well aware of what the law required. PrimeTime's attempt to comply with the SHVA was largely ineffectual and has led to "systematic violation of SHVA's white area restriction." ABC, Inc. v. PrimeTime 24 Joint Venture, 17 F. Supp. 2d 467,

---

1. Before asking the third question, PrimeTime suggests that its distributors tell potential subscribers that, if they say that they receive an acceptable quality picture, they will not be eligible to receive network service.

477 (M.D.N.C. 1998). Accordingly, the Court finds that PrimeTime has engaged in a nationwide willful or repeated pattern or practice of infringements.

Id. at 1349–57.

PrimeTime 24 turned out to be the prelude to a storm.

The district court went on to grant a permanent injunction against PrimeTime's unauthorized use of the copyrighted material. Once applied to all relevant DBS customers, the injunction promised to deprive three million Americans of access to the programming of the major networks. But such an injunction never went into effect.

Following the district court's decision, the satellite, cable, and broadcast industries took their arguments to Congress. Leaders in Congress made clear that they did not want to see three million Americans lose access to valued TV programming. At the same time, Congress recognized an opportunity to rationalize the regulation of DBS providers. In November 1999 (before a negotiated standstill was about to expire), Congress enacted the Satellite Home Viewer Improvement Act of 1999 (SHVIA), Pub. L. No. 106-113, 113 Stat. 1501 (codified at scattered sections of 17 U.S.C. and 47 U.S.C.).[2] To address the relevant issues, SHVIA amended both federal copyright law (those changes codified at 17 U.S.C.) and the Communications Act of 1934 (the changes codified at 47 U.S.C.).

The general purpose of the Act was to make DBS regulation more consistent with cable regulation and, in that way, to promote competition between the two media platforms. In particular, the Congressional reports suggested frustration with increased cable television prices but an unwillingness to re-impose the rate regulation on cable services that largely ceased April 1, 1999. SHVIA was therefore intended to increase competition by leveling the playing field and allowing DBS to offer local stations. *See, e.g.,* The Satellite Television Act of 1999, Sen. Rpt. 106-51 (May 20, 1999).

SHVIA made several important changes. First, in § 1002(a), it amended federal copyright law by adding a new section, 17 U.S.C. § 122, which made clear that "a secondary transmission of a performance or display of a work embodied in a primary transmission of a television broadcast station in the station's local market shall be subject to statutory licensing." In other words, DBS providers would enjoy a compulsory license to retransmit even copyrighted local broadcast content back into the local market. Subsection 1002(c) further provided that DBS providers do not have to pay any royalty in exchange for this compulsory license. Other provisions in this section established rules comparable to those in effect with respect to cable, for example prohibiting DBS providers from willfully altering the retransmitted signal.

Note that the compulsory license created by § 1002(a) does not perfectly mirror the compulsory license created by the Copyright Act of 1976 for the benefit of cable providers. Most importantly, the SHVIA license applies only to the retransmission of local content back into the local market; it is explicitly not a license to retransmit distant signals. The provisions relating to cable's compulsory license, in contrast, do apply to distant programming—both distant network programming (for which there is no royalty) and distant non-network programming (for which there is a royalty). The license granted to DBS operators, then, is considerably narrower than the one granted to cable providers back in 1976.

Second, in § 1005, SHVIA addressed the issue of distant signal importation for the benefit of unserved households. The provision allowed the importation of distant sig-

---

2. Be careful with your acronyms: SHVIA is an entirely different statute from SHVA, discussed above.

nals for households not within the Grade B contour (the same technical test as applied under SHVA, without the requirement of a 90-day noncable waiting period). The section also grandfathered, but only until 2004, the households caught up in litigation like the *PrimeTime 24* case.

Third, §§ 1008 and 1009 of the Act created a retransmission consent requirement and a "carry one, carry all" rule for local stations. We will discuss these provisions in some detail later in this chapter, along with comparable rules that apply to cable.

In enacting SHVIA, Congress set an expiration date at the end of 2004. Thus, in 2004, Congress revisited the basic questions related to satellite television and, in December, ultimately enacted the Satellite Home Viewer Extension and Reauthorization Act of 2004 (SHVERA), Pub. L. No. 108-447, 118 Stat. 2809, 3393. For the most part, SHVERA closely followed SHVIA. For example, SHVERA continued to grant DBS providers a compulsory license that authorized the retransmission of local broadcast content back into the relevant local market. The legislation also continued to recognize in DBS providers a right to import distant signals to "unserved" households. And the legislation still subjected DBS providers to must-carry obligations, albeit still only in instances where the relevant provider had invoked the aforementioned local-into-local compulsory license. But SHVERA created a new compulsory license, this one applying to "significantly viewed" signals that originate outside the local market. The idea was to level the playing field as compared to cable television, which already had special compulsory licenses in place to deal with stations that were widely viewed within a local market even though they did not originate there.

In 2009, the issue arose once again, ultimately leading to another extension of SHVIA's basic provisions in the Satellite Television Extension and Localism Act of 2010 (STELA), Pub. L. No. 111-151, 124 Stat. 1027. In STELA, Congress set forth the relevant criteria for DBS providers to maintain access to local programming in the wake of the transition to digital television. Most notably, STELA required the FCC to "prescribe a point-to-point predictive model for determining the ability of individual locations to receive an over-the-air digital television broadcast signal at the intensity level needed for service through the use of an antenna." Establishment of a Model for Predicting Digital Broadcast Television Field Strength Received at Individual Locations, Notice of Proposed Rulemaking, 25 FCC Rcd. 10,474 (2010). Under STELA, this model provides the basis for determining whether network affiliates are available over the air in a particular market.

Notes and Questions

1. Justifiable Differences? Should cable and DBS providers be subject to different compulsory license regimes? What should be the basis for such differences?

2. Borrowing from MVPD. Our discussion thus far has focused exclusively on situations where MVPD providers want to borrow content that has already aired on broadcast outlets. But what about situations where one MVPD provider wants to borrow content that has been transmitted by another MVPD provider? In particular, should a start-up DBS provider be entitled to carry the programming developed by an incumbent cable provider at nondiscriminatory terms and conditions? Chapter Ten addresses this issue—in particular, the possibility of program access rules under which an upstart MVPD provider would carry a network owned by an incumbent cable operator.

§9.A.2. What Constitutes a Performance under Copyright Law?

The Copyright Act of 1976 granted broad exclusive rights to copyright holders that clearly applied to cable television service and thus effectively reversed *Fortnightly* and *Teleprompter*, but it did not disrupt the ability of viewers to use antennas to receive programs free of copyright obligations. What is the line between the viewer function of using an antenna and a public performance via antenna? Enter Aereo, Inc., which was designed to exploit *Fortnightly* and allow subscribers to stream broadcast content over the Internet. Aereo attached many small antennas to an Internet service that allowed anyone with an Internet connection to select one of the antennas to receive broadcast content. Broadcast television networks were not amused (or compensated) and sued on copyright grounds, ultimately resulting in the opinion below.

AMERICAN BROADCASTING COMPANIES, INC. v. AEREO, INC.
134 S. Ct. 2498 (2014)

BREYER, J., delivered the opinion of the Court, in which ROBERTS, C. J., and KENNEDY, GINSBURG, SOTOMAYOR, and KAGAN, JJ., joined. SCALIA, J., filed a dissenting opinion, in which THOMAS and ALITO, JJ., joined.

Justice BREYER delivered the opinion of the Court.

The Copyright Act of 1976 gives a copyright owner the "exclusive right[]" to "perform the copyrighted work publicly." 17 U.S.C. § 106(4). The Act's Transmit Clause defines that exclusive right as including the right to "transmit or otherwise communicate a performance ... of the [copyrighted] work ... to the public, by means of any device or process, whether the members of the public capable of receiving the performance ... receive it in the same place or in separate places and at the same time or at different times." § 101.

We must decide whether respondent Aereo, Inc., infringes this exclusive right by selling its subscribers a technologically complex service that allows them to watch television programs over the Internet at about the same time as the programs are broadcast over the air. We conclude that it does.

I

A

For a monthly fee, Aereo offers subscribers broadcast television programming over the Internet, virtually as the programming is being broadcast. Much of this programming is made up of copyrighted works. Aereo neither owns the copyright in those works nor holds a license from the copyright owners to perform those works publicly.

Aereo's system is made up of servers, transcoders, and thousands of dime-sized antennas housed in a central warehouse. It works roughly as follows: First, when a subscriber wants to watch a show that is currently being broadcast, he visits Aereo's website and selects, from a list of the local programming, the show he wishes to see.

Second, one of Aereo's servers selects an antenna, which it dedicates to the use of that subscriber (and that subscriber alone) for the duration of the selected show. A server then tunes the antenna to the over-the-air broadcast carrying the show. The antenna begins to receive the broadcast, and an Aereo transcoder translates the signals received into data that can be transmitted over the Internet.

Third, rather than directly send the data to the subscriber, a server saves the data in a subscriber-specific folder on Aereo's hard drive. In other words, Aereo's system creates a subscriber-specific copy—that is, a "personal" copy—of the subscriber's program of choice.

Fourth, once several seconds of programming have been saved, Aereo's server begins to stream the saved copy of the show to the subscriber over the Internet. The subscriber can watch the streamed program on the screen of his personal computer, tablet, smart phone, Internet-connected television, or other Internet-connected device. The streaming continues, a mere few seconds behind the over-the-air broadcast, until the subscriber has received the entire show.

Aereo emphasizes that the data that its system streams to each subscriber are the data from his own personal copy, made from the broadcast signals received by the particular antenna allotted to him. Its system does not transmit data saved in one subscriber's folder to any other subscriber. When two subscribers wish to watch the same program, Aereo's system activates two separate antennas and saves two separate copies of the program in two separate folders. It then streams the show to the subscribers through two separate transmissions—each from the subscriber's personal copy.

II

This case requires us to answer two questions: First, in operating in the manner described above, does Aereo "perform" at all? And second, if so, does Aereo do so "publicly"? We address these distinct questions in turn.

Does Aereo "perform"? See § 106(4) ("[T]he owner of [a] copyright ... has the exclusive right[] ... to *perform* the copyrighted work publicly" (emphasis added)); § 101 ("To *perform* ... a work 'publicly' means [among other things] to transmit ... a performance ... of the work ... to the public ..." (emphasis added)). Phrased another way, does Aereo "transmit ... a performance" when a subscriber watches a show using Aereo's system, or is it only the subscriber who transmits? In Aereo's view, it does not perform. It does no more than supply equipment that "emulate[s] the operation of a home antenna and [digital video recorder (DVR)]." Brief for Respondent 41. Like a home antenna and DVR, Aereo's equipment simply responds to its subscribers' directives. So it is only the subscribers who "perform" when they use Aereo's equipment to stream television programs to themselves.

Considered alone, the language of the Act does not clearly indicate when an entity "perform[s]" (or "transmit[s]") and when it merely supplies equipment that allows others to do so. But when read in light of its purpose, the Act is unmistakable: An entity that engages in activities like Aereo's performs.

B

In 1976 Congress amended the Copyright Act in large part to reject the Court's holdings in Fortnightly Corp. v. United Artists Television, Inc., 392 U.S. 390 (1968) and CBS v. Teleprompter, 415 U.S. 394 (1974). Congress enacted new language that erased the Court's line between broadcaster and viewer, in respect to "perform[ing]" a work. The amended statute clarifies that to "perform" an audiovisual work means "to show its images in any sequence or to make the sounds accompanying it audible." § 101. Under this new language, *both* the broadcaster *and* the viewer of a television program "perform," because they both show the program's images and make audible the program's sounds.

Congress also enacted the Transmit Clause, which specifies that an entity performs publicly when it "transmit[s] ... a performance ... to the public." § 101. Cable system activities, like those of the CATV systems in *Fortnightly* and *Teleprompter,* lie at the heart of the activities that Congress intended this language to cover. The Clause thus makes clear that an entity that acts like a CATV system itself performs, even if when doing so, it simply enhances viewers' ability to receive broadcast television signals.

Congress further created a new section of the Act to regulate cable companies' public performances of copyrighted works. *See* § 111. Section 111 creates a complex, highly detailed compulsory licensing scheme that sets out the conditions, including the payment of compulsory fees, under which cable systems may retransmit broadcasts.

Congress made these three changes to achieve a similar end: to bring the activities of cable systems within the scope of the Copyright Act.

C

This history makes clear that Aereo is not simply an equipment provider. Rather, Aereo, and not just its subscribers, "perform[s]" (or "transmit[s]"). Aereo's activities are substantially similar to those of the CATV companies that Congress amended the Act to reach. *See id.,* at 89 ("[C]able systems are commercial enterprises whose basic retransmission operations are based on the carriage of copyrighted program material"). Aereo sells a service that allows subscribers to watch television programs, many of which are copyrighted, almost as they are being broadcast. In providing this service, Aereo uses its own equipment, housed in a centralized warehouse, outside of its users' homes. By means of its technology (antennas, transcoders, and servers), Aereo's system "receive[s] programs that have been released to the public and carr[ies] them by private channels to additional viewers." *Fortnightly,* 392 U.S., at 400. It "carr[ies] ... whatever programs [it] receive[s]," and it offers "all the programming" of each over-the-air station it carries. *Id.,* at 392, 400.

Aereo's equipment may serve a "viewer function," *Teleprompter,* 415 U.S. at 408; it may enhance the viewer's ability to receive a broadcaster's programs. It may even emulate equipment a viewer could use at home. But the same was true of the equipment that was before the Court, and ultimately before Congress, in *Fortnightly* and *Teleprompter.*

We recognize, and Aereo and the dissent emphasize, one particular difference between Aereo's system and the cable systems at issue in *Fortnightly* and *Teleprompter.* The systems in those cases transmitted constantly; they sent continuous programming to each subscriber's television set. In contrast, Aereo's system remains inert until a subscriber indicates that she wants to watch a program. Only at that moment, in automatic response to the subscriber's request, does Aereo's system activate an antenna and begin to transmit the requested program.

This is a critical difference, says the dissent. It means that Aereo's subscribers, not Aereo, "select[] the copyrighted content" that is "perform[ed]," *post,* at 4 (opinion of SCALIA, J.), and for that reason they, not Aereo, "transmit" the performance. Aereo is thus like "a copy shop that provides its patrons with a library card." *Post,* at 5. A copy shop is not directly liable whenever a patron uses the shop's machines to "reproduce" copyrighted materials found in that library. And by the same token, Aereo should not be directly liable whenever its patrons use its equipment to "transmit" copyrighted television programs to their screens.

In our view, however, the dissent's copy shop argument, in whatever form, makes too much out of too little. Given Aereo's overwhelming likeness to the cable companies targeted by the 1976 amendments, this sole technological difference between Aereo and traditional cable companies does not make a critical difference here. The subscribers of the *Fortnightly* and *Teleprompter* cable systems also selected what programs to display on their receiving sets. Indeed, as we explained in *Fortnightly,* such a subscriber "could choose any of the ... programs he wished to view by simply turning the knob on his own television set." 392 U.S., at 392. The same is true of an Aereo subscriber. Of course, in *Fortnightly* the television signals, in a sense, lurked behind the screen, ready to emerge when the subscriber turned the knob. Here the signals pursue their ordinary course of travel through the universe until today's "turn of the knob"—a click on a website—activates machinery that intercepts and reroutes them to Aereo's subscribers over the Internet. But this difference means nothing to the subscriber. It means nothing to the broadcaster. We do not see how this single difference, invisible to subscriber and broadcaster alike, could transform a system that is for all practical purposes a traditional cable system into "a copy shop that provides its patrons with a library card."

In other cases involving different kinds of service or technology providers, a user's involvement in the operation of the provider's equipment and selection of the content transmitted may well bear on whether the provider performs within the meaning of the Act. But the many similarities between Aereo and cable companies, considered in light of Congress' basic purposes in amending the Copyright Act, convince us that this difference is not critical here. We conclude that Aereo is not just an equipment supplier and that Aereo "perform[s]."

III

Next, we must consider whether Aereo performs petitioners' works "publicly," within the meaning of the Transmit Clause. Under the Clause, an entity performs a work publicly when it "transmit[s] ... a performance ... of the work ... to the public." § 101. Aereo denies that it satisfies this definition. It reasons as follows: First, the "performance" it "transmit[s]" is the performance created by its act of transmitting. And second, because each of these performances is capable of being received by one and only one subscriber, Aereo transmits privately, not publicly.

We assume *arguendo* that Aereo's first argument is correct. But what about the Clause's further requirement that Aereo transmit a performance "to the public"? One and only one subscriber has the ability to see and hear each Aereo transmission. The fact that each transmission is to only one subscriber, in Aereo's view, means that it does not transmit a performance "to the public."

In terms of the Act's purposes, these differences do not distinguish Aereo's system from cable systems, which do perform "publicly." Viewed in terms of Congress' regulatory objectives, why should any of these technological differences matter? They concern the behind-the-scenes way in which Aereo delivers television programming to its viewers' screens. They do not render Aereo's commercial objective any different from that of cable companies. Nor do they significantly alter the viewing experience of Aereo's subscribers. Why would a subscriber who wishes to watch a television show care much whether images and sounds are delivered to his screen via a large multisubscriber antenna or one small dedicated antenna, whether they arrive instantaneously or after a few seconds' delay, or whether they are transmitted directly or after a personal copy is made? And why, if Aereo is right, could not modern CATV systems simply continue the same commercial and consumer-oriented activities, free of copyright restrictions, provided they substitute such new technologies for old? Congress would as much have intended to protect a copyright holder from the unlicensed activities of Aereo as from those of cable companies.

The Act applies to transmissions "by means of any device or process." § 101. And retransmitting a television program using user-specific copies is a "process" of transmitting a performance. A "cop[y]" of a work is simply a "material object[] ... in which a work is fixed ... and from which the work can be perceived, reproduced, or otherwise communicated." *Id.* So whether Aereo transmits from the same or separate copies, it performs the same work; it shows the same images and makes audible the same sounds. Therefore, when Aereo streams the same television program to multiple subscribers, it "transmit[s] ... a performance" to all of them.

Moreover, the subscribers to whom Aereo transmits television programs constitute "the public." Aereo communicates the same contemporaneously perceptible images and sounds to a large number of people who are unrelated and unknown to each other. This matters because, although the Act does not define "the public," it specifies that an entity performs publicly when it performs at "any place where a substantial number of persons outside of a normal circle of a family and its social acquaintances is gathered." *Id.* The Act thereby suggests that "the public" consists of a large group of people outside of a family and friends.

Neither the record nor Aereo suggests that Aereo's subscribers receive performances in their capacities as owners or possessors of the underlying works. This is relevant because when an entity performs to a set of people, whether they constitute "the public" often depends upon their relationship to the underlying work. When, for example, a valet parking attendant returns cars to their drivers, we would not say that the parking service provides cars "to the public." We would say that it provides the cars to their owners. We would say that a car dealership, on the other hand, does provide cars to the public, for it sells cars to individuals who lack a pre-existing relationship to the cars. Similarly, an entity that transmits a performance to individuals in their capacities as owners or possessors does not perform to "the public," whereas an entity like Aereo that transmits to large numbers of paying subscribers who lack any prior relationship to the works does so perform.

Finally, we note that Aereo's subscribers may receive the same programs at different times and locations. This fact does not help Aereo, however, for the Transmit Clause expressly provides that an entity may perform publicly "whether the members of the public capable of receiving the performance ... receive it in the same place or in separate places and at the same time or at different times." *Id.* In other words, "the public" need not be situated together, spatially or temporally. For these reasons, we conclude that Aereo transmits a performance of petitioners' copyrighted works to the public, within the meaning of the Transmit Clause.

IV

Aereo and many of its supporting amici argue that to apply the Transmit Clause to Aereo's conduct will impose copyright liability on other technologies, including new technologies, that Congress could not possibly have wanted to reach. We agree that Congress, while intending the Transmit Clause to apply broadly to cable companies and their equivalents, did not intend to discourage or to control the emergence or use of different kinds of technologies. But we do not believe that our limited holding today will have that effect.

For one thing, the history of cable broadcast transmissions that led to the enactment of the Transmit Clause informs our conclusion that Aereo "perform[s]," but it does not determine whether different kinds of providers in different contexts also "perform." For another, an entity only transmits a performance when it communicates contemporaneously perceptible images and sounds of a work.

Further, we have interpreted the term "the public" to apply to a group of individuals acting as ordinary members of the public who pay primarily to watch broadcast television programs, many of which are copyrighted. We have said that it does not extend to those who act as owners or possessors of the relevant product. And we have not considered whether the public performance right is infringed when the user of a service pays primarily for something other than the transmission of copyrighted works, such as the remote storage of content. *See* Brief for United States as Amicus Curiae 31 (distinguishing cloud-based storage services because they "offer consumers more numerous and convenient means of playing back copies that the consumers have *already* lawfully acquired" (emphasis in original)). In addition, an entity does not transmit to the public if it does not transmit to a substantial number of people outside of a family and its social circle.

We also note that courts often apply a statute's highly general language in light of the statute's basic purposes. Finally, the doctrine of "fair use" can help to prevent inappropriate or inequitable applications of the Clause.

We cannot now answer more precisely how the Transmit Clause or other provisions of the Copyright Act will apply to technologies not before us. We agree with the Solicitor General that "[q]uestions involving cloud computing, [remote storage] DVRs, and other novel issues not before the Court, as to which 'Congress has not plainly marked [the] course,' should await a case in which they are squarely presented." Brief for United States as Amicus Curiae 34 (quoting *Sony, supra,* at 431 (alteration in original)). And we note that, to the extent commercial actors or other interested entities may be concerned with the relationship between the development and use of such technologies and the Copyright Act, they are of course free to seek action from Congress.

Justice SCALIA, with whom Justice THOMAS and Justice ALITO join, dissenting.

I. Legal Standard

There are two types of liability for copyright infringement: direct and secondary. As its name suggests, the former applies when an actor personally engages in infringing conduct. Secondary liability, by contrast, is a means of holding defendants responsible for infringement by third parties, even when the defendants "have not themselves engaged in the infringing activity." Sony Corp. of America v. Universal City Studios, Inc., 464 U.S. 417, 435 (1984).

Most suits against equipment manufacturers and service providers involve secondary-liability claims. This suit, or rather the portion of it before us here, is fundamentally different. The Networks claim that Aereo *directly* infringes their public-performance right. Accordingly, the Networks must prove that Aereo "perform[s]" copyrighted works, § 106(4), when its subscribers log in, select a channel, and push the "watch" button. That process undoubtedly results in a performance; the question is *who* does the performing. If Aereo's subscribers perform but Aereo does not, the claim necessarily fails.

The Networks' claim is governed by a simple but profoundly important rule: A defendant may be held directly liable only if it has engaged in volitional conduct that violates the Act. This requirement is firmly grounded in the Act's text, which defines "perform" in active, affirmative terms: One "perform[s]" a copyrighted "audiovisual work," such as a movie or news broadcast, by "show[ing] its images in any sequence" or "mak[ing] the sounds accompanying it audible." § 101. And since the Act makes it unlawful to copy or perform copyrighted works, not to copy or perform in general, *see* § 501(a), the volitional-act requirement demands conduct directed to the plaintiff's copyrighted material.

The volitional-conduct requirement is not at issue in most direct-infringement cases; the usual point of dispute is whether the defendant's conduct is infringing (e.g., Does the defendant's design copy the plaintiff's?), rather than whether the defendant has acted at all (e.g., Did this defendant create the infringing design?). But it comes right to the fore when a direct-infringement claim is lodged against a defendant who does nothing more than operate an automated, user-controlled system. Internet-service providers are a prime example. When one user sends data to another, the provider's equipment facilitates the transfer automatically. Does that mean that the provider is directly liable when the transmission happens to result in the "reproduc[tion]," § 106(1), of a copyrighted work? It does not. The provider's system is "totally indifferent to the material's content," whereas courts require "some aspect of volition" directed at the copyrighted material before direct liability may be imposed. CoStar Group, Inc. v. LoopNet, Inc., 373 F.3d 544, 550–51 (4th Cir. 2004). The defendant may be held directly liable only if the defendant *itself* "trespassed on the exclusive domain of the copyright owner." *Id.*, at 550. Most of the time that issue will come down to who selects the copyrighted content: the defendant or its customers.

A comparison between copy shops and video-on-demand services illustrates the point. A copy shop rents out photocopiers on a per-use basis. One customer might copy his 10-year-old's drawings—a perfectly lawful thing to do—while another might duplicate a famous artist's copyrighted photographs—a use clearly prohibited by § 106(1). Either way, *the customer* chooses the content and activates the copying function; the photocopier does nothing except in response to the customer's commands. Because the shop plays no role in selecting the content, it cannot be held directly liable when a customer makes an infringing copy. *See CoStar, supra,* at 550.

Video-on-demand services, like photocopiers, respond automatically to user input, but they differ in one crucial respect: *They choose the content.* That selection and arrangement by the service provider constitutes a volitional act directed to specific copyrighted works and thus serves as a basis for direct liability.

II. Application to Aereo

So which is Aereo: the copy shop or the video-on-demand service? In truth, it is neither. Rather, it is akin to a copy shop that provides its patrons with a library card. Aereo offers access to an automated system consisting of routers, servers, transcoders, and dime-sized antennae. Like a photocopier or VCR, that system lies dormant until a subscriber activates it. When a subscriber selects a program, Aereo's system picks up the relevant broadcast signal, translates its audio and video components into digital data, stores the data in a user-specific file, and transmits that file's contents to the subscriber via the Internet—at which point the subscriber's laptop, tablet, or other device displays the broadcast just as an ordinary television would. The result of that process fits the statutory definition of a performance to a tee: The subscriber's device "show[s]" the broadcast's "images" and "make[s] the sounds accompanying" the broadcast "audible." § 101. The only question is whether those performances are the product of Aereo's volitional conduct.

They are not. Unlike video-on-demand services, Aereo does not provide a prearranged assortment of movies and television shows. Rather, it assigns each subscriber an antenna that—like a library card—can be used to obtain whatever broadcasts are freely available. Some of those broadcasts are copyrighted; others are in the public domain. The key point is that subscribers call all the shots: Aereo's automated system does not relay any program, copyrighted or not, until a subscriber selects the program and tells Aereo to relay it. Aereo's operation of that system is a volitional act and a but-for cause of the resulting performances, but, as in the case of the copy shop, that degree of involvement is not enough for direct liability.

In sum, Aereo does not "perform" for the sole and simple reason that it does not make the choice of content. And because Aereo does not perform, it cannot be held directly liable for infringing the Networks' public-performance right. That conclusion does not necessarily mean that Aereo's service complies with the Copyright Act. Quite the contrary. The Networks' complaint alleges that Aereo is directly *and* secondarily liable for infringing their public-performance rights (§ 106(4)) *and also* their reproduction rights (§ 106(1)). Their request for a preliminary injunction—the only issue before this Court—is based exclusively on the direct-liability portion of the public-performance claim (and further limited to Aereo's "watch" function, as opposed to its "record" function). Affirming the judgment below would merely return this case to the lower courts for consideration of the Networks' remaining claims.

* * *

We are told that nothing less than "the very existence of broadcast television as we know it" is at stake. Brief for Petitioners 39. Aereo and its amici dispute those forecasts and make a few of their own, suggesting that a decision in the Networks' favor will stifle technological innovation and imperil billions of dollars of investments in cloud-storage services. We are in no position to judge the validity of those self-interested claims or to foresee the path of future technological development. Hence, the proper course is not to bend and twist the Act's terms in an effort to produce a just outcome, but to apply the law as it stands and leave to Congress the task of deciding whether the Copyright Act needs an upgrade.

Notes and Questions

1. The Threat to Broadcast Television. The petitioners' brief Justice Scalia quotes (joined by all major television broadcasters) presented Aereo's reading of copyright law as "threaten[ing] the very existence of broadcast television as we know it," because "Aereo has built an entire business around the unauthorized exploitation of broadcasters' copyrighted content. It seeks to siphon off cable and satellite subscribers by offering this content for a lower fee, which it can do only because, unlike its competitors, Aereo does not compensate copyright owners for its use." Petitioners' Brief at 39, American Broadcasting Companies, Inc. v. Aereo, Inc., 134 S. Ct. 2498 (2014). On what constructions of copyright law should that affect the Supreme Court's holding?

2. The Threat to the Cloud. For its part, Aereo warned that acceptance of the broadcasters' reading of copyright law "would pervasively threaten the use of cloud technologies to store and access copyrighted content." Respondents' brief at 49, American Broadcasting Companies, Inc. v. Aereo, Inc., 134 S. Ct. 2498 (2014). What implications does the Supreme Court's ruling have for new and developing methods of storage and retrieval? Should the Supreme Court have said more about technologies beyond Aereo's? If so, what should it have said?

3. If It Looks Like Cable.... In a section of his dissent not excerpted above entitled "Guilt by Resemblance," Justice Scalia criticizes the majority for creating a "cable-TV-lookalike rule," i.e., that a service that looks too much like cable "performs" under the statute. The majority gives some ammunition for this characterization when it rejects the dissent's copy shop analogy by emphasizing "Aereo's overwhelming likeness to the cable companies targeted by the 1976 amendments." In part this disagreement reflects difference emphases on text and purpose—and, as a general matter, the dissenters are often more sympathetic to textual statutory interpretation and those in the majority more sympathetic to purposivist statutory interpretation. But this also has significant consequences for future technologies. If you were advising a company that was devising a system for remote storage and retrieval of broadcast television shows, would you advise them to be unlike cable? What would that entail?

4. Does This Mean Aereo Is Entitled to a Compulsory License? In light of the holding that Aereo closely resembles a cable operator, is Aereo entitled to a compulsory license under 17 U.S.C. § 111? After all, § 111 creates a compulsory license for a "cable system," which it broadly defines as a facility that "receives signals transmitted or programs broadcast by one or more television broadcast stations licensed by the Federal Communications Commission, and makes secondary transmissions of such signals or programs by wires, cables, microwave, or other communications channels to subscribing members of the public who pay for such service." 17 U.S.C. § 111(f)(3). Unfortunately for Aereo, Congress designated the Copyright Office as the agency that administers § 111 (and thus courts look to its interpretations of § 111), and the Copyright Office has stated that "[e]xamination of the overall operation of section 111 proves that the compulsory license applies only to localized retransmission services regulated as cable systems by the FCC." 57 Fed. Reg. 3284, 3292 (1992); *see* WPIX, Inc. v. ivi, Inc., 691 F.3d 275 (2d Cir. 2012) (relying on the Copyright Office's construction of § 111 in concluding that an Internet streaming service was not a "cable system" under § 111). And, in fact, shortly after losing in the Supreme Court, Aereo attempted to rely on 17 U.S.C. § 111, but the Copyright Office rejected that attempt, invoking the language quoted above from its regulation and the *WPIX* holding. Letter from Jacqueline C. Charlesworth, General Counsel and Associate Register of Copyrights, to Matthew Calabro, Aereo, Inc. (July 16, 2014), available at http://www.nab.org/documents/newsRoom/pdfs/071614_Aereo_Copyright_Office_letter.pdf. So unless the FCC regulates companies like Aereo as cable operators, the Copyright Office changes its interpretation, or a court rejects the Copyright Office's interpretation, companies like Aereo will not be entitled to compulsory licenses.

---

§ 9.A.3. Syndicated Exclusivity and Network Nonduplication

Overall, the Copyright Act of 1976 represented a compromise: cable operators had to pay for some of the content they retransmitted, but neither broadcasters nor copyright holders were able to deny cable operators the right to carry previously broadcast programming. Section 111, however, had an important exception: secondary transmissions were subject to compulsory licenses only "where the carriage of the signals comprising the secondary transmission [was also] permissible under the rules, regulations, or authorizations" of the FCC.

Prior to the 1976 Act, many FCC rules governed the respective rights of cable operators, broadcasters, and copyright holders. After the Act was passed, the FCC repealed most of those rules so as to not interfere with the compulsory licensing scheme devised by Congress. In 1988, the FCC reinstated the syndicated exclusivity rules. *See* Amendment of Parts 73 and 76 of the Commission's Rules Relating to Program Exclusivity in the Cable and Broadcast Industries, Report and Order, 3 FCC Rcd. 5299 (1988).

The syndicated exclusivity rules (sometimes called syndex) are companion rules to the network nonduplication rules (sometimes called network nondupe), which the FCC never lifted and which address closely related concerns. The FCC refers to these rules collectively as the exclusivity rules. The syndicated exclusivity rules apply to the syndicated programs that are distributed to and aired by independent broadcast stations. By contrast, the network nonduplication rules apply to programs that are distributed within and aired by the networks. In short, the syndicated exclusivity rules enable a local broadcaster to prevent a cable system from exhibiting that part of an imported distant broadcaster's signal that contains programs (or episodes from a television series) for which the local broadcaster has obtained exclusive broadcast rights, in that local area, from the copyright holder. The network nonduplication rules operate in a related fashion to give local broadcasters similar rights with respect to network programming for which they have obtained local exclusivity. (There are also similar rules protecting sports leagues' efforts to establish partial exclusivity in local markets.) The rules provide for FCC enforcement of these contractual arrangements. As the FCC explained, the rules "are grounded in the private contractual arrangements that exist between a station and the provider of network or syndicated programming. The Commission's rules do not create these rights but rather provide a means for the parties to the exclusive contracts to enforce them through the Commission rather than through the courts." Amendment of the Commission's Rules Related to Retransmission Consent, Notice of Proposed Rulemaking, 26 FCC Rcd. 2718 ¶ 42 (2011).

Congress did not mandate syndicated exclusivity and network nonduplication rules for cable television, but a section of SHVIA not discussed above requires the FCC to apply rules like those developed for cable to DBS. Specifically, the Commission was directed to establish regulations applying network nonduplication, syndicated exclusivity, and sports blackout rules to DBS. Congress ordered the FCC to apply the network nonduplication and syndicated exclusivity rules to DBS only with respect to superstations (broadcasters, such as WTBS and WGN, that had established themselves as nationally distributed stations). 47 U.S.C. §§ 339(b) & (d). In the cable context, by contrast, the FCC's rules for cable television apply to any imported signal, be it superstation or not.

Why have these rules? As summarized by a D.C. Circuit opinion upholding the FCC's reinstatement of the syndicated exclusivity rules,

> [t]he Commission's decision to reinstate syndex rests on its finding that syndex rules will promote diversity in syndicated programming. In the report accompanying the rules, the Commission found that unrestricted importation of distant signals (i.e., no syndex protection) leads to duplication of programming in local broadcasting areas; this duplication lessens the value of syndicated programs to broadcast stations; that loss of value in turn lowers the price syndicated program suppliers will receive for their programs; and all of this ultimately reduces the incentive for syndicated program suppliers to produce programs, which translates into a reduction in the diversity of programming available to the public. On the basis of this scenario, the Commission concluded that syndex rules should be reinstated in order to promote diversity of programming.

United Video v. FCC, 890 F.2d 1173, 1178 (D.C. Cir. 1989).

That said, in 2011, and again in 2014, the Commission issued notices of proposed rulemaking asking whether the rules' benefits outweigh their costs and thus whether they should be eliminated. The Commission itself asked some of the key questions about the rules:

> Do these rules serve a useful purpose in today's marketplace? Should exclusivity in this area be left entirely to the private marketplace, without providing any means of enforcement through the Commission? Would there be a beneficial impact to removing these rules if the contractual provisions that the rules enforce stay in place? Would the elimination of the network non-duplication and syndicated exclusivity rules have a negative impact on localism? We seek comment on the impact of our network non-duplication and syndicated exclusivity rules

on the distribution of programming by television stations. Do these rules provide stations and networks with any rights that cannot be secured through a combination of network-affiliate contracts and retransmission consent?

Amendment of the Commission's Rules Related to Retransmission Consent, Notice of Proposed Rulemaking, 26 FCC Rcd. 2718 ¶ 44 (2011).

Notes and Questions

1. **The Logic of the Exclusivity Rules.** What interests are these rules designed to protect? Suppose a major-market independent station (say, a non-network station in Washington, D.C.) is imported into a small market (Quincy, Illinois) by the Quincy cable system. Suppose further that both the imported D.C. station and a Quincy station hold rights to exhibit episodes of "The Big Bang Theory." Is the D.C. station harmed by the importation of its signal? How about the Quincy station? Although the Quincy station may lose audience members to the Quincy cable system, won't it also be able, as a consequence, to obtain "The Big Bang Theory" rights for a smaller fee? How about the producer of "The Big Bang Theory"? Won't that firm now be able to charge higher prices to the D.C. station due to its expanded audience in Quincy?

2. **Why Have *Rules*?** The rules provide for FCC enforcement of contractual arrangements. Why not leave this up to the parties and courts? Is private enforcement via courts too inefficient or expensive? Whatever are the reasons for FCC rules enforcing these contractual arrangements, wouldn't those reasons apply to other contractual arrangements? That is, why shouldn't the FCC set up rules that will create enforcement mechanisms for a host of contractual arrangements, thus providing a comprehensive alternative to courts?

3. **Relationship to Retransmission Consent.** The FCC's consideration of the exclusivity rules has arisen in its consideration of retransmission consent (discussed in the next section), as the title of the proceeding indicates: Amendment of the Commission's Rules Related to Retransmission Consent. Indeed, the paragraph excerpted immediately above these notes and questions begins as follows: "We seek comment on whether eliminating the Commission's network non-duplication and syndicated exclusivity rules, without abrogating any private contractual provisions, would have a beneficial impact on retransmission consent negotiations. Would eliminating these rules help to minimize regulatory intrusion in the market, thus better enabling free market negotiations to set the terms for retransmission consent?" *Id.* ¶ 44. We will examine retransmission consent in the next section, but the quotation above raises larger questions. Examining rules in light of other rules seems to make sense, so that a regulator can try to craft coherent policies. But how far should that go? Should the FCC attempt to review all rules relevant to cable television in one big proceeding? All rules relevant to the provision of video (including broadcasters and MVPDs)? All rules relevant to telecommunications?

---

§ 9.B. Programs Grouped into Signals

While both copyright law and the exclusivity rules focus primarily on program content, Congress created two additional rights under federal telecommunications law, both of which benefit TV broadcasters (at the expense of cable and DBS providers). First, 47

U.S.C. § 325(b) states that an MPVD (which includes cable and DBS operators) cannot retransmit a broadcaster's signal without that broadcaster's explicit permission. This is known as "retransmission consent" and provides a right for broadcasters to withhold the signals from cable and DBS providers, even if they enjoy the right of access under copyright law. This system allows broadcasters with desirable content to charge cable companies for the right to carry that content. Second, 47 U.S.C. §§ 534 and 535 give certain broadcasters the right to insist that their local signals be carried by the local cable system free of charge. This is known as the "must-carry" obligation. Note that the must-carry obligations for DBS providers are different from those for cable providers. Section 338 provides that if a DBS operator carries a local broadcaster pursuant to a statutory compulsory license, it must carry all the local stations. This DBS provision is known as "carry one, carry all," and we will discuss it in more detail later in this chapter.

§ 9.B.1. Retransmission Consent

Retransmission consent refers to the permission a cable operator must receive in order to carry the signal of almost any broadcast station. The only stations for which consent is not needed are the superstations. Retransmission consent is required in addition to any permissions needed under copyright law. That is, retransmission consent recognizes a property right in the signal that is independent of, and in addition to, the intellectual property rights already recognized in the copyrighted content being transmitted by the signal. The provision gives broadcasters the power to negotiate with cable operators for a share of the revenues generated by the retransmission of broadcast signals.

So whose interests does retransmission consent protect? That, unfortunately, is not entirely clear. The copyright, syndicated exclusivity and network nonduplication rules seem to already protect program suppliers. And if retransmission consent was designed to protect the additional value in a station's signal that is contributed by the station—for example, the value created when a station assembles a package of programs that provides a continuous sequence of entertainment—one still must explain why broadcasters could not be adequately compensated for this value in other ways, such as in the value of the advertising revenue they collect. The history of the retransmission consent right underscores that it provides broadcasters with a valuable threat to withhold programming in return for payments by cable companies (in dollars or in kind).

Retransmission consent took effect in 1993. In that year, the major networks had their first experience negotiating with cable providers and took different stances. CBS took a hard line and attempted to hold out for huge fees. Cable operators refused to pay, and ultimately CBS caved in and authorized retransmission at no charge. Meanwhile, NBC and ABC granted retransmission consent, but not for money. Instead, these networks gave their consent in exchange for space on the various cable systems. NBC used that space for an ultimately unsuccessful cable channel called America's Talking. ABC more profitably used its space for the sports channel ESPN2. (Fox also traded retransmission consent for system capacity, using its cable capacity to launch the cable channel FX.) The principal benefit to the broadcasters from this right (excepting CBS) was that they were able to introduce new cable channels that immediately reached upwards of 18 million subscribers.

Bargaining over retransmission consent grew increasingly contentious in subsequent rounds of these triennial negotiations. For example, in 1999, ABC took an aggressive stance with respect to retransmission consent, trying both to increase subscribership for its affiliated Lifetime network and to introduce a new movie channel. Negotiations went well past the expiration date of the then-existing retransmission consent agreement, and so for several weeks ABC's status on a number of major cable systems was precariously maintained through ad hoc extensions of the old deal. Indeed, in some negotiations, the two sides failed to make a deal by the expiration of their previous agreement and the broadcaster vanished from the cable lineup until the two sides reached an agreement. In 2004, EchoStar (then owner of DISH Network) and Viacom similarly failed to reach an agreement by the relevant date, meaning that for a while Viacom's channels (CBS, MTV, and Nickelodeon, among others) were not available to EchoStar/DISH Network's DBS customers. In all of these cases, the disputes were ultimately settled, but it is worth noting that, without retransmission consent, such battles could not take place, as the compulsory license would set the terms of access.

Negotiations over retransmission consent have routinely involved broadcasters demanding a higher price and MVPDs complaining that the price is too high. Broadcasters say that they are merely demanding what they are worth. Cable and satellite companies complain that providing automatic carriage rights for some (must-carry) and the threat of hold-out for others (under retransmission consent) leaves them in the worst of all worlds. They particularly feel the pressure after the pre-existing agreement expires and valuable content is not available to their customers. In 2010, for example, Cablevision did not carry Fox for the first two games of the World Series because of a dispute over retransmission fees.

Why have these negotiations been so fraught? Should the must-carry/retransmission consent regime be changed? In 2011, the FCC issued a Notice of Proposed Rulemaking on this topic, seeking comment on the issues involved in retransmission negotiations (and reconsidering the exclusivity rules). Then, as discussed below, in 2014, the FCC revised the retransmission consent rules, prohibiting "joint negotiation" on the part of certain broadcasters. The 2011 notice is both a useful summary of the current rules and an opportunity to consider the question of how regulations may affect (or not) the relative bargaining power of the companies in a retransmission consent dispute.

AMENDMENT OF THE COMMISSION'S RULES RELATED TO RETRANSMISSION CONSENT

Notice of Proposed Rulemaking, 26 FCC Rcd. 2718 (2011)

I. Introduction

1. In this Notice of Proposed Rulemaking (NPRM), we seek comment on a series of proposals to streamline and clarify our rules concerning or affecting retransmission consent negotiations. Our primary objective is to assess whether and how the Commission rules in this arena are ensuring that the market-based mechanisms Congress designed to govern retransmission consent negotiations are working effectively and, to the extent possible, minimize video programming service disruptions to consumers.

2. The Communications Act of 1934, as amended (the Act), prohibits cable systems and other multichannel video programming distributors (MVPDs) from retransmitting a broadcast station's signal without the station's consent. This consent is what is known as "retransmission consent." The law requires broadcasters and MVPDs to negotiate for retransmission consent in good faith. 47 U.S.C. § 325(b)(3)(C). Since Congress enacted the retransmission consent regime in 1992, there have been significant changes in the video programming marketplace. One such change is the form of compensation sought by broadcasters. Historically, cable operators typically compensated broadcasters for consent to retransmit the broadcasters' signals through in-kind compensation, which might

include, for example, carriage of additional channels of the broadcaster's programming on the cable system or advertising time. Today, however, broadcasters are increasingly seeking and receiving monetary compensation from MVPDs in exchange for consent to the retransmission of their signals. Another important change concerns the rise of competitive video programming providers. In 1992, the only option for many local broadcast television stations seeking to reach MVPD customers in a particular Designated Market Area (DMA) was a single local cable provider. Today, in contrast, many consumers have additional options for receiving programming, including two national direct broadcast satellite (DBS) providers, telephone providers that offer video programming in some areas, and, to a degree, the Internet. One result of such changes in the marketplace is that disputes over retransmission consent have become more contentious and more public, and we recently have seen a rise in negotiation impasses that have affected millions of consumers.

3. Accordingly, we have concluded that it is appropriate for us to reexamine our rules relating to retransmission consent. We consider below revisions to the retransmission consent and related rules that we believe could allow the market-based negotiations contemplated by the statute to proceed more smoothly, provide greater certainty to the negotiating parties, and help protect consumers.

II. Background

A. Retransmission Consent

4. The current regulatory scheme for carriage of broadcast television stations was established by the Cable Television Consumer Protection and Competition Act of 1992 (1992 Cable Act). In 1992, unlike today, local broadcast television stations seeking to reach viewers in a particular DMA through an MVPD service often had only one option—namely, a single local cable provider. While broadcasters benefited from cable carriage, Congress recognized that broadcast programming "remains the most popular programming on cable systems, and a substantial portion of the benefits for which consumers pay cable systems is derived from carriage of the signals of network affiliates, independent television stations, and public television stations." In adopting the retransmission consent provisions of the 1992 Cable Act, Congress found that cable operators obtained great benefit from the local broadcast signals that they were able to carry without broadcaster consent or copyright liability, and that this benefit resulted in an effective subsidy to cable operators. Accordingly, Congress adopted its retransmission consent provisions to allow broadcasters to negotiate to receive compensation for the value of their signals. Through the 1992 Cable Act, Congress modified the Communications Act, inter alia, to provide television stations with certain carriage rights on cable television systems in their local market.

5. Pursuant to the statutory provisions enacted in 1992, television broadcasters elect every three years whether to proceed under the retransmission consent requirements of Section 325 of the Act, or the mandatory carriage ("must carry") requirements of Sections 338 and 614 of the Act [codified at 47 U.S.C. §§ 325, 338 & 534, respectively]. There are important differences between the retransmission consent and must carry regimes. Specifically, a broadcaster electing must carry status is guaranteed carriage on cable systems in its market, and the cable operator is generally prohibited from accepting or requesting compensation for carriage, whereas a broadcaster who elects carriage under the retransmission consent rules may insist on compensation. In order to reach MVPD customers, most broadcasters elected carriage under the must carry rules in the early years following enactment of the new regime.

6. Since 2001, broadcasters have also had mandatory carriage rights on DBS systems. The Satellite Home Viewer Improvement Act of 1999 (SHVIA) gives satellite carriers a statutory copyright license to retransmit local broadcast stations to subscribers in the station's market, also known as "local-into-local" service. Generally, when a satellite carrier provides local-into-local service pursuant to the statutory copyright license, the satellite carrier is obligated to carry any qualified local television station in the particular DMA that has made a timely election for mandatory carriage, unless the station's programming is duplicative of the programming of another station carried by the carrier in the DMA or the station does not provide a good quality signal to the carrier's local receive facility.

7. As an alternative to seeking mandatory carriage, a broadcaster may elect carriage under the retransmission consent rules, which allow for negotiations with cable operators and other MVPDs for carriage. A broadcaster electing retransmission consent may accept or request compensation for carriage in retransmission consent negotiations. The legislative history of Section 325 indicates that Congress intended "to establish a marketplace for the disposition of the rights to retransmit broadcast signals; it is not the Committee's intention in this bill to dictate the outcome of the ensuing marketplace negotiations." S. Rep. No. 92, 102d Cong., 2d Sess. 92 (1991). Under Section 325(b)(1)(A) of the Act, if a broadcaster electing retransmission consent and an MVPD are unable to reach an agreement, or do not agree to the extension of an existing agreement prior to its expiration, then the MVPD may not retransmit the broadcasting station's signal because the signal cannot be carried without the broadcast station's consent.

B. Good Faith Negotiations

8. Initially, Section 325 of the Act did not include any standards governing retransmission consent negotiations between broadcasters and MVPDs. That changed in 1999 when Congress adopted SHVIA, which contained provisions concerning the satellite industry, as well as television broadcast stations and terrestrial MVPDs. Specifically, Congress required broadcast television stations engaging in retransmission consent negotiations with any MVPD to negotiate in good faith.

10. The Commission adopted a two-part framework to determine whether broadcasters and MVPDs negotiate retransmission consent in good faith. First, the Commission established a list of seven objective good faith negotiation standards, the violation of which is considered a per se breach of the good faith negotiation obligation. Second, even if the seven specific standards are met, the Commission may consider whether, based on the totality of the circumstances, a party failed to negotiate retransmission consent in good faith. The Commission has stated that, where "a broadcaster is determined to have failed to negotiate in good faith, the Commission will instruct the parties to renegotiate the agreement in accordance with the Commission's rules and Section 325(b)(3)(C)." Implementation of the Satellite Home Viewer Improvement Act of 1999, Report and Order, 15 FCC Rcd. 5445, 5480 ¶ 84 (2000). While the Commission did not find any statutory authority to impose damages, it noted "that, as with all violations of the Communications Act or the Commission's rules, the Commission has the authority to impose forfeitures for violations of Section 325(b)(3)(C)." In discussing remedies for a violation of the good faith negotiation requirement, the Commission did not reference continued carriage as a potential remedy, and stated that it could not adopt regulations permitting retransmission during good faith negotiation or while a good faith complaint is pending before the Commission, absent broadcaster consent to such retransmission.

11. The Commission concluded that Congress did not intend for it to sit in judgment of the terms of every executed retransmission consent agreement. Rather, the Commis-

sion said, "[w]e believe that, by imposing the good faith obligation, Congress intended that the Commission develop and enforce a process that ensures that broadcasters and MVPDs meet to negotiate retransmission consent and that such negotiations are conducted in an atmosphere of honesty, purpose and clarity of process."

12. There have been very few complaints filed alleging violations of the Commission's good faith rules. Accordingly, there is little Commission precedent regarding the good faith rules, and there has only been one finding that a party to a retransmission consent agreement negotiated in bad faith.

D. Consumer Impact

15. In the past year, we have seen high profile retransmission consent disputes result in carriage impasses. When Cablevision Systems Corp. (Cablevision) and News Corp.'s agreement for two Fox-affiliated television stations and one MyNetwork TV-affiliated television station expired on October 15, 2010 and the parties did not reach an extension or renewal agreement, Cablevision was forced to discontinue carriage of the three stations until agreement was reached on October 30, 2010. The carriage impasse resulted in affected Cablevision subscribers being unable to view on cable the baseball National League Championship Series, the first two games of the World Series, a number of NFL regular season games, and other regularly scheduled programs. Previously, on March 7, 2010, Walt Disney Co. (Disney) and Cablevision were unable to reach agreement on carriage of Disney's ABC signal for nearly 21 hours after a previous agreement expired. As a result, the approximately 3.1 million households served by Cablevision were unable to view the first 14 minutes of the Academy Awards through their cable provider.

16. In addition, consumers have been concerned about other high profile retransmission consent negotiations that seemed close to an impasse. We are concerned about the uncertainty that consumers have faced regarding their ability to continue receiving certain broadcast television stations during recent contentious retransmission consent negotiations.

III. Discussion

17. Our goal in this proceeding is to take appropriate action, within our existing authority, to protect consumers from the disruptive impact of the loss of broadcast programming carried on MVPD video services. Subscribers are the innocent bystanders adversely affected when broadcasters and MVPDs fail to reach an agreement to extend or renew their retransmission consent contracts.

18. As a threshold matter, we note that the Petition proposed, among other suggestions, that the Commission adopt a mandatory arbitration mechanism for retransmission consent disputes, and provide for mandatory interim carriage while an MVPD negotiates in good faith or while dispute resolution proceedings are pending. We do not believe that the Commission has authority to adopt either interim carriage mechanisms or mandatory binding dispute resolution procedures applicable to retransmission consent negotiations. First, regarding interim carriage, examination of the Act and its legislative history has convinced us that the Commission lacks authority to order carriage in the absence of a broadcaster's consent due to a retransmission consent dispute. Rather, Section 325(b) of the Act expressly prohibits the retransmission of a broadcast signal without the broadcaster's consent. Furthermore, consistent with the statutory language, the legislative history of Section 325(b) states that the retransmission consent provisions were not intended "to dictate the outcome of the ensuing marketplace negotiations" and that broadcasters would retain the "right to control retransmission and to be compensated for others' use

of their signals." We thus interpret Section 325(b) to prevent the Commission from ordering carriage over the objection of the broadcaster, even upon a finding of a violation of the good faith negotiation requirement. Consistent with this interpretation, the Commission previously found that it has "no latitude ... to adopt regulations permitting retransmission during good faith negotiation or while a good faith or exclusivity complaint is pending before the Commission where the broadcaster has not consented to such retransmission." Contrary to the suggestion of some commenters, Section 4(i) of the Act does not authorize the Commission to act in a manner that is inconsistent with other provisions of the Act, and thus does not support Commission-ordered carriage in this context. Second, we believe that mandatory binding dispute resolution procedures would be inconsistent with both Section 325 of the Act, in which Congress opted for retransmission consent negotiations to be handled by private parties subject to certain requirements, and with the Administrative Dispute Resolution Act, which authorizes an agency to use arbitration "whenever all parties consent." 5 U.S.C. § 575(a)(1).

A. Strengthening the Good Faith Negotiation Standards of Section 76.65(b)(1)

20. When the Commission originally adopted the good faith standards in 2000, the circumstances were different from the conditions industry and consumers face today. At that time programming disruptions due to retransmission consent disputes were rare. The Commission's approach then was to provide broad standards of what constitutes good faith negotiation but generally leave the negotiations to the parties.

21. As discussed above, in implementing the reciprocal good faith negotiation requirement of Section 325 of the Act, the Commission established a list of seven objective good faith negotiation standards. Violation of any of these standards by a broadcast station or MVPD is considered a per se breach of its obligation to negotiate in good faith.

22. First, we seek comment on whether it should be a per se violation for a station to agree to give a network with which it is affiliated the right to approve a retransmission consent agreement with an MVPD or to comply with such an approval provision. Interested parties have argued that, in recent retransmission consent negotiations, a network's exercise of its contractual approval right has hindered the progress of the negotiations. The good faith rules currently require the Negotiating Entity to designate a representative with authority to make binding representations on retransmission consent and not unreasonably delay negotiations. If a station has granted a network a veto power over any retransmission consent agreement with an MVPD, then it has arguably impaired its own ability to designate a representative who can bind the station in negotiations, contrary to our rules. Do provisions in network affiliation agreements giving the network approval rights over the grant of retransmission consent by its affiliate represent a reasonable exercise by a network of its distribution rights in network programming? If so, in considering revisions to the good faith rules, how should the Commission balance the networks' rights against the stations' obligation to negotiate in good faith and the regulatory goal of protecting consumers from service disruptions? In our consideration of the role of the network in its affiliates' retransmission consent negotiations, we do not intend to interfere with the flow of revenue between networks and their affiliates. We recognize the special value of broadcast network programming to local broadcast television stations and to MVPDs. Accordingly, we do not propose to prevent a network from contracting to receive a portion of its affiliates' retransmission consent fees. Rather, we seek comment on the permissible scope of a network's involvement in the negotiations or right to approve an agreement. If the Commission decides to prohibit stations from granting networks the right to approve their affiliates' retransmission consent agreements, should we, on a

going-forward basis, abrogate any provisions restricting an affiliate's power to grant retransmission consent without network approval that appear in existing agreements?

23. Second, we seek comment on whether it should be a per se violation for a station to grant another station or station group the right to negotiate or the power to approve its retransmission consent agreement when the stations are not commonly owned. Such consent might be reflected in local marketing agreements (LMAs), Joint Sales Agreements (JSAs), shared services agreements, or other similar agreements. The Commission believes that, when a station relinquishes its responsibility to negotiate retransmission consent, there may be delays to the negotiation process, and negotiations may become unnecessarily complicated if an MVPD is forced to negotiate with multiple parties with divergent interests, potentially including interests that extend beyond a single local market. The proposal on which we seek comment would effectively prohibit joint retransmission consent negotiations by stations that are not commonly owned.

24. Third, we seek comment on whether it should be a per se violation for a Negotiating Entity to refuse to put forth bona fide proposals on important issues.

25. Fourth, we seek comment on whether it should be a per se violation for a Negotiating Entity to refuse to agree to non-binding mediation when the parties reach an impasse within 30 days of the expiration of their retransmission consent agreement.

26. Fifth, we seek comment on what it means to "unreasonably" delay retransmission consent negotiations. Section 76.65(b)(1)(iii) currently provides that "[r]efusal by a Negotiating Entity to meet and negotiate retransmission consent at reasonable times and locations, or acting in a manner that unreasonably delays retransmission consent negotiations," constitutes a violation of the Negotiating Entity's duty to negotiate retransmission consent in good faith. Commenters report that negotiations have been adversely affected by a party—either a broadcaster or an MVPD—delaying the commencement or progress of a negotiation as a tactic to gain advantage rather than out of necessity. We believe that delaying retransmission consent negotiations could predictably and intentionally lead to the type of impasse and threat of disruption that inconveniences consumers.

27. Sixth, we seek comment on whether a broadcaster's request or requirement, as a condition of retransmission consent, that an MVPD not carry an out-of-market "significantly viewed" (SV) station violates Section 76.65(b)(1)(vi) of our rules. Section 76.65(b)(1)(vi) provides that "[e]xecution by a Negotiating Entity of an agreement with any party, a term or condition of which[] requires that such Negotiating Entity not enter into a retransmission consent agreement with any other television broadcast station or multichannel video programming distributor" is a violation of the Negotiating Entity's duty to negotiate in good faith. Despite the existence of this rule, in the Commission's proceeding implementing Section 203 of the Satellite Television Extension and Localism Act of 2010 (STELA), DISH Network L.L.C. requested that the Commission adopt a rule to "clarify that tying retransmission consent to restrictions on SV station carriage" violates the requirement that parties negotiate retransmission consent in good faith. DISH Network stated that some "local stations have tied the grant of their retransmission consent for local-into-local service to concessions from satellite carriers that the carriers will not introduce any SV stations of the same network." We note that the Commission previously interpreted Section 76.65(b)(1)(vi) narrowly, as involving collusion between a broadcaster and an MVPD.

B. *Specification of the Totality of the Circumstances Standard of Section 76.65(b)(2)*

31. We seek comment on revising the "totality of the circumstances" standard for determining whether actions in the negotiating process are taken in good faith, in an effort to improve the standard's utility and to better serve innocent consumers. [W]e invite

comment on how the Commission can more effectively evaluate complaints that do not allege per se violations but involve behavior calculated to threaten disruption of consumer access as a negotiating tactic.

Notes and Questions

1. Subscribers' Interests? The Commission states that MVPD subscribers are "innocent bystanders" (¶ 17) to a dispute between their MVPD and a broadcaster. Why, for example, might MVPDs have or not have the proper incentive to protect subscribers' interests?

2. How Many Suspensions? Does the NPRM read as if the Commission thinks that the optimal number of failed negotiations is zero? Is that correct? In an era of multiple MVPDs as well as the availability of much programming on the Internet, should the baseline be that every broadcast channel is carried on every MVPD? Stated differently, is TV special, warranting regulatory protection akin to those preventing air traffic controllers from going on strike?

3. Regulation and Bargaining Power? Think through each of the FCC's proposals and requests for comments and consider how each of them might alter the bargaining power of the MVPD or of the broadcasters. If you think the regulation has no effect on bargaining power, what is the purpose of the regulation? Could it be that some of them embody the terms that would prevail in the market anyway, and therefore save on the multiparty negotiation costs that would otherwise be necessary to create them?

4. Joint Negotiation. After receiving comments, in 2014 the Commission issues an order pursuant to the notice of proposed rulemaking excerpted above. The order implemented only one of the proffered possibilities in the 2011 notice of proposing rulemaking—the suggestion in ¶ 17 regarding joint retransmission consent negotiations. The Commission did not promulgate rules regarding the other possibilities. Below is an excerpt explaining the rationale behind the order.

AMENDMENT OF THE COMMISSION'S RULES RELATED TO RETRANSMISSION CONSENT

Report and Order and Further Notice of Proposed Rulemaking, 29 FCC Rcd. 3351 (2014)

3. Section 325 of the Act prohibits broadcast television stations and MVPDs from "failing to negotiate [retransmission consent] in good faith," and it provides that entering "into retransmission consent agreements containing different terms and conditions, including price terms" is not a violation of the duty to negotiate in good faith "if such different terms and conditions are based on competitive marketplace considerations." 47 U.S.C. § 325(b)(3)(C).

6. We amend our rules to provide that it is a violation of the Section 325(b)(3)(C)(ii) duty to negotiate in good faith for a television broadcast station that is ranked among the top four stations as measured by audience share to negotiate retransmission consent jointly with another such station, if the stations are not commonly owned and serve the same geographic market ("joint negotiation"). We conclude that adopting a prohibition on joint negotiation is authorized by Section 325 of the Act and serves the public interest by promoting competition among Top Four broadcast stations for MVPD carriage of their signals and the associated retransmission consent revenues.

11. Our decision to adopt a rule addressing joint negotiation by Top Four stations is consistent with the Commission's previous determination, in implementing Section

325(b)(3)(C) of the Act, that agreements not to compete or to fix prices are "inconsistent with competitive marketplace considerations and the good faith negotiation requirement." *See* Implementation of the Satellite Home Viewer Improvement Act of 1999, Report and Order, 15 FCC Rcd. 5445, 5470 ¶ 58 (2000) [(hereinafter Good Faith Order)]. In the Good Faith Order, the Commission stated:

> It is implicit in Section 325(b)(3)(C) that any effort to stifle competition through the negotiation process would not meet the good faith negotiation requirement. Considerations that are designed to frustrate the functioning of a competitive market are not 'competitive marketplace considerations.' Conduct that is violative of national policies favoring competition—that is, for example... an agreement not to compete or to fix prices... is not within the competitive marketplace considerations standard included in the statute.

Id.

13. We conclude that joint negotiation by same market, separately owned Top Four stations is not consistent with "competitive marketplace considerations" within the meaning of Section 325(b)(3)(C) because it eliminates price rivalry between and among stations that otherwise would compete directly for carriage on MVPD systems and the associated retransmission consent revenues. Specifically, we find that joint negotiation gives such stations both the incentive and the ability to impose on MVPDs higher fees for retransmission consent than they otherwise could impose if the stations conducted negotiations for carriage of their signals independently. Because same market, Top Four stations are considered by an MVPD seeking carriage rights to be at least partial substitutes for one another, their joint negotiation prevents an MVPD from taking advantage of the competition or substitution between or among the stations to hold retransmission consent payments down. The record also demonstrates that joint negotiation enables Top Four stations to obtain higher retransmission consent fees because the threat of simultaneously losing the programming of the stations negotiating jointly gives those stations undue bargaining leverage in negotiations with MVPDs. This leverage is heightened because MVPDs may be prohibited from importing out-of-market broadcast stations carrying the same network programming as the broadcast stations at issue in the negotiations.

14. Analyses in the record draw on basic economic principles to explain why coordinated conduct such as joint negotiation results in higher retransmission consent fees:

> [I]f two broadcasters can collectively threaten to withdraw their signals unless they are each satisfied, then they will be able to negotiate higher fees for everyone than if each broadcaster can only threaten to withdraw its own signal unless the broadcaster is satisfied.... [I]t is the ability to threaten collective withdrawal that creates the power to raise retransmission consent fees.

See Rogerson, Coordinated Negotiation Analysis at 3, 11. The proposition that, when providers of inputs that are at least partial substitutes for one another bargain jointly with a downstream user of the inputs, the returns to the input providers are higher than if the input providers negotiated separately with the downstream user, has been validated in other economic contexts. This general proposition is also reflected in the Federal Trade Commission and Department of Justice merger and collaboration guidelines. The Department of Justice has recognized that collaboration by competing broadcast stations could "harm competition by increasing the potential for firms to coordinate over price or other strategic dimensions, and/or by reducing incentives of firms to compete with one another." Ex Parte Filing of the Department of Justice, MB Docket Nos. 09-182, 07-294, 04-256, February 20, 2014, at 17.

16. Empirical data in the record lends support to the theory that joint negotiation by Top Four stations leads to increases in retransmission consent fees. In particular, the American Cable Association references an example indicating that, where a single entity controls retransmission consent negotiations for more than one Top Four station in a single market, the average retransmission consent fees paid for such stations was more than twenty percent higher than the fees paid for other Top Four stations in those same markets. Data filed in the record from three cable operators also lends support to our conclusion that joint negotiation between or among separately owned, same market Top Four stations leads to supracompetitive increases in retransmission consent fees. We find these empirical data to be persuasive evidence of how joint negotiation can affect the level of retransmission consent fees in cases involving Top Four stations operating in the same market. In view of the apparent widespread nature of joint negotiation involving Top Four stations and the expected growth of retransmission consent fees, we find that the record provides ample support for our decision to adopt a rule barring joint negotiation by same market, separately owned Top Four stations.

17. We believe that a rule barring joint negotiation may, by preventing supracompetitive increases in retransmission consent fees, tend to limit any resulting pressure for retail price increases for subscription video services. While there is an argument that at least a part of retransmission fee increases likely will be passed on to consumers, our decision to adopt a prohibition on joint negotiation is not premised on rate increases at the retail level. Cable operators are not required to pass through any savings derived from lower retransmission consent fees, and fee increases resulting from joint negotiation may not compare in magnitude to other costs that MVPDs incur. But artificially higher retransmission rates do increase input costs for MVPDs, and anticompetitive harm can be found at any level of distribution. Nor is the possibility that supracompetitive retransmission consent fees derived from joint negotiation might enable broadcasters to invest in higher quality programming, as some parties assert, a valid basis for permitting an anticompetitive arrangement that generates those fees. We reject the suggestion that the public interest is served merely because an arrangement generally increases the funds available to broadcasters, if that arrangement otherwise is anticompetitive and potentially harmful to consumers.

20. We reject assertions that the Commission should permit joint negotiation because it promotes a level playing field for stations in small and medium sized markets where an MVPD has significant bargaining leverage. The size and bargaining power of individual broadcasters and MVPDs vary significantly from market to market, depending on market size, concentration, popularity of programming, and many other factors. We do not consider it the Commission's role in the retransmission consent process to adjust bargaining power between suppliers and their customers by countenancing anti-competitive practices. But we do see it as our role to prohibit arrangements among competitors that eliminate competition among them and thereby generate supracompetitive retransmission consent fees, because "any effort to stifle competition through the negotiation process would not meet the good faith negotiation requirement" imposed by Congress. Good Faith Order, 15 FCC Rcd. at 5470 ¶ 58.

22. We believe that prohibiting joint negotiation is harmonious with antitrust law, which generally prohibits contracts or combinations in restraint of trade. In particular, we find that joint negotiation between or among Top Four stations that are not commonly owned and that serve the same market is akin to the type of coordinated conduct disfavored by antitrust law because, as discussed above, the stations negotiating jointly are programming inputs for an MVPD that are at least partially substitutable. In other words, absent their coordination, such stations would compete head-to-head for distribution on MVPD systems and the associated retransmission consent revenues.

23. The Commission on multiple occasions has drawn on antitrust principles in exercising its responsibility under the Act to regulate broadcasting in the public interest. Indeed, the Commission's authority under Title III of the Act to regulate broadcasting in the public interest empowers us to prescribe regulation that not only prevents anticompetitive practices, but also affirmatively promotes competition. And we have concluded that conduct that violates our national policies favoring competition is "not within the competitive marketplace considerations standard" set forth in Section 325(b)(3)(C) of the Act.

Notes and Questions

1. The Commission's Rationale. The proffered rationale is economic in nature, and indeed (as the Commission notes) related to the competition analysis performed by other agencies. Should the Commission have been persuaded by non-economic considerations? If so, which ones? If, on the other hand, its economic focus was appropriate, should Congress have the Federal Trade Commission or the Department of Justice perform this analysis, given that they are the government's main antitrust enforcers?

2. Why Stop There? If joint negotiations cause so many problems, why limit the rule to negotiations involving Top Four stations? Why not prohibit all joint negotiations?

3. What About the Other Proposals? The 2011 notice of proposed rulemaking contained a range of possibilities for comment. Does the fact that the Commission implemented only one indicate that the Commission put too much on the table in 2011? That it was too timid in 2014? That it changed its mind between 2011 and 2014? Or is it a sign of good governance for the Commission to put many ideas on the table and ultimately implement only one?

4. Relationship to the Exclusivity Rules. Cable operators, and the FCC, have connected retransmission consent with the exclusivity rules discussed in the previous section. As the Commission noted in the 2014 order excerpted above, cable operators claim that broadcasters use these rules to "extract supracompetitive prices for retransmission from small companies," whereas "broadcasters assert that eliminating the exclusivity rules would give MVPDs unfair leverage in retransmission consent negotiations" *Id.* ¶¶ 54 & 65 (internal quotation omitted). On what basis should the FCC determine what constitutes unfair leverage, or supracompetitive prices?

In its 2014 order, the Commission stated that "We note that upon elimination of our exclusivity rules, free market negotiations between broadcasters and networks or syndicated program suppliers would continue to determine the exclusivity terms of affiliation and syndicated programming agreements, and broadcasters and MVPDs would continue to conduct retransmission consent negotiations in light of these privately negotiated agreements, but without Commission intrusion in the form of a regulatory enforcement mechanism." *Id.* ¶ 66. Is this important? Does it undermine the broadcasters' defense of the exclusivity rules (because they can achieve exclusivity without the rules) or the cable operators' attack against the exclusivity rules (because eliminating the rules will not change contractual exclusivity)?

§ 9.B.2. Must-Carry

The must-carry provisions are in some ways the converse of the retransmission consent provision. Under must-carry, certain TV broadcasters can relinquish their rights to demand retransmission consent and instead insist that the local cable provider retransmit their broadcast signals at no charge. This option is only available for broadcasters in the local area covered by the cable system and, in practice, is only used for those broadcasters that do not offer highly desirable programming (for which they will demand compensation using their retransmission consent rights). The logic behind must-carry is that the protected broadcasters could be significantly harmed were the cable operator to decide not to retransmit their signals and instead to devote that channel capacity to other programming. Must-carry in these cases works to force the cable provider's hand; even if the cable provider does not want to retransmit these signals, it has no choice. (While it is unlikely that any cable provider would drop all broadcast stations, it is easy to imagine a cable provider opting not to carry one channel, and thereby putting that one channel at an extraordinary disadvantage in the local market.)

To be more specific, the must-carry provisions apply to two types of broadcast channels: local commercial television stations including both network affiliates and independents, 47 U.S.C. §534(a), and noncommercial educational television stations, 47 U.S.C. §535(a). Cable operators are not required to carry all local commercial stations nor are they required to carry all noncommercial educational stations. Instead, §§534(b) and 535(b) establish specific numeric requirements for commercial and educational channels, respectively, that are tied to the number of subscribers the cable system has and the maximum number of channels it is capable of delivering. Cable operators are of course free to carry more stations than this on a voluntary basis and, by FCC rule, local stations carried pursuant to retransmission consent agreements count toward the numeric requirements for must-carry channels. *See* Implementation of the Cable Television Consumer Protection and Competition Act of 1992, Report and Order, 8 FCC Rcd. 2965 (1993). Section 534(b)(6) stipulates that any station carried in fulfillment of the must-carry provision for local commercial stations must be carried on the cable system at the same channel number on which the local commercial station is broadcast over the air unless the parties otherwise agree. Section 535(b)(5) establishes the same right for educational channels. Once every three years, broadcasters must elect to either invoke the must-carry obligation or pursue fees under retransmission consent. 47 C.F.R. §76.64(f).

§9.B.2.a. First Amendment Challenges to Cable Must-Carry

The must-carry provisions have twice been considered by the Supreme Court. Opinions from both cases are excerpted below.

TURNER BROADCASTING SYSTEM, INC. v. FCC [*TURNER I*]
512 U.S. 622 (1994)

KENNEDY, J., announced the judgment of the Court and delivered the opinion for a unanimous Court with respect to Part I, the opinion of the Court with respect to Parts II-A and II-B, in which REHNQUIST, C.J., and BLACKMUN, O'CONNOR, SCALIA, SOUTER, THOMAS, and GINSBURG, JJ., joined, the opinion of the Court with respect to Parts II-C, II-D, and III-A, in which REHNQUIST, C.J., and BLACKMUN, STEVENS, and SOUTER, JJ., joined, and an opinion with respect to Part III-B, in which REHNQUIST, C.J., and BLACKMUN and SOUTER, JJ., joined. BLACKMUN, J., filed a concurring opinion. STEVENS, J., filed an opinion concurring in part and concurring in the judgment. O'CONNOR, J., filed an opinion concurring in part and dissenting in part, in which SCALIA and GINSBURG, JJ., joined, and in Parts I and III of which THOMAS, J., joined. GINSBURG, J., filed an opinion concurring in part and dissenting in part.

JUSTICE KENNEDY announced the judgment of the Court and delivered the opinion of the Court, except as to Part III-B.

I

B

Section 4 of the Cable Television Consumer Protection and Competition Act of 1992 requires carriage of "local commercial television stations," defined to include all full power television broadcasters, other than those qualifying as "noncommercial educational" stations under §5, that operate within the same television market as the cable system. §4, 47 U.S.C. §§534 (b)(1)(B), (h)(1)(A). Cable systems with more than 12 active channels, and more than 300 subscribers, are required to set aside up to one-third of their channels for commercial broadcast stations that request carriage. Cable systems with more than 300 subscribers, but only 12 or fewer active channels, must carry the signals of three commercial broadcast stations.[3]

If there are fewer broadcasters requesting carriage than slots made available under the Act, the cable operator is obligated to carry only those broadcasters who make the request. If, however, there are more requesting broadcast stations than slots available, the cable operator is permitted to choose which of these stations it will carry. The broadcast signals carried under this provision must be transmitted on a continuous, uninterrupted basis and must be placed in the same numerical channel position as when broadcast over the air. Further, subject to a few exceptions, a cable operator may not charge a fee for carrying broadcast signals in fulfillment of its must-carry obligations.

Section 5 of the Act imposes similar requirements regarding the carriage of local public broadcast television stations, referred to in the Act as local "noncommercial educational television stations." 47 U.S.C. §535(a). A cable system with 12 or fewer channels must carry one of these stations; a system of between 13 and 36 channels must carry between one and three; and a system with more than 36 channels must carry each local public broadcast station requesting carriage. As with commercial broadcast stations, §5 requires cable system operators to carry the program schedule of the public broadcast station in its entirety and at its same over-the-air channel position.

Taken together, therefore, §§4 and 5 subject all but the smallest cable systems nationwide to must-carry obligations, and confer must-carry privileges on all full power broadcasters operating within the same television market as a qualified cable system.

C

Congress enacted the 1992 Cable Act after conducting three years of hearings on the structure and operation of the cable television industry. The conclusions Congress drew from its factfinding process are recited in the text of the Act itself. *See* §§2 (a)(1)–(21). In brief, Congress found that the physical characteristics of cable transmission, compounded by the increasing concentration of economic power in the cable industry, are endangering the ability of over-the-air broadcast television stations to compete for a viewing audience and thus for necessary operating revenues. Congress determined that regulation of the market for video programming was necessary to correct this competitive imbalance.

---

3. If there are not enough local full power commercial broadcast stations to fill the one-third allotment, a cable system with up to 35 active channels must carry one qualified low power station and an operator with more than 35 channels must carry two of them. *See* §534(c)(1). Low power television stations are small broadcast entities that transmit over a limited geographic range. They are licensed on a secondary basis and are permitted to operate only if they do not interfere with the signals of full power broadcast stations.

In particular, Congress found that over 60 percent of the households with television sets subscribe to cable, and for these households cable has replaced over-the-air broadcast television as the primary provider of video programming. This is so, Congress found, because "[m]ost subscribers to cable television systems do not or cannot maintain antennas to receive broadcast television services, do not have input selector switches to convert from a cable to antenna reception system, or cannot otherwise receive broadcast television services." §2(a)(17). In addition, Congress concluded that due to "local franchising requirements and the extraordinary expense of constructing more than one cable television system to serve a particular geographic area," the over-whelming majority of cable operators exercise a monopoly over cable service. §2(a)(2). "The result," Congress determined, "is undue market power for the cable operator as compared to that of consumers and video programmers." Id.

According to Congress, this market position gives cable operators the power and the incentive to harm broadcast competitors. The power derives from the cable operator's ability, as owner of the transmission facility, to "terminate the retransmission of the broadcast signal, refuse to carry new signals, or reposition a broadcast signal to a disadvantageous channel position." §2(a)(15). The incentive derives from the economic reality that "[c]able television systems and broadcast television stations increasingly compete for television advertising revenues." §2(a)(14). By refusing carriage of broadcasters' signals, cable operators, as a practical matter, can reduce the number of households that have access to the broadcasters' programming, and thereby capture advertising dollars that would otherwise go to broadcast stations. §2(a)(15).

Congress found, in addition, that increased vertical integration in the cable industry is making it even harder for broadcasters to secure carriage on cable systems, because cable operators have a financial incentive to favor their affiliated programmers. §2(a)(5). Congress also determined that the cable industry is characterized by horizontal concentration, with many cable operators sharing common ownership. This has resulted in greater "barriers to entry for new programmers and a reduction in the number of media voices available to consumers." §2(a)(4).

In light of these technological and economic conditions, Congress concluded that unless cable operators are required to carry local broadcast stations, "[t]here is a substantial likelihood that ... additional local broadcast signals will be deleted, repositioned, or not carried," §2(a)(15); the "marked shift in market share" from broadcast to cable will continue to erode the advertising revenue base which sustains free local broadcast television, §§2(a)(13)–(14); and that, as a consequence, "the economic viability of free local broadcast television and its ability to originate quality local programming will be seriously jeopardized." §2(a)(16).

II

There can be no disagreement on an initial premise: Cable programmers and cable operators engage in and transmit speech, and they are entitled to the protection of the speech and press provisions of the First Amendment. Leathers v. Medlock, 499 U.S. 439, 444 (1991). Through "original programming or by exercising editorial discretion over which stations or programs to include in its repertoire," cable programmers and operators "seek[] to communicate messages on a wide variety of topics and in a wide variety of formats." Los Angeles v. Preferred Communications, Inc., 476 U.S. 488, 494 (1986). By requiring cable systems to set aside a portion of their channels for local broadcasters, the must-carry rules regulate cable speech in two respects: The rules reduce the number of channels over which cable operators exercise unfettered control, and they render it more difficult for cable programmers to compete for carriage on the limited channels remaining. Nevertheless, because not every interference with speech triggers the same degree of scrutiny under the First Amendment, we must decide at the outset the level of scrutiny applicable to the must-carry provisions.

A

We address first the Government's contention that regulation of cable television should be analyzed under the same First Amendment standard that applies to regulation of broadcast television. It is true that our cases have permitted more intrusive regulation of broadcast speakers than of speakers in other media. *Compare* Red Lion Broadcasting Co. v. FCC, 395 U.S. 367 (1969) (television), and National Broadcasting Co. v. United States, 319 U.S. 190 (1943) (radio), *with* Miami Herald Publishing Co. v. Tornillo, 418 U.S. 241 (1974) (print), and Riley v. National Federation of Blind of N.C., Inc., 487 U.S. 781 (1988) (personal solicitation). But the rationale for applying a less rigorous standard of First Amendment scrutiny to broadcast regulation, whatever its validity in the cases elaborating it, does not apply in the context of cable regulation.

Although courts and commentators have criticized the scarcity rationale since its inception, we have declined to question its continuing validity as support for our broadcast jurisprudence, and see no reason to do so here. The broadcast cases are inapposite in the present context because cable television does not suffer from the inherent limitations that characterize the broadcast medium. Indeed, given the rapid advances in fiber optics and digital compression technology, soon there may be no practical limitation on the number of speakers who may use the cable medium. Nor is there any danger of physical interference between two cable speakers attempting to share the same channel. In light of these fundamental technological differences between broadcast and cable transmission, application of the more relaxed standard of scrutiny adopted in *Red Lion* and the other broadcast cases is inapt when determining the First Amendment validity of cable regulation.

[W]hatever relevance these physical characteristics [of cable transmission] may have in the evaluation of particular cable regulations, they do not require the alteration of settled principles of our First Amendment jurisprudence.

[T]he Government and some appellees maintain that the must-carry provisions are nothing more than industry-specific antitrust legislation, and thus warrant rational basis scrutiny under this Court's "precedents governing legislative efforts to correct market failure in a market whose commodity is speech," such as Associated Press v. United States, 326 U.S. 1 (1945), and Lorain Journal Co. v. United States, 342 U.S. 143 (1951). *See* Brief for Federal Appellees 17. This contention is unavailing. *Associated Press* and *Lorain Journal* both involved actions against members of the press brought under the Sherman Antitrust Act, a law of general application. But while the enforcement of a generally applicable law may or may not be subject to heightened scrutiny under the First Amendment, laws that single out the press, or certain elements thereof, for special treatment "pose a particular danger of abuse by the State," Arkansas Writers' Project, Inc. v. Ragland, 481 U.S. 221, 228 (1987), and so are always subject to at least some degree of heightened First Amendment scrutiny. Because the must-carry provisions impose special obligations upon cable operators and special burdens upon cable programmers, some measure of heightened First Amendment scrutiny is demanded.

B

As a general rule, laws that by their terms distinguish favored speech from disfavored speech on the basis of the ideas or views expressed are content based. By contrast, laws that confer benefits or impose burdens on speech without reference to the ideas or views expressed are in most instances content neutral.

C

Insofar as they pertain to the carriage of full power broadcasters, the must-carry rules, on their face, impose burdens and confer benefits without reference to the content of speech. Although the provisions interfere with cable operators' editorial discretion by compelling them to offer carriage to a certain minimum number of broadcast stations, the extent of the interference does not depend upon the content of the cable operators' programming. The rules impose obligations upon all operators, save those with fewer than 300 subscribers, regardless of the programs or stations they now offer or have offered in the past. Nothing in the Act imposes a restriction, penalty, or burden by reason of the views, programs, or stations the cable operator has selected or will select. The number of channels a cable operator must set aside depends only on the operator's channel capacity; hence, an operator cannot avoid or mitigate its obligations under the Act by altering the programming it offers to subscribers. *Cf. Tornillo*, 418 U.S. at 256–57 (newspaper may avoid access obligations by refraining from speech critical of political candidates).

The must-carry provisions also burden cable programmers by reducing the number of channels for which they can compete. But, again, this burden is unrelated to content, for it extends to all cable programmers irrespective of the programming they choose to offer viewers. And finally, the privileges conferred by the must-carry provisions are also unrelated to content. The rules benefit all full power broadcasters who request carriage — be they commercial or noncommercial, independent or network affiliated, English or Spanish language, religious or secular.

It is true that the must-carry provisions distinguish between speakers in the television programming market. But they do so based only upon the manner in which speakers transmit their messages to viewers, and not upon the messages they carry: Broadcasters, which transmit over the airwaves, are favored, while cable programmers, which do not, are disfavored. Cable operators, too, are burdened by the carriage obligations, but only because they control access to the cable conduit. So long as they are not a subtle means of exercising a content preference, speaker distinctions of this nature are not presumed invalid under the First Amendment.

That the must-carry provisions, on their face, do not burden or benefit speech of a particular content does not end the inquiry. Our cases have recognized that even a regulation neutral on its face may be content based if its manifest purpose is to regulate speech because of the message it conveys.

Our review of the Act and its various findings persuades us that Congress' overriding objective in enacting must-carry was not to favor programming of a particular subject matter, viewpoint, or format, but rather to preserve access to free television programming for the 40 percent of Americans without cable.

In unusually detailed statutory findings, Congress explained that because cable systems and broadcast stations compete for local advertising revenue, §§ 2(a)(14)–(15), and because cable operators have a vested financial interest in favoring their affiliated programmers over broadcast stations, § 2(a)(5), cable operators have a built-in "economic incentive ... to delete, reposition, or not carry local broadcast signals." § 2(a)(16). Congress concluded that absent a requirement that cable systems carry the signals of local broadcast stations, the continued availability of free local broadcast television would be threatened. *Id.* Congress sought to avoid the elimination of broadcast television because, in its words, "[s]uch programming is ... free to those who own television sets and do not require cable transmission to receive broadcast television signals," §2(a)(12), and because "[t]here is a substantial governmental interest in promoting the continued availability of such free television programming, especially for viewers who are unable to afford other means of receiving programming." *Id.*

By preventing cable operators from refusing carriage to broadcast television stations, the must-carry rules ensure that broadcast television stations will retain a large enough potential audience to earn necessary advertising revenue—or, in the case of noncommercial broadcasters, sufficient viewer contributions—to maintain their continued operation. In so doing, the provisions are designed to guarantee the survival of a medium that has become a vital part of the Nation's communication system, and to ensure that every individual with a television set can obtain access to free television programming.

The design and operation of the challenged provisions confirm that the purposes underlying the enactment of the must-carry scheme are unrelated to the content of speech. The rules, as mentioned, confer must-carry rights on all full power broadcasters, irrespective of the content of their programming. They do not require or prohibit the carriage of particular ideas or points of view. They do not penalize cable operators or programmers because of the content of their programming. They do not compel cable operators to affirm points of view with which they disagree. They do not produce any net decrease in the amount of available speech. And they leave cable operators free to carry whatever programming they wish on all channels not subject to must-carry requirements.

Appellants and Justice O'Connor make much of the fact that, in the course of describing the purposes behind the Act, Congress referred to the value of broadcast programming. In particular, Congress noted that broadcast television is "an important source of local news[,] public affairs programming, and other local broadcast services critical to an informed electorate," §2(a)(11), and that noncommercial television "provides educational and informational programming to the Nation's citizens." §2(a)(8). We do not think, however, that such references cast any material doubt on the content-neutral character of must-carry. That Congress acknowledged the local orientation of broadcast programming and the role that noncommercial stations have played in educating the public does not indicate that Congress regarded broadcast programming as *more* valuable than cable programming. Rather, it reflects nothing more than the recognition that the services provided by broadcast television have some intrinsic value and, thus, are worth preserving against the threats posed by cable.

We likewise reject the suggestion, advanced by appellants and by Judge Williams in dissent, that the must-carry rules are content-based because the preference for broadcast stations "*automatically* entails content requirements." 819 F. Supp., at 58. It is true that broadcast programming, unlike cable programming, is subject to certain limited content restraints imposed by statute and FCC regulation. But it does not follow that Congress mandated cable carriage of broadcast television stations as a means of ensuring that particular programs will be shown, or not shown, on cable systems.

As an initial matter, the argument exaggerates the extent to which the FCC is permitted to intrude into matters affecting the content of broadcast programming. The FCC is forbidden by statute from engaging in "censorship" or to promulgate any regulation "which shall interfere with the [broadcasters'] right of free speech." 47 U.S.C. §326. In particular, the FCC's oversight responsibilities do not grant it the power to ordain any particular type of programming that must be offered by broadcast stations.

[G]iven the minimal extent to which the FCC and Congress actually influence the programming offered by broadcast stations, it would be difficult to conclude that Congress enacted must-carry in an effort to exercise content control over what subscribers view on cable television. In a regime where Congress or the FCC exercised more intrusive control over the content of broadcast programming, an argument similar to appellants' might carry greater weight. But in the present regulatory system, those concerns are without foundation.

D

Appellants advance three additional arguments to support their view that the must-carry provisions warrant strict scrutiny. In brief, appellants contend that the provisions (1) compel speech by cable operators, (2) favor broadcast programmers over cable programmers, and (3) single out certain members of the press for disfavored treatment. None of these arguments suffices to require strict scrutiny in the present case.

1

Appellants maintain that the must-carry provisions trigger strict scrutiny because they compel cable operators to transmit speech not of their choosing. Relying principally on *Tornillo*, appellants say this intrusion on the editorial control of cable operators amounts to forced speech which, if not per se invalid, can be justified only if narrowly tailored to a compelling government interest.

The same principles [invoked in *Tornillo*] led us to invalidate a similar content-based access regulation in Pacific Gas & Elec. Co. v. Public Util. Comm'n of Cal., 475 U.S. 1 (1986). At issue was a rule requiring a privately owned utility to include with its monthly bills an editorial newsletter published by a consumer group critical of the utility's ratemaking practices. [T]he plurality held that the same strict First Amendment scrutiny [as in *Tornillo*] applied. Like the statute in *Tornillo*, the regulation conferred benefits to speakers based on viewpoint, giving access only to a consumer group opposing the utility's practices.

Tornillo and *Pacific Gas & Electric* do not control this case for the following reasons. First, unlike the access rules struck down in those cases, the must-carry rules are content neutral in application. They are not activated by any particular message spoken by cable operators and thus exact no content-based penalty. Likewise, they do not grant access to broadcasters on the ground that the content of broadcast programming will counterbalance the messages of cable operators.

Second, appellants do not suggest, nor do we think it the case, that must-carry will force cable operators to alter their own messages to respond to the broadcast programming they are required to carry. Given cable's long history of serving as a conduit for broadcast signals, there appears little risk that cable viewers would assume that the broadcast stations carried on a cable system convey ideas or messages endorsed by the cable operator.

Finally, the asserted analogy to *Tornillo* ignores an important technological difference between newspapers and cable television. Although a daily newspaper and a cable operator both may enjoy monopoly status in a given locale, the cable operator exercises far greater control over access to the relevant medium. A daily newspaper, no matter how secure its local monopoly, does not possess the power to obstruct readers' access to other competing publications—whether they be weekly local newspapers, or daily newspapers published in other cities. Thus, when a newspaper asserts exclusive control over its own news copy, it does not thereby prevent other newspapers from being distributed to willing recipients in the same locale.

The same is not true of cable. When an individual subscribes to cable, the physical connection between the television set and the cable network gives the cable operator bottleneck, or gatekeeper, control over most (if not all) of the television programming that is channeled into the subscriber's home. Hence, simply by virtue of its ownership of the essential pathway for cable speech, a cable operator can prevent its subscribers from obtaining access to programming it chooses to exclude. A cable operator, unlike speakers in other media, can thus silence the voice of competing speakers with a mere flick of the switch.

The potential for abuse of this private power over a central avenue of communication cannot be overlooked. The First Amendment's command that government not impede the freedom of speech does not disable the government from taking steps to ensure that private interests not restrict, through physical control of a critical pathway of communication, the free flow of information and ideas.

2

Second, appellants urge us to apply strict scrutiny because the must-carry provisions favor one set of speakers (broadcast programmers) over another (cable programmers). Appellants maintain that as a consequence of this speaker preference, some cable programmers who would have secured carriage in the absence of must-carry may now be dropped. Relying on language in Buckley v. Valeo, 424 U.S. 1 (1976), appellants contend that such a regulation is presumed invalid under the First Amendment.

At issue in *Buckley* was a federal law prohibiting individuals from spending more than $1,000 per year to support or oppose a particular political candidate. We rejected that [regulation] with the observation that Congress may not "abridge the rights of some persons to engage in political expression in order to enhance the relative voice of other segments of our society." *Id.* at 49 n.55.

Our holding in *Buckley* does not support appellants' broad assertion that all speaker-partial laws are presumed invalid. Rather, it stands for the proposition that speaker-based laws demand strict scrutiny when they reflect the Government's preference for the substance of what the favored speakers have to say (or aversion to what the disfavored speakers have to say).

The question here is whether Congress preferred broadcasters over cable programmers based on the content of programming each group offers. The answer, as we explained above, is no.

3

Finally, appellants maintain that strict scrutiny applies because the must-carry provisions single out certain members of the press—here, cable operators—for disfavored treatment. In support, appellants point out that Congress has required cable operators to provide carriage to broadcast stations, but has not imposed like burdens on analogous video delivery systems, such as multichannel multipoint distribution (MMDS) systems and satellite master antenna television (SMATV) systems. Relying upon our precedents invalidating discriminatory taxation of the press, appellants contend that this sort of differential treatment poses a particular danger of abuse by the government and should be presumed invalid. But such heightened scrutiny is unwarranted when the differential treatment is "justified by some special characteristic of" the particular medium being regulated. Minneapolis Star and Tribune Co. v. Minnesota Com'r of Revenue, 460 U.S. 575, 585 (1983).

The must-carry provisions, as we have explained above, are justified by special characteristics of the cable medium: the bottleneck monopoly power exercised by cable operators and the dangers this power poses to the viability of broadcast television. Appellants do not argue, nor does it appear, that other media—in particular, media that transmit video programming such as MMDS and SMATV—are subject to bottleneck monopoly control, or pose a demonstrable threat to the survival of broadcast television. It should come as no surprise, then, that Congress decided to impose the must-carry obligations upon cable operators only.

In addition, the must-carry provisions are not structured in a manner that carries the inherent risk of undermining First Amendment interests. The regulations are broad-based, applying to almost all cable systems in the country, rather than just a select few.

III

A

In sum, the must-carry provisions do not pose such inherent dangers to free expression, or present such potential for censorship or manipulation, as to justify application of the most exacting level of First Amendment scrutiny. We agree with the District Court that the appropriate standard by which to evaluate the constitutionality of must-carry is the intermediate level of scrutiny applicable to content-neutral restrictions that impose an incidental burden on speech. *See* Ward v. Rock Against Racism, 491 U.S. 781 (1989); United States v. O'Brien, 391 U.S. 367 (1968).

B

That the Government's asserted interests are important in the abstract does not mean that the must-carry rules will in fact advance those interests. When the Government defends a regulation on speech as a means to redress past harms or prevent anticipated harms, it must do more than simply "posit the existence of the disease sought to be cured." Quincy Cable TV, Inc. v. FCC, 768 F.2d 1434, 1455 (D.C. Cir. 1985). It must demonstrate that the recited harms are real, not merely conjectural, and that the regulation will in fact alleviate these harms in a direct and material way.

Thus, in applying *O'Brien* scrutiny we must ask first whether the Government has adequately shown that the economic health of local broadcasting is in genuine jeopardy and in need of the protections afforded by must-carry. Assuming an affirmative answer to the foregoing question, the Government still bears the burden of showing that the remedy it has adopted does not "burden substantially more speech than is necessary to further the government's legitimate interests." *Ward*, 491 U.S. at 799. On the state of the record developed thus far, and in the absence of findings of fact from the District Court, we are unable to conclude that the Government has satisfied either inquiry.

Because of the unresolved factual questions, the importance of the issues to the broadcast and cable industries, and the conflicting conclusions that the parties contend are to be drawn from the statistics and other evidence presented, we think it necessary to permit the parties to develop a more thorough factual record, and to allow the District Court to resolve any factual disputes remaining, before passing upon the constitutional validity of the challenged provisions.

[Concurring opinion of JUSTICE BLACKMUN is omitted.]

JUSTICE STEVENS, concurring in part and concurring in the judgment.

While I agree with most of Justice Kennedy's reasoning, and join Parts I, II-C, II-D, and III-A of his opinion, I part ways with him on the appropriate disposition of this case. In my view the District Court's judgment sustaining the must-carry provisions should be affirmed.

An industry need not be in its death throes before Congress may act to protect it from economic harm threatened by a monopoly. Congress did not have to find that all broadcasters were at risk before acting to protect vulnerable ones, for the interest in preserving access to free television is valid throughout the Nation. Indeed, the Act is well tailored to assist those broadcasters who are most in jeopardy. Because thriving commercial broadcasters will likely avail themselves of the remunerative "retransmission consent" procedure of § 6, those broadcasters who gain access via the § 4 must-carry route are apt to be the most economically vulnerable ones. Precisely how often broadcasters will secure carriage through § 6 rather than § 4 will depend upon future developments; the very unpredictability of this and other effects of the new regulatory scheme militates in favor of allowing the scheme to proceed rather than requiring a perfectly documented or entirely complete ex ante justification.

It is thus my view that we should affirm the judgment of the District Court. Were I to vote to affirm, however, no disposition of this appeal would command the support of a majority of the Court. An accommodation is therefore necessary. Accordingly, because I am in substantial agreement with Justice Kennedy's analysis of the case, I concur in the judgment vacating and remanding for further proceedings.

JUSTICE O'CONNOR, with whom JUSTICE SCALIA and JUSTICE GINSBURG join, and with whom JUSTICE THOMAS joins as to Parts I and III, concurring in part and dissenting in part.

I

A

The 1992 Cable Act implicates the First Amendment rights of two classes of speakers. First, it tells cable operators which programmers they must carry, and keeps cable operators from carrying others that they might prefer. Though cable operators do not actually originate most of the programming they show, the Court correctly holds that they are, for First Amendment purposes, speakers. Selecting which speech to retransmit is, as we know from the example of publishing houses, movie theaters, bookstores, and "Reader's Digest," no less communication than is creating the speech in the first place.

Second, the Act deprives a certain class of video programmers—those who operate cable channels rather than broadcast stations—of access to over one-third of an entire medium. Cable programmers may compete only for those channels that are not set aside by the must-carry provisions. It is as if the government ordered all movie theaters to reserve at least one-third of their screening for films made by American production companies, or required all bookstores to devote one-third of their shelf space to nonprofit publishers. As the Court explains in Parts I, II-A, and II-B of its opinion, which I join, cable programmers and operators stand in the same position under the First Amendment as do the more traditional media.

But looking at the statute at issue, I cannot avoid the conclusion that its preference for broadcasters over cable programmers is justified with reference to content. The findings, enacted by Congress as § 2 of the Act, and which I must assume state the justifications for the law, make this clear. "There is a substantial governmental and First Amendment interest in promoting a diversity of views provided through multiple technology media." § 2(a)(6). "[P]ublic television provides educational and informational programming to the Nation's citizens, thereby advancing the Government's compelling interest in educating its citizens." § 2(a)(8)(A). "A primary objective and benefit of our Nation's system of regulation of television broadcasting is the local origination of programming. There is a substantial governmental interest in ensuring its continuation." § 2(a)(10). "Broadcast television stations continue to be an important source of local news and public affairs programming and other local broadcast services critical to an informed electorate." § 2(a)(11).

Similar justifications are reflected in the operative provisions of the Act. In determining whether a broadcast station should be eligible for must-carry in a particular market, the FCC must "afford particular attention to the value of localism by taking into account such factors as ... whether any other [eligible station] provides news coverage of issues of concern to such community or provides carriage or coverage of sporting and other events of interest to the community." § 4.

Preferences for diversity of viewpoints, for localism, for educational programming, and for news and public affairs all make reference to content. They may not reflect hostility to particular points of view, or a desire to suppress certain subjects because they are controversial or offensive. They may be quite benignly motivated. But benign motivation, we have consistently held, is not enough to avoid the need for strict scrutiny of content based justifications. The First Amendment does more than just bar government from intentionally suppressing speech of which it disapproves. It also generally prohibits the government from excepting certain kinds of speech from regulation because it thinks the speech is especially valuable.

This is why the Court is mistaken in concluding that the interest in diversity—in "access to a multiplicity" of "diverse and antagonistic sources"—is content neutral. The interest in ensuring access to a multiplicity of diverse and antagonistic sources of information, no matter how praiseworthy, is directly tied to the content of what the speakers will likely say.

B

The Court dismisses the findings quoted above by speculating that they do not reveal a preference for certain kinds of content; rather, the Court suggests, the findings show "nothing more than the recognition that the services provided by broadcast television have some intrinsic value and, thus, are worth preserving against the threats posed by cable." The controversial judgment at the heart of the statute is not that broadcast television has some value—obviously it does—but that broadcasters should be preferred over cable programmers. The best explanation for the findings, it seems to me, is that they represent Congress' reasons for adopting this preference; and, according to the findings, these reasons rest in part on the content of broadcasters' speech.

It may well be that Congress also had other, content-neutral, purposes in mind when enacting the statute. But we have never held that the presence of a permissible justification lessens the impropriety of relying in part on an impermissible justification. [W]hen a content-based justification appears on the statute's face, we cannot ignore it because another, content-neutral justification is present.

C

Content-based speech restrictions are generally unconstitutional unless they are narrowly tailored to a compelling state interest. This is an exacting test. It is not enough that the goals of the law be legitimate, or reasonable, or even praiseworthy. There must be some pressing public necessity, some essential value that has to be preserved; and even then the law must restrict as little speech as possible to serve the goal.

The interest in localism, either in the dissemination of opinions held by the listeners' neighbors or in the reporting of events that have to do with the local community, cannot be described as "compelling" for the purposes of the compelling state interest test. It is a legitimate interest, perhaps even an important one—certainly the government can foster it by, for instance, providing subsidies from the public fisc—but it does not rise to the level necessary to justify content-based speech restrictions. It is for private speakers and listeners, not for the government, to decide what fraction of their news and entertainment ought to be of a local character and what fraction ought to be of a national (or international) one. And the same is true of the interest in diversity of viewpoints: While the government may subsidize speakers that it thinks provide novel points of view, it may not restrict other speakers on the theory that what they say is more conventional.

The interests in public affairs programming and educational programming seem somewhat weightier, though it is a difficult question whether they are compelling enough to justify restricting other sorts of speech. We have never held that the Government could impose educational content requirements on, say, newsstands, bookstores, or movie theaters; and it is not clear that such requirements would in any event appreciably further the goals of public education.

But even assuming, *arguendo,* that the Government could set some channels aside for educational or news programming, the Act is insufficiently tailored to this goal. To benefit the educational broadcasters, the Act burdens more than just the cable entertainment programmers. It equally burdens CNN, C-SPAN, the Discovery Channel, the New Inspirational Network, and other channels with as much claim as PBS to being educational or related to public affairs.

Finally, my conclusion that the must-carry rules are content based leads me to conclude that they are an impermissible restraint on the cable operators' editorial discretion as well as on the cable programmers' speech. For reasons related to the content of speech, the rules restrict the ability of cable operators to put on the programming they prefer, and require them to include programming they would rather avoid. This, it seems to me, puts this case squarely within the rule of *Pacific Gas & Electric.*

II

Even if I am mistaken about the must-carry provisions being content based, however, in my view they fail content neutral scrutiny as well.

If Congress wants to protect those stations that are in danger of going out of business, or bar cable operators from preferring programmers in which the operators have an ownership stake, it may do that. But it may not, in the course of advancing these interests, restrict cable operators and programmers in circumstances where neither of these interests is threatened.

III

Having said all this, it is important to acknowledge one basic fact: The question is not whether there will be control over who gets to speak over cable—the question is who will have this control. Under the FCC's view, the answer is Congress, acting within relatively broad limits. Under my view, the answer is the cable operator.

I have no doubt that there is danger in having a single cable operator decide what millions of subscribers can or cannot watch. And I have no doubt that Congress can act to relieve this danger. In other provisions of the Act, Congress has already taken steps to foster competition among cable systems. Congress can encourage the creation of new media, such as inexpensive satellite broadcasting, or fiber-optic networks with virtually unlimited channels, or even simple devices that would let people easily switch from cable to over-the-air broadcasting. And of course Congress can subsidize broadcasters that it thinks provide especially valuable programming.

Congress may also be able to act in more mandatory ways. If Congress finds that cable operators are leaving some channels empty—perhaps for ease of future expansion—it can compel the operators to make the free channels available to programmers who otherwise would not get carriage. Congress might also conceivably obligate cable operators to act as common carriers for some of their channels, with those channels being open to all through some sort of lottery system or time-sharing arrangement. Setting aside any possible Takings Clause issues, it stands to reason that if Congress may demand that telephone companies operate as common carriers, it can ask the same of cable companies; such an approach would not suffer from the defect of preferring one speaker to another.

But the First Amendment as we understand it today rests on the premise that it is government power, rather than private power, that is the main threat to free expression; and as a consequence, the Amendment imposes substantial limitations on the Government even when it is trying to serve concededly praiseworthy goals.

[Concurring and dissenting opinion of JUSTICE GINSBURG is omitted.]

Notes and Questions

1. Overlooked Elements? What explains the failure of the Court to acknowledge that (1) broadcast stations and cable systems compete in a wide variety of different local markets; (2) broadcast stations differ greatly in their ability to reach large numbers of viewers without the aid of cable transmission (especially in size of market and quality of over-the-air signal reception); and (3) cable operators may compete with commercial stations, but not with noncommercial stations, for advertising revenues?

2. Content Neutral? Precisely why do the majority and dissenting opinions differ on the key question of whether the must-carry provisions are content neutral? Are you convinced by the majority's argument that the content-neutral criterion Congress used was "the manner in which speakers transmit their messages to viewers"? The Cable Act does not direct cable systems to carry all broadcasters or even a number of randomly selected broadcasters; only local broadcasters were selected for must-carry status. On the other hand, are the dissenting justices straining in finding a content-based explanation for must-carry provisions that appear more plainly to rest on an economic premise: that cable operators control a facility to which their rival broadcast stations need access in order to compete?

3. Valuable Speech. The dissent argues that "[t]he First Amendment does more than just bar government from intentionally suppressing speech of which it disapproves. It also generally prohibits the government from excepting certain kinds of speech from regulation because it thinks the speech is especially valuable." Does the majority agree with this proposition? Does it explain why it is not applicable in this case?

4. Taxation by Regulation. In Part I-C, the dissent draws a distinction between forcing cable operators to carry stations under a must-carry regime and, instead, using tax revenues to pay cable operators to carry particular stations. Specifically, while strenuously objecting to the must-carry provisions, Justice O'Connor writes that the government could "certainly" foster its interest in the case by "providing subsidies from the public fisc." Is O'Connor's distinction a good one? Defensible? This relates to the notion of "taxation by regulation," which we discuss again in Chapter Fifteen, where government imposes certain content requirements on broadcasters as licensing conditions. What would O'Connor say is the best way to encourage, for example, the development of children's television?

5. Why Must-Carry in Addition to Retransmission Consent? What is the policy rationale for giving local commercial television broadcast stations both a right to insist on retransmission consent and a right to must-carry status? Is Justice Stevens correct that, once local TV stations are afforded retransmission consent rights, the sole or principal function of must-carry will be to protect those stations that are most "economically vulnerable"? If so, what is the public policy justification for mandating carriage of these not-so-successful stations instead of using that channel capacity for other programming? Does your answer to this question change if you assume that, in the absence of a must-carry obligation, the cable capacity at issue would be used for (a) C-SPAN or (b) The Cartoon Network?

6. The Constitutional Status of Broadcast. The opinion of the Court may also be important for what it says about the constitutional status of content regulation of broadcasting. Part II-A seems to reaffirm the notion that broadcasters enjoy diminished protection under the First Amendment. (If this is the Court's intention, is it noteworthy that the defense of this notion seems rather sketchy and flimsy?) On the other hand, at the conclusion of Part II-C, the Court seems to portray television broadcasters as being legally protected against most forms of censorship. Might *Turner I*, as a whole, be read as a tentative first step toward reordering the First Amendment jurisprudence that applies to broadcast regulation?[4]

7. Round Two. Justice Blackmun retired the day after *Turner I* was handed down. Although *Turner II* technically raised questions not resolved in *Turner I*, it turned out that the only vote that mattered was that of Justice Breyer, Blackmun's replacement. With Breyer's decisive fifth vote, a majority upheld the law.

TURNER BROADCASTING SYSTEM, INC. v. FCC [*TURNER II*]
520 U.S. 180 (1997)

KENNEDY, J., announced the judgment of the Court and delivered the opinion of the Court, except as to a portion of Part II-A-1. REHNQUIST, C.J., and STEVENS and SOUTER, JJ., joined that opinion in full, and BREYER, J., joined except insofar as Part II-A-1 relied on an anticompetitive rationale. STEVENS, J., filed a concurring opinion. BREYER, J., filed an opinion concurring in part. O'CONNOR, J., filed a dissenting opinion, in which SCALIA, THOMAS, and GINSBURG, JJ., joined.

JUSTICE KENNEDY delivered the opinion of the Court, except as to a portion of Part II-A-1.

On appeal from the District Court's grant of summary judgment for appellees, the case now presents the two questions left open during the first appeal: First, whether the record as it now stands supports Congress' predictive judgment that the must-carry provisions further important governmental interests; and second, whether the provisions do not burden substantially more speech than necessary to further those interests. We answer both questions in the affirmative, and conclude the must-carry provisions are consistent with the First Amendment.

II

We begin where the plurality ended in *Turner I*, applying the standards for intermediate scrutiny enunciated in [United States v.] O'Brien, 391 U.S. 367 (1968). A content-

---

4. Note that the Court's statement in Part II-C that "the FCC's oversight responsibilities do not grant it the power to ordain any particular type of programming that must be offered by broadcast stations" is hard to square with the result in *Red Lion* enforcing an FCC order that a radio station air a particular program—in that case a response to a "personal attack." Further, that same statement is at least in some tension with the premises underlying the present regulation of children's television (discussed in Chapter Fifteen of this book).

neutral regulation will be sustained under the First Amendment if it advances important governmental interests unrelated to the suppression of free speech and does not burden substantially more speech than necessary to further those interests. As noted in *Turner I*, must-carry was designed to serve "three interrelated interests: (1) preserving the benefits of free, over-the-air local broadcast television, (2) promoting the widespread dissemination of information from a multiplicity of sources, and (3) promoting fair competition in the market for television programming." We decided then, and now reaffirm, that each of those is an important governmental interest.

The Congressional findings do not reflect concern that, absent must-carry, "a few voices" would be lost from the television marketplace. In explicit factual findings, Congress expressed clear concern that the "marked shift in market share from broadcast television to cable television services" resulting from increasing market penetration by cable services, as well as the expanding horizontal concentration and vertical integration of cable operators, combined to give cable systems the incentive and ability to delete, reposition, or decline carriage to local broadcasters in an attempt to favor affiliated cable programmers. Congress predicted that "absent the reimposition of [must-carry], additional local broadcast signals will be deleted, repositioned, or not carried," with the end result that "the economic viability of free local broadcast television and its ability to originate quality local programming will be seriously jeopardized."

At the same time, Congress was under no illusion that there would be a complete disappearance of broadcast television nationwide in the absence of must-carry. Congress was concerned not that broadcast television would disappear in its entirety without must-carry, but that without it, "significant numbers of broadcast stations will be refused carriage on cable systems," and those "broadcast stations denied carriage will either deteriorate to a substantial degree or fail altogether."

We have noted that "'it has long been a basic tenet of national communications policy that "the widest possible dissemination of information from diverse and antagonistic sources is essential to the welfare of the public."'" *Turner I*, at 663–64. "'[I]ncreasing the number of outlets for community self-expression'" represents a "'long-established regulatory goal[] in the field of television broadcasting.'" United States v. Midwest Video Corp., 406 U.S. 649, 667–68 (1972) (plurality opinion). Consistent with this objective, the [1992] Cable Act's findings reflect a concern that Congressional action was necessary to prevent "a reduction in the number of media voices available to consumers." Congress identified a specific interest in "ensuring [the] continuation" of "the local origination of [broadcast] programming," an interest consistent with its larger purpose of promoting multiple types of media, and found must-carry necessary "to serve the goals" of the original Communications Act of 1934 of "providing a fair, efficient, and equitable distribution of broadcast services." In short, Congress enacted must-carry to "preserve the existing structure of the Nation's broadcast television medium while permitting the concomitant expansion and development of cable television." *Turner I*, at 652.

Although Congress set no definite number of broadcast stations sufficient for these purposes, the Cable Act's requirement that all cable operators with more than 12 channels set aside one-third of their channel capacity for local broadcasters, §4, 47 U.S.C. §534(b)(1)(B), refutes the notion that Congress contemplated preserving only a bare minimum of stations. Congress's evident interest in "preserv[ing] the existing structure" of the broadcast industry discloses a purpose to prevent any significant reduction in the multiplicity of broadcast programming sources available to noncable households. To the extent the appellants question the substantiality of the Government's interest in preserving something more than a minimum number of stations in each community, their position is meritless. It is for Congress to decide how much local broadcast television should be preserved for noncable households, and the validity of its determination "'does not turn on a judge's agreement with the responsible decision-maker' ... concerning the degree to which [the Government's] interests should be promoted." Ward v. Rock Against Racism, 491 U.S. 781, 800 (1989).

The dissent proceeds on the assumption that must-carry is designed solely to be (and can only be justified as) a measure to protect broadcasters from cable operators' anticompetitive behavior. Federal policy, however, has long favored preserving a multiplicity of broadcast outlets regardless of whether the conduct that threatens it is motivated by anticompetitive animus or rises to the level of an antitrust violation. Broadcast television is an important source of information to many Americans. Though it is but one of many means for communication, by tradition and use for decades now it has been an essential part of the national discourse on subjects across the whole broad spectrum of speech, thought, and expression. Congress has an independent interest in preserving a multiplicity of broadcasters to ensure that all households have access to information and entertainment on an equal footing with those who subscribe to cable.

A

The expanded record permits us to consider whether the must-carry provisions were designed to address a real harm, and whether those provisions will alleviate it in a material way. We turn first to the harm or risk which prompted Congress to act. The Government's assertion that "the economic health of local broadcasting is in genuine jeopardy and in need of the protections afforded by must-carry" rests on two component propositions: First, "significant numbers of broadcast stations will be refused carriage on cable systems" absent must-carry. Second, "the broadcast stations denied carriage will either deteriorate to a substantial degree or fail altogether."

1

We have no difficulty in finding a substantial basis to support Congress' conclusion that a real threat justified enactment of the must-carry provisions.

As to the evidence before Congress, there was specific support for its conclusion that cable operators had considerable and growing market power over local video programming markets. As Congress noted, § 2(a)(2), cable operators possess a local monopoly over cable households.

Evidence indicated the structure of the cable industry would give cable operators increasing ability and incentive to drop local broadcast stations from their systems, or reposition them to a less-viewed channel. Horizontal concentration was increasing as a small number of multiple system operators (MSO's) acquired large numbers of cable systems nationwide.

Vertical integration in the industry also was increasing. Extensive testimony indicated that cable operators would have an incentive to drop local broadcasters and to favor affiliated programmers.

After hearing years of testimony, and reviewing volumes of documentary evidence and studies offered by both sides, Congress concluded that the cable industry posed a threat to broadcast television. The Constitution gives to Congress the role of weighing conflicting evidence in the legislative process. Even when the resulting regulation touches on First Amendment concerns, we must give considerable deference, in examining the evidence, to Congress' findings and conclusions, including its findings and conclusions with respect to conflicting economic predictions. Furthermore, much of the testimony, though offered by interested parties, was supported by verifiable information and citation to independent sources.

In addition, evidence before Congress, supplemented on remand, indicated that cable systems would have incentives to drop local broadcasters in favor of other programmers less likely to compete with them for audience and advertisers. Empirical studies indicate that cable-carried broadcasters so enhance competition for advertising that even modest increases in the numbers of broadcast stations carried on cable are correlated with significant decreases in advertising revenue to cable systems. Thus, operators stand to benefit by dropping broadcast stations.

Cable systems also have more systemic reasons for seeking to disadvantage broadcast stations: Simply stated, cable has little interest in assisting, through carriage, a competing medium of communication. The cap on carriage of affiliates included in the Cable Act, 47 U.S.C. §533(f)(1)(B); 47 C.F.R. §76.504(a) (1995), and relied on by the dissent is of limited utility in protecting broadcasters.

It was more than a theoretical possibility in 1992 that cable operators would take actions adverse to local broadcasters; indeed, significant numbers of broadcasters had already been dropped. The record before Congress contained extensive anecdotal evidence about scores of adverse carriage decisions against broadcast stations.

Substantial evidence demonstrated that absent must-carry the already "serious" problem of noncarriage would grow worse because "additional local broadcast signals will be deleted, repositioned, or not carried," §2(a)(15). The record included anecdotal evidence showing the cable industry was acting with restraint in dropping broadcast stations in an effort to discourage reregulation. A contemporaneous FCC report noted that "[c]able operators' incentive to deny carriage ... appears to be particularly great as against local broadcasters." Defendants' Joint Statement of Evidence Before Congress ¶ 155 (JSCR).

Additional evidence developed on remand supports the reasonableness of Congress' predictive judgment. Approximately 11 percent of local broadcasters were not carried on the typical cable system in 1989. The figure had grown to even more significant proportions by 1992. According to one of appellants' own experts, between 19 and 31 percent of all local broadcast stations, including network affiliates, were not carried by the typical cable system.

The dissent cites evidence indicating that many dropped broadcasters were stations few viewers watch. [But] the broadcasters added by must-carry had ratings greater than or equal to the cable programs they replaced. If cable systems refused to carry certain local broadcast stations because of their subscribers' preferences for the cable services carried in their place, one would expect that all cable programming services would have ratings exceeding those of broadcasters not carried. That is simply not the case.

The evidence on remand also indicated that the growth of cable systems' market power proceeded apace. By 1994, the 10 largest MSO's controlled 63 percent of cable systems, a figure projected to have risen to 85 percent by the end of 1996.

The issue before us is whether, given conflicting views of the probable development of the television industry, Congress had substantial evidence for making the judgment that it did. We need not put our imprimatur on Congress' economic theory in order to validate the reasonableness of its judgment.

2

The harm Congress feared was that stations dropped or denied carriage would be at a "serious risk of financial difficulty" and would "deteriorate to a substantial degree or fail altogether." *Turner I*, at 666. Congress had before it substantial evidence to support its conclusion. Congress was advised the viability of a broadcast station depends to a material extent on its ability to secure cable carriage.

Considerable evidence, consisting of statements compiled from dozens of broadcasters who testified before Congress and the FCC, confirmed that broadcast stations had fallen into bankruptcy, curtailed their broadcast operations, and suffered serious reductions in operating revenues as a result of adverse carriage decisions by cable systems. Congress thus had ample basis to conclude that attaining cable carriage would be of increasing importance to ensuring a station's viability. We hold Congress could conclude from the substantial body of evidence before it that "absent legislative action, the free local off-air broadcast system is endangered." Senate Report, at 42.

To be sure, the record also contains evidence to support a contrary conclusion. Appellants (and the dissent in the District Court) make much of the fact that the number of broadcast stations and their advertising revenue continued to grow during the period without must-carry, albeit at a diminished rate. Evidence introduced on remand indicated that only 31 broadcast stations actually went dark during the period without must-carry (one of which failed after a tornado destroyed its transmitter), and during the same period some 263 new stations signed on the air. New evidence appellants produced on remand indicates the average cable system voluntarily carried local broadcast stations accounting for about 97 percent of television ratings in noncable households. Appellants, as well as the dissent in the District Court, contend that in light of such evidence, it is clear "the must-carry law is not necessary to assure the economic viability of the broadcast system as a whole." NCTA Brief 18.

This assertion misapprehends the relevant inquiry. The question is not whether Congress, as an objective matter, was correct to determine must-carry is necessary to prevent a substantial number of broadcast stations from losing cable carriage and suffering significant financial hardship. Rather, the question is whether the legislative conclusion was reasonable and supported by substantial evidence in the record before Congress.

Although evidence of continuing growth in broadcast could have supported the opposite conclusion, a reasonable interpretation is that expansion in the cable industry was causing harm to broadcasting. Growth continued, but the rate of growth fell to a considerable extent during the period without must-carry (from 4.5 percent in 1986 to 1.7 percent by 1992), and appeared to be tapering off further. At the same time, "in an almost unprecedented development," 5 FCC Rcd., at 5041, ¶¶ 153–154, stations began to fail in increasing numbers. Broadcast advertising revenues declined in real terms by 11 percent between 1986 and 1991, during a period in which cable's real advertising revenues nearly doubled. While these phenomena could be thought to stem from factors quite separate from the increasing market power of cable (for example, a recession in 1990–1992), it was for Congress to determine the better explanation.

Despite the considerable evidence before Congress and adduced on remand indicating that the significant numbers of broadcast stations are at risk, the dissent believes yet more is required before Congress could act. It demands more information about which of the dropped broadcast stations still qualify for mandatory carriage; about the broadcast markets in which adverse decisions take place; and about the features of the markets in which bankrupt broadcast stations were located prior to their demise. The level of detail in factfinding required by the dissent would be an improper burden for courts to impose on the Legislative Branch.

We think it apparent must-carry serves the Government's interests "in a direct and effective way." *Ward*, 491 U.S. at 800. Must-carry ensures that a number of local broadcasters retain cable carriage, with the concomitant audience access and advertising revenues needed to support a multiplicity of stations. Appellants contend that even were this so, must-carry is broader than necessary to accomplish its goals. We turn to this question.

B

Under intermediate scrutiny, the Government may employ the means of its choosing "'so long as the ... regulation promotes a substantial governmental interest that would be achieved less effectively absent the regulation,'" and does not "'burden substantially more speech than is necessary to further'" that interest. *Turner I*, at 662 (quoting *Ward, supra*, at 799).

The must-carry provisions have the potential to interfere with protected speech in two ways. First, the provisions restrain cable operators' editorial discretion in creating programming packages by "reduc[ing] the number of channels over which [they] exercise unfettered control." Second, the rules "render it more difficult for cable programmers to compete for carriage on the limited channels remaining."

Appellants say the burden of must-carry is great, but the evidence adduced on remand indicates the actual effects are modest. Significant evidence indicates the vast majority of cable operators have not been affected in a significant manner by must-carry. Appellees note that only 1.18 percent of the approximately 500,000 cable channels nationwide is devoted to channels added because of must-carry; weighted for subscribership, the figure is 2.4 percent. Appellees contend the burdens of must-carry will soon diminish as cable channel capacity increases, as is occurring nationwide.

We do not understand appellants to dispute in any fundamental way the accuracy of those figures, only their significance. They note national averages fail to account for greater crowding on certain (especially urban) cable systems and contend that half of all cable systems, serving two-thirds of all cable subscribers, have no available capacity. Appellants argue that the rate of growth in cable programming outstrips cable operators' creation of new channel space, that the rate of cable growth is lower than claimed, and that must-carry infringes First Amendment rights now irrespective of future growth. Finally, they say that regardless of the percentage of channels occupied, must-carry still represents "thousands of real and individual infringements of speech." Br. of Time Warner 44.

While the parties' evidence is susceptible of varying interpretations, a few definite conclusions can be drawn about the burdens of must-carry. It is undisputed that broadcast stations gained carriage on 5,880 channels as a result of must-carry. While broadcast stations occupy another 30,006 cable channels nationwide, this carriage does not represent a significant First Amendment harm to either system operators or cable programmers because those stations were carried voluntarily before 1992, and even appellants represent that the vast majority of those channels would continue to be carried in the absence of any legal obligation to do so. The 5,880 channels occupied by added broadcasters represent the actual burden of the regulatory scheme. Appellants concede most of those stations would be dropped in the absence of must-carry, so the figure approximates the benefits of must-carry as well.

Because the burden imposed by must-carry is congruent to the benefits it affords, we conclude must-carry is narrowly tailored to preserve a multiplicity of broadcast stations for the 40 percent of American households without cable. Congress took steps to confine the breadth and burden of the regulatory scheme. For example, the more popular stations (which appellants concede would be carried anyway) will likely opt to be paid for cable carriage under the "retransmission consent" provision of the Cable Act; those stations will nonetheless be counted towards systems' must-carry obligations. Congress exempted systems of 12 or fewer channels, and limited the must-carry obligation of larger systems to one-third of capacity; allowed cable operators discretion in choosing which competing and qualified signals would be carried; and permitted operators to carry public stations on unused public, educational, and governmental channels in some circumstances.

Our precedents establish that when evaluating a content-neutral regulation which incidentally burdens speech, we will not invalidate the preferred remedial scheme because some alternative solution is marginally less intrusive on a speaker's First Amendment interests.

In any event, after careful examination of each of the alternatives suggested by appellants, we cannot conclude that any of them is an adequate alternative to must-carry for promoting the Government's legitimate interests. [One] alternative appellants urge is the use of input selector or "A/B" switches, which, in combination with antennas, would permit viewers to switch between cable and broadcast input, allowing cable subscribers to watch broadcast programs not carried on cable. Congress examined the use of A/B switches as an alternative to must-carry and concluded it was "not an enduring or feasible method of distribution and ... not in the public interest." § 2(a)(18). The data showed that: many households lacked adequate antennas to receive broadcast signals; A/B switches suffered from technical flaws; viewers might be required to reset channel settings repeatedly in order to view both UHF and cable channels; and installation and use of the switch with other common video equipment (such as videocassette recorders) could be "cumbersome or impossible." Senate Report, at 45, and nn.115–16.

Appellants also suggest a leased-access regime, under which both broadcasters and cable programmers would have equal access to cable channels at regulated rates. Because this alternative is aimed solely at addressing the bottleneck control of cable operators, it would not be as effective in achieving Congress's further goal of ensuring that significant programming remains available for the 40 percent of American households without cable. Furthermore, Congress was specific in noting that requiring payment for cable carriage was inimical to the interests it was pursuing, because of the burden it would impose on small broadcasters.

Appellants next suggest a system of subsidies for financially weak stations. [A] system of subsidies would serve a very different purpose than must-carry. Must-carry is intended not to guarantee the financial health of all broadcasters, but to ensure a base number of broadcasters survive to provide service to noncable households. Must-carry is simpler to administer and less likely to involve the Government in making content based determinations about programming.

Appellants also suggest a system of antitrust enforcement or an administrative complaint procedure to protect broadcasters from cable operators' anticompetitive conduct. Congress could conclude, however, that the considerable expense and delay inherent in antitrust litigation, and the great disparities in wealth and sophistication between the average independent broadcast station and average cable system operator, would make these remedies inadequate substitutes for guaranteed carriage. The record suggests independent broadcasters simply are not in a position to engage in complex antitrust litigation, which involves extensive discovery, significant motions practice, appeals, and the payment of high legal fees throughout. An administrative complaint procedure, although less burdensome, would still require stations to incur considerable expense and delay before enforcing their rights.

III

Judgments about how competing economic interests are to be reconciled in the complex and fast-changing field of television are for Congress to make. Those judgments "cannot be ignored or undervalued simply because [appellants] cast[] [their] claims under the umbrella of the First Amendment." Columbia Broadcasting v. Democratic National Committee, 412 U.S. 94, 103 (1974). The judgment of the District Court is affirmed.

[Concurring opinion of JUSTICE STEVENS is omitted.]

JUSTICE BREYER, concurring in part.

I join the opinion of the Court except insofar as Part II-A-1 relies on an anticompetitive rationale. My conclusion rests not upon the principal opinion's analysis of the statute's efforts to "promot[e] fair competition," but rather upon its discussion of the statute's other objectives, namely "'(1) preserving the benefits of free, over-the-air local broadcast television,'" and "'(2) promoting the widespread dissemination of information from a multiplicity of sources.'" Whether or not the statute does or does not sensibly compensate for some significant market defect, it undoubtedly seeks to provide over-the-air viewers who *lack* cable with a rich mix of over-the-air programming by guaranteeing the over-the-air stations that provide such programming with the extra dollars that an additional cable audience will generate. I believe that this purpose—to assure the over-the-air public "access to a multiplicity of information sources"—provides sufficient basis for rejecting appellants' First Amendment claim.

I do not deny that the compulsory carriage that creates the "guarantee" extracts a serious First Amendment price. It interferes with the protected interests of the cable operators to choose their own programming; it prevents displaced cable program providers from obtaining an audience; and it will sometimes prevent some cable viewers from watching what, in its absence, would have been their preferred set of programs. This "price" amounts to a "suppression of speech."

But there are important First Amendment interests on the other side as well. The statute's basic noneconomic purpose is to prevent too precipitous a decline in the quality and quantity of programming choice for an ever-shrinking non-cable-subscribing segment of the public. This purpose reflects what "has long been a basic tenet of national communications policy," namely that "the widest possible dissemination of information from diverse and antagonistic sources is essential to the welfare of the public." *Turner I*, at 663 (internal quotations omitted). That policy, in turn, seeks to facilitate the public discussion and informed deliberation, which, as Justice Brandeis pointed out many years ago, democratic government presupposes and the First Amendment seeks to achieve. Whitney v. California, 274 U.S. 357, 375–76 (1927) (Brandeis, J., concurring). *See also* New York Times Co. v. Sullivan, 376 U.S. 254, 270 (1964); Red Lion Broadcasting Co. v. FCC, 395 U.S. 367, 390 (1969).

With important First Amendment interests on both sides of the equation, the key question becomes one of proper fit. In particular, I note (and agree) that a cable system, physically dependent upon the availability of space along city streets, at present (perhaps less in the future) typically faces little competition, that it therefore constitutes a kind of bottleneck that controls the range of viewer choice (whether or not it uses any consequent economic power for economically predatory purposes), and that *some* degree—at least a limited degree—of governmental intervention and control through regulation can prove appropriate when justified under *O'Brien* (at least when not "content based"). I also agree that, without the statute, cable systems would likely carry significantly fewer over-the-air stations, that station revenues would therefore decline, and that the quality of over-the-air programming on such stations would almost inevitably suffer. I agree further that the burden the statute imposes upon the cable system, potential cable programmers, and cable viewers, is limited and will diminish as typical cable system capacity grows over time.

Finally, I believe that Congress could reasonably conclude that the statute will help the typical over-the-air viewer (by maintaining an expanded range of choice) more than it will hurt the typical cable subscriber (by restricting cable slots otherwise available for preferred programming). The latter's cable choices are many and varied, and the range of choice is rapidly increasing. The former's over-the-air choice is more restricted; and, as cable becomes more popular, it may well become still more restricted insofar as the over-the-air market shrinks and thereby, by itself, becomes less profitable. In these circumstances, I do not believe the First Amendment dictates a result that favors the cable viewers' interests.

These and other similar factors discussed by the majority lead me to agree that the statute survives "intermediate scrutiny," whether or not the statute is properly tailored to Congress' purely economic objectives.

JUSTICE O'CONNOR, with whom JUSTICE SCALIA, JUSTICE THOMAS, and JUSTICE GINSBURG join, dissenting.

I

Perhaps because of the difficulty of defending the must-carry provisions as a measured response to anticompetitive behavior, the Court asserts an "independent" interest in preserving a "multiplicity" of broadcast programming sources. In doing so, the Court posits the existence of "conduct that threatens" the availability of broadcast television outlets, quite apart from anticompetitive conduct. We are left to wonder what precisely that conduct might be. Moreover, when separated from anticompetitive conduct, this interest in preserving a "multiplicity of broadcast programming sources" becomes poorly defined. Whether cable poses a "significant" threat to a local broadcast market depends first on how many broadcast stations in that market will, in the absence of must-carry, remain available to viewers in noncable households. It also depends on whether viewers actually watch the stations that are dropped or denied carriage. The Court provides some raw data on adverse carriage decisions, but it never connects those data to markets and viewership. Instead, the Court proceeds from the assumptions that adverse carriage decisions nationwide will affect broadcast markets in proportion to their size; and that all broadcast programming is watched by viewers. Neither assumption is logical or has any factual basis in the record.

As discussed below, the must-carry provisions cannot be justified as a narrowly tailored means of addressing anticompetitive behavior. As a result, the Court's inquiry into whether must-carry would prevent a "significant reduction in the multiplicity of broadcast programming sources" collapses into an analysis of an ill-defined and generalized interest in maintaining broadcast stations, wherever they might be threatened and whatever their viewership. Neither the principal opinion nor the partial concurrence ever explains what kind of conduct, apart from anticompetitive conduct, threatens the "multiplicity" of broadcast programming sources. Indeed, the only justification advanced by the parties for furthering this interest is heavily content based. It is undisputed that the broadcast stations protected by must-carry are the "marginal" stations within a given market; the record on remand reveals that any broader threat to the broadcast system was entirely mythical. Pressed to explain the importance of preserving noncable viewers' access to "vulnerable" broadcast stations, appellees emphasize that the must-carry rules are necessary to ensure that broadcast stations maintain "diverse," "quality" programming that is "responsive" to the needs of the local community. Brief for Federal Appellees 13, 30; *see also* Breyer, J., concurring in part (justifying must-carry as a means of preventing a decline in "quality and quantity of programming choice"). Undoubtedly, such goals are reasonable and important, and the stations in question may well be worthwhile targets of Government subsidies. But appellees' characterization of must-carry as a means of protecting these stations, like the Court's explicit concern for promoting "'community self-expression'" and the "'local origination of broadcast programming,'" reveals a content-based preference for broadcast programming. This justification of the regulatory scheme is, in my view, wholly at odds with the *Turner I* Court's premise that must-carry is a means of preserving "access to free television programming—*whatever its content*," *Turner I*, at 649 (emphasis added).

I do not read Justice Breyer's opinion—which analyzes the must-carry rules in part as a "speech-enhancing" measure designed to ensure a "rich mix" of over-the-air programming—to treat the content of over-the-air programming as irrelevant to whether the Government's interest in promoting it is an important one. The net result appears to be that five Justices of this Court *do not view* must-carry as a narrowly tailored means of serving a substantial governmental interest in preventing anticompetitive behavior; and that five Justices of this Court *do* see the significance of the content of over-the-air programming to the Government's and appellees' efforts to defend the law. Under these circumstances, the must-carry provisions should be subject to strict scrutiny, which they surely fail.

II

The principal opinion goes to great lengths to avoid acknowledging that preferences for "quality," "diverse," and "responsive" local programming underlie the must-carry scheme, although the partial concurrence's reliance on such preferences is explicit. I take the principal opinion at its word and evaluate the claim that the threat of anticompetitive behavior by cable operators supplies a content neutral basis for sustaining the statute. It does not.

On whether must-carry furthers a substantial governmental interest, the *Turner I* Court remanded the case to test two essential and unproven propositions: "(1) that unless cable operators are compelled to carry broadcast stations, *significant numbers* of broadcast stations will be refused carriage on cable systems; and (2) that the broadcast stations denied carriage will either *deteriorate to a substantial degree or fail altogether.*" *Turner I*, at 666 (emphasis added). As for whether must-carry restricts no more speech than essential to further Congress' asserted purpose, the *Turner I* plurality found evidence lacking on the extent of the burden that the must-carry provisions would place on cable operators and cable programmers.

A

What was not resolved in *Turner I* was whether "reasonable inferences based on substantial evidence" *Turner I*, at 666 (plurality opinion), supported Congress' judgment that the must-carry provisions were necessary "to prevent cable operators from exploiting their economic power to the detriment of broadcasters," *id*. at 649. Because I remain convinced that the statute is not a measured response to congressional concerns about monopoly power, in my view the principal opinion's discussion on this point is irrelevant. But even if it were relevant, it is incorrect.

1

The principal opinion appears to accept two related arguments on this point: first, that vertically integrated cable operators prefer programming produced by their affiliated cable programming networks to broadcast programming; and second, that potential advertising revenues supply cable system operators, whether affiliated with programmers or not, with incentives to prefer cable programming to broadcast programming.

Even accepting as reasonable Congress's conclusion that cable operators have incentives to favor affiliated programmers, Congress has already limited the number of channels on a cable system that can be occupied by affiliated programmers. 47 U.S.C. §533(f)(1)(B); 47 C.F.R. §76.504 (1995). Once a cable system operator reaches that cap, it can no longer bump a broadcaster in favor of an affiliated programmer. If Congress were concerned that cable operators favored too many affiliated programmers, it could simply adjust the cap. Must-carry simply cannot be justified as a response to the allegedly "substantial" problem of vertical integration.

Appellees claim that since cable operators compete directly with broadcasters for some advertising revenue, operators will profit if they can drive broadcasters out of the market and capture their advertising revenue. There is no dispute that a cable system depends primarily upon its subscriber base for revenue. A cable operator is therefore unlikely to drop a widely viewed station in order to capture advertising revenues—which, according to the figures of appellees' expert, account for between one and five percent of the total revenues of most large cable systems. In doing so, it would risk losing subscribers. Even assuming that, at the margin, advertising revenues would drive cable systems to drop some stations—invariably described as "vulnerable" or "smaller" independents—the strategy's success would depend upon the additional untested premise that the advertising revenues freed by dropping a broadcast station will flow to cable operators rather than to *other* broadcasters.

2

Under the standard articulated by the *Turner I* plurality, the conclusion that must-carry serves a substantial governmental interest depends upon the "essential propositio[n]" that, without must-carry, "significant numbers of broadcast stations will be refused carriage on cable systems." *Turner I*, at 666. In analyzing whether this undefined standard is satisfied, the Court focuses almost exclusively on raw numbers of stations denied carriage or "repositioned"—that is, shifted out of their traditional channel positions.

The Court discounts the importance of whether dropped stations now qualify for mandatory carriage, on the ground that requiring any such showing places an "improper burden" on the Legislative Branch. It seems obvious, however, that if the must-carry rules will not reverse those adverse carriage decisions on which appellees rely to illustrate the Government "interest" supporting the rules, then a significant question remains as to whether the rules in fact serve the articulated interest. Without some further analysis, I do not see how the Court can, in the course of its independent scrutiny on a question of constitutional law, deem Congress' judgment "reasonable."

Nor can we evaluate whether must-carry is necessary to serve an interest in preserving broadcast stations without examining the value of the stations protected by the must-carry scheme to viewers in noncable households. The *only* analysis in the record of the relationship between carriage and noncable viewership favors the appellants. A 1991 study by Federal Trade Commission staff concluded that most cable systems voluntarily carried broadcast stations with any reportable ratings in noncable households and that most instances of noncarriage involved "relatively remote (and duplicated) network stations, or local stations that few viewers watch."

Appellees—who bear the burden of proof in this case—offer no alternative measure of the viewership in noncable households of stations dropped or denied carriage. Instead, appellees and their experts repeatedly emphasize the importance of preserving "vulnerable" or "marginal" independent stations serving "relatively small" audiences. When appellees are pressed to explain the Government's "substantial interest" in preserving noncable viewers' access to "vulnerable" or "marginal" stations with "relatively small" audiences, it becomes evident that the interest has nothing to do with anticompetitive behavior, but has everything to do with content—preserving "quality" local programming that is "responsive" to community needs. Brief for Federal Appellees 13, 30. Indeed, Justice Breyer expressly declines to accept the anticompetitive rationale for the must-carry rules embraced by the principal opinion, and instead explicitly relies on a need to preserve a "rich mix" of "quality" programming.

3

I turn now to the evidence of harm to broadcasters denied carriage or repositioned. The record on remand does not permit the conclusion, at the summary judgment stage, that Congress could reasonably have predicted serious harm to a significant number of stations in the absence of must-carry.

The purported link between an adverse carriage decision and severe harm to a station depends on yet another untested premise. Even accepting the conclusion that a cable system operator has a monopoly over *cable* services to the home, it does not necessarily follow that the operator also has a monopoly over all *video* services to cabled households. Cable subscribers using an input selector switch and an antenna can receive broadcast signals. Widespread use of such switches would completely eliminate any cable system "monopoly" over sources of video input. Growing use of direct broadcast satellite television also tends to undercut the notion that cable operators have an inevitable monopoly over video services entering cable households.

The Court notes the importance of deferring to congressional judgments about the "interaction of industries undergoing rapid economic and technological change." But this principle does not require wholesale deference to judgments about rapidly changing technologies that are based on unquestionably outdated information.

The Court concludes that the evidence on remand meets the threshold of harm established in *Turner I*. The Court begins with the "considerable evidence" that broadcast stations denied carriage have fallen into bankruptcy. The "considerable evidence" relied on by the Court consists of repeated references to the bankruptcies of the same 23 commercial independent stations—apparently, new stations. Because the must-carry provisions have never been justified as a means of *enhancing* broadcast television, I do not understand the relevance of this evidence, or of the evidence concerning the difficulties encountered by *new* stations seeking financing.

All but *one* of the commercial broadcast stations cited as claiming a curtailment in operations or a decline in revenue was broadcasting within [a broadcast market] that experienced net growth, or at least no net reduction, in the number of commercial broadcast stations operating during the non-must-carry era.

The Court acknowledges that the record contains much evidence of the health of the broadcast industry. But the Court dismisses such evidence, emphasizing that the question is not whether Congress correctly determined that must-carry is necessary to prevent significant financial hardship to a substantial number of stations, but whether "the legislative conclusion was reasonable and supported by substantial evidence in the record before Congress." Even accepting the Court's articulation of the relevant standard, it is not properly applied here. The principal opinion disavows a need to closely scrutinize the logic of the regulatory scheme at issue on the ground that it "need not put [its] imprimatur on Congress' economic theory in order to validate the reasonableness of its judgment." That approach trivializes the First Amendment issue at stake in this case. A highly dubious economic theory has been advanced as the "substantial interest" supporting a First Amendment burden on cable operators and cable programmers.

B

I turn now to the second portion of the *O'Brien* inquiry, which concerns the fit between the Government's asserted interests and the means chosen to advance them. Even assuming that the Court is correct that the 5,880 channels occupied by added broadcasters "represent the actual burden of the regulatory scheme," the Court's leap to the conclusion that must-carry "is narrowly tailored to preserve a multiplicity of broadcast stations" is nothing short of astounding. The Court's logic is circular. Surmising that most of the 5,880 channels added by the regulatory scheme would be dropped in its absence, the Court concludes that the figure also approximates the "benefit" of must-carry. Finding the scheme's burden "congruent" to the benefit it affords, the Court declares the statute narrowly tailored. The Court achieves this result, however, only by equating the *effect* of the statute — requiring cable operators to add 5,880 stations — with the governmental *interest* sought to be served. Without a sense whether *most* adverse carriage decisions are anticompetitively motivated, it is improper to conclude that the statute is narrowly tailored simply because it prevents *some* adverse carriage decisions.

In my view, the statute is not narrowly tailored to serve a substantial interest in preventing anticompetitive conduct. I do not understand Justice Breyer to disagree with this conclusion. Congress has commandeered up to one-third of each cable system's channel capacity for the benefit of local broadcasters, without any regard for whether doing so advances the statute's alleged goals. To the extent that Congress was concerned that anticompetitive impulses would lead vertically integrated operators to prefer those programmers in which the operators have an ownership stake, the Cable Act is overbroad, since it does not impose its requirements solely on such operators. Moreover, Congress has placed limits upon the number of channels that can be used for affiliated programming. 47 U.S.C. §533(f)(1)(B). The principal opinion does not suggest why these limits are inadequate or explain why, once a system reaches the limit, its remaining carriage decisions would also be anticompetitively motivated. Even if the channel limits are insufficient, the principal opinion does not explain why requiring carriage of *broadcast* stations on *one-third* of the system's channels is a measured response to the problem.

[As to less-speech-restrictive alternatives,] it is one thing to say that a regulation need not be the *least*-speech-restrictive means of serving an important governmental objective. It is quite another to suggest, as I read the majority to do here, that the availability of less-speech-restrictive alternatives cannot establish or confirm that a regulation is substantially broader than necessary to achieve the Government's goals. The availability of less intrusive approaches to a problem serves as a benchmark for assessing the reasonableness of the fit between Congress' articulated goals and the means chosen to pursue them.

If Congress truly sought to address anticompetitive behavior by cable system operators, it passed the wrong law. Nevertheless, the availability of less restrictive alternatives — a leased-access regime and subsidies — reinforces my conclusion that the must-carry provisions are overbroad.

Consider first appellants' proposed leased-access scheme, under which a cable system operator would be required to make a specified proportion of the system's channels available to broadcasters and independent cable programmers alike at regulated rates. Leased access would directly address both vertical integration and predatory behavior, by placing broadcasters and cable programmers on a level playing field for access to cable. Must-carry quite clearly does not respond to the problem of vertical integration. In addition, the must-carry scheme burdens the rights of cable programmers *and* cable operators; there is no suggestion here that leased access would burden cable *programmers* in the same way as must-carry does. In both of these respects, leased access is a more narrowly tailored guard against anticompetitive behavior. Finally, if, as the Court suggests, Congress were concerned that a leased access scheme would impose a burden on "small broadcasters" forced to pay for access, subsidies would eliminate the problem.

The Court suggests that a subsidy scheme would involve the Government in making "content based determinations about programming." Even if that is so, it does not distinguish subsidies from the must-carry provisions. In light of the principal opinion's steadfast adherence to the position that a preference for "diverse" or local-content broadcasting is not a content based preference, the argument is ironic indeed.

I therefore respectfully dissent, and would reverse the judgment below.

Notes and Questions

1. Deference to Congress. Is there any fact, or set of facts, that opponents of the law might have submitted to the Court that would have persuaded the majority to change its mind? Or is the majority's point that the factual disputes underlying must-carry policies are for Congress to resolve? If so, what task, if any, remained for the Court?

2. The Importance of Technology. Suppose that, at an appropriate moment in the litigation, researchers at MIT had come forward to show the Court a relatively inexpensive remote control unit that would allow television viewers to switch from cable to broadcast and back again without climbing out of their chairs. Suppose further that economists had testified that, if the Court were to strike down the must-carry provisions, demand for this technology would be significant and would lead, among other things, to even better variations of the technology and even cheaper prices. Would that have changed the Court's ultimate decision in the case? If so, how does the Court deal with its implicit reliance on the state of existing technology? Is this a normal problem faced by courts, or an aberrational one peculiar to this controversy?

3. Predictive Harms. In both *Turner I* and *Turner II*, the Court suggested that the asserted harms to broadcast television had not yet occurred and that the legislative assertions of such harms were therefore predictions. Should the predictive nature of these harms affect the constitutional analysis, and if so, how? In this regard, note that *Turner I* emphasized that the harms on which the must-carry legislation rested must be "real, not merely conjectural," but in *Turner II* the "not merely conjectural" language fell out of the equation (the Court simply referred to "a real harm" and "a real threat"). What is the difference between these formulations? Which one makes more sense?

4. Understanding the Standard. Is it the position of the *Turner II* dissenters that every remedy for—or protection against—anticompetitive behavior by a cable operator must be closely tailored to achieve no more competition or protection than is necessary?

§ 9.B.2.b. DBS Carry One, Carry All

Congress could have decided to give DBS carriers a station-by-station copyright license that could be used free of carriage obligations. Under such a license, satellite carriers could pick the stations they wanted in each local market. The smaller broadcasters' fear was that this would result in satellite carriers carrying only the major network affiliates, and not the local broadcasters with fewer viewers. Congress instead decided to impose the "carry one, carry all" rule. So § 1008 of SHVIA, codified at 47 U.S.C. § 338, states that if a DBS provider chooses to retransmit the signal of a local television station pursuant to the statutory copyright license made available under § 1002 of SHVIA, 17 U.S.C. § 122, the provider will have the obligation to carry the signals of all television broadcast stations located within that same local market.

The Fourth Circuit upheld § 338 against a First Amendment challenge. *See* Satellite Broadcasting and Communications Ass'n v. FCC, 275 F.3d 337 (4th Cir. 2001). In challenging the law, the satellite carriers argued that § 338 violated the First Amendment by interfering with their editorial discretion to choose their own content. They contended that § 338 was content based or, alternatively, that it was unconstitutional even if content neutral. Moreover, they argued that § 338 served only to promote the interests of some speakers (independent broadcasters in large markets) at the expense of others (major network affiliates in small and medium-sized markets), and that this was not even a legitimate—let alone a substantial or important—government interest.

The Fourth Circuit rejected all of those arguments. It held that § 338 was content neutral and that it satisfied intermediate scrutiny because it was a narrowly tailored means of advancing two substantial government interests: (1) preserving a multiplicity of local broadcast outlets for over-the-air viewers who do not subscribe to satellite or cable service, and (2) preventing the government's grant of a statutory copyright license to satellite carriers from undermining competition in local markets for broadcast television advertising. 275 F.3d at 356–63.

The Fourth Circuit further explained the operation of and policy rationale behind the provision in upholding its constitutionality:

> This kind of license forces satellite carriers to expand their local-into-local service one market at a time, beginning with the carriage of all requesting local stations in the largest markets and expanding from there. In sum, Congress either could have allowed satellite carriers to cherry pick by retransmitting *some* stations (the major network affiliates) in *many* markets, or it could have allowed satellite carriers to retransmit *all* of the stations in *some* markets. While satellite carriers would have preferred (and now argue for) the first result, Congress chose the second because it feared that cherry picking of major network affiliates within local markets would make it more difficult for non-carried stations in those markets to reach their audiences:
>
>> Although the conferees expect that subscribers who receive no broadcast signals at all from their satellite service may install antennas or subscribe to cable service in addition to satellite service, the Conference Committee is less sanguine that subscribers who receive network signals and hundreds of other programming choices from their satellite carrier will undertake such trouble and expense to obtain over-the-air signals from independent broadcast stations.
>
> SHVIA Conf. Rep. at 102. Non-carried stations in cherry-picked markets would "face the same loss of viewership Congress previously found with respect to cable noncarriage." *Id.* at 101. Congress therefore concluded that the carry one, carry all rule would protect the ability of all local broadcasters to reach their audiences and thereby "preserve free television for those not served by satellite or cable systems and ... promote widespread dissemination of information from a multiplicity of sources." *Id.*

275 F.3d at 337.

Notes and Questions

1. Linking the Two Provisions. Why did Congress link the compulsory license provision with the must-carry provision? For example, could Congress have structured the must-carry requirement such that it applied in the largest thirty metropolitan areas, irrespective of whether a given satellite provider had invoked the compulsory license provision? Would such a rule be more consistent with the First Amendment, or less so?

2. Who Loses? The must-carry provisions benefit local broadcasters at the expense of would-be specialty channels. That is, every slot used up by a local station carried under must-carry is a slot that might otherwise have gone to the next Discovery Channel, ESPN, or Cartoon Network. Why should these marginal channels lose out to the equally marginal broadcast channels that must-carry protects? Are these channels even considered in the Fourth Circuit's First Amendment analysis? What about the small-market broadcast channels that also will be squeezed out due to the must-carry provisions? That is, in the absence of must-carry, DirecTV might have carried the biggest station in each market. In the presence of must-carry, by contrast, DirecTV will likely carry every station in Los Angeles or Cleveland, reflecting the fact that DBS providers have limited capacity and must transmit all stations that are accessible to its viewers, although local TV programs will be blocked outside of their metropolitan service areas. Is this a superior outcome?

3. Comparison to Cable. Section 338 differs from the cable must-carry regime in a number of notable respects. For one thing, its effective date was set at January 1, 2002, which means that Congress gave DBS providers a period of a little more than two years after passage of SHVIA during which there would be no must-carry obligations. More importantly, the must-carry obligation is triggered only if a DBS provider retransmits a station through reliance on the compulsory license created by § 1002. As the FCC noted in a notice of proposed rulemaking on SHVIA, "if satellite carriers provide local television signals pursuant to private copyright arrangements, the [must-carry] obligations do not apply." *See* Implementation of the Satellite Home Viewer Improvement Act of 1999: Broadcast Signal Carriage Issues, Notice of Proposed Rulemaking, 15 FCC Rcd. 12,147 ¶ 10 (2000). What this means is simply that, if in a given local market a DBS provider makes its own arrangements without relying on the compulsory license, or chooses not to retransmit local signals at all, then that carrier will have no must-carry obligations in that local market. Lastly, note that—unlike the 1992 Cable Act—SHVIA does not create a "basic tier" of service that must include all broadcast stations that opt for must-carry.

In all these ways, the DBS requirements might be seen as less onerous than the must-carry regime for cable discussed above. Other differences, however, may pose a greater burden on DBS providers. Most notably, in contrast to the provision in the 1992 Cable Act that tied the number of local stations that had to be carried to the total number of channels a cable provider offered, § 338 does not by its own terms limit the number of local stations that DBS providers must carry. Section 338 does allow a DBS provider to refuse to carry more than one network affiliate in any given market unless the affiliates for the same network are in different states, and also to refuse to carry a signal that "substantially duplicates" the signal of a local station it is already retransmitting. But unless the FCC decides to limit the DBS must-carry obligation to a specified percentage of local stations, the requirement, when it applies at all, will apply to all local stations.

Also note that cable operators must carry local broadcast channels and specified public, educational, or governmental (PEG) channels. DBS providers are not required to carry

PEG channels or local broadcast channels. On the other hand, Congress did require that each DBS provider reserve between 4 and 7 percent of its channel "exclusively for noncommercial programming of an educational or informational nature," 47 U.S.C. § 335(b)(1) (discussed in Chapter Fifteen), and no similar requirement applies to cable operators. Can you justify these differences between the regulations applicable to cable and DBS? If you cannot, does that indicate that either the cable or the DBS provisions should be modified? Or would regulatory consistency be a false consistency in this case since the same regulation might have very different implications for DBS as opposed to cable?

4. Cable Must-Carry and Digital Broadcasts. During the transition to digital broadcast television (DTV), there was a period when broadcasters transmitted both digital and analog signals. This raised the question of what cable providers would have to carry under the must-carry rule. The FCC issued a notice of proposed rulemaking in 1998 asking for comment on the extent to which cable operators should be required to carry broadcasters' digital signals. In Carriage of Digital Television Broadcast Signals: Amendments to Part 76 of the Commission's Rules: Implementation of the Satellite Home Viewer Improvement Act of 1999, First Report and Order and Further Notice of Proposed Rulemaking, 16 FCC Rcd. 2598 (2001), the Commission tentatively decided not to require dual carriage of digital and analog signals, and determined that a cable operator need carry only a single stream from each broadcaster. Four years later, in Carriage of Digital Television Broadcast Signals: Amendments to Part 76 of the Commission's Rules, Second Report and Order and First Order on Reconsideration, 20 FCC Rcd. 4516 (2005), the FCC formally decided not to impose a dual carriage requirement on the cable operators.

On carriage of digital and analog signals, the 2005 order (like the 2001 order) found that "[t]he statute neither mandates nor precludes the mandatory simultaneous carriage of both a television station's digital and analog signals. Further, we do not believe that mandating dual carriage is necessary either to advance the governmental interests identified by Congress in enacting [the must-carry provisions] and upheld in *Turner II* or to effectuate the DTV transition." *Id.* ¶ 13. In its 2001 order, the FCC based its tentative rejection of the dual carriage requirement on its "tentative[] conclu[sion] that, based on the existing record evidence, a dual carriage requirement appears to burden cable operators' First Amendment interests substantially more than is necessary to further the government's substantial interests," but it sought additional information from interested parties. 16 FCC Rcd. 2598 ¶ 3. In its 2005 order, the FCC concluded that First Amendment considerations were dispositive, and that they militated against dual carriage:

> After close examination of the information submitted, we find nothing in the record that would allow us to conclude that mandatory dual carriage is necessary to further the governmental interests identified in *Turner I*, or other potential governmental interests put forward by commenters. In addition, even if it could be shown that dual carriage could further any of the governmental interests based on the current record, the burden that mandatory dual carriage places on cable operators' speech appears to be greater than is necessary to achieve the interests that must carry was meant to serve. Mandatory dual carriage would essentially double the carriage rights and substantially increase the burdens on free speech beyond those upheld in *Turner I*. *Turner II* found the benefits and burdens of must carry to be congruent, such that must carry is narrowly tailored to preserve the multiplicity of broadcast stations for households that do not subscribe to cable.

20 FCC Rcd. 4516 ¶ 15.

5. Multiple Digital Stream Carriage? In the DTV world, many broadcasters use their 6 MHz channel to provide a number of different digital channels rather than the single channel offered in the analog environment. In the face of this technological change, the TV broadcasters suggested that they should be afforded must-carry rights on any additional digital channels they broadcast over-the-air. The Commission, as in the dual carriage case, concluded that it had discretion on this matter. On the merits of the question, the Commission concluded that "multi-cast carriage" was not necessary to advance Congress's goals (as articulated in *Turner II*) of "preserving the benefits of free, over-the-air local broadcast television for viewers, and promoting 'the widespread dissemination of information from a multiplicity of sources.'" *Id.* ¶ 37 (quoting *Turner II*).

6. Satellite "Carry One, Carry All" and Digital Broadcasts. In a parallel order to the one excerpted above, the Commission adopted a comparable set of requirements for satellite providers in the wake of the digital transition. *See* Carriage of Digital Television Broadcast Signals: Amendment to Part 76 of the Commission's Rules, Second Report and Order, Memorandum Opinion and Order, and Second Further Notice of Proposed Rulemaking, 23 FCC Rcd. 5351 (2008). Notably, those rules provide that if a satellite provider carries the high definition signal of any local broadcast station, it is subject to the "carry one, carry all" requirement. In so doing, the Commission made clear that any digital-only station (whether a new one or one that returned its analog spectrum) was entitled to must-carry rights. Finally, the order provides that, if a satellite provider carries a high definition channel from one local broadcast station in a particular market, it must carry all the other digital stations in that market.

7. The Single-Dish Requirement. SHVERA amended 47 U.S.C. § 338 to provide that "each satellite carrier that retransmits the analog signals of local television broadcast stations in a local market shall retransmit such analog signals in such market by means of a single reception antenna and associated equipment." 47 U.S.C. § 338(g)(1). This provision was designed to stop a practice whereby satellite providers were shunting disfavored broadcast stations onto secondary home receiving equipment. DBS providers were doing so in order to conserve space on the primary equipment for more popular or more profitable fare, but the result was that it became more onerous for subscribers to receive the disfavored channels—to do so, a subscriber had to allow some secondary piece of equipment to be installed on her premises. 47 U.S.C. § 338(g)(2) provides an exception to this requirement by allowing satellite carriers to retransmit local digital channels by means of a separate dish if they transmit all local digital channels to the same dish.

---

§ 9.C. Programming Delivered à la Carte

Television viewers mostly choose which channels to watch but not which ones to buy. That is, as part of the established business model, cable and DBS providers bundle a large number of channels into a limited number of "tiers" of service and then let customers make more fine-grained choices later—when they are actually watching television. The reasons for this practice are complex, including the requirements of supplier contracts (ESPN insists on inclusion in the expanded basic tier, for example); a judgment by the operators that bundling channels will increase viewership and advertising revenue while also lowering costs; the lack of more developed technology to facilitate à la carte choices;

and, in the opinion of some consumer advocates, the conclusion that this model forces consumers to pay more for video programming than they otherwise would.

After Congress prodded the FCC under Michael Powell to study the economics of à la carte, the Commission released a report generally criticizing the concept of an à la carte mandate. Once Kevin Martin became Chairman of the FCC, he decided to develop a new report. That report, which the Commission conducted on its own motion, differed sharply from the earlier report, concluding that à la carte "could" be good for consumers and enable easier entry of new cable channels. Further Report on the Packaging and Sale of Video Programming Services to the Public, 37 Communications Reg. (P & F) 979 (2006). This later report came in for substantial criticism as well. *See, e.g.*, Charles B. Goldfarb, Cong. Research Serv., RL 33,338, The FCC's "à la Carte Reports" (2006).

The debate over mandatory unbundling of MVPD channels has both economic and noneconomic aspects. On the economic front, one can argue (as Chairman Martin did) that consumers are hurt by being "forced to buy" channels that they do not want. On the other hand, consumers are, in fact, paying a price that they are willing to pay, even if the bundle includes channels that they will never watch. The more direct economic issue is that bundling may facilitate price-discrimination. We discussed price discrimination generally in Chapter One and described how price discrimination may help or may hurt consumers. To see how channel bundling facilitates price-discrimination, consider a ridiculously simplified example. Suppose that Aviva loves the HBO Family channel — in particular enjoying family-friendly movies about dogs — and would be willing to pay up to $20 per month for that channel. Suppose that Aviva likes the HBO New Release channel much less; Aviva would pay $5 per month for that one, but no more. Meanwhile, her friend Sammy is the opposite: he loves his new releases and would pay $20 per month for those, but he values the family-friendly fare only at $5. If HBO had to sell these two channels à la carte, it would be hard to price them. There is no easy way for HBO to figure out whether they are selling to someone like Aviva or someone like Sammy, thus the best option would be to offer each channel at $20 per month and, in this example, earn a total of $40. Aviva would pay for and enjoy HBO Family but would neither pay for nor be allowed to watch HBO New Releases, and vice versa for Sammy.

If HBO could bundle the two channels as a combined HBO package offering, however, the best price for the combined offering would be $25. HBO would earn $50—$10 more than under à la carte—as both Sammy and Aviva would purchase the package. More important, HBO would be better off, and arguably so would Aviva and Sammy, in that both would have access to both channels. It would be as if Aviva paid $20 for HBO Family and $5 for HBO New Releases, while Sammy paid $20 for HBO New Releases and $5 for HBO Family — yet in actuality HBO would have simply charged $25 to each and been done with it. This is an implicit form of price discrimination, but it has many of the same implications as would a more explicit form. *See* Yannis Bakos, Erik Brynjolfsson & Douglas Lichtman, Shared Information Goods, 42 J.L. & Econ. 117 (1999).

MVPDs may also argue that bundling actually grows the entire market, by inducing viewing the consumers did not initially know they would want. "Channel flipping" exposes consumers to additional channels and programs. MVPDs also argue that the infrastructure for implementing separate billing would be very expensive.

On the noneconomic front, some argue that bundling forces consumers to have in their home content to which they object, for example on religious grounds. On the other hand, niche programming networks rely on being bundled with more popular channels so that some consumers will end up watching them and thereby boost their subscriber base (and advertising revenues). The alliances here can cross traditional lines. Evangelical and self-styled family and consumer groups have strongly supported a requirement that programming be offered à la carte, but many niche broadcasters—prominently including religious broadcasters—have opposed such regulations. One religious broadcaster emphasized the importance of viewers finding their program by happenstance and said, "If you obligate viewers to pre-select religious service, you are essentially going to find yourself witnessing to the choir." Piet Levy, Evangelicals vs. Christian Cable: Under 'à la Carte' Plan, Viewers Could Bar Certain Channels, Washington Post, June 10, 2006, at B9. Representatives of a family group countered that à la carte makes sense because, "Unfortunately, the number of inappropriate programs far outweighs the number of good." Id.

The last consideration (although not perhaps least for the MVPDs) is a First Amendment question: Do cable and DBS providers have a First Amendment right to select how they package their programming? How would a challenge to an à la carte mandate fare under *Turner I*? How would an incentive-based bill (say, one that lowered required franchise fees) fare under First Amendment scrutiny?

§ 9.D. The FCC's Role in Digital Copyright Policy

What, if any, role should the FCC play with respect to copyright policy? This issue arose with particular force when the Commission was promoting the transition to digital television. Content providers made clear in that context that they were worried about losing income because of unauthorized sharing, and they threatened to withhold digital programming altogether if measures were not adopted to protect it from piracy. The FCC found itself in an uncomfortable position because, as then-Chairman Powell noted, digital copyright issues were the "Achilles' heel of [the] overall digital transition" and the agency "grop[ed] its way through what role it can play." Fixing Spectrum Policy Is Among Powell's Top Priorities, Communications Daily, Jan. 13, 2003.

To a generation familiar with online copyright piracy opportunities, it will come as no surprise that the transition to digital television stoked content providers' fears of losing control over their products. Digital content is vulnerable to unauthorized distribution and duplication, particularly because, unlike copies of analog content, a digital copy maintains the full sound and picture quality of the original. Content owners were thus understandably nervous about the transition to digital distribution; the question for the Commission was whether and how telecommunications regulation—as opposed to or in addition to copyright law—should respond.

A primary issue has been whether hardware manufacturers will be obligated to, allowed to, or barred from helping content producers protect their work. That is, should the Commission mandate hardware-based copy protection, stopping unauthorized duplication and distribution at its source and thereby protecting the incentive structure created by federal copyright law? Should the Commission instead leave these details to the market, allowing the content and consumer electronics industries to negotiate their own arrangements in the shadow of existing copyright rules and remedies? Or should the Commission forbid hardware manufacturers from implementing copy protection, on the rationale that such a rule would leave the most flexibility for hardware design and innovation?

With respect to broadcasting, the Commission answered these questions by promulgating rules to implement the so-called "broadcast flag," which is in essence a copy control mechanism. The broadcast flag is just a series of bits embedded in the digital content and designed to mark the content as content that comes from broadcast television. In 2003, the FCC issued an order that adopted a particular mechanism for marking broadcast content and required that devices capable of receiving DTV signals over the air had to comply with this broadcast flag requirement by July 1, 2005. Digital Broadcast Content Protection, Report and Order and Further Notice of Proposed Rulemaking, 18 FCC Rcd. 23,550 (2003). The rule did not apply to devices that are incapable of receiving over-the-air DTV—and existing televisions would not have been affected by the rule—but devices capable of receiving DTV broadcasts built after July 1, 2005, were to be required to watch for this broadcast flag and, upon seeing it, restrict distribution of the relevant content. *Id.*

The justification for the broadcast flag—here, in the words of Jack Valenti, then-president of the Motion Picture Association of America—was that it would place "free, over-the-air broadcasters on a level playing field in terms of their ability to protect high-value digital content from massive unauthorized redistribution on the Internet and other digital networks. If free TV cannot protect high-value content from unauthorized digital redistribution, that content will be forced to migrate to subscription cable and satellite delivery systems which now have the technical capacity to prevent Internet redistribution." Stephen Labaton, Rules Near on TV Piracy, N.Y. Times, Oct. 27, 2003, at C5 (quoting Valenti). The chief criticisms, by contrast, were that the regulations would stifle innovation and that they would unavoidably restrict legitimate downstream uses of digital broadcast content.

The FCC's decision to require the broadcast flag was overturned by the D.C. Circuit on the ground that the FCC did not have jurisdiction to regulate the use of content *after* that content was broadcast. See American Library Ass'n v. FCC, 406 F.3d 689 (D.C. Cir. 2005). But jurisdiction was not the only objection to the FCC's order. At the time, the order did not apply to analog broadcasting, which created a substantial gap in its effectiveness and, in all events, even proponents of the broadcast flag acknowledge that it created only a "speed bump" that would encumber but not completely thwart unauthorized digital distribution. *See* 18 FCC Rcd. 23,550 ¶ 14.

A broader question raised by the broadcast flag matter is whether the FCC is the right institution to set digital copyright policy. On that point it bears noting that, during the broadcast flag regime's time in effect, the FCC did approve a number of devices that, according to some, posed a risk of copyright infringement. One of those devices was TiVo's "ToGo" product—which enabled viewers to transport recorded programs to their computers for later viewing—that the FCC approved over the objections of a number of parties, including the NFL. *See* Digital Output Protection Technology and Recording Method Certifications, Order, 19 FCC Rcd. 15,876 (2004). Whether this was a desirable role for the Commission is a matter open to debate.

PART FOUR
Antitrust and Structural Regulation of Media

Chapter Ten

Structural Regulation of Media

Introduction

This chapter considers various regulatory limitations on the common ownership and control of content distribution and production. Over time, structural rules have evolved separately in various telecommunications sectors. Those rules have shared the underlying policy objectives of preventing concentration of market power in the hands of a few owners of media distribution and promoting content diversity by preserving access to distribution for independent content producers. The rules therefore typically limit the extent to which one entity may own multiple communications providers and govern vertical relationships between the systems that distribute content and the enterprises that produce content.

The FCC's structural regulations—by which we mean rules affecting ownership and control of networks and content—are not the only forces affecting the scope of joint ownership or vertical relationships in the telecommunications industry. Antitrust authorities, for example, review mergers and acquisitions among communications firms while both public and private antitrust suits have targeted allegedly anticompetitive conduct by telecommunications providers. The application of antitrust law to telecommunications will be discussed in Chapter Eleven. Other regulations impose various requirements on the level and quality of access that particular distribution networks provide to unaffiliated content providers. Examples of such rules are the cable must-carry obligations discussed in Chapter Nine and the open Internet rules examined in Chapter Fourteen.

In this chapter, our focus is on FCC rules that have affected horizontal and vertical ownership structures among firms engaged in media distribution. We begin with a discussion of regulations specifically governing broadcast networks' relationships with affiliated stations and program suppliers before moving on to the FCC's broader media ownership rules and, then, to structural and behavioral regulation of cable providers, including the evolution from the one (structural) to the other (behavioral). The last regulatory topic is spectrum caps—limits on the total amount of spectrum that a given mobile carrier may own. This chapter concludes with discussions by Cass Sunstein and Richard Posner, and an FCC staff report on program choice and quality.

§ 10.A. Structural Regulation of Broadcasting

The FCC has over time promulgated a large number of regulations that are designed in various ways to preserve competition in broadcast markets. Here, we look at two sets of rules written with this aim in mind. The first are rules to constrain the power of television networks like ABC, NBC, and CBS, with a particular eye toward increasing the viability of unaffiliated broadcast licensees and independent content producers. The second are rules that focus on the number of broadcast outlets owned by a single party and that impose various limits on the number of stations that can come under combined control.

§ 10.A.1. Television Networks and Vertical Integration

Broadcast television—or any other good—could be provided by a single integrated entity that both creates the products (television shows) and then delivers them to consumers (viewers) via a network of integrated distributors (wholly owned local affiliates). FCC regulations, however, did not allow for such complete vertical integration, and broadcast television therefore developed differently. Broadcast television networks were permitted to own some local television licensees, but the majority had to be owned by separate entities. The networks could produce some of their own programming, but much had to come from independent producers. The results were that networks bought many of their programs from unaffiliated producers and produced other programming in-house; and they owned some local television stations and entered into affiliation contracts with other, separately owned local stations under which the network agreed to provide programming and the local stations agreed to air it.

The restrictions on television networks' relationships with affiliates grew out of similar rules for radio and were originally promulgated in 1941 as the "chain broadcasting rules" (upheld in NBC v. United States, 319 U.S. 190 (1943)). Like most FCC rules, they rely on the FCC's power over licensees (i.e., the local stations themselves). Some of these rules have been repealed.[1] Many of the other rules have been modified and weakened over the years but remain in effect. Under the rules, licensees may not enter into agreements, express or implied, with networks that prohibit them from acquiring programs from another network; that hinder other local stations from airing programs offered by the network that the licensee has declined to air; that allow a network to control when a program is aired; that prevent the licensee from rejecting a network program "which the station reasonably believes to be unsatisfactory or unsuitable or contrary to the public interest" or from replacing a network program with one of greater local interest; or that bar the licensee from fixing or altering its rates for the sale of non-network broadcast time.[2]

The economic relationship between networks and program suppliers is, on a basic level, similar to the relationship between networks and local stations (and, for that matter, between any two entities): each party considers its alternatives in determining what prices to bid or ask and reaches an agreement (whether one-time, short-term, or long-term) only if it believes that it is gaining value from the arrangement. Unlike the market

---

1. In 1995 the FCC repealed the network station ownership rule, which prohibited the major television networks (then ABC, CBS, and NBC) from owning TV stations in markets with "so few stations, or stations of such unequal desirability (in terms of coverage, power, frequency, or other related matters), that 'competition would be substantially restrained' by permitting network ownership." Review of the Commission's Regulations Governing Television Broadcasting, Report and Order, 10 FCC Rcd. 4538, ¶ 1 (1995). It also repealed the secondary affiliation rule, which had prevented the major networks from establishing a secondary affiliation in markets where two stations had network affiliations and there was at least one independent unaffiliated station. The FCC "conclude[d] that changes in the marketplace have made both rules obsolete." Id.

2. 47 C.F.R. § 73.658. Other rules limit dual network operations, networks' representation of local stations, and territorial exclusivity in non-network arrangements. Id.

for affiliates, which is limited by the number of governmentally conferred licenses, would-be program suppliers are not limited by governmentally created entry barriers. Anyone with sufficient time and talent can write a script and then turn to the market to acquire cameras, film, actors, camera operators, and so forth—all of which can be rented and are available in abundant supply at competitive prices. The program supply industry, in short, is much more decentralized and structurally competitive than the broadcasting industry itself. These differences do not mean that programs will be available at marginal cost; certain programs garner large followings, and the sellers of those particular programs surely enjoy some degree of market power. But it does mean that, in contrast to the broadcast industry, there is no reason to believe that the program supply industry has inherent limits on competition among rival providers.

Despite the comparatively competitive structure of the market for programming, the FCC opted in the early 1970s to regulate the relationship between program suppliers and television networks on the ground that the television networks could use their leverage as distributors to distort competition in the program supply market. In particular, the Commission adopted two types of rules. First, the prime time access rule (PTAR) limited ABC, CBS, and NBC to supplying their affiliates with only three hours of programming for use during the four-hour "primetime" block. This rule meant that, for one primetime hour each night, even network affiliates had to turn to third-party suppliers or in-house talent for program content. Notably, children's programs, half-hour newscasts, and the Rose Bowl were excepted from this prohibition—the first two exemptions have obvious policy allure while the third seems to be the result of parochial interests influencing policy. The PTAR was defended largely on the grounds that (1) it carved out a market for independent producers to sell their programs directly to network affiliates and (2) it increased the profits of unaffiliated (especially UHF) stations since, during that one prime-time hour, affiliates and independents were on equal footing. In 1995, the Commission repealed the PTAR, summarizing its reasoning as follows:

> The three major networks do not dominate the markets relevant to PTAR. There are large numbers of sellers and buyers of video programming. Entry, even by small businesses, is relatively easy. There are a substantially greater number of broadcast programming outlets today than when PTAR was adopted in 1970 due to the growth in numbers of independent stations. In addition, nonbroadcast media have proliferated. Viewers can choose from program offerings on cable, so-called "wireless" cable, satellite television systems, and VCRs. Under these market conditions, PTAR is no longer needed to promote the development of non-network sources of television programming. We also find, given these market conditions, and the record before us, that the rule is not warranted as a means of promoting the growth of independent stations and new networks, or of safeguarding affiliate autonomy. Indeed, the rule generates costs and inefficiencies that are not now offset by substantial, if any, benefits.

Review of the Prime Time Access Rule, Section 73.658(k) of the Commission's Rules, Report and Order, 11 FCC Rcd. 546, ¶ 3 (1995).

The second type of rule, and the focus of this section, were the so-called financial interest and syndication rules (sometimes called "fin-syn" for short). These rules and their subsequent evolution are described in more detail in Schurz Communications, Inc. v. FCC, 982 F.2d 1043 (7th Cir. 1992), below. For simplicity, however, we can summarize the rules as follows: the fin-syn rules prohibited the major networks (ABC, CBS, and NBC) from (1) acquiring profit-sharing positions in network programs produced by independent companies and (2) engaging in the business (called off-network syndication) of licensing to independent stations the rights to show reruns of program series that have concluded their network runs. The rules respond to two fears. First, the FCC worried that networks would employ their power to extract from program suppliers excessively low fees or excessively generous grants of subsidiary rights. Second, the Commission thought that networks might seek to control the off-network syndication market in order to prevent competition from reruns (especially since these programs are typically telecast, in competition with network affiliates, by independent stations and cable networks).

SCHURZ COMMUNICATIONS, INC. V. FCC
982 F.2d 1043 (7th Cir. 1992)

Opinion for the court filed by Circuit Judge POSNER, in which BAUER, Chief Judge, and FAIRCHILD, Senior Circuit Judge, concur.

POSNER, Circuit Judge:

In 1970 the Federal Communications Commission adopted "financial interest and syndication" rules designed to limit the power of the then three television networks—CBS, NBC, and ABC—over television programming. 47 C.F.R. §73.658(j) (1990); see Network Television Broadcasting, Report and Order, 23 F.C.C. 2d 382, 387 (1970), aff'd under the name of Mt. Mansfield Television, Inc. v. FCC, 442 F.2d 470 (2d Cir. 1971). Each of the three networks consisted (as they still do) of several television stations, in key markets, owned and operated by the network itself, plus about two hundred independently owned stations electronically connected to the network by cable or satellite. In exchange for a fee paid them by the network, these affiliated stations broadcast programs that the network transmits to them, as well as to its owned and operated stations. The networking of programs intended for the early evening hours that are the "prime time" for adult television viewing gives advertisers access to a huge number of American households simultaneously, which in turn enables the networks to charge the high prices for advertising time that are necessary to defray the cost of obtaining the programming most desired by television viewers.

The financial interest and syndication rules adopted in 1970 forbade a network to syndicate (license) programs produced by the network for rebroadcast by independent television stations—that is, stations that were not owned by or affiliated with the network—or to purchase syndication rights to programs that it obtained from outside producers, or otherwise to obtain a financial stake in such programs. If the network itself had produced the program it could sell syndication rights to an independent syndicator but it could not retain an interest in the syndicator's revenues or profits.

Many syndicated programs are reruns, broadcast by independent stations, of successful comedy or dramatic series first shown on network television. Very few series are sufficiently successful in their initial run to be candidates for syndication. Independent stations like to air five episodes each week of a rerun series that originally had aired only once a week or less, so unless a series has a first run of several years—which few series do—it will not generate enough episodes to sustain a rerun of reasonable length. The financial interest and syndication rules thus severely limited the networks' involvement in supplying television programs other than for their own or their affiliated stations.

The concern behind the rules was that the networks, controlling as they did through their owned and operated stations and their affiliates a large part of the system for distributing television programs to American households, would unless restrained use this control to seize a dominating position in the production of television programs. That is, they would lever their distribution "monopoly" into a production "monopoly." They would, for example, refuse to buy programs for network distribution unless the producers agreed to surrender their syndication rights to the network. For once the networks controlled those rights, the access of independent television stations, that is, stations not owned by or affiliated with one of the networks, to reruns would be at the sufferance of the networks, owners of a competing system of distribution.

The Commission hoped the rules would strengthen an alternative source of supply (to the networks) for independent stations—the alternative consisting of television producers not owned by networks. The rules would do this by curtailing the ability of the networks to supply the program market represented by the independent stations, and by protecting the producers for that market against being pressured into giving up potentially valuable syndication rights. And the rules would strengthen the independent stations (and so derivatively the outside producers, for whom the independent stations were an important market along with the networks themselves) by securing them against having to purchase reruns from their competitors the networks.

The basis for this concern was never very clear. If the networks insisted on buying syndication rights along with the right to exhibit a program on the network itself, they would be paying more for their programming. (So one is not surprised that in the decade before the rules were adopted, the networks had acquired syndication rights to no more than 35 percent of their prime-time series, although they had acquired a stake in the syndicator's profits in a considerably higher percentage of cases.) If the networks then turned around and refused to syndicate independent stations, they would be getting nothing in return for the money they had laid out for syndication rights except a long-shot chance—incidentally, illegal under the antitrust laws—to weaken the already weak competitors of network stations. Nor was it clear just how the financial interest and syndication rules would scotch the networks' nefarious schemes. If forbidden to buy syndication rights, networks would pay less for programs, so the outside producers would not come out clear winners—indeed many would be losers. Production for television is a highly risky undertaking, like wildcat drilling for gas and oil. Most television entertainment programs are money losers. The losses are offset by the occasional hit that makes it into syndication after completing a long first run. The sale of syndication rights to a network would enable a producer to shift risk to a larger, more diversified entity presumptively better able to bear it. The resulting reduction in the risks of production would encourage new entry into production and thus give the independent stations a more competitive supply of programs. Evidence introduced in this proceeding showed that, consistent with this speculation, networks in the pre-1970 era were more likely to purchase syndication rights from small producers than from large ones.

Whatever the pros and cons of the original financial interest and syndication rules, in the years since they were promulgated the structure of the television industry has changed profoundly. The three networks have lost ground, primarily as a result of the expansion of cable television, which now reaches 60 percent of American homes, and videocassette recorders, now found in 70 percent of American homes. Today each of the three networks buys only 7 percent of the total video and film programming sold each year, which is roughly a third of the percentage in 1970. (The inclusion of films in the relevant market is appropriate because videocassettes enable home viewers to substitute a film for a television program.) And each commands only about 12 percent of total television advertising revenues. Where in 1970 the networks had 90 percent of the prime-time audience, today they have 62 percent, and competition among as well as with the three networks is fierce.

They are, moreover, challenged today by a fourth network, the Fox Broadcasting Corporation, which emerged in the late 1980s.

Notwithstanding the fourth network, which might have been expected to reduce the number of independent stations by converting many of them to Fox network stations, the number of independent stations has increased fivefold since 1970. At the same time, contrary to the intention behind the rules yet an expectable result of them because they made television production a riskier business, the production of primetime programming has become more concentrated. There are 40 percent fewer producers of primetime programming today than there were two decades ago. And the share of that programming accounted for directly or indirectly by the eight largest producers, primarily Hollywood studios — companies large enough to bear the increased risk resulting from the Commission's prohibition against the sale of syndication rights to networks — has risen from 50 percent to 70 percent.

The evolution of the television industry, sketched above, suggested that the rules, if they were having any effect at all, were working perversely from a competitive standpoint. An extensive staff study ordered by the Commission concluded that the rules were obsolete and recommended that they be abandoned. Final Report of Network Inquiry Special Staff, FCC (1980). In 1983 the Commission issued a tentative decision agreeing with the staff, proposing radical revisions in the rules leading to their eventual repeal, but inviting further public comments on the details of its proposals. Tentative Decision and Request for Further Comments in Docket 82-345, 94 F.C.C. 2d 1019 (1983). The networks, the Commission found in the tentative decision, had lost any significant monopoly or market power that they may once have had. The financial interest and syndication rules were hampering the entry of new firms into production by blocking an important mechanism (the sale of syndication rights) by which new firms might have shifted the extraordinary risks of their undertaking to the networks.

Mainly as a result of congressional pressure, Hearings before the Subcomm. on Communications of the S. Comm. on Commerce, Science & Transportation on S. 1707, 98th Cong., 1st Sess. 6, 9 (1984), there was no follow-up to the tentative decision. The question what to do about the rules remained in limbo until 1990, when the Commission at the request of the Fox network initiated a fresh notice-and-comment rulemaking proceeding. After receiving voluminous submissions from the various segments of the television industry, the Commission held a one-day hearing, after which it issued an opinion, over dissents by two of the five commissioners, including the chairman, promulgating a revised set of financial interest and syndication rules. Evaluation of the Syndication and Financial Interest Rules, 56 Fed. Reg. 26,242 (1991), on reconsideration, 56 Fed. Reg. 64,207 (1991). The new rules (published at 47 C.F.R. §§ 73.658(k), 73.659–73.662, 73.3526(a)(11) (1991)) are different from the old and also more complicated. They define "network" as an entity that supplies at least 15 hours [per week] of prime-time programming to interconnected affiliates. They take off all restrictions on non-entertainment programming (that is, news and sports), and most restrictions on non-prime-time programming and on syndication for the foreign as distinct from the domestic market. But in a provision that has no counterpart in the old rules, the new ones provide that no more than 40 percent of a network's own prime-time entertainment schedule may consist of programs produced by the network itself. The new rules unlike the old permit a network to buy domestic syndication rights from outside producers of prime-time entertainment programming — provided, however, that the network does so pursuant to separate negotiations begun at least 30 days after the network and the producer have agreed on the fee for licensing the network to exhibit the program on the network itself. Even then the network may not arrange for the distribution of the programming to the independent stations; it must hire an independent syndicator for that. And it may acquire syndication rights only in reruns, not in first-run programs, and thus it may not distribute first-run programming other than to its network stations.

Although the Commission conceded that the networks may already have lost so much of their market power as no longer to pose a threat to competition as it is understood in antitrust law, it concluded that some restrictions remain necessary to assure adequate diversity of television programming.

The networks have petitioned this court to invalidate [the new rules] as arbitrary and capricious. 5 U.S.C. §706(2)(A). They argue that the only administrative order supportable by the record compiled by the Commission would be a total repeal of the 1970 rules.

The difficult question presented by the petitions to review is not whether the Commission is authorized to restrict the networks' participation in program production and distribution. It is whether the Commission has said enough to justify, in the face of the objections lodged with it, the particular restrictions that it imposed in the order here challenged. It is not enough that a rule might be rational; the statement accompanying its promulgation must show that it is rational—must demonstrate that a reasonable person upon consideration of all the points urged pro and con the rule would conclude that it was a reasonable response to a problem that the agency was charged with solving.

The new rules flunk this test. The Commission's articulation of its grounds is not adequately reasoned. Key concepts are left unexplained, key evidence is overlooked, arguments that formerly persuaded the Commission and that time has only strengthened are ignored, contradictions within and among Commission decisions are passed over in silence. The impression created is of unprincipled compromises of Rube Goldberg complexity among contending interest groups viewed merely as clamoring suppliants who have somehow to be conciliated. The Commission said that it had been "confronted by alternative views of the television programming world so starkly and fundamentally at odds with each other that they virtually defy reconciliation." The possibility of resolving a conflict in favor of the party with the stronger case, as distinct from throwing up one's hands and splitting the difference, was overlooked. The opinion contains much talk but no demonstration of expertise, and a good deal of hand-wringing over the need for prudence and the desirability of avoiding "convulsive" regulatory reform, yet these unquestioned goods are never related to the particulars of the rules—rules that could have a substantial impact on an industry that permeates the daily life of this nation and helps shape, for good or ill, our culture and our politics.

Stripped of verbiage, the Commission's majority opinion, like a Persian cat with its fur shaved, is alarmingly pale and thin. It can be paraphrased as follows. The television industry has changed since 1970. There is more competition—cable television, the new network, etc. No longer is it clear that the networks have market power in an antitrust sense, which they could use to whipsaw the independent producers and strangle the independent stations. So there should be some "deregulation" of programming—some movement away from the 1970 rules. But not too much, because even in their decline the networks may retain some power to extort programs or program rights from producers. The networks offer advertisers access to 98 percent of American households; no competing system for the distribution of television programming can offer as much. Anyway the Commission's concern, acknowledged to be legitimate, is not just with market power in an antitrust sense but with diversity, and diversity is promoted by measures to assure a critical mass of outside producers and independent stations. So the networks must continue to be restricted—but less so than by the 1970 rules. The new rules will give the networks a greater opportunity to participate in programming than the old ones did, while protecting outside producers and independent stations from too much network competition.

All this is, on its face, plausible enough, but it is plausible only because the Commission, ostrich fashion, did not discuss the most substantial objections to its approach, though the objections were argued vigorously to it, by its own chairman among others. To begin with, the networks object that the new rules do not in fact increase their access to the programming market and may decrease it, in the face of the Commission's stated objective. The 40 percent limitation on the amount of primetime entertainment that a network can supply from its in-house production is a new restriction on the networks, having no counterpart in the original rules. The carving out of nonentertainment programming from the restrictions imposed by the new rules is a throwaway, because there is no syndication market for news and sports programs. Also illusory, the networks argue, is the newly granted right to acquire syndication rights from outside producers, given the restrictions with which the new right is hedged about. A producer cannot wait until 30 days after negotiating the network license fee to sell off syndication rights, because the sale of those rights, the networks contend, is critical to obtaining the financing necessary to produce the program in the first place. These arguments may be right or wrong; our point is only that the Commission did not mention them. We are left in the dark about the grounds for its belief that the new rules will give the networks real, not imaginary, new opportunities in programming.

The new rules, like their predecessors, appear to harm rather than to help outside producers as a whole (a vital qualification) by reducing their bargaining options. It is difficult to see how taking away a part of a seller's market could help the seller. One of the rights in the bundle of rights that constitutes the ownership of a television program is the right to syndicate the program to nonnetwork stations. The new rules restrict—perhaps, as a practical matter, prevent—the sale of that right to networks. How could it help a producer to be forbidden to sell his wares to a class of buyers that may be the high bidders for them? Since syndication is the riskiest component of a producer's property right—for its value depends on the distinctly low-probability event that the program will be a smash hit on network television—restricting its sale bears most heavily on the smallest, the weakest, the newest, the most experimental producers, for they are likely to be the ones least able to bear risk. It becomes understandable why the existing producers support the financial interest and syndication rules: the rules protect these producers against new competition both from the networks (because of the 40 percent cap) and from new producers. The ranks of the outside producers of prime-time programming have been thinned under the regime of financial interest and syndication rules. The survivors are the beneficiaries of the thinning. They consent to have their own right to sell syndication rights curtailed as the price of a like restriction on their potential competitors, on whom it is likely to bear more heavily.

This analysis of risk and its bearing on competition in the program industry is speculative, theoretical, and may for all we know be all wet—though it is corroborated by the increasing concentration of the production industry since the rules restricting the sale of syndication rights were first imposed in 1970. The Commission was not required to buy the analysis. But as the analysis was more than plausible and had been pressed upon it by a number of participants in the rulemaking proceeding, the Commission majority was not entitled to ignore it. Not even to consider the possibility that the unrestricted sale of syndication rights to networks would strengthen the production industry (the industry—

not necessarily its present occupants) and thereby increase programming diversity by enabling a sharing between fledgling producers and the networks of the risks of new production was irresponsible. For if the argument about risk sharing is correct, the rules are perverse; by discouraging the entry of new producers into the high-risk prime-time entertainment market, they are likely to reduce the supply of programs to the independent stations and so reduce diversity both of program sources and of program outlets. The Commission's stated desiderata are competition and diversity. The rules adopted by the Commission in order to achieve these desiderata have the remarkable property—if the risk-sharing argument that the Commission did not deign to address is correct—of disserving them both.

If the networks do have market power, the new rules (in this respect like the old) do not seem rationally designed to prevent its exercise. A rule telling a person he may not do business with some firm believed to have market power is unlikely to make the person better off. Suppose that in a competitive market a network would pay $2 million for first-run rights to some program and $1 million for syndication rights, for a total of $3 million, but that because of the lack of perfect substitutes for using this network to distribute his program the producer is willing to sell each of these rights to the network for half their competitive market value (i.e., for $1 million and $500,000 respectively). The producer is made no better off by being forbidden to sell the syndication rights to the network. He gets the same meager first-run license fee ($1 million) and now must cast about for another buyer for the syndication rights. That other buyer is unlikely to pay more than the network would ($500,000); otherwise the producer would have sold the syndication rights to him in the first place. It is no answer that the network would not have given the producer the option of selling it only first-run rights, that it would have insisted on the whole package so that it could control the program supply of the independent stations, which are heavily dependent on reruns and hence on syndication. The producer might indeed be desperate for network distribution, but that desperation would be reflected in the low price at which he was willing to sell the network whatever rights the network wanted. He cannot do better by being forbidden to make such a deal. If he could do better by selling syndication rights to someone else he would not accede to such unfavorable terms as the network offered.

If this is right, the new rules, at least insofar as they restrict network syndication, cannot increase the prices that producers receive. All they can do is increase the costs of production by denying producers the right to share risks with networks.

Finally, while the word diversity appears with incantatory frequency in the Commission's opinion, it is never defined. At argument one of the counsel helpfully distinguished between source diversity and outlet diversity. The former refers to programming sources, that is, producers, and the latter to distribution outlets, that is, television stations. The two forms of diversity are related because the station decides what programs to air and therefore affects producers' decisions about what to produce. A third, and one might suppose the critical, form of diversity is diversity in the programming itself; here "diversity" refers to the variety or heterogeneity of programs. The Commission neither distinguished among the types of diversity nor explained the interrelation among them. As it is very difficult to see how sheer number of producers or outlets could be thought a good thing—and anyway the rules seem calculated, however unwittingly, to decrease, or at least to freeze, but certainly not to increase, the number of producers—we assume that the Commission thinks of source diversity and outlet diversity as means to the end of programming diversity.

Are they? It has long been understood that monopoly in broadcasting could actually promote rather than retard programming diversity. If all the television channels in a particular market were owned by a single firm, its optimal programming strategy would be to put on a sufficiently varied menu of programs in each time slot to appeal to every substantial group of potential television viewers in the market, not just the largest group. For that would be the strategy that maximized the size of the station's audience. Suppose, as a simple example, that there were only two television broadcast frequencies (and no cable television), and that 90 percent of the viewers in the market wanted to watch comedy from 7 to 8 p.m. and 10 percent wanted to watch ballet. The monopolist would broadcast comedy over one frequency and ballet over the other, and thus gain 100 percent of the potential audience. If the frequencies were licensed to two competing firms, each firm would broadcast comedy in the 7 to 8 p.m. time slot, because its expected audience share would be 45 percent (one half of 90 percent), which is greater than 10 percent. Each prime-time slot would be filled with "popular" programming targeted on the median viewer, and minority tastes would go unserved. Some critics of television believe that this is a fair description of prime-time network television. Each network vies to put on the most popular programs and as a result minority tastes are ill served.

Well, so what? Almost everyone in this country either now has or soon will have cable television with 50 or 100 or even 200 different channels to choose among. With that many channels, programming for small audiences with specialized tastes becomes entirely feasible. It would not have been surprising, therefore, if the Commission had taken the position that diversity in prime-time television programming, or indeed in over-the-air broadcasting generally, was no longer a value worth promoting. It did not take that position. Instead it defended its restrictions on network participation in programming on the ground that they promote diversity. But it made no attempt to explain how they do this. It could have said, but did not, that independent television stations depend on reruns, which they would prefer to get from sources other than the networks with which they compete, and—since reruns are the antithesis of diversity—they use their revenue from reruns to support programming that enhances programming diversity. It could have said that programs produced by networks' in-house facilities are somehow more uniform than programs produced by Hollywood studios. It didn't say that either. It never drew the link between the rules, which on their face impede the production of television programs and the interest in diverse programming. The Commission may have thought the link obvious, but it is not. The rules appear to handicap the networks and by handicapping them to retard new entry into production; how all this promotes programming diversity is mysterious, and was left unexplained in the Commission's opinion.

That opinion, despite its length, is unreasoned and unreasonable, and therefore, in the jargon of judicial review of administrative action, arbitrary and capricious. The Commission's order is therefore vacated and the matter is returned to the Commission for further proceedings.

Notes and Questions

1. Subsequent Events. On remand, the Commission essentially repealed the financial interest and syndication rules as well as its newer limitation on networks producing their own programming. *See* Evaluation of the Syndication and Financial Interest Rules, Second Report and Order, 8 FCC Rcd. 3282 (1993). The agency removed all restrictions on network acquisition of financial interests and syndication rights, and the agency eliminated entirely the cap on in-house production. Retained were the prohibitions on active network domestic syndication, whether in first-run or off-network syndication, but only as to primetime entertainment programming, only for a limited period, and only as to ABC, CBS, and NBC. The Seventh Circuit affirmed in Capital Cities/ABC, Inc. v. FCC, 29 F.3d 309 (7th Cir. 1994).

2. Promoting Competition. The 1991 rules were to some extent justified on the grounds that they would promote competition. The court, however, opines that "a rule telling a person he may not do business with some firm believed to have market power is unlikely to make the person better off." Of course, the 1991 rules did not tell program suppliers they could not do business with the networks, only that they could not sell certain rights to them absent certain protections. Didn't the Commission adequately explain why producers might be harmed if, as a consequence of selling syndication rights to the networks, they eventually confronted a syndication market that was dominated by those networks? Precisely what flaw(s) in this argument does the court identify?

3. The First Amendment. Can you imagine any conceivable public interest rationale for the 1991 limit on the number of programs networks could produce for themselves? A rationale that would survive First Amendment objections? Might this aspect of the new rules have been a prime source of the court's "impression ... of unprincipled compromises ... among contending interest groups"?

4. Understanding Monopoly Incentives. Is it really true that "monopoly in broadcasting [can] actually promote rather than retard programming diversity"? Posner's simple example seems to work, but are important complexities left out of his discussion that undermine this claim? What assumptions about viewer tastes drive the model? Does the point still have force when we consider viewers who have first, second, and third choices in terms of their viewing preferences? What other refinements help us to evaluate this claim and its implications?

5. More Networks, Less Cash? Consider one more economic wrinkle relevant to understanding the market for program supply. One might suspect that, by increasing the number of networks or supporting the continued development of cable and satellite as distribution technologies, the FCC could increase profits in the program supply industry. The argument would be that the added competition would yield higher bids for any particular program. This is not necessarily true, however, since, as the number of outlets increases, the average audience per outlet likely decreases. Each outlet therefore attracts less advertising revenue and quite possibly ends up bidding less on content. Does this mean that increasing competition among outlets decreases competition among program suppliers? If so, now what?

6. The Internet Changes Everything. As the Internet becomes an increasingly viable medium for distributing programming, the concern that the financial interests of the networks will not be aligned with that of the affiliates becomes even more powerful. When networks first began Internet distribution of popular shows after they were aired, the affiliates were up in arms and demanded some form of compensation. Can the market be expected to resolve this tension?

7. Irrational Networks? Another reason to worry that networks may not look after affiliates' interests is that they, in a post-fin-syn rules world, are vertically integrated into the programming supply market. That is, most networks—ABC, Fox, and NBC—own programming arms—respectively, Disney Television Animation, 20th Century Fox Television, and Universal Media Studios. Is it reasonable to expect that network executives will recognize talent when they see it, even if it is from independent programming suppliers? This concern about vertical integration animates many media critics' attacks on "big media."

§ 10.A.2. Ownership Restrictions

Another method the FCC employs to foster competition in broadcasting is limiting the number of telecommunications platforms any single entity can own or control. There are two main categories of such limitations. First, there are "multiple ownership" rules that restrict ownership within the same service or closely connected services. These rules can apply nationally or locally, and they can set caps by stipulating a maximum number of licenses, a maximum percent of the relevant audience, or both. So, for example, the local television ownership rules limit the number of television broadcast licenses that a single entity can hold in a given market, and the "national television ownership rules" limit the percent of the national audience that a single television broadcaster can reach through stations it owns or controls. (Note that network affiliates—other than those that are owned and operated by the networks—are not necessarily controlled by their associated network because an independently owned affiliate has the right to refuse to air particular network programs. This most often happens when an affiliate preempts national programming to focus on an event of local importance, but it also happens when a local owner decides that a program put out by the network is inappropriate given local tastes.)

Second, the Commission promulgates various "cross ownership" rules that restrict ownership across different communications services. For example, the Commission has regulations preventing a single entity from owning both a television station and more than a specified number of radio stations in a given locality. Cross-ownership rules can include nonbroadcast properties as well. For instance, Commission regulations restrict an entity's ownership of broadcast facilities and a newspaper in the same local market.

The Commission is by no means the only player in the struggle over ownership restrictions, however. Congress and the courts have also played an important role. As for the former, in the Telecommunications Act of 1996, Congress reduced the FCC's power to control the market structure of broadcasting, particularly of radio broadcasting, by raising the number of stations a single licensee could own in a given geographic market. Pub. L. No. 104-104, § 202(b), 110 Stat. 56 (1996). It similarly raised the ceiling on the percent of viewing households that a single owner of television stations could serve nationwide. Id. §§ 202(c)(1), 202(e). In 1999, the FCC followed Congress's initiative by eliminating the strict prohibition against consolidation of broadcasters in the same market and allowed local station mergers under certain conditions. Review of the Commission's Regulations Governing Television Broadcasting, Report and Order, 14 FCC Rcd. 12,903 (1999). And in 2001, the Commission amended its rules to permit one of the four major television networks (ABC, CBS, Fox, and NBC) to own, operate, maintain, or control one or both of the emerging networks, which were defined in the Telecommunications Act of 1996, and specifically identified in the legislative history of that Act, as the UPN and WB television networks. Amendment of Section 73.658(g) of the Commission's Rules—The Dual Network Rule, Report and Order, 16 FCC Rcd. 11,114 (2001). Significantly, the 1996 Act also contained a provision—§ 202(h)—that ordered the FCC to undertake biennial (now quadrennial) reviews of its media ownership regulations and to "repeal or modify any regulation it determines to be no longer in the public interest."[3]

Turning to the courts, the U.S. Court of Appeals for the D.C. Circuit rejected and remanded media ownership regulations in two different 2002 cases. In Fox Television Stations, Inc. v. FCC, 280 F.3d 1027 (D.C. Cir. 2002), the court found that the FCC failed to provide any basis for retaining either the national television station ownership (NTSO) limit or the cable/broadcasting cross-ownership prohibition. The court's interpretation of § 202(h) bears particular notice:

---

3. Congress modified this provision in 2004 to call for quadrennial as opposed to biennial reviews. See Consolidated Appropriations Act, Pub. L. No. 108-199, § 629, 118 Stat. 3, 99–100 (2004).

The Commission's wait-and-see approach cannot be squared with its statutory mandate promptly—that is, by revisiting the matter biennially—to "repeal or modify" any rule that is not "necessary in the public interest." ... [In short], the statute imposed upon the Commission a duty to examine critically the new 35% NTSO Rule and to retain it only if it continued to be necessary; for the Commission to defer to the Congress's choice of 35% as of 1996 is to default upon this ongoing duty.... [T]he mandate of §202(h) might better be likened to Farragut's order at the battle of Mobile Bay ("Damn the torpedoes! Full speed ahead.") than to the wait-and-see attitude of the Commission.

Id. at 1042–44.

With respect to the national broadcast ownership cap, the court found that the FCC did not take into account recent data on the number of stations in operation. Furthermore, it found that the FCC failed to reconcile its refusal to loosen national ownership limits with its earlier decision to loosen local station ownership limitations—a step of perhaps greater consequence because it could reduce the number of owners serving a given locality rather than simply reduce the number of owners nationwide. The court remanded the national ownership cap for further consideration of whether to repeal or modify it. By contrast, the court found that the Commission had utterly failed to justify its cable/broadcasting cross-ownership prohibition on either competition or diversity grounds. It concluded that the likelihood of the FCC justifying this rule on remand was sufficiently low that it simply vacated, rather than remanded, the rule.

Shortly after *Fox*, a different panel of the D.C. Circuit decided in Sinclair Broadcast Group, Inc. v. FCC, 284 F.3d 148 (D.C. Cir. 2002), that the FCC had failed to justify its remaining local broadcast station ownership limits; in particular, the court held that the FCC had erred by insufficiently justifying its exclusion of nonbroadcast media from the eight "voices" that must be left in a market in order for a local station merger to be permitted. *Id.* at 152. The court clarified that neither the precedent recognizing the FCC's "wide discretion" to draw administrative lines nor the difficulty of defining "diversity" freed the FCC from its obligation to explain why and provide evidence that its rules are necessary to promote diversity. *Id.* at 161–62. As with the national broadcast ownership cap, it remanded the rule to the FCC for further consideration of whether to repeal or modify it. *Fox* and *Sinclair* thus refused to allow rules to stand absent an administrative record containing unambiguous, convincing evidence, not just theory, that a rule was needed.

The Commission had for many years typically responded to judicial remands of its ownership rules by opening narrow proceedings designed to address the specific ownership restriction at issue. When a court rejected and remanded some national cap, for example, the Commission responded by issuing a new NPRM with respect to that specific cap. This led to the predictable complaint that the Commission's ownership restrictions were an incoherent hodgepodge of regulations updated at different times and subject to different pressures, rather than a comprehensive network of rules designed to promote competition in the marketplace of ideas. In September 2002, with several of the media ownership rules in flux and at various stages of administrative review, the FCC determined that "it is appropriate for the Commission to consider these rules collectively, as any change to one rule may affect the need for other rules to be retained, modified, or eliminated." 2002 Biennial Regulatory Review—Review of Commission's Broadcast Ownership Rules and Other Rules Adopted Pursuant to Section 202 of the Telecommunications Act of 1996, Notice of Proposed Rulemaking, 17 FCC Rcd. 18,503, ¶8 (2002).

The Commission issued its media ownership order in 2003. 2002 Biennial Regulatory Review—Review of the Commission's Broadcast Ownership Rules and Other Rules Adopted Pursuant to Section 202 of the Telecommunications Act of 1996, Report and Order and Notice of Proposed Rulemaking, 18 FCC Rcd. 13,620 (2003). The order covered several rules: (1) the national television multiple ownership rule, which caps the number of television stations a single entity may own nationwide; (2) the local television multiple ownership rule, which limits the number of stations a single entity may own in a local viewing market; (3) the radio/television cross-ownership rule, which limits multiple holdings among those media; (4) the dual network rule, which prohibits combinations among the four major TV networks; (5) the newspaper/broadcast rule, which limits cross-ownership of television stations and daily newspapers; and (6) the local radio ownership rule, which governs the amount of consolidation permissible in a local listening market. 47 C.F.R. §§ 73.3555(a)–(d), 73.658(g).

The FCC's 2003 media ownership order did not eliminate or make changes to all these rules. In some cases the FCC essentially repealed regulations while in others it made more incremental changes. With regard to the national television ownership rule, for example, the FCC increased the limit on audience reach from 35% to 45% nationwide. The FCC also relaxed the local television station multiple ownership rule, allowing an entity to own two local stations in markets with five or more stations or to own three local stations in markets with eighteen or more stations, so long as only one of the stations involved is within the top four in ratings. The FCC retained its ban on mergers among the top four national television networks (NBC, ABC, CBS, and Fox).

The FCC made the biggest changes to its cross-ownership rules. It substantially repealed the prior ban on newspaper/broadcast and broadcast/radio cross-ownership and retained the ban (subject to waiver) only in markets with three or fewer television stations. In markets with four to eight television stations, the order permitted cross-ownership between a daily paper and one television station as well as cross-ownership between either a daily paper or a television station and a limited number of radio stations. The FCC completely repealed the cross-ownership rules in markets with nine or more television stations. Finally, the FCC retained its caps on local radio station ownership but refined its method for defining radio markets.

In each case in which the FCC relaxed its ownership rules, its action had the effect of lifting or weakening ex ante prohibitions rather than supplying ex ante approvals. Thus, the fact that the FCC's rules no longer blocked higher television market concentration did not necessarily mean that mergers up to the new maximum levels would be approved. The antitrust agencies would weigh in on significant transactions. Similarly, the relaxation and repeal of the FCC's cross-ownership rules did not exempt any acquisitions among different media platforms from antitrust scrutiny. The rule changes from the FCC's 2003 media ownership order would therefore have the effect of expanding the scope of general antitrust law into areas where specific administrative rules previously did the work.

The new rules met a storm of opposition. Indeed, during the course of the rulemaking proceeding, the FCC received more than 1,000,000 comments, nearly all of which opposed changes that would have allowed for greater media consolidation. The opponents spanned the political spectrum. Such disparate groups as the ACLU, the National Rifle Association, the AFL-CIO, the Parents Television Council, the National Organization for Women, the Family Research Council, and MoveOn.org argued against relaxation of the ownership limits. 2002 Biennial Regulatory Review, Report and Order and Notice of Proposed Rulemaking, 18 FCC Rcd. 13,620 app. A (2003). After the FCC issued its new rules, the fight moved to Capitol Hill and to the public sphere. Perhaps most interestingly, at that moment even the FCC leadership thought it necessary to address the public directly. *See* Michael K. Powell, Op-Ed., New Rules, Old Rhetoric, N.Y. Times, July 28, 2003, at A17.

Ultimately, only one part of the FCC's order was legislatively altered: the national television ownership cap. On this, Congress served the FCC with a striking rebuke with broad bipartisan majorities voting to rescind the FCC's increase in the national television cap and codifying a 35% limit. This provision was included in the omnibus spending bill for the 2004 fiscal year. The Bush Administration responded by threatening to veto the omnibus bill (full of spending initiatives dear to both the President and to members of Congress) if the 35% provision remained in the bill. Eventually, Republican leaders in the House and Senate agreed to change the legislated national ownership level to 39%. That, too, provoked outrage: many members of the House and Senate (of both parties) denounced the move from 35% to 39%. They noted that broad majorities in both houses wanted a 35% limit, and they vociferously opposed any increase. By late January 2004 (almost four months after fiscal year 2004 started), the pressure to pass the omnibus spending bill was too great, and the 39% compromise was enacted—though a significant number of Senators restated their outrage at the increase to 39%. The legislation also specifically denies the FCC the power to use its forbearance authority (normally available under 47 U.S.C. § 160) and requires divestiture within two years for entities exceeding the 39% cap. Consolidated Appropriations Act, 2004, Pub. L. No. 108-199, tit. VI, § 629, 118 Stat. 3 (2004).

Meanwhile, opponents of the new FCC rules brought suit challenging them as arbitrary or capricious and therefore in violation of § 706 of the Administrative Procedure Act, 5 U.S.C. § 706(2)(A). Challenges were filed in a number of federal circuits, and the cases were consolidated and assigned by lottery to the Court of Appeals for the Third Circuit. The resulting opinion is excerpted below. It summarizes the Commission's new approach before addressing the various challenges raised. As with other materials on this topic, we urge you not to focus too heavily on the details of the rules—those change with such regularity that memorizing the current numbers is probably a waste of time—but instead to consider the broader issues raised. Why is the Commission designing these rules rather than deferring to antitrust law and its enforcement authorities? What types of diversity are important: national? local? viewpoint? source? And how much evidence or explanation should courts demand from the Commission in cases, such as this, in which there clearly are no bright-line "right" answers and thus everything in the end is a complicated balance of competing policy factors?

Prometheus Radio Project v. FCC [*Prometheus I*]
373 F.3d 372 (3d Cir. 2004)

Opinion for the court filed by Circuit Judge AMBRO, in which Circuit Judge FUENTES concurs. Opinion concurring and dissenting in part filed by Chief Judge SCIRICA.

AMBRO, Circuit Judge:

On July 2, 2003, the Commission announced a comprehensive overhaul of its broadcast media ownership rules. It increased the number of television stations a single entity may own, both locally and nationally; revised various provisions of the regulations governing common ownership of radio stations in the same community; and replaced two existing rules limiting common ownership among newspapers and broadcast stations (the newspaper/broadcast cross-ownership rule and the radio/television cross-ownership rule) with a single set of "Cross-Media Limits." *See* 2002 Biennial Regulatory Review—Review of the Commission's Broadcast Ownership Rules and Other Rules Adopted Pursuant to Section 202 of the Telecommunications Act of 1996, Report and Order and Notice of Proposed Rulemaking, 18 FCC Rcd. 13,620 (2003) (the Order).

Several public interest and consumer advocacy groups (collectively, the Citizen Petitioners) petitioned for judicial review of the Order in various courts of appeals, contending that its deregulatory provisions contravened the Commission's statutory mandates as well as the Administrative Procedure Act, 5 U.S.C. §§ 551 *et seq.* (the APA). Associations of networks, broadcasters, and newspaper owners also challenged the Order, arguing that pro-regulatory revisions as well as the absence of further deregulation violate the Telecommunications Act of 1996, Pub. L. No. 104-104, 110 Stat. 56 (1996) (the 1996 Act), the APA, and the United States Constitution. The Judicial Panel on Multidistrict Litigation consolidated the petitions in this Court. On September 3, 2003, we stayed implementation of the rules pending our review.

For the reasons stated below, we affirm the power of the Commission to regulate media ownership. In doing so, we reject the contention that the Constitution or § 202(h) of the 1996 Act somehow provides rigid limits on the Commission's ability to regulate in the public interest. But we must remand certain aspects of the Commission's Order that are not adequately supported by the record. Most importantly, the Commission has not sufficiently justified its particular chosen numerical limits for local television ownership, local radio ownership, and cross-ownership of media within local markets. Accordingly, we partially remand the Order for the Commission's additional justification or modification, and we partially affirm the Order. The stay will continue pending our review of the Commission's action on remand.

II. Jurisdiction and Standard of Review

Our standard of review is governed by the APA and the 1996 Act provision authorizing the Commission's periodic regulatory review.

A. Standard of Review Under the Administrative Procedure Act

Our standard of review in the agency rulemaking context is governed first by the judicial review provision of the APA, 5 U.S.C. § 706. Under it, we "hold unlawful or set aside agency action, findings, and conclusions" that are found to be "arbitrary, capricious, an abuse of discretion, or otherwise not in accordance with the law ... [or] unsupported by substantial evidence." *Id.* § 706(2)(a), (e).

The traditional APA standard of review is even more deferential "where the issues involve 'elusive' and 'not easily defined' areas such as programming diversity in broadcasting." *Sinclair Broad. Grp.*, 284 F.3d at 159. Yet even when an administrative order involves policy determinations on such elusive goals, a "rationality" standard is appropriate. *See* FCC v. Nat. Citizens Comm. for Broad., 436 U.S. 775, 796–97 (*NCCB*) (finding that the Commission acted rationally in determining that diversification of ownership would enhance the possibility of increasing diverse viewpoints). Additionally, when an agency has engaged in line-drawing determinations and our review is necessarily deferential to agency expertise, its decisions may not be "patently unreasonable" or run counter to the evidence before the agency. *Sinclair*, 284 F.3d at 162.

B. Standard of Review Considerations Under Section 202(h)

The Order was promulgated as part of the periodic review requirements of § 202(h) of the 1996 Act. Consequently, our review standard is informed by that provision, which, at the time of the Order's release, read:

(h) Further Commission Review. The Commission shall review its rules adopted pursuant to this section and all of its ownership rules biennially as part of its regulatory reform review under section 11 of the Communications Act of 1934 and shall determine whether any of such rules are necessary in the public interest as the result of competition. The Commission shall repeal or modify any regulation it determines to be no longer in the public interest.

110 Stat. 111–12. Section 11 of the Communications Act, to which § 202(h) refers, was also added by the 1996 Act to ensure that the Commission review periodically its regulations governing telecommunications services to "determine whether any such regulation is no longer necessary in the public interest as a result of meaningful economic competition between providers of such service" and "repeal or modify any regulation it determines to be no longer necessary in the public interest." 47 U.S.C. § 161.

The text and legislative history of the 1996 Act indicate that Congress intended periodic reviews to operate as an "ongoing mechanism to ensure that the Commission's regulatory framework would keep pace with the competitive changes in the marketplace" resulting from that Act's relaxation of the Commission's regulations, including the broadcast media ownership regulations. 2002 Biennial Regulatory Review, Report, 18 FCC Rcd. 4726, ¶¶ 16, 17 (2003) (citing preamble to the 1996 Act; H.R. Conf. Rep. No. 104-458 (1996)). Put another way, the periodic review provisions require the Commission to "monitor the effect of ... competition ... and make appropriate adjustments" to its regulations. *Id.* ¶ 5.

As noted, the first sentence of § 202(h) requires the Commission to "determine" whether media concentration rules are "necessary in the public interest as the result of competition." The second sentence contains a separate instruction to the Commission: to "repeal or modify" those rules "no longer in the public interest." 110 Stat. 111–12. We analyze each of these instructions in turn.

1. *"Determine whether any such rules are necessary in the public interest."*

Recognizing that competitive changes in the media marketplace could obviate the public necessity for some of the Commission's ownership rules, the first instruction requires the Commission to take a fresh look at its regulations periodically in order to ensure that they remain "necessary in the public interest." This raises the question of what is "necessary."

In the context of § 11 of the Communications Act, 47 U.S.C. § 161 — which, like § 202(h), requires the Commission periodically to review its telecommunications regulations and determine whether they "remain necessary in the public interest" — the Commission has interpreted "necessary" to mean "useful," "convenient" or "appropriate" rather than "required" or "indispensable." Setting out its rationale for this interpretation in the 2002 Biennial Regulatory Review, 18 FCC Rcd. 4726, ¶¶ 14–22, the Commission determined that the 1996 Act's legislative history indicated that Congress meant "no longer necessary" to mean "no longer in the public interest" and "no longer meaningful." 18 FCC Rcd. 4726, ¶ 17 (citing H.R. Conf. Rep. No. 104-458, at 185 (1996)).

Next, the Commission found that an "indispensable" construction of "necessary" as to § 11 would be unreasonably inconsistent with the Communications Act's grant of general rulemaking authority to the Commission. *Id.* ¶ 18 n.31. Under 47 U.S.C. § 201(b), the Commission is authorized to "prescribe such rules and regulations [regarding services and charges of communications common carriers] as may be necessary in the public interest to carry out the provisions of this Act." The Commission reasoned that the same standard must also apply to the review process required under § 11 in order to avoid absurd results. If the rulemaking and review standards were different, the Commission could promulgate any rule that is useful, but then, at the next periodic review, would have to revoke any of those rules that do not also meet a higher standard of "indispensable." *Id.* ¶ 18 & n.33. Under such a system, periodic review would either be inefficient or irrelevant, as the Commission could effectively sidestep the more stringent review standard by subsequently reissuing any "useful" rule that it had to repeal for failing to be "indispensable." *Id.* ¶ 18.

Lastly, the Commission rejected arguments that there is controlling judicial precedent for an "indispensable" construction of "necessary." It acknowledged that the Supreme Court and the D.C. Circuit Court of Appeals have upheld such constructions, but countered that these cases "simply demonstrate that terms such as 'necessary'... must be read in their statutory context." *Id.* ¶ 19.

For these reasons, the Commission determined that § 11's requirement that it review its telecommunications regulations to determine whether they remain "necessary in the public interest" does not require it to employ a more stringent standard than "plain public interest" found in other parts of the Communications Act. *Id.* ¶¶ 18, 22 (citing 47 U.S.C. § 201(b) as an example).

Recently, the D.C. Circuit Court upheld, in the context of § 11, the Commission's interpretation of "necessary" contained in the 2002 Biennial Regulatory Review. Cellco P'ship v. FCC, 357 F.3d 88 (D.C. Cir. 2004). Recognizing that "necessary" is a "chameleon-like" word whose "meaning... may be influenced by its context," the *Cellco* Court determined that it would uphold any reasonable interpretation that did not contravene the express provisions of the Communications Act. *Id.* at 94, 96.

Cellco also acknowledged that the Commission's interpretation of "necessary" is consistent with the many courts that have endorsed a "useful" or "appropriate" interpretation over an "essential" or "indispensable" one. *Id.* at 97 (citing, *inter alia*, NCCB, 436 U.S. at 795–96; McCulloch v. Maryland, 17 U.S. (4 Wheat.) 316, 413, (1819); Cellular Telecomm. & Internet Ass'n v. FCC, 330 F.3d 502, 510 (D.C. Cir. 2003) (specifically rejecting an "indispensable" connotation of "necessary" as used in the Communications Act's enforcement forbearance provision, § 10(a))).

For the same reasons proffered by the Commission and endorsed by the D.C. Circuit Court to reject the "indispensable" definition of "necessary" under § 11, we do so under § 202(h). Though § 11 and § 202(h) are separate statutory provisions, they are both periodic review provisions from the same statute. We see no reason to adopt a different definition of "necessary" under § 202(h) than under § 11. Moreover, interpreting § 202(h)'s first sentence to require the Commission to review its rules to determine whether they are indispensable in the public interest would lead to incongruous results when compared to the instruction in § 202(h)'s second sentence, which requires the Commission to "repeal or modify any regulation it determines to be no longer in the public interest." For the "determine" instruction to be meaningful, "necessary" must embody the same "plain public interest" standard that Congress set out in the "repeal or modify" instruction.

2. *"Repeal or modify any regulations it determines to be no longer in the public interest."*

Turning to the second instruction of § 202(h), the Commission is required to "repeal or modify" rules that are "no longer in the public interest." Having concluded that the first instruction requires the Commission to determine whether any existing rule fails to satisfy the "plain public interest" standard, the relationship between the first and second instruction is evident. Under the second instruction, the Commission must repeal or modify the regulations that it has determined under the first instruction do not satisfy that same standard.

While we acknowledge that § 202(h) was enacted in the context of deregulatory amendments (the 1996 Act) to the Communications Act, *see Fox I*, 280 F.3d at 1033; *Sinclair*, 284 F.3d at 159, we do not accept that the "repeal or modify in the public interest" instruction must therefore operate only as a one-way ratchet, i.e., the Commission can use the review process only to eliminate then-extant regulations. For starters, this ignores both "modify" and the requirement that the Commission act "in the public interest." What if the Commission reasonably determines that the public interest calls for a more stringent regulation? Did Congress strip it of the power to implement that determination? The obvious answer is no, and it will continue to be so absent clear congressional direction otherwise.

What, then, makes § 202(h) "deregulatory"? It is this: Section 202(h) requires the Commission periodically to justify its existing regulations, an obligation it would not otherwise have. A regulation deemed useful when promulgated must remain so. If not, it must be vacated or modified.

Misguided by the *Fox* and *Sinclair* Courts' "deregulatory presumption" characterization and lacking the benefit of *Cellco*'s subsequent clarification, the Commission concluded that § 202(h) "appears to upend traditional administrative law principles" by not requiring it to justify affirmatively a rule's repeal or modification. Order ¶ 11. This overstates the case. Rather than "upending" the reasoned analysis requirement that under the APA ordinarily applies to an agency's decision to promulgate new regulations (or modify or repeal existing regulations), § 202(h) *extends* this requirement to the Commission's decision to retain its existing regulations. This interpretation avoids a crabbed reading of the statute under which we would have to infer, without express language, that Congress intended to curtail the Commission's rulemaking authority and to contravene "traditional administrative law principles."

C. Conclusion

Though our standard of review analysis is lengthy, it is in the end amenable to a straightforward summing-up: In a periodic review under § 202(h), the Commission is required to determine whether its then-extant rules remain useful in the public interest; if no longer useful, they must be repealed or modified. Yet no matter what the Commission decides to do to any particular rule—retain, repeal, or modify (whether to make more or less stringent)—it must do so in the public interest and support its decision with a reasoned analysis. We shall evaluate each aspect of the Commission's Order accordingly.

IV. Cross-Ownership Rules

The Commission's decision to repeal its newspaper/broadcast cross-ownership rules in favor of new Cross-Media Limits has been attacked on all fronts. Some petitioners support the repeal but argue that the Cross-Media Limits are too restrictive. Others challenge the repeal decision and argue that the new limits are too lenient. We conclude that the Commission's decision to replace its cross-ownership rules with the Cross-Media Limits is not of itself constitutionally flawed and does not violate § 202(h). But we cannot uphold the Cross-Media Limits themselves because the Commission does not provide a reasoned analysis to support the limits that it chose.

A. Regulatory Background and the 2002 Biennial Review

Since the 1970s, the Commission has enforced two separate limits on the common ownership of different-type media outlets in local markets. One cross-ownership rule prohibits the common ownership of a full-service television broadcast station and a daily public newspaper in the same community. The other limits the number of television and radio stations to the following combinations: (1) in markets where at least 20 independently owned media voices would remain post-merger, two television stations and six radio stations or one television station and seven radio stations; (2) in markets where at least 10 independent voices would remain, two television stations and four radio stations; and (3) in other markets, two television stations (subject to the local television ownership rule) and one radio station.

The Commission considered both cross-ownership rules during its 2002 biennial review under § 202(h). In the Order, the Commission announced that because neither rule remained necessary in the public interest, it was repealing them and replacing them with a single set of Cross-Media Limits. The three-tiered Cross-Media Limits regulate common ownership depending on the size of the market: small (those with three or fewer full-power commercial or noncommercial television stations), mid-sized (between four and eight television stations), and large (more than eight television stations). In small markets, newspaper/broadcast combinations and radio/television combinations are prohibited. In medium-sized markets, an entity may own a newspaper and either (a) one television station and up to 50% of the radio stations that may be commonly owned in that market under the local radio rule or (b) up to 100% of the radio stations allowed under the local rule. In large markets, cross-ownership is unrestricted.

B. The Commission's decision not to retain a ban on newspaper/broadcast cross-ownership is justified under § 202(h) and is supported by record evidence.

The Commission determined that the rule prohibiting newspaper/broadcast cross-ownership was no longer necessary in the public interest for three primary reasons: (1) the ban is not necessary to promote competition in local markets because most advertisers do not view newspapers and television stations as close substitutes; (2) the ban undermines localism by preventing efficient combinations that would allow for the production of high-quality local news; and (3) there is not enough evidence to conclude that ownership influences viewpoint to warrant a blanket cross-ownership ban, thus making it unjustifiable on diversity grounds (and moreover, the presence of other media sources—such as the Internet and cable—compensate for the viewpoint diversity lost to consolidation), *id.* ¶ 365. The Citizen Petitioners object to the localism and diversity components of the Commission's rationale. We conclude differently, as reasoned analysis supports the Commission's determination that the blanket ban on newspaper/broadcast cross-ownership was no longer in the public interest.

1. Newspaper/broadcast combinations can promote localism.

The Commission measured the promotion of localism by considering "the selection of programming responsive to local needs and interests, and local news quantity and quality." Order ¶ 78. Evidence that existing (grandfathered) newspaper-owned broadcast stations produced local news in higher quantity with better quality than other stations convinced the Commission that the ban on newspaper/broadcast combinations undermined its localism interest.

2. A blanket prohibition on newspaper/broadcast combinations is not necessary to protect diversity.

The Commission offered two rationales for its conclusion that a blanket prohibition on newspaper/broadcast combinations is no longer necessary to ensure diversity in local markets. First, it found that "[c]ommonly-owned newspapers and broadcast stations do not necessarily speak with a single, monolithic voice." *Id.* ¶ 361. Given conflicting evidence in the record on whether ownership influences viewpoint, the Commission reasonably concluded that it did not have enough confidence in the proposition that commonly owned outlets have a uniform bias to warrant sustaining the cross-ownership ban.

Second, the Commission found that diverse viewpoints from other media sources in local markets (such as cable and the Internet) compensate for viewpoints lost to newspaper/broadcast consolidations. We agree record evidence suggests that cable and the Internet supplement the viewpoint diversity provided by broadcast and newspaper outlets in local markets. As discussed more fully below, we believe that the Commission gave too much weight to the Internet in deriving the Cross-Media Limits. But separate from the question of degree, we conclude that it was acceptable for the Commission to find that cable and the Internet contribute to viewpoint diversity.

C. The Commission's decision to retain some limits on common ownership of different-type media outlets was constitutional and did not violate § 202(h).

The Deregulatory Petitioners support the Commission's repeal of the newspaper/broadcast cross-ownership ban but object to its decision to retain any restriction on the common ownership of newspaper and broadcast media outlets. First they argue that any limits on newspaper/broadcast cross-ownership violate § 202(h), because, as the Commission acknowledges, the evidence suggests that the cross-ownership restrictions are not in the public interest. They also argue that the Cross-Media Limits violate the First and Fifth Amendments of the United States Constitution. We disagree on all counts.

1. Continuing to regulate cross-media ownership is in the public interest.

The Commission's finding that a blanket prohibition on newspaper/broadcast cross-ownership is no longer in the public interest does not compel the conclusion that no regulation is necessary. As described above, the Commission found evidence to undermine the premise that ownership always influences viewpoint, but it did not find the opposite to be true. And while the Commission found that other media sources contributed to viewpoint diversity in local markets, it could not have found that the Internet and cable were complete substitutes for the viewpoints provided by newspapers and broadcast stations. *See* Gregory S. Crawford, Television Station Ownership Structure and the Quantity and Quality of Programming, FCC Media Ownership Working Group (2007) (*MOWG Study No. 3*) (finding that the Internet and cable rank as sources of local news, but they do not outrank newspapers and broadcast television). Given the Commission's goal of balancing the public's interests in competition, localism, and diversity, it reasonably concluded that repealing the cross-ownership ban was necessary to promote competition and localism, while retaining some limits was necessary to ensure diversity.

3. Continuing to regulate cross-media ownership does not violate the First Amendment.

The Deregulatory Petitioners argue that the Commission's decision to retain restrictions on the common ownership of newspapers and broadcast stations contravenes the First Amendment because it limits the speech opportunities of newspaper owners and broadcast station owners, and hence limits the public's access to information. Yet again their challenge is foreclosed by *NCCB*, where the Supreme Court affirmed the Commission's authority, despite a First Amendment challenge, to regulate broadcast/newspaper cross-ownership in the public interest. Due to the "physical scarcity" of the broadcast spectrum, the Court scrutinized the regulation to discern a rational basis. 436 U.S. at 799. The Commission's action, it held, was "a reasonable means of promoting the public interest in diversified mass communications." *Id.* at 802.

The Deregulatory Petitioners suggest, as they did in mounting their Fifth Amendment challenge, that the expansion of media outlets since *NCCB*'s day requires a rethinking of the scarcity rationale and the lower level of constitutional review it entails. Again we decline their invitation to disregard precedent, and we are not alone. *See* FCC v. League of

Women Voters of Cal., 468 U.S. 364, 376 & n.11 (1984) (upholding the scarcity rationale until Congress speaks to the issue); *Fox I*, 289 F.3d at 1046 ("First, contrary to the implication of the networks' argument, this court is not in a position to reject the scarcity rationale even if we agree that it no longer makes sense. The Supreme Court has already heard the empirical case against that rationale and still 'declined to question its continuing validity.'" (citing Turner v. FCC, 512 U.S. 622, 638 (1994))).

Even were we not constrained by Supreme Court precedent, we would not accept the Deregulatory Petitioners' contention that the expansion of media outlets has rendered the broadcast spectrum less scarce. In *NCCB*, the Court referred to the "physical scarcity" of the spectrum—the fact that many more people would like access to it than can be accommodated. 436 U.S. at 799. The abundance of non-broadcast media does not render the broadcast spectrum any less scarce.

In this context, we will apply a rational basis standard to the Commission's restrictions on the common ownership between newspaper and broadcast stations, and uphold them if they are rationally related to a substantial government interest. *See NCCB*, 436 U.S. at 799–800. In *NCCB*, the Supreme Court endorsed a substantial government interest in promoting diversified mass communications. *Id.* at 795, 802. The Supreme Court held that the Commission had "acted rationally in finding that diversification of ownership would enhance the possibility of achieving greater diversity of viewpoints." *Id.* at 796. Here, as in *NCCB*, the Commission justified its continued restrictions on common ownership of newspapers and broadcast stations as promoting the public interest in viewpoint diversity. The Court has said that limiting common ownership is a reasonable means of promoting the public interest in viewpoint diversity. *NCCB*, 436 U.S. at 796. Therefore, applying *NCCB*, we hold that the Commission's continued regulation of the common ownership of newspapers and broadcasters does not violate the First Amendment rights of either.

D. The Commission did not provide reasoned analysis to support the specific Cross-Media Limits that it chose.

The Commission concluded that cross-ownership limits were necessary in specific situations to guard against "an elevated risk of harm to the range and breadth of viewpoints that may be available to the public." Order ¶ 442. But recognizing that ownership limits impede the speech opportunities for both broadcasters and newspapers, the Commission endeavored to craft new limits "as narrowly as possible." *Id.* ¶ 441. In that vein, the Commission sought to identify "at risk" local markets—those with high levels of viewpoint concentration— where continued regulation was necessary. By focusing its regulation on those markets, the Commission hoped to avoid needlessly over-regulating markets with already ample viewpoint diversity.

But for all of its efforts, the Commission's Cross-Media Limits employ several irrational assumptions and inconsistencies. We do not object in principle to the Commission's reliance on the Department of Justice and Federal Trade Commission's antitrust formula, the Herfindahl-Hirschmann Index (HHI), as its starting point for measuring diversity in local markets. In converting the HHI to a measure for diversity in local markets, however, the Commission gave too much weight to the Internet as a media outlet, irrationally assigned outlets of the same media type equal market shares, and inconsistently derived the Cross-Media Limits from its Diversity Index results. For these reasons, detailed below, we remand for the Commission to justify or modify further its Cross-Media Limits.

[The court then went through a lengthy examination of the FCC's "diversity index," which the agency used to measure how diverse the content offerings were in a given market. This index was based, as the passage above mentions, on the Herfindahl-Hirschman Index that the federal antitrust enforcement agencies use to measure competitiveness in relevant markets. The FCC calculated its diversity index by first determining which kind of media (it chose television, radio, newspapers, Internet) should be included as contributors to viewpoint diversity. Next, it assigned relative weights to each of those kinds of media, with broadcast television receiving the highest weight (33.8%), followed in order by daily newspapers (22%), radio (24.9%), weekly newspapers (8.6%) and the Internet (the remainder). The Commission then would determine how many outlets of each media type existed in a given geographic market (e.g., how many television stations, etc.) and assign each of those outlets an equal share of its particular market (so if there were 10 TV stations in a local area, each would be assigned a 10% share of that local market). The ownership share of a given media provider would consist of the number of stations it owned times the market share attributed to each of those media outlets (so an owner of 3 stations in our hypothetical market would be assumed to have 30% of the local TV market). Finally, to get the particular owner's share of diversity in the local market, that 30% above would be multiplied by the diversity weight the Commission had assigned to the type of media in the second step above. So for a broadcaster with 30% market share, the diversity share would be 30% × 33.8% = 10.14. The FCC would do this calculation for each media owner in the market, then square each media owner's share and add them together to get a "diversity index" of media ownership in that market. The lower the index, the more diffuse the ownership and hence the more diverse the content in the local market. The Third Circuit rejected this complicated approach not in theory but in its particulars. The court was especially critical of the FCC's decision to attribute equal market shares to each kind of media outlet, regardless of what share of viewership or readership the outlet actually had, saying instead the agency should have applied actual usage data for media outlets or done a better job of justifying why it did not.]

V. Local Television Ownership Rule

Both the Citizen Petitioners and the Deregulatory Petitioners challenge the Commission's modification to the local television ownership rule, which would allow triopolies in markets of 18 stations or more and duopolies in other markets, subject to a restriction on combinations of the four largest stations in any market. We uphold the top-four restriction but remand the numerical limits for the Commission to harmonize certain inconsistencies and better support its assumptions and rationale. We also remand for the Commission to reconsider or justify its decision to expand the rule's waiver provision—applicable to sales of failed, failing, or unbuilt television stations—by eliminating the requirement that waiver applicants notice the station's availability to out-of-market buyers.

2. Media other than broadcast television may contribute to viewpoint diversity in local markets.

Recognizing that allowing more television concentration in local markets could detract from viewpoint diversity, the Commission rationalized its decision to deregulate with its finding that media other than broadcast television contribute to viewpoint diversity. This is a departure from the Commission's rationale for the existing rule—the issue remanded by the *Sinclair* Court—that only television stations are relevant to its diversity analysis.

We agree with the Commission's conclusion that broadcast media are not the only media outlets contributing to viewpoint diversity in local markets. Yet because we remand the Commission's numerical limits, as explained in Part V.D below, we need not decide the degree to which non-broadcast media compensate for lost viewpoint diversity to justify the modified rule. Rather, we leave it for the Commission to demonstrate that there is ample substitutability from non-broadcast media to warrant the particular numerical limits that it chooses on remand.

C. We uphold the Commission's decision to retain the top-four restriction.

Though the Commission recognized that the combination of television stations within the same market could yield efficiencies that benefit consumers, the Commission also recognized that station combinations only have an overall public "welfare-enhancing" effect when the consolidation does not create a "new largest" entity. Order ¶ 194. Thus, the Commission determined that it had to limit allowable station combinations to those that would not create excessive market power in a "new largest" entity. Finding that a significant "cushion" of audience share percentage points generally separates top-four stations from the fifth-ranked stations, the Commission decided that a top-four restriction would ensure that station consolidations did not lead to excessive market power. The Commission also recognized that efficiencies are less prevalent when financially strong stations merge with each other. For example, top-four stations are already more likely to be originating local news and to have made the transition to digital television.

Here there is ample evidence in the record to support the Commission's restriction on combinations among the top-four stations as opposed to the top-three or some other number. The Commission found a "cushion" of audience share percentage points between the fourth- and fifth-ranked stations in most markets. Networks' national audience statistics, which are generally reflected in local market rankings of affiliated stations, also show a substantial 60% drop in audience share between the fourth- and fifth-ranked networks. In the ten largest markets, the top-four stations combined control at least 69% (and an average of 83%) of the local commercial share in their respective markets, and in all of the ten largest markets a combination between the third- and fourth-ranked stations would produce a new largest station. Furthermore, the Commission found that permitting mergers among top-four ranked stations generally leads to large HHI increases.

Thus we conclude that the Commission's decision to retain the top-four restriction is supported by record evidence. Accordingly, we extend deference. *See Sinclair*, 284 F.3d at 162.

D. We remand the specific numerical limits for the Commission's further consideration.

The Commission decided to construct its numerical limits to ensure that most markets would have six equal-sized competitors because the HHI score of a six-member market — 1667 ($6 \times (100/6)^2$) — is below the Department of Justice and Federal Trade Commission's 1800 threshold for highly concentrated markets for antitrust purposes. Thus the Commission decided to allow triopolies in markets of 18 stations or more (18/3 = 6 equal-sized competitors) and duopolies in markets of 17 or fewer (both limits subject to the restriction on a combination of top-four stations).

The Commission's assumption of equal market shares received flak from both ends of the objecting spectrum. The Citizen Petitioners point out that television stations' market shares vary widely and argue that it is arbitrary for the Commission to base its numerical limits on a rudimentary station "head count" of outlets. The Commission's rationale for its triopoly rule requires that we accept a combination of the first-, fifth-, and sixth-ranked stations as the competitive equal of a combination of the 16th-, 17th-, and 18th-ranked stations, just because each combination consists of the same number of stations.

While the Citizen Petitioners demonstrate the Commission's flawed rationale with examples of what the modified rule allows, the Deregulatory Petitioners demonstrate the same flaw by pointing out what the modified rule forbids. There is no logical reason, they argue, why it should be impermissible to have five duopolies and one triopoly (a total of six competitors) in a market with 13 stations when it is possible that the triopoly could have a lower combined market share than any or all of the duopolies.

The Commission defends its equal market shares approach with the suggestion that market share, which varies with each season's new programs, is too "fluid" to be the basis for its regulations. But elsewhere in the local television ownership rule the Commission found that the market share was stable enough to rely on for support of its top-four restriction. And not only is the Commission's "market share is too fluid" rationale inconsistent with other aspects of the rule, it is unsupported. The Order cites no evidence to support its assumption that market share fluctuates more in television broadcasting than in other industries. Nor does it refute the Citizen Petitioners' suggestion that this is unlikely to be the case because, unlike most other industries, television station owners face a barrier to market entry (requirement of a license) and the number of market participants (television station owners) is in decline.

The deference with which we review the Commission's line-drawing decisions extends only so far as the line-drawing is consistent with the evidence or is not "patently unreasonable." *Sinclair*, 284 F.3d at 162. The Commission's numerical limits are neither. No evidence supports the Commission's equal market share assumption, and no reasonable explanation underlies its decision to disregard actual market share. The modified rule is similarly unreasonable in allowing levels of concentration to exceed further its own benchmark for competition (1800)—a glaring inconsistency between rationale and result. We remand the numerical limits for the Commission to support and harmonize its rationale.

VI. Local Radio Ownership Rule

Petitioners challenge the Commission's decision to modify its local radio ownership rule, which limits the number of commercial radio stations that a party may own in local markets of different sizes, by, among other changes, adopting a new method for determining the size of local markets. They also argue that the Commission failed to justify its decision to retain the rule's specific numerical limits. We affirm the Commission's decision to modify the rule (including modifying its method for determining local market size), but we agree that its decision to retain the numerical limits was arbitrary and capricious, and hence remand for the Commission's further consideration.

1. The Commission's numerical limits approach is rational and in the public interest.

The Commission's decision to retain a numerical limits approach to radio station ownership regulation is "in the public interest." Without numerical limits, radio markets risk becoming "locked up" in the hands of a few owners (or even one owner) because all of the available radiofrequency spectrum has been licensed—a high barrier to new market entrants. Based on record evidence, the Commission justifiably concluded that numerical limits are necessary "to guard against consolidation ... and to ensure a market structure that fosters opportunities for new entry into radio broadcasting." Order ¶ 291. For example, a MOWG study found that, since the existing limits were imposed in 1996, the number of radio station owners declined by 34% even though the number of stations increased by 5.4%. George Williams & Scott Roberts, Radio Industry Review 2002: Trends in Ownership, Format, and Finance, FCC Media Ownership Working Group 3 (2002) (*MOWG Study No. 11*). Additionally, the record shows that today 10 parent companies—the largest of which, Clear Channel Communications, owns 1200 stations nationwide, or 10%—dominate the radio industry and control about two-thirds of both listeners and radio revenues nationwide. In contrast, prior to the 1996 Act's deregulation, the largest nationwide radio station combinations had fewer than 65 stations each.

Furthermore, the record shows how increased consolidation has increased station prices, which limits opportunities for new market entrants and as a result limits diversity in station ownership and output. Consolidation has also reduced the amount of locally produced radio content, as large group-owners often broadcast remotely from national offices instead of having local employees produce programming. The record contains examples of consolidated stations that eliminated local news production. The evidence thus supports the Commission's conclusion that, by continuing to limit the consolidation of radio stations, numerical limits are "in the public interest" as required under § 202(h).

2. The Commission did not support its decision to retain the existing numerical limits with reasoned analysis.

Both the Citizen Petitioners and the Deregulatory Petitioners argue that the Commission's decision to retain the existing numerical limits was arbitrary and capricious. Predictably, the Citizen Petitioners argue that the Commission should have tightened the existing limits, and the Deregulatory Petitioners argue that the Commission should have relaxed them. But both sides' predominant argument is essentially the same: the numerical limits are not supported by the Commission's theory that they ensure five equal-sized competitors in most markets. While, as discussed above, substantial evidence supports the Commission's decision to retain the numerical limits structure of its local radio ownership rule, we also agree with the Petitioners that the Order lacks a reasoned analysis for retaining these specific numerical limits. We thus remand for the Commission's additional justification.

a. The Commission did not sufficiently justify "five equal-sized competitors" as the right benchmark.

The Commission relied on game theory to support its premise that five equal-sized competitors ensure that local markets are fragmented and structurally competitive. Order ¶ 289 n.609 (citing Louis Philips, Competition Policy: A Game Theory Perspective 23–38 (1995); Timothy F. Bresnahan & Peter C. Reiss, Entry and Competition in Concentrated Markets, 99 J. Pol. Econ. 997 (1991); Reinhard Selten, A Simple Model of Imperfect Competition Where Four Are Few and Six Are Many, 2 Int'l J. Game Theory 141 (1973)). The Citizen Petitioners and the Deregulatory Petitioners both dispute that these articles support the Commission's selection of five equal-sized competitors as the appropriate benchmark. The Deregulatory Petitioners argue that the articles fall short because they do not rule out market structures other than equal-sized competitors (such as one large firm and many small ones) as equally competitive markets. This argument, unanswered by the Commission, warrants a response because (as discussed below) the record evidence supports neither actual nor potential existence of equal-sized competitors.

b. The Commission did not sufficiently justify that the existing numerical limits actually ensure that markets will have five equal-sized competitors.

Regardless whether five equal-sized competitors is the right benchmark for competition, the Commission did not sufficiently justify that five equal-sized competitors would emerge or actually have emerged under the numerical limits. It defies logic to assume that a combination of top-ranked stations is the competitive equal to a combination of low-ranked stations just because the two combinations have the same number of stations. The Commission itself acknowledges that "radio station groups with similar numbers of radio stations [can] have vastly different levels of market power." Order ¶ 290.

Furthermore, evidence shows that the existing numerical limits do not ensure five equal-sized competitors. According to the record, most markets are dominated by one or two large station owners. And the top-four station owners together control the lion's share of the market. Even if these four station-owners were "equal-sized" (they are not), the HHI score of such a market would be 2500, well above the Merger Guidelines' 1800 threshold for highly concentrated markets.

The Commission does not explain why it could not take actual market share into account when deriving the numerical limits. Had it proffered the "market share is too fluid" rationale, we have already rejected that explanation in the context of the local television ownership rule and the Cross-Media Limits. We also note that the Commission has in the past extolled the value of audience share data for measuring diversity and competition in local radio markets. So the Commission's reliance on the fiction of equal-sized competitors, as opposed to measuring their actual competitive power, is even more suspect in the context of the local radio rule.

For these reasons, the Commission's numerical limits cannot rationally be derived from a "five equal-sized competitor" premise. We thus remand for the Commission to develop numerical limits that are supported by a rational analysis.

VII. Conclusion

Though we affirm much of the Commission's Order, we have identified several provisions in which the Commission falls short of its obligation to justify its decisions to retain, repeal, or modify its media ownership regulations with reasoned analysis. The Commission's derivation of new Cross-Media Limits, and its modification of the numerical limits on both television and radio station ownership in local markets, all have the same essential flaw: an unjustified assumption that media outlets of the same type make an equal contribution to diversity and competition in local markets. We thus remand for the Commission to justify or modify its approach to setting numerical limits. We also remand for the Commission to reconsider or better explain its decision to repeal the FSSR. The stay currently in effect will continue pending our review of the Commission's action on remand, over which this panel retains jurisdiction.

SCIRICA, Chief Judge, dissenting in part, concurring in part.

Although I concur in some parts of the Court's comprehensive analysis of this complex agency order, including its rejection of the constitutional challenges, I respectfully dissent from its decision to vacate and remand. In my view, the Court's decision has upended the usual way the judiciary reviews agency rulemaking. Whether the standard is "arbitrary or capricious," "reasonableness," or some variant of a "deregulatory presumption," the Court has applied a threshold that supplants the well-known principles of deference accorded to agency decision-making. In so doing, the Court has substituted its own policy judgment for that of the Federal Communications Commission and upset the ongoing review of broadcast media regulation mandated by Congress in the Telecommunications Act of 1996.

Notes and Questions

1. How Much Evidence? What sorts of evidence does the Third Circuit expect the Commission to produce on remand? What explains the Commission's failure to produce that support in the first instance? After all, the FCC had to know that its actions would likely face judicial review. So why didn't the FCC produce more support right away? Is the problem that the court is demanding more justification than the FCC can produce? Is the problem that the Commission commits analytical errors rather than merely failing to gather needed empirical evidence? Does it make sense as a matter of social policy to force the Commission to spend so much time and effort explaining itself and writing bullet-proof regulations instead of focusing on more substantive issues? Do you have any doubt that the Commission can produce a record that will support its favored rules, whatever they turn out to be?

2. Mixed Messages. Note that *Prometheus I* emerged from the Third Circuit whereas the *Fox* decision came from the D.C. Circuit. Do you think the Third Circuit adopts a different interpretation of § 202(h)'s mandate to reevaluate ownership restrictions? After all, the D.C. Circuit analogized this provision to a "Damn the torpedoes! Full speed ahead," approach toward deregulation.

3. Antitrust. Note that, whatever the FCC did or does, antitrust laws still put limits on an entity's ability to buy up all its competitors. Even if the FCC blesses a single company's purchase of most of the players in a given market, the Department of Justice would likely step in to prevent it. Antitrust laws are, of course, laws of general applicability. They apply to all products and markets—whether widgets or bits. In light of the presence of antitrust laws, are telecommunications-specific ownership rules appropriate? Does the Commission have adequate understanding of market structure to implement telecommunications-specific rules?

4. Equal Market Shares. The court makes much of the Commission's strategy for determining market share. Consider in contrast the following comments from the economist Bruce Owen:

> In the marketplace of ideas, what matters is the number of alternative information outlets available to consumers, not the current popularity, much less the technology of transmission, of the ideas communicated by each outlet. Each source of ideas available to a given consumer is equally significant from a First Amendment perspective. The rational way to measure the "share" of each source of ideas available to a given set of consumers, therefore, is to give each source equal weight. To discount media that are available to all but that garner small audiences because consumers prefer other content would understate the level of diversity from the perspective of any coherent public policy theory of the *purpose* of promoting diversity. It would be remarkable indeed for the Commission to adopt an ownership concentration metric that implies, as a social ideal, that all ideas should be equally popular.

Bruce M. Owen, Statement on Media Ownership Rules (2003) (available at: http://transition.fcc.gov/ownership/enbanc022703_docs/Owen.pdf). Are you persuaded that the availability of an idea is what is important, rather than its market share? If the Commission had adopted this argument in the documentation supporting its media ownership rules, would the Third Circuit have come out differently on any of its analysis?

5. Diversity. What kinds of diversity does the Commission pursue in its original media ownership rules? In the 2003 media ownership order, the Commission identifies five types of diversity that it says are relevant to media ownership rules: (1) viewpoint diversity ("the availability of media content reflecting a variety of perspectives"); (2) program diversity (a variety of program formats); (3) outlet diversity ("in a given market, there are multiple independently-owned firms"); (4) source diversity ("the availability of media content from a variety of content producers"); and (5) minority and female ownership diversity. 18 FCC Rcd. 13,620, ¶¶ 19, 26, 38, 42 & 46. Which of these forms of diversity is important and why? Which forms is the Commission constrained from directly pursuing? Are there other types of diversity worth pursuing, for example diversity in the type of technology used in a given market? And which of these types of diversity can be accomplished through regulations other than ownership restrictions?

6. No Good Deed Goes Unpunished. Under the statute, the Commission must repeal or modify media rules no longer in the public interest. Could the Commission, instead of promulgating the modified rules here remanded, simply have repealed the rules altogether and thereby escaped the scrutiny the Third Circuit gives in this opinion? How would the court have reviewed repeals instead of modifications? Having found it constitutional for the FCC to repeal and modify its media ownership rules and, moreover, having found the FCC's underlying reasons for scrapping the old rules to be valid, how could the court have overturned the Commission had it taken the more radical step of outright repeal instead of modification?

7. Ownership Limits for Nonbroadcast Spectrum. The FCC's move away from spectrum ownership limits has not been confined to broadcasting. The Commission has also eliminated limits on the ownership of non-broadcast spectrum. Most notably, in 2001 the Commission jettisoned two types of multiple ownership restrictions applicable to spectrum used for Commercial Mobile Radio Service, or CMRS (a generic term for commercial wireless services such as cellular telephony, paging, and digital PCS). 2000 Biennial Regulatory Review: Spectrum Aggregation Limits for Commercial Mobile Radio Services, Report and Order, 16 FCC Rcd. 22,668 (2001). One of the rules at issue forbade any single entity from controlling more than a certain number of cellular telephony licenses in a given area. The other rule was more general, capping the total amount of CMRS spectrum a given entity could control, whether it was all licensed for cellular traffic (and hence regulated under the first rule) or was instead licensed for some mixture of CMRS services. The Commission noted that the rules were promulgated when there was a duopoly on cellular service in most markets (a duopoly that the FCC had created by choosing to grant spectrum licenses to only two cellular providers in each market) but that there was now robust competition among CMRS providers and thus no need for the rules.

8. Proceedings on Remand. After *Prometheus I* remanded the media ownership regulations, the FCC commissioned several new empirical studies but took no formal actions on the rules for several years. But in 2008 the Commission voted 3–2 (with all three Republicans in favor and both Democrats opposed) to relax the newspaper/broadcast cross-ownership rule. The following order contains the Commission's ruling and discussion.

2006 QUADRENNIAL REGULATORY REVIEW — REVIEW OF THE COMMISSION'S BROADCAST OWNERSHIP RULES AND OTHER RULES ADOPTED PURSUANT TO SECTION 202 OF THE TELECOMMUNICATIONS ACT OF 1996

Report and Order and Order on Reconsideration, 23 FCC Rcd. 2010 (2008)

III. NEWSPAPER/BROADCAST CROSS-OWNERSHIP

13. The 1975 cross-ownership ban is the only Commission media ownership rule that has remained in effect without modification for over three decades. Today, we make a modest change in the rule that has the primary effect of presuming that certain limited combinations of newspaper and broadcast facilities in the largest markets are in the pub-

lic interest. In this order, we take a modest step in loosening the complete ban on cross-ownership. We adopt a presumption, in the top 20 Designated Market Areas (DMAs), that it is not inconsistent with the public interest for one entity to own a daily newspaper and a radio station or, under the following limited circumstances, a daily newspaper and a television station, if (1) the television station is not ranked among the top four stations in the DMA and (2) at least eight independent "major media voices" remain in the DMA. In all other instances, we adopt a presumption that a newspaper/broadcast station combination would not be in the public interest, with two limited exceptions, and therefore emphasize that the Commission is unlikely to approve such transactions. Taking into account these respective presumptions, in determining whether the grant of a transaction that would result in newspaper/broadcast cross-ownership is in the public interest, the Commission will consider the following factors: (1) whether the cross-ownership will increase the amount of local news disseminated through the affected media outlets in the combination; (2) whether each affected media outlet in the combination will exercise its own independent news judgment; (3) the level of concentration in the Nielsen DMA; and (4) the financial condition of the newspaper or broadcast outlet, and if the newspaper or broadcast station is in financial distress, the proposed owner's commitment to invest significantly in newsroom operations. Our cautious approach addresses the need to support the availability and sustainability of local news while not significantly increasing local concentration or harming diversity.

B. Discussion

18. As an initial matter, we reaffirm the Commission's decision to eliminate the blanket ban on newspaper/broadcast cross-ownership and replace it with a presumption that waivers of the ban are in the public interest in certain limited circumstances set forth below. The *Prometheus I* court agreed that the ban is not necessary to promote competition, diversity, or localism. First, the court agreed that the ban is not necessary to promote competition in local markets because most advertisers do not view newspapers and television stations as close substitutes. Second, the court agreed that the ban could undermine localism by preventing efficient combinations that would allow for the production of high-quality local news. Third, the court found that the ban is not necessary on grounds of diversity because of insufficient evidence that ownership influences viewpoint. Finally, the court affirmed that a complete ban is unwarranted due to the presence of other media sources in local markets, such as the Internet and cable.

21. *Relevant Marketplace Developments.* The Commission has tailored its approach to common ownership of newspapers and broadcast stations several times in its history as the media marketplace evolved. As discussed below, the current ban prohibiting the cross-ownership of newspapers and broadcast stations arose 32 years ago in an era when two mature industries—daily newspapers and broadcasting—constituted the only "mass media" providing local news and information to most American communities. In 1975, moved by a newly heightened concern about media diversity at the local level, the Commission reversed what had been its decades-old policy of encouraging newspaper/broadcast combinations. The data before us now show that the media environment has changed considerably over the past three decades. The emergence of new forms of electronic media in recent years has come at the expense of traditional media, and of newspapers in particular. Changes include a diminished number of newspaper outlets, ebbing popularity with consumers, and a notable shift in the role that traditional media outlets play in gathering and disseminating news and information. Faced with these facts, we find that the state of the marketplace today warrants a measured readjustment of the newspaper/broad-

cast rule. We believe that our revised regulation will continue to serve our goal of preserving media diversity in local markets while also providing some flexibility for new, efficient combinations in appropriate circumstances.

31. Aside from declining circulations, the Internet has also had a particularly noteworthy effect in taking away advertising from newspapers, particularly classified advertising. Advertising-oriented websites such as craigslist, eBay, and Zillow have siphoned off a large amount of revenue that newspapers large and small have counted on for decades to provide a significant and relatively stable flow of revenue. For instance, there was a $2.3 billion decline in classified revenues over five years, as reported by the [Newspaper Association of America (NAA)], from $19.6 billion in 2000 to $17.3 billion in 2005.

32. The newspaper industry faces other problems as well. At the same time that advertising revenues have flattened and circulation has declined, newspaper operational expenses have continued to rise. An index of input costs for the industry has risen steadily in recent years, climbing from 106.3 in 2000 to 122.9 in 2005 (on an index that sets 1992 input costs at 100). This means that total input costs rose by 6.3 percent in the eight years from 1992 to 2000 and by 15.6 percent in the five years from 2000 to 2005. Newspaper managers responded with renewed cost-cutting efforts, including reductions in professional staff.

38. The nearly instantaneous speed with which consumers can now communicate via the Internet has created a vastly improved two-way flow in the sharing of ideas between traditional news gatherers and news consumers, with a consequent power to affect the priority that the traditional media place on coverage of certain events and topics. Many previously passive consumers of news are already taking advantage of the opportunities the Internet allows to influence the newsgathering process. More than ever before, readers and audiences are themselves communicating with news gatherers to demand, directly and indirectly, coverage of specific topics. There are many high-profile examples of news organizations slow to pick up on a story which, after percolating among bloggers and others in the online arena, grows into an issue that traditional news media eventually cover. The erosion of newspapers' traditional gatekeeping power convinces us that newspaper combinations no longer pose the same threat to diversity that they once did. For this reason as well, a total ban on cross-ownership can no longer be justified as necessary to protect viewpoint diversity.

39. *Policy Goals.* In the 2002 Biennial Regulatory Review, Report and Order and Notice of Proposed Rulemaking, 18 FCC Rcd. 13,620 (2003), *aff'd in part and remanded in part*, *Prometheus I*, 373 F.3d at 435, *stay modified on rehearing*, No. 03-3388 (3d Cir. 2004) (*Prometheus* Rehearing Order), *cert. denied*, 545 U.S. 1123 (2005) (2002 Biennial Review Order), the Commission concluded that efficiencies from the common ownership of two media outlets may increase the amount of diverse, competitive news and local information available to the public. We continue to find evidence that cross-ownership in the largest markets can preserve the viability of newspapers without threatening diversity by allowing them to spread their operational costs across multiple platforms. In doing so, they can improve or increase the news offered by the broadcaster and the newspaper. Numerous media owners provide examples of cost savings and shared resources leading to more local coverage and better quality news coverage.

42. We have a considerable amount of empirical evidence in the record on both sides concerning the relationship between newspaper/broadcast combinations and localism. On balance, we believe the evidence suggests that some newspaper/broadcast cross-ownership combinations can enhance localism. [The Commission then summarized the results of three studies showing different, yet net positive effects of newspaper/broadcast cross-ownership on television news coverage and local content.]

46. We recognize that there is disagreement in the studies. On balance, however, we conclude that the weight of evidence indicates that cross-ownership can promote localism by increasing the amount of news and information transmitted by the co-owned outlets. The inconclusiveness of some of the data and disagreement as to the outcome of the studies, however, supports our decision to undertake a case-by-case review of particular combinations in particular markets, rather than providing hard, across-the-board limits. Under our method, we can consider facts in a particular case, with a presumption in favor of allowing newspaper and radio station or non-top four television station combinations in the top 20 markets, and a presumption against combinations in all other markets. A case-by-case approach will enable the Commission to make a more fully informed assessment that a proposed transaction in a particular market actually will increase the total amount of local news generated by the combined outlets.

IV. RADIO/TELEVISION CROSS-OWNERSHIP RULE

A. Background

81. In adopting the current rule in 1999, the Commission explained that it balanced diversity and competition concerns with the desire to permit broadcasters and the public to realize the benefits of common ownership. In the 2002 Biennial Review Order, the Commission eliminated the radio/television cross-ownership rule in its entirety by finding that it no longer remained "necessary in the public interest to ensure competition, diversity or localism." 18 FCC Rcd. at 13,768, ¶ 371. The Commission reasoned that the removal was warranted because "diversity and competition goals [would] be adequately protected by the local ownership rules" adopted in that proceeding. These rules included cross-media limits that were "specifically designed to protect diversity of viewpoint in those markets [where] consolidation of media ownership could jeopardize such diversity." The cross-media limits were challenged in *Prometheus I*. The *Prometheus I* court concluded that although "the Commission's decision to replace its cross-ownership rules with cross-media limits" was "not of itself constitutionally flawed and [did] not violate § 202(h)," it would not uphold the cross-media limits because the "Commission [did] not provide a reasoned analysis to support the limits that it chose." 373 F.3d at 397.

B. Discussion

82. We retain the radio/television cross-ownership rule currently in effect to provide protection for diversity goals in local markets and thereby serve the public interest. Our conclusion in the 2002 Biennial Review Order that the radio/television cross-ownership rule was no longer necessary to ensure viewpoint diversity was based in large part on our adoption of the cross-media limits in that proceeding. Now that the court has invalidated the cross-media limits, we must adopt diversity protection provisions to act in their place, and therefore retain the current radio/television cross-ownership rule.

V. LOCAL TELEVISION OWNERSHIP RULE

87. We find that restrictions on common ownership of television stations in local markets continue to be necessary in the public interest to protect competition for viewers and in local television advertising markets. As discussed below, we conclude that, in order to preserve adequate levels of competition within local television markets, the local television ownership rule as it is currently in effect should be retained. Accordingly, an entity may own two television stations in the same DMA if: (1) the Grade B contours of the stations do not overlap; or (2) at least one of the stations in the combination is not ranked among the top four stations in terms of audience share, *and* at least eight independently owned and operating commercial or non-commercial full-power broadcast television sta-

tions would remain in the DMA after the combination. To determine the number of voices remaining after the merger, the Commission counts those broadcast television stations whose Grade B signal contours overlap with the Grade B signal contour of at least one of the stations that would be commonly owned.

B. Discussion

97. We base our decision on our assessment that the Commission's local television ownership rule promotes competition for viewers and advertisers within local television markets. The public is best served when numerous rivals compete for a viewing audience. In the video programming market, competitors profit by attracting new audiences and by attracting existing audiences away from their competitors. Competition thus provides an incentive to television stations to invest in better programming and to provide programming that is preferred by viewers. The local community benefits from competition among broadcast television stations in the form of higher quality programming provided to viewers. As the Commission concluded in the 2002 Biennial Review Order, we cannot rely on competition from cable programmers to respond to local needs and interests because most cable programming is provided by cable networks, and those networks respond primarily to national and regional forces. Local broadcast television stations have incentives to respond to conditions in local markets, and those incentives may be diminished by mergers between stations that reduce competition to anticompetitive levels. Competition among local broadcast television stations is also necessary to preserve competition for advertising by local businesses that want to advertise their products on television. Lower advertising costs benefit consumers by promoting efficiency and by allowing firms to pass the savings on to consumers of the advertised products. In the 2002 Biennial Review Order, the Commission determined that the exercise of market power in broadcast television markets would result in targeted and non-uniform price increases to those advertisers that do not have good substitutes for broadcast television, without raising prices for those advertisers that do have good substitutes for broadcast television.

98. We decline to tighten the local television ownership rule, as requested by some commenters. We recognize that owning a second in-market station can result in substantial savings in overhead and management costs and can allow the local broadcaster to innovate by spreading its fixed costs and operating capital over a larger number of operating units and to better compete with non-broadcast content providers for advertising dollars. We find that these potential significant benefits of duopolies permitted under the parameters of the rule, in markets with a plethora of diverse voices, outweigh commenters' speculative claims that duopolies harm diversity and competition.

99. We find that a minimum of eight independently owned-and-operated television stations is appropriate to ensure that there will be robust competition in the local television marketplace. As an initial matter, the "eight voices" test will ensure that each market includes four stations affiliated with the four major networks in each market (i.e., ABC, NBC, CBS, and Fox), plus at least an equal number of independently owned-and-operated broadcast television stations that are not affiliated with a major network. Preserving the independent ownership in each local market of four stations that are neither owned by or affiliated with a major network nor commonly owned with a network affiliate in that market will help to ensure that local television stations, spurred by competition, will provide dynamic and vibrant alternative fare, including local news and public affairs programming. In addition, we believe that the eight voices test is supported by the general structure of the local television marketplace. While our 2003 rule was premised on maintaining the presence of six equal-sized competitors in the marketplace, the Third Circuit

in *Prometheus* pointed out that this assumption of equal-sized competitors was flawed. Indeed, the Commission itself has found that there is generally a significant gap between the top four stations in a market and the remaining stations. In light of this concentration among the top four stations in most markets, we believe that it is prudent to require the presence of at least four (rather than two) competitors not affiliated with a major network in order to ensure vibrant competition in the local television marketplace. We believe that such competition will ultimately benefit the public by spurring more innovative programming and more programming responsive to local needs and interests.

101. We recognize that the Commission concluded in the 2002 Biennial Review Order that the current local television ownership rule was not necessary to protect competition given "the competitive impact of other video programming outlets" on local broadcasters. 18 FCC Rcd. at 13,668, 13,671, ¶¶ 133, 140. We now reverse that determination because we find that eliminating the rule could harm competition among broadcast television stations in local markets. Because we are retaining the rule primarily to foster competition among local television stations, our determination regarding the continued need for the rule does not depend on the competitive impact of other video programming outlets. While other outlets contribute to the diversity of voices in local markets, we still find that it is necessary in the public interest to ensure that there are at least eight independently owned local television stations in order to ensure robust competition for local television viewers and the continued provision of video programming responsive to the needs and interest of viewers in local markets.

102. As we found in the 2002 Biennial Review Order, we continue to believe that combinations of top four stations should be prohibited because mergers of those stations would be the most deleterious to competition. The top four prohibition minimizes the likelihood that the market share of two merged stations will significantly overtake the market share of the largest station in a local market, which, as discussed in the 2002 Biennial Review Order, could create welfare harms. We also find that, in general, a significant "cushion" of audience share percentage points continues to separate the top four stations from the fifth-ranked stations. As noted above, the number of locally owned stations remained fairly constant, with only a slight increase in the number of stations and a slight decrease in the number of owners, from 2002 to 2005. In addition, allowing two top four stations to merge would harm competition in the local broadcast television advertising market because the top four networks (whose affiliates tend to be the top four broadcasters in a given market) enjoy a large and growing advantage over other broadcasters with regard to advertising volume and prices. Accordingly, we find that comments suggesting that the rule is no longer justified are unpersuasive. Prohibiting mergers between the top four television stations in a market prevents well-established competitive harms.

103. In the 2002 Biennial Review Order, we also concluded that the current rule potentially threatens local programming and that the efficiencies to be gained by relaxing the rule could result in a higher quantity and quality of local news and public affairs programming. We find that the record now before us is unpersuasive regarding the effects of multiple ownership on local programming. Given our finding that there is insufficient evidence to conclude that the current rule threatens local programming, we conclude that it serves the public interest to retain it in order to preserve vigorous competition among local television stations.

VI. LOCAL RADIO OWNERSHIP RULE

110. [W]e conclude that the current local radio ownership rule, including the market definition as revised in the 2002 Biennial Review Order, remains "necessary in the pub-

lic interest" to protect competition in local radio markets. As directed by the *Prometheus I* court, we also provide a reasoned justification for our decision to retain the existing numerical limits on local radio ownership rule in the 2002 Biennial Review Order. Accordingly, an entity may own, operate, or control (1) up to eight commercial radio stations, not more than five of which are in the same service (i.e., AM or FM), in a radio market with 45 or more full-power, commercial and noncommercial radio stations; (2) up to seven commercial radio stations, not more than four of which are in the same service, in a radio market with between 30 and 44 (inclusive) full-power, commercial and noncommercial radio stations; (3) up to six commercial radio stations, not more than four of which are in the same service, in a radio market with between 15 and 29 (inclusive) full-power, commercial and noncommercial radio stations; and (4) up to five commercial radio stations, not more than three of which are in the same service, in a radio market with 14 or fewer full-power, commercial and noncommercial radio stations, except that an entity may not own, operate, or control more than 50 percent of the stations in such a market.

Dissenting Statement of Commissioner Michael J. Copps

Let's be careful not get too carried away with the supposed premise for all this contortionism, namely the poor state of local newspapers. The death of the traditional news business is often greatly exaggerated. The truth remains that the profit margins for the newspaper industry last year averaged around 17.8%; the figure is even higher for broadcast stations. As the head of the Newspaper Association of America put it in a Letter to the Editor of the Washington Post on July 2 of this year: "The reality is that newspaper companies remain solidly profitable and significant generators of free cash flow." John Sturm, Healthy Newspapers, N.Y. Times, July 2, 2007. And as Member after Member [of] Congress has reminded us, our job is not to ensure that newspapers are profitable—which they mostly are. Our job is to protect the principles of localism, diversity and competition in our media.

Were newspapers momentarily discombobulated by the rise of the Internet? Probably so. Are they moving now to turn threat into opportunity? Yes, and with signs of success. Far from newspapers being gobbled up by the Internet, we ought to be far more concerned with the threat of big media joining forces with big broadband providers to take the wonderful Internet we know down the same road of consolidation and control by the few that has already inflicted such heavy damage on our traditional media.

Despite all the talk you may hear today about the threat to newspapers from the Internet and new technologies, today's Order actually deals with something quite old-fashioned. Powerful companies are using political muscle to sneak through rule changes that let them profit at the expense of the public interest. They are seeking to improve their economic prospects by capturing a larger percentage of the news business in communities all across the United States.

When I think about where the FCC has been and where it is today, two conclusions:

First, the consolidation we have seen so far and the decision to treat broadcasting as just another business has *not* produced a media system that does a better job serving most Americans. Quite the opposite. Rather than reviving the news business, it has led to *less* localism, *less* diversity of opinion and ownership, *less* serious political coverage, *fewer* jobs for journalists, and the list goes on.

Second, I think we have learned that the purest form of commercialism and high quality news make uneasy bedfellows. As my own hero, Franklin Delano Roosevelt, put it in a letter to Joseph Pulitzer, "I have always been firmly persuaded that our newspapers cannot be edited in the interests of the general public from the counting room." Letter from

Franklin Delano Roosevelt, U.S. President, to Joseph Pulitzer, Editor (Nov. 1938). So, too, for broadcast journalism. This is not to say that good journalism is incompatible with making a profit—I believe that both interests can and must be balanced. But when TV and radio stations are no longer required by law to serve their local communities, and are owned by huge national corporations dedicated to cutting costs through economies of scale, it should be no surprise that, in essence, viewers and listeners have become the products that broadcasters sell to advertisers.

We could have been—should have been—here today lauding the best efforts of government to reverse these trends and to promote a media environment that actually strengthens American democracy rather than weakens it.

Last time a lot of insiders were surprised by the country's reaction. This time they should be forewarned. I hope, I really hope, that today's majority decision will be consigned to the fate it deserves and that one day in the not too distant future we can look back upon it as an aberration from which we eventually recovered. We have had a dangerous, decades-long flirtation with media consolidation. I would welcome a little romance with the public interest for a change.

Notes and Questions

1. Better Now? In contrast to the 2002 Order, which relaxed a number of media ownership rules, this 2008 Order changed only the newspaper/broadcast cross-ownership rule. What do you think explains the Commission's decision to change only that one rule? The negative public reaction to the 2002 Order? The negative congressional reaction? *Prometheus I*? Something else?

2. Senate Disapproval. If the FCC thought that relaxing just the newspaper/broadcast cross-ownership rule would avoid significant political opposition, it was mistaken. In May 2008, the Senate passed by voice vote Senate Joint Resolution 28, which provided in its entirety: "Congress disapproves the rule submitted by the Federal Communications Commission relating to broadcast media ownership (Report and Order FCC 07-216), received by Congress on February 22, 2008, and such rule shall have no force or effect." S.R.J. Res. 28, 110th Cong., (2008). This provision was not enacted into law.

3. Why This Rule? Did the Commission adequately explain why it singled out this particular rule to change? It emphasized that newspapers are losing readers and thus revenue streams, but the same thing is true for conventional broadcasters, whose viewership has been steadily decreasing for more than thirty years (as cable's percent of viewers has been increasing). And, as Commissioner Copps notes in his dissent, newspapers were still earning profits.

4. Empirics. How much of the debate is an empirical one—whether newspapers will in fact serve as gatekeepers for most readers, whether consolidation will produce more local news coverage or less, etc.? The FCC sought to shed light on these questions by commissioning not only studies but also peer reviews of those studies (we deleted the FCC's discussions of those peer reviews for space reasons). But the studies and peer reviews did not resolve matters to the satisfaction of Commissioner Copps and many other critics. Is the answer that we need more empirical data? If so, exactly what sort of data? Is the answer that empirical data do not tell us very much? But why not? Each side is, after all, making factual claims about what has happened and will happen in a world of media consolidation. Is the answer that empirical data could resolve the questions for fair-minded people but that one or both sides are so entrenched that they will refuse to acknowledge data with which they disagree? If so, is that an indictment of the FCC? Of the entire political process?

5. "The death of the traditional news business is often greatly exaggerated." That was the view of Commissioner Copps in his dissent from the relaxation of the newspaper/broadcast cross-ownership rules. The year immediately after the FCC issued its 2008 Order saw serious financial difficulties for many newspapers, leading to cutbacks in coverage and major cuts in staff. Some major newspapers ceased publication (e.g., the Rocky Mountain News and the Seattle Post-Intelligencer), and others had near-death experiences (e.g., the San Francisco Chronicle and the Boston Globe). And many commentators—including newspaper publishers—expressed skepticism about the long-term viability of newspapers. Does this mean that Commissioner Copps's more optimistic view of the economic position of newspapers should now be jettisoned? If so, cross-ownership or other forms of consolidation are not the only means the government could use to help newspapers. And it is always possible that the naysayers are wrong and that in fact newspapers are on the verge of a great upswing in their economic prospects. So what, if any, effect should newspapers' current difficulties have on FCC ownership policies?

6. *Prometheus II. Prometheus I* was followed by *Prometheus II*, which involved a challenge to the order excerpted above (and to an order addressing broadcast ownership diversity issued the same day, discussed in Chapter Five). Prometheus Radio Project v. FCC, 652 F.3d 431 (3d Cir. 2011). In large part, the court affirmed the FCC's new rules. The court remanded on two grounds. The first, as noted in Chapter Five, was that the Commission had failed to demonstrate how its preference for small businesses in media markets would further a goal of fostering minority and women ownership of stations. The second was that the FCC had not given sufficient notice of the manner in which it would address newspaper/broadcast cross-ownership. The FCC's notice following the court's 2004 decision did say that the FCC was reconsidering the issue, but the court found it deficient because it did not provide a specific draft rule (or a range of possible options) that the agency was proposing. 2006 Quadrennial Regulatory Review—Review of the Commission's Broadcast Ownership Rules and Other Rules Adopted Pursuant to Section 202 of the Telecommunications Act of 1996, Further Notice of Proposed Rulemaking, 21 FCC Rcd. 8834 (2006).

---

§ 10.B. Structural Regulation of Cable Providers

In this section, we turn our attention to the structural rules that have tried to shape the cable television market by limiting the market power enjoyed both by particular cable operators and by the cable industry overall. These rules are intended to protect two groups: firms that supply program content to cable operators and firms that distribute program content by technologies other than cable.

Consider first the restrictions designed to benefit firms that supply programs. Many firms create and produce informational, educational, and entertainment programming that they then supply to cable operators—as well as to broadcasters, operators of direct broadcast satellite (DBS) television, and so on. Among these firms are the major Hollywood production studios, companies that operate specialized cable networks such as USA and MTV, and the major professional sports leagues. These firms worry about two threats. First, they worry that a given cable operator might grow so large that it will have monopolistic purchasing power and be able to demand content at particularly low prices or under particularly favorable terms. Second, they worry that cable providers will start to produce and favor their own content, effectively blocking independent program suppliers from their wires.

As always, these concerns could be addressed in part by antitrust law, as we discuss in Chapter Eleven. But they have also been addressed by cable-specific regulation. The first concern is addressed by the FCC's rules on horizontal ownership. Section 11(c)(2) of the 1992 Cable Act requires the Commission to promulgate rules "establishing reasonable limits on the number of cable subscribers" a given cable operator can reach through commonly owned or controlled cable systems. Cable Television Consumer Protection and Competition Act of 1992, Pub. L. No. 102-385, § 11(c)(2), 106 Stat. 1460, 1487–88. In implementing this law, the FCC developed a rule that forbids a single cable provider from serving, through owned or controlled cable systems, more than 30% of all multiple video programming distribution (MVPD) subscribers nationwide. Note that the latter number includes not just cable subscribers (which would have constrained cable operators more) but all subscribers to services comparable to cable, such as DBS and video services delivered over the telephone network. (As we shall see, the D.C. Circuit invalidated the FCC rule and remanded the matter to the FCC for reconsideration.)

The second concern—the worry that cable providers will favor content produced in-house or by affiliated firms—is addressed by the FCC's rules limiting vertical integration, again promulgated under the authority of § 11(c)(2) of the 1992 Cable Act. Other provisions of the 1992 Act focus less on possible harms to program suppliers than on possible harms to competing program distribution technologies. The must-carry provisions discussed in Chapter Nine fit into this category, protecting as they do conventional broadcasters. So, too, does § 628 of the Communications Act, codified at 47 U.S.C. § 548, an umbrella provision designed to increase "competition and diversity in the multichannel video programming market." 47 U.S.C. § 548(a). In fact, § 628 requires the FCC to issue regulations that, among other things, prohibit cable operators from causing affiliated content providers to discriminate against other players in the multichannel video programming market. *Id.* § 548(c)(2)(B). These regulations are often referred to as the "program access rules" because they ensure that MVPD rivals to the cable incumbents have access to programming affiliated with established cable providers.

The materials that follow consider in greater detail these efforts to protect program suppliers as reflected in the FCC's regulations affecting the size (by market share of subscribers) and degree of vertical integration of cable operators. In studying these materials, be sure to ask yourself what specific fears each regulation addresses, whether those fears are well founded, to what extent each regulation is likely to be effective in mitigating the identified problem, and what alternatives the FCC might have considered.

§ 10.B.1. Judicial Review of the FCC's Cable Ownership Rules

Section 11(c)(2) of the 1992 Cable Act required the Commission to conduct a proceeding

(A) to prescribe rules and regulations establishing reasonable limits on the number of cable subscribers a person is authorized to reach through cable systems owned by such person, or in which such person has an attributable interest;

(B) to prescribe rules and regulations establishing reasonable limits on the number of channels on a cable system that can be occupied by a video programmer in which a cable operator has an attributable interest; and

(C) to consider the necessity and appropriateness of imposing limitations on the degree to which multichannel video programming distributors may engage in the creation or production of video programming.

Id. § 11(c)(2) (codified at 47 U.S.C. § 533(f)(1)).

The Commission implemented these statutory provisions by prescribing both national subscriber limits (in response to subsection (A)) and channel occupancy limits (in response to subsection (B)). The Commission declined, however, to impose any limitations on cable operators' creation or production of video programming. In 2001, the D.C. Circuit evaluated the FCC rules, invalidating them in the opinion reproduced below.

TIME WARNER ENTERTAINMENT CO. v. FCC [*TIME WARNER II*]
240 F.3d 1126 (D.C. Cir. 2001)

Opinion for the Court filed by Circuit Judge WILLIAMS, in which Circuit Judges RANDOLPH and TATEL concur.

WILLIAMS, Circuit Judge:

Section 11(c) of the Cable Television Consumer Protection and Competition Act of 1992, Pub. L. No. 102-385, 106 Stat. 1460 (1992 Cable Act), amends 47 U.S.C. § 533 to direct the Federal Communications Commission to set two types of limits on cable operators. The first type is horizontal, addressing operators' scale: "limits on the number of cable subscribers a person is authorized to reach through cable systems owned by such person, or in which such person has an attributable interest." 47 U.S.C. § 533(f)(1)(A). The second type is vertical, addressing operators' integration with "programmers" (suppliers of programs to be carried over cable systems): "limits on the number of channels on a cable system that can be occupied by a video programmer in which a cable operator has an attributable interest." 47 U.S.C. § 533(f)(1)(B). The FCC has duly promulgated regulations. Petitioners Time Warner and AT&T challenge the horizontal limit as in excess of statutory authority, as unconstitutional infringements of their freedom of speech, and as products of arbitrary and capricious decision making which violate the Administrative Procedure Act. Time Warner similarly challenges the vertical limit. Together with AT&T, Time Warner also challenges as arbitrary and capricious the rules for determining what counts as an "attributable interest." Concluding that the FCC has not met its burden under the First Amendment and, in part, lacks statutory authority for its actions, we remand for further consideration of both limits. In addition we vacate specific portions of the attribution rules as lacking rational justification.

* * *

The horizontal rule imposes a 30% limit on the number of subscribers that may be served by a multiple cable system operator (MSO). *See* 47 C.F.R. § 76.503; Implementation of Section 11(c) of the Cable Television Consumer Protection and Competition Act of 1992, Horizontal Ownership Limits, Third Report and Order, 14 FCC Rcd. 19,098, ¶ 55 (1999) (Third Report). Both the numerator and denominator of this fraction include only current subscribers to multichannel video program distributor (MVPD) services. Subscribers include not only users of traditional cable services but also subscribers to non-cable MVPD services such as Direct Broadcast Satellite (DBS), a rapidly growing segment of the MVPD market. The Commission pointed out that under this provision the nominal 30% limit would allow a cable operator to serve 36.7% of the nation's cable subscribers if it served none by DBS. In an express effort to encourage competition through new provision of cable, the Commission excluded from any MSO's numerator all new subscribers signed up by virtue of "overbuilding," the industry's term for cable laid in competition with a pre-existing cable operator. Further, subscribers to a service franchised after the rule's adoption (October 20, 1999) do not go into an MSO's numerator, even if not the result of an overbuild. As a result, the rule's main bite is on firms obtaining subscribers through merger or acquisition.

The vertical limit is currently set at 40% of channel capacity, reserving 60% for programming by non-affiliated firms. *See* 47 C.F.R. § 76.504; Implementation of Sections 12 and 19 of the Cable Television Consumer Protection and Competition Act of 1992, Horizontal and Vertical Ownership Limits, Second Report and Order, 8 FCC Rcd. 8565, ¶ 68 (1993) (Second Report); Implementation of Section 11(c) of the Cable Television Consumer Protection and Competition Act of 1992, Vertical Ownership Limits, Memorandum Opinion and Order on Reconsideration of the Second Report and Order, 10 FCC Rcd. 7364, ¶ 14 (1995). Channels assigned to broadcast stations, leased access, and for public, educational, or governmental uses are included in the calculation of channel capacity. Capacity over 75 channels is not subject to the limit, so a cable operator is never required to reserve more than 45 channels for others (.60 × 75 = 45).

As cable operators, Time Warner and AT&T "exercise[] editorial discretion in selecting the programming [they] will make available to [their] subscribers," Time Warner Ent-m't Co. v. United States, 211 F.3d 1313, 1316 (D.C. Cir. 2000) (*Time Warner I*), and are "entitled to the protection of the speech and press provisions of the First Amendment," Turner Broad. Sys., Inc. v. FCC, 512 U.S. 622, 636 (1994) (*Turner I*). The horizontal limit interferes with petitioners' speech rights by restricting the number of viewers to whom they can speak. The vertical limit restricts their ability to exercise their editorial control over a portion of the content they transmit.

In *Time Warner I* we upheld the statutory provisions against a facial attack, after finding them subject to intermediate rather than, as the cable firms argued, strict scrutiny. The regulations here present a related but independent set of questions. Constitutional authority to impose some limit is not authority to impose any limit imaginable.

Under the formula set forth in United States v. O'Brien, 391 U.S. 367, 377 (1968), and reaffirmed by Turner Broadcasting System, Inc. v. Federal Communications Commission, 520 U.S. 180, 189 (1997) (*Turner II*), a governmental regulation subject to intermediate scrutiny will be upheld if it "advances important governmental interests unrelated to the suppression of free speech and does not burden substantially more speech than necessary to further those interests." *Id.* (quoting *O'Brien*, 391 U.S. at 377).

The interests asserted in support of the horizontal and vertical limits are the same interrelated interests that we found sufficient to support the statutory scheme in *Time Warner I*: "the promotion of diversity in ideas and speech" and "the preservation of competition." *Time Warner I*, 211 F.3d at 1319; *see also Turner I*, 512 U.S. at 662–64 (concluding that both qualify as important governmental interests).

* * *

The FCC asserts that a 30% horizontal limit satisfies its statutory obligation to ensure that no single "cable operator or group of cable operators can unfairly impede ... the flow of video programming from the video programmer to the consumer," 47 U.S.C. § 533(f)(2)(A), while adequately respecting the benefits of clustering [i.e., the strategy under which MSOs concentrate their operations within a particular geographic region] and the economies of scale that are thought to come with larger size. *See* Third Report ¶ 61. In setting the limit at 30%, it assumed there was a serious risk of collusion. But while collusion is a form of anti-competitive behavior that implicates an important government interest, the FCC has not presented the "substantial evidence" required by *Turner I* and *Turner II* that such collusion has in fact occurred or is likely to occur; so its assumptions are mere conjecture.

Part VI of the Third Report lays out the calculations that lead the FCC to the 30% limit. First the FCC determines that the average cable network needs to reach 15 million subscribers to be economically viable. This is 18.56% of the roughly 80 million MVPD subscribers, and the FCC rounds it up to 20% of such subscribers. The FCC then divines that the average cable programmer will succeed in reaching only about 50% of the subscribers linked to cable companies that *agree* to carry its programming, because of channel capacity, "programming tastes of particular cable operators," or other factors. Third Report ¶ 49. The average programmer therefore requires an "open field" of 40% of the market to be viable (.20/.50 = .40).

Finally, to support the 30% limit that it says is necessary to assure this minimum, the Commission reasons as follows: With a 30% limit, a programmer has an "open field" of 40% of the market even if the two largest cable companies deny carriage, acting "individually or collusively." *Id.* ¶ 53. A 50% rule is inadequate because, if a duopoly were to result, "[t]he probability of tacit collusion is higher with 2 competitors than 3 competitors." *Id.* ¶ 51. Even if collusion were not to occur, *independent* rejections by two MSOs could doom a new programmer, thwarting congressional intent as the Commission saw it. See *id.* A 40% limit is insufficient for the same reason: "two MSOs, ... representing a total of 80% of the market, might decline to carry the new network" and leave only 20% "open," which by hypothesis is not enough (because of the 50% success rate). *Id.* ¶ 52. Although the Commission doesn't spell out the intellectual process, it is necessarily defining the requisite "open field" as the residue of the market after a programmer is turned down either (1) by one cable company acting alone, or (2) by a set of companies acting either (a) collusively or (b) independently but nonetheless in some way that, because of the combined effect of their choices, threatens fulfillment of the statutory purposes. We address the FCC's authority to regulate each of these scenarios in turn.

The Commission is on solid ground in asserting authority to be sure that no single company could be in a position single-handedly to deal a programmer a death blow. Statutory authority flows plainly from the instruction that the Commission's regulations "ensure that no cable operator or group of cable operators can unfairly impede, either because of *the size of any individual operator* or because of joint actions of operators of sufficient size, the flow of video programming from the video programmer to the consumer." 47 U.S.C. §533(f)(2)(A) (emphasis added). Constitutional authority is equally plain. As the Supreme Court said in *Turner II*: "We have identified a corresponding 'governmental purpose of the highest order' in ensuring public access to 'a multiplicity of information sources.'" 520 U.S. at 190 (quoting *Turner I*, 512 U.S. at 663). If this interest in diversity is to mean anything in this context, the government must be able to ensure that a programmer have at least two conduits through which it can reach the number of viewers needed for viability—independent of concerns over anticompetitive conduct.

Assuming the validity of the premises supporting the FCC's conclusion that a 40% "open field" is necessary (a question that we need not answer here), the statute's express concern for the act of "any individual operator" would justify a horizontal limit of 60%. To reach the 30% limit, the FCC's action necessarily involves one or the other of two additional propositions: Either there is a material risk of collusive denial of carriage by two or more companies, or the statute authorizes the Commission to protect programmers against the risk of completely *independent* rejections by two or more companies leaving less than 40% of the MVPD audience potentially accessible. Neither proposition is sound.

First, we consider whether there is record support for inferring a non-conjectural risk of collusive rejection. Either Congress or the Commission could supply that record, and we take them in that order. We give deference to the predictive judgments of Congress, see *Turner II*, 520 U.S. at 195–96, but Congress appears to have made no judgment regarding collusion. The statute plainly alludes to the *possibility* of collusion when it authorizes regulations to protect against "*joint* actions by a group of operators of sufficient size." 47 U.S.C. §533(f)(2)(A) (emphasis added). But this phrase, while granting the Commission authority to take action in the event that it finds collusion extant or likely, is not itself a congressional finding of actual or probable collusion. Such findings have not been made. No reference to collusion appears in the Act's findings or policy, nor in the legislative history discussing the horizontal or vertical limits. *See* H.R. Rep. No. 102-628, at 40–43 (1992) (House Report); S. Rep. No. 102-92, at 24–29, 32–34, reprinted in 1992 U.S.C.C.A.N. 1133, at 1156–62, 1165–67 (Senate Report). It was thus appropriate for the FCC to describe Congress's reference to "joint" action as merely a "legislative *assumption*." Third Report ¶ 43 (emphasis added).

The Commission's own findings amount to precious little. It says only:

> The legislative assumption [about joint action] is not unreasonable given an environment in which all the larger operators in the industry are vertically integrated so that all are both buyers and sellers of programming and have mutual incentives to reach carriage decisions beneficial to each other. Operators have incentives to agree to buy their programming from one another. Moreover, they have incentives to encourage one another to carry the same non-vertically integrated programming in order to share the costs of such programming.

Id. None of these assertions is supported in the record. The Commission never explains why the vertical integration of MSOs gives them "mutual incentive to reach carriage decisions beneficial to each other," what may be the firms' "incentives to buy ... from one another," or what the probabilities are that firms would engage in reciprocal buying (presumably to reduce each other's average programming costs). After all, the economy is filled with firms that, like MSOs, display partial upstream vertical integration. If that phenomenon implies the sort of collusion the Commission infers, one would expect the Commission to be able to point to examples. Yet it names none. Further, even if one accepts the proposition that an MSO could benefit from sharing the services of specific programmers, programming is not more attractive for this purpose merely because it originates with another MSO's affiliate rather than with an independent.

The only justification that the FCC offers in support of its collusion hypothesis is the economic commonplace that, all other things being equal, collusion is less likely when there are more firms. This observation will always be true, although marginally less so for each additional firm; but by itself it lends no insight into the question of what the appropriate horizontal limit is. *Turner I* demands that the FCC do more than "simply 'posit the existence of the disease sought to be cured.'" *Turner I*, 512 U.S. at 664. It requires that the FCC draw "reasonable inferences based on substantial evidence." *Turner I*, 512 U.S. at 666. Substantial evidence does not require a complete factual record—we must give appropriate deference to predictive judgments that necessarily involve the expertise and experience of the agency. *See Turner II*, 520 U.S. at 196. But the FCC has put forth no evidence at all that indicates the prospects for collusion.

That having been said, we do not foreclose the possibility that there are theories of anti-competitive behavior other than collusion that may be relevant to the horizontal limit and on which the FCC may be able to rely on remand. *See* 47 U.S.C. §533(f)(1). Indeed, Congress considered, among other things, the ability of MSOs dominant in specific cable markets to extort equity from programmers or force exclusive contracts on them. A single MSO, acting alone rather than "jointly," might perhaps be able to do so while serving somewhat less than the 60% of the market (i.e., less than the fraction that would allow it unilaterally to lock out a new cable programmer) despite the existence of antitrust laws and specific behavioral prohibitions enacted as part of the 1992 Cable Act, *see* 47 U.S.C. § 536, and the risk might justify a prophylactic limit under the statute. *See Time Warner I*, 211 F.3d at 1322–23. So the absence of any showing of a serious risk of collusion does not *necessarily* preclude a finding of a sufficient governmental interest in preventing unfair competition. (We express no opinion on whether exploitation of a monopoly position in a specific cable market to extract rents that would otherwise flow to programmers alone gives rise to an "important governmental interest" justifying a burden on speech.) But the FCC made no attempt to justify its regulation on these grounds.

With the risk of collusion inadequately substantiated to support the 30% limit and no attempt to find other anticompetitive behavior, there remains the Commission's alternative ground—that programming choices made "unilaterally" by multiple cable companies, Third Report ¶ 51, might reduce a programmer's "open field" below the 40% benchmark. The only support the Commission offered for regulation based on this possibility was the idea that every additional chance for a programmer to secure access would enhance diversity:

> [T]he 30% limit serves the salutary purpose of ensuring that there will be at least 4 MSOs in the marketplace. The rule thus maximizes the potential number of MSOs that will purchase programming. With more MSOs making purchasing decisions, this increases the likelihood that the MSOs will make different programming choices and a greater variety of media voices will therefore be available to the public.

Id. ¶ 54. Petitioners challenge the FCC's authority to regulate for this purpose on both constitutional and statutory grounds.

We have some concern how far such a theory may be pressed against First Amendment norms. Everything else being equal, each additional "voice" may be said to enhance diversity. And in this special context, every additional splintering of the cable industry increases the number of *combinations* of companies whose acceptance would in the aggregate lay the foundations for a programmer's viability. But at some point, surely, the marginal value of such an increment in "diversity" would not qualify as an "important" governmental interest. Is moving from 100 possible combinations to 101 "important"? It is not clear to us how a court could determine the point where gaining such an increment is no longer important. And it would be odd to discover that although a newspaper that is the only general daily in a metropolitan area cannot be subjected to a right of reply, *see* Miami Herald Publishing Co. v. Tornillo, 418 U.S. 241 (1974), it could in the name of diversity be forced to self-divide. Certainly the Supreme Court has not gone so far.

We need not face that issue, however, because we conclude that Congress has not given the Commission authority to impose, solely on the basis of the "diversity" precept, a limit that does more than guarantee a programmer two possible outlets (each of them a market adequate for viability). We analyze the agency action under the familiar framework of Chevron USA, Inc. v. Natural Resources Defense Council, Inc., 467 U.S. 837 (1984). If we find (using traditional tools of statutory interpretation) that Congress has resolved the question, that is the end of the matter.

We begin with the statutory language. The relevant section requires the FCC to ensure that no cable operator or group of cable operators can unfairly impede, either because of the size of any individual operator or because of joint actions by a group of operators of sufficient size, the flow of video programming from the video programmer to the consumer.

47 U.S.C. §533(f)(2)(A).

The language addresses only "unfair[]" impediments to the flow of programming. The word "unfair" is of course extremely vague. Certainly, the action of several firms that is "joint," in the sense of collusive, may often entail unfairness of a conventional sort. The statute goes further, plainly treating exercise of editorial discretion by a single cable operator as "unfair" simply because that operator is the only game in town. (And *Time Warner I* authoritatively determines that the government may constitutionally impose limits solely on that ground.) But we cannot see how the word unfair could plausibly apply to the legitimate, independent editorial choices of multiple MSOs. A broad interpretation is plausible *only* for actions that impinge at least to some degree on the interest in competition that lay at the heart of Congress's concern. The Commission's reading of the clause effectively deletes the word "joint" and opens the door to illimitable restrictions in the name of diversity.

On the record before us, we conclude that the 30% horizontal limit is in excess of statutory authority. While a 60% limit might be appropriate as necessary to ensure that programmers had an adequate "open field" even in the face of rejection by the largest company, the present record supports no more. In addition, the statute allows the Commission to act prophylactically against the risk of "unfair" conduct by cable operators that might unduly impede the flow of programming, either by the "joint" actions of two or more companies or the independent action of a single company of sufficient size. But the Commission has pointed to nothing in the record supporting a non-conjectural risk of anticompetitive behavior, either by collusion or other means. Accordingly, we reverse and remand with respect to the 30% rule.

* * *

The FCC presents its 40% vertical limit as advancing the same interests invoked in support of its statutory authority to adopt the rule: diversity in programming and fair competition. As with the horizontal rules the FCC must defend the rules themselves under intermediate scrutiny and justify its chosen limit as not burdening substantially more speech than necessary. Far from satisfying this test, the FCC seems to have plucked the 40% limit out of thin air.

The FCC relies almost exclusively on the congressional findings that vertical integration in the cable industry could "make it difficult for non-cable affiliated ... programmers to secure carriage on vertically integrated cables systems" and that "vertically integrated program suppliers have the incentive and the ability to favor their affiliated cable operators ... and program distributors." Second Report ¶41 (citing 1992 Cable Act §2(a)(5)). Regulatory limits in response to these consequences would "increase the diversity of voices available to the public." Second Report ¶42 (citing Senate Report at 80).

We recognize that in drawing a numerical line an agency will ultimately indulge in some inescapable residue of arbitrariness; even if 40% is a highly justifiable pick, no one could expect the Commission to show why it was materially better than 39% or 41%. But to pass even the arbitrary and capricious standard, the agency must at least reveal "'a rational connection between the facts found and the choice made.'" Dickson v. Sec'y of Def., 68 F.3d 1396, 1404–05 (D.C. Cir. 1995) (quoting Motor Vehicle Mfrs. Ass'n v. State Farm Mut. Auto. Ins. Co., 463 U.S. 29, 43 (1983)). Here the FCC must also meet First Amendment intermediate scrutiny. Yet it appears to provide nothing but the conclusion that "we believe that a 40% limit is appropriate to balance the goals." *See* Second Report ¶ 68. What are the conditions that make 50% too high and 30% too low? How great is the risk presented by current market conditions? These questions are left unanswered by the Commission's discussion.

In fairness, the FCC does make an attempt to review some relevant conditions. The FCC cites the House Report's conclusion that "some" vertically integrated MSOs favor their affiliates and "may" discriminate against others. *Id.* ¶ 42 (citing House Report at 43). But it also notes a report that none of the top five MSOs "showed a pattern" of favoring their affiliates. *Id.* ¶ 43. Indeed, the FCC concludes that "vertical relationships had increased both the quality and quantity of cable programming services." *Id.* ¶ 44. But still it settled on a limit of 40%. There is no effort to link the numerical limits to the benefits and detriments depicted. Further, given the pursuit of diversity, one might expect some inquiry into whether innovative independent originators of programming find greater success selling to affiliated or to unaffiliated programming firms, but there is none.

We find that the FCC has failed to justify its vertical limit as not burdening substantially more speech than necessary. Accordingly, we reverse and remand to the FCC for further consideration.

Notes and Questions

1. Why Horizontal and Vertical Restrictions? As the opinion notes, Congress mandated both horizontal and vertical restrictions. Why both? Once effective horizontal restrictions exist, what public purpose is achieved by the rules limiting vertical integration? How, for example, could an MSO that accounted for, say, ten percent of cable subscribers nationwide hope to benefit by favoring programming in which it has an "attributable interest" over programming that the market prefers? Conversely, once effective vertical restrictions exist, what purpose is served by horizontal restrictions? And what of those leased access channels? Even putting the horizontal limitations aside, isn't leased access sufficient to protect unaffiliated programmers? If not, then why have the leased access rules in the first place?

2. Prophylactic Regulation versus Antitrust. In theory, an expert agency can institute prophylactic rules that can make case-by-case antitrust oversight unnecessary. But one question is whether, in practice, such rules operate effectively. In the case of the cable ownership restrictions, they have yet to take effect. In light of the experience of these rules and the media ownership rules, what are the merits of such rules as opposed to simply relying on antitrust law?

3. Market Power. As the opinion notes, market power can be exercised either unilaterally or collectively (i.e., collusion). The opinion suggests, however, that arguments based on prophylactic concerns must be developed with considerable care—i.e., the FCC is not entitled to presume that a limited number of providers will collude. Was the court too harsh on the FCC's "open field" analysis?

4. The First Amendment and Deference. Courts, as in *Turner II*, insist that, when subjecting statutes to First Amendment scrutiny, they defer to congressional judgments. Does the same level of deference apply when Congress delegates to the FCC the authority to make the relevant policy judgment? Would the analysis in *Time Warner II* differ if the court simply engaged in the usual review of administrative decisions (under the Administrative Procedure Act) as opposed to under the First Amendment? Does the court's approach represent a misuse of the First Amendment?

5. Diversity. The court attaches little weight to the FCC's claim that diversity concerns supported the imposition of the ownership restrictions. Do you think that the court is responding to the concern, also evinced in the *Schurz* case (which invalidated the financial interest and syndication rules), that the FCC invokes diversity as a "fudge factor"?

6. Limits on Creating Programming. Section 11(c)(2) of the 1992 Cable Act not only required the Commission to promulgate rules regarding vertical integration and horizontal concentration but also required the Commission to "consider the necessity and appropriateness of imposing limitations on the degree to which multichannel video programming distributors may engage in the creation or production of video programming." 1992 Cable Act §§ 11(c)(2), 613(f)(1)(C). Interestingly, in just a few small paragraphs of its first order on vertical integration limits, the Commission determined that no restrictions were necessary. "In view of the structural and behavioral restrictions already required under the 1992 Act, we do not believe that additional restrictions on the ability of multichannel distributors to engage in the creation or production of video programming are warranted at the present time. We conclude that at the present time the objectives of such a restriction are fully addressed by the other provisions ... of the 1992 Cable Act." Implementation of Sections 11 and 13 of the Cable Television Consumer Protection and Competition Act of 1992: Horizontal and Vertical Ownership Limits, Second Report and Order, 8 FCC Rcd. 8565, ¶ 106 (1993). This category was the only category for which the Commission had the discretion to decide not to regulate. Given its decision, do you think the Commission would also have chosen not to promulgate vertical or horizontal restraints, were those options available? If so, what, if anything, should that tell Congress?

7. "As Applied" Challenge versus Facial Challenge. The *Time Warner II* case above ended an almost decade-long litigation. Immediately after the 1992 Cable Act was passed, cable providers challenged the ownership restriction provision on First Amendment grounds, claiming that, on its face, the statute was unconstitutional. After a series of decisions, the D.C. Circuit ultimately concluded, in *Time Warner I*, that neither the subscriber limits provision nor the channel occupancy provision facially violated the First Amendment. Nonetheless, in the case above, the D.C. Circuit concluded that the regulations could not survive an "as applied" challenge. What, if anything, does this long course of litigation tell us?

8. Remand Proceedings. In 2007, the FCC finally acted on the D.C. Circuit's remand order in the Commission's Cable Horizontal and Vertical Ownership Limits and Attribution Rules, Fourth Report & Order and Further Notice of Proposed Rulemaking, 23 FCC Rcd. 2134 (2008). The matter, predictably, returned to the D.C. Circuit, which in 2009 again vacated the Commission's rules.

COMCAST CORP. v. FCC
579 F.3d 1 (D.C. Cir. 2009)

Opinion for the Court filed by Circuit Judge GINSBURG, in which Circuit Judge KAVANAUGH and Senior Circuit Judge RANDOLPH concur.

GINSBURG, Circuit Judge:

Comcast Corporation and several intervenors involved in the cable television industry petition for review of a rule in which the Federal Communications Commission capped at 30% of all subscribers the market share any single cable television operator may serve. We agree with Comcast that the 30% subscriber limit is arbitrary and capricious. We therefore grant the petition and vacate the Rule.

I. Background

The Cable Television Consumer Protection and Competition Act of 1992 directed the FCC, "[i]n order to enhance effective competition," 47 U.S.C. §533(f)(1), to

> prescrib[e] rules and regulations ... [to] ensure that no cable operator or group of cable operators can unfairly impede, either because of the size of any individual operator or because of joint actions by a group of operators of sufficient size, the flow of video programming from the video programmer to the consumer.

Id. §533(f)(2)(A). The Commission is to "make such rules and regulations reflect the dynamic nature of the communications marketplace." *Id.* §533(f)(2)(E).

In 2001 we considered a petition for review of a then newly revised version of the 30% subscriber limit. Time Warner Entm't Co. v. FCC (*Time Warner II*), 240 F.3d 1126 (D.C. Cir. 2001).

In establishing the subscriber limit we reviewed in *Time Warner II*, the Commission had sought to ensure a minimum open field of 40% and reasoned that a 30% cap, rather than the seemingly obvious 60% cap, was necessary because the Commission was concerned about the viability of a video programming network if the two largest cable operators denied it carriage. We granted the petition because the record contained no evidence of cable operators' colluding to deny a video programmer carriage and "the legitimate, independent editorial choices" of two or more cable operators, could not be said to "unfairly impede, either because of the size of any individual operator or because of joint actions by a group of operators of sufficient size, the flow of video programming from the video programmer to the consumer," 47 U.S.C. §533(f)(2)(A). We directed the agency on remand to consider how the increasing market share of direct broadcast satellite (DBS) companies, such as DirecTV and Dish Network, diminished cable operators' ability to determine the economic fate of programming networks.

On remand, the Commission adopted the current version of the 30% subscriber limit. The Rule here under review was designed to ensure that no single cable operator "can, by simply refusing to carry a programming network, cause it to fail." The Comm'n's Cable Horizontal and Vertical Ownership Limits, Fourth Report and Order and Further Notice of Proposed Rulemaking, 23 FCC Rcd. 2134, ¶39 (2008) (Fourth Report). Based upon the record before the court in *Time Warner II*, the subscriber limit under this standard could not have been lower than 60%. Based upon the present record, however, the Commission concluded no cable operator could safely be allowed to serve — *mirabile dictu* — more than 30% of all subscribers. *Plus ça change, plus c'est la même chose?*

In re-calculating the minimum viable scale, the Commission relied upon a study's finding regarding the number of viewers a cable network needed to reach in order to have a 70% chance of survival after five years, using data on the survival of cable networks between 1984 and 2001. Based upon the study, the FCC found the minimum viable scale was 19.03 million subscribers, about four million more than the agency had found were necessary in 1999.

To determine the total number of subscribers, the FCC counted all cable subscribers and DBS customers, totaling approximately 96 million (up from 80 million in 1999). In re-calculating the penetration rate, the Commission observed, "many, if not most, new cable networks are placed on a digital tier. A consequence of being placed on a digital tier versus one of the basic levels of service ... is a much lower penetration rate." *Id.* ¶60. Using an in-house study of the tiering and subscribership data for a sample of cable operators and a linear regression model, the Commission determined the penetration rate of the average network was 27.42%, or slightly more than half the 50% penetration rate it found in 1999. *Id.* ¶ 61.

From these data, the Commission calculated that a video programming network, to be viable, required an open field of 70% (up from 40% in 1999). Therefore, no cable operator could serve more than 30% of all subscribers.

Although the Commission recognized "that competition in the downstream market [especially from DBS companies] may affect the ability of a large cable operator to prevent successful entry by a programming network, and that [the] open field analysis does not directly measure this," it decided not to adjust the subscriber limit to account for such competition because doing so would be "quite difficult." The FCC then gave four reasons it did not regard competition from DBS companies as significant: Customers are reluctant to switch from cable service to DBS because (1) switching is costly; and (2) cable operators offer non-video services, such as telephone and internet access, that are not available with DBS; and (3) "video programming is a product, the quality of which cannot be known with certainty until it is consumed." *Id.* ¶ 70. Additionally, (4) "[c]ompetitive pressures from DBS will not provide any assistance to networks that," not having a contract with the largest cable operator, are unable to "launch due to a lack of financing." *Id.* ¶ 71.

II. Analysis

B. The 30% Subscriber Limit

We may set aside the Commission's decision "only if [it] was 'arbitrary, capricious, an abuse of discretion, or otherwise not in accordance with law.'" Mission Broad. Corp. v. FCC, 113 F.3d 254, 259–60 (D.C. Cir. 1997) (quoting 5 U.S.C. § 706(2)(A)).

Whether a cable operator serving more than 30% of subscribers can exercise "bottleneck monopoly power," depends, as we observed in *Time Warner II*, "not only on its share of the market, but also on the elasticities of supply and demand, which in turn are determined by the *availability* of competition." 240 F.3d at 1134. A cable operator faces competition primarily from non-cable companies, such as those providing DBS service and, increasingly, telephone companies providing fiber optic service. As Comcast points out, DBS companies alone now serve approximately 33% of all subscribers. Recognizing the growing importance particularly of DBS, in *Time Warner II* we said in no uncertain terms that "in revisiting the horizontal rules the Commission will have to take account of the impact of DBS on [cable operators'] market power." *Id.*

Of the three aspects of the Commission's open field model—minimum viable scale, total number of subscribers, and penetration rate—only the total subscribers measure fully takes account of the competition from DBS companies and companies offering fiber optic services. As Comcast points out, the measure of minimum viable scale relies upon data from 1984–2001 and, as a result, fails to consider the impact of DBS companies' growing market share (from 18% to 33%) over the six years immediately preceding issuance of the Rule, as well as the growth of fiber optic companies. The penetration rate calculation, by the Commission's own admission, leaves out data regarding DBS penetration— an omission the FCC attempts to justify with the question-begging assertion that such data would not have materially changed the penetration rate.

Comcast argues the Commission has offered no plausible reason for its failure to heed our explicit direction in *Time Warner II* to consider the competitive impact of DBS companies. Instead the Commission made the four non-empirical observations we enumerated above. As for the first, transaction costs undoubtedly do deter some cable customers from switching to satellite services, but Comcast points to record evidence that almost 50% of all DBS customers formerly subscribed to cable; in the face of that evidence, the Commission's observation that cost may deter some customers from switching to DBS is feeble indeed. With regard to the second—that some cable consumers may be reluctant to switch to a satellite television service because, unlike cable companies, DBS companies do not offer internet and telephone services—the Commission does not point to any evidence tending to show these inframarginal customers are numerous enough to confer upon cable operators their supposed bottleneck power over programming. Moreover, as Comcast points out, both DirecTV and Dish Network have partnered with telephone companies to offer bundled DBS and telephone services.

The Commission's third justification—that consumers will not switch providers to access new programming because they cannot know the quality of the programming before consuming it—warrants little discussion. As Comcast points out, there is no record support for this conjecture. In any event, it is common knowledge that new video programming is advertised on other television stations and in other media, and can be previewed over the Internet, thus providing consumers with information about the quality of competing services. The FCC's fourth reason—that without its subscriber cap an upstart network will have trouble securing financing unless it has a contract with a cable company serving more than 30% of the market—is no more convincing than the other three when one recalls DBS companies already serve more than 30% of the market.

Finally, we note the Commission's observation that assessing competition from DBS companies is difficult—possibly true even if unexplained—does not justify the agency's failure to consider competition from DBS companies in important aspects of its model. That a problem is difficult may indicate a need to make some simplifying assumptions, but it does not justify ignoring altogether a variable so clearly relevant and likely to affect the calculation of a subscriber limit—not to mention one the court had directed the agency to consider.

Comcast, on the other hand, points beyond DBS companies' growing market share to their exclusive arrangements with certain highly sought after programmers as evidence that competition has led and will likely continue to lead subscribers to switch services. Indeed, Commissioner McDowell pointed out in dissent that, as of the date of the Fourth Report, DirecTV and Dish Network each served more customers than any cable company save Comcast itself. Comcast also points to evidence that the number of cable networks has increased by almost 500% since 1992 and has grown at an ever faster rate since 2000, and that a much lower percentage of cable networks are vertically integrated with cable operators than was the case when the Congress passed the 1992 Act. There can be no doubt that consumers are now able to receive far more channels than they could in 1999, let alone 1992.

In sum, the Commission has failed to demonstrate that allowing a cable operator to serve more than 30% of all cable subscribers would threaten to reduce either competition or diversity in programming. First, the record is replete with evidence of ever increasing competition among video providers: Satellite and fiber optic video providers have entered the market and grown in market share since the Congress passed the 1992 Act, and particularly in recent years. Cable operators, therefore, no longer have the bottleneck power over programming that concerned the Congress in 1992. Second, over the same period there has been a dramatic increase both in the number of cable networks and in the programming available to subscribers.

In view of the overwhelming evidence concerning "the dynamic nature of the communications marketplace," 47 U.S.C § 533(f)(2)(E), and the entry of new competitors at both the programming and the distribution levels, it was arbitrary and capricious for the Commission to conclude that a cable operator serving more than 30% of the market poses a threat either to competition or to diversity in programming. Considering the marketplace as it is today and the many significant changes that have occurred since 1992, the FCC has not identified a sufficient basis for imposing upon cable operators the "special obligations," *Turner I*, 512 U.S. at 641, represented by the 30% subscriber limit. We conclude the Commission has failed to "examine[] the relevant data and articulate[] a satisfactory explanation for its action," Fresno Mobile Radio, Inc. v. FCC, 165 F.3d 965, 968 (D.C. Cir. 1999), and hold the 30% subscriber cap is arbitrary and capricious.

C. Remedy

[The Court decides to vacate the FCC's rule, instead of remanding the matter to the agency for further proceedings.]

Notes and Questions

1. Standard of Review. What standard of review does the court apply? Was the Commission's decision so devoid of basis in evidence that it deserved no deference? The D.C. Circuit clearly disagrees with the FCC's conclusions, but were those conclusions on which reasonable people could disagree and, therefore, ones on which the court should have upheld the Commission?

2. Switching Costs. The court rejects the FCC's conclusion that subscribers unhappy with their cable service would face switching costs sufficiently high to impede their migration from cable to DBS. On what basis does the court reject that conclusion? Is the evidence the court relies upon persuasive?

3. Do We Need a Cap? Putting aside questions about administrative law and standard of review, is the court right that the changing video marketplace has rendered the FCC's proposed cap unnecessary? Is there really a need for a cable subscriber cap at all?

§ 10.C. Regulation of Vertical Foreclosure by MVPDs

A principal purpose of the 1992 Cable Act was to encourage the continued deployment of multichannel technologies (such as DBS) that might ultimately compete with cable television. One barrier facing those rival technologies was the possibility that cable operators might make it difficult for them to obtain high-quality programming, either through exclusive contracts with content providers or through vertical integration into cable programming. Congress thus forbade cable operators, their affiliated "satellite cable programming vendor[s]," and "satellite broadcast programming vendor[s]" from "engag[ing] in unfair methods of competition or unfair or deceptive acts or practices, the purpose or effect of which is to hinder significantly or to prevent any multichannel video programming distributor from providing satellite cable programming or satellite broadcast programming to subscribers or consumers." 47 U.S.C. § 548(b) (§ 628 of the Communications Act).[4] Congress also specifically required the FCC to promulgate rules

---

4. The statute's use of the terms "satellite cable programming or satellite broadcast programming," § 548(b), meant that the statute applied only to that content distributed by cable companies to their individual systems using satellites. The initial effect of this provision was to limit the § 628 require-

on program supply contracts between cable operators and their affiliated programming vendors with the goal of intervening on behalf of rival MVPDs and ensuring equal access to program content. 47 U.S.C. §548(c). As the FCC summarized the rulemaking requirements:

> Section 628(c) instructs the Commission to adopt regulations to specify particular conduct that is prohibited by subsection (b). Specifically, the regulations are to:
>
> (1) establish safeguards to prevent undue influence by cable operators upon actions by affiliated program vendors related to the sale of programming to unaffiliated distributors;
>
> (2) prohibit price discrimination by vertically integrated satellite cable programming vendors and satellite broadcast programming vendors; and
>
> (3) prohibit exclusive contracts between a cable operator and a vertically integrated programming vendor in areas that are not served by a cable operator and any such exclusive arrangements in areas served by cable that are not found in the public interest by the Commission.
>
> The statute provides parties aggrieved by conduct alleged to violate the program access provisions the right to commence an adjudicatory proceeding before the Commission.

Implementation of Sections 12 and 19 of the Cable Television Consumer Protection and Competition Act of 1992: Development of Competition and Diversity in Video Programming Distribution and Carriage, First Report and Order, 8 FCC Rcd. 3359, ¶ 3 (1993).

§ 10.C.1. The Initial Program Access Rules

The initial FCC action under §628 addressed both the substantive standards that would govern complaints concerning "unfair methods of competition" and "unfair or deceptive acts or practices" and the FCC's own procedures for handling such complaints. As to substance, the decision addressed two main areas: (1) exclusive contracting practices between cable providers and affiliated content providers and (2) price discrimination in content offerings to noncable MVPDs. The FCC defined affiliated content providers to be those content providers who own more than five percent of a cable operator or were more than five percent owned by a cable operator. The FCC specifically forbade exclusive contract terms between cable companies and affiliated programming vendors that covered areas where the cable operator did not provide service. *Id.* ¶¶ 59–61. In areas where cable systems operated, the FCC did not forbid exclusive contracts but found that although "[a]s a general matter, the public interest in exclusivity in the sale of entertainment programming is widely recognized," in this situation "Congress has clearly placed a higher value on new competitive entry than on the continuation of exclusive distribution practices that impede this entry." *Id.* ¶ 63. The FCC therefore required "any vertically integrated programmer or any cable operator seeking to execute an exclusive contract to seek and obtain our public interest judgment before doing so." *Id.* ¶ 67. If the competing MVPD complains of price discrimination, the FCC held that the burden will be on the pro-

---

ment to national cable programming (in effect exempting locally generated programming). But as cable companies began to distribute programming to their local systems by fiber optic cables, this limiting language rendered the provision underinclusive, as we will see.

gramming vendor to establish that any price difference is justified by cost, volume, creditworthiness, or other service-based differences among distributors. *Id.* ¶¶ 99, 105.

The key practical effect of the Commission's implementation of § 628 has been to render invalid most exclusive programming contracts for well-established programs, although not all exclusivity is forbidden. These rules raise several institutional and policy issues. First, the rules appear to treat content as an essential facility in the provision of multichannel video, and moreover, they limit the content providers' ability (which is protected by copyright) to decide exactly how to distribute their works. Second, the need for program access rules appears to concede that the statutory and regulatory restrictions on vertical and horizontal ownership concentration, discussed above, are not sufficient to solve all competitive problems. Or is this simply the best multidimensional balance—that is, that horizontal and vertical integration produce some efficiencies and that the best balance is to allow those efficiencies while attempting to address program access issues with these behavioral rules? Third, the role of the FCC itself is interesting. The key statutory language—forbidding "unfair methods of competition" and "unfair or deceptive acts or practices"—mirrors the language of § 5 of the Federal Trade Commission Act. 15 U.S.C. § 45(a)(1) ("Unfair methods of competition in or affecting commerce, and unfair or deceptive acts or practices in or affecting commerce, are hereby declared unlawful."). And the rules affect not only the cable television companies, which are under the FCC's supervision, but also the content industry more generally. As implemented by the FCC, the rules are more generous to those challenging allegedly unfair arrangements than general antitrust law. As noted, § 628 and the Commission's rules place the burden of proof on the parties seeking exclusive arrangements, while antitrust would place the burden on the challenger to prove that the exclusivity has the effect of injuring competition. Similarly, § 628 and the rules place the burden on the party seeking non–cost-based price discrimination, while antitrust would again place it on the challenger.

§ 10.C.2. Extensions of the Program Access Rules

The 1992 Act required the program access rules to sunset in 2002 unless the Commission found that the rules "continue[] to be necessary to preserve and protect competition and diversity in the distribution of video programming." 47 U.S.C. § 548(c)(5). In 2002, the FCC found exactly that and extended the rules through 2007. Implementation of the Cable Television Consumer Protection and Competition Act of 1992, Report and Order, 17 FCC Rcd. 12,124 (2002). The FCC found that "vertically integrated programmers retain the incentive to favor their affiliated cable operators over competitive MVPDs such that competition and diversity in the distribution of video programming would not be preserved and protected"—especially as there remains "'must have' vertically integrated programming for which there are no good substitutes." *Id.* ¶ 4. Commissioner Kathleen Q. Abernathy dissented, arguing that increased competition in both the programming and distribution markets rendered the rules unnecessary: "In enacting the 1992 Cable Act, Congress stated that it was its policy to 'rely on the marketplace, to the maximum extent feasible[,] to achieve' the 'availability to the public of a diversity of views and information through cable television and other video distribution media.'" *Id.* at 12,175 (Abernathy, Comm'r, dissenting) (quoting 1992 Cable Act § 2(b)(1)–(2)).

The Commission similarly extended the rules in 2007 for an additional five years. Implementation of the Cable Television Consumer Protection and Competition Act of 1992, Report and Order and Notice of Proposed Rulemaking, 22 FCC Rcd. 17,791 (2007). In 2007, seventy percent of MVPD subscribers were still cable subscribers. The FCC also found:

[T]hree additional developments since 2002 provide cable-affiliated programmers with an even greater economic incentive to withhold programming from competitive MVPDs: (i) the increase in horizontal concentration in the industry; (ii) the increase in clustering of cable systems; and (iii) the recent emergence of new entrants in the video market place, such as telephone companies.

Id. ¶ 53. The D.C. Circuit upheld this extension. Cablevision Sys. Corp. v. FCC, 597 F.3d 1306 (D.C. Cir. 2010). Judge Kavanaugh dissented on the ground that the regulation failed intermediate scrutiny under the First Amendment. *Id.* at 1315–16 (Kavanaugh, J., dissenting).

In 2012, the FCC issued an order in which it "decline[d] to extend the exclusive contract prohibition section of the program access rules beyond its October 5, 2012 sunset date." Revision of the Commission's Program Access Rules, Report and Order, Further Notice of Proposed Rulemaking, and Order on Reconsideration, 27 FCC Rcd. 12,605, ¶ 1 (2012). The Commission summarized its decision and approach for the future as follows:

2. We find that a preemptive prohibition on exclusive contracts is no longer "necessary to preserve and protect competition and diversity in the distribution of video programming" considering that a case-by-case process will remain in place after the prohibition expires to assess the impact of individual exclusive contracts. 47 U.S.C. § 548(c)(5). [B]ecause the current market presents a mixed picture (with the cable industry now less dominant at the national level than it was when the exclusive contract prohibition was enacted, but prevailing concerns about cable dominance and concentration in various individual markets), we find that extending a preemptive ban on exclusive contracts sweeps too broadly. Rather, this mixed picture justifies a case-by-case approach in applying our program access rules (consistent with the case-by-case inquiries we undertake in the terrestrial programming and program carriage contexts), with special account taken of the unique characteristics of Regional Sports Network (RSN) programming. In addition to allowing us to assess any harm to competition resulting from an exclusive contract, this case-by-case approach will also allow us to consider the potentially procompetitive benefits of exclusive contracts in individual cases, such as promoting investment in new programming, particularly local programming, and permitting MVPDs to differentiate their service offerings. Accordingly, consistent with Congress's intention that the exclusive contract prohibition would not remain in place indefinitely and its finding that exclusive contracts can have procompetitive benefits in some markets, we decline to extend the preemptive prohibition beyond its October 5, 2012 sunset date.

3. We recognize that the potential for anticompetitive conduct resulting from vertical integration between cable operators and programmers remains a concern. For example, in some markets, vertical integration may result in exclusive contracts between cable operators and their affiliated programmers that preclude competitors in the video distribution market from accessing critical programming needed to attract and retain subscribers and thus harm competition. While the amount of satellite-delivered, cable-affiliated programming among the most popular cable networks has declined since 2007, some of that programming may still be critical for MVPDs to compete in the video distribution market. Congress has provided the Commission with the authority to address exclusive contracts on a case-by-case basis. We thus conclude that, in the context of present market conditions, such an individualized assessment of exclusive contracts in response to complaints is a more appropriate

regulatory approach than the blunt tool of a prohibition that preemptively bans all exclusive contracts between satellite-delivered, cable-affiliated programmers and cable operators. This case-by-case consideration of exclusive contracts involving satellite-delivered, cable-affiliated programming will mirror our treatment of terrestrially delivered, cable-affiliated programming, including the establishment of a rebuttable presumption that an exclusive contract involving a cable-affiliated RSN has the purpose or effect prohibited in Section 628(b) of the Act. As demonstrated by our recent actions on complaints involving withholding of terrestrially delivered, cable-affiliated programming, the Commission is committed to exercising its authority under Section 628 of the Act to require cable-affiliated programmers to license their programming to competitors in appropriate cases.

Notes and Questions

1. Sports Are Special. Note the "rebuttable presumption that an exclusive contract involving a cable-affiliated RSN has the purpose or effect prohibited in Section 628(b) of the Act" (established in an earlier order and broadened here). Why the focus on these sports networks? As an empirical matter, it turns out that for many viewers, watching their local sports teams is must-have programming.

2. Case-by-Case. In its 2012 order the FCC replaces a broad prohibition with a case-by-case approach. Should the FCC move towards more flexible approaches in general? That is, what are the advantages and disadvantages of the Commission replacing bright-line rules with more flexible standards? Are there reasons why the move to a case-by-case approach is more attractive here than in other contexts?

§ 10.C.3. Expansion of the Program Access Theory

Over the past decade, the program access rules and the FCC's underlying theory of competition have expanded in several dimensions. First, the FCC has extended them to entities and programming not originally covered by the rules. Through merger review, the FCC extended them to an integrated satellite provider, and then the FCC, by rule, extended them to cover programming distributed by MVPDs through terrestrial means. The FCC also used its § 628 authority to forbid exclusive contracts between MVPDs and the owners of apartment buildings and other multitenant dwellings. This last move of course had nothing to do with program exclusivity, but it operated on a similar theory: that exclusive contracts between MVPDs and building owners foreclosed an important area of competition among MVPDs (and thereby injured consumers). Because these FCC actions are in the progression of the Commission's § 628 theory, we include the relevant orders below.

§ 10.C.3.a. Extension of the Program Access Rules to DirecTV

In 2004, News Corp. purchased DirecTV, thereby creating the first vertically integrated DBS provider. In approving the merger between News Corp. and DirecTV, the FCC imposed a set of conditions on the merged firm in order to address what it viewed as potential competitive concerns arising from this vertical integration. News Corp. later spun off DirecTV, selling it to Liberty Media Corporation. We nonetheless include the order approving the original acquisition by News Corp. because it clearly describes the FCC's underlying competition theory for program access rules. As it happens, Liberty also owns programming interests, and the FCC went on to impose a similar set of requirements as a condition of approving that merger.

General Motors Corp. and Hughes Electronics Corp., Transferors, and the News Corp. Ltd, Transferee, for Authority to Transfer Control

Memorandum Opinion and Order, 19 FCC Rcd. 473 (2004)

V. INTRODUCTION TO THE VIDEO PROGRAMMING AND MVPD MARKETS

A. Background

39. The proposed transaction involves the acquisition by News Corp., a major owner of both broadcast and cable video programming content and programming-related technologies, of a 34% interest in Hughes Electronics, owner of DirecTV, a DBS provider that is the second largest MVPD in the United States and the largest MVPD that has a national service footprint. News Corp. presently has no MVPD assets in the United States; its primary domestic business is the provision of video programming to MVPDs in every area of the country. Similarly, Hughes currently does not participate in the video programming market as a programming supplier; rather, its DirecTV subsidiary functions as a purchaser and distributor of multichannel video programming to subscribing customers. By acquiring DirecTV, News Corp. immediately transforms itself from a supplier of video programming MVPDs to a vertically integrated MVPD competitor. News Corp. thus becomes a vertically integrated supplier of broadcast and cable video programming to all of its MVPD competitors in every region of the country.

B. Applicable Regulatory Framework

1. Program Access Requirements

41. The program access provisions, contained in section 628 of the Communications Act, were adopted as part of the Cable Television Consumer Protection and Competition Act of 1992. At the time, Congress was concerned that most cable operators enjoyed a monopoly in program distribution at the local level. Congress found that vertically integrated program suppliers had the incentive and ability to favor their affiliated cable operators over nonaffiliated cable operators and programming distributors using other technologies. Section 628 is intended to foster the development of competition to traditional cable systems by governing the access of competing MVPDs to cable programming services. DBS was among the technologies that Congress intended to foster through the program access provisions.

42. The program access rules specifically prohibit cable operators, a satellite cable programming vendor in which a cable operator has an attributable interest, or a satellite cable programming vendor from:

- Engaging in unfair acts or practices which hinder significantly or prohibit an MVPD from providing satellite cable programming to subscribers or consumers.
- Discriminating in the prices, terms and conditions of sale or delivery of satellite cable programming.
- Entering into exclusive contracts with cable operators unless the Commission finds the exclusivity to be in the public interest.

43. Aggrieved entities can file a complaint with the Commission. Remedies for violations of the rules may include the imposition of damages and the establishment of rea-

sonable prices, terms and conditions for the sale of programming. Broadcast programming is not subject to the program access rules.

44. The Commission's 2002 examination of whether the exclusivity prohibition should sunset placed substantial weight on whether, in the absence of the exclusivity prohibition, vertically integrated programmers would currently have the incentive and ability to favor their affiliated cable operators over nonaffiliated cable operators and program distributors using other technologies and, if they would, whether such behavior would result in a failure to protect and preserve competition and diversity in the distribution of video programming. The Commission held that access to all vertically integrated satellite cable programming continues to be necessary in order for competitive MVPDs to remain viable in the marketplace. The Commission further found that an MVPD's ability to provide service that is competitive with an incumbent cable operator is significantly harmed if denied access to "must have" vertically integrated programming for which there are no good substitutes, such as regional news and sports networks. The Commission also found that vertically integrated programmers retain the incentive to favor their affiliated cable operators over competing MVPDs. In that regard, the Commission found that cable operators continue to dominate the MVPD marketplace and that horizontal consolidation and clustering combined with affiliation with regional programming, have contributed to cable's overall market dominance. In addition, the Commission determined that an economic basis for denial of access to vertically integrated programming to competitive MVPDs continues, and that such denial would harm such competitors' ability to compete for subscribers. The prohibition on exclusive contracts for satellite-delivered cable or satellite-delivered broadcast programming was therefore extended for five years, until October 5, 2007.

69. Transactions involving the acquisition of a full or partial interest in another company may give rise to concerns regarding "horizontal" concentration and/or "vertical" integration, depending on the lines of business engaged in by the two firms. A transaction is said to be horizontal when the firms in the transaction sell products that are in the same relevant markets and are therefore viewed as reasonable substitutes by purchasers of the products. Horizontal transactions are of antitrust concern because they eliminate competition between the firms and increase concentration in the relevant markets. The reduction in overall competition in the relevant markets may lead to substantial increases in prices paid by purchasers of products in the markets.

70. Vertical transactions raise slightly different competitive concerns. At the outset, it is important to note that antitrust law and economic analysis have viewed vertical transactions more favorably in part because vertical mergers, standing alone, do not increase concentration in either the upstream or downstream markets. In addition, vertical mergers may generate significant efficiencies. For example, a vertical transaction may produce a more efficient organization form, which can reduce transaction costs, limit free-riding by internalizing incentives, and take advantage of technological economies.

71. Nevertheless, as discussed in greater detail below, vertical transactions also have the potential for anticompetitive effects. In particular, a vertically integrated firm that competes both in an upstream input market and a downstream output market, such as post-transaction News Corp., may have the incentive and ability to: (1) discriminate against particular rivals in either the upstream or downstream markets (e.g., by foreclosing rivals from inputs or customers); or (2) raise the costs to rivals generally in either of the markets.

80. There is an additional reason why temporary foreclosure may be profitable. Specifically, by temporarily foreclosing supply of the input to a downstream competitor or by

threatening to engage in temporary foreclosure, the integrated firm may improve its bargaining position so as to be able to extract a higher input price from the downstream competitor than it could have negotiated if it were a non-integrated input supplier. In order for an integrated firm successfully to employ temporary foreclosure or the threat of temporary foreclosure as a strategy to increase its bargaining position, the foreclosure strategy must be credible. This means that competitors must believe that temporary foreclosure is profitable (whether or not it actually is) in order to extract a higher input price. For example, if the vertically integrated firm, by temporarily withholding an input from a competitor, can cause the competitor to lose sufficient revenue or suffer other competitive harms, the competitor might agree to pay a higher price for the input, which could lead to higher prices for the output, thus injuring consumers. Even if the vertically integrated firm suffered a loss in profits from engaging in a specific instance of temporary foreclosure, it might nevertheless find it to be a profitable strategy over the longer run. Specifically, if by temporarily foreclosing certain competitors, the vertically integrated firm may signal to other downstream competitors its willingness to foreclose, which may cause other downstream competitors to agree to a higher price without the vertically integrated firm's having to actually engage in repeated foreclosures.

107. [In response to alleged competitive concerns, a]pplicants have offered that "neither News Corp. nor DirecTV will discriminate against unaffiliated programming services in the selection, price, terms or conditions of carriage." Consolidated Application of Gen. Motors Corp. and Hughes Elecs. Corp., Transferors, and the News Corp. Ltd., Transferee, for Auth. to Transfer Control, 53, Attachment G, MB Dkt. No. 03-124 (May 2003) (May 2003 Filing). We conclude that Applicants' proposed commitment to allow unaffiliated programmers access to the DirecTV platform on nondiscriminatory terms and conditions adequately addresses concerns raised regarding unaffiliated video programmers' access to the DirecTV platform. We will therefore condition our grant of the Application on compliance with this access commitment.

114. In addition, Applicants commit to not entering into exclusive arrangements for the distribution of an affiliated programming rights holder's satellite cable programming.

132. In conclusion, we believe as a general matter that the Commission's program access rules are satisfactory to address any imbalance of power between News Corp. and competing MVPDs with respect to national and non-sports regional cable programming networks. Likewise, our acceptance of the offered conditions ensures that any imbalance that may exist between DirecTV and some of its competitors in the MVPD market is remedied in the same manner as with vertically integrated MVPDs that use cable technology to deliver their product to consumers, regardless of the effect of any post-closing changes in the corporate relationships between News Corp. and its various cable programming affiliates. In contrast, as described below, the record indicates that News Corp. has considerable market power with respect to its regional sports networks and its local broadcast station signals, that the transaction is likely to increase its incentive and ability to use that market power to obtain substantially greater fee increases and other carriage concessions for such programming than it can today, and that additional remedial actions are therefore warranted for such video programming.

133. Since the Commission first began tracking regional cable programming networks in 1998, it has repeatedly recognized the importance of regional sports programming to MVPD offerings. This acknowledgement is based, in part, on the finding that for such programming, there are no readily acceptable close substitutes. The basis for the lack of adequate substitutes for regional sports programming lies in the unique nature of its core component: regional sports networks (RSNs) typically purchase exclusive rights to show

sporting events and sports fans believe that there is no good substitute for watching their local and/or favorite team play an important game. The Commission's extension of the sunset date for the exclusivity program access rules last year was intended, in part, to ensure that competing MVPDs would have continued access to the satellite-delivered regional sports programming owned by vertically integrated cable operators. We also have long recognized that the terrestrial distribution of programming—particularly RSN programming—by vertically integrated cable operators could competitively disadvantage competing MVPDs if they were denied access to the terrestrially delivered programming.

147. We conclude that News Corp. currently possesses significant market power with respect to its RSNs within each of their specific geographic regions, and that the proposed transaction will enhance News Corp.'s incentive and ability to temporarily withhold or threaten to withhold access to its RSN programming to increase the fees it receives for the programming, over and above what it could negotiate absent the transaction, to the ultimate detriment of the public. Moreover, we find that in contrast to the situation with respect to access to national and non-sports regional programming, neither our program access rules nor Applicants' proposed program access commitments are sufficient to protect against these likely transaction-specific harms.

173. We [believe] that a neutral dispute resolution forum would provide a useful backstop to prevent News Corp. from exercising its increased market power to force rival MVPDs to either accept inordinate affiliate fee increases for access to RSN programming and/or other unwanted programming concessions or potentially to cede critical content to their most powerful DBS competitor, DirecTV. We therefore create a mechanism whereby an aggrieved MVPD may choose to submit a dispute with News Corp. over the terms and conditions of carriage of RSNs to commercial arbitration to constrain News Corp.'s increased incentive to use temporary foreclosure strategies during carriage negotiations for RSN programming in each region in which News Corp. owns or holds a controlling interest or manages any non-broadcast RSN, and require News Corp. to permit the MVPD to continue to carry the RSN while the dispute is being resolved.

175. Thus, our remedy is to allow MVPDs to demand commercial arbitration when they are unable to come to a negotiated "fair" price for the programming. The staff analysis has found that the allure of temporary with-holding to News Corp. is substantial, even after the ability invariably to obtain supracompetitive affiliate fee increases is eliminated. Accordingly we do not allow News Corp. to deauthorize carriage of the RSN after an MVPD has chosen to avail itself of the arbitration condition. We also specify that expedited arbitration procedures be used and that the final offers submitted to the arbitrator by each side may not include any compensation for RSN carriage in the form of the MVPD's agreement to carry any video programming networks or any other service other than the RSN.

Dissenting Statement of Commissioner Jonathan S. Adelstein

Deciding whether a fox should guard a hen house is a far more serious exercise than this Order reflects. Granted, the birds in this case are not hens but valuable satellites with a national footprint from which nearly 12 million people receive video programming through DirecTV. And the Fox in this case is already one of the world's largest media conglomerates, with a vast array of global content and distribution assets. The acquisition of Hughes Electronics Corporation by News Corporation (News Corp.) will result in unprecedented control over local and national media properties in one global media empire. Its shockwaves will undoubtedly recast our entire media landscape.

Never before has a single corporation been armed with a national video distribution platform; a major broadcast network; television stations in nearly every major media market—reaching more than 44 percent of the country—with guaranteed carriage rights on other distribution platforms; multiple cable networks (11 national and 22 regional, including sports networks with exclusive rights); a major film and television studio; newspaper, magazine and book publishing operations; significant video programming and broadcasting satellite backhaul capacity; and the leading program guide and programming-related technologies to facilitate a consumer's viewing experience. With this unprecedented combination, News Corp. could be in a position to raise programming prices for consumers, harm competition in video programming and distribution markets nationwide, and decrease the diversity of media voices. I wish the full dangers of this combination would have been more thoroughly examined and confronted.

News Corp. is now in a position to distribute programs or sporting events either on its broadcast network, cable networks, regional networks, television stations, or even over pay-per-view. Imagine the increased bargaining power of News Corp. as it sits at various negotiating tables in these interconnected industries, finding itself on all sides at once, and with an increased arsenal of weapons against rival programmers or distributors. News Corp. will be in a position to demand higher programming fees or demand concessions without fear of losing distribution.

This merger also threatens disruptive effects for competing programmers, particularly independent programmers and producers. Even without the merger, through the use of retransmission consent, News Corp. has been able to expand its cable networks faster than any other cable programmer. I will continue to monitor closely whether News Corp. provides opportunities for both established and new networks, particularly new entrants, to negotiate carriage on fair and reasonable terms on DirecTV. New Spanish-language networks, for example, have reached agreement with cable providers and are attempting to negotiate carriage on DirecTV. Given DirecTV's history of promoting a diversity of programming, I would be concerned if its acquisition by News Corp. resulted in a loss of diverse, independent or minority-owned programming to an eager public in order to favor networks it owns.

These many concerns call for a more serious examination of the concentration resulting from the merger, or other more comprehensive structural or behavioral conditions. While this Order does contain some important protections, not all the effects on consumers and competition have been fully analyzed or remedied to assure fair competition and protection of consumer interests. I dissent.

Notes and Questions

1. Merger Review-Based Rulemaking. In reviewing the DirecTV matter, the Commission developed a series of new regulations that, nominally at least, were "voluntary undertakings" by News Corp. As we discuss in Chapter Eleven, the Commission's merger review authority is controversial. In this case, the conditions did address competitive harms that the Department of Justice was not in a good position to remedy. Notably, after the Commission issued its decision, the Justice Department closed its investigation of this matter, explaining that the Commission's action addressed its concerns. Should the fact that this decision resolved concerns shared by the Justice Department distinguish it from other cases, in which the "voluntary conditions" often pursue policy objectives only distantly related to a merger?

2. Vertical Integration Redux. For Commissioner Adelstein, the prospect of greater vertical integration creates heartburn. In the Commission's order, however, vertical integration is cited as a source of valuable economic efficiencies. Are vertical integration concerns, even if not grounded in economic theory, sufficient to reject combinations like DirecTV and News Corp.?

3. Meet the New Boss. News Corp., as part of unwinding its relationship with Liberty Media Corporation, sold DirecTV to Liberty. As such, News Corp.'s cable channels are no longer subject to the above regime. But Liberty Media owns a number of cable channels. Consequently, the order approving the transaction explained that the combination

> presents potential public interest harms similar to those the Commission sought to mitigate when it conditionally approved News Corp.'s acquisition of an interest in DirecTV. As the Commission did in approving that transaction, we grant the instant Application subject to certain conditions to address our concerns. Specifically, we require the Applicants to abide by program access, program carriage, RSN arbitration, and retransmission consent arbitration conditions modeled on the conditions imposed in the News Corp.-Hughes proceeding.

News Corp. & the DirecTV Group, Inc., Transferors, & Liberty Media Corp., Transferee, for Authority to Transfer Control, Memorandum Opinion and Order, 23 FCC Rcd. 3265, ¶ 5 (2008).

§ 10.C.3.b. MVPD Access to Buildings

May an MVPD provider, such as a cable company, enter into an exclusive service arrangement with a condominium or apartment complex (known generically as a multiple-dwelling unit), thereby excluding competing providers' access to the individual customers living there? The FCC concluded that such contracts were impermissible in 2007. The FCC reasoned that under § 628(b) such exclusive contracts also represented unfair competition. Cable companies challenged this interpretation, and the D.C. Circuit upheld it in the opinion below.

NATIONAL CABLE & TELECOMMUNICATIONS ASS'N v. FCC
567 F.3d 659 (D.C. Cir. 2009)

Opinion of the Court issued by Circuit Judge TATEL, in which Circuit Judge GARLAND and Senior Circuit Judge SILBERMAN concur.

TATEL, Circuit Judge.

Finding that exclusivity agreements between cable companies and owners of apartment buildings and other multi-unit developments have an anti-competitive effect on the cable market, the Federal Communications Commission banned such contracts. The Commission believes that these deals—which involve a cable company exchanging a valuable service like wiring a building for the exclusive right to provide service to the residents—may be regulated under section 628 of the Communications Act as cable company practices that significantly impair the ability of their competitors to deliver programming to consumers. The Commission thus forbade cable operators not only from entering into new exclusivity contracts, but also from enforcing old ones. Petitioners, associations representing cable operators and apartment building owners, argue that the Commission exceeded its statutory authority, arbitrarily departed from precedent, and otherwise violated the Administrative Procedure Act. Having carefully considered the parties' excellent submissions, we disagree and conclude that the Commission acted well within the bounds of both section 628 and general administrative law.

I.

Understanding this controversy requires that we begin by explaining a few unintuitive statutory terms. The provision at issue here, section 628(b) of the Communications Act, makes it unlawful "for a cable operator ... to engage in unfair methods of competition or unfair or deceptive acts or practices, the purpose or effect of which is to hinder significantly or to prevent any multichannel video programming distributor from providing satellite cable programming or satellite broadcast programming to subscribers or consumers." 47 U.S.C. § 548(b). "Cable operators" are just companies that deliver video programming by cable, like Comcast and Time-Warner. *See* 47 U.S.C. § 522(5)–(7). "Multichannel video programming distributors" (MVPDs) are a broader set of companies that provide video programming to subscribers. MVPDs include not only cable operators like Comcast but also direct broadcast satellite companies like DirecTV. *See* § 522(13). Although "satellite cable programming" and "satellite broadcast programming" differ somewhat—they originate from slightly different kinds of entities, *compare* § 548(i)(1), *and* 47 U.S.C. § 605(d)(1), *with* § 548(i)(3)—both terms essentially refer to programming (i.e., television shows) transmitted to MVPDs via satellite for retransmission to subscribers. For our purposes, the important point about them is this: petitioners nowhere dispute the Commission's finding that "most programming is delivered via satellite" and so falls within one of these two categories. Exclusive Service Contracts for Provision of Video Services in Multiple Dwelling Units and Other Real Estate Developments, Report and Order and Further Notice of Proposed Rulemaking, 22 FCC Rcd. 20,235, 20,255, ¶ 43 n.132 (2007) (Order). Section 628(b)'s plain terms thus prohibit cable company practices with the purpose or effect of preventing competing MVPDs, including other cable companies, from providing the two predominant types of programming to consumers.

The Commission first considered exclusivity contracts between cable operators and so-called multiple dwelling units (MDUs) as an ancillary part of its 2003 Inside Wiring Order. *See* Telecommunications Services Inside Wiring, First Order on Reconsideration and Section Report and Order, 18 FCC Rcd. 1342, 1366–70, ¶¶ 63–71 (2003). That proceeding primarily concerned the ownership status of certain wiring inside MDUs, and the Commission's order considered some thirteen different issues presented by its new wiring rules. But the Commission also addressed a related issue raised in a separate notice of proposed rulemaking, namely "whether it would be appropriate to cap exclusive contracts to open up MDUs to potential competition on a building-wide or unit-to-unit basis, and, if so, what would represent a reasonable cap." Id. ¶ 63. Reviewing the evidence then available, the Commission found that there was no "sufficient basis in this record to ban or cap the term of exclusive contracts." Id. ¶ 68; *see also* ¶¶ 69–71.

Four years later, the Commission returned to exclusivity contracts in a rulemaking devoted solely to that question. Analyzing the competitive harms and benefits of exclusivity clauses, the Commission this time concluded that "exclusivity clauses cause significant harm to competition and consumers that the record did not reflect at the time of our 2003 Inside Wiring Order." Order ¶¶ 26–29. And because the Commission found that the record now supports regulation, this time it extensively analyzed its authority to ban such contracts, concluding that both section 628 and its "ancillary authority" empower it to act. The Commission accordingly prohibited cable companies from "enforcing existing exclusivity clauses and executing contracts containing new ones," *id.* ¶ 30, rejecting more limited remedial options.

II.

Conceding that on a literal reading of the statute exclusivity contracts do have the "effect" of preventing competing MVPDs from "providing satellite cable programming or satellite broadcast programming to subscribers or consumers," § 548(b), petitioners nonetheless argue that section 628's text, structure, and history demonstrate that it was addressed to a different evil altogether. Congress, they argue, was concerned not with barriers to *service* but with practices that prevent cable competitors from obtaining certain kinds of *programming* that the American public wants to watch. Textually, they emphasize Congress's identification of "satellite cable programming" and "satellite broadcast programming" in particular, arguing that the Commission has read these well-defined terms out of the statute. Structurally, they emphasize section 628(c), which directs the Commission to implement subsection (b) with rules and procedures focused on fair dealing between programming vendors and MVPDs, not on anti-competitive barriers to service generally. Petitioners thus argue that in enacting section 628(b), Congress intended to prevent the cable industry from starving its competition of programming—nothing more, nothing less.

For its part, the Commission concedes that Congress's primary purpose in enacting section 628 was indeed to expand competition for programming, not service. But this primary purpose is hardly dispositive, it argues, because "statutory prohibitions often go beyond the principal evil to cover reasonably comparable evils, and it is ultimately the provisions of our laws rather than the principal concerns of our legislators by which we are governed." Oncale v. Sundowner Offshore Servs., Inc., 523 U.S. 75, 79, (1998). Reviewing the same text, structure, and legislative history, the Commission interprets section 628 to permit regulation of exclusive service agreements as an evil that easily falls within the literal terms of the statute and is reasonably comparable to the paradigmatic anti-competitive practices that section 628 specifically targets. We agree.

Beginning, "as always, with the plain language of the statute," Citizens Coal Council v. Norton, 330 F.3d 478, 482 (D.C. Cir. 2003), we find nothing in section 628 that unambiguously forecloses the Commission's interpretation. What the Commission forbade lies within the literal terms of section 628(b)'s proscription. Indeed, exclusivity agreements have both the proscribed "purpose" and the proscribed "effect"—cable operators execute them precisely so that they can be the sole company serving a building, and as petitioners themselves put it, "if you can't serve a building then you can't deliver satellite cable programming and satellite broadcast programming." Oral Arg. 3:29–3:34.

In the end, petitioners are unable to satisfy their heavy burden. To prevail at *Chevron* step one, they must show that section 628(b) is unambiguously limited to Congress's principal concern with unfair program hoarding. Because Section 628's actual words reach the behavior the Commission prohibited, petitioners are left to argue "that the Commission relies almost entirely on a literal reading of the statutory language—not the most damning criticism when it comes to statutory interpretation." Consumer Elecs. Ass'n v. FCC, 347 F.3d 291, 297 (D.C. Cir. 2003). And while the statute's text, structure, and history do support the proposition that Congress was, in fact, principally concerned with program hoarding, none suggests that Congress chose its language to limit the Commission to regulating that evil alone. Indeed, having employed all available tools of statutory construction, we find little that suggests any congressional intent to limit section 628(b) to competition for programming, and so are unable to conclude that a reading literally permitted is nonetheless unambiguously foreclosed. At the very best, petitioners have demonstrated some ambiguity as to whether Congress intended to allow regulation of exclusivity contracts along with unfair dealing over programming—ambiguity the Commission reasonably resolved in favor of its own interpretation. Thus, concluding that section 628(b) authorizes the Commission's action, we need not consider the Commission's ancillary authority.

Real estate petitioners' separate attack on the Commission's authority has little merit. They argue that the exclusivity ban impermissibly regulates the real estate industry, which lies outside the Commission's jurisdiction. The terms of the challenged prohibition apply only to cable companies, however, and they neither require nor prohibit any action by MDUs. We decline to put issues relating to their cable service outside the Commission's authority simply because those issues also matter to their landlords.

III.

For their primary Administrative Procedure Act claim, petitioners argue that in deciding "to bar [exclusivity contracts] now, after affirmatively permitting them in 2003," the Commission failed to explain its change of heart and thus acted arbitrarily and capriciously. Of course, "it is axiomatic that agency action must either be consistent with prior action or offer a reasoned basis for its departure from precedent." Williams Gas Processing–Gulf Coast Co. v. FERC, 475 F.3d 319, 326 (D.C. Cir. 2006). Yet it is equally axiomatic that an agency is free to change its mind so long as it supplies "a reasoned analysis." Petitioners believe that the Commission has neither reasonably disavowed the logic of the 2003 Inside Wiring Order nor explained how that logic could fail to produce the same outcome on the record now presented. Finding the Commission's extensive discussion of its change in approach more than equal to our forgiving standard of review, we disagree.

To be sure, as petitioners emphasize, the 2003 Inside Wiring Order does conclude with the following two sentences: "We note that competition in the MDU market is improving, even with the existence of exclusive contracts. Accordingly, we decline to intervene." 2003 Inside Wiring Order ¶ 71. But context matters, and here it makes clear that petitioners have confused a mere contributing factor with a sufficient condition. The uncited portions of that same paragraph note that commenters "identified both pro-competitive and anti-competitive aspects of exclusive contracts," and that the Commission was unable to "state, *based on the record*, that exclusive contracts [were] predominantly anti-competitive." *Id.* (emphasis added). Indeed, reading the four short paragraphs the Commission devoted to the issue in their entirety, we think it quite clear that the Commission based its unwillingness to intervene in 2003 primarily on the absence of a sufficient record. In short, the Commission acknowledged in its 2003 Inside Wiring Order that exclusivity contracts could either foster competition over entire buildings or foil competition over individual units, and that decision indicates only that the record then available was insufficient to resolve this question. Contrary to petitioners' claim, nothing about this logic commits the Commission to abstaining from regulation whenever competition is increasing—one could easily imagine that, however much competition improved despite exclusivity agreements, it would have improved more without them.

Conversely, petitioners give the Commission far too little credit for its extensive analysis of this issue in the order before us today. Rather than merely observing, as it did in 2003, that exclusivity agreements could theoretically have both pro-competitive and anti-competitive effects, in 2007 the Commission extensively analyzed the question, and concluded that "the harms significantly outweigh the benefits in ways they did not at the time of the Commission's 2003 Inside Wiring Order." *Id.* ¶ 16. The Commission found that exclusivity agreements would likely raise prices, limit access to certain programming, and delay deployment of fiber optic and broadband technologies.

IV.

The final issue presented concerns the Commission's decision to apply its rule to existing contracts. According to petitioners, this amounts to "directly retroactive" action barred by the APA's requirement that "legislative rules ... be given future effect only," or, alternatively, to agency action with harmful, secondarily retroactive effects that the Commission failed to consider. Neither argument persuades.

First, we think it readily apparent that the Commission's action has only "future effect" as the APA and our precedents use that term. The exclusivity ban purports to alter only the present situation, not "'the past legal consequences of past actions.'" Mobile Relay Assocs. v. FCC, 457 F.3d 1, 11 (D.C. Cir. 2006). Petitioners insist that under our precedent, "[t]he critical question" is only whether the Commission's rule "changes the legal landscape." Nat'l Mining Ass'n v. Dep't of Labor, 292 F.3d 849, 859 (D.C. Cir. 2002). Of course, if that were all it took to render a rule impermissible under the APA, it would spell the end of informal rulemaking. We have thus repeatedly made clear that an agency order that only "upsets expectations based on prior law is not retroactive." Mobile Relay, 457 F.3d at 11. That describes precisely this case.

Petitioners' alternative argument regarding secondary retroactivity fares somewhat better, but not well enough. Our case law does require that agencies balance the harmful "secondary retroactivity" of upsetting prior expectations or existing investments against the benefits of applying their rules to those preexisting interests. And by significantly altering the bargained-for benefits of now-unenforceable exclusivity agreements, the Commission has undoubtedly created the kinds of secondary retroactive effects that require agency attention and balancing. Petitioners' argument nonetheless fails for an obvious reason: the Commission did expressly consider the relative benefits and burdens of applying its rule to existing contracts and, after extensive analysis, concluded that banning enforcement of existing contracts was essential. The Commission found it "strongly in the public interest" to prevent the harms from existing contracts "to continue for years," or to "continue indefinitely in the cases of exclusivity clauses that last perpetually." Order ¶ 35.

V.

In sum, we see the challenged order as fully authorized by section 628 and the product of careful agency reconsideration. The petitions for review are denied.

[Concurring opinion by Senior Circuit Judge SILBERMAN omitted.]

Notes and Questions

1. Regulatory Flexibility. The D.C. Circuit notes that "Congress had a particular manifestation of a problem in mind, but in no way expressed an unambiguous intent to limit the Commission's power solely to that version of the problem." Nat'l Cable & Telecomm. Ass'n, 567 F.3d at 665. When should courts read statutes as embodying greater flexibility for agency action? What in §628 connotes that such flexibility is appropriate?

2. Retroactivity. Federal agencies often consider whether their decisions should apply to existing contracts, past conduct, or future conduct. Here, existing contracts—including bargained-for consideration—were implicated by the FCC's rule. Should agencies hesitate to adopt such rules? Why or why not?

3. The "Terrestrial Loophole." The program access rules applied, in the first instance, only to satellite-delivered programming, which meant that cable operators could avoid their application if the programming were delivered terrestrially (by fiber optic cable or otherwise). Section 628(b), as the D.C. Circuit noted in the case above, was written fairly broadly. In 2010, the Commission relied on §628 to address aspects of this seeming gap (often called the terrestrial loophole).

§ 10.C.3.c. Extension of the Program Access Rules to Terrestrially Distributed Programming

Review of the Commission's Program Access Rules and Examination of Programming Tying Arrangements
First Report and Order, 25 FCC Rcd. 746 (2010)

I. Introduction

1. In this First Report and Order, we take an important step to further promote competition in the video distribution market. We establish rules to address unfair acts, including exclusive contracts, involving terrestrially delivered, cable-affiliated programming. These rules will provide competitors to incumbent cable operators with an opportunity to obtain access to certain cable-affiliated programming that they are currently unable to offer to their subscribers, thereby promoting competition in the delivery of video to consumers. Our existing program access rules have been a boon to such competition, and we anticipate that the rules we adopt today will have similar procompetitive effects. Our efforts to spur competition in the marketplace for video programming are also aimed at increasing consumer benefits, including better services, innovations in technology, and lower prices. Moreover, we believe broadband adoption to be a further benefit from increased competition and diversity in video programming distribution. Specifically, today we adopt rules permitting complainants to pursue program access claims involving terrestrially delivered, cable-affiliated programming similar to the claims that they may pursue with respect to satellite-delivered, cable-affiliated programming, where the purpose or effect of the challenged act is to significantly hinder or prevent the complainant from providing satellite cable programming or satellite broadcast programming. The types of claims potentially involved include challenges to: (i) exclusive contracts between a cable operator and a cable-affiliated programmer that provides terrestrially delivered programming; (ii) discrimination in the prices, terms, and conditions for the sale of programming among multichannel video programming distributors (MVPDs) by a provider of terrestrially delivered programming that is wholly owned by, controlled by, or under common control with one or more of the following: a cable operator or operators, a satellite cable programming vendor or vendors in which a cable operator has an attributable interest, or a satellite broadcast programming vendor or vendors; and (iii) efforts by a cable operator to unduly influence the decision of its affiliated provider of terrestrially delivered programming to sell its programming to a competitor.

II. Background

A. Section 628

11. Congress enacted section 628 as part of the 1992 Cable Act to "promote the public interest, convenience, and necessity by increasing competition and diversity in the multichannel video programming market, to increase the availability of satellite cable programming and satellite broadcast programming to persons in rural and other areas not currently able to receive such programming, and to spur the development of communications technologies." 47 U.S.C. § 548(c)(1). To advance these goals, sections 628(b) and 628(c)(1) grant the Commission broad authority to adopt rules to prohibit unfair acts of cable operators that have the purpose or effect of preventing or hindering significantly an MVPD from providing satellite cable programming or satellite broadcast programming to subscribers or consumers. Section 628(b) provides that:

> [I]t shall be unlawful for a cable operator, a satellite cable programming vendor in which a cable operator has an attributable interest, or a satellite broadcast

programming vendor to engage in unfair methods of competition or unfair or deceptive acts or practices, the purpose or effect of which is to hinder significantly or to prevent any multichannel video programming distributor from providing satellite cable programming or satellite broadcast programming to subscribers or consumers.

Section 628(c)(1) provides that "the Commission shall, in order to promote the public interest, convenience, and necessity by increasing competition and diversity in the multichannel video programming market and the continuing development of communications technologies, prescribe regulations to specify particular conduct that is prohibited by" section 628(b). 47 U.S.C. § 548(c)(1). A federal court of appeals recently held that section 628(b) is written in "broad and sweeping terms" and therefore "'should be given broad, sweeping application.'" Nat'l Cable & Telecomms. Ass'n, 567 F.3d 659 (D.C. Cir. 2009) (*NCTA*).

12. In addition to this broad grant of authority, Congress in section 628(c)(2) directed the Commission to include "minimum contents" in its regulations specifying certain unfair acts, relating to satellite-delivered programming, that are among those prohibited by section 628(b). First, Congress required the Commission to prohibit efforts by cable operators to unduly influence the decision of cable-affiliated programming vendors that provide satellite-delivered programming to sell their programming to competitors ("undue or improper influence"). Second, Congress required the Commission to address discrimination by cable-affiliated programming vendors that provide satellite-delivered programming in the prices, terms, and conditions for sale of programming among MVPDs ("discrimination"). Third, Congress required the Commission to prohibit exclusive contracts between cable operators and cable-affiliated programming vendors that provide satellite-delivered programming subject to certain exceptions in areas served by a cable operator as of October 5, 1992 (the "exclusive contract prohibition"). These exceptions are: (i) exclusive contracts entered into prior to June 1, 1990 are not subject to the exclusive contract prohibition; (ii) exclusive contracts that the Commission deems to be in the public interest based on the factors set forth in the statute are not subject to the exclusive contract prohibition; and (iii) the exclusive contract prohibition will cease to be effective after October 5, 2002 unless the Commission finds that it "continues to be necessary to preserve and protect competition and diversity in the distribution of video programming." 47 U.S.C. § 548(c)(5); *see also* 47 C.F.R. § 76.1002(c)(6).

13. Section 628 was intended to address Congress' concern that cable operators or their affiliates would engage in unfair acts, including acts involving programming they own, that impede competition in the video distribution market.

III. Discussion

A. The Commission's Statutory Authority to Address Unfair Acts Involving Terrestrially Delivered, Cable-Affiliated Programming

19. Section 628(b) gives the Commission authority to promulgate rules applicable to unfair acts of cable operators (and certain other entities), including acts involving terrestrially delivered programming that have the purpose or effect of hindering significantly or preventing an MVPD from providing satellite cable programming or satellite broadcast programming to subscribers or consumers. Section 628(c)(1) authorizes the Commission to prescribe regulations to specify particular conduct prohibited by section 628(b). Our analysis reflects the Commission's interpretation of section 628(b) in the MDU Order, where the Commission held that it has authority pursuant to section 628(b) to adopt rules prohibiting exclusive contracts between cable operators and owners of multiple

dwelling units (MDUs) because those contracts prevent or significantly hinder the ability of competing MVPDs to provide all programming, including "satellite cable programming" and "satellite broadcast programming," in those markets. This interpretation was recently upheld by a federal court of appeals.

20. Vertically integrated cable operators note that section 628(c)(2) requires the Commission to prohibit unfair acts involving only satellite-delivered programming and assert that this specific mandate precludes the Commission from addressing terrestrially delivered programming pursuant to the general authority provided in section 628(b). While section 628(c)(2) lists specific unfair acts that the Commission is required to address as "minimum contents" in its regulations, the United States Court of Appeals for the District of Columbia Circuit has explained that this list does not preclude the Commission from adopting rules to address additional conduct that also is prohibited under section 628(b). As the court stated, "Congress had a particular manifestation of a problem in mind, but in no way expressed an unambiguous intent to limit the Commission's power solely to that version of the problem." *NCTA*, 567 F.3d at 664–65.

21. Here, we find that unfair acts involving cable-affiliated programming, regardless of whether that programming is satellite-delivered or terrestrially delivered, pose the danger of significantly hindering MVPDs from providing satellite cable programming or satellite broadcast programming, thereby harming competition in the video distribution market and limiting broadband deployment.

B. *The Need for Commission Action to Address Unfair Acts Involving Terrestrially Delivered, Cable-Affiliated Programming*

25. Having established that we possess authority to address unfair acts involving terrestrially delivered, cable-affiliated programming, in this section we discuss whether there is a need for such action. As discussed below, we find three reasons for taking action in this area: (i) cable operators continue to have an incentive and ability to engage in unfair acts or practices involving their affiliated programming, regardless of whether this programming is satellite-delivered or terrestrially delivered; (ii) our judgment regarding this incentive and ability is supported by real-world evidence that vertically integrated cable operators have withheld certain terrestrially delivered, cable-affiliated programming from their MVPD competitors; and (iii) there is evidence that, in some cases, this withholding may significantly hinder MVPDs from providing satellite cable programming and satellite broadcast programming to subscribers.

1. Incentive and Ability to Engage in Unfair Acts

26. Cable operators continue to have the incentive and ability to withhold or take other unfair acts with their affiliated programming in order to hinder competition in the video distribution market. This incentive and ability do not vary based on whether the cable-affiliated programming is delivered to cable operators by satellite or by terrestrial means. A vertically integrated cable operator may raise the costs of its MVPD competitors by increasing the price of its affiliated programming or may choose not to sell its affiliated programming to rival MVPDs. As the Commission noted in the *Adelphia Order*, "the integrated firm may be able to harm its rivals' competitive positions, enabling it to raise prices and increase its market share in the downstream market, thereby increasing its profits while retaining lower prices for itself or for firms with which it does not compete." Applications for Consent to the Assignment and/or Transfer of Control of Licenses, Adelphia Commc'ns Corp., Assignors, to Time Warner Cable, Inc., Assignees, et al., Memorandum Opinion and Order, 21 FCC Rcd. 8203, ¶ 117 (2006) (*Adelphia Order*). Unfair acts involving cable-affiliated programming may harm the ability of MVPDs to compete with incumbent cable

operators, thereby resulting in less competition in the marketplace to the detriment of consumers.

27. In the 2007 Program Access Order, the Commission analyzed the incentive and ability of cable operators and their affiliates to engage in one type of unfair act—withholding of affiliated programming from rival MVPDs. If the vertically integrated cable operator engages in withholding, it can recoup profits lost at the upstream level (i.e., by licensing programming) by increasing the number of subscribers of its downstream MVPD division. The Commission explained that, particularly "where competitive MVPDs are limited in their market share, a cable-affiliated programmer will be able to recoup a substantial amount, if not all, of the revenues foregone by pursuing a withholding strategy." Implementation of the Cable Television Consumer Protection and Competition Act of 1992, 22 FCC Rcd. 17,791, 17,827–29, ¶ 53 (2007) (2007 Program Access Order). Although the cable industry's share of MVPD subscribers nationwide has decreased since the 1992 Cable Act was passed, the Commission in the 2007 Program Access Order concluded that the cable industry's 67 percent market share remained sufficient to enable vertically integrated cable firms to make withholding a profitable strategy. There is no evidence in this proceeding that market shares have changed materially since that time. To the contrary, the cable industry has elsewhere stated that its share of MVPD subscribers nationwide has declined only slightly since the 2007 Program Access Order, to approximately 63.5 percent at the end of 2008. Moreover, the Commission observed that the regional market shares of cable operators sometimes exceed the national average. This makes withholding of local and regional programming, which is often terrestrially delivered and therefore beyond the reach of the program access rules, potentially an even more profitable strategy.

2. Evidence of Unfair Acts

30. Our judgment that cable operators continue to have the incentive and ability to withhold or take other unfair acts with their affiliated programming, including terrestrially delivered programming, is supported by real-world evidence. Because the program access rules currently apply only to satellite-delivered programming, terrestrial distribution allows a cable-affiliated programmer to bypass the program access rules. The record here, as well as our discussion in the 2007 Program Access Order, reflects substantial evidence that cable firms withhold affiliated programming from competitors when not barred from doing so. Moreover, the record reflects that terrestrial distribution is becoming more cost effective, and that its use is likely to continue and possibly increase in the future.

3. Evidence of the Impact of Unfair Acts

31. As discussed below, Commission action to address unfair acts involving terrestrially delivered, cable-affiliated programming is also needed because (i) there is evidence suggesting that such conduct has significantly hindered MVPDs from providing satellite cable programming and satellite broadcast programming in some cases and (ii) by significantly hindering MVPDs from providing video programming to subscribers, such conduct may significantly hinder the ability of competitive MVPDs to provide broadband services, particularly in rural areas.

a. Impact on Competition in the Video Distribution Market

33. While the Commission concluded in the 1998 Program Access Order that the record developed in that proceeding did not demonstrate that unfair acts involving terrestrially delivered, cable-affiliated programming were having a "significant anticompetitive effect," that conclusion was based on the limited data that were available more than ten years ago.

We now have evidence that unfair acts involving terrestrially delivered, cable-affiliated programming may well have the effect in some cases of significantly hindering MVPDs from providing all programming to subscribers and consumers. Moreover, while the Commission concluded in the 1998 Program Access Order that the record developed in that proceeding did not demonstrate that programming was being shifted from satellite to terrestrial delivery, the record here demonstrates that the MVPD marketplace has evolved, such that terrestrial distribution is becoming more cost effective and its use is likely to increase for new as well as established programming networks. Indeed, the record reflects that competitively significant networks, such as RSNs, are being delivered terrestrially today.

34. Vertically integrated cable operators argue that MVPDs are not dependent on vertically integrated cable programming because multiple programming options exist. But that is not always the case. As the Commission concluded in the 2007 Program Access Order, cable operators own programming for which there may be no good substitutes, and this "must-have" programming is necessary for viable competition in the video distribution market. The Commission explained that this includes both satellite-delivered and terrestrially delivered programming. As the Commission stated in the 2002 Program Access Order, "cable programming—be it news, drama, sports, music, or children's programming—is not akin to so many widgets." *Id.* ¶ 33. The salient point for purposes of section 628(b) is not the total number of programming networks available or the percentage of these networks that are vertically integrated with cable operators, but rather the popularity of the particular programming that is withheld and how the inability of competitive MVPDs to access that programming in a particular local market may impact their ability to provide a commercially attractive MVPD service.

b. Impact on Ability to Provide Broadband Services

36. Commission action to address unfair acts involving terrestrially delivered, cable-affiliated programming will have additional benefits, not specifically envisioned by Congress in 1992, because such acts have the potential to limit the ability of MVPDs to provide broadband services, particularly in rural areas. The Commission has previously concluded that a wireline firm's decision to deploy broadband is linked to its ability to offer video. Thus, by impeding the ability of MVPDs to provide video service, unfair acts involving terrestrially delivered, cable-affiliated programming can also impede the ability of MVPDs to provide broadband services. Allowing unfair acts involving terrestrially delivered, cable-affiliated programming to continue where they have this effect would undermine the goal of promoting the deployment of advanced services that Congress established as a priority for the Commission. This secondary effect heightens the urgency for Commission action.

c. Impact on Investment in Programming and Product Differentiation

37. Vertically integrated cable operators argue that the Commission should refrain from addressing denials of terrestrially delivered, cable-affiliated programming because exclusive distribution contracts for this programming can promote investment in programming and product differentiation.

38. We note that the Commission in the 2007 Program Access Order found unpersuasive arguments that the program access rules, including the exclusive contract prohibition, have reduced the incentives for cable operators and competitive MVPDs to create and invest in programming. The Commission noted that the number of vertically integrated satellite-delivered national programming networks has in fact more than doubled since 1994 when the rule implementing the exclusive contract prohibition took effect. While evidence was submitted in that proceeding that the percentage of vertically integrated satellite-delivered national programming networks had decreased over time, competitive

MVPDs characterized the decrease as "meaningless because it is attributable to an increase in the number of total programming networks available, most of which they contend have minimal subscriber bases and are targeted towards niche markets." *Id.* ¶ 32. Competitive MVPDs argued that the more relevant fact was the control of cable MSOs over "must have" programming, access to which is necessary to compete in the video distribution market. The Commission agreed: "What is most significant to our analysis is not the percentage of total available programming that is vertically integrated with cable operators, but rather the popularity of programming that is vertically integrated and how the inability of competitive MVPDs to access this programming will affect the preservation and protection of competition in the video distribution marketplace." *Id.* ¶ 37. A similar analysis applies to the present matter, given our goal of increasing competition and diversity in the video distribution market. In addition, while vertically integrated cable operators claim that exclusive deals and other unfair acts are justified because they allow a cable operator to differentiate its services from other MVPDs, section 628(b) specifically precludes such acts where they have the purpose or effect set forth in section 628(b).

39. In sum, sections 628(b) and 628(c)(1) of the Act give the Commission authority to address unfair acts of cable operators that have the purpose or effect of hindering significantly or preventing any MVPD from providing "satellite cable programming or satellite broadcast programming to subscribers or consumers." The focus of the statute is not on the ability of an MVPD to provide a particular terrestrially delivered programming network, but on the ability of the MVPD to compete in the video distribution market by selling satellite cable and satellite broadcast programming to subscribers and consumers. To be sure, unfair acts involving terrestrially delivered, cable-affiliated programming generally do not absolutely bar an MVPD from providing satellite cable programming or satellite broadcast programming to subscribers or consumers. For example, an incumbent cable operator's exclusive contract with a terrestrially delivered, cable-affiliated RSN does not totally preclude a rival MVPD from providing other programming, including satellite cable programming and satellite broadcast programming, to subscribers or consumers. As discussed above, however, in some cases the effect of denying an MVPD the ability to provide certain terrestrially delivered, cable-affiliated programming may be to significantly hinder the MVPD from providing video programming in general, including satellite cable programming and satellite broadcast programming, as well as terrestrially delivered programming. The result of this conduct may be to discourage MVPDs from entering new markets or to limit the ability of MVPDs to provide a competitive alternative to the incumbent cable operator. The reduction in robust competition in the video distribution market that results may allow cable operators to raise rates and to refrain from innovating, thereby adversely impacting consumers.

40. In addition to satisfying the plain language of section 628(b), our action here will also further the goals established by Congress in sections 628(a) and 628(c)(1) of the Act. First, our action will increase competition and diversity in the video distribution market by providing MVPDs with an opportunity to obtain access to certain cable-affiliated programming that they are currently unable to offer. Second, our action will increase the availability of satellite cable programming and satellite broadcast programming to persons in rural and unserved areas by eliminating a barrier to entry in the video distribution market. Third, our action will spur the development of communications technologies by promoting the provision of broadband services by MVPDs.

C. Constitutional Issues

41. We conclude that addressing unfair acts involving terrestrially delivered, cable-affiliated programming on a case-by-case basis comports with the First Amendment. As

the D.C. Circuit explained in rejecting a facial challenge to the constitutionality of the program access provisions dictated by section 628(c)(2) and applicable to satellite-delivered, cable-affiliated programming, these provisions will survive intermediate scrutiny if they "further an important or substantial governmental interest; if the governmental interest is unrelated to the suppression of free expression; and if the incidental restriction on alleged First Amendment freedoms is no greater than is essential to the furtherance of that interest." Time Warner Entm't Co., L.P. v. FCC, 93 F.3d 957, 978 (D.C. Cir. 1996). We conclude that the rules we adopt today with respect to terrestrially delivered, cable-affiliated programming comport with the First Amendment.

42. First, in *Time Warner v. FCC* the court found that the governmental interest Congress intended to serve in enacting the program access provisions was "the promotion of fair competition in the video marketplace," and that this interest was substantial. Moreover, the court noted Congress' conclusion that "the benefits of these provisions—the increased speech that would result from fairer competition in the video programming marketplace—outweighed the disadvantages the possibility of reduced economic incentives to develop new programming." We find that this governmental interest remains substantial today. 93 F.3d at 979.

43. Second, in *Time Warner v. FCC*, the court held that the governmental objective served by the statutory program access provisions was unrelated to the suppression of free expression. Similarly, our decision to address unfair acts involving terrestrially delivered, cable-affiliated programming on a case-by-case basis is not based on programming content but is instead intended to address significant hindrances to competition in the video distribution market. It responds to concerns about competition, not content. Thus, the regulations are content-neutral and unrelated to the suppression of free speech.

44. Third, any alleged restriction on speech resulting from our decision "is no greater than is essential to the furtherance" of Congress' interest in promoting competition in the video distribution market. *Id.* The analysis in *Time Warner v. FCC* applies here as well. Indeed, *Time Warner v. FCC* upheld as narrowly tailored the categorical, prophylactic program access rules, whereas here we adopt a tailored case-by-case approach that examines actual competitive harms in each instance. Noting the Commission's decision in the 2007 Program Access Order, Comcast contends that applying an exclusive contract prohibition to all cable-affiliated programming is overinclusive because it regulates at least some programming that is not competitively significant. But that argument misconceives the action we take today. In the 2007 Program Access Order, the Commission was implementing section 628(c)(2)(D), which establishes a broad prophylactic rule that subjects all satellite-delivered, cable-affiliated programming to an exclusive contract prohibition, subject to a procedure whereby individual programmers can seek Commission approval to enter into exclusive arrangements. Here, we are not implementing the statutory scheme set forth in section 628(c)(2)(D). Rather, we act pursuant to sections 628(b) and 628(c)(1), which give the Commission broad authority to adopt rules to address unfair acts of cable operators that have the purpose or effect of hindering significantly any MVPD from providing satellite cable programming or satellite broadcast programming. We decline to adopt a broad prophylactic rule that subjects all terrestrially delivered, cable-affiliated programming to the program access rules because we lack sufficient record evidence to reach general conclusions that unfair acts involving terrestrially delivered, cable-affiliated programming will always prevent or significantly hinder an MVPD from providing video services. Rather, we adopt rules whereby the Commission will consider on a case-by-case basis whether an unfair act involving terrestrially delivered, cable-affiliated programming has the purpose or effect of preventing or significantly hindering an MVPD from providing satellite cable programming or satellite broadcast programming to subscribers or

consumers, as required by section 628(b). The complaint process we establish today requires showings over and above those required by the program access rules applicable to satellite-delivered programming, and these additional showings (including a purpose or effect of preventing or significantly hindering an MVPD from providing satellite cable or satellite broadcast programming) prevent overinclusiveness. In short, our action today addresses any legitimate concerns about tailoring by adopting a case-by-case evaluation rather than a broad prophylactic rule.

D. *Complaint Filing Requirements*

1. *Types of Claims*

49. We thus conclude that actions by cable operators, satellite cable programming vendors in which a cable operator has an attributable interest, or satellite broadcast programming vendors involving terrestrially delivered, cable-affiliated programming that would be prohibited by the program access rules under section 628(c)(2) but for the terrestrial loophole (i.e., exclusive contracts, discrimination, and undue or improper influence) are "unfair methods of competition or unfair or deceptive acts or practices" within the meaning of section 628(b). Accordingly, an MVPD may initiate a complaint proceeding alleging that a cable operator, a satellite cable programming vendor in which a cable operator has an attributable interest, or a satellite broadcast programming vendor has engaged in one or more of these three unfair acts involving terrestrially delivered, cable-affiliated programming, with the purpose or effect of preventing or significantly hindering an MVPD from providing satellite cable programming or satellite broadcast programming to subscribers or consumers. While our program access procedural rules provide a defendant with 20 days after service to file an Answer to a complaint, we will provide the defendant with 45 days from the date of service of the complaint to file an Answer to a complaint involving terrestrially delivered programming to ensure that the defendant has adequate time to develop a response. We believe that additional time is appropriate because program access complaints involving terrestrially delivered programming, unlike complaints involving satellite-delivered programming, entail an additional factual inquiry regarding whether the unfair act has the purpose or effect set forth in section 628(b). With the exception of the additional burdens described below and the additional time for defendants to file an Answer, these proceedings will be subject to the same procedures set forth in sections 76.7 and 76.1003 of the Commission's rules that apply to program access complaints involving satellite-delivered, cable-affiliated programming. Among other things, these rules provide for pre-filing notices, discovery, remedies, potential defenses, and the required contents of and deadlines for filing the complaint, answer, and reply.

2. *Additional Burdens in Program Access Complaint Proceedings Alleging Unfair Acts Involving Terrestrially Delivered, Cable-Affiliated Programming*

51. For most terrestrially delivered, cable-affiliated programming, the record contains no evidence that unfair acts involving such programming generally have the purpose or effect of significantly hindering or preventing MVPDs from providing satellite cable programming or satellite broadcast programming. Nonetheless, such an act may have the purpose or effect set forth in section 628(b) in a particular case, especially given predictions that programming will increasingly shift to terrestrial delivery. Accordingly, in a program access complaint alleging an unfair act involving terrestrially delivered, cable-affiliated programming, the complainant will have the burden of proving that the unfair act has the purpose or effect of significantly hindering or preventing the MVPD from providing satellite cable programming or satellite broadcast programming. This burden

under section 628(b) is in addition to any other burdens imposed by the Commission's rules on a complainant pursuing a program access complaint regarding an exclusive contract, discrimination, or undue or improper influence.

52. We do identify one class of programming that, as shown by both Commission precedent and record evidence in this proceeding, is very likely to be both non-replicable and highly valued by consumers. We recognize the weight of the existing precedent and categorical evidence concerning RSNs by allowing complainants to invoke a rebuttable presumption that an unfair act involving a terrestrially delivered, cable-affiliated RSN has the purpose or effect set forth in section 628(b).

Notes and Questions

1. Statutory Language. Look at § 628(b). Is the Commission's reading the best reading of that provision? The only reading? A permissible reading?

2. Assumptions. Under what circumstances would it be in an MVPD's interest to refuse to accept a fair market price from competitors who want to show the MVPD's "must-have" programming? Under what circumstances would it be in an MVPD's interest to accept a fair market price for such programming?

3. Presumptions. Should the FCC have adopted a conclusive presumption that an unfair act involving an RSN violates § 628(b)? Conversely, should it have adopted no presumption at all with respect to RSNs? Why do you think the FCC struck the balance it chose?

4. Appellate Review. The D.C. Circuit upheld the key elements of the order excerpted above in the case excerpted below.

CABLEVISION SYSTEMS CORP. v. FCC
649 F.3d 695 (D.C. Cir. 2011)

Opinion for the Court filed by Circuit Judge TATEL, in which Circuit Judges ROGERS and GRIFFITH concur.

TATEL, Circuit Judge.

II.

Starting with petitioners' statutory argument, we apply the familiar *Chevron* framework to the Commission's interpretation of its governing statute. Chevron U.S.A. Inc. v. Natural Res. Def. Council, 467 U.S. 837, 842–43 (1984). We begin by asking "whether Congress has directly spoken to the precise question at issue." *Id.* at 842. If it has, we "give effect to the unambiguously expressed intent of Congress." *Id.* at 842–43. But if Congress has not unambiguously foreclosed the agency's construction of the statute, we defer to the agency provided its construction is reasonable. *See* Nat'l Cable & Telecomms. Ass'n v. Brand X Internet Servs., 545 U.S. 967, 980 (2005).

Petitioners face an uphill climb in arguing that the Commission's interpretation of section 628(b) fails under *Chevron* step one. In *National Cable & Telecommunications Ass'n v. FCC (NCTA)*, we described section 628(b)'s prohibition as "broad and sweeping," observing that its language bars unfair "practices 'the purpose or effect of which is to hinder significantly or to prevent any multichannel video programming distributor from providing satellite ... programming ... to subscribers or consumers.'" 567 F.3d 659, 664

(D.C. Cir. 2009) (quoting 47 U.S.C. § 548(b)). This broad language, we pointed out, "comports" with section 628's similarly expansive "express purpose of 'promot[ing] the public interest, convenience, and necessity by increasing competition and diversity in the multichannel video programming market.'" *Id.* (quoting 47 U.S.C. § 548(a)).

Petitioners' first argument—that section 628(c)(2)'s limitations implicitly restrict the scope of section 628(b)'s general prohibition—fails for the same reason we rejected a similar argument in *NCTA*. "By its terms, section 628(c)[(2)] describes only the '[m]inimum contents of regulations....'" *NCTA*, 567 F.3d at 664–65 (quoting 47 U.S.C. § 548(c)(2)). Indeed, "Congress's enumeration of specific, required regulations in subsection (c) actually suggests that Congress intended subsection (b)'s generic language to cover a broader field." *Id.* at 665. Petitioners' reliance on cases holding that agencies may not use their general rulemaking authority to override a more specific statutory directive is thus misplaced. Because section 628(c)(2) establishes a floor rather than a ceiling, the Commission's reliance on subsections (b) and (c)(1) to regulate conduct that subsection (c)(2) leaves unrestricted in no way contravenes congressional intent.

Hardly clairvoyant, especially with respect to rapidly evolving technologies, Congress may well have targeted satellite programming in section 628(c)(2) simply because it was at the time far and away the dominant form of video programming and thus the focus of concerns about anticompetitive withholding. The legislative history sheds no light on Congress's intent, as there is neither any explanation in the House committee reports concerning its decision to use the term "satellite programming" rather than "video programming" nor any indication in the conference report that Congress adopted the House language to restrict the statute's coverage. To the contrary, the conference report emphasizes the statute's expansive goals, explaining that "the conferees expect the Commission to address and resolve the problems of unreasonable cable industry practices, including restricting the availability of programming and charging discriminatory prices to non-cable technologies." *See* H.R. Rep. No. 102-862, at 93 [(1991)]. We thus see no justification for construing Congress's reference to satellite programming withholding in subsection (c)(2) as an effort to prevent the Commission from addressing similar unfair practices that—two decades later—have either the purpose or effect that subsection (b) proscribes.

Moreover, even were there reason to believe that Congress deliberately phrased subsection (c)(2) to exclude terrestrial programming, as opposed to simply using a term that captured the overwhelming majority of video programming at the time, we still see nothing in the statute that would unambiguously preclude the Commission from extending its rules to terrestrial programming on a case-by-case basis. Congress may well have wanted to avoid dictating the rules the Commission must adopt for a nascent technology while leaving it with authority to act should regulation prove necessary.

[W]e are unpersuaded by petitioners' contention that the Commission lacks authority to regulate terrestrial programming withholding under section 628(b) because, in their view, the effect of such withholding on the provision of satellite programming is too attenuated. According to petitioners and their supporting intervenor, section 628(b) gives the Commission authority to regulate practices that prevent or significantly impair an MVPD from either *obtaining* satellite programming (which the subsection (c)(2) program access rules address) or *delivering* satellite programming to customers (which the MDU order in *NCTA* dealt with). Terrestrial programming withholding, they insist, has no effect on a rival MVPD's ability either to obtain satellite programming or to deliver such programming because even when cable-affiliated terrestrial programmers refuse to share, the MVPD remains fully able to make satellite programming available to interested customers. Acknowledging that terrestrial programming withholding may limit the number of customers an MVPD can attract, thus reducing its market share, petitioners contend that commercial attractiveness has nothing to do with whether the MVPD can provide satellite programming.

The problem with petitioners' argument is that it wrongly assumes an MVPD's lack of commercial attractiveness will never prevent or significantly hinder it from providing satellite programming. Indeed, as explained above, Congress enacted section 628 largely on the theory that "exclusive arrangements" for programming "may tend to establish a barrier to entry and inhibit the development of competition in the market." S. Rep. No. 102–92, at 28 (1991). When a vertically integrated cable programmer limits access to programming that customers want and that competitors are unable to duplicate—like the games of a local team selling broadcast rights to a single sports network—competitor MVPDs will find themselves at a serious disadvantage when trying to attract customers away from the incumbent cable company. To use a concrete example, we doubt that Philadelphia baseball fans would switch from cable to an alternative MVPD if doing so would mean they could no longer watch Roy Halladay, Cliff Lee, Roy Oswalt, and Cole Hamels take the mound, even if they thought the alternative MVPD was otherwise superior in terms of price and quality. Facing such a structural disadvantage, a potential MVPD competitor might realistically conclude that expanding its presence in the Philadelphia market would be uneconomical, thus limiting its ability to provide video programming—and hence satellite video programming—to customers.

Another hypothetical proves the point. Suppose the impact of withholding a particular cable-affiliated terrestrial programming network in a particular market is so great that it drives existing non-cable MVPDs completely out of the market and keeps others from entering. In that case, no one would doubt that terrestrial programming withholding prevented MVPDs from providing satellite programming. Just as "if you can't serve a building then you can't deliver satellite ... programming," *NCTA*, 567 F.3d at 664 (internal quotation marks omitted), if you can't enter or survive in a market, then you can't deliver satellite programming in that market. Petitioners conceded at oral argument that the Commission would possess section 628(b) authority in such a case, but they insisted there is no evidence that terrestrial withholding has ever made it completely impossible for potential competitors to enter or survive in a market. Of course, petitioners are right about this: the Commission has never suggested that there are situations in which terrestrial withholding has completely prevented an MVPD from serving a market. But given petitioners' concession that the Commission can in principle regulate terrestrial withholding when such withholding completely prevents an MVPD from competing, thus preventing that MVPD from providing satellite programming, they have no basis for arguing that section 628 unambiguously precludes the Commission from regulating where it has evidence that such withholding "hinder[s] significantly," 47 U.S.C. § 548(b), an MVPD from competing with the incumbent cable operator to deliver satellite programming to customers.

Having rejected petitioners' arguments that section 628(b) unambiguously forecloses the Commission's interpretation, we are left to decide whether that interpretation is reasonable under *Chevron* step two's "highly deferential standard." Nat'l Rifle Ass'n of Am., Inc. v. Reno, 216 F.3d 122, 137 (D.C. Cir. 2000). It is. As the Commission explained, through section 628 "Congress intended to encourage entry and facilitate competition in the video distribution market by existing or potential competitors to traditional cable systems by, among other things, making available to those entities the programming they need to compete in the video distribution market." Review of the Comm'n's Program Access Rules & Examination of Programming Tying Arrangements, First Report and Order, 25 FCC Rcd. at 754 ¶ 13 (2010 Order). And according to the Commission, terrestrially delivered programming, or at least some kinds of terrestrial programming like RSNs that are both nonreplicable and highly coveted, have become necessary for MVPDs to compete fully with vertically integrated cable companies. *Id.* at 768–71, ¶¶ 32–35. Petitioners have given us no reason to disturb the Commission's effort to pursue Congress's objectives as the video distribution industry evolves.

Relying on language from *NCTA*, petitioners argue that the Commission's interpretation of section 628(b) creates "the specter of a statutory grant without bounds" because by interpreting a statute focused on the provision of satellite programming to authorize terrestrial withholding regulations, the Commission has "stray[ed] so far from the paradigm case as to render its interpretation unreasonable, arbitrary, or capricious." 567 F.3d at 665. In our view, however, the Commission has "barely reached beyond the paradigm case at all." *Id.* at 666. Indeed, the order at issue here actually aligns more closely with Congress's core purpose in enacting section 628 than did the MDU order. After all, preventing vertically integrated cable companies from engaging in unfair dealing over programming, precisely the conduct the challenged order addresses, was the primary reason Congress enacted section 628. *See id.* at 663 (acknowledging that "Congress's primary purpose in enacting section 628 was ... to expand competition for programming, not service").

III.

Petitioners next contend that the Commission's order violates the First Amendment, both on its face and as applied, because the program access rules for terrestrial programming burden the speech and association rights of cable operators and video programmers. As to that claim, this court has already done much of the heavy lifting. In Time Warner Entm't Co. v. FCC, 93 F.3d 957, 977–78 (D.C. Cir. 1996) (*per curiam*), we held that intermediate scrutiny applied to a facial challenge to the Commission's satellite programming access rules established pursuant to section 628(c)(2). Under that standard, we will sustain a regulation if "'it furthers an important or substantial governmental interest; if the governmental interest is unrelated to the suppression of free expression; and if the incidental restriction on alleged First Amendment freedoms is no greater than is essential to the furtherance of that interest.'" Turner Broad. Sys., Inc. v. FCC, 512 U.S. 622, 662 (1994) (quoting United States v. O'Brien, 391 U.S. 367, 377 (1968)) (*Turner I*). Concluding that regulating vertically integrated programmers and operators to promote competition in the video marketplace "furthers an important government interest [that] is unrelated to the suppression of free expression" and that subsection (c)(2)'s restrictions did not "burden substantially more speech than is necessary to further" that interest, we upheld the Commission's program access rules against a facial challenge. *Time Warner v. FCC*, 93 F.3d at 978–79 (internal quotation marks omitted).

In this case, therefore, we apply intermediate scrutiny to the Commission's order, recognizing that we have already concluded that its asserted justification—promoting competition in the MVPD market—represents an important governmental interest. Of course, just because the government's "asserted interests are important in the abstract does not mean" that the Commission's terrestrial programming withholding rules "will in fact advance those interests." *Turner I*, 512 U.S. at 664. "When the [g]overnment defends a regulation on speech as a means to redress past harms or prevent anticipated harms, it must ... demonstrate that the recited harms are real, not merely conjectural, and that the regulation will in fact alleviate these harms in a direct and material way." *Id.* Pointing to dramatic changes in the video programming industry since Congress passed the Cable

Act in 1992, and in particular to significant gains in market share enjoyed by MVPD competitors to cable, petitioners contend that the Commission's imposition of any program access obligations no longer serves an important governmental interest and therefore violates the First Amendment. "At a minimum," they assert, the extension of program access rules to terrestrially delivered programming fails intermediate scrutiny because "competition in the MVPD industry has flourished even though terrestrial programming was never required to be shared." Pet'rs' Br. 32.

The video programming industry does indeed look very different today than it did when Congress passed the Cable Act in 1992. Although cable operators then controlled approximately 95% of the national market for video programming, by 2007 their share had decreased to 67%, and it has apparently continued dropping in the face of competition from DBS providers and, more recently, from telephone companies offering fiber optic services, see 2010 Order, 25 FCC Rcd. at 763, ¶ 27. In addition, the number of programming networks has increased dramatically while the percentage of networks vertically integrated with cable operators has declined.

Contrary to petitioners' argument, however, these market changes do not mean that the Commission's order fails intermediate scrutiny. By imposing liability only when complainants demonstrate that a company's unfair act has "the purpose or effect" of "hinder[ing] significantly or ... prevent[ing]" the provision of satellite programming, 47 U.S.C. § 548(b), the Commission's terrestrial programming rules specifically target activities where the governmental interest is greatest. Accordingly, to survive intermediate scrutiny in this facial challenge, the Commission need show only that vertically integrated cable operators remain dominant in some video distribution markets, that the withholding of highly desirable terrestrially delivered cable programming, like RSNs, inhibits competition in those markets, and that providing other MVPDs access to such programming will "promot[e] ... fair competition in the video marketplace." *Time Warner v. FCC*, 93 F.3d at 978. The Commission has no obligation to establish that vertically integrated cable companies retain a stranglehold on competition nationally or that all withholding of terrestrially delivered programming negatively affects competition. For these reasons, petitioners' reference to the Commission's extending its program access rules by closing the terrestrial loophole is a red herring. Although it is true that competition in the MVPD industry has generally increased even absent rules restricting terrestrial withholding, nothing prevents the Commission from addressing any remaining barriers to effective competition with appropriately tailored remedies.

With our inquiry thus focused, we believe that the Commission's order serves an important governmental interest and that the Commission has satisfied its constitutional burden under intermediate scrutiny. As we observed in *Cablevision Systems Corp. v. FCC*, the transformation in the MVPD market, although significant, presents a "mixed picture" when considered as a whole. 597 F.3d 1306, 1314 (D.C. Cir. 2010). Relying on the record from the Commission's 2007 program access order extension for satellite programming, we observed that not only do cable operators still control some two-thirds of the market nationally, but also that they enjoy higher shares in several markets. *See Cablevision*, 597 F.3d at 1314. We further recognized that clustering and consolidation in the industry bolsters the market power of cable operators because "a single geographic area can be highly susceptible to near-monopoly control by a cable company." *Id.* at 1309. On the programming side, we cited the Commission's finding that despite major gains in the amount and diversity of programming, as of 2007 "the four largest cable operators [were] still vertically integrated with six of the top 20 national networks, some of the most popular premium networks, and almost half of all regional sports networks." *Id.* at 1314. In the order at issue here, the Commission reaffirmed these observations about the MVPD market, finding "no evidence ... that market shares have changed materially since" 2007, and concluding that "cable operators still have a dominant share of MVPD subscribers," that "there is evidence that cable prices have risen in excess of inflation," and that "cable operators still own significant programming." 2010 Order, 25 FCC Rcd. at 763, 776 ¶¶ 27, 42. Petitioners have given us no reason to question these findings.

Moreover, the Commission's 2006 regression analysis concerning the withholding of terrestrially delivered, cable-affiliated RSN programming in the Philadelphia and San Diego markets demonstrates that vertically integrated cable companies can in fact withhold terrestrially delivered programming to limit the market share of rival MVPDs. Applying APA review, we relied on this study in *Cablevision* to reject a challenge to the Commission's five-year extension of its prohibition on exclusive contracts for satellite programming between cable operators and cable-affiliated programmers for satellite programming. First Amendment intermediate scrutiny is, of course, substantially more demanding than arbitrary and capricious review of agency action. But given how directly this study supports the Commission's present order, which adopts case-by-case restrictions on terrestrial programming, as compared to the Commission's earlier decision, which extended the general ban on exclusive contracts for cable-affiliated satellite programming, we give the study significant weight here as well.

Notes and Questions

1. Revisiting *NCTA v. FCC*. Does anything in this excerpt cast doubt on the D.C. Circuit's reasoning in *NCTA v. FCC*? That is, do the ramifications of *NCTA v. FCC*, as reflected in the excerpt above, suggest that *NCTA v. FCC* interpreted § 628(b) too broadly?

2. Purposes. Do you think that Congress's purpose in enacting § 628(b) encompasses measures like the order at issue in this case? Are you persuaded by the court's statement that the order at issue "actually aligns more closely with Congress's core purpose in enacting § 628 than did the MDU order" at issue in *NCTA v. FCC*? Again, should that tell us anything about *NCTA v. FCC*?

3. First Amendment, Antitrust, and Regulatory Institutions? The court says that the First Amendment objection is overcome because the FCC will order carriage only when it can show that the withholding company is dominant and that the withholding injures competition. Is the court's view that the First Amendment requires an antitrust standard? Should it? If so, why have the FCC rather than the antitrust institutions administer this? And, if this is the standard for FCC enforcement, who won the war here?

§ 10.D. MVPD Non-Discrimination Obligations

The structural and behavioral rules that addressed the integration of programming and distribution were designed to facilitate entry in the MVPD market—that is, to ensure that that new distribution companies would have access to sufficient programming to enter the market. By contrast, the rules discussed earlier limiting horizontal ownership were structural rules designed directly to benefit content providers, by giving them multiple outlets for their programming. Congress and the FCC have also adopted behavioral rules addressed at that same concern. Thus, in the 1992 Cable Act, § 616, Congress said that the FCC must adopt regulations designed to prevent a multichannel video programming distributor from engaging in conduct the effect of which is to unreasonably restrain the ability of an unaffiliated video programming vender to compete fairly by discriminating in video programming distribution on the basis of affiliation or nonaffiliation of vendors in the selection, terms, or conditions for carriage of video programming by such vendors.

47 U.S.C. § 536(a)(3). The FCC's regulations mirrored this language, and created a complaint mechanism for programmers that believed they had been subject of such discrimination. In the FCC's nomenclature, these are the "program carriage rules" (to distinguish them from the "program access rules" just discussed). 47 C.F.R. § 76.1302.

In 2011, the FCC described the prima facie case that a programmer must make. Revision of the Commission's Program Carriage Rules, Report and Order, 26 FCC Rcd. 11,494 (2011). In brief, the FCC said that a complainant must show that it was treated differently from the way in which an MVPD treats similarly situated, affiliated programming and that this different treatment had the effect of "unreasonably restraining" its ability "to compete fairly." Id. ¶ 15. The D.C. Circuit's most important decision interpreting the FCC's regulations and discussing the programmer's burden of proof is excerpted below.

COMCAST CABLE COMMUNICATIONS, LLC v. FCC
717 F.3d 982 (D.C. Cir. 2013)

Opinion for the Court filed by Senior Circuit Judge WILLIAMS, in which Circuit Judge KAVANAUGH and Senior Circuit Judge EDWARDS concur.

WILLIAMS, Senior Circuit Judge.

Regulations of the Federal Communications Commission, adopted under the mandate of § 616 of the Communications Act of 1934 and virtually duplicating its language, bar a multichannel video programming distributor (MVPD) such as a cable company from discriminating against unaffiliated programming networks in decisions about content distribution. More specifically, the regulations bar such conduct when the effect of the discrimination is to "unreasonably restrain the ability of an unaffiliated video programming vendor to compete fairly." 47 C.F.R. § 76.1301(c); see also 47 U.S.C. § 536(a)(3). Tennis Channel, a sports programming network and intervenor in this suit, filed a complaint against petitioner Comcast Cable, an MVPD, alleging that Comcast violated § 616 and the Commission's regulations by refusing to broadcast Tennis as widely (i.e., via the same relatively low-priced "tier") as it did its own affiliated sports programming networks, Golf Channel and Versus. An administrative law judge ruled against Comcast, ordering that it provide Tennis carriage equal to what it affords Golf and Versus, and the Commission affirmed. See Tennis Channel, Inc. v. Comcast Cable Commc'ns, LLC, Memorandum Opinion and Order, 27 FCC Rcd. 8508 (2012) (Order).

Comcast's arguments on appeal are, broadly speaking, threefold. First, it contends that Tennis's complaint was untimely filed. Second, Comcast poses a number of issues as to the meaning of § 616, including an argument that the Commission reads it so broadly as to violate Comcast's free speech rights under the First Amendment. We need not reach those issues, as Comcast prevails with its third set of arguments—that even under the Commission's interpretation of § 616 (the correctness of which we assume for purposes of this decision), the Commission has failed to identify adequate evidence of unlawful discrimination.

Many arguments within this third set involve complex and at least potentially sophisticated disputes. But Comcast also argued that the Commission could not lawfully find discrimination because Tennis offered no evidence that its rejected proposal would have afforded Comcast any benefit. If this is correct, as we conclude below, the Commission has nothing to refute Comcast's contention that its rejection of Tennis's proposal was simply "a straight up financial analysis," as one of its executives put it.

* * *

Comcast, the largest MVPD in the United States, offers cable television programming to its subscribers in several different distribution "tiers," or packages of programming services, at different prices. Since Versus's and Golf's launches in 1995, Comcast—which originally had a minority interest in the two networks, and now has 100% ownership—has generally carried the networks on its most broadly distributed tiers, Expanded Basic or the digital counterpart Digital Starter.

Tennis Channel, launched in 2003, initially sought distribution of its content on Comcast's less broadly distributed sports tier, a package of 10 to 15 sports networks that Comcast's subscribers can access for an extra $5 to $8 per month. In 2005, Tennis entered a carriage contract that gave Comcast the "right to carry" Tennis "on any ... tier of service," subject to exclusions irrelevant here. Comcast in fact placed Tennis on the sports tier.

In 2009, however, Tennis approached Comcast with proposals that Comcast reposition Tennis onto a tier with broader distribution. Tennis's proposed agreement called for Comcast to pay Tennis for distribution on a per-subscriber basis. [E]ven with the discounts that Tennis offered, the amounts are substantial. Neither the analysis provided at the time, nor testimony received in this litigation, made (much less substantiated) projections of any resulting increase in revenue for Comcast, let alone revenue sufficient to offset the increased fees.

Comcast entertained the proposal, checking with "division and system employees to gauge local and subscriber interest." After those consultations, and based on previous analyses of interest in Tennis, Comcast rejected the proposal in June 2009. Tennis then filed its complaint with the Commission in January 2010, which led to the order now under review. By way of remedy, the ALJ ordered, and the Commission affirmed, that Comcast must "carry [Tennis] on the same distribution tier, reaching the same number of subscribers, as it does [Golf] and Versus." Order ¶ 92.

The parties agree that Comcast distributes the content of affiliates Golf and Versus more broadly than it does that of Tennis. The question is whether that difference violates § 616 and the implementing regulations. There is also no dispute that the statute prohibits only discrimination based on affiliation. Thus, if the MVPD treats vendors differently based on a reasonable business purpose (obviously excluding any purpose to illegitimately hobble the competition from Tennis), there is no violation. The Commission has so interpreted the statute, and the Commission's attorney conceded as much at oral argument.

In contrast with the detailed, concrete explanation of Comcast's additional costs under the proposed tier change, Tennis showed no corresponding benefits that would accrue to Comcast by its accepting the change. Testimony from one of Comcast's executives identifies some of the factors it considers when deciding whether to move a channel to broader distribution:

> In deciding whether to carry a network and at what cost, Comcast Cable must balance the costs and benefits associated with a wide range of factors, including: the amount of the licensing fees (which is generally the most important factor); the nature of the programming content involved; the intensity and size of the fan

base for that content; the level of service sought by the network; the network's carriage on other MVPDs; the extent of [most favored nation] protection provided; the term of the contract sought; and a variety of other operational issues.

Of course the record is very strong on the proposed increment in licensing fees, in itself a clear negative. The question is whether the other factors, and perhaps ones unmentioned by Comcast, establish reason to expect a net benefit.

But neither Tennis nor the Commission offers such an analysis on either a qualitative or a quantitative basis. Instead, the best the Commission offers, both in the Order and at oral argument, is that Tennis charges less per "rating point" than does either Golf or Versus. But those differentials are not affirmative evidence that acceptance of Tennis's 2009 proposal could have offered Comcast any net gain.

In the absence of evidence that the lower cost per ratings point is correlated with changes in revenues to offset the proposed cost increase for Tennis's broader distribution, the discussion of cost per ratings point is mere handwaving.

A rather obvious type of proof would have been expert evidence to the effect that X number of subscribers would switch to Comcast if it carried Tennis more broadly, or that Y number would leave Comcast in the absence of broader carriage, or a combination of the two, such that Comcast would recoup the proposed increment in cost. There is no such evidence. (Conceivably Tennis could have shown that the incremental losses from carrying Tennis in a broad tier would be the same as or less than the incremental losses Comcast was incurring from carrying Golf and Versus in such tiers. The parties do not even hint at this possibility, nor analyze its implications.)

Not only does the record lack affirmative evidence along these lines, there is evidence that no such benefits exist. After Tennis proposed the broader distribution of its content on Comcast's network, Comcast executives surveyed employees in various geographic divisions to gauge interest in the proposal. The executive in charge of the northern division reported that there was "[n]o interest whatsoever" in moving Tennis to a broader distribution, because there had never been "a request or a complaint to move Tennis Channel to a more available tier." Perhaps more telling is the natural experiment conducted in Comcast's southern division. There Comcast had in 2007 or 2008 acquired a distribution network from another MVPD that had distributed Tennis more broadly than did Comcast. When Comcast repositioned Tennis to the sports tier (a "negative repo" in MVPD lingo), thereby making it available to Comcast's general subscribers only for an additional fee, not one customer complained about the change.

Neither Tennis nor the Commission has invoked the concept that an otherwise valid business consideration is here merely pretextual cover for some deeper discriminatory purpose. Without showing any benefit for Comcast from incurring the additional fees for assigning Tennis a more advantageous tier, the Commission has not provided evidence that Comcast discriminated against Tennis on the basis of affiliation.

The petition is therefore Granted.

KAVANAUGH, Circuit Judge, concurring:

As the Court's opinion explains, the FCC erred in concluding that Comcast discriminated against the Tennis Channel on the basis of affiliation. I join the Court's opinion in full. I write separately to point out that the FCC also erred in a more fundamental way. Section 616's use of the phrase "unreasonably restrain"—an antitrust term of art—establishes that the statute applies only to discrimination that amounts to an unreasonable restraint under antitrust law. Vertical integration and vertical contracts—for example, between a video programming distributor and a video programming network—become potentially problematic under antitrust law only when a company has market power in the relevant market. It follows that Section 616 applies only when a video programming distributor possesses market power. But Comcast does not have market power in the national video programming distribution market, the relevant market analyzed by the FCC in this case. Therefore, as I will explain in Part I of this opinion, Section 616 does not apply here.

Applying Section 616 to a video programming distributor that lacks market power not only contravenes the terms of the statute, but also violates the First Amendment as it has been interpreted by the Supreme Court. As I will explain in Part II of this opinion, the canon of constitutional avoidance thus strongly reinforces the conclusion that Section 616 applies only when a video programming distributor possesses market power.

I

Congress enacted Section 616 (over the veto of President George H.W. Bush) as part of the Cable Television Consumer Protection and Competition Act of 1992, known as the Cable Act. The Cable Act included numerous provisions designed to curb abuses of cable operators' bottleneck monopoly power and to promote competition in the cable television industry. When the Act was passed, however, the video programming market looked quite different than it looks today. At the time, most households subscribed to cable in order to view television programming. And as Congress noted, "most cable television subscribers [had] no opportunity to select between competing cable systems." Cable Television Consumer Protection and Competition Act of 1992, Pub. L. No. 102-385, § 2(a)(2), 106 Stat. 1460, 1460 (1992). Congress decided to proactively counteract the bottleneck monopoly power that cable operators possessed in many local markets.

The Cable Act employs a variety of tools to advance competition. Some provisions directly prohibit practices that Congress viewed as anticompetitive in the market at the time. For example, the Act prohibits local franchising authorities from granting exclusive franchises to cable operators. *See id.* § 7(a), 106 Stat. at 1483. Similarly, the Act's "must-carry" provisions require cable operators to carry a specified number of local broadcast stations. *See id.* § 4, 106 Stat. at 1471.

In other parts of the Act, Congress borrowed from antitrust law, authorizing the FCC to regulate cable operators' conduct in accordance with antitrust principles. For example, the Act requires the FCC, when prescribing limits on the number of cable subscribers or affiliated channels, to take account of "the nature and market power of the local franchise." *See id.* § 11(c), 106 Stat. at 1488. Similarly, the Act allows rate regulation only of those cable systems that are not subject to effective competition. *See id.* § 3, 106 Stat. at 1464.

The provision at issue in this case, Section 616, incorporates traditional antitrust principles. Section 616 does not categorically forbid a video programming distributor from extending preferential treatment to affiliated video programming networks or lesser treatment to unaffiliated video programming networks. Rather, to violate Section 616, a video programming distributor must discriminate among video programming networks on the basis of affiliation, and the discrimination must "unreasonably restrain" an unaffiliated network's ability to compete fairly. 47 U.S.C. § 536(a)(3).

The phrase "unreasonably restrain" is of course a longstanding term of art in antitrust law. *See, e.g.,* Leegin Creative Leather Products, Inc. v. PSKS, Inc., 551 U.S. 877, 885 (2007) ("[T]he Court has repeated time and again that § 1 outlaws only unreasonable restraints."). When a statute uses a term of art from a specific field of law, we presume that Congress adopted "the cluster of ideas that were attached to each borrowed word in the body of learning from which it was taken." FAA v. Cooper, 132 S. Ct. 1441, 1449 (2012).

From the "term of art" canon and Section 616's use of the antitrust term of art "unreasonably restrain," it follows that Section 616 incorporates antitrust principles governing unreasonable restraints.

So what does antitrust law tell us? In antitrust law, certain activities are considered per se anticompetitive. Otherwise, however, conduct generally can be considered unreasonable only if a firm, or multiple firms acting in concert, have market power.

This case involves vertical integration and vertical contracts. Beginning in the 1970s (well before the 1992 Cable Act), the Supreme Court has recognized the legitimacy of vertical integration and vertical contracts by firms without market power. Vertical integration and vertical contracts become potentially problematic only when a firm has market power in the relevant market. That's because, absent market power, vertical integration and vertical contracts are procompetitive. Vertical integration and vertical contracts in a competitive market encourage product innovation, lower costs for businesses, and create efficiencies—and thus reduce prices and lead to better goods and services for consumers.

Now back to Section 616: Because Section 616 incorporates antitrust principles and because antitrust law holds that vertical integration and vertical contracts are potentially problematic only when a firm has market power in the relevant market, it follows that Section 616 applies only when a video programming distributor has market power in the relevant market.

How, then, did the FCC reach the opposite conclusion in this case? The short answer is that the FCC badly misread the statute. Contrary to the plain language of Section 616, the FCC stated that the term "unreasonably" modified "discriminating" not "restrain"—even though Section 616 says it applies only to discriminatory conduct that "unreasonably restrain[s]" the ability of a competitor to compete fairly. Because the FCC did not read Section 616 as written, it did not recognize the antitrust term of art "unreasonably restrain" that is apparent on the face of the statute. That erroneous reading of the text, in turn, led the FCC to mistakenly focus on the effects of Comcast's conduct on a competitor (the Tennis Channel) rather than on overall competition. That was a mistake because the goal of antitrust law (and thus of Section 616) is to promote consumer welfare by protecting competition, not by protecting individual competitors.

It is true that Section 616 references discrimination against competitors. But again, the statute does not ban such discrimination outright. It bans discrimination that unreasonably restrains a competitor from competing fairly. By using the phrase "unreasonably restrain," the statute incorporates an antitrust term of art, and that term of art requires that the discrimination in question hinder overall competition, not just competitors.

In sum, Section 616 targets instances of preferential program carriage that are anticompetitive under the antitrust laws. Section 616 thus may apply only when a video programming distributor possesses market power in the relevant market. Comcast has only about a 24% market share in the national video programming distribution market; it does not possess market power in the market considered by the FCC in this case. Therefore, the FCC erred in finding that Comcast violated Section 616.

II

To the extent there is uncertainty about whether the phrase "unreasonably restrain" in Section 616 means that the statute applies only in cases of market power or instead may have a broader reach, we must construe the statute to avoid "serious constitutional concerns." Edward J. DeBartolo Corp. v. Florida Gulf Coast Building & Construction Trades Council, 485 U.S. 568, 577 (1988). That canon strongly supports limiting Section 616 to cases of market power. Applying Section 616 to a video programming distributor that lacks market power would raise serious First Amendment questions under the Supreme Court's case law. Indeed, applying Section 616 to a video programming distributor that lacks market power would violate the First Amendment as it has been interpreted by the Supreme Court.

To begin with, the Supreme Court has squarely held that a video programming distributor such as Comcast both engages in and transmits speech, and is therefore protected by the First Amendment. *See* Turner Broadcasting System, Inc. v. FCC, 512 U.S. 622, 636 (1994). Just as a newspaper exercises editorial discretion over which articles to run, a video programming distributor exercises editorial discretion over which video programming networks to carry and at what level of carriage.

In its 1994 decision in *Turner Broadcasting*, the Supreme Court ruled that the Cable Act's must-carry provisions might satisfy intermediate First Amendment scrutiny, but the Court rested that conclusion on "special characteristics of the cable medium: the bottleneck monopoly power exercised by cable operators and the dangers this power poses to the viability of broadcast television." *Id.* at 661. When a cable operator has bottleneck power, the Court explained, it can "silence the voice of competing speakers with a mere flick of the switch." *Id.* at 656. In subsequently upholding the must-carry provisions, the Court reiterated that cable's bottleneck monopoly power was critical to the First Amendment calculus. *See* Turner Broadcasting System, Inc. v. FCC, 520 U.S. 180, 197–207 (1997) (controlling opinion of Kennedy, J.). The Court stated that "cable operators possess[ed] a local monopoly over cable households," with only one percent of communities being served by more than one cable operator. *Id.* at 197.

In 1996, when this Court upheld the Cable Act's exclusive-contract provisions against a First Amendment challenge, we likewise pointed to the "special characteristics" of the cable industry. *See* Time Warner Entertainment Co. v. FCC, 93 F.3d 957 (D.C. Cir. 1996). Essential to our decision were "both the bottleneck monopoly power exercised by cable operators and the unique power that vertically integrated companies have in the cable market." *Id.* at 978.

But in the 16 years since the last of those cases was decided, the video programming distribution market has changed dramatically, especially with the rapid growth of satellite and Internet providers. This Court has previously described the massive transformation, explaining that cable operators "no longer have the bottleneck power over programming that concerned the Congress in 1992." Comcast Corp. v. FCC, 579 F.3d 1, 8 (D.C. Cir. 2009).

In today's highly competitive market, neither Comcast nor any other video programming distributor possesses market power in the national video programming distribution market. To be sure, beyond an interest in policing anticompetitive behavior, the FCC may think it preferable simply as a communications policy matter to equalize or enhance the voices of various entertainment and sports networks such as the Tennis Channel. But as the Supreme Court stated in one of the most important sentences in First Amendment history, "the concept that government may restrict the speech of some elements of our society in order to enhance the relative voice of others is wholly foreign to the First Amendment." Buckley v. Valeo, 424 U.S. 1, 48–49 (1976).

The Supreme Court's precedents amply demonstrate that the FCC's interpretation of Section 616 violates the First Amendment. At a minimum, the Supreme Court's precedents raise serious First Amendment questions about the FCC's interpretation of Section 616. Under the constitutional avoidance canon, those serious constitutional questions require that we construe Section 616 to apply only when a video programming distributor possesses market power.

* * *

The FCC erred in concluding that Section 616 may apply to a video programming distributor without market power. For that reason, in addition to the reasons given by the Court, the FCC's Order cannot stand.

[Concurring opinion by Senior Circuit Judge EDWARDS omitted.]

Notes and Questions

1. The First Amendment. In 2013, the Second Circuit rejected a facial constitutional challenge to the FCC's 2011 regulations. That court stated, in some tension with Judge Kavanaugh, that, "[w]hile rapidly increasing competition in the video programming industry may undermine [the conclusion that the FCC's rules are constitutional] in the not-to-distant future, that time has not yet come." Time Warner Cable Inc. v. FCC, 729 F.3d 137, 155 (2d Cir. 2013). Does the First Amendment really require that the courts determine the level of competition in video distribution markets, instead of the legislature or the FCC?

2. Regulation or Antitrust. This situation of course raises the recurring theme of regulation or antitrust as the best approach. As an initial matter, are you convinced that the FCC could not interpret the statute as permitting a more prophylactic approach than antitrust? Does § 616 merely reinforce the application of longstanding antirust principles (for of course antitrust law existed at the time of the 1992 Cable Act)? If so, then why did Congress enact § 616?

3. Practical Effects. The practical effect of the D.C. Circuit's decision has been to make a complaint very difficult to bring. How could an unaffiliated programmer practically show that its programming will benefit the cable operator, when most of the relevant information will be in the cable operator's hands? Could the FCC address this issue by revising its regulations? Consistently with the First Amendment?

§ 10.E. Spectrum Caps

The FCC has also used regulation to affect market structure in mobile markets. Initially, the FCC made choices concerning eligibility for licenses in order to promote and maintain competition in mobile services, much as it did in setting licensing policy in television. Later, the FCC turned to limits on the amount of spectrum that mobile carriers could acquire, initially by setting absolute limits and later by setting screens that would require specific transactions to be reviewed in greater detail by the agency. These spectrum limits directly affect the number and viability of competitors in local markets. In its most recent consideration of the issue, the FCC reviewed the history of its actions, the competition theory, and its policy for the future.

POLICIES REGARDING MOBILE SPECTRUM HOLDINGS: EXPANDING THE ECONOMIC AND INNOVATION OPPORTUNITIES OF SPECTRUM THROUGH INCENTIVE AUCTIONS

Report and Order, 29 FCC Rcd. 6133 (2014)

I. INTRODUCTION

1. Every American should be able to enjoy the benefits of a competitive mobile wireless marketplace. Competition among mobile wireless providers leads to lower prices,

more innovation, and greater investment. Competition, however, depends critically upon the availability of suitable spectrum as a necessary input in the provision of mobile wireless services. Rules are needed to facilitate access to necessary inputs if competition, and the benefits it provides, are to be enjoyed by all. Today, 92 percent of non-rural consumers, but only 37 percent of rural consumers, are covered by at least four 3G or 4G mobile wireless providers' networks. The policies that we adopt today aim to address this discrepancy and ensure that all Americans, regardless of whether they live in an urban, suburban, or rural area, can enjoy the benefits that competition provides.

2. Spectrum is a necessary input in the provision of mobile wireless services, including mobile broadband. Skyrocketing consumer demand for high-speed data is increasing providers' need for spectrum at an unprecedented rate. Consumers today expect mobile broadband at home, at work, and while on the go. To meet this increasing consumer demand, service providers need access to more spectrum. Accordingly, in recent years, we have made substantially more spectrum available for the provision of mobile wireless services. And we have two large auctions planned in the near future: Advanced Wireless Services-3 (AWS-3), which will auction 65 megahertz of high-band spectrum; and the 600 MHz Incentive Auction, which is a once-in-a-generation opportunity to auction significant amounts of greenfield low-band spectrum.

3. Especially in light of these two upcoming auctions, we must ensure that our policies and rules facilitate access to spectrum in a manner that promotes competition. Specifically, we must update the spectrum screen used in our competitive review of secondary market spectrum acquisitions to reflect the current suitability and availability of spectrum for the provision of mobile telephony/broadband services. As mentioned above, the growth in consumer demand for mobile broadband has led to a growing need for spectrum. But not all spectrum is created equal. Spectrum below 1 GHz has, compared to spectrum above 1 GHz, distinct propagation advantages for network deployment over long distances, while also reaching deep into buildings and urban canyons. High-band spectrum is more plentiful and possesses certain technical advantages allowing for the transmission of large amounts of information. In this sense, spectrum below 1 GHz may be thought of as "coverage" spectrum, and high-band spectrum may be thought of as "capacity" spectrum. While other cost-related factors exist, ensuring that multiple providers are able to access a sufficient amount of low-band spectrum is a threshold requirement for extending and improving service in both rural and urban areas.

4. In this Report and Order, we update our spectrum screen and establish the following rules for our upcoming auctions of high- and low-band spectrum in light of the growing demand for spectrum, the differences between spectrum bands, and in accordance with our desire to preserve and promote competition. Specifically, we:

- Update our spectrum screen for our competitive review of proposed secondary market transactions to reflect current suitability and availability of spectrum for mobile wireless services.
    - Add to our spectrum screen:
        - 40 megahertz of AWS-4;
        - 10 megahertz of H Block;
        - 65 megahertz of AWS-3, when it becomes available on a market-by-market basis;
        - 12 megahertz of BRS;
        - 89 megahertz of EBS; and

- The total amount of 600 MHz spectrum auctioned in the Incentive Auction.
  ◦ Subtract from our spectrum screen:
    - 12.5 megahertz of SMR; and
    - 10 megahertz that was the Upper 700 MHz D Block.
- Establish a market-based spectrum reserve of up to 30 megahertz in the Incentive Auction in each license area that is designed to ensure against excessive concentration in holdings of low-band spectrum while including safeguards to ensure that all bidders bear a fair share of the cost of the Incentive Auction.
- Adopt limits on secondary market transactions of 600 MHz spectrum licenses for six years post-auction.
- Decline to adopt auction-specific limits for AWS-3.
- Treat certain further concentrations of below-1-GHz spectrum as an enhanced factor in our case-by-case analysis of the potential competitive harms posed by individual transactions.

5. We conclude that, together, these actions advance the public interest by helping to ensure that American consumers can enjoy the benefits of a competitive wireless marketplace, regardless of whether they live in urban, suburban, or rural areas. These actions will furnish opportunities for additional access to spectrum to all providers, while adopting measures to protect against the risk that further concentration of spectrum, particularly low-band spectrum, would have significant effects on competition in the marketplace in the foreseeable future. Indeed, we find that the policies we adopt today will preserve and promote competitive choices, enabling all Americans to enjoy the benefits that a competitive wireless marketplace can bring.

II. Background

A. Statutory Authority

6. The Communications Act requires the Commission to examine closely the impact of spectrum aggregation on competition, innovation, and the efficient use of spectrum to ensure that spectrum is assigned in a manner that serves the public interest, convenience, and necessity. In particular, Section 309(j)(3) of the Communications Act provides that, in designing systems of competitive bidding, the Commission must (1) "include safeguards to protect the public interest in the use of the spectrum," and must seek to promote various objectives, including (2) "promoting economic opportunity and competition and ensuring that new and innovative technologies are readily accessible to the American people by avoiding excessive concentration of licenses and by disseminating licenses among a wide variety of applicants," (3) encouraging rapid deployment "including ... in rural areas," and (4) promoting "efficient and intensive use" of spectrum. 47 U.S.C. § 309(j)(3). Additionally, under the Communications Act, when reviewing a proposed license assignment or transfer application, the Commission must determine whether the applicant has demonstrated that the proposed assignment or transfer of control of licenses will serve the public interest, convenience, and necessity. Section 309(j)(3)(B) is forward-looking, and requires the Commission to rely upon its predictive judgment to proactively guard against potential harms. In Section 6404 of the Spectrum Act, Pub. L. 112-96, tit. VI, § 6404, Congress reaffirmed the extent of the Commission's existing (and well established) authority in future auctions and under future market conditions "to adopt and enforce rules of general applicability, including rules concerning spectrum aggregation that promote competition." 47 U.S.C. § 309(j)(17)(b).

B. History of Spectrum Aggregation Limits

7. Title III of the Communications Act requires the Commission to assign frequencies for radio stations "as public convenience, interest, or necessity requires," to "generally encourage the larger and more effective use of radio in the public interest," and to "[m]ake such rules and regulations and prescribe such restrictions, not inconsistent with law, as may be necessary to carry out the provisions of this chapter." 47 U.S.C. §§ 303(c), 303(g), 303(r). Our competitive analysis, "which has always formed a vital part of this public interest mandate, is informed by, but not limited to, traditional antitrust principles." Applications of Cellco Partnership d/b/a Verizon Wireless and SpectrumCo LLC and Cox TMI, LLC for Consent to Assign AWS-1 Licenses, Memorandum Opinion and Order, 27 FCC Rcd. 10,698, 10,710, ¶ 29 (2012). As the courts have made clear, "... the competitive consequences of proposals before the FCC 'must be read in the light of the special considerations that have influenced Congress to make specific provision for the particular industry.'" United States v. FCC, 652 F.2d 72, 85, 88 (D.C. Cir. 1980) (en banc) (quoting FCC v. RCA Communs., Inc., 346 U.S. 86 (1953)). As noted above, those specific provisions include Section 309(j)(3) of the Communications Act in designing systems of competitive bidding, and Section 310(d)'s public interest mandate with respect to secondary market transactions.

8. Our authority to adopt "rules concerning spectrum aggregation that promote competition" is longstanding. 47 U.S.C. § 309(j)(17)(B). In particular, avoiding undue aggregation of spectrum in particular geographic markets has long been a bedrock principle of our wireless policy. Since the advent of commercial mobile services in the early 1980s, the Commission has consistently considered and adopted policies designed to prevent undue concentration of spectrum licenses necessary to provide those services, and thereby to further consumer welfare by promoting the competitive provision of those services. The tools that the Commission has used to achieve its overall policy goals have changed over time, depending on the marketplace characteristics at specific points in time. Over the years, those tools have included the cellular cross-interest rule, the Personal Communications Service (PCS) spectrum aggregation limit, the PCS cross-ownership rule, the Commercial Mobile Radio Services (CMRS) spectrum cap, and the current case-by-case review.

9. *Cellular Service*. In 1981, the Commission established the rules for the licensing of 800 MHz cellular radiotelephone ("cellular") service. In doing so, it acknowledged the D.C. Circuit's concern that the Commission's 40 megahertz allocation plan, which had initially provided for only one licensee per market, led to assertions with "significant plausibility" that "AT&T will operate most, if not all, of the cellular systems eventually put in operation." Use of the Bands 825-845 MHz and 870-890 MHz for Cellular Communications Systems; and Amendment of Parts 2 and 22 of the Commission's Rules Relative to Cellular Communications Systems, Report and Order, 86 F.C.C. 2d 469, 472, ¶ 6 (1981) (quoting NARUC v. FCC, 525 F.2d 630, 636 (D.C. Cir. 1976)). The court had upheld that allocation five years earlier, "strongly influenced by the position of the Justice Department," while also upholding the allocation only "at this time" and imposing on the Commission a "duty of continual supervision" that "includes being on the lookout for possible anticompetitive effects." *NARUC v. FCC*, 525 F.2d at 638. Consistent with that mandate, the Commission changed its policy, and instead sought to create head-to-head competition by licensing cellular spectrum to two service providers, one of which was the incumbent wireline provider, in each geographic area. In 1991, the Commission issued the cellular cross-interest rule, which prohibited any entity with an attributable interest in one licensee, from having a material ownership interest in the other licensee.

10. *PCS Cap, PCS Cross-Ownership Rule, and PCS Set Asides.* The Commission subsequently determined in the early 1990s that the duopolistic nature of the cellular-services marketplace rendered it less than fully competitive. Accordingly, in 1993, as it established rules for making additional spectrum available in the Broadband PCS band, the Commission adopted two PCS spectrum caps that limited the amount of spectrum that a service provider could hold in individual markets. Specifically, PCS licensees were prohibited from holding an ownership interest in frequency blocks that totaled more than 40 megahertz and served the same geographic area. In addition, a cellular licensee was prohibited from holding a license of more than 10 megahertz of broadband PCS spectrum if the PCS license area would significantly overlap with the cellular license area. This PCS cap and the PCS cross-ownership rule were eliminated in 1996 in favor of a modified CMRS spectrum cap.

11. The Commission has also exercised its authority under Section 309(j) to reserve certain spectrum for a limited class of auction bidders. In auctions conducted from 1996 to 1999, the Commission initially made available licenses for 40 out of 120 megahertz of PCS spectrum through bidding open only to small "entrepreneurs." The Commission defined "entrepreneurs" as bidders with gross revenues of less than $125 million in each of the previous two years and total assets of less than $500 million at the time the auction application was filed. The Commission sought to promote auction participation by these entrepreneurs by allowing them to make installment payments for awarded licenses. Starting in 2000, the Commission determined that licenses for certain of these blocks would remain restricted to entrepreneurs in Auction 35 and in subsequent auctions, while others would no longer be restricted. Accordingly, from 2000 through the most recent Broadband PCS auction in 2008, a subset of the PCS licenses that was initially restricted to entrepreneurs continued to be so restricted.

12. *CMRS Spectrum Cap.* In 1994, the Commission instituted a new spectrum limit that prohibited a provider of commercial mobile radio service from holding attributable interests in CMRS licenses—defined to include broadband PCS, cellular, and certain Specialized Mobile Radio (SMR) licenses—exceeding 45 megahertz in any licensed geographic service area. As implemented, the Commission attributed all controlling interests and many non-controlling interests, including in most cases equity ownership of 20 percent or more. In 1999, the Commission modified the CMRS spectrum cap by, among other things, adopting a 55 megahertz spectrum aggregation limit for licensees serving RSAs. In 2001, in response to the growth of competition in the provision of mobile wireless services in the 1990s, the Commission initiated a transition away from the CMRS spectrum cap in favor of case-by-case review by scheduling the cap for elimination as of January 1, 2003.

13. *Case-by-Case Review.* In analyzing the *Cingular-AT&T Wireless* transaction in 2004, the Commission for the first time articulated its framework for a case-by-case review of spectrum aggregation (and market share concentration, if appropriate). *See* Applications of AT&T Wireless Inc. and Cingular Wireless Corporation For Consent To Transfer of Control of Licenses and Authorizations, Memorandum Opinion and Order, 19 FCC Rcd. 21,522, 21,525, ¶ 4 (2004) (*Cingular-AT&T Wireless Order*) ("[F]or the first time in this sector, we articulate and apply our public interest standard by undertaking a case-by-case analysis of a large transaction without the presence of a bright-line rule related to spectrum aggregation."). In that context and in its analysis of subsequent proposed transactions, the Commission applied an initial screen to help identify for case-by-case review local markets where changes in spectrum holdings resulting from the transaction may be of particular concern. In its application of a spectrum screen to the *Cingular-AT&T Wire-*

less transaction, the Commission included cellular, PCS, and SMR spectrum for a total of approximately 200 megahertz of spectrum, and established a screen "trigger" of 70 megahertz, or approximately one-third of the total suitable and available spectrum. In 2008, the Commission articulated that its case-by-case review also would apply to the initial licensing of spectrum post-auction. In the past decade, in its application of the spectrum screen to various secondary market transactions, the Commission has determined that additional bands of spectrum were suitable and available for use and should be included in the spectrum screen. In addition, the Commission has indicated that it would not limit its analysis of potential competitive harms to solely those markets identified by the initial screen, when encountering other factors that may bear on the public interest inquiry.

14. For example, the Commission has placed a significant emphasis on increased below-1-GHz spectrum concentration as a factor in its case-by-case review because below-1 GHz spectrum possesses favorable propagation characteristics and is relatively scarce as compared to higher band spectrum. [I]n its last three annual Mobile Wireless Competition Reports, the Commission has focused on the importance to competitors of the superior propagation characteristics of spectrum below 1 GHz, stating that "[g]iven these different spectrum characteristics [of low- and high-band spectrum], a licensee's particular mix of spectrum holdings may affect its ability to provide efficient mobile wireless services." Implementation of Section 6002(B) of the Omnibus Budget Reconciliation Act of 1993, Annual Report and Analysis of Competitive Market Conditions with Respect to Mobile Wireless Including Commercial Mobile Services, Fourteenth Report, 25 FCC Rcd. 11,407, 11,573, ¶ 274 (2010).

16. *Mobile Spectrum Holdings Rulemaking.* In September 2012, the Commission initiated this proceeding to review the mobile spectrum holdings policies that currently apply to both secondary market transactions and auctions. Intending to take a fresh look at all facets of its rules concerning spectrum aggregation, the Commission sought comment on whether the Commission should, in the context of both auctions and transactions, retain or modify its current case-by-case approach to evaluating mobile spectrum holdings, adopt proposed bright-line limits on spectrum aggregation, reevaluate the spectrum bands included in any evaluation of mobile spectrum holdings, and distinguish between different bands of spectrum.

III. PRESERVING AND PROMOTING COMPETITION IN THE MOBILE WIRELESS MARKETPLACE

A. Overview

17. The Commission has long recognized that "spectrum is an input in CMRS markets," and that "the state of control over the spectrum input is a relevant factor" in its competitive analysis. 2000 Biennial Regulatory Review Spectrum Aggregation Limits for Commercial Radio Servs., WT Dkt. No. 01-14, Report and Order, 16 FCC Rcd. 22,668, 22,679–80, ¶ 27 (2001) (*CMRS Cap Sunset Order*). Ensuring that sufficient spectrum is available for multiple existing mobile service providers as well as potential entrants is crucial to promoting consumer choice and competition throughout the country, including in rural areas, and is similarly crucial to fostering innovation in the marketplace. As the Commission has found, in order for there to be robust competition, multiple competing service providers must have access to or hold sufficient spectrum to be able to enter a marketplace or expand output rapidly in response to any price increase or reduction in quality, or other change that would harm consumer welfare.

18. Since the Commission's last comprehensive review of its mobile spectrum holdings policies more than a decade ago, the marketplace for mobile wireless services has

evolved significantly—both in consumer demand for services and market structure—as has the role of low-band spectrum for coverage purposes and high-band spectrum for capacity purposes in the deployment of providers' networks. As late as 2001, as the Commission recognized in the *CMRS Cap Sunset Order*, consumers primarily demanded reliable mobile voice services; today consumers demand access to high-quality mobile broadband services at myriad locations at any time of day, and for extended periods of use—"anywhere, anytime." As providers deploy next-generation mobile networks, the engineering properties and deployment capabilities of the mix of particular spectrum bands in providers' holdings have become increasingly important, particularly as multi-band phones allow users to take advantage of the different properties of different spectrum bands. Moreover, while the mobile wireless marketplace a decade ago consisted of six near-nationwide providers and a substantial number of regional and small providers, since then, there has been a significant degree of consolidation resulting in a market with four nationwide providers and a smaller number of regional and more local service providers.

19. Reflecting this evolution in the mobile wireless marketplace, the Commission, in recent years, has considered in more detail the technical distinctions among spectrum bands used to deploy next-generation mobile networks. These considerations largely have been undertaken in the context of our Annual Mobile Wireless Competition Reports, as well as our case-by-case analysis of transactions. Commenters have argued that we should address these issues in a rulemaking to provide increased clarity and certainty. We agree. Accordingly, we adopt mobile spectrum holdings policies in this rulemaking that address how the differences among spectrum bands may affect our overall competitive analysis of spectrum acquisitions and therefore our decision making for both auctions and secondary market transactions.

21. Consistent with the evolution of the marketplace and the Commission's statutory directives and policy goals, and in light of the evolution of wireless services demanded by consumers, we must ensure that multiple service providers have access to spectrum in the foreseeable future. Existing marketplace conditions, including concerns about the potential for anticompetitive behavior, inform our predictive judgment but are not determinative as to whether we need to act. For the reasons stated below, the mobile spectrum holdings policies we adopt today are necessary to preserve and promote consumer choice and competition among multiple service providers, promote the efficient and intensive use of spectrum, maximize economic opportunity, and foster the deployment of innovative technologies.

B. Evolution of the Mobile Wireless Marketplace

22. Starting in the early 1990s, digital technologies were deployed in the wireless marketplace that were more efficient and offered improved service quality over the existing analog technologies deployed in the cellular bands at the time. These improvements in operating efficiency and quality, combined with the presence of new entrants and lower prices, facilitated the growth and development of a more competitive mobile wireless marketplace, with increased investment, innovation, and network expansion by both new entrants and existing service providers. By 1998, for example, 87 percent of the U.S. population was covered by three or more mobile wireless providers, and 54 percent by five or more providers. Cumulative investment in the industry more than tripled from $19 billion to more than $70 billion from 1994 to 2000, and for the same time period the number of cell sites more than quadrupled, from 18,000 to more than 80,000. Further, marketplace dynamics continued to evolve, with multiple providers of wireless services offering new pricing plans, and smaller and more powerful handsets, thus facilitating the mass-market acceptance of mobile wireless services.

23. During the past decade, provider supply and consumer demand for wireless services has exploded, with the industry focus changing from the provision of mobile voice services to the provision of mobile broadband services. The rapid adoption of smartphones, as well as tablet computers and the widespread use of mobile applications, combined with the increasing deployment of high-speed 3G and now 4G technologies, is driving significantly more intensive use of mobile networks. In 2013, a single smartphone generated 48 times more mobile data traffic than a feature phone, and average smartphone usage grew 50 percent in 2013. The adoption of smartphones increased from 27 percent to 54 percent of U.S. subscribers from December 2010 to December 2012. In addition, global mobile data traffic grew 81 percent in 2013, and is anticipated to grow elevenfold between 2013 and 2018. Moreover, the percentage of adults and children living in wireless-only households has increased from approximately three percent in 2003 to approximately 38 percent (adults) and 45 percent (children) by June 2013. Consequently, service providers generally need access to more spectrum to meet the increasing demand for mobile broadband, which consumes far greater amounts of bandwidth than did mobile phones just a short time ago. Indeed, a 2012 study by the Council of Economic Advisors found that "the spectrum currently allocated to wireless is not sufficient to handle the projected growth in demand, even with technological improvements allowing for more efficient use of existing spectrum and significant investment in new facilities." Council of Economic Advisors, The Economic Benefits of New Spectrum for Wireless Broadband at 5 (Feb. 2012), available at: http://www.whitehouse.gov/sites/default/files/cea_spectrum_report_2-21-2012.pdf.

24. The wireless industry has also undergone significant consolidation during the past decade. In 2003, at the sunset of the spectrum cap, there were six facilities-based wireless service providers that analysts then described as nationwide: AT&T Wireless, Sprint PCS, Verizon Wireless, T-Mobile, Cingular Wireless, and Nextel. Since that time, the number of nationwide facilities-based wireless service providers has decreased by a third from six to four—Verizon Wireless, AT&T, Sprint, and T-Mobile. In addition, there have been several significant spectrum-only transactions that have resulted in increased spectrum aggregation among the remaining providers.

25. Concentration in the market share of the major providers has also increased during that time period. As of December 2003, the top six facilities-based nationwide providers accounted for approximately 79 percent of total mobile wireless subscribers in the country. By December 2013, the top four facilities-based nationwide providers had increased their combined market share to 97 percent of all subscribers. Moreover, Verizon Wireless and AT&T together accounted for 68 percent of the nation's subscribers as of year-end 2013, compared to 51 percent in 2004. Some regional and local service providers have achieved significant market shares within particular local markets, often the most rural markets, but they typically rely on roaming agreements with nationwide facilities-based providers to extend the geographic reach of their networks.

C. Ensuring that All Americans Benefit from Mobile Wireless Competition

28. The Commission's competition-related decision making is designed to advance the public interest by preserving and promoting competition that benefits consumers. Specific competitors may prefer one proposed policy to another, but the Commission must consider the totality of the circumstances and choose policies that are most likely to allow competition to flourish for the public benefit. Accordingly, we recognize the important tradeoffs in the policy decision at hand. Policies that would limit the ability of major providers to acquire additional spectrum licenses may limit their ability to provide new

services or serve new customers. At the same time, policies that would allow these service providers to acquire all or substantially all of the spectrum licenses to be auctioned in the near future, particularly spectrum licenses being auctioned in the Incentive Auction, or that would allow further concentration in below-1-GHz spectrum in secondary market transactions without enhanced scrutiny, would raise significant competitive issues.

29. The Commission has examined these tradeoffs as part of its wholesale review of its spectrum aggregation policies. In the course of our current review, several parties, including the Antitrust Division of the Department of Justice (DOJ), have expressed specific concerns about potential threats to competition in the mobile wireless marketplace, and in particular, the need for access to spectrum as a critical factor to ensure competition in the future. Based upon current marketplace conditions, DOJ concludes that mobile wireless providers possess "the ability and, in some cases, the incentive to exercise at least some degree of market power, particularly given that there is already significant nationwide concentration in the wireless industry." *Ex Parte* Submission of the United States Department of Justice, WT Dkt. No. 12-269, filed Apr. 11, 2013 at 8. DOJ therefore recommends that "the Commission should consider the potential that the acquisition of specific blocks of spectrum may have to foreclose or raise the costs of competitors in its policies on spectrum acquisition." *Id.* at 11.

31. *Advantages of Different Types of Spectrum Holdings.* Commenters in this proceeding consistently recognize that different frequencies possess different characteristics for the provision of mobile wireless services. Their agreement on the fundamentals of spectrum notwithstanding, commenters draw highly divergent policy conclusions from these differences [with some arguing that the technical differences require accounting for different spectrum bands different, and others arguing that the differences in technical characteristics are irrelevant to a competition analysis].

41. *Raising Rivals' Costs and Foreclosure.* In 2001, while not observing specific evidence of foreclosure by wireless providers of their competitors' access to spectrum, the Commission nonetheless recognized that "it is at least a threshold possibility that because the supply of suitable spectrum is limited, firms in CMRS markets might choose to overinvest in spectrum in order to deter entry, depending on the costs of doing so." *CMRS Cap Sunset Order,* 16 FCC Rcd. at 22,691–92, ¶ 44. Various commenters in this proceeding address the potential for harm to consumers as a result of anticompetitive actions by the largest providers in the market, in particular actions related to raising rivals' costs and foreclosure. In certain situations, a dominant firm may raise rivals' costs by a variety of means, including input monopolization. As rivals' costs are raised, the competiveness of the marketplace is likely to diminish. Foreclosure can occur when competitors have an incentive and ability to acquire an input not only to put it to their own use, but also to withhold it from their rivals. While there is general consensus among commenters that increased concentration of an essential input, in this case, spectrum, could in theory lead to anti-competitive effects in downstream markets, commenters disagree about the relative risk that such strategies would be utilized in today's wireless marketplace, the costs associated with such a strategy, and whether low-band spectrum is sufficiently distinct from high-band spectrum to form the basis for a successful strategy to raise rivals' costs or foreclose competition.

42. AT&T and Verizon Wireless argue that while anticompetitive behavior to raise rivals' cost or foreclose competition is theoretically possible, the risk of such action is virtually nonexistent, as marketplace conditions will make it irrational for any firm to pursue such strategies. Specifically, AT&T and Verizon Wireless argue that a firm would have to ensure that no other existing spectrum holder sells or leases spectrum to a potential entrant.

Further, they claim that while the costs of such anticompetitive strategies would be borne by a few, the benefits would be enjoyed by all existing providers, thus reducing the pay-off and effectively precluding such strategies from occurring. Finally, AT&T and Verizon Wireless argue that the Commission's build-out requirements would impose additional, preclusive costs on such strategies without requiring as much intervention in the market.

43. In contrast, DOJ expresses concern that larger service providers may possess the incentive and ability to foreclose or raise the costs of smaller service providers by obtaining the spectrum that their smaller rivals or potential rivals need to compete. DOJ remarks that "[i]n a highly concentrated industry with large margins between the price and incremental cost of existing wireless broadband services, the value of keeping spectrum out of competitors' hands could be very high." DOJ Apr. 11, 2013 *Ex Parte* at 11. DOJ explains that "when market power is *not* an issue," it would normally expect the highest use value for new spectrum to come from the highest bidders. *Id.* at 10. Absent compelling evidence that the largest incumbent providers are already using their existing spectrum licenses efficiently and their networks are still capacity-constrained, the highest bidder may be relying on the profits from foreclosure strategy and is not necessarily the bidder that will "generate the greatest benefits to consumers." *Id.* DOJ concludes that the Commission should "consider the potential that the acquisition of specific blocks of spectrum may have to foreclose or raise the costs of competitors in its policies on spectrum acquisition" and advises that "[t]he Commission's policies, particularly regarding auction of new low-frequency spectrum, can potentially improve the competitive landscape by preventing the leading carriers from foreclosing their rivals from access to low-frequency spectrum." *Id.* at 11, 14.

44. *Discussion.* In our review of the evolution of the mobile wireless marketplace, its current state, and the potential future effects on consumers, we are required to consider a number of concerns to advance the public interest. In particular, Section 309(j) requires the Commission to balance a number of specific statutory objectives including competition, diversity and the avoidance of excessive concentration in designing its rules regarding spectrum licenses and the competitive bidding assignment process. Bearing this in mind, we find that, under the totality of circumstances, the public interest will be advanced by the decisions we make today, namely: reaffirming the current case-by-case review of proposed transactions, with continued use of a spectrum screen triggered at aggregations of approximately one third or more of the spectrum suitable and available for mobile telephony/broadband; updating the spectrum screen to include spectrum currently suitable and available for mobile telephony/broadband; treating certain levels of increased aggregations of below-1-GHz spectrum as an enhanced factor during case-by-case review of secondary market transactions involving below-1-GHz spectrum; and establishing a market-based spectrum reserve in the upcoming 600 MHz auction.

45. There are three independent bases for our conclusion, each of which we find warrants the policies we adopt today: (1) the importance of access to low-band spectrum to promote variety in licensees and the advancement of rural deployment as directed by Section 309(j), (2) the benefits to consumers associated with robust competition among multiple providers having access to low-band spectrum, and (3) the potential for competitive harm if we do not provide safeguards to mitigate against the possibility of providers raising rivals' costs or foreclosing competition by denying competitors access to low-band spectrum. In accordance with our statutory mandate under 47 U.S.C. 309(j), we adopt policies to ensure that the spectrum we are auctioning will be used to promote robust competition and to limit the potential for future excessive concentration of low-band spectrum holdings.

46. Our findings are compelled by the changing circumstances posed by the marketplace today: increased consolidation, the growth in demand for mobile broadband, and the significance of the upcoming 600 MHz auction. First, we recognize that the mobile wireless marketplace has undergone considerable consolidation, both in terms of number of firms and relative market shares, as well as increased concentration of low-band spectrum. Recent acquisitions have exacerbated this concentration. While limited amounts of low-band spectrum might theoretically be acquired in secondary market transactions, as noted below the vast bulk of that spectrum has already been acquired. In considering secondary-market acquisitions, the Commission is barred by the Communications Act from considering "whether the public interest, convenience, and necessity might be served by the transfer" to any other party outside the application presented. 47 U.S.C. § 310(d). There is also significantly less low-band spectrum than there is high-band spectrum: after our decisions today, there will be 134 megahertz of spectrum below 1 GHz suitable and available for the provision of mobile broadband services and 446.5 megahertz of suitable and available spectrum above 1 GHz. Concentration in spectrum holdings by service providers of low-band spectrum has become particularly pronounced, with Verizon Wireless and AT&T together having aggregated more than 90 percent of all cellular spectrum. Generally speaking, Verizon Wireless and AT&T each were the beneficiaries from their predecessors in interest of one of the two initial cellular licenses that were granted to an incumbent local exchange carrier and a new entrant in the 1980s, and have since further increased their spectrum holdings within this band. In addition, these two service providers together currently hold approximately 72 percent of 700 MHz spectrum. By comparison, variation in spectrum holdings of higher-frequency spectrum in the range of 1 to 2 GHz is more evenly distributed: of the PCS spectrum, Verizon Wireless holds 16 percent, AT&T holds 29 percent, Sprint holds 28 percent and T-Mobile holds 22 percent; of the AWS-1 spectrum, Verizon Wireless holds 37 percent, AT&T holds 13 percent, and T-Mobile holds 42 percent.

47. Second, our findings are informed by the skyrocketing consumer demand for mobile broadband. Today, consumers are demanding more data at higher speeds, while at home, at work, and in transit. We find that to provide this level of service in the marketplace to the benefit of consumers, providers will need to deploy more spectrum that can provide both coverage and in-building penetration, as well as spectrum that can provide the increased throughput for mobile broadband applications. In the next few decades, the demands on wireless networks and the need for access to spectrum will continue to increase.

48. Third, our findings are based on the recognition that the 600 MHz spectrum that will be made available in the Incentive Auction will be the last offering of a significant amount of nationwide greenfield low-band spectrum for the foreseeable future. This is particularly important because of the very different characteristics of low-band spectrum. There is a large frequency gap between the below-1-GHz spectrum (in the 700 and 800 MHz bands now largely held by the leading providers, and the 600 MHz Incentive Auction spectrum) and the remaining spectrum currently suitable and available for mobile broadband use, beginning with the AWS-1 band at 1710 MHz. Low-band spectrum possesses distinct propagation advantages for network deployment, particularly in rural areas and indoors. As a result, the auction of spectrum below 1 GHz presents a once-in-a-generation opportunity to promote competition as specifically required by Section 309(j). Based upon current trends in consumer demand for mobile broadband services, we conclude that the decisions we make here will have a significant impact on the extent to which competition may flourish for years to come.

54. In short, our experience, consistent with the substantial record evidence that includes theoretical and empirical RF propagation models, actual network design and meas-

urement studies, and customer surveys, is that—while other factors may affect the value of spectrum (both low-band and high-band)—low-band spectrum has significantly greater propagation advantages both in wide-area coverage and in serving the growing number of wireless uses within buildings. In addition, providers with both low-band and high-band spectrum have greater flexibility and capability to vigorously compete in the marketplace to better serve consumers.

56. *Variety of Licensees and Rural Deployment.* Under Section 309(j), Congress mandated that we design auctions to "include safeguards to protect the public interest in the use of the spectrum," including the objectives to disseminate licenses "among a wide variety of applicants" and to promote deployment of new technologies, products, and services to "those residing in rural areas." 47 U.S.C. §309(j)(a)–(b). The limited restrictions we impose today on spectrum holdings will promote both of these statutory policies. A variety of licensees is particularly important in light of the lack of competitive offerings in rural America today. Currently, 92 percent of non-rural consumers, but only 37 percent of rural consumers, are covered by at least four 3G or 4G mobile wireless providers' networks.

57. Increasing the number of providers who have access to low-band spectrum can increase the competitive offerings of mobile wireless service for consumers, particularly in rural areas. Today, two nationwide providers control the vast majority of low-band spectrum, and this disparity makes it difficult for rural consumers to have access to the competition and choice that would be available if more wireless competitors also had access to low-band spectrum. Low-band spectrum, given its unique propagation characteristics, can serve as a foundation for expansion of an existing network or a new or upcoming service providers' network deployment as it builds a customer base to support further growth. [L]ow-band spectrum is particularly well suited to deployment in rural areas. We find that our spectrum holdings policies will promote variety in licensees and deployment of new technologies to those residing in rural areas.

58. *Benefits to Consumers from Promotion of Competition in Mobile Wireless Markets.* Rigorous competition among providers having access to low-band spectrum will result in significant benefits that may be realized by consumers. While we cannot predict with absolute certainty future marketplace conditions, under our Title III mandate, the question we consider is whether there is a rational basis for finding that our limited restrictions "would enhance the possibility of achieving" our public interest goals, including preserving and promoting competition in this marketplace. FCC v. Nat'l Citizens Comm. for Broad., 436 U.S. 775, 796–97 (1978). The superior propagation of spectrum below-1-GHz means that larger geographic areas may be served more cost effectively through use of fewer transmitters.

59. In addition, we believe that holding a mix of spectrum bands is advantageous to providers and that consumers benefit when multiple providers have access to a mix of spectrum bands. The continually evolving marketplace makes having a mix of low- and high-band spectrum more important for the deployment of robust high quality networks by multiple service providers, which in turn can increase competition, drive down prices, and ensure continued innovation and investment. In planning their network buildout, service providers consider many factors, including the cost of the spectrum licenses, the type of spectrum, coverage and quality requirements which affect the capital and operating costs of the network infrastructure, as well as the time and regulatory requirements. We find that a service provider holding a mix of low- and high-band spectrum licenses would have greater flexibility and would be better able to optimize its network costs for a given quality level, thus promoting the efficient and intensive use of spectrum. Consumers of

wireless services benefit from multiple providers having access to a mix of spectrum bands. The benefits to consumers from competition between multiple providers and increased deployment to rural areas outweigh the costs of the limited restrictions described below. Accordingly, we find our public interest goal of promoting consumer welfare would be advanced by the policies we adopt today.

60. *Potential for Competitive Harm from Increased Aggregation of Spectrum.* We also find that in the absence of additional below-1-GHz spectrum on a nationwide basis, there is a substantial likelihood of competitive harm if providers that currently lack sufficient access to such spectrum cannot acquire it. Under Section 309(j), we have mandates to promote competition, promote efficient use of spectrum, and avoid the excessive concentration of licenses. As indicated above, low-band spectrum is less costly to deploy and provides higher coverage quality. The leading providers have most of the low-band spectrum available today. If they were to acquire all or substantially all of the remaining low-band spectrum, they would benefit independently of any deployment of this newly acquired spectrum to the extent that their rivals are denied its use. Without access to this low-band spectrum, their rivals would be less able to provide a competitive alternative. Deploying high-band spectrum is more costly, more time-consuming, and more subject to variation given the increased number of cell sites required for deployment to achieve similar service quality and the accompanying need for cell tower siting authorizations and zoning approvals. As noted above, it is also far less effective in providing for the growing demand for in-building use, which as we have recently noted now involves 56 percent of all wireless calls and 80 percent of smartphone usage. Although alternative methods to increase rural and in-building coverage to serve additional customers are available, such as adding towers, splitting cells, or acquiring roaming rights on other networks, these substitute inputs are not nearly as cost effective and likely would increase costs.

61. Along with an attenuated ability to increase output or service quality in response to price increases, providers that lack access to low-band spectrum may lack the ability quickly to expand coverage or provide new or innovative services, which would have a significant impact on competition in the mobile wireless marketplace. The consumer harms from the raising of rivals' costs from increased concentration of low-band spectrum outweigh the potential benefits of unlimited spectrum aggregation. Accordingly, we find that the limited restrictions we adopt today will reasonably balance our goals of promoting competition, ensuring the efficient use of spectrum, and avoiding an excessive concentration of licenses in accord with Section 309(j).

62. *Foreclosure.* We agree with the Antitrust Division of the DOJ, one of our nation's expert antitrust agencies: there is a risk of foreclosure in downstream wireless markets. Today's mobile wireless marketplace is characterized by factors that, according to DOJ, increase the potential for anticompetitive conduct, including high market concentration, highly concentrated holdings of low-band spectrum, high margins, and high barriers to entry. These risk factors increase the incentive and ability for a provider with low-band spectrum to bid for the spectrum in an attempt to stifle competition that may arise if multiple licensees were to hold low frequency spectrum. As a result, such a provider might be the highest bidder in a spectrum auction, not because it will put the spectrum to its highest use, but because it is motivated to engage in a foreclosure strategy.

63. We find unpersuasive, particularly as applied to the specific limits that we are adopting today, various arguments by AT&T and Verizon Wireless that the possibility of future limits on the ability of providers to compete should not be considered in our evaluation of whether to limit their acquisition of low-band spectrum given current market

conditions. This is a forward-looking rulemaking that must consider the potential for competitive harms in the future.

64. We also disagree with AT&T's argument that any potential for competitive harm from concentrated spectrum holdings will be addressed by market prices reflecting the total cost of deploying with different bands, such that the greater costs associated with high-band spectrum will result in lower prices for it. Initially, these arguments, as presented, are theoretical and speculative, and not necessarily predictive of actual pricing in spectrum markets in the future. In fact, there is substantial evidence in the record that AT&T's equilibrium pricing model does not apply in the marketplace for acquiring wireless spectrum. As a threshold matter, the model ignores the likelihood of foreclosure. But it also ignores that this particular market is very illiquid. Unlike a fluid and active commodities market, spectrum is made available for initial licensing at irregular times and in irregular amounts. The secondary market for spectrum licenses in any geographic area has very few buyers and sellers. Providers often hold onto spectrum for decades for a number of reasons, including the value they may assign to keeping spectrum out of the hands of potential competitors. This lack of liquidity necessarily limits the accuracy of spectrum pricing.

65. We also note that spectrum transactions occur with imperfect information regarding the costs and timing of deployment, neither of which is entirely within a provider's control. Thus, while providers that value high-band spectrum less than low-band spectrum will offer to pay relatively less for high-band spectrum, this does not mean that spectrum markets will accurately price spectrum to fully reflect deployment costs, particularly low-band spectrum that is relatively scarce. In any event, the record contains substantial evidence that the disadvantages of high band spectrum resulting from poor in-building coverage and increased obstacles today to siting of new wireless facilities are more than mere cost disadvantages. Accordingly, we acknowledge that there are many factors that may determine the price of spectrum, and we find that we cannot rely on price differentials alone to address competitive concerns.

66. We also reject AT&T's and Verizon Wireless's argument that the Commission must prove a significant reduction of downstream competition will occur in the future in order to limit their acquisition of spectrum. There is no basis for this standard in the Communications Act, and these parties do not offer any such basis. As discussed above, Congress mandated the Commission to act prospectively to promote competition and protect the public interest. Our conclusion, which accords with the DOJ's, is that there is a risk of foreclosure. In light of this risk and balancing the inherent tradeoffs, we find that the limited restrictions we enact today are a reasonable balance of the Section 309(j) and public interest factors that form our statutory mandate, including the goals to promote competition, disseminate licenses among a wide variety of applicants, ensure high quality service to those in rural areas and avoid the excessive concentration of licenses, while also promoting the efficient and intensive use of the spectrum.

D. Conclusion

67. For the reasons set forth above, spectrum is a limited and essential input for the provision of mobile wireless telephony and broadband services, and ensuring access to, and the availability of, sufficient spectrum is critical to promoting the competition that drives innovation and investment. The Communications Act has long required the Commission to examine closely the impact of spectrum aggregation on competition, innovation, and the efficient use of spectrum to ensure that spectrum is allocated and assigned in a manner that serves the public interest, convenience and necessity, and avoids the excessive concentration of licenses. In recent years, the Commission has considered in more

detail and largely in the context of our case-by-case analysis of secondary market transactions how distinctions among spectrum bands affect competition in the provision of next-generation mobile broadband services.

68. In today's marketplace, in many service areas currently suitable and available below-1-GHz spectrum is disproportionately concentrated in the hands of larger nationwide service providers: the two largest providers hold 73 percent of the low-band spectrum. Particularly in the context of the once-in-a-generation Incentive Auction, we find that there is a reasonably foreseeable risk of not achieving our various Section 309(j) goals whether or not leading providers are motivated by foreclosure strategies. We conclude that if we do not act at this time to ensure the highest use of low-band spectrum, the competitive choices available to wireless consumers will likely be substantially less attractive. We therefore find it essential to establish clear and transparent policies that will preserve and promote competition in the future, promote the efficient use of spectrum, ensure competitive mobile broadband service in rural areas, and avoid an excessive concentration of licenses. We find that excessive concentration in the allocation of relatively scarce below-1-GHz spectrum, given ever increasing consumer demand for more bandwidth-intensive services, would substantially harm the public interest and indeed, would create a significant risk in the future of an insufficient number of service providers with a network capable of satisfying consumer demand.

69. We find that the promotion of competition, variety of licensees, rural coverage, and consumer choice in the mobile marketplace, as well as in the future, crucially depends upon multiple providers having access to the low-band spectrum they need to operate and vigorously compete. We also find that we must consider the potential for anticompetitive results if the concentrated holdings of below-1-GHz spectrum are not addressed. We cannot ignore the possibility of diminished competition in the future, both from rivals' costs being raised and from foreclosure. Further, we find that the burden that some providers may experience by limits on their ability to acquire increasing amounts of below-1-GHz spectrum, when tailored to the minimum we believe necessary to promote competition as described below, will be outweighed by the public interest benefits that will flow from the preservation and promotion of robust and sustainable competition. By adopting clear and transparent spectrum aggregation limits, we aim to ensure that American consumers have meaningful choices among multiple service providers in the future.

Notes and Questions

1. Horizontal and Vertical. Although the FCC's order focuses on the manner in which spectrum acquisition limits may promote competition among carriers, it appears that the same vertical concerns that were present in the horizontal ownership limits for cable companies are also present in this context—especially as mobile phones increasing are used for applications and services offered by third-party providers, as most smartphones today are.

2. Antitrust? The FCC's screens simply set a threshold at which the agency will scrutinize a transaction more closely to ascertain competitive effects. What is the value of these screens, above and beyond the case-by-case inquiry the FCC (and the antitrust authorities) could apply to any transaction? For one, the screens may work to provide safe harbors (although the FCC has not described the screens explicitly in that manner), creating some market certainty. Second, as an administrative agency, the FCC will receive from the court deference in its factfinding, while the antitrust authorities must prove their competition case in court.

3. Incentive Auctions. The most controversial part of the FCC's action here is its hard set-aside (not just a presumptive screen) for acquisitions in the incentive auctions, which are discussed in Chapter Five. The FCC's action depends most crucially on its finding that this spectrum is different from all other spectrum, and that the difference affects competition enough that a limit specific to it should be set. Are you persuaded by the FCC's reasoning? Do you think that technology may change those considerations over time, and, if so, what does that mean for the FCC's policy choice for this auction?

4. **A Theory of Market Structure?** Does the FCC put forward a clear theory of what a competitive market structure would look like? Is it the FCC's expectation that mobile carriers need to be roughly equal in size in order to compete? Do they have to have nationwide footprints? (The FCC notes that certain regional carriers have significant market share but then appears to dismiss their significance by noting that they must rely on roaming agreements outside of their home regions.) Usual competition theory asks the economic question (whether two services exert pricing constraint on each other), not the functional question (whether the services operate in the same manner). If regional carriers, or smaller national carriers, constrain the pricing power of the larger national carriers, then the market is competitive despite perhaps being lopsided. Similarly, at several points in the order, the FCC suggests that carriers are "warehousing" spectrum to keep it out of competitors' hands. Given what the Commission itself has said about the explosive growth of mobile data demand, how does the Commission know that the carriers don't simply have different projections of future need?

---

§ 10.F. Choice

The increased competition, choice, and responsibility that consumers now face trouble many media critics who see an increasingly coarse, shrill, and impoverished set of viewing options in the midst of a competitive "market for eyeballs." Regarding TV news in particular, media critics decry sensationalism and the blurring line between news and entertainment. The next two excerpts, one from Cass Sunstein and the other from Judge Richard Posner, address these questions. We conclude with a staff study from the FCC that asks whether developments that appear to expand the range of information options actually meet the needs of communities.

§ 10.F.1. Is More Always Better?

THE FIRST AMENDMENT IN CYBERSPACE
Cass R. Sunstein, 104 Yale L.J. 1757 (1995)

II. THE PRESENT: MARKETS AND MADISON

There are two free speech traditions in the United States, not simply one. There have been two models of the First Amendment, corresponding to the two free speech traditions. The first emphasizes well-functioning speech markets. It can be traced to Justice Holmes' great *Abrams* dissent, where the notion of a "market in ideas" received its preeminent exposition. The market model emerges as well from *Miami Herald Publishing Co. v. Tornillo*, invalidating a "right of reply" law as applied to candidates for elected office. It finds its most recent defining statement not in judicial decisions, but in an FCC opinion rejecting the fairness doctrine. Syracuse Peace Council v. Television Station WTVH, 2 FCC Rcd. 5043, 5054–55 (1987).

The second tradition, and the second model, focuses on public deliberation. The second model can be traced from its origins in the work of James Madison, with his attack on the idea of seditious libel, to Justice Louis Brandeis, with his suggestion that "the greatest menace to freedom is an inert people," through the work of Alexander Meiklejohn, who associated the free speech principle not with laissez-faire economics, but with ideals of democratic deliberation. The Madisonian tradition culminated in the reaffirmation of the fairness doctrine in the *Red Lion* case, Red Lion Broad. Co. v. FCC, 395 U.S. 367 (1969), with the Supreme Court's suggestion that governmental efforts to encourage diverse views and attention to public issues are compatible with the free speech principle—even if they result in regulatory controls on the owners of speech sources.

Those who endorse the marketplace model do not claim that government may not do anything at all. Of course government may set up the basic rules of property and contract; it is these rules that make markets feasible. Without such rules, markets cannot exist at all. Government is also permitted to protect against market failures, especially by preventing monopolies and monopolistic practices. Structural regulation is acceptable so long as it is a content-neutral attempt to ensure competition. It is therefore important to note that advocates of marketplaces and democracy might work together in seeking to curtail monopoly. Of course, the prevention of monopoly is a precondition for well-functioning information markets.

Many people think that there is now nothing distinctive about the electronic media or about modern communications technologies that justifies an additional governmental role. *See, e.g., Syracuse Peace Council.* If such a role was ever justified, they would argue, it was because of problems of scarcity. When only three television networks exhausted the available options, a market failure may have called for regulation designed to ensure that significant numbers of people were not left without their preferred programming. But this is no longer a problem. With so dramatic a proliferation of stations, most people can obtain the programming they want, or will be able to soon. With cyberspace, people will be able to make, or to participate in, their own preferred programming in their own preferred "locations" on the Internet. With new technologies, perhaps there are no real problems calling for governmental controls, except for those designed to establish the basic framework.

The second model emphasizes that our constitutional system is one of deliberative democracy. This system prizes both political (not economic) equality and a shared civic culture. It seeks to promote, as a central democratic goal, reflective and deliberative debate about possible courses of action. The Madisonian model sees the right of free expression as a key part of the system of public deliberation.

On this view, even a well-functioning information market is not immune from government controls. Government is certainly not permitted to regulate speech however it wants; it may not restrict speech on the basis of viewpoint. But it may regulate the electronic media or even cyberspace to promote, in a sufficiently neutral way, a well-functioning democratic regime. It may attempt to promote attention to public issues. It may try to ensure diversity of view. It may promote political speech at the expense of other forms of speech. In particular, educational and public-affairs programming, on the Madisonian view, has a special place.

Some people think that the distinction between marketplace and Madisonian models is now an anachronism. Perhaps the two models conflicted at an earlier stage in history; but in one view, Madison has no place in an era of limitless broadcasting options and cyberspace. Perhaps new technologies now mean that Madisonian goals can best be satisfied in a system of free markets. Now that so many channels, e-mail options, and discussion "places" are available, cannot everyone read or see what they wish? If people want to spend their time on public issues, are there not countless available opportunities? Is this not especially true with the emergence of the Internet? Is it not hopelessly paternalistic, or anachronistic, for government to regulate for Madisonian reasons?

I do not believe that these questions are rhetorical. We know enough to know that even in a period of limitless options, our communications system may fail to promote an educated citizenry and political equality. Madisonian goals may be severely compromised even under technologically extraordinary conditions. There is no logical or *a priori* connection between a well-functioning system of free expression and limitless broadcasting or Internet options.

It is foreseeable that free markets in communications will be a mixed blessing. They could create a kind of accelerating "race to the bottom," in which many or most people see low-quality programming involving trumped-up scandals or sensationalistic anecdotes calling for little in terms of quality or quantity of attention. It is easily imaginable that well-functioning markets in communications will bring about a situation in which many of those interested in politics merely fortify their own unreflective judgments, and are exposed to little or nothing in the way of competing views. It is easily imaginable that the content of the most widely viewed programming will be affected by the desires of advertisers, in such a way as to produce shows that represent a bland, watered-down version of conventional morality, and that do not engage serious issues in a serious way for fear of offending some group in the audience.

It is easily imaginable that the television—or the personal computer carrying out communications functions—will indeed become what former FCC Chair Mark Fowler described as "just another appliance ... a toaster with pictures," and that the educative or aspirational goals of the First Amendment will be lost or even forgotten.

V. SPEECH, EMERGING MEDIA, AND CYBERSPACE

It is possible to describe certain categories of regulation and to set out some general guidelines about how they might be approached. I would suggest that existing law provides principles and analogies on which it makes sense to draw. An exploration of new problems confirms this suggestion. It shows that current categories can be invoked fairly straightforwardly to make sense of likely future dilemmas.

A large lesson may emerge from the discussion. Often participants in legal disputes, and especially in constitutional disputes, disagree sharply with respect to high-level, abstract issues; the debate between Madisonians and marketplace advocates is an obvious illustration. But sometimes such disputants can converge, or narrow their disagreement a great deal, by grappling with highly particular problems. In other words, debate over abstractions may conceal a potential for productive discussion and even agreement over particulars. Perhaps this is a strategy through which we might make much progress in the next generation of free speech law.

1. Requiring Competition

Many actual and imaginable legislative efforts are designed to ensure competition in the new communications markets. There is no constitutional problem with such efforts. The only qualification is that some such efforts might be seen as subterfuge for content regulation, disguised by a claimed need to promote monopoly; but this should be a relatively rare event. If government is genuinely attempting to prevent monopolistic practices, and to offer a structure in which competition can take place, there is no basis for constitutional complaint. Here First Amendment theorists of widely divergent views might be brought into agreement.

2. Subsidizing New Media

It is predictable that government might seek to assist certain technologies that offer great promise for the future. Some such efforts may in fact be a result of interest-group pressure. But in general, there is no constitutional obstacle to government efforts to subsidize preferred communications sources. Perhaps government believes that some technological innovations are especially likely to do well, or that they could receive particularly valuable benefits from national assistance. At least so long as there is no reason to believe that government is favoring speech of a certain content, efforts of this kind are unobjectionable as a matter of law. They may be objectionable as a matter of policy, since government may make bad judgments reflecting confusion or factional influence, but that is a different issue.

3. Subsidizing Particular Programming or Particular Broadcasters

In her dissenting opinion in *Turner [I]*, Justice O'Connor suggested that the appropriate response to government desire for programming of a certain content is not regulation but instead subsidization. This idea fits well with the idea that the government is unconstrained in its power to subsidize such speech as it prefers. Hence there should be no constitutional objection to government efforts to fund public broadcasting, to pay for high-quality fare for children, or to support programming that deals with public affairs. Perhaps government might do this for certain uses of the Internet.

To be sure, it is doubtful that [this] would be taken to its logical extreme. Could the government fund the Democratic Convention but not the Republican Convention? Could the government announce that it would fund only those public-affairs programs that spoke approvingly of current government policy? If we take the First Amendment to ban viewpoint discrimination, funding of this kind should be held to be improperly motivated. On the other hand, government subsidies of educational and public-affairs programming need not raise serious risks of viewpoint discrimination. It therefore seems unexceptionable for government, short of viewpoint discrimination, to subsidize those broadcasters whose programming it prefers, even if any such preference embodies content discrimination. So too, government might promote "conversations" or fora on e-mail that involve issues of public importance, or that attempt to promote educational goals for children or even adults.

4. Leaving Admittedly "Open" Channels Available to Others Who Would Not Otherwise Get Carriage

Suppose that a particular communications carrier has room for five hundred channels; suppose that four hundred channels are filled, but that one hundred are left open. Would it be legitimate for government to say that the one hundred must be filled by stations that would otherwise be unable be pay for carriage? Let us suppose that the stations would be chosen through a content neutral system, such as a lottery. From the First Amendment point of view, this approach seems acceptable. The government would be attempting to ensure access for speakers who would otherwise be unable to reach the audience. It is possible that as a matter of policy, government should have to provide some payment to the carrier in return for the access requirement. But there does not seem to be a First Amendment problem.

5. Requiring Carriers To Be Common Carriers for a Certain Number of Stations, Filling Vacancies with a Lottery System or Timesharing

In her dissenting opinion in *Turner [I]*, Justice O'Connor suggested the possibility that carriers could be required to set aside certain channels to be filled by a random method.

The advantage of this approach is that it would promote access for people who would otherwise be denied carriage, but without involving government in decisions about preferred content. This approach should raise no First Amendment difficulties.

6. Imposing Structural Regulation Designed Not To Prevent a Conventional Market Failure, But To Ensure Universal or Near-Universal Consumer Access to Networks

The protection of broadcasters in *Turner [I]* was specifically designed to ensure continued viewer access to free programming. Notably, the Court permitted the government to achieve this goal through regulation rather than through subsidy. Of course subsidy is the simpler and ordinarily more efficient route. If government wants to make sure that all consumers have access to communications networks, why should government not be required to pay to allow such access, on a kind of analogue to the food stamp program? The ordinary response to a problem of access is not to fix prices but instead to subsidize people who would otherwise be without access. The *Turner [I]* Court apparently believed that it is constitutionally acceptable for the government to ensure that industry (and subscribers), rather than taxpayers, provide the funding for those who would otherwise lack access.

The precise implications of this holding remain to be seen. It is impossible to foresee the range of structural regulations that might be proposed in an effort to ensure that all or almost all citizens have access to free programming or to some communications network, including any parts of the "informational superhighway." Some such regulations might in fact be based on other, more invidious motives, such as favoritism toward a particular set of suppliers; this may well be true of the measure in *Turner [I]* itself. The *Turner [I]* decision means that courts should review with some care any governmental claim that regulation is actually based on an effort to promote free access. But the key point here is that if the claim can be made out on the facts, structural regulation should be found acceptable.

7. Protecting Against Obscene, Libelous, Violent, Commercial, or Harassing Broadcasting or Messages

New technologies have greatly expanded the opportunity to communicate obscene, libelous, violent, or harassing messages—perhaps to general groups via stations on (for example) cable television, perhaps to particular people via electronic mail. Invasions of privacy are far more likely. The Internet poses special problems on these counts. As a general rule, any restrictions should be treated like those governing ordinary speech, with ordinary mail providing the best analogy. If restrictions are narrowly tailored, and supported by a sufficiently strong record, they should be upheld.

What of a regulatory regime designed to prevent invasion of privacy, libel, unwanted commercial messages, and obscenity, harassment, or infliction of emotional distress? Some such regulatory regime will ultimately make a great deal of sense. The principal obstacles are that the regulations should be both clear and narrow. It is easy to imagine a broad or vague regulation, one that would seize upon the sexually explicit or violent nature of communication to justify regulation that is far broader than necessary. Moreover, it is possible to imagine a situation in which liability was extended to any owner or operator who could have no knowledge of the particular materials being sent. The underlying question, having to do with efficient risk allocation, involves the extent to which a carrier might be expected to find and to stop unlawful messages; that question depends upon the relevant technology.

Some of the services that provide access to the Internet should not themselves be treated as speakers; they are providers of speech, but their own speech is not at issue. This point is closely related to the debate in *Turner [I]* about the speech status of cable carriers. But whether or not a carrier or provider is a speaker, a harmful effect on speech would raise First Amendment issues. We can see this point with an analogy. Certainly it would not be constitutional to say that truck owners will be criminally liable for carrying newspapers containing articles critical of the President. Such a measure would be unconstitutional in its purposes and in its effects, even if the truck owners are not speakers. From this we can see that a criminal penalty on carriers of material that is independently protected by the First Amendment should be unconstitutional. Thus a criminal penalty could not be imposed for providing "filthy" speech, at least if "filthy" speech is otherwise protected.

But a penalty imposed on otherwise unprotected materials raises a different question. Suppose that the government imposes criminal liability on carriers or providers of admittedly obscene material on the Internet. The adverse effect on unprotected speech should not by itself be found to offend the Constitution, even if there would be a harmful economic effect, and even unfairness, for the provider of the service. Instead the constitutional question should turn on the extent of the adverse effects on the dissemination of materials that are protected by the Constitution. If, for example, the imposition of criminal liability for the distribution of unprotected speech had serious harmful effects for the distribution of protected speech, the First Amendment issue would be quite severe. But that question cannot be answered in the abstract; it depends on what the relevant record shows with respect to any such adverse effects.

To answer that question, we need to know whether carrier liability, for unprotected speech, has a significant adverse effect on protected speech as well. We need to know, in short, whether the proper analogy is to a publisher or instead to a carrier of mail. It is therefore important to know whether a carrier could, at relatively low expense, filter out constitutionally unprotected material, or whether, on the contrary, the imposition of criminal liability for unprotected material would drive legitimate carriers out of business, or force them to try to undertake impossible or unrealistically expensive "searches." The answer to this question will depend in large part on the state of technology.

8. Imposing Content Based Regulation Designed To Ensure Public-Affairs and Educational Programming

It can readily be imagined that Congress might seek to promote education via regulation or subsidy of new media. It might try to ensure attention to public affairs. Suppose, for example, that Congress sets aside a number of channels for public-affairs and educational programming, on the theory that the marketplace provides too much commercial programming. This notion has in fact been under active consideration in Congress. Thus a recent bill would have required all telecommunications carriers to provide access at preferential rates to educational and health care institutions, state and local governments, public broadcast stations, libraries and other public entities, community newspapers, and broadcasters in the smallest markets.

Turner [I] certainly does not stand for the proposition that such efforts are constitutional. By hypothesis, any such regulation would be content based. It would therefore meet with a high level of judicial skepticism. On the other hand, *Turner [I]* does not authoritatively suggest that such efforts are unconstitutional. The Court did not itself say whether it would accept content discrimination designed to promote Madisonian goals. Certainly the opinion suggests that the government's burden would be a significant one. But it does not resolve the question.

It is notable that Justice O'Connor's opinion appears quite sensible on this point, and she leaves the issue open. Her principal argument is that the "must-carry" rules are too crude. Certainly crudely tailored measures give reason to believe that interest-group pressures, rather than a legitimate effort to improve educational and public-affairs programming, are at work. But if the relevant measures actually promote Madisonian goals, they should be upheld. There is of course reason to fear that any such measures have less legitimate purposes and functions, and hence a degree of judicial skepticism is appropriate. But narrow measures, actually promoting those purposes, are constitutionally legitimate.

VI. MADISON IN CYBERSPACE?

Do Madisonian ideals have an enduring role in American thought about freedom of speech? The existence of new technologies makes the question different and far more complex than it once was. It is conceivable that in a world of newly emerging and countless options, the market will prove literally unstoppable, as novel possibilities outstrip even well-motivated government controls.

If so, this result should not be entirely lamented. It would be an under-statement to say that a world in which consumers can choose from limitless choices has many advantages, not least from the Madisonian point of view. If choices are limitless, people interested in politics can see and listen to politics; perhaps they can even participate in politics, and in ways that were impossible just a decade ago. But that world would be far from perfect. It may increase social balkanization. It may not promote deliberation, but foster instead a series of referenda in cyberspace that betray constitutional goals.

My central point here has been that the system of free expression is not an aimless abstraction. Far from being an outgrowth of neoclassical economics, the First Amendment has independent and identifiable purposes. Free speech doctrine, with its proliferating tests, distinctions, and subparts, should not lose touch with those purposes. Rooted in a remarkable conception of political sovereignty, the goals of the First Amendment are closely connected with the founding commitment to a particular kind of polity: a deliberative democracy among informed citizens who are political equals. It follows that instead of allowing new technologies to use democratic processes for their own purposes, constitutional law should be concerned with harnessing those technologies for democratic ends—including the founding aspirations to public deliberation, citizenship, political equality, and even a certain kind of virtue. If the new technologies offer risks on these scores, they hold out enormous promise as well. I have argued here that whether that promise will be realized depends in significant part on judgments of law, including judgments about the point of the First Amendment.

BAD NEWS

Richard A. Posner, N.Y. Times Book Rev., July 31, 2005, at 1

The conventional news media are embattled. Attacked by both left and right in book after book, rocked by scandals, challenged by upstart bloggers, they have become a focus of controversy and concern. Their audience is in decline, their credibility with the public in shreds. In a recent poll conducted by the Annenberg Public Policy Center, 65 percent of the respondents thought that most news organizations, if they discover they've made a mistake, try to ignore it or cover it up, and 79 percent opined that a media company would hesitate to carry negative stories about a corporation from which it received substantial advertising revenues.

The industry's critics agree that the function of the news is to inform people about social, political, cultural, ethical and economic issues so that they can vote and otherwise express themselves as responsible citizens. They agree on the related point that journalism is a profession rather than just a trade and therefore that journalists and their employers must not allow profit considerations to dominate, but must acknowledge an ethical duty to report the news accurately, soberly, without bias, reserving the expression of political preferences for the editorial page and its radio and television counterparts. The critics further agree, as they must, that 30 years ago news reporting was dominated by newspapers and by television network news and that the audiences for these media have declined with the rise of competing sources, notably cable television and the Web.

The audience decline is potentially fatal for newspapers. Not only has their daily readership dropped from 52.6 percent of adults in 1990 to 37.5 percent in 2000, but the drop is much steeper in the 20-to-49-year-old cohort, a generation that is, and as it ages, will remain much more comfortable with electronic media in general and the Web in particular than are the current elderly.

At this point the diagnosis splits along political lines. Liberals, including most journalists (because most journalists are liberals), believe that the decline of the formerly dominant "mainstream" media has caused a deterioration in quality. They attribute this decline to the rise of irresponsible journalism on the right, typified by the Fox News Channel (the most-watched cable television news channel), Rush Limbaugh's radio talk show and right-wing blogs by Matt Drudge and others. But they do not spare the mainstream media, which, they contend, provides in the name of balance an echo chamber for the right. To these critics, the deterioration of journalism is exemplified by the attack of the "Swift boat" Vietnam veterans on Senator John Kerry during the 2004 election campaign. The critics describe the attack as consisting of lies propagated by the new right-wing media and reported as news by mainstream media made supine by anxiety over their declining fortunes.

Critics on the right applaud the rise of the conservative media as a long-overdue corrective to the liberal bias of the mainstream media, which, according to Jim A. Kuypers, the author of "Press Bias and Politics," are "a partisan collective which both consciously and unconsciously attempts to persuade the public to accept its interpretation of the world as true." Fourteen percent of Americans describe themselves as liberals, and 26 percent as conservatives. The corresponding figures for journalists are 56 percent and 18 percent. This means that of all journalists who consider themselves either liberal or conservative, 76 percent consider themselves liberal, compared with only 35 percent of the public that has a stated political position.

So politically one-sided are the mainstream media, the right complains (while sliding over the fact that the owners and executives, as distinct from the working journalists, tend to be far less liberal), that not only does it slant the news in a liberal direction; it will stop at nothing to defeat conservative politicians and causes. The right points to the "60 Minutes II" broadcast in which Dan Rather paraded what were probably forged documents concerning George W. Bush's National Guard service, and to Newsweek's erroneous report, based on a single anonymous source, that an American interrogator had flushed a copy of the Koran down the toilet (a physical impossibility, one would have thought).

Strip these critiques of their indignation, treat them as descriptions rather than as denunciations, and one sees that they are consistent with one another and basically correct. The mainstream media are predominantly liberal—in fact, more liberal than it used to be, but not because the politics of journalists have changed. Rather, because the rise of new media, itself mainly an economic rather than a political phenomenon, has caused polarization, pushing the already liberal media farther left.

The news media have also become more sensational, more prone to scandal and possibly less accurate. But note the tension between sensationalism and polarization: the trial of Michael Jackson got tremendous coverage, displacing a lot of political coverage, but it had no political valence.

The interesting questions are: first, the why of these trends, and, second, so what?

The why is the vertiginous decline in the cost of electronic communication and the relaxation of regulatory barriers to entry, leading to the proliferation of consumer choices. Thirty years ago the average number of television channels that Americans could receive was seven; today, with the rise of cable and satellite television, it is 71. Thirty years ago there was no Internet, therefore no Web, hence no online newspapers and magazines, and no blogs. The public's consumption of news and opinion used to be like sucking on a straw; now it's like being sprayed by a fire hose.

To see what difference the elimination of a communications bottleneck can make, consider a town that before the advent of television or even radio had just two newspapers because economies of scale made it impossible for a newspaper with a small circulation to break even. Each of the two, to increase its advertising revenues, would try to maximize circulation by pitching its news to the median reader, for that reader would not be attracted to a newspaper that flaunted extreme political views. There would be the same tendency to political convergence that is characteristic of two-party political systems, and for the same reason, attracting the least committed is the key to obtaining a majority.

One of the two newspapers would probably be liberal and have a loyal readership of liberal readers, and the other conservative have a loyal conservative readership. That would leave a middle range. To snag readers in that range, the liberal newspaper could not afford to be too liberal or the conservative one too conservative. The former would strive to be just liberal enough to hold its liberal readers, and the latter just conservative enough to hold its conservative readers. If either moved too close to its political extreme, it would lose readers in the middle without gaining readers from the extreme, since it had them already.

But suppose cost conditions change, enabling a newspaper to break even with many fewer readers than before. Now the liberal newspaper has to worry that any temporizing of its message in an effort to attract moderates may cause it to lose its most liberal readers to a new, more liberal newspaper; for with small-scale entry into the market now economical, the incumbents no longer have a secure base. So the liberal newspaper will tend to become even more liberal and, by the same process, the conservative newspaper more conservative. (If economies of scale increase, and as a result the number of newspapers grows, the opposite ideological change will be observed, as happened in the 19th century. The introduction of the "penny press" in the 1830s enabled newspapers to obtain large circulations and thus finance themselves by selling advertising; no longer did they have to depend on political patronage.)

The current tendency to political polarization in news reporting is thus a consequence of changes not in underlying political opinions but in costs, specifically the falling costs of new entrants. The rise of the conservative Fox News Channel caused CNN to shift to the left. CNN was going to lose many of its conservative viewers to Fox anyway, so it made sense to increase its appeal to its remaining viewers by catering more assiduously to their political preferences.

The tendency to greater sensationalism in reporting is a parallel phenomenon. The more news sources there are, the more intense the struggle for an audience. One tactic is to occupy an overlooked niche—peeling away from the broad-based media, a segment of the consuming public whose interests were not catered to previously. That is the tactic that produces polarization. Another is to "shout louder" than the competitors, where shouting takes the form of a sensational, attention-grabbing discovery, accusation, claim, or photograph. According to James T. Hamilton in his valuable book "All the News That's Fit to Sell," this even explains why the salaries paid news anchors have soared: the more competition there is for an audience, the more valuable is a celebrity newscaster.

The argument that competition increases polarization assumes that liberals want to read liberal newspapers and conservatives conservative ones. Natural as that assumption is, it conflicts with one of the points on which left and right agree—that people consume news and opinion in order to become well informed about public issues. Were this true, liberals would read conservative newspapers, and conservatives liberal newspapers, just as scientists test their hypotheses by confronting them with data that may refute them. But that is not how ordinary people (or, for that matter, scientists) approach political and social issues. The issues are too numerous, uncertain and complex, and the benefit to an individual of becoming well informed about them too slight, to invite sustained, disinterested attention. Moreover, people don't like being in a state of doubt, so they look for information that will support rather than undermine their existing beliefs. They are also uncomfortable seeing their beliefs challenged on issues that are bound up with their economic welfare, physical safety or religious and moral views.

So why do people consume news and opinion? In part it is to learn of facts that bear directly and immediately on their lives—hence the greater attention paid to local than to national and international news. They also want to be entertained, and they find scandals, violence, crime, the foibles of celebrities and the antics of the powerful all mightily entertaining. And they want to be confirmed in their beliefs by seeing them echoed and elaborated by more articulate, authoritative and prestigious voices. So they accept, and many relish, a partisan press. Forty-three percent of the respondents in the poll by the Annenberg Public Policy Center thought it "a good thing if some news organizations have a decidedly political point of view in their coverage of the news." Press Release, Annenberg Public Policy Center, Public and Press Differ About Partisan Bias, Accuracy and Press Freedom (May 14, 2005).

Being profit-driven, the media respond to the actual demands of their audience rather than to the idealized "thirst for knowledge" demand posited by public intellectuals and deans of journalism schools. They serve up what the consumer wants, and the more intense the competitive pressure, the better they do it. We see this in the media's coverage of political campaigns. Relatively little attention is paid to issues. Fundamental questions, like the actual difference in policies that might result if one candidate rather than the other won, get little play. The focus instead is on who's ahead, viewed as a function of campaign tactics, which are meticulously reported. Candidates' statements are evaluated not for their truth but for their adroitness; it is assumed, without a hint of embarrassment, that a political candidate who levels with voters disqualifies himself from being taken seriously, like a racehorse that tries to hug the outside of the track. News coverage of a political campaign is oriented to a public that enjoys competitive sports, not to one that is civic-minded.

We saw this in the coverage of the selection of Justice Sandra Day O'Connor's successor. It was played as an election campaign; one article even described the jockeying for the nomination by President Bush as the "primary election" and the fight to get the nominee confirmed by the Senate the "general election" campaign. With only a few exceptions, no attention was paid to the ability of the people being considered for the job or the actual consequences that the appointment was likely to have for the nation.

Does this mean that the news media was better before competition polarized them? Not at all. A market gives people what they want, whether they want the same thing or different things. Challenging areas of social consensus, however dumb or even vicious the consensus, is largely off limits for the media, because it wins no friends among the general public. The mainstream media do not kick sacred cows like religion and patriotism.

Not that the media lie about the news they report; in fact, they have strong incentives not to lie. Instead, there is selection, slanting, decisions as to how much or how little prominence to give a particular news item. Giving a liberal spin to equivocal economic data when conservatives are in power is, as the Harvard economists Sendhil Mullainathan and Andrei Shleifer point out, a matter of describing the glass as half empty when conservatives would describe it as half full.

Journalists are reluctant to confess to pandering to their customers' biases; it challenges their self-image as servants of the general interest, unsullied by commerce. They want to think they inform the public, rather than just satisfying a consumer demand no more elevated or consequential than the demand for cosmetic surgery in Brazil or bullfights in Spain. They believe in "deliberative democracy"—democracy as the system in which the people determine policy through deliberation on the issues. In his preface to "The Future of Media" (a collection of articles edited by Robert W. McChesney, Russell Newman and Ben Scott), Bill Moyers writes that "democracy can't exist without an informed public." Bill Moyers, The Future of Media: Resistance and Reform in the 21st Century (Robert W. McChesney, Russell Newman & Ben Scott eds., 2005). If this is true, the United States is not a democracy (which may be Moyers's dyspeptic view). Only members of the intelligentsia, a tiny slice of the population, deliberate on public issues.

The public's interest in factual accuracy is less an interest in truth than a delight in the unmasking of the opposition's errors. Conservatives were unembarrassed by the errors of the Swift Boat veterans, while taking gleeful satisfaction in the exposure of the forgeries on which Dan Rather had apparently relied, and in his resulting fall from grace. They reveled in Newsweek's retracting its story about flushing the Koran down a toilet yet would prefer that American abuse of prisoners be concealed. Still, because there is a market demand for correcting the errors and ferreting out the misdeeds of one's enemies, the media exercise an important oversight function, creating accountability and deterring wrongdoing. That, rather than educating the public about the deep issues, is its great social mission. It shows how a market produces a social good as an unintended byproduct of self-interested behavior.

The limited consumer interest in the truth is the key to understanding why both left and right can plausibly denounce the same media for being biased in favor of the other. Journalists are writing to meet a consumer demand that is not a demand for uncomfortable truths. So a newspaper that appeals to liberal readers will avoid exposés of bad behavior by blacks or homosexuals, as William McGowan charges in "Coloring the News"; similarly, Daniel Okrent, the first ombudsman of The New York Times, said that the news pages of The Times "present the social and cultural aspects of same-sex marriage in a tone that approaches cheerleading." William McGowan, Coloring the News: How Political Correctness has Corrupted American Journalism (2002); Daniel, Okrent, The Public Editor; Is the New York Times a Liberal Newspaper?, N.Y. Times, July 25, 2004. Not only would such exposés offend liberal readers who are not black or homosexual; many blacks and homosexuals are customers of liberal newspapers, and no business wants to offend a customer.

But the same liberal newspaper or television news channel will pull some of its punches when it comes to reporting on the activities of government, even in Republican administrations, thus giving credence to the left critique, as in Michael Massing's "Now They Tell Us," about the reporting of the war in Iraq. A newspaper depends on access to officials for much of its information about what government is doing and planning, and is reluctant to bite too hard the hand that feeds it. Michael Massing, Now They Tell Us: The American Press in Iraq (2004). Nevertheless, it is hyperbole for Eric Alterman to claim in "What Liberal Media?" that "liberals are fighting a near-hopeless battle in which they are enormously outmatched by most measures" by the conservative media, or for Bill Moyers to say that "the marketplace of political ideas" is dominated by a "quasi-official partisan press ideologically linked to an authoritarian administration." Eric Alterman, What Liberal Media?: The Truth About Bias in the News (2003). In a sample of 23 leading newspapers and news magazines, the liberal ones had twice the circulation of the conservative. The bias in some of the reporting in the liberal media, acknowledged by Okrent, is well documented by McGowan, as well as by Bernard Goldberg in "Bias" and L. Brent Bozell III in "Weapons of Mass Distortion." Bernard Goldberg, Bias: A CBS Insider Exposes How the Media Distort the News (2002); L. Brent Bozell III, Weapons of Mass Distortion: The Coming Meltdown of the Liberal Media (2004).

Journalists minimize offense, preserve an aura of objectivity and cater to the popular taste for conflict and contests by—in the name of "balance"—reporting both sides of an issue, even when there aren't two sides. So "intelligent design," formerly called by the oxymoron "creation science," though it is religious dogma thinly disguised, gets almost equal billing with the theory of evolution. If journalists admitted that the economic imperatives of their industry overrode their political beliefs, they would weaken the right's critique of liberal media bias.

The latest, and perhaps gravest, challenge to the journalistic establishment is the blog. Journalists accuse bloggers of having lowered standards. But their real concern is less highminded—it is the threat that bloggers, who are mostly amateurs, pose to professional journalists and their principal employers, the conventional news media. A serious newspaper, like The Times, is a large, hierarchical commercial enterprise that interposes layers of review, revision and correction between the reporter and the published report and that to finance its large staff depends on advertising revenues and hence on the good will of advertisers and (because advertising revenues depend to a great extent on circulation) readers. These dependences constrain a newspaper in a variety of ways. But in addition, with its reputation heavily invested in accuracy, so that every serious error is a potential scandal, a newspaper not only has to delay publication of many stories to permit adequate checking but also has to institute rules for avoiding error—like requiring more than a single source for a story or limiting its reporters' reliance on anonymous sources—that cost it many scoops.

Blogs don't have these worries. Their only cost is the time of the blogger, and that cost may actually be negative if the blogger can use the publicity that he obtains from blogging to generate lecture fees and book royalties. Having no staff, the blogger is not expected to be accurate. Having no advertisers (though this is changing), he has no reason to pull his punches. And not needing a large circulation to cover costs, he can target a segment of the reading public much narrower than a newspaper or a television news channel could aim for. He may even be able to pry that segment away from the conventional media. Blogs pick off the mainstream media's customers one by one, as it were.

And bloggers thus can specialize in particular topics to an extent that few journalists employed by media companies can, since the more that journalists specialized, the more of them the company would have to hire in order to be able to cover all bases. A newspaper will not hire a journalist for his knowledge of old typewriters, but plenty of people in the blogosphere have that esoteric knowledge, and it was they who brought down Dan Rather. Similarly, not being commercially constrained, a blogger can stick with and dig into a story longer and deeper than the conventional media dare to, lest their readers become bored. It was the bloggers' dogged persistence in pursuing a story that the conventional media had tired of that forced Trent Lott to resign as Senate majority leader.

What really sticks in the craw of conventional journalists is that although individual blogs have no warrant of accuracy, the blogosphere as a whole has a better error-correction machinery than the conventional media do. The rapidity with which vast masses of information are pooled and sifted leaves the conventional media in the dust. Not only are there millions of blogs, and thousands of bloggers who specialize, but, what is more, readers post comments that augment the blogs, and the information in those comments, as in the blogs themselves, zips around blogland at the speed of electronic transmission.

This means that corrections in blogs are also disseminated virtually instantaneously, whereas when a member of the mainstream media catches a mistake, it may take weeks to communicate a retraction to the public. This is true not only of newspaper retractions—usually printed inconspicuously and in any event rarely read, because readers have forgotten the article being corrected—but also of network television news. It took CBS so long to acknowledge Dan Rather's mistake because there are so many people involved in the production and supervision of a program like "60 Minutes II" who have to be consulted.

The charge by mainstream journalists that blogging lacks checks and balances is obtuse. The blogosphere has more checks and balances than the conventional media; only they are different. The model is Friedrich Hayek's classic analysis of how the economic market pools enormous quantities of information efficiently despite its decentralized character, its lack of a master coordinator or regulator, and the very limited knowledge possessed by each of its participants.

In effect, the blogosphere is a collective enterprise—not 12 million separate enterprises, but one enterprise with 12 million reporters, feature writers and editorialists, yet with almost no costs. It's as if The Associated Press or Reuters had millions of reporters, many of them experts, all working with no salary for free newspapers that carried no advertising.

How can the conventional news media hope to compete? Especially when the competition is not entirely fair? The bloggers are parasitical on the conventional media. They copy the news and opinion generated by the conventional media, often at considerable expense, without picking up any of the tab. The degree of parasitism is striking in the case of those blogs that provide their readers with links to newspaper articles. The links enable the audience to read the articles without buying the newspaper. The legitimate gripe of the conventional media is not that bloggers undermine the overall accuracy of news reporting, but that they are free riders who may in the long run undermine the ability of the conventional media to finance the very reporting on which bloggers depend.

Some critics worry that "unfiltered" media like blogs exacerbate social tensions by handing a powerful electronic platform to extremists at no charge. Bad people find one another in cyberspace and so gain confidence in their crazy ideas. The conventional media filter out extreme views to avoid offending readers, viewers and advertisers; most bloggers have no such inhibition.

The argument for filtering is an argument for censorship. (That it is made by liberals is evidence that everyone secretly favors censorship of the opinions he fears.) But probably there is little harm and some good in unfiltered media. They enable unorthodox views to get a hearing. They get 12 million people to write rather than just stare passively at a screen. In an age of specialization and professionalism, they give amateurs a platform. They allow people to blow off steam who might otherwise adopt more dangerous forms of self-expression. They even enable the authorities to keep tabs on potential troublemakers; intelligence and law enforcement agencies devote substantial resources to monitoring blogs and Internet chat rooms.

And most people are sensible enough to distrust communications in an unfiltered medium. They know that anyone can create a blog at essentially zero cost that most bloggers are uncredentialed amateurs, that bloggers don't employ fact checkers and don't have editors and that a blogger can hide behind a pseudonym. They know, in short, that until a blogger's assertions are validated (as when the mainstream media acknowledge an error discovered by a blogger), there is no reason to repose confidence in what he says. The mainstream media, by contrast, assure their public that they make strenuous efforts to prevent errors from creeping into their articles and broadcasts. They ask the public to trust them, and that is why their serious errors are scandals.

A survey by the National Opinion Research Center finds that the public's confidence in the press declined from about 85 percent in 1973 to 59 percent in 2002, with most of the decline occurring since 1991. Over both the longer and the shorter period, there was little change in public confidence in other major institutions. So it seems there are special factors eroding trust in the news industry. One is that the blogs have exposed errors by the mainstream media that might otherwise have gone undiscovered or received less publicity. Another is that competition by the blogs, as well as by the other new media, has pushed the established media to get their stories out faster, which has placed pressure on them to cut corners. So while the blogosphere is a marvelous system for prompt error correction, it is not clear whether its net effect is to reduce the amount of error in the media as a whole.

But probably the biggest reason for declining trust in the media is polarization. As media companies are pushed closer to one end of the political spectrum or the other, the trust placed in them erodes. Their motives are assumed to be political. This may explain recent Pew Research Center poll data that show Republicans increasingly regarding the media as too critical of the government and Democrats increasingly regarding them as not critical enough.

Thus the increase in competition in the news market that has been brought about by lower costs of communication (in the broadest sense) has resulted in more variety, more polarization, more sensationalism, more healthy skepticism and, in sum, a better matching of supply to demand. But increased competition has not produced a public more oriented toward public issues, more motivated and competent to engage in genuine self-government, because these are not the goods that most people are seeking from the news media. They are seeking entertainment, confirmation, reinforcement, and emotional satisfaction; and what consumers want, a competitive market supplies, no more, no less. Journalists express dismay that bottom-line pressures are reducing the quality of news coverage. What this actually means is that when competition is intense, providers of a service are forced to give the consumer what he or she wants, not what they, as proud professionals, think the consumer should want, or more bluntly, what they want.

Yet what of the sliver of the public that does have a serious interest in policy issues? Are these people less well served than in the old days? Another recent survey by the Pew Research Center finds that serious magazines have held their own and that serious broadcast outlets, including that bane of the right, National Public Radio, are attracting ever larger audiences. And for that sliver of a sliver that invites challenges to its biases by reading The New York Times and The Wall Street Journal, that watches CNN and Fox, that reads Brent Bozell and Eric Alterman and everything in between, the increased polarization of the media provides a richer fare than ever before.

So when all the pluses and minuses of the impact of technological and economic change on the news media are toted up and compared, maybe there isn't much to fret about.

Notes and Questions

1. **"The Daily Me."** In Being Digital (1995), technologist Nicholas Negroponte suggested that, in the new media environment, each person could use digital technology to select news stories based on that person's tastes, producing personalized news he called "The Daily Me." Cass Sunstein has argued (in his book Republic.com (2001)) that such technologies—now being used, for example, to facilitate the reading of blogs—threaten the core of our democracy. Were we better off as a nation when everyone watched Walter Cronkite and "All in the Family"?

2. **Brand Names and New Video Options.** What the blogosphere represents to print journalism, video entertainment via websites such as YouTube might be to network-developed programming. In The Wealth of Networks (2006), Yochai Benkler champions the model of peer production and argues that individually created programming will increasingly command attention and credibility. Do you agree? What are the implications of an affirmative or negative answer to this question?

---

§ 10.F.2. What Could the FCC Do About It?

Judge Posner, in the excerpt above, poses some empirical questions (and makes some empirical claims) concerning the nature of the change in media in the Internet age. The FCC too has considered these issues, attempting to assess the "information needs of communities" and possible regulatory responses to the changing landscape. The excerpt below is from a wide-ranging FCC staff study that attempts to address these questions and to consider appropriate regulatory responses. The following excerpt focuses on the study's finding that increased outlets and opinions do not necessarily compensate for the loss of traditional reporting by news entities.

THE INFORMATION NEEDS OF COMMUNITIES: THE CHANGING MEDIA LANDSCAPE IN A BROADBAND AGE

Steven Waldman & the Working Group on Information Needs of Communities,
FCC (2011), *available at* http://www.fcc.gov/info-needs-communities

The enormous challenges facing traditional media would be of less concern if the vibrant new digital media were filling the gap. Is it?

It is important to appreciate that the Internet has not only allowed for new forms of self-expression but has improved news in many ways. Lower barriers to entry and the vast amount of available space online have led to a greater diversity of voices, increased depth of some types of coverage, more consumer choices.

Technology has reduced the costs of gathering, producing and distributing news, in some cases substantially. Reporters can use computerized databases to pull together stories in hours that would have previously taken weeks. The cost of producing and publishing images, sound, and text has fallen sharply. And most obviously, and most dramatically, the search-engine-driven Internet has made it infinitely easier to find a wide range of information rapidly.

Citizens are more empowered than ever. They choose where to get their content, how to share it, and are reporting it themselves. Billions of hours of volunteer labor have helped bring important information online and make it accessible on a grand scale. With 76 percent of cell phone owners using their phone to take pictures, we may conclude that, as remarkable as it is that most Americans now carry around a minicomputer, it is just as significant that most now carry a camera. Indeed, it has become a staple of modern news coverage to include photos and videos from citizens who captured images with their phones. Perhaps the most important piece of citizen journalism in this new era was the video taken by an Iranian doctor on his cell phone of a woman named Neda Agha-Soltan being murdered on the street in Tehran.

Citizens can customize what news they want and when. There is not a topic that does not have aggregators providing headlines from around the world. We can get it on demand (when we're ready to consume) or in real time; through desktop, tablet, phone, or TV; in text, video, still images, audio or an infinite combination. Even data has become infinitely customizable. For instance, the Texas Tribune, a news startup in Austin, Texas, offers online readers the ability to sort through data about Texas lawmakers, prisoners, and public employees. Readers can set the parameters as they wish, based on their particular interests—say, information about their particular town—and the gizmo tailors the results to them. Built as one feature—a database—from a consumer perspective it actually provides thousands of different "stories."

Citizens can now play a much greater role in holding institutions accountable. Whether it's snapping photos of potholes that the city hasn't fixed and posting it to a website, or scouring documents to help a news website uncover a scandal, a broad range of Americans can now more easily scrutinize government, companies and other powerful organizations. These attributes are not just enriching born-on-the-Internet websites but the digital operations of traditional media as well. Newspapers and TV stations are now, on their websites or other digital platforms, making use of citizen submissions of reporting, images, and video; statistical databases; photo galleries; crowd-sourcing; interactive maps; user-comment areas; aggregation of information from around the web; Twitter feeds; live video streaming; and many other information tools.

Perhaps no area has been more dramatically transformed than "hyperlocal"—coverage on the neighborhood or block by block level. Even in the fattest-and-happiest days of traditional media, they could not regularly provide news on such a granular level. Professional media have been joined by a wide range of local blogs, email lists, websites and the proliferation of local groups on national websites like Facebook or Yahoo! For the most part, hyperlocally-oriented websites and blogs do not operate as profitable businesses, but they do not need to. This is journalism as voluntarism—a thousand points of news.

The number and variety of websites, blogs, and tweets contributing to the news and information landscape is truly stunning. Yet this abundance can obscure a parallel trend: the shortage of full-time reporting.

For instance, the Pew case study of Baltimore revealed a profusion of media outlets. Between new media (blogs and websites) and traditional media (TV, radio, newspapers), researchers counted 53 different outlets—considerably more than existed 10 years ago. But when Pew's researchers analyzed the content they were providing, particularly regarding the city budget and other public affairs issues, they discovered that 95 percent of the stories—including those in the new media—were based on reporting done by traditional media (mostly the Baltimore Sun). And those sources were doing less than they had done in the past. Several other studies have had similar findings.

This is not a criticism of citizen media or web-based news aggregators and commentators. Even when they are working primarily with the reporting of others, they often add tremendous value—distributing the news through alternate channels or offering new interpretations of its meaning. But we are seeing a decline in the media with a particular strength—gathering the information—and seeing it replaced by a media that often exhibits a different set of strengths (for instance, distributing and interpreting it).

This problem became evident several years ago, prompting a flood of former newspaper journalists and concerned citizens to start web operations dedicated to serious reporting, especially about local civic affairs. More than a hundred impressively creative websites—such as MinnPost in Minneapolis, voiceofsandiego.org, the Texas Tribune, the Bay Citizen in San Francisco, the Sacramento Press, and the Chicago News Cooperative—now populate the cyberscape. Some are nonprofits, some for-profits—and many have brought new energy to the local journalism scene. Some are even becoming profitable and self-sufficient.

But so far these new websites are not large enough or self-sustaining enough to fill the gaps left by newspaper layoffs. In a recent survey of 66 local news websites, half reported that their organizations drew in annual income of less than $50,000, and three-quarters reported annual income of less than $100,000. That is not a typographical error; it is *annual* income for the whole website.

The nonprofit online news sector may be vibrant, but it is small in scale. The Knight Foundation hosted a recent gathering of leaders from 12 of the most influential and well-funded websites. Together they employ 88 full-time staffers, which seems quite encouraging until one remembers that more than 13,000 reporters have left the newspaper industry in the last decade. Another point of reference: while newspapers have been suffering an estimated $1.6 billion drop in editorial spending per year, foundations have contributed an estimated $180 million to fund new online ventures *over a period of five years*. Billions out, millions in.

In addition to the local websites, there are a handful of national Internet companies making major efforts to serve local communities. Examiner.com has sites in 233 cities, deploying 67,000 "examiners" to write on local topics. But these part-timers focus on lifestyle topics, such as entertainment, retail, and sports—not on hard news. AOL's Patch has created local websites in 800 communities, hiring a reporter-editor in each location—meaning that Patch has likely hired more reporters than any other media organization in the past two years. In the wake of the AOL merger with Huffington Post, founder Arianna Huffington maintained that a major reason for her interest in this deal was to do more for local news and information. On the other hand, AOL executives in the past have stressed that to succeed financially, they must focus their efforts on affluent areas. And a single editor wearing many hats, even working with volunteer contributors, will usually not have time to do full-time enterprise reporting on par with the best of traditional urban dailies—though he or she may well match or better the efforts of local community newspapers. In other words, Examiner, Patch, and companies like them add tremendous value to the media ecosystem, but they also leave many crucial gaps unfilled.

Michele McLellan, who has studied the digital news scene comprehensively for the University of Missouri journalism school, writes, "The tired idea that born-on-the-Web news sites will replace traditional media is wrong-headed, and it's past time that academic research and news reports reflect that." Michele McLellan, Debunking the Replacement Myth, Knight Digital Media Center (July 26, 2010) http://www.knightdigitalmediacenter.org/leadership_blog/comments/20100726_the_replacement_myth/.

Why has the Internet not so far spawned business models that can sustain large numbers of reporters? To answer that, we review some of the most important ways that the digital revolution has changed the economics of news production.

The great unbundling: During the news media's most profitable days, in many towns, there was only one newspaper, leaving consumers with limited choice. And, though we may not have thought of it this way, purchasing a paper meant having to buy a bundle of goods, even readers only wanted certain parts. A cross-subsidy system had developed, in which a consumer who bought the paper for the box scores was helping to pay the salary of the city hall reporter. Today, however, a reader can get a mobile app that provides only box scores (with second-by-second updates!). The bundle is broken — and so is the cross-subsidy.

Advertisers have benefited from unbundling, too. Remember the saying attributed to department store executive John Wanamaker: "Half the money I spend on advertising is wasted; the trouble is I don't know which half"? On the Internet, the executive *can* know which half is wasted, and spend it elsewhere.

Downward pressure on online advertising rates: It is a myth that local newspapers suffered because they did not grow traffic online. From 2005 to 2009, newspapers' online traffic skyrocketed — from 43.7 million unique monthly users to 70 million, from 1.6 billion monthly page views to 3 billion page views. But in financial terms, that growth was shockingly meaningless. During that period, online advertising revenue — for the entire newspaper industry — grew $716 million, while the print advertising side of the business lost $22.6 billion. This led to the saying in the newspaper world that "print dollars were being replaced by digital dimes." The constant growth of Internet page views — fueled in part by social media — has resulted in online advertising rates that are a fraction of TV and newspaper ad rates.

Advertising is increasingly disconnected from content: While billions of ad dollars have shifted from TV and newspapers to the Internet, many of those dollars do not go to websites that produce their own content, like newspaper and magazine sites. In 2000, one percent of online ad dollars went to the purchase of advertising units appearing in search engine results. In 2009, 47 percent did. On mobile devices, advertisers can increasingly geo-target ads based on where the consumer is located at a particular moment. Through social media and direct-to-consumer discount services like Groupon, advertisers can reach consumers without having to search for an appropriate editorial context for their ads. To reach consumers, advertisers need content less and less.

Mobile has brought huge innovation to news distribution, but not to news media business models: The fastest growing platform for accessing news and information is the mobile device. Fifty six percent of all mobile device users, and 47 percent of the population, now use such devices to get local news via an Internet connection. Increasingly, the mobile device is a news media platform — just like a newspaper or a TV set — as much as it is a two-way communication device. Publishers have expressed some optimism about the iPad and other tablets fundamentally altering the economics of digital news, making it far more likely that consumers will pay to access content. But the jury is still out regarding whether they, or other mobile devices, will have that impact. A review of Apple's App Store revealed that approximately 72 percent of iPad news apps and 71 percent of iPhone news apps were available for free.

The nature of news as a public good: To some degree, the struggles of traditional media flow from fundamental economic principles related to certain types of news that are essentially "public goods." Economists say that many people simply will not pay for news, since they know they can "free ride" and still get the benefits of the news. If you want an apple, you have to pay for it, and the benefits go only to you. By contrast, education reporting can generate stories that benefit an entire community, and yet people get the benefits of better schools even if they do not subscribe to the paper. The result: lots of apples sold, but few education reporters employed.

Consider: In a three-day December 2008 series about the probation system, the Raleigh (NC) News & Observer established that 580 North Carolina probationers had killed people since the start of 2000. The series occupied several staff over six months, costing roughly $200,000 to produce. It prompted the governor to try to fix the program. In the future, there will probably be people walking the streets of Raleigh who were not murdered because of the reforms. But local residents have no way of knowing who among them is alive due to the newspaper series. To have benefited from it, one did not need to have read the series or subscribed to the News & Observer (which was available for free on the Internet). It is a terrific deal for citizens: tremendous benefit, without the cost or even the bother of reading.

Of course the catch is that if too many people free ride, media outlets cannot pay the salaries of the reporters who painstakingly gather the information. One of the most famous phrases of the Internet era is "Information wants to be free." There is some truth to that. People want to distribute and receive information for free. But what that leaves out is reality that in some cases the information will not come to the fore without the work of professional reporters. And while information may want to be free, labor wants to be paid.

Notes and Questions

1. The FCC's Role. The report itself states that "[g]overnment is not the main player in this drama." Nevertheless, the report includes several recommendations, from increasing the transparency of data currently filed by media companies with the FCC to ensuring that innovative approaches to news in the commercial and nonprofit sectors face low barriers to entry. The report also concludes that the trends it identifies further support the need for universal broadband to ensure widespread, democratic access to new information sources.

2. Universal Service for Local News or Media? The report does not go exactly this far, but it notes that substantial government expenditures in the media space (such as advertising expenditures and funding for educational programs) are not targeted towards local outlets. Of course, the government could go further and simply provide grants to news organizations. Just how far can the government go in providing funding for particular types of media before it threatens core First Amendment values?

Chapter Eleven

Antitrust and Merger Review

Introduction

An important aspect of government intervention in telecommunications—one that transcends the many different telecommunications services and markets that we examine in this book—is competition policy and enforcement. Antitrust stands as an alternative or a complement to sector-specific regulation in the control of monopoly. We have already seen several instances in which the Department of Justice (DOJ) has used antitrust law to curb monopoly excesses and to affect telecommunications market structure, the most dramatic example being the divestiture of AT&T. The FCC can also engage in antitrust-like enforcement: one example was the Commission's ultimately failed effort to take action against Comcast for discrimination against BitTorrent (which is discussed in Chapter Fourteen). And, of course, the FCC reviews telecommunications mergers and may impose remedies that add to or differ from any imposed by the antitrust agencies, as several transactions discussed below will demonstrate. In this chapter, we will discuss the role of antitrust in telecommunications regulation and examine the interplay between the enforcement of the antitrust laws and regulation under the Communications Act. This chapter will focus mostly on merger review. Merger review and antitrust enforcement differ from the structural regulation discussed in the previous chapter; whereas structural regulation involves ex ante rules that govern categories of conduct by categories of firms without reference to the facts of a particular case, merger and antitrust enforcement involve case-by-case determinations of the actual or potential competitive effects of specific conduct by specific firms. Broadcast ownership caps, for example, ban combinations by certain broadcasters above a certain cap, while merger review asks whether the particular combination of two given broadcasters would be likely to harm consumers. Waivers from rules narrow the gap between the ex ante approach of regulation and the ex post approach of merger and antitrust review, but the approaches differ in that the firm seeking a waiver bears the burden of persuading the FCC that the rule should not apply while the FCC or antitrust agencies bear the burden of showing merger or other antitrust harm in the case-by-case context.

After discussing mergers, this chapter looks at the continuing use of antitrust in telecommunications markets and discusses single-firm conduct through the case of *Verizon v. Trinko*.

§ 11.A. Merger Enforcement and Telecommunications Regulation

In each sector of the U.S. telecommunications industry, market structure has changed over time. In broadcast, for example, the number of radio and television stations has increased over the decades, but ownership of those stations, particularly radio, came to be concentrated in fewer hands. In wireless communications, the market expanded from the original cellular duopoly (a market with only two competing firms) to a market with six nationwide carriers, later becoming more concentrated with the AT&T Wireless/Cingular and Sprint/Nextel mergers. Similarly, cable operators Comcast and AT&T merged while DBS providers EchoStar and DirecTV scuttled their proposed merger in the face of FCC and Justice Department opposition. Subsequently, the FCC and Justice Department approved the merger between DirecTV and News Corp. (which owns Fox).

Changes in the ownership structure of local telephony were particularly dramatic in the aftermath of the 1996 Act. In 1984, just after the Bell divestiture, there were seven Regional Holding Companies (RHCs): Ameritech, Bell Atlantic, BellSouth, NYNEX, Pacific Telesis, Southwestern Bell, and US West. There were also two large ILECs not associated with the former Bell System: GTE and Southern New England Telephone (SNET). By 2011, only three large local exchange carriers remained. This change in number reflected the merging of Southwestern Bell, Pacific Telesis, SNET, and Ameritech into SBC Communications and the merging of Bell Atlantic, NYNEX, and GTE into Verizon Communications. (The third was Qwest, which acquired US West, but no longer exists under that name.) By the end of 2005 AT&T and MCI no longer existed as independent firms. SBC merged with AT&T (and took its name before also acquiring BellSouth), and Verizon acquired MCI.

As you read the materials that follow, think about two separate but related issues. First, consider the substance of the various mergers at issue. Should we be worried when two large LECs, wireless carriers, or other communications entities combine forces, on the theory that the resulting markets will see less vigorous competition? Should we instead celebrate because mergers likely make possible new efficiencies? Are vertical mergers—e.g., the one between News Corp. and DirecTV—less objectionable than horizontal ones—e.g., the one between EchoStar and DirecTV? Is competition among a smaller number of larger firms better or worse than competition among a larger number of smaller firms? Where should we draw the line? Second, focus on the FCC's merger review procedure itself. On what authority does the FCC get involved in telecommunications mergers? Does the FCC overstep this authority when it imposes conditions on mergers it then approves, or is this an example of the healthy application of administrative expertise? In short, given that other federal agencies (in particular the Department of Justice) already engage in merger review, why is the Commission involved, and what exactly is it trying to accomplish?

§ 11.A.1. Background on Merger Policy

Mergers, acquisitions, and general concerns about industry concentration have long been on the regulatory agenda in U.S. telecommunications. The Bell breakup in 1984 was neither the beginning nor the end. Regulators and antitrust officials had been worried about consolidation in telecommunications markets since long before divestiture, and those concerns continue to be salient today. Indeed they may be of increasing importance as policymakers focus on helping telecommunications markets transition to increasingly competitive structures.

As we have already briefly discussed, the Justice Department filed an antitrust suit in 1913 alleging that Bell had improperly used its dominance in the long-distance market to pressure competing local carriers to merge into the Bell System. As part of the "Kingsbury Commitment" (the agreement that settled that case) Bell agreed to stop acquiring independent competitors. The Department of Justice nonetheless approved most of Bell's special applications to acquire local companies in the years the consent decree was in force, mostly on the grounds that those acquisitions helped resolve inefficient fragmentation of the phone system by noninterconnecting local carriers. In 1918, Congress and the President gave the Postmaster General emergency wartime powers over the phone system; that led to further consolidations that would remain even after control of the phone system was returned to private parties.

In 1921, Congress suspended the nonacquisition provisions of the Kingsbury Commitment for good and gave the Interstate Commerce Commission authority to exempt telephone company mergers from the antitrust laws. The resulting statute, the Willis-Graham Act, was expressly aimed at eliminating the inefficient fragmentation of the phone system caused by the lack of local interconnection. Willis-Graham Act, Pub. L. No. 67-15, 42 Stat. 27 (1921), *repealed by* Telecommunications Act of 1996, Pub. L. No. 104-104, §601(b)(2), 110 Stat. 56, 143. On its face, of course, the Willis-Graham Act did not announce an open season for acquisitions. The Act only withheld antitrust enforcement for consolidations that were "of advantage to the persons to whom service is to be rendered and in the public interest." *Id.* In practice, however, the hurdle proved a low one.

When Congress enacted the Communications Act of 1934, it retained the core of the Willis-Graham Act: the relevant agency—now the FCC—had the power to exempt local telephone company mergers from antitrust scrutiny. The FCC could thus trump both the Department of Justice and the Federal Trade Commission (FTC), the agencies normally empowered to review mergers of this sort. Specifically, §221(a) of the 1934 Act gave the Commission authority to exempt mergers from "any Act or Acts of Congress making the proposed transaction unlawful." Communications Act of 1934, Pub. L. No. 73-416, §221(a), 48 Stat. 1064, 1080. This authority remained with the Commission for over 50 years, until §601(b)(2) of the Telecommunications Act of 1996 expressly repealed §221(a). The Act now states that the FCC has no authority "to modify, impair, or supersede the applicability of any of the antitrust laws." 47 U.S.C. §152 note.

The fact that the FCC can no longer exempt mergers from antitrust review does not mean that the Commission has no role in reviewing these transactions, nor does it mean that the Commission is without power to block them. The Clayton Antitrust Act, for example, grants the FCC concurrent jurisdiction with the Justice Department to act on transactions among "common carriers engaged in wire or radio communications." 15 U.S.C. §21(a). The FCC has not availed itself of this authority, however, because it has found authority to review transactions under its public interest authority in §§214(a) and 310(d) of the Communications Act itself. Section 214(a) requires the Commission to certify that any acquisition of lines by a common carrier will serve the present and future "public convenience and necessity." Similarly, no transfer of a spectrum license can occur without a finding by the Commission that the transfer will serve the "public interest, convenience, and necessity." 47 U.S.C. §310(d).

The FCC thus has the authority and indeed the obligation to review transfers of licenses that are part of a proposed merger or acquisition. Exactly how it reviews mergers and articulates the standard of review of §310(d) has evolved over time. In 2011 the Commission explained how it reviews mergers in its order conditionally approving Comcast's acquisition of NBC Universal.

Applications of Comcast Corp., General Electric Co., and NBC Universal, Inc. for Consent To Assign Licenses and Transfer Control of Licensees

Memorandum Opinion and Order, 26 FCC Rcd. 4238 (2011)

IV. Standard of Review and Public Interest Framework

22. Pursuant to Section 310(d) of the Act, we must determine whether the proposed assignment and transfer of control of certain licenses and authorizations held and controlled by Comcast and NBCU will serve "the public interest, convenience, and necessity." In making this determination, we must assess whether the proposed transaction complies with the specific provisions of the Act, other applicable statutes, and the Commission's Rules. If the transaction would not violate a statute or rule, the Commission considers whether a grant could result in public interest harms by substantially frustrating or impairing the objectives or implementation of the Act or related statutes. The Commission then employs a balancing test, weighing any potential public interest harms of the proposed transaction against any potential public interest benefits. The Applicants bear the burden of proving, by a preponderance of the evidence, that the proposed transaction, on balance, serves the public interest. If we are unable to find that the proposed transaction serves the public interest for any reason, or if the record presents a substantial and material question of fact, we must designate the Application for hearing.

23. Our public interest evaluation necessarily encompasses the "broad aims of the Communications Act," Michael Katz, Jonathan Orszag, & Theresa Sullivan, An Economic Analysis of Consumer Harm from the Current Retransmission Consent Regime, Nov. 12, 2009, at ¶¶ 30–36, which include, among other things, a deeply rooted preference for preserving and enhancing competition in relevant markets, accelerating private-sector deployment of advanced services, ensuring a diversity of information sources and services to the public, and generally managing spectrum in the public interest. Our public interest analysis may also entail assessing whether the transaction will affect the quality of communications services or will result in the provision of new or additional services to consumers. In conducting this analysis, the Commission may consider technological and market changes as well as trends within the communications industry, including the nature and rate of change.

24. Our competitive analysis, which forms an important part of the public interest evaluation, is informed by but not limited to traditional antitrust principles. The DOJ reviews communications transactions pursuant to Section 7 of the Clayton Act, and if it wishes to block a transaction, it must demonstrate to a court that the transaction may substantially lessen competition or tend to create a monopoly. The Commission's competitive analysis under the public interest standard is somewhat broader. For example, the Commission considers whether a transaction will enhance, rather than merely preserve, existing competition, and often takes a more expansive view of potential and future competition in analyzing that issue.

25. Our analysis recognizes that a proposed transaction may have both beneficial and harmful consequences. Our public interest authority enables us, where appropriate, to impose and enforce transaction-related conditions targeted to ensure that the public interest is served by the transaction. Section 303(r) of the Act authorizes the Commission to prescribe restrictions or conditions, not inconsistent with the law, which may be necessary to carry out the provisions of the Act. Indeed, unlike the role of antitrust enforcement authorities, our public interest authority enables us to rely upon our extensive

regulatory and enforcement experience to impose and enforce conditions to ensure that a transaction will yield overall public interest benefits. In exercising this broad authority, the Commission generally has imposed conditions to confirm specific benefits or remedy specific harms likely to arise from transactions and that are related to the Commission's responsibilities under the Act and related statutes.

Notes and Questions

1. A Flexible Standard. The Commission has elsewhere interpreted its public interest standard to be "a flexible one that encompasses the broad aims of the Communications Act." Applications of Teleport Commc'ns Grp. Inc., Transferor, & AT&T Corp., Transferee, for Consent to Transfer of Control of Corps. Holding Point-to-Point Microwave Licenses and Authorizations to Provide Int'l Facilities-Based and Resold Commc'ns Servs., Memorandum Opinion and Order, 13 FCC Rcd. 15,236, ¶ 11 (1998) (internal quotation marks omitted). In judging common carrier mergers, the Commission has typically focused on competition issues and Commission goals regarding the equitable build-out of new services. Meanwhile, in transactions involving broadcast licenses, the Commission has typically focused on issues related to diversity (which, as we saw in Chapter Five, has been defined in different ways). Importantly, however, under the public interest standard as interpreted by the FCC, the Commission need not show that a transaction is likely to reduce competition in order to challenge that transaction. Under the "broad aims" of the Act, the FCC could instead decide that a merger might affect any of the Act's goals (as the FCC interprets them) and, for any of those reasons, block, condition, or approve a transaction regardless of its competitive effects.

2. Broader Than Antitrust Review. As the above excerpt makes clear, the FCC's merger review standards are potentially much broader than the standards applied under the antitrust laws by either the Justice Department's Antitrust Division or the Federal Trade Commission. Section 7 of the Clayton Antitrust Act, 15 U.S.C. § 18, bars mergers where the effect "may be substantially to lessen competition, or to tend to create a monopoly." In interpreting that statute, the federal antitrust authorities look principally at whether a transaction will lead to the accumulation of "market power." "A merger enhances market power if it is likely to encourage one or more firms to raise price, reduce output, diminish innovation, or otherwise harm customers as a result of diminished competitive constraints or incentives." DOJ & FTC, Horizontal Merger Guidelines § 1, at 2 (2010), http://www.justice.gov/atr/public/guidelines/hmg-2010.pdf. On this basis the DOJ and FTC have promulgated guidelines for analyzing when a merger is likely to reduce competition and lead to higher prices for consumers. *See id.* The sine qua non of merger review under the federal antitrust statutes is thus market power in the sale of a given product or service. In contrast, under the FCC's public interest analysis, even a merger that would not harm consumers might be challenged because, for example, it would not create "affirmative" benefits for consumers or would make regulatory oversight more difficult.

§ 11.A.2. The SBC/Ameritech Proceeding

The Commission's broad interpretation of its authority has created much controversy, but this controversy arises only in an extremely small fraction of the Commission's license transfer proceedings. Indeed, the Commission processes enormous numbers of license transfers that attract no notice whatsoever. The fact that a vast number of license transfers have passed smoothly and routinely through the Commission has not, however, insulated the Commission from criticism. The reason is that in some very large mergers, mostly among common carriers but also among MVPDs, license transfer review has been anything but routine. It should not be surprising that the Commission would engage in a much broader and more stringent review of a major merger among carriers than it does to a sale of a typical wireless license from one operator to another. The primary points of controversy have been the scope of the Commission's review, the standard it applies on review, and the means it uses to resolve its concerns about a merger. The following excerpts from the Commission's decision allowing RHCs Ameritech and SBC to merge—or, more precisely, allowing Ameritech to transfer its FCC licenses to SBC—exemplifies the Commission's approach to large telecommunications mergers and makes clear why there is such fierce debate over the FCC's role in merger approval.

APPLICATIONS OF AMERITECH CORP., TRANSFEROR, AND SBC COMMUNICATIONS, INC., TRANSFEREE, FOR CONSENT TO TRANSFER CONTROL OF CORPORATIONS HOLDING COMMISSION LICENSES AND LINES PURSUANT TO SECTIONS 214 AND 310(D) OF THE COMMUNICATIONS ACT AND PARTS 5, 22, 24, 25, 63, 90, 95 AND 101 OF THE COMMISSION'S RULES

Memorandum Opinion and Order, 14 FCC Rcd. 14,712 (1999)

I. INTRODUCTION

2. We conclude that approval of the applications to transfer control of Commission licenses and lines from Ameritech to SBC is in the public interest because such approval is subject to significant and enforceable conditions designed to mitigate the potential public interest harms of their merger, to open up the local markets of these Regional Bell Operating Companies (RBOCs), and to strengthen the merged firm's incentives to expand competition outside its regions. We believe that the proposed voluntary commitments by SBC and Ameritech substantially mitigate the potential public interest harms while providing public interest benefits that extend beyond those contained in the original applications.

3. Specifically, we conclude in this Order that the proposed merger of these RBOCs threatens to harm consumers of telecommunications services by: (a) denying them the benefits of future probable competition between the merging firms; (b) undermining the ability of regulators and competitors to implement the pro-competitive, deregulatory framework for local telecommunications that was adopted by Congress in the Telecommunications Act of 1996; and (c) increasing the merged entity's incentives and ability to raise entry barriers to, and otherwise discriminate against, entrants into the local markets of these RBOCs. Furthermore, the asserted benefits of the proposed merger, absent conditions, do not outweigh these significant harms, as described herein.

4. The proposed conditions, however, change the public interest balance. We expect that with these conditions, competition in the provision of local exchange services, including advanced services, will increase both inside and outside the merged firm's region. Accordingly, assuming the Applicants' ongoing compliance with the conditions described in this Order, we find that the Applicants have demonstrated that the proposed transfer of licenses and lines from Ameritech to SBC serves the public interest, convenience, and necessity.

II. EXECUTIVE SUMMARY

5. To implement the dismantling of the Bell System, seven Regional Bell Operating Companies were created in 1984. After the mergers of SBC with Pacific Telesis, and Bell Atlantic with NYNEX, five RBOCs remain. The instant proceeding concerns the proposed transfer of licenses and lines attendant upon a proposed merger of two RBOCs, SBC and Ameritech. We conclude that, with the conditions adopted by this Order, the Applicants have demonstrated that the proposed transfer of licenses and lines from Ameritech to SBC will serve the public interest, convenience, and necessity. We also make the following determinations in support of this conclusion:

- Harms—The proposed merger of these RBOCs threatens to harm consumers of telecommunications services in three distinct, but interrelated, ways.

  1) The merger will remove one of the most significant potential participants in local telecommunications mass markets both within and outside of each company's region.

  2) The merger will substantially reduce the Commission's ability to implement the market-opening requirements of the 1996 Act by comparative practice oversight methods. Contrary to the deregulatory, competitive purpose of the 1996 Act, this will, in turn, increase the duration of the entrenched firms' market power and raise the costs of regulating them.

  3) The merger will increase the incentive and ability of the merged entity to discriminate against its rivals, particularly with respect to the provision of advanced telecommunications services. This is likely to frustrate the Commission's ability to foster advanced services as it is directed to do by the 1996 Act.

- Benefits—The asserted benefits of the proposed merger do not outweigh the significant harms, detailed above. Specifically:

  1) The Applicants have failed to demonstrate that the merger is necessary in order to obtain the benefits to local competition of the National-Local Strategy, a plan in which the merged firm will enter 30 out-of-region markets as a competitive LEC.

  2) Only a small portion of the Applicants' claimed cost-saving efficiencies, including procurement savings, consolidation efficiencies, implementation of best practices, faster and broader roll-out of new products and services, and benefits to employees and communities, are merger-specific, likely and verifiable.

  3) The only merger-specific benefits to product markets other than local wireline telecommunications markets, such as wireless services, Internet services, long distance and international services, and global seamless services for large business customers, relate to a somewhat increased pace of expansion and modest reductions in unit costs. Any benefits in these regards are both speculative and small.

62. In short, absent stringent conditions, we would be forced to conclude that this merger does not serve the public interest, convenience or necessity because it would inevitably retard progress in opening local telecommunications markets, thereby requiring us to engage in more regulation. Standing alone, without conditions, the initial application proposed a license transfer that would have been inconsistent with the approach to telecommunications regulation and telecommunications markets that the Congress es-

tablished in the 1996 Act, ratifying the fundamental approaches enshrined in the MFJ. For that reason, we conclude that it would be inconsistent with the public interest, convenience and necessity to permit this license transfer in the absence of significant and enforceable conditions.

VII. CONDITIONS

349. As noted above, on July 1, 1999, the Applicants supplemented their initial Application to include a package of voluntary commitments that they intended would alter the public interest balance in their favor.

A. Open Process

350. As a threshold matter, we affirm that considering conditions in license and line transfer proceedings is an appropriate and, in circumstances such as this merger, a necessary process in our application review. It is seductively simple, yet short-sighted, to believe that our role is limited to voting an application up or down, measuring an application solely against whether it violates a specific provision of the Act or a specific Commission rule. Such a view rests on the assumption that our market-opening rules will work equally well regardless of the number of major incumbent LECs or RBOCs and of who owns them. [T]his would be an incorrect view of our rules, and the current realities of the telecommunications industry.

1. Promoting Equitable and Efficient Advanced Services Deployment

363. <u>Separate Affiliate for Advanced Services</u>. Under this condition, SBC and Ameritech will create, prior to closing the merger, one or more separate affiliates to provide all advanced services in the combined SBC/Ameritech region on a phased-in basis. At present, we note that SBC and Ameritech are only permitted to provide intraLATA advanced services. Establishing an advanced services separate affiliate will provide a structural mechanism to ensure that competing providers of advanced services receive effective, nondiscriminatory access to the facilities and services of the merged firm's incumbent LECs that are necessary to provide advanced services. Because the merged firm's own separate advanced services affiliate will use the same processes as competitors, and pay an equivalent price for facilities and services, the condition should ensure a level playing field between SBC/Ameritech and its advanced services competitors. Given this expectation, we anticipate that this condition will greatly accelerate competition in the advanced services market by lowering the costs and risks of entry and reducing uncertainty, while prodding all carriers, including the Applicants, to hasten deployment.

376. <u>Nondiscriminatory Rollout of xDSL Services</u>. As a means of ensuring that the merged firm's rollout of advanced services reaches some of the least competitive market segments and is more widely available to low income consumers, SBC and Ameritech will target their deployment of xDSL services to include low income groups in rural and urban areas. Specifically, for each SBC/Ameritech in-region state, SBC/Ameritech will ensure that at least 10 percent of the rural wire centers where it, or its separate advanced services affiliate, deploys xDSL service will be low income rural wire centers, meaning those wire centers with the greatest number of low income households. Similarly, at least 10 percent of the urban wire centers where the merged firm or its separate advanced services affiliate deploys xDSL service in each in-region state will be low income urban wire centers.

2. Ensuring Open Local Markets

377. <u>Carrier-to-Carrier Performance Plan</u>. As a means of ensuring that SBC/Ameritech's service to telecommunications carriers will not deteriorate as a result of the merger and

the larger firm's increased incentive and ability to discriminate and to stimulate the merged entity to adopt "best practices" that clearly favor public rather than private interests, SBC/Ameritech will publicly file performance measurement data for each of the 13 SBC/Ameritech in-region states with this Commission and the relevant state commission on a monthly basis. The data will reflect SBC/Ameritech incumbent LECs' performance of their obligations toward telecommunications carriers in 20 different measurement categories. These categories cover key aspects of pre-ordering, ordering, provisioning, maintenance and repair associated with UNEs, interconnection, and resold services.

390. Carrier-to-Carrier Promotions. To offset the loss of probable competition between SBC and Ameritech for residential services in their regions and to facilitate market entry, the Applicants propose three promotions designed specifically to encourage rapid development of local competition in residential and less dense areas. [The three promotions involve various pricing discounts that have to be offered to rival firms. These promotions do not have to be offered to all requesting firms; instead, there are caps as to the number of firms that must be allowed to purchase at these lower rates, and there are also specific windows of opportunity during which interested firms must request to participate in the promotions.]

3. Fostering Out-of-Territory Competition

398. Out-of-Territory Competitive Entry (National-Local Strategy). As a condition of this merger, within 30 months of the merger closing date the combined firm will enter at least 30 major markets outside SBC's and Ameritech's incumbent service area as a facilities-based provider of local telecommunications services to business and residential customers. This will ensure that residential consumers and business customers outside of SBC/Ameritech's territory benefit from facilities-based competitive service by a major incumbent LEC. This condition effectively requires SBC and Ameritech to redeem their promise that their merger will form the basis for a new, powerful, truly nationwide multi-purpose competitive telecommunications carrier. We also anticipate that this condition will stimulate competitive entry into the SBC/Ameritech region by the affected incumbent LECs.

4. Improving Residential Phone Service

400. Pricing of InterLATA Services. As a direct benefit to consumers, particularly low income consumers and low-volume long distance callers, this condition provides that SBC/Ameritech will not charge residential customers a minimum monthly or minimum flat rate charge for long distance service for a period of not less than three years.

419. We conclude that, with the conditions that we adopt in this Order, the merger of SBC and Ameritech is likely to be beneficial for consumers and spur competition in the local and advanced services markets. Given that the conditions will substantially mitigate the potential public interest harms of the proposed merger and will result in affirmative public benefit, we conclude that the Applicants have demonstrated that the proposed merger, on balance, will serve the public interest, convenience and necessity.

Notes and Questions

1. Preventing Harms or Extracting Benefits? To what extent do you think the above conditions are aimed at mitigating competitive harms from the merger and to what extent are they aimed at achieving affirmative, but perhaps logically unrelated, benefits from the merger? Does the FCC arrogate to itself too much authority here?

2. Overlapping Jurisdiction. Where the conditions are designed to resolve competitive harms, are these harms that the other federal agencies would have overlooked? If we assume that the DOJ or FTC also reviewed this merger with care, does the above document suggest any reasons why the FCC should also analyze the merger? Is the argument that there are distinct benefits that come from the Commission's expertise, just as the DOJ and FTC bring antitrust expertise to the process? Is the argument instead simply that two agencies are better than one with respect to review of proposed mergers? What costs do you see from all this overlapping jurisdiction?

3. Limitations to FCC Review. What practical and/or legal concerns are raised by the Commission's use of merger conditions to obtain benefits from, rather than avoid harms from, the transaction? Review §§ 214(a) and 310(d) of the Act. What are the possible arguments for and against reading those provisions to support the FCC's broad merger inquiry? What might be the objectives of a narrower inquiry under the language of those provisions?

4. The Debate at the FCC. The next excerpt is from the separate statement of FCC Commissioner Harold Furchtgott-Roth dissenting in part from the order excerpted above. This separate statement highlights the major issues in the debate over the FCC's merger review authority.

SEPARATE STATEMENT OF COMMISSIONER HAROLD FURCHTGOTT-ROTH CONCURRING IN PART, DISSENTING IN PART

14 FCC Rcd. 14,712, 15,174–96 (1999)

I concur only in the narrow decision to grant SBC and Ameritech authorization to transfer lines pursuant to § 214 and licenses pursuant to section 310(d). I cannot support the reasoning of the Order and must dissent in full from the adoption of the conditions on these license and authorization transfers.

I. The Conditions Are Inconsistent with the Communications Act

The conditions imposed in this Order are, in my opinion, of highly questionable legal validity. In particular, many of the conditions are inconsistent with specific sections of the Communications Act.

To be sure, the Communications Act grants the Commission authority to condition license transfer and § 214 authorizations. This authority is *not* without its limits, however. Rather, § 303(r) provides that "except as otherwise provided in this Act, the Commission ... shall ... prescribe such ... conditions, *not inconsistent with law*, as may be necessary to carry out *the provisions of this Act*." 47 U.S.C. § 303(r) (emphasis added). And § 214(c) states that the Commission "may attach to the issuance of [a § 214] certificate such terms and conditions as in its judgment the public convenience and necessity may require." Although this provision contains no express language limiting conditions to enforcement of the Act, it is certainly not in the public interest to adopt conditions violative of federal communications law. At a minimum, then, we cannot impose conditions under either § 303(r) or § 214(c) that contradict the Act itself.

The conditions in this Order do just that, however. Of especial legal concern are those related to carrier-to-carrier promotions. These conditions limit the number of services and facilities that may be offered to competitive local exchange carriers (CLECs) on a promotional basis. Once the caps are reached, some CLECs will be unable to obtain the same promotional deals as other CLECs. Quite simply, carrier-to-carrier promotions will not be available on an equal basis to all requesting carriers. In this way, then, the conditions violate the "nondiscriminatory access" requirement of § 251(c)(3), as well as the resale nondiscrimination requirement of § 251(c)(4)(B).

II. The Conditions Are Disproportionate to the Alleged Potential Harms

A. The Transaction Does Not Violate the Specific Terms of Any Extant Communications Statute or Regulation

Commission regulations take up many bookcases. For a license transfer to run afoul of a specific administrative rule therefore is not an improbable outcome. Given the breadth of our regulation in this area, it is remarkable that the Order never asserts that the transfer of licenses between SBC and Ameritech would violate any specific substantive provision of the Communications Act or any Commission regulation. Remedies for such harms, of course, would be easily and clearly prescribed: the transferee would be obliged to bring the license transfers into compliance with existing rules.

B. The Alleged Harms Are Speculative and Do Not Flow From the Merger

The Commission foresees three potential harms in the consummation of the license transfers. *First*, that the merger will remove significant potential participants in the local exchange market within, and outside of, each company's current region. *Second*, that the merger will impair this Commission's ability to engage in comparative practice oversight and consequently extend the entrenchment of certain firms and raise the cost of regulating them. *Third*, that the merged entity will have increased incentive and ability to discriminate against competitors, and that this increased incentive and ability will have particular force with respect to the provision of advanced telecommunications services.

The first harm is premised on the Commission's "precluded competitor" doctrine. According to this theory, the license transfers will result in reduced or precluded competition both inside the RBOC territories and outside the SBC/Ameritech regions. The record, however, presents no clear evidence that either SBC or Ameritech had developed plans to provide substantial in-region competition for local exchange services in the other company's territory. Whether plans that might have been developed at some future date are affected by the proposed license transfers is idle speculation.

The second harm is similarly conjectural. Can the Commission really defend the proposition that a reduction from six to five local exchange carriers creates a significant, material, and appreciable difference in its ability to make comparative evaluations? Or that the elimination of one company will "severely restrict" the behaviors that regulators can observe in the local exchange market? That is a hard case to make indeed. Currently, the FCC has no duly promulgated rules that depend on benchmarking performance to industry levels, much less benchmarking performance to industry levels that must be derived from a minimum of six major carriers. Accordingly, this harm is based at most on the possibility that the Commission will, assuming statutory authority to do so, in the future adopt rules benchmarking performance to industry standards.

The third alleged harm is based on an especially large ratio of speculation to actual likelihood. First, the Order does not demonstrate why the combined firm has any more incentive and ability to discriminate against competitors than do the separate companies. SBC is a large and powerful company in its territory, as is Ameritech. On this record, there is little compelling evidence that whatever market power either company may exercise in its region would be significantly enhanced by the license transfers. Moreover, incentives to discriminate in a market—as opposed simply to treating all customers either equally well or equally poorly for administrative, financial, legal, and regulatory convenience — depend on many technical factors of market demand and supply. Even for a single service in a narrow geographic market, it would be difficult, even with substantial empirical evidence, to conclude with certainty whether a regulatory action would increase, decrease, or leave unaltered incentives to discriminate. It is breathtaking to conclude that the proposed license transfers at issue would have a perceptible effect on incentives to discriminate.

Moreover, all these alleged harms bear a common characteristic: the merger itself does not increase the likelihood of any of them. That is, they are things that the individual companies would be equally likely to do if the merger never took place. The merger does not in any *appreciable* way make, say, discrimination more likely or benchmarking harder than it is now. Nor are these companies, on a stand-alone basis, distinguishable from other local exchange carriers in terms of their incentives and abilities to engage in these sorts of behaviors. Even if one could quantify it, the differential in the Commission's ability now and post-merger to make such judgments is negligible in comparison to the heavy duties that have been imposed as a remedy for that purported impact.

When it comes to the *benefits* of the merger, the Commission abruptly switches to a more exacting standard of proof and becomes concerned with merger-specificity. It finds that "only a small portion of the Applicants' claim cost-saving efficiencies ... are merger-specific, likely and verifiable," and that "the only merger-specific benefits to product markets ... are both speculative and small." 14 FCC Rcd. 14,712, 14,717, ¶ 5. A scouring of this record will show, however, that applicants' evidence of their asserted benefits is no weaker than the Commission's evidence of its posited harms. It is every bit as, if not more so, founded in empirical and economic reality.

C. *The Conditions Do Not Materially Remediate the Alleged Harms*

Even if one assumes that the harms have been predicted with adequate certainty, the conditions do not really address those harms. In some instances, there is a complete lack of nexus between the posited harm and the adopted conditions, and in others the conditions will simply not remediate in any direct way the purported harm.

IV. *The Conditions Are Either Voluntary and Unenforceable, or Involuntary and Judicially Reviewable*

As I have previously explained:

- The use of voluntary standards allows administrative agencies better to skirt statutory limits on their authority, an offense to the concept of administrative agencies in possession of only those powers delegated to them by Congress.... It is no coincidence that the commitments extracted from regulated entities in the guise of voluntary standards tend to be things that the agency lacks statutory authority straightforwardly to require. Voluntary standards, as opposed to duly promulgated rules, can all too easily be used to bootstrap jurisdictional issues: got jurisdiction to approve or disprove the transfer of licenses but no express statutory authority to require unbundling of the licensee's product offerings? Just make it an "optional" condition of the license transfer, add water, mix, and you have fresh jurisdiction to regulate a whole new area. The problem with this approach ... is that it renders superfluous Congressional attempts to delineate our areas of responsibility.

- There is another reason that agencies might prefer voluntary standards to rules: they are harder to challenge in a court of law. Judicial review of the statutory basis for "voluntary" standards may be difficult to obtain because such guidelines, being technically non-binding, may never formally be announced or enforced against any regulatee.

Voluntary Standards Are Neither, Speech Before the Media Institute (Nov. 17, 1998).

In this Order, the Commission tries to walk a tightrope between the two alternatives as to the legal status of the conditions, referring to the conditions as "voluntary commitments" but hinting elsewhere that it fully expects SBC/Ameritech to carry them out. It is simply not possible to have it both ways, however: either the commitments are *de facto* standards and subject to judicial review, or they are legally unenforceable and thus meaningless as a practical matter.

V. The Commission Lacks "Merger" Review Authority

In addition to the legal problems associated with the nature of the conditions themselves, it is important to step back and recall that, as I have repeatedly pointed out, this Commission possesses no statutory authority to review "mergers" writ large.

Rather, the Communications Act charges the Commission with a much narrower task: review of the proposed transfer of licenses under Title III from Ameritech to SBC, and consideration of the transfer of common carrier lines between those parties. Nothing in § 310(d) or § 214—the provisions pursuant to which these applications were filed—speaks of jurisdiction to approve or disapprove the merger that has occasioned Ameritech's desire to transfer licenses and § 214 authorizations. [The remainder of this paragraph is relocated from footnote 15 of the original document.] The Commission does possess authority under the Clayton Act, which prohibits combinations in restraint of trade, to review mergers *per se. See* 15 U.S.C. § 21 (granting FCC authority to enforce Clayton Act where applicable to common carriers engaged in wire or radio communication or radio transmission of energy). If the Commission intends to exercise authority over mergers and acquisitions as such, it ought to do so pursuant to the Clayton Act, with its carefully prescribed procedures and standards of review, not the broad licensing provisions of the Communications Act.

To be sure, the transfer of the licenses and authorizations is an important part of the merger. But it is simply not the same thing. The merger is a much larger and more complicated set of events than the transfer of FCC permits. It includes, to name but a few things, the passage of legal title for many assets other than Title III licenses, corporate restructuring, stock swaps or purchases, and the consolidation of corporate headquarters and personnel. Clearly, then, asking whether the particularized transactions of license transfers and section 214 transfers would serve the public interest, convenience, and necessity entails a significantly more limited focus than contemplating the industry-wide effects of a merger between the transferee and transferor.

For instance, in considering the transfer of licenses, one might ask whether there is any reason to think that the proposed transferee would not put the relevant spectrum to efficient use or comply with applicable Commission regulations; one would not, by contrast, consider how the combination of the two companies might affect other competitors in the industry. One might also consider the benefits of the transfer, but not of the merger generally. And one might consider the transferee's proposed use and disposition of the actual Title III licenses, but one would not venture into an examination of services provided by the transferee that do not even involve the use of those licenses.

By using §§ 214 and 310 to assert jurisdiction over the entire merger of two companies that happen to be the transferee and transferor of radio licenses and international resale authorizations, the Commission greatly expands its regulatory authority under the Act. Because the very premise of this Order is that it must analyze the competitive effects of the "merger," in contravention of the plain language of §§ 214 and 310, I cannot sign on to its reasoning.

Notes and Questions

1. Furchtgott-Roth. Which of Furchtgott-Roth's arguments do you find most compelling? Least compelling? Does he find the greatest problems to be procedural or substantive?

2. Sui Generis Review. Furchtgott-Roth suggests that the Commission's approach to the SBC/Ameritech merger is ad hoc and made up for the purposes of this one transaction ("sui generis," in his words). Is he right? Has the Commission pulled its substantive approach from thin air, or is its approach grounded in, and perhaps even required by, established regulatory concerns? Do ¶¶ 12–17 of the Commission's order justify the Commission's actions?

3. Donkeys and Elephants. The author of the partial dissent above was a Republican appointee to the Commission, as was the other partial dissenter, Michael Powell. The three Commissioners concurring in full with the order were Democrats. Does this mean that shifts in political administration are likely to lead to radical shifts in merger review and the kinds of scrutiny firms can expect? Is there some reason this should be more true for FCC merger review than for review by the Department of Justice or the Federal Trade Commission?

4. The DOJ and the FCC. How do procedural differences affect the position of merging parties before the FCC as compared to their position before the DOJ? Both the DOJ and the FCC have the burden of going to court to block a disputed merger. The FCC, though, can prevent a *license transfer* without going to court, and the burden is then on the merging parties to seek judicial review if they want to go ahead with the disapproved transfer. But that difference may in the end have only limited practical implications. It is very expensive in terms of time and money for parties to fight a suit by the DOJ, so more often than not they either negotiate a settlement that will allow the merger or else abandon the transaction. Similarly, the delays inherent in challenging an FCC license transfer decision could be so costly that often the preferred path from the parties' perspective is to bargain with the FCC on "conditions" that will allow the agency to approve the transfer. An important difference, however, is that an FCC decision to approve a license transfer can be challenged in a U.S. Court of Appeals by third parties (e.g., competitors of the merging parties) whereas decisions by the DOJ or FTC not to contest a merger cannot be so challenged.

5. Rulemaking versus Merger Review. One criticism raised by the partial dissents is that the Commission uses its merger review process to impose policies that it could not impose generally through a rulemaking procedure. For example, SBC and Ameritech agreed to provide advanced services through a separate subsidiary that will deal on nondiscriminatory terms with the parent companies. But there is no general requirement that ILECs provide advanced services in this manner, and the Commission had indeed backed off from earlier proposals for such a requirement (mainly due to intense political pressure from Congress). Does it raise concern that the Commission now imposes such a requirement as a merger condition? Does this create an opportunity for the FCC to turn a condition on particular parties into a general rule—the Commission's argument being that, once SBC/Ameritech is subject to the condition, it becomes "unfair" to allow SBC/Ameritech's rivals to operate under the normal, less restrictive rules? How might the dynamics of promulgating a particular rule change after the rule's requirements have been imposed through merger conditions on particular carriers?

6. Summary. The FCC's merger review process raises several important issues of law and policy. Questions about the FCC's statutory authority, the vagueness of the public interest standard, coercion of merging parties, the lack of judicial review, the social costs of merger conditions, and delay due to duplication of activities among the various federal agencies have all factored into the debate over the Commission's proper role in mergers. The debate has led to calls for reform.

§ 11.A.3. Reconsidering the FCC's Merger Review Process

In March 2000, within two weeks of each other, the FCC and Congress held public proceedings on merger policy in telecommunications. The proximity in timing was not accidental. The Commerce Committee of the U.S. House of Representatives had drafted legislation entitled the "Telecommunications Merger Review Act of 2000," the purpose of which was to curtail the Commission's authority to impose conditions outside the formal rulemaking process and to accelerate the FCC's review by requiring final action within 60 to 90 days from the filing of a merger application. H.R. 4019, 106th Cong. (2000). The Commission, in an effort to preempt some of the concerns raised by the proposed bill and in anticipation of Congressional hearings on the legislation, held a public forum at which it presented its own proposal for streamlining FCC review of merger-related applications.

At the Congressional hearings, FCC Chairman William Kennard testified that the FCC brought industry specific expertise to telecommunications mergers and provided the only forum in which the public had a meaningful opportunity to comment on such mergers. He moreover argued that the FCC provides a broader kind of review that is not duplicative of review by the antitrust agencies. Commissioner Furchtgott-Roth offered opposing testimony largely echoing his critiques of the SBC/Ameritech merger decree.

§ 11.A.4. The FCC's Own Institutional Reforms

At about the same time as the above hearings in Congress, the FCC streamlined its merger review process by committing to a timeline that would culminate in a final Commission order within 180 days of the filing of a transfer request. The steps in the proposed timeline were: (1) issuance of a public notice on the day of filing; (2) a public comment period lasting until day 30; (3) a reply-comment period lasting until day 45; (4) review by the agency for completeness of the filing lasting until day 75; (5) analysis of the record and discussions with parties until day 110; (6) major changes to the transaction at issue could be submitted by the parties on day 110, followed on day 130 by a public forum on any such changes; and (7) issuance of a final decision by day 180. *See* Issues Memorandum for March 1, 2000 Transactions Team Public Forum on Streamlining FCC Review of Applications Relating to Mergers, FCC (March 1, 2000), http://www.fcc.gov/transaction/issuesmemo.html. Although the FCC established this internal timeline, it is not formally binding, and the Commission may (and sometimes does) "stop the clock" during a proceeding for a variety of reasons.

In addition to addressing the question of timing, the Commission's Issues Memorandum also addressed several other issues that have given rise to concern about the Commission's role in reviewing mergers. Two particularly important issues addressed in the memorandum were: (1) variability in standards from transaction to transaction and (2) coordination with the federal antitrust agencies. With respect to the first point, the Commission's Issues Memorandum states:

The Commission's review process has sometimes been characterized as imposing different levels or even different "standards" of review. For example, in many cases "routine" applications may be granted fairly rapidly; others require more detailed and lengthy consideration; and still others are subject to intensive analysis of competition and other public interest issues on the basis of an extensive record. These differences in procedure do not result from a difference in the applicable standards for Commission review under the Communications Act and the implementing regulations. That Act applies a similar "public interest" test to transfers, assignments, or authorizations relating to mergers. The circumstances of a particular case, however, may present issues that require a more thorough analysis to determine whether the public interest standard is met. For example, (1) the transaction to which the application relates may create a level of horizontal concentration in a market for communications services where the FCC under the 1996 Act is relying on vigorous competition to meet the goals of the Communications Act, (2) granting the application may arguably result in a violation of either the Act or the Commission's rules, (3) the applicant may be seeking a waiver of the Commission's rules, or (4) the transaction may result in a substantial degree of vertical integration that may have a substantial impact on the health of competition with respect to one or more communications services. There may be substantial public comments filed in the review process addressing these or other issues for which the FCC is given responsibility under the public interest standard in the Communications Act. Cases involving circumstances such as these require more attention than those that can be processed easily under established rules and precedents.

With respect to coordination and potential overlap issues, the Issues Memorandum distinguished the Commission's role from that played by the other federal agencies and, indeed, suggested that the inquiries might be complementary:

> The Department of Justice or the Federal Trade Commission reviews the competitive impacts of a number of the transactions that require changes in FCC licenses or authorizations under the antitrust laws. Those reviews differ from the FCC review in substance and procedure. They involve narrower issues than the public interest standard established by the Communications Act. In addition, the process of review by these agencies is an investigation largely hidden from public view that most often results in either no action (with no explanation), a consent decree that is presented to a court after negotiations with the government have been completed, or (rarely) a full trial of a law suit in federal court. The agencies have prosecutorial discretion and no obligation to explain the basis of their decision if they take no enforcement action. In contrast, the FCC review process is a public adjudication, with full opportunity for public participation, which results in a decision that must be agreed to by at least a majority of a five member Commission (or be made on delegated authority), that must explain its basis and address the arguments made by the parties, and that is subject to judicial review.
>
> Despite the substantive differences, the issues addressed in antitrust review and the FCC's public interest review overlap to some degree. Similarly, despite the procedural differences, the reviews must take place roughly simultaneously. With the increase in these transactions over the last several years, the federal agencies have gained experience in coordinating their efforts to avoid duplication, increase efficient use of the limited government resources, and avoid reaching results that would impose inconsistent requirements on the applicants. Thus,

the agencies have found it useful to request waivers from the applicants and other parties to permit FCC review of documents and discussions among the personnel involved in reviewing the transactions in the respective agencies. Discussions and efforts to improve this coordination continue.

Notes and Questions

1. A Good Alternative? How well do the Commission's proposals in the Issues Memorandum address the various concerns about the merger process? Which of the issues raised in the separate statement by Commissioner Furchtgott-Roth do they resolve?

2. Substance or Procedure? Are the proposals by the FCC and Congress truly substantive reforms, or are these reforms merely aimed at speeding up the merger review process without changing merger review standards? Do the proposed reforms go far enough? Too far? Who should make that determination? Based on what yardstick and what level of deference to the FCC?

3. Streamlining Some Transactions. In 2002, the Commission went beyond informal guidelines and promulgated rules designed to streamline the agency's review of transfers of control of domestic transmission lines; the FCC must approve such transfers under §214 of the Communications Act. The purpose of the new rules is to allow certain transactions to qualify for expedited review. *See* Implementation of Further Streamlining Measures for Domestic Section 214 Authorizations, Report and Order, 17 FCC Rcd. 5517 (2002). The principal achievement of this order has been to implement a 30-day review process for certain transactions. As the FCC explained in its news release announcing the new merger rules:

> Applications meeting specified criteria—such as certain small incumbent local exchange carrier (LEC) transactions, or transactions involving only non-facilities-based carriers, or those in which the acquiring party is not a telecommunications provider—are automatically granted 30 days after public notice unless applicants are otherwise notified by the Commission. By doing so, the Commission establishes, for the first time, specific rules limiting the amount of time it will take to review transactions that do not normally raise public interest concerns.

Press Release, FCC, FCC Updates Merger Review Process (March 14, 2002), *available at* http://transition.fcc.gov/Bureaus/CommonCarrier/News_Releases/2002/nrcc0206.html. This is clearly an effort to reduce the number of mergers that the Commission reviews and to introduce a systematic distinction between the kinds of mergers the Commission really scrutinizes and the kinds it will let through without proceedings.

§11.A.5. The Elusive Effort to Restrict the Scope of FCC Merger Review

The reforms discussed above tightened the timeframe for review by the Commission and also tried to clarify the FCC's standards. They say little about the remedies and conditions the Commission will seek or accept, however, and therefore leave open questions at the heart of Commissioner Furchtgott-Roth's partial dissent above: to what standard of proof should the Commission's predictions of harm have to rise before the agency imposes or accepts conditions addressing those harms? Will the agency impose or accept conditions that address policy goals other than those directly implicated by the merger?

For a time after the FCC's reforms, Chairman Powell pressed for a limited use of the FCC's merger review authority, and the agency appeared to be limiting the imposition of conditions on the merging parties. Under his successor (Kevin Martin), however, the FCC once again engaged in accepting "voluntary" conditions that went beyond arguable competitive harms. Two instances of merger review are particularly instructive about the agency's approach and raise some interesting questions. The first is the FCC's approval of the SBC/AT&T and Verizon/MCI mergers; the second is its approval of the merger of satellite radio carriers XM and Sirius.

In 2005, the FCC simultaneously approved SBC's acquisition of what remained of AT&T and Verizon's acquisition of MCI. The agency examined the effects of those transactions on six different service markets (special-access competition, retail-enterprise competition, mass-market competition, Internet-backbone competition, wholesale long-distance competition, and international competition). In each of those markets the FCC concluded that the mergers were not likely to harm competition or lead to any harms. Moreover, the agency concluded that the transactions would in fact yield affirmative public interest benefits. *See* Press Release, FCC, FCC Approves SBC/AT&T and Verizon/MCI Mergers (Oct. 31, 2005), 2005 WL 2850037. Despite these conclusions the agency did not simply close its investigation and approve the mergers. Instead, it accepted a set of "voluntary conditions," sparking a partial dissent from Commissioner Abernathy:

> I would perhaps be less concerned about this aspect of today's decisions if either (a) the Department of Justice had outlined problems arising from the larger competitive impacts of these mergers; or (b) these remedies were clearly needed to cure palpable existing problems. But neither is the case here. While I recognize that the Commission's merger review mandate implicates a broader standard of review than that of DOJ, it remains nevertheless true that DOJ's review was focused on the same issues we are asked to examine: competition in the various markets involved. And all the expert economists, lawyers, and other professionals reviewing these issues for DOJ found no significant cause for concern in most of the areas subject to the conditions.
>
> I am not suggesting that DOJ's evaluation is, or should be, co-extensive with ours. But what I would suggest is that it effectively places on the Commission the burden of showing the existence of other problems so grave and immediate that conditioning the merger agreement is the only effective remedy. It should not be standard operating procedure to craft company-specific merger conditions to address unknown and hypothetical competitive threats. After all, the customary administrative weaponry in the Commission's arsenal — rulemaking, enforcement, and so on — does not suddenly evaporate once a merger is approved. We always have these tools and we can always use them when and if necessary.
>
> The competition unleashed by the convergence of formerly separate lines of business places an additional premium on taking a more circumspect approach to conditioning mergers. Competition is a *process,* not a *product.* This new competitive market is still developing, and it needs to be given reasonable regulatory elbow-room to do so. Imposing ad hoc conditions that do not reflect the reali-

ties of today's market hamstrings this development rather than helps it and creates market distortions. Therefore, it is my view that we should resort to imposing such conditions only *first*, where the perceived harm is an obvious consequence of the merger, not merely a prediction about what might go wrong; and *second*, where other administrative remedies are inadequate to address this harm. That simply isn't the case in these mergers, with these conditions.

Verizon Comm'ns Inc. and MCI, Inc., Applications for Approval and Transfer of Control, 20 FCC Rcd. 18,433 (2005) (statement of Commissioner Kathleen Abernathy).

Commissioner Abernathy points out two notable things in her partial dissent. First, a number of the merger conditions address issues that could be resolved via industry-wide rulemaking. For example, there was a condition regarding the provision of DSL without the provision of circuit-switched telephone service (so-called "naked DSL"), an issue on which the FCC in fact had an open proceeding. Was it appropriate for the Commission to impose that condition, given the open proceeding?

Second, Commissioner Abernathy notes the difference in result at the Department of Justice. Indeed, the Department of Justice found no evidence of likely harm in the above mergers and simply approved them. The FCC found no evidence of likely harm and imposed conditions. This to some degree may reflect differences in the balance of risks in each agency's review, partly driven by the standard of proof each could be called upon to meet. The DOJ would bear the burden in court of proving a likelihood of anticompetitive effects in order to block a merger. Absent such proof of likelihood, the DOJ closes its investigation, and there is some likelihood that a bad merger would be allowed to occur. The FCC typically does not go to court in merger cases, and the merging parties have a higher incentive to offer conditions because the FCC does not have the statutory time limitations on its review that the antitrust agencies have; moreover, the merging parties are likely to be repeat players before the FCC and therefore less willing to develop an adversarial relationship with the agency.

Thus, the FCC may condition a merger even absent evidence that harmful effects are likely. The risk here is not of allowing a bad merger but of placing unnecessary burdens on a good merger. That appears to have been Commissioner Abernathy's concern in the above statement. These different approaches of the antitrust agencies and the FCC were highlighted even more starkly in the 2008 XM/Sirius merger. Satellite radio carriers XM and Sirius announced their intention to merge in March 2007. The merger sparked substantial debate and controversy. The Department of Justice issued its decision approving the merger in March 2008; the FCC issued its approval four months later. An excerpt of the DOJ's decision follows.

STATEMENT OF THE DEPARTMENT OF JUSTICE ANTITRUST DIVISION ON ITS DECISION TO CLOSE ITS INVESTIGATION OF XM SATELLITE RADIO HOLDINGS INC.'S MERGER WITH SIRIUS SATELLITE RADIO INC.

Press Release, DOJ (Mar. 24, 2008), *available at*
http://www.usdoj.gov/opa/pr/2008/March/08_at_226.html

After a careful and thorough review of the proposed transaction, the Division concluded that the evidence does not demonstrate that the proposed merger of XM and Sirius is likely to substantially lessen competition, and that the transaction therefore is not likely to harm consumers.

ANALYSIS

Extent of Likely Future Competition between XM and Sirius

The Division's analysis considered the extent to which the two satellite radio providers compete with one another. Although the firms in the past competed to attract new subscribers, there has never been significant competition between them for customers who have already subscribed to one or the other service and purchased the requisite equipment. Also, competition for new subscribers is likely to be substantially more limited in the future than it was in the past.

As to existing subscribers, the Division found that satellite radio equipment sold by each company is customized to each network and will not function with the other service. XM and Sirius made some efforts to develop an interoperable radio capable of receiving both sets of satellite signals. Depending on how such a radio would be configured, it could enable consumers to switch between providers without incurring the costs of new equipment. The Division's investigation revealed, however, that no such interoperable radio is on the market and that such a radio likely would not be introduced in the near term. Data analyzed by the Division confirmed that subscribers rarely switch between XM and Sirius.

As to new subscribers, XM and Sirius sell satellite radios and service primarily through two distribution channels: (1) car manufacturers that install the equipment in new cars and (2) mass-market retailers that sell automobile aftermarket equipment and other stand-alone equipment. Car manufacturers account for an increasingly large portion of XM and Sirius sales, and the parties have focused more and more of their resources on attracting subscribers through the car manufacturer channel. However, XM and Sirius have entered into sole-source contracts with all the major automobile manufacturers that fix the amount of these subsidies and other pertinent terms through 2012 or beyond. Moreover, there was no evidence that competition between XM or Sirius beyond the terms of these contracts would affect customers' choices of which car to buy. As a result, there is not likely to be significant competition between XM and Sirius for satellite radio equipment and service sold through the car manufacturer channel for many years.

The Division's investigation identified the mass-market retail channel as an arena in which XM and Sirius would compete with one another for the foreseeable future. Both XM and Sirius devote substantial effort and expense to attracting subscribers in this arena, with both companies offering discounts, most commonly in the form of equipment rebates, to attract consumers. Retail channel sales have dropped significantly since 2005, and the parties contended that the decline was accelerating. However, retail outlets still account for a large portion of the firms' sales, and the Division was unable to determine with any certainty that this channel would not continue to be important in the future.

Effect on Competition in the Retail Channel

Because XM and Sirius would no longer compete with one another in the retail channel following the merger, the Division examined what alternatives, if any, were available to consumers interested in purchasing satellite radio service, and specifically whether the relevant market was limited to the two satellite radio providers, such that their combination would create a monopoly. The parties contended that they compete with a variety of other sources of audio entertainment, including traditional AM/FM radio, HD Radio, MP3 players (e.g., iPods®), and audio offerings delivered through wireless telephones.

The Division found that evidence developed in the investigation did not support defining a market limited to the two satellite radio firms, and similarly did not establish that the combined firm could profitably sustain an increased price to satellite radio consumers. XM and Sirius seek to attract subscribers in a wide variety of ways, including by offering commercial-free music (with digital sound quality), exclusive programming (such as Howard Stern on Sirius and "Oprah & Friends" on XM), niche music formats, out-of-market sporting events, and a variety of news and talk formats in a service that is accessible nationwide. The variety of these offerings reflects an effort to attract consumers with highly differentiated interests and tastes. Thus, while the satellite radio offerings of XM and Sirius likely are the closest substitutes for some current or potential customers, the two offerings do not appear to be the closest substitutes for other current or potential customers. For example, a potential customer considering purchasing XM service primarily to listen to Major League Baseball games or one considering purchasing Sirius service primarily to listen to Howard Stern may not view the other satellite radio service, which lacks the desired content, as a particularly close substitute. Similarly, many customers buying radios in the retail channel are acquiring an additional receiver to add to an existing XM or Sirius subscription for their car radio, and these customers likely would not respond to a price increase by choosing a radio linked to the other satellite radio provider. The evidence did not demonstrate that the number of current or potential customers that view XM and Sirius as the closest alternatives is large enough to make a price increase profitable. Importantly in this regard, the parties do not appear to have the ability to identify and price discriminate against those actual or potential customers that view XM and Sirius as the closest substitutes.

Likely Efficiencies

To the extent there were some concerns that the combined firm might be able profitably to increase prices in the mass-market retail channel, efficiencies flowing from the transaction likely would undermine any such concern. The Division's investigation confirmed that the parties are likely to realize significant variable and fixed cost savings through the merger. It was not possible to estimate the magnitude of the efficiencies with precision due to the lack of evidentiary support provided by XM and Sirius, [but] the merger is likely to allow the parties to consolidate development, production and distribution efforts on a single line of radios and thereby eliminate duplicative costs and realize economies of scale. These efficiencies alone likely would be sufficient to undermine an inference of competitive harm.

Effect of Technological Change

Any inference of a competitive concern was further limited by the fact that a number of technology platforms are under development that are likely to offer new or improved alternatives to satellite radio. Most notable is the expected introduction within several years of next-generation wireless networks capable of streaming Internet radio to mobile devices. [C]onsumers are likely to have access to new alternatives, including mobile broadband Internet devices, by the time the current long-term contracts between the parties and car manufacturers expire.

Notes and Questions

1. Internal Contradictions? The DOJ states in the introduction to the statement that it finds no evidence that the merger will substantially lessen competition. The DOJ later states that XM and Sirius devoted "substantial effort" to competing with each other in the mass-market retail channel, a channel whose future importance the DOJ could not discount. Does the Antitrust Division reconcile its overall conclusion of no harm to competition with the harm to competition in the mass-market retail channel? If so, how?

2. Betting on Innovation. The DOJ places heavy reliance on future technological events that will transform the marketplace in which satellite radio operates. On what technologies does the DOJ rely, and upon what evidence does it do so? Is there any evidence cited to take the DOJ's emphasis on future technology beyond mere speculation?

3. Intermodal Competition. The DOJ concludes that "satellite radio" is not a market in and of itself. What other kinds of competitors does the DOJ include in the market? Do you think it was correct to do so?

4. Hard to Assess. As the DOJ notes, closing statements like the one above are short on factual specifics, often due to confidentiality concerns for both the merging parties and third-party witnesses. This makes closing statements hard to assess, although one can wonder whether, on key points like market definition and innovation, the DOJ could have provided more public facts to make their analysis more convincing.

5. The FCC's Turn. After the DOJ concluded its investigation, the FCC approved the XM/Sirius merger on July 25, 2008. The Commission approval came with several conditions: that the merged company cap prices for three years, that it set aside 8% of its channel capacity for minority and noncommercial programming, and that it pay nearly $20 million in fines for past violations of FCC rules. Applications for Consent to the Transfer of Control of Licenses: XM Satellite Radio Holdings Inc., Transferor, to Sirius Satellite Radio Inc., Transferee, Memorandum Opinion and Order and Report and Order, 23 FCC Rcd. 12,348 (2008).

COMMISSION APPROVES TRANSACTION BETWEEN SIRIUS SATELLITE RADIO HOLDINGS INC. AND XM SATELLITE RADIO HOLDINGS, INC. SUBJECT TO CONDITIONS

Press Release, FCC (July 28, 2008), 2008 WL 2902112

On July 25, 2008, the Commission voted to approve the application of Sirius Satellite Radio Inc. (Sirius) and XM Satellite Radio Holdings Inc. (XM; jointly, the Applicants) to transfer control of the licenses and authorizations held by Sirius and XM and their subsidiaries for the provision of satellite digital audio radio service (or SDARS) in the United States. The Commission found that grant of the application, with the voluntary commitments made by the Applicants and other conditions, is in the public interest. The transaction will benefit consumers by making available to them a wider array of programming choices at various price points and by affording them greater choice and control over the programming to which they subscribe.

Highlights of the Commission's action are noted below:

- After reviewing the empirical data available as part of its competitive analysis, the Commission determined there was insufficient evidence in the record to predict the likelihood of anticompetitive harms. It therefore evaluated the application under "worst-case" assumptions, i.e., that the relevant market is limited to SDARS. This approach permitted the Commission to protect consumers from potential adverse effects of the transaction while also allowing the Commission to balance potential harms against potential public interest benefits. The Commission concluded that the merger, absent the Applicants' voluntary commitments and other conditions, would result in potential harms. With those commitments and conditions to mitigate the harms, however, the Commission found the transaction to be in the public interest. All of the voluntary commitments must continue in effect at least three years after consummation of the merger.

- The Commission accepted the Applicants' voluntary commitments to:
  - Cap prices for 36 months after consummation of the transaction, subject to certain cost pass-throughs after one year. In addition, six months prior to the end of commitment period, the Commission will seek public comment on whether the cap continues to be necessary in the public interest and will determine whether it should be extended, removed, or modified. The merger approval is conditioned on the Commission's ability to modify or extend the price cap beyond the three-year commitment period.
  - Offer to consumers, within three months of consummation of the transaction, the ability to receive a number of new programming packages, including the ability to select programming on an a la carte basis.
  - Make available 4 percent of its capacity for use by certain Qualified Entities, and an additional 4 percent of capacity for the delivery of noncommercial educational or informational (NCE) programming, which will enhance the diversity of programming available to consumers.
  - Offer interoperable receivers in the "retail after-market," i.e., receivers available at retail outlets for installation in consumers' automobiles or homes, within nine months of consummation of the merger.
  - Refrain from entering into any agreement that would grant an equipment manufacturer an exclusive right to manufacture, market, and sell SDARS receivers. Applicants also commit to refrain from barring any manufacturer from including in any receiver non-interfering hybrid digital terrestrial radio functionality, iPod compatibility, or other audio technology. In addition, Applicants commit to make available the intellectual property needed to allow any device manufacturer to develop equipment that can deliver SDARS.
  - File the applications needed to provide Sirius satellite service to Puerto Rico via terrestrial repeaters within three months of the consummation of the merger.
- Although the Commission found it unnecessary to impose a condition requiring the inclusion of hybrid digital radio technology in SDARS receivers, it recognized that important questions have been raised about hybrid digital radio that warrant further examination in a separate proceeding. The Commission therefore committed to initiating a notice of inquiry within 30 days after adoption of the merger order to gather additional information on the issues.
- The Commission reiterated that SDARS licensees are already prohibited, independent of the merger, from using terrestrial repeaters to distribute local content—including both programming and advertising—that is distinct from that provided to subscribers nationwide via satellite.
- The Commission prohibited the merged entity from entering into agreements that would bar any terrestrial radio station from broadcasting live local sporting events.

Notes and Questions

1. "Worst-Case" Assumptions. The FCC agrees with the DOJ that there is insufficient evidence to show a likelihood of harmful effects. The agency then says it will therefore review the merger under "worst-case" assumptions. In some ways this is startling: Is the FCC saying that even absent likelihood of harm, it will challenge or condition a merger to address the worst possible outcome of the transaction? If so, by what standard will this "worst-case" assumption be judged? Must it be reasonably supported by the evidence? Merely plausible? It is unimaginable that in a trial, even a civil one, legal liability would be explicitly determined by the worst possible interpretation of the facts as opposed to the interpretation supported by the preponderance of the evidence. Under what authority or logic is the FCC allowing itself to proceed under an assumption of harm from the merger even while acknowledging that the evidence does not support the likelihood of harm?

2. The Pricing Condition. One might argue that the Commission's worst-case assumption was just a reasonable way to protect consumers in the face of an uncertain prediction about the effects of the merger. In that light, the three-year pricing cap might not look so bad even if imposed under a worst-case assumption. Although the evidence did not allow the agencies to predict that the merger would *likely* lead to price increases, neither did it rule out the possibility that such effects *could* occur. So perhaps the FCC was just using its ability to obtain a pricing commitment from the parties to protect the public interest. What do you think of that interpretation and its implications for the FCC's role in merger review?

3. The Channel Set-Aside Condition. Do you see a distinction between the logic behind the FCC's channel set-aside condition and that of the pricing condition? Which do you think is more defensible? Which condition is more vulnerable to the kinds of concerns that Commissioners Furchtgott-Roth and Abernathy have raised in the past about the scope of merger review?

---

§ 11.A.6. The Comcast/NBCU Proceeding

Much of the debate over the FCC's approach to mergers came to a head in the Comcast/NBCU merger. Here, we set out an excerpt of the FCC's decision that describes the great scope of the merger and the multiple considerations that the FCC addressed. The merger implicated terrestrial television, cable television, video content, broadband Internet, and emerging business possibilities combining these assets. The FCC approved the merger, but again, conditions played a central role. But the FCC was not, this time, the only source of conditions. The Department of Justice also cleared the merger, but significant conditions were imposed through the device of a consent decree, where the Department sues to block the transaction but simultaneously enters with the court a settlement with the merging parties, which is embodied (if the court finds it to be in the public interest) in a final judgment (the consent decree). Many of the DOJ's conditions were the same as the FCC's and, in fact, relied on the FCC's processes for enforcement (at least in the first instance).

APPLICATIONS OF COMCAST CORP., GENERAL ELECTRIC CO. AND NBC UNIVERSAL, INC. FOR CONSENT TO ASSIGN LICENSES AND TRANSFER CONTROL OF LICENSEES

Memorandum Opinion and Order, 26 FCC Rcd. 4238 (2011)

I. Introduction

1. In this proceeding, Comcast Corporation (Comcast), General Electric Company (GE), and NBC Universal, Inc. (NBCU) — collectively referred to as "the Applicants" —

seek authorization to assign and transfer control of broadcast, satellite, and other radio licenses from GE to Comcast. The proposed transaction would combine, in a single joint venture (Comcast-NBCU or the JV), the broadcast, cable programming, online content, movie studio, and other businesses of NBCU with some of Comcast's cable programming and online content businesses. The JV's assets would include two broadcast television networks (NBC and Telemundo), 26 broadcast television stations, and NBCU's cable programming (such as CNBC, MSNBC, Bravo, and USA Network), all of which would be under the control of Comcast, the nation's largest cable operator and Internet service provider.

3. This transaction would effectuate an unprecedented aggregation of video programming content with control over the means by which video programming is distributed to American viewers offline and, increasingly, online as well. The harms that could result are substantial. For example, Comcast-NBCU would have both greater incentive and greater ability to raise prices for its popular video programming to disadvantage Comcast's rival multichannel distributors (such as telephone companies and direct broadcast satellite (DBS) providers). It would also have the incentive and ability to hinder the development of rival online video offerings and inhibit potential competition from emerging online video distributors that could challenge Comcast's cable television business. Moreover, the transaction presents concerns with respect to our statutory mandate to promote diversity and localism in broadcast television and video programming distribution.

4. Because of these and other threats posed by the proposed transaction to competition, innovation, and consumer welfare, the Commission has developed a number of targeted, transaction-related conditions and Comcast has offered a number of voluntary commitments to mitigate the potential harms the proposed combination might otherwise cause. These conditions and voluntary commitments, as discussed in further detail below, fall into three main categories as they relate to competition issues:

- *Ensuring Reasonable Access to Comcast-NBCU Programming for Multichannel Distribution.* Building on successful requirements adopted in prior, similar transactions, we make available to rival multichannel video programming distributors (MVPDs) an improved commercial arbitration process for resolving disputes about prices, terms, and conditions for licensing Comcast-NBCU's video programming. We believe that this remedy, designed to prevent harms from integrating content and distribution market power, will be even more effective and less costly than previous procedures. We apply the arbitration and standstill remedies to *all* Comcast-NBCU affiliated programming.

- *Protecting the Development of Online Competition.* Recognizing the danger this transaction could present to the development of innovative online video distribution, we adopt conditions designed to guarantee *bona fide* online distributors the ability to obtain Comcast-NBCU programming in appropriate circumstances. These conditions respond directly to the concerns voiced by commenters—including consumer advocates, online video distributors (OVDs) and MVPDs—while respecting the legitimate business interests of the Applicants. Among other things, the Commission:

  ○ Requires Comcast-NBCU to provide to all MVPDs, at fair market value and non-discriminatory prices, terms, and conditions, any affiliated content that Comcast makes available online to its own subscribers or to other MVPD subscribers.

  ○ Requires Comcast-NBCU to offer its video programming to any requesting OVD on the same terms and conditions that would be available to an MVPD.

- Obligates Comcast-NBCU to make comparable programming available on economically comparable prices, terms, and conditions to an OVD that has entered into an arrangement to distribute programming from one or more of Comcast-NBCU's peers.
- Restricts Comcast-NBCU's ability to enter into agreements to hamper online distribution of its own video programming or programming of other providers.
- Requires the continued offering of standalone broadband Internet access services at reasonable prices and of sufficient bandwidth so that customers can access online video services without the need to purchase a cable television subscription from Comcast.
- Prevents Comcast from disadvantaging rival online video distribution through its broadband Internet access services and/or set-top boxes.
- Addresses threats to Hulu, an emerging OVD to which NBCU provides programming, that arise from the transaction.

- *Access to Comcast's Distribution Systems.* In light of the significant additional programming Comcast will control—programming that may compete with third-party programming Comcast carries on its MVPD service—we require that Comcast not discriminate in video programming distribution on the basis of affiliation or non-affiliation with Comcast-NBCU. Moreover, we require that, if Comcast "neighborhoods" its news (including business news) channels, it must include all unaffiliated news (or business news) channels in that neighborhood. We also adopt as a condition of the transaction Comcast's voluntary commitment to provide 10 new independent channels within eight years on its digital tier.

5. We also impose conditions and accept voluntary commitments concerning a number of other public interest issues, including diversity, localism, and broadcasting, among others. For example, to protect the integrity of over-the-air broadcasting, network-affiliate relations, and fair and equitable retransmission consent negotiations with the JV, we adopt a series of conditions that were independently negotiated between the Applicants and various network affiliates.

6. In addition to these and other conditions, which are designed to remedy potential harms, we also look to the affirmative benefits of the proposed transaction, both those inherent in the combination as well as additional voluntary commitments made by the Applicants, in order to ensure that this transaction serves the public interest. These commitments, which we make enforceable through this Order, include but are not limited to:

- *Broadband Adoption and Deployment.* Comcast will make available to approximately 2.5 million low income households: (i) high-speed Internet access service for less than $10 per month, (ii) personal computers, netbooks, or other computer equipment at a purchase price below $150, and (iii) an array of digital-literacy education opportunities. Comcast will also expand its existing broadband networks to reach approximately 400,000 additional homes, provide broadband Internet access service in six additional rural communities, and provide free video and high-speed Internet service to 600 new anchor institutions, such as schools and libraries, in underserved, low income areas.
- *Localism.* To further broadcast localism, Comcast-NBCU will maintain at least the current level of news and information programming on NBCU's owned-and-

operated (O&O) broadcast stations, and in some cases expand news and other local content. Comcast-NBCU's O&O NBC and Telemundo stations also will provide thousands of additional hours of local news and information programming to their viewers, and some of its NBC stations will enter into cooperative arrangements with locally focused nonprofit news organizations. Additional free, on-demand local programming will be made available as well.

- *Children's Programming.* Comcast-NBCU will increase the availability of children's programming on its NBC and Telemundo broadcast stations, and add at least 1,500 more choices to Comcast's on-demand offerings for children. It will provide additional on-screen ratings information for original entertainment programming on the Comcast-NBCU broadcast and cable television channels and improved parental controls. Comcast-NBCU also will restrict interactive advertising aimed at children 12 years old and younger and provide public service announcements addressing children's issues.
- *Programming Diversity.* Building on Comcast's voluntary commitments in this area, we require Comcast-NBCU to increase programming diversity by expanding its over-the-air programming to the Spanish language-speaking community, and by making NBCU's Spanish-language broadcast programming available via Comcast's on demand and online platforms. As noted above, Comcast also will add at least 10 new independent channels to its cable offerings.
- *Public, Educational, and Governmental (PEG) Programming.* Comcast will safeguard the continued accessibility and signal quality of PEG channels on its cable television systems and introduce new on demand and online platforms for PEG content.

8. We therefore find that the grant of the proposed assignments and transfers of control of broadcast, satellite, and other radio licenses by the Commission will serve the public interest and, accordingly, the proposed transaction should be approved, as conditioned, pursuant to Section 310(d) of the Communications Act of 1934, as amended (Act).

[The Commission then turned in Section IV of the order to the "Standard of Review and Public Interest Framework." That section, which the reader might at this point want to review, is excerpted earlier in this chapter. Eds.]

V. Analysis of Potential Harms

A. Potential Competitive Harms Arising From Vertical Elements of the Transaction

28. We have found that the vertical integration from the proposed transaction raises three potential areas of anticompetitive concern that require further analysis. First, we consider program access issues as they relate to existing MVPD markets. That is, we consider whether the Applicants could use their control over video programming to harm competing MVPDs by withholding content or raising programming prices. Second, we address the emerging market in online video programming distribution, evaluating whether the Applicants could use their control over video programming, broadband, or set-top boxes to harm current and emerging online rivals. Finally, we address program carriage issues, which involve the Applicants' potential anticompetitive use of their control over video distribution to deny unaffiliated video programmers access to Comcast subscribers or impose unreasonable terms for distribution on Comcast's systems.

1. MVPD Access to Comcast-NBCU Programming

a. Potential for Exclusionary Conduct

29. The proposed transaction creates the possibility that Comcast-NBCU, either temporarily or permanently, will block Comcast's video distribution rivals from access to the

video programming content the JV would come to control or raise programming costs to its video distribution rivals. These exclusionary strategies could raise distribution competitors' costs or diminish the quality of the content available to them. As a result, Comcast could obtain or (to the extent it may already possess it) maintain market power in video distribution, and charge higher prices to its video distribution subscribers than those consumers would have paid absent the transaction. To address this potential harm, we impose an arbitration remedy, with a number of procedural improvements from arbitration remedies in previous transactions, that applies to all Comcast-NBCU programming.

34. *Discussion.* Congress and the Commission have long been concerned about the possibility that an integrated video firm may exploit its ability to exclude its distribution rivals from access to its programming, or raise programming prices to harm competition in video distribution.

36. Our analysis adapts an analytical framework employed in antitrust law. First, we agree with commenters who assert that this transaction gives Comcast an increased ability to disadvantage some or all of its video distribution rivals by exclusion, causing them to become less effective competitors. The record shows that the loss of Comcast-NBCU programming, including the programming contributed by NBCU, would harm rival video distributors, reducing their ability or incentive to compete with Comcast for subscribers. This is particularly true for marquee programming, which includes a broad portfolio of national cable programming in addition to RSN [Regional Sports Network] and local broadcast programming; such programming is important to Comcast's competitors and without good substitutes from other sources.

37. This conclusion is consistent with our previous finding that Comcast's withholding of the terrestrially delivered Comcast SportsNet Philadelphia RSN from DBS operators caused the percentage of television households subscribing to DBS in Philadelphia to be 40 percent lower than what it otherwise would have been.

40. The Commission has analyzed the possible competitive harms of past vertical transactions on the distribution of video programming with relevant markets defined as all MVPD services within local cable franchise areas. We adopt the same definition here. We decline to include broadcast television in the definition of MVPD services. The Commission has previously held that broadcast television is not sufficiently substitutable with the services provided by MVPDs to constrain attempted MVPD price increases, and hence declined to broaden the MVPD product market. This conclusion was based on factors including the degree of specialized programming provided, the number and diversity of channels offered, the fee charged for MVPD service, and the provision of premium movie channels, video on demand, and pay-per-view programming.

41. We do not determine at this time whether online video competes with MVPD services. In the last few years, the Internet has evolved into a powerful method of video programming distribution. We recognize that the amount of video content available on the Internet continues to increase significantly each year, and consumers are increasingly turning to the Internet to view video programming. As discussed below, we conclude that regardless of whether online video is a complement or substitute to MVPD service today, it is potentially a substitute product. When identifying market participants, therefore, we will include online video distributors as potential competitors into MVPD services markets.

46. In the extensive record before us now, many credible concerns have been raised that post-vertical integration price increases will result for Comcast-NBCU national cable programming—as well as for O&O programming and RSN programming. Video pro-

gramming has evolved over time—today certain national cable programming networks produce programming that is more widely viewed and commands higher advertising revenue than certain broadcast or RSN programming. Based on our analysis in the Technical Appendix, we also believe that the bargaining model used in the economic expert reports submitted by ACA and DISH supports the conclusion that the transaction could lead to price increases that target MVPD rivals.

48. We therefore conclude that conditions are necessary to ameliorate these potential harms for all categories of programming, as explained in more detail below.

b. Remedial Conditions

49. As a threshold matter, we conclude that our program access rules are insufficient to remedy the potential harm identified above. As the Commission found in the News Corp.-Hughes Order, a strategy of uniform price increases for video programming would not necessarily violate our current rules because the price increases would not involve discriminatory conduct. To facilitate the combined entity's exercise of a uniform-price-increase strategy, Comcast could pay the same fees as its MVPD rivals or could choose to pay the highest fee that NBCU charges a competing MVPD. Therefore, our program access rules, which address discriminatory pricing, inadequately address the potential harms presented by the increased ability and incentive of Comcast-NBCU to uniformly raise Comcast's rivals' fees.

50. To address this concern in prior transactions, the Commission has imposed baseball-style arbitration to maintain the pre-integration balance of bargaining power between vertically integrated programming networks and rival MVPDs. We do so here, with modifications. We establish a mechanism whereby an aggrieved MVPD may choose to submit a dispute with Comcast-NBCU over the terms and conditions of carriage of Comcast-NBCU affiliated programming to commercial arbitration. As in prior transactions, the arbitrator is directed to pick between the final contract offers submitted by Comcast-NBCU and the complainant MVPD based on which offer best reflects the fair market value of the programming at issue. This neutral dispute resolution forum will prevent Comcast-NBCU from exercising its increased market power to force Comcast's MVPD rivals to accept either inordinate fee increases for access to affiliated programming or other unwanted programming concessions, and will effectively address price increase strategies that could otherwise be used to circumvent our program access rules.

51. After considering the record in this proceeding, we have modified our arbitration procedures from past transactions in order to make them more effective and less costly, for example by limiting the discovery that is presumptively available. We also require Comcast- NBCU to permit the MVPD to continue to carry the programming that is the subject of arbitration while the dispute is being resolved.

2. Online Video Content

[This portion of the FCCs order, which discusses the competition issues involving online video distribution, is excerpted in Chapter Fourteen. In brief, the FCC found that the merged NBC/Comcast would have the ability and incentive both to use online content to disadvantage other MVPDs and to disadvantage other, unaffiliated OVDs. The Commission imposed several nondiscrimination conditions directed at these potential foreclosures.]

D. Broadband Internet Access Service

91. *Positions of the Parties.* Several commenters raise concerns that Comcast, in its capacity as a provider of Internet access services, will have an increased incentive to degrade the delivery of, or block entirely, traffic from the websites of other content providers or OVDs, or speed up access to their own content and aggregation websites. These com-

menters argue that Comcast has demonstrated its ability to engage in network management practices that have a discriminatory effect on selected content, and retains the ability to use technologies such as deep packet inspection to discriminate between packets. Some commenters argue that Comcast would also have an increased incentive to set usage caps that would penalize Comcast's broadband subscribers for viewing unaffiliated content, or for viewing content delivered by an unaffiliated OVD.

93. *Discussion.* Although we agree with the Applicants that these concerns affect all ISPs, we also identify particular transaction-related harms that arise from the increased risk that Comcast will engage in blocking or discrimination when transmitting network traffic over its broadband service. Specifically, we find that Comcast's acquisition of additional programming content that may be delivered via the Internet, or for which other providers' Internet-delivered content may be a substitute, will increase Comcast's incentive to discriminate against unaffiliated content and distributors in its exercise of control over consumers' broadband connections. Post-transaction, Comcast will gain control of NBCU [REDACTED], which is composed primarily of video programming assets. Comcast-NBCU will also control a 32 percent interest in Hulu, the second most-watched source of online video and the [REDACTED]. Comcast-NBCU will have a roughly five percent share of the market in online video distribution sites. Few other OVDs control such a high percentage of the content they distribute, and no others are vertically integrated with the nation's largest residential broadband provider. Furthermore, if Comcast or Comcast-NBCU were to discriminate against disfavored online content or distributors after the transaction, that conduct could render our online program access conditions ineffective.

94. To address these transaction-related concerns, the Applicants have offered a number of voluntary commitments. The Applicants have agreed that, in their provision of broadband Internet access services, neither Comcast nor Comcast-NBCU shall prioritize affiliated Internet content over unaffiliated Internet content. In addition, any Comcast or Comcast-NBCU broadband Internet access service offering that involves caps, tiers, metering, or other usage-based pricing shall not treat affiliated network traffic differently from unaffiliated network traffic. Comcast and Comcast-NBCU shall also comply with all relevant FCC rules, including the rules adopted by the Commission in GN Docket No. 09-191, and, in the event of any judicial challenge affecting the latter, Comcast-NBCU's voluntary commitments concerning adherence to those rules will be in effect.

3. Program Carriage Issues

116. *Discussion.* Based on the record, and consistent with the concerns about vertical integration addressed by Congress in section 616 of the Cable Act, we find that the combination of Comcast, the nation's largest cable service provider and a producer of its own content, with NBCU, the nation's fourth largest owner of national cable networks, will result in an entity with increased ability and incentive to harm competition in video programming by engaging in foreclosure strategies or other discriminatory actions against unaffiliated video programming networks. Comcast's extensive cable distribution network affords it the ability to use its video distribution market position to harm other competing video programming firms and harm competition in video programming. Comcast is the nation's largest multiple system operator (MSO), with nearly 24 percent of MVPD subscribers nationwide. Furthermore, Comcast's market share in some of the nation's highest-ranked DMAs is considerably greater—for example, Comcast's market share is as much as 62 percent in the Chicago DMA and 67 percent in the Philadelphia DMA. While the transaction does not increase this significant share that Comcast has in distribution, that share gives Comcast an ability not possessed by pre-transaction NBCU to disadvantage rival networks that compete

with NBCU networks. Comcast's large subscriber base potentially allows it to limit access to customers for any network it wishes to disadvantage by either denying carriage or, with a similar but lesser competitive effect, placing the network in a less penetrated tier or on a less advantageous channel number (making it more difficult for subscribers to find the programming). In doing so, Comcast can reduce the viewership of competing video programming networks, which in turn could render these networks less attractive to advertisers, thus reducing their revenues and profits. As a result, these unaffiliated networks may compete less aggressively with NBCU networks, allowing the latter to obtain or (to the extent they may already possess it) maintain market power with respect to advertisers seeking access to their viewers.

118. The transaction also increases Comcast's incentives to discriminate in favor of its affiliated programming. Upon consummation of the transaction, Comcast will compete with an increased pool of unaffiliated programming vendors offering content that viewers might consider substitutes for its affiliates' programming content and against which it could potentially pursue foreclosure or discrimination strategies in order to favor that content. NBCU's content offerings include both broadcast and cable networks including the USA Network, the top-rated basic cable network, CNBC, the number one business news channel, and MSNBC, the second-rated cable news channel. In addition, Telemundo is the second-largest global provider of Spanish language content. Post-transaction, content will be a significant source of revenue for Comcast. Comcast acknowledges that the transaction "[b]rings together outstanding content creation and distribution capabilities," and that "[c]able channels represent 82% of the new joint venture's [operating cash flow] and drive its profitability." Comcast, Creating a Premier Media and Entertainment Company 4 (Dec. 3, 2009) *available at* http://files.shareholder.com/downloads/CMCSA/0x0x336728/546b65cb-9493-4289-aeba-5bfa6eb7cf6e/Comcast_PDF(4)12.03.09.pdf. Five of NBCU's cable channels generate over $200 million in annual operating cash flow.

120. In an effort to address commenters' concerns, the Applicants voluntarily commit to several carriage obligations. Among its voluntary commitments, Comcast commits to add at least ten new independently owned and operated programming services to the digital (D1) tier over the eight years following closing of the transaction. Comcast has assured the Commission that this commitment creates "floors, not ceilings," and that it will add additional independent channels and/or add them faster if possible. Further, for seven years after the closing of the transaction, Comcast commits that it will not discriminate "against local, in-market non-NBCU stations in favor of NBCU stations with respect to certain technical signal carriage matters." Letter from Michael H. Hammer, Counsel for Comcast, and David H. Solomon, Counsel for NBCU, to Marlene H. Dortch, Sec'y, FCC (Aug. 6, 2010).

121. Although these commitments are helpful, they are not sufficient to allay our concerns. We believe it is in the public interest to adopt additional remedies regarding program carriage disputes. Specifically, we condition the approval of this transaction on the requirement that Comcast not discriminate in video programming distribution on the basis of affiliation or nonaffiliation of vendors in the selection of, or terms or conditions for, carriage, including in decisions regarding tiering and channel placement. If program carriage disputes arise based on this non-discrimination condition, it will be sufficient for the aggrieved vendor to show that it was discriminated against on the basis of its affiliation or non-affiliation. A vendor proceeding under this condition will not need to also prove that it was unreasonably restrained from competing, as it would under our program carriage rules. This non-discrimination requirement will be binding on Comcast independent of the Commission's rules, and will extend to non-discriminatory treat-

ment in placement within search menus as well as channel placement. We also prohibit retaliation for bringing a program carriage complaint.

122. In addition, although we decline to adopt a requirement that Comcast affirmatively undertake neighborhooding, in accordance with the special importance of news programming to the public interest, we adopt a narrowly tailored condition related to channel placement for independent news channels. Specifically, we require that if Comcast now or in the future carries news and/or business news channels in a neighborhood, defined as placing a significant number or percentage of news and/or business news channels substantially adjacent to one another in a system's channel lineup, Comcast must carry all independent news and business news channels in that neighborhood.

B. Potential Competitive Harms Arising from Horizontal Elements of the Transaction

125. In analyzing the horizontal elements of the proposed transaction, we examine the effects of the joint venture on competition in: (1) local distribution markets in which Comcast is the dominant cable provider and NBCU owns broadcast television stations; (2) the sale of video programming to MVPDs; (3) content production; and (4) online video content. We also examine the effects of the proposed transaction on advertising in video programming on both cable and broadcast television and on the Internet.

1. Linear Programming

a. Distribution

129. *Discussion.* The Commission previously has found that MVPD services and broadcast television are not sufficiently close substitutes to warrant including them in the same product market. No evidence has been submitted in this proceeding suggesting otherwise. Accordingly, we continue to view MVPD services and broadcast television as different relevant product markets. In light of the fact that NBCU does not own any MVPD properties and Comcast does not hold an interest in any broadcast television stations, the transaction will neither increase concentration in the MVPD services in any geographic market nor increase concentration in the 9.5 percent of homes that rely solely on over-the-air delivery of broadcast signals in any region. Consequently, the combination of Comcast's MVPD assets with NBCU's broadcast television station assets is unlikely to harm competition in any video distribution market.

b. Video Programming

135. *Discussion.* The ability of a company to obtain greater bargaining power because of a horizontal transaction is a well-established concern in antitrust enforcement, and the theoretical possibility that this could occur here is accepted by the Applicants. In order for the transaction to allow Comcast-NBCU to raise the prices for its programming, the price must be set by negotiation, as opposed to settings in which transactions occur at market prices not resulting from bargaining between buyers and sellers. That is certainly true here. Comcast-NBCU and the MVPDs to which it will sell programming negotiate over the terms and conditions of the programming carriage agreements.

138. We conclude that commenters have raised a legitimate concern about the effect the combination of Comcast's RSNs and the NBC O&O stations will have on carriage prices for both of those networks. Nonetheless, we find that this potential harm will be mitigated in the context of this transaction because the program access-related conditions we impose will prevent Comcast-NBCU from using any increased bargaining power it might obtain to raise rates above market levels for each of the Comcast RSNs and the NBC O&Os individually.

140. We do not accept the other arguments made by commenters regarding increased market power over certain categories of programming. Our record is insufficient to reach the conclusion that the horizontal combination of programming within these categories—sports programming, local news networks, and programming viewed by women—would substantially lessen the alternatives available to MVPDs seeking to attract subscribers interested in programming in these categories. In each of these categories, comparable programming will remain available on numerous unaffiliated broadcast networks and national cable networks. In the absence of other evidence suggesting that the combination of networks with programming in these categories will increase the bargaining leverage the joint venture has in negotiating the price for such programming with MVPDs, we have no basis for requiring conditions to address these specific concerns, beyond the relief afforded by the program access conditions we impose.

VI. Analysis of Potential Public Interest Benefits

A. Analytical Framework

226. In determining whether approval of a transaction is in the public interest, the Commission evaluates whether the transaction is likely to produce public interest benefits. The Commission applies several criteria in deciding whether a claimed benefit should be considered and weighed against potential harms. First, the claimed benefit must be transaction specific. That is, the claimed benefit must be likely to occur as a result of the transaction but unlikely to be realized by other practical means having fewer anticompetitive effects. Second, the claimed benefit must be verifiable. The Applicants, who possess much of the information relating to the potential benefit of a transaction, are required to provide sufficient supporting evidence to permit us to verify the likelihood and magnitude of each claimed benefit. Benefits expected to occur only in the distant future are inherently more speculative than more immediate benefits. Third, the Commission calculates the magnitude of benefits net of the cost of achieving them. Fourth, the benefits must flow through to consumers, and not inure solely to the benefit of the company.

227. The Commission applies a "sliding scale approach" to its ultimate evaluation of benefit claims. Where potential harms appear both substantial and likely, the Applicants' demonstration of claimed benefits must reveal a higher degree of magnitude and likelihood than the Commission would otherwise demand. On the other hand, where potential harms appear less likely and less substantial, we will accept a lesser showing.

B. Alleged Benefits

1. Cooperation and Agreement Between the Parties

228. *Positions of the Parties.* The Applicants argue their vertical integration will reduce the barriers or friction preventing them from reaching agreements over content distribution, and that greater access to content will promote the creation of new programming and the accelerated deployment of new media distribution services. They state it is difficult to structure long-term contracts with unaffiliated content providers who are reluctant to commit their content to, or invest in new content for, new and unproven distribution models. They cite the difficulties Comcast experienced in launching its VOD, "day-and-date" movie releases, Fancast Xfinity TV/TV Everywhere, and advanced advertising services, and argue Comcast's eventual success with VOD (after acquiring an interest in MGM) exemplifies the synergies likely to arise from the joint venture. They anticipate content gained through the transaction will accelerate developments in the business model for in-home on demand movies, as well as online video, and encourage Comcast's investment in the joint venture's programming assets.

229. Parties opposing the proposed transaction argue reduced transactional friction does not result in a transaction-specific benefit given that launch of the aforementioned services is likely, and indeed continues, even absent vertical integration. They also argue it is too speculative to draw the inference that Comcast would invest in NBCU properties in the same way it has invested in its own underperforming networks given the two sets of networks are not similarly situated.

231. *Discussion.* We agree that the transaction will likely reduce some of the barriers and friction that exist when unaffiliated content providers and distributors negotiate to reach agreements. Particularly in a time of uncertainty and change, the difficulty of accurately predicting (and therefore allocating) the risks and rewards in agreements that involve departures from standard business models can inhibit the bargaining process and slow innovation. While we recognize this benefit, it is difficult to quantify aside from specific commitments and contexts. Nevertheless, we will give it some weight, since it is a transaction-related change in structure that will change incentives, while acknowledging its potential impacts, *e.g.*, on introduction of novel products and services, are hard to specify in advance.

2. Facilitate Broadband Goals

232. *Positions of the Parties.* This transaction holds the promise of promoting the growth of video on the Internet and accelerating broadband adoption. The Applicants state that given the intense competition in the entertainment environment, it is reasonable to expect that the Applicants' investments and innovations will spur advancements by others in order to maintain their ability to compete effectively. As discussed in this Order, online video does encourage the demand for broadband, and to support competition in the online video marketplace, we impose certain conditions to check the Applicants' enhanced ability and incentive to thwart innovation and new developments in online video services.

233. *Discussion.* We note that the Applicants have made commitments to expand broadband deployment to unserved areas, including rural communities, and to facilitate increased broadband adoption by low income households. Specifically, Comcast will expand its existing broadband networks to reach approximately 400,000 additional homes. Comcast also will provide Internet access service in additional rural communities and provide courtesy video and HSI service to 600 new locations (such as schools and libraries) in underserved, low-income areas. To further encourage broadband adoption, Comcast will make available to low-income households HSI access service for less than $10 per month, and personal computers, netbooks, or other computer equipment at a purchase price below $150. We find that these commitments will lead to greater broadband demand, deployment and adoption, and thus adopt them as conditions so that the public will realize these considerable benefits.

234. In addition, in the National Broadband Plan, in order to fill the critical need for more spectrum for wireless broadband, the Commission proposed to recover up to 120 MHz of spectrum from broadcast television through incentive auctions in which licensees would have the option of participating by contributing all or a portion of their stations' allocated spectrum. Comcast has agreed, subject to certain conditions, to continue to carry on its cable systems the programming of non-commercial educational television stations that have must-carry rights and that it currently carries, either pursuant to the signal carriage obligations under section 76.55(a) of the Rules, or pursuant to a digital carriage agreement, in the event that the station opts to relinquish all of its spectrum in such an auction. Comcast's agreement to do so will provide the licensees of such stations an additional incentive to choose to participate in such auctions by enabling them to continue to provide programming to the public. We adopt this commitment as a condition of the transaction so that the public interest objective of acquiring much-needed additional

spectrum for mobile broadband will be served, but not at the expense of our policy goals of program diversity and localism. Accordingly, we also find that, through this condition, the transaction will assist in meeting the Commission's broadband objectives.

VII. Balancing Potential Public Interest Harms and Benefits

251. Our task under the Act is to determine whether the "public interest, convenience and necessity will be served," *see* 47 U.S.C. §§ 310(d), 309(a), (d), by the grant of the Application. Once we are satisfied that a proposed transaction will not violate a statutory provision or rule, the public interest standard involves a balancing of potential public interest harms of the proposed transaction and the potential public interest benefits. The Applicants bear the burden of proving, by a preponderance of the evidence that the proposed transaction, on balance, serves the public interest. Our options at this stage are to grant the Application without conditions, grant it with conditions, or designate the Application for hearing if we are unable to make the findings required by the Act for its grant.

256. We balance the potential public interest harms and benefits with due attention to the context and structure of the current marketplace. The Applicants have chosen vertical integration as their path forward through a marketplace in transition driven by technological change. Joining control over a major distribution channel on one hand and over marquee programming on the other creates potential for public interest harms—most notably to slow down or skew competition and innovation that promises substantial benefits for consumers—but the conditions we impose in this Order are designed to neutralize those possible negative impacts. On the positive side, the transaction will create an entity with a broader range of assets, more potential flexibility for innovation, and some efficiencies of scale and scope. On balance, we conclude that the proposed transaction, as conditioned, should be approved as serving the public interest.

Notes and Questions

1. Why Approve? Given its concerns, why did the FCC approve the merger? The Commission's bottom line was that the conditions eliminated most of the possibility for anticompetitive behavior and that "the transaction will create an entity with a broader range of assets, more potential flexibility for innovation, and some efficiencies of scale and scope." *Comcast/NBC Order* ¶ 256. Are you persuaded?

2. More Disciplined Analysis or Just More Elaborate Explanation? The FCC again imposes a large number of conditions on the merging parties, including a set of "voluntary" commitments. Compared to the other cases reviewed in this chapter, do the conditions seem more closely tied to predicted harms from the specific transaction, or is the FCC engaging in the kind of overreaching that Commissioner Furchtgott-Roth criticized in his earlier discussed partial dissent? On one hand, the Commission seems careful to examine predicted effects of the merger and to adopt remedies tailored to those harms. On the other hand, the Commission also imposes remedies related to issues—like localism and diversity—that the introduction to the order indicates are designed not to remedy harms but to create positive benefits from the merger. Is this the kind of benefit of which ¶ 226 says the Commission should take account? Or is this the FCC taking advantage of the merger application to create benefits that are unrelated to the transaction? Look at ¶ 6 of the order: Does anything constrain the nature and number of "affirmative benefits" the FCC might seek from merging parties? If so, what? If not, is that cause for concern?

3. Basis for Predicted Harms. On what basis does the FCC predict harms from the transaction? The agency often refers to the parties' incentives to undertake some kind of anticompetitive conduct. How convincing do you find those arguments to be? What empirical evidence does the FCC advance? On the whole, does the FCC make a good case for the likelihood of harm from the merger and for the conditions it has imposed?

4. Actual and Potential Competitors. In its analysis of the transaction, the FCC does not include online video in the relevant product market. In ¶ 41 the agency reserves judgment on whether online video providers compete with MVPDs. But later in that paragraph the FCC says that online video is "potentially a substitute product" and that it will include online video distributors as "potential competitors" with MVPD markets. What does it mean to say that online video is a potential competitor but not enough of one to impose competitive discipline? One possibility is that the FCC is just being forward-looking and showing that while competition today from online video is not enough to discipline Comcast's behavior the agency recognizes the future importance of the medium. But beyond showing that it recognizes the video market to be dynamic, the FCC also benefits from this categorization of online video services in its analysis of the merged venture's incentives and ability to discriminate. Do you see how?

---

§ 11.B. Antitrust in a Regulatory Thicket

At issue in the section above was whether the Commission should be involved in merger review given that other federal agencies also review mergers and arguably have more expertise on matters of market structure. Our point is that telecommunications law seems to overlap with antitrust law as applied to mergers, and the question is whether the Commission ought to in such cases simply defer to the traditional antitrust mechanisms. In 2004, the Supreme Court addressed what is in some sense the opposite question: namely, are there instances in which telecommunications law is so involved with a given set of relationships that antitrust law ought to step aside and leave the telecommunications mechanisms free to resolve any disputes?

VERIZON COMMUNICATIONS INC. v. LAW OFFICES OF CURTIS V. TRINKO, LLP
540 U.S. 398 (2004)

SCALIA, J., delivered the opinion of the Court, in which REHNQUIST, C.J., and O'CONNOR, KENNEDY, GINSBURG, and BREYER, JJ., joined. STEVENS, J., filed an opinion concurring in the judgment, in which SOUTER and THOMAS, JJ., joined.

Justice SCALIA delivered the opinion of the Court.

The Telecommunications Act of 1996 imposes certain duties upon incumbent local telephone companies in order to facilitate market entry by competitors, and establishes a complex regime for monitoring and enforcement. In this case we consider whether a complaint alleging breach of the incumbent's duty under the 1996 Act to share its network with competitors states a claim under § 2 of the Sherman Act, 26 Stat 209.

I

Respondent, a New York City law firm, was a local telephone service customer of AT&T. According to the complaint, Verizon "has filled orders of [competitive LEC] customers after filling those for its own local phone service, has failed to fill in a timely manner, or not at all, a substantial number of orders for [competitive LEC] customers..., and has systematically failed to inform [competitive LECs] of the status of their customers' orders." Pl.'s Amended Comp., 2001 WL 34765802, ¶ 21 (S.D.N.Y. Jan. 19, 2001). It asserted that the result of Verizon's improper "behavior with respect to providing access to its local loop" was to "deter potential customers [of rivals] from switching." *Id.* ¶ 57. The complaint sought damages and injunctive relief for violation of § 2 of the Sherman Act, 15 U.S.C. § 2, pursuant to the remedy provisions of §§ 4 and 16 of the Clayton Act, 38 Stat. 731, as amended, 15 U.S.C. §§ 15, 26. The complaint also alleged violations of the 1996 Act, and state law.

The District Court dismissed the complaint in its entirety. As to the antitrust portion, it concluded that respondent's allegations of deficient assistance to rivals failed to satisfy the requirements of § 2. The Court of Appeals for the Second Circuit reinstated the complaint in part, including the antitrust claim. We granted certiorari, limited to the question whether the Court of Appeals erred in reversing the District Court's dismissal of respondent's antitrust claims.

II

To decide this case, we must first determine what effect (if any) the 1996 Act has upon the application of traditional antitrust principles. The Act imposes a large number of duties upon incumbent LECs—above and beyond those basic responsibilities it imposes upon all carriers, such as assuring number portability and providing access to rights-of-way, *see* 47 U.S.C. §§ 251(b)(2), (4). Under the sharing duties of § 251(c), incumbent LECs are required to offer three kinds of access. Already noted, and perhaps most intrusive, is the duty to offer access to UNEs on "just, reasonable, and nondiscriminatory" terms, § 251(c)(3), a phrase that the FCC has interpreted to mean a price reflecting long-run incremental cost. *See* Verizon Commc'ns Inc. v. FCC, 535 U.S. 467, 495–96 (2002). A rival can interconnect its own facilities with those of the incumbent LEC, or it can simply purchase services at wholesale from the incumbent and resell them to consumers. *See* §§ 251(c)(2), (4). The Act also imposes upon incumbents the duty to allow physical "collocation"—that is, to permit a competitor to locate and install its equipment on the incumbent's premises—which makes feasible interconnection and access to UNEs. *See* § 251(c)(6).

That Congress created these duties, however, does not automatically lead to the conclusion that they can be enforced by means of an antitrust claim. Indeed, a detailed regulatory scheme such as that created by the 1996 Act ordinarily raises the question whether the regulated entities are not shielded from antitrust scrutiny altogether by the doctrine of implied immunity. In some respects the enforcement scheme set up by the 1996 Act is a good candidate for implication of antitrust immunity, to avoid the real possibility of judgments conflicting with the agency's regulatory scheme "that might be voiced by courts exercising jurisdiction under the antitrust laws." United States v. Nat'l Ass'n of Sec. Dealers, Inc., 422 U.S. 694, 734 (1975).

Congress, however, precluded that interpretation. Section 601(b)(1) of the 1996 Act is an antitrust-specific saving clause providing that "nothing in this Act or the amendments made by this Act shall be construed to modify, impair, or supersede the applicability of any of the antitrust laws." 47 U.S.C. § 152. This bars a finding of implied immunity. As the FCC has put the point, the saving clause preserves those "claims that satisfy established antitrust standards."

But just as the 1996 Act preserves claims that satisfy existing antitrust standards, it does not create new claims that go beyond existing antitrust standards; that would be equally inconsistent with the saving clause's mandate that nothing in the Act "modify, impair, or supersede the applicability" of the antitrust laws. We turn, then, to whether the activity of which respondent complains violates pre-existing antitrust standards.

III

The complaint alleges that Verizon denied interconnection services to rivals in order to limit entry. If that allegation states an antitrust claim at all, it does so under § 2 of the Sherman Act, which declares that a firm shall not "monopolize" or "attempt to monopolize." *Id.* It is settled law that this offense requires, in addition to the possession of monopoly power in the relevant market, "the willful acquisition or maintenance of that power as distinguished from growth or development as a consequence of a superior product, business acumen, or historic accident." United States v. Grinnell Corp., 384 U.S. 563, 570–71 (1966). The mere possession of monopoly power, and the concomitant charging of monopoly prices, is not only not unlawful; it is an important element of the free-market system. The opportunity to charge monopoly prices—at least for a short period—is what attracts "business acumen" in the first place; it induces risk taking that produces innovation and economic growth. To safeguard the incentive to innovate, the possession of monopoly power will not be found unlawful unless it is accompanied by an element of anticompetitive conduct.

Firms may acquire monopoly power by establishing an infrastructure that renders them uniquely suited to serve their customers. Compelling such firms to share the source of their advantage is in some tension with the underlying purpose of antitrust law, since it may lessen the incentive for the monopolist, the rival, or both to invest in those economically beneficial facilities. Enforced sharing also requires antitrust courts to act as central planners, identifying the proper price, quantity, and other terms of dealing—a role for which they are ill-suited. Moreover, compelling negotiation between competitors may facilitate the supreme evil of antitrust: collusion. Thus, as a general matter, the Sherman Act "does not restrict the long recognized right of [a] trader or manufacturer engaged in an entirely private business, freely to exercise his own independent discretion as to parties with whom he will deal." United States v. Colgate & Co., 250 U.S. 300, 307 (1919).

However, "[t]he high value that we have placed on the right to refuse to deal with other firms does not mean that the right is unqualified." Aspen Skiing Co. v. Aspen Highlands Skiing Corp., 472 U.S. 585, 601 (1985). Under certain circumstances, a refusal to cooperate with rivals can constitute anticompetitive conduct and violate § 2. We have been very cautious in recognizing such exceptions, because of the uncertain virtue of forced sharing and the difficulty of identifying and remedying anticompetitive conduct by a single firm.

IV

Finally, we do not believe that traditional antitrust principles justify adding the present case to the few existing exceptions from the proposition that there is no duty to aid competitors. Antitrust analysis must always be attuned to the particular structure and circumstances of the industry at issue. Part of that attention to economic context is an awareness of the significance of regulation. As we have noted, "careful account must be taken of the pervasive federal and state regulation characteristic of the industry." United States v. Citizens & S. Nat. Bank, 422 U.S. 86, 91 (1975).

One factor of particular importance is the existence of a regulatory structure designed to deter and remedy anticompetitive harm. Where such a structure exists, the additional benefit to competition provided by antitrust enforcement will tend to be small, and it will be less plausible that the antitrust laws contemplate such additional scrutiny. Where, by contrast, "[t]here is nothing built into the regulatory scheme which performs the antitrust function," Silver v. New York Stock Exch., 373 U.S. 341, 358 (1963), the benefits of antitrust are worth its sometimes considerable disadvantages. Just as regulatory context may in other cases serve as a basis for implied immunity, it may also be a consideration in deciding whether to recognize an expansion of the contours of §2. The regulatory framework that exists in this case demonstrates how, in certain circumstances, "regulation significantly diminishes the likelihood of major antitrust harm." Concord v. Boston Edison Co., 915 F.2d 17, 25 (1st Cir. 1990) (Breyer, C.J.).

Against the slight benefits of antitrust intervention here, we must weigh a realistic assessment of its costs. Under the best of circumstances, applying the requirements of §2 "can be difficult" because "the means of illicit exclusion, like the means of legitimate competition, are myriad." United States v. Microsoft Corp., 253 F.3d 34, 58 (D.C. Cir. 2001) (en banc) (per curiam). Mistaken inferences and the resulting false condemnations "are especially costly, because they chill the very conduct the antitrust laws are designed to protect." Matsushita Elec. Indus. Co. v. Zenith Radio Corp., 475 U.S. 574 (1986). The cost of false positives counsels against an undue expansion of §2 liability. One false-positive risk is that an incumbent LEC's failure to provide a service with sufficient alacrity might have nothing to do with exclusion. Allegations of violations of §251(c)(3) duties are difficult for antitrust courts to evaluate, not only because they are highly technical, but also because they are likely to be extremely numerous, given the incessant, complex, and constantly changing interaction of competitive and incumbent LECs implementing the sharing and interconnection obligations. As [one amicus brief points out,] competitive LECs are threatened with "death by a thousand cuts," Brief for New York et al. as Amici Curiae 10 (internal quotation marks omitted)—the identification of which would surely be a daunting task for a generalist antitrust court. Judicial oversight under the Sherman Act would seem destined to distort investment and lead to a new layer of interminable litigation, atop the variety of litigation routes already available to and actively pursued by competitive LECs.

Even if the problem of false positives did not exist, conduct consisting of anticompetitive violations of §251 may be, as we have concluded with respect to above-cost predatory pricing schemes, "beyond the practical ability of a judicial tribunal to control." Brooke Grp. Ltd. v. Brown & Williamson Tobacco Corp., 509 U.S. 209, 223 (1993). Effective remediation of violations of regulatory sharing requirements will ordinarily require continuing supervision of a highly detailed decree. We think that Professor Areeda got it exactly right: "No court should impose a duty to deal that it cannot explain or adequately and reasonably supervise. The problem should be deemed irremedia[ble] by antitrust law when compulsory access requires the court to assume the day-to-day controls characteristic of a regulatory agency." Areeda, Essential Facilities: An Epithet in Need of Limiting Principles, 58 Antitrust L.J. 841, 853 (1989). In this case, respondent has requested an equitable decree to "[p]reliminarily and permanently enjoi[n] [Verizon] from providing access to the local loop market ... to [rivals] on terms and conditions that are not as favorable" as those that Verizon enjoys. Pl's Comp., at (v). An antitrust court is unlikely to be an effective day-to-day enforcer of these detailed sharing obligations.

The 1996 Act is in an important respect much more ambitious than the antitrust laws. It attempts "*to eliminate the monopolies* enjoyed by the inheritors of AT&T's local franchises." *Verizon Comm'ns Inc.*, 535 U.S. at 476 (emphasis added). Section 2 of the Sherman Act, by contrast, seeks merely to prevent unlawful monopolization. It would be a serious mistake to conflate the two goals. The Sherman Act is indeed the "Magna Carta of free enterprise," United States v. Topco Assocs., Inc., 405 U.S. 596, 610 (1972), but it does not give judges carte blanche to insist that a monopolist alter its way of doing business whenever some other approach might yield greater competition. We conclude that respondent's complaint fails to state a claim under the Sherman Act.

[Concurring opinion of JUSTICE STEVENS is omitted.]

Notes and Questions

1. **Scope of Antitrust.** What does this case say about the scope of antitrust in a highly regulated industry absent preemption by a specific statutory provision? Does the case say that antitrust then applies with nothing more or less than its full force? Or did the existence of the 1996 Act actually argue against the application of antitrust oversight in this case, the implication being that the scope of antitrust enforcement is indeed reduced in the context of regulated industries?

2. **Importance of a Savings Clause.** The Court notes that allowing the 1996 Act to increase the range of conduct that constitutes an antitrust violation would be inconsistent with §601's statement that the Act does not "modify" existing antitrust law. Suppose that §601 did not use the word *modify* but said only that the Act would not "impair or supersede the applicability" of the antitrust laws. Would the case still come out the same way?

3. **Costs and Benefits of Antitrust.** The Court states that the costs of antitrust enforcement may offset its benefits in the context of regulation that itself addresses and promotes competition. How does this argument square with the more textual argument based on the §601 savings clause? Is the Court implying that even a cause of action recognized under existing antitrust law might not be allowed when another statute overlaps or provides its own safeguards for competition?

4. **Standing.** Our focus thus far has been on the potential overlap and conflict between antitrust enforcement and the 1996 Act writ large. But note the many more detailed conflicts at issue as well. For example, should an individual CLEC subscriber like the law firm that brought this case actually have standing to litigate this sort of alleged antitrust violation? On the facts here, the CLEC that was allegedly harmed had already voiced its objections to state and federal authorities, and that CLEC had been party to a settlement in which Verizon paid a sizeable fine and promised to correct its ways. Given that, can you think of any reason to allow a customer of the wronged CLEC to persevere in the litigation? How will that change the various parties' incentives to sue and settle? How will it change their powers to resolve disputes and allow providers to move forward with the business of providing service?

5. **The *Trinko* Trigger.** Under what circumstances does *Trinko*'s rule of deference to telecommunications regulators apply? Does it apply if the FCC is not specifically acting in an area or if it has set forth only broad standards? In the area of broadband regulation, discussed in Chapter Fourteen, for example, the FCC first proceeded by issuing a Policy Statement and even later, when it moved towards rules, those rules had substantial room for interpretation and application.

6. **Institutional Competence Revisited.** Justice Scalia's opinion strongly suggests that overseeing interconnection arrangements is beyond the purview of antitrust courts. Does such a view suggest that antitrust law is incapable of replacing regulation in a network industry in which interconnection issues are likely to be contested? Alternatively, can you envision a role for antitrust law whereby the respective roles of the FCC, Justice Department, and FTC will need to be reconceived over time?

PART FIVE
THE INTERNET

Chapter Twelve

Introduction and Evolution

The Internet has risen from obscurity to ubiquity with astonishing speed. Indeed, it has become almost too obvious to say that the Internet has profoundly transformed the world of telecommunications—and the world more generally. The Internet's ability to make every person a "broadcaster" and every person a "publisher," combined with increases in its global reach, the volume of information it can access, and the speeds at which people can interconnect, portend an even bigger impact in the future. From a regulatory perspective, the Internet has enabled the convergence we discussed in Chapter One, under which all communications services can be provided by a single underlying infrastructure—a big change from the original structure of telecommunications markets in which different types of services were by and large provided by different technologies and thus by different companies.

This chapter introduces the basic structure and history of the Internet and provides a vocabulary for discussing the technology of the Internet as it relates to Internet regulation. As with telephone technology, this will be important when we turn to the interactions between technology, market structure, competition, and regulation. Then, the chapter turns to several early, overarching statements of Internet policy, and a brief mention of the now diminishing role of the United States in maintaining the domain name system, the addressing system of the Internet.

§ 12.A. The History and Architecture of the Internet

A discussion of the birth of the Internet begins to sound as remote today as does the Cretaceous period ("In 1960, when computers were the size of houses, and the mighty behemoth IBM ruled the earth . . ."). But this history is nevertheless important because, for better or worse, it will for the foreseeable future continue to affect how the U.S. government views the Internet. The idea of a computer "network of networks" was conceived by J.C.R. Licklider at MIT in 1962. Licklider was also the first head of computing research at the Defense Advanced Research Projects Agency (DARPA), an agency of the U.S. Department of Defense. It was at DARPA that Licklider's ideas germinated most fruitfully, and it was under DARPA that scientists and engineers first developed the technology we recognize today as the Internet. At this time, the network was known as the ARPANET.

ARPANET's purpose was to permit units within the Department of Defense (DOD) and various DOD contractors to share information with one another easily and quickly, regardless of the distance between them. The ARPANET was first publicly demonstrated in 1972. In this, and many other ways that will be discussed below, the U.S. Government can be said to have paid for and built much of the U.S. portions of the (initial) Internet. Contrast this with, for example, the telephone and cable television plant, which have been largely built by private entities using private funds.

New technology, such as the ARPANET, will often flourish when it provides consumers with an application that makes the technology too attractive to pass up, sometimes referred to as the killer application, or killer app. For television viewers, the killer app may have been the entertainment value of seeing Milton Berle in a dress from their living rooms. For personal computers, perhaps the first killer app to ignite user interest was the VISI-CALC spreadsheet. The first killer app for the ARPANET was email, which was introduced in 1972. Once the utility of ARPANET and email had been demonstrated, it was not long before other constituencies that had ready access to computers began to push for their own networks. By the mid-1970s, networks such as BITNET (research and education users), MFENET (U.S. Department of Energy magnetic fusion energy researchers), and SPAN (NASA space physics researchers) began to spring up, often using government funding, though sometimes using private funds.

Networks that sprang up in this era typically relied on disparate networking protocols. That is, each of these networks organized its information differently and so, for the most part, information could not easily move from one of these networks to another. The fundamental principle underlying the Internet, by contrast, is that individual computers and local networks are able to communicate easily regardless of the type of equipment employed. Such a "network of networks" obviously depends on the presence of a single set of communication rules that are followed by every affiliated computer. Two researchers developed such a set of generic rules and made them public in 1973; those rules became what we now know as "TCP/IP"—the Transmission Control Protocol/Internet Protocol.[1] TCP/IP is in many ways the heart of the Internet; the goal of the Internet is connectivity, and the tools used are TCP and IP.[2] In 1974, DARPA contracted with three groups to implement TCP/IP. On January 1, 1983, a milestone event occurred: on that day every host computer on the ARPANET switched to TCP/IP for internetworking.

DARPA was not the only government agency to play a central role in the creation of the Internet. In the mid-1980s, the National Science Foundation (NSF) undertook a major new government-funded networking initiative when it began work on the NSFNET, a "network of networks" intended to serve the higher education community. In 1985, a second milestone event occurred—the NSF decided to adopt TCP/IP for the NSFNET and announced that it would from that point onward work with DARPA to ensure interoperability between the two national networks. The NSF also contracted with IBM, MCI, and Merit Network, Inc. to manage the NSFNET backbone. Some $200 million was spent on developing the NSFNET between 1986 and 1995.

A different federal entity (the National Science and Technology Council) formed the Federal Networking Council to coordinate the various government agencies involved and also to coordinate with international organizations supporting the global Internet. The Federal Networking Council passed a resolution providing a definition of the Internet that has become commonly used:

---

1. *See* V.G. Cerf and R.E. Kahn, A Protocol for Packet Network Interconnection, 22 IEEE Trans. on Comm. 637 (1974). The creators of these protocols were Robert Kahn (then at DARPA) and Vinton Cerf (then at Stanford).
2. *See* Internet Architecture Board, RFC 1958, June 1996, *available at* http://www.faqs.org/rfcs/rfc1958.html; Internet Activities Board, RFC 791, September 1981, *available at* http://www.faqs.org/rfcs/rfc791.html.

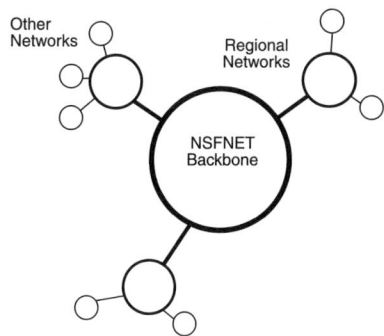

The NSFNET. The NSF helped to build the Internet by providing much of the original backbone infrastructure that connected regional networks into the giant network of networks that would mature into today's Internet. This diagram is based on a figure in Kevin Werbach, Digital Tornado: The Internet and Telecommunications Policy (1997).

"Internet" refers to the global information system that—

(i) is logically linked together by a globally unique address space based on the Internet Protocol (IP) or its subsequent extensions/follow-ons;

(ii) is able to support communications using the Transmission Control Protocol/Internet Protocol (TCP/IP) suite or its subsequent extensions/follow-ons, and/or other IP-compatible protocols; and

(iii) provides, uses or makes accessible, either publicly or privately, high level services layered on the communications and related infrastructure described herein.[3]

§ 12.A.1. Basic Characteristics

The Internet's basic architecture reflects a series of choices made over decades, beginning with the development of a distributed packet switching network. A goal of this architecture, owing to its DARPA roots, was survivability in the case of an attack. A second important feature of the Internet was its reliance on open, nonproprietary protocols. Capturing both points, a working paper for the FCC's Office of Plans and Policy lays out the central features of the Internet this way:

> The fundamental operational characteristics of the Internet are that it is a distributed, interoperable, packet-switched network.
>
> A distributed network has no one central repository of information or control, but is comprised of an interconnected web of "host" computers, each of which can be accessed from virtually any point on the network. Thus, an Internet user can obtain information from a host computer in another state or another country just as easily as obtaining information from across the street, and there is no hierarchy through which the information must flow or be monitored. Routers throughout the network regulate the flow of data at each connection point. (By contrast, in a centralized network, all users would connect to a single location.) The distributed nature of the Internet gives it robust survivability

---

3. FNC Resolution: Defining "Internet" (1995), http://www.nitrd.gov/fnc/Internet_res.html.

characteristics, because there is no one point of failure for the network, but it makes measurement and governance difficult.

An interoperable network uses open protocols so that many different types of networks and facilities can be transparently linked together, and allows multiple services to be provided to different users over the same network. The Internet can run over virtually any type of facility that can transmit data, including copper and fiber optic circuits of telephone companies, coaxial cable of cable companies, and various types of wireless connections. The Internet also interconnects users of thousands of different local and regional networks, using many different types of computers. The interoperability of the Internet is made possible by the TCP/IP protocol, which defines a common structure for Internet data and for the routing of that data through the network.

Distributed Networks. The Internet is not a centralized network (panel a), nor a decentralized network (panel b), but instead a distributed network (panel c). Among other virtues, a distributed network can continue to operate even if a given node on the network fails, and a distributed network can easily route traffic around congested areas, thus increasing speed of service.

A packet-switched network means that data transmitted over the network is split up into small chunks, or "packets." Unlike "circuit-switched" networks such as the public switched telephone network (PSTN), a packet-switched network is "connectionless."[4] In other words, a dedicated end-to-end transmission path (or circuit) does not need to be opened for each transmission.[5] Rather, each router calculates the best routing for a packet at a particular moment in time, given current traffic patterns, and sends the packet to the next router. Thus, even two packets from the same message may not travel the same physical path through

---

4. Some newer technologies, such as Multiprotocol Label Switching (MPLS), allow for the creation of "paths" through the Internet, which allow traffic to follow a defined route through the network. Such technologies are closer to the mode of how circuit switching operates, but they still transmit information in the form of packets.

5. In actuality, much of the PSTN, especially for long distance traffic, uses digital multiplexing to increase transmission capacity. Thus, beyond the truly dedicated connection along the subscriber loop to the local switch, the "circuit" tied up for a voice call is a set of time slices or frequency assignments in multiplexing systems that send multiple calls over the same wires and fiber optic circuits.

the network. When packets arrive at the destination point, they must be reassembled, and packets that do not arrive for whatever reason must generally be re-sent. This system allows network resources to be used more efficiently, as many different communications can be routed simultaneously over the same transmission facilities. On the other hand, the inability of the sending computer to ensure that sufficient bandwidth will be available between the two points creates difficulties for services that require constant transmission rates, such as streaming video and voice applications.[6]

Kevin Werbach, FCC Office of Plans & Policy, OPP Working Paper No. 29, The Digital Tornado (1997), *available at* http://www.fcc.gov/working-papers/digital-tornado-internet-and-telecommunications-policy.

§ 12.A.2. Network Elements

Although the Internet works as a seamless whole no matter the distance between the end user and the service that he or she is trying to access, one can usefully identify different transport functions in the network. Sometimes these different pieces of transport are provided by different companies, which hand off traffic between them, and sometimes they are provided by the same company. The FCC has found it useful to create such a taxonomy because different transport markets may have different competitive characteristics.

Advanced services are provided using a variety of public and private networks that rely on different network architectures and transmission paths. Some of these networks, like the Internet, are public in the sense that access to the network is open to all users. Other networks, like those built and maintained by corporations for their internal use, are private in the sense that access to the network may be restricted to a particular class of users, often the corporation's employees. Moreover, depending on the network, data may travel from the sender to the recipient over various architectures and transmission paths such as copper wire, cable, terrestrial wireless radio spectrum, satellite radio spectrum, or a combination of these and other media. In addition, data may be transmitted using different communications protocols that manage and direct traffic at different layers of a particular network.

Although advanced services are provided over myriad combinations of public and private networks using a variety of transmission paths and protocols, [f]or simplicity, we have divided network infrastructure into four general categories: backbone, middle mile, last mile, and last 100 feet. In addition, we refer to the points of connection between these components of the network as connection points.

In conceptualizing the categories of network infrastructure identified above, we find it helpful to analogize network infrastructure to a system of roads. In our simplified analogy, each of the categories corresponds to a different type of road:

Backbone—Multi-lane Interstate Highway: Backbone provides a long-distance, high-capacity, high-speed transmission path for transporting massive quantities of data, much like the way a large multi-lane interstate highway allows large amounts of traffic quickly to travel long distances. Most backbone

---

6. "Streaming" voice and video applications are those in which the data available to the receiving user is updated as data packets are received, rather than waiting until an entire image or sound file is downloaded to the recipient's computer.

consists of fiber optic lines, either buried in the ground or laid under the sea. In addition, backbone can be provided using satellite systems and radio spectrum.

Middle Mile—Divided Highway: As its name suggests, middle mile facilities provide relatively fast, large-capacity connections between backbone and last mile, similar to the way a divided highway may connect local roads to multi-lane interstate highways. Middle mile facilities can range from a few miles to a few hundred miles. They are often constructed of fiber optic lines, but microwave and satellite links can be used as well.

Last Mile—Local Road: The last mile is the link between the middle mile and the last 100 feet to the end user's terminal. The last mile is analogous to the local road between a larger, divided highway and a traveler's driveway. A last mile with advanced telecommunications capability provides speeds in excess of 200 kbps in each direction. Last miles may consist of cable modem service, digital subscriber line (DSL) service, terrestrial wireless service, or satellite service.

Last 100 Feet—Driveway: The last 100 feet is the link between the last mile and the end user's terminal, which is similar to the way a driveway connects a traveler's home or office to a local road. The last 100 feet includes the in-house wiring found in a consumer's residence, the wiring in an apartment or office building, the more complex wiring in a wireline local area network, or the wireless links in a local wireless network.

Connection Points—Intersections, On-Ramps, and Interchanges: Connection points are the places at which the various components of the network interconnect, often with the aid of an electronic or optical device (e.g., switches and routers between the middle mile and backbone), so that data can move across the network. Connection points are analogous to the intersections, on-ramps, and interchanges between local roads, divided highways, and multi-lane interstate highways.

Deployment of Advanced Telecommunications to all Americans in a Reasonable and Timely Fashion, and Possible Steps to Accelerate Such Deployment Pursuant to Section 706 of the Telecommunications Act of 1996, Second Report, 15 FCC Rcd. 20,913 (2000).

§ 12.A.3. Packet Switching and Addressing

As the excerpts above suggest, in terms of structure the Internet is, in many ways, the antithesis of the PSTN. Indeed, the Internet is sometimes described as the PSTN "turned inside out." The PSTN is a circuit-switched network, which means, in somewhat oversimplified terms, that when you dial a number a pathway is dedicated to that call and remains dedicated to that call until you hang up. Even when no one on the call is speaking, the phone system is still reserving a pathway for the call. The Internet works quite differently. When a request is made by a client computer for a document, the server holding the document responds by sending the requested information across the Internet. No circuit is dedicated to this "call." Instead, the IP protocol breaks the information (whether voice, video, or some other form of data) into "packets," each of which can be thought of as a payload (a small piece of the requested data) and a guidance system (a destination IP address).[7]

---

7. Because no particular route must be used, the Internet is relatively stable to an outage on one part of the network. For example, if one connection in the network goes off line, remaining network traffic will continue to be routed via whatever route is efficient at the time.

More specifically, each packet includes a header that indicates where the data originates and where it is being sent. In order for the packet to arrive, each computer must be given a unique address, analogous to the unique telephone number used to route phone calls to a given phone. TCP/IP solves this problem by defining locations on the Internet through the use of numerical labels known as IP addresses. Fortunately for humans, IP-addressable computers can be represented by alphanumeric domain and host names, which allow Internet addresses to be rendered into more easily recognizable (and memorable) forms such as the ubiquitous "www.EnglishWordHere.com."[8]

The usability of these alphanumeric addresses depends on a system for cross-referencing host names with their associated IP addresses. This translation of host names to the appropriate IP addresses is accomplished via the domain name system (DNS). Thus a user's host computer relies on the domain name system to translate a host name into a numeric address that can be understood by the routers that make the Internet work. The domain name system was initially managed by Jon Postel at UCLA (later at the University of Southern California's Information Sciences Institute) under contract with DARPA, and provided to the networking community by SRI International, also under contract with DARPA. When the ARPANET was phased out, the NSF assumed responsibility for the domain name system and, in 1992, entered into a contract with Network Solutions, Inc., to manage the registration of domain names. In 1992, NSI registered 200 domain names per month; by 1998, this number had reached 120,000 names per month. By 2010, the total number of domain names passed 200 million.

This association of host names with IP addresses highlights a deeper addressing issue: for there to be an "Internet" through which all computers can connect, there must be a generally accepted system that tells computers where they can find a given IP address on the network. At the top of (and in some senses above) the domain name system is a set of "root" servers, each of which lists the IP addresses of the computers containing the authoritative files for each of the top-level domains. This system is central to the smooth operation of the Internet. It, and the domain name system more generally, is considered in greater detail in the next section's discussion of the regulation of the Internet.

§ 12.A.4. Services

The actual services provided to end users through the Internet are not defined by the TCP/IP protocols, but depend instead on higher-level application protocols that enable particular services. These protocols are not embedded in the Internet itself. This means that a new application layer protocol, and the new service that it enables, can be added at any time and without seeking a license to use the Internet protocols or permission of the network operators to provide an application that "rides on the Internet." In short, any application can be operated over the Internet as long as one server computer can transmit data in the proper format and one client computer can receive and interpret the data.

---

8. These names can be broken down into the following components: a "host name," i.e., the name of a specific machine; a "domain name," i.e., the name of a specific local network where the host resides; and a "top-level domain name." Top-level domains mainly fall into two categories: generic top-level domains (e.g., .com, .edu, and .gov), and country code top-level domains (e.g., .uk for the United Kingdom, .de for Germany), which are, as the name suggests, designed to host particular countries' networks.

Prominent examples of these protocols are the hypertext transfer protocol (HTTP), file transfer protocol (FTP), and simple mail transfer protocol (SMTP).

The early Internet pioneers consciously adopted an open architecture that welcomed innovative applications of all kinds. Unlike the circuit-switched telephone network, which is optimized to support voice communications, the Internet is a "dumb" network that can support all sorts of applications—ranging from email to the World Wide Web to streaming video. The lack of intelligence built into the network itself was no accident; it reflected what engineers call an end-to-end design principle; all packets are delivered on a "best efforts" basis and managed at the ends of the network. This feature, however, offers end users no quality assurance that downloaded applications will work effectively. In short, the general ethos of the Internet's original design was to allow a blossoming of ideas and inventions. As a result, the network is service agnostic and is not designed to optimize the provision of even valuable services.

As late as the early 1990s, most Americans were not aware of the Internet (except, perhaps, as a research tool for scientists). For the Internet to explode as a mass medium, the public needed a killer app to adopt this new technology. In 1992, the U.S. Congress turned an important corner by granting the NSF the statutory authority to permit commercial traffic on NFSNET. With the authorization for commercial providers to market Internet-related products and services, the stage was set for the Internet's second killer application (after email): the World Wide Web and the Web browser.

Building on the idea of hypermedia, Tim Berners-Lee created the concept of the World Wide Web in 1989. The Web contains documents, typically with embedded links to various other documents, written in a standard format such as "hypertext markup language" (HTML). HTML is code that describes the structure of a page that a browser can then render as a screen image in the form of a virtual document. The Web browser provides a "smart" interface that can interpret the page for display without any need for the user to know anything about the underlying data structure.

Berners-Lee also wrote the first Internet browser, but it was the creation of a different browser, Mosaic, by Marc Andreessen and Eric Bina in 1992 while at the National Center for Supercomputer Applications (NCSA) in Illinois, that led to the Web we know today. Browsers rely on standard protocols (FTP, NNTP, or HTTP for example) layered on top of TCP/IP to retrieve and display documents. This means that browsers can combine text and graphical material—and can incorporate all of the other major Internet services, ranging from video traffic to music to pictures—into one standard interface. With browsers like Mosaic, however, Web use was limited to relatively sophisticated users running some flavor of the Unix operating system. The Web finally left the computer science world and entered popular culture when several Mosaic developers left the NCSA to start Netscape Communications. Netscape developed a browser that was easily installable on personal computers and (relatively) freely available. The availability of a browser that offered easy use, installation, and access to a world of linked documents provided the killer app to drive the widespread growth of the Internet.

§ 12.A.5. Layers

This hierarchy—of the networks, the protocols that coordinate transmissions on and between the networks, and the applications that the networks enable—has been described as "layering." The notion of layers in a network is not new to the Internet; telecommunications engineers have long utilized the separation of function into distinct layers. What is new is the extent to which a seemingly technical description has penetrated the policy discussion. Because the description has potential policy implications, there is no universally accepted model. The most basic model has four layers: the physical layer, representing the transmission networks; the logical layer, representing the TCP/IP protocol suite; the applications layer, representing all of the services that are offered through and over the Internet; and the content layer, which covers the information (in whatever form accessed by users) made available by the particular application.

What is at stake in all of these discussions is how the various pieces interact with one another. The provision of an Internet service to a consumer is usually a problem of joint production—the consumer uses his or her Internet service to access a service or application provided by another company. The actual delivery of the service will therefore require all of the parties to coordinate with one another. From a regulatory perspective, the existence of market power at one or more of the layers may create the opportunity for a company at one layer to charge monopoly prices or to engage in strategic behavior against other companies. Even apart from issues of market power, the government may be involved in standard-setting that governs the interfaces between the various layers. Chapter Fourteen, in discussing the debate over network neutrality, returns to these themes.

§ 12.B. Initial Principles of Internet Policy

What strategy should the government adopt towards Internet regulation? In the context of the other technologies we have addressed in the book, we have seen examples of laws that do not merely marginally affect a telecommunications technology but instead put the government in the position of squarely regulating some aspect of that technology. Such laws make up the centerpiece of the government's responses to technologies like broadcast, cable, and satellite. To what extent does the government play such a direct role in the regulation of the Internet?

One obvious and often discussed aspect of Internet governance is the management of the addressing system and the government's role (or lack thereof) in overseeing it. As we discussed above, crucial to the existence of the Internet as a single coherent network is a routing system whereby a message from any point on the network can reach its intended destination elsewhere on the network. With some simplification not relevant here, this requires that each computer have an associated IP address, and a mechanism to resolve the address from an alphanumeric name (e.g., www.fcc.gov). When someone sends a message to "fcc.gov," her computer needs to ask a server where to find "fcc.gov," and if servers point in different directions (i.e., to different computers) then some messages will not go to the proper place. The difficulties that would result from such conflicting address systems have been avoided on the Internet because a given server gets its information about where to look for the FCC's IP address from a server above it in the hierarchy, culminating in information at the top from the central root server (known as the "A" root server).

Control of the databases in these servers, and in particular in the "A" root server, is thus in some ways akin to centralized governance. It is not true governance, because users could always direct their computers to servers that look to a different address list; but it would probably take a coordinated defection to topple this hierarchy, and such a defection has never occurred and would be difficult to achieve. Indeed, the U.S. government helps to insure the primacy of the "A" root server by playing a role in the operation of many of the root servers at the next level of the hierarchy. *See* National Telecommunications and Information Administration, Statement of Policy, Management of Internet Names and Addresses, 63 Fed. Reg. 31,741, 31,742 (1998).

The government in this way helps to cement the position of the "A" root server database, but, interestingly, it has abjured direct control over that server. For most of the 1990s, the "A" root server database and the domain name system that rested upon it were maintained by Network Solutions, a private firm. In 1998, the government issued a statement of policy proposing a privatization of the management of Internet names and addresses. The statement articulated four principles: stability, representation, competition, and—where coordination was necessary—"private, bottom-up coordination" (because "a private coordinating process is likely to be more flexible than government and to move rapidly enough to meet the changing needs"). *Id.* at 31,749. The policy statement called for the creation of a private nonprofit corporation that would take over responsibility for allocating the IP address space; that entity would also oversee operation of the root server system and determine whether to add new top-level domains to the root system. *Id.* Shortly thereafter, a nonprofit entity called the Internet Corporation for Assigned Names and Numbers (ICANN) was incorporated, and the government (through the Department of Commerce) signed a memorandum of understanding with ICANN transferring these functions to ICANN.[9]

This arrangement with ICANN has generated quite a bit of controversy in the Internet community, with particularly heated concerns raised about its broad powers and its perceived lack of democratic accountability.[10] Space considerations prevent us from doing justice to these issues in this book, but one point bears emphasizing: the U.S. government chose not to exercise operational control over the root server and domain name system itself, although it retained important contractual rights with ICANN under which it had some ultimate control. It may well be that the government believed that direct governmental control was not a viable option—and that it was correct in so believing—based on, for example, the greater expertise existing outside the government, the increasing internationalization of the Internet, the advantages of decentralized, bottom-up coordination, and so on. The point is simply that, for whatever reason, the government chose not to arrogate this authority to itself. The United States government helped to create the Internet, and it had an opportunity to attempt to manage it, but it refrained from doing so. Indeed, in 2014, the United States announced that it would eliminate the contractual arrangement with ICANN, and ICANN (assuming it adopted governance principles for this activity) would entirely control this activity.

The government's 1998 decision to privatize the management of Internet names and addresses did not come out of the blue. In fact, it flowed from (and was in many senses preordained by) the Clinton Administration's central statement on Internet policy, the Framework for Global Electronic Commerce.

---

9. *See* Memorandum of Understanding Between the U.S. Department of Commerce and Internet Corporation for Assigned Names and Numbers (1998), *available at* http://www.ntia.doc.gov/page/1998/memorandum-understanding-between-us-department-commerce-and-internet-corporation-assigned-.

10. *See, e.g.,* A. Michael Froomkin, Wrong Turn in Cyberspace: Using ICANN to Route Around the APA and the Constitution, 50 Duke L.J. 17 (2000); materials collected by ICANNWatch, www.icannwatch.org. The article by Professor Froomkin also presents a comprehensive background on the domain name system and ICANN.

A Framework for Global Electronic Commerce

http://clinton4.nara.gov/WH/New/Commerce/read.html (1997)

PRINCIPLES

1. The private sector should lead.

Though government played a role in financing the initial development of the Internet, its expansion has been driven primarily by the private sector. For electronic commerce to flourish, the private sector must continue to lead. Innovation, expanded services, broader participation, and lower prices will arise in a market-driven arena, not in an environment that operates as a regulated industry.

Accordingly, governments should encourage industry self-regulation wherever appropriate and support the efforts of private sector organizations to develop mechanisms to facilitate the successful operation of the Internet. Even where collective agreements or standards are necessary, private entities should, where possible, take the lead in organizing them. Where government action or intergovernmental agreements are necessary, on taxation for example, private sector participation should be a formal part of the policy making process.

2. Governments should avoid undue restrictions on electronic commerce.

Parties should be able to enter into legitimate agreements to buy and sell products and services across the Internet with minimal government involvement or intervention. Unnecessary regulation of commercial activities will distort development of the electronic marketplace by decreasing the supply and raising the cost of products and services for consumers the world over. Business models must evolve rapidly to keep pace with the breakneck speed of change in the technology; government attempts to regulate are likely to be outmoded by the time they are finally enacted, especially to the extent such regulations are technology-specific.

Accordingly, governments should refrain from imposing new and unnecessary regulations, bureaucratic procedures, or taxes and tariffs on commercial activities that take place via the Internet.

3. Where governmental involvement is needed, its aim should be to support and enforce a predictable, minimalist, consistent and simple legal environment for commerce.

In some areas, government agreements may prove necessary to facilitate electronic commerce and protect consumers. In these cases, governments should establish a predictable and simple legal environment based on a decentralized, contractual model of law rather than one based on top-down regulation. This may involve states as well as national governments. Where government intervention is necessary to facilitate electronic commerce, its goal should be to ensure competition, protect intellectual property and privacy, prevent fraud, foster transparency, support commercial transactions, and facilitate dispute resolution.

4. Governments should recognize the unique qualities of the Internet.

The genius and explosive success of the Internet can be attributed in part to its decentralized nature and to its tradition of bottom-up governance. These same characteristics pose significant logistical and technological challenges to existing regulatory models, and governments should tailor their policies accordingly.

Electronic commerce faces significant challenges where it intersects with existing regulatory schemes. We should not assume, for example, that the regulatory frameworks established over the past sixty years for telecommunications, radio and television fit the

Internet. Regulation should be imposed only as a necessary means to achieve an important goal on which there is a broad consensus. Existing laws and regulations that may hinder electronic commerce should be reviewed and revised or eliminated to reflect the needs of the new electronic age.

5. *Electronic Commerce over the Internet should be facilitated on a global basis.*

The Internet is emerging as a global marketplace. The legal framework supporting commercial transactions on the Internet should be governed by consistent principles across state, national, and international borders that lead to predictable results regardless of the jurisdiction in which a particular buyer or seller resides.

Notes and Questions

1. Deference to the Private Sector. Do these principles give short shrift to problems with private sector leadership? Do they lean too far toward private leadership? Do they not go far enough?

2. Comparisons to Broadcast, Cable, and Telephone. Are these principles consistent with the government's regulation of broadcast, cable, and telephony? If not, was the government wrong in those other contexts? Further, note the irony: the government played a crucial role in funding and helping to create the Internet, but it says that it will refrain from regulating the Internet. Meanwhile, the government did not create the broadcast spectrum or pay for cable and telephone wire, and the broadcasting, cable, and telephone industries developed with few direct financial contributions from government sources,[11] and yet each of those technologies is heavily regulated. Which approach makes more sense? Could both be right?

3. The Domain Name System. Is this statement of principles consistent with the decision made in 1998 to privatize the system of managing Internet names and addresses? What would be a less regulatory position than the one the government adopted in 1998?

4. Electronic Commerce. The above principles, and in fact the entire document of which they are a part, focus on electronic commerce. Is that an appropriate focus? Would it have been better for the Clinton administration to have focused on how to improve the content available on the Internet?

5. A More International Approach? The principles suggest that "electronic commerce over the Internet should be facilitated on a global basis." In 2011, the Organization for Economic Cooperation and Development (OECD) issued a Communiqué on Principles for Internet Policy-Making. An excerpt of that document is set out below.

COMMUNIQUÉ ON PRINCIPLES FOR INTERNET POLICY-MAKING: OECD HIGH LEVEL MEETING ON THE INTERNET ECONOMY

http://www.oecd.org/dataoecd/40/21/48289796.pdf (2011)

The Internet has grown and diffused extremely rapidly across the globe, and continues to bring significant benefits to economies and societies. Individual innovators, and a co-operative multi-stakeholder environment, have played significant roles in this process.

---

11. There was a major nonmonetary contribution to broadcast, of course, in the granting of spectrum licenses to broadcasters free of explicit fees. *See* Chapter Four.

Enhancing access and participation in the Internet Economy through the deployment of high speed broadband Internet networks can also help in increasing the availability of legitimate content, in addition to supporting the free flow of information and knowledge, the freedom of expression, association and assembly, the protection of individual liberties, as critical components of a democratic society and cultural diversity.

The policy-making principles in this communiqué are designed to help preserve the fundamental openness of the Internet while concomitantly meeting certain public policy objectives, such as the protection of privacy, security, children online, and intellectual property, as well as the reinforcement of trust in the Internet. Effective protection of intellectual property rights plays a vital role in spurring innovation and furthers the development of the Internet economy. Internet policy making principles need to take into account the unique social, technical and economic aspects of the Internet environment. It is clear that the open and accessible nature of the Internet needs to be supported for the benefit of freedom of expression, and to facilitate the legitimate sharing of information, knowledge and exchange of views by users including research and development that has brought about widespread innovation to our economies.

Recognizing the reliance of our economies on the Internet, the global nature of the Internet, and the various approaches implemented to stimulate the Internet economy, including innovative governance strategies in convening diverse groups of stakeholders to forge consensus-based policies, we agreed as governments, private sector stakeholders and civil society to the following basic principles for Internet policy-making:

Promote and protect the global free flow of information:

The Internet economy, as well as individuals' ability to learn, share information and knowledge, express themselves, assemble and form associations, depend on the global free flow of information. To encourage the free flow of information online, it is important to work together to advance better global compatibility across a diverse set of laws and regulations. While promoting the free flow of information, it is also essential for governments to work towards better protection of personal data, children online, consumers, intellectual property rights, and to address cybersecurity. In promoting the free flow of information governments should also respect fundamental rights.

Promote the open, distributed and interconnected nature of the Internet:

As a decentralized network of networks, the Internet has achieved global interconnection without the development of any international regulatory regime. The development of such a formal regulatory regime could risk undermining its growth. The Internet's openness to new devices, applications and services has played an important role in its success in fostering innovation, creativity and economic growth. This openness stems from the continuously evolving interaction and independence among the Internet's various technical components, enabling collaboration and innovation while continuing to operate independently from one another. This independence permits policy and regulatory changes in some components without requiring changes in others or impacting on innovation and collaboration. The Internet's openness also stems from globally accepted, consensus driven technical standards that support global product markets and communications. The roles, openness, and competencies of the global multi-stakeholder institutions that govern standards for different layers of Internet components should be recognized and their contribution should be sought on the different technical elements of public policy objectives. Maintaining technology neutrality and appropriate quality for all Internet services is also important to ensure an open and dynamic Internet environment. Provision of open Internet access services is critical for the Internet economy.

Promote investment and competition in high speed networks and services:

High speed networks and services are essential for future economic growth, job creation, greater competitiveness and for people to enjoy a better life. Public policies should promote robust competition in the provision of high speed broadband Internet that is available to users at affordable prices and promote investment also to attain the greatest geographic coverage of broadband Internet. They should also promote an optimal level of investment by creating demand for high speed broadband networks and services, in particularly in areas where governments play a key role such as in education, health, energy distribution and transport. Public policies should help foster a diversity of content, platforms, applications, online services, and other user communication tools that will create demand for networks and services, as well as to allow users to fully benefit from those networks and services and to access a diversity of content, on non-discriminatory terms, including the cultural and linguistic content of their choice.

Promote and Enable the Cross-Border Delivery of Services:

Suppliers should have the ability to supply services over the Internet on a cross-border and technologically neutral basis in a manner that promotes interoperability of services and technologies, where appropriate. Users should have the ability to access and generate lawful content and run applications of their choice. To ensure cost effectiveness and other efficiencies, other barriers to the location, access and use of cross-border data facilities and functions should be minimized, providing that appropriate data protection and security measures are implemented in a manner consistent with the relevant OECD Guidelines and reflecting the necessary balance among all fundamental rights, freedoms and principles.

Encourage multi-stakeholder co-operation in policy development processes:

The Internet's complexity, global reach, and constant evolution require timely, scalable, and innovation-enabling policies. Due to the rapidly changing technological, economic and social environment within which new policy challenges emerge, multi-stakeholder processes have been shown to provide the flexibility and global scalability required to address Internet policy challenges. These multi-stakeholder processes should involve the participation of all interested stakeholders and occur in a transparent manner. In particular, continued support is needed for the multi-stakeholder environment, which has underpinned the process of Internet governance and the management of critical Internet resources (such as naming and numbering resources) and these various stakeholders should continue to fully play a role in this framework. Governments should also work in multi-stakeholder environments to achieve international public policy goals and strengthen international co-operation in Internet governance.

Notes and Questions

1. Compare and Contrast. How do the OECD policy-making principles compare to those of the 1997 Clinton Administration report? How are they different?

2. The OECD. The OECD, unlike the International Telecommunications Union and the World Trade Organization, is not a treaty-based organization. As such, the principles set out in its Communiqué are a call to action (or inaction, in many cases) for governments around the world. Will a strategy of norm-building—or "soft law," as it is often called—be effective in developing compatible approaches for Internet policy?

3. Multistakeholder Bodies and Governance. The principles set out above focus on the role of multistakeholder institutions. ICANN, discussed above, is one such body. Given the criticisms of ICANN (most notably as not being democratically legitimate), why do you think the OECD embraces such bodies as a tool of governance?

4. The End of Residual U.S. Control. In March 2014, the U.S. Department of Commerce, National Telecommunications & Information Administration (NTIA), announced that it would transition the last of the Internet Domain Name Functions to ICANN within a year, and ICANN began a process of adopting governance principles for this function. Below is an excerpt of the NTIA's reasoning.

NTIA Announces Intent to Transition Key Internet Domain Name Functions

Press Release (March 14, 2014) (available at http://www.ntia.doc.gov/press-release/2014/ntia-announces-intent-transition-key-internet-domain-name-functions)

To support and enhance the multistakeholder model of Internet policymaking and governance, the U.S. Commerce Department's National Telecommunications and Information Administration (NTIA) today announces its intent to transition key Internet domain name functions to the global multistakeholder community. As the first step, NTIA is asking the Internet Corporation for Assigned Names and Numbers (ICANN) to convene global stakeholders to develop a proposal to transition the current role played by NTIA in the coordination of the Internet's domain name system (DNS).

NTIA's responsibility includes the procedural role of administering changes to the authoritative root zone file—the database containing the lists of names and addresses of all top-level domains—as well as serving as the historic steward of the DNS. NTIA currently contracts with ICANN to carry out the Internet Assigned Numbers Authority (IANA) functions and has a Cooperative Agreement with Verisign under which it performs related root zone management functions. Transitioning NTIA out of its role marks the final phase of the privatization of the DNS as outlined by the U.S. Government in 1997.

ICANN is uniquely positioned, as both the current IANA functions contractor and the global coordinator for the DNS, as the appropriate party to convene the multistakeholder process to develop the transition plan. NTIA has informed ICANN that it expects that in the development of the proposal, ICANN will work collaboratively with the directly affected parties, including the Internet Engineering Task Force, the Internet Architecture Board, the Internet Society, the Regional Internet Registries, top level domain name operators, VeriSign, and other interested global stakeholders.

NTIA has communicated to ICANN that the transition proposal must have broad community support and address the following four principles:
- Support and enhance the multistakeholder model;
- Maintain the security, stability, and resiliency of the Internet DNS;
- Meet the needs and expectation of the global customers and partners of the IANA services; and,
- Maintain the openness of the Internet.

Consistent with the clear policy expressed in bipartisan resolutions of the U.S. Senate and House of Representatives (S.Con.Res.50 and H.Con.Res.127), which affirmed the United States support for the multistakeholder model of Internet governance, NTIA will not accept a proposal that replaces the NTIA role with a government-led or an inter-governmental organization solution.

From the inception of ICANN, the U.S. Government and Internet stakeholders envisioned that the U.S. role in the IANA functions would be temporary. The Commerce Department's June 10, 1998 Statement of Policy stated that the U.S. Government "is committed to a transition that will allow the private sector to take leadership for DNS management." http://www.ntia.doc.gov/files/ntia/publications/6_5_98dns.pdf. ICANN as an organization has matured and taken steps in recent years to improve its accountability and transparency and its technical competence. At the same time, international support continues to grow for the multistakeholder model of Internet governance as evidenced by the continued success of the Internet Governance Forum and the resilient stewardship of the various Internet institutions.

While stakeholders work through the ICANN-convened process to develop a transition proposal, NTIA's current role will remain unchanged.

Notes and Questions

1. The Broader Context. The NTIA's announcement was made while the United States was receiving substantial international criticism in reaction to the disclosure of electronic surveillance techniques by former National Security Agency contractor Edward Snowden. Predictably, several other countries pointed to this as reason for the United States to have no role in the Internet. In the United States, the NTIA announcement was greeted with congressional hearings and protests that ICANN's processes allow too much influence by foreign governments.

2. Process versus Performance. Much of the debate about and within ICANN is about the structure of its processes — how much weight to give to governments, how to resolve disputes among stakeholders, who counts as a stakeholder? Are there any obvious metrics by which to measure whether certain of the processes are "better," or does it come down to ideological predisposition? Alternatively, are there any performance metrics for the Internet that would reveal whether process changes improved matters or not?

3. Internet Openness and Nation States. How can ICANN, the United States, or any other body ensure the openness of the Internet, which is one of the criteria on which the NTIA says that it will judge the ICANN transition? We still live in a world of sovereigns, and many of those sovereigns have not committed to provide an open Internet within their own borders, much less permit international content to flow freely to their citizens. *See, e.g.*, Jack Goldsmith & Tim Wu, Who Controls the Internet?: Illusions of a Borderless World (2008). Nor is there an international regime, similar to the World Trade Organization, to which complaints may be brought. Some have proposed that the International Telecommunications Union (ITU), an arm of the United Nations, play a role in Internet governance, as it has played a role in coordinating spectrum uses and policies. The ITU, however, is a government-centric organization, which has given others pause over empowering it to regulate the Internet. *See, e.g.*, Joe Waz & Phil Weiser, Internet Governance: The Role of Multistakeholder Organizations, 10 J. Telecom & High Tech. L. 331 (2012).

Chapter Thirteen

Universal Service: From Telephony to Broadband

The first section of the Communications Act of 1934 declares the purpose to be "to make available, so far as possible, to all the people of the United States, ... a rapid, efficient, Nation-wide, and world-wide wire and radio communication service with adequate facilities at reasonable charges." 47 U.S.C. § 151. In this chapter, we examine how regulation has been used to ensure universal service of telecommunications, and how the specific techniques have changed over time. Assuming that universal service is good policy (on which there has been occasional debate), one must ask what particular services should be covered by the guarantee and how any such program should be funded. The chapter discusses both questions through the evolution of universal service policy into the broadband age. As to the first, the FCC has had to specifically determine whether to commit to broadband universal service. As to the second, the evolution to competition in telecommunications markets has, since the Bell Divestiture, required an evolving set of strategies to raise the necessary universal service funds. At the end of the chapter, we note the IP transition—the predicted retirement of the PSTN in total—and note the FCC's tentative moves to reconsider some of the fundamental values of communications policy.

§ 13.A. Origins of Universal Service Policy

Universal service has been something of a catch-all phrase in telecommunications regulation, lumping together a variety of regulatory programs, each designed to manipulate prices in a way that furthers some public policy goal. Universal service was easy to implement back when Bell ran a unified national phone system. After all, at that time, the prices charged for any one service did not necessarily have to reflect the costs of providing that service. The only constraint was that the integrated provider needed to make a profit overall. An integrated provider could therefore be told to price its services such that some were priced artificially low as compared to their actual costs whereas others were priced artificially high. The latter would in essence "cross-subsidize" the former.

Regulators took advantage of this easy price manipulation and over time built into the telephone system a large number of implicit cross-subsidies. For instance, business users subsidized the costs of residential service. Bell charged business customers higher rates than it charged residential customers for the same services, and those extra profits in the business sector were used to keep prices low for residential customers. Thus, in a neighborhood in which two identical structures sat side by side, each containing one telephone and one telephone line, if the only difference between them was that one was a barbershop and the other was a residence, the barbershop would still have paid a higher monthly fee. Note that this cross-subsidy takes the form of charging different prices for services with identical costs.

To take another example, urban customers subsidized rural ones. In general, the per customer cost of providing telephone service decreases as population density increases. More people can be served by one switch, and the phone lines from the residences to the switch need not be so long. Nevertheless, policymakers thought it good policy to set monthly subscriber fees such that they were generally equal regardless of whether the area was densely or sparsely populated. This served to overcharge urban customers and undercharge rural ones. Note that, unlike the cross-subsidy for residential over business services, this cross-subsidy involved charging identical prices for services that had very different costs.

A third example involves the use of long distance rates to subsidize local service. The Communications Act of 1934 vested jurisdiction over interstate rates in the FCC but left intrastate telephone rates to state regulation. This required federal and state regulators to decide jointly which parts of the telephone system to allocate to interstate and which parts to intrastate service. This process of "separations and settlements" gave government officials a great deal of discretion because many costs (for example, the basic connection of a home to the network) were not obviously allocable to either service exclusively. In order to keep residential rates low—presumably so that more low income consumers would join the network—in the early days there was strong policy support for erring on the side of allocating costs to the interstate system. This artificially raised long distance rates but correspondingly lowered the rates charged for basic telephone service.

Universal service was thus something of a jumble. It was mostly implemented implicitly through the rate approval process, and it came into being in part because it was so easy to do when there was a single, unified telephone service provider. As we will discuss below, universal service became much more complicated as competition began to take hold in certain markets.

Notes and Questions

1. Other Cross-Subsidies. While the cross-subsidies outlined in the text were the ones with the strongest political appeal, a variety of other implicit cross-subsidies have long been built into telephone rates. For example, long distance calls tend to be more costly the longer they travel and the longer they last because, in both cases, more system capacity is occupied by the call. Rates were and are set on both of these bases. But, time and distance being equal, frequency of infrastructure use also affects the cost of a call. If the line from, say, St. Louis to Chicago is used more frequently than another line of about the same length (say, Quincy, Illinois, to South Bend, Indiana) then the cost per call on the heavily used route is lower. Due to a policy of "nationwide rate averaging" in effect throughout the early history of telephone regulation, these cost differences were not reflected in long distance prices and, hence, St. Louis/Chicago callers subsidized their Quincy/South Bend peers.

2. An Explicit Tax Alternative. Why was the desire to subsidize certain services by raising the rates on other services a good reason to favor an integrated telephone service provider?

Couldn't these same policies have been achieved in a world with multiple carriers simply by implementing a targeted system of telecommunications taxes? Suppose, for example, that it is good policy to have business users subsidize residential ones. Why not just impose a tax on all business telephone service, no matter which firm provides it, and then use that money to subsidize the purchase of residential service? Phrased another way, are there reasons why an implicit subsidy scheme (the cross-subsidies) would be more desirable than an explicit equivalent (taxation)? Is it because implicit subsidies are somehow easier for politicians to slip into legislation? Does that mean that the subsidies serve special interests? But what do you make of the fact that the implicit subsidy scheme hurt constituencies like business and urban users but helped constituencies like residential and rural users? Should cross-subsidies be understood as a means by which elected officials pandered to powerful special interests?

3. Entry Problems. Think ahead to the development of competition in telecommunications markets, to which we will turn shortly. How do these implicit cross-subsidies affect entry? Which markets will competitors seek to enter? What is the effect on the incumbent if new companies engage in selective entry? Should the incumbent be able to resist that selective entry? How could the system be reformed to meet both universal service and competition goals?

§ 13.B. Equity and Efficiency in Subsidizing Universal Service: Ramsey Pricing versus Distributional Policy

Universal service policies distort prices: they keep some prices artificially high in order to keep other prices artificially low. This raises the concern that universal service policies cause firms and individuals to make inefficient decisions—consuming too much of the goods priced below cost while consuming too little of the goods priced above cost. For example, if long distance rates overstate the actual costs of providing long distance service, consumers will see those higher rates and react by making fewer long distance calls. Conversely, if residential rates are subsidized by business rates, residential users will underestimate the burden their calls impose on the telephone network and thus residential users will make inefficiently many calls. Equity and efficiency are thus in tension when it comes to setting prices in the telephone system; policies that manipulate rates on pure policy grounds often inadvertently lead to inefficient use of the telephone network.

The tension between equity and efficiency is actually a much broader problem in the telephone network. To see why, consider the following simple example.

Suppose that, in order to offer two services—say, local service and long distance service—a telephone company must incur a significant fixed cost of $20,000. This figure represents the costs of laying the necessary telephone lines, purchasing and deploying routers, and so on. Suppose, further, that having made that initial infrastructure investment, the firm can offer local service to its customers at a cost of $20 per month and long distance service at a cost of $25 per month. What price should the firm set for these two services in a purely efficiency-driven world?

Our initial inclination might be to suggest marginal cost, in this case $20 for local service and $25 for long distance service. Were that feasible, that would of course be the right answer. By charging marginal cost, the firm would ensure that every consumer who values either service above its cost would buy that service, and, conversely, the firm would also ensure that service would be denied to any consumer for whom the benefits did not exceed the costs. This would be efficient, but, again, this is not practical. Marginal cost pricing would not allow the firm to in any way recoup its upfront fixed cost investment of $20,000.

It is clear, then, that the prices of one or both of these services must be set above the level of marginal cost. But by how much? One possibility would be to price local service at its marginal cost ($20) but raise the price of long distance until the revenues there covered both long distance costs and the fixed cost investment. Another possibility would be to price long distance at its marginal cost ($25) but raise the price of local service until those revenues covered both the costs of local service and the fixed cost investment. But there are an infinite number of other possibilities between these two extremes, and the puzzle here is to identify the most efficient choice.

British economist and mathematician Frank Ramsey considered this sort of problem back in 1927.[1] Ramsey found that the best approach is to raise the prices of both products such that each experiences the same percent reduction in demand. In other words, if marginal cost pricing would have led 4,000 consumers to purchase local service and 5,000 consumers to purchase long distance service, then the most efficient prices that nevertheless allow the firm to recoup its fixed cost investment will result in the same 4:5 ratio in the consumption of the two goods. So, if the firm found that it could recover its fixed costs by raising prices such that, in the end, 3,600 people purchased local service and 4,500 purchased long distance, we would know that it had raised prices in the most efficient way possible because the ratio of the quantities demanded is the same before and after the price increase.

The intuition here is as follows. Marginal cost pricing would be the most efficient option were it plausible but, because of the fixed cost expenditure, it is not. We thus have to raise prices and, in turn, reduce consumption. Ramsey pricing suggests that, in raising prices, we should at least maintain the desirable relative output level as between the two services. That is, if a 4:5 ratio was the ratio of local service demanded versus long distance service demanded under marginal cost pricing, the 4:5 ratio is still the best outcome in a world where prices must exceed marginal cost. The absolute levels of demand unavoidably must change; given that, the best option is to at a minimum avoid skewing the relative consumption levels.

Ramsey's insight has an important policy implication, one that significantly sharpens the tension between equity and efficiency in this setting: under Ramsey pricing, price is raised more for the product that has the less "elastic" demand. Elasticity measures how sensitive consumers are to price. It is defined to be the percent change in quantity demanded that results from a 1 percent change in price. The more elastic the demand, the more output changes for a given price change. What this means is that, because Ramsey pricing requires that both services experience the same percent decrease in quantity demanded, the most efficient price pair will raise the price more on the good for which consumers are less sensitive to price. If consumers have a strong desire for local telephone service no matter what its price, but are more sensitive to price when it comes to long distance calling, Ramsey pricing would suggest that the fixed costs of the telephone system be recovered mainly by increasing the price of local phone service. Long distance prices should stay near marginal cost—at least according to Ramsey's theory.

---

1. Frank Ramsey, A Contribution to the Theory of Taxation, 37 Econ. J. 47 (1927). An accessible and helpful explanation of Ramsey pricing can be found in Kenneth Train, Optimal Regulation 117–40 (1991).

On other policy grounds, of course, this outcome is distinctly unappealing. Indeed, it runs in the exact opposite direction of the relevant universal service subsidy. Remember, universal service keeps local service inexpensive by raising the price of long distance service. Hence, efficiency and equity really are in sharp tension in the telephone setting. Not only do universal service cross-subsidies cause inefficient overuse and underuse of particular telephone services, but more broadly, universal service policies tend to push prices in one direction whereas efficiency concerns would move them in the exact opposite direction.

This sort of tension between efficiency and public policy is not unique to telephone pricing: Ramsey pricing is often unattractive on policy grounds. For example, demand for clean drinking water is not very sensitive to price, yet it is unlikely that policymakers would be willing to raise the costs of drinking water as a way to fund the sewage and water treatment infrastructure. Similarly, people without cars likely have relatively inelastic demand for public transportation, yet few policymakers would be willing to pay for highway maintenance by raising the prices charged for public transportation. The question here is whether local phone service is so like drinking water (and public transportation) that equity concerns should trump Ramsey's efficiency-based logic.

Notes and Questions

1. How Broad a Principle? Above we consider increasing the prices of various telephone services as a way of paying for the telephone infrastructure. But would anything change if, instead of trying to pay for the telephone infrastructure, we were trying to pay for something completely unrelated to telephone service? Suppose, for instance, that a local politician wants to subsidize school lunches and has decided to do so by taxing telephone usage. Does Ramsey pricing tell us anything about how that tax should be collected, or is Ramsey irrelevant because school lunches are not logically related to telephone service?

2. Cross-Subsidies and Ramsey. How would Ramsey suggest that policymakers resolve the tension between universal service policies on the one hand, and economic efficiency on the other? Can equity and efficiency goals both be satisfied simultaneously? Can the tension at least be mitigated?

3. Test Your Understanding. In order to raise money for new computers, the law school dean has decided to increase the prices charged for law textbooks at the bookstore, food at the law school cafeteria, and candy at a vending machine located in the law school basement. What do the economics behind Ramsey pricing suggest about which of these prices should be increased most significantly? Should the dean instead just charge for computer access?

4. Paying the Fixed Costs. We could avoid the difficult tradeoffs inherent in Ramsey pricing by having the government pay the fixed costs of telephone service. Would this be a better approach? If the fixed costs were paid in this manner, would there still be an argument in favor of cross-subsidies in telephone pricing? Would those cross-subsidies still raise efficiency concerns?

§ 13.C. Universal Service After Divestiture

It was only in the decade before the MFJ (discussed in Chapter Six) that universal service policies received explicit and systematic attention from federal regulators. Before then, universal service was a catch-all, referring rather vaguely to the wide array of cross-subsidies and policy goals surveyed above. In 1970, however—just before the final antitrust prosecution of the Bell System began—the Commission made universal service more explicit by implementing the so-called "Ozark Plan" for federal universal service support. Prescriptions of Procedures for Separating and Allocating Plant Investment, Operating Expenses, Taxes and Reserve Between the Intrastate and Interstate Operations of Telephone Companies, Report and Order, 26 F.C.C. 2d 247 (1970).

The Ozark Plan disproportionately allocated the fixed costs of the local telephone network to long distance traffic. In particular, for every 1 percent of traffic consisting of long distance calls, the plan required that 3.3 percent of local network costs be covered through long distance prices. So, if there were 1000 total calls on a network, 900 of which were local and 100 of which were long distance, the costs of the network would be recovered 33 percent through long distance rates and only 67 percent through local rates. It was in this way that the Ozark Plan expressly subsidized local rates; the Plan was implemented in 1971 and, by 1980, long distance calls paid for approximately 25 percent of the common local line infrastructure even though those calls made up only 8 percent of traffic on the local networks. *See* Peter W. Huber, et al., Federal Telecommunications Law 133 (2d ed. 1999).

One might have thought that this highly disproportionate rate structure would have led to court challenge, but it did not. Bell, after all, was providing both local and long distance service at this time, and so (as we have pointed out before) it did not much matter whether money was coming into its left pocket or its right pocket. Further, Bell might have thought that these sorts of cross-subsidies would, as a political matter, protect it from antitrust challenge. After all, just as having a single integrated telephone service provider made it easy for Bell to engage in the sorts of cross-subsidization challenged in the antitrust litigation, having a single integrated telephone service provider made these sorts of policy-motivated cross-subsidies easy to accomplish as well.

The 1984 breakup required the Commission to revisit its universal service policies, however, because long distance and local rates would no longer be paid to the same firm. In the post-divestiture world, raising the price on long distance service to subsidize local service would not work without a mechanism by which AT&T and the other long distance carriers could be forced to transfer funds to the Bell Operating Companies and other local exchange carriers. At the same time, and in obvious tension with the Ozark Plan, the Commission during this period was ready to reduce long distance rates and allocate costs more accurately, the policy motivation being that the exaggerated long distance rates were causing inefficient underutilization of long distance service.

The Commission's post-divestiture universal service plan thus had two parts. The first was to create "access charges" paid by long distance companies to local carriers for originating and terminating long distance calls. *See* MTS and WATS Market Structure, Phase I, Third Report and Order, 93 F.C.C. 2d 241 (1983). The second was to allocate more of the fixed costs of the local network to local rates through a subscriber line charge (SLC) that would be paid by local phone service customers. The original plan was to peg the SLC at a fixed $6 per month, which would be offset by an immediate decrease in long distance rates of five to ten cents a minute. However, in the face of virulent opposition from Congress, consumer advocates, and state regulators—all of whom liked the idea of keeping local rates low and who either did not factor long distance spending into their assessment of consumer welfare or did not believe long distance prices would actually fall—the FCC backed off. In the end, the Commission left the $6 SLC in place only for business users and capped the residential SLC at $3.50 per month. The FCC did not alter those charges until 2000, when it raised the residential SLC to $4.35 with conditional provision for increases up to $6.50 over the following three years. Access Charge Reform, Sixth Report and Order, 15 FCC Rcd. 12,962 (2000).

The important post-divestiture changes in universal service policies were thus (1) the shifting of a greater proportion of the costs of local service onto the charges for those services through the creation of the subscriber line charge; and (2) the creation of interstate access charges through which revenues from interexchange service could be transferred to local exchange carriers. Both changes faced controversy. Controversy surrounding the former is discussed above; as for the latter, long distance companies claimed that access charges were significantly in excess of the local exchange companies' costs of originating and terminating traffic, thereby improperly inflating the local companies' profits while raising long distance prices for consumers. Access charge reform thus became an important policy issue—one that would ultimately take center stage in the Telecommunications Act of 1996.

§ 13.D. Universal Service After the 1996 Act

The 1996 Act addressed universal service within its general purpose of introducing competition into all communications markets, most notably the local exchange markets that had been left as monopolies after divestiture. The implicit cross-subsidies that became difficult after divestiture in 1984 became even more so as the potential for multiple local carriers was introduced in 1996. The central provision of the Act, 47 U.S.C. § 254, maintained a commitment to universal service but made two substantial changes to the status quo. The first was to broaden the definition of services that might be supported under a universal service regime both to include additional providers and to include advanced telecommunications services, a topic we will turn to later in this chapter. The second was to require that universal service support mechanisms be made explicit. As the Fifth Circuit said in a case reviewing important FCC first steps to implement § 254: "To attain the goal of local competition while preserving universal service, Congress directed the FCC to replace the patchwork of explicit and implicit subsidies with 'specific, predictable and sufficient Federal and State mechanisms to preserve and advance universal service.' 47 U.S.C. § 254(b)(5)." Texas Office of Publi Utilities Counsel v. FCC, 183 F.3d 393, 406 (5th Cir. 1999). Similarly, § 254(e) provides that any universal service support received by a carrier "should be explicit and sufficient to achieve the purposes of this section." 47 U.S.C. § 254(e).[2]

Universal service and access charge reform instituted after the Bell break up are therefore interrelated, and § 254 refers to such fees at several points. Access charges overcompensated the LECs, the idea being that the charges not only should cover the real expenses associated with origination and termination but also should represent a contribution by the IXCs to the universal service infrastructure provided by the LECs. In short, above-cost access charges funded some of the costs of the local exchange and thereby offset the costs of LEC universal service obligations.

---

2. The courts, however, have given the FCC significant leeway in implementing the "goal" of explicit support mechanisms, saying that "there is no timetable on *realization* of the reform." Competitive Telecomm. Ass'n v. FCC, 309 F.3d 8, 15 (D.C. Cir. 2002).

§ 13.D.1. Access Charge Reform

In 1997, the FCC began the process of changing the regulation of access charges. Access Charge Reform, First Report and Order, 12 FCC Rcd. 15,982 (1997). The FCC noted that the "patchwork of implicit and explicit subsidies [inherent in the traditional system] generates inefficient and undesirable economic behavior." *Id.* ¶ 30. For example, the access charge regime results in significantly higher long-distance rates, distorting demand, and may even induce some customers to bypass traditional telephone carriers, even if those carriers were the most efficient. *Id.* The FCC took important steps to implement the 1996 Act's new requirements, adopting rules that would take implicit subsidies out of access charges and, eventually, move access charges to competitive rates. *Id.* Litigation over the details of this transition were substantial, and eventually the FCC sought a more comprehensive solution.

In May 2000, the FCC adopted a combined access charge reform and universal service proposal filed by the Coalition for Affordable Local and Long Distance Service (CALLS). *See* Access Charge Reform, Report and Order, 15 FCC Rcd. 12,962 (2000). The coalition consisted of AT&T, Bell Atlantic, BellSouth, GTE, SBC, and Sprint. The principal goals of the CALLS proposal were to (1) reduce access charges and thereby reduce long distance calling rates; (2) require local exchange companies to recover more of the universal service subsidy directly from end users rather than indirectly through charges imposed on long distance calling; and (3) make the universal service subsidy previously received implicitly through interstate access charges explicit and "portable" to different local carriers. The proposal, which is highly technical and covers many issues, also established price cap reductions aimed at reaching target rates within five years for a variety of services and network elements.

Notably, in adopting CALLS, the FCC agreed to do something it refused to do in the First Report and Order on access charge reform: it agreed to gradually raise the subscriber line charge (SLC) on primary lines above the longtime level of $3.50. Because telephone network costs are substantial while variable costs are low (*see* Chapter One), an efficient pricing system could include a substantial fixed fee for simply having a connection to the network. But such a pricing structure is politically controversial because then customers who make few calls may still be required to pay a (significant?) monthly fee simply to remain connected.

The Commission's universal service and access charge reforms were subject to continued judicial review. The most important challenge came in Texas Office of Public Utilities Counsel v. FCC, 265 F.3d 313 (5th Cir. 2001), a broad assault on the CALLS order. There, the court found that two important elements of the plan lacked a rational basis. The first was the Commission's plan to create a temporary $650 million universal service fund that was designed to subsidize poor and rural end users until more permanent access charge reform was complete. The court held that the Commission had "failed to exercise sufficiently independent judgment" in setting the fund size (i.e., it was too influenced by the proposals in the record) and thus remanded to the FCC for further explanation. *See id.* at 327–28. The second element rejected by the court was the Commission's plan to use a so-called X-factor to gradually lower telephone rates. X-factors had traditionally been used in this setting as a way of adjusting telephone rates for the increases in productivity that are expected to occur over time. In CALLS, however, the X-factor was not linked to expected productivity improvements; it was instead just a built-in gradual rate adjustment, unconnected to any particular real world phenomenon. This the court would not accept, on grounds that the Commission could use such an argument to support any X-factor it chose. *See id.* at 328–29. As discussed immediately below, the FCC moved towards a more comprehensive solution to the issue of carriers charging each other for the completion of calls.

§ 13.D.2. Intercarrier Compensation Reform

The Commission decided to wrap the issue of access charge reform together with other issues of carrier-to-carrier compensation (e.g., reciprocal compensation payments between local carriers), under the more general heading of "intercarrier compensation" reform, in order to achieve a comprehensive solution (one that also takes account of changing universal service goals). In February 2011, the Commission released a Notice of Proposed Rulemaking designed to address both universal service and intercarrier compensation, promising fast action. Connect America Fund, Notice of Proposed Rulemaking and Further Notice of Proposed Rulemaking, 26 FCC Rcd. 4554 (2011). And the Commission did act quickly, issuing a comprehensive order in November that same year. Connect America Fund, Report and Order and Further Notice of Proposed Rulemaking, 26 FCC Rcd. 17,663 (2011). This order addressed both issues of intercarrier compensation and of universal service. On appeal, the Tenth Circuit issued two opinions, one on the intercarrier compensation issues and one on the universal service issues—both affirming the FCC's action. We excerpt here the Tenth Circuit's decision on the intercarrier compensation parts of the order.

IN RE FCC 11-161
753 F.3d 1015 (10th Cir. 2014)

Opinion for the court filed by Circuit Judge BACHARACH, in which BRISCOE, Chief Judge, and HOLMES, Circuit Judge, concur.

BACHARACH, Circuit Judge:

Issues Involving Intercarrier Compensation

Exercising its rulemaking authority under the Communications Act of 1934 and the Telecommunications Act of 1996, the FCC overhauled the intercarrier compensation regime and adopted a "uniform national bill-and-keep framework ... for all telecommunications traffic exchanged with a [local exchange carrier]." Connect America Fund, Report and Order and Further Notice of Proposed Rulemaking, 26 FCC Rcd. 17,663, ¶ 34 (2011) (Order). To ease the transition to a new regime of bill-and-keep, the FCC also adopted a comprehensive plan to phase out the old intercarrier compensation system. The Petitioners challenge the plan on grounds that it exceeded the FCC's authority, was arbitrary and capricious, and resulted in a denial of due process. These challenges are rejected.

I. The FCC's Restructuring of the Telecommunications Market

A. The Old Regime

The FCC adopted the plan against the backdrop of two types of arrangements. One provided reciprocal compensation for local calls, and the other involved charges for long-distance carriers to connect to a local carrier's network. In the Order, the FCC revamped this regime, exercising authority over all traffic exchanged with a local exchange carrier (LEC), including intrastate calls.

Before 1996, regulation of telecommunications was generally divided between the FCC and state commissions. The FCC regulated interstate service, and state commissions regulated intrastate service. Under this division of authority, states granted exclusive franchises to LECs within their designated service areas. Through these franchises, the LECs owned the local telecommunications networks.

In 1996, Congress set out to restructure the market to enhance competition. These efforts led to enactment of the Telecommunications Act of 1996. In this statute, Congress empowered the FCC and created a new breed of competitors (called Competitive LECs or CLECs).

Under the new statute, all LECs would assume certain duties. One of these duties involved the establishment of arrangements for "reciprocal compensation" in the "transport and termination of telecommunications." 47 U.S.C. §251(b)(5). This statutory duty includes two key terms underlying the present litigation: "reciprocal compensation" and "telecommunications." In the Order, the FCC recently interpreted these terms to cover all traffic, including intrastate service and use of local networks by long-distance carriers.

This interpretation reflects a departure from the FCC's previous reading of the 1996 Act. In the past, for example, the FCC had narrowly read the phrase "reciprocal compensation" as limited to local traffic. *See* Bell Atlantic Telephone Companies v. FCC, 206 F.3d 1, 4 (D.C. Cir. 2000). Under the FCC's previous interpretation, the parties or state commissions set the charges for intrastate traffic between two LECs.

The charges were called "access charges" because long-distance carriers (called IXCs) paid LECs for the opportunity to use their networks at the start- and end-points of the calls. This system is known as "exchange access." 47 U.S.C. §153(20).

In exchange access, long-distance calls start (or "originate") on an LEC's network, continue on the IXC's network to another local telephone exchange, and end (or "terminate") on the network of another LEC.

The three different combinations led to three different types of access charges, each with its own mode of regulation:

- Interstate IXC–LEC Traffic: For this kind of traffic, the IXC paid an access charge to the originating LEC and a terminating interstate access charge to the terminating LEC. The access charges were regulated by the FCC.
- Intrastate IXC–LEC Traffic: For traffic within a single state by an IXC and LEC, the IXC paid an access charge to the originating LEC and an access charge to the terminating LEC. The access charge was governed by state law and was typically set above interstate rates.
- Local LEC–LEC Traffic: For local traffic between two LECs, the LECs paid each other consistently with their reciprocal compensation arrangement. The arrangement was either negotiated by the parties or set by the states using a methodology prescribed by the FCC under 47 §§201(b) and 251(b)(5).

Each arrangement assumed that the calling party should pay for the call. This assumption was based on the view that the callers were the only persons that benefited from the call and that they should bear all of the costs. Thus, callers paid their own carriers, which in turn paid other carriers for access to their networks to reach the person being called.

B. The New Regime

In the Order, the FCC restructured this system in three ways. First, the FCC reinterpreted the 1996 law to cover all traffic, including traffic subject to charges for access to a network. Second, the FCC claimed that it could prevent state commissions from approving access charges for intrastate calls in the absence of an agreement between the parties. Third, the FCC rejected the idea that a caller should bear the full cost of the call; thus, the FCC prescribed a new system, known as "bill-and-keep," for all traffic.

"Bill-and-keep" anticipates that carriers will recover their costs from their end-user customers rather than from other carriers. In moving to "bill-and-keep," the FCC reasoned that the parties to a call should split the costs because both enjoy the benefits. Once bill-and-keep is fully implemented for all traffic exchanged with an LEC, the calling party and the called party will divide the costs.

C. *The Transition from the Old Regime to the New Regime*

Recognizing that the change would disrupt the market, the FCC opted to gradually transition to bill-and-keep. In the transition period, incumbent LECs (ILECs) could recover some, but not all, of their lost intercarrier compensation revenue through the FCC's funding mechanisms.

D. *The Types of Challenges*

The Petitioners challenge four aspects of the reforms: (1) implementation of bill-and-keep for all traffic; (2) limitations on funding mechanisms during the transitional period; (3) irregularities in the rule-making process; and (4) application of the reforms to particular circumstances. We reject all of the challenges.

II. *Challenges to the FCC's Authority to Implement a National Bill–and–Keep Framework for All Traffic*

In the Order, the FCC concluded that 47 U.S.C. § 251(b)(5) applied to all telecommunications traffic exchanged with an LEC. Based on this conclusion, the FCC prescribed bill-and-keep as the default methodology for that traffic. The Petitioners challenge not only the FCC's authority to regulate the traffic, but also the way in which the FCC chose to exercise this authority. Thus, we must address both challenges: the FCC's authority and the content of the new regulations.

The FCC claims authority under 47 U.S.C. §§ 251(b)(5) and 201(b) to implement bill-and-keep as the default intercarrier compensation framework for all traffic exchanged with an LEC. For traffic between LECs and wireless providers, the FCC also invokes authority under 47 U.S.C. § 332. And for interstate traffic, the FCC relies on 47 U.S.C. § 201.

A. *Standard of Review*

Congress has unambiguously authorized the FCC to administer the Communications Act through rulemaking and adjudication. Thus, we apply *Chevron* deference to the FCC's interpretation of the statute and its own authority. *Chevron* involves a two-step inquiry. Chevron U.S.A., Inc. v. Natural Res. Def. Council, Inc., 467 U.S. 837, 842–43 (1984).

In the first step, we ask whether Congress has spoken on the issue. When the statute is unambiguous, we look no further. "[I]f the statute is silent or ambiguous with respect to the specific issue," we must decide "whether the agency's answer is based on a permissible construction of the statute." *Chevron*, 467 U.S. at 843.

B. *The FCC's Authority Over Access Charges on All Traffic*

The FCC interprets 47 U.S.C. § 201(b) and § 251(b)(5) to apply to all traffic, including access given to long-distance carriers, intrastate traffic, and origination. This interpretation is reasonable.

1. *Traffic Between LECs and Long–Distance Carriers*

In adopting the new regulations, the FCC concluded that it had jurisdiction over all traffic between LECs and long-distance carriers.

a. *The FCC's Rationale*

This interpretation flows in part from the language in § 251(b)(5). This section provides that each LEC must "establish reciprocal compensation arrangements for the transport and termination of telecommunications." 47 U.S.C. § 251(b)(5). The term "telecommunications" is defined in the statute and "encompasses communications traffic of any geographic scope ... or regulatory classification." 47 U.S.C. § 153(50). Because the term is untethered to geographic or regulatory limits, the FCC regards its authority under § 251(b)(5) to cover all traffic regardless of geography or regulatory classification. In addition, the FCC relies on 47 U.S.C. § 201(b), which authorizes the adoption of regulations as necessary to carry out §§ 251 and 252.

Based on the broad definition of "telecommunications" and the text of § 201, the FCC recently concluded that § 251(b)(5) covers all traffic between IXCs and LECs. In doing so, the FCC recognized that it had changed its interpretation of § 251(b)(5). But the FCC reasoned that its earlier reading of the law had been "inconsistent" with the text.

c. Traffic Between LECs and IXCs as "Reciprocal Compensation"

The FCC broadly interprets the phrase "reciprocal compensation" to encompass any intercarrier compensation agreements between carriers. The Petitioners raise two challenges to this conclusion under the first step of *Chevron*: (1) Congress used the term "reciprocal compensation" as a technical term of art to denote local traffic between two LECs; and (2) the plain meaning of "reciprocal compensation" cannot include traffic between IXCs and LECs because the payments go only one way (to the LECs).

i. "Reciprocal Compensation" as a Term of Art

Under step one of *Chevron*, we start with the statutory text to determine whether the phrase "reciprocal compensation" is a term of art. At this step, we give technical terms of art their established meaning absent a contrary indication in the statute.

The Petitioners rely on two pieces of evidence: (1) an FCC website description of the term "reciprocal compensation," which limited its application to local calls; and (2) accounts in the trade press, which discussed state-imposed reciprocal compensation requirements for local traffic. The two pieces of evidence do not eliminate ambiguity in the phrase.

ii. Plain Meaning of the Term "Reciprocal Compensation"

The Petitioners also argue that the FCC has distorted the plain meaning of the term "reciprocal compensation." Joint Intercarrier Compensation Principal Br. of Pet'rs at 25–26. According to the Petitioners, traffic between an LEC and IXC is not "reciprocal" because the charges and traffic go only one way. For this position, the Petitioners contend that for compensation to be "reciprocal," both carriers must pay each other. Relying on this definition, the Petitioners argue that access charges "are never reciprocal" because the IXC pays the LECs on both ends to originate and terminate the traffic. *Id*.

Section 251(b)(5) requires LECs to establish arrangements for "reciprocal compensation." 47 U.S.C. § 251(b)(5). Thus, we could adopt the Petitioners' interpretation only if the statute requires traffic and compensation to "actually flow to and from both carriers ... to be a 'reciprocal compensation arrangement.'" Pac. Bell v. Cook Telecom, Inc., 197 F.3d 1236, 1244 (9th Cir. 1999). This is a reasonable reading of the statute. But the statute can also be read to simply require the existence of reciprocal obligations. A carrier can have a reciprocal entitlement to compensation for transporting and terminating traffic even if it does not ultimately transport or terminate a call.

The statutory term "reciprocal compensation" is ambiguous; thus, we reach the second step of *Chevron*. At step two, we conclude that the FCC reasonably interpreted the term "reciprocal compensation" for "telecommunications" to include the traffic between IXCs and LECs.

d. The Petitioners' Reliance on §§ 252(d)(2)(A) and 251(c)(2)(A)

The Petitioners argue that two other statutory sections (§§ 252(d)(2)(A) and 251(c)(2)(A)) would prevent application of § 251(b)(5) to access traffic. We disagree.

i. Section 252(d)(2)(A)

The Petitioners invoke § 252(d)(2)(A), arguing that it precludes an expansive reading of § 251(b)(5) because traffic never originates on an IXC's network. This argument is invalid.

Section 252(d)(2)(A) applies to state commission arbitrations of interconnection agreements between an ILEC and another telecommunications carrier. *See* 47 U.S.C. § 252. Under this section, state commissions can consider reciprocal compensation terms just and reasonable only if they "provide for the mutual and reciprocal recovery by each carrier of costs associated with the transport and termination on each carrier's network facilities of calls that originate on the network facilities of the other carrier." *Id.* at § 252(d)(2)(A). Because IXCs do not originate calls, the Petitioners contend that reciprocal compensation arrangements cannot apply to traffic between LECs and IXCs.

The FCC rejected this argument, reasoning that § 252(d)(2)(A) does not limit § 251(b)(5). In rejecting the argument, the FCC found that § 252(d)(2)(A) "'deals with the mechanics of who owes what to whom,'" but "'does not define the scope of traffic to which § 251(b)(5) applies.'" Order ¶ 768 (quoting In re High–Cost Universal Serv. Support, 24 FCC Rcd. 6475, 6481, ¶ 12 (2008)). With this finding, the FCC reiterated that Congress did not intend "'the pricing standards in section 252(d)(2) to limit the otherwise broad scope of section 251(b)(5).'" *Id.* (quoting High–Cost Universal Serv. Support, 24 FCC Rcd. 6475, 6480, ¶ 11 (2008)). Instead, the FCC concluded that § 252(d)(2)'s pricing rules do "not address what happens when carriers exchange traffic that originates or terminates on a third carrier's network." In re High–Cost Universal Serv. Support, 24 FCC Rcd. at 6481, ¶ 12.

The FCC's interpretation is reasonable. Section 251(b)(5) broadly refers to "the transport and termination of telecommunications." 47 U.S.C. § 251(b)(5). This section is incorporated into § 252(d)(2), but not the other way around. Consequently, there is nothing in § 252(d)(2) to suggest that it limits the scope of § 251(b)(5). In these circumstances, the FCC reasonably relied on the breadth of § 251(b)(5) to conclude that it is not narrowed by § 252(d)(2).

ii. Section 251(c)(2)(A)

The Petitioners also rely on § 251(c)(2)(A), which distinguishes between "exchange access" and "exchange service." This section requires ILECs to provide telecommunications carriers with interconnection to their networks "for the transmission and routing of telephone exchange service [local calls] and exchange access [long-distance calls]." 47 U.S.C. § 251(c)(2)(A). Because the section distinguishes between "exchange service" and "exchange access," the Petitioners argue that "reciprocal compensation" must refer to something other than "exchange access." Joint Intercarrier Compensation Principal Br. of Pet'rs at 11–12 (July 17, 2013). We reject this argument.

The Petitioners' argument does not render § 251(b)(5) unambiguous or vitiate the reasonableness of the FCC's interpretation. For this argument, the Petitioners incorrectly conflate "exchange service" and "reciprocal compensation." Section 251(c)(2)(A) refers to an ILEC's duty to allow others to interconnect for local- and long-distance calls. This duty is distinct from the duty in § 251(b)(5) to establish arrangements for reciprocal compensation. Thus, § 251(c)(2)(A) does not unambiguously shed light on how the FCC should interpret § 251(b)(5).

2. Preemption of State Regulatory Authority Over Intrastate Access Charges

The Petitioners argue that even if the FCC can regulate IXC–LEC traffic, this authority would include calls that were interstate, but not intrastate. [T]he Petitioners argue that § 152(b) and § 601(c)(1) require the FCC to narrowly interpret § 251(b)(5) to avoid interference with state regulation of intrastate traffic. We disagree. Otherwise, we would be interpreting §§ 152(b) and 601(c)(1) in a way that would upset the regulatory scheme envisioned in the 1996 Act.

Section 152(b) simply limits the FCC's ancillary jurisdiction. *See* AT&T Corp. v. Iowa Utilities Bd., 525 U.S. 366, 380–81 & n. 7 (1999) (stating that § 152(b) serves only to limit the FCC's ancillary authority). And, § 601(c)(1) does not limit Congress's actual delegation of authority to the FCC. Because §§ 152(b) and 601(c)(1) do not unambiguously narrow the scope of § 251(b)(5), we proceed to *Chevron*'s second step.

At that step, we defer to the FCC's interpretation of a statutory ambiguity that concerns the scope of its regulatory authority. Administrative deference is suitable here. Congress appears to grant plenary authority to the FCC through § 251, and §§ 152(b) and 601(c)(1) do not preclude the FCC from interpreting § 251(b)(5) to allow preemption of state regulation over intrastate access charges.

The Petitioners further rely on 47 U.S.C. § 251(d)(3) to rebut the FCC's interpretation that § 251(b)(5) includes intrastate traffic between IXCs and LECs. Section 251(d)(3), entitled "Preservation of State access regulations," prevents the FCC from preempting state commissions' regulations, orders, or policies that: (1) establish LEC access and interconnection obligations, (2) are consistent with the requirements of § 251, and (3) do not substantially prevent implementation of the requirements of § 251 and the purposes of the Communications Act of 1934. 47 U.S.C. § 251(d)(3). According to the Petitioners, § 251(d)(3) prevents the FCC from preempting state access charges.

This argument is unpersuasive. The FCC reasonably concluded that § 251(d)(3) does not speak to the preemptive effect of § 251(b)(5) or limit the permissible interpretations of the statute or the FCC's rulemaking authority. The FCC has interpreted intrastate traffic as subject to § 251(b)(5); and, in exercising the grant of power under § 251(b)(5), the FCC is establishing a national bill-and-keep policy for all access traffic.

C. Bill–and–Keep as a Default Methodology

The FCC not only extended its regulations to all access traffic, but also began a transition to bill-and-keep as the default standard for reciprocal compensation. According to the FCC's interpretation of its authority, § 201(b) allows the adoption of rules and regulations to implement § 251(b)(5). In implementing § 251(b)(5), the FCC considers bill-and-keep to be "just and reasonable" under § 201(b); thus, the FCC concluded it has statutory authority to implement bill-and-keep as the default reciprocal compensation standard for all traffic subject to § 251(b)(5).

In arriving at this conclusion, the FCC addressed opposition based on §§ 252(c) and 252(d)(2). Section 252 does two things: (1) It preserves state rate- setting authority in state commission arbitrations involving ILECs and other carriers; and (2) it defines "just and reasonable" rates. 47 U.S.C. § 252.

For two reasons, the FCC concluded that these provisions did not prevent adoption of a bill-and-keep methodology. First, the FCC pointed to *AT&T*, 525 U.S. at 384, which authorizes the FCC to establish a pricing methodology for state commissions to apply in these arbitrations. In choosing among pricing methodologies, the FCC found specific approval of bill-and-keep in 47 U.S.C. § 252(d)(2)(B). Second, the FCC found that bill-

and-keep is just and reasonable under § 252(d)(2) because it allows carriers to recover their transport and termination costs from their end-users.

Both conclusions are criticized by the Petitioners. They argue that: (1) bill-and-keep effectively sets a zero rate that infringes on state rate-setting authority under § 252(d), and (2) bill-and-keep does not lead to just and reasonable intercarrier compensation rates under §§ 252(d)(2)(A) and 201(b).

Because the statute expressly authorizes bill-and-keep arrangements along with state rate-setting authority, we believe the FCC's interpretation of § 252(d)(2) is reasonable and entitled to deference under *Chevron*.

Under section 252(d)(2), states continue to enjoy authority to arbitrate "terms and conditions" in reciprocal compensation. *See* 47 U.S.C. § 252(d)(2). For example, even under bill-and-keep arrangements, states must arbitrate the "edge" of carrier's networks. This reservoir of state authority can be significant.

The "edge" of a carrier's network consists of the points "at which a carrier must deliver terminating traffic to avail itself of bill-and-keep." *Id.* The location of the "edge" of a carrier's network determines the transport and termination costs for the carrier.

The FCC reasonably determined that by continuing to set the network "edge," states retain their role under § 252(d) in "determin[ing] the concrete result in particular circumstances." Order ¶ 776.

In *AT&T*, the Supreme Court upheld the FCC's rule-making authority over §§ 251 and 252. *AT&T*, 525 U.S. at 378. Interpreting § 252(c)(2)'s reservation of rate-setting authority to state commissions, the Court upheld the FCC's requirement that state commissions use a particular methodology for prices involving interconnection and unbundled access. *See id.* at 384–85. In doing so, the Supreme Court concluded that the FCC has rule-making authority to implement a pricing methodology for the states to implement, "determining the concrete result in particular circumstances. That is enough to constitute the establishment of rates." *Id.* at 384.

The Petitioners [also] point to 47 U.S.C. §§ 201(b) and 252(d)(2), arguing that they require rates to be "just and reasonable." Joint Intercarrier Compensation Principal Br. of Pet'rs at 39–40 (July 17, 2013). Invoking these sections, the Petitioners argue that the FCC's bill-and-keep methodology is not "just and reasonable." Joint Intercarrier Compensation Principal Br. of Pet'rs at 39–42 (July 17, 2013). This argument is invalid under *Chevron*.

According to the FCC, bill-and-keep allows for just and reasonable rates by providing for the "mutual and reciprocal recovery of costs through the offsetting of reciprocal obligations." Federal Resp'ts' Final Resp. to the Joint Intercarrier Compensation Principal Br. of Pet'rs at 33–34 (July 29, 2013). Under a bill-and-keep arrangement, each carrier obtains an "in kind" exchange.

The FCC reasoned that under this methodology, a carrier that terminates a call that originates with another carrier performs a service for its end-user, the call's recipient. Because both end-users benefit from the call, the end-users should split the cost and pay their respective carriers for the call. Through this in-kind exchange of services, bill-and-keep allows carriers to obtain compensation for the call from their own customers.

III. Challenges to Cost Recovery as Arbitrary and Capricious

The Petitioners have challenged not only the ultimate goal of the reforms, but also the way in which the FCC chose to transition toward a national bill-and-keep methodology.

A. The Transitional Plan

Perceiving that an immediate change would unduly disrupt the market, the FCC elected to gradually move toward a bill-and-keep methodology. The FCC decided to transition terminating access charges to bill-and-keep over a six-year period for price cap carriers and over a nine-year period for rate-of-return carriers. The FCC limited interstate originating access charges to existing levels, but has not yet decided how to transition these charges to bill-and-keep.

The FCC created a federal recovery mechanism to ease the transition to bill-and-keep for incumbent LECs. This recovery mechanism is not revenue neutral, for the FCC helps incumbent LECs recover only part of their lost revenues. The amount of the recovery will be based on existing trends that show declining revenues. For price-cap carriers, the recovery generally starts at 90% of 2011 revenues and declines 10% per year. For rate-of-return carriers, the recovery starts at 2011 revenues for switched access and net reciprocal compensation. When the FCC acted, rate-of-return carriers were experiencing yearly drops in revenue of: (1) 3% for interstate switched access, and (2) 10% for intrastate intercarrier compensation. Choosing a benchmark between 3% and 10%, the FCC chose to reduce the eligible recovery for rate-of-return carriers by 5% each year.

Under the FCC's recovery mechanism, carriers can recover part of their lost revenues through: (1) a federally tariffed Access Recovery Charge on end-users, and (2) supplemental support from the Connect America Fund. The Access Recovery Charge is limited to prevent individual end-users from paying excessive rates and is allocated at a carrier's holding-company level. To obtain supplemental support from the Connect America Fund, carriers must meet certain broadband obligations.

[The Court rejected these challenges, as well as challenges to the FCC's procedures and many, more limited challenges brought by various industry segments.]

VI. Conclusion

We deny all of the petitions for review involving the FCC's regulations regarding intercarrier compensation.

Notes and Questions

1. The End of the End? The FCC's clear direction is to eliminate access charges and other vestiges of the intercarrier compensation regime that traditionally supported universal service. What were the forces that drove the FCC in this direction? Local competition? Regulatory arbitrage? Better economics?

2. A New Beginning. Although we have separated the issues of intercarrier compensation reform and the funding of broadband universal service, keep in mind that they are intimately related—indeed, they are two parts of the very same order. The FCC in following the National Broadband Plan placed a high priority on broadband networks, and even said that plain old voice services will be provided over broadband networks. That may be correct generally, but deploying new broadband networks is more expensive than continuing in place plain old voice service, which may do the job just fine (depending of course on what the "job" is). Is the FCC being paternalistic? Is there an appropriate way to gauge what the market wants?

3. Legal Authority and the States. The Supreme Court held in AT&T Corp. v. Iowa Utilities Board, 525 U.S. 366 (1999), that the FCC, and not the states, had primary authority to implement the local competition provisions of the 1996 Telecommunications Act (47 U.S.C. §§ 251 & 252). But this order is an important further step. The FCC's scheme of intercarrier compensation applies to intrastate traffic, and this is a significant change from the traditional scheme in which the FCC regulated interstate access charges and left the matter of intrastate access charges to the States. What role is left for the States after this order? Should the States have any continuing role?

4. Bill-and-Keep. The court approves the FCC's move to bill-and-keep for all intercarrier compensation, after a transition period. Under bill-and-keep, carriers do not pay one another for the termination of traffic, even if traffic flows are imbalanced. Rather, to the extent that a carrier needs capital to increase capacity due to traffic flowing into it—traffic that it must terminate for its customers—the carrier must increase its charges to its own customers who, as the FCC says, benefit from receiving calls.

5. Phantom Traffic and Access Stimulation. Two of the FCC's motivations (although by no means its only motivations) for moving to a single, unified bill-and-keep scheme for intercarrier compensation were phantom traffic and access stimulation. Phantom traffic was that traffic in which the sending network masked its true origination in order to take advantage of a lower-priced termination fee, for example masking long-distance traffic as local. The problem of access stimulation arose where a LEC made an arrangement with an entity that received many calls but made few (such as a "free" conference call service) and then raised its terminating access fees significantly. Long-distance carriers did not raise their rates on a call-by-call basis to their subscribers, and so they unhappily absorbed the very-high termination fees. In an earlier phase of the Connect America Fund proceeding, the FCC adopted rules designed to limit both of these practices. Connect America Fund, Report and Order and Further Notice of Proposed Rulemaking, 26 FCC Rcd. 17,663 (2011). The move to universal bill-and-keep eliminates the incentive to engage in either practice.

---

§ 13.E. Broadband Universal Service

As discussed above, the 1996 Act required a transition from implicit cross-subsidies to explicit charges that could be distributed to meet the traditional goals of telephone universal service. But although the Act did not, in general, address the Internet, its universal service reforms were somewhat more forward-looking. Thus, § 254(b)(3) expressly stated the policy that "[c]onsumers in all regions of the Nation, including low-income consumers and those in rural, insular, and high cost areas, should have access to telecommunications and information services, including interexchange and advanced telecommunications and information services, that are reasonably comparable to those services provided in urban areas and that are available at rates that are reasonably comparable to rates charged for similar services in urban areas." This broad policy of access to advanced telecommunications and information services was made more specific for schools, libraries, and health care providers. In § 254(h), the 1996 Act required the FCC to create a specific universal service policy to ensure that each of these would have "access to advanced telecommunications and information services." § 254(h)(2).

The 1996 Act amendments also allowed the FCC to expand the base of providers to which universal service payments were made (such as allowing it to make universal service payments to wireless companies) and to expand the base of companies that would contribute to universal service funds. In Vonage Holdings Corp. v. FCC, 489 F.3d 1232 (D.C. Cir. 2007), the D.C. Circuit held that § 254(d) authorized the FCC to require "interconnected VoIP" providers to contribute to the universal service fund. Interconnected VoIP providers are those companies offering Voice-over-Internet-Protocol telephony whose services allow customers to receive calls from and make calls to traditional telephone lines.[3] In recognition of the need to modernize its universal service policies for a broadband world, the FCC's Broadband Plan calls for expanding support for such connections beyond the realm of schools, libraries, and rural health care providers. The first excerpt below outlines the FCC's decision to provide support for broadband connections to schools, libraries, and rural health care providers; the second is from the FCC's Broadband Plan.

FEDERAL-STATE JOINT BOARD ON UNIVERSAL SERVICE
Report and Order, 12 FCC Rcd. 8776 (1997)

I. INTRODUCTION

1. In the Telecommunications Act of 1996, Congress directed the Commission and states to take the steps necessary to establish support mechanisms to ensure the delivery of affordable telecommunications service to all Americans, including low income consumers, eligible schools and libraries, and rural health care providers. Specifically, Congress directed the Commission and the states to devise methods to ensure that "consumers in all regions of the Nation, including low income consumers and those in rural, insular, and high cost areas ... have access to telecommunications and information services ... at rates that are reasonably comparable to rates charged for similar services in urban areas." 47 U.S.C. § 254(b)(3) (2006). Congress further directed the Commission to define additional services for support for eligible schools, libraries, and health care providers, and directed the Commission to "establish competitively neutral rules ... to enhance, to the extent technically feasible and economically reasonable, access to advanced telecommunications and information services for all public and non-profit elementary and secondary school classrooms, health care providers, and libraries."[4]

2. Consistent with the explicit statutory principles, our immediate implementation of § 254 is shaped by our commitment to achieve four critical goals. First, we must implement all of the universal service objectives established by the Communications Act of 1934, including those for low income individuals, consumers in rural, insular, and high cost areas, schools, libraries, and rural health care providers. *See, e.g.,* 47 U.S.C. §§ 254(b), (h), and (i). Second, we must maintain rates for basic residential service at affordable levels. We believe that the rates for this service are generally at affordable levels today. Third, we must ensure affordable basic service continues to be available to all users through an explicit universal service funding mechanism. For the present, we believe we can

---

3. Section 254(d) has two layers concerning contributions. Its "mandatory" provision states that "[e]very telecommunications carrier that provides interstate telecommunications services shall contribute" to the universal service fund. The section also has a permissive component, that provides that "[a]ny other provider of interstate telecommunications may be required to contribute to the preservation and advancement of universal service in the public interest." The FCC was required to utilize its permissive authority because, as discussed in the next chapter, it had previously characterized VoIP has an "information service." VoIP providers therefore used (and offered) telecommunications, but they did not offer "telecommunications services."

4. 47 U.S.C. § 254(h)(2)(A). Telecommunications carriers are required to provide service to rural health care providers "at rates that are reasonably comparable to rates charged for similar services in urban areas." 47 U.S.C. § 254(h)(1)(A). Schools and libraries now are entitled under federal law to service "at rates less than the amounts charged for similar services to other parties." 47 U.S.C. § 254(h)(1)(B). In addition, Congress directed the Commission to "enhance ... access to advanced telecommunications and information services for all public and non-profit elementary and secondary school classrooms, health care providers, and libraries." 47 U.S.C. § 254(h)(2).

achieve this goal by maintaining our existing high cost mechanism at current funding levels, picking a platform mechanism by December 1997, and implementing a forward-looking economic cost mechanism for universal service for non-rural carriers starting January 1, 1999. Fourth, we must bring the benefits of competition to as many consumers as possible.

3. Today, we adopt rules that reflect virtually all of the Joint Board's recommendations and fulfill the universal service goals established by Congress. *See* Federal-State Joint Board on Universal Service, CC Docket No. 96-45, Recommended Decision, 12 FCC Rcd. 87 (1996).

G. Support for Schools and Libraries

29. We concur with the Joint Board's recommendation to provide schools and libraries with discounts on all commercially available telecommunications services, Internet access, and internal connections. This program provides schools and libraries with the maximum flexibility to purchase the package of services they believe will meet their communications needs most effectively. We conclude that sections 254(c)(3) and 254(h)(1)(B) authorize us to permit eligible schools and libraries to receive telecommunications services, Internet access, and internal connections at discounted rates from telecommunications carriers.

30. Fiscal responsibility compels us to require schools and libraries to seek competitive bids for all services eligible for § 254(h) discounts. Competitive bidding is the most efficient means for ensuring that schools and libraries are informed about all of the choices available to them. In addition, we agree with the Joint Board that the lowest corresponding price, defined for each telecommunications carrier bidding to serve a school or library as the lowest price that carrier charges to similarly situated non-residential customers in its geographic service area for similar services, shall constitute the ceiling for that carrier's competitively bid pre-discount price for interstate rates.

31. We adopt discounts from 20 percent to 90 percent for all telecommunications services, Internet access, and internal connections, with the level of discounts correlated to indicators of poverty and high cost for schools and libraries. We also establish an annual cap of $2.25 billion on the amount of funds available to schools and libraries.

H. Support for Health Care Providers

35. Sections 254(c) and 254(h) add health care providers to the list of entities that may benefit from universal service support. Recognizing that § 254 requires that universal service support mechanisms be specific, predictable, and sufficient, we establish support for health care providers subject to a $400 million annual cap.

36. Section 254(h)(2)(A) directs the Commission to establish "competitively neutral rules to enhance, to the extent technically feasible and economically reasonable, access to advanced telecommunications and information services for all public and nonprofit health care providers." To meet the goals of this section, and, based on our review of comments filed in response to the Recommended Decision, we adopt mechanisms to provide support for limited toll-free access to an Internet service provider. Each health care provider that lacks toll-free access to an Internet service provider may receive the lesser of the toll charges incurred for 30 hours of access to an Internet service provider or $180 per month in toll charge credits for toll charges imposed for connecting to the Internet.

Notes and Questions

1. **Why Selective Subsidies?** What is the rationale for subsidizing some telecommunications services for some people and institutions? The 1996 Act extends universal service ben-

efits to elite prep schools and wealthy rural landowners. Is this because Congress believes that, absent the subsidy, many such schools and landowners would not buy the services? If not, why include them in the program? That is, why should some rich and poor telecommunications service consumers be taxed to provide cheap telecommunications services to other rich and poor telecommunications service consumers? Should the programs be limited, then, to low income consumers? To consumers who would not purchase without the subsidy but would purchase with it? (Note that these last two categories will likely have some, but by no means complete, overlap.)

2. Money Is Money. What if people in rural areas, low income consumers, and/or high school principals decide that, rather than subsidized telephone service or Internet access, what they'd really like is subsidies for clothing? Or simply more disposable income? Should we devote funds to telecommunications services because of the network externality even if the beneficiaries of those funds would vastly prefer to use the money for other purposes? Why does Congress know better than rural and low income consumers what are those consumers' most compelling unfulfilled wants?

3. Controversy Over School and Library Subsidies. Paragraphs 29–31 of the above order created a program adopting discounts ranging from 20 percent to 90 percent for all telecommunications services, Internet access, and internal connections for schools and libraries. The level of the discount increased with the percentage of students who received subsidized school lunches, and rural schools received a slightly bigger discount than urban ones. *See* 47 C.F.R. §54.505(c). This discount, known as the "E-rate," is funded by telecommunications carriers (who generally pass that fee on to consumers), and administered by the FCC.

The FCC's own Inspector General has issued several reports criticizing the FCC's oversight of the E-rate program. Its random audits of some recipients found instances of payments made for goods and services that were not provided, and the Inspector General concluded that there was a real concern about waste, fraud, and abuse but insufficient oversight by the FCC to prevent it. *See, e.g.*, FCC Office of the Inspector General, Semiannual Report to Congress, April 1, 2004 to September 30, 2004, available at http://transition.fcc.gov/oig/SAR32_final_revise_112204.pdf. This spurred Congress to look into the program, resulting in several hearings in 2004 that took a critical look at the E-rate program. In response to these developments, the FCC issued Schools and Libraries Universal Service Support Mechanism, Fifth Report and Order and Order, 19 FCC Rcd. 15,808 (2004), which was designed to enhance oversight and respond to concerns about waste, fraud, and abuse. The order stated flatly at the outset: "In this order, we adopt measures to protect against waste, fraud, and abuse in the administration of the schools and libraries universal service support mechanism (also known as the E-rate program). In particular, we resolve a number of issues that have arisen from audit activities conducted as part of ongoing oversight over the administration of the universal service fund, and we address programmatic concerns raised by our Office of Inspector General." *Id.* ¶1. The Government Accountability Office (GAO) nonetheless still found in a 2005 report that "major issues remain[ed] unresolved," and dangers of waste, fraud, and abuse remained. *See* U.S. Gov't Accountability Office, GAO-05-151, Greater Involvement Needed by FCC in the Management and Oversight of the E-rate Program 6 (2005), *available at* http://www.gao.gov/new.items/d05151.pdf.

One big area of concern stems from the fact that some schools and libraries pay only 10% of the costs of the goods and services, leaving them with relatively little incentive to economize (and leaving a large pool of funds contractors could offer as kickbacks to schools and libraries). The GAO suggests that some of the problem stems from the fact that the funding of the program is not treated as a tax and is not subject to all the requirements that ordinarily apply to funds in the U.S. Treasury, but instead is administered by the FCC in an ad hoc way. As the GAO stated in one of its headings, "FCC Established an Unusual Program Structure without Comprehensively Addressing the Applicability of Governmental Standards and Fiscal Controls." GAO Report at 11. The GAO contends that the FCC could have, and should have, created such controls. The GAO also suggests that the FCC failed to develop useful performance goals and measures, and (like the FCC's Inspector General) contends that it failed to engage in appropriate oversight. Id. at 19–36.

4. National Broadband Plan on Universal Service. The overall goal of the National Broadband Plan was to develop a strategy to ensure that all Americans would have access to broadband technology. As a result, a significant portion of the Plan addresses universal service policy for broadband.

NATIONAL BROADBAND PLAN: CONNECTING AMERICA
FCC (2010)
(available at http://transition.fcc.gov/national-broadband-plan/national-broadband-plan.pdf)
Chapter 8

SECTION 8.1: THE BROADBAND AVAILABILITY GAP

At present, there are 14 million people living in 7 million housing units that do not have access to terrestrial broadband infrastructure capable of meeting the National Broadband Availability Target. [In an earlier portion of the report, the FCC identified an availability target of 4 Mbps service.]

This broadband availability gap is greatest in areas with low population density. Because service providers in these areas cannot earn enough revenue to cover the costs of deploying and operating broadband networks, including expected returns on capital, there is no business case to offer broadband services in these areas. As a result, it is unlikely that private investment alone will fill the broadband availability gap. The question, then, is how much public support will be required to fill the gap.

An FCC analysis finds that the level of additional funding required is approximately $24 billion (present value in 2010 dollars). Adding initial capital expenditures (capex) and continuing costs and subtracting revenue yields a gap of approximately $24 billion.

The support needs of different geographic areas are distinct and depend on many factors, including the existing network infrastructure and household density. In some areas, subsidizing all or part of the initial capex will allow a service provider to have a sustainable business. Elsewhere, subsidizing initial capex will not be enough; service providers will need support for continuing costs. Support for one-time deployment or upgrades will likely be enough to provide broadband to 46% of the seven million unserved housing units. Closing the gap for the remaining 54% of housing units will probably require support for both one-time and recurring costs.

Moreover, serving the 250,000 housing units with the highest gaps accounts for $14 billion of the broadband availability gap. This represents less than two-tenths of 1% of all housing units in the United States. The average amount of funding per housing unit to close the gap for these units with terrestrial broadband is $56,000.

SECTION 8.3: UNIVERSAL SERVICE

Universal service has been a national objective since the Communications Act of 1934, in which Congress stated its intention to "make available, so far as possible, to all the people of the United States ... a rapid, efficient, Nation-wide, and world-wide wire and radio communication service with adequate facilities at reasonable charges." 47 U.S.C. § 151. The current federal universal service programs were created in the aftermath of the Telecommunications Act of 1996—at a time when only 23% of Americans had dial-up Internet access at home, and virtually no one had broadband. While the federal USF and earlier programs have played a critical role in the universalization of voice service in the last century, the current USF was not designed to support broadband directly, other than for schools, libraries and rural health care providers.

In 2010, the federal USF is projected to make total outlays of $8.7 billion through four programs. The High-Cost program, which subsidizes telecommunications services in areas where costs would otherwise be prohibitively high, will spend $4.6 billion. E-rate, which supports voice and broadband connectivity for schools and libraries, will spend $2.7 billion. The Low Income program, which subsidizes the cost of telephone service for low-income people, will spend $1.2 billion, and the Rural Health Care program, which supports connectivity for health care providers, will spend $214 million.

At least 21 states have high-cost funds that collectively distribute over $1.5 billion. Thirty-three states have a state low-income program, nine states have a state subsidy program for schools and libraries, and at least 27 states support state telehealth networks. In addition, a number of states have established specific programs to fund broadband deployment. Some states provide tax credits for investment in broadband infrastructure.

Accelerating the pace of investment in broadband networks in high-cost areas will also require consideration of related policy issues that affect the revenue streams of existing carriers. The [Intercarrier Compensation (ICC)] system provides a positive revenue stream for certain carriers, which in turn affects their ability to upgrade their networks during the transition from voice telephone service to broadband service. In rural America USF and ICC represent a significant portion of revenues for some of the smallest carriers— i.e., 60% or more of their regulated revenues. The rules governing special access services also affect the economics of deployment and investment, as middle-mile transmission often represents a significant cost for carriers that need to transport their traffic a significant distance to the Internet backbone. For that reason, the FCC needs to consider the middle mile in any discussion of government support to high-cost areas.

USF and ICC regulations were designed for a telecommunications industry that provided voice service over circuit-switched networks. State and federal ratemaking created implicit subsidies at both the state and federal levels and were designed to shift costs from rural to urban areas, from residential to business customers, and from local to long distance service.

Unfortunately, the current regulatory framework will not close the broadband availability gap. A comprehensive reform program is required to shift from primarily supporting voice communications to supporting a broadband platform that enables many applications, including voice. This reform must be staged over time to realign these systems to support broadband and minimize regulatory uncertainty for investment.

The goal of reform is to provide everyone with affordable voice and broadband. The reforms must be achieved over time to manage the impact on consumers, who ultimately pay for universal service. The FCC should target areas that are currently unserved, while taking care to ensure that consumers continue to enjoy broadband and voice services that are available today. Given that USF is a finite resource, the FCC should work to maximize the number of households that can be served quickly, focusing first on those areas that require lower amounts of subsidy to achieve that goal, and over time addressing those areas that are the hardest to serve, recognizing that the subsidy required may decline in the future as technology advances and costs decline. Ongoing support should be provided where necessary.

Sudden changes in USF and ICC could have unintended consequences that slow progress. Success will come from a clear road map for reform, including guidance about the timing and pace of changes to existing regulations, so that the private sector can react and plan appropriately.

Stage One of this comprehensive reform program starts with building the institutional foundation for reform, identifying funding that can be shifted immediately to jump start broadband deployment in unserved areas, creating the framework for a new Connect America Fund and a Mobility Fund, establishing a long-term vision for ICC, and examining middle-mile costs and pricing. In Stage Two, the FCC will begin disbursements from the CAF and Mobility Fund, while implementing the first step in reducing intercarrier compensation rates and reforming USF contribution methodology. Stage Three completes the transformation of the legacy High-Cost program, ends support for voice-only networks and completes reforms of ICC.

Notes and Questions

1. How Much to Spend? The Broadband Plan notes that bringing service to the 250,000 housing units with the highest gaps (less than 0.2% of houses in America) costs an average of $56,000 per house. Should the government tell some Americans that it is just too expensive for the government to pay to give them broadband service? If so, where should it draw the line?

2. How Much Broadband? The FCC's measure of universal service need is driven in part by its definition of broadband as 4 Mbps service, which came from the FCC's assessment of how consumers are using broadband for video and other advanced services. Should the FCC have a different measure for essential service? Or a measure that varies based on the expense of providing universal service?

3. Implementing the National Broadband Plan's Proposals. In 2011, the FCC issued an order implementing the goals of the National Broadband Plan. The excerpt below is from that portion of the Tenth Circuit's opinion discussing and affirming the FCC's broadband universal service program, the Connect America Fund.

In re FCC 11-161

753 F.3d 1015 (10th Cir. 2014)

Opinion for the court filed by Chief Judge BRISCOE, in which HOLMES, Circuit Judge, concurs. BACHARACH, Circuit Judge, concurring in part and dissenting in part.

BRISCOE, Chief Judge:

In late 2011, the Federal Communications Commission issued an order comprehensively reforming and modernizing its universal service and intercarrier compensation systems. Connect America Fund, Report and Order and Further Notice of Proposed Rulemaking, 26 FCC Rcd. 17,663 (2011) (Order). Petitioners, each of whom were parties to the FCC's rulemaking proceeding below, filed petitions for judicial review of the FCC's Order. [P]etitioners assert a host of challenges to the portions of the Order revising how universal service funds are to be allocated to and employed by recipients. After carefully considering those claims, we find them either unpersuasive or barred from judicial review. Consequently, we deny the petitions to the extent they are based upon those claims.

II. Background

G. The FCC's Report and Order of November 18, 2011

On November 18, 2011, the FCC released its 752-page Order. The Order stated that "[t]he universal service challenge of our time is to ensure that all Americans are served by networks that support high-speed Internet access—in addition to basic voice service—where they live, work, and travel." Order ¶ 5. In turn, the Order stated that the "existing universal service and intercarrier compensation systems [we]re based on decades-old assumptions that fail[ed] to reflect today's networks, the evolving nature of communications services, or the current competitive landscape." Order ¶ 6. In light of these factors, the Order purported to "comprehensively reform[ ] and modernize[ ] the universal service and intercarrier compensation systems to ensure that robust, affordable voice and broadband service, both fixed and mobile, [we]re available to Americans throughout the nation." Order ¶ 1.

The Order summarized the key components of the universal service reform the FCC would be implementing. Because the vast majority of Americans "that lack access to residential fixed broadband at or above the [FCC]'s broadband speed benchmark live in areas served by price cap carriers," i.e., "Bell Operating Companies and other large and mid-sized carriers," the FCC stated that it "w[ould] introduce targeted, efficient support for broadband in two phases" for these areas. Order ¶ 21. Phase I of this plan, intended "[t]o spur immediate broadband buildout," would freeze "all existing high-cost support to price cap carriers" and make "an additional $300 million in CAF funding ... available." Order ¶ 22. "Frozen support w[ould] be immediately subject to the goal of achieving universal availability of voice and broadband, and subject to obligations to build and operate broadband-capable networks in areas unserved by an unsubsidized competitor over time." *Id.* Phase II of the plan "w[ould] use a combination of a forward-looking broadband cost model and competitive bidding to efficiently support deployment of networks providing both voice and broadband service for five years." Order ¶ 23.

With respect to rate-of-return carriers, which "serve[d] less than five percent of access lines in the U.S.," but received "total support from the high-cost fund ... approaching $2 billion annually," the Order imposed substantial reforms. Order ¶ 26. In particular, any such carriers "receiving legacy universal service support, or CAF support to offset lost ICC revenues," were required to "offer broadband service meeting initial CAF requirements ... upon their customers' reasonable requests." *Id.* The Order noted that, because of "the economic challenges of extending service in the high-cost areas of the country served by rate-of-return carriers, this flexible approach [would] not require rate-of-return companies to extend service to customers absent such a request." *Id.*

The Order indicated that a CAF Mobility Fund would be created to "promot[e] the universal availability" of "mobile voice and broadband services." Order ¶ 28. Phase I of the CAF Mobility Fund would "provide up to $300 million in one-time support to immediately accelerate deployment of networks for mobile voice and broadband services in unserved areas." *Id.* at 402. This support, the Order indicated, would "be awarded through a nationwide reverse auction." *Id.* Phase II of the Mobility Fund would "provide up to $500 million per year in ongoing support" in order to "expand and sustain mobile voice and broadband services in communities in which service would be unavailable absent federal support." *Id.* Included in this $500 million annual budget was "ongoing support for Tribal areas of up to $100 million per year." *Id.* Phase II also anticipated "eliminat[ing] the identical support rule that determines the amount of support for mobile, as well as wireline, competitive ETCs [(eligible telecommunications carriers)]," Order ¶ 29, and the creation of a "Remote Areas Fund" designed "to ensure that Americans living in the most remote areas in the nation, where the cost of deploying traditional terrestrial broadband networks is extremely high, can obtain affordable access through alternative technology platforms, including satellite and unlicensed wireless services," Order ¶ 30.

IV. Universal Service Fund Issues

  A. Joint Universal Service Fund Principal Brief

  1. Did the FCC's broadband requirement exceed its authority under 47 U.S.C. § 254?

[T]he resolution of this issue hinges, in substantial part, on the interpretation of two subsections of § 254: subsection (c)(1) and subsection (e). Addressing these subsections in order, it is beyond dispute that subsection (c)(1) expressly authorizes the FCC to define "periodically" the types of telecommunications services that are encompassed by "universal service" and thus "supported by Federal universal service support mechanisms." Further, there is no question that the FCC, to date, has interpreted the term "telecommunications services" to include only telephone services and not VoIP or other broadband internet services. All that said, however, nothing in the language of subsection (c)(1) serves as an express or implicit limitation on the FCC's authority to determine what a USF recipient may or must do with those funds. More specifically, nothing in subsection (c)(1) expressly or implicitly deprives the FCC of authority to direct that a USF recipient, which necessarily provides some form of "universal service" and has been deemed by a state commission or the FCC to be an eligible telecommunications carrier under 47 U.S.C. § 214(e), use some of its USF funds to provide services or build facilities related to services that fall outside of the FCC's current definition of "universal service." In other words, nothing in the statute limits the FCC's authority to place conditions, such as the broadband requirement, on the use of USF funds.

That leaves § 254(e), the second sentence of which the FCC asserts authorizes it to direct that USF recipients provide broadband Internet access to customers upon reasonable request. The threshold question we must address, under *Chevron*, is whether Congress in § 254(e) "has directly spoken to the precise question at issue," Chevron U.S.A., Inc. v. Natural Res. Def. Council, Inc., 467 U.S. 837, 842 (1984), i.e., did Congress in the second sentence of § 254(e) delegate authority to the FCC to identify precisely what a recipient of USF funds must do with those funds, *id.* at 844.

As noted above, the second sentence of subsection (e) provides that "[an eligible telecommunications] carrier [designated under 47 U.S.C. § 214(e)] that receives [Federal universal service] support shall use that support only for the provision, maintenance, and upgrading of facilities and services for which the support is intended." 47 U.S.C. § 254(e). Quite clearly, this language does not explicitly delegate any authority to the FCC. But the question remains whether this language can reasonably be construed, as the FCC suggests, as an implicit grant of authority to specify what a USF recipient may or must do with the funds?

Upon careful examination, we conclude that the FCC's interpretation of § 254(e) is not "arbitrary, capricious, or manifestly contrary to the statute." *Chevron*, 467 U.S. at 844. Congress clearly intended, by way of the second sentence of § 254(e), to mandate that USF funds be used by recipients "only for the provision, maintenance, and upgrading of facilities and services for which the support is intended." And it seems highly unlikely that Congress would leave it to USF recipients to determine what "the support is intended" for. Instead, as the FCC suggests, it is reasonable to conclude that Congress left a gap to be filled by the FCC, i.e., for the FCC to determine and specify precisely how USF funds may or must be used.

The FCC also, in our view, reasonably concluded that Congress's use of the terms "facilities" and "service" in the second sentence of § 254(e) afforded the FCC "the flexibility not only to designate the types of telecommunications services for which support would be provided, but also to encourage the deployment of the types of facilities that will best achieve the principles set forth in section 254(b)." Order ¶ 64.

(d) Does Section 706 of the Act, 47 U.S.C. § 1302, serve as an independent grant of authority to the FCC to impose the broadband requirement?

In a related attack on the FCC's broadband requirement, petitioners argue that section 706 of the Communications Act of 1934 (the Act), 47 U.S.C. § 1302, does not, contrary to the conclusion reached by the FCC in the Order, serve as an independent grant of authority to the FCC.

We reject petitioners' arguments. To be sure, both section 706(a) and section 706(b) focus on "the deployment ... of advanced telecommunications capability to all Americans." Further, both sections make reference, in terms of achieving such deployment, to the removal of "barriers to infrastructure investment." But that is where the similarities end. As noted, section 706(a) is a general directive stating that the FCC "shall encourage the deployment ... of advanced telecommunications capability to all Americans ... by utilizing ... price cap regulation, regulatory forbearance, measures that promote competition in the local telecommunications market, or other regulating methods that remove barriers to infrastructure investment." The FCC has concluded "that section 706(a) gives [it] an affirmative obligation to encourage the deployment of advanced services, relying on [its] authority established elsewhere in the [1996] Act." In re Deployment of Wireline Servs. Offering Advanced Telecomms. Capability, 13 FCC Rcd. 24,012, 24,046, ¶ 74 (1998). In other words, the FCC has concluded that section 706(a) is "not ... an independent grant of authority, but rather, ... a direction to the [FCC] to use the forbearance [and other] authority granted elsewhere in the Act." *Id.* at 24,047 (¶ 76).

In contrast, section 706(b) requires the FCC to perform two related tasks. First, the FCC must conduct an annual inquiry to "determine whether advanced telecommunications capability is being deployed to all Americans in a reasonable and timely fashion." Second, and most importantly for purposes of this appeal, if the FCC's annual "determination is negative," it is required to "take immediate action to accelerate deployment of such capability by removing barriers to infrastructure investment and by promoting competition in the telecommunications market." Unlike section 706(a), section 706(b) does not specify how the FCC is to accomplish this latter task, or otherwise refer to forms of regulatory authority that are afforded to the FCC in other parts of the Act. As the FCC concluded in the Order, section 706(b) thus appears to operate as an independent grant of authority to the FCC "to take steps necessary to fulfill Congress's broadband deployment objectives," and "it is hard to see what additional work section 706(b) does if it is not an independent source of authority." Order ¶ 70.

2. Did the FCC act arbitrarily in simultaneously imposing the broadband requirement and reducing USF support?

Petitioners next complain that the FCC's broadband requirement was "impose [d] ... in the face of a *net reduction* to USF and related intercarrier compensation revenues for rural carriers." Pet'r Br. 3 at 29 (emphasis in original). They argue, in turn, that "[t]his 'do more with less' directive flies in the face of Congress's interrelated requirements under section 254(b) that the FCC use USF to keep quality service 'affordable,' that consumers in high cost areas receive services comparable to those available to their urban counterparts at 'reasonably comparable' rates, that USF support mechanisms be 'predictable and sufficient' to preserve and advance universal service, and that telecommunications service providers contribute equitably to achieve that objective." *Id.* (citing 47 U.S.C. §§ 254(b)(1), (3), (5)). And, they argue, the FCC "made no attempt to measure whether reduced support, coupled with the added costs of the broadband obligation, will allow carriers to meet the universal service objectives of section 254(b)." *Id.* at 30.

This is not the first time we have analyzed § 254(b). In *Qwest Corp.*, we noted that "[t]he plain text of the statute ... indicates a mandatory duty on the FCC" to "base its universal policies on the principles listed in § 254(b)." Qwest Corp. v. FCC, 258 F.3d 1191, 1200 (10th Cir. 2001). "However," we emphasized, "each of the principles in § 254(b) internally is phrased in terms of 'should,'" which "indicates a recommended course of action, but does not itself imply the obligation associated with 'shall.'" *Id.* Consequently, we held, "the FCC must base its policies on the principles, but any particular principle can be trumped in the appropriate case." *Id.* In other words, "the FCC may exercise its discretion to balance the principles against one another when they conflict, but may not depart from them altogether to achieve some goal." *Id.*

a) Does the Order fail to ensure that USF support for rural carriers is sufficient to preserve and advance universal service?

Petitioners argue that the FCC failed to ensure that USF support for rural carriers is "'sufficient'... to achieve Congress's goals." Pet'r Br. 3 at 30. "The overarching problem," petitioners assert, "is that the [FCC] improperly limited its analysis to whether, without reform [i.e., a fixed budget], USF support would be *excessive*." *Id.* at 31 (emphasis in original). As a result, petitioners assert, "[t]he Order leaves unanalyzed whether reduced USF support will be sufficient to preserve and enhance traditional voice services." *Id.*

The term "sufficient" is mentioned in both § 254(b)(5) ("There should be specific, predictable and sufficient Federal and State mechanisms to preserve and advance universal service.") and § 254(e) ("Any such support should be ... sufficient to achieve the purposes of this section."). The Fifth Circuit has concluded, however, that "§ 254(b) [simply] identifies a set of principles and does not lay out any specific commands for the FCC," and that "[e]ven § 254(e), which is framed as a direct, statutory command, is ambiguous as to what constitutes 'sufficient' support." Texas Office of Public Util. Counsel v. FCC, 183 F.3d 393, 425 (5th Cir. 1999). Consequently, the Fifth Circuit concluded, a reviewing court need "not consider the language an expression of Congress's 'unambiguous intent' allowing *Chevron* step-one review," and instead need only "review [the FCC's] interpretation for reasonability under *Chevron* step-two." *Id.* at 425–26. Because we agree with the Fifth Circuit, we need determine in this case only that the FCC's "sufficiency" analysis was not arbitrary, capricious, or manifestly contrary to the statute.

In setting the overall budget for the Connect America Fund (CAF), the FCC expressed a "commitment to controlling the size of the universal service fund," and, consequently, it "sought comment on setting an overall budget for the CAF such that the sum of the CAF and any existing legacy high-cost support mechanisms ... in a given year would remain equal to current funding levels." Order ¶ 121. "[A] broad cross-section of interested stakeholders ... agreed" with this proposal, "with many urging the [FCC] to set that budget at $4.5 billion per year, the estimated size of the program in fiscal year (FY) 2011." Order ¶ 122. After considering these comments, the FCC concluded that the "establish[ment]

[of] a defined budget for the high-cost component of the universal service fund" would "best ensure that [it] ha[d] in place 'specific, predictable, and sufficient' funding mechanisms to ensure [its] universal service objectives." Order ¶ 123. In reaching this conclusion, the FCC expressed concern that, "were the CAF to significantly raise the end-user cost of services, it could undermine [the FCC's] broader policy objectives to promote broadband and mobile deployment and adoption." Order ¶ 124. And, consistent with many of the comments it received, the FCC "establish[ed] an annual funding target, set at the same level as [its] current estimate for the size of the high-cost program for FY 2011, of no more than $4.5 billion." Order ¶ 125. The FCC found "that amount [was not] excessive given" its decision to "expand the high-cost program in important ways to promote broadband and mobility; facilitate intercarrier compensation reform; and preserve universal voice connectivity." *Id.* "At the same time," the FCC found that "a higher budget [was not] warranted, given the substantial reforms [it was] adopt[ing] to modernize [its] legacy funding mechanisms to address long-standing inefficiencies and wasteful spending." *Id.* The FCC also noted that it would need "to evaluate the effect of these reforms before adjusting [its] budget," *id.*, and it specifically stated that it "anticipate[d] ... revisit[ing] and adjust[ing] accordingly the appropriate size of each of [its] programs by the end of the six-year period, based on market developments," Order ¶ 18.

In sum, the FCC determined that budgetary "sufficiency" for price cap and rate-of-return carriers could be achieved through a combination of measures, including, but not limited to: (1) maintaining current USF funding levels while reducing or eliminating waste and inefficiencies that existed in the prior USF funding scheme; (2) affording carriers the authority to determine which requests for broadband service are reasonable; (3) allowing carriers, when necessary, to use the waiver process; and (4) conducting a budgetary review by the end of six years. And, relatedly, the FCC quite clearly rejected any notion that budgetary "sufficiency" is equivalent to "complete" or "full" funding for carrying out the broadband and other obligations imposed upon carriers who are voluntary recipients of USF funds. In our view, these determinations were not arbitrary, capricious, or manifestly contrary to the directives outlined in § 254. To contrary, the FCC's determinations, particularly when considered in light of the other statutory directives the FCC was charged with achieving, were reasonable and sufficient to survive scrutiny under *Chevron* step-two analysis.

c) Does the Order's establishment of a budget cap, without widening the contribution base, fail to protect affordability or ensure equitable fund contributions?

Petitioners argue that the Order's imposition of a USF budget cap, "[w]ithout widening the contribution base, ... will do nothing to ensure affordability." Pet'r Br. 3 at 34. "The problem," according to petitioners, "is that telecommunications voice revenues are declining." *Id.* As a result, they argue, "[e]ven a fixed budget will have to be recovered from fewer customers, whose individual charges will *go up* (become *less* affordable), unless the contribution base is widened." *Id.* at 34–35 (emphasis in original). In turn, petitioners argue that, even assuming that the FCC acted within its authority in imposing the broadband mandate, "it is inequitable to exempt telecommunications providers who also offer broadband from being required to contribute to universal service from the revenues they receive for such services, particularly since rural carriers assuming a broadband obligation will incur added costs." *Id.* at 35. And, they argue, it is not enough for the FCC to "decide at some unspecified future date ... whether to expand its contribution base." *Id.*

Two points are clear from the Order and the parties' briefs. First, the Order concluded that the existing contribution framework (which is comprised of assessments paid by interstate telecommunications service providers) was sufficient to satisfy the annual USF budget established in the Order. Second, the FCC chose to address potential changes to the contribution framework in a separate proceeding. More specifically, the FCC in a separate rulemaking docket has sought comment on proposals to reform and modernize how USF contributions are assessed and recovered. *See* Universal Service Contribution Methodology; A National Broadband Plan for Our Future, 27 FCC Rcd. 5357, 5358 (2012).

As the FCC correctly notes in its appellate response brief, 47 U.S.C. § 154(j) affords it the discretion to "conduct its proceedings in such manner as will best conduce to the proper dispatch of business and to the ends of justice." FCC Br. 3 at 68. And we agree with the FCC that its decision to address USF contributions not in the Order, but rather in a separate proceeding, falls well within that discretion.

3. Does the FCC's use of auctions to distribute USF violate § 214(e)?

Petitioners contend that the FCC's use of auctions to distribute USF violates 47 U.S.C. § 214(e). According to petitioners, "Congress," by way of § 214(e), "expressly gave State commissions the job of deciding *who* would receive universal service support and *where* supported services would be advertised and provided by the carrier." Pet'r Br. 3 at 40 (emphasis in original). More specifically, petitioners assert, § 214(e) "provides that only ETCs may receive USF support and that, with narrow exceptions, only states may designate ETCs and their service areas." *Id.* at 39. And, they assert, "[o]nce an ETC is designated by a state commission to serve a particular service area under section 214(e)(2), it is eligible to receive funding and must offer and advertise the supported services throughout its service area." *Id.*

Petitioners complain that "[t]he Order contravenes this statutory scheme in two respects." *Id.* "First," petitioners assert, the Order "adopted various competitive bidding mechanisms to distribute USF support, and provided that the [FCC] will define the geographic areas to be auctioned off." *Id.* at 39–40. "Second," petitioners assert, "the FCC created an entirely new 'conditional designation,' nowhere mentioned in the statute, that will require state commissions to conditionally designate 'ETCs' before auctions to distribute Mobility Fund support are concluded." *Id.* at 40.

The key flaw in petitioners' argument, as the FCC correctly notes in its response brief, is that "it conflates eligibility for subsidies with the right to receive subsidies." FCC Br. 3 at 62. To be sure, § 214(e) authorizes state commissions to decide which entities will be designated as ETCs and, relatedly, to determine the service areas served by those ETCs. But nothing in § 214(e) gives authority to the state commissions to allocate USF funds, nor does § 214(e) give a designated ETC the absolute right to receive USF funds. Rather, as the language of § 214(e)(1) makes clear, "[a] common carrier designated as an eligible telecommunications carrier under paragraph (2), (3), or (6) shall be *eligible* to receive universal service support in accordance with section 254 [47 USCS § 254]." 47 U.S.C. § 214(e) (emphasis added). Had Congress intended designated ETCs to automatically receive USF funds, it could and should have omitted the phrase "be eligible to" from the language of § 214(e)(1).

4. Was the FCC's decision to reduce USF support in areas with "artificially low" end user rates unlawful or arbitrary?

Petitioners contend that the FCC's decision to reduce USF support in areas with "artificially low" end user rates was both unlawful and arbitrary.

The portion of the Order being challenged by petitioners is a section entitled "Reducing High Cost Loop Support for Artificially Low End–User Rates." Therein, the Order "adopt[ed] a rule," applicable "to both rate-of-return carriers and price cap companies," "to limit high-cost support where end-user rates do not meet a specified local floor." Order ¶ 235. In doing so, the Order noted there was "evidence in the record" indicating that "there [were] a number of carriers with local rates that [we]re significantly lower than rates that urban consumers pay." Order ¶ 235. "For example," the Order noted, there were "two carriers in Iowa and one carrier in Minnesota [that] offer[ed] local residential rates below $5 per month." *Id.* The Order concluded that Congress did not "intend[ ] to create a regime in which universal service subsidizes artificially low local rates in rural areas when it adopted the reasonably comparable principle in section 254(b); rather, [the Order concluded], it [wa]s clear from the overall context and structure of the statute that its purpose [wa]s to ensure that rates in rural areas not be significantly higher than in urban areas." *Id.*.

Petitioners argue that "the de facto effect of the Order "is that the FCC is setting local rates." Pet'r Br. 3 at 41. "And," they argue, "since local rate setting is exclusively the province of state commissions under the Act, 47 U.S.C. § 152(b), the Order unlawfully usurps a power reserved to the states." *Id.* "The perverse result of this portion of the Order, petitioners argue, is that to avoid depriving local carriers of needed USF support, states must raise some local rates above levels they would have deemed reasonable." *Id.* at 41–42.

The FCC asserts, however, and we agree, that we are not bound to examine the "practical effect" of an agency order. As the District of Columbia Circuit has noted, "no canon of administrative law requires [a reviewing court] to view the regulatory scope of agency actions in terms of their practical or even foreseeable effects." *Id.* As the District of Columbia Circuit noted, "[o]therwise, [a reviewing court] would have to conclude, for example, that the Environmental Protection Agency regulates the automobile industry when it requires states and localities to comply with national ambient air quality standards, or that the Department of Commerce regulates foreign manufacturers when it collects tariffs on foreign-made goods." *Id.* Thus, we summarily reject the petitioners' argument regarding the practical effect of the Order's new rate floors.

In any event, to the extent the Order encourages states to adjust local rates to ensure that they are not excessively low in comparison to urban rates, that appears to be permissible under, and indeed is consistent with, the universal service principles outlined in the Act. As we noted in *Qwest Corp.*, "the FCC may not simply assume that the states will act on their own to preserve and advance universal service." 258 F.3d at 1204. Rather, the FCC "remains obligated to create some inducement ... for the states to assist in implementing the goals of universal service," i.e., in this case to ensure that rural rates are not artificially low. *Id.* The portion of the Order at issue appears to serve that purpose by encouraging states to set rural rates that are least comparable to urban rates.

5. Does the Order unlawfully deprive rural carriers of a reasonable opportunity to recover their prudently-incurred costs?

Petitioners argue that the Order unlawfully deprives rural carriers of a reasonable opportunity to recover their prudently-incurred costs. In support, petitioners assert that "they are required to continue to provide current services and, at considerable additional expense, to provide broadband service as well." Pet'r Br. 3 at 43. "At the same time," they assert, "their ICC revenue streams are being narrowed and their USF support will be capped, reduced or eliminated outright (depending on their regulatory status)." *Id.* In turn, petitioners argue that "[i]t would be one thing if the [FCC] had tied the reductions in USF support to a determination that the individual carriers had imprudently incurred costs, or that they were recovering the costs of investments not 'used and useful' in delivering regulated services, or that these costs could somehow be recovered from end users without violating the statutory universal service principle calling for rural service rates to be reasonably comparable with those in urban areas." *Id.* at 44. "But," they assert, "the FCC made none of these findings." *Id.* at 45. Lastly, petitioners acknowledge that the Order contains a waiver provision, but they argue that that provision applies only in narrow circumstances and does not reflect "[t]he constitutional test," which they assert "is whether the carrier has been afforded a reasonable opportunity to recover its costs." *Id.*

The FCC asserts, in response, that all of this amounts to an "unsubstantiated takings claim" that "is not ripe." FCC Br. 3 at 39. The FCC notes that the Order made clear that if "any rate-of-return carrier can effectively demonstrate that it needs additional support to avoid constitutionally confiscatory rates, the [FCC] will consider a waiver request for additional support." Order ¶ 294. The FCC thus argues that "[n]o takings claim is ripe until a party has invoked that process and been denied." FCC Br. 3 at 39.

In any event, however, it is clear to us that the FCC did not act arbitrarily in implementing changes to the USF mechanisms. Notably, the Order includes a section expressly discussing the "Impact of These Reforms on Rate–of–Return Carriers and the Communities They Serve." In that section, the FCC concluded that its "intercarrier compensation reforms" would provide rate-of-return carriers with "greater certainty and a more predictable flow of revenues than the status quo." Order ¶ 286. The FCC further noted that the Order's "package of universal service reforms [wa]s targeted at eliminating inefficiencies and closing gaps in [the] system, not at making indiscriminate industry-wide reductions." Order ¶ 287. Relatedly, the FCC noted that its "reforms w[ould] not affect all carriers in the same manner or in the same magnitude," but it expressed confidence "that carriers that invest and operate in a prudent manner will be minimally affected." Order ¶ 289. In support, the FCC stated that its "analysis show[ed] that nearly 9 out of 10 rate-of-return carriers w[ould] see reductions in high-cost universal service receipts of less than 20 percent annually, ... approximately 7 out of 10 w[ould] see reductions of less than 10 percent, ... almost 34 percent ... w[ould] see no reductions whatsoever, and more than 12 percent ... w[ould] see an increase in high-cost universal service receipts." Order ¶ 290. The FCC also "reject[ed] the sweeping argument that the rule changes ... would unlawfully necessarily affect a taking." Order ¶ 293. And it emphasized "that carriers have no vested property interest in USF." *Id.* More specifically, it noted "there [wa]s no statutory provision or Commission rule that provides companies with a vested right to continued receipt of support at current levels, and we are not aware of any other, independent source of law that gives particular companies an entitlement to ongoing USF support." Order ¶ 293. Lastly, the FCC concluded that "carriers ha[d] not shown that elimination of USF support w[ould] result in confiscatory end-user rates." Order ¶ 294. In reaching this conclusion, the FCC noted that, "[t]o the extent that any rate-of-return carriers can effectively demonstrate that it needs additional support to avoid constitutionally confiscatory rates, the Commission will consider a waiver request for additional support." *Id.*

Nothing about this analysis is remotely arbitrary or capricious. Rather, we conclude the FCC's analysis is both reasoned and reasonable. Further, the FCC's analysis is entirely consistent with the overarching universal service principles outlined in 47 U.S.C. § 254(b), including the principle that "[t]here should be specific, predictable and sufficient Federal and State mechanisms to preserve and advance universal service." 47 U.S.C. § 254(b)(5).

8. Does eliminating USF support for the highest-cost areas defeat the very purpose of universal service?

Petitioners complain that the Order delays indefinitely, and thereby effectively eliminates, support for remote, so-called "extremely high-cost areas," and thus defeats the very purpose of universal service. Pet'r Br. 3 at 52.

We begin our analysis of this claim by outlining the Order's treatment of universal funding for "extremely high-cost" service areas. The Order, in pertinent part, "adopt[s] Phase II of the Connect America Fund: a framework for extending broadband to millions of unserved locations over a five-year period, including households, businesses, and community anchor institutions, while sustaining existing voice and broadband services." Order ¶ 156. The primary focus of CAF Phase II is to provide "increased support to areas served by price cap carriers." Order ¶ 159. Those areas, the Order noted, accounted for "more than 83 percent of the unserved locations in the nation" in 2010, but only "receive[d] approximately 25 percent of high-cost support." Order ¶ 158.

"CAF Phase II will have an annual budget of no more than $1.8 billion," which will be distributed "us[ing] a combination of competitive bidding and a new forward-looking model of the cost of constructing modern multi-purpose networks." *Id.* "Using th[is] [forward-looking] model," the FCC "will estimate the support necessary to serve areas where costs are above a specified benchmark, but below a second 'extremely high-cost' benchmark." *Id.* The FCC "delegate[d] to the Wireline Competition Bureau the responsibility for setting the extremely high-cost threshold in conjunction with adoption of a final-cost model." Order ¶ 169.

Relatedly, the Order created a "Remote Areas Fund" intended "to ensure that the less than one percent of Americans living in remote areas where the cost of deploying traditional terrestrial broadband networks is extremely high can obtain affordable broadband." Order ¶ 1224. The Remote Areas Fund, the Order indicated, will receive "$100 million in annual CAF funding to maximize the availability of affordable broadband in such areas." Order ¶ 168. In the FNPRM portion of the Order, the FCC "s[ought] comment on how best to utilize" the Remote Areas Fund. *Id.* The Order proposed that the "universal service goals [could be fulfilled in extremely high-cost areas] by taking advantage of services such as next-generation broadband satellite service or wireless internet service provider (WISP)." *Id.* The Order also sought "comment on how to structure the Remote Areas Fund." Order ¶ 1225. In doing so, the Order proposed several alternative structures, including "a portable consumer subsidy," *id.*, "a competitive bidding process," Order ¶ 1226, and "a competitive proposal evaluation process," Order ¶ 1227.

As the FCC notes in its response brief, until the Remote Areas Fund distribution rules "are in place, extremely high-cost areas will continue to receive support under existing mechanisms for price cap and rate-of-return carriers." FCC Br. 3 at 64 (citing Order ¶¶ 133 (freezing support for price-cap carriers), 195 (maintaining support for rate-of-return carriers)).

In light of these undisputed facts, it is readily apparent that the Order neither "indefinitely" delays distribution of the Remote Areas Fund, nor effectively denies USF funding to extremely high-cost areas. Further, any specific challenges that petitioners may seek to assert against the manner in which the Remote Areas Fund is distributed are not yet ripe.

V. Conclusion

We deny the petitions for review.

BACHARACH, Circuit Judge, concurring in part and dissenting in part.

I join virtually all of Chief Judge Briscoe's thorough, persuasive opinion. But, I respectfully dissent on Part IV(A)(2). There, the majority rejects the Petitioners' challenge to the sufficiency of the budget for the Universal Service Fund. On this limited issue, I respectfully dissent. In my view, the FCC failed to supply a rational basis for its conclusion that an annual budget of $4.5 billion would suffice with the new requirements for broadband capability. In this respect, I believe the FCC acted arbitrarily in violation of the Administrative Procedure Act.

Notes and Questions

1. Other Challenges. The Tenth Circuit rejected a number of other challenges that we have not excerpted here, including specific and vigorous (but ultimately unsuccessful) challenges brought by wireless carriers, rural LECs, and tribal entities.

2. Public Interest Obligations. Note that the FCC now requires that carriers, as a condition of receiving support, commit to providing both voice service and broadband service (under specific metrics). The Commission is ensuring the maintenance of voice service, but notes that such service will be provided over broadband network infrastructure. Is that a sensible approach? On what basis would you argue for a different one?

3. Section 706. Does the Commission need to rely on §706 in addition to §254 for authority to reorient universal service to support broadband deployment? Note that the Commission's authority under §706 is also controversial in the network neutrality context, as is discussed in Chapter Fourteen. There, the argument is parallel—whether the section gives the Commission general authority to regulate and promote Internet services, or whether the Commission is limited to the specific (deregulatory) tools identified in §706(a).

4. Even Less for the States. Recall the significant shrinking of the states' role under the intercarrier compensation part of the order, discussed above. Here, the court affirms the FCC's decision to impose service requirements and limit funding through the auction mechanism. The states still have a role (the court says) by designating eligible telecommunications carriers, but now not all ETCs will receive universal service funds. Could Congress, in the 1996 Act, really have intended such a diminished role for the states? Does that mean the FCC is wrong?

3. Why Not a Broad-Based Tax? The obvious alternative to USF payments is to collect funds for broadband universal service via a broad-based tax. (After all, assuming that we want to subsidize telecommunications for particular groups, there is no requirement that the funds come from telecommunications services.) Broad-based taxes exist of course—notably, taxes on all income, from whatever source derived. Why not raise the broadband universal service funds through such a tax, thereby ending the regulatory arbitrage opportunities created by a more narrowly focused tax?

Is the answer that money to fund a service should come from users of that service? After all, governments often fund highway construction from highway tolls. But, if that is so, is it consistent with the goals of expanding the network? The answer might be yes, if we assume that the number of net givers who will abandon the network because of higher fees will be smaller than the number of net receivers who will join the network because of the subsidies they will receive. But that takes us back to the question of evaluating the effect of the universal service program, which might be difficult to do. And, in any event, wouldn't we achieve greater expansion of telecommunications service if the fee were not levied on that service?

Is the answer instead that voters would not support an increase in income taxes to fund these programs, but they will not complain as loudly about fees on broadband services because they are not as aware of the taxes they effectively pay on such services? On this reasoning, a program that might be politically untenable if funded via a broad-based tax becomes politically viable if funded via a fee on telecommunications services. If that is not the explanation, why not move to a broad-based tax? If it is the explanation, does it cast doubt on the wisdom of the program? To put the point differently, if a program would be unpopular if voters were aware of it and thus is viable only because voters are unaware of it, should that tell members of Congress who support the programs that maybe they have a faulty sense of what is in the public interest? Or would continuation of the program be an example of legislators appropriately acting in the public's best interest, even if the public (or a majority of it, anyway) does not believe that it is in their interest?

§ 13.F. A New Blank Slate: The IP Transition

The final stage in the evolution from the PSTN will be its replacement with an all-IP network. As carriers make this technology transition, the FCC will be confronted again with fundamental issues, including the development of competition, the need for interconnection regulation, and the extent to which universal service will be mandated. As only one example, the Bell System's implicit deal with regulators saw it provide universal wiring—that mandate is no longer part of the system as we now know. The FCC is now considering these issues, in the context of permitting voluntary experiments. One could see this as a greenfield exercise, in which the FCC has the opportunity to write new rules on a blank slate. This excerpt from the FCC's initial order gives a sense of the stakes.

TECHNOLOGY TRANSITIONS
Order, Report and Order and Further Notice of Proposed Rulemaking, Report and Order, Order and Further Notice of Proposed Rulemaking,
Proposal for Ongoing Data Initiative, 29 FCC Rcd. 1433 (2014)

I. Introduction

1. Today's Orders, Report and Orders, Further Notices of Proposed Rulemaking, and Proposal for Ongoing Data Initiative (Order) kickstart the process for a diverse set of experiments and data collection initiatives that will allow the Commission and the public to evaluate how customers are affected by the historic technology transitions that are transforming our nation's voice communications services—from a network based on time-division multiplexed (TDM) circuit-switched voice services running on copper loops to an all-Internet Protocol (IP) network using copper, co-axial cable, wireless, and fiber as physical infrastructure. Americans have come to expect secure, reliable, and innovative communications services. The purpose of these experiments is to speed market-driven technological transitions and innovations by preserving the core statutory values as codified by Congress—public safety, ubiquitous and affordable access, competition, and consumer protection—that exist today. The experiments and initiatives will collect data that will permit service providers and their customers, and independent analysts and commentators—as well as the federal, State, local, and Tribal officials charged with oversight—to make data-driven decisions about these technology transitions. By using an open and deliberative process to identify and address challenges, all stakeholders will ben-

efit as we together learn how we may ensure that our values flourish as providers implement new technologies at scale and, ultimately, seek to discontinue legacy services and facilities.

2. We must act with dispatch. Technology transitions are already underway. These ongoing transitions have brought new and improved communications services to the marketplace. Network providers have invested billions of dollars to transition legacy networks and services to next generation technologies, and over the next several years will invest many billions more. Modernizing communications networks can dramatically reduce network costs, allowing providers to serve customers with increased efficiencies that can lead to improved and innovative product offerings and lower prices. It also catalyzes further investments in innovation that both enhance existing products and unleash new services, applications and devices, thus powering economic growth. The lives of millions of Americans could be improved by the direct and spillover effects of the technology transitions, including innovations that cannot even be imagined today. The proceeding we initiate today is designed to position all the players—innovators (including those in existing lines of business), legacy service providers and manufacturers, government regulators and the general public—to prepare for, maintain, and facilitate the momentum of technological advances that are already occurring.

3. Today, these technology transitions bring additional choices to consumers by largely supplementing, rather than supplanting, the legacy copper circuit-switched voice services in the marketplace. In the context of voice communications, for example, most consumers may choose to "cut-the-cord" by using only wireless voice services, or may opt for digital, packet-based voice services by relying on IP-based services. To date, these consumers by and large could revert to legacy services if their chosen alternative does not meet their needs or expectations. But, in the natural course of progress, we expect there will come a tipping point, a point where the adoption of new communications technologies reaches a critical mass and most providers wish to cease offering legacy services. This is a reflection of technological innovation and in that respect is a good thing. But it also removes a choice from the marketplace: the choice that has been the source of the enduring values for generations and the service that Congress beyond question marked as essential to all Americans. From this perspective, we stand today at the precipice of a very different technology transition—the turning off of the legacy suite of services that has served our nation well.

4. Our mission and statutory responsibility are to ensure that the core statutory values endure as we embrace modernized communications networks. Fulfilling this mission requires that we learn much more about how the modernization of communications networks affects consumers. Today's Order does this along three broad directions.

5. First, we open a proceeding and invite any and all interested providers to submit detailed proposals to test real-world applications of planned changes in technology that are likely to have tangible effects on consumers. These voluntary service-based experiments will examine the impacts of replacing existing customer services with IP-based alternatives in discrete geographic areas or ways. We identify below and in the Appendix the types of information that will be useful to us in evaluating applicants' proposals, the conditions, presumptions, and relevant factors on which proposals will be evaluated, and principles for the collection and reporting of data from any experiment. We also establish below the process and timeframe for submitting proposals. To ensure transparency and maximize public input, we will seek comment on each proposal.

6. Second, in parallel with seeking proposals for the service-based experiments, we are moving forward with targeted experiments and cooperative research to explore the im-

pact of technology transitions that focus on universal access, one of our enduring values that must be protected and enhanced in the technology transition. These proof-of-concept initiatives are focused on new technologies for particular groups of consumers, aspects of network functions, or more effective ways to reach all Americans. One of these experiments explores ways to examine the impact of technology transitions on rural Americans, including those living on Tribal lands, and ensure that, as networks transition, they are not left behind. We seek additional comment in a Further Notice of Proposed Rulemaking on a number of issues relating to this rural broadband experiment. We also further universal access by taking the next step in developing and funding an interagency collaborative research program into IP-based technologies for individuals with disabilities. In addition, we seek to facilitate the development of a numbering testbed to address concerns raised about number assignment and databases in an all-IP world, without disrupting current systems.

7. Third, we initiate a proposal for ongoing data initiative and seek feedback below on a number of other efforts to improve our collection of data about how technological evolutions are impacting network values—data that the Commission needs to make informed decisions and speed the technology transitions. For example, we intend to reform our consumer complaint and inquiry processes and collaborate with State, local, and Tribal governments and leaders to develop a better understanding of the transition from the consumer's perspective. In addition, we intend to conduct a structured data collection and analysis of next generation 911 (NG911) transition deployment projects in coordination with the Department of Transportation's National 911 Office and various other public safety associations. We seek comment on these proposals and, more broadly, on our efforts to assess what data we collect, where there are information gaps, and how we can work with outside parties to enhance our information about the technology transitions and their impact on our network values.

8. We emphasize that the goal of all of these experiments and initiatives is to learn about the impact of the technology transitions on the customers—and communities—that rely on communications networks. We are not proposing technology experiments designed to resolve technical questions. Nor are we seeking to resolve the legal and policy questions arising from the technology transitions in the context of an experiment. Rather, we endeavor to learn in diverse ways how the modernization of communications networks is affecting the achievement of our statutory responsibilities. And for that we need real-world data. These data will fuel the ongoing public dialogue about the technology transitions, ensuring that it is fact-based and data-driven. Having a robust and factually-informed public discussion will help guide the Commission as we make legal and policy choices that advance and accelerate the technology transitions while ensuring that consumers and the enduring values established by Congress are not adversely affected.

9. Although there of course remains much to do, the important mileposts described above will help guide us in the historic journey from a voice-focused communications network that would have been easily recognizable to Alexander Graham Bell to the very different all-IP networks that collectively will comprise the global multimedia communications infrastructure of the future. Though the task before us is daunting, we take comfort that we are not alone in our efforts to encourage technology transitions while protecting the enduring values established by Congress for our nation's communication networks. State, local, and Tribal governments and leaders share this challenge, along with other federal entities. We will work alongside each other to ensure that, as networks transition, public safety is assured, access is universal, competition is promoted, consumers are protected, and the nation remains well-served by its critical communications infrastructure.

II. BACKGROUND

A. Network Evolution

10. As we begin the process of exploring what the technology transitions mean for customers and our enduring values, we pause to take stock. America's first great national network was the railroad. Early railroad passengers compared their experience to being inside a projectile shot through the landscape, disorienting their sense of space and time. To some, it seemed that "[s]pace is killed by the railroad and we are left with time alone." Wolfgang Schivelbusch, The Railway Journey: The Industrialization of Time and Space in the 19th Century 53–54, 129 (1986). The telegraph would annihilate time as well. The copper wire that carried the famous words "what hath God wrought" from Washington, D.C. to Baltimore in 1844 did so, then as now, at about two-thirds the speed of light. *Id.* at 37. Even in 1988, describing the Internet, the Washington Post marveled: "It enables a user sitting at one machine, with permission, actually to operate another machine on the network, just as if the person were in the same room." Barton Gellman, Here's How the Post Covered the 'Grand Social Experiment' of the Internet in 1988, Wash. Post (Nov. 4, 2013). But as networks spread and interconnected to form networks of networks, we have come to rely on them not as marvels but as necessities, and have come to expect that they will serve the public interest, bring help in emergencies, and keep us and the nation safe.

11. The economic consequences of deploying network infrastructure that can conquer space and time are enormous. The day after the final spike was driven in the Transcontinental railroad, a shipment of Japanese tea left San Francisco for St. Louis. Within ten years, the railroad carried $50 million worth of freight per year across the country, and a book published in San Francisco could reach New York shops within a week. In 1850, a mere 9,021 miles of American railway existed; by 1890, tracks covered 129,774 miles. Economic historians credit the railroad with the largest contribution to American gross national product of any single innovation before 1900, even when its incalculable spillover effects are ignored.

12. The economic impact of telephone networks is equally dramatic. Alexander Graham Bell patented the telephone on March 7, 1876. Most Americans saw little use for the telephone at first—and with reason, as so few people had one. By the early 1900s, Bell System local exchanges competed briskly for customers with rival, non-interconnecting local exchanges. And by 1983, more than 90 percent of America's 85.8 million households had a telephone. Economic investment powered this growth. Merely developing the first usable electronic switching system was "found to have required a staggering four thousand man-years of work at Bell Labs" and to have cost $500 million. John Brooks, Telephone—The First Hundred Years 279 (1975). Between 1996, when the telephone network was broadly opened to competition, and 2001, a torrent of new investment deployed over 200,000 miles of trenches and approximately 18 million miles of fiber—enough fiber to circle the equator 750 times.

13. The growth of our nation's wireless infrastructure tells a similar story. Since 1997, wireless use has grown from 5.8 billion minutes per month to 187.8 billion minutes per month in 2012; the number of cell sites has grown from 51,600 cell sites in 1997 to 301,779 cell sites in 2012; and industry annual revenue has grown from $27.4 billion in 1997 to $185 billion in 2012. "Wireless only" households have grown from "n/a" in 1997 to 38.2 percent in 2012. More impressive still, the wireless industry reports a penetration rate of "102.2 percent," meaning our nation now has more wireless devices than people.

14. But progress does not stop once a network is built. Technology continues to evolve, and networks incorporate these innovations. The result is better and faster services for con-

sumers, thus changing expectations and creating demand for more. Most of these innovations are unremarkable—incremental improvements that may not even be perceptible to network users. But over time, the accretion of thousands of technological improvements sometimes raises questions as to whether one service is being discontinued in favor of another—a modern day version of the Ship of Theseus. In addition, some technologies improve to the point where they come to displace other technologies outright. When this happens, providers may overbuild their legacy networks with new networks, and may seek to turn off their legacy services and retire their legacy facilities in favor of the modern alternatives.

15. Technology transitions mark progress and are a good thing—sometimes even a triumph. But change on this scale can also be disruptive. Customer expectations may become unsettled, established business models may crumble as the assumptions on which they are built become outdated, and the rules of the road may be called into question through the uncertain application of existing rules to new technologies. These changes can ripple throughout society, requiring accommodations and investments by those affected. While technology transitions always risk unsettling particular expectations, such changes also pose societal risks. If technology transitions are implemented with insufficient regard for customers, the enduring and shared network values may be sacrificed—a result that should be unacceptable to all.

16. We are focused on three key technology transitions that significantly affect customers. These changes are ongoing, and will continue for years. First, providers are migrating to new general-purpose transport networks—that is, providers are migrating to underlying infrastructures that are different from the equipment found in the legacy networks that were designed initially with voice communications in mind. In particular, circuit-switched providers are increasingly transitioning switched voice services from legacy TDM and Signaling System No. 7 (SS7) networks to Session Initiation Protocol (SIP)/IP networks.

17. Second, the transition to SIP/IP-based transport and signaling enables an ongoing technological transition at the application layer: specifically, providers, and third parties, are transitioning customers' services from purpose-built networks to new applications that can ride over more general broadband transport networks. Most notably, TDM-based switched voice services are being replaced in many places by interconnected Voice over Internet Protocol (VoIP) services that rely on SIP/IP networks, and Voice over LTE (VoLTE) services will soon be widely available on LTE wireless networks.

18. Third, the physical layer of last-mile technology is changing. Historically, the physical medium over which fixed end-user communications were predominantly transmitted consisted of twisted pairs of copper wire, which have served us well for over a century. Now providers in many places are sending communications over a diversity of physical platforms. In addition to twisted copper pair, providers today are increasingly using fiber optic cable, co-axial cable, and wireless technologies for fixed end-user voice and data transmissions.

B. Procedural History

19. On November 7, 2012, AT&T filed a petition asking the Commission to consider conducting trial runs of the transition to next generation services, including the retirement of TDM facilities and service offerings and their replacement with IP-based alternatives. AT&T's Petition further requests the Commission to invite incumbent local exchange carriers (LECs) to propose individual wire centers for these experiments. The proposals would submit plans identifying in each wire center the steps the carrier would

take, and the modifications each carrier would make to its network, to transition from TDM- to IP-based facilities and services.

III. VOLUNTARY SERVICE-BASED EXPERIMENTS

22. To the extent described below, we grant AT&T's petition. Specifically, we initiate a proceeding and establish a framework within which providers can conduct what we will call "service-based" experiments. Service-based experiments are experiments in which incumbent providers seek to substitute new communications technologies for the TDM-based services over copper lines that they currently are providing to customers, with an eye toward discontinuing those legacy services and in which others may propose new and innovative services that bring benefits to consumers while preserving the enduring values of our nation's communications networks. As requested by AT&T, we hereby solicit prompt, detailed proposals for service-based experiments in diverse but limited arenas. We set forth below what information we believe will be relevant and useful in evaluating any proposal; the values-based conditions, presumptions, and relevant factors on which proposed experiments will be evaluated; the data we would expect providers to collect and report; and a process for proposal submission, public comment, and Commission evaluation and decision at the May Commission meeting.

A. Experiments to Examine Potential Impacts on Network Values

23. Our over-arching purpose in soliciting these service-based experiment proposals is to speed technological advances by preserving the positive attributes of network services that customers have come to expect. These statutory values include "four enduring values that have always informed communications law—public safety, universal service, competition, and consumer protection."

24. The values themselves are interdependent and mutually reinforcing. For example, the existence of a network that reliably allows users to dial 911 in an emergency to obtain help reinforces the importance of universal access to that network. Moreover, there is no choice between embracing technological transitions and protecting values. Rather, preserving network values advances the technological progress. By the same example, a new communications technology that failed to provide reliable 911 service would not be widely adopted as a replacement for legacy technologies that offer that functionality.

25. We state again that these service-based experiments are not intended to test technologies *per se* or to resolve legal or policy debates. Rather, we seek to create arenas of innovation where providers and their competitors, and the customers of each, are free to explore a variety of approaches to resolving any operational challenges that result from transitioning to new technology and that may impact users. We believe that such an environment is more likely to emerge if applicants are freed, to the extent possible, from the necessity of calculating the rippling legal and policy ramifications of each new action. We therefore emphasize that decisions about how to address or resolve a problem or dispute during an experiment will not constitute a determination by the Commission or service providers that such an approach represents binding legal or policy obligations outside the context of the experiment. For example, if a provider exchanges VoIP traffic in a wire center without first converting it to TDM, that provider shall not be deemed to have conceded—nor will the Commission have determined—that VoIP traffic is subject to interconnection obligations. The data generated as a result of these experiments will deepen our understanding of the effects of the technology transitions on consumers with respect to core statutory objectives. This understanding will enable the Commission to make data-driven legal and policy choices that protect consumers and our enduring values, while also advancing and accelerating the technology transitions.

26. To protect the enduring values, we set forth criteria for experiments below along the following framework:

- **Conditions.** We provide below a basic set of values-based conditions that any proposed experiment must satisfy. For example, applicants must ensure reliable and uninterrupted 911 service during an experiment. We expect experiments to comply with the Commission's existing rules.

- **Presumptions.** In addition to these set conditions, we provide rebuttable presumptions that will guide our evaluation of proposed experiments. In this regard, applicants might submit evidence to demonstrate that the experiments will satisfy the statutory objectives in other ways and that full compliance with all applicable rules would impede the experiment and is unnecessary to protect the public interest. For example, we presume below that applicants will adhere to existing intercarrier compensation requirements in any experiment, but will consider applications that argue that a deviation from those rules is justified and in the public interest in the context of a particular experiment.

- **Relevant Factors.** Finally, there are values-based areas of interest and relevant factors that the public and the Commission will have to consider in order to evaluate and provide feedback on a particular experiment. We discuss these considerations below in order to provide guidance to applicants in preparing their applications, so that they can readily identify the types of information that we will find useful and necessary to guide our review.

27. By adopting this framework of mandatory conditions, rebuttable presumptions, and relevant factors, we hope to create a transparent and efficient process that will afford applicants flexibility, ensure public input, and allow us to move swiftly.

28. We re-emphasize that our adoption of conditions and presumptions does not dictate what specific requirements the Commission might apply long-term, outside the narrow context of technology transition experiments. The conditions and presumptions we set forth below shall not have specific binding legal or policy effect outside the context of the experiments except insofar as the Commission subsequently determines otherwise.

Notes and Questions

1. Innovation by Permission? Why should telecommunications companies need FCC approval to change technologies, so long as service standards are maintained? As the FCC notes, it has performance regulations, such as for 911 service. If a carrier can change its technology and still meet these standards, why should it need government permission? One part of the answer is that, sometimes, the carrier might abandon service that it was previously providing. Section 214 of the Communications Act, 47 U.S.C. § 214, requires Commission approval for the "discontinuance" of a "line," which provides much of the source of the Commission's authority. But identifying this legal authority does not necessarily justify its exercise. Section 214 is a vestige of the common carrier model, under which service could not be started without permission and, if approved, service had to be maintained for all customers in an area. Given that the 1996 Act's theory was to point telecommunications markets in the direction of other, unregulated markets, isn't this a jarring reminder that telecommunications markets remain quite controlled?

2. Universal Service Again. Is there much more at stake here than universal service? Is it possible to imagine that a communications provider would not provide connection to

911 centers, or other quality of service that consumers want? Indeed, if the FCC's policies provide universal broadband, won't an abundance of voice and other apps expand to fill those roles? What is the FCC's mission other than universal service at this point?

3. No Landlines. Many households do not have traditional landline service, relying instead on a combination of cell phone and Internet services for whatever voice they might use. Given that the FCC in the Connect America Fund order stated that voice would be provided over broadband, isn't the transition away from a PSTN all but inevitable? Does the FCC's order make it seem as if the FCC wants to slow down that transition? Is the FCC acting as if it has more time than it might?

Chapter Fourteen

Broadband Jurisdiction and Structural Regulation

Introduction

The Telecommunications Act of 1996, as we discussed in Chapter Twelve, did not entirely anticipate the Internet as a technological force that would disrupt the legacy telecommunications system. The Internet, however, has emerged as the ultimate form of convergence—broadband Internet service providers can support video programming, voice telephone calls, and a range of other services. The next chapter will consider regulations aimed at Internet content. This chapter will address structural broadband regulation, in particular the legal and policy challenges that have emerged regarding the classification of broadband service under the Communications Act and the decisions whether and how to regulate it. We do so in the context of two contested policy issues: (1) the debate over network neutrality for broadband Internet access service[1] and (2) the conflict over the proper regulatory treatment of Voice over Internet Protocol (VoIP) applications. We conclude the chapter by applying this discussion to the phenomenon of "over-the-top" video.

The issues in this chapter can profitably be broken into three questions. First, what, if any, authority does the FCC have to regulate broadband providers? Here, the essential conflict is one of statutory interpretation of the Communications Act. On the one hand is the view that the FCC has authority to regulate all "interstate ... communication by wire or radio" so long as its regulations fit within the general purposes of the Act, 47 U.S.C. § 151; on the other hand is the view that the FCC has authority only to regulate the types of services specifically described in the main titles of the Act (i.e., common carrier, spectrum, and cable services). Under the broader view, the FCC has regulatory authority over broadband transmission because broadband is undoubtedly communications and is taking the place of the traditional common carrier, broadcast, and cable services. Under the narrower view, the FCC does not have authority over broadband transmission unless the service provided via broadband is itself a common carrier, broadcast, or cable service over which Congress has expressly granted the FCC authority. In between these

---

1. The particular focus of regulatory concern in the net neutrality proceeding, and thus a major focus of this chapter, is broadband Internet access service, which the FCC defines as "[a] mass-market retail service by wire or radio that provides the capability to transmit data to and receive data from all or substantially all Internet endpoints, including any capabilities that are incidental to and enable the operation of the communications service, but excluding dial-up Internet access service." Preserving the Open Internet, Report and Order, 25 FCC Rcd. 17,905 ¶ 44 (2010).

views is the position finally adopted by the FCC and partially endorsed by the D.C. Circuit, that Congress did grant the FCC at least some specific authority over Internet communications.

This leads naturally to the second question: What kind of communications service is broadband transmission service? Under the narrow view of the FCC's regulatory authority, classification means a great deal because it ties broadband service into the specific regulatory scheme created by Congress in one of the titles of the Act. Even under the broader view, classification is important, for the constraints on the FCC's authority may depend on whether a service falls within an established category or within the FCC's residual authority over all interstate communications.

The third question is simply what should the appropriate policies be? Apart from the question of the FCC's authority to regulate, one must ask what the appropriate regulation of broadband networks should be. Congress could give the FCC additional authority (if the FCC lacks it), the Federal Trade Commission could exert authority under its broad statutes, or the Antitrust Division of the Department of Justice could attack certain problems through competition law.

Although we break them out, the questions have inevitably developed in an interrelated fashion. Different agencies are historically and statutorily associated with different regulatory approaches, meaning that the locus and substance of regulation are driven by the type of problems one is trying to solve. And the inquiries may interact: for instance, classification decisions (question two) may be affected by one's view of the appropriate regulation to be applied (question three).

§ 14.A. The Ancillary Jurisdiction Doctrine and the Past as Prologue?

When confronting the questions above, a historical case study is instructive: the rise of cable television, which created a conundrum for the FCC. As discussed in Chapter Two, under the Communications Act of 1934, the FCC enjoys authority under Title II to regulate common carrier telecommunications by wire and under Title III to regulate broadcasting by air. The delivery of television signals by wire did not fall within either mandate, and the FCC initially concluded that it lacked jurisdiction to regulate this emerging medium. In the early 1960s (at the behest of broadcasters), the FCC reconsidered this decision and concluded that, under what has become known as Title I authority, the FCC could regulate cable television because such regulations were ancillary to its charge to regulate broadcasting. Notably, the theory of Title I jurisdiction rejects the suggestion that the provisions in Title I of the 1934 Act were mere housekeeping measures. Instead, this argument views the relevant provisions as charging the FCC with a common-law-like authority to develop new rules for evolving technologies. In particular, the first two provisions of Title I establish the FCC "[f]or the purpose of regulating interstate and foreign commerce in communication by wire and radio" and make clear that "[t]he provisions of this chapter shall apply to," among other things, "all interstate and foreign communication by wire or radio." 47 U.S.C. §§ 151, 152(a). Moreover, § 4(i) of the Act, which is sometimes called the FCC's "necessary and proper" clause,[2] authorizes the Com-

---

2. *See, e.g.*, Motion Picture Ass'n of Am., Inc. v. FCC, 309 F.3d 796, 807 (D.C. Cir. 2002) (quoting Implementation of Video Description of Video Programming, Report and Order, 15 FCC Rcd. 15,230, 15,276 (2000) (Powell, Comm'r, dissenting in part and concurring in part)).

mission to "perform any and all acts, make such rules and regulations, and issue such orders, not inconsistent with this chapter, as may be necessary in the execution of its functions." 47 U.S.C. § 154(i).

In a series of cases the Supreme Court addressed the FCC's authority over cable (before, of course, Congress amended the Communications Act specifically to include Title VI, the cable provisions), and the Court's decisions established the framework for the FCC's more general authority over "communication" not covered by the Act's specific titles. In United States v. Southwestern Cable Co., 392 U.S. 157 (1968), the Supreme Court embraced a broad view of Title I authority and concluded that the FCC had jurisdiction over cable television providers to the extent necessary to promulgate rules "reasonably ancillary to the effective performance of the Commission's various responsibilities for the regulation of television broadcasting." *Id.* at 178. Following the Supreme Court's approval in *Southwestern Cable*, the FCC possessed the authority to regulate cable television. After *Southwestern Cable*, the Commission continued to expand its efforts to regulate cable television. Ultimately, it went too far. In FCC v. Midwest Video Corp. (*Midwest Video II*), 440 U.S. 689 (1979), the Supreme Court rejected an FCC rule that would have required cable systems to carry "public access" channels. According to the Court, the rule was not "reasonably ancillary" to the Commission's mandate to regulate broadcasting because broadcasters themselves could not be regulated as common carriers. *Id.* at 708–09.

Set out below are very brief excerpts from the key decisions.

United States v. Southwestern Cable Co.
392 U.S. 157 (1968)

HARLAN, J., delivered the opinion of the Court. WHITE, J., filed an opinion concurring in the result. DOUGLAS and MARSHALL, JJ., took no part in the consideration or decision of the case.

Justice HARLAN delivered the opinion of the Court.

We must first emphasize that questions as to the validity of the specific rules promulgated by the Commission for the regulation of community antenna television (CATV) are not now before the Court. The issues in these cases are only two: whether the Commission has authority under the Communications Act to regulate CATV systems, and, if it has, whether it has, in addition, authority to issue the prohibitory order here in question.

The Commission's authority to regulate broadcasting and other communications is derived from the Communications Act of 1934, as amended. The Act's provisions are explicitly applicable to "all interstate and foreign communication by wire or radio...." 47 U.S.C. § 152(a). The Commission's responsibilities are no more narrow: it is required to endeavor to "make available ... to all the people of the United States a rapid, efficient, Nation-wide, and world-wide wire and radio communication service...." 47 U.S.C. § 151. The Commission was expected to serve as the "single Government agency" with "unified jurisdiction" and "regulatory power over all forms of electrical communication, whether by telephone, telegraph, cable, or radio." It was for this purpose given "broad authority." As this Court emphasized in an earlier case, the Act's terms, purposes, and history all indicate that Congress "formulated a unified and comprehensive regulatory system for the (broadcasting) industry." FCC v. Pottsville Broadcasting Co., 309 U.S. 134, 137 (1940).

Respondents do not suggest that CATV systems are not within the term "communication by wire or radio." Indeed, such communications are defined by the Act so as to encompass "the transmission of ... signals, pictures, and sounds of all kinds," whether by radio or cable, "including all instrumentalities, facilities, apparatus, and services (among other things, the receipt, forwarding, and delivery of communications) incidental to such transmission." 47 U.S.C. §§ 153(a), (b). These very general terms amply suffice to reach respondents' activities.

Nor can we doubt that CATV systems are engaged in interstate communication, even where, as here, the intercepted signals emanate from stations located within the same State in which the CATV system operates. We may take notice that television broadcasting consists in very large part of programming devised for, and distributed to, national audiences. Nonetheless, respondents urge that the Communications Act, properly understood, does not permit the regulation of CATV systems. First, they emphasize that the Commission in 1959 and again in 1966 sought legislation that would have explicitly authorized such regulation, and that its efforts were unsuccessful. In the circumstances here, however, this cannot be dispositive. The Commission's requests for legislation evidently reflected in each instance both its uncertainty as to the proper width of its authority and its understandable preference for more detailed policy guidance than the Communications Act now provides.

Second, respondents urge that § 152(a) does not independently confer regulatory authority upon the Commission, but instead merely prescribes the forms of communication to which the Act's other provisions may separately be made applicable. Respondents emphasize that the Commission does not contend either that CATV systems are common carriers, and thus within Title II of the Act, or that they are broadcasters, and thus within Title III. They conclude that CATV, with certain of the characteristics both of broadcasting and of common carriers, but with all of the characteristics of neither, eludes altogether the Act's grasp.

We cannot construe the Act so restrictively. Nothing in the language of § 152(a), in the surrounding language, or in the Act's history or purposes limits the Commission's authority to those activities and forms of communication that are specifically described by the Act's other provisions. The section itself states merely that the "provisions of (the Act) shall apply to all interstate and foreign communication by wire or radio...." Similarly, the legislative history indicates that the Commission was given "regulatory power over all forms of electrical communication." S. Rep. No. 781, 73d Cong., 2d Sess., 1. Certainly Congress could not in 1934 have foreseen the development of community antenna television systems, but it seems to us that it was precisely because Congress wished "to maintain, through appropriate administrative control, a grip on the dynamic aspects of radio transmission," *Pottsville Broadcasting*, 309 U.S. at 138, that it conferred upon the Commission a "unified jurisdiction" and "broad authority." Thus, "(u)nderlying the whole (Communications Act) is recognition of the rapidly fluctuating factors characteristic of the evolution of broadcasting and of the corresponding requirement that the administrative process possess sufficient flexibility to adjust itself to these factors." *Id*. We have found no reason to believe that § 152 does not, as its terms suggest, confer regulatory authority over "all interstate ... communication by wire or radio."

Moreover, the Commission has reasonably concluded that regulatory authority over CATV is imperative if it is to perform with appropriate effectiveness certain of its other responsibilities. Congress has imposed upon the Commission the "obligation of providing a widely dispersed radio and television service," with a "fair, efficient, and equitable distribution" of service among the "several States and communities." 47 U.S.C. § 307(b). The Commission has, for this and other purposes, been granted authority to allocate broadcasting zones or areas, and to provide regulations "as it may deem necessary" to prevent interference among the various stations. 47 U.S.C. §§ 303(f), (h). The Commission has concluded, and Congress has agreed, that these obligations require for their satisfaction the creation of a system of local broadcasting stations, such that "all communities of appreciable size (will) have at least one television station as an outlet for local self-expression." In turn, the Commission has held that an appropriate system of local broadcasting may be created only if two subsidiary goals are realized. First, significantly wider use must be made of the available ultra-high-frequency channels. Second, communities must be encouraged "to launch sound and adequate programs to utilize the television channels now reserved for educational purposes." These subsidiary goals have received the endorsement of Congress.

The Commission has reasonably found that the achievement of each of these purposes is "placed in jeopardy by the unregulated explosive growth of CATV." H.R. Rep. No. 1635, 89th Cong., 2d Sess., 7. Although CATV may in some circumstances make possible "the realization of some of the (Commission's) most important goals," First Report and Order, 38 F.C.C. 683, 699, its importation of distant signals into the service areas of local stations may also "destroy or seriously degrade the service offered by a television broadcaster," *id.* at 700, and thus ultimately deprive the public of the various benefits of a system of local broadcasting stations. In particular, the Commission feared that CATV might, by dividing the available audiences and revenues, significantly magnify the characteristically serious financial difficulties of UHF and educational television broadcasters. The Commission acknowledged that it could not predict with certainty the consequences of unregulated CATV, but reasoned that its statutory responsibilities demand that it "plan in advance of foreseeable events, instead of waiting to react to them." *Id.* at 701. We are aware that these consequences have been variously estimated, but must conclude that there is substantial evidence that the Commission cannot "discharge its overall responsibilities without authority over this important aspect of television service." Staff of Senate Comm. on Interstate and Foreign Commerce, 85th Cong., 2d Sess., The Television Inquiry: The Problem of Television Service for Smaller Communities 19 (Comm. Print 1959).

There is no need here to determine in detail the limits of the Commission's authority to regulate CATV. It is enough to emphasize that the authority which we recognize today under § 152(a) is restricted to that reasonably ancillary to the effective performance of the Commission's various responsibilities for the regulation of television broadcasting. The Commission may, for these purposes, issue "such rules and regulations and prescribe such restrictions and conditions, not inconsistent with law," as "public convenience, interest, or necessity requires." 47 U.S.C. § 303(r). We express no views as to the Commission's authority, if any, to regulate CATV under any other circumstances or for any other purposes.

[Concurring opinion of JUSTICE WHITE is omitted.]

FCC v. MIDWEST VIDEO CORP. [*MIDWEST VIDEO II*]
440 U.S. 689 (1979)

WHITE, J., delivered the opinion of the Court. STEVENS, J., filed a dissenting opinion in which BRENNAN and MARSHALL, JJ., joined.

JUSTICE WHITE delivered the opinion of the Court.

In May 1976, the Federal Communications Commission promulgated rules requiring cable television systems that have 3,500 or more subscribers and carry broadcast signals to develop, at a minimum, a 20-channel capacity by 1986, to make available certain channels for access by third parties, and to furnish equipment and facilities for access purposes. Report and Order, 59 F.C.C. 2d 294 (1976 Order). The issue here is whether these rules are "reasonably ancillary to the effective performance of the Commission's various responsibilities for the regulation of television broadcasting," United States v. Southwestern Cable Co., 392 U.S. 157, 178 (1968), and hence within the Commission's statutory authority.

The Commission derives its regulatory authority from the Communications Act of 1934, 48 Stat. 1064, as amended, 47 U.S.C. § 151 *et seq.* The Act preceded the advent of cable television and understandably does not expressly provide for the regulation of that medium. But it is clear that Congress meant to confer "broad authority" on the Commission, H.R. Rep. No. 1850, 73d Cong., 2d Sess., 1 (1934), so as "to maintain, through appropriate administrative control, a grip on the dynamic aspects of radio transmission." FCC v. Pottsville Broadcasting Co., 309 U.S. 134, 138 (1940). To that end, Congress subjected to regulation "all interstate and foreign communication by wire or radio." Communications Act of 1934, § 2(a), 47 U.S.C. § 152(a). In *Southwestern Cable*, we construed § 2(a) as conferring on the Commission a circumscribed range of power to regulate cable television, and we reaffirmed that determination in United States v. Midwest Video Corp., 406 U.S. 649 (1972) (*Midwest Video I*). The question now before us is whether the Act, as construed in these two cases, authorizes the capacity and access regulations that are here under challenge.

Soon after our decision in *Southwestern*, the Commission resolved "to condition the carriage of television broadcast signals ... upon a requirement that the CATV system also operate to a significant extent as a local outlet by originating." Notice of Proposed Rulemaking and Notice of Inquiry, 15 F.C.C. 2d 417, 422 (1968). It stated that its "concern with CATV carriage of broadcast signals [was] not just a matter of avoidance of adverse effects, but extend[ed] also to requiring CATV affirmatively to further statutory policies." *Id.* Accordingly, the Commission promulgated a rule providing that CATV systems having 3,500 or more subscribers may not carry the signal of any television broadcast station unless the system also operates to a significant extent as a local outlet by originating its own programs—or cablecasting—and maintains facilities for local production and presentation of programs other than automated services. 47 C.F.R. § 74.1111(a) (1970). This Court, by a 5 to 4 vote but without an opinion for the Court, sustained the Commission's jurisdiction to issue these regulations in *Midwest Video I*.

Four Justices, in an opinion by Mr. Justice Brennan, reaffirmed the view that the Commission has jurisdiction over cable television and that such authority is delimited by its statutory responsibilities over television broadcasting. They thought that the reasonably-ancillary standard announced in *Southwestern* permitted regulation of CATV "with a view not merely to protect but to promote the objectives for which the Commission had been assigned jurisdiction over broadcasting." 406 U.S. at 667. The Commission had reasonably determined, Mr. Justice Brennan's opinion declared, that the origination requirement would "'further the achievement of long-established regulatory goals in the field of television broadcasting by increasing the number of outlets for community self-expression and augmenting the public's choice of programs and types of services.... '" *Id.* at 667–68, quoting First Report and Order, 20 F.C.C. 2d 201, 202 (1969). The conclusion was that the "program-origination rule [was] within the Commission's authority recognized in *Southwestern*." 406 U.S. at 670.

The Chief Justice, in a separate opinion concurring in the result, admonished that the Commission's origination rule "strain[ed] the outer limits" of its jurisdiction. *Id.* at 676. Though not "fully persuaded that the Commission ha[d] made the correct decision in [the] case," he was inclined to defer to its judgment. *Id.*

B

Because its access and capacity rules promote the long-established regulatory goals of maximization of outlets for local expression and diversification of programming—the objectives promoted by the rule sustained in *Midwest Video I*—the Commission maintains that it plainly had jurisdiction to promulgate them. Respondents, in opposition, view the access regulations as an intrusion on cable system operations that is qualitatively different from the impact of the rule upheld in *Midwest Video I*. Specifically, it is urged that by requiring the allocation of access channels to categories of users specified by the regulations and by depriving the cable operator of the power to select individual users or to control the programming on such channels, the regulations wrest a considerable degree of editorial control from the cable operator and in effect compel the cable system to provide a kind of common-carrier service. Respondents contend, therefore, that the regulations are not only qualitatively different from those heretofore approved by the courts but also contravene statutory limitations designed to safeguard the journalistic freedom of broadcasters, particularly the command of § 3(h) of the Act that "a person engaged in ... broadcasting shall not ... be deemed a common carrier." 47 U.S.C. § 153(h).

We agree with respondents that recognition of agency jurisdiction to promulgate the access rules would require an extension of this Court's prior decisions. Our holding in *Midwest Video I* sustained the Commission's authority to regulate cable television with a purpose affirmatively to promote goals pursued in the regulation of television broadcasting; and the plurality's analysis of the origination requirement stressed the requirement's nexus to such goals. But the origination rule did not abrogate the cable operators' control over the composition of their programming, as do the access rules. It compelled operators only to assume a more positive role in that regard, one comparable to that fulfilled by television broadcasters. Cable operators had become enmeshed in the field of television broadcasting, and, by requiring them to engage in the functional equivalent of broadcasting, the Commission had sought "only to ensure that [they] satisfactorily [met] community needs within the context of their undertaking." 406 U.S. at 670 (Brennan, J.).

With its access rules, however, the Commission has transferred control of the content of access cable channels from cable operators to members of the public who wish to communicate by the cable medium. Effectively, the Commission has relegated cable systems, pro tanto, to common-carrier status. A common-carrier service in the communications context is one that "makes a public offering to provide [communications facilities] whereby all members of the public who choose to employ such facilities may communicate or transmit intelligence of their own design and choosing...." Report and Order, Industrial Radiolocation Service, 5 F.C.C. 2d 197, 202 (1966); *see* National Ass'n of Regulatory Utility Comm'rs v. FCC, 424, 525 F.2d 630, 641, *cert. denied*, 425 U.S. 992 (1976); Multipoint Distribution Service, 45 F.C.C. 2d 616, 618 (1974). A common carrier does not "make individualized decisions, in particular cases, whether and on what terms to deal." 525 F.2d at 641.

Congress, however, did not regard the character of regulatory obligations as irrelevant to the determination of whether they might permissibly be imposed in the context of broadcasting itself. The Commission is directed explicitly by § 3(h) of the Act not to treat persons engaged in broadcasting as common carriers. We considered the genealogy and the meaning of this provision in Columbia Broadcasting System, Inc. v. Democratic National Committee, 412 U.S. 94 (1973).

We now reaffirm that view of § 3(h): The purpose of the provision and its mandatory wording preclude Commission discretion to compel broadcasters to act as common carriers, even with respect to a portion of their total services. As we demonstrate in the following text, that same constraint applies to the regulation of cable television systems.

Of course, §3(h) does not explicitly limit the regulation of cable systems. But without reference to the provisions of the Act directly governing broadcasting, the Commission's jurisdiction under §2(a) would be unbounded. *See Midwest Video I*, 406 U.S. at 661 (opinion of Brennan, J.). Though afforded wide latitude in its supervision over communication by wire, the Commission was not delegated unrestrained authority. The Court regarded the Commission's regulatory effort at issue in *Southwestern* as consistent with the Act because it had been found necessary to ensure the achievement of the Commission's statutory responsibilities. Specifically, regulation was imperative to prevent interference with the Commission's work in the broadcasting area. And in *Midwest Video I* the Commission had endeavored to promote long-established goals of broadcasting regulation. Petitioners do not deny that statutory objectives pertinent to broadcasting bear on what the Commission might require cable systems to do. Indeed, they argue that the Commission's authority to promulgate the access rules derives from the relationship of those rules to the objectives discussed in *Midwest Video I*. But they overlook the fact that Congress has restricted the Commission's ability to advance objectives associated with public access at the expense of the journalistic freedom of persons engaged in broadcasting.

That limitation is not one having peculiar applicability to television broadcasting. Its force is not diminished by the variant technology involved in cable transmissions. Cable operators now share with broadcasters a significant amount of editorial discretion regarding what their programming will include. As the Commission, itself, has observed, "both in their signal carriage decisions and in connection with their origination function, cable television systems are afforded considerable control over the content of the programming they provide." Report and Order, 69 F.C.C. 2d 1324, 1330 (1978).

In determining, then, whether the Commission's assertion of jurisdiction is "reasonably ancillary to the effective performance of [its] various responsibilities for the regulation of television broadcasting," *Southwestern Cable*, 392 U.S. at 178, we are unable to ignore Congress's stern disapproval — evidenced in §3(h) — of negation of the editorial discretion otherwise enjoyed by broadcasters and cable operators alike. Though the lack of congressional guidance has in the past led us to defer — albeit cautiously — to the Commission's judgment regarding the scope of its authority, here there are strong indications that agency flexibility was to be sharply delimited.

The exercise of jurisdiction in *Midwest Video I*, it has been said, "strain[ed] the outer limits" of Commission authority. 406 U.S. at 676 (Burger, C.J., concurring in result). In light of the hesitancy with which Congress approached the access issue in the broadcast area, and in view of its outright rejection of a broad right of public access on a common-carrier basis, we are constrained to hold that the Commission exceeded those limits in promulgating its access rules. The Commission may not regulate cable systems as common carriers, just as it may not impose such obligations on television broadcasters. We think authority to compel cable operators to provide common carriage of public-originated transmissions must come specifically from Congress.

[Dissenting opinion of JUSTICE STEVENS is omitted.]

Notes and Questions

1. The Path Not Taken? In *Southwestern Cable*, the Supreme Court's theory was that the FCC should have the ability to regulate emerging technologies based on its legacy authority. *Southwestern Cable*'s principal ground was a positive one: that Congress in fact had that intent in the Communications Act. How plausible do you find that interpretation? There is of course a normative dimension as well. In a dynamic sector such as telecommunications, the FCC could find itself greatly limited in its effectiveness—based on addressing legacy policies, such as overseeing the broadcast industry—if it lacked such authority. But suppose that the Supreme Court held that no such Title I authority existed? What could the FCC have done as a result? What about Congress?

2. A Two-Part Test for Ancillary Jurisdiction. The test for ancillary jurisdiction that emerged from *Southwestern Cable* might be distilled as follows: The FCC has jurisdiction over (a) communications by wire or radio (b) to impose regulations "reasonably ancillary" to the Communications Act—with *Midwest Video II* adding that a regulation cannot be ancillary to the Act if its substance is contrary to the most analogous provisions of the Act. In *Southwestern Cable* and *Midwest Video II*, the first part of this test was fairly obviously met. In several other cases, however, it has proved important. Thus, in Illinois Citizens Committee for Broadcasting v. FCC, 467 F.2d 1397 (7th Cir. 1972), the court affirmed the FCC's decision that it did not have jurisdiction over the construction of the Sears Tower in Chicago, notwithstanding arguments that the Tower would seriously disrupt broadcasting coverage (and that the FCC therefore had ancillary jurisdiction to further its broadcasting policy by limiting skyscraper construction). More recently and in a more difficult decision, the D.C. Circuit decided in American Library Ass'n v. FCC, 406 F.3d 689 (D.C. Cir. 2005), that the FCC could not require a "broadcast flag"—a code inserted in broadcasts to help protect the broadcasts from copying—because the regulation extended FCC jurisdiction beyond "wire or radio" to TV sets and recording equipment.

3. Public Choice Theory and Ancillary Jurisdiction. One risk of ancillary jurisdiction is that today's incumbents can seek regulation of tomorrow's entrants and extend a legacy regulatory regime into a new technological reality. Indeed, this dynamic has occurred in many contexts, including efforts to regulate trucking so that legacy efforts to regulate the railroads could remain effective and intact. As we see below, there are echoes of this dynamic in the advent of cable broadband services.

§ 14.B. Regulatory Characterization of Broadband Services

One of the linchpin requirements of common carrier regulation is that the carrier provide service on a nondiscriminatory basis. 47 U.S.C. § 202(a). Although the matter was in some doubt early on, U.S. regulators and courts long ago established that federal common carrier law requires carriers to treat their competitors the same as other customers—that is, to sell to competitors any service made generally available, even if the competitor would turn around and use that service as part of an offering that competed with the carrier itself. In the *Computer Inquiries* discussed in Chapter Six, the FCC adopted rules that confirmed these general principles in the context of "information services" (then called "enhanced services") offered by facilities-based common carriers. That is, these dominant providers were required to provide nondiscriminatory access to any underlying transport services that the carriers used to provide their own information services, so that the information services market could develop in a competitive fashion. This requirement ensured that rival, unaffiliated information service providers could gain equal access to such essential inputs.

As dial-up Internet access services began sprouting up in the early to mid-1990s, Internet service providers (ISPs) took advantage of the right to gain access to telecommunications infrastructure on the same terms that incumbents applied to other services, including the incumbents' own. That form of "open access," among other things, enabled over 3,000 providers to provide dial-up Internet access, with companies such as AOL becoming major Internet sensations. In the mid- to late 1990s, however, cable companies began to offer cable broadband services and suggested that they faced no comparable requirement to unbundle access to their underlying infrastructure and provide it to would-be competitors. Needless to say, dial-up ISPs complained, calling on the FCC to make clear that the Communications Act required cable companies to provide such access.

The initial stance of the FCC was to take no action on the so-called "open access" controversy. Chairman William Kennard famously suggested that the Commission's goal would be to "first, do no harm" and that the cable broadband marketplace was not a monopoly or duopoly (with DSL connections being a competitor) but a "no-opoly."[3] Consequently, the FCC declined to classify cable modem services under the Communications Act, leaving open to debate whether they were cable services (under Title VI), telecommunications services (under Title II), or information services (under Title I).

Like nature, regulatory policy abhors a vacuum. Thus, this dispute before long found its way into a judicial forum. The case below involves an action by the City of Portland to condition its approval of AT&T's (then a standalone long distance and wireless telephone company) acquisition of TCI (then a cable company getting into the broadband services arena) on the company's provision of "open access" to its cable modem service, so that competitors could provide competing broadband Internet services. The opinion of the Ninth Circuit Court of Appeals is excerpted below.

AT&T CORP. v. CITY OF PORTLAND
216 F.3d 871 (9th Cir. 2000)

Opinion for the court filed by Circuit Judge THOMAS, in which Circuit Judges LEAVY and FERNANDEZ concur.

THOMAS, Circuit Judge:

This appeal presents the question of whether a local cable franchising authority may condition a transfer of a cable franchise upon the cable operator's grant of unrestricted access to its cable broadband transmission facilities for Internet service providers other than the operator's proprietary service. We conclude that the Communications Act prohibits a franchising authority from doing so and reverse the judgment of the district court.

The race to acquire broadband transmission systems has, in part, prompted a number of corporate mergers. This appeal concerns the merger between AT&T, at the time the nation's largest long distance telephone provider, and Telecommunications, Inc. (TCI),

---

3. William E. Kennard, Chairman, FCC, Remarks Before the National Cable Television Association (June 15, 1999), *available at* http://transition.fcc.gov/Speeches/Kennard/spwek921.html.

one of the nation's largest cable television operators. In addition to providing traditional cable television programming, TCI provided cable broadband Internet access to consumers in certain geographic areas. Since acquiring TCI, AT&T has continued to offer cable broadband access as part of its "@Home" service, which bundles its cable conduit with Excite, an Internet service provider (ISP) under an exclusive contract. Like many other ISPs, @Home supplements its Internet access with user e-mail accounts and a Web portal site, a default home page gateway offering Internet search capabilities and proprietary content devoted to chat groups, interactive gaming, shopping, finance, news, and other topics. @Home subscribers also may "click-through" to other free Web portal sites, and may access other Internet service providers if they are willing to pay for an additional ISP; however, subscribers cannot purchase cable broadband access separately from an unaffiliated ISP, and have no choice over terms of Internet service such as content and bandwidth restrictions.

To effect the merger, AT&T and TCI sought three types of regulatory approval. The Department of Justice approved the merger on antitrust grounds, subject to TCI's divestiture of its interest in Sprint PCS wireless services. The Federal Communications Commission approved the transfer of federal licenses from TCI to AT&T, after addressing public interest concerns in four service areas, including residential Internet access. *See* Applications for Consent to the Transfer of Licenses and Section 214 Authorizations from TCI to AT&T, Memorandum Opinion and Order, 14 FCC Rcd. 3160 (1999).

The last regulatory hurdle that AT&T and TCI faced was the approval of local franchising authorities where required by local franchising agreements. *See* 47 U.S.C. § 537 (permitting franchising authority approval of cable system sales when the franchise agreement so requires). TCI's franchises with Portland and Multnomah County (collectively, "Portland") permitted the city to "condition any Transfer upon such conditions, related to the technical, legal, and financial qualifications of the prospective party to perform according to the terms of the Franchise, as it deems appropriate." This language parallels the text of 47 U.S.C. § 541(a)(4)(C), which describes the conditions a locality may impose on a franchise.

Portland referred the transfer application for recommendation by the Mount Hood Cable Regulatory Commission, an intergovernmental agency overseeing cable affairs in the Portland region. On December 17, 1998, Portland and Multnomah County voted to approve the transfer, subject to an open access condition expressed in a written acceptance:

> Non-discriminatory access to cable modem platform. Transferee shall provide, and cause the Franchisees to provide, non-discriminatory access to the Franchisees' cable modem platform for providers of Internet and on-line services, whether or not such providers are affiliated with the Transferee or the Franchisees, unless otherwise required by applicable law. So long as cable modem services are deemed to be "cable services," as provided under Title VI of the Communications Act of 1934, as amended, Transferee and the Franchisees shall comply with all requirements regarding such services, including but not limited to, the inclusion of revenues from cable modem services and access within the gross revenues of the Franchisees' cable franchises, and commercial leased access requirements.

AT&T refused the condition, which resulted in a denial of the request to transfer the franchises. AT&T then brought this action, seeking declarations that the open access condition violated the Communications Act of 1934, the franchise agreements, and the Constitution's Commerce Clause, Contract Clause, and First Amendment. The district court rejected all of AT&T's claims and granted summary judgment to Portland. We review de novo a grant of summary judgment; there being no disputed factual issues, we face only a question of statutory interpretation.

II
A

Because Portland premised its open access condition on its position that @Home is a "cable service" governed by the franchise, we begin with the question of whether the @Home service truly is a "cable service" as Congress defined it in the Communications Act. We conclude that it is not.

Subject to limited exceptions, the Communications Act provides that "a cable operator may not provide cable service without a franchise." 47 U.S.C. §541(b)(1). The Act defines "cable service" as "(A) the one-way transmission to subscribers of (i) video programming, or (ii) other programming service, and (B) subscriber interaction, if any, which is required for the selection or use of such video programming or other programming service." 47 U.S.C. §522(6). For the purposes of this definition, "video programming" means "programming provided by, or generally considered comparable to programming provided by, a television broadcast station," 47 U.S.C. §522(20), and "other programming service" means "information that a cable operator makes available to all subscribers generally." 47 U.S.C. §522(14). The essence of cable service, therefore, is one-way transmission of programming to subscribers generally.

This definition does not fit @Home. Internet access is not one-way and general, but interactive and individual beyond the "subscriber interaction" contemplated by the statute. Accessing Web pages, navigating the Web's hypertext links, corresponding via e-mail, and participating in live chat groups involve two-way communication and information exchange unmatched by the act of electing to receive a one-way transmission of cable or pay-per-view television programming. And unlike transmission of a cable television signal, communication with a Web site involves a series of connections involving two-way information exchange and storage, even when a user views seemingly static content. Thus, the communication concepts are distinct in both a practical and a technical sense. Surfing cable channels is one thing; surfing the Internet over a cable broadband connection is quite another.

Further, applying the carefully tailored scheme of cable television regulation to cable broadband Internet access would lead to absurd results, inconsistent with the statutory structure. For example, cable operators like AT&T may be required by a franchising authority to set aside cable channels for public, educational or governmental use, *see* 47 U.S.C. §531, must designate some of their channels for commercial use by persons unaffiliated with the operator, *see* 47 U.S.C. §532, and must carry the signals of local commercial and non-commercial educational television stations, *see* 47 U.S.C. §§534 & 535. We cannot rationally apply these cable television regulations to a non-broadcast interactive medium such as the Internet.

Thus, because the Internet services AT&T provides through @Home cable modem access are not "cable services" under the Communications Act, Portland may not directly regulate them through its franchising authority.

[The Ninth Circuit then went on to find that cable modem service constituted "telecommunications" under the Act and, consequently, that cable operators were providing a "telecommunications service" when offering cable modem Internet access. This finding was important to the court's final jurisdictional conclusion because under 47 U.S.C.

§ 253(a) no state or local law can have the effect of prohibiting any entity from providing telecommunications service. Once the Ninth Circuit found cable modem service to be a telecommunications service, it had to find the merger condition that Portland imposed to be invalid under § 253(a).]

Notes and Questions

1. Implications. In the end, the court does not say that cable operators are immune from open access rules. It says only that, because the transmission of Internet access constitutes a "telecommunications service" rather than a "cable service," a cable license transfer cannot under the Act be conditioned on anything to do with cable modem service. What are the possible outcomes for open access under this decision? Would state regulators be obligated to develop "interconnection agreements" for access to cable broadband infrastructure? Would the FCC be free to classify cable broadband connections as "interstate telecommunications services," as the FCC had already done for DSL connections? Could the FCC forbear from the regulation of such services, as it had done for wireless services?

2. Policy. The Ninth Circuit did not, of course, address the pure policy question of whether open access requirements are in the public interest. The court simply noted that several policy options were open to the Commission, including forbearance, and struck down Portland's ordinance as being outside the city's powers. Several months after the Ninth Circuit's decision, although not specifically in response to the case, the FCC opened an inquiry into the broader policy question of open access regulation. The results of that inquiry and its subsequent extension to DSL service follow.

3. Subsequent Action. Once the Ninth Circuit ruled that cable modem service is best understood as an "information service" that contains an underlying "telecommunications service," the FCC undertook to decide for itself how to treat cable modem service. In Inquiry Concerning High-Speed Access to the Internet Over Cable and Other Facilities, Declaratory Ruling and Notice of Proposed Rulemaking, 17 FCC Rcd. 4798 (2002), the Commission reached a different result from the Ninth Circuit. In particular, it differed from the Ninth Circuit over whether cable modem service is a "telecommunications service" under the Act:

> As currently provisioned, cable modem service supports such functions as email, newsgroups, maintenance of the user's World Wide Web presence, and the DNS [domain name system]. Accordingly, we find that cable modem service, an Internet access service, is an information service. This is so regardless of whether subscribers use all of the functions provided as part of the service, such as email or web-hosting, and regardless of whether every cable modem service provider offers each function that could be included in the service. As currently provisioned, cable modem service is a single, integrated service that enables the subscriber to utilize Internet access service through a cable provider's facilities and to realize the benefits of a comprehensive service offering.

Id. at 4822–23, ¶ 38 (footnotes omitted). Several parties appealed the FCC's order (which we do not excerpt because it is discussed in detail in the following opinion) to the Ninth Circuit, which rejected the FCC's position, relying on its earlier decision in *Portland*. Brand X Internet Services v. FCC, 345 F.3d 1120 (9th Cir. 2003). The Supreme Court granted certiorari and reversed the Ninth Circuit in the case excerpted below.

NATIONAL CABLE & TELECOMMUNICATIONS ASS'N V. BRAND X INTERNET SERVICES
545 U.S. 967 (2005)

THOMAS, J., delivered the opinion of the Court, in which REHNQUIST, C.J., and STEVENS, O'CONNOR, KENNEDY, and BREYER, JJ., joined. STEVENS, J., and BREYER, J., filed concurring opinions. SCALIA, J., filed a dissenting opinion, in which SOUTER and GINSBURG, JJ., joined as to Part I.

JUSTICE THOMAS delivered the opinion of the Court.

Title II of the Communications Act of 1934 subjects all providers of "telecommunications servic[e]" to mandatory common-carrier regulation, § 153(44). In the order under review, the Federal Communications Commission concluded that cable companies that sell broadband Internet service do not provide "telecommunications servic[e]" as the Communications Act defines that term, and hence are exempt from mandatory common-carrier regulation under Title II. We must decide whether that conclusion is a lawful construction of the Communications Act under Chevron U.S.A., Inc. v. Natural Resources Defense Council, Inc., 467 U. S. 837 (1984), and the Administrative Procedure Act, 5 U.S.C. § 555 et seq. We hold that it is.

II

At issue in these cases is the proper regulatory classification under the Communications Act of broadband cable Internet service. The Act, as amended by the Telecommunications Act of 1996, defines two categories of regulated entities relevant to these cases: telecommunications carriers and information-service providers. The Act regulates telecommunications carriers, but not information-service providers, as common carriers. Telecommunications carriers, for example, must charge just and reasonable, nondiscriminatory rates to their customers, 47 U.S.C. §§ 201–209, design their systems so that other carriers can interconnect with their communications networks, § 251(a)(1), and contribute to the federal "universal service" fund, § 254(d). These provisions are mandatory, but the Commission must forbear from applying them if it determines that the public interest requires it. §§ 160(a), (b). Information-service providers, by contrast, are not subject to mandatory common-carrier regulation under Title II, though the Commission has jurisdiction to impose additional regulatory obligations under its Title I ancillary jurisdiction to regulate interstate and foreign communications, see §§ 151–161.

These two statutory classifications originated in the late 1970s, as the Commission developed rules to regulate data-processing services offered over telephone wires. That regime, the "Computer II" rules, distinguished between "basic" service (like telephone service) and "enhanced" service (computer-processing service offered over telephone lines). Amendment of Section 64.702 of the Commission's Rules and Regulations (Second Computer Inquiry), 77 F.C.C. 2d 384, 417–23, ¶¶ 86–101 (1980) (hereinafter *Computer II*). The *Computer II* rules defined both basic and enhanced services by reference to how the consumer perceives the service being offered.

The definitions of the terms "telecommunications service" and "information service" established by the 1996 Act are similar to the *Computer II* basic- and enhanced-service classifications. "Telecommunications service" — the analog to basic service — is "the offering of telecommunications for a fee directly to the public ... regardless of the facilities used." 47 U.S.C. § 153(46). "Telecommunications" is "the transmission, between or among points specified by the user, of information of the user's choosing, without change in the form or content of the information as sent and received." § 153(43). "Telecommunications carrier[s]"—those subjected to mandatory Title II common-carrier regulation—are defined as "provider[s] of telecommunications services." § 153(44). And "information service"—the analog to enhanced service—is "the offering of a capability for generating, acquiring, storing, transforming, processing, retrieving, utilizing, or making available information via telecommunications...." § 153(20).

In September 2000, the Commission initiated a rulemaking proceeding to, among other things, apply these classifications to cable companies that offer broadband Internet service directly to consumers. In March 2002, that rulemaking culminated in the Declaratory Ruling under review in these cases. Inquiry Concerning High-Speed Access to the Internet Over Cable and Other Facilities, Declaratory Ruling and Notice of Proposed Rulemaking, 17 FCC Rcd. 4798 (2002) (hereinafter Declaratory Ruling). In the Declaratory Ruling, the Commission concluded that broadband Internet service provided by cable companies is an "information service" but not a "telecommunications service" under the Act, and therefore not subject to mandatory Title II common-carrier regulation. In support of this conclusion, the Commission relied heavily on its Universal Service Report. *See* Declaratory Ruling 4821–22, ¶¶ 36–37 (citing Federal-State Joint Board on Universal Service, 13 FCC Rcd. 11,501 (1998) (hereinafter Universal Service Report or Report)). The Universal Service Report classified "non-facilities-based" ISPs—those that do not own the transmission facilities they use to connect the end user to the Internet—solely as information-service providers. *See* Universal Service Report 11,533, ¶ 67. Unlike those ISPs, cable companies own the cable lines they use to provide Internet access. Nevertheless, in the Declaratory Ruling, the Commission found no basis in the statutory definitions for treating cable companies differently from non-facilities-based ISPs: Both offer "a single, integrated service that enables the subscriber to utilize Internet access service ... and to realize the benefits of a comprehensive service offering." Declaratory Ruling 4823, ¶ 38. Because Internet access provides a capability for manipulating and storing information, the Commission concluded that it was an information service. *Id.*

The integrated nature of Internet access and the high-speed wire used to provide Internet access led the Commission to conclude that cable companies providing Internet access are not telecommunications providers. This conclusion, the Commission reasoned, followed from the logic of the Universal Service Report. The Report had concluded that, though Internet service "involves data transport elements" because "an Internet access provider must enable the movement of information between customers' own computers and distant computers with which those customers seek to interact," it also "offers end users information-service capabilities inextricably intertwined with data transport." Universal Service Report 11,539–40, ¶ 80. ISPs, therefore, were not "offering ... telecommunications ... directly to the public," § 153(46), and so were not properly classified as telecommunications carriers, *see id.* at 11,540, ¶ 81. In other words, the Commission reasoned that consumers use their cable modems not to transmit information "transparently," such as by using a telephone, but instead to obtain Internet access.

The Commission applied this same reasoning to cable companies offering broadband Internet access. Its logic was that, like non-facilities-based ISPs, cable companies do not "offe[r] telecommunications service to the end user, but rather ... merely us[e] telecommunications to provide end users with cable modem service." Declaratory Ruling 4824, ¶ 41. Though the Commission declined to apply mandatory Title II common-carrier regulation to cable companies, it invited comment on whether under its Title I jurisdiction it should require cable companies to offer other ISPs access to their facilities on common-carrier terms. *Id.* at 4839, ¶ 72.

The Court of Appeals vacated the ruling to the extent it concluded that cable modem service was not "telecommunications service" under the Communications Act. It held that the Commission could not permissibly construe the Communications Act to exempt cable companies providing Internet service from Title II regulation. Rather than analyzing the permissibility of that construction under the deferential framework of *Chevron*, however, the Court of Appeals grounded its holding in the stare decisis effect of AT&T Corp. v. Portland, 216 F.3d 871 (9th Cir. 2000). *Portland* held that cable modem service was a "telecommunications service," though the court in that case was not reviewing an administrative proceeding and the Commission was not a party to the case. Nevertheless, *Portland*'s holding, the Court of Appeals reasoned, overrode the contrary interpretation reached by the Commission in the Declaratory Ruling.

IV

[*Chevron*'s framework applies to the Commission's interpretation of "telecommunications service."] We next address whether the Commission's construction of the definition of "telecommunications service," 47 U.S.C. § 153(46), is a permissible reading of the Communications Act under the *Chevron* framework. *Chevron* established a familiar two-step procedure for evaluating whether an agency's interpretation of a statute is lawful. At the first step, we ask whether the statute's plain terms "directly addres[s] the precise question at issue." 467 U.S. at 843. If the statute is ambiguous on the point, we defer at step two to the agency's interpretation so long as the construction is "a reasonable policy choice for the agency to make." *Id.* at 845. The Commission's interpretation is permissible at both steps.

A

We first set forth our understanding of the interpretation of the Communications Act that the Commission embraced. The issue before the Commission was whether cable companies providing cable modem service are providing a "telecommunications service" in addition to an "information service."

The Commission first concluded that cable modem service is an "information service," a conclusion unchallenged here. The Act defines "information service" as "the offering of a capability for generating, acquiring, storing, transforming, processing, retrieving, utilizing, or making available information via telecommunications...." § 153(20). Cable modem service is an information service, the Commission reasoned, because it provides consumers with a comprehensive capability for manipulating information using the Internet via high-speed telecommunications. That service enables users, for example, to browse the World Wide Web, to transfer files from file archives available on the Internet via the "File Transfer Protocol," and to access e-mail and Usenet newsgroups. Like other forms of Internet service, cable modem service also gives users access to the Domain Name System (DNS). DNS, among other things, matches the Web page addresses that end users type into their browsers (or "click" on) with the Internet Protocol (IP) addresses of the servers containing the Web pages the users wish to access. All of these features, the Commission concluded, were part of the information service that cable companies provide consumers. Declaratory Ruling at ¶¶ 36–38.

At the same time, the Commission concluded that cable modem service was not "telecommunications service." "Telecommunications service" is "the offering of telecommunications for a fee directly to the public." 47 U.S.C. § 153(46). "Telecommunications," in turn, is defined as "the transmission, between or among points specified by the user, of information of the user's choosing, without change in the form or content of the information as sent and received." § 153(43). The Commission conceded that, like all information-service providers, cable companies use "telecommunications" to provide consumers with Internet service; cable companies provide such service via the high-speed wire that transmits signals to and from an end user's computer. Declaratory Ruling at ¶ 40. For the Commission, however, the question whether cable broadband Internet providers "offer" telecommunications involved more than whether telecommunications was one necessary component of cable modem service. Instead, whether that service also includes a telecommunications "offering" "tur[ned] on the nature of the functions the *end user* is offered," *id.* at 4822, ¶ 38 (emphasis added), for the statutory definition of "telecommunications service" docs not "res[t] on the particular types of facilities used," *id.* at 4821, ¶ 35; *see* § 153(46) (definition of "telecommunications service" applies "regardless of the facilities used").

Seen from the consumer's point of view, the Commission concluded, cable modem service is not a telecommunications offering because the consumer uses the high-speed wire always in connection with the information-processing capabilities provided by Internet access, and because the transmission is a necessary component of Internet access: "As provided to the end user the telecommunications is part and parcel of cable modem service and is integral to its other capabilities." Declaratory Ruling 4823, ¶ 39. The wire is used, in other words, to access the World Wide Web, newsgroups, and so forth, rather than "transparently" to transmit and receive ordinary-language messages without computer processing or storage of the message. The integrated character of this offering led the Commission to conclude that cable modem service is not a "stand-alone," transparent offering of telecommunications. *Id.* 4823–25, ¶¶ 41–43.

B

This construction passes *Chevron*'s first step. Respondents argue that it does not, on the ground that cable companies providing Internet service necessarily "offe[r]" the underlying telecommunications used to transmit that service. The word "offering" as used in § 153(46), however, does not unambiguously require that result. Instead, "offering" can reasonably be read to mean a "stand-alone" offering of telecommunications, i.e., an offered service that, from the user's perspective, transmits messages unadulterated by computer processing. That conclusion follows not only from the ordinary meaning of the word "offering," but also from the regulatory history of the Communications Act.

1

Cable companies in the broadband Internet service business "offe[r]" consumers an information service in the form of Internet access and they do so "via telecommunications," § 153(20), but it does not inexorably follow as a matter of ordinary language that they also "offe[r]" consumers the high-speed data transmission (telecommunications) that is an input used to provide this service, § 153(46). We have held that where a statute's plain terms admit of two or more reasonable ordinary usages, the Commission's choice of one of them is entitled to deference. The term "offe[r]" as used in the definition of telecommunications service, 47 U.S.C. § 153(46), is ambiguous in this way.

It is common usage to describe what a company "offers" to a consumer as what the consumer perceives to be the integrated finished product, even to the exclusion of discrete components that compose the product, as the dissent concedes. *See post* (opinion of SCALIA, J.). One might well say that a car dealership "offers" cars, but does not "offer" the integrated major inputs that make purchasing the car valuable, such as the engine or the chassis. It would, in fact, be odd to describe a car dealership as "offering" consumers the car's components in addition to the car itself. Even if it is linguistically permissible to say that the car dealership "offers" engines when it offers cars, that shows, at most, that the term "offer," when applied to a commercial transaction, is ambiguous about whether it describes only the offered finished product, or the product's discrete components as well. It does not show that no other usage is permitted.

The question, then, is whether the transmission component of cable modem service is sufficiently integrated with the finished service to make it reasonable to describe the two as a single, integrated offering. *See id.* We think that they are sufficiently integrated, because "[a] consumer uses the high-speed wire always in connection with the information-processing capabilities provided by Internet access, and because the transmission is a necessary component of Internet access." *Supra* at 16. In the telecommunications context, it is at least reasonable to describe companies as not "offering" to consumers each discrete input that is necessary to providing, and is always used in connection with, a finished service. We think it no misuse of language, for example, to say that cable companies providing Internet service do not "offer" consumers DNS, even though DNS is essential to providing Internet access. Declaratory Ruling 4810, n.74, 4822–4823, ¶ 38. Likewise, a telephone company "offers" consumers a transparent transmission path that conveys an ordinary-language message, not necessarily the data transmission facilities that also "transmi[t] ... information of the user's choosing," § 153(43), or other physical elements of the facilities used to provide telephone service, like the trunks and switches, or the copper in the wires. What cable companies providing cable modem service and telephone companies providing telephone service "offer" is Internet service and telephone service respectively—the finished services, though they do so using (or "via") the discrete components composing the end product, including data transmission. Such functionally integrated components need not be described as distinct "offerings."

In response, the dissent argues that the high-speed transmission component necessary to providing cable modem service is necessarily "offered" with Internet service because cable modem service is like the offering of pizza delivery service together with pizza, and the offering of puppies together with dog leashes. *Post* (opinion of SCALIA, J.). The dissent's appeal to these analogies only underscores that the term "offer" is ambiguous in the way that we have described. The entire question is whether the products here are functionally integrated (like the components of a car) or functionally separate (like pets and leashes). That question turns not on the language of the Act, but on the factual particulars of how Internet technology works and how it is provided, questions *Chevron* leaves to the Commission to resolve in the first instance. As the Commission has candidly recognized, "the question may not always be straightforward whether, on the one hand, an entity is providing a single information service with communications and computing components, or, on the other hand, is providing two distinct services, one of which is a telecommunications service." Universal Service Report 11,530, ¶ 60. Because the term "offer" can sometimes refer to a single, finished product and sometimes to the "individual components in a package being offered" (depending on whether the components "still possess sufficient identity to be described as separate objects," *post*), the statute fails unambiguously to classify the telecommunications component of cable modem service as a distinct offering. This leaves federal telecommunications policy in this technical and complex area to be set by the Commission, not by warring analogies.

We also do not share the dissent's certainty that cable modem service is so obviously like pizza delivery service and the combination of dog leashes and dogs that the Commission could not reasonably have thought otherwise. For example, unlike the transmission component of Internet service, delivery service and dog leashes are not integral components of the finished products (pizzas and pet dogs). One can pick up a pizza rather than having it delivered, and one can own a dog without buying a leash. By contrast, the Commission reasonably concluded, a consumer cannot purchase Internet service without also purchasing a connection to the Internet and the transmission always occurs in connection with information processing. In any event, we doubt that a statute that, for example, subjected offerors of "delivery" service (such as Federal Express and United Parcel Service) to common-carrier regulation would unambiguously require pizza-delivery companies to offer their delivery services on a common-carrier basis.

2

The Commission's traditional distinction between basic and enhanced service also supports the conclusion that the Communications Act is ambiguous about whether cable companies "offer" telecommunications with cable modem service.

The Commission has long held that "all those who provide some form of transmission services are not necessarily common carriers." *Computer II*, 77 F.C.C. 2d at 431, ¶ 122. For example, the Commission did not subject to common-carrier regulation those service providers that offered enhanced services over telecommunications facilities, but that did not themselves own the underlying facilities—so-called "non-facilities-based" providers. *See* Universal Service Report 11,530, ¶ 60. Examples of these services included database services in which a customer used telecommunications to access information, such as Dow Jones News and Lexis, as well as "value added networks," which lease wires from common carriers and provide transmission as well as protocol-processing service over those wires. *See* Amendment to Sections 64.702 of the Commission's Rules and Regulations (Third Computer Inquiry), 3 FCC Rcd. 1150, 1153, n.23 (1988) (*Computer III*). These services "combin[ed] communications and computing components," yet the Commission held that they should "always be deemed enhanced" and therefore not subject to common-carrier regulation. Universal Service Report 11,530, ¶ 60. Following this traditional distinction, the Commission in the Universal Service Report classified ISPs that leased rather than owned their transmission facilities as pure information-service providers. *Id.* at 11,540, ¶ 81.

Respondents' statutory arguments conflict with this regulatory history. They claim that the Communications Act unambiguously classifies as telecommunications carriers all entities that use telecommunications inputs to provide information service. As respondent MCI concedes, this argument would subject to mandatory common-carrier regulation all information-service providers that use telecommunications as an input to provide information service to the public. For example, it would subject to common-carrier regulation non-facilities-based ISPs that own no transmission facilities. Those ISPs provide consumers with transmission facilities used to connect to the Internet, and so, under respondents' argument, necessarily "offer" telecommunications to consumers. Respondents' position that all such entities are necessarily "offering telecommunications" therefore entails mandatory common-carrier regulation of entities that the Commission never classified as "offerors" of basic transmission service, and therefore common carriers, under the *Computer II* regime. We doubt that the parallel term "telecommunications service" unambiguously worked this abrupt shift in Commission policy.

In the *Computer II* rules, the Commission subjected facilities-based providers to common-carrier duties not because of the nature of the "offering" made by those carriers, but rather because of the concern that local telephone companies would abuse the monopoly power they possessed by virtue of the "bottleneck" local telephone facilities they owned. The differential treatment of facilities-based carriers was therefore a function not of the definitions of "enhanced service" and "basic service," but instead of a choice by the Commission to regulate more stringently, in its discretion, certain entities that provided enhanced service. The Act's definitions, however, parallel the definitions of enhanced and basic service, not the facilities-based grounds on which that policy choice was based, and the Commission remains free to impose special regulatory duties on facilities-based ISPs under its Title I ancillary jurisdiction. In fact, it has invited comment on whether it can and should do so.

In sum, if the Act fails unambiguously to classify non-facilities-based information-service providers that use telecommunications inputs to provide an information service as "offer[ors]" of "telecommunications," then it also fails unambiguously to classify facilities-based information-service providers as telecommunications-service offerors; the relevant definitions do not distinguish facilities-based and non-facilities-based carriers. That silence suggests, instead, that the Commission has the discretion to fill the consequent statutory gap.

C

We also conclude that the Commission's construction was "a reasonable policy choice for the [Commission] to make" at *Chevron*'s second step. 467 U.S. at 845.

Respondents argue that the Commission's construction is unreasonable because it allows any communications provider to "evade" common-carrier regulation by the expedient of bundling information service with telecommunications. Respondents argue that under the Commission's construction a telephone company could, for example, offer an information service like voice mail together with telephone service, thereby avoiding common-carrier regulation of its telephone service.

We need not decide whether a construction that resulted in these consequences would be unreasonable because we do not believe that these results follow from the construction the Commission adopted. As we understand the Declaratory Ruling, the Commission did not say that any telecommunications service that is priced or bundled with an information service is automatically unregulated under Title II. The Commission said that a telecommunications input used to provide an information service that is not "separable from the data-processing capabilities of the service" and is instead "part and parcel of [the information service] and is integral to [the information service's] other capabilities" is not a telecommunications offering. Declaratory Ruling 4823, ¶ 39.

This construction does not leave all information service offerings exempt from mandatory Title II regulation. "It is plain," for example, that a local telephone company "cannot escape Title II regulation of its residential local exchange service simply by packaging that service with voice mail." Universal Service Report 11,530, ¶ 60. That is because a telephone company that packages voice mail with telephone service offers a transparent transmission path — telephone service — that transmits information independent of the information-storage capabilities provided by voice mail. For instance, when a person makes a telephone call, his ability to convey and receive information using the call is only trivially affected by the additional voice-mail capability. By contrast, the high-speed transmission used to provide cable modem service is a functionally integrated component of that service because it transmits data only in connection with the further processing of information and is necessary to provide Internet service. The Commission's construction therefore was more limited than respondents assume.

Respondents answer that cable modem service does, in fact, provide "transparent" transmission from the consumer's perspective, but this argument, too, is mistaken. Respondents characterize the "information-service" offering of Internet access as consisting only of access to a cable company's e-mail service, its Web page, and the ability it provides consumers to create a personal Web page. When a consumer goes beyond those offerings and accesses content provided by parties other than the cable company, respondents argue, the consumer uses "pure transmission" no less than a consumer who purchases phone service together with voice mail.

This argument, we believe, conflicts with the Commission's understanding of the nature of cable modem service, an understanding we find to be reasonable. When an end user accesses a third-party's Web site, the Commission concluded, he is equally using the information service provided by the cable company that offers him Internet access as when he accesses the company's own Web site, its e-mail service, or his personal Web page. For example, as the Commission found below, part of the information service cable companies provide is access to DNS service. A user cannot reach a third-party's Web site without DNS, which (among other things) matches the Web site address the end user types into his browser (or "clicks" on with his mouse) with the IP address of the Web page's host server. It is at least reasonable to think of DNS as a "capability for ... acquiring ... retrieving, utilizing, or making available" Web site addresses and therefore part of the information service cable companies provide. 47 U.S.C. §153(20). Similarly, the Internet service provided by cable companies facilitates access to third-party Web pages by offering consumers the ability to store, or "cache," popular content on local computer servers. *See* Declaratory Ruling 4810, ¶17, and n.76. Caching obviates the need for the end user to download anew information from third-party Web sites each time the consumer attempts to access them, thereby increasing the speed of information retrieval. In other words, subscribers can reach third-party Web sites via "the World Wide Web, and browse their contents, [only] because their service provider offers the 'capability for ... acquiring, [storing,] ... retrieving [and] utilizing ... information.'" Universal Service Report 11,538, ¶76 (quoting 47 U.S.C. §153(20)). "The service that Internet access providers offer to members of the public is Internet access," Universal Service Report 11,539, ¶79, not a transparent ability (from the end user's perspective) to transmit information. We therefore conclude that the Commission's construction was reasonable.

V

Respondent MCI, Inc., urges that the Commission's treatment of cable modem service is inconsistent with its treatment of DSL service, and therefore is an arbitrary and capricious deviation from agency policy. MCI points out that when local telephone companies began to offer Internet access through DSL technology in addition to telephone service, the Commission applied its *Computer II* facilities-based classification to them and required them to make the telephone lines used to transmit DSL service available to competing ISPs on nondiscriminatory, common-carrier terms. MCI claims that the Commission's decision not to regulate cable companies similarly under Title II is inconsistent with its DSL policy.

We conclude, however, that the Commission provided a reasoned explanation for treating cable modem service differently from DSL service. As we have already noted, the Commission is free within the limits of reasoned interpretation to change course if it adequately justifies the change. It has done so here. The traditional reason for its *Computer II* common-carrier treatment of facilities-based carriers (including DSL carriers), as the Commission explained, was "that the *telephone network* [was] the primary, if not exclusive, means through which information service providers can gain access to their customers." Declaratory Ruling 4825, ¶44 (emphasis in original; internal quotation marks omitted). The Commission applied the same treatment to DSL service based on that history, rather than on an analysis of contemporaneous market conditions.

The Commission in the order under review, by contrast, concluded that changed market conditions warrant different treatment of facilities-based cable companies providing Internet access. Unlike at the time of *Computer II*, substitute forms of Internet transmission exist today: "[R]esidential high-speed access to the Internet is evolving over multiple electronic platforms, including wireline, cable, terrestrial wireless and satellite." *Id.* 4802, ¶ 6. The Commission concluded that "broadband services should exist in a minimal regulatory environment that promotes investment and innovation in a competitive market." *Id.* 4802, ¶ 5. This, the Commission reasoned, warranted treating cable companies unlike the facilities-based enhanced-service providers of the past. *Id.* at 4825, ¶ 44. We find nothing arbitrary about the Commission's providing a fresh analysis of the problem as applied to the cable industry, which it has never subjected to these rules. This is adequate rational justification for the Commission's conclusions.

Respondents argue, in effect, that the Commission's justification for exempting cable modem service providers from common-carrier regulation applies with similar force to DSL providers. We need not address that argument. The Commission's decision appears to be a first step in an effort to reshape the way the Commission regulates information-service providers; that may be why it has tentatively concluded that DSL service provided by facilities-based telephone companies should also be classified solely as an information service. *See* Appropriate Framework for Broadband Access to the Internet over Wireline Facilities, 17 FCC Rcd. 3019, 3030, ¶ 20 (2002). The Commission need not immediately apply the policy reasoning in the Declaratory Ruling to all types of information-service providers. It apparently has decided to revisit its longstanding *Computer II* classification of facilities-based information-service providers incrementally. Any inconsistency between the order under review and the Commission's treatment of DSL service can be adequately addressed when the Commission fully reconsiders its treatment of DSL service and when it decides whether, pursuant to its ancillary Title I jurisdiction, to require cable companies to allow independent ISPs access to their facilities. We express no view on those matters. In particular, we express no view on how the Commission should, or lawfully may, classify DSL service.

The questions the Commission resolved in the order under review involve a "subject matter [that] is technical, complex, and dynamic." National Cable & Telecommunications Ass'n v. Gulf Power Co., 534 U.S. 327, 339 (2002). The Commission is in a far better position to address these questions than we are. Nothing in the Communications Act or the Administrative Procedure Act makes unlawful the Commission's use of its expert policy judgment to resolve these difficult questions. The judgment of the Court of Appeals is reversed, and the cases are remanded for further proceedings consistent with this opinion.

[Concurring opinions of JUSTICE STEVENS and JUSTICE BREYER are omitted.]

JUSTICE SCALIA, with whom JUSTICE SOUTER and JUSTICE GINSBURG join as to Part I, dissenting.

The Federal Communications Commission (FCC or Commission) has once again attempted to concoct "a whole new regime of regulation (or of free-market competition)" under the guise of statutory construction. MCI Telecommunications Corp. v. American Telephone & Telegraph Co., 512 U.S. 218, 234 (1994). Actually, in these cases, it might be more accurate to say the Commission has attempted to establish a whole new regime of *non*-regulation, which will make for more or less free-market competition, depending upon whose experts are believed. The important fact, however, is that the Commission has chosen to achieve this through an implausible reading of the statute, and has thus exceeded the authority given it by Congress.

I

The first sentence of the FCC ruling under review reads as follows: "Cable modem service provides high-speed access to the Internet, *as well as* many applications or functions that can be used with that access, over cable system facilities." Inquiry Concerning High-Speed Access to the Internet Over Cable and Other Facilities, Declaratory Ruling and

Notice of Proposed Rulemaking, 17 FCC Rcd. 4798, 4799, ¶ 1 (2002) (hereinafter Declaratory Ruling) (emphasis added, footnote omitted). Does this mean that cable companies "offer" high-speed access to the Internet? Surprisingly not, if the Commission and the Court are to be believed.

It happens that cable-modem service is popular precisely because of the high-speed access it provides, and that, once connected with the Internet, cable-modem subscribers often use Internet applications and functions from providers other than the cable company. Nevertheless, for purposes of classifying what the cable company does, the Commission (with the Court's approval) puts all the emphasis on the rest of the package (the additional "applications or functions"). It does so by claiming that the cable company does not "offe[r]" its customers high-speed Internet access because it offers that access only in conjunction with particular applications and functions, rather than "separate[ly]," as a "stand-alone offering." *Id.* at 4802, ¶ 7, 4823, ¶ 40.

The Court concludes that the word "offer" is ambiguous in the sense that it has "alternative dictionary definitions" that might be relevant. *Ante* (quoting National Railroad Passenger Corporation v. Boston & Maine Corp., 503 U.S. 407, 418 (1992)). It seems to me, however, that the analytic problem pertains not really to the meaning of "offer," but to the identity of what is offered. The relevant question is whether the individual components in a package being offered still possess sufficient identity to be described as separate objects of the offer, or whether they have been so changed by their combination with the other components that it is no longer reasonable to describe them in that way.

If, for example, I call up a pizzeria and ask whether they offer delivery, both common sense and common "usage," *ante*, would prevent them from answering: "No, we do not offer delivery—but if you order a pizza from us, we'll bake it for you and then bring it to your house." The logical response to this would be something on the order of, "so, you *do* offer delivery." But our pizzaman may continue to deny the obvious and explain, paraphrasing the FCC and the Court: "No, even though we bring the pizza to your house, we are not actually 'offering' you delivery, because the delivery that we provide to our end users is 'part and parcel' of our pizzeria-pizza-at-home service and is 'integral to its other capabilities.'" *Cf.* Declaratory Ruling 4823, ¶ 39; *ante*. Any reasonable customer would conclude at that point that his interlocutor was either crazy or following some too-clever-by-half legal advice.

Despite the Court's mighty labors to prove otherwise, the telecommunications component of cable-modem service retains such ample independent identity that it must be regarded as being on offer—especially when seen from the perspective of the consumer or the end user, which the Court purports to find determinative. The Commission's ruling began by noting that cable-modem service provides *both* "high-speed access to the Internet" *and* other "applications and functions," Declaratory Ruling 4799, ¶ 1, because that is exactly how any reasonable consumer would perceive it: as consisting of two separate things.

The consumer's view of the matter is best assessed by asking what other products cable-modem service substitutes for in the marketplace. Broadband Internet service provided by cable companies is one of the three most common forms of Internet service, the other two being dial-up access and broadband Digital Subscriber Line (DSL) service. In each of the other two, the physical transmission pathway to the Internet is sold—indeed, *is legally required* to be sold—separately from the Internet functionality. With dial-up access, the physical pathway comes from the telephone company and the Internet service provider (ISP) provides the functionality.

"In the case of Internet access, the end user utilizes two different and distinct services. One is the transmission pathway, a telecommunications service that the end user purchases from the telephone company. The second is the Internet access service, which is an enhanced service provided by an ISP.... Th[e] functions [provided by the ISP] are separate from the transmission pathway over which that data travels. The pathway is a regulated telecommunications service; the enhanced service offered over it is not." Oxman, The FCC and the Unregulation of the Internet (FCC, Office of Plans and Policy, Working Paper No. 31, July 1999), 13.

As the Court acknowledges, DSL service has been similar to dial-up service in the respect that the physical connection to the Internet must be offered separately from Internet functionality. Thus, customers shopping for dial-up or DSL service will not be able to use the Internet unless they get both someone to provide them with a physical connection and someone to provide them with applications and functions such as e-mail and Web access. It is therefore inevitable that customers will regard the competing cable-modem service as giving them *both* computing functionality *and* the physical pipe by which that functionality comes to their computer—both the pizza and the delivery service that non-delivery pizzerias require to be purchased from the cab company.

Since the delivery service provided by cable (the broadband connection between the customer's computer and the cable company's computer-processing facilities) is downstream from the computer-processing facilities, there is no question that it merely serves as a conduit for the information services that have already been "assembled" by the cable company in its capacity as ISP. This is relevant because of the statutory distinction between an "information service" and "telecommunications." The former involves the capability of getting, processing, and manipulating information. § 153(20). The latter, by contrast, involves no "change in the form or content of the information as sent and received." § 153(43). When cable-company-assembled information enters the cable for delivery to the subscriber, the information service is already complete. The information has been (as the statute requires) generated, acquired, stored, transformed, processed, retrieved, utilized, or made available. All that remains is for the information in its final, unaltered form, to be delivered (via telecommunications) to the subscriber.

This reveals the insubstantiality of the fear invoked by both the Commission and the Court: the fear of what will happen to ISPs that do not provide the physical pathway to Internet access, yet still use telecommunications to acquire the pieces necessary to assemble the information that they pass back to their customers. According to this reductio, if cable-modem-service providers are deemed to provide "telecommunications service," then so must *all* ISPs because they all "use" telecommunications in providing Internet functionality (by connecting to other parts of the Internet, including Internet backbone providers, for example). In terms of the pizzeria analogy, this is equivalent to saying that, if the pizzeria "offers" delivery, *all* restaurants "offer" delivery, because the ingredients of the food they serve their customers have come from other places; no matter how their customers get the food (whether by eating it at the restaurant, or by coming to pick it up themselves), they still consume a product for which delivery was a necessary "input." This is nonsense. Concluding that delivery of the finished pizza constitutes an "offer" of delivery does not require the conclusion that the serving of prepared food includes an "offer" of delivery. And that analogy does not even do the point justice, since "telecommunications service" is defined as "the offering of telecommunications for a fee *directly to the public.*" 47 U.S.C. § 153(46) (emphasis added). The ISPs' use of telecommunications in their processing of information is not offered directly to the public.

The "regulatory history" on which the Court depends so much provides another reason why common-carrier regulation of all ISPs is not a worry. Under its *Computer Inquiry* rules, which foreshadowed the definitions of "information" and "telecommunications" services the Commission forbore from regulating as common carriers "value-added networks" — non-facilities-based providers who leased basic services from common carriers and bundled them with enhanced services; it said that they, unlike facilities-based providers, would be deemed to provide only enhanced services. That same result can be achieved today under the Commission's statutory authority to forbear from imposing most Title II regulations. 47 U.S.C. § 160. In fact, the statutory criteria for forbearance—which include what is "just and reasonable," "necessary for the protection of consumers," and "consistent with the public interest," §§ 160(a)(1), (2), (3)—correspond well with the kinds of policy reasons the Commission has invoked to justify its peculiar construction of "telecommunications service" to exclude cable-modem service.

Finally, I must note that, notwithstanding the Commission's self-congratulatory paean to its deregulatory largesse, it concluded the Declaratory Ruling by asking, as the Court paraphrases, "whether under its Title I jurisdiction [the Commission] should require cable companies to offer other ISPs access to their facilities on common-carrier terms." *Ante.* In other words, what the Commission hath given, the Commission may well take away—unless it doesn't. This is a wonderful illustration of how an experienced agency can (with some assistance from credulous courts) turn statutory constraints into bureaucratic discretions. The main source of the Commission's regulatory authority over common carriers is Title II, but the Commission has rendered that inapplicable in this instance by concluding that the definition of "telecommunications service" is ambiguous and does not (in its current view) apply to cable-modem service. It contemplates, however, altering that (unnecessary) outcome, not by changing the law (i.e., its construction of the Title II definitions), but by reserving the right to change the facts. Under its undefined and sparingly used "ancillary" powers, the Commission might conclude that it can order cable companies to "unbundle" the telecommunications component of cable-modem service. And presto, Title II will then apply to them, because they will finally be "offering" telecommunications service! Of course, the Commission will still have the statutory power to forbear from regulating them under § 160 (which it has already tentatively concluded it would do, Declaratory Ruling 4847–48, ¶¶ 94–95). Such Mobius-strip reasoning mocks the principle that the statute constrains the agency in any meaningful way.

After all is said and done, after all the regulatory cant has been translated, and the smoke of agency expertise blown away, it remains perfectly clear that someone who sells cable-modem service is "offering" telecommunications. For that simple reason set forth in the statute, I would affirm the Court of Appeals.

Notes and Questions

1. Substance and Semantics. As the majority notes, the common carrier provisions of Title II "are mandatory but the Commission must refrain from applying them if it determines that the public interest requires it." Could the FCC have avoided all the definitional wrangling over "telecommunications service" and "information service" by saying that, whatever cable modem service is, in the Commission's opinion the public interest requires forbearance from common carrier regulation? Had *Brand X* come out the other way, could the FCC forbear from applying Title II and create the same substantive policy result of nonregulation? Forbearance would likely require the Commission to have a substantial evidentiary record to justify its public interest conclusions (*see* 47 U.S.C. § 160) whereas defining cable modem service to be outside Title II imposes a burden of reasonable interpretation but less of an evidentiary issue for the Commission.

2. Telecommunications versus Telecommunications Service. One of the most confusing aspects of the *Brand X* case and the regulatory battles that preceded it is the difference between "telecommunications" and a "telecommunications service." As Justice Thomas explains, a firm offers a "telecommunications service" if that is the product sold to the public. By contrast, a firm can sell an "information service" that relies on and even includes a "telecommunications" component. The essential regulatory question — and what Justices Thomas and Scalia argue over — is whether a product that provides telecommunications along with some additional functionality should be characterized as a "telecommunications service" or an "information service." As we shall see, this issue returned with a vengeance in the battles over how to characterize VoIP.

3. The Consumer Perspective. The majority and dissent part ways over what the consumer is buying under the label of "cable modem service." Justice Thomas, writing for the majority, defines the product as "Internet access" with the emphasis on *Internet*. The transport aspect of such Internet service is merely an integral component. Justice Scalia, in dissent, also defines the service as "Internet access" but puts the emphasis on high-speed *access*. To him consumers are not buying the Internet, so to speak, but high-speed transport *to* the Internet. Who is right? Should it matter that the Internet exists independently of cable systems and that it is neither owned by nor dependent on cable systems? If that is the case, what are the cable operators selling other than transport? What exactly are the cable operators selling to which transport is (as the majority finds) a mere component?

4. Parity for DSL? Near the end of the opinion the Court states that "[a]ny inconsistency between the order under review and the Commission's treatment of DSL service can be adequately addressed when the Commission fully reconsiders its treatment of DSL service and when it decides whether, pursuant to its ancillary Title I jurisdiction, to require cable companies to allow independent ISPs access to their facilities." *Brand X*, 545 U.S. at 1002. In 2005, the FCC addressed the regulatory classification of DSL and concluded that it too should be treated as an information service. Appropriate Framework for Broadband Access to the Internet Over Wireline Facilities, Report and Order and Notice of Proposed Rulemaking, 20 FCC Rcd. 14,853 (2005) (Wireline Broadband Order).

As it had in the case of cable modem service, the FCC held that wireline broadband service in general "combines computer processing, information provision, and computer interactivity with data transport, enabling end users to run a variety of applications (e.g., email, web pages, and newsgroups). These applications encompass the capability for generating, acquiring, storing, transforming, processing, retrieving, utilizing, or making available information via telecommunications, and taken together constitute an information service as defined by the Act." *Id.* at 14,863–64, ¶ 14 (footnote omitted) (quoting Inquiry Concerning High- Speed Access to the Internet Over Cable and Other Facilities, Declaratory Ruling and Notice of Proposed Rulemaking, 17 FCC Rcd. 4798, 4823–24, ¶ 41) (internal quotation marks omitted)). The agency acknowledged that many users did not take such services from their broadband ISP but still concluded that Internet access was an information service:

> The information service classification applies regardless of whether subscribers use all of the functions and capabilities provided as part of the service (e.g., e-mail or web-hosting), and whether every wireline broadband Internet access service provider offers each function and capability that could be included in that service. Indeed, as with cable modem service, an end user of wireline broadband Internet access service cannot reach a third party's web site without access to the Domain Naming Service (DNS) capability "which (among other things)

matches the Web site address the end user types into his browser (or 'clicks' on with his mouse) with the IP address of the Web page's host server." The end user therefore receives more than transparent transmission whenever he or she accesses the Internet.

Id. at 14,864, ¶ 15 (footnotes omitted) (quoting *Brand X*, 545 U.S. at 999).

The FCC also eliminated the *Computer II* and *Computer III* requirements to the extent that they would require wireline broadband providers to offer transport to unaffiliated companies. The FCC characterized these rules as unnecessary and inappropriate given the fast-developing and more competitive nature of the Internet access market.

> We base our decision to eliminate these requirements on a number of factors.... First, broadband Internet access services in most parts of the country are offered by two established platform providers, which continue to expand rapidly, and by several existing and emerging platforms and providers, intermodal and intramodal alike. Second, the record shows that the existing regulations constrain technological advances and deter broadband infrastructure investment by creating disincentives to the deployment of facilities capable of providing innovative broadband Internet access services. Third, fast-paced technological changes and new consumer demands are causing a rapid evolution in the marketplace for these services. Wireline broadband carriers are constrained in their ability to respond to these changes in an efficient, effective, or timely manner as a result of the limitations imposed by these regulations. Fourth, the marketplace should create incentives for facilities-based wireline broadband providers to make broadband transmission available on a wholesale basis without these requirements. Finally, the directives of section 706 of the 1996 Act, 47 U.S.C. § 1302, require that we ensure that our broadband policies promote infrastructure investment, consistent with our other obligations under the Act.

Id. at 14,865, ¶¶ 18–19.

5. Forbearance versus Reclassification. We mentioned above that the FCC enjoys the authority to forbear from Title II regulation. In the case of wireline broadband facilities, the FCC chose to reclassify those facilities as information services governed by Title I. In other cases, however, the FCC has used its forbearance authority. In particular, the FCC granted Verizon's request that its broadband services be exempt from all *Computer III* requirements (mandating access on a nondiscriminatory basis to underlying telecommunications facilities that support information services) and Title II requirements more generally. *See* Verizon Telephone Companies' Petition for Forbearance from Title II and Computer Inquiry Rules with Respect to Their Broadband Services Is Granted by Operation of Law, No. 04-440, 2006 WL 707632 (FCC Mar. 20, 2006). What relief emerges from this decision that is not already granted by the Wireline Broadband Order?

6. Naked DSL. Some consumers want broadband service over the telephone grid but not voice service. For instance, a consumer might want to use a mobile phone for all voice communications but still want DSL service for Internet access. Will the local ILEC provide DSL without an accompanying voice service subscription? This kind of service, often called "naked DSL," came into the market as ILECs realized that cable companies could gain broadband market share through a broadband-only offering. At the same time, some states began to require that ILECs provide naked DSL to CLEC voice subscribers if those subscribers wished to purchase such a stripped-down service. In March 2005, the FCC ruled that states could not require ILECs to provide naked DSL. BellSouth Telecommunications, Inc. Request for Declaratory Ruling that State Commissions May Not Regulate Broadband Internet Access Services by Requiring BellSouth to Provide Wholesale or Retail Broadband Services to Competitive LEC UNE Voice Customers, Memorandum Opinion and Order and Notice of Inquiry, 20 FCC Rcd. 6830 (2005). The FCC argued that such state intervention would be inconsistent with the Act and interfere with the FCC's implementation of unbundling regulations as broadband policy. Some ILECs are nonetheless experimenting with naked DSL offerings. What do such offerings say about the competitive state of the telecommunications market?

§ 14.C. Net Neutrality

The *Brand X* decision and the follow-on Wireline Broadband Order effectively rejected the application of "open access" regulations to broadband Internet access providers. But whereas access to underlying transport infrastructure faded as a regulatory policy issue, the question of whether broadband providers can discriminate as to *applications* and *content* that ride on their network remains a heated controversy.

We now turn to the debate over the policy merits of the net neutrality issue—i.e., whether such rules should be adopted, either by the Commission or otherwise. As an initial matter, we must define the concept of net neutrality, which is no easy task. In the words of two economists studying the debate, "[n]et neutrality has no widely accepted precise definition, but usually means that broadband service providers charge consumers only once for Internet access, do not favor one content provider over another, and do not charge content providers for sending information over broadband lines to end users." Robert Hahn & Scott Wallsten, The Economics of Net Neutrality, Economists' Voice, June 2006, at 1, http://dx.doi.org/10.2202/1553-3832.1194. At the heart of the debate, therefore, is the ability of cable operators or telephone networks to charge a content or applications provider— say an Internet voice service provider, travel reservation company, or online merchant— different prices for different levels of transmission quality. For example, consider a provider of video programming over the Internet that wishes to ensure that its customers will always receive their videos quickly. Can that content provider purchase such assured quality from the cable system or telephone company that owns the underlying network? Advocates of net neutrality say no: such "tiering" of service quality would force new innovators to "pay to play" and in that way effectively relegate them to lower quality connections. The long-run concern is that the public Internet will become a repository of second-rate service while high-quality transmission will become the province of increasingly private, pay-to-play networks.

Opponents argue that the ability of network owners to charge content providers simply requires that those services imposing costs on the network bear those costs; the charges, in turn, allow content providers to get the quality they need to launch successful new services that require particular levels of transmission quality. Charging for tiers of service thereby fosters innovation in applications and ensures efficient use of the Internet infrastructure. It also provides additional revenue that might encourage further deployment of high-speed networks.

§ 14.C.1. The Broadband Internet Access Marketplace

One fundamental factor in suggesting whether regulation of broadband networks is appropriate to protect competition in applications and content markets is whether the level of competition in broadband markets is sufficient to punish the behavior of a firm that engages in anticompetitive practices. If, for example, there are a number of rival providers and one of them engages in anticompetitive discrimination, that behavior will degrade its offerings and lead consumers to turn to its rivals. By contrast, if only one or two firms provide broadband Internet access, the risks of such behavior would be greater.

To be sure, the level of competition in the Internet access marketplace is not the only factor; one must also consider the extent to which an Internet access provider would have the incentive to engage in anticompetitive activity directed at the application or content markets. That issue is raised in the following section—you should immediately see the parallel to the question of the Bell System's incentives and ability to use power in the local market to discriminate in the long-distance market and any other number of earlier controversies. Nevertheless, access-marketplace competition is an important factor in the policy analysis.

In its Broadband Plan, the FCC reviewed the state of the marketplace. We include this excerpt not for specific data or findings on the current state of the market; those numbers evolve after all. Rather, the FCC here provides a framework for thinking about the state of competition, both as a static and a dynamic matter.

NATIONAL BROADBAND PLAN: CONNECTING AMERICA
FCC (2010)
(available at http://transition.fcc.gov/national-broadband-plan/national-broadband-plan.pdf)
Chapter 4

4.1 NETWORKS

Competition in industries with high fixed costs

Building broadband networks—especially wireline—requires large fixed and sunk investments. Consequently, the industry will probably always have a relatively small number of facilities-based competitors, at least for wireline service. Bringing down the cost of entry for facilities-based wireline services may encourage new competitors to enter in a few areas, but it is unlikely to create several new facilities-based entrants competing across broad geographic areas. Bringing down the costs of entry and expansion in wireless broadband by facilitating access to spectrum, sites and high-capacity backhaul may spur additional facilities-based competition. Whether wireless competition is sustainable in driving innovation, investment and consumer welfare will depend on the evolution of technology and consumer behavior among many other factors.

The lack of a large number of wireline, facilities-based providers does not necessarily mean competition among broadband providers is inadequate. While older economic models of competition emphasized the danger of tacit collusion with a small number of rivals, economists today recognize that coordination is possible but not inevitable under such circumstances. Moreover, modern analyses find that markets with a small number of participants can perform competitively; however, those analyses do not tell us what degree of competition to expect in a market with a small number of wireline broadband providers combined with imperfect competition from wireless providers. Given that approximately 96% of the population has at most two wireline providers, there are reasons to be concerned about wireline broadband competition in the United States. Whether sufficient competition exists is unclear and, even if such competition presently exists, it is surely fragile. To ensure that the right policies are put in place so that the broadband ecosystem benefits from meaningful competition as it evolves, it is important to have an ongoing, data-driven evaluation of the state of competition.

In general, broadband subscribers appear to have benefited from the presence of multiple providers. Broadband providers have invested in network upgrades to deliver faster broadband speeds and enter new product markets—cable companies providing telephony and telephone companies offering multichannel video—but the data available only provide limited evidence of price competition among providers.

Fixed broadband service

Unlike many countries, the majority of U.S. broadband subscribers do not connect to the Internet via local-access infrastructure owned by an incumbent telephone company. The U.S. cable infrastructure was advanced and ubiquitous enough to allow cable companies to offer broadband access services to large portions of the country, in many cases before the telephone companies. As a result, the U.S. market structure is relatively unique in that people in most parts of the country have been able to choose from two wireline, facilities-based broadband platforms for many years. Approximately 4% of housing units are in areas with three wireline providers (either DSL or fiber, the cable incumbent and a cable over-builder), 78% live in areas with two wireline providers, about 13% are in areas with a single wireline provider and 5% have no wireline provider.

These data do not necessarily mean that 82% (78% + 4%) of housing units have two or three competitive options for wireline broadband service—the data used here do not provide adequate information on price and performance to determine if multiple providers present in a given area compete head-to-head.

Additionally, the data show that rural areas are less likely to have access to more than one wireline broadband provider than other areas. The data also show that low-income areas are on average somewhat less likely to have more than one provider than higher-income areas.

There are other types of fixed broadband providers. For instance, satellite-based broadband service is available in most areas of the country from two providers, while hundreds of small fixed wireless Internet service providers (WISPs) offer service to more than 2 million people and Clearwire offers WiMAX service in a number of cities. These providers compete for customers as well, although their services tend to be either more expensive or offer a lower range of speeds than today's wireline offerings.

The presence of a facilities-based competitor impacts investment. Indeed, broadband providers appear to invest more heavily in network upgrades in areas where they face competition. [C]ontrolling for housing density, household income and state-specific factors that affect supply and demand, providers of broadband over any given wireline technology—Digital Subscriber Line (DSL), cable or fiber—generally offer faster speeds when competing with other wireline platforms. So, for example, available cable speeds are higher in areas in which cable competes with DSL or fiber than in areas where cable is the only option. DSL and fiber show similar results. Available speeds are even higher where three wireline providers compete (e.g., where a cable over-builder is also present).

In principle, providers can compete on price as well as on service. Unfortunately, the dearth of consistent, comprehensive and detailed price data makes it difficult to evaluate price competition. Some international comparisons suggest the number of retail broadband providers may be positively correlated with advertised download speeds, at least at the high end of the market, and with affordability. Others rank the United States high in affordability of broadband, despite the fact that 96% of consumers have two or fewer choices, and suggest that consumers may not be willing to pay as much for high speeds as they are for other functionality.

Mobile broadband competition

As of November 2009, according to data from American Roamer, third-generation (3G) wireless service covers roughly 60% of U.S. landmass. In addition, approximately 77% of the U.S. population lived in an area served by three or more 3G service providers, 12% lived in an area served by two, and 9% lived in an area served by one. About 2% lived in an area with no provider.

These measures likely overstate the coverage actually experienced by consumers, since American Roamer reports *advertised* coverage as reported by many carriers who all use different definitions of coverage. In addition, these measures do not take into account other factors such as signal strength, bitrate or in-building coverage, and they may convey a false sense of consistency across geographic areas and service providers. As with fixed broadband, most areas without mobile broadband coverage are in rural or remote areas. Nonetheless, the data can help benchmark mobile broadband availability nationwide. In total, while U.S. service providers are building out mobile broadband coverage, the United States is far from having "complete" coverage.

Mobile data users typically receive download speeds ranging from hundreds of kilobits per second to about one megabit per second. Several competing firms offer mobile broadband. In addition to the nationwide service providers AT&T, Verizon, Sprint and T-Mobile (two of which are also leading providers of wireline broadband), new competitors such as Leap Wireless and MetroPCS have emerged in metropolitan areas in recent years. Like wireline broadband providers, these firms may compete along many dimensions including coverage, device selection, roaming and services.

Wireline-wireless competition

Whether wireless broadband, either fixed or mobile, can compete with wireline broadband is an important question in evaluating the status of broadband services competition. The answer depends on how technology, costs and consumer preferences evolve, as well as on the strategic choices of firms that control wireline and wireless assets, including firms that offer both fixed and mobile broadband.

Consumers' preferences differ depending on how they use their broadband connections and how much they are willing to pay for such use. Some value download speeds more than any other attribute, some value mobility and new converts from dial-up may still even value the simple "always on" connection. A user who values little more than e-mail and browsing news sites has, in principle, many choices — nearly any broadband access technology will do. But a user who streams high-definition video and enjoys gaming probably requires high download and upload speeds and low latency. That user will likely have few choices.

Wireless broadband may not be an effective substitute in the foreseeable future for consumers seeking high-speed connections at prices competitive with wireline offers. Given enough spectrum, however, a variety of engineering techniques — including higher transmitter power, high-gain directional antennas and multiple externally mounted antennae — may make wireless a viable price/performance competitor to wired solutions at far higher speeds than are possible today, further increasing consumer choice.

The ongoing upgrade of the wireless infrastructure is promising because of its potential to be a closer competitor to wireline broadband, especially at lower speeds. For example, if wireless providers begin to advertise, say, 4 Mbps home broadband service, wireline providers may be forced to respond by lowering prices of their broadband offerings. This could be true even if wireless services are more expensive, especially if the service is also mobile. Further, as with most goods, consumers choose broadband by trading off price and features. Providers offering a product with fewer features may have to reduce prices in order to remain competitive, even if the superior product charges more.

There is no guarantee, however, that competition will necessarily evolve this way. Technologies, costs and consumer preferences are changing too quickly in this dynamic part of the economy to make accurate predictions. Regardless of how those develop, affordability will remain a principal policy concern. The FCC should therefore carefully monitor affordability of low-end offerings and, if affordability does not improve in light of ongoing wireless upgrades, take further steps beyond those already described in this plan to address the issue.

Potential future issues for fixed broadband competition

[I]n 2004 the mean advertised download peak speeds of cable and DSL were similar, and the maximum and minimum advertised peak speeds were identical. By 2009, the mean advertised cable speed was about 2.5 times higher than DSL, while the maximum peak advertised speed was three times higher than DSL. The minimum advertised peak speeds remained identical. While the [data] does not contain information about demand or uptake of the higher-speed offers, or actual speeds delivered, it shows that the upgrade in network performance for cable companies from DOCSIS 3.0 is likely to continue or accelerate the trend where offers to end-users of traditional DSL cannot keep pace.

As with fixed-mobile substitution, how the evolution of network capabilities affects competition depends on how pricing, consumer demand, technology and costs evolve over time. For example, if users continue to value primarily applications that do not require very high speeds (e.g., speeds in excess of 20 Mbps), and are not willing to pay much for vastly increased speeds, then a provider may not gain much of an advantage by offering those higher speeds. In contrast, if typical users require high speeds and only one provider can offer those speeds and expected returns to telephone companies do not justify fiber upgrades, then users may face higher prices, fewer choices and less innovation. Because of this risk, it is crucial that the FCC track and compare the evolution of pricing in areas where two service providers offer very high peak speeds with pricing in areas where only one provider can offer very high peak speeds. The FCC should benchmark prices and services and include these in future reports on the state of broadband deployment.

Competition in Wholesale Broadband Markets

Residential broadband competition—as important as it is—is not the only type of competition we must foster to lay the foundation for America's broadband future. Ensuring robust competition not only for American households but also for American businesses requires particular attention to the role of wholesale markets, through which providers of broadband services secure critical inputs from one another. Because of the economies of scale, scope and density that characterize telecommunications networks, well functioning wholesale markets can help foster retail competition, as it is not economically or practically feasible for competitors to build facilities in all geographic areas. Therefore, the nation's regulatory policies for wholesale access affect the competitiveness of markets for retail broadband services provided to small businesses, mobile customers and enterprise customers.

Unfortunately, the FCC's current regulatory approach is a hodgepodge of wholesale access rights and pricing mechanisms that were developed without the benefit of a consistent, rigorous analytic framework. Similar network functionalities are regulated differently, based on the technology used. Therefore, while networks generally have been converging to integrated, packet-mode, largely-IP networks, regulatory policy regarding wholesale access has followed the opposite trajectory. This situation undermines longstanding competition policy objectives. In some cases it limits the ability of smaller carriers—often those specializing in serving niche markets such as small and medium sized business—to gain access to the necessary inputs to compete.

While facilities such as end-user loops and other point-to-point data circuits often serve as critical inputs to retail broadband services for business, mobile and residential customers, competitors' access to those inputs currently depends on factors that have little bearing on the economics of facilities-based competitive entry. For example, some wholesale access policies vary based on technology—including whether the facility or service operates using a circuit- or packet-based mode or is constructed from copper or fiber—regardless of the economic viability of replicating the physical facility. Similarly, the FCC's wireless roaming policies vary based on the services offered; roaming is only required for voice telephone calls and not mobile data services. As a result, mobile customers may not be able to use all functions of their smartphone devices when roaming, even in situations where it is technically feasible for all of those functions to work.

In other cases, FCC rules draw distinctions based on the capacity of the facility, or by using various proxies to measure existing or potential competitive entry. FCC has also been criticized for not collecting better data or monitoring the impact of its current approach to competition. The lack of a consistent analytical framework hinders the FCC's ability to promote competition. Accordingly, the FCC should comprehensively review its current policies and develop a cohesive and effective approach to advancing competition through its wholesale access policies

Notes and Questions

1. Workable Competition? What level of competition exists in the residential marketplace according to the Broadband Plan? On what basis should policymakers determine the degree to which wireless broadband offerings are an effective substitute for wireline offerings?

2. Wholesale Broadband Offerings. The Broadband Plan notes that "some wholesale access policies vary based on technology—including whether the facility or service operates using a circuit- or packet-based mode or is constructed from copper or fiber—regardless of the economic viability of replicating the physical facility." The technical term for wholesale access is "special access," or "dedicated access," which refers to the legacy type of tariff that made dedicated capacity available to major businesses and other carriers. Such facilities, according to smaller carriers, are not subject to competition, and the FCC has failed to develop effective oversight in this market. Moreover, as the quotation indicates, whatever oversight exists depends on the type of underlying technology used in those offerings.

§ 14.C.2. Net Neutrality Policy (and Jurisdiction, Again)

The FCC's first discussion of net neutrality issues came in a policy statement that it issued in tandem with its Wireline Broadband Order. In so doing, the FCC formalized a policy that former chairman Michael Powell had discussed previously in speeches. But a policy statement, like a speech, is not enforceable.

Appropriate Framework for Broadband Access to the Internet Over Wireline Facilities

Policy Statement, 20 FCC Rcd. 14,986 (2005)

DISCUSSION

4. The Communications Act charges the Commission with "regulating interstate and foreign commerce in communication by wire and radio." 47 U.S.C. § 151. The Communications Act regulates telecommunications carriers, as common carriers, under Title II. National Cable & Telecommunications Ass'n v. Brand X Internet Services, 545 U.S. 967, 973 (2005). Information service providers, "by contrast, are not subject to mandatory common-carrier regulation under Title II." Id. at 976. The Commission, however, "has jurisdiction to impose additional regulatory obligations under its Title I ancillary jurisdiction to regulate interstate and foreign communications."[4] As a result, the Commission has jurisdiction necessary to ensure that providers of telecommunications for Internet access or Internet Protocol-enabled (IP-enabled) services are operated in a neutral manner. Moreover, to ensure that broadband networks are widely deployed, open, affordable, and accessible to all consumers, the Commission adopts the following principles:

- *To encourage broadband deployment and preserve and promote the open and interconnected nature of the public Internet,* consumers are entitled to access the lawful Internet content of their choice.

- *To encourage broadband deployment and preserve and promote the open and interconnected nature of the public Internet,* consumers are entitled to run applications and use services of their choice, subject to the needs of law enforcement.

- *To encourage broadband deployment and preserve and promote the open and interconnected nature of the public Internet,* consumers are entitled to connect their choice of legal devices that do not harm the network.[5]

- *To encourage broadband deployment and preserve and promote the open and interconnected nature of the public Internet,* consumers are entitled to competition among network providers, application and service providers, and content providers.

CONCLUSION

5. The Commission has a duty to preserve and promote the vibrant and open character of the Internet as the telecommunications marketplace enters the broadband age. To foster creation, adoption and use of Internet broadband content, applications, services and attachments, and to ensure consumers benefit from the innovation that comes from competition, the Commission will incorporate the above principles into its ongoing policymaking activities.[6]

---

4. We also note that the Enforcement Bureau recently entered into a consent decree to resolve an investigation with respect to the blocking of ports used for Voice over Internet Protocol (VoIP). See Madison River Communications, LLC and Affiliated Companies, Order, 20 FCC Rcd. 4295 (Enf. Bur. 2005).

5. [The statement refers to Hush-A-Phone Corp. v. United States, 238 F.2d 266 (D.C. Cir. 1956), and Use of the Carterfone Device in Message Toll Telephone Service, Decision, 13 F.C.C. 2d 420 (1968), each of which is discussed in Chapter Six. Eds.]

6. Accordingly, we are not adopting rules in this policy statement. The principles we adopt are subject to reasonable network management.

Notes and Questions

1. Why a Policy Statement? If the FCC genuinely thought that the principles embedded in the policy statement should be followed by Internet access carriers, why did it proceed in this manner? A policy statement does not create binding law; its office in administrative law is that of an internal statement meant to guide agency enforcement discretion and, if announced, to give the regulated community notice of the agency's intentions. Why did the agency here decide to proceed by nonbinding policy statement?

2. Rules versus Case by Case. One of the reasons for the policy statement was to induce cooperation from the Internet community. But it was also meant to signal that the FCC did not want to limit legitimate freedom of action in a fast-moving market. How would you assess this balancing act? Based on what metrics?

3. "Reasonable Network Management." The FCC states in the policy statement that "[t]he principles [it] adopt[s] are subject to reasonable network management." But that is all that is said on the matter. How was the regulated community to know what was and was not "reasonable network management"? In the *Comcast* decision, Formal Complaint of Free Press and Public Knowledge Against Comcast Corp. for Secretly Degrading Peer-to-Peer Applications, Memorandum Opinion and Order, 23 FCC Rcd. 13,028 (2008), *rev'd*, Comcast Corp. v. FCC, 600 F.3d 642 (D.C. Cir. 2010), the FCC ruled that Comcast's practice of blocking certain BitTorrent applications was not reasonable network management. But should companies have a better idea in advance? In fact, what is reasonable network management?

4. Wireless Broadband and Open Platforms. The second major initiative that the FCC took regarding neutrality among networks came in connection with its oversight of wireless broadband services. In particular, the question of open wireless platforms arose as the agency developed the rules for its 700 MHz band plan. In that context, the legal issues are different from those in the case of wireline broadband. First, the FCC's Title III authority over spectrum licenses is quite broad, enabling it to regulate the use of wireless spectrum in a manner necessary to serve the "public convenience, interest, or necessity." 47 U.S.C. § 307(a). Second, in the case of the 700 MHz band plan, the FCC imposed what it called open platform conditions on only one block of spectrum, the so-called "C Block," and firms unwilling to comply with the relevant terms did not have to bid on such spectrum.

The context of the C Block conditions was the transition from analog to digital television, which opened up new spectrum for wireless broadband services and a new venue for debates about how to structure spectrum rights. In 1996, Congress granted TV broadcasters an extra set of frequencies for digital television signals, but in 2005 Congress passed legislation setting February 17, 2009 (later pushed back to June 12, 2009), as the date when full-power broadcasters would stop analog broadcasting and relinquish one of those assignments. This created the prospect of freeing a substantial amount of spectrum in 2009. The biggest swath of such frequencies is the 108 MHz that historically were used for UHF broadcasting on channels 52 through 69 (each channel was assigned 6 MHz). This spectrum attracted enormous interest, as it presented the first reallocation of "beachfront spectrum"—i.e., frequencies with very desirable propagation characteristics—in many years and in greater amounts than were likely to become available for years to come.

Congress provided the FCC with limited direction on how to manage this spectrum. It did direct that the FCC dedicate 24 MHz of this spectrum for public safety, but it left 84 MHz to be auctioned for commercial and other uses based on whatever restrictions the FCC decided were in the public interest. In the early 2000s, the FCC auctioned 22 MHz for commercial uses, leaving licenses for 62 MHz of very valuable spectrum to be auctioned along the lines spelled out in the 700 MHz band plan. That band plan, as noted above, included an open platforms requirement, as outlined in the following excerpt from that order.

Service Rules for the 698–746, 747–762 & 777–792 MHz Bands

Second Report and Order, 22 FCC Rcd. 15,289 (2007)

I. Introduction

1. In this Second Report and Order, we establish rules governing wireless licenses in the 698–806 MHz Band (herein, the "700 MHz Band"). This spectrum currently is occupied by television broadcasters in TV Channels 52–69. It is being made available for wireless services, including public safety and commercial services, as a result of the digital television ("DTV") transition.

7. [W]e determine that for one commercial spectrum block in the 700 MHz Band, the Upper 700 MHz Band C Block, licensees will be required to allow customers, device manufacturers, third-party application developers, and others to use devices and applications of their choice, subject to certain conditions. We conclude, however, that at this time it would not serve the public interest to mandate broader requirements, such as a wholesale requirement for the unauctioned 700 MHz Band spectrum.

III. Discussion

A. *Commercial 700 MHz Band, Including 700 MHz Guard Bands*

2. Service Rules

a. *Commercial Services (Excluding Guard Bands and Upper 700 MHz D Block)*

iii. *Open Platforms for Devices and Applications*

189. *Background.* In [an earlier notice in this proceeding], we sought comment on a proposal filed by the Ad Hoc Public Interest Spectrum Coalition (PISC) that licenses for at least 30 MHz of the unauctioned commercial 700 MHz Band spectrum bear a condition requiring a licensee to provide open platforms for devices and applications.[7] PISC described its proposal as including the right of a consumer to use any equipment, content, application, or service on a non-discriminatory basis.

190. PISC argues that "incumbent wireless carriers ... routinely choke bandwidth to users, cripple features, and control the user experience" in order to protect their wireline broadband offerings (e.g., DSL and cable modem). Supporters offer many examples of such restrictions, including restrictions on the use of Voice over Internet Protocol (VoIP), webcams, and other media devices. [Another commenter] cites the Apple iPhone device, which is designed to work exclusively on one provider's network.

191. Proponents argue that without mandated open access, wireless broadband service is unlikely to develop into a vigorous competitor for existing wireline broadband serv-

---

7. The Ad Hoc Public Interest Spectrum Coalition [PISC] consists of the Consumer Federation of America, Consumers Union, Free Press, Media Access Project, New America Foundation, and Public Knowledge.

ices, because incumbent wireless service providers owned by wireline companies will instead limit the quality of their wireless broadband offerings to protect their wireline broadband offerings. These commenters credit the open access model with creating a competitive environment in which independent service and equipment providers flourished in this country under the *Carterfone* decision, the Computer Proceedings, and the 1996 Telecommunications Act.[8] They argue that the 700 MHz open access policies they advocate will facilitate competitive entry for both wireless service providers and Internet service providers, which will foster innovation, enhance services, and lower prices. For example, Google maintains that the only way to guarantee new broadband platforms is through open platform requirements: open applications, open devices, open services, and open networks.

192. On the other hand, opponents dispute the need for open access requirements and argue that these requirements could have adverse consequences. They maintain that, unlike the monopoly wireline market in which the *Carterfone* decision was based, there is effective competition in the mobile wireless market and that auction of the remaining commercial 700 MHz Band spectrum will provide opportunities for additional competitors. Opponents assert that open access advocates exaggerate the restrictions wireless providers impose on consumers, and to the extent providers do engage in such practices, such practices are reasonable measures to protect the integrity and efficiency of wireless networks. In addition, some commenters argue that imposing open access requirements would directly contradict Commission findings that bundling mobile handsets with wireless service contracts increases wireless penetration, and that subjecting wireless broadband Internet access service providers to access, price, or unbundling mandates is a disservice to consumers. Verizon Wireless maintains that the "incumbent advantages" cited by Google are not anticompetitive, and result from high-risk capital investments in a competitive market.

195. *Discussion.* Although we generally prefer to rely on marketplace forces as the most efficient mechanism for fostering competition, we conclude that the 700 MHz spectrum provides an important opportunity to apply requirements for open platforms for devices and applications for the benefit of consumers, without unduly burdening existing services and markets. For the reasons described below, we determine that for one commercial spectrum block in the 700 MHz Band—the Upper 700 MHz Band C Block—we will require licensees to allow customers, device manufacturers, third-party application developers, and others to use or develop the devices and applications of their choice, subject to certain conditions, as described further below. We conclude, however, that it would not serve the public interest to mandate, at this time, requirements for open platforms for devices and applications for all unauctioned commercial 700 MHz spectrum, or to impose broader requirements, such as wholesale or interconnection requirements, for the C Block.

198. Although wireless broadband services have great promise, we have become increasingly concerned that certain practices in the wireless industry may constrain consumer access to wireless broadband networks and limit the services and functionalities provided

---

8. *See, e.g.,* PISC, 700 MHz Further Notice Comments at 16–19; Google, June 9, 2007 Ex Parte at 5–6. In addition, approximately 250,000 individual citizens filed brief comments both during and after the formal comment periods asking the Commission to ensure that large corporations will not stifle competition and innovation in Internet markets over U.S. airwaves, and to set aside at least 30 MHz of spectrum for open and non-discriminatory Internet access. [*Carterfone* and the Computer Proceedings are discussed in Chapter Six. Eds.]

to consumers by these networks. In [an earlier order], we recognized that wireless IP-based multimedia content and services are typically sold through a service provider-branded, service provider-controlled portal. We also noted that "in some cases, providers use filters to limit the web sites that a customer can access, and, in other cases, subscribers can enter any URL using a handset but the site may not be viewable due to software, processing, or other constraints of the device."[9] In contrast, wireless broadband Internet access services for laptop computers typically allow consumers to access the same applications that would be available had they chosen a cable or wireline broadband Internet access connection.

200. The Commission generally relies on the competitive marketplace to deliver the benefits of choice, innovation and affordability to American consumers, and regulates only when market driven forces alone may not achieve broader social goals. The Commission has found that the Commercial Mobile Radio Services (CMRS) market is effectively competitive, and that competitive pressures continue to result in the introduction of innovative pricing plans and service offerings. We have not found, however, that competition in the CMRS marketplace is ensuring that consumers drive handset and application choices, especially in the emerging wireless broadband market. For example, while it is easy for consumers to differentiate among providers by price, most consumers are unaware when carriers block or degrade applications and of the implications of such actions, thus making it difficult for providers to differentiate themselves on this score. As a result, while many commenters assert that market forces require that wireless providers support handsets and applications that consumers want, there is evidence that wireless service providers nevertheless block or degrade consumer-chosen hardware and applications without an appropriate justification.

202. To promote innovation in this spectrum band from the outset, we find it is reasonable to impose certain conditions on the C Block in the Upper 700 MHz Band to provide open platforms for devices and applications. While the Commission strives to apply a consistent regulatory framework to like services, that does not obligate us to treat all spectrum-based services identically. The Commission has applied different spectrum regulatory models as warranted by different market conditions, ranging from licenses that largely grant exclusive rights to use the spectrum to unlicensed approaches in which access to the spectrum is open and subject to minimal rules. Particularly in developing markets, regulatory policies have played an important role in encouraging new competitive services to emerge. Many technologies, such as Wi-Fi services, have developed as a result of regulatory policies established by the Commission in particular spectrum bands.

203. In these circumstances, we conclude that prohibiting a provider's ability to unreasonably limit applications and devices on its network in a portion of the 700 MHz Band is both appropriate and feasible.

204. We believe that the C Block is the most reasonable block for applying a new regulatory model that attempts to give consumers additional choices. The C Block is a large 22-megahertz block (comprised of paired 11-megahertz blocks). [W]e believe that a block of this size and scope will provide an environment conducive to the development and deployment of 4G services designed to compete with wireline broadband alternatives. Imposing such a requirement on a band with these characteristics should provide an opportunity for innovators and entrepreneurs to develop equipment and applications that require substantial bandwidth to realize their full potential. It should also provide sufficient potential market penetration to attract investment and achieve economies of scale in the equipment marketplace. Without access to a block capable of supporting high data

---

9. *See* Appropriate Regulatory Treatment for Broadband Access to the Internet Over Wireless Networks, Declaratory Ruling, 22 FCC Rcd. 5901, 5908 ¶ 16 (2007).

rates and the potential for substantial market penetration, the requirements we impose here would be less likely to result in rapid innovation at the edge of the network. Thus, more than any other spectrum block in the 700 MHz Band, it is the C Block that would benefit from our intervention to help ensure that access to anticipated 4G services is not unduly inhibited or foreclosed.

205. While we adopt a requirement for the C Block licensees to provide open platforms for devices and applications, we decline at this time to impose these same principles or other openness obligations broadly in the 700 MHz Band, as recommended in PISC's open access and Google's broader proposals. Given the state of the record, we believe that a more measured approach is appropriate. While the open platform requirement for devices and applications in the C Block holds the potential to foster innovation, we cannot rule out the possibility that such a requirement may have unanticipated drawbacks as well. Therefore, we think that it is appropriate to impose the open platform requirement only on a limited basis. While the record in this proceeding regarding the potential merits or drawbacks of the open platform requirement for devices and applications is not so clear as to warrant adopting such conditions for the entire 700 MHz Band, the approach that we take today will allow both the Commission and industry to observe the real-world effects of such a requirement. Moreover, we note that to the extent the results of our C Block requirements prove attractive to consumers, we would anticipate that providers in other 700 MHz Band blocks and other bands will have competitive incentives to offer similar choices. We disagree with PISC's suggestions that the wireless market is not competitive. We also reject Google's argument that mandatory wholesale and other broad regulatory models are necessary at this time to provide incentives for new entry and innovation. We have not established wireless regulatory policies based solely on "leveling the playing field" against incumbent operators, as suggested by Google, and we decline to do so here. In addition, the record is not sufficient to adopt broader obligations here or even to decide the specifics of such mandates.

206. Accordingly, consistent with the broadband principles set out above, we will require only C Block licensees to allow customers, device manufacturers, third-party application developers, and others to use or develop the devices and applications of their choosing in C Block networks, so long as they meet all applicable regulatory requirements and comply with reasonable conditions related to management of the wireless network (i.e., do not cause harm to the network). Specifically, a C Block licensee may not block, degrade, or interfere with the ability of end users to download and utilize applications of their choosing on the licensee's C Block network, subject to reasonable network management. We anticipate that wireless service providers will address this requirement by developing reasonable standards, including through participation in standards setting organizations, as discussed below. Finally, for the reasons noted above, we will not impose additional requirements on the C Block, including wholesale and interconnection requirements.

207. *Commission's Authority to Impose Requirements for Open Platforms for Devices and Applications.* As a general matter, the Commission has the authority to establish license conditions and operational obligations, such as the requirements we adopt here, if the condition or obligation will further the goals of the Communications Act without contradicting any basic parameters of the agency's authority. As we have demonstrated above, the record is sufficient to conclude that current practices in the industry may be impeding the development and deployment of devices and applications that consumers want to use. Thus, a requirement to allow consumer use of any such devices and applications (limited by reasonable requirements to protect the network and to enable the wireless service provider to comply with its regulatory obligations) in a band like the C Block holds the potential to foster the development of innovative devices and applications, and

as a result, promises to benefit consumers. This type of initiative — in terms of purpose, scope, and method of implementation — falls squarely within a number of the Commission's statutory sources of authority.

222. *Scope of the requirement for open platforms for devices and applications.* Wireless service providers subject to this requirement will not be allowed to disable features or functionality in handsets where such action is not related to reasonable network management and protection, or compliance with applicable regulatory requirements. For example, providers may not "lock" handsets to prevent their transfer from one system to another. We also prohibit standards that block Wi-Fi access, MP3 playback ringtone capability, or other services that compete with wireless service providers' own offerings. Standards for third-party applications or devices that are more stringent than those used by the provider itself would likewise be prohibited. In addition, C Block licensees cannot exclude applications or devices solely on the basis that such applications or devices would unreasonably increase bandwidth demands. We anticipate that demand can be adequately managed through feasible facility improvements or technology-neutral capacity pricing that does not discriminate against subscribers using third-party devices or applications. In that regard, we emphasize that C Block licensees may not impose any additional discriminatory charges (one-time or recurring) or conditions on customers who seek to use devices or applications outside of those provided by the licensee. Finally, C Block licensees may not deny access to a customer's device solely because that device makes use of other wireless spectrum bands, such as cellular or PCS spectrum. However, we also note that, in accepting a multi-band device for use on its network, a C Block licensee is not required to extend the requirement for open platforms for devices and applications to other spectrum bands on which the provider operates.

223. We emphasize that we are not requiring wireless service providers to allow the unrestricted use of *any* devices or applications on their networks. In particular, we are mindful of the risks network operators face in protecting against harmful devices and malicious software. Wireless service providers may continue to use their own certification standards and processes to approve use of devices and applications on their networks so long as those standards are confined to reasonable network management. For example, providers are free to choose their air interface technology, and to deny service to devices or applications that cannot operate on the same technology, since such a restriction permits significant network efficiencies without significantly reducing consumer access to services and features. We also recognize that wireless providers have legitimate technical reasons to restrict particular non-carrier devices and applications on their networks, specifically to ensure the safety and integrity of their networks. In particular, we believe that it is reasonable for wireless service providers to maintain network control features that permit dynamic management of network operations, including the management of devices operating on the network, and to restrict use of the network to devices compatible with these network control features. Standards to ensure that network performance will not be significantly degraded would also be appropriate.

224. We will not at this time specify a particular process for C Block licensees to develop reasonable network management and openness standards, but we will require certain minimum steps to ensure that device manufacturers and application developers have the ability to design products for this spectrum in a timely manner. Specifically, a C Block licensee must publish standards no later than the time at which it makes such standards available to any preferred vendors (i.e., vendors with whom the provider has a relationship to design products for the provider's network). We also require the C Block licensee to provide to potential customers notice of the customers' rights to request the attachment of a device or application to the licensee's network, and notice of the licensee's process for

customers to make such requests, including the relevant network criteria. We expect that any standards adopted by a C Block licensee will be non-proprietary, such that they would be open to any third party vendors and that the standards applied to third parties will be no more restrictive than those applied to the provider's preferred vendors.

Notes and Questions

1. Competition and Nondiscriminatory Access. The Commission declines, in authorizing the auction of available spectrum, to impose any limits on what entities could bid for spectrum licenses. If the Commission is concerned about an absence of competition, which presumably explains its focus on the need for open platforms conditions, should it have restricted who could bid for available spectrum? What impact would have resulted from such restrictions?

2. *Carterfone*. The excerpt above discusses the proposal to implement a "*Carterfone*" requirement. As discussed in Chapter Six, *Carterfone* was a 1968 FCC ruling, Use of the Carterfone Device in Message Toll Telephone Service, Decision, 13 F.C.C. 2d 420 (1968), that the then-Bell monopoly could not restrict what customer premises equipment (CPE) could be used in conjunction with the local telephone network. Before that ruling went into effect, Bell required all of its customers to lease telephones and barred any "foreign attachments" to the network. The impact of the *Carterfone* regime was considerable, with consumers getting more choice, higher quality, and cheaper phones as a result. It also enabled new technologies, such as the modem, to be developed and marketed without having to receive Bell's permission first. At the time of the excerpted order, the FCC had opened a more wide-ranging wireless *Carterfone* proceeding. Rather than act in that docket, the FCC opted to move only on the C Block front. What justifications can you suggest for pursuing this strategy? What criticisms of it can you offer?

3. Bidding. The auction for the 700 MHz spectrum concluded in March 2008 and yielded winning bids totaling more than $19.5 billion. The bidders who won the most frequencies were Verizon Wireless and AT&T. The most common way of measuring the price of spectrum is in dollars per MHz passing one person in the coverage area of the license (or POP). The C Block sold (to Verizon Wireless) for 76 cents per MHz POP. By contrast, the B Block sold for $2.68 per MHz POP, the A Block $1.16 per MHz POP, and the E Block 74 cents per MHz POP.[10] Do the relatively lower bids for the C Block than for the A and B Blocks tell us anything about the conditions the FCC imposed? One way of thinking about the question is as follows: assuming that the bids for the C Block were lower because of the nondiscrimination requirements the FCC imposed, who will be the beneficiary of that foregone revenue?

4. Evasion. How easy (or difficult) do you think it is for the winning bidders (Verizon Wireless, as it turns out) to evade the nondiscrimination requirements contained in this order? The order leaves licensees with some ability to manage their networks. Does the FCC leave the winning bidders with too much wiggle room? Not enough? Raising these very questions, Google filed a complaint at the FCC in the spring of 2008—before Verizon Wireless even gained control of the relevant spectrum—alleging that its plans fail to comply with the FCC's order.

---

10. Relatedly, each block had a reserve price (below which the block would not sell). For the A Block, the winning bids totaled $3.96 billion, or 2.2 times the reserve, for the B Block it was $9.14 billion, or 6.7 times the reserve, and for the C Block it was $4.75 billion, or 1.02 times the reserve.

5. Net Neutrality Enforcement. The next important development in the debate over the FCC's ancillary jurisdiction came explicitly over its ability to regulate broadband Internet service. In 2007, some Comcast subscribers alleged that the company was secretly degrading peer-to-peer traffic. The FCC investigated the claims. Comcast initially denied the allegations, but it eventually admitted to degrading the traffic. This led to an FCC order (the culmination of an adjudication). Formal Complaint of Free Press & Public Knowledge Against Comcast Corp. for Secretly Degrading Peer-to-Peer Applications, Memorandum Opinion and Order, 23 FCC Rcd. 13,028 (2008). In its order, the FCC found that Comcast had violated the principles embodied in the FCC's Internet Policy Statement, and it ordered Comcast to cease and desist certain practices (which Comcast agreed to do). Comcast challenged the FCC's authority to issue this order, leading to the following opinion.

Comcast Corp. v. FCC
600 F.3d 642 (D.C. Cir. 2010)

Opinion for the Court filed by Circuit Judge TATEL, in which Circuit Judge SENTELLE and Senior Circuit Judge RANDOLPH concur.

TATEL, Circuit Judge:

I.

In 2007 several subscribers to Comcast's high-speed Internet service discovered that the company was interfering with their use of peer-to-peer networking applications. Peer-to-peer programs allow users to share large files directly with one another without going through a central server. Such programs also consume significant amounts of bandwidth.

Challenging Comcast's action, two non-profit advocacy organizations, Free Press and Public Knowledge, filed a complaint with the Federal Communications Commission and, together with a coalition of public interest groups and law professors, a petition for declaratory ruling. Both filings argued that Comcast's actions "violat[ed] the FCC's Internet Policy Statement." Issued two years earlier, that statement "adopt[ed] the ... principles" that "consumers are entitled to access the lawful Internet content of their choice ... [and] to run applications and use services of their choice." Appropriate Framework for Broadband Access to the Internet Over Wireline Facilities, Policy Statement, 20 FCC Rcd. 14,986, 14,988, ¶ 4 (2005). Comcast defended its interference with peer-to-peer programs as necessary to manage scarce network capacity.

Following a period of public comment, the Commission issued the order challenged here. Formal Compl. of Free Press & Public Knowledge Against Comcast Corp. for Secretly Degrading Peer-to-Peer Applications, Memorandum Opinion and Order, 23 FCC Rcd. 13,028 (2008) (Order). The Commission began by concluding not only that it had jurisdiction over Comcast's network management practices, but also that it could resolve the dispute through adjudication rather than through rulemaking. On the merits, the Commission ruled that Comcast had "significantly impeded consumers' ability to access the content and use the applications of their choice," and that because Comcast "ha[d] several available options it could use to manage network traffic without discriminating" against peer-to-peer communications, its method of bandwidth management "contravene[d] ... federal policy." Because by then Comcast had agreed to adopt a new system for managing bandwidth demand, the Commission simply ordered it to make a set of disclosures describing the details of its new approach and the company's progress toward implementing it. The Commission added that an injunction would automatically issue should Comcast either fail to make the required disclosures or renege on its commitment.

II.

Through the Communications Act of 1934, as amended over the decades, 47 U.S.C. § 151 et seq., Congress has given the Commission express and expansive authority to regulate common carrier services, including landline telephony, *id.* § 201 et seq. (Title II of the Act); radio transmissions, including broadcast television, radio, and cellular telephony, *id.* § 301 et seq. (Title III); and "cable services," including cable television, *id.* § 521 et seq. (Title VI). In this case, the Commission does not claim that Congress has given it express authority to regulate Comcast's Internet service. Indeed, in its still-binding 2002 Cable Modem Order, the Commission ruled that cable Internet service is neither a "telecommunications service" covered by Title II of the Communications Act nor a "cable service" covered by Title VI. High-Speed Access to the Internet Over Cable and Other Facilities, Declaratory Ruling and Notice of Proposed Rulemaking, 17 FCC Rcd. 4798, 4802, ¶ 7 (2002), *aff'd,* Nat'l Cable & Telecomms. Ass'n v. Brand X Internet Servs., 545 U.S. 967 (2005). The Commission therefore rests its assertion of authority over Comcast's network management practices on the broad language of section 4(i) of the Act: "The Commission may perform any and all acts, make such rules and regulations, and issue such orders, not inconsistent with this chapter, as may be necessary in the execution of its functions," 47 U.S.C. § 154(i).

Courts have come to call the Commission's section 4(i) power its "ancillary" authority, a label that derives from three foundational Supreme Court decisions: United States v. Southwestern Cable Co., 392 U.S. 157 (1968), United States v. Midwest Video Corp., 406 U.S. 649 (1972) (*Midwest Video I*), and FCC v. Midwest Video Corp., 440 U.S. 689 (1979) (*Midwest Video II*). All three cases dealt with Commission jurisdiction over early cable systems at a time when, as with the Internet today, the Communications Act gave the Commission no express authority to regulate such systems. (Title VI, which gives the Commission jurisdiction over "cable services," was not added to the statute until 1984.)

In the first case, *Southwestern Cable*, the Supreme Court considered a challenge to a Commission order restricting the geographic area in which a cable company could operate. The Supreme Court sustained that order, explaining that even though the then-existing Communications Act gave the Commission no express authority over cable television, the Commission could nonetheless regulate cable television to the extent "reasonably ancillary to the effective performance of the Commission's various responsibilities for the regulation of television broadcasting." Four years later, in *Midwest Video I*, the Court again sustained the Commission's use of its ancillary authority, this time to support issuance of a regulation that required cable operators to facilitate the creation of new programs and to transmit them alongside broadcast programs they captured from the air. In *Midwest Video II*, the Court rejected the Commission's assertion of ancillary authority, setting aside regulations that required cable systems to make certain channels available for public use.

We recently distilled the holdings of these three cases into a two-part test. In American Library Assocation v. FCC, 406 F.3d 689 (D.C. Cir. 2005), we wrote: "The Commission ... may exercise ancillary jurisdiction only when two conditions are satisfied: (1) the Commission's general jurisdictional grant under Title I [of the Communications Act] covers the regulated subject and (2) the regulations are reasonably ancillary to the Commission's effective performance of its statutorily mandated responsibilities."

406 F.3d at 691–92. Comcast concedes that the Commission's action here satisfies the first requirement because the company's Internet service qualifies as "interstate and foreign communication by wire" within the meaning of Title I of the Communications Act. 47 U.S.C. § 152(a). Whether the Commission's action satisfies *American Library*'s second requirement is the central issue in this case.

IV.
A.

The Commission relies principally on section 230(b), part of a provision entitled "Protection for private blocking and screening of offensive material," 47 U.S.C. § 230, that grants civil immunity for such blocking to providers of interactive computer services, *id.* § 230(c)(2). Setting forth the policies underlying this protection, section 230(b) states, in relevant part, that "[i]t is the policy of the United States ... to promote the continued development of the Internet and other interactive computer services" and "to encourage the development of technologies which maximize user control over what information is received by individuals, families, and schools who use the Internet." In this case the Commission found that Comcast's network management practices frustrated both objectives.

In addition to section 230(b), the Commission relies on section 1, in which Congress set forth its reasons for creating the Commission in 1934: "For the purpose of regulating interstate and foreign commerce in communication by wire and radio so as to make available, so far as possible, to all the people of the United States ... a rapid, efficient, Nation-wide, and world-wide wire and radio communication service ... at reasonable charges, ... there is created a commission to be known as the 'Federal Communications Commission'...." 47 U.S.C. § 151. The Commission found that "prohibiting unreasonable network discrimination directly furthers the goal of making broadband Internet access service both 'rapid' and 'efficient.'"

Comcast argues that neither section 230(b) nor section 1 can support the Commission's exercise of ancillary authority because the two provisions amount to nothing more than congressional "statements of policy." Such statements, Comcast contends, "are not an operative part of the statute, and do not enlarge or confer powers on administrative agencies. As such, they necessarily fail to set forth 'statutorily mandated responsibilities'" within the meaning of *American Library*.

The Commission acknowledges that section 230(b) and section 1 are statements of policy that themselves delegate no regulatory authority. Still, the Commission maintains that the two provisions, like all provisions of the Communications Act, set forth "statutorily mandated responsibilities" that can anchor the exercise of ancillary authority. "The operative provisions of statutes are those which *declare the legislative will*," the Commission asserts. "Here, the legislative will has been declared by Congress in the form of a policy, along with an express grant of authority to the FCC to perform all actions necessary to execute and enforce all the provisions of the Communications Act."

In support of its reliance on congressional statements of policy, the Commission points out that in both *Southwestern Cable* and *Midwest Video I* the Supreme Court linked the challenged Commission actions to the furtherance of various congressional "goals," "objectives," and "policies." In particular, the Commission notes that in *Midwest Video I*, the plurality accepted its argument that the Commission's "concern with CATV carriage of broadcast signals ... extends ... to requiring CATV affirmatively to further statutory *policies*." According to the Commission, since congressional statements of policy were sufficient to support ancillary authority over cable television, it may likewise rely on such statements—section 230(b) and section 1—to exercise ancillary authority over the network management practices of Internet providers.

We read *Southwestern Cable* and *Midwest Video I* quite differently. In those cases, the Supreme Court relied on policy statements not because, standing alone, they set out "statutorily mandated responsibilities," but rather because they did so in conjunction with an express delegation of authority to the Commission, i.e., Title III's authority to regulate broadcasting.

The teaching of *Southwestern Cable, Midwest Video I,* [and] *Midwest Video II*—that policy statements alone cannot provide the basis for the Commission's exercise of ancillary authority—derives from the "axiomatic" principle that "administrative agencies may [act] only pursuant to authority delegated to them by Congress." Policy statements are just that—statements of policy. They are not delegations of regulatory authority. To be sure, statements of congressional policy can help delineate the contours of statutory authority. Consider, for example, the various services over which the Commission enjoys express statutory authority. When exercising its Title II authority to set "just and reasonable" rates for phone service, 47 U.S.C. § 201(b), or its Title III authority to grant broadcasting licenses in the "public convenience, interest, or necessity," *id.* § 307(a), or its Title VI authority to prohibit "unfair methods of competition" by cable operators that limit consumer access to certain types of television programming, *id.* § 548(b), the Commission must bear in mind section 1's objective of "Nation-wide ... wire and radio communication service ... at reasonable charges," *id.* § 151. In all three examples, section 1's policy goal undoubtedly illuminates the scope of the "authority delegated to [the Commission] by Congress,"—though it is Titles II, III, and VI that do the delegating. So too with respect to the Commission's section 4(i) ancillary authority. Although policy statements may illuminate that authority, it is Title II, III, or VI to which the authority must ultimately be ancillary.

In this case the Commission cites neither section 230(b) nor section 1 to shed light on any express statutory delegation of authority found in Title II, III, VI, or, for that matter, anywhere else. That is, unlike the way it successfully employed policy statements in *Southwestern Cable* and *Midwest Video I*, the Commission does not rely on section 230(b) or section 1 to argue that its regulation of an activity over which it concededly has no express statutory authority (here Comcast's Internet management practices) is necessary to further its regulation of activities over which it does have express statutory authority (here, for example, Comcast's management of its Title VI cable services).

Instead, the Commission maintains that congressional policy by itself creates "statutorily mandated responsibilities" sufficient to support the exercise of section 4(i) ancillary authority. Not only is this argument flatly inconsistent with *Southwestern Cable, Midwest Video I,* [and] *Midwest Video II*, but if accepted it would virtually free the Commission from its congressional tether. As the Court explained in *Midwest Video II*, "without reference to the provisions of the Act" expressly granting regulatory authority, "the Commission's [ancillary] jurisdiction ... would be unbounded." Indeed, Commission counsel told us at oral argument that just as the Order seeks to make Comcast's Internet service more "rapid" and "efficient," the Commission could someday subject Comcast's Internet service to pervasive rate regulation to ensure that the company provides the service at "reasonable charges," 47 U.S.C. § 151. Were we to accept that theory of ancillary authority, we see no reason why the Commission would have to stop there, for we can think of few examples of regulations that apply to Title II common carrier services, Title III broadcast services, or Title VI cable services that the Commission, relying on the broad policies articulated in section 230(b) and section 1, would be unable to impose upon Internet service providers.

Because the Commission has failed to tie its assertion of ancillary authority over Comcast's Internet service to any "statutorily mandated responsibility," we grant the petition for review and vacate the Order.

Notes and Questions

1. **What Is the Difference?** How different was the Commission's losing argument in *Comcast* from its winning arguments in the cases the court discusses? Was the court trying to rein in ancillary jurisdiction? If so, is that because the Commission's power would otherwise seem unlimited, and unlimitable? What remains of ancillary jurisdiction, and in particular, the Commission's authority under Title I?

2. **Deference?** The Commission is usually entitled to deference for its interpretations of the Communications Act, under the *Chevron* doctrine discussed in *Brand X* and elsewhere. *See* Chevron U.S.A. Inc. v. Natural Resources Defense Council, Inc., 467 U.S. 837 (1984). Why did the court not discuss the notion of deference?

3. **More Than a Bump in the Road.** The impact of this decision was not limited to net neutrality. The Commission (in the Broadband Plan and other initiatives) had articulated a wide range of possible actions with respect to broadband, for all of which it planned to rely on ancillary jurisdiction. This included changes to universal service, consumer protection, privacy, cyber security, and access for people with disabilities. As we saw in Chapter Thirteen, the Tenth Circuit found that the Commission's universal service rules were authorized. In re FCC 11-161, 753 F.3d 1015 (10th Cir. 2014). Is the Tenth Circuit's reasoning in tension with the opinion above?

4. **The FCC's Policy Reasoning.** In its decision against Comcast, the FCC held that Comcast blocked peer-to-peer traffic because it was acting to protect revenues that it earned through its video services (traditional channels and especially video-on-demand). Assuming that the FCC is correct that Comcast would have such an incentive, is that only because Comcast (by virtue of net neutrality norms or otherwise) is not permitted to apply a premium charge to other video providers using the Internet platform (e.g., YouTube or Netflix)? Such premium charges are common in traditional video markets.

5. **Next Steps.** As a result of the court's decision, the FCC was faced with a choice (unless and until Congress passed new legislation): leave Internet services unregulated, attempt to revive its theory of ancillary jurisdiction, or revisit its classification of Internet access service as an information service regulated under Title I rather than a common carrier service regulated under Title II. In the wake of the D.C. Circuit's decision, the FCC proceeded to adopt a more comprehensive regime without classifying Internet access service under Title II. The D.C. Circuit's decision summarizes the FCC's action.

Verizon v. FCC
740 F.3d 623 (D.C. Cir. 2014)

Opinion for the Court filed by Circuit Judge TATEL. Opinion concurring in part and dissenting in part filed by Senior Circuit Judge SILBERMAN.

TATEL, Circuit Judge.

For the second time in four years, we are confronted with a Federal Communications Commission effort to compel broadband providers to treat all Internet traffic the same regardless of source—or to require, as it is popularly known, "net neutrality." In Comcast Corp. v. FCC, 600 F.3d 642 (D.C. Cir. 2010), we held that the Commission had failed to cite any statutory authority that would justify its order compelling a broadband provider to adhere to open network management practices. After *Comcast,* the Commission issued the order challenged here—In re Preserving the Open Internet, Report and Order, 25 FCC Rcd. 17,905 (2010) ("the Open Internet Order")—which imposes disclosure, anti-blocking, and anti-discrimination requirements on broadband providers. As we explain in this opinion, the Commission has established that section 706 of the Telecommunications Act of 1996 vests it with affirmative authority to enact measures encouraging the deployment of broadband infrastructure. The Commission, we further hold, has reasonably interpreted section 706 to empower it to promulgate rules governing broadband providers' treatment of Internet traffic, and its justification for the specific rules at issue here—that they will preserve and facilitate the "virtuous circle" of innovation that has driven the explosive growth of the Internet—is reasonable and supported by substantial evidence. That said, even though the Commission has general authority to regulate in this arena, it may not impose requirements that contravene express statutory mandates. Given that the Commission has chosen to classify broadband providers in a manner that exempts them from treatment as common carriers, the Communications Act expressly prohibits the Commission from nonetheless regulating them as such. Because the Commission has failed to establish that the anti-discrimination and anti-blocking rules do not impose per se common carrier obligations, we vacate those portions of the Open Internet Order.

I.

While the *Comcast* matter was pending, the Commission sought comment on a set of proposed rules that, with some modifications, eventually became the rules at issue here. In support, it relied on the same theory of ancillary jurisdiction it had asserted in the Comcast Order. But after our decision in *Comcast* undermined that theory, the Commission sought comment on whether and to what extent it should reclassify broadband Internet services as telecommunications services. Ultimately, however, rather than reclassifying broadband, the Commission adopted the Open Internet Order that Verizon challenges here.

The Open Internet Order establishes two sets of "prophylactic rules" designed to "incorporate longstanding openness principles that are generally in line with current practices." 25 FCC Rcd. at 17,907, ¶ 4. One set of rules applies to "fixed" broadband providers—i.e., those furnishing residential broadband service and, more generally, Internet access to end users "primarily at fixed end points using stationary equipment." *Id.* at 17,934, ¶ 49. The other set of requirements applies to "mobile" broadband providers—i.e., those "serv[ing] end users primarily using mobile stations," such as smart phones. *Id.*

The Order first imposes a transparency requirement on both fixed and mobile broadband providers. They must "publicly disclose accurate information regarding the network management practices, performance, and commercial terms of [their] broadband Internet access services." *Id.* at 17,937, ¶ 54 (fixed providers); *see also id.* at 17,959, ¶ 98 (mobile providers).

Second, the Order imposes anti-blocking requirements on both types of broadband providers. It prohibits fixed broadband providers from "block[ing] lawful content, applications, services, or non-harmful devices, subject to reasonable network management." *Id.* at 17,942, ¶ 63. Similarly, the Order forbids mobile providers from "block[ing] consumers from accessing lawful websites" and from "block[ing] applications that compete with the provider's voice or video telephony services, subject to reasonable network management." *Id.* at 17,959, ¶ 99. The Order defines "reasonable network management" as practices designed to "ensur[e] network security and integrity," "address [ ] traffic that is unwanted by end users," "and reduc[e] or mitigat[e] the effects of congestion on the network." *Id.* at 17,952, ¶ 82. The anti-blocking rules, the Order explains, not only prohibit broadband providers from preventing their end-user subscribers from accessing a particular edge provider altogether, but also prohibit them "from impairing or degrading particular content, applications, services, or non-harmful devices so as to render them effectively unusable." *Id.* at 17,943, ¶ 66.

Third, the Order imposes an anti-discrimination requirement on fixed broadband providers only. Under this rule, such providers "shall not unreasonably discriminate in transmitting lawful network traffic over a consumer's broadband Internet access service. Reasonable network management shall not constitute unreasonable discrimination." *Id.* at 17,944, ¶ 68. The Commission explained that "[u]se-agnostic discrimination"—that is, discrimination based not on the nature of the particular traffic involved, but rather, for example, on network management needs during periods of congestion—would generally comport with this requirement. *Id.* at 17,945–46, ¶ 73. Although the Commission never expressly said that the rule forbids broadband providers from granting preferred status or services to edge providers who pay for such benefits, it warned that "as a general matter, it is unlikely that pay for priority would satisfy the 'no unreasonable discrimination' standard." *Id.* at 17,947, ¶ 76. Declining to impose the same anti-discrimination requirement on mobile providers, the Commission explained that differential treatment of such providers was warranted because the mobile broadband market was more competitive and more rapidly evolving than the fixed broadband market, network speeds and penetration were lower, and operational constraints were higher. *See id.* at 17,956–57, ¶¶ 94–95.

As authority for the adoption of these rules, the Commission invoked a plethora of statutory provisions. *See id.* at 17,966–81, ¶¶ 115–37. In particular, the Commission relied on section 706 of the 1996 Telecommunications Act, which directs it to encourage the deployment of broadband telecommunications capability. *See* 47 U.S.C. § 1302(a), (b). According to the Commission, the rules furthered this statutory mandate by preserving unhindered the "virtuous circle of innovation" that had long driven the growth of the Internet. Open Internet Order, 25 FCC Rcd. at 17,910–11, ¶ 14. Internet openness, it reasoned, spurs investment and development by edge providers, which leads to increased end-user demand for broadband access, which leads to increased investment in broadband network infrastructure and technologies, which in turn leads to further innovation and development by edge providers. If, the Commission continued, broadband providers were to disrupt this "virtuous circle" by "[r]estricting edge providers' ability to reach end users, and limiting end users' ability to choose which edge providers to patronize," they would "reduce the rate of innovation at the edge and, in turn, the likely rate of improvements to network infrastructure." *Id.* at 17,911, ¶ 14.

Two members of the Commission dissented. As they saw it, the Open Internet Order rules not only exceeded the Commission's lawful authority, but would also stifle rather than encourage innovation. *See* Open Internet Order, 25 FCC Rcd. at 18,049–81 (Dissenting Statement of Commissioner McDowell); *id.* at 18,084–98 (Dissenting Statement of Commissioner Baker).

II.

The Commission cites numerous statutory provisions it claims grant it the power to promulgate the Open Internet Order rules. But we start and end our analysis with section 706 of the 1996 Telecommunications Act, which, as we shall explain, furnishes the Commission with the requisite affirmative authority to adopt the regulations.

Section 706(a) provides:

> The Commission and each State commission with regulatory jurisdiction over telecommunications services shall encourage the deployment on a reasonable and timely basis of advanced telecommunications capability to all Americans (including, in particular, elementary and secondary schools and classrooms) by utilizing, in a manner consistent with the public interest, convenience, and necessity, price cap regulation, regulatory forbearance, measures that promote competition in the local telecommunications market, or other regulating methods that remove barriers to infrastructure investment.

47 U.S.C. § 1302(a). Section 706(b), in turn, requires the Commission to conduct a regular inquiry "concerning the availability of advanced telecommunications capability." *Id.* § 1302(b). It further provides that should the Commission find that "advanced telecommunications capability is [not] being deployed to all Americans in a reasonable and timely fashion," it "shall take immediate action to accelerate deployment of such capability by removing barriers to infrastructure investment and by promoting competition in the telecommunications market." *Id.* The statute defines "advanced telecommunications capability" to include "broadband telecommunications capability." *Id.* § 1302(d)(1).

Verizon contends that neither subsection (a) nor (b) of section 706 confers any regulatory authority on the Commission. As Verizon sees it, the two subsections amount to nothing more than congressional statements of policy. Verizon further contends that even if either provision grants the Commission substantive authority, the scope of that grant is not so expansive as to permit the Commission to regulate broadband providers in the manner that the Open Internet Order rules do. In addressing these questions, we apply the familiar two-step analysis of Chevron, U.S.A., Inc. v. Natural Resources Defense Council, Inc., 467 U.S. 837 (1984). As the Supreme Court has recently made clear, *Chevron* deference is warranted even if the Commission has interpreted a statutory provision that could be said to delineate the scope of the agency's jurisdiction. *See* City of Arlington v. FCC, 133 S.Ct. 1863, 1874 (2013).

A.

This is not the first time the Commission has asserted that section 706(a) grants it authority to regulate broadband providers. Advancing a similar argument in *Comcast*, the Commission contended that section 706(a) provided a statutory hook for its exercise of ancillary jurisdiction. Although we thought that section 706(a) might "arguably be read to delegate regulatory authority to the Commission," we concluded that the Commission could not rely on this provision to justify the Comcast Order because it had previously determined, in the still-binding Advanced Services Order, that the provision "'does not constitute an independent grant of authority.'" *Comcast*, 600 F.3d at 658 (quoting Deployment of Wireless Services Offering Advanced Telecommunications Capability, 13 FCC Rcd. 24,012, 24,047, ¶ 77 (1998)).

But the Commission need not remain forever bound by the Advanced Services Order's restrictive reading of section 706(a). So long as an agency "adequately explains the reasons for a reversal of policy," its new interpretation of a statute cannot be rejected simply because it is new. *Brand X*, 545 U.S. at 981. At the time we issued our *Comcast* opinion, the Commission failed to satisfy this requirement, as its assertion that section 706(a) gave it regulatory authority represented, at that point, an attempt to "depart from a prior policy sub silentio." *Comcast*, 600 F.3d at 659.

In the Open Internet Order, however, the Commission has offered a reasoned explanation for its changed understanding of section 706(a). To be sure, the Open Internet

Order evinces a palpable reluctance to accept this court's interpretation of the Advanced Services Order, as the Commission again attempts to reconcile its current understanding of section 706(a) with its prior interpretation.

In any event, the Commission expressly declared: "To the extent that the Advanced Services Order can be construed as having read Section 706(a) differently, we reject that reading of the statute for the reasons discussed in the text." Open Internet Order, 25 FCC Rcd. at 17,969, ¶ 119 n.370 . The question, then, is this: Does the Commission's current understanding of section 706(a) as a grant of regulatory authority represent a reasonable interpretation of an ambiguous statute? We believe it does.

Recall that the provision directs the Commission to "encourage the deployment ... of advanced telecommunications capability ... by utilizing ... price cap regulation, regulatory forbearance, measures that promote competition in the local telecommunications market, or other regulating methods that remove barriers to infrastructure investment." 47 U.S.C. § 1302(a). As Verizon argues, this language could certainly be read as simply setting forth a statement of congressional policy, directing the Commission to employ "regulating methods" already at the Commission's disposal in order to achieve the stated goal of promoting "advanced telecommunications" technology. But the language can just as easily be read to vest the Commission with actual authority to utilize such "regulating methods" to meet this stated goal. As the Commission put it in the Open Internet Order, one might reasonably think that Congress, in directing the Commission to undertake certain acts, "necessarily invested the Commission with the statutory authority to carry out those acts." Open Internet Order, 25 FCC Rcd. at 17,969, ¶ 120.

Section 706(a)'s reference to state commissions does not foreclose such a reading. Observing that the statute applies to both "[t]he Commission and each State commission with regulatory jurisdiction over telecommunications services," 47 U.S.C. § 1302(a), Verizon contends that Congress would not be expected to grant both the FCC and state commissions the regulatory authority to encourage the deployment of advanced telecommunications capabilities. But Congress has granted regulatory authority to state telecommunications commissions on other occasions, and we see no reason to think that it could not have done the same here. *See, e.g., id.* § 251(f) (granting state commissions the authority to exempt rural local exchange carriers from certain obligations imposed on other incumbents); *id.* § 252(e) (requiring all interconnection agreements between incumbent local exchange carriers and entrant carriers to be approved by a state commission). Thus, Congress has not "directly spoken" to the question of whether section 706(a) is a grant of regulatory authority simply by mentioning state commissions in that grant. *Chevron*, 467 U.S. at 842.

This case, moreover, is a far cry from FDA v. Brown & Williamson Tobacco Corp., 529 U.S. 120 (2000), on which Verizon principally relies. There, the Supreme Court held that "Congress ha[d] clearly precluded the [Food and Drug Administration] from asserting jurisdiction to regulate tobacco products." *Id.* at 126. The Court emphasized that the FDA had not only completely disclaimed any authority to regulate tobacco products, but had done so for more than eighty years, and that Congress had repeatedly legislated against this background. The Court also observed that the FDA's newly adopted conclusion that it did in fact have authority to regulate this industry would, given its findings regarding the effects of tobacco products and its authorizing statute, logically require the agency to ban such products altogether, a result clearly contrary to congressional policy. Furthermore, the Court reasoned, if Congress had intended to "delegate a decision of such economic and political significance" to the agency, it would have done so far more clearly. *Id.* at 160.

The circumstances here are entirely different. Although the Commission once disclaimed authority to regulate under section 706(a), it never disclaimed authority to regulate the Internet or Internet providers altogether, nor is there any similar history of congressional reliance on such a disclaimer. To the contrary, when Congress passed section 706(a) in 1996, it did so against the backdrop of the Commission's long history of subjecting to common carrier regulation the entities that controlled the last-mile facilities over which end users accessed the Internet. In fact, section 706(a)'s legislative history suggests that Congress may have, somewhat presciently, viewed that provision as an affirmative grant of authority to the Commission whose existence would become necessary if other contemplated grants of statutory authority were for some reason unavailable. The Senate Report describes section 706 as a "necessary fail-safe" "intended to ensure that one of the primary objectives of the [Act]—to accelerate deployment of advanced telecommunications capability—is achieved." S.Rep. No. 104-23 at 50-51. As the Commission observed in the Open Internet Order, it would be "odd ... to characterize Section 706(a) as a 'fail-safe' that 'ensures' the Commission's ability to promote advanced services if it conferred no actual authority." 25 FCC Rcd. at 17,970, ¶ 120.

Of course, we might well hesitate to conclude that Congress intended to grant the Commission substantive authority in section 706(a) if that authority would have no limiting principle. But we are satisfied that the scope of authority granted to the Commission by section 706(a) is not so boundless as to compel the conclusion that Congress could never have intended the provision to set forth anything other than a general statement of policy. The Commission has identified at least two limiting principles inherent in section 706(a). First, the section must be read in conjunction with other provisions of the Communications Act, including, most importantly, those limiting the Commission's subject matter jurisdiction to "interstate and foreign communication by wire and radio." 47 U.S.C. § 152(a). Any regulatory action authorized by section 706(a) would thus have to fall within the Commission's subject matter jurisdiction over such communications—a limitation whose importance this court has recognized in delineating the reach of the Commission's ancillary jurisdiction. Second, any regulations must be designed to achieve a particular purpose: to "encourage the deployment on a reasonable and timely basis of advanced telecommunications capability to all Americans." 47 U.S.C. § 1302(a). Section 706(a) thus gives the Commission authority to promulgate only those regulations that it establishes will fulfill this specific statutory goal—a burden that, as we trust our searching analysis below will demonstrate, is far from "meaningless." Dissenting Op. at 662.

B.

Section 706(b) has a less tortured history. Until shortly before the Commission issued the Open Internet Order, it had never considered whether the provision vested it with any regulatory authority. The Commission had no need to do so because prior to that time it had made no determination that advanced telecommunications technologies, including broadband Internet access, were not "being deployed to all Americans in a reasonable and timely fashion," the prerequisite for any purported invocation of authority to "take immediate action to accelerate deployment of such capability" under section 706(b). 47 U.S.C. § 1302(b).

In July 2010, however, the Commission concluded that "broadband deployment to all Americans is not reasonable and timely." Sixth Broadband Deployment Report, 25 FCC Rcd. at 9558, ¶ 2. This conclusion, the Commission recognized, represented a deviation from its five prior assessments. According to the Commission, the change was driven by its decision to raise the minimum speed threshold qualifying as broadband. "Broadband," as defined in the 1996 Telecommunications Act, is Internet service furnished at speeds that "enable[] users to originate and receive high-quality voice, data, graphics, and video telecommunications using any technology." 47 U.S.C. § 1302(d)(1). In 1999, the Commission found this requirement satisfied by services "having the capability of supporting ... a speed ... in excess of 200 kilobits per second (kbps) in the last mile." In re Inquiry Concerning the Deployment of Advanced Telecommunications Capability to All Americans in a Reasonable and Timely Fashion, 14 FCC Rcd. 2398, 2406, ¶ 20 (1999).

In the Sixth Broadband Deployment Report, the Commission explained that consumers now regularly use their Internet connections to access high-quality video and expect to be able at the same time to check their email and browse the web. Two hundred kbps, the Commission determined, "simply is not enough bandwidth" to permit such uses. Sixth Broadband Deployment Report, 25 FCC Rcd. at ¶ 9562, ¶ 10. The Commission thus adopted a new threshold more appropriate to current consumer behavior and expectations: four megabytes per second (mbps) for end users to download content from the Internet—twenty times as fast as the prior threshold—and one mbps for end users to upload content.

Applying this new benchmark, the Commission found that "roughly 80 million American adults do not subscribe to broadband at home, and approximately 14 to 24 million Americans do not have access to broadband today." Sixth Broadband Deployment Report, 25 FCC Rcd. at 9574, ¶ 28. Given these figures and the "ever-growing importance of broadband to our society," the Commission was unable to find "that broadband is being reasonably and timely deployed" within the meaning of section 706(b). *Id.* This conclusion, it explained, triggered section 706(b)'s mandate that the Commission "take immediate action to accelerate deployment." *Id.* at 9558, ¶ 3 (quoting 47 U.S.C. § 1302(b)) (internal quotation marks omitted).

Subsequently, in the Open Internet Order the Commission made clear that this statutory provision does not limit the Commission to using other regulatory authority already at its disposal, but instead grants it the power necessary to fulfill the statute's mandate. *See* Open Internet Order, 25 FCC Rcd. at 17,972, ¶ 123. Emphasizing the provision's "shall take immediate action" directive, the Commission concluded that section 706(b) "provides express authority" for the rules it adopted. *Id.*

Contrary to Verizon's arguments, we believe the Commission has reasonably interpreted section 706(b) to empower it to take steps to accelerate broadband deployment if and when it determines that such deployment is not "reasonable and timely." To be sure, as with section 706(a), it is unclear whether section 706(b), in providing that the Commission "shall take immediate action to accelerate deployment of such capability by removing barriers to infrastructure investment and by promoting competition in the telecommunications market," vested the Commission with authority to remove such barriers to infrastructure investment and promote competition. 47 U.S.C. § 1302(b). But the provision may certainly be read to accomplish as much, and given such ambiguity we have no basis for rejecting the Commission's determination that it should be so understood.

C.

This brings us, then, to Verizon's alternative argument that even if, as we have held, sections 706(a) and 706(b) grant the Commission affirmative authority to promulgate rules governing broadband providers, the specific rules imposed by the Open Internet Order fall outside the scope of that authority. The Commission's theory, to reiterate, is that its regulations protect and promote edge-provider investment and development, which in turn drives end-user demand for more and better broadband technologies, which in turn stimulates competition among broadband providers to further invest in broadband.

Thus, the Commission claims, by preventing broadband providers from blocking or discriminating against edge providers, the rules "encourage the deployment on a reasonable and timely basis of advanced telecommunications capability to all Americans," 47 U.S.C. § 1302(a), and "accelerate deployment of such capability," *id.* § 1302(b), by removing "barriers to infrastructure investment" and promoting "competition," *id.* § 1302(a), (b). That is, contrary to the dissent, the Commission made clear—and Verizon appears to recognize—that the Commission found broadband providers' potential disruption of edge-provider traffic to be itself the sort of "barrier" that has "the potential to stifle overall investment in Internet infrastructure," and could "limit competition in telecommunications markets." Open Internet Order, 25 FCC Rcd. at 17,970, ¶ 120.

Verizon mounts a twofold challenge to this rationale. It argues that the Open Internet Order regulations will not, as the Commission claims, meaningfully promote broadband deployment, and that even if they do advance this goal, the manner in which they do so is too attenuated from this statutory purpose to fall within the scope of authority granted by either statutory provision.

We begin with the second, more strictly legal, question of whether, assuming the Commission has accurately predicted the effect of these regulations, it may utilize the authority granted to it in sections 706(a) and 706(b) to impose regulations of this sort on broadband providers. As we have previously acknowledged, "in proscribing ... practices with the statutorily identified effect, an agency might stray so far from the paradigm case as to render its interpretation unreasonable, arbitrary, or capricious." National Cable & Telecommunications Ass'n v. FCC, 567 F.3d 659, 665 (D.C. Cir. 2009). Here, Verizon has given us no reason to conclude that the Open Internet Order's requirements "stray" so far beyond the "paradigm case" that Congress likely contemplated as to render the Commission's understanding of its authority unreasonable. The rules not only apply directly to broadband providers, the precise entities to which section 706 authority to encourage broadband deployment presumably extends, but also seek to promote the very goal that Congress explicitly sought to promote.

Whether the Commission's assessment of the likely effects of the Open Internet Order deserves credence presents a slightly more complex question. Verizon attacks the reasoning and factual support underlying the Commission's theory, advancing these arguments both as an attack on the Commission's statutory interpretation and as an APA arbitrary and capricious challenge. Given that these two arguments involve similar considerations, we address them together. In so doing, "we must uphold the Commission's factual determinations if on the record as a whole, there is such relevant evidence as a reasonable mind might accept as adequate to support [the] conclusion." Secretary of Labor, MSHA v. Federal Mine Safety & Health Review Comm'n, 111 F.3d 913, 918 (D.C. Cir. 1997). We evaluate the Commission's reasoning to ensure that it has "examine[d] the relevant data and articulate[d] a satisfactory explanation for its action including a rational connection between the facts found and the choice made." National Fuel Gas Supply Corp. v. FERC, 468 F.3d 831, 839 (D.C. Cir. 2006). Under these standards, the Commission's prediction that the Open Internet Order regulations will encourage broadband deployment is, in our view, both rational and supported by substantial evidence.

To begin with, the Commission has more than adequately supported and explained its conclusion that edge-provider innovation leads to the expansion and improvement of broadband infrastructure. The Internet, the Commission observed in the Open Internet Order, is, "[l]ike electricity and the computer," a "'general purpose technology' that enables new methods of production that have a major impact on the entire economy." Open Internet Order, 25 FCC Rcd. at 17,909, ¶ 13. The rise of streaming online video is perhaps the best and clearest example the Commission used to illustrate that the Internet constitutes one such technology: higher-speed residential Internet connections in the late 1990s "stimulated" the development of streaming video, a service that requires particularly high bandwidth, "which in turn encouraged broadband providers to increase network speeds." Open Internet Order, 25 FCC Rcd. at 17,911, ¶ 14 n.23. The Commission's emphasis on this connection between edge-provider innovation and infrastructure development is uncontroversial.

The Commission's finding that Internet openness fosters the edge-provider innovation that drives this "virtuous cycle" was likewise reasonable and grounded in substantial evidence. Continued innovation at the edge, the Commission explained, "depends upon low barriers to innovation and entry by edge providers," and thus restrictions on edge providers' "ability to reach end users ... reduce the rate of innovation." Open Internet Order, 25 FCC Rcd. at 17,911, ¶ 14. This conclusion finds ample support in the economic literature on which the Commission relied, as well as in history and the comments of several edge providers. For one prominent illustration of the relationship between openness and innovation, the Commission cited the invention of the World Wide Web itself by Sir Tim Berners-Lee, who, although not working for an entity that operated the underlying network, was able to create and disseminate this enormously successful innovation without needing to make any changes to previously developed Internet protocols or securing "any approval from network operators." Open Internet Order, 25 FCC Rcd. at 17,910, ¶ 13.

Equally important, the Commission has adequately supported and explained its conclusion that, absent rules such as those set forth in the Open Internet Order, broadband providers represent a threat to Internet openness and could act in ways that would ultimately inhibit the speed and extent of future broadband deployment. First, nothing in the record gives us any reason to doubt the Commission's determination that broadband providers may be motivated to discriminate against and among edge providers. The Commission observed that broadband providers—often the same entities that furnish end users with telephone and television services—"have incentives to interfere with the operation of third-party Internet-based services that compete with the providers' revenue-generating telephone and/or pay-television services." Open Internet Order, 25 FCC Rcd. at 17,916, ¶ 22. As the Commission noted, Voice–over–Internet–Protocol (VoIP) services such as Vonage increasingly serve as substitutes for traditional telephone services, *id.*, and broadband providers like AT&T and Time Warner have acknowledged that online video aggregators such as Netflix and Hulu compete directly with their own "core video subscription service," *id.* at 17,917, ¶ 22 & n.54. Broadband providers also have powerful incentives to accept fees from edge providers, either in return for excluding their competitors or for granting them prioritized access to end users. Indeed, at oral argument Verizon's counsel announced that "but for [the Open Internet Order] rules we would be exploring those commercial arrangements." Oral Arg. Tr. 31. And although broadband providers might not adopt pay-for-priority agreements or other similar arrangements if, according to the Commission's analysis, such agreements would ultimately lead to a decrease in end-user demand for broadband, the Commission explained that the resultant harms to innovation and demand will largely constitute "negative externalities": any given broadband provider will "receive the benefits of ... fees but [is] unlikely to fully account for the detrimental impact on edge providers' ability and incentive to innovate and invest." Open Internet Order, 25 FCC Rcd. at 17,919–20, ¶ 25 & n.68.

Moreover, as the Commission found, broadband providers have the technical and economic ability to impose such restrictions. Verizon does not seriously contend otherwise. Because all end users generally access the Internet through a single broadband provider, that provider functions as a "'terminating monopolist,'" *id.* at 17,919, ¶ 24 n.66, with power to act as a "gatekeeper" with respect to edge providers that might seek to reach its end-user subscribers, *id.* at 17,919, ¶ 24. As the Commission reasonably explained, this ability to act as a "gatekeeper" distinguishes broadband providers from other participants in the Internet marketplace—including prominent and potentially powerful edge providers such as Google and Apple—who have no similar "control [over] access to the Internet for their subscribers and for anyone wishing to reach those subscribers." *Id.* at 17,935, ¶ 50.

To be sure, if end users could immediately respond to any given broadband provider's attempt to impose restrictions on edge providers by switching broadband providers, this gatekeeper power might well disappear. For example, a broadband provider like Comcast would be unable to threaten Netflix that it would slow Netflix traffic if all Comcast subscribers would then immediately switch to a competing broadband provider. But we see no basis for questioning the Commission's conclusion that end users are unlikely to react in this fashion. According to the Commission, "end users may not know whether charges or service levels their broadband provider is imposing on edge providers vary from those of alternative broadband providers, and even if they do have this information may find it costly to switch." *Id.* at 17,921, ¶ 27.

The dissent focuses on this latter aspect of the Commission's reasoning, arguing at some length that the Commission's failure to expressly find that broadband providers have market power with respect to end users is "fatal to its attempt to regulate." Dissenting Op. at 665. But Verizon has never argued that the Commission's failure to make a market power finding somehow rendered its understanding of its statutory authority unreasonable or its decision arbitrary and capricious. Verizon does fleetingly mention the market power issue once in its opening brief, asserting as part of its First Amendment claim that Turner Broadcasting System, Inc. v. FCC, 520 U.S. 180 (1997)—in which the Supreme Court, applying intermediate scrutiny, upheld a congressional statute compelling cable companies to carry local broadcast television stations, *id.* at 185—is distinguishable in part because, unlike the Commission here, Congress had found "evidence of 'considerable and growing market power.'" Verizon Br. 46 (quoting *Turner I*, 520 U.S. at 197). But to say, as Verizon does, that an allegedly speech-infringing regulation violates the First Amendment because of the absence of a market condition that would increase the need for that regulation is hardly to say that the absence of this market condition renders the regulation wholly irrational.

In any event, it seems likely that the reason Verizon never advanced this argument is that the Commission's failure to find market power is not "fatal" to its theory. Broadband providers' ability to impose restrictions on edge providers does not depend on their benefiting from the sort of market concentration that would enable them to impose substantial price increases on end users—which is all the Commission said in declining to make a market power finding. Rather, broadband providers' ability to impose restrictions on edge providers simply depends on end users not being fully responsive to the imposition of such restrictions. *See supra* at 646. If the dissent believes that broadband providers' ability to restrict edge-provider traffic without having their end users react would itself represent an exercise of market power, then the dissent's dispute with the Commission's reasoning appears to be largely semantic: the Commission expressly found that end users are not responsive in this fashion even if it never used the term "market power" in doing so. *See* Open Internet Order, 25 FCC Rcd. at 17,924–25, ¶ 34.

III.

Even though section 706 grants the Commission authority to promote broadband deployment by regulating how broadband providers treat edge providers, the Commission may not, as it recognizes, utilize that power in a manner that contravenes any specific prohibition contained in the Communications Act.

We think it obvious that the Commission would violate the Communications Act were it to regulate broadband providers as common carriers. Given the Commission's still-binding decision to classify broadband providers not as providers of "telecommunications services" but instead as providers of "information services," such treatment would run afoul of section 153(51): "A telecommunications carrier shall be treated as a common carrier under this [Act] only to the extent that it is engaged in providing telecommunications services." 47 U.S.C. § 153(51). Likewise, because the Commission has classified mobile broadband service as a "private" mobile service, and not a "commercial" mobile service, treatment of mobile broadband providers as common carriers would violate section 332: "A person engaged in the provision of a service that is a private mobile service shall not, insofar as such person is so engaged, be treated as a common carrier for any purpose under this [Act]." 47 U.S.C. § 332(c)(2).

Thus, we must determine whether the requirements imposed by the Open Internet Order subject broadband providers to common carrier treatment. If they do, then given the manner in which the Commission has chosen to classify broadband providers, the regulations cannot stand.

A.

Offering little guidance as to the meaning of the term "common carrier," the Communications Act defines that phrase, somewhat circularly, as "any person engaged as a common carrier for hire." 47 U.S.C. § 153(11). Courts and the Commission have therefore resorted to the common law to come up with a satisfactory definition.

Although the nature and scope of the duties imposed on common carriers have evolved over the last century, the core of the common law concept of common carriage has remained intact. In National Association of Regulatory Utility Commissioners v. FCC, 525 F.2d 630, 642 (D.C. Cir. 1976) (*NARUC I*), we identified the basic characteristic that distinguishes common carriers from "private" carriers—i.e., entities that are not common carriers—as "[t]he common law requirement of holding oneself out to serve the public indiscriminately." "[A] carrier will not be a common carrier," we further explained, "where its practice is to make individualized decisions, in particular cases, whether and on what terms to deal." *Id.* at 641. Similarly, in National Association of Regulatory Utility Commissioners v. FCC, 533 F.2d 601, 608 (1976) (*NARUC II*), we concluded that "the primary sine qua non of common carrier status is a quasi-public character, which arises out of the undertaking to carry for all people indifferently." (Internal quotation marks omitted).

For our purposes, perhaps the seminal case applying this notion of common carriage is *Midwest Video II*. At issue in *Midwest Video II* was a set of regulations compelling cable television systems to operate a minimum number of channels and to hold certain channels open for specific users. 440 U.S. at 692–93. Cable operators were barred from exercising any discretion over who could use those latter channels and what those users could transmit. They were also forbidden from charging users any fee for some of the channels and limited to charging an "appropriate" fee for the remaining channels. *Id.* at 693–94. Because at that time the Commission had no express statutory authority over cable systems, it sought to justify these rules as ancillary to its authority to regulate broadcasting. *Id.* at 696–99.

Rejecting this argument, the Supreme Court held that the Commission had no power to regulate cable operators in this fashion. The Court reasoned that if the Commission sought to exercise such ancillary jurisdiction over cable operators on the basis of its authority over broadcasters, it must also respect the specific statutory limits of that authority, as "without reference to the provisions of the Act directly governing broadcasting, the Commission's jurisdiction ... would be unbounded." *Midwest Video II*, 440 U.S. at 706. Congress had expressly prohibited the Commission from regulating broadcasters as common carriers, a limitation that must then, according to the Court, also extend to cable operators. *Id.* at 707. And the challenged regulations, the Court held, "plainly impose common-carrier obligations on cable operators." *Id.* at 701. In explaining this conclusion, the Court largely reiterated the nature of the obligations themselves: "Under the rules, cable systems are required to hold out dedicated channels on a first-come, nondiscriminatory basis. Operators are prohibited from determining or influencing the content of access programming. And the rules delimit what operators may charge for access and use of equipment." *Id.* at 701–02.

In *Cellco*, we recently confronted the similar question of whether a Commission regulation compelling mobile telephone companies to offer data roaming agreements to one another on "commercially reasonable" terms impermissibly regulated these providers as common carriers. 700 F.3d at 537. From the history and decisions surveyed above, we distilled "several basic principles" that guide our analysis here. *Id.* at 547. First, "[i]f a carrier is forced to offer service indiscriminately and on general terms, then that carrier is being relegated to common carrier status." *Id.* We also clarified, however, that "there is an important distinction between the question whether a given regulatory regime is consistent with common carrier or private carrier status, and the *Midwest Video II* question whether that regime necessarily confers common carrier status." *Id.* Thus, "common carriage is not all or nothing—there is a gray area in which although a given regulation might be applied to common carriers, the obligations imposed are not common carriage per se." *Id.* In this "space between per se common carriage and per se private carriage," we continued, "the Commission's determination that a regulation does or does not confer common carrier status warrants deference." *Id.*

Given these principles, we concluded that the data roaming rule imposed no per se common carriage requirements because it left "substantial room for individualized bargaining and discrimination in terms." *Cellco*, 700 F.3d at 548. The rule "expressly permit[ted] providers to adapt roaming agreements to 'individualized circumstances without having to hold themselves out to serve all comers indiscriminately on the same or standardized terms.'" *Id.* That said, we cautioned that were the Commission to apply the "commercially reasonable" standard in a restrictive manner, essentially elevating it to the traditional common carrier "just and reasonable" standard, *see* 47 U.S.C. §201(b), the rule might impose obligations that amounted to common carriage per se, a claim that could be brought in an "as applied" challenge. *Cellco*, 700 F.3d at 548–49.

B.

The Commission's explanation in the Open Internet Order for why the regulations do not constitute common carrier obligations and its defense of those regulations here largely rest on its belief that, with respect to edge providers, broadband providers are not "carriers" at all. Stating that an entity is not a common carrier if it may decide on an individualized basis "'whether and on what terms to deal' with potential customers," the Commission asserted in the Order that "[t]he customers at issue here are the end users who subscribe to broadband Internet access services." Open Internet Order, 25 FCC Rcd. at 17,950–51, ¶79 (quoting *NARUC I*, 525 F.2d at 641). It explained that because broadband providers would remain able to make "individualized decisions" in determining on what terms to deal with end users, the Order permitted the providers the "flexibility to customize service arrangements for a particular customer [that] is the hallmark of private carriage." *Id.* at 17,951, ¶ 79. Here, the Commission reiterates that "as long as [a broadband provider] is not required to serve end users indiscriminately, rules regarding blocking or charging edge providers do not create common carriage." Commission's Br. 61. We disagree.

It is true, generally speaking, that the "customers" of broadband providers are end users. But that hardly means that broadband providers could not also be carriers with respect to edge providers. "Since it is clearly possible for a given entity to carry on many types of activities, it is at least logical to conclude that one may be a common carrier with regard to some activities but not others." *NARUC II*, 533 F.2d at 608. Because broadband providers furnish a service to edge providers, thus undoubtedly functioning as edge providers' "carriers," the obligations that the Commission imposes on broadband providers may well constitute common carriage per se regardless of whether edge providers are broadband providers' principal customers. This is true whatever the nature of the preexisting commercial relationship between broadband providers and edge providers. In contending otherwise, the Commission appears to misunderstand the nature of the inquiry in which we must engage. The question is not whether, absent the Open Internet Order, broadband providers would or did act as common carriers with respect to edge providers; rather, the question is whether, given the rules imposed by the Open Internet Order, broadband providers are now obligated to act as common carriers.

Midwest Video II is indistinguishable. The *Midwest Video II* cable operators' primary "customers" were their subscribers, who paid to have programming delivered to them in their homes. There, as here, the Commission's regulations required the regulated entities to carry the content of third parties to these customers—content the entities otherwise could have blocked at their discretion. Moreover, much like the rules at issue here, the *Midwest Video II* regulations compelled the operators to hold open certain channels for use at no cost—thus permitting specified programmers to "hire" the cable operators' services for free. Given that the cable operators in *Midwest Video II* were carriers with respect to these third-party programmers, we see no basis for concluding that broadband providers are not similarly carriers with respect to third-party edge providers.

C.

We have little hesitation in concluding that the anti-discrimination obligation imposed on fixed broadband providers has "relegated [those providers], pro tanto, to common carrier status." *Midwest Video II*, 440 U.S. at 700–01. In requiring broadband providers to serve all edge providers without "unreasonable discrimination," this rule by its very terms compels those providers to hold themselves out "to serve the public indiscriminately." *NARUC I*, 525 F.2d at 642.

Significantly for our purposes, the Commission never argues that the Open Internet Order's "no unreasonable discrimination" standard somehow differs from the nondiscrimination standard applied to common carriers generally—the argument that salvaged the data roaming requirements in *Cellco*. In a footnote in the Order itself, the Commission suggested that it viewed the rule's allowance for "reasonable network management" as establishing treatment that was somehow inconsistent with per se common carriage. But the Commission has forfeited this argument by failing to raise it in its briefs here.

In any event, the argument is without merit. The Order defines the "reasonable network management" concept as follows: "A network management practice is reasonable if it is appropriate and tailored to achieving a legitimate network management purpose, taking into account the particular network architecture and technology of the broadband Internet access service." Open Internet Order, 25 FCC Rcd. at 17,952, ¶ 82. This provision, the Commission explained, would permit broadband providers to do two things, neither of which conflict with per se common carriage. First, "the reasonable network management" exception would permit broadband providers to "address [] traffic that is unwanted by end users ... such as by providing services or capabilities consistent with an end user's choices regarding parental controls or security capabilities." Id. Because the relevant service broadband providers furnish to edge providers is the ability to access end users if those end users so desire, a limited exception permitting end users to direct broadband providers to block certain traffic by no means detracts from the common carrier nature of the obligations imposed on broadband providers. Second, the Order defines "reasonable network management" to include practices designed to protect the network itself by "addressing traffic that is harmful to the network" and "reducing or mitigating the effects of congestion." Id. at 17,952, ¶ 82. As Verizon correctly points out, however, this allowance "merely preserves a common carrier's traditional right to 'turn [] away [business] either because it is not of the type normally accepted or because the carrier's capacity has been exhausted.'" Verizon's Br. 20 (quoting NARUC I, 525 F.2d at 641). Railroads have no obligation to allow passengers to carry bombs on board, nor need they permit passengers to stand in the aisles if all seats are taken. It is for this reason that the Communications Act bars common carriers from engaging in "unjust or unreasonable discrimination," not all discrimination. 47 U.S.C. § 202 (emphasis added).

The Commission has provided no basis for concluding that in permitting "reasonable" network management, and in prohibiting merely "unreasonable" discrimination, the Order's standard of "reasonableness" might be more permissive than the quintessential common carrier standard. See Cellco, 700 F.3d at 548 (characterizing the "just and reasonable" standard as being that "applicable to common carriers"). To the extent any ambiguity exists regarding how the Commission will apply these rules in practice, we think it is best characterized as ambiguity as to how the common carrier reasonableness standard applies in this context, not whether the standard applied is actually the same as the common carrier standard. Unlike the data roaming requirement at issue in Cellco, which set forth a "commercially reasonable" standard, see id. at 537, the language of the Open Internet Order's anti-discrimination rule mirrors, almost precisely, section 202's language establishing the basic common carrier obligation not to "make any unjust or unreasonable discrimination." 47 U.S.C. § 202. Indeed, confirming that the two standards are equivalent, the Commission responded to commenters who argued that the "no unreasonable discrimination" requirement was too vague by quoting another commenter who observed that "[s]eventy-five years of experience have shown [the 'unreasonable' qualifier in Section 202] to be both administrable and indispensable to the sound administration of the nation's telecommunications laws." Open Internet Order, 25 FCC Rcd. at 17,949, ¶ 77 n.240.

Whether the Open Internet Order's anti-blocking rules, applicable to both fixed and mobile broadband providers, likewise establish per se common carrier obligations is somewhat less clear. According to Verizon, they do because they deny "broadband providers discretion in deciding which traffic from ... edge providers to carry," and deny them "discretion over carriage terms by setting a uniform price of zero." Verizon's Br. 16–17. This argument has some appeal. The anti-blocking rules establish a minimum level of service that broadband providers must furnish to all edge providers: edge providers' "content, applications [and] services" must be "effectively []usable." Open Internet Order, 25 FCC Rcd. at 17,943, ¶ 66.

At oral argument, however, Commission counsel asserted that "[i]t's not common carriage to simply have a basic level of required service if you can negotiate different levels with different people." Oral Arg. Tr. 86. This contention rests on the fact that under the anti-blocking rules broadband providers have no obligation to actually provide any edge provider with the minimum service necessary to satisfy the rules. Viewed this way, the relevant "carriage" broadband providers furnish might be access to end users more generally, not the minimum required service. In delivering this service, so defined, the anti-blocking rules would permit broadband providers to distinguish somewhat among edge providers, just as Commission counsel contended at oral argument. For example, Verizon might, consistent with the anti-blocking rule—and again, absent the anti-discrimination rule—charge an edge provider like Netflix for high-speed, priority access while limiting all other edge providers to a more standard service. In theory, moreover, not only could Verizon negotiate separate agreements with each individual edge provider regarding the level of service provided, but it could also charge similarly-situated edge providers completely different prices for the same service. Thus, if the relevant service that broadband providers furnish is access to their subscribers generally, as opposed to access to their subscribers at the specific minimum speed necessary to satisfy the anti-blocking rules, then these rules, while perhaps establishing a lower limit on the forms that broadband providers' arrangements with edge providers could take, might nonetheless leave sufficient "room for individualized bargaining and discrimination in terms" so as not to run afoul of the statutory prohibitions on common carrier treatment. *Cellco*, 700 F.3d at 548.

Whatever the merits of this view, the Commission advanced nothing like it either in the underlying Order or in its briefs before this court. Instead, it makes no distinction at all between the anti-discrimination and anti-blocking rules, seeking to justify both types of rules with explanations that, as we have explained, are patently insufficient. We are unable to sustain the Commission's action on a ground upon which the agency itself never relied.

The disclosure rules are another matter. Verizon does not contend that these rules, on their own, constitute per se common carrier obligations, nor do we see any way in which they would. Also, because Verizon does not direct its First Amendment or Takings Clause claims against the disclosure obligations, we have no need to address those contentions here.

Verizon does argue that the disclosure rules are not severable, insisting that if the anti-discrimination and anti-blocking rules fall so too must the disclosure requirements. We disagree.

IV.

For the forgoing reasons, although we reject Verizon's challenge to the Open Internet Order's disclosure rules, we vacate both the anti-discrimination and the anti-blocking rules. We remand the case to the Commission for further proceedings consistent with this opinion.

SILBERMAN, Senior Circuit Judge, concurring in part and dissenting in part:

I am in general agreement with the majority's conclusion that the Open Internet Order impermissibly subjects broadband providers to treatment as common carriers, but I disagree with the majority's conclusion that § 706 otherwise provides the FCC with affirmative statutory authority to promulgate these rules. I also think the Commission's reasoning violates the Administrative Procedure Act. These differences are important since the majority opinion suggests possible regulatory modifications that might circumvent the prohibition against common carrier treatment.

I.

I quite agree with the majority that the relevant statutory language is §706 of the Communications Act. 47 U.S.C. §1302. Although the FCC purports to rely on a scatter shot of other provisions of the statute, as well as §706, none of those other provisions truly bear on the issue. "Emanations from the penumbra" may once have served to justify constitutional interpretation, but it hasn't caught on as legitimate statutory interpretation. I also agree with the majority—and disagree with Verizon—that §706 is a grant of positive regulatory authority, but it doesn't come close to sanctioning the Commission's regulation.

The statute directs the Commission to "encourage the deployment on a reasonable and timely basis of advanced telecommunications capability to all Americans ... by utilizing ... price cap regulation, regulatory forbearance, measures that promote competition in the local telecommunications market, or other regulating methods that remove barriers to infrastructure investment." 47 U.S.C. §1302(a).

The FCC contends for, and the majority grants, *Chevron* deference as to the interpretation of this language. I don't disagree that *Chevron* is called for, but *Chevron* "is not a wand by which courts can turn an unlawful frog into a legitimate prince." Associated Gas Distributors v. F.E.R.C., 824 F.2d 981, 1001 (D.C. Cir. 1987).

The key words obviously are "measures that promote competition in the local telecommunications market or other regulating methods that remove barriers to infrastructure investment." Those are the words that grant actual authority. Yet the Commission does not ground its regulation on this language. Indeed, both the Commission and the majority conflate these two clauses, though they have distinct functions. "Promoting competition in the telecommunications market" implies a regulation that encourages broadband providers to compete with each other, head-to-head, on price and quality. Removing "barriers to infrastructure investment," on the other hand, does not necessarily require any increased competition in the telecommunications market. For example, if a particular broadband provider were a monopolist, then by regulating its prices, the Commission might encourage it to expand supply to increase profits, rather than artificially restrict supply so as to charge supracompetitive rates. Such a regulation would not increase competition, but it would at least potentially remove a barrier to investment. This is, essentially, the theory that the Commission purportedly relies on: If the Commission theoretically could spur demand for broadband, the Commission would encourage further infrastructure investment regardless of head-to-head competition. Thus, it is on the "removing barriers" clause, primarily, that the Order must stand or fall. Yet, the Commission never actually identifies any practices of the broadband providers as "barriers to investment"—not once in over 100 pages—probably because it would be so far fetched an interpretation of those words.

Nor does the Commission state (or argue in its brief), contrary to the majority's opinion, that the "triple cushion shot"—the means by which the Commission hopes to stimulate demand for better broadband—is designed to increase competition in the broadband market.

Indeed, the Commission frankly admits its purpose is much wider than the statutory objectives. It claims it must regulate broadly, so as to "protect [] consumer choice, free expression, end-user control, and the ability to innovate without permission," 25 FCC Rcd. at 17,949, ¶78, which certainly indicates a Commission objective that exceeds the statutory authority granted in §706.

The majority takes the statutory language even further; it states that the Commission's authority to promulgate regulations that promote broadband deployment encompasses the power to regulate broadband providers' economic relationships with edge providers if, in fact, the nature of those relationships influences the rate and extent to which broadband providers develop and expand services for end users.

Majority Op. at 643. So much for the terms "promote competition in the local telecommunications market" or "remove barriers to infrastructure investment." Presto, we have a new statute granting the FCC virtually unlimited power to regulate the Internet. This reading of §706, as we said in Comcast Corp. v. FCC, "would virtually free the Commission from its congressional tether." 600 F.3d 642, 655 (D.C. Cir. 2010). The limiting principles the majority relies on are illusory.

The majority claims that the Commission cannot exceed its subject-matter jurisdiction over "interstate and foreign communication by wire and radio." 25 FCC Rcd. at 17,970, ¶ 121 (citing 47 U.S.C. § 152(a)). This is obviously true, but it is not a limitation on the Commission's interpretation of this specific statutory provision. The question is not whether the statute permits the Commission to do absolutely anything—of course it does not—but, rather, whether § 706 contains any intrinsic limitations. If the Commission's subject matter jurisdiction is a "limiting principle," then we might as well call the First Amendment a limiting principle, for surely the Commission could not censor the Internet, even if doing so did somehow increase broadband deployment.

According to the majority, the Commission is also restrained because it may only regulate pursuant to §706 if it does so to achieve a particular purpose: to "encourage the deployment on a reasonable and timely basis of advanced telecommunications capability to all Americans." 25 FCC Rcd. at 17,970, ¶ 121 (citing 47 U.S.C. § 1302(a)). This is an almost meaningless limitation, as demonstrated by the Open Internet Order itself. The Commission's theory is that an open Internet will spur demand for broadband infrastructure. But any regulation that, in the FCC's judgment might arguably make the Internet "better," could increase demand. I do not see how this "limitation" prevents § 706 from being carte blanche to issue any regulation that the Commission might believe to be in the public interest.

To sum up, §706 requires the Commission to identify a "barrier [] to infrastructure investment" or a measure that "promote[s] competition" in the broadband market—which it has not.

II.

Verizon alternatively argues that, even assuming that §706 grants the Commission its claimed authority, the regulation is arbitrary and capricious because its findings—such as they are—lack substantial evidence. I agree.

The Commission purports to fear that broadband providers might discriminate against, or even block, the Internet traffic of specific edge providers or classes of edge providers, perhaps because broadband providers offer some competing services or because they might charge certain edge providers for premium services. The majority puts it even more starkly, asserting that the Commission "found that broadband providers have the technical and economic ability to impose restrictions on edge providers." Majority Op. at 646 (emphasis added). But the Commission never actually made such a finding. Its conclusions are littered with "may," "if," and "might." For example, according to the Commission, a broadband provider:

- "may have economic incentives to block or otherwise disadvantage specific edge providers"

- "might use this power to benefit its own or affiliated offerings at the expense of unaffiliated offerings"
- "may act to benefit edge providers that have paid it to exclude rivals"
- "may have incentives to increase revenues by charging edge providers"
- "might withhold or decline to expand capacity in order to 'squeeze' non-prioritized traffic"

25 FCC Rcd. at 17,915–22, ¶¶ 21–29. To be sure, the majority correctly observes that we should defer to an agency's "predictive judgments as to the economic effect of a rule," National Telephone Cooperative Ass'n v. FCC, 563 F.3d 536, 541 (D.C. Cir. 2009), but deference to such a judgment must be based on some logic and evidence, not sheer speculation. That a party "may" do something is hardly a finding—at least in American law—that a party has done or will do something. Moreover, whether or not the "triple cushion shot" theory is rational economics (and I have my doubts), it rests, as I have noted, on a false factual premise—that the evidence supports a finding that broadband providers across the board, in all markets, enjoy sufficient economic clout to take the above actions.

The Commission asserts—and the majority accepts—that broadband providers act as "gatekeepers" because each one has a so-called "terminating monopoly" over access to particular end users. These are terms, largely invented, the economic significance of which the Commission does not explain. All retail stores, for instance, are "gatekeepers." The term is thus meaningful only insofar as the gatekeeper by means of a powerful economic position vis-a-vis consumers gains leverage over suppliers. The Commission made no effort to construct an analytic framework to measure this supposed gateway advantage—it is a rather slippery concept—nor did it adduce evidence to establish the economic power it would supposedly afford all broadband providers against all edge providers.

Without broadband provider market power, consumers, of course, have options; they can go to another broadband provider if they want to reach particular edge providers or if their connections to particular edge providers have been degraded. The Commission implicitly recognizes this, because it justifies exempting dial-up Internet providers from the Order by noting that "telephone service has historically provided the easy ability to switch among competing dial-up Internet access services." 25 FCC Rcd. at 17,935, ¶ 51. The Commission also exempts "backbone" Internet providers—which interconnect between broadband providers—obviously for the same reason.

The majority does contend that four possible instances of broadband providers restricting users' access to certain edge providers are sufficient evidence of broadband providers' "incentives and ability to restrict Internet traffic." Majority Op. at 649. That the Commission was able to locate only four potential examples of such conduct is, frankly, astonishing. In such a large industry where, as Verizon notes, billions of connections are formed between users and edge providers each year, one would think there should be ample examples of just about any type of conduct. But even if examples of such conduct were more numerous, it would still not be evidence that broadband providers are economically capable of restricting consumer choice. And, as the Commission noted, there are potentially efficient, pro-consumer reasons that an individual broadband provider might wish to restrict access to some edge providers. *See* 25 FCC Rcd. at 17,921, ¶ 28 n.80 ("Economics literature recognizes that access charges could be harmful under some circumstances and beneficial under others.... [T]he economic literature on two-sided markets is at an early stage of development."). The Commission's anecdotes then do not show that any broadband providers are capable of actually causing the harm about which the Commission is concerned.

My view, then, is that the Commission's failure to conduct a market power analysis is fatal to its attempt to regulate, because it means that there is inadequate evidence to support the lynchpin of the Commission's economic theory. The Commission actually recognized that a finding of market power would enhance its theory. 25 FCC Rcd. at 17,923, ¶ 32. Indeed! But such a finding would, of course, have to be made market to market (indeed the statute specifically references local telecommunications markets), and if so, it would be a finding of a barrier to broadband investment without the mental gymnastics of the triple cushion shot. If one (or two) broadband providers have market power in any particular market and thereby could raise prices while restricting supply, the Commission could well conclude that was a barrier to broadband investment.

Of course, before the Commission could determine whether a particular broadband provider possesses market power, it would have to first define the relevant market. Instead, the Commission, in this case, simply cited a 2009 study that found that "nearly 70 percent of households lived in census tracts where only one or two wireline or fixed wireless firms provided advertised download speeds of at least 3 Mbps and upload speeds of at least 768 Kbps." 25 FCC Rcd. at 17,923, ¶ 32. Why are these speeds relevant? Because the Commission has previously, as part of its statutory duty to assess the state of broadband deployment, defined "broadband" to mean download speeds of at least 4 Mbps and upload speeds of at least 1 Mbps. According to the Commission, it is the minimum speed necessary to stream high quality video while simultaneously browsing the Internet and using email. I don't dispute the legitimacy of that definition. Yet, while the Commission is free to rely on technical considerations in defining the statutory term "broadband," such considerations are irrelevant when it comes to defining the market in economic terms. A broadband provider offering a 2 Mbps connection is not, according to the FCC, really offering broadband. But it is quite likely that consumers, in deciding which Internet service to purchase, will compare products at varying speeds and price points. Slower service providers can still exert competitive pressure on faster service providers. So, too, can mobile broadband providers. Before the Commission can conclude that a market is concentrated, it must first define that market. It has made no effort to do so.

The Commission, moreover, does not address whether the trend in the broadband market is towards more or less competition. Obviously the deployment of broadband infrastructure is a capital-intensive process, and it should not be surprising if, during a period of expansion, some areas are served by fewer competitors than others. But there is no evidence in the record suggesting that broadband providers are carving up territory or avoiding head-to-head competition.

The Commission apparently wanted to avoid a disciplined inquiry focused on market power, notwithstanding the warning it received from the Justice Department less than a year before the regulation issued—which, as I noted, Verizon cited—a warning that unless the FCC's focus was on market power, any regulation could actually discourage broadband development, thus frustrating the statutory objective:

> Although enacting some form of regulation to prevent certain providers from exercising monopoly power may be tempting with regard to ... areas [served by only one or two broadband providers], care must be taken to avoid stifling the infrastructure investments needed to expand broadband access. In particular, price regulation would be appropriate only where necessary to protect consumers from the exercise of monopoly power and where such regulation would not stifle incentives to invest in infrastructure deployment.

Ex Parte Submission of the U.S. DOJ at 28, Docket No. 09–51 (Jan. 4, 2010).

The Commission did postulate one other economic theory supposedly establishing a "barrier to infrastructure investment" that does not depend on the broadband providers possessing market power. It argued, essentially, that innovation among edge providers is a public good in that every broadband provider benefits from an open Internet, but each broadband provider has an individual incentive to charge edge providers for service because, if broadband providers were to forego that revenue stream, they would be unable to internalize all of the supposed benefits to innovation. In short, the Commission speculates that the Open Internet Order prevents a classic "tragedy of the commons"—a situation in which each economic actor, behaving in his own self-interest, contributes to the destruction of a public good. In such a situation, each actor would be better off if a central regulator prevented them from doing what would be in their private interest if they were acting unilaterally. Again, however, the Commission fails to make any real economic findings regarding whether these rules are actually necessary to prevent such a situation. As such, it is the sheerest of fanciful speculation.

Indeed, if a tragedy of the commons were likely in the broadband market, then one would expect Verizon and other broadband providers to support the Open Internet Order, because such a situation would be economically harmful to them in the long run.

Perhaps most troubling, the Commission fails to appreciate the long-term impact of its own regulations. An unwarranted government interference in a functioning market is likely to persist indefinitely, whereas a failure to intervene, even when regulation would be helpful, is likely to be only temporarily harmful because new innovations are constantly undermining entrenched industrial powers.

III.

Because the Open Internet Order obviously imposes common carrier obligations on broadband providers, I join generally the opinion of the Court with respect to Part III. Indeed, even noted proponents of "net neutrality" acknowledge as much: "[N]et neutrality is the twenty-first century's version of common carriage.... In the case of the Internet, common carriage under the name of net neutrality amounts to an FCC rule that bans any degree of blocking individual sites, [or] transmission of data." Tim Wu, The Master Switch 236 (2010).

I have, however, one quibble with the majority's analysis of the anti-blocking rules. Although ultimately concluding that the anti-blocking rules are unlawful, the majority says that whether those rules "likewise establish per se common carrier obligations is somewhat less clear." Majority Op. at 657. Although the Order states that, under the anti-blocking rules, broadband providers may not degrade content so as to make it "effectively unusable," the majority supposes that a broadband provider might voluntarily choose to offer service that is faster than the anti-blocking rules require, i.e., faster than the minimum speed necessary to make each edge provider effectively usable by consumers. By exceeding the minimum level of service, the majority suggests, the broadband providers would have wide latitude to engage in individualized bargaining, which might take this rule outside of common carriage per se. My concern with this hypothesis is that the phrase "effectively unusable" is subject to manipulation. I think it should mean that whatever speed is generally offered to most edge providers is the minimum necessary to be effectively usable. After all, it is artificial to distinguish between what is "effective" and what consumers expect. If a faster speed were to become standard, we would likely consider a slower speed to be effectively unusable. Thus, while there is a possibility that a "fast lane" Internet service might be offered on a non-common carriage basis, the service that most users receive under this rule would still have to be offered as common carriage, at a regulated price of zero. In any event, as the majority recognizes, the Commission did not make this argument, so the anti-blocking rules must fall.

This regulation essentially provides an economic preference to a politically powerful constituency, a constituency that, as is true of typical rent seekers, wishes protection against market forces. The Commission does not have authority to grant such a favor.

Notes and Questions

1. Another Leveraging Example. Although broadband infrastructure and, therefore, the net neutrality debate are "new," we have seen this concern arise throughout the history and across the breadth of communications regulation: from the concerns over broadcaster and cable company control over content to the Bell System's control over manufacturing and long distance. What is different about this debate? What is the same?

2. Mobile Antidiscrimination and Open Platforms. As the opinion notes, the Commission declined to apply its antidiscrimination rules to mobile providers. The Commission earlier applied a different set of rules, mandating open platforms, to mobile providers in one block of the 700 MHz Band. Service Rules for the 698–746, 747–762 & 777–792 MHz Bands, Second Report and Order, 22 FCC Rcd. 15,289 (2007) (excerpted above). How would you compare and contrast the antidiscrimination and open platform rules? At what harms is each aimed? Who will benefit from each set of rules, and who will be burdened by them? Which set of rules is likely to be less costly? Which is likely to be more effective? Did the FCC make the right decision in applying open platform mandates to one block of spectrum and not applying the antidiscrimination rules to mobile providers?

3. Market Structure and Net Neutrality. To what extent would the existence of a third, ubiquitous broadband network resolve net neutrality concerns? Many opponents of such regulation argue that networks themselves have strong incentives not to block or impede valuable content for consumers. Notably, any such impediment makes the access service less desirable to consumers, driving them to the service of a rival. The economic literature on oligopoly (competition among a small group of firms) suggests that collusion and monopoly-like outcomes diminish significantly when the number of competitors goes from two to three, although they do not vanish entirely. The evidence does strongly suggest, however, that one of the best broadband policies society could have right now would be to encourage the development of new networks.

4. Backbone Non-Regulation. As the dissent notes, the FCC has not regulated the providers of Internet backbone services—the long-distance carriers of the Internet. The policy is long-standing. *See* Jason Oxman, The FCC and the Unregulation of the Internet (FCC OPP Working Paper Series, no. 31, 1999) (available at: http://transition.fcc.gov/Bureaus/OPP/working_papers/oppwp31.pdf); Michael Kende, The Digital Handshake: Connecting Internet Backbones (FCC OPP Working Paper Series, no. 32, 2000). In 2011, in approving the acquisition of one Internet backbone by another, the Wireline Competition Bureau found there to be at least 12 Tier-1 backbones and at least 38 nationwide providers of transit arrangements. Applications Filed by Global Crossing Ltd. and Level 3 Communs., Inc. for Consent to Transfer Control, 26 FCC Rcd. 14,056 (Wireline Comp. Bur. 2011).

5. Discrimination, Good and Bad. Discrimination in terms of access can be good or bad, depending on how it is structured. To be sure, new innovators would be harmed if networks had a premium stratum of transmission that they made available only to a few, favored firms. But how much of the concern over net neutrality goes away if networks charge content providers for different levels of access but make that menu of access alternatives available to all providers on an equal basis (in a manner akin to common carriage)?

6. Section 706. As the dissent notes, despite rejecting aspects of the net neutrality rules, the majority's construction of § 706 was fairly broad. Do you agree with the majority (and the FCC) that § 706 gives the FCC authority to regulate the Internet, so long as it does not violate any specific prohibition in the Communications Act and so long as it can describe the action as one that promotes adoption of the Internet, or do you agree with the dissent that § 706 is more limited? What limits does the majority's construction of § 706 impose on the FCC? How much greater are the limits the dissent's interpretation would impose?

7. Net Neutrality but not Common Carriage. What room is left for the FCC to address its concerns of discrimination by broadband ISPs? In Cellco Partnership v. FCC, 700 F.3d 534 (D.C. Cir. 2012), a case much discussed in the *Verizon* opinions, the D.C. Circuit reviewed an FCC rulemaking "requiring all mobile-data providers to offer roaming agreements to other such providers on 'commercially reasonable' terms." *Id.* at 537. As noted in *Verizon*, the D.C. Circuit approved because "the data roaming rule leaves substantial room for individualized bargaining and discrimination in terms." *Cellco*, 700 F.3d at 548.

Following the *Verizon* decision, the FCC acted quickly to issue a new Notice of Proposed Rulemaking, and the Commission attempted to walk exactly this line. Protecting and Promoting the Open Internet, Notice of Proposed Rulemaking, 29 FCC Rcd. 5561 (2014). First, the FCC proposed to "enhance" its transparency rule, by requiring more detailed disclosures targeted to each of "individual end users, edge providers, the broader Internet community, and the Commission." *Id.* ¶ 68. Second, the FCC re-adopted its "no blocking" rule, "with a clarification that it does not preclude broadband providers from negotiating individualized, differentiated arrangements with similarly situated edge providers (subject to the separate commercial reasonableness rule or its equivalent)." *Id.* ¶ 89. In this regard, the FCC proposed to adopt a "minimum level of access," *id.* ¶ 97, and the requirement that all individualized arrangements nevertheless be "commercially reasonable," *id.* ¶ 116. The FCC sought comment on the manner in which disputes over individual arrangements should be presented and decided.

Do you think that these proposals satisfy *Verizon*?

---

§ 14.D. Voice over Internet Protocol

Earlier in this chapter, we saw that the FCC has concluded that Internet access services such as DSL and cable modem are not "telecommunications services" within the meaning of the Communications Act. A separate question arises as to whether particular Internet-based services that consumers choose to reach themselves constitute "telecommunications services." In no area is this question more important and knotty than in the area of VoIP. VoIP services, such as those provided by Skype or Vonage, refer generally to services that allow customers to use the Internet to make voice calls. But within that general basket of services exist real differences in how various services operate. Some services, such as Skype, allow consumers to talk from computer to computer without ever going through a switch in the public switched telephone network (PSTN). Other services, such as Vonage or those provided by cable companies, use the existing broadband infrastructure to carry telephone calls over IP networks and connect to the PSTN so that consumers make telephone calls using a phone and to ordinary telephone numbers without any clear indication that Internet technology is involved.

The advent of VoIP has raised a number of regulatory challenges. Voice telephony has long been a heavily regulated service under Title II of the Communications Act. Internet services, on the other hand, have been developing in a deliberately unregulated, or at least less regulated, environment. So when the bits that travel over the Internet happen to constitute voice rather than some other form of data, voice services can escape their regulated sphere. Think of what that could mean: voice service that exists without retail rate regulation, access charges, universal service contributions, and so on. Voice could become just another service, like email, that customers get over the Internet. VoIP thus puts significant pressure on traditional telephone regulation and policy goals.

Consider the position of a state regulatory agency that controls retail rates for local phone service and manages state universal service objectives. If consumers use their computers to make phone calls, the regulator may have no way to know whether those calls are being made, never mind what they cost. If enough consumers stop subscribing to local phone service, instead using their cable modem connections to make phone calls over the Internet, how can cross subsidies that contribute to state universal service policies be maintained? These are just examples of the fundamental regulatory issues that VoIP raises and explains why Internet voice services have come to command the FCC's attention.

At the heart of the regulatory issues related to VoIP is which, if any, Internet voice services should be considered "telecommunications services." In a 1998 report to Congress, Federal-State Joint Board on Universal Service, 13 FCC Rcd. 11,501 (1998), the FCC considered whether IP telephony is "telecommunications" under the Communications Act. The FCC noted that "phone-to-phone" IP telephony "bear[s] the characteristics of [a] 'telecommunications service[],'" id. at 11,544, ¶ 89, but it decided to "defer a more definitive resolution of these issues pending the development of a more fully-developed record." Id. at 11,544, ¶ 90. Strikingly, the FCC then ignored IP telephony—now known as VoIP—for several years. In 2004, however, the FCC began devoting substantial attention to the subject.

In 2004, the FCC adopted a notice of proposed rulemaking on voice services over the Internet. See IP-Enabled Services, Notice of Proposed Rulemaking, 19 FCC Rcd. 4863 (2004). That NPRM discussed the classification of various aspects of VoIP services without placing VoIP in either the "telecommunications services" or "information services" category. In the 2011 NPRM noted in Chapter Thirteen on universal service proposing the Connect America Fund, the Commission again "invite[d] comment on whether we should consider classifying interconnected voice over Internet protocol as a telecommunications service or an information service."[11] Connect America Fund, Notice of Proposed Rulemaking and Further Notice of Proposed Rulemaking, 26 FCC Rcd. 4554, ¶ 73 (2011).

Although it has not placed all interconnected VoIP services into one category or the other, the FCC has issued several orders that constitute a regulatory approach to VoIP. The FCC

---

11. 47 C.F.R. § 9.3 defines interconnected VoIP as a "service that:
    (1) Enables real-time, two-way voice communications;
    (2) Requires a broadband connection from the user's location;
    (3) Requires Internet protocol-compatible customer premises equipment (CPE); and
    (4) Permits users generally to receive calls that originate on the public switched telephone network and to terminate calls to the public switched telephone network."

released the first of these orders at the same time it issued its 2004 NPRM, declaring that one Internet service—Pulver.com's "Free World Dialup"—is not a "telecommunications service" under the Communications Act and hence is not subject to Title II regulation. Petition for Declaratory Ruling That Pulver.com's Free World Dialup Is Neither Telecommunications nor a Telecommunications Service, Memorandum Opinion and Order, 19 FCC Rcd. 3307 (2004). The Commission decided that Pulver.com's service was not telecommunications because it did not interconnect with the PSTN—it was solely computer-to-computer. The Commission also determined that AT&T's somewhat distinct phone-to-phone VoIP service was, on the other hand, not exempt from access-charge rules that apply to conventional long-distance calls. Petition for Declaratory Ruling That AT&T's Phone-to-Phone IP Telephony Services Are Exempt from Access Charges, Order, 19 FCC Rcd. 7457 (2004).

The Commission also imposed some obligations on providers of interconnected VoIP similar to those imposed on telecommunications providers, including local number portability, universal service contribution, and 911 emergency calling capability. Telephone Number Requirements for IP-Enabled Service Providers, Report and Order, 22 FCC Rcd. 19,531 (2007) (number portability); Universal Service Contribution Methodology, Report and Order and NPRM, 21 FCC Rcd. 7518 (2006) (universal service); IP-Enabled Services, First Report and Order and NPRM, 20 FCC Rcd. 10,245 (2005) (911 calling). Although the local number portability order was not challenged in court, the other two were. In Vonage Holdings Corp. v. FCC, 489 F.3d 1232 (D.C. Cir. 2007), the D.C. Circuit upheld as reasonable the Commission's central determination that it had authority to require interconnected VoIP providers to make universal service contributions, but rejected specific aspects of its implementation. And the order on 911 emergency calling capability was affirmed in Nuvio Corp. v. FCC, 473 F.3d 302 (D.C. Cir. 2007), excerpted below.

Additionally, in a very important decision, the FCC limited state jurisdiction over certain VoIP services. Vonage Holdings Corp. Petition for Declaratory Ruling Concerning an Order of the Minnesota Public Utilities Commission, Memorandum Opinion and Order, 19 FCC Rcd. 22,404 (2004). We excerpt the judicial decision upholding this order immediately below.

And finally, the FCC made clear in a consent decree with a local exchange carrier that the Commission would not tolerate efforts by conventional LECs to block entry by VoIP carriers. Madison River Communications, LLC, Order, 20 FCC Rcd. 4295 (Enf. Bur. 2005). Taken together, these orders provide the basic contours of the FCC's approach to VoIP.

Minnesota Public Utilities Commission v. FCC
483 F.3d 570 (8th Cir. 2007)

Opinion for the court filed by Circuit Judge BYE, in which Circuit Judges HEANEY and COLLOTON concur.

BYE, Circuit Judge:

Before the court are consolidated petitions for review which challenge an order of the Federal Communications Commission (FCC) preempting state regulation of telecommunication services which utilize a relatively new technology called Voice over Internet Protocol (VoIP). The FCC preempted state regulation after determining it would be impractical, if not impossible, to separate the intrastate portions of VoIP service from the interstate portions, and state regulation would conflict with federal rules and policies. We affirm the FCC's order and deny the petitions for review.

II.

On July 15, 2003, the Minnesota Department of Commerce (MDOC) filed a complaint with the Minnesota Public Utilities Commission (MPUC) alleging the DigitalVoice services being offered by Vonage Holdings Corporation (Vonage), which utilized VoIP technology, were "telephone services." The complaint further alleged Vonage was offering such services without complying with the state regulations governing telephone services—such as obtaining a service permit and filing a tariff listing the prices, terms, and conditions applicable to DigitalVoice. As a result of the MDOC's complaint, the MPUC ordered Vonage to comply with the Minnesota regulations applicable to telephone service and to cease and desist offering DigitalVoice services within the state until it did so.

In response to the MPUC's order, Vonage filed a petition with the FCC requesting it to preempt the order on the grounds Vonage was a provider of "information services," rather than a "telecommunications carrier," and thus exempt from state regulation for its DigitalVoice service. In the alternative, Vonage invoked the "impossibility exception" of 47 U.S.C. § 152(b), which allows the FCC to preempt state regulation of a service which would otherwise be subject to dual federal and state regulation where it is impossible or impractical to separate the service's intrastate and interstate components, and the state regulation interferes with valid federal rules or policies. *See* Louisiana Public Service Comm'n v. FCC, 476 U.S. 355, 368 (1986) (indicating the FCC can preempt state law "where compliance with both federal and state law is in effect physically impossible"); *see also id.* at 375 n.4 ("FCC pre-emption of state regulation [should be] upheld where it [is] not possible to separate the interstate and the intrastate components of the asserted FCC regulation.").

Vonage also filed suit against the MPUC in federal district court seeking to enjoin enforcement of the cease and desist order. The district court granted a permanent injunction which barred the MPUC from enforcing its order, concluding Vonage was providing "information services" rather than "telecommunication services" and therefore not subject to state regulation. Vonage Holdings Corp. v. Minnesota Public Utilities Comm'n, 290 F. Supp. 2d 993, 999 (D. Minn. 2003). The MPUC appealed the ruling to the Eighth Circuit.

While the MPUC's appeal was pending, the FCC issued an order addressing Vonage's petition. In its order, the FCC adopted Vonage's alternative position, which is, irrespective of whether Vonage's services should be characterized as "telecommunication services" or "information services," the FCC determined it was appropriate to preempt state regulation because it was impossible or impractical to separate the intrastate components of VoIP service from its interstate components. The FCC stated: "[T]he practical inseverability of other types of IP-enabled services having basic characteristics similar to DigitalVoice *would* likewise preclude state regulation.... Accordingly, to the extent other entities, such as cable companies, provide VoIP services, we *would* preempt state regulation to an extent comparable to what we have done in this Order." Vonage Holdings Corp., Memorandum Opinion & Order, 19 FCC Rcd. 22,404, 22,424, ¶ 32 (2004) (emphasis added).

The four primary issues raised in the consolidated petitions are whether the FCC's order is arbitrary and capricious because it (1) failed to make a threshold determination about whether VoIP services were "information services" or "telecommunications services," (2) determined it is impractical or impossible to separate the intrastate components of VoIP service from its interstate components, (3) determined state regulation of VoIP service conflicts with federal regulatory policies, and (4) preempted emergency 911 telephone service requirements.

III.

This court reviews a federal agency's decision under the Administrative Procedure Act (APA) and will set aside the decision only when it is "arbitrary, capricious, an abuse of discretion, or otherwise not in accordance with law." 5 U.S.C. § 706(2)(a).

The first issue is whether the FCC arbitrarily or capriciously failed to classify VoIP service as either an "information service" or a "telecommunications service." The FCC concluded state regulation of VoIP service should be preempted regardless of its regulatory classification because it was impossible or impractical to separate the intrastate components of VoIP service from its interstate components. The FCC deferred resolution of the regulatory classification of VoIP service in its order because the issue was already "the subject of [its] IP-Enabled Services Proceeding where the Commission is comprehensively examining numerous types of IP-enabled services, including services like DigitalVoice." As to this order, the FCC contends the dispositive nature of the impossibility exception made it unnecessary to first classify VoIP service.

In National Cable & Telecommunications Ass'n v. Gulf Power Co., 534 U.S. 327, 338 (2002), the Supreme Court described as "sensible" the FCC's decision not to determine "whether [Internet services] are cable services" under the Communications Act, given the FCC's decision that such a determination was unnecessary for the FCC to assert jurisdiction over pole-attachment rates for Internet traffic. This case is similar to *Gulf Power*. The impossibility exception, if applicable, is dispositive of the issue whether the FCC has authority to preempt state regulation of VoIP services. It was therefore sensible for the FCC to address that question first without having to determine whether VoIP service should be classified as a telecommunication service or an information service.

The next issue is whether the FCC arbitrarily or capriciously concluded the impossibility exception applies to VoIP services. As already discussed, the "impossibility exception" of 47 U.S.C. § 152(b) allows the FCC to preempt state regulation of a service if (1) it is not possible to separate the interstate and intrastate aspects of the service, and (2) federal regulation is necessary to further a valid federal regulatory objective, i.e., state regulation would conflict with federal regulatory policies. We address each of the components of the impossibility exception in turn.

The FCC determined on the basis of the record before it that there was no "practical means ... of directly or indirectly identifying the geographic location of a DigitalVoice subscriber." The FCC further emphasized

> the significant costs and operational complexities associated with modifying or procuring systems to track, record and process geographic location information as a necessary aspect of the service would substantially reduce the benefits of using the Internet to provide the service, and potentially inhibit its deployment and continued availability to consumers.... The Internet's inherently global and open architecture obviates the need for any correlation between Vonage's DigitalVoice service and its end users' geographic locations.

Additionally, the FCC recognized communications over the Internet were very different from traditional landline-to-landline telephone calls because of the multiple service features which might come into play during a VoIP call, i.e., "access[ing] different websites or IP addresses during the same communication and [] perform[ing] different types of communications simultaneously, none of which the provider has a means to separately track or record [by geographic location]."

It was proper for the FCC to consider the economic burden of identifying the geographic endpoints of VoIP communications in determining whether it was impractical or impossible to separate the service into its interstate and intrastate components. Service providers are not required to develop a mechanism for distinguishing between interstate and intrastate communications merely to provide state commissions with an intrastate communication they can then regulate. In addition, the issue whether VoIP services can be separated into interstate and intrastate components is a largely fact-driven inquiry requiring a high level of technical expertise. As noted above, in such situations we accord a high level of deference to the informed decision of the agency charged with making those fact findings. After carefully examining the record in this case, as well as the parties' arguments, we conclude the FCC did not arbitrarily or capriciously determine it was impractical or impossible to separate the intrastate components of VoIP service from its interstate components.

Because of the high level of deference we owe to the FCC on this fact-specific issue, it is unnecessary to justify our decision by countering all of the petitioners' challenges to the FCC's fact-findings, and instead we focus our attention on the primary contention raised on appeal—the alleged inconsistency between the FCC order challenged here and a subsequent order issued by the FCC addressing VoIP 911 service. *See* IP-Enabled Servs. & E911 Requirements for IP-Enabled Serv. Providers, First Report & Order & Notice of Proposed Rulemaking, 20 FCC Rcd. 10,245 (2005) (911 Order). The petitioners contend the two orders are inconsistent—while the first finds it impractical or impossible to identify the geographic end-points of VoIP communications, the second requires VoIP providers to do just that for the purpose of ensuring customers using VoIP service can obtain 911 services when the need arises. The petitioners contend the 911 Order requires Vonage to pinpoint the geographic source of the call. They argue it necessarily follows that the intrastate and interstate components of the service can then be separated.

The 911 Order does not provide a basis for concluding the order before us is arbitrary and capricious. Contrary to the assertions of the state public utilities commissions, the 911 Order also recognizes the practical difficulties of accurately determining the geographic location of VoIP customers when they place a phone call. *See* 911 Order, 20 FCC Rcd. 10,245, 10,259, ¶ 25 ("VoIP service providers often have no reliable way to discern from where their customers are accessing VoIP service."); *see also* Nuvio Corp. v. FCC, 473 F.3d 302, 303–304 (D.C. Cir. 2007) (denying a petition for review challenging the 911 Order and noting "there are no means yet available to easily determine the location of a caller using interconnected VoIP service [and] it is not yet technologically feasible to detect automatically the location of nomadic VoIP callers."). Recognizing this practical difficulty, the FCC devised a temporary solution requiring VoIP service providers to have their customers register the physical location at which they would first utilize VoIP service, and to also provide a means for customers to update these registered locations. Under this temporary fix, responses to 911 calls would be routed to the registered location, which may not be the same as the actual location where the call was placed. Thus, in both the order before us and the 911 Order, the FCC recognized the practical difficulties of determining the geographic location of nomadic VoIP phone calls.

Similarly, we emphasize the limited scope of our review of the FCC's decision. Our review is limited to the issue whether the FCC's determination was reasonable based on the record existing before it at the time. If, in the future, advances in technology undermine the central rationale of the FCC's decision, its preemptive effect may be reexamined.

The FCC also determined state regulation of VoIP service would interfere with valid federal rules or policies. Because the FCC deferred the regulatory classification of VoIP service to its IP-Enabled Services Proceeding, the FCC examined whether state and federal policies would conflict regardless of whether DigitalVoice were classified as an information service or a telecommunications service. The FCC determined conflicts would exist in either event.

With respect to the conflicts which would exist if DigitalVoice were classified as a telecommunications service, the FCC explained "Vonage would be considered a non-dominant, competitive telecommunications provider for which the Commission has eliminated entry and tariff filing requirements." In contrast, Minnesota law would compel a tariffed offering. Similarly, Minnesota law has entry requirements under which Vonage would be required to obtain a certificate of authority from the MPUC before offering its services in Minnesota. The FCC noted it eliminated tariff requirements for the purpose of promoting competition and the public interest, and Minnesota's tariff requirement "*may actually harm consumers* by impeding the development of vigorous competition."

With respect to the conflicts which would develop if DigitalVoice were classified as an information service, the FCC referred to its "long-standing national policy of nonregulation of information services." The FCC has promoted a market-oriented policy allowing providers of information services to "burgeon and flourish in an environment of free give-and-take of the marketplace without the need for and possible burden of rules, regulations and licensing requirements." Thus, any state regulation of an information service conflicts with the federal policy of nonregulation.

The FCC's conclusions regarding the conflicts between state regulation and federal policy deserve "weight"—the agency has a "thorough understanding of its own [regulatory framework] and its objectives and is uniquely qualified to comprehend the likely impact of state requirements." Geier v. American Honda Motor Co., 529 U.S. 861, 883 (2000). Competition and deregulation are valid federal interests the FCC may protect through preemption of state regulation. After carefully considering the positions presented by both sides of this dispute, we conclude the FCC did not arbitrarily or capriciously determine state regulation of VoIP service would interfere with valid federal rules or policies.

The next issue is whether the FCC arbitrarily or capriciously preempted Minnesota's 911 requirements. Minnesota "includes as one of its entry conditions the approval of a 911 service plan 'comparable to the provision of 911 service by the [incumbent] local exchange carrier.'" Vonage Holdings Corp., Memorandum Opinion and Order, 19 FCC Rcd. 22,404, 22,430, ¶42 (quoting Minn. R. §7812.0550, Subpt. 1). The FCC determined this requirement "inextricably links pre-approval of a 911 plan to becoming certificated to offer services in the state" and thus "operates as an entry regulation." *Id.* Because the FCC had already determined there was no practical way for Vonage to identify the geographic location of the calls placed by its customers, Vonage could not comply with this entry regulation and thus the requirement effectively barred Vonage from entry into Minnesota. As a consequence, the FCC preempted "this requirement along with all other entry requirements contained in Minnesota's 'telephone company' regulations."

Relying upon the obligations imposed upon VoIP providers under FCC's subsequent 911 Order (issued June 3, 2005), the MPUC contends Vonage could have complied with Minnesota's 911 requirement. We disagree. The FCC's VoIP 911 requirements did not exist when the MPUC asserted jurisdiction over Vonage, or when the FCC issued the order at issue here. As a consequence, it is improper for the MPUC to rely upon the 911 Order to challenge the reasonableness of the FCC decision now before us. *See* 47 U.S.C. §405(a) (providing that a party must file a petition for agency reconsideration before it may seek judicial review of an issue over which the FCC has had no "opportunity to pass"). Moreover, there is no guarantee Minnesota would accept as sufficient for its purposes the requirements imposed upon VoIP providers under the 911 Order. As the FCC noted in the 911 Order, there are a variety of "differences in state laws and regulations governing the provision of 911 service." Because of the nomadic nature of VoIP service, we agree with the FCC there is a need for "setting national rules for 911/E911 service[]." The FCC did not arbitrarily or capriciously preempt Minnesota's 911 requirements.

Notes and Questions

1. **Fish or Fowl?** As we noted above, the FCC has refused to classify interconnected VoIP as either an information or telecommunications service. This reluctance to classify VoIP parallels the earlier reluctance to classify broadband as either an information or telecommunications service. In the *Vonage* case above, however, the FCC does not want to allow the court to make the decision for the agency (as occurred with respect to broadband when the Ninth Circuit took the first crack at the issue in *Portland*). Consequently, the FCC decided that VoIP was either an "interstate telecommunications service" or an "information service" and that, in either case, state regulation was preempted.

2. **Fixed-Line VoIP.** The FCC's decision classified both "nomadic VoIP providers" — i.e., ones like Vonage that allow individuals to bring their VoIP phones with them when they travel — and fixed-line VoIP services, such as those provided by cable companies. The Eighth Circuit, however, declined to rule on this classification, concluding that the FCC's decision was pure dicta and that the facts of the case before the court did not require it to either uphold or reject that classification. How would you rule on fixed-line VoIP? Does the rationale for classifying it as either an interstate telecommunications service or an information service hold up?

3. **Consumer Protection.** State utility commissions traditionally have protected consumers from all sorts of telecommunications-related scams. Are they prohibited from exercising any form of oversight over VoIP? How about state attorneys general or state courts authorized to enforce common law fraud claims?

4. **Impediments to Competition.** The FCC states that Minnesota's rules would impede entry by VoIP providers. Meanwhile, the FCC was developing its own rules for VoIP providers. As you read the excerpts below, ask yourself how the rules the FCC applies differ in their implications for competition from the rules preempted in the order above.

5. **E911 Calls.** As we noted above, the Commission issued an order requiring interconnected VoIP providers to transmit 911 calls to a local emergency authority. The Commission set a 120-day deadline for VoIP providers to meet that requirement. Nuvio, a VoIP provider, challenged the 120-day requirement, resulting in the opinion below.

NUVIO CORP. v. FCC
473 F.3d 302 (D.C. Cir. 2006)

Opinion for the court filed by Circuit Judge GRIFFITH, in which Chief Judge GINSBURG and Circuit Judge KAVANAUGH concur. Concurring opinion filed by Judge KAVANAUGH.

GRIFFITH, Circuit Judge:

Petitioners, providers of the newly-emerging technology of Internet telephone service, challenge an order of the Federal Communications Commission that gave them only 120 days to do what is already required of providers of traditional telephone service: transmit 911 calls to a local emergency authority. We deny their consolidated petition for review because we conclude that the Commission adequately considered not only the technical and economic feasibility of the deadline, inquiries made necessary by the bar against arbitrary and capricious decision-making, but also the public safety objectives the Commission is required to achieve.

I.

One of the many dramatic changes the Internet has brought to telecommunications has been the development of interconnected Voice over Internet Protocol ("VoIP") service, which allows a caller using a broadband Internet connection to place calls to and receive calls from other callers using either VoIP or traditional telephone service. E911 Requirements for IP-Enabled Serv. Providers, First Report & Order & Notice of Proposed Rulemaking, 20 FCC Rcd. 10,245, 10,246 n.1 (2005) (Order). From a caller's perspective, interconnected VoIP service is, for the most part, similar to traditional telephone service, and its users reasonably expect it to function the same. But two additional capabilities of VoIP service undermine those expectations when callers try to use 911 emergency services. VoIP service allows callers to choose what are called "non-native" area codes. For example, a customer living in the District of Columbia can use an area code from anywhere in the country. Some interconnected VoIP providers ("IVPs") also offer "nomadic" service, which allows a VoIP telephone call to be made and received from wherever the user can establish a broadband connection. (By contrast, "fixed" VoIP telephone service can only be used from a dedicated, fixed connection—typically in a home or office.) As attractive as these two features may be, each makes it difficult for IVPs to provide the local callers the 911 emergency service they expect and upon which they rely. Routers designed to direct 911 calls cannot recognize non-native area codes, and unlike traditional and wireless telephone service, there are no means yet available to easily determine the location of a caller using interconnected VoIP service. IVPs, which were not required to do otherwise, failed to use dedicated trunks (communications paths connecting two switching systems, used to establish an end-to-end connection) set aside for routing calls to a local emergency call center (known as a public safety answering point or "PSAP") and instead routed 911 calls to administrative lines that had not been designed and were not staffed to handle emergency calls. The resulting tragedies gave rise to the Order at issue.

The Commission, which had previously been reluctant to regulate this nascent industry for fear of hindering its development, *see, e.g.*, IP-Enabled Servs., Notice of Proposed Rulemaking, 19 FCC Rcd. 4863, 4864 (2004) (Notice of Proposed Rulemaking or NPRM) (noting that IP-enabled services had developed "in an environment that is free of many of the regulatory obligations applied to traditional telecommunication services"), decided that an immediate solution was required to "discharge [] the Commission's statutory obligation to promote an effective nationwide 911/E911 emergency access system." The Commission thus ordered that

> within 120 days of the effective date of this Order, an interconnected VoIP provider must transmit all 911 calls, as well as a call back number and the caller's "Registered Location" for each call, to the PSAP, designated statewide default answering point, or appropriate local emergency authority that serves the caller's Registered Location.

In effect, the Order requires that all IVPs, including those that offer nomadic service using non-native area codes, ensure that their users are able to reach local emergency services when making 911 calls. The Order only requires that IVPs ensure that 911 calls are routed to the *registered* and not the *actual* location of each 911 caller. IVPs, however, must provide a way for consumers to update their registered locations in a timely fashion.

The Commission did not dictate a specific manner for IVPs to provide E911 access. Instead, the Commission noted that IVPs could satisfy these requirements by interconnecting directly with the E911 network through incumbent local exchange carriers (ILECs), by interconnecting indirectly through a third party, or by any other solution that results in E911 access.

II.

Petitioners' argument that the Commission overlooked the economic cost of implementing the Order's 120-day deadline highlights that our task under the arbitrary or capricious standard is to determine only whether an agency's decision "'was based on a consideration of the relevant factors and whether there has been a clear error of judgment,'" Motor Vehicle Mfrs. Ass'n of U.S., Inc. v. State Farm Mut. Auto. Ins. Co., 463 U.S. 29, 43 (1983) (quoting Bowman Transp., Inc. v. Ark.-Best Freight System, Inc., 419 U.S. 281, 285 (1974)). Petitioners overlook a countervailing interest that the Commission must consider and we must respect—the threat to public safety. When, as is the case with the FCC, Congress has given an agency the responsibility to regulate a market such as the telecommunications industry that it has repeatedly deemed important to protecting public safety, the agency's judgments about the economic cost of its regulations must take into account its duty to protect the public. The Commission is required to consider public safety by both its enabling act, see Communications Act of 1934 § 1, 47 U.S.C. § 151 ("so as to make available, so far as possible ... [a] world-wide wire and radio communication service with adequate facilities at reasonable charges ... *for the purpose of promoting safety of life and property through the use of wire and radio communications*") (emphasis added), and the Wireless Communication and Public Safety Act of 1999 § 3, 47 U.S.C. § 615 ("shall encourage and support efforts by States to deploy comprehensive end-to-end emergency communications infrastructure and programs, based on coordinated statewide plans, including seamless, ubiquitous, reliable wireless telecommunications networks and enhanced wireless 9-1-1 service"). The Commission here weighed public safety against the economic cost of compliance with the Order and found that, "[w]hile 120 days is an aggressively short amount of time in which to comply with these requirements, *the threat to public safety if we delay further is too great* and demands near immediate action." Order, 20 FCC Rcd. at 10,266-67, ¶ 37 (emphasis added).

Because the Commission has reasonably determined that nomadic, non-native VoIP E911 access is technologically feasible, any argument about the time period required for implementation is nothing more than a quarrel over relative costs and benefits. In this case, the Commission has weighed the cost of an "aggressive" implementation scheme—a 120-day deadline—against the cost in human lives, and found in favor of public safety. We may not disturb its determination where, as here, the Commission has considered relevant factors and has articulated a reasoned basis for its conclusion. When viewed in this light, we cannot agree that the 120-day deadline is arbitrary or capricious.

Petitioners' final challenge to the 120-day deadline is that it represents an unexplained departure from longstanding precedent. The precedent, so the argument goes, was established when the FCC gave more time for wireless and satellite phones and other new technologies to implement 911 capabilities than the aggressive deadline it has imposed on the new VoIP telephone service market. Petitioners are right that an agency departing from precedent "must provide a principled explanation for its change of direction." But surely different technologies may reasonably bear different regulatory burdens. It is not apparent to us that the regulation of satellite or wireless phones is clear precedent for the regulation of information technology service providers.

Because petitioners acknowledge that some type of E911 regulation is necessary, this petition for review is, in essence, a challenge only to where the FCC has drawn the regulatory "line," and we have previously and repeatedly given the Commission "wide discretion to determine where to draw administrative lines." Based on the record evidence, the demonstrated safety concerns, and our deference to the Commission's predictive judgments, we conclude that the Order's 120-day deadline was neither arbitrary nor capricious.

[Concurring opinion of Judge Kavanaugh is omitted.]

Notes and Questions

1. What Alternatives? In acknowledging that some E911 mandate was warranted, what do the petitioners want instead of the FCC's policy? Would their alternatives serve the public as well? Consider how the FCC could have been stricter in its regulation. Did it strike a good balance between avoiding competitive impediments and protecting the public?

2. Wireless versus VoIP E911. Wireless providers were afforded considerable leeway as they developed technologies to enable consumers to access 911 from their phones and for "automatic location information" (ALI) to be delivered to the public safety answer points (PSAPs). In the order upheld above, VoIP providers were mandated to adopt such technologies within 120 days. Why the difference in treatment? Do you agree with the FCC's rationale?

3. Caveat Emptor. Should the FCC be in the business of requiring all telephone services to provide emergency contacts? If, for example, consumers use VoIP services in a way complementary to conventional or wireless telephone services that already provide 911 service, then to what extent is the FCC benefiting consumers? Why not let VoIP providers differentiate themselves, with some offering E911 in an effort to displace other forms of telephony and some not providing it but offering a lower cost in an effort to become a more complementary service? In such cases, a requirement of disclosure about the existence of 911 connectivity might suffice. Is the FCC effectively prejudging the role that VoIP will eventually play in the marketplace?

4. PSAPs and ALI. The FCC exercises jurisdiction over the carriers, not over the PSAPs. Many PSAPs have limited funding sources and thus have not upgraded from their antiquated systems, meaning that, in some cases, they are not able to process the ALI even when delivered to them. Should carriers be required to adopt the capability of delivering such information even if it will not be useful to individual PSAPs?

5. Public Choice Theory in Action? One popular theory of regulation is that the regulatory process is used by particular firms to gain an advantage over their competitors. This theory, which is often termed "public choice theory" or "rent-seeking explanations," could be used to suggest that the E911 mandate foisted upon VoIP providers reflected an effort by incumbent phone companies to make life more difficult for their competitors. Is that a fair characterization?

6. VoIP and Old Regulations. Law enforcement views telecommunications as a vital asset in the efforts to fight crime (by making wiretapping technology feasible) and to respond to emergencies (by providing E911 capability). In the case below, consider the FCC's argument and how the court views its persuasiveness in justifying a general "information services" treatment toward broadband and VoIP while still justifying the imposition of the wiretapping obligations under the Communications Assistance in Law Enforcement Act (CALEA), 47 U.S.C. §§ 1001–1010.

American Council on Education v. FCC
451 F.3d 226 (D.C. Cir. 2006)

Opinion for the Court filed by Circuit Judge SENTELLE, in which Circuit Judge BROWN concurs. Dissenting opinion filed by Senior Circuit Judge EDWARDS.

SENTELLE, Circuit Judge:

In 2004, several law-enforcement agencies petitioned the Federal Communications Commission ("FCC" or "the Commission") to clarify the scope of the Communications Assistance for Law Enforcement Act, 47 U.S.C. §§ 1001–1010 ("CALEA" or "the Act"), with respect to certain broadband Internet services. In response, the Commission ruled that providers of broadband Internet access and Voice over Internet Protocol ("VoIP") services are regulable as "telecommunications carriers" under the Act. As "telecommunications carriers," broadband and VoIP providers must ensure that law-enforcement officers are able to intercept communications transmitted over the providers' networks. The American Council on Education and various other interested parties (collectively "ACE") petition for review, arguing that the Commission's interpretation of CALEA was unlawful. Because we disagree, we deny the petition.

I.

Before the dawn of the digital era, there were few technological obstacles to the government's wiretapping capabilities: Eavesdropping on a phone call was as easy as finding the copper wires that ran into every caller's home. With the advent of the digital age, however, the architecture of the world's communications networks changed drastically. In the place of physical copper wires that connected individual end-users, new communications technologies (such as digital subscriber line ("DSL"), cable modems, and VoIP) substituted ethereal and encrypted digital signals that were much harder to intercept and decode using old-fashioned call-interception techniques.

Responding to these changing technologies, in 1994 Congress passed CALEA, which requires "telecommunications carriers" to "ensure" that their networks are technologically "capable" of being accessed by authorized law enforcement officials. 47 U.S.C. § 1002(a). While CALEA's substantive provisions apply to "telecommunications carrier[s]," they do not apply to "information services." *See id.* § 1002(a), (b). Determining which communications services fall where is the crux of this case.

A

CALEA applies only to "telecommunications carriers." *See id.* § 1002(a). The Act defines a "telecommunications carrier" as an "entity engaged in the transmission or switching of wire or electronic communications as a common carrier for hire." *Id.* § 1001(8)(A). However, in addition to providers of "transmission or switching," CALEA's definition of a "telecommunications carrier" also includes:

> [1] a person or entity engaged in providing wire or electronic communication switching or transmission service to the extent that [2] *the Commission finds that such service is a replacement for a substantial portion of the local telephone ex-*

change service and that [3] it is in the public interest to deem such a person or entity to be a telecommunications carrier for purposes of this subchapter....

CALEA does not apply to "persons or entities insofar as they are engaged in providing information services." *Id.* § 1001(8)(C)(i) (the "information-services exclusion"). The Act defines an "information service" as "the offering of a capability for generating, acquiring, storing, transforming, processing, retrieving, utilizing, or making available information via telecommunications." *Id.* § 1001(6)(A). Because information-service providers are not subject to CALEA, they need not make their networks accessible to law-enforcement agencies. *See id.* § 1002(b)(2)(A).

B

In 2004, the United States Department of Justice, the Federal Bureau of Investigation, and the United States Drug Enforcement Administration (collectively, "the DOJ") filed a joint petition for expedited rulemaking before the FCC. The DOJ explained that "[t]he ability of federal, state, and local law enforcement to carry out critical electronic surveillance is being compromised today by providers who have failed to implement CALEA-compliant intercept capabilities." In response, the Commission issued a notice of proposed rulemaking and invited comments on whether certain communications providers—including broadband and VoIP providers—must comply with CALEA.

After receiving thousands of pages of comments from more than 40 interested parties, the Commission ruled that broadband and VoIP providers are covered (at least in part) by CALEA's definition of "telecommunications carriers." *See* Communications Assistance for Law Enforcement Act and Broadband Access and Services, First Report and Order and Further Notice of Proposed Rulemaking, 20 FCC Rcd. 14,989, ¶ 8 (2005) (Order). To avoid an "irreconcilable tension" between CALEA's [Substantial Replacement Provision] SRP and the information-services exclusion, the Commission concluded that the Act creates three categories of communications services: pure telecommunications (which plainly fall within CALEA), pure information (which plainly fall outside CALEA), and hybrid telecommunications-information services (which are only partially governed by CALEA). *Id.* ¶ 18.

The FCC then concluded that broadband and VoIP are hybrid services that contain both "telecommunications" and "information" components. *Id.* ¶¶ 24–45. The Commission explained that CALEA applies to providers of those hybrid services only to the extent they qualify as "telecommunications carriers" under the three prongs of the SRP. First, providers of both technologies must perform switching and transport functions. Second, providers of both technologies serve as replacements for a substantial functionality of local telephone exchange service: Broadband replaces the transmission function previously used to reach dial-up Internet service providers ("ISPs"), and VoIP replaces traditional telephone service's voice capabilities. Third, the public interest requires application of CALEA to the "telecommunications" component of both technologies: The even-handed application of CALEA across technologies will not impede competition or innovation, and "[t]he overwhelming importance of CALEA's assistance capability requirements to law enforcement efforts to safeguard homeland security and combat crime weighs heavily in favor" of applying CALEA broadly. *Id.* ¶ 35.

The Commission recognized that it had separately adopted a different interpretation of a similar term ("telecommunications *service*") under a different statute. Interpreting the Telecommunications Act of 1996, Pub. L. No. 104-104, 110 Stat. 56, 47 U.S.C. §§ 251–276 ("the Telecom Act" or "the 1996 Act"), the FCC previously concluded that broadband Internet service is *not* a "telecommunications service," and it therefore falls outside the ambit of the 1996 Act. *See* Inquiry Concerning High-Speed Access to the Internet over Cable and Other Facilities, Internet Over Cable Declaratory Ruling, 17 FCC Rcd. 4798, 4823 (2002) ("Broadband Declaratory Ruling"). To reconcile the Order (promulgated under CALEA) with the Broadband Declaratory Ruling (promulgated under the 1996 Act), the Commission emphasized that both CALEA and the Telecom Act are silent regarding how (or whether) the FCC should regulate mixed services that have both "telecommunications" and "information" components. Order, 20 FCC Rcd. 14,989 ¶ 17. Thus, the FCC concluded that both statutes vest it with discretion to interpret Congress's ambiguous treatment of hybrid telecommunications-information services.

In the context of the 1996 Act, the Commission concluded that hybrid services fall entirely outside the statute's scope. Because the 1996 Act defines both "telecommunications service" and "information service" in terms of an "offering" to consumers, *see* Broadband Declaratory Ruling, 17 FCC Rcd. at 4820, ¶ 34, and because consumers perceive broadband Internet access to be a single "offer" for an integrated "information service," *id.* at 4821–24, ¶¶ 35–41, the FCC concluded that cable-modem service is exclusively an "information service," which is unregulable under the 1996 Act, *id.* at 4832, ¶ 59. The Commission further emphasized that its interpretation of the Telecom Act is consistent with Congress's deregulatory goals. *See id.* at 4802, ¶ 5; *id.* at 4823–24, ¶¶ 40–41. The Supreme Court upheld the FCC's Broadband Declaratory Ruling as a "reasonable" interpretation of the 1996 Act. *See* National Cable & Telecommunications Ass'n v. Brand X Internet Services, 545 U.S. 967, 997 (2005).

However, the Telecom Act differs significantly from CALEA. Unlike CALEA, the 1996 Act does *not* contain an analogue to CALEA's SRP: While an entity is covered by CALEA if it provides transmission, switching, or the functional equivalent thereof, an entity is covered by the Telecom Act only if it provides "transmission." *See* 47 U.S.C. § 153(43). Also unlike CALEA, the Telecom Act does *not* contain an analogue to CALEA's "insofar as" clause: While an entity is excluded from CALEA only "insofar as" it provides "information services," the 1996 Act categorically excludes "information services" en toto. *See id.* § 153(44). Finally, unlike CALEA, the Telecom Act refers to *two* "service offerings": While CALEA refers only to an "offering" of "information services," the Telecom Act refers to "offerings" of both "telecommunications services" and "information services." *Id.* § 153(20), (46); *see also* Broadband Declaratory Ruling, 17 FCC Rcd. at 4823, ¶ 40 (emphasizing the fact that the 1996 Act—unlike CALEA—contains separate definitions for "telecommunications" and "telecommunications service").

EDWARDS, Senior Circuit Judge, dissenting:

In determining that broadband Internet providers are subject to CALEA as "telecommunications carriers," and not excluded pursuant to the "information services" exemption, the Commission apparently forgot to read the words of the statute. CALEA does not give the FCC unlimited authority to regulate every telecommunications service that might conceivably be used to assist law enforcement. Quite the contrary. Section 1002 is precise and limited in its scope. It expressly states that the statute's assistance capability requirements "do not apply to [...] information services." *Id.* Broadband Internet is an "information service"—indeed, the Commission does not dispute this. Therefore, broadband Internet providers are exempt from the substantive provisions of CALEA.

The FCC apparently believes that law enforcement will be better served if broadband Internet providers are subject to CALEA's assistance capability requirements. Although the agency may be correct, it is not congressionally authorized to implement this view. In fact, the "information services" exemption prohibits the FCC from subjecting broadband service providers to CALEA's assistance capability requirements. If the FCC wants the additional authority that Congress withheld, it must lobby for a new statute. Until Congress decides that the "information services" exemption is ill-advised, the agency is bound to respect the legislature's will and we are bound to enforce it.

What we see in this case is an agency attempting to squeeze authority from a statute that does not give it. The FCC's interpretation completely nullifies the information services exception and manufactures broad new powers out of thin air.

It seems that the Commission had little interest in reading CALEA in a manner that is consistent with the statute's language and structure. The Commission's argument is quite revealing. By emphasizing the need to construe CALEA to "ensur[e] that technological change [does] not erode lawful surveillance authority," FCC's Br. at 30, the Commission betrays its true objective: administrative amendment of the statute. Our standard for reviewing an agency's interpretation of congressional commands does not permit us to ratify the FCC's unauthorized attempt to legislate new and better tools for law enforcement.

The question here is whether the FCC has identified a statutory predicate for enlarging CALEA's scope to encompass providers of broadband access. It has not. Merely saying that broadband is not an information service does not make it so, certainly not in light of all that the FCC has said in the past. And merely invoking *law enforcement*, "as though it were a talisman under which any agency decision is by definition unimpeachable," *State Farm*, 463 U.S. at 50, offends good sense.

The FCC can no more contend that "information service" providers are really "telecommunications carriers" because their regulation can facilitate the law enforcement purposes of CALEA, than the agency could assert that those who operate "movie theaters" are really "radio broadcasters" because their regulation would facilitate control of indecent material pursuant to 18 U.S.C. § 1464. There is absolutely no permissible basis for this court to sustain the FCC's convoluted attempt to infer broad new powers under CALEA. The agency has simply abandoned the well-understood meaning of "information services" without offering any coherent alternative interpretation in its place. The net result is that the FCC has altogether gutted the "information services" exemption from CALEA. Only Congress can modify the statute in this way.

Notes and Questions

1. Deference and New Technologies. As in the *Southwestern Cable* case discussed previously, the FCC continues to enjoy leeway—for example, in the *American Council on Education* and *Brand X* cases—as to the implementation of a statute that, by all accounts, did not appreciate how the Internet would revolutionize telecommunications. Should courts, as both Justice Scalia and Judge Edwards suggest, be less deferential to the FCC's effort to adapt the statute to new technologies and require a more active role by Congress in the process?

2. The Internet and Wiretaps. The architecture of the Internet, for reasons explained in Chapter Twelve, does not lend itself to central control and easy oversight. For this reason, some technologists are skeptical that wiretaps will operate effectively in the Internet context. Is the effectiveness or cost of CALEA relevant under the statute? Is that something the FCC should take into account when applying an established law to new technologies?

§ 14.E. "Over the Top" Online Video Competition

Just as VOIP challenged the notion of a "voice network," the Internet challenges the entire notion of video channels—which have become known as "linear" programming—where a network (either broadcast or MVPD) puts together a schedule of programs to be transmitted one after another. The Internet's architecture (assuming sufficient bandwidth) allows video to be stored on servers and for individual programs to be streamed or downloaded to users on demand.

Internet video is sometimes called "over the top" video because, as with other Internet content and applications, delivery is not tied to any particular legacy architecture. Customers can access the content from any Internet-connected device, over any Internet access platform.

The increased popularity of online video services and their bandwidth demands have given rise to a number of related controversies. First, of course, is the issue of net neutrality, writ large. As discussed above, the FCC's theory in the *Comcast* decision was that Comcast interrupted peer-to-peer sessions in part to protect its own video revenues (both linear video and video-on-demand, which most closely competes with Internet video platforms).

Second, vertical integration of content and distribution providers may heighten these incentives, as ownership may increase the returns to discrimination and foreclosure. Vertical integration also raises the concern that a company would deny content to unaffiliated over-the-top providers, to diminish their portfolio and therefore their ability to compete with the combined company's own offerings. The worry that a cable company would deny content to other MVPDs was behind the Program Access Rules, discussed in Chapter Ten, and this same competitive concern could arise with respect to Internet video. Just this issue arose directly in the FCC and DOJ's consideration of the NBC/Comcast merger. Challengers to the merger contended that the combined company would have the ability and the incentive to retard the development of online video businesses, in order to protect Comcast's revenues from traditional cable channels. In its order approving the transaction, the FCC imposed a variety of conditions designed to meet this concern. The Department of Justice imposed similar conditions in a consent decree entered under its antitrust authority. The FCC said:

> 2. *Online Video Content*
>
> 60. In this section, we examine the role of the Internet in the delivery of video programming, which has progressed from negligible just a few years ago to an increasingly mainstream role today. Major companies deliver video content over the Internet to consumers over websites and other applications. Consumers are more and more able to view this content not just on their television sets, but also on a multitude of other devices, such as PCs, tablets, and mobile phones.
>
> 61. We find that, as a vertically integrated company, Comcast will have the incentive and ability to hinder competition from other OVDs [online video distributors], both traditional MVPDs and standalone OVDs, through a variety of anticompetitive strategies. These strategies include, among others: (1) restricting access to or raising the price of affiliated online content; (2) blocking, degrading, or otherwise violating open Internet principles with respect to the delivery of unaffiliated online video to Comcast broadband subscribers; and (3) using Comcast set-top boxes to hinder the delivery of unaffiliated online video.
>
> 62. We impose a set of measures carefully tailored to safeguard against these potential harms. The online video market is expanding, and has the potential

to increase consumers' choice of video providers, enhance the mix and availability of content, drive innovation, and lower prices for OVD and MVPD services. A robust OVD market also will encourage broadband adoption, consistent with the goals of the Commission's National Broadband Plan.

a. Background

65. Internet video viewing is growing. One half of American consumers watch some video over the Internet. Although the amount of viewing is still relatively small—one estimate is that it makes up nine percent of all viewing—it is clearly increasing. The number of United States-based viewers in 2009 who watched video online grew 19 percent over 2008, and the number of "videos" watched increased 95 percent. By 2010, the average user was online almost 97 hours per month, with "real-time entertainment" comprising almost half (45 percent) of all downstream Internet traffic. During evening hours, this represented a 45 percent increase over 2009. Netflix estimates that by the end of 2010, a majority of its subscribers will watch more content streamed over the Internet than delivered on physical DVDs. Usage on mobile devices shows a similar pattern, with entertainment accounting for 45 percent of all data use and users staying online for almost 24 hours per month.

66. Not surprisingly, then, the Internet figures prominently in the plans of many MVPDs and other OVDs. The Applicants and the commenters agree that consumers want to watch programming "anytime, anywhere"—and that there is every reason to believe this trend will continue. It is against this backdrop that we evaluate the claims of many commenters that the transaction will increase the Applicants' incentive and ability to take a variety of anticompetitive actions against other MVPDs and OVDs.

b. Online Video Content to MVPDs

70. We conclude that, without conditions, the transaction would cause competitive harms to rival MVPDs and, ultimately, consumers. Online viewing is indisputably becoming an important service demanded by consumers—one that every major MVPD is offering its subscribers. Without access to online content on competitive terms, an MVPD would suffer a distinct competitive disadvantage compared to Comcast, to the detriment of competition and consumers. This reality will give Comcast-NBCU the incentive, similar to that discussed above, to withhold or otherwise discriminate in providing online rights to video programming in order to prevent Comcast's MVPD rivals from competing aggressively with it. And Comcast will gain an increased ability to act on this anticompetitive incentive through the acquisition of NBCU's video content.

72. As a condition of our approval of the transaction, we require Comcast-NBCU to provide to all other MVPDs, at fair market value and non-discriminatory prices, terms and conditions, any affiliated content that it makes available online to Comcast's own subscribers or to other MVPD subscribers.

73. We also conclude that Comcast-NBCU will have increased leverage to negotiate restrictive online rights from third parties, again to the detriment of competition. Comcast-NBCU's demand of restrictive online rights in exchange for carriage may also cause harms to consumer choice, diversity, and broadband investment. The Applicants emphasize that the distribution of online rights is non-exclusive, and that a content provider is free to license its content to the online platforms of other MVPDs. They have reiterated in this proceeding that they will adhere to this principle. To ensure that the Applicants adhere

to their commitments in this proceeding, and as a condition of our approval, we prohibit Comcast-NBCU from entering into restrictive agreements with third-party content providers regarding online rights, except under limited circumstances. We also prohibit Comcast-NBCU from impeding access to its own content by entering into overly restrictive agreements for online rights to that content.

c. Online Video Content to Non-MVPDs

78. We conclude that Comcast-NBCU will have the incentive and ability to discriminate against, thwart the development of, or otherwise take anticompetitive actions against OVDs. OVDs offer a tangible opportunity to bring customers substantial benefits. They can provide and promote more programming choices, viewing flexibility, technological innovation and lower prices. The availability of OVD choices may also drive consumers to purchase broadband services where they have not already. New OVD services and new deals are announced seemingly daily. Comcast has an incentive to prevent these services from developing to compete with it and to hinder the competition from those that do develop.

79. Whether viewers are "cutting the cord" has been examined by a multitude of studies. Although the amount of online viewing is growing, the record indicates that cord-cutting is relatively infrequent. We therefore agree with the Applicants that most consumers *today* do not see OVD service as a substitute for their MVPD service, but as an additional method of viewing programming. We nonetheless conclude that Comcast has an incentive and ability to diminish the potential competitive threat from these new services.

85. Finally, despite their arguments in this proceeding, the Applicants' internal documents and public statements demonstrate that they consider OVDs to be at least a potential competitive threat. The record here is replete with e-mails from Comcast executives and internal Comcast documents showing that Comcast believes that OVDs pose a potential threat to its businesses, that Comcast is concerned about this potential threat, and that Comcast makes investments in reaction to it. The record also contains NBCU emails and documents showing that many of the other cable companies are similarly concerned about the OVD threat and that NBCU feels pressure to avoid upsetting those companies with respect to any actions it might take regarding the online distribution of its content.

86. For all these reasons, we find that OVDs pose a potential competitive threat to Comcast's MVPD service, and that the Applicants therefore will have an incentive to take actions to hinder that competition.

87. Accordingly, we adopt targeted conditions to ensure that OVDs retain non-discriminatory access to Comcast-NBCU video programming, while permitting the continued evolution of the online market. First, we require Comcast-NBCU to offer its video programming to any requesting OVD on the same terms and conditions that would be available to a traditional MVPD. To take advantage of this condition, an OVD will have to make the Comcast-NBCU programming available to its users as an MVPD would, which we expect typically will require the OVD to provide a linear video stream alongside any VOD content. By granting OVDs substantially similar rights to video programming as MVPDs, this condition generally protects them from discriminatory treatment aimed at keeping OVDs from competing directly with Comcast for video subscribers.

88. We also recognize, however, that many OVDs may wish to offer video services that differ from traditional MVPD service. Because the terms by which video programming vendors offer their programming to such services are unsettled and likely to change rapidly, we conclude that the best way to ensure that Comcast-NBCU treats such services fairly is to require it to offer its programming on terms comparable to those offered by its non-vertically integrated peers, which lack Comcast-NBCU's incentive to harm online providers. Specifically, once an OVD has entered into an arrangement to distribute programming from one or more Comcast-NBCU peers, we require Comcast-NBCU to make comparable programming available to that OVD on economically comparable terms. This market-driven approach will ensure access to programming by OVDs as the online services develop, without prejudging the direction that dynamic market will take.

Applications of Comcast Corp., General Electric Co. and NBC Universal, Inc. for Consent to Assign Licenses and Transfer Control of Licenses, Memorandum Opinion and Order, 26 FCC Rcd. 4238 (2011).

Third, the importance of over-the-top video raises questions about interconnection policy, which is related to (but not identical to) the question of nondiscrimination put forward by net neutrality. An online video provider—or, more likely, the content distribution network (CDN) that distributes its content—will seek arrangements that enhance the quality of service of its video product. A CDN is a service such as Akamai or Level 3 that hosts content in distributed data centers and has its own distribution backbone to optimize delivery of content throughout the country (or the world). One way of conceptualizing net neutrality is that it should prohibit carriers from selling preferential speeds inside their networks to certain video services. Such rules would also prohibit the carriers from selling preferential speeds to all video services, preferring video traffic to non-video traffic. But there is another way in which an access network (such as a cable system) can influence a content-provider's quality of service, without necessarily treating traffic differently on its own network. Specifically, an access network may agree to "peer" with a CDN or a video provider, meaning that the connection and routing between the access network and the CDN is much more direct. The favored CDN might then avoid one source of congestion that other CDNs or content providers would suffer. And the access provider might charge for that preferred form of interconnection. Again, once the traffic "hits" the access network, there is no discrimination—the only discrimination (if that is the right description) is in the interconnection arrangement. Noting that "recent disputes between Netflix and ISPs such as Comcast and Verizon [which have allegedly demanded that Netflix pay for peering] have highlighted this issue," FCC Chairman Tom Wheeler noted in 2014 that the Commission was collecting information on the issue "to understand precisely what is happening in order to understand whether consumers are being harmed." Statement by FCC Chairman Tom Wheeler on Broadband Consumers and Internet Congestion (June 13, 2014) (available at: http://www.fcc.gov/document/chairman-statement-broadband-consumers-and-internet-congestion).

Notes and Questions

1. **What Innovation?** Given the conditions in the Comcast/NBC merger, can you see any online video products or services that the combined company could offer without making the identical content available to competitors? If not, why did the parties agree to the merger under the imposed conditions? The most skeptical observers of the merger have

offered the view that seven years is not a long time—that is, the conditions sunset by their own terms after seven years, and Comcast will simply bide its time until then. The somewhat less skeptical observers have posited that the merger closed simply because it was better than failure.

2. Bundling and Windowing. In most video markets, content providers have released their products through different channels at different times (called "windows"), allowing the providers to engage in price discrimination. A movie, for example, would be released through first-run theaters, then through cable exclusivity, then through DVDs, and then finally through online services. A television show might be first released by a broadcast channel, and then released in summer reruns, then perhaps syndicated, and then released on DVD. The online model of content distribution challenges this ability to price discriminate and online distributors have had difficulty charging the same total prices as traditional distributors. Moreover, traditional multichannel distribution was built around the idea of bundling channels together, at least at the first several basic tiers, in a way that brought more content to consumers than perhaps the consumers would order on an a la carte basis. What should regulators conclude about the future of video revenues, and on what basis?

3. Interconnection v. Nondiscrimination. Is there any analytical difference between discrimination in interconnection arrangements and discrimination in treatment of traffic internal to a network? Chairman Wheeler's Statement, while calling for further investigation, acknowledged that the net neutrality rules the Commission adopted in 2010 did not address the interconnection issue. Was that a mistake? On what basis should a regulator so conclude?

4. Legal Authority Redux. The FCC has significant authority over the interconnection of telecommunications networks, in 47 U.S.C. §§ 201, 251. But, under the D.C. Circuit's *Verizon* decision, the FCC may not impose common carrier-like nondiscrimination rules using § 706. Consider a standard that draws the line at what is "commercially reasonable." Do you think it would be commercially reasonable for an access provider to charge more for direct connections, especially to video providers whose services generate significant traffic flows to the access provider?

PART SIX
DIRECT REGULATION OF CONTENT

Chapter Fifteen

Direct Regulation of Content Deemed Valuable

Introduction

Many telecommunications regulations have an indirect impact on content. Often this is by design. One justification of the minority preference policies at issue in Metro Broadcasting v. FCC, 497 U.S. 547 (1990), for example, was that they increased program diversity. Sometimes, though, the government regulates content directly, obliging providers to increase content the government deems to be valuable and/or decrease content it deems harmful. In this and the next chapter, we consider such regulations. This chapter addresses regulations mandating (or effectively mandating, as we shall see) carriage of valuable programming. The next chapter will turn to laws limiting content deemed harmful.

Congressional legislation aimed at harmful content has focused on one specific category—indecency. So the story of legislation to stop bad content is largely the story of indecency regulation. And Congress has enacted indecency legislation with respect to every communications platform. Thus the central content regulation of cable television, telephony, and the Internet has been indecency regulation. Laws aimed at increasing valuable content generally fall into two categories: regulations aimed at providing access for views contrasting with those presented, for people who were attacked, and for political candidates; and regulations designed to increase children's programming. The apparent concern underlying these regulations is that an unregulated market might underproduce such content, because this content is not as remunerative as what it would replace, and (in the case of regulations aimed at providing access) perhaps because the owners' political views lead them to want to deny access to some people or viewpoints. Broadcasters have been the focus of most of these laws to increase valuable content.

This special treatment of broadcasters was encapsulated in the idea that broadcasters were "public trustees." From the start, the FCC adopted the view that broadcast stations should operate as public trustees and that an important function of the Commission would be to ensure that broadcasters perform that role. "Public trustee" was and is an amorphous phrase. In general, it signifies that one has a special duty to subordinate one's own interests to the public good. For purposes of this discussion, we might say that a broadcaster acts as a public trustee when it sacrifices financial gain to serve the interests of the viewing and listening public—or, more precisely, to serve what the government perceives to be the interests of the viewing and listening public.

In the first days of broadcasting, the public trustee notion seemed easy to justify. Broadcasters employed an essential input, use of the spectrum, which the government gave them free of charge. Further, in determining who would be allowed to use that input, the government chose the most meritorious applicants via comparative hearings, and merit was defined in large measure by public interest criteria. Thus, it seemed only natural that the government should impose upon those who won broadcast licenses a special obligation to use them to serve the public.

Today, by contrast, comparative hearings are no more—replaced, as we discussed in Chapter Five, by auctions and lotteries—yet public trustee obligations persist. There are fewer of them, to be sure, and those that remain are typically less onerous than their predecessors. Still, broadcasters are regulated as public trustees. Does it matter, for this purpose, that almost all broadcast licenses were distributed via comparative hearing (i.e., before auctions were mandated for all licenses)? Or that most broadcast licenses have been sold by the original licensee, with the new holder paying the previous holder for the license?

Our study of these content-based public trustee obligations begins with *Miami Herald Publishing Co. v. Tornillo*, a case that concerns a newspaper, not a broadcast station. The Supreme Court's opinion there makes clear that, as applied to newspaper content, the public trustee concept is not permitted (let alone embraced) by the First Amendment. In fact, *Tornillo* goes so far as to suggest that the First Amendment requires that the government permit publishers to "do good by doing well"—that is, to fulfill their public functions of educating, informing, and arousing the populace by whatever means they choose in the pursuit of their own self-interest, subject only to content-neutral laws of general applicability. *Tornillo* stands in sharp contrast to the case that immediately follows it in the materials, *Red Lion*, in which the Supreme Court seems to reach fully opposite conclusions about the same sort of content-based public trustee obligations. The central difference is that *Red Lion* involves broadcasting.

§ 15.A. The Fairness Doctrine and Related Obligations

§ 15.A.1. *Tornillo* and *Red Lion*

MIAMI HERALD PUBLISHING CO. V. TORNILLO
418 U.S. 241 (1974)

BURGER, C.J., delivered the opinion of the Court. BRENNAN, J., filed a concurring opinion in which REHNQUIST, J., joined. WHITE, J., filed a concurring opinion.

CHIEF JUSTICE BURGER delivered the opinion of the Court.

In the fall of 1972, Tornillo, Executive Director of the Classroom Teachers Association, was a candidate for the Florida House of Representatives. On September 20, 1972, and again on September 29, 1972, the Miami Herald printed editorials critical of Tornillo's candidacy. In response to these editorials Tornillo demanded that the Herald print verbatim his replies. The Herald declined to print Tornillo's replies, and Tornillo brought suit. The action was premised on [a] Florida "right of reply" statute which provides that if a candidate for nomination or election is assailed regarding his personal character or official record by any newspaper, the candidate has the right to demand that the newspaper print, free of cost to the candidate, any reply the candidate may make to the newspaper's charges. The reply must appear in as conspicuous a place and in the same kind of type as the charges which prompted the reply, provided it does not take up more space than the charges. Failure to comply with the statute constitutes a first-degree misdemeanor. The Herald contends the statute is void on its face because it purports to regulate the content of a newspaper in violation of the First Amendment.

Tornillo and supporting advocates of an enforceable right of access to the press vigorously argue that government has an obligation to ensure that a wide variety of views reach the public. Newspapers have become big business and there are far fewer of them to serve a larger literate population. Chains of newspapers, national newspapers, national wire and news services, and one-newspaper towns are the dominant features of a press that has become noncompetitive and enormously powerful and influential in its capacity to manipulate popular opinion and change the course of events. The result of these vast changes has been to place in a few hands the power to inform the American people and shape public opinion. In effect, it is claimed, the public has lost any ability to respond or to contribute in a meaningful way to the debate on issues.

The obvious solution, which was available to dissidents at an earlier time when entry into publishing was relatively inexpensive, today would be to have additional newspapers. But the same economic factors which have caused the disappearance of vast numbers of metropolitan newspapers have made entry into the marketplace of ideas served by the print media almost impossible. It is urged that the claim of newspapers to be "surrogates for the public" carries with it a concomitant fiduciary obligation to account for that stewardship. From this premise it is reasoned that the only effective way to insure fairness and accuracy and to provide for some accountability is for government to take affirmative action. The First Amendment interest of the public in being informed is said to be in peril because the "marketplace of ideas" is today a monopoly controlled by the owners of the market.

However much validity may be found in these arguments, at each point the implementation of a remedy such as an enforceable right of access necessarily calls for some mechanism, either governmental or consensual. If it is governmental coercion, this at once brings about a confrontation with the express provisions of the First Amendment and the judicial gloss on that Amendment developed over the years.

The clear implication [of our previous cases] has been that any compulsion exerted by government to publish that which "reason tells newspapers should not be published" is unconstitutional. A responsible press is an undoubtedly desirable goal, but press responsibility is not mandated by the Constitution and like many other virtues it cannot be legislated.

Tornillo's argument that the Florida statute does not amount to a restriction of the Herald's right to speak because "the statute in question here has not prevented the Miami Herald from saying anything it wished" begs the core question. The Florida statute operates as a command in the same sense as a statute or regulation forbidding the Herald to publish specified matter. The Florida statute exacts a penalty on the basis of the content of a newspaper. The first phase of the penalty resulting from the compelled printing of a reply is exacted in terms of the cost in printing and composing time and materials and in taking up space that could be devoted to other material the newspaper may have preferred to print. It is correct, as Tornillo contends, that a newspaper is not subject to the finite technological limitations of time that confront a broadcaster but it is not correct to say that, as an economic reality, a newspaper can proceed to infinite expansion of its column space to accommodate the replies that a government agency determines or a statute commands the readers should have available.

Faced with the penalties that would accrue to any newspaper that published news or commentary arguably within the reach of the right-of-access statute, editors might well conclude that the safe course is to avoid controversy. Therefore, under the operation of the Florida statute, political and electoral coverage would be blunted or reduced. Government-enforced right of access inescapably "dampens the vigor and limits the variety of public debate," New York Times Co. v. Sullivan, 376 U.S. 254, 279 (1964).

Even if a newspaper would face no additional costs to comply with a compulsory access law and would not be forced to forgo publication of news or opinion by the inclusion of a reply, the Florida statute fails to clear the barriers of the First Amendment because of its intrusion into the function of editors. A newspaper is more than a passive receptacle or conduit for news, comment, and advertising. The choice of material to go into a newspaper, and the decisions made as to limitations on the size and content of the paper, and treatment of public issues and public officials—whether fair or unfair—constitute the exercise of editorial control and judgment. It has yet to be demonstrated how governmental regulation of this crucial process can be exercised consistent with First Amendment guarantees of a free press as they have evolved to this time.

[Concurring opinions of JUSTICES BRENNAN and WHITE are omitted.]

RED LION BROADCASTING CO. v. FCC
395 U.S. 367 (1969)

WHITE, J., delivered the opinion of the Court. DOUGLAS, J., took no part in the Court's decision.

JUSTICE WHITE delivered the opinion of the Court.

The Federal Communications Commission has for many years imposed on radio and television broadcasters the requirement that discussion of public issues be presented on broadcast stations, and that each side of those issues must be given fair coverage. This is known as the fairness doctrine. It is distinct from the statutory requirement of §315 of the Communications Act that equal time be allotted all qualified candidates for public office. Two aspects of the fairness doctrine, relating to personal attacks in the context of controversial public issues and to political editorializing, were codified more precisely in the form of FCC regulations in 1967. The two cases before us now, which were decided separately below, challenge the constitutional and statutory bases of the doctrine and component rules. *Red Lion* involves the application of the fairness doctrine to a particular broadcast, and *RTNDA* [the companion case] arises as an action to review the FCC's 1967 promulgation of the personal attack and political editorializing regulations, which were laid down after the *Red Lion* litigation had begun.

I

The Red Lion Broadcasting Company is licensed to operate a Pennsylvania radio station, WGCB. On November 27, 1964, WGCB carried a 15-minute broadcast by the Reverend Billy James Hargis as part of a 'Christian Crusade' series. A book by Fred J. Cook entitled "Goldwater—Extremist on the Right" was discussed by Hargis, who said that Cook had been fired by a newspaper for making false charges against city officials; that Cook had then worked for a Communist-affiliated publication; that he had defended Alger Hiss and attacked J. Edgar Hoover and the Central Intelligence Agency; and that he had now written a "book to smear and destroy Barry Goldwater." When Cook heard of the broadcast he concluded that he had been personally attacked and demanded free reply time, which the station refused. After an exchange of letters among Cook, Red Lion, and the FCC, the FCC declared that the Hargis broadcast constituted a personal attack on Cook; that Red Lion had failed to meet its obligation under the fairness doctrine to send a tape, transcript, or summary of the broadcast to Cook and offer him reply time; and that the station must provide reply time whether or not Cook would pay for it. On review in the Court of Appeals for the District of Columbia Circuit, the FCC's position was upheld as constitutional and otherwise proper.

Not long after the *Red Lion* litigation was begun, the FCC [adopted rules] making the personal attack aspect of the fairness doctrine more precise and more readily enforceable, and specifying its rules relating to political editorials. [T]he rules were held unconstitutional in the *RTNDA* litigation by the Court of Appeals for the Seventh Circuit, on review of the rule-making proceeding, as abridging the freedoms of speech and press.

As they now stand amended, the regulations read as follows:

"Personal attacks; political editorials.

"(a) When, during the presentation of views on a controversial issue of public importance, an attack is made upon the honesty, character, integrity or like personal qualities of an identified person or group, the licensee shall, no later than 1 week after the attack, transmit to the person or group attacked (1) notification of the date, time and identification of the broadcast; (2) a script or tape (or an accurate summary if a script or tape is not available) of the attack; and (3) an offer of a reasonable opportunity to respond over the licensee's facilities.

"(b) The provisions of paragraph (a) shall not be applicable (1) to attacks on foreign groups or foreign public figures; (2) to personal attacks which are made by legally qualified candidates on other such candidates and (3) to bona fide newscasts....

"(c) Where a licensee, in an editorial, (i) endorses or (ii) opposes a legally qualified candidate or candidates, the licensee shall, within 24 hours after the editorial, transmit to respectively (i) the other qualified candidate or candidates for the same office or (ii) the candidate opposed in the editorial (1) notification of the date and the time of the editorial; (2) a script or tape of the editorial; and (3) an offer of a reasonable opportunity for a candidate or a spokesman of the candidate to respond over the licensee's facilities."

II

Before 1927, the allocation of frequencies was left entirely to the private sector, and the result was chaos. It quickly became apparent that broadcast frequencies constituted a scarce resource whose use could be regulated and rationalized only by the Government. Without government control, the medium would be of little use because of the cacophony of competing voices, none of which could be clearly and predictably heard. Consequently, the Federal Radio Commission was established to allocate frequencies among competing applicants in a manner responsive to the public "convenience, interest, or necessity."

Very shortly thereafter the Commission expressed its view that the "public interest requires ample play for the free and fair competition of opposing views, and the commission believes that the principle applies to all discussions of issues of importance to the public." Great Lakes Broadcasting Co., 3 F.R.C. Ann. Rep. 32, 33 (1929), *rev'd on other grounds*, 59 App. D.C. 197, *cert. dismissed*, 281 U.S. 706 (1930). This doctrine was applied through denial of license renewals or construction permits, both by the FRC and its successor FCC. After an extended period during which the licensee was obliged not only to cover and to cover fairly the views of others, but also to refrain from expressing his own personal views, Mayflower Broadcasting Corp., 8 F.C.C. 333 (1940), the latter limitation on the licensee was abandoned and the doctrine developed into its present form.

There is a twofold duty laid down by the FCC's decisions and described by the 1949 Report on Editorializing by Broadcast Licensees, 13 F.C.C. 1246 (1949). The broadcaster must give adequate coverage to public issues, United Broadcasting Co., 10 F.C.C. 515 (1945), and coverage must be fair in that it accurately reflects the opposing views. New Broadcasting Co., 6 Rad. Reg. (P & F) 258 (1950). This must be done at the broadcaster's own expense if sponsorship is unavailable. Cullman Broadcasting Co., 25 Rad. Reg. (P & F) 895 (1963).

III

The broadcasters challenge the fairness doctrine and its specific manifestations in the personal attack and political editorial rules on conventional First Amendment grounds, alleging that the rules abridge their freedom of speech and press. Their contention is that the First Amendment protects their desire to use their allotted frequencies continuously to broadcast whatever they choose, and to exclude whomever they choose from ever using that frequency. No man may be prevented from saying or publishing what he thinks, or from refusing in his speech or other utterances to give equal weight to the views of his opponents. This right, they say, applies equally to broadcasters.

A

Although broadcasting is clearly a medium affected by a First Amendment interest, differences in the characteristics of new media justify differences in the First Amendment standards applied to them. Just as the Government may limit the use of sound-amplifying equipment potentially so noisy that it drowns out civilized private speech, so may the Government limit the use of broadcast equipment. The right of free speech of a broadcaster, the user of a sound truck, or any other individual does not embrace a right to snuff out the free speech of others.

[O]nly a tiny fraction of those with resources and intelligence can hope to communicate by radio at the same time if intelligible communication is to be had, even if the entire radio spectrum is utilized in the present state of commercially acceptable technology. Where there are substantially more individuals who want to broadcast than there are frequencies to allocate, it is idle to posit an unabridgeable First Amendment right to broadcast comparable to the right of every individual to speak, write, or publish. If 100 persons want broadcast licenses but there are only 10 frequencies to allocate, all of them may have the same "right" to a license; but if there is to be any effective communication by radio, only a few can be licensed and the rest must be barred from the airwaves. It would be strange if the First Amendment, aimed at protecting and furthering communications, prevented the Government from making radio communication possible by requiring licenses to broadcast and by limiting the number of licenses so as not to overcrowd the spectrum.

By the same token, as far as the First Amendment is concerned those who are licensed stand no better than those to whom licenses are refused. A license permits broadcasting, but the licensee has no constitutional right to be the one who holds the license or to monopolize a radio frequency to the exclusion of his fellow citizens. There is nothing in the First Amendment which prevents the Government from requiring a licensee to share his frequency with others and to conduct himself as a proxy or fiduciary with obligations to present those views and voices which are representative of his community and which would otherwise, by necessity, be barred from the airwaves.

[T]he people as a whole retain their interest in free speech by radio and their collective right to have the medium function consistently with the ends and purposes of the

First Amendment. It is the right of the viewers and listeners, not the right of the broadcasters, which is paramount. It is the purpose of the First Amendment to preserve an uninhibited marketplace of ideas in which truth will ultimately prevail, rather than to countenance monopolization of that market, whether it be by the Government itself or a private licensee. It is the right of the public to receive suitable access to social, political, esthetic, moral, and other ideas and experiences which is crucial here. That right may not constitutionally be abridged either by Congress or by the FCC.

B

Rather than confer frequency monopolies on a relatively small number of licensees, in a Nation of 200,000,000, the Government could surely have decreed that each frequency should be shared among all or some of those who wish to use it, each being assigned a portion of the broadcast day or the broadcast week. The ruling and regulations at issue here do not go quite so far. They assert that under specified circumstances, a licensee must offer to make available a reasonable amount of broadcast time to those who have a view different from that which has already been expressed on his station. The expression of a political endorsement, or of a personal attack while dealing with a controversial public issue, simply triggers this time sharing. As we have said, the First Amendment confers no right on licensees to prevent others from broadcasting on "their" frequencies and no right to an unconditional monopoly of a scarce resource which the Government has denied others the right to use.

Otherwise, station owners and a few networks would have unfettered power to make time available only to the highest bidders, to communicate only their own views on public issues, people and candidates, and to permit on the air only those with whom they agreed. There is no sanctuary in the First Amendment for unlimited private censorship operating in a medium not open to all.

C

It is strenuously argued, however, that if political editorials or personal attacks will trigger an obligation in broadcasters to afford the opportunity for expression to speakers who need not pay for time and whose views are unpalatable to the licensees, then broadcasters will be irresistibly forced to self-censorship and their coverage of controversial public issues will be eliminated or at least rendered wholly ineffective. Such a result would indeed be a very serious matter, for should licensees actually eliminate their coverage of controversial issues, the purposes of the doctrine would be stifled.

At this point, however, that possibility is at best speculative. The communications industry, and in particular the networks, have taken pains to present controversial issues in the past, and even now they do not assert that they intend to abandon their efforts in this regard. And if experience with the administration of those doctrines indicates that they have the net effect of reducing rather than enhancing the volume and quality of coverage, there will be time enough to reconsider the constitutional implications. The fairness doctrine in the past has had no such overall effect.

That this will now occur seems unlikely, however, since if present licensees should suddenly prove timorous, the Commission is not powerless to insist that they give adequate and fair attention to public issues. It does not violate the First Amendment to treat licensees given the privilege of using scarce radio frequencies as proxies for the entire community, obligated to give suitable time and attention to matters of great public concern. Congress need not stand idly by and permit those with licenses to ignore the problems which beset the people or to exclude from the airways anything but their own views of fundamental questions.

The statute mandates the issuance of licenses if the "public convenience, interest, or necessity will be served thereby." 47 U.S.C. § 307(a). In applying this standard the Commission for 40 years has been choosing licensees based in part on their program proposals. The Court [has previously recognized] that the Commission was more than a traffic policeman concerned with the technical aspects of broadcasting and that it neither exceeded its powers under the statute nor transgressed the First Amendment in interesting itself in general program format and the kinds of programs broadcast by licensees. NBC v. United States, 319 U.S. 190 (1943).

D

There is no question here of the Commission's refusal to permit the broadcaster to carry a particular program or to publish his own views; of a discriminatory refusal to require the licensee to broadcast certain views which have been denied access to the airwaves; of government censorship of a particular program contrary to § 326; or of the official government view dominating public broadcasting. Such questions would raise more serious First Amendment issues.

E

It is argued that even if at one time the lack of available frequencies for all who wished to use them justified the [fairness doctrine], this condition no longer prevails so that continuing control is not justified. To this there are several answers.

Scarcity is not entirely a thing of the past. Advances in technology, such as microwave transmission, have led to more efficient utilization of the frequency spectrum, but uses for that spectrum have also grown apace. Among the various uses for radio frequency space, including marine, aviation, amateur, military, and common carrier users, there are easily enough claimants to permit use of the whole with an even smaller allocation to broadcast radio and television uses than now exists.

Comparative hearings between competing applicants for broadcast spectrum space are by no means a thing of the past. Nothing in this record, or in our own researches, convinces us that the resource is no longer one for which there are more immediate and potential uses than can be accommodated, and for which wise planning is essential.

In view of the scarcity of broadcast frequencies, the Government's role in allocating those frequencies, and the legitimate claims of those unable without governmental assistance to gain access to those frequencies for expression of their views, we hold the regulations and ruling at issue here are both authorized by statute and constitutional.

Notes and Questions

1. A Precursor. *Red Lion* cites an important precursor on scarcity—NBC v. United States, 319 U.S. 190 (1943), in which the Court faced its first serious challenge to the regulation of broadcasting. At issue were the chain broadcasting rules, which limited the ability of radio networks to control the programming of their broadcast affiliates. NBC's arguments to the Court focused on the First Amendment. NBC contended that "[r]adio is no less entitled to the protection of the guaranties of the First Amendment than is the press." Brief for Appellant NBC at 38, *NBC*, 319 U.S. 190 (1943) (No. 554). Concerns about interference, NBC argued, could not justify the government's regulatory regime.

The Supreme Court rejected NBC's arguments, finding that government control of the spectrum, and the rules it implemented pursuant to that control, were justified by the scarcity of the spectrum. Its main reasoning about scarcity appeared in a single paragraph:

> [There are] certain basic facts about radio as a means of communication — its facilities are limited; they are not available to all who may wish to use them; the radio spectrum simply is not large enough to accommodate everybody. There is a fixed natural limitation upon the number of stations that can operate without interfering with one another. Regulation of radio was therefore as vital to its development as traffic control was to the development of the automobile. In enacting the Radio Act of 1927, the first comprehensive scheme of control over radio communication, Congress acted upon the knowledge that if the potentialities of radio were not to be wasted, regulation was essential.

319 U.S. at 213. Its direct discussion of the First Amendment argument likewise occupied a single paragraph, the bulk of which follows:

> We come, finally, to an appeal to the First Amendment. The Regulations, even if valid in all other respects, must fall because they abridge, say the appellants, their right of free speech. If that be so, it would follow that every person whose application for a license to operate a station is denied by the Commission is thereby denied his constitutional right of free speech. Freedom of utterance is abridged to many who wish to use the limited facilities of radio. Unlike other modes of expression, radio inherently is not available to all. That is its unique characteristic, and that is why, unlike other modes of expression, it is subject to governmental regulation. Because it cannot be used by all, some who wish to use it must be denied. But Congress did not authorize the Commission to choose among applicants upon the basis of their political, economic or social views, or upon any other capricious basis. If it did, or if the Commission by these Regulations proposed a choice among applicants upon some such basis, the issue before us would be wholly different. The question here is simply whether the Commission, by announcing that it will refuse licenses to persons who engage in specified network practices (a basis for choice which we hold is comprehended within the statutory criterion of "public interest"), is thereby denying such persons the constitutional right of free speech. The right of free speech does not include, however, the right to use the facilities of radio without a license.

Id. at 226–27. Note that *NBC* treated the chain broadcasting rules at issue as content-neutral. The regulation at issue in *Red Lion* was triggered by content and thus presented a different constitutional question. Still, its focus on scarcity laid some of the groundwork for *Red Lion*.

2. Missing Citation. The Court's decision in *Tornillo* is strong and sweeping, written as if the result flows inexorably from deeply established precedent under the First Amendment. Interestingly, the opinion contains no discussion of — or even citations to — *Red Lion*, which had been decided five years before. Is this because the two cases cannot be reconciled? Because a case about broadcast has no bearing on a case about print media? Was this irresponsible behavior on the part of the Supreme Court, or was the Court simply exercising restraint by, in each instance, deciding only the case before it?

3. Reconciling *Tornillo* and *Red Lion*. At first blush, at least, all the arguments rejected in *Red Lion* seem to be the very ones accepted in *Tornillo*. More specifically, the *Tornillo* Court overturned the Florida statute for two reasons. First, any government "compulsion to publish that which 'reason tells [newspapers] should not be published' is unconstitutional." Second, "under the operation of the Florida statute, political and electoral coverage would be blunted or reduced." These arguments seem to reflect precisely the issues addressed by the *Red Lion* Court. The broadcasters in that case contend "that the First Amendment protects their desire to use their allocated frequencies continuously to broadcast whatever they choose, and to exclude whomever they choose from ever using that frequency" and "that if political editorials or personal attacks will trigger an obligation in broadcasters to afford the opportunity for expression to speakers who need not pay for time and whose views are unpalatable to the licensees, then broadcasters will be irresistibly forced to self-censorship and their coverage of controversial public issues will be eliminated or at least rendered wholly ineffective."

4. Scarcity. *Red Lion* suggests that the basis for special First Amendment treatment of broadcasters is the scarcity of the broadcast spectrum. Chapter Three considers the general question of spectrum scarcity in some detail, so that discussion need not be repeated here. But consider the specific reasoning offered by *Red Lion* in the last two paragraphs of the opinion as edited above. Can you think of any "resource" (including paper and ink) for which there are *not* "more immediate and potential uses than can be accommodated, and for which wise planning is [not] essential"? Moreover, similar arguments were raised and rejected in *Tornillo*. Indeed, as the *Tornillo* Court itself reported, there are only a few owners of newspapers; entry into the newspaper market is "almost impossible"; and, just like broadcasts, newspapers are subject to limits on how much information they can transmit. Yet in *Tornillo* none of these considerations softened the First Amendment protection recognized.

5. Print versus Broadcast. Are there other bases for distinguishing broadcast from print that would justify the lesser First Amendment protection afforded to broadcasters? One commonly noted rationale is that the government licenses the spectrum, and for many years distributed licenses without charge, so public interest obligations like a mandated right of reply were perhaps permissible conditions on the use of government resources. But, given our discussion of scarcity and interference in Chapter Three, is that argument convincing? And how does the argument change now that licenses are distributed by auction, not hearing? Are there other bases for distinguishing broadcasting from print? That broadcasting is an unusually powerful medium? That it is ubiquitous? That it greatly influences our culture? But none of these attributes fits only broadcasting, does it? And if broadcasting is unique in one or more of these manners, why would that suggest that broadcasters should receive less rather than more First Amendment protection?

6. Choosing an Approach. It seems, then, that one must choose between the First Amendment jurisprudence of *Tornillo* and that of *Red Lion*. Which makes more sense? Does *Tornillo* overstate the dangers of government regulation and the extent to which editors will be chilled by it? Why did the *Tornillo* Court fail to conclude that "it is the right of the [readers], not the right of the [publishers], which is paramount"? Does *Red Lion* fail to appreciate that the fairness doctrine is enforced by unelected bureaucrats? Does it fail to appreciate the fact that even a minor threat against a very valuable broadcasting license can be weighty? Is *Red Lion* flawed by its failure to subject a content-specific speech regulation to strict scrutiny, or is *Tornillo* flawed because it uses such a high standard of review that a beneficial regulation was needlessly found unconstitutional?

7. Multiple First Amendment Constituencies. Consider *Red Lion*'s suggestion that the First Amendment rights of broadcast licensees are counterbalanced by the First Amendment rights of viewers and listeners. In particular, consider the Court's reference to "the right of the public to receive suitable access to social, political, esthetic, moral, and other ideas and experiences." Is such a reading of the First Amendment persuasive? Is it necessary to accept this reading in order to uphold a right-of-reply statute? And what are the implications of the quoted language? For example, does this language suggest that the fairness doctrine is not merely permissible but is in fact constitutionally *required*? That is, does it indicate that, by creating a licensing regime but not creating any explicit fairness obligation, the 1934 Act itself violated the First Amendment? Similarly, does the public's right to suitable access mean that television networks are acting unconstitutionally when they imitate each other's most popular programming and thereby fail to provide a wide range of programming alternatives? Does the First Amendment thus justify a rule forbidding a radio station to switch from a unique, financially viable format to another format already employed by several stations in the same market? Recall that this issue arose in FCC v. WNCN Listeners Guild, 450 U.S. 582 (1981), excerpted in Chapter Five. Justice White, who wrote the opinion in both *WNCN Listeners Guild* and *Red Lion*, addressed the point as follows:

> [The Listeners Guild contends that] the Policy Statement conflicts with the First Amendment rights of listeners "to receive suitable access to social, political, esthetic, moral, and other ideas and experiences." Red Lion Broadcasting Co. v. FCC, 395 U.S. 367, 390 (1969). Although observing that the interests of the people as a whole were promoted by debate of public issues on the radio, we did not imply [in *Red Lion*] that the First Amendment grants individual listeners the right to have the Commission review the abandonment of their favorite entertainment programs. The Commission seeks to further the interests of the listening public as a whole by relying on market forces to promote diversity in radio entertainment formats and to satisfy the entertainment preferences of radio listeners. This policy does not conflict with the First Amendment.

450 U.S. 582, 603–04. Are you persuaded?

8. Implications. Would *Red Lion* permit: (a) a prohibition on speech that the government determines to be of little or no "social, political, esthetic, [or] moral" value?; (b) a rule requiring each television broadcaster to provide a minimum amount of programming per day or per week for pre-school age children?; (c) awarding, in comparative hearing cases, a preference for applicants who are women or members of minority races?; or (d) application of the fairness doctrine to a cable television system?

---

§ 15.A.2. The FCC Abandons the Fairness Doctrine

Although the Supreme Court has not abandoned *Red Lion*, the FCC did abandon the fairness doctrine. The path to that abandonment was a complicated one, in the course of which the FCC rejected most of the justifications asserted in the *Red Lion* opinion. In fact, the FCC cast doubt on the standard enunciated in *Red Lion* itself, although more recently it has attempted to revive *Red Lion*. Consider, in reading the FCC materials that follow, whether one of the decisions, or *Red Lion*, or none of these, provides sound policy analysis.

§ 15.A.2.a. The Fairness Doctrine Report

INQUIRY INTO THE COMMISSION'S RULES AND REGULATIONS CONCERNING THE GENERAL FAIRNESS DOCTRINE OBLIGATIONS OF BROADCAST LICENSEES

Report, 102 F.C.C. 2d 142 (1985)

I. INTRODUCTION

1. Before the Commission for consideration are the matters raised by the Notice of Inquiry (Notice) in the above-captioned proceeding in which the Commission solicited

comments on the statutory, constitutional, and policy implications underlying the fairness doctrine. 49 Fed. Reg. 20317 (1984).

3. The fairness doctrine imposes upon broadcasters a two-pronged obligation. Broadcast licensees are required to provide coverage of vitally important controversial issues of interest in the community served by the licensees and to provide a reasonable opportunity for the presentation of contrasting viewpoints on such issues.

4. Our past judgment that the fairness doctrine comports with the public interest was predicated upon three factors. First, in light of the limited availability of broadcast frequencies and the resultant need for government licensing, we concluded that the licensee is a public fiduciary, obligated to present diverse viewpoints representative of the community at large. We determined that the need to effectuate the right of the viewing and listening public to suitable access to the marketplace of ideas justifies restrictions on the rights of broadcasters. Second, we presumed that a governmentally imposed restriction on the content of programming is a viable mechanism—indeed the best mechanism—by which to vindicate this public interest. Third, we determined, as a factual matter, that the fairness doctrine, in operation, has the effect of enhancing the flow of diverse viewpoints to the public.

5. On the basis of the voluminous factual record compiled in this proceeding, our experience in administering the doctrine and our general expertise in broadcast regulation, we no longer believe that the fairness doctrine, as a matter of policy, serves the public interest. We believe that the interest of the public in viewpoint diversity is fully served by the multiplicity of voices in the marketplace today and that the intrusion by government into the content of programming occasioned by the enforcement of the doctrine unnecessarily restricts the journalistic freedom of broadcasters. Furthermore, we find that the fairness doctrine, in operation, actually inhibits the presentation of controversial issues of public importance to the detriment of the public and in degradation of the editorial prerogatives of broadcast journalists.

6. We believe that the same factors which demonstrate that the fairness doctrine is no longer appropriate as a matter of policy also suggest that the doctrine may no longer be permissible as a matter of constitutional law.

7. [T]he fairness doctrine has been a longstanding administrative policy and central tenet of broadcast regulation that Congress has chosen not to eliminate. Moreover, there are proposals pending before Congress to repeal the doctrine. As a consequence, we believe that it would be inappropriate at this time for us to either eliminate or significantly restrict the scope of the doctrine. Instead, we will afford Congress an opportunity to review the fairness doctrine in light of the evidence adduced in this proceeding.

II. THE CONSTITUTIONALITY OF THE FAIRNESS DOCTRINE IS SUSPECT

19. As demonstrated *infra*, the compelling evidence in this proceeding demonstrates that the fairness doctrine, in operation, inhibits the presentation of controversial issues of public importance. As a consequence, we believe that the fairness doctrine can no longer be justified on the grounds that it is necessary to promote the First Amendment rights of the viewing and listening public. Indeed, the chilling effect on the presentation of controversial issues of public importance resulting from our regulatory policies affirmatively disserves the interest of the public in obtaining access to diverse viewpoints. In addition, we believe that the fairness doctrine, as a regulation which directly affects the content of speech aired over broadcast frequencies, significantly impairs the journalistic freedom of broadcasters. As set forth in detail below, in light of the substantial increase in the number and types of information sources, we believe that the artificial mechanism

of interjecting the government into an affirmative role of overseeing the content of speech is unnecessary to vindicate the interest of the public in obtaining access to the marketplace of ideas.

20. While it is true that the limited availability of the electromagnetic spectrum may constitute a per se justification for certain types of government regulation, such as licensing, it does not follow that all other types of governmental regulation, particularly rules which affect the constitutionally sensitive area of content regulation, are similarly justified.

III. A NUMBER OF FACTORS JUSTIFY A REASSESSMENT OF THE FAIRNESS DOCTRINE

B. The Fairness Doctrine in Operation Lessens the Amount of Diverse Views Available to the Public

1. Broadcasters Perceive That the Fairness Doctrine Involves Significant Burdens

26. A licensee may be inhibited from presenting controversial issues of public importance by operation of the fairness doctrine even though the first prong of that doctrine affirmatively requires the licensee to broadcast such issues. The reason underlying this apparent paradox is that the two parts of the fairness doctrine differ markedly in the scope of the controversial issues that they encompass, the ease by which a licensee can meet the requirements embodied in the two prongs and the degree to which the Commission, in the past, has taken affirmative action to enforce compliance with them.

27. It is well-established that a licensee, in complying with the first prong of the fairness doctrine, has broad discretion in determining the specific controversial issues of public importance that it chooses to present. Indeed, in our 1974 Fairness Report, we stated that "we have no intention of becoming involved in the selection of issues to be discussed, nor do we expect a broadcaster to cover each and every important issue which may arise in his community." 48 F.C.C. 2d 1, 10. Rather, with respect to the affirmative obligation to cover controversial issues of public importance, "[a] presumption of compliance exists," The Handling of Public Issues under the Fairness Doctrine and the Public Interest Standards of the Communications Act, Memorandum Opinion and Order, 89 F.C.C. 2d 916, 925 (1982), and only "in rare instances, where a licensee has failed to give coverage to an issue found to be of critical importance to its particular community, would questions be raised as to whether a licensee had fulfilled its fairness obligations." Complaint of Brent Buell, et al. against Station WCBS-TV New York, New York, 97 F.C.C. 2d 55, 57 (1984)

28. The responsive programming obligation embodied in the second prong of the fairness doctrine arises whenever the licensee airs any controversial issue of public importance, even in situations where the issue broadcast is not "so critical or of such great public importance," 1974 Fairness Report, 48 F.C.C. 2d at 10, to trigger a requirement under the first part of the fairness doctrine. An overwhelming majority of the complaints we receive and virtually all our orders directing licensees to take corrective action to conform to the requirements of the fairness doctrine involve the second prong of that doctrine.

29. As a result of the asymmetry between its two components, the fairness doctrine in its operation encourages broadcasters to air only the minimal amount of controversial issue programming sufficient to comply with the first prong. By restricting the amount and type of controversial programming aired, a broadcaster minimizes the potentially substantial burdens associated with the second prong of the doctrine while remaining in compliance with the strict letter of its regulatory obligations. Therefore, despite the first

prong obligation, in net effect the fairness doctrine often discourages the presentation of controversial issue programming.[1]

37. Certain parties take issue with the contention that the fear of fairness doctrine litigation can have an inhibiting effect on the presentation of controversial issues of public importance. [T]hese parties argue that the Commission requests broadcasters to respond to only a small number of the complaints it receives annually and, as a consequence, most broadcasters do not in fact incur such costs. The evidence of record in this proceeding, however, reflects that broadcasters are convinced that these costs can in fact be a significant inhibiting factor in the presentation of controversial issues. Moreover, while it may be true that most broadcasters may not be confronted with actual fairness doctrine litigation, virtually all broadcasters do incur administrative and financial costs which result from presenting responsive programming and negotiating with complainants. Furthermore, in light of the fact that the costs involved in fairness doctrine cases which do proceed beyond the complaint stage can be prohibitively expensive, particularly to smaller stations, we believe that there is a substantial danger that many broadcasters are inhibited from providing controversial issues of public importance by operation of the fairness doctrine.

2. The Record Demonstrates that the Fairness Doctrine Causes Broadcasters to Restrict Their Coverage of Controversial Issues.

42. The record reflects that, in operation, the fairness doctrine — in stark contravention of its purpose — operates as a pervasive and significant impediment to the broadcasting of controversial issues of public importance. [T]he requirement that broadcasters provide balance in their overall coverage of controversial public issues in fact makes them more timid than they would otherwise be in airing programming that involves such issues.

44. [T]he record is replete with descriptions from broadcasters who have candidly recounted specific instances in which they decided not to air controversial matters of public importance because such broadcasts might trigger fairness doctrine obligations.

46. Equally or perhaps even more disturbing than the self-censorship of individual broadcasts is the fact that the avoidance of fairness doctrine burdens has precipitated specific "policies" on the part of broadcast stations which have the direct effect of diminishing, on a routine basis, the amount of controversial material presented to the public on broadcast stations. For example, the owner of a broadcast station and two newspapers regularly prints editorials in his newspapers but, inhibited by regulatory restrictions, is reluctant to repeat the same editorials on his radio station.

49. The most compelling evidence of the existence of a "chilling effect" with respect to ballot advertising is presented in the Comments of the Public Media Center (PMC), an organization actively involved in prosecuting complaints under the fairness doctrine. In its Comments, PMC vividly illustrates the manner in which a complainant can successfully pressure broadcasters into refusing to sell advertising on ballot issues. For example, PMC recounts the tactics of a pro-bottle bill coalition as follows: "Ads opposing the beverage deposit — sponsored by an industry front group ... hit the air in early August.

---

1. We do not believe that more stringent enforcement of the first prong would be an appropriate remedial response to the existence of a "chilling effect." [C]ontrary to the principles of the First Amendment, a stricter regulatory approach would increase the government's intrusion into the editorial decisionmaking process of broadcast journalists. It would enlarge the opportunity for governmental officials to abuse the doctrine for partisan political purposes. Were the chilling effect of the government sanction removed, the result might well be greater coverage of issues and thus more satisfaction of the policy behind the fairness doctrine's first prong.

Within ten days, the [pro-bottle bill coalition] sent a letter to all 500 California stations asking for a 2 to 1 ratio in free spot time. [The coalition] urged broadcasters to refuse to sell time and therefore avoid a fairness situation at all." PMC Comments at 1, n.1. The majority of the California stations followed the coalition's exhortation. Less than one-third of the stations contacted by the coalition sold ballot advertising to the industry group.

56. A number of parties characterize the statements made by broadcasters that document the existence of "chilling effect" as mere "self-serving" utterances to which the Commission should accord little probative value.

57. We disagree. Because the existence of a "chilling effect" is a subjective perception, the statements of broadcasters who are personally subject to its requirements on a daily basis are able to present some of the best evidence on whether or not the doctrine, in operation, inhibits the presentation of controversial issues of public importance.

58. In addition, we reject the proposition that the evidentiary value of these statements is undercut by their alleged "self-serving" nature. A statement by a broadcaster that he or she is inhibited from presenting controversial issues of public importance is, in a very real sense, an admission against interest.

60. Some parties assert that any inhibiting effect of the fairness doctrine is not attributable to the actual requirements of the doctrine itself but rather to the misperception of broadcasters as to their precise obligations under the doctrine. However, broadcasters are not lawyers. A broadcaster may be uncertain as to the precise boundaries of our detailed and complex regulatory scheme or may be uncertain as to whether he or she will be able to convince us, in the course of fairness doctrine litigation, that the station's overall programming complies with our regulatory requirements. As a consequence, a broadcaster, in order to avoid even the possibility of litigation, may be deterred from airing material even though the Commission, after hearing all the evidence, would have concluded that the program did not trigger fairness doctrine obligations.

68. In sum, we find that the evidence, derived from the record as a whole, leads us to conclude that the fairness doctrine chills speech. Because the fairness doctrine inhibits the presentation of controversial and important issues, in operation, it actually disserves the purpose it was designed to achieve. In our view, an elimination of the doctrine would result in greater discussion of controversial and important public issues on broadcast facilities.

C. The Administration of the Fairness Doctrine Operates to Inhibit the Expression of Unorthodox Opinions

69. While the fairness doctrine has the laudatory purpose of encouraging the presentation of diverse viewpoints, we fear that in operation it may have the paradoxical effect of actually inhibiting the expression of a wide spectrum of opinion on controversial issues of public importance. In this regard, our concern is that the administration of the fairness doctrine has unintentionally resulted in stifling viewpoints which may be unorthodox, unpopular or unestablished.

70. First, the requirement to present balanced programming under the second prong of the fairness doctrine is in itself a government regulation that inexorably favors orthodox viewpoints. As we stated in our 1974 Fairness Report, it is only "major" or "significant" opinions which are within the scope of the regulatory obligation to provide contrasting viewpoints. As a consequence, the fairness doctrine makes a regulatory distinction between two different categories of opinions: those which are "significant enough to warrant broadcast coverage [under the fairness doctrine]" and opinions which do not rise to

the level of a major viewpoint of sufficient public importance that triggers responsive programming obligations. 1974 Fairness Report, 48 F.C.C. 2d at 15. As a consequence, the fairness doctrine in operation inextricably involves the Commission in the dangerous task of evaluating the merits of particular viewpoints.

71. Second, [b]roadcasters who have been denied or threatened with a denial of the renewal of their licenses due to fairness doctrine violations have generally not been those which have provided only minimal coverage of controversial and important public issues. Indeed, some licensees that we have not renewed or threatened with non-renewal have presented controversial issue programming far in excess of that aired by the typical licensee. In a number of situations it was the licenses of broadcasters who aired opinions which many in society found to be abhorrent or extreme which were placed in jeopardy due to allegations of fairness doctrine violations.[2] [W]e are extremely concerned over the potential of the fairness doctrine, in operation, to interject the government, even unintentionally, into the position of favoring one type of opinion over another.

E. *The Fairness Doctrine Creates the Opportunity for Intimidation of Broadcasters by Governmental Officials*

74. [T]he broadcast industry is characterized by pervasive regulation. [T]his pervasive regulatory authority, including the intrusive power over program content occasioned by the fairness doctrine, provides governmental officials with the dangerous opportunity to abuse their position of power in an attempt either to stifle opinion with which they disagree or to coerce broadcasters to favor particular viewpoints which further partisan political objectives.

75. For example, a White House official during the Nixon Administration suggested to the President's Chief of Staff that the Administration respond to the alleged "unfair coverage" of the broadcast media by showing "favorites within the media," establishing "an official monitoring system through the FCC" and making "official complaints from the FCC." David Bazelon, FCC Regulation of the Telecommunications Press, 1975 Duke L.J. 213, 248 (1975) (quoting from Memorandum to H.R. Haldeman from Jeb S. Magruder). The attempts to coerce broadcast journalists, moreover, have not been restricted to specific partisan viewpoints or politicians of a particular political party. As described in the Notice, a government official in another Administration was reported to state that the "massive strategy [of the Administration] was to use the fairness doctrine to challenge and harass the right-wing broadcasters and hope that the challenges would be so costly to them that they would be inhibited, and decide that it was too expensive to continue."

G. *Need for the Fairness Doctrine in Light of the Increase in the Amount and Type of Information Sources in the Marketplace*

85. [I]n a proceeding revising its national multiple ownership rules, the Commission noted:

> The record in this proceeding supports the conclusion that the information market relevant to diversity includes not only TV and radio outlets, but cable, other

---

2. *See, e.g.*, Lamar Life Broadcasting Co., 38 F.C.C. 1143 (1965), *rev'd sub nom.* Off. of Comm. of United Church of Christ v. FCC, 359 F.2d 994 (D.C. Cir. 1966) (FCC refusal to grant a full term license to a station which espoused racially segregationist viewpoints); Trinity Methodist Church v. FRC, 62 F.2d 850, 851 (D.C. Cir. 1932) (Federal Radio Commission denied license renewal in a situation in which "the station had been used to attack a religious organization ... [and where] the broadcasts [aired by the licensee] were sensational rather than instructive....").

video media and numerous print media as well. [T]hese other media compete with broadcast outlets for the time that citizens devote to acquiring the information they desire. That is, cable, newspapers, magazines and periodicals are substitutes in the provision of such information.

Amendment of the Commission's Rules Relating to Multiple Ownership of AM, FM, and Television Broadcast Stations, Report and Order, 49 Fed. Reg. 31,877, 31,880 (1984). That the various media are in fact information substitutes in the marketplace of ideas is further reflected in our local cable and television, newspaper and broadcast, radio and television cross-ownership rules.

128. On the record before us, we cannot find that there are an insufficient number of voices in local markets to warrant continuation of the fairness doctrine. [I]ncreases in signal availability from traditional broadcasting facilities—television and radio—by themselves attenuate the need for a government imposed obligation to provide coverage to controversial issues. The existence of a plethora of alternate electronic voices, as well as numerous locally oriented print voices, augments this argument.

H. The Fairness Doctrine Cannot Be Justified on the Basis that It Protects Either Broadcasters or the Public from Undue Influence

133. Several commenters contend that retention of the fairness doctrine is useful as a "protection against outside pressures" by groups within the community which would otherwise exert undue influence on the editorial decisionmaking of broadcasters. Absent the fairness doctrine, these parties contend that broadcasters will simply "cave-in" to the pressures of advertisers, political action committees, or other powerful groups in the community who do not wish to have particular controversial viewpoints expressed.

134. We take issue with the assumption that intrusive governmental regulation is necessary to "protect" broadcasters from groups which allegedly attempt to influence their programming decisions. The First Amendment forbids governmental intervention in order to "protect" print journalists and we believe that broadcast journalists are in no greater need of "protection" than their counterparts in the print media. We think it telling, in this regard, that broadcasters themselves are not seeking this protection.

135. In addition, several commenters, in support of the fairness doctrine, argue that the doctrine serves to safeguard the public against unwarranted influence by what they perceive as biased broadcast reporting. Although the commenting parties differ among themselves in their perception of the bias to which they object, they believe that retention of the fairness doctrine is appropriate to prevent broadcasters from presenting biased or one-sided programming. The argument apparently is predicated upon the presumption that the requirement to provide "balanced" controversial issue programming is not merely a means to assure access to the marketplace of ideas but is itself a valid regulatory objective.

136. Balance may be a laudable editorial goal, but there are grave dangers when the government tries to strike that balance. First, as we have just noted above, determining what constitutes balanced programming is a very subjective endeavor. Second, as we have described, having the government attempt to achieve balance by means of enforcing the fairness doctrine results in a chilling effect to the ultimate detriment of the listening public. Third, there are the inherent dangers of an arm of the federal government influencing the content of programming in an attempt to guarantee balance. Further, the First Amendment does not require and may well not permit a neat apportionment, dictated by the government, in the marketplace of ideas, with equal space assigned to every viewpoint. The fact that a particular viewpoint may have the

capability to be extremely influential or offensive does not mean that it is accorded a lesser degree of First Amendment protection than the expression of less influential or more reasonable opinions.

VI. CONCLUSION

176. Notwithstanding these conclusions, we have decided not to eliminate the fairness doctrine at this time. The doctrine has been a longstanding administrative policy and a central tenet of broadcast regulation in which Congress has shown a strong although often ambivalent interest. Because of the intense Congressional interest in the fairness doctrine and the pendency of legislative proposals, we have determined that it would be inappropriate at this time to eliminate the fairness doctrine. [W]e will continue to administer and enforce the fairness doctrine obligations of broadcasters and [expect] that broadcast licensees will continue to satisfy these requirements.

Notes and Questions

1. Regulatory Capture. In ¶¶ 56–57, the Commission considers allegations that much of the evidence on which it relies—namely, testimony from broadcast licensees—is biased since broadcasters have an obvious interest in convincing the Commission that the fairness doctrine should be eliminated. As the Commission puts it, "A number of parties characterize the statements made by broadcasters ... as mere 'self-serving' utterances to which the Commission should accord little probative value." The Commission responds that these subjective perceptions are the best evidence available since the question of chill is itself a question about broadcasters' subjective perceptions of the fairness doctrine. Is this a convincing retort? Or does it suggest that the agency has perhaps grown too sympathetic to broadcasters' perspectives?

The phrase "regulatory capture" is used to describe a situation where the regulatory agency has fallen under the influence of a powerful interest group. The paradigmatic case of capture arises when an agency does the bidding of the very parties it was originally designed to regulate, and therefore stops regulating in the public's interest and starts, instead, regulating for the benefit of the regulated parties. This is not an uncommon allegation, especially because regulators necessarily do work closely with the parties they regulate— for example, in gathering information from them—and thus at least some form of a relationship is bound to develop. Moreover, regulators and regulatees in some sense rely on one another for their survival: should the industry disappear or become fully competitive, the regulators might find themselves without work;[3] should the regulators become too strict, the regulatees might find themselves losing considerable profits and freedoms. All this intuitively could cloud a regulator's judgment—but is that what happened in the above proceeding? If so, why didn't the Commission fully abandon the doctrine? If not, why didn't the Commission more explicitly discount the testimony referred to in ¶ 56?

---

3. Another issue that might lead to some degree of capture: when regulatory officials leave government and return to the private sector, they often choose to stay involved with the very industry they once regulated. While there are limitations on what those former regulators can do—for example, there is typically a period during which they are not allowed to appear before their former agency on behalf of private clients—regulators might nevertheless foresee this shift in their own interests and thus have some tendency to treat the regulatee/possible future employer better than a regulator otherwise would.

2. Different Rules for Different Markets. The 1985 report seems to lump together all broadcasters and all markets. But wouldn't the case for retention be stronger in some markets than in others? For instance, isn't the case for retaining the fairness doctrine stronger for VHF television than for AM or FM radio? What is the significance of the fact that the FCC did not draw such a distinction? Would it have been wiser to retain the fairness doctrine for certain markets? If so, how should such markets be identified and defined?

3. Powerful Media. Is the controversy over the fairness doctrine a debate about broadcasting or about speech? Do proponents of the fairness doctrine believe that there is something unusual about encoded electromagnetic radiation (would they apply the fairness doctrine to citizens band radio?), or do they instead believe that the government ought to ensure the fairness of very powerful media? Would proponents have applied the fairness doctrine to book publishing in the 16th century and to weekly newspapers in the 18th?

4. Chill. The main concern raised in all of these materials is that the fairness doctrine might chill speech, and the main advantage of the fairness doctrine is that it might lead to more balanced presentations of controversial issues. With respect to the chill, could this concern have been mitigated by the adoption of a new, more detailed fairness doctrine that gave licensees clear touchstones as to which broadcasts would (and would not) trigger fairness doctrine obligations? With respect to the desire for balanced coverage, given the increase in broadcast outlets today, is that goal now so well accomplished through competition that the doctrine loses its allure?

---

§ 15.A.2.b. *Syracuse Peace Council*

An issue edited out of the excerpt of the Commission's 1985 report is whether the Communications Act required the FCC to enforce the fairness doctrine. In 1986, the D.C. Circuit held that Congress had not codified the doctrine, finding it to be "an administrative construction, not a binding statutory directive." Telecommunications Research & Action Center v. FCC, 801 F.2d 501, 517 (D.C. Cir. 1986), *cert. denied*, 482 U.S. 919 (1987).

That step squarely raised the issue of the fairness doctrine's status in light of the FCC's peculiar decision that the doctrine was inconsistent with the public interest but the Commission would administer and enforce it anyway. In 1987, the D.C. Circuit remanded a case to the FCC for the Commission either to abandon the fairness doctrine as against the public interest, or to defend the doctrine's constitutionality, and thus retain and enforce it. Meredith Corp. v. FCC, 809 F.2d 863 (D.C. Cir. 1987). Backed into a corner by the D.C. Circuit and its own 1985 report, the FCC took the next step and repealed the fairness doctrine in Complaint of Syracuse Peace Council against Television Station WTVH Syracuse, New York, Memorandum Opinion and Order, 2 FCC Rcd. 5043 (1987) (*Syracuse Peace Council*). In this Order, the Commission first "evaluate[d] the constitutionality of the fairness doctrine under the standard enunciated in *Red Lion* and its progeny," *id.* ¶ 36, concluding that

> the fairness doctrine in operation disserves both the public's right to diverse sources of information and the broadcaster's interest in free expression. Its chilling effect thwarts its intended purpose, and it results in excessive and unnecessary government intervention into the editorial processes of broadcast journalists. We hold, therefore, that under the constitutional standard established by *Red*

Lion and its progeny, the fairness doctrine contravenes the First Amendment and its enforcement is no longer in the public interest.

Id. ¶ 61. The order then went on to articulate its preferred constitutional approach, stating in part:

> 86. While the objective underlying the fairness doctrine is that of the First Amendment itself—the promotion of debate on important controversial issues—the means employed to achieve this objective, government coercion, is the very one which the First Amendment is designed to prevent. [T]he fairness doctrine *uses* government intervention in order to foster diversity of viewpoints, while the scheme established by the framers of our Constitution *forbids* government intervention for fear that it will stifle robust debate. In this sense, the underlying rationale of the fairness doctrine turns the First Amendment on its head.
>
> 89. The type of speech regulated by the fairness doctrine involves opinions on controversial issues of public importance. This type of expression is "precisely that ... which the Framers of the Bill of Rights were most anxious to protect—speech that is 'indispensable to the discovery and spread of political truth'...." FCC v. League of Women Voters, 468 U.S. 364, 383 (1984), quoting Whitney v. California, 274 U.S. 357, 375 (1927) (Brandeis, J., concurring). Yet, instead of safeguarding this type of speech from regulatory intervention, the doctrine anomalously singles it out for governmental scrutiny.
>
> 94. Finally, we believe that under the First Amendment, the right of viewers and listeners to receive diverse viewpoints is achieved by guaranteeing them the right to receive speech unencumbered by government intervention. The *Red Lion* decision, however, apparently views the notion that broadcasters should come within the free press and free speech protections of the First Amendment as antagonistic to the interest of the public in obtaining access to the marketplace of ideas. As a result, it is squarely at odds with the general philosophy underlying the First Amendment, *i.e.*, that the individual's interest in free expression and the societal interest in access to viewpoint diversity are both furthered by proscribing governmental regulation of speech. The special broadcast standard applied by the Court in *Red Lion*, which sanctions restrictions on speakers in order to promote the interest of the viewers and listeners, contradicts this fundamental constitutional principle.
>
> 97. We believe that the role of the electronic press in our society is the same as that of the printed press. Both are sources of information and viewpoint. Accordingly, the reasons for proscribing government intrusion into the editorial discretion of print journalists provide the same basis for proscribing such interference into the editorial discretion of broadcast journalists. The First Amendment was adopted to protect the people *not from journalists, but from government.* It gives the people the right to receive ideas that are unfettered by government interference. We fail to see how that right changes when individuals choose to receive ideas from the electronic media instead of the print media. There is no doubt that the electronic media is powerful and that broadcasters can abuse their freedom of speech. But the framers of the Constitution believed that the potential for abuse of private freedoms posed far less a threat to democracy than the potential for abuse by a government given the power to control the press. We concur. We therefore believe that full First Amendment protections against content regulation should apply equally to the electronic and the printed press.

Notes and Questions

1. Judicial Review. The D.C. Circuit affirmed the FCC's repeal of the fairness doctrine in its *Syracuse Peace Council* order. The court did so without reaching the constitutional grounds, instead finding the public interest determination to be sufficient. Syracuse Peace Council v. FCC, 867 F.2d 654 (D.C. Cir. 1989), *cert. denied*, 493 U.S. 1019 (1990). In a separate opinion, Chief Judge Wald concurred in the elimination of the second prong of the fairness doctrine, but dissented from the decision to eliminate the first prong. Finding this portion of the decision both unsupported by the record and procedurally deficient (no notice was given prior to the prong's elimination, so there was no opportunity for public comment), Chief Judge Wald categorized the action as "deregulation running riot." *Id.* at 673.

2. Principle or Pragmatism? Does the FCC mean to oppose the fairness doctrine as a matter of principle or as a matter of pragmatic regulatory strategy? Suppose that, during the 21st century, an entirely new medium of communication arises (say, communication through ground waves); that initially very few firms are willing to invest the large sums of money required for this strange and untested technology; and that the medium becomes an extraordinary success with the public. If Congress sought to impose a fairness doctrine on the few owners of this new medium of communication, which, if any, of the arguments in the 1985 report or the *Syracuse Peace Council* order would be relevant to that issue?

3. Other Public Trustee Obligations. Is it possible to agree with the FCC's conclusions in the 1985 report and its order in *Syracuse Peace Council* and still believe that broadcast licensees should be regulated in some other matters as "public trustees"? If so, on what basis?

4. Empirical Evidence. Recall that in *Red Lion* the Court indicated a willingness to reconsider its approval of the challenged doctrines "if experience with the administration of those doctrines indicates that they have the net effect of reducing rather than enhancing the volume and quality of coverage."[4] In its 1985 report, the FCC had anecdotal support for its assertion that the fairness doctrine produced a reduction in coverage of controversial subjects, but it lacked the kind of comparative evidence that would be ideal — for instance, a showing that when broadcasters are not subject to the fairness doctrine they carry more news programming. The absence of such comparative data is not surprising: the fairness doctrine had been in effect for more than forty years, so there was no period free of the fairness doctrine that could be used for purposes of comparison.

The FCC's repeal of the fairness doctrine did afford such an opportunity, however, as researchers could compare pre- and post-1987 broadcasting. Thomas Hazlett and David Sosa undertook just such a study. They examined data on the U.S. radio market from 1975 to 1995 and found that elimination of the fairness doctrine was followed by sig-

---

4. The Supreme Court quoted this language in making the point more forcefully in FCC v. League of Women Voters of California, 468 U.S. 364 (1984). In that case the Court declined an invitation to reconsider the constitutionality of the fairness doctrine but stated that, "[a]s we recognized in *Red Lion*, were it to be shown by the Commission that the fairness doctrine '[has] the net effect of reducing rather than enhancing' speech, we would then be forced to reconsider the constitutional basis of our decision in that case." *Id.* at 379 n.12 (quoting *Red Lion*, 395 U.S. at 393).

nificant changes in radio station formats—including, notably, an increase in informational programming. Their key chart for AM radio is reproduced below. (They found similar trends for both AM and FM radio.) It is of course not clear whether the legal change

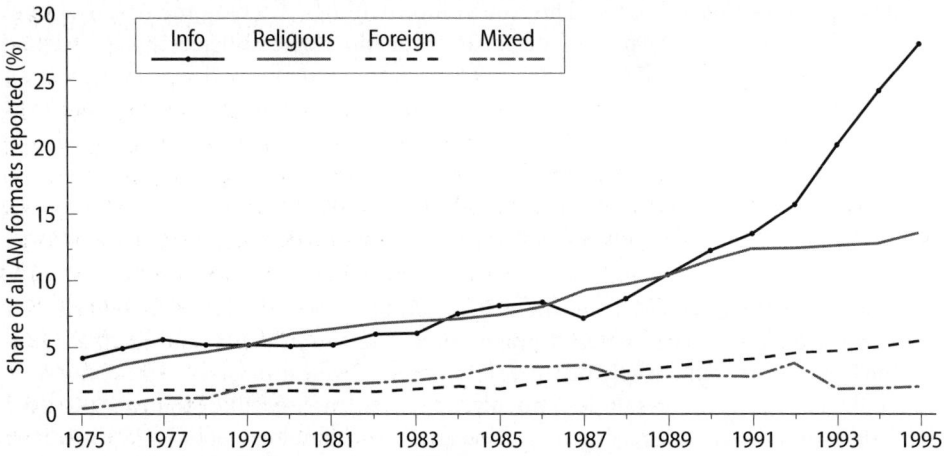

caused the content change; as the authors put it, "[c]orrelation is not causality, but the correlation is very strong." Thomas W. Hazlett & David W. Sosa, Was the Fairness Doctrine a "Chilling Effect"? Evidence from the Postderegulation Radio Market, 26 J. Legal Stud. 279, 299 (1997).

5. Congress and the President. In 1987, just after the FCC repealed the fairness doctrine, a statute passed both houses of Congress that would have reinstated the doctrine by congressional mandate. President Reagan refused to sign the measure, explaining in a statement to the press that, in his view, the fairness doctrine was unconstitutional. Veto of the Fairness in Broadcasting Act of 1987, 23 Weekly Comp. Pres. Doc. 715 (June 19, 1987) (vetoing S. 742-100 (1987), reprinted in 133 Cong. Rec. H4160 (daily ed. June 3, 1987)). Given this pattern of events, should the FCC have reinstated the doctrine of its own accord, following Congress and thus implicitly out-voting Reagan? And what of Reagan's explanation; did he have the authority to deem the doctrine unconstitutional given that the Court had already ruled in *Red Lion* that this sort of regulation of broadcasting was constitutional?

§ 15.A.3. The Personal Attack and Political Editorial Rules

The FCC's decision in *Syracuse Peace Council* repealed the fairness doctrine. The focus of *Red Lion*, however, was not the fairness doctrine generally but instead the specific rules mandating that broadcasters provide airtime for responses to any "personal attacks" or "political editorials" that are broadcast. Attempts to repeal those rules have taken their own tortured path, which is significant both in its own right and as an example of the tangled relationships among the Commission, the courts, and private parties.

In response to a 1980 petition by the National Association of Broadcasters (NAB) requesting repeal of the personal attack and political editorial rules, the FCC in 1983 proposed eliminating or substantially modifying those rules, noting its doubts about their consistency with First Amendment objectives. Nothing happened in direct response to that petition, and after the FCC issued *Syracuse Peace Council*, the NAB, the Radio-Television News Directors Association (RTNDA), and other interested groups filed a "petition for expedited rulemaking" to eliminate the personal attack and political editorial rules and clarify *Syracuse Peace Council*'s effect on those rules. After repeated unsuccessful attempts (including another petition in 1990) to prod the FCC to take some sort of action, in 1996 the RTNDA filed a petition in the D.C. Circuit for a writ of mandamus to order the FCC to act on the RTNDA's petition to eliminate the rules. On February 7, 1997, the court ordered that "the petition be denied without prejudice to its renewal should the Federal Communications Commission fail to make significant progress, within the next six months, toward the possible repeal or modification of the personal attack and political editorial rules." Radio-Television News Directors Ass'n, 1997 WL 150084 (D.C. Cir. 1997). Six months and a day later, on August 8, 1997, the Commission announced that a majority of the Commission could not agree on any resolution, as two commissioners voted to repeal the rules, two voted to keep them and commence a full inquiry into their continued value, and the final Commission seat was vacant. Commission Proceeding Regarding the Personal Attack and Political Editorial Rules, Public Notice, 12 FCC Rcd. 11,956 (1997). Shortly thereafter, four new commissioners were confirmed by the Senate, and in May 1998 the Commission voted anew, but again the Commission was deadlocked. This time, there were no open seats, but William Kennard (who had participated in the challenge to the personal attack and political editorial rules when he represented the NAB) recused himself and the remaining four split two in favor of repeal and two in favor of retention. Two weeks later, the D.C. Circuit ordered the FCC to submit the 2–2 vote as a final agency action, along with a statement of reasons by the Commissioners who wanted to keep the rule.

The D.C. Circuit issued an opinion but did not resolve the underlying debate. In Radio-Television News Directors Ass'n v. FCC, 184 F.3d 872 (D.C. Cir. 1999), the D.C. Circuit declined to review the rules on their merits and instead remanded the matter to the FCC for further consideration. The court rejected the argument (put forward by the RTNDA and NAB, as well as Commissioners Powell and Furchtgott-Roth in a joint dissenting statement) that the repeal of the fairness doctrine necessarily entailed the repeal of the personal attack and political editorial rules. The court stated that it could be theoretically consistent for the agency to repeal the broader fairness doctrine while leaving the more specific rules in place. The court went on to conclude, however, that the joint statement of the Commissioners who favored the rule (Ness and Tristani) failed to present an adequate basis for concluding that these rules were in the public interest and thus was "insufficient to permit judicial review." *Id.* at 885. The reasoning on which Ness and Tristani relied (that the "'scarcity of broadcast frequencies provides a rationale for imposing public interest obligations on broadcasters,'" *id.* at 883), after all, was the very same reasoning that the FCC had rejected when it repealed the fairness doctrine. Having found that the FCC (through the joint statement of Commissioners Ness and Tristani) had not provided an adequate justification for keeping the personal attack and political editorial rules, the court ordered the FCC "to provide a more detailed defense — and possibly modifications as well — sufficient to permit meaningful judicial review." *Id.* at 888.

The D.C. Circuit ended its 1999 opinion by stating that "the FCC need act expeditiously," but months passed with no FCC action. So, in July 2000, the petitioners filed yet another motion for a writ of mandamus. In September 2000, Chairman Kennard decided to reverse his prior decision to recuse and thus began to participate in the proceeding. Shortly thereafter, on October 4, 2000, the Commission voted 3–2 (with Kennard joining Ness and Tristani, and Powell and Furchtgott-Roth dissenting) to suspend the personal attack and political editorial rules for 60 days—which, the Commission noted, would correspond with the final month of the 2000 election season. The reason given for this suspension was to see what happened on the airwaves and thus "to enable us to obtain a better record on which to review the rules." Repeal or Modification of the Personal Attack and Political Editorial Rules, Order and Request to Update Record, 15 FCC Rcd. 19,973 ¶ 1 (2000).

Notably, in this order suspending the personal attack and political editorial rules, the FCC repudiated "the dicta in *Syracuse Peace Council* regarding the appropriate level of First Amendment scrutiny" for broadcast. *Id.* ¶ 17. The Commission stated:

> The fundamental error of the Commission's decision in *Syracuse Peace Council* was its confusion of the rationale underlying the fairness doctrine with the basis for public interest regulation of the broadcast spectrum. The fairness doctrine originated at a time when there were only three major television networks, and the proliferation of television stations and the development of cable television reasonably led the Commission to reevaluate the need for the fairness doctrine. The standard of *Red Lion*, however, was not based on the absolute number of media outlets, but on the fact that the spectrum is a public resource and "there are substantially more individuals who want to broadcast than there are frequencies to allocate." [*Red Lion*,] 395 U.S. at 388. As both the U.S. Supreme Court and the D.C. Circuit have explained, "[a] licensed broadcaster is 'granted the free and exclusive use of a valuable part of the public domain; when he accepts that franchise it is burdened by enforceable public obligations.'" CBS v. FCC, 453 U.S. 367, 395 (1981) (quoting Office of Communication of the United Church of Christ v. FCC, 359 F.2d 994, 1003 (D.C. Cir. 1966)). [T]he long-standing basis for the regulation of broadcasting is that "the radio spectrum simply is not large enough to accommodate everybody." NBC v. FCC, 319 U.S. 190, 213 (1943). Under our Nation's system for allocating spectrum, some are granted the "exclusive use" of a portion of this "public domain," even though others would use it if they could. CBS v. FCC, 453 U.S. at 395. That is why "it is idle to posit an unabridgeable First Amendment right to broadcast comparable to the right of every individual to speak, write or publish." *Red Lion*, 395 U.S. at 388.

15 FCC Rcd. 19,973 ¶ 18.

A few days later, the D.C. Circuit rebuffed the FCC's planned suspension and ordered instead that the rules be repealed. The court did not reach the question of whether the rules were consistent with the First Amendment, and it stated that the FCC could still institute a new rulemaking proceeding "to determine whether, consistent with constitutional constraints, the public interest requires the public attack and political editorial rules." Radio-Television News Directors Ass'n v. FCC, 229 F.3d 269, 272 (D.C. Cir. 2000). The D.C. Circuit instead based its decision on the FCC's response (or lack thereof) to the court's orders. The court emphasized that "the Commission still has not provided adequate justification for the rules, and in its [October 4] Order provides no assurance that it will do so. Incredibly, the Order reinstates the rules before the Commission will have received any of the updated information that the Commission states it requires in order to evaluate the rules. [I]t is folly to suppose that the 60-day suspension and call to update the record cures anything." On this basis, the court issued a writ of mandamus directing the Commission to immediately repeal the personal attack and political editorial rules. *Id.* at 271–72.

§ 15.A.4. Political Broadcasting[5]

In 1970, the Commission addressed the applicability of fairness rules to situations in which supporters of political candidate A purchased broadcast air time that they used to support candidate A, or to criticize candidate B. The Commission concluded that "the fairness doctrine is plainly applicable in [those] circumstances," and that the broadcaster would be required to sell time to supporters of candidate B comparable to that bought on behalf of candidate A. Request by Nicholas Zapple, Communications Counsel, Committee on Commerce for Interpretative Ruling Concerning Section 315 Fairness Doctrine, 23 F.C.C. 2d 707, 707 (1970). This became known as the Zapple doctrine.

In 2012, supporters of a Wisconsin gubernatorial candidate filed a complaint alleging a violation of the Zapple doctrine. The Commission delegates responses to such complaints to the chief of its Media Bureau. In 2014, the chief responded, stating in relevant part that "we have no basis to enforce the Zapple doctrine. The doctrine was based on an interpretation of the fairness doctrine, which the Commission abrogated in *Syracuse Peace Council*. Given the fact that the Zapple doctrine was based on an interpretation of the fairness doctrine, which has no current legal effect, we conclude that the Zapple doctrine similarly has no current legal effect." WISN(AM), Milwaukee, WI, Letter (Media Bureau, May 8, 2014), *available at* http://transition.fcc.gov/Daily_Releases/Daily_Business/2014/db0508/DA-14-621A1.pdf.

The rejection of the Zapple doctrine seems straightforward: in creating the doctrine, the Commission relied on the defunct fairness doctrine and also invoked the now-repealed personal attack and political editorial rules. But the rejection of the Zapple doctrine sits somewhat uneasily alongside existing political broadcasting rules, and in particular § 315 of the Communications Act, which the Commission's 1970 Zapple ruling also invoked. Section 315 contains the so-called "equal time" rule, which provides that if a broadcaster allows "a legally qualified candidate for any public office" (city, state or federal) to gain air time, the station must allow the candidate's opponent(s) a like opportunity. Thus, if candidate A is given free broadcast time, A's opponent(s) must be given free broadcast time; and if A bought air time, A's opponent(s) must be allowed to buy an equal amount at the same rate.

The equal time rule seems inconsistent with the theory of free speech on which *Tornillo* rests and the reasoning that led to the rejection of the fairness doctrine. But the Commission has vigorously enforced it, and courts have concluded that *Red Lion* forecloses any First Amendment challenges to it. *See* Branch v. FCC, 824 F.2d 37, 49–50 (D.C. Cir. 1987). This underscores the fact that although the FCC disavowed the fairness doctrine, it has never completely dropped its reliance on the general theory of broadcasting and the First Amendment espoused in *Red Lion*—as the above excerpt from *Repeal or Modification of the Personal Attack and Political Editorial Rules* reminds us. The Commission's insistence that broadcast licensees should be deemed to surrender editorial discretion in return for access to valuable spectrum is nowhere more evident today than in the Commission's control over political broadcasting.

The equal time rule has been part of broadcast regulation from regulation's earliest days, originally appearing as § 18 of the 1927 Radio Act. The legislators who wrote the Radio Act did not want the new medium to be turned against them. *See* Hugh Carter Donahue, The Battle to Control Broadcast News 9–18 (1989); David H. Ostroff, Equal Time: Ori-

---

5. Scattered paragraphs in this section are based on materials in the "Political Broadcasting" section of Thomas G. Krattenmaker & Lucas A. Powe, Jr., Regulating Broadcast Programming 66–69 (1994).

gins of Section 18 of the Radio Act of 1927, 24 J. Broad. 367 (1980). The Commission found enforcement of § 315 rather simple until it encountered a twist in 1959. In February of that year, two Chicago stations included in their evening newscast footage of Mayor Richard Daley greeting the president of Argentina at Midway Airport during a snowstorm. Mayor Daley was at that time running for reelection. One of his opponents, Lar "America First" Daly, demanded equal free air time because of Mayor Daley's "use" of the two stations. The stations refused. They reasoned that Mayor Daley's greeting was news, while Lar Daly, a perennial candidate who went about in public in an "Uncle Sam" costume, was a joke. The FCC thought differently. It ordered the stations to grant Daly equal time. Petitions of Columbia Broadcasting System, Inc., and National Broadcasting Co. for Reconsideration and Motions for Declaratory Rulings or Orders Relating to the Applicability of Section 315 of the Communications Act of 1934, as amended, to Newscasts by Broadcast Licensees, Interpretive Opinion, 26 F.C.C. 715 (1959).

Congress—perhaps acting in its members' self-interest—quickly overruled the agency's interpretation. Within three months, § 315 was amended to exempt both on-the-spot coverage of bona fide news events and bona fide newscasts from the equal-time constraints. Donahue, *supra*, at 55–66. That, of course, raised a new question: what is a bona fide news program? Answering that question with respect to any given program requires a case-by-case analysis, which again the FCC delegates to the chief of its Media Bureau. As the following order reveals, however, the FCC has developed (or thinks it has developed) a set of criteria that provides meaningful guidance as to what constitutes a bona fide news program.

REQUEST OF ABC, INC. FOR DECLARATORY RULING
Staff Ruling, 15 FCC Rcd. 1355 (1999)

1. The Commission has before it a request for declaratory ruling filed by ABC, Inc. (ABC) on behalf of Buena Vista Television, Inc. (Buena Vista"), the producer of the program "Politically Incorrect with Bill Maher" ("Politically Incorrect"). ABC seeks a ruling that "Politically Incorrect" is exempt from the "equal opportunities" provision of Section 315(a) of the Communications Act of 1934, as amended (the "Act"). 47 U.S.C. § 315(a).

I. FACTUAL BACKGROUND

3. ABC explains that "Politically Incorrect" is hosted by "satirist and humorist" Bill Maher, who begins each program with a "monologue" on current news-related issues. He then introduces a panel of four persons from various fields including the media, academia, politics, and popular culture. Mr. Maher poses an issue from his monologue and asks for his guests' opinions. Occasionally, the program will focus on a single issue; more typically it will involve discussion of several current issues of the day. ABC contends that the satirical aspect of Mr. Maher's monologue should not be an impediment to an exemption because satire has long been recognized as an important and serious part of the American political landscape.[6]

4. ABC argues that "Politically Incorrect" fully satisfies the Commission's established criteria for exempt *bona fide* news interview programs in that: (1) it has been a regularly scheduled half-hour program, broadcast by the ABC television network each weekday evening since January 6, 1997; (2) the producer, Buena Vista, controls all aspects of the

---

6. ABC notes that the U.S. Supreme Court has recognized satire as constitutionally protected, citing Hustler Magazine v. Falwell, 485 U.S. 46, 51 (1988) (*Falwell*), in which a cartoon satirizing the Rev. Jerry Falwell was deemed fully protected by the First Amendment. The Court also stated its view that satirical cartoons had played an important role in political debate throughout our history.

program, ensuring that decisions as to format, content, and participants are based on *bona fide* journalistic judgment and not motivated by partisan purposes; (3) Buena Vista selects the guests from a variety of fields based on the guests' "involvement in newsworthy events," "competence to discuss current issues," and "represent[ation] [of] a cross-section of ideologies to stimulate a lively exchange of views";[7] (4) prior to the taping of each show, "the producers meet with the guests to review the pre-selected issues and their positions on the issues" and intervene during commercial breaks as they deem necessary to give direction to the participants; and (5) Mr. Maher exercises control over discussions by preventing speechmaking and steering straying comments back to the main topics.

II. DISCUSSION

5. Section 315(a) of the Act provides that if a broadcaster permits a legally qualified candidate for public office to "use" a broadcast station, it must afford equal opportunities to all legally qualified opponents for the same office.[8] In 1959, Congress amended Section 315 so that appearances by legally qualified candidates on the following types of news programs would be exempt from equal opportunities requirements:

1) *bona fide* newscast,

2) *bona fide* news interview,

3) *bona fide* news documentary (if the appearance of the candidate is incidental to the presentation of the subject or subjects covered by the news documentary), or

4) on-the-spot coverage of *bona fide* news events (including but not limited to political conventions and activities incidental thereto).

47 U.S.C. §315(a)(1–4).

6. Congress's fundamental purpose in enacting these exemptions was to encourage increased news coverage of political campaigns and to give broadcasters the discretion to exercise their good faith news judgment in deciding which candidates to cover and in what formats. The legislative history emphasizes the congressional intention:

> [T]o enable what probably has become the most important medium of political information to give the news concerning political races to the greatest number of citizens, and to make it possible to cover the political news to the fullest degree.

105 Cong. Rec. 14,451 (1959) (Holland); *see also* Chisholm v. FCC, 538 F.2d 349 (1976). Neither the explicit terms of the statute nor the legislative history of the news exemption amendments, however, reveal the specific format characteristics envisioned by Congress for any of the exemptions. Indeed, the legislative history demonstrates that Congress chose to leave to the Commission the task of interpreting which kinds of programming properly fit the scope of each exemption. In affirming the Commission's 1975 decision that candidate debates should be exempt under Section 315(a)(4) ("on-the-spot coverage of *bona fide* news events"), the *Chisholm* court observed:

> In creating a broad exemption to the equal time requirements in order to facilitate broadcast coverage of political news, Congress knowingly faced risks of political favoritism by broadcasters, and opted in favor of broader coverage and

---

7. ABC states that from the political realm the program often includes elected officials and persons aspiring to be elected.

8. In general, a use is any "positive" identified or identifiable appearance of a legally qualified candidate. This excludes disparaging depictions by opponents or third-party adversaries. *See* Report and Order, 7 FCC Rcd. 678, 684 (1991).

increased broadcaster discretion. Rather than enumerate specific exempt and non-exempt "uses," Congress opted in favor of legislative generality, preferring to assign that task to the Commission.

Chisholm, 538 F.2d at 366. Although Congress did not specifically detail exempt formats, nor define exactly what it meant by "news,"[9] the legislative history indicates that, in general, the common characteristic envisioned of each exemption is "*bona fide* news value." Thus, Congress qualified each exemption with the term "*bona fide*" to emphasize that, to be exempt from the equal opportunities requirement, news programming should be genuinely newsworthy and not designed for the partisan purpose of advancing or harming any particular candidate. The legislative history also shows that Congress expected *bona fide* news interview programs to be regularly scheduled and under broadcaster control.

7. Thus, in deciding whether a program qualifies as a "*bona fide* news interview" under Section 315(a)(2), a three-prong test evolved:

(1) whether the program is regularly scheduled;

(2) whether the broadcaster or an independent producer controls the program;[10] and

(3) whether the broadcaster's or independent producer's decisions on format, content and participants are based on newsworthiness rather than on an intention to advance or harm an individual's candidacy.

8. The Commission remained conservative in its analysis of news interview exemption requests under this test for over twenty-five years, essentially limiting the news interview exemption to what it viewed as more traditional question and answer formats like those cited in the legislative history ("Meet the Press," "Face the Nation" and "Youth Wants to Know"). In 1984, however, the Commission reversed an earlier denial of a news interview exemption to the "Donahue" program. Multimedia Entertainment, Inc., 56 Rad. Reg. (P & F) 143, 146 (1984) (*Donahue*). The *Donahue* decision signaled the Commission's willingness to recognize varying less conventional interview formats as being consistent with Congress' overriding intent to increase news coverage of the political campaign process.[11]

9. In *Donahue*, with respect to the second prong of the test, whether sufficient control over the program is present, the Commission concluded that:

[I]t would be unsound to rule that a program involving a unique or innovative approach to interviewing its guests somehow lacks sufficient licensee control evident in more traditional news interview programs like "Meet the Press" or "Face

---

9. While the legislative history lacks any specific discussion of the format of exempt news interviews, there is reference to three programs, "Meet the Press," "Face the Nation" and "Youth Wants To Know" as the kind of interview programming it envisioned.

10. In 1992, the Commission expanded the test to allow exemptions to independently-produced news interview programs. In doing so, the Commission emphasized that a licensee who chooses to carry such programming must still assure itself that the format is nonpartisan and under sufficient producer control to assure against abuse. Request for Declaratory Ruling on Independently Produced News Interviews, Independently Produced News Interview Programs, 7 FCC Rcd. 4681 (1992), *aff'd sub nom.* TRAC v. FCC, 26 F.3d 185 (D.C. Cir. 1994).

11. *Donahue* also discussed the format of "Youth Wants To Know," one of the three programs mentioned in the legislative history and concluded that it too was not a traditional question and answer format. Rather, the Commission stated that it was "an innovative program of its time involving questions posed by students, not professional journalists ... To argue that such a format guaranteed adherence to a licensee's journalistic judgment any more than the 'Donahue' format cannot be justified and appears to be inconsistent with the legislative history." 56 Rad. Reg. 2d (P & F) at 146.

the Nation" when the licensee has implemented reasonable techniques to ensure control. To do so would discourage programming innovation by sending a signal to broadcasters that to be exempt an interview program should adhere only to the format of certain programs mentioned by Congress over twenty-five years ago.

56 Rad. Reg. 2d (P & F) 146.

As to the third prong, good faith news judgment, the Commission reasoned that it should not second-guess broadcasters about the relative newsworthiness of the interviewees or the topics of discussion. The Commission concluded that it should confine its analysis to whether the broadcaster acted reasonably and in good faith. *Donahue* stressed that "reasonable persons may differ" about the newsworthiness of particular topics or guests, and that absent bad faith or unreasonableness, the Commission should follow Congress in its willingness to take risks with the exemptions and thus defer substantially to broadcasters' good faith journalistic judgment.[12]

10. We believe that ABC has satisfied each prong of the test. First, "Politically Incorrect" has been regularly scheduled for almost two years, clearly meeting this requirement. Second, as to control, ABC has identified various reasonable mechanisms Buena Vista has implemented for exercising control throughout the production of "Politically Incorrect" and those structural safeguards appear reasonably designed to assure that good faith news judgment can be adequately protected. Third, ABC represents that Buena Vista's decisions about format, content and selection of participants are based on newsworthiness and not motivated by any partisan purpose. The presence of satire as an element of "Politically Incorrect" should not prevent the program from being considered *bona fide* in terms of good faith news judgment absent an indication that the satire is utilized to advance or harm any particular candidate for public office. The Supreme Court in the *Falwell* decision noted the importance of satire in political speech, stating that, "Despite their sometimes caustic nature, from the early cartoon portraying George Washington as an ass down to the present day, graphic depictions and satirical cartoons have played a prominent role in public and political debate." 485 U.S. 46, 54. Satire in the form of a broadcast monologue about news of the day or during discussion of such issues does not appear less important in the realm of political debate than political cartoons.

III. CONCLUSION

11. Congress knowingly gave the Commission substantial discretion to interpret the news exemptions to the equal opportunities requirement and decided that the risk of some broadcasters abusing the exemption for partisan purposes was outweighed by the benefit to the public inherent in increased news coverage of political campaigns. In attempting to fulfill the letter and the spirit of the law, the Commission's decisions in this area have

---

12. Since *Donahue* the Commission has continued to grant exemptions to news interview programs similar to the Donahue program or with other unique and innovative format elements. *See, e.g.*, Pacifica Radio Town Hall Meetings, 9 FCC Rcd. 2817 (Mass Media Bureau (MMB) 1994); Face to Face, 9 FCC Rcd. 2813 (1994); Larry King, 56 Rad. Reg. 2d (P & F) 956 (MMB 1984). The Commission has also determined that different areas of news coverage are eligible for exemption under 315(a). In 1988, the Mass Media Bureau granted the "Entertainment Tonight" program an exemption (under 315(a)(1), bona fide newscast), stating that no controlling distinction can be made between various kinds of "news" such as entertainment, business, sports, and religion. The Bureau said that "a determination [of whether a program is *bona fide*] should not be predicated on the subject matter reported on, but rather should be judged on a basis of whether the program reports news of some area of current events." Paramount Communications, Inc., 3 FCC Rcd. 245 (MMB 1988).

continued to expand the kinds of programming eligible for exemption in recognition of change and innovation in broadcast production. Granting an exemption to "Politically Incorrect" is consistent with these principles.

Notes and Questions

1. **Less Conventional Interview Formats.** The declaratory ruling notes that in 1984 the Commission signaled a willingness to expand its definition of bona fide news interview programs to include "less conventional interview formats." ¶ 8. Was that a wise decision? Was it constitutionally compelled? Note that the *Donahue* decision came one year before the 1985 Fairness Report, and the same year that the Commission issued a major report eliminating many broadcast regulations, Revision of Programming and Commercialization Policies, Ascertainment Requirements, and Program Log Requirements for Commercial Television Stations, Report and Order, 98 F.C.C. 2d 1075 (1984) (also referred to as the Deregulation of Commercial Television Order). Are those actions consistent with the *Donahue* decision? At cross-purposes with it?

2. **Defining Bona Fide News Programming.** Did the decision to expand the definition of bona fide news interview programs increase or decrease the rigor of that definition? Does the definition have meaningful criteria that give it real substance and predictability? If not, does that raise First Amendment concerns? Is such clarity achievable? If not, does *that* raise First Amendment concerns?

3. **Section 315 and the Zapple Doctrine.** The thrust behind § 315 was to balance different candidates' access to the airwaves. But note that § 315 applies to the use of a broadcast station by "any person who is a legally qualified candidate for any public office." So if supporters of candidate A, instead of the candidate herself, purchase air time, the language of § 315 is not implicated. The rule that responded to this possibility was the Zapple doctrine. As we noted above, there does not appear to be any difference in the rationales behind § 315 and the Zapple doctrine. Their legal status appears to account for the different treatment: the Zapple doctrine was an FCC-created doctrine that relied on another FCC-created doctrine (the fairness doctrine), and the rejection of the latter left the former without a legal foundation. Both of those doctrines might rely on the same justifications as the equal time rule, but the equal time rule arises out of a federal statute that governs the FCC. Rejecting the application of a federal statute is quite different from finding one of one's own doctrines unenforceable.

4. **When an Actor Is a Candidate.** In 2003, California prepared for a recall election that had 135 announced candidates. One of those candidates (and the eventual winner) was Arnold Schwarzenegger, and another was former child actor Gary Coleman. When the candidates were certified, the National Association of Broadcasters (which represents local broadcasters) sent an alert to its members warning them that any broadcaster in California or in a nearby state with California viewers that aired a Schwarzenegger movie or an episode of Coleman's "Diff'rent Strokes" would open itself up to a claim under § 315 from one or more of the other candidates. *See* Gary Gentile, Arnold's Films Likely to Be Kept Off Air, Wash. Post, Aug. 13, 2003. Meanwhile, CBS lawyers informed Craig Kilborn of "The Late Show" that he could not show a picture of Schwarzenegger (even to make fun of it) unless he showed pictures of the 134 other candidates. *See* Craig Kilborn, My Couch Is Too Small for 135 Candidates, N.Y. Times, Aug. 30, 2003. Similarly, NBC stopped airing episodes of "Law and Order" featuring Fred Thompson during his Presidential candidacy in 2007–08. *See* Mr. Thompson in Repeat, Wall St. Journal, Sept. 8, 2007. There was precedent for these

positions. Most notably, in 1972 comedian Pat Paulsen launched a satirical run for the Presidency that included getting his name on the New Hampshire primary ballot. When NBC wanted to air a show in which Paulsen appeared, the FCC ruled that Paulsen was indeed a candidate and that his appearance would constitute a "use" of the broadcasters under § 315, so "any national television appearances by Paulsen would impose equal opportunities obligations upon broadcast licensees." Paulsen v. FCC, 491 F.2d 887, 889 (9th Cir. 1974); *see also* Primer, Political Broadcasting, 100 F.C.C. 2d 1476 ¶ 34(d) (1984) ("If an actor becomes a legally qualified candidate for public office, his appearances on telecasts of his movies thereafter will be uses, entitling his opponents to equal time, if the actor is identifiable in the movies"); *id.* ¶¶ 34(e) & 34(h) (taking the same position for appearances by "the host of a teenage dance show," "a radio disc jockey," and a minister on a religious program).

This rigid implementation of equal time might seem silly to some (it certainly did to Kilborn). But the FCC has to give meaning to "use," and bright-line rules have the advantage of clarity. And other bright-line rules (e.g., allowing the airing of any movie or show involving the candidate as an actor) could easily be manipulated (e.g., a TV show featuring Schwarzenegger as a strong leader). If the FCC instead decided to make case-by-case determinations about particular movies or shows, it would become immersed in judgment calls about how a given appearance might help a candidate. And how would the FCC make those determinations? It is hard to imagine that it could provide sufficiently meaningful guideposts that broadcasters would know in advance what would, and would not, trigger the equal time rules. Then again, would such an inquiry about a particular program's benefit to a candidate be more or less clear than the question of what constitutes a "bona fide news interview program" or what constitutes a personal attack or political editorial?

5. Howard Stern and Clarity. Another person who wanted to feature Arnold Schwarzenegger in 2003 without providing equal time for his 134 opponents was Howard Stern. In September 2003, the Commission (again, through the chief of its Media Bureau) issued a five-paragraph ruling declaring that "The Howard Stern Show" (then on broadcast radio) was a bona fide news interview program and therefore exempt from the equal opportunities requirement of § 315. Its first three paragraphs briefly outlined the provision and the FCC's past treatment of it. The entirety of the discussion specific to the Howard Stern show follows:

> 4. Infinity states that the news interview segments of "The Howard Stern Show" satisfy the Commission's requirements for exempt *bona fide* news interview programming because the program is regularly scheduled; Infinity, which broadcasts the program, has control over all aspects of the show; Infinity's decisions on format, content, and participants are based on newsworthiness; and guests that happen to be political candidates are not selected to advance their candidacies.
>
> 5. Based on the record before us, we conclude that the news interview segments of "The Howard Stern Show" qualify for the bona fide news interview exemption under Section 315(a)(2), and that news interviews conducted on that program are exempt from the equal opportunities requirements of Section 315(a) of the Act. Although we take this action in response to Infinity's request, we emphasize that licensees airing programs that meet the statutory news exemption, as clarified in our case law, need not seek formal declaration from the Commission that such programs qualify as news exempt programming under Section 315(a).

Request of Infinity Broadcasting Operations Inc., Declaratory Ruling (Media Bureau, September 9, 2003), *available at* http://hraunfoss.fcc.gov/edocs_public/attachmatch/DA-03-2865A1.pdf.

Does the FCC too blithely accept Infinity's assertions about the show? Andrew Schwartzman, CEO of the Media Access Project, objected to the FCC's conclusion that Stern's show was a bona fide news interview program, stating "When guests are selected by the size of their bust, it is not bona fide news programming." FCC Says Shock-Jock Stern Qualifies as Newsman, USA Today, Sept. 10, 2003. If "newsworthiness" describes the basis on which Stern's guests are chosen, what programs wouldn't satisfy this criterion?

Note the FCC's pointed statement that programs need not seek declaratory rulings from the FCC. Coupled with the ruling's flat acceptance of Infinity's assertions, does this mean that any company that can plausibly claim to meet the criteria will in fact be regarded as a news interview program? If so, this both reduces the meaningfulness of the criteria and makes application of § 315 more straightforward. Does it represent an abandonment of the statutory requirements? Is there a better way?

6. Televised Political Debates. The amendment to § 315 exempting bona fide news programs has further significance, as it created a new opportunity: televised political debates. Everyone had understood that one effect of § 315 as originally written was that it covered minor party candidates as well as those on the Democratic or Republican tickets. Thus, before the 1959 amendment of § 315, no one knew of a way to hold televised debates among candidates for public office without letting all candidates for the position onto the podium. But in 1975, the FCC ruled that debates between candidates could be covered as bona fide news events if they were scheduled by a third party.[13] Under the exception Congress enacted to overrule the *Lar Daly* rule, covering the debates as news events would not trigger an obligation to give equal time to those candidates not represented at the debates. Subsequently, the FCC dropped the window dressing of sponsorship by a third party, ruling that debates are news events within the meaning of § 315 no matter how they come about. Petitions of Henry Geller and National Association of Broadcasters and the Radio-Television News Directors Association to Change Commission Interpretation of Subsections 315(a)(3) and (4) of the Communications Act, Report and Order, 54 Rad. Reg. 2d (P & F) 1246 (1983), *aff'd*, League of Women Voters Educ. Fund v. FCC, 731 F.2d 995 (D.C. Cir. 1984).

7. Candidate Access to the Airwaves. Section 315 does not prevent a station from refusing to sell air time to any and all candidates. Congress has also enacted, however, § 312(a)(7) of the Act. It grants candidates for federal office the right to purchase broadcast time for their advertisements at the broadcaster's lowest unit charge. Specifically, the statute states that: (1) candidates must be allowed to purchase broadcast time whether the broadcaster in question wants to sell it or not; and (2) the purchase price must be the station's lowest unit charge for the particular class of advertisement. The FCC determines when a campaign has begun (thus triggering the two-pronged obligation),[14] and the rule applies

---

13. Petitions of the Aspen Institute Program on Communications and Society and CBS, Inc., for Revision or Clarification of Commission Rulings Under Section 315(a)(2) & 315(a)(4), Memorandum Opinion and Order, 55 F.C.C. 2d 697 (1975). The 1960 debates between candidates Kennedy and Nixon were made possible by Congress suspending § 315 for that one election season. Later, Lyndon Johnson and Richard Nixon both saw to it that § 315 was not suspended for their campaigns, as they did not wish to debate their opponents on national television.

14. In Complaint of Carter-Mondale Presidential Committee, Inc. against the ABC, CBS and NBC Television Networks, Memorandum Opinion and Order, 74 F.C.C. 2d 631 (1979), the Carter/Mondale campaign had wanted to purchase 30 minutes of air time from the major television broadcasters, but the broadcasters refused. The FCC concluded that the campaign had begun for purposes of § 312(a)(7), and thus that the networks were indeed obliged to comply with the statute's requirements regarding selling air time at the lowest unit charge. The D.C. Circuit and Supreme Court both upheld the FCC's decision.

only to federal candidates. The statute was held to be constitutional in CBS v. FCC, 453 U.S. 367 (1981).

8. Proposals for Reform. Rules about purchasing air time do little good for candidates who cannot afford the time. Thus, some politicians have embraced the idea of requiring broadcasters to provide candidates with free television time. *See, e.g.*, Heather Fleming, Clinton Calls for Free Airtime, 127 Broadcasting & Cable 18 (March 17, 1997). One variant here would require broadcasters to donate commercial time to a "political time bank" that would be available free of charge to candidates for elective office. Another proposal would mandate that candidates be offered thirty minutes of free television time and discounted time at fifty percent below the lowest unit charge for additional ads. A third proposal would require that, in the weeks leading up to a federal election, broadcasters set aside five minutes each night for election messages, with the candidates taking turns filling those five-minute periods.

Proponents of this last idea have suggested that the broadcasters be required to provide those five-minute blocks free of charge. But, failing that, they have argued that broadcasters at least be required to sell commercial time in nonstandard commercial blocks (like five-minute periods) instead of only selling time in the shorter increments currently used for traditional commercial advertising. The allure of the longer segments from a policy perspective is that they might lead to more substantive messages; the concern is that 30- and 60-second commercials quickly devolve into sound bites. Broadcasters of course do not relish the prospect of modifying their normal programming schedule in order to allow for five-minute messages, and they have argued that they should not be required to provide special time periods for candidates. The FCC ruled in 1994 that there was no such obligation. Request for Declaratory Ruling of National Association of Broadcasters Regarding Section 312(a)(7) of the Communications Act, Memorandum Opinion and Order, 9 FCC Rcd. 5778 (1994). In 1999, it granted a petition to reconsider that ruling and concluded that "a broadcast station should not be allowed to refuse a request for political advertising time *solely* on the ground that the station does not sell or program such lengths of time." Petition for Reconsideration by People for the American Way and Media Access Project of Declaratory Ruling Regarding Section 312(a)(7) of the Communications Act, Memorandum Opinion and Order, 17 Communications Reg. (P & F) 186 (1999). The NAB then petitioned the FCC to reconsider its 1999 reconsideration, fearing that its implementation would lead to programming disruptions. In 2003 the Commission issued an order rejecting the request for reconsideration, stating that the NAB's fears of disruption were overblown, because the Commission's multifactor test allowed a broadcaster to consider "the potentially disruptive impact on the station's regular programming" in deciding whether to accept a request for nonstandard length advertisements. Petition for Reconsideration by National Association of Broadcasters of Memorandum Opinion and Order Regarding Section 312(a)(7) of the Communications Act, Memorandum Opinion and Order, 18 FCC Rcd. 24,414 (2003).

9. The First Amendment. Would a requirement of free air time be vulnerable to First Amendment challenge? Would *Tornillo* be distinguishable because the hypothetical regulation operates without regard to what the broadcaster has (or has not) said? Would *Red Lion* be distinguishable on the grounds that, unlike the fairness doctrine, this hypothetical regulation is not designed to counter misinformation or partial information that the listener or viewer would otherwise receive?

Note that, interestingly, neither *Red Lion* nor *Tornillo* makes any reference to the extensive regulation of political broadcasting, even though it constitutes some of the most intensive political speech in America. Nevertheless, it is no secret that the FCC is charged with enforcing the "equal time," "lowest unit charge," and "guaranteed access" rules, that it enforces these rules with vigor, and that its enforcement has significant effects on political elections across the country in every campaign season. Is there an adequate justification in the *Red Lion* opinion for this kind of administrative oversight of political contests? Can the theory underlying *Tornillo* be reconciled with FCC regulation of political broadcasting? Does the explosion of new audio and video technologies since the enactments of §§ 312(a)(7) and 315 make it easier or harder to defend the FCC's efforts against First Amendment challenges?

10. Beyond Fairness. The equal time, lowest unit charge, and guaranteed access rules discussed above might seem to suggest that, absent regulation, broadcasters will not treat politicians well. But isn't the real worry here that broadcasters *will* treat particular politicians well—politicians who might then reciprocate with sweetheart regulations or legislation?

In July 1999, broadcasters began airing a series of 30-second public service announcements on topics like literacy, drunk driving, and breast cancer. The ads began in familiar ways, say with a man and a woman talking in an office or a couple having a conversation over their kitchen table. But then, about 10 seconds before each advertisement ended, the spouse of a local Congressman or Senator would come on camera and say something like, "Hello, I'm Simone-Marie Meeks. My husband, Congressman Gregory Meeks, and I urge you to read with your children. Because literacy is a gift for life." The spouse's face would then fade away and the narrator would announce, "This message brought to you by the National Association of Broadcasters." David Rosenbaum, TV Ads by Congressional Wives Are a Sweet Deal for All Involved, N.Y. Times, July 13, 1999, at A1.

The ads were an obvious boon for all the involved parties. The politicians enjoyed low-risk, favorable public exposure for their names and their families, all without (at least thus far) triggering equal time obligations in favor of their political rivals. The broadcasters meanwhile (arguably) satisfied part of their public trustee obligation by airing public service announcements and, at the same time, surely ingratiated themselves with the featured politicians. But what of the public's interest? Assuming that the spots did indeed represent an attempt by the NAB to ingratiate itself with members of Congress, what changes in the existing regulatory regime would eliminate the NAB's incentive to do so? Would such changes be a good idea, as a policy matter? Is there an argument that these changes are constitutionally compelled? *Cf.* Matthew L. Spitzer, The Constitutionality of Licensing Broadcasters, 64 N.Y.U. L. Rev. 990 (1989).

11. Gore/Bush 2000. As of October 2000, the Presidential contest between Democratic nominee Al Gore and Republican nominee George W. Bush was a statistical dead heat. The first presidential debate, then, would possibly affect the election outcome significantly. That debate took place on Tuesday, October 3, and it was aired live on CBS, ABC, and PBS. Fox and NBC, however—the other two major broadcast television networks—broke with tradition and chose to compete with the debate: Fox aired the series premiere of James Cameron's science-fiction/adventure program, "Dark Angel," and NBC took the unusual step of giving its affiliates a choice: either air the debate or air a Major League Baseball playoff game, with the debate available on tape-delay after the game was over.

Should the FCC have punished the affiliates who failed to air the debate live for violating their public trustee obligation? Should it have revoked their licenses? Does it matter that, according to the Nielsen ratings, "Dark Angel" drew an audience of over 17 million viewers, while the debate on ABC and CBS drew a combined audience of roughly 30 million? Shauna Snow, Morning Report, L.A. Times, October 5, 2000, at F52. Which way does that fact cut? Should the FCC distinguish between the NBC affiliates who chose to show the baseball game and the Fox affiliates, who were not given the option of carrying the debate live? Should the FCC reward the NBC affiliates who did choose to show the debate live? Does it matter whether other affiliates aired the debate later that same evening?

12. Other Media: Political Broadcasting. This section has focused on broadcasters. Do the regulations discussed in this section apply to cable and satellite operators as well?

As to cable operators, § 312(a)(7) does not apply because it applies only to spectrum licensees. *See* Codification of the Commission's Political Programming Policies, Report and Order, 7 FCC Rcd. 678, 680 n.11 (1991). Congress amended § 315, however, to include cable operators. *See* Pub. L. No. 92-225, 86 Stat. 3 (1972). Note that the requirements of § 315 apply only to the programming that a given cable operator exclusively controls. Use of Broadcast and Cablecast Facilities by Candidates for Public Office, Public Notice, 34 F.C.C. 2d 510 (1972); 47 C.F.R. § 76.5(p). This requirement of exclusive control (called "origination") is quite significant, because cable operators largely transmit programming (and advertising) that they do not exclusively control. Cable operators choose whether or not to carry traditional cable channels (e.g., CNN or ESPN), but the owners of those channels, not the system operators, choose what content to include. Cable operators are legally required to carry particular channels ("must-carry" and PEG channels, which we discuss in Chapter Eight), but again they do not choose their content. Separate from these channels, cable operators sometimes choose to create, program, and distribute their own channels (e.g., a local cable channel focused on local news, sports, and weather). These are generally the only channels that cable operators directly control, and thus are the only ones subject to § 315.

Turning to direct broadcast satellite television (DBS), Congress required the Commission to apply the requirements of §§ 312(a)(7) and 315 to DBS providers. Cable Television Consumer Protection and Competition Act of 1992, Pub. L. No. 102-385, 106 Stat. 1460, codified at 47 U.S.C. § 335. With respect to § 315, the Commission implemented the same rule to DBS as to cable—the statute applies, but only to content controlled by the DBS provider. The Commission further decided that the requirements of § 312(a)(7) apply to DBS providers and are not limited to content they control (but recall that § 312(a)(7) applies only to advertising). *See* Implementation of Section 25 of the Cable Television Consumer Protection and Competition Act of 1992: Direct Broadcast Satellite Public Interest Obligations, Sua Sponte Reconsideration, Second Order on Reconsideration of First Report and Order, 19 FCC Rcd. 5647 ¶ 30 (2004); 47 C.F.R. § 25.701(b).

One other nonbroadcast programming source bears mention—satellite radio. In Establishment of Rules and Policies for the Digital Audio Radio Satellite Service in the 2310–2360 MHz Frequency Band, Report and Order, Memorandum Opinion and Order, and Further Notice of Proposed Rulemaking, 12 FCC Rcd. 5754 (1997), the Commission considered what, if any, public interest programming obligations it would impose on satellite radio providers. Commenters (mainly potential competitors) proposed a range of such obligations. (National Public Radio, for example, "advocate[d] either a specific reservation of channel capacity for noncommercial or educational programming or a commitment to provide a minimum amount of educational[,] cultural, and informational programming to unserved or underserved areas." *Id.* ¶ 89.) With little explanation, the Commission decided to impose §§ 312(a)(7) and 315, but not to impose additional mandates. *Id.* ¶¶ 92–93.

Finally, the fairness doctrine and personal attack and political editorial rules have of course been repealed, but a form of these rules did apply to programming exclusively controlled by cable operators. *See* Amendment of the Commission's Rules Concerning the Fairness Doctrine and Political Cablecasting Requirements for Cable Television Systems, Proposed Rule, 48 Fed. Reg. 26,472-01 (1983).

---

§ 15.A.5. The Scarcity Rationale in Other Media

In *Red Lion*, the Supreme Court found that spectrum scarcity justified reduced First Amendment scrutiny in the broadcasting context. As we saw in Chapter Nine, the Supreme Court rejected application of *Red Lion* to cable television in Turner Broadcasting System, Inc. v. FCC, 512 U.S. 622 (1994). The Supreme Court has never considered the applicability of *Red Lion* to satellite services, but the D.C. Circuit had occasion to do so in Time Warner Entertainment Co. v. FCC, 93 F.3d 957 (D.C. Cir. 1996).

The brief background is that the same legislation that applied §§ 312(a)(7) and 315 to DBS providers also mandated that each DBS provider "reserve a portion of its channel capacity, equal to not less than 4 percent nor more than 7 percent, exclusively for noncommercial programming of an educational or informational nature." Section 25 of the Cable Television Consumer Protection and Competition Act of 1992, Pub. L. No. 102-385, 106 Stat. 1460, codified at 47 U.S.C. § 335(b)(1). As part of the massive litigation challenging various provisions of the 1992 Cable Act (part of which was split off and became *Turner Broadcasting v. FCC*), companies challenged § 25 as violating the First Amendment. In the following opinion, the Court of Appeals for the District of Columbia Circuit upheld the provision.

TIME WARNER ENTERTAINMENT CO. v. FCC
93 F.3d 957 (D.C. Cir. 1996)

Before BUCKLEY, RANDOLPH, and TATEL, Circuit Judges. Opinion for the Court filed PER CURIAM. Opinion concurring in part and dissenting in part filed by Circuit Judge TATEL.

PER CURIAM:

Time Warner insists, for a variety of reasons, that the DBS set-aside provisions must be subjected to strict scrutiny; it also maintains that we may not consider the government's argument that DBS systems are analogous to broadcast television and therefore subject to no more than heightened scrutiny, because that argument had not been raised before the district court. [But] for us to ignore the obvious similarity between DBS and broadcasting would do nothing to preserve the integrity of the judicial process.

The Supreme Court recognized, in 1969, that because of the limited availability of the radio spectrum for broadcast purposes, "only a tiny fraction of those with resources and intelligence can hope to communicate by radio at the same time." Red Lion Broadcasting Co., Inc. v. FCC, 395 U.S. 367, 388 (1969). The same is true for DBS today. Because the United States has only a finite number of satellite positions available for DBS use, the opportunity to provide such services will necessarily be limited. Even before the first DBS communications satellite was launched in 1994, the FCC found that "the demand for channel/orbit allocations far exceeds the available supply." Recently, the last DBS license was auctioned off for $682.5 million, the largest sum ever received by the FCC for any single license to use the airwaves. As the Supreme Court observed,

> [w]here there are substantially more individuals who want to broadcast than there are frequencies to allocate, it is idle to posit an unabridgeable First Amend-

ment right to broadcast comparable to the right of every individual to speak, write, or publish.

Red Lion, 395 U.S. at 388.

In such cases, the Court applies a "less rigorous standard of First Amendment scrutiny," based on a recognition that

> the inherent physical limitation on the number of speakers who may use the ... medium has been thought to require some adjustment in traditional First Amendment analysis to permit the Government to place limited content restraints, and impose certain affirmative obligations, on broadcast licensees.

Turner Broadcasting Sys., Inc. v. FCC, 512 U.S. 622, 637, 638 (1994). Because the new DBS technology is subject to similar limitations, we conclude that section 25 should be analyzed under the same relaxed standard of scrutiny that the court has applied to the traditional broadcast media.

Both broadcasters and the public have First Amendment rights that must be balanced when the government seeks to regulate access to the radio spectrum. Nonetheless, the Supreme Court has held that "[i]t is the right of the viewers and listeners, not the right of the broadcasters, which is paramount.... It is the right of the public to receive suitable access to social, political, esthetic, moral and other ideas and experiences which is crucial here." *Red Lion*, 395 U.S. at 390. An essential goal of the First Amendment is to achieve "the widest possible dissemination of information from diverse and antagonistic sources." FCC v. National Citizens Comm. for Broadcasting, 436 U.S. 775, 799 (1978) (*NCCB*). Broadcasting regulations that affect speech have been upheld when they further this First Amendment goal. For example, in *NCCB*, the Supreme Court recognized that "efforts to enhance the volume and quality of coverage of public issues through regulation of broadcasting may be permissible where similar efforts to regulate the print media would not be." *Id.* at 800.

The government asserts an interest in assuring public access to diverse sources of information by requiring DBS operators to reserve four to seven percent of their channel capacity for noncommercial educational and informational programming. Indeed, a stated policy of the 1992 Act is to "promote the availability to the public of a diversity of views and information through cable television and other video distribution media." 1992 Act, §2(b)(1), 106 Stat. at 1463. This interest lies at the core of the First Amendment: "Assuring that the public has access to a multiplicity of informational sources is a governmental purpose of the highest order, for it promotes values central to the First Amendment." *Turner*, 512 U.S. at 663.

Section 25 represents nothing more than a new application of a well-settled government policy of ensuring public access to noncommercial programming. The section achieves this purpose by requiring DBS providers to reserve a small portion of their channel capacity for such programs as a condition of their being allowed to use a scarce public commodity. The set-aside requirement of from four to seven percent of a provider's channel capacity is hardly onerous, especially in light of the instruction, in the Senate Report, that the FCC "consider the total channel capacity of DBS systems operators" so that it may "subject DBS systems with relatively large total channel capacity to a greater reservation requirement than systems with relatively less total capacity." S. Rep. No. 92, 102d Cong., 2d Sess. 92 (1991). Furthermore, a DBS provider "may utilize for any purpose any unused channel capacity required to be reserved under this subsection pending the actual use of such channel capacity for noncommercial programming of an educational or informational nature." 47 U.S.C. §335(b)(2).

[Separate opinion of Judge TATEL, concurring in this portion of the opinion and dissenting from a different portion, is omitted.]

Time Warner sought a rehearing en banc (by the full court of appeals) but that request was denied. Although there were many different issues in the case, only the DBS provision drew a written dissent from the decision to deny the en banc rehearing.

TIME WARNER ENTERTAINMENT CO. v. FCC
On Suggestions for Rehearing *In Banc*, 105 F.3d 723 (D.C. Cir. 1997)

Before EDWARDS, Chief Judge, WALD, SILBERMAN, WILLIAMS, GINSBURG, SENTELLE, HENDERSON, RANDOLPH, ROGERS and TATEL, Circuit Judges.

PER CURIAM:

The Suggestions for Rehearing *In Banc* and the response thereto have been circulated to the full court. The taking of a vote was requested. Thereafter, a majority of the judges of the court in regular active service did not vote in favor of the suggestions. Upon consideration of the foregoing, it is ordered that the suggestions be denied.

Circuit Judges WALD and HENDERSON did not participate in this matter.

WILLIAMS, Circuit Judge, with whom Chief Judge EDWARDS, Judge SILBERMAN, Judge GINSBURG and Judge SENTELLE concur, dissenting from the denial of rehearing in banc:

Although I dissent from the denial of the suggestion for rehearing *in banc*, I do so with genuine uncertainty about the correct outcome. But I believe there were fatal defects in the panel's legal *theory* for upholding the 1992 Cable Act's requirement that direct broadcast satellite (DBS) providers set aside several channels for noncommercial programming of an educational or informational nature. DBS is not subject to anything remotely approaching the "scarcity" that the Court found in conventional broadcast in 1969 and used to justify a peculiarly relaxed First Amendment regime for such broadcast. Accordingly *Red Lion* should not be extended to this medium.

If the 1992 Act's content rules for DBS can be sustained at all, in my view it would only be on the theory that the government is entitled to more leeway in setting the terms on which it supplies "property" to private parties for speech purposes (or for purposes that include speech).

1. Red Lion

The panel concluded that DBS is more like broadcasting than like cable, and that therefore *Red Lion* applied. As the *Red Lion* doctrine relies on an idea of extreme physical scarcity, I disagree. The new DBS technology already offers more channel capacity than the cable industry, and far more than traditional broadcasting.[15]

DBS is more than an order of magnitude less scarce than traditional broadcasting. Over 50% of the conventional broadcast markets receive fewer than five commercial

---

15. Even in its heartland application, *Red Lion* has been the subject of intense criticism. Partly this rests on the perception that the "scarcity" rationale never made sense—in either its generic form (the idea that an excess of demand over supply at a price of zero justifies a unique First Amendment regime) or its special form (that broadcast channels are peculiarly rare). And partly the criticism rests on the growing number of available broadcast channels. While *Red Lion* is not in such poor shape that an intermediate court of appeals could properly announce its death, we can think twice before extending it to another medium.

broadcast channels (including UHF channels), and only 20% receive seven or more. While this number of channels is greater than those available in 1969 when *Red Lion* was decided, it pales in comparison to cable or DBS. Cable operators currently offer about fifty channels, but compression techniques and new technology may eventually lead to 500 channels or more.

DBS has even greater channel capacity. The three orbital slots that permit broadcast throughout the continental United States can accommodate at least 120 video channels each, using existing compression technology, for a total of 360 channels. This does not include the other five orbital slots (4 usable for west coast broadcasting and 1 for east coast broadcasting), which raise the number of channels available to 480 (4 X 20) for the east coast, and 840 (7 X 120) for the west coast. DBS compression is expected to increase the number of channels fivefold by the year 2000. Currently, there are four DBS providers, each providing between 45 and 75 video channels and up to 30 music channels. Thus, even in its nascent state, DBS provides a given market with four times as many channels as cable, which (even without predicted increases in compression) offers about 10 times as many channels as broadcast.

Accordingly, *Red Lion*'s factual predicate—scarcity of channels—is absent here. And the *Red Lion* Court implied that its result would have been different in the absence of such a predicate. Similarly, to the extent that *Turner* distinguishes *Red Lion* on grounds of lack of scarcity in cable, *see* Turner Broadcasting System, Inc. v. FCC, 512 U.S. 622, 637 (1994) (observing that "distinct approach to broadcast regulation rests upon the unique physical limitations of the broadcast medium"), DBS falls on the cable rather than the broadcast side of the line.

Turner, to be sure, appears in part to ground its distinction between cable and broadcast on technological characteristics independent of sheer numbers. "[I]f two broadcasters were to attempt to transmit over the same frequency in the same locale, they would interfere with one another's signals, so that neither could be heard at all." *Id.* But this can hardly be controlling. Alleviation of interference does not necessitate government content management; it requires, as do most problems of efficient use of resources, a system for allocation and protection of exclusive property rights. A cable operator enjoys property rights in the cables in which he transmits his signal (as well, of course, as in the structures he uses to make the transmission). That is the reason would-be cable operators do not interfere with each other's "signals." If I were to burst into Time Warner's studio full of zest to run my program or attempt to transmit signals through wires owned by a cable operator, I would be guilty of trespass and Time Warner could have me ejected. There is no technological obstacle to applying this regime to the broadcast spectrum; indeed, under the current regime a licensee is subject to legal sanctions if he broadcasts outside the wavelengths covered by his license.

Accordingly, it seems to me more reasonable to understand *Red Lion* as limited to cases where the number of channels is genuinely low.

3. Rust v. Sullivan, et al.

The government may subsidize some activities and not others. In *Rust v. Sullivan*, the Court held that Congress could prohibit grantees of federal funds for certain family planning services from using those funds for the "counseling, referral, and the provision of information regarding abortion..." 500 U.S. 173, 193 (1991). Rejecting arguments that the requirement was unconstitutionally viewpoint-based, the Court stated that the government was "simply insisting that public funds be spent for the purposes for which they are authorized." *Id.* at 196. In its response to the petition for rehearing, the government makes an oblique allusion to this analysis, suggesting that it was within the government's power to retain control over the "public domain" to have reserved 4-to-7% of channel capacity for itself.

Echoes of this idea can be found in the various opinions in the recent case of Denver Area Educational Telecommunications Consortium v. FCC, 518 U.S. 727 (1996). And in *Red Lion* itself, the Court used the language of conditioned grants:

> To condition the granting or renewal of licenses on a willingness to present representative community views on controversial issues is consistent with the ends and purposes of those constitutional provisions forbidding the abridgment of freedom of speech and freedom of the press.

395 U.S. at 394.

On the other hand, the Court has not clearly committed itself to treating spectrum licenses as conditioned grants. For example, when in FCC v. League of Women Voters, 468 U.S. 364 (1984), it struck down Congress's ban on editorializing by stations receiving monetary grants from the Corporation for Public Broadcasting, it considered only those grants and found them inadequate to justify the restriction. It did not consider the stations' positions as holders of broadcast licenses.

There is, perhaps, good reason for the Court to have hesitated to give great weight to the government's property interest in the spectrum. First, unallocated spectrum is government property only in the special sense that it simply has not been allocated to any real "owner" in any way. Thus it is more like unappropriated water in the western states, which belongs, effectively, to no one. Indeed, the common law courts had treated spectrum in this manner before the advent of full federal regulation. *See* Chicago Tribune Co. v. Oak Leaves Broadcasting Station, Ill. Circuit Ct., Cook County, Nov. 17, 1926, reprinted in 68 Cong. Rec. 215–19 (1926) (recognizing rights in spectrum acquired by reason of investment of time and money in application of the resource to productive use, and drawing on analogy to western water rights law).

Further, the way in which the government came to assert a property interest in spectrum has obscured the problems raised by government monopoly ownership of an entire medium of communication. We would see rather serious First Amendment problems if the government used its power of eminent domain to become the only lawful supplier of newsprint and then sold the newsprint only to licensed persons, issuing the licenses only to persons that promised to use the newsprint for papers satisfying government-defined rules of content. The government asserted its monopoly over broadcast spectrum long before the medium attained dominance, making the assertion of power seem modest and, by the time dominance was manifest, normal. While this sequence veiled the size and character of the asserted monopoly, it is not clear why it should justify an analysis any different from what would govern the newsprint hypo.

If the subsidy model is suitable for spectrum, the DBS licenses are properly viewed as subsidies, even though there is no cash transfer to the DBS providers for the support of educational programming. The character varies depending on whether the license was granted free, or in an auction occurring after the enactment of the 1992 Act. (There appear to be no licenses auctioned before the 1992 Act.) As for DBS providers that received their licenses gratis, the subsidy is clear, although it is troubling that all the DBS providers that did so received them before the condition was attached.

There is also a subsidy in the auction setting. Those bidding for the DBS channels necessarily discounted their bids in light of the known prospect that a portion of the channels would be allocated for educational programming (and that the DBS provider would bear at least some of the operating costs and overhead). This differential—money that the government could have received had it not imposed the programming requirement—constitutes a subsidy exactly matching the pecuniary burden imposed by the provision. Thus the government may be said to have given the educational channels to the DBS providers.

Analogizing from *Rust v. Sullivan*, then, the government may argue that it has not required "the [licensee] to give up [non-educational speech]...," but simply to use those channels granted by the government for educational and informational programming for that "specific and limited purpose." 500 U.S. at 196.

Because I can see no principled basis for upholding the requirements imposed on DBS operators without resolving these questions, I dissent from the denial of the petition for rehearing *in banc*.

Notes and Questions

1. Implications. Which opinion has the more persuasive reading of *Red Lion*? Did *Red Lion* rely on the scarcity of broadcast television channels, or the scarcity of spectrum more broadly? Does the panel's reasoning mean that any regulation of a service that uses spectrum will be subject to less rigorous First Amendment scrutiny than would regulation of a similar service that uses wires?

2. Contrasting Bases. The panel opinion extends *Red Lion* to DBS. The dissent from the denial of rehearing en banc rejects the application of *Red Lion* to DBS, but suggests that a governmental subsidy model might justify regulation of DBS. What are the implications of extending *Red Lion* versus finding regulation justified because of a subsidy? Which line of reasoning would trouble you more if you were the lawyer for: (a) a cable television provider; (b) a wireless paging service (would it matter whether your service used satellites to transmit messages?); (c) a rural incumbent local exchange carrier; (d) a company hoping to gain FCC approval for the use of previously unusable spectrum to transmit information to home appliances (would you need more knowledge about what kind of information and/or what kind of appliances?); or (e) a newspaper?

§ 15.B. Children's Television

The Commission has long struggled to identify the best way to encourage broadcast licensees to air educational children's television. As the documents that follow will reveal, the agency has wavered considerably in its approach over the last twenty years. Should licensees be given explicit requirements—told, for example, exactly what constitutes an "educational program" and how many hours of such programming are required per week? Should educational television instead be handled more subtly, with licensees simply warned that they have an obligation to serve the educational needs of children and told that performance on this score will be evaluated come renewal time? Are educational goals best served by requiring every broadcast licensee to provide suitable content? Might they be better served by a regulatory regime where only a small number of licensees develop expertise in this area and then provide all the content needed? On these and related issues, the Commission's answer has been both "yes" and "no"—and, at that, all in a relatively short time period.

As you work through these documents, see if you can understand why the Commission's position has changed so much over time. Are these adjustments the result of pressure from Congress and interest groups? Are we witnessing an agency that is learning from its early attempts and making adjustments in response? Did the agency in the beginning overestimate how cooperative licensees would be when it came to furthering this public interest goal and then, in the later proceedings, adopt regulations that better reflect a more cynical view? Overall, are the conflicting policy pronouncements that follow evidence that children's television is so far outside the Commission's areas of core competence that the Commission is bound to have trouble defining the problem, let alone crafting a sensible solution? Or does the evidence more charitably suggest that the administrative process here has been a success, providing a forum for continued examination of (and flexible responses to) what is an inherently complex and contentious public policy issue?

CHILDREN'S TELEVISION PROGRAMMING AND ADVERTISING PRACTICES

Report and Order, 96 F.C.C. 2d 634 (1983)

1. Now before the Commission for consideration are the comments filed in response to the Notice of Proposed Rule Making (Notice) in the above-captioned proceeding concerning television programming for children. 75 F.C.C. 2d 138 (1980). The Notice is the most recent step in a thirteen year inquiry into television programming and advertising addressed to children.

2. In 1970, Action for Children's Television (ACT) submitted a petition proposing a rule requiring commercial television broadcasters to provide, on a weekly basis, minimum amounts of age-specific programming for children. In 1971, we adopted our First Notice of Inquiry to explore and define the fundamental issues in children's television. A Children's Television Task Force (Task Force) was set up at that time to help achieve these goals. We concluded the inquiry in 1974 with the issuance of a Report and Policy Statement, 50 F.C.C. 2d 1 (1974) (Policy Statement). The Policy Statement specifically asked commercial television licensees to: (1) make a "meaningful effort" to increase the amount of programming for children; (2) air a "reasonable amount" of programming for children designed to educate and inform and not simply to entertain; (3) air informational programming separately targeted for both preschool and school-age children; and (4) air programming for children scheduled during weekdays as well as on weekends. Commercial television broadcasters also were expected to: (1) limit the amount of advertising in children's programming; (2) insure an adequate separation between program content and commercial messages; and (3) eliminate host-selling and tie-in practices.

4. In 1978, the Commission re-established the Children's Television Task Force to inquire into the effectiveness of broadcast industry self-regulation under the Policy Statement. The Task Force presented its report to the Commission on October 30, 1979. It concluded that broadcasters had not complied with the programming guidelines of the Policy Statement but, in general, had complied with the advertising guidelines.

6. In the opinion of the Task Force, the economic incentives of the advertiser-supported broadcasting system do not encourage the provision of specialized programming for children. Advertisers desire the largest possible audience of potential buyers for their advertised products, but young children have an influence on decisions to buy only a relatively few advertised products. Thus, the amount of money spent on children's advertising appears to be small relative to the amount spent advertising to adults. The Task Force believed that the small numbers of children and the limited appeal of the children's

market to advertisers, combined with the small number of outlets in most markets, create incentives for the commercial television system to neglect the specific needs of the child audience.

10. On March 28, 1983, the Commission reopened the children's television proceeding. We sought to update the record to enable us better to resolve the important questions raised by the Notice.

23. The Task Force, believing that greater attention to the needs of the child audience was desirable, focused on three broad options to improve the situation: 1) mandatory programming requirements, 2) increased governmental funding (or other incentives) for the production and distribution of such programming, and 3) increasing the number of video outlets so as to improve the commercial incentives for serving subgroups in the audience and to increase the available distribution paths for children's programming. The recommended mandatory programming requirement could be enforced either through a specific rule or through processing guidelines applied to the renewal of station licenses.[16]

24. Our weighing of what we think are the relevant considerations in this proceeding leads us to believe that the recommended mandatory programming obligations are undesirable and should not be adopted. The other recommendations of the Task Force, relating to public funding for the production and distribution of informational and instructional children's programming and for the creation of additional video outlets and commercial funding mechanisms, we agree with fully. While issues relating to public funding are beyond our jurisdiction, we have moved aggressively to create new video outlets.

Availability of Children's Programming

26. In several important respects we disagree with the predicate upon which the Task Force based its recommendations and on which many parties base arguments supporting mandatory programming requirements. The first of these disagreements relates to the issue of the actual availability of programming for the child audience. In particular, we find the Task Force conclusion erroneous for its failure to properly consider: (1) the growth in number of commercial stations and their increased receivability; (2) programming on noncommercial stations; (3) cable program services; and (4) child viewing of "family" oriented television. These failures undermine the conclusions drawn by the Report. The second disagreement concerns practical, legal, and policy problems with our ability to adopt and enforce programming obligations.

27. With respect to the first of these concerns, the Task Force focused its attention on the amount and scheduling of children's programming by the average commercial station. We must, of course, exercise our regulatory authority with respect to individual licensees. The objective of the Commission's involvement, however, is to assure that the telecommunications system as a whole is responsive to the needs of the public. It is therefore appropriate to look to that system as a whole in reviewing developments relating to the accessibility of programming for the child audience.

---

16. [The use of these processing guidelines is discussed more fully in section V. of the Commission's 1996 Children's Television rules, *infra*. The basic idea is that the Commission establishes guidelines, in this case a minimum amount of children's programming. Broadcasters who do not meet these guidelines would not break any FCC rule, but would face different procedures at license renewal time. For licensees whose past performance and proposed future programming met or exceeded the guidelines, the Commission's staff would be delegated authority to renew their licenses. Stations not meeting these guidelines would have their applications referred to the Commission for full review. Eds.]

28. The data developed by the Task Force reveal a 7.2 percent increase, during the years studied (1973–74 and 1977–78), in the amount of time commercial broadcast stations, on average, devoted to children's programming. Not focused on, however, was the fact that since this docket was commenced, the total number of licensed commercial stations increased from 668 (1971) to 844 (1983), an increase of approximately 25 percent. Moreover, the reach of these stations was being constantly increased through more efficient operations (increased power and antenna height), through reductions in the UHF handicap, and through increased cable television carriage. Summary data show the average television household now receives 9.8 signals, an increase of 3 (44 percent) since 1970. Thus, not only was the average output of children's programming per station increasing but the average number of stations accessible to the child viewer was increasing as well.

29. Even this broader focus, which includes the totality of programming from all commercial stations however, is unduly narrow since it excludes from the product available to the child audience that which by almost any measure must be the most significant programming—that produced and distributed by the public broadcasting system. This system was created precisely for the purpose of supplementing the commercial broadcasting system and in specific recognition of the desirability of providing public support to increasing the availability of programming that might not be fully supported by commercial incentives. The public broadcasting system has recognized this mandate with respect to the broadcasting of children's programming and its successes in this field have been broadly recognized. The Corporation for Public Broadcasting has recently recognized children's programming as the number one priority in its Program Fund guidelines. We do not expect the public broadcasting system to bear the sole responsibility for meeting the needs of the child television audience or its existence to provide an excuse for the failings of the commercial broadcasting system. But we do not believe it appropriate to exclude its output from consideration as a significant factor in measuring the extent to which the needs of this audience are being served. The Commission has reserved channels in its television broadcast table of allotments for the specific use of noncommercial broadcasting stations so that the public would have access to the kinds of informational, instructional, and cultural programming that these stations deliver. Today, almost 300 stations—more than a quarter of all the licensed television stations—are of the noncommercial variety. The Public Broadcasting System, during the 1982–83 season, provided stations in the public broadcasting system, reaching over 90 percent of all television households, with some 2,050 hours of children's programming.

30. An additional important component of the national children's television programming market consists of the programming available to the child audience from nonbroadcast sources, including in particular that programming available over the facilities of cable television systems. Cable television now passes some 54 percent of all homes and cannot be avoided in any assessment of the accessibility of programming to the child audience. Millions of households have access to children's program services by cable, including "Nickelodeon," (14 million subscribers) and the recently inaugurated Disney Channel.

31. [The Task Force's] concern was principally with that programming defined in the Commission's rules as children's programming. This definition covers only programs "originally produced and broadcast primarily for a child audience twelve years old and under." Explicitly excluded from coverage are programs that might be appealing to children and significantly viewed by them but which were, when produced, intended for a broader audience as well. This exclusion of what has been broadly referred to as "family" programming, clearly resulted in an unduly narrowed definition of the programming of interest

and value to the child audience. [B]y using limitations that excluded programs such as "The Wonderful World of Disney," relevant programming of value could not be fully comprehended by the study. Such a definitional limitation serves to encourage the broadcasting of programming that is likely, given the dynamics of program selection within the household, to have not only a smaller total audience but a smaller child audience. Moreover, it suggests that positive values should be associated with programs, directed to the child audience, whatever the social utility of those programs, while programs specifically designed to bridge age levels and be shared by parents and children are of lesser value on the regulatory scale.

32. In sum, the adequacy of the programming to which children have access must be based on a consideration of the whole of the video distribution system. Viewing that system broadly, there is no national failure of access to children's programming that requires an across-the-board, national quota for each and every licensee to meet.

Issues of Law and Policy

33. Much of the discussion has addressed the overall quantity and scheduling of programming created for children. Yet, in fact, much of the actual concern has only to do with the availability of "quality" children's programming, programming that through its educational, intellectual, or cultural content is mentally or developmentally uplifting to the child audience.

34. Any analysis of the service received by the child audience that is entirely content neutral—which equates hours of television viewing with needs satisfaction—must conclude that this audience is well served. [C]hildren watch enough television, and no regulatory initiative need be introduced to get them to watch more. Thus, we are not persuaded that efforts to adopt specific mandatory program hours obligations can achieve their intended objective in the absence of some control over or attention to the issue of quality.

36. Because of concerns with problems of this type, we have believed, with only the rarest of exceptions, that selection of programming is a matter that should be decided by station licensees and by the audience through its viewing pattern voting. Program quota systems have been viewed historically as fundamentally in conflict with the statutory scheme of broadcast regulation.

41. In a statement with which we agree, the [D.C. Circuit] stated that it failed to see the logic in policies that imply that a regular schedule of cartoons would satisfy the public interest when a more limited schedule of educational specials would not. Washington Association for Television and Children v. FCC, 712 F.2d 677, 684 (D.C. Cir. 1983). This raises again the issue of program quality. If it is assumed that station licensees will provide children's programming only involuntarily, then there is no logical way to disassociate quantity and quality. At a given cost, a specific regulatory requirement to respond to the needs and interests of children could be responded to either by the broadcasting of a limited number of more costly programs (more costly either in terms of production cost or lost audience) or a larger number of less costly programs. Although from the point of view of the station enterprise both approaches are equal in cost, rules that require or reward quantity create a strong bias to follow the "more programs lower cost" approach. Proponents of mandatory requirements urge, however, that with mandatory time requirements at least some programming would be available and, having to provide that programming, stations would then have an incentive to make their best efforts to produce attractive programming. While we agree that stations would attempt to maximize their returns within the constraints imposed, the hypothetical example posed by the Court of

Appeals—regularly scheduled cartoons receiving more credit than less frequently scheduled better quality programs—would still seem to be the likely result.

42. As the Children's Television Task Force has suggested, such specialization as is made possible by the development of more programming outlets provides the surest long run chance of providing better service to all segments of society, including children. No sophisticated survey is required to observe that such specialization is occurring. During weekday mornings, independent (as well as public) stations in many markets compete for the child audience. Network affiliated stations concentrate on news and public affairs. On weekends, when network stations target the child audience, the independent (and the public) stations do not. As predicted, market segmentation leads to station specialization better serving the needs of the entire viewing public.

43. Recognizing that a balance must be reached, we believe this balance is best struck through a continued stress on the general licensee obligations emphasized by the Commission in its 1974 Children's Television Policy Statement and through the general requirement that stations provide programming responsive to the needs and interests of the communities they serve. We continue to believe "that the broadcasters' public service obligation includes a responsibility to provide diversified programming designed to meet the varied needs and interests of the child audience."

44. We do not believe it desirable, however, to mandate programming quotas or impose more specific program or scheduling requirements nor do we interpret the Policy Statement as imposing such obligations.

46. In summary, we do not wish this decision to be an endorsement of a "raised eyebrow" approach to regulation. No cryptic message will be found between the lines of this decision. Simply put, we find no basis in the record to apply a national mandatory quota for children's programming. But, there is a continuing duty, under the public interest standard, on each licensee to examine the program needs of the child part of the audience and to be ready to demonstrate at renewal time its attention to those needs. This duty is part of the public interest requirement that a licensee consider the needs of all significant elements of its community. A licensee may consider what other children's program service is available in its market in executing its response to those needs. But a licensee who fails to consider those needs, in light of its particular market situation, will find no refuge in this order.

Notes and Questions

1. The Commission's Rationale. The Commission majority's rationale seems to incorporate two key arguments. First, the majority argues that the extent to which the public interest is being served should be measured by the performance of the entire market—including all video services, not simply free broadcast services. This is, of course, the usual method of evaluating the performance of an industry. For example, no one would say that the shoe industry is performing badly if some stores do not carry all makes of all brands of shoes for men, women, and children. Rather, the question would be whether the shoe market, as a whole, provided quality shoes at reasonable prices that were responsive to people's various needs and tastes. But, as applied to television (or radio), isn't this approach completely inconsistent with the concept of the licensee as public trustee? What can remain of a public trustee obligation, in any programming area, under the FCC's rationale in this proceeding?

Second, the majority makes clear that, in their view, the real issue here is quality, not quantity. Is this assertion inconsistent with the previous one? If video markets function well, shouldn't a requirement to program for children lead to competition to capture a large children's audience with quality programming? Is the FCC's discussion of this issue in ¶ 41 convincing?

2. What Must a Broadcaster Do? What is the nature of the duty the Commission articulates in ¶ 46? What should broadcasters have concluded they were required to do under this order?

3. The Next Round. The 1983 Report and Order was not the final word on children's television. Congress changed the legal landscape by passing the Children's Television Act of 1990, Pub. L. No. 101-437, 104 Stat. 996. That legislation required that each commercial broadcast licensee and cable operator "shall limit the duration of advertising in children's television programming to not more than 10.5 minutes per hour on weekends and not more than 12 minutes per hour on weekdays." 47 U.S.C. § 303a(b). The 1990 Act also required the FCC to consider other children's television measures. The Commission did so in the following order.

Policies and Rules Concerning Children's Television Programming
Report and Order, 6 FCC Rcd. 2111 (1991)

I. INTRODUCTION

1. On November 8, 1990, the Commission adopted a Notice of Proposed Rulemaking (Notice), 5 FCC Rcd. 7199, initiating the process of implementing the Children's Television Act of 1990.

III. PROGRAMMING RENEWAL REVIEW REQUIREMENTS

14. The Children's Television Act [of 1990] requires that, in reviewing television license renewal applications, we consider whether the licensee has served "the educational and informational needs of children through the licensee's overall programming, including programming specifically designed to serve such needs." We may "in addition" consider (1) "any special nonbroadcast efforts ... which enhance the educational and informational value of such programming" and (2) any "special effort" to produce or support programming broadcast by another station in the licensee's market that is "specifically designed to serve the educational and informational needs of children." [W]e will implement this programming provision by reviewing a licensee's renewal application to determine whether, over the course of its license term, it has served the educational and informational needs of children in its overall programming, including programming specifically designed to serve such needs.

A. Age Range of "Children"

15. The Act does not define "children" for purposes of the educational and informational programming renewal review requirement. [O]lder as well as younger children have unique needs and can benefit from programming directed to them. Teenagers are undergoing a transition to adulthood. They are still very influenced by adult role models and peers, including those portrayed on television. They are generally inexperienced and yet face many crucial decisions concerning sex, drugs, and their own identities. [W]e believe that we must interpret the programming renewal review requirement to apply to programs originally produced and broadcast for an audience of children 16 years of age and under.

18. Requiring each broadcaster to serve all age groups in order to pass our renewal review would probably result in less expensive and lower quality programming, possibly

engendering what the Association of Independent Television Stations describes as "sameness and mediocrity." We thus decline to adopt suggestions that broadcasters program to all ages or to each subset of children within the under 16 range. Stations may select the age groups they can most effectively serve.

B. *Standard*

1. *Programming*

19. Although we stated the desire to avoid any de facto system of "precensorship" and to leave it to licensees to interpret the meaning of educational and informational programming, the Notice asked those commenters desiring a delineation of the Act's programming renewal review requirement to address what definition of "educational and informational" programming we might use. The Notice specifically referred to a description, used by Senator Inouye, as programming which furthers a child's intellectual, emotional and social development.

21. Programming that furthers the positive development of the child in any respect, including the child's cognitive/intellectual or emotional/social needs, can contribute to satisfying the licensee's obligation to serve the educational and informational needs of children.

22. The Notice proposed to require each licensee to assess the needs of children given (1) the circumstances within the community, (2) other programming on the station, (3) programming aired on other broadcast stations within the community, and (4) other programs for children available in the broadcaster's community of license. Licensees would then air programs intended to meet "the educational and informational needs of children" responding to this assessment. In order to avoid unnecessary burdens, we are not requiring use of the proposed assessment criteria. We do, however, adopt them as permissive guidelines for exercise of licensee discretion in applying this definition. These factors can serve to make licensees' decisionmaking process more objective and may make it easier for licensees to justify programming decisions that are questioned. We therefore encourage their use.

24. The Act imposes no quantitative standards and the legislative history suggests that Congress meant that no minimum amount criterion be imposed. Given this strong legislative direction, and the latitude afforded broadcasters in fulfilling the programming requirement, we believe that the amount of "specifically designed" programming necessary to comply with the Act's requirement is likely to vary according to other circumstances, including but not limited to, the type of programming aired and other nonbroadcast efforts made by the station. We thus decline to establish any minimum programming requirement for licensees for renewal review independent of that established in the Act.

2. *Nonbroadcast efforts*

27. Section 103(b) of the Act permits the Commission, in evaluating compliance with the broadcaster's obligation to demonstrate at renewal time that it served the educational and informational needs of children, to consider "in addition" to its programming (1) "any special nonbroadcast efforts ... which enhance the educational and informational value" of programming meeting such needs and (2) any "special effort" to produce or support programming broadcast by another station in the licensee's market that is specifically designed to meet such needs.

29. If a station produces or buys children's programs broadcast on another station, so as to qualify under section 103(b)(2) of the Act, we hold that both stations may rely on such programming in their renewal applications. The extent of support, measured in

both time and money, given to another station's programming will determine the weight afforded it. Nonprogramming efforts, however, will not entirely eliminate the obligation to air some "specifically designed" educational and informational programming.

D. Record-keeping and Reporting

36. We do not adopt proposed processing guidelines based on percentages of children's programming, as these would conflict with Congress' rejection of quantitative standards.

IV. PENALTIES

39. We will assess forfeitures for violations of rules implementing the Act if violations are "willful or repeated" within the meaning of 47 U.S.C. § 503. Given that the Act's programming requirement is to be measured over the course of the license term, however, forfeitures for violation of that requirement would be appropriately considered only at renewal. Similarly, violations of the Act should be considered along with a licensee's overall performance in determining whether it is entitled to a renewal.

Notes and Questions

1. The Commission's Interpretation. Did the Commission's implementation of the Act substantially reduce its force? Just what did the 1991 rules require of licensees with respect to children's programming? A public interest group reported that, in the year after the FCC's Report and Order, licensees seeking renewals filed such descriptions of their children's programming as: (a) Program: "Bucky O'Hare" (animation), Description: "Gooddoer Bucky fights off the evil toads from aboard his ship. Issues of social consciousness and responsibility are central themes of the program." (b) Program: "Leave It to Beaver," Description: "Eddie misunderstands Wally's help to girlfriend, Cindy, and confronts Wally with his fist. Communication and trust are shown in this episode." Harry F. Waters, On Kid TV, Ploys R Us, Newsweek, Nov. 30, 1992, at 88.

2. Another Round. In March 1993, shortly after the Clinton Administration took office, the FCC issued a Notice of Inquiry on Children's Television. A Notice of Proposed Rulemaking followed in 1995. These formed the basis for the Commission's dramatic reversal of course in 1996.

POLICIES AND RULES CONCERNING CHILDREN'S TELEVISION PROGRAMMING

Report and Order, 11 FCC Rcd. 10,660 (1996)

I. INTRODUCTION

2. [O]ur initial regulations implementing the [Children's Television Act of 1990 (CTA)] have not been fully effective in prompting broadcasters "to increase the amount of educational and informational broadcast television programming available to children." Senate Report at 1. Our review of the record in this proceeding reveals several problems. First, because of their imprecision in defining the scope of a broadcaster's obligation under the Children's Television Act, our rules have led to a variation in the level and nature of broadcasters' compliance efforts that is incompatible with the intent of the CTA. In so doing, our rules fail to adequately counterbalance the marketplace disincentives as Congress intended when it enacted the CTA. Indeed, some broadcasters are carrying very

little regularly scheduled standard length programming specifically designed to educate and inform children. Second, some broadcasters are claiming to have satisfied their statutory obligations with shows that, by any reasonable benchmark, cannot be said to be "specifically designed" to educate and inform children within the meaning of the CTA. Third, parents and others frequently lack timely access to information about the availability of programming in their communities specifically designed to educate and inform children, exacerbating market disincentives. Therefore, as proposed in the Notice of Proposed Rulemaking (NPRM) we released in 1995, we refine our policies and rules implementing the CTA to remedy these problems.[17]

3. First, we adopt a number of proposals designed to provide better information to the public about the shows broadcasters air to fulfill their obligation to air educational and informational programming under the CTA. Such information will assist parents who wish to guide their children's television viewing and, if large numbers of parents use that information to choose educational programming for their children, increase the likelihood that the market will respond with more educational programming. In addition, better information should help parents and others have an effective dialogue with broadcasters in their community about children's programming and, where appropriate, to urge programming improvements without resorting to government intervention.

4. Second, we adopt a definition of programming "specifically designed" to educate and inform children (or "core" programming) that provides better guidance to broadcasters concerning programming that fulfills their statutory obligation to air such programming. In order to qualify as core programming, a show must have serving the educational and informational needs of children as a significant purpose. The Commission will ordinarily rely on the good faith judgments of broadcasters as to whether programming satisfies this test and will evaluate compliance of individual programs with this definition only as a last resort. Our new definition of core programming includes other objective elements. A core program must be a regularly scheduled, weekly program of at least 30 minutes, and aired between 7:00 a.m. and 10:00 p.m. The program must also be identified as educational and informational for children when it is aired and must be listed in the children's programming report placed in the broadcaster's public inspection file.

5. Third, we adopt a processing guideline that will provide certainty for broadcasters about how to comply with the CTA and facilitate our processing efforts. As described more fully below, under this guideline, broadcasters will receive staff-level approval of the CTA portion of their renewal applications if they air three hours per week of core programming or if, while providing somewhat less than three hours per week of core programming, they air a package of programming that demonstrates a level of commitment to educating and informing children that is at least equivalent to airing three hours per week of core programming. Broadcasters that do not meet this guideline will be referred to the full Commission for consideration, where they will have a full opportunity

---

17. The actions we take today are consistent with a proposal submitted by President Clinton on behalf of "a group including educators, child advocates, and broadcast industry representatives" on how to revise our rules "to provide educational programming for America's children in fulfillment of the purpose of the 1990 Children's Television Act." Letter from President Clinton to Chairman Reed Hundt (July 31, 1996). The National Association of Broadcasters (NAB) participated in this group and submitted the identical proposal in supplemental comments. See NAB Supplemental Comments (filed July 29, 1996).

to demonstrate compliance with the CTA, including through efforts other than "core" programming and through nonbroadcast efforts.[18]

6. [A] processing guideline will help ensure that broadcasters who wish to provide an ample amount of children's educational programming will not find themselves at an unfair disadvantage in the market relative to competing broadcasters who do not, and will not find themselves facing competitive pressure to forgo airing educational programs. A processing guideline will also facilitate speedy and consistent application processing by Commission staff. In short, a processing guideline is a clear, fair and efficient way to implement the Children's Television Act.

II. BACKGROUND

A. The Importance of Children's Educational Television Programming

10. Studies confirm, and many commenters in this proceeding agree, that children can benefit substantially from viewing educational television. In one such study, children who watch "Barney" showed greater counting skills, knowledge of colors and shapes, vocabulary, and social skills, than children who did not watch the program. Although all children can benefit from educational television, it has been found to be particularly beneficial to children from lower income families. Thus, there is substantial information before us showing that television can educate children.

11. That television has the power to teach is important because nearly all American children have access to television and spend considerable time watching it. Recent data show that television reaches 98 percent of all American homes, including well over 90 percent of households with annual incomes below $5,000. Data also show that children from ages 2 to 17 watch on average more than 3 hours of television each day. The significance of over-the-air television for children is reinforced by the fact that fewer children have access to cable television than to over-the-air television. Hence, over-the-air broadcasting is an important source of video programs for children and for all members of low income families, including children.

12. Television reaches children earlier and for more hours per day than any other educational influence except perhaps family. Many children watch television before they are exposed to any formal education. Nearly 70 percent of day-care facilities have a television on for several hours each day. By the time most American children begin the first grade, they will have spent the equivalent of three school years in front of the television set.

13. Some have argued that children will not watch educational programming. But there are studies that show that, where educational programming is available, a large percentage of children watch. The Westat study found that the majority of young children in all demographic groups watch "Sesame Street." Another study submitted by [Children's Television Workshop (CTW)] suggests that children do not distinguish between educational and non-educational programming, and that they do not find educational programming less appealing. Fox Broadcasting Company, Fox Children's Network (FCN), and Fox Affiliates Association (collectively referred to herein as "Fox") submitted evidence that the educational programs developed by the FCN receive high ratings.

---

18. *See* 47 U.S.C. § 303b(b) (providing that, in addition to considering educational and informational programming aired on the licensee's station, the Commission may consider "any special non-broadcast efforts" by the licensee to enhance the value of such programming, and "any special efforts" by the licensee to sponsor programming on another station in its market).

D. The Supply of Children's Educational Television Programming

29. *The Economics of Children's Educational Programming.* [I]n enacting the CTA, Congress found that market forces were not sufficient to ensure that commercial stations would provide children's educational and information programming.

30. A number of factors explain the marketplace constraints on providing such programming. Over-the-air commercial broadcast television stations earn their revenues from the sale of advertising time. Revenues received from the sale of advertising depend on the size and the socio-demographic characteristics of the audience reached by the broadcaster's programming. Broadcasters thus have a reduced economic incentive to promote children's programming because children's television audiences are smaller than general audiences.

31. Broadcasters have even less economic incentive to provide educational programs for children. Educational programming generally must be targeted at segments of the child audience. An educational program for children aged 2–5, however, may well be of little interest to children aged 6–11 or children aged 12–17. By contrast, an entertainment program for children is more likely to appeal to a broader range of children.[19] Thus the market for children's educational television may be segmented by age in ways that do not characterize children's entertainment programming or adult programming. Additionally, the adult audience is much larger than the child audience. There are 59.5 million children in the television audience: 16.0 million children aged 2–5, 22.2 million aged 6–11, and 21.3 million children aged 12–17. Adults aged 18–49 number 122.2 million. Because the adult audience is so much larger than the children's audience, the potential advertising revenues are also much larger and therefore provide broadcasters with an incentive to focus on adult programming rather than children's educational television programming. And within the category of children's programming, broadcasters have an economic incentive to select entertainment programs that appeal to a broader range of children rather than educational programs that appeal to a narrower group.

32. If stations are required to provide some educational programming for children, we believe that the same incentives could cause station owners to prefer to show such programming when relatively few adults would likely be in the audience. For example, it is less costly for broadcasters to show children's educational programs very early in the morning than to show them at later hours because the number of adult viewers lost, and hence the advertising revenues lost, will be relatively low. [A] significant portion of children's programming is currently aired before 7:00 a.m. and few children's programs are shown in prime time, which draws the largest adult audiences.

33. Furthermore, in the broadcasting marketplace it may be difficult for a small number of parents and others with strong demands for children's educational programming to signal the intensity of their demand for such programming. In other retail markets, consumers can demonstrate the intensity of their preferences by the amount of money they spend, i.e., their dollar "votes." However, broadcasting rating services basically register only one "vote" per viewer. But the signal that matters to the broadcaster is the dollar amount of advertising revenues. Small audiences with little buying power, such as children's educational tel-

---

19. Nielsen data indicate that children ages 6 to 11 are much more likely to watch general audience or adult-oriented entertainment programs than they are to watch children's programs. Moreover, when asked to name their favorite programs, children ages 10 to 17 were much more likely to include adult-oriented or general audience programs than child-specific shows. The State of Children's Television: An Examination of Quantity, Quality, and Industry Beliefs, conducted by Amy B. Jordan for the Annenberg Public Policy Center of the University of Pennsylvania under the Direction of Kathleen Hall Jamieson, June 17, 1996, *citing* Nielsen Media Research, March, 1996.

evision audiences, are unlikely to be able to signal the intensity of their demand for such programming in the broadcasting market. Therefore, broadcasters will have little incentive to provide such programming because the small audiences and small resulting advertising revenues means that there will be a substantial cost to them (the so-called "opportunity cost") of forgoing larger revenues from other types of programs not shown.

34. These and the other factors described above tend to lead to an underprovision of children's educational and informational television programming, as Congress found in the CTA.

36. *The amount of educational programming on broadcast television.* [T]he studies submitted [in this proceeding] are inconclusive in establishing the exact amount of educational programming that currently is being provided by broadcasters. Despite their deficiencies, however, the studies do allow us to conclude that some broadcasters are providing a very limited amount of programming specifically designed to educate and inform children and that broadcasters vary widely in their understanding of the type of programming that the CTA requires. This evidence, viewed together with the rest of the record, leads us to conclude that it is necessary to take the actions adopted here to achieve the goals of the CTA. [A lengthy review of the studies is omitted.]

43. *Availability of educational programming on nonbroadcast media.* A number of broadcasters submitted comments arguing that the Commission should assess not just the educational programming being provided over-the-air by broadcast stations, but rather the overall availability of educational programming in the video marketplace. We believe, however, that the proper focus in this proceeding should be on the provision of children's educational programming by broadcast stations, not by cable systems and other subscription services such as direct broadcast satellite systems that, in contrast to broadcast service, require the payment of a subscription fee. The CTA itself expressly focuses on broadcast licensees. In enacting this statute, Congress found that, as part of their public interest obligations, "*television station operators and licensees* should provide programming that serves the special needs of children," 47 U.S.C. § 303a (emphasis added), and the Act applies only to television broadcast stations, *id.* at § 303b(a). Thus, the statute focuses on the provision of children's educational programming through broadcasting, a ubiquitous service, which may be the only source of video programming for some families that cannot afford, or do not have access to, cable or other subscription services. While noting an increase in the number of nonbroadcast outlets available for children to receive video programming, the House Report states that "the new marketplace for video programming does not obviate the public interest responsibility of individual broadcast licensees to serve the child audience." House Report at 6.

III. PUBLIC INFORMATION INITIATIVES

47. We conclude that the market inadequacies that led Congress to pass the Children's Television Act can be addressed, in part, by enhancing parents' knowledge of children's educational programming.

48. Commercial television is advertiser supported. Parents can increase the audience of an educational program by encouraging their children to watch the show, but can only do so if they know in advance when the show will air and that the show is educational. Increasing the audience size for educational programs increases the incentive of broadcasters to air, and producers to supply, more such programs.

49. In considering the options to improve the information available regarding educational programming, we seek to maximize the access to such information by the public while minimizing the cost to the licensee. [W]e [adopt] three basic methods to improve

the public's access to information: commercial broadcasters should identify core programming at the time those programs are aired in a form that is at the sole discretion of the licensee; they should identify such programs to publishers of program guides; and, as detailed below, they should provide improved access to information to the public through standardized reporting and other means. We note that disclosure requirements of the sort we adopt today promote First Amendment interests by increasing the flow of information to the public.

IV. DEFINITION OF PROGRAMMING "SPECIFICALLY DESIGNED" TO SERVE CHILDREN'S EDUCATIONAL AND INFORMATIONAL NEEDS

80. The definition of core programming that we adopt is designed to provide licensees with clear guidance regarding how we will evaluate renewal applications. The elements of our proposed definition are also designed to be as objective as possible so that they are more easily understood by licensees and the Commission staff and to avoid injecting the Commission unnecessarily into sensitive decisions regarding program content. [P]rogramming specifically designed to serve children's educational and informational needs is the only category of programming the CTA expressly requires each licensee to provide. Adopting a definition of such programming will promote this statutory objective by more precisely defining the programming that qualifies and, consequently, provide appropriate incentives to increase the amount of such programming. We further believe that the definition we adopt today will continue to provide broadcasters ample discretion in designing and producing such programming. We emphasize that the test of whether programming qualifies as core does not depend in any way on its topic or viewpoint. The test is whether it is "specifically designed" to serve the educational and informational needs of children. We now turn to the specific elements of the new definition of core programming.

Significant Purpose

81. We propose[] that core programming have serving the educational and informational needs of children as a "significant" instead of "primary" purpose as suggested in the NOI, in response to the widely-held view that such programming must be entertaining to be successful. We belie[ve] that this terminology makes clear that education need not be the only purpose of programming specifically designed to meet the educational and informational needs of children, but must be more than an incidental goal.

84. [T]o qualify as core programming, a show must have serving the educational and informational needs of children ages 16 and under as a significant purpose. The "significant purpose" standard appropriately acknowledges the point advanced by broadcasters and others that to be successful, and thus to serve children's needs as mandated by the CTA, educational and informational programming must also be entertaining and attractive to children. Accordingly, we will require that core programming be specifically designed to meet the educational and informational needs of children ages 16 and under and have educating and informing children as a significant purpose.

87. Several commenters asked us to clarify that our definition of core programming includes educational and informational programs that further children's social and emotional development as well as their cognitive and intellectual development. The CTA speaks of programming specifically designed to serve "the educational and informational needs of children." 47 U.S.C. §303b(a)(2). It does not draw a distinction between educational and informational programming that furthers children's cognitive and intellectual development and educational and informational programming that furthers children's

social and emotional development. We decline to draw that distinction ourselves and accordingly conclude that both fall within the scope of our definition.

Educational and Informational Objective and Target Child Audience Specified in Writing

90. With respect to the second element of our core programming definition, we require licensees to specify in writing in their children's programming report the educational and informational objective of a core program, as well as its target child audience.

96. [W]e decline to require broadcasters to serve particular segments of the child audience. [W]e recognize the possibility that licensees may be induced to air programming for children over 12 because (1) this group has greater spending power than young children, (2) shows for older children may attract general audiences as well as children, and (3) programming designed for children 12 and under is subject to commercial limits, while programming for older children is not. Nonetheless, we conclude[] that it would be undesirable to require broadcasters to serve particular segments of the child audience, in part because we do not have adequate data showing that in fact younger age groups are underserved relative to other children.

Times Core Programming May Be Aired

99. To qualify as core, a program must air between the hours of 7:00 a.m. and 10:00 p.m. In specifying this time period, our intention is to encourage broadcasters to air educational programming at times the maximum number of child viewers will be watching. [The Commission then recounted data suggesting that child viewing increases substantially after 7 a.m. and drops considerably after 10 p.m.]

Regularly Scheduled

105. [Q]ualifying core programming should be regularly scheduled, particularly in view of our emphasis on improving the flow of information to parents through published program guides and other means to enable them to select educational and informational programs for their children. Programming that is aired on a regular basis is more easily anticipated and located by viewers, and can build loyalty that will improve its chance for commercial success. We agree with those commenters who argue that programs that air regularly can reinforce lessons from episode to episode. We also believe that regularly scheduled programs can develop a theme which enhances the impact of the educational and informational message. Accordingly, to be considered as core, we will require that educational and informational programs air on a regular basis.

Substantial Length

110. [C]ore programming should be at least 30 minutes in length. [T]he dominant broadcast television format is 30 minutes or longer in length. Programs in these standard formats are more likely than shorter programming to be regularly scheduled and to be listed in program guides, and thus are easier for parents to identify for their child's viewing. In addition, programs that are 30 minutes or longer allow more time for educational and informational material to be presented. There was no evidence presented to support claims by some parties that children have short attention spans and thus will not benefit from substantial length programming.

112. We emphasize that programming with a significant purpose of educating and informing children that is less than 30 minutes in length, although not credited as core programming, can contribute to serving children's needs pursuant to the CTA. Such programming can count toward meeting the three-hour processing guideline when broadcasters air somewhat less than 3 hours per week of core programming, as described below.

Identified as Educational and Informational

113. [S]tations [will] be required to identify core programs as educational and informational at the beginning of the program, and to make available the necessary information for listing these programs as educational and informational in program guides. [W]e adopt both of these [rules] in order to improve the information available to parents regarding programming specifically designed for children's educational and informational needs, and to assist them in selecting these programs for their children. We also believe this measure will make broadcasters more accountable in classifying programming as specifically designed to educate and inform.

V. PROCESSING GUIDELINE

115. In the NPRM, we sought comment on several proposals for evaluating a licensee's compliance with the Children's Television Act at renewal. Specifically, we proposed to adopt one of three alternative options: (1) Commission monitoring of the amount of educational and informational programming on the air during a period of time following the adoption of measures to improve the flow of programming information to the public and adoption of a definition of "core" programming; (2) adoption of a safe harbor processing guideline specifying an amount of programming specifically designed to serve children's educational and informational needs that would represent one means of satisfying the CTA's programming obligation; and (3) adoption of a programming standard that would require broadcasters to air a specified average number of hours per week of programming specifically designed to serve the educational and informational needs of children. We also sought comment on whether we should adopt "program sponsorship" rules or guidelines, giving licensees the option of satisfying a portion of the prescribed amount by providing financial or other "in kind" support for programming aired on other stations in their market.

120. Based on our review of the record, as well as our experience in enforcing the CTA over the past five years, we have decided to adopt a three-hour processing guideline. [U]nder this guideline, the Mass Media Bureau[20] will be authorized to approve the Children's Television Act portions of a broadcaster's renewal application where the broadcaster has aired three hours per week (averaged over a six month period) of educational and informational programming that has as a significant purpose serving the educational and informational needs of children ages 16 and under. Renewal applications that do not meet this guideline will be referred to the Commission, where the applicant will have a full opportunity to demonstrate compliance with the CTA by, for example, relying in part on sponsorship of core educational and informational programs on other stations in the market that increases the amount of core educational or informational programming on the station airing the sponsored program and/or on special nonbroadcast efforts which enhance the value of children's educational and informational television programming.

124. In the context of the CTA, a processing guideline is clear, fair and efficient. First, our experience in reviewing the children's programming portions of renewal applications teaches us that a processing guideline is desirable as a matter of administrative efficiency in enforcing the CTA and provides desirable clarity about the extent of a broadcaster's programming responsibilities under the statute. Due to the volume of broadcast television renewal applications received by the Commission—approximately 1500 commercial and noncommercial

---

20. [The Mass Media Bureau, now called the Media Bureau, is a subdivision of the FCC that focuses on mass media issues. The FCC has other specialized units, for example the Wireless Telecommunications Bureau and the Wireline Competition Bureau. Eds.]

applications during each renewal cycle—the Commission has for many years delegated to the Mass Media Bureau the authority to act on applications that do not present difficult issues. In the absence of an articulated guideline regarding CTA compliance that the Bureau would use to distinguish applications that are properly processed at the staff level from those that must be sent to the full Commission, a *de facto* processing guideline likely would develop. But this *de facto* guideline, if unpublished, would not provide clear and timely notice of what a licensee can do to guarantee renewal under the CTA. By adopting a safe harbor processing guideline in this order, the Commission is simply giving public notice of the procedures it will use to evaluate a broadcaster's children's educational and informational programming performance.[21] Licensees and the public will consequently know with certainty and in advance what a licensee can do to ensure that it meets its CTA obligations.

129. We recognize that this is contrary to our earlier interpretation of the CTA as precluding quantification of the CTA obligation. We reached this conclusion in 1991 on the grounds that the statute itself "impos[ed] no quantitative standard" and the "legislative history suggest[ed] that Congress meant that no minimum amount criterion be imposed." In reaching a contrary conclusion today, we begin with the fact that nothing in the statutory language of the CTA forbids the use of a processing guideline. Furthermore, although there is specific language in the legislative history, cited in our 1991 Report and Order and by parties in this proceeding, stating the "Committee does not intend that the FCC interpret this section as requiring or mandating a quantification standard," this language does not prohibit us from seeking to provide greater clarity and guidance through a processing guideline. Rather, this language simply makes clear that the CTA does not *require* quantitative standards or guidelines. It is not our conclusion today that we *must* adopt a quantitative guideline, but that the processing guideline approach we adopt will clarify the imprecision of our current rules that has led to a variation in the level and nature of broadcasters' compliance efforts that is incompatible with the intent of the CTA. Thus, because of its clarity, fairness, and ease of administration, a processing guideline will remedy the shortcomings of our initial rules and thereby provide the appropriate counterweight to the market forces identified by Congress that tend to discourage broadcasters from airing children's educational and informational programming.

136. If we find that a broadcaster has not complied with the CTA, we will apply the same remedies that we use in enforcing our other rules. These remedies will vary depending on the severity of the deficiency based on objective criteria. For less serious deficiencies, we will consider letters of admonition or reporting requirements. For more serious violations, we will consider other sanctions, including forfeitures and short-term renewals. In extreme cases, we will consider designating the license for hearing to determine whether the licensee's violations of the CTA and our implementing rules warrant nonrenewal under the standards set forth in section 309(k) of the Communications Act.

138. *Special Sponsorship Efforts.* The CTA states that, "[i]n addition to consideration of the licensee's [educational] programming, the Commission may consider ... any special efforts by the licensee to produce or support programming broadcast by another sta-

---

21. The Commission in the past has adopted processing guidelines to achieve similar purposes. For example, the Commission's non-entertainment programming processing guidelines provided that the applications of licensees that offered less than certain amounts of non-entertainment programming had to be acted upon by the Commission rather than by the Bureau. *See* Deregulation of Radio, Report and Order, 84 F.C.C. 2d 968, 975 (1981), *recon.*, Deregulation of Radio, Memorandum Opinion and Order, 87 F.C.C. 2d 797 (1981), *aff'd in part, remanded in part*, Off. of Comm. of the United Church of Christ v. FCC, 707 F.2d 1413, 1432 (D.C. Cir. 1983). It is universally accepted that these guidelines were "purely procedural." 707 F.2d at 1432.

tion in the licensee's marketplace which is specifically designed to serve the educational and informational needs of children." Some parties supported giving credit to a sponsoring station in assessing its CTA performance at renewal time, while others opposed the idea. We will allow a licensee to present evidence at the Commission level of such special sponsorship efforts. To receive credit under this provision for a "special" sponsorship effort, a broadcaster must demonstrate that its production or support of core programming aired on another station in its market increased the amount of core programming on the station airing the sponsored core programming. Also, we note again that the text of section 103(b) does not relieve a broadcaster of the obligation to air programming specifically designed to serve the educational and informational needs of children. It permits the Commission to consider sponsorship nonbroadcast efforts only "in addition to consideration of the licensee's [educational] programming."

VII. FIRST AMENDMENT ISSUES

147. To the extent that some commenters argue that the CTA is unconstitutional, Congress itself addressed that issue. It specifically concluded that "it is well within the First Amendment strictures to require the FCC to consider, during the license renewal process, whether a television licensee has provided information specifically designed to serve the educational and informational needs of children in the context of its overall programming." Senate Report at 16. As the Senate Report noted, broadcasters, in exchange for "the free and exclusive use of a valuable part of the public domain," can be expected to serve as a public fiduciary, obliged to serve the needs and interests of their viewers. [*Id.* (*citing* Red Lion Broadcasting Co. v. FCC, 395 U.S. 367 (1969)).] That obligation includes the obligation to serve the needs of children. Even more specifically, as the FCC, the courts, and Congress have concluded, a broadcaster's public interest obligation properly includes an obligation to serve the educational and informational needs of children. The question in this proceeding is not *whether* the Commission should give effect to the CTA, but *how* it should do so.

149. "It does not violate the First Amendment to treat licensees given the privilege of using scarce radio frequencies as proxies for the entire community, obligated to give suitable time and attention to matters of great public concern." *Red Lion*, 395 U.S. at 394. Congress's authority to order "suitable time and attention to matters of great public concern" includes the authority to require broadcasters to air programming specifically designed to further the educational needs of children. The airwaves belong to the public, not to any individual broadcaster. The fact that Congress elected to retain public ownership of the broadcast spectrum and to lease it for free to private licensees for limited periods carries significant First Amendment consequences.

150. In CBS v. FCC, 453 U.S. 367 (1981), the Supreme Court upheld a challenge to the statute (47 U.S.C. §312(a)(7)) that requires broadcasters to provide reasonable access to individual candidates seeking federal elective office. Similarly, here, the CTA requires broadcasters to serve the educational and informational needs of children through programming specifically designed for those needs. Both provisions require broadcasters to air certain types of programming they might not otherwise choose to provide. However, the obligation imposed by section 312(a)(7) appears to be significantly more burdensome than the obligation imposed by the CTA. Under section 312(a)(7), broadcasters have no control over the content of the political advertising. In contrast, under the CTA broadcasters are obligated to provide children's educational programming, yet they retain wide discretion in choosing what programs to provide, a fact little changed by the clarifying measures we adopt today.

153. The CTA and our regulations directly advance the government's substantial, and indeed compelling, interest in the education of America's children. As Congress recognized, "[i]t is difficult to think of an interest more substantial than the promotion of the welfare of children who watch so much television and rely upon it for so much of the information they receive." Senate Report at 17; *see also* House Report at 11.

154. [T]he Children's Television Act is designed to promote programming that *educates and informs* children. The framers of the First Amendment understood that "the greatest menace to freedom is an inert people," as Justice Brandeis wrote [in Whitney v. California, 274 U.S. 357, 372 (1927) (concurring opinion)]. It is entirely consistent with the First Amendment to ask trustees of the public airwaves to pursue reasonable, viewpoint-neutral measures designed to increase the likelihood that children will grow into adults capable of fully participating in our deliberative democracy.

155. Such a requirement also is supported by the Supreme Court's decision in FCC v. Pacifica Foundation, 438 U.S. 726 (1978). In that case the Court recognized that "broadcasting is uniquely accessible to children" and that "the broadcast media have established a uniquely pervasive presence in the lives of all Americans." *Id.* at 748, 749–750. Both of those factors support Congress' decision to require broadcasters to serve the educational needs of children. [T]elevision has an influence on children in our society rivalled only by family and school. It would be accurate to blend the two factors noted in *Pacifica* and conclude that television has a pervasive presence in the lives of American children. The Court in *Pacifica* upheld restrictions on the broadcast of indecent material. [T]he government's interest in the intellectual development of our nation's children is at least as significant as its interest in protecting them from exposure to indecent material.

156. *Pacifica* upheld a complete ban on a particular type of programming (indecent programming) during hours when children are likely to be in the audience. The measures we adopt today do not ban programming of any type, they simply notify broadcasters that compliance with the CTA can be achieved with, on average, less than half an hour a day of programming expressing any viewpoint on any topic that broadcasters desire.

Notes and Questions

1. Reversal of Course. With adoption of these 1996 Children's Television rules, the FCC—with some prodding from Congress—had now come full circle. What factor(s) account for the switch in policy? As we asked at the start of this section, can the Commission's changes in policy be explained simply on the grounds that it learned a great deal from its early attempts and regulation and acted later to correct those early errors? Or are these policies more fundamentally inconsistent?

2. Careful Looks. In reviewing the various children's television proceedings, it is helpful to consider the variety of specific policies that are proposed and debated. What seems to determine whether a policy is considered seriously or brushed aside? Does the Commission overlook any policy angles that might have proven fruitful upon further consideration?

3. Defining Children's Television. What do advocates of regulation mean by "children's programming"? Is it television that children watch? Television that is targeted for children? Television that children should watch? Does the Commission adopt a consistent, complete definition of this term? Does it need to in order to regulate, or is that itself one of the issues being debated in these proceedings?

4. Why Intervene? What is the basic rationale for government intervention? That government should see to it that young children spend more time watching TV? Is the rationale based on the assertion that the television marketplace has failed or that the entire economic and political system has failed? Is the claim that TV uniquely underserves children or that all of society undervalues youngsters' needs and that television is an appropriate or easily available candidate for reform?

5. Children of Different Ages. Recall that, in *ACT III*, the D.C. Circuit did not distinguish teenagers from younger children for purposes of approving the regulations at issue there. Is that consistent with the FCC's emphasis in the 1996 Children's Television rules (see, for example, ¶ 31) on the different interests and resulting market segmentation of children based on their age? How might you argue that they are consistent?

6. Taxation by Regulation. Why did Congress choose to pursue its educational goals by empowering the FCC to regulate licensees instead of taking a more direct approach, for example taxing broadcasters and using those revenues to pay for the production and distribution of high-quality children's programming? That is, doesn't the current approach in essence operate as a tax on broadcasters, causing them to forfeit the opportunity to engage in their preferred (more profitable) broadcasts and instead air children's television? Why does this make sense? Wouldn't broadcasters be just as happy to buy their way out of this requirement, perhaps airing NBA games and then splitting the revenues with the U.S. Department of Education which could then, in turn, use those monies both to produce quality children's programming and to purchase time on local stations? Indeed, wouldn't such an approach be better for all parties concerned? Surely the U.S. Department of Education can develop better educational content than can some unwilling broadcaster. Further, a tax-and-spend approach would make all the relevant policy choices more explicit, perhaps forcing Congress to consider even better options—like perhaps spending all this money on teacher salaries instead of regularly scheduled "educational" cartoons.

As a general matter, the phrase taxation by regulation refers to any situation where the government imposes a financial burden on a regulated party not directly, but instead by requiring a particular unprofitable behavior. The phrase is designed to remind policymakers to consider the explicit alternative—namely, actually taxing the regulated parties in that same amount and then using those monies to further the policy goal at issue. There are myriad examples of taxation by regulation in this book. An important question to consider throughout your study of telecommunications, then, is whether taxation by regulation is a particularly efficient manner of governing in the public interest or, rather, an inefficient option that cases like *Red Lion* unfortunately make easily available to regulators.

7. The 1990 Children's Television Act. The 1990 Children's Television Act is a particularly interesting case study in taxation by regulation since the statute expressly permits stations to buy their way out of certain burdens that they would otherwise bear. Specifically, the Act, as implemented in the 1996 Children's Television rules, allows a licensee to receive credit for sponsoring children's programming on another station. Such sponsorship cannot, however, fully "relieve a broadcaster of the obligation to air programming specifically designed to serve the educational and informational needs of children." ¶ 138. What assumptions about television viewing are reflected in this refusal to allow sponsorship to discharge fully a licensee's children's television obligations? If licensees were allowed to discharge all of their children's television obligations by sponsoring programs on other stations, whose interests would be served? Whose sacrificed?

8. Regulation by Raised Eyebrow. The 1996 Children's Television rules also nicely illustrate the phenomenon of regulation by raised eyebrow, a concept first introduced in Chapter

Two. When regulating by raised eyebrow, a regulatory agency announces that it would be pleased if the regulated firm does so-and-so but that the firm is not legally required to do it. The firm, of course, ignores such "advice" at its peril, but at the same time has no apparent basis on which to contest the legality of the agency's announcement since no particular legal penalty attaches to a firm's decision not to comply. Consider, in this regard, ¶ 22 of the FCC's 1991 Report and Order. How would you advise a licensee that was inclined not to follow the "assessment criteria" set out there? Processing guidelines, such as those adopted in the 1996 Report and Order, are of course classic "raised eyebrow" approaches. The agency simply announces that licensees who follow the recommended guidelines will breeze through come renewal time, whereas licensees that ignore the guidelines will be subject to full Commission review. Any guesses as to how many licensees opt for full Commission review?

9. The First Amendment. Does the "raised eyebrow" argument dispose of a First Amendment objection to the 1996 rules? Are you persuaded by the Commission's response to the argument that its rules violate the Constitution? Would all of the Commission's arguments apply as well to the imposition of comparable rules on any other medium of expression? Or is the Commission repudiating not only the policy conclusions of its 1983 Children's Television Report, but also the conclusion in its 1985 Fairness Doctrine Report and 1987 *Syracuse Peace Council* Order that television is not a unique medium for constitutional purposes?

Note, too, that the FCC's constitutional argument (in Part VII of the 1996 Report and Order) does not fully reflect the content of its rules. Part VII appears to describe vague processing guidelines designed to encourage licensees to serve the needs of children. But the rules in fact manage the programming process to a significant degree, providing at least six conditions that must be met before a program is a "core" program for purposes of the rules. And this management takes place in every television market, for every television station, regardless of the number of stations or children's program networks in the market. Suppose the Commission sought to publish a document that justified the constitutionality of the rules which the agency in fact promulgated. This would require, for example, explaining why a highly informative program that is not part of a regularly scheduled series or is twenty-five minutes long is officially disfavored. How might the Commission argue that such rules do not abridge the freedom of speech?

10. The Economics of Children's Educational Programming. Consider the Commission's arguments in its 1996 Report and Order concerning the economics of children's educational television programming. *See* ¶¶ 29–34. If what is said there is accurate, what accounts for the fact that bookstores routinely carry substantial quantities of books geared specifically at "the educational and informational needs of children" and that both PBS and certain cable television networks carry programming of the same sort? Is the Commission's point that none of these other services or media are supported by advertisers? Does the Commission mean to assert that Americans have a right to advertiser-supported television *and* that the exercise of this right also entitles the FCC to enact content regulations that the First Amendment would otherwise forbid? If a conventional television broadcast station were to shift from "free" to "pay" status by scrambling its signal, would it then be able to argue successfully that the 1996 rules cannot be constitutionally applied to it?

11. Evaluating the Programming. How should the Commission measure the success and value of these regulations? Should it look to the quality of the programming? The quantity? The times it airs? In this regard, a group called Children Now released a report in 2008 that analyzed 120 episodes of 40 programs identified as children's programming, and rated 63% "moderately educational," 23% "minimally educational," and only 13% as "highly educational" (a decrease from studies in the 1990s, which had found 20% to 33% "highly educational"). The study also found that 59% of stations aired only the minimum three hours per week, that 75% of stations aired children's educational programming exclusively on weekends, and that the shows on commercial stations received significantly lower scores than programs on PBS. http://www.childrennow.org/uploads/documents/eireport_2008.pdf. Does this suggest that the regulations have failed and should be abandoned? That they are insufficiently specific and rigorous?

12. Broader Metrics. Perhaps the metrics above, focusing on particular shows, are too narrow. Should the Commission instead look to broader metrics? If so, what should they be? Should the Commission ask whether children are spending more time watching television? Whether children have shifted their viewing patterns from "Sesame Street" to more expensive educational fare produced by commercial networks? Whether preschoolers engage in more "imaginative play"? ¶ 9.

13. Application to Digital Broadcasts and Internet Websites. In 2004, the FCC issued an order entitled Children's Television Obligations of Digital Television Broadcasters, Report and Order and Further Notice of Proposed Rulemaking, 19 FCC Rcd. 22,943 (2004). Parts of the order updated the 1996 Report and Order: most notably, it revised the definition of "commercial matter" to include promotions for non-children's television programming and added a new requirement that broadcasters identify children's programming with the symbol "E/I." 19 FCC Rcd. at ¶¶ 41, 46, 57.

More interestingly for our purposes, it addressed two issues that were not relevant in 1996 but became meaningful later. The first arises from the transition to digital television, and specifically the fact that the FCC permits a broadcast licensee to multicast—i.e., transmit video signals, paid or free, in addition to the one free digital signal it is obligated to transmit. As the Commission stated in the order, "[t]he current 3 hours per week processing guideline was adopted with the one channel per broadcaster analog model in mind." *Id.* ¶ 18. The question before the Commission was whether it would impose children's television requirements on additional digital signals. The Commission decided that "[d]igital broadcasters will continue to be subject to the existing three hours per week core programming processing guideline on their main program stream. DTV broadcasters that choose to provide additional streams or channels of free video programming will, in addition, have the following guideline applied to the additional programming: 1/2 hour per week of additional core programming for every increment of 1 to 28 hours of free video programming provided in addition to the main program stream." *Id.* ¶ 19. The order gives broadcasters the choice whether to air this additional programming on a single free digital channel or on multiple channels, as long as at least three hours per week are shown on their main channel, and "as long as the stream/s on which the core programming is aired has comparable carriage on multichannel video programming distributors as the stream whose programming generates the core programming obligation under the revised processing guideline." *Id.* ¶ 24.

The order also deals with the relationship of the Internet to children's programming. It provides that for programs directed at children ages twelve and under, the display of Internet website addresses during program material is permitted "only if the website: (1) offers a substantial amount of *bona fide* program-related or other noncommercial content; (2) is not primarily intended for commercial purposes, including either e-commerce or advertising; (3) the website's home page and other menu pages are clearly labeled to distinguish the noncommercial from the commercial sections; and (4) the page of the website to which viewers are directed by the website address is not used for e-commerce, advertising, or other commercial purposes (e.g., contains no links labeled "store" and no links to another page with commercial material)." *Id.* ¶ 50. This restriction applies to all broadcasters, both analog and digital, as well as cable operators. (The order found "little if any use" of direct, interactive, links to commercial Internet sites in children's programming, so the Commission decided to forego issuing any decision on such linking, but to consider the issue in a future order. *Id.* ¶ 53.) This puts the FCC in the position of evaluating not only broadcast content but also Internet content. Is this a case of the FCC inappropriately aggrandizing its power, or wisely eliminating a loophole by recognizing the role of the Internet in television programming?

14. Stakeholders' Agreement. Several broadcasters pushed for changes to the 2004 order mentioned above. After the FCC declined to modify its order, they filed lawsuits challenging the order on First Amendment and administrative law grounds. *See* The Walt Disney Co., No. 05-1393 (filed D.C. Cir. Oct. 11, 2005); Viacom Inc. v. FCC, No. 05-1387 (filed D.C. Cir. Oct. 3, 2005). The Commission urged the broadcasters to reach an agreement with children's television advocates over changes to the order. The two groups announced a joint proposal to modify the rules in 2006, and the FCC immediately announced its intention to accept that proposal. Children's Television Obligations of Digital Television Broadcasters, Second Further Notice of Proposed Rulemaking, 21 FCC Rcd. 3642 (2006).

Most notably, under the joint proposal the restrictions on the display of Web addresses would not apply to portions of children's programming demarcated as commercial time (which would be "clearly separated from programming material"). And "commercial matter" would not include "promotions for children's or other age-appropriate programming appearing on the same channel, or promotions for children's E/I programming on any channel"—so cross-promotions by, say, Disney would not count as commercials. Joint Proposal of Industry and Advocates on Reconsideration of Children's Television Rules, https://apps.fcc.gov/edocs_public/attachmatch/FCC-06-33A2.pdf.

The joint proposal required FCC approval, of course. If that approval was not foreordained, then why would broadcasters and children's television advocates spend their time on this? If the FCC's approval was foreordained, why would the FCC effectively outsource rule modifications to broadcasters and children's television advocates? Does this represent an abdication of the FCC's role? Relatedly, were there important interests (or interest groups) who were not represented in this negotiation?

15. Other Media and Children's Television. As we noted above, 47 U.S.C. § 303a limits the time devoted to advertising that broadcast stations and cable operators may air during children's programming. The Commission extended those limits to DBS operators in Implementation of Section 25 of the Cable Television Consumer Protection and Competition Act of 1992: Direct Broadcast Satellite Public Interest Obligations, Sua Sponte Reconsideration, Second Order on Reconsideration of First Report and Order, 19 FCC Rcd. 5647 (2004). The Commission has not extended the guidelines in the 2006 order discussed in number 14, above, to cable or DBS operators or channels.

As we noted earlier in this chapter, Congress did require that each DBS provider reserve between 4 and 7 percent of its channels "exclusively for noncommercial programming of an educational or informational nature," and the D.C. Circuit upheld that provision against a First Amendment challenge. 47 U.S.C. § 335(b)(1); Time Warner Entertainment Co. v. FCC, 93 F.3d 957 (D.C. Cir. 1996).

Chapter Sixteen

Direct Regulation of Content Deemed Harmful

Introduction

The previous chapter focuses on regulations obligating providers (mainly broadcasters) to provide content that the government believes is valuable and likely to be underproduced absent regulation. In this chapter, we address laws limiting content deemed harmful. As we noted in the previous chapter, the laws have focused on one particular kind of content deemed harmful—indecency. Congress has enacted legislation regulating indecency on broadcast, cable television, telephony, and the Internet, and each category has produced at least one major Supreme Court opinion. Indecency thus has the distinction of being the only area that Congress has seen fit to regulate, and the Supreme Court has seen fit to address, with respect to all four of the basic forms of communication that make up telecommunications. In this way, indecency presents an interesting cross-cutting case study. In considering the Supreme Court's treatment of broadcasting, cable television, telephony, and the Internet, we can see what differences it identifies as constitutionally significant among them.

One other point bears noting. Many of the regulations addressed in this casebook involve the Commission crafting its own regulations pursuant to broad or ambiguous congressional legislation; the key elements of the regulation were created by the Commission. The FCC's approach to comparative hearings (discussed in Chapter Five) are a good example. With respect to indecency, however, Congress has seen fit to legislate with more specificity than the broad legislative language we have seen elsewhere. Indeed, as the cases below reveal, Congress has not only mandated limits on indecency but has returned to the issue if its first foray was rejected. Congress has focused on legislating against indecency more than it has focused on any other area of telecommunications regulation. This may reflect in part the courts' rejection of so many congressional efforts at indecency regulation. Courts have never invalidated the Sherman Antitrust Act, so Congress has not needed to pass new legislation to achieve its antitrust aims. But it also reflects the popularity, at least in Congress, of regulations aimed at indecency. Are there other areas of telecommunications that merit such congressional focus?

We begin with regulation of indecency. Below are cases involving broadcast indecency, cable indecency, indecency over the telephone, and Internet indecency. We then turn to the other form of harmful content that has been the subject of regulatory focus (though much less than indecency)—violence.

§ 16.A. Indecency

§ 16.A.1. Regulation of Broadcast Indecency

FCC v. Pacifica Foundation
438 U.S. 726 (1978)

STEVENS, J., delivered the opinion of the Court (Parts I, II, III, and IV-C) and an opinion in which BURGER, C.J., and REHNQUIST, J., joined (Parts IV-A and IV-B). POWELL, J., filed an opinion concurring in part and concurring in the judgment, in which BLACKMUN, J., joined. BRENNAN, J., filed a dissenting opinion, in which MARSHALL, J., joined. STEWART, J., filed a dissenting opinion in which BRENNAN, WHITE, and MARSHALL, JJ., joined.

JUSTICE STEVENS delivered the opinion of the Court (Parts I, II, III and IV-C) and an opinion in which CHIEF JUSTICE BURGER and JUSTICE REHNQUIST joined (Parts IV-A and IV-B).

A satiric humorist named George Carlin recorded a 12-minute monologue entitled "Filthy Words" before a live audience in a California theater. He began by referring to his thoughts about "the words you couldn't say on the public, ah, airwaves, um, the ones you definitely wouldn't say, ever." He proceeded to list those words and repeat them over and over again in a variety of colloquialisms.[1] The transcript of the recording indicates frequent laughter from the audience.

At about 2 o'clock in the afternoon on Tuesday, October 30, 1973, a New York radio station, owned by respondent Pacifica Foundation, broadcast the "Filthy Words" monologue. A few weeks later a man, who stated that he had heard the broadcast while driving with his young son, wrote a letter complaining to the Commission. He stated that, although he could perhaps understand the "record's being sold for private use, I certainly cannot understand the broadcast of same over the air that, supposedly, you control."

The complaint was forwarded to the station for comment. In its response, Pacifica explained that the monologue had been played during a program about contemporary society's attitude toward language and that, immediately before its broadcast, listeners had been advised that it included "sensitive language which might be regarded as offensive to some." Pacifica characterized George Carlin as "a significant social satirist" who "like Twain and Sahl before him, examines the language of ordinary people.... Carlin is not mouthing obscenities, he is merely using words to satirize as harmless and essentially silly our attitudes towards those words." Pacifica stated that it was not aware of any other complaints about the broadcast.

On February 21, 1975, the Commission issued a declaratory order granting the complaint. [T]he Commission concluded that certain words depicted sexual and excretory activities in a patently offensive manner, noted that they "were broadcast at a time when children were undoubtedly in the audience (i. e., in the early afternoon)," and that the prerecorded language, with these offensive words "repeated over and over," was "deliberately broadcast." Citizen's Complaint Against Pacifica Foundation, 56 F.C.C. 2d 94, 99. In summary, the Commission stated: "We therefore hold that the language as broadcast was indecent and prohibited by 18 U.S.C. [§] 1464."

---

1. [Carlin identified the seven words as shit, piss, fuck, cunt, cocksucker, motherfucker, and tits. At the time, the FCC had seven commissioners. In the aftermath of *Pacifica*, industry rumor had it that, for future enforcement efforts, each commissioner was assigned one word. Eds.]

II

[Here, the Court concluded that § 326 of the Communications Act, which forbids the Commission to engage in censorship, "does not limit the Commission's authority to impose sanctions on licensees who engage in obscene, indecent, or profane broadcasting." The Court found that the section forbids censorship in advance of broadcast. And, "[e]ntirely apart from the fact that the subsequent review of program content is not the sort of censorship at which the statute was directed, its history makes it perfectly clear that it was not intended to limit the Commission's power to regulate the broadcast of obscene, indecent, or profane language."]

III

The only other statutory question presented by this case is whether the afternoon broadcast of the "Filthy Words" monologue was indecent within the meaning of 18 U.S.C. § 1464. [The section forbids "any obscene, indecent, or profane language by means of radio communications." The Court held that "obscene" and "indecent," as those words are employed in § 1464, have different meanings. To be obscene, language must appeal to the prurient interest and lack serious value.] Prurient appeal is an element of the obscene, but the normal definition of "indecent" merely refers to nonconformance with accepted standards of morality.

IV

Pacifica makes two constitutional attacks on the Commission's order. First, it argues that the Commission's construction of the statutory language broadly encompasses so much constitutionally protected speech that reversal is required even if Pacifica's broadcast of the "Filthy Words" monologue is not itself protected by the First Amendment. Second, Pacifica argues that inasmuch as the recording is not obscene, the Constitution forbids any abridgment of the right to broadcast it on the radio.

A

The first argument fails because our review is limited to the question whether the Commission has the authority to proscribe this particular broadcast.

It is true that the Commission's order may lead some broadcasters to censor themselves. At most, however, the Commission's definition of indecency will deter only the broadcasting of patently offensive references to excretory and sexual organs and activities.[2] While some of these references may be protected, they surely lie at the periphery of First Amendment concern.

B

When the issue is narrowed to the facts of this case, the question is whether the First Amendment denies government any power to restrict the public broadcast of indecent language in any circumstances.[3] For if the government has any such power, this was an appropriate occasion for its exercise.

---

2. A requirement that indecent language be avoided will have its primary effect on the form, rather than the content, of serious communication. There are few, if any, thoughts that cannot be expressed by the use of less offensive language.

3. Pacifica's position would, of course, deprive the Commission of any power to regulate erotic telecasts unless they were obscene under Miller v. California, 413 U.S. 15 (1973). Anything that could be sold at a newsstand for private examination could be publicly displayed on television. We are assured by Pacifica that the free play of market forces will discourage indecent programming. "Smut may," as Judge Leventhal put it, "drive itself from the market and confound *Gresham*," 556

[T]he fact that society may find speech offensive is not a sufficient reason for suppressing it. If there were any reason to believe that the Commission's characterization of the Carlin monologue as offensive could be traced to its political content—or even to the fact that it satirized contemporary attitudes about four-letter words—First Amendment protection might be required. But that is simply not this case. These words offend for the same reasons that obscenity offends.[4] "Such utterances are no essential part of any exposition of ideas, and are of such slight social value as a step to truth that any benefit that may be derived from them is clearly outweighed by the social interest in order and morality." Chaplinsky v. New Hampshire, 315 U.S. 568, 572 (1942).

In this case it is undisputed that the content of Pacifica's broadcast was "vulgar," "offensive," and "shocking." Because content of that character is not entitled to absolute constitutional protection under all circumstances, we must consider its context in order to determine whether the Commission's action was constitutionally permissible.

C

We have long recognized that each medium of expression presents special First Amendment problems. And of all forms of communication, it is broadcasting that has received the most limited First Amendment protection. Thus, although other speakers cannot be licensed except under laws that carefully define and narrow official discretion, a broadcaster may be deprived of his license and his forum if the Commission decides that such an action would serve "the public interest, convenience, and necessity." 47 U.S.C. §§ 309(a), 312(a)(2). Similarly, although the First Amendment protects newspaper publishers from being required to print the replies of those whom they criticize, Miami Herald Publishing Co. v. Tornillo, 418 U.S. 241 (1974), it affords no such protection to broadcasters; on the contrary, they must give free time to the victims of their criticism. Red Lion Broadcasting Co. v. FCC, 395 U.S. 367 (1969).

The reasons for these distinctions are complex, but two have relevance to the present case. First, the broadcast media have established a uniquely pervasive presence in the lives of all Americans. Patently offensive, indecent material presented over the airwaves confronts the citizen, not only in public, but also in the privacy of the home, where the individual's right to be left alone plainly outweighs the First Amendment rights of an intruder. Because the broadcast audience is constantly tuning in and out, prior warnings cannot completely protect the listener or viewer from unexpected program content. To say that one may avoid further offense by turning off the radio when he hears indecent language is like saying that the remedy for an assault is to run away after the first blow. One may hang up on an indecent phone call, but that option does not give the caller a constitutional immunity or avoid a harm that has already taken place.

Second, broadcasting is uniquely accessible to children, even those too young to read. Although Cohen's written message [referring to Cohen v. California, 403 U.S. 15 (1971)] might have been incomprehensible to a first grader, Pacifica's broadcast could have enlarged a child's vocabulary in an instant. Other forms of offensive expression may be withheld from the young without restricting the expression at its source. Bookstores and

---

F.2d at 35; the prosperity of those who traffic in pornographic literature and films would appear to justify skepticism.

4. The Commission stated: "Obnoxious, gutter language describing these matters has the effect of debasing and brutalizing human beings by reducing them to their mere bodily functions." 56 F.C.C. 2d at 98. Our society has a tradition of performing certain bodily functions in private, and of severely limiting the public exposure or discussion of such matters. Verbal or physical acts exposing those intimacies are offensive irrespective of any message that may accompany the exposure.

motion picture theaters, for example, may be prohibited from making indecent material available to children. We held in Ginsberg v. New York, 390 U.S. 629 (1968), that the government's interest in the "well-being of its youth" and in supporting "parents' claim to authority in their own household" justified the regulation of otherwise protected expression.[5] The ease with which children may obtain access to broadcast material, coupled with the concerns recognized in *Ginsberg*, amply justify special treatment of indecent broadcasting.

It is appropriate, in conclusion, to emphasize the narrowness of our holding. This case does not involve a two-way radio conversation between a cab driver and a dispatcher, or a telecast of an Elizabethan comedy. We have not decided that an occasional expletive in either setting would justify any sanction or, indeed, that this broadcast would justify a criminal prosecution. The Commission's decision rested entirely on a nuisance rationale under which context is all-important. The concept requires consideration of a host of variables. The time of day was emphasized by the Commission. The content of the program in which the language is used will also affect the composition of the audience,[6] and differences between radio, television, and perhaps closed-circuit transmissions, may also be relevant. As Mr. Justice Sutherland wrote, a "nuisance may be merely a right thing in the wrong place—like a pig in the parlor instead of the barnyard." Euclid v. Ambler Realty Co., 272 U.S. 365, 388 (1926). We simply hold that when the Commission finds that a pig has entered the parlor, the exercise of its regulatory power does not depend on proof that the pig is obscene.

APPENDIX TO OPINION OF THE COURT

The following is a verbatim transcript of "Filthy Words" prepared by the Federal Communications Commission.

Aruba-du, ruba-tu, ruba-tu. I was thinking about the curse words and the swear words, the cuss words and the words that you can't say, that you're not supposed to say all the time, [']cause words or people into words want to hear your words. Some guys like to record your words and sell them back to you if they can, (laughter) listen in on the telephone, write down what words you say. A guy who used to be in Washington, knew that his phone was tapped, used to answer, Fuck Hoover, yes, go ahead. (laughter) Okay, I was thinking one night about the words you couldn't say on the public, ah, airwaves, um, the ones you definitely wouldn't say, ever, [']cause I heard a lady say bitch one night on television, and it was cool like she was talking about, you know, ah, well, the bitch is the first one to notice that in the litter Johnie right (murmur) Right. And, uh, bastard you can say, and hell and damn so I have to figure out which ones you couldn't and ever and it came down to seven but the list is open to amendment, and in fact, has been changed, uh, by now, ha, a lot of people pointed things out to me, and I noticed some myself. The original seven words were, shit, piss, fuck, cunt, cocksucker, motherfucker, and tits. Those are the ones that will curve your spine, grow hair on your hands and (laughter) maybe, even bring us, God help us, peace without honor (laughter) um, and a bourbon. (laugh-

---

5. The Commission's action does not by any means reduce adults to hearing only what is fit for children. *Cf.* Butler v. Michigan, 352 U.S. 380, 383 (1957). Adults who feel the need may purchase tapes and records or go to theaters and nightclubs to hear these words. In fact, the Commission has not unequivocally closed even broadcasting to speech of this sort; whether broadcast audiences in the late evening contain so few children that playing this monologue would be permissible is an issue neither the Commission nor this Court has decided.

6. Even a prime-time recitation of Geoffrey Chaucer's Miller's Tale would not be likely to command the attention of many children who are both old enough to understand and young enough to be adversely affected by passages such as: "And prively he caughte hire by the queynte." The Canterbury Tales, Chaucer's Complete Works (Cambridge ed. 1933), p. 58.

ter) And now the first thing that we noticed was that word fuck was really repeated in there because the word motherfucker is a compound word and it's another form of the word fuck. (laughter) You want to be a purist it doesn't really—it can't be on the list of basic words. Also, cocksucker is a compound word and neither half of that is really dirty. The word—the half sucker that's merely suggestive (laughter) and the word cock is a half-way dirty word, 50% dirty—dirty half the time, depending on what you mean by it. (laughter) Uh, remember when you first heard it, like in 6th grade, you used to giggle. And the cock crowed three times, heh (laughter) the cock—three times. It's in the Bible, cock in the Bible. (laughter) And the first time you heard about a cock-fight, remember—What? Huh? naw. It ain't that, are you stupid? man. (laughter, clapping) It's chickens, you know, (laughter) Then you have the four letter words from the old Angle-Saxon fame. Uh, shit and fuck. The word shit, uh, is an interesting kind of word in that the middle class has never really accepted it and approved it. They use it like, crazy but it's not really okay. It's still a rude, dirty, old kind of gushy word. (laughter) They don't like that, but they say it, like, they say it like, a lady now in a middle-class home, you'll hear most of the time she says it as an expletive, you know, it's out of her mouth before she knows. She says, Oh shit oh shit, (laughter) oh shit. If she drops something, Oh, the shit hurt the broccoli. Shit. Thank you. (footsteps fading away) (papers ruffling)

Read it! (from audience)

Shit! (laughter) I won the Grammy, man, for the comedy album. Isn't that groovy? (clapping, whistling) (murmur) That's true. Thank you. Thank you man. Yeah. (murmur) (continuous clapping) Thank you man. Thank you. Thank you very much, man. Thank, no, (end of continuous clapping) for that and for the Grammy, man, [']cause (laughter) that's based on people liking it man, yeh, that's ah, that's okay man. (laughter) Let's let that go, man. I got my Grammy. I can let my hair hang down now, shit. (laughter) Ha! So! Now the word shit is okay for the man. At work you can say it like crazy. Mostly figuratively, Get that shit out of here, will ya? I don't want to see that shit anymore. I can't *cut* that shit, buddy. I've had that shit up to here. I think you're full of shit myself. (laughter) He don't know shit from Shinola. (laughter) you know that? (laughter) Always wondered how the Shinola people felt about that (laughter) Hi, I'm the new man from Shinola, (laughter) Hi, how are ya? Nice to see ya. (laughter) How are ya? (laughter) Boy, I don't know whether to shit or wind my watch. (laughter) Guess, I'll shit on my watch. (laughter) Oh, *the* shit is going to hit *de* fan. (laughter). Built like a brick shit-house. (laughter) Up, he's up shit's creek. (laughter) He's had it. (laughter) He hit me, I'm sorry. (laughter) Hot shit, holy shit, tough shit, eat shit. (laughter) shit-eating grin. Uh, whoever thought of that was ill. (murmur laughter) He had a shit-eating grin! He had a what? (laughter) Shit on a stick. (laughter) Shit in a handbag. I always like that. He ain't worth shit in a handbag. (laughter) Shitty. He acted real shitty. (laughter) You know what I mean? (laughter) I got the money back, but a real shitty attitude. Heh, he had a shit-fit. (laughter) Wow! Shit-fit. Whew! Glad I wasn't there. (murmur, laughter) All the animals—Bull shit, horseshit, cow shit, rat shit, bat shit. (laughter) First time I heard bat shit, I really came apart. A guy in Oklahoma, Boggs, said it, man. Aw! Bat shit. (laughter) Vera reminded me of that last night, ah (murmur). Snake shit, slicker than owl shit. (laughter) Get your shit together. Shit or get off the pot. (laughter) I got a shit-load full of them. (laughter) I got a shit-pot full, all right. Shit-head, shit-heel, shit in your heart, shit for brains, (laughter) shit-face, heh (laughter) I always try to think how that could have originated; the first guy that said that. Somebody got drunk and fell in some shit, you know. (laughter) Hey, I'm shit-face. (laughter) Shit-face, *today*. (laughter) Anyway, enough of that shit. (laughter) The big one, the word fuck that's the one that hangs them up the most. [']Cause in a lot of cases that's the very act that hangs them up the most. So, it's natural that the word would, uh, have the same effect. It's a great word, fuck, nice word, easy word, cute word, kind of. Easy word to say. One syllable, short u. (laughter) Fuck. (murmur) You know, it's easy. Starts with a nice soft sound fuh ends with a *kuh*. Right? (laughter) A little something for everyone. Fuck (laughter) Good word. Kind of a proud word, too. Who are you? I am *FUCK*, (laughter) *FUCK OF THE MOUNTAIN*. (laughter) Tune in again next week to FUCK OF THE MOUNTAIN. (laughter) It's an interesting word too, [']cause it's got a double kind of a life—personality—dual, you know, whatever the right phrase is. It leads a double life, the word fuck. First of all, it means, sometimes, most of the time, fuck. What does it mean? It means to make love. Right? We're going to make love, yeh, we're going to fuck, yeh, we're going to fuck, yeh, we're going to make love. (laughter) we're really going to fuck, yeh, we're going to make love. Right? And it also means the beginning of life, it's the act that begins life, so there's the word hanging around with words like love, and life, and yet on the other hand, it's also a word that we really use to hurt each other with, man. It's a heavy. It's one that you have toward the end of the argument. (laughter) Right? (laughter) You finally can't make out. Oh, fuck you man. I said, fuck you. (laughter, murmur) Stupid fuck. (laughter) Fuck you and everybody that looks like you. (laughter) man. It would be nice to change the movies that we already have and substitute the word fuck for the word kill, wherever we could, and some of those movie cliches would change a little bit. Madfuckers still on the loose. Stop me before I fuck again. Fuck the ump, fuck the ump, fuck the ump, fuck the ump, fuck the ump. Easy on the clutch Bill, you'll fuck that engine again. (laughter) The other shit one was, I don't give a shit. Like it's worth something, you know? (laughter) I don't give a shit. Hey, well, I don't take no shit, (laughter) you know what I mean? You know why I don't take no shit? (laughter) [']Cause I don't give a shit. (laughter) If I give a shit, I would have to pack shit. (laughter) But I don't pack no shit cause I don't give a shit. (laughter) You wouldn't shit me, would you? (laughter) That's a joke when you're a kid with a worm looking out the bird's ass. You wouldn't shit me, would you? (laughter) It's an eight-year-old joke but a good one. (laughter) The additions to the list. I found three more words that had to be put on the list of words you could never say on television, and they were fart, turd and twat, those three. (laughter) Fart, we talked about, it's harmless. It's like tits, it's a cutie word, no problem. Turd, you can't say but who wants to, you know? (laughter) The subject never comes up on the panel so I'm not worried about that one. Now the word twat is an interesting word. Twat! Yeh, right in the twat. (laughter) Twat is an interesting word because it's the only one I know of, the only slang word applying to the, a part of the sexual anatomy that doesn't have another meaning to it. Like, ah, snatch, box and pussy all have other meanings, man. Even in a Walt Disney movie, you can say, We're going to snatch that pussy and put him in a box and bring him on the airplane. (murmur, laughter) Everybody loves it. The twat stands alone, man, as it should. And two-way words. Ah, ass is okay providing you're riding into town on a religious feast day. (laughter) You can't say, up your *ass*. (laughter) You can say, stuff it! (murmur) There are certain things you can say its weird but you can just come so close. Before I cut, I, uh, want to, ah, thank you for listening to my words, man, fellow, uh space travelers. Thank you man for tonight and thank you also. (clapping whistling)

JUSTICE POWELL, with whom JUSTICE BLACKMUN joins, concurring in part and concurring in the judgment.

I join Parts I, II, III, and IV-C of Justice Stevens' opinion.

I do not subscribe to the theory that the Justices of this Court are free generally to decide on the basis of its content which speech protected by the First Amendment is most "valuable" and hence deserving of the most protection, and which is less "valuable" and hence deserving of less protection. In my view, the result in this case does not turn on whether Carlin's monologue, viewed as a whole, or the words that constitute it, have more or less "value" than a candidate's campaign speech. This is a judgment for each person to make, not one for the judges to impose upon him.

The result turns instead on the unique characteristics of the broadcast media, combined with society's right to protect its children from speech generally agreed to be inappropriate for their years, and with the interest of unwilling adults in not being assaulted by such offensive speech in their homes.

JUSTICE BRENNAN, with whom JUSTICE MARSHALL joins, dissenting.

Without question, the privacy interests of an individual in his home are substantial and deserving of significant protection. In finding these interests sufficient to justify the content regulation of protected speech, however, the Court commits two errors. First, it misconceives the nature of the privacy interests involved where an individual voluntarily chooses to admit radio communications into his home. Second, it ignores the constitutionally protected interests of both those who wish to transmit and those who desire to receive broadcasts that many—including the FCC and this Court—might find offensive.

I believe that an individual's actions in switching on and listening to communications transmitted over the public airways and directed to the public at large do not implicate fundamental privacy interests, even when engaged in within the home. Instead, because the radio is undeniably a public medium, these actions are more properly viewed as a decision to take part, if only as a listener, in an ongoing public discourse.

[U]nlike other intrusive modes of communication, such as sound trucks, "[t]he radio can be turned off," Lehman v. Shaker Heights, 418 U.S. 298, 302 (1974)—and with a minimum of effort. Whatever the minimal discomfort suffered by a listener who inadvertently tunes into a program he finds offensive during the brief interval before he can simply extend his arm and switch stations or flick the "off" button, it is surely worth the candle to preserve the broadcaster's right to send, and the right of those interested to receive, a message entitled to full First Amendment protection.

The Court's balance, of necessity, fails to accord proper weight to the interests of listeners who wish to hear broadcasts the FCC deems offensive. It permits majoritarian tastes completely to preclude a protected message from entering the homes of a receptive, unoffended minority.

[P]arents, *not* the government, have the right to make certain decisions regarding the upbringing of their children. As surprising as it may be to individual Members of this Court, some parents may actually find Mr. Carlin's unabashed attitude towards the seven "dirty words" healthy, and deem it desirable to expose their children to the manner in which Mr. Carlin defuses the taboo surrounding the words.[7]

I would place the responsibility and the right to weed worthless and offensive communications from the public airways where it belongs and where, until today, it resided: in a public free to choose those communications worthy of its attention from a marketplace unsullied by the censor's hand.

---

7. The opinions of my Brothers POWELL and STEVENS rightly refrain from relying on the notion of "spectrum scarcity" to support their result. As Chief Judge Bazelon noted below, "although scarcity has justified *increasing* the diversity of speakers and speech, it has never been held to justify censorship." Pacifica Foundation v. FCC, 556 F.2d 9, 29 (1977).

II

The idea that the content of a message and its potential impact on any who might receive it can be divorced from the words that are the vehicle for its expression is transparently fallacious. A given word may have a unique capacity to capsule an idea, evoke an emotion, or conjure up an image. Indeed, for those of us who place an appropriately high value on our cherished First Amendment rights, the word "censor" is such a word.

My Brother Stevens finds relevant to his First Amendment analysis the fact that "[a]dults who feel the need may purchase tapes and records or go to theaters and nightclubs to hear [the tabooed] words." My Brother Powell agrees: "The Commission's holding does not prevent willing adults from purchasing Carlin's record, from attending his performances, or, indeed, from reading the transcript reprinted as an appendix to the Court's opinion." The opinions of my Brethren display both a sad insensitivity to the fact that these alternatives involve the expenditure of money, time, and effort that many of those wishing to hear Mr. Carlin's message may not be able to afford, and a naive innocence of the reality that in many cases, the medium may well be the message.

The airways are capable not only of carrying a message, but also of transforming it. A satirist's monologue may be most potent when delivered to a live audience; yet the choice whether this will in fact be the manner in which the message is delivered and received is one the First Amendment prohibits the government from making.

III

[I]n our land of cultural pluralism, there are many who think, act, and talk differently from the Members of this Court, and who do not share their fragile sensibilities. It is only an acute ethnocentric myopia that enables the Court to approve the censorship of communications solely because of the words they contain. The words that the Court and the Commission find so unpalatable may be the stuff of everyday conversations in some, if not many, of the innumerable subcultures that compose this Nation. As one researcher concluded, "[w]ords generally considered obscene like 'bullshit' and 'fuck' are considered neither obscene nor derogatory in the [black] vernacular except in particular contextual situations and when used with certain intonations." C. Bins, Toward an Ethnography of Contemporary African American Oral Poetry, Language and Linguistics Working Papers No. 5, p. 82 (Georgetown Univ. Press 1972).

Today's decision will thus have its greatest impact on broadcasters desiring to reach, and listening audiences composed of, persons who do not share the Court's view as to which words or expressions are acceptable and who, for a variety of reasons, including a conscious desire to flout majoritarian conventions, express themselves using words that may be regarded as offensive by those from different socio-economic backgrounds. In this context, the Court's decision may be seen for what, in the broader perspective, it really is: another of the dominant culture's inevitable efforts to force those groups who do not share its mores to conform to its way of thinking, acting, and speaking.

JUSTICE STEWART, with whom JUSTICE BRENNAN, JUSTICE WHITE, and JUSTICE MARSHALL join, dissenting.

The statute pursuant to which the Commission acted, 18 U.S.C. § 1464, makes it a federal offense to utter "any obscene, indecent, or profane language by means of radio communication." The Commission held, and the Court today agrees, that "indecent" is a broader concept than "obscene" as the latter term was defined in Miller v. California, 413 U.S. 15 (1973), because language can be "indecent" although it has social, political, or artistic value and lacks prurient appeal. But this construction of § 1464, while perhaps plausible, is by no means compelled. To the contrary, I think that "indecent" should properly be read as meaning no more than "obscene." Since the Carlin monologue concededly was not "obscene," I believe that the Commission lacked statutory authority to ban it.

Notes and Questions

1. Uniquely Pervasive, Accessible Speech? The Supreme Court's opinion in *Pacifica* was not a surprise, but it did require the Court to juggle precedent somewhat, as a number of precedents outside the broadcasting field seemed to cut against the FCC. The *Pacifica* Court had to distinguish four major cases: (1) Butler v. Michigan, 352 U.S. 380 (1957), which held that the state could not enforce an obscenity statute focused on corrupting children that "reduce[d] the adult population of Michigan to reading only what is fit for children"; (2) Cohen v. California, 403 U.S. 15 (1971), which overturned a conviction for wearing a jacket inscribed with the statement "Fuck the Draft" and which appeared to leave the government equally helpless to regulate the language of speech and its content on the grounds that there was no legitimate distinction between the two; (3) Miller v. California, 413 U.S. 15 (1973), which held that the government had wide-ranging powers to regulate "obscene" speech but defined obscene speech to be speech that (a) described sexual conduct in a patently offensive way, (b) appealed to the prurient interest, and (c) lacked serious literary, artistic, scientific, or political value; and (4) Erznoznik v. City of Jacksonville, 422 U.S. 205 (1975), which held unconstitutional a municipal regulation barring drive-in movies from exhibiting motion pictures visible from public streets in which "the human male or female bare buttocks, human female bare breasts, or human bare pubic areas are shown." When the city sought to justify the *Erznoznik* regulation as designed to protect children, the Court stated that the law invaded minors' First Amendment rights. "Speech that is neither obscene as to youths nor subject to some other legitimate proscription cannot be suppressed solely to protect the young from ideas or images that a legislative body thinks unsuitable for them." *Id.* at 213–14.

The *Pacifica* Court thus needed to assert that Carlin's speech was of peculiarly low value, notwithstanding these precedents, or to pronounce broadcasting "unique" in order to justify the result. Is the Court convincing in asserting that broadcasting is uniquely pervasive and uniquely accessible to children? That such uniqueness justifies FCC censorship? Of this broadcast? (Are these claims more convincing than the correlative claim in *Red Lion* that broadcasting is unique because it employs scarce resources?)

2. Scarcity. Neither Justice Stevens' opinion nor Justice Powell's concurrence placed any weight on the scarcity rationale, and Justice Brennan's dissent stated flatly that scarcity could not support censorship. The argument for this position is fairly straightforward: the theory of scarcity seeks to justify regulations that expand voices, not those that contract them. But could the scarcity argument apply more broadly? If scarcity justifies requirements that broadcasters provide favored programming, why wouldn't it also justify prohibiting them from wasting that scarce resource on disfavored programming, especially because such a prohibition would then make room for more valuable programming? After all, if the government prohibited all low-value programming, it would not be replaced with silence but with other programs that presumably would be of greater value.

In this regard, consider the statement in *Red Lion* regarding the "right of the public to receive suitable access to social, political, esthetic, moral, and other ideas and experiences." *Red Lion*, 395 U.S. at 390. If, as Justice Stevens' opinion suggests, indecency is "no essential part of any exposition of ideas" and its social value is outweighed by the harms that it imposes, wouldn't the right of the public articulated in *Red Lion* be vindicated by the replacement of indecency with speech that is more likely to be an essential part of an exposition of ideas?

3. Indecent Speech. Notice that two of the five Justices in the *Pacifica* majority (Powell and Blackmun) relied exclusively on the unique status of broadcasting. For the others (Stevens, Burger, and Rehnquist), it was also important—indeed, perhaps most important—that what was being regulated was "indecent" speech. (*See* Part IV-B of the Stevens opinion, which Powell and Blackmun declined to join.) What, if any, limits do you suppose the Powell-Blackmun view would place on the ability of the FCC to censor? If AM radio broadcasting is "unique," is it possible that other media are similarly unique? If other media are similarly unique—an oxymoron—does this suggest that AM broadcasting is not unique after all?

4. Implications. How far does the *Pacifica* rationale reach? The FCC's briefs emphasized that its indecency regulation was aimed at protecting children under the age of twelve from indecent material. *See* Action for Children's Television v. FCC, 852 F.2d 1332, 1341– 42 (D.C. Cir. 1988) (*ACT I*). Does *Pacifica* suggest that its lenient review standard applies only to protections of "children ... too young to read"? Conversely, would its reasoning apply if the FCC defined "children" as everyone under the age of eighteen? Does *Pacifica* authorize a total ban on indecency or simply a limitation on its broadcast, say to certain times of the day? When implementing restrictions on indecency, does the government need to produce evidence of harm to children or of the likelihood that children would be in the listening or viewing audience? As to the latter, does the government need to show a risk that children were watching the specific show broadcast or only that some children were listening to some radio show somewhere? Is the Commission required to adopt a reasonably precise definition of "indecent programming" in order to clarify licensees' responsibilities and confine the FCC's discretion?

5. *Action for Children's Television*. Through press announcements shortly after *Pacifica*, the Commission stated that it believed the decision applied only to the repeated use, solely for shock value, of the words Carlin employed, when broadcast before 10:00 p.m. The FCC brought no further indecency cases until, on a single day in 1987, it issued three indecency opinions and announced that it was broadening its interpretation of indecency.[8] The Commission stated that "notwithstanding any prior contrary indications, ... [w]e find that the definition of indecent broadcast material set forth in *Pacifica* appropriately includes a broader range of material than the seven specific words at issue in *Pacifica*." Pacifica Foundation, Memorandum Opinion and Order, 2 FCC Rcd. 2698 ¶ 12. The Commission then said that "speech involving the description or depiction of sexual or excretory functions must be examined in context to determine whether it is patently offensive under contemporary community standards applicable to the broadcast medium." *Id.* ¶ 13.

---

8. Pacifica Foundation, Memorandum Opinion and Order, 2 FCC Rcd. 2698 (1987); Infinity Broadcasting Corp. of Pa., Memorandum Opinion and Order, 2 FCC Rcd. 2705 (1987); Regents of the University of California, Memorandum Opinion and Order, 2 FCC Rcd. 2703 (1987). To avoid any doubt on this score, the FCC also issued a public notice summarizing the three orders released that day and "put[ting] all broadcast and amateur radio licensees on notice as to new standards that the Commission will apply in enforcing the prohibition against obscene and indecent transmissions." New Indecency Enforcement Standards to be Applied to All Broadcast and Amateur Radio Licensees, Public Notice, 2 FCC Rcd. 2726 (1987); *see ACT I*, 852 F.2d at 1336.

Pacifica asked the FCC to reconsider its ruling in that order, putting in motion a legal process that ultimately involved the Commission, the courts, and Congress. That process culminated in the following en banc decision by the Court of Appeals for the D.C. Circuit.

Action for Children's Television v. FCC [ACT III]
58 F.3d 654 (D.C. Cir. 1995) (en banc), *cert. denied* 516 U.S. 1043 (1996)

Opinion for the court filed by Circuit Judge BUCKLEY, in which Circuit Judges SILBERMAN, WILLIAMS, GINSBURG, SENTELLE, HENDERSON, and RANDOLPH concur. Dissenting opinion filed by Chief Judge EDWARDS. Dissenting opinion filed by Circuit Judge WALD, in which Circuit Judges ROGERS and TATEL join.

BUCKLEY, Circuit Judge:

I. Background

In Infinity Broadcasting Corp. of Pa., 3 FCC Rcd. 930 (1987) (Reconsideration Order), the Commission reviewed its decisions in three cases: Pacifica Foundation, 2 FCC Rcd. 2698 (1987), Infinity Broadcasting Corp. of Pa., 2 FCC Rcd. 2705 (1987), and Regents of the University of California, 2 FCC Rcd. 2703 (1987). In each of them, the agency found that a radio station had introduced particularly offensive pigs into American parlors in violation of section 1464.

The FCC reaffirmed the Government interest in safeguarding children from exposure to such speech and placed broadcasters on notice that because

> at least with respect to the particular markets involved, available evidence suggested there were still significant numbers of children in the audience at 10:00 p.m.[,] ... broadcasters should no longer assume that 10:00 p.m. is automatically the time after which indecent broadcasts may safely be aired. Rather, ... indecent material would be actionable (that is, would be held in violation of 18 U.S.C. § 1464) if broadcast when there is a reasonable risk that children may be in the audience....

3 FCC Rcd. at 930–31. The Commission noted, however, that it was its "current thinking" that midnight marked the time after which "it is reasonable to expect that it is late enough to ensure that the risk of children in the audience is minimized and to rely on parents to exercise increased supervision over whatever children remain in the viewing and listening audience." *Id.* at 937 n.47.

In our review of the Reconsideration Order in Action for Children's Television v. FCC, 852 F.2d 1332 (D.C. Cir. 1988) (*ACT I*), we rejected the argument that the Commission's definition of indecency was unconstitutionally vague and overbroad. But although we affirmed the declaratory ruling that found portions of the morning broadcast to be in violation of section 1464, we vacated the Commission's rulings with respect to the two post-10:00 p.m. broadcasts. *Id.* In those instances, we considered the findings on which the Commission rested its decision to be "more ritual than real," *id.*, because the Commission had relied on data as to the number of teenagers in the total radio audience rather than the number of them who listened to the radio stations in question. We further concluded that "the FCC's midnight advice, indeed its entire position on channeling, was not adequately thought through." *Id.* at 1342.

Two months after our decision in *ACT I*, Congress instructed the Commission to promulgate regulations "enforce[ing] the provisions of ... section [1464] on a 24 hour per day basis." Pub. L. No. 100-459, §608, 102 Stat. 2186, 2228 (1988). The Commission complied by issuing a regulation banning all broadcasts of indecent material. We reviewed the 24-hour ban in Action for Children's Television v. FCC, 932 F.2d 1504 (D.C. Cir. 1991) (*ACT II*). We again rejected petitioners' vagueness and overbreadth arguments, but we struck down the total ban on indecent broadcasts because "[o]ur previous holding in *ACT I* that the Commission must identify some reasonable period of time during which indecent material may be broadcast necessarily means that the Commission may not ban such broadcasts entirely." 932 F.2d at 1509.

Shortly after the Supreme Court denied certiorari in *ACT II*, 503 U.S. 913 (1992), Congress again intervened, passing the Public Telecommunications Act of 1992, Pub. L. No. 102-356, 106 Stat. 949. Section 16(a) of the Act requires the Commission to

> promulgate regulations to prohibit the broadcasting of indecent programming—
>
> (1) between 6 a.m. and 10 p.m. on any day by any public radio station or public television station that goes off the air at or before 12 midnight; and
>
> (2) between 6 a.m. and 12 midnight on any day for any radio or television broadcasting station not described in paragraph (1).

47 U.S.C. § 303 note (Supp. IV 1992). Pursuant to this congressional mandate, the Commission issued regulations implementing section 16(a). Enforcement of Prohibitions Against Broadcast Indecency in 18 U.S.C. §1464, Report and Order, 8 FCC Rcd. 704, 711 (1993); 47 C.F.R. §73.3999 (1994). These are challenged in the petition now before us.

II. Discussion

A. The First Amendment Challenge

It is common ground that "[s]exual expression which is indecent but not obscene is protected by the First Amendment." Sable Communications of California, Inc. v. FCC, 492 U.S. 115, 126 (1989). The Government may, however, "regulate the content of constitutionally protected speech in order to promote a compelling interest if it chooses the least restrictive means to further the articulated interest." *Id.* Thus, a restriction on indecent speech will survive First Amendment scrutiny if the "Government's ends are compelling [and its] means [are] carefully tailored to achieve those ends." *Id.*

The Supreme Court has "long recognized that each medium of expression presents special First Amendment problems.... [O]f all forms of communication, it is broadcasting that has received the most limited First Amendment protection." FCC v. Pacifica Foundation, 438 U.S. 726, 748 (1978) (citation omitted).

Unlike cable subscribers, who are offered such options as "pay-per-view" channels, broadcast audiences have no choice but to "subscribe" to the entire output of traditional broadcasters. Thus they are confronted without warning with offensive material. *See Pacifica*, 438 U.S. at 748–49. This is "manifestly different from a situation" where a recipient "seeks and is willing to pay for the communication...." *Sable*, 492 U.S. at 128.

In light of these differences, radio and television broadcasts may properly be subject to different—and often more restrictive—regulation than is permissible for other media under the First Amendment. While we apply strict scrutiny to regulations of this kind regardless of the medium affected by them, our assessment of whether section 16(a) survives that scrutiny must necessarily take into account the unique context of the broadcast medium.

1. The Compelling Government Interests

The Commission identifies three compelling Government interests as justifying the regulation of broadcast indecency: support for parental supervision of children, a concern for children's well-being, and the protection of the home against intrusion by offensive broadcasts. Because we find the first two sufficient to support such regulation, we will not address the third.

Petitioners do not contest that the Government has a compelling interest in supporting parental supervision of what children see and hear on the public airwaves. While conceding that the Government has an interest in the well-being of children, petitioners argue that because "no causal nexus has been established between broadcast indecency and any physical or psychological harm to minors," Joint Brief for Petitioners at 32, that interest is "too insubstantial to justify suppressing indecent material at times when parents are available to supervise their children." *Id.* at 33. That statement begs two questions: The first is how effective parental supervision can actually be expected to be even when parent and child are under the same roof; the second, whether the Government's interest in the well-being of our youth is limited to protecting them from clinically measurable injury.

As Action for Children's Television argued in an earlier FCC proceeding, "parents, no matter how attentive, sincere or knowledgeable, are not in a position to really exercise effective control" over what their children see on television. Action for Children's Television, 50 F.C.C. 2d 1, 26 (1974). This observation finds confirmation from a recent poll conducted by Fairbank, Maslin, Maullin & Associates on behalf of Children Now. The survey found that 54 percent of the 750 children questioned had a television set in their own rooms and that 55 percent of them usually watched television alone or with friends, but not with their families. Sixty-six percent of them lived in a household with three or more television sets. Studies described by the FCC in its 1989 Notice of Inquiry suggest that parents are able to exercise even less effective supervision over the radio programs to which their children listen. According to these studies, each American household had, on average, over five radios, and up to 80 percent of children had radios in their own bedrooms, depending on the locality studied; two-thirds of all children ages 6 to 12 owned their own radios, more than half of whom owned headphone radios. It would appear that Action for Children's Television had a firmer grasp of the limits of parental supervision 20 years ago than it does today.

With respect to the second question begged by petitioners, the Supreme Court has never suggested that a scientific demonstration of psychological harm is required in order to establish the constitutionality of measures protecting minors from exposure to indecent speech. In Ginsberg v. New York, 390 U.S. 629, 634 (1968), the Court considered a New York State statute forbidding the sale to minors under the age of 17 of literature displaying nudity even where such literature was "not obscene for adults...." *Id.* at 634. The Court observed that while it was "very doubtful" that the legislative finding that such literature impaired "the ethical and moral development of our youth" was based on "accepted scientific fact," a causal link between them "had not been disproved either." *Id.* at 641–42. The Court then stated that it "d[id] not demand of legislatures scientifically certain criteria of legislation. We therefore cannot say that [the statute] ... has no rational relation to the objective of safeguarding such minors from harm." *Id.* at 642–43. In *Ginsberg*, of course, the protection of children did not require simultaneous restraints on the access of adults to indecent speech. The Court, however, has made it abundantly clear that the Government's interest in the "well-being of its youth" justified special treatment of indecent broadcasting.

Finally, we think it significant that the Supreme Court has recognized that the Government's interest in protecting children extends beyond shielding them from physical and psychological harm. The statute that the Court found constitutional in *Ginsberg* sought to protect children from exposure to materials that would "impair[] [their] ethical and moral development." *Id.* at 641. Furthermore, although the Court doubted that this legislative finding "expresse[d] an accepted scientific fact," *id.*, it concluded that the legislature could properly support the judgment of "parents and others, teachers for example, who have [the] primary responsibility for children's well-being ... [by] ... assessing sex-related material harmful to minors according to prevailing standards in the adult community as a whole with respect to what is suitable material for minors." *Id.* at 639.

Congress does not need the testimony of psychiatrists and social scientists in order to take note of the coarsening of impressionable minds that can result from a persistent exposure to sexually explicit material just this side of legal obscenity. The Supreme Court has reminded us that society has an interest not only in the health of its youth, but also in its quality. *See* Prince v. Massachusetts, 321 U.S. 158, 168 (1944) ("A democratic society rests, for its continuance, upon the healthy, well-rounded growth of young people into full maturity as citizens, with all that implies."). As Irving Kristol has observed, it follows "from the proposition that democracy is a form of self-government[] ... that if you want it to be a meritorious polity, you have to care about what kind of people govern it." Irving Kristol, On the Democratic Idea in America 41–42 (1972).

We are not unaware that the vast majority of States impose restrictions on the access of minors to material that is not obscene by adult standards. In light of Supreme Court precedent and the social consensus reflected in state laws, we conclude that the Government has an independent and compelling interest in preventing minors from being exposed to indecent broadcasts.

Petitioners argue, nevertheless, that the Government's interest in supporting parental supervision of children and its independent interest in shielding them from the influence of indecent broadcasts are in irreconcilable conflict. The basic premise of this argument appears to be that the latter interest potentially undermines the objective of facilitating parental supervision for those parents who wish their children to see or hear indecent material. The Supreme Court has not followed this reasoning. Rather, it treats the Government interest in supporting parental authority and its "independent interest in the well-being of its youth," *Ginsberg*, 390 U.S. at 640, as complementary objectives mutually supporting limitations on children's access to material that is not obscene for adults. *Id.* at 639–40.

Today, of course, parents who wish to expose their children to the most graphic depictions of sexual acts will have no difficulty in doing so through the use of subscription and pay-per-view cable channels, delayed-access viewing using VCR equipment, and the rental or purchase of readily available audio and video cassettes. Thus the goal of supporting "parents' claim to authority in their own household to direct the rearing of their children," *id.* at 639, is fully consistent with the Government's own interest in shielding minors from being exposed to indecent speech by persons other than a parent. Society "may prevent the general dissemination of such speech to children, leaving to parents the decision as to what speech of this kind their children shall hear and repeat." *Pacifica*, 438 U.S. at 758 (Powell, J., concurring in part and concurring in the judgment).

The Government's dual interests in assisting parents and protecting minors necessarily extend beyond merely channeling broadcast indecency to those hours when parents can be at home to supervise what their children see and hear. It is fanciful to believe that the vast majority of parents who wish to shield their children from indecent material can effectively do so without meaningful restrictions on the airing of broadcast indecency.

2. Least Restrictive Means

[Petitioners] contend that the "safe harbor" is not narrowly tailored because it fails to take proper account of the First Amendment rights of adults and because of the chilling effect of the 6:00 a.m. to midnight ban on the programs aired during the evening "prime time" hours.

The data on broadcasting that the FCC has collected reveal that large numbers of children view television or listen to the radio from the early morning until late in the evening, that those numbers decline rapidly as midnight approaches, and that a substantial portion of the adult audience is tuned into television or radio broadcasts after midnight. We find this information sufficient to support the safe harbor parameters that Congress has drawn.

We conclude that there is a reasonable risk that large numbers of children would be exposed to any indecent material broadcast between 6:00 a.m. and midnight.

Petitioners suggest that Congress should have used station-specific and program-specific data in assessing when children are at risk of being exposed to broadcast indecency. We question whether this would have aided the analysis. Children will not likely record, in a Nielsen diary or other survey, that they listen to or view programs of which their parents disapprove. Furthermore, changes in the program menu make yesterday's findings irrelevant today. Finally, to borrow the Commission's phrase, such station- and program-specific data do not take "children's grazing" into account.

The remaining question, then, is whether Congress, in enacting section 16(a), and the Commission, in promulgating the regulations, have taken into account the First Amendment rights of the very large numbers of adults who wish to view or listen to indecent broadcasts. We believe they have. The data indicate that significant numbers of adults view or listen to programs broadcast after midnight. Based on information provided by Nielsen indicating that television sets in 23 percent of American homes are in use at 1:00 a.m., the Commission calculated that between 21 and 53 million viewers were watching television at that time. Comments submitted to the FCC by petitioners indicate that approximately 11.7 million adults listen to the radio between 10:00 p.m. and 11:00 p.m., while 7.4 million do so between midnight and 1:00 a.m. With an estimated 181 million adult listeners, this would indicate that approximately 6 percent of adults listen to the radio between 10:00 p.m. and 11:00 p.m. while 4 percent of them do so between midnight and 1:00 a.m.

While the numbers of adults watching television and listening to radio after midnight are admittedly small, they are not insignificant. Furthermore, as we have noted above, adults have alternative means of satisfying their interest in indecent material at other hours in ways that pose no risk to minors. We therefore believe that a midnight to 6:00 a.m. safe harbor takes adequate account of adults' First Amendment rights.

Petitioners argue, nevertheless, that delaying the safe harbor until midnight will have a chilling effect on the airing of programs during the evening "prime time" hours that are of special interest to adults. They cite, as examples, news and documentary programs and dramas that deal with such sensitive contemporary problems as sexual harassment and the AIDS epidemic and assert that a broadcaster might choose to refrain from presenting relevant material rather than risk the consequences of being charged with airing broadcast indecency. Whatever chilling effects may be said to inhere in the regulation of indecent speech, these have existed ever since the Supreme Court first upheld the FCC's enforcement of section 1464 of the Radio Act. The enactment of section 16(a) does not add to such anxieties; to the contrary, the purpose of channeling, which we mandated in *ACT I* and reaffirmed in *ACT II*, and which Congress has now codified, is to provide a period in which radio and television stations may let down their hair without worrying whether they have stepped over any line other than that which separates protected speech from obscenity. Thus, section 16(a) has ameliorated rather than aggravated whatever chilling effect may be inherent in section 1464.

Petitioners also argue that section 16(a)'s midnight to 6:00 a.m. channeling provision is not narrowly tailored because, for example, Congress has failed to take into consideration the fact that it bans indecent broadcasts during school hours when children are presumably subject to strict adult supervision, thereby depriving adults from listening to such broadcasts during daytime hours when the risk of harm to minors is slight. The Government's concerns, of course, extend to children who are too young to attend school. *See Pacifica*, 438 U.S. at 749 ("broadcasting is uniquely accessible to children, even those too young to read"). But more to the point, even if such fine tuning were feasible, we do not believe that the First Amendment requires that degree of precision.

[W]e believe that deciding where along the bell curves of declining adult and child audiences it is most reasonable to permit indecent broadcasts is the kind of judgment that is better left to Congress, so long as there is evidence to support the legislative judgment. Extending the safe harbor for broadcast indecency to an earlier hour involves "a difference only in degree, not a less restrictive alternative in kind." Burson v. Freeman, 504 U.S. 191 (1992) (reducing campaign-free boundary around entrances to polling places from 100 feet to 25 feet is a difference in degree, not a less restrictive alternative in kind); *see also* Buckley v. Valeo, 424 U.S. 1, 30 (1976) (if some limit on campaign contributions is necessary, court has no scalpel to probe whether $2,000 ceiling might not serve as well as $1,000). It follows, then, that in a case of this kind, which involves restrictions in degree, there may be a range of safe harbors, each of which will satisfy the "narrowly tailored" requirement of the First Amendment. We are dealing with questions of judgment; and here, we defer to Congress's determination of where to draw the line just as the Supreme Court did when it accepted Congress's judgment that $1,000 rather than some other figure was the appropriate limit to place on campaign contributions.

Recognizing the Government's compelling interest in protecting children from indecent broadcasts, Congress channeled indecent broadcasts to the hours between midnight and 6:00 a.m. in the hope of minimizing children's exposure to such material. Given the substantially smaller number of children in the audience after midnight, we find that section 16(a) reduces children's exposure to broadcast indecency to a significant degree. We also find that this restriction does not unnecessarily interfere with the ability of adults to watch or listen to such materials both because substantial numbers of them are active after midnight and because adults have so many alternative ways of satisfying their tastes at other times. Although the restrictions burden the rights of many adults, it seems entirely appropriate that the marginal convenience of some adults be made to yield to the imperative needs of the young. We thus conclude that, standing alone, the midnight to 6:00 a.m. safe harbor is narrowly tailored to serve the Government's compelling interest in the well-being of our youth.

B. *The Public Broadcaster Exception*

Section 16(a) permits public stations that sign off the air at or before midnight to broadcast indecent material after 10:00 p.m. *See* 47 U.S.C. § 303 note. Petitioners argue that section 16(a) is unconstitutional because it allows the stations to present indecent material two hours earlier than all others.

Whatever Congress's reasons for creating it, the preferential safe harbor has the effect of undermining both the argument for prohibiting the broadcasting of indecent speech before that hour and the constitutional viability of the more restrictive safe harbor that appears to have been Congress's principal objective in enacting section 16(a). Congress has failed to explain what, if any, relationship the disparate treatment accorded certain public stations bears to the compelling Government interest—or to any other legislative value—that Congress sought to advance when it enacted section 16(a). Congress and the Commission have backed away from the consequences of their own reasoning, leaving us with no choice but to hold that the section is unconstitutional insofar as it bars the broadcasting of indecent speech between the hours of 10:00 p.m. and midnight.

EDWARDS, Chief Judge, dissenting:

In this case, the majority upholds as constitutional a *total ban* of "indecent" speech on *broadcast* television and radio between the hours of 6 a.m. and midnight. The majority readily acknowledges that *indecent* speech (as distinguished from *obscene* speech) is fully protected by the Constitution, and that the Government may not regulate such speech based on its content except when it chooses the least restrictive means to effectively promote an articulated compelling interest. In this case, the Government fails to satisfy the acknowledged constitutional strictures.

The Government advances three goals in support of the statute: first, it claims that the statute facilitates parental supervision of the programming their children watch and hear; second, it claims that the ban promotes the well-being of minors by protecting them from indecent programming assumed to be harmful; and, finally, it contends that the ban preserves the privacy of the home. The majority finds the first two interests compelling, and so finds it unnecessary to address the third. I, too, will focus on the first two interests, which I find to be unsupported.

As an initial matter, I do not comprehend how the two interests can stand *together*. "Congress may properly pass a law to *facilitate parental supervision of their children, i.e.*, a law that simply segregates and blocks indecent programming and thereby helps parents control whether and to what extent their children are exposed to such programming. However, a law that effectively *bans* all indecent programming—as does the statute at issue in this case—does not facilitate parental supervision. In my view, my right as a parent has been preempted, not facilitated, if I am told that certain programming will be banned from my ... television. Congress cannot take away my right to decide what my children watch, absent some showing that my children are in fact at risk of harm from exposure to indecent programming." Alliance for Community Media v. FCC, 56 F.3d 105, 145 (D.C. Cir. 1995) (Edwards, C.J., dissenting).

Furthermore, the two interests—facilitating parental supervision and protecting children from indecent material—fare no better if considered alone. With respect to the alleged interest in protecting children, although the majority strains mightily to rest its finding of harm on intuitive notions of morality and decency (notions with which I have great sympathy), the simple truth is that "[t]here is not one iota of evidence in the record ... to support the claim that exposure to indecency is harmful—indeed, the nature of the alleged 'harm' is never explained." *Id.* There *is* significant evidence suggesting a causal connection between viewing *violence* on television and antisocial violent behavior; but, as was conceded by Government counsel at oral argument in this case, the FCC has pointed to no such evidence addressing the effects of *indecent* programming. With respect to the interest in facilitating parental supervision, the statute is not tailored to aid parents' control over what their children watch and hear; it does not, for example, "segregate" indecent programming on special channels, as was the case in *Alliance for Community Media*,[9] nor does it promote a blocking device which individuals control. Rather, section 16(a) involves a *total ban* of disfavored programming during hours when adult viewers are most likely to be in the audience.

Because the statutory ban imposed by section 16(a) is not the least restrictive means to further compelling state interests, the majority decision must rest primarily on a perceived distinction between the First Amendment rights of *broadcast media* and *cable* (and all other non-broadcast) media. The majority appears to recognize that section 16(a) could not withstand constitutional scrutiny if applied against *cable* television operators; nonetheless, the majority finds this irrelevant because it believes that "there can be no doubt that the traditional broadcast media are properly subject to more regulation than is generally permissible under the First Amendment." This is the heart of the case, plain and simple.

Respectfully, I find the majority's position flawed. First, because I believe it is no longer responsible for courts to provide lesser First Amendment protection to broadcasting based on its alleged "unique attributes," I would scrutinize section 16(a) in the same manner that courts scrutinize speech restrictions of cable media.

Second, I find it incomprehensible that the majority can so easily reject the "public broadcaster exception" to section 16(a), and yet be blind to the utterly irrational distinction that Congress has created between *broadcast* and *cable* operators. No one disputes that cable exhibits more and worse indecency than does broadcast. And cable television is certainly pervasive in our country. Today, a majority of television households have cable, and over the last two decades, the percentage of television households with cable has increased every year. However, the Government does not even attempt to regulate cable with the same heavy regulatory hand it applies to the broadcast media. There is no ban between 6 a.m. and midnight imposed on cable. Rather, the Government relies on viewer subscription and individual discretion instead of regulating commercial cable. Viewers may receive commercial cable, with all of its indecent material, to be seen by adults and children at any time, subject only to the viewing discretion of the cable subscriber.

If exposure to "indecency" really is harmful to children, then one wonders how to explain congressional schemes that impose iron-clad bans of indecency on *broadcasters*, while simultaneously allowing a virtual free hand for the real culprits—*cable operators*. And the greatest irony of all is that the majority holds that section 16(a) is constitutional in part because, in allowing parents to subscribe to cable television as they see fit, Congress has facilitated parental supervision of children. In other words, Congress may ban indecency on broadcast television because parents can easily purchase all the smut they please on cable! I find this rationale perplexing.

At bottom, I dissent for three reasons: First, the Government's asserted interests in facilitating parental supervision and protecting children from indecency are irreconcilably in conflict in this case. Second, the Commission offers no evidence that indecent broad-

---

9. *Alliance for Community Media* involved the Cable Television Consumer Protection and Competition Act of 1992, Pub. L. No. 102-385, § 10, 106 Stat. 1460, 1468 and Implementation of Section 10 of the Cable Consumer Protection and Competition Act of 1992, Second Report and Order, 8 FCC Rcd. 2638 (1993), which included a segregate-and-block scheme. [The Supreme Court granted the petition for certiorari in *Alliance for Community Media*, and affirmed in part and reversed in part in Denver Area Educational Telecommunications Consortium, Inc. v. FCC, 518 U.S. 727 (1996). Eds.]

casting harms children. And although it is an easy assumption to make—that indecent broadcasting is harmful to minors—Supreme Court doctrine suggests that the Government must provide some evidence of harm before enacting speech-restrictive regulations. Finally, the Government has made no attempt to search out the least speech-restrictive means to promote the interests that have been asserted. For these reasons, section 16(a) should be struck down as unconstitutional.

I. First Amendment Protections for the Broadcast Media

Whatever the merits of *Pacifica* when it was issued almost 20 years ago, it makes no sense now.

The [Supreme Court's] justifications—spectrum scarcity, intrusiveness, and accessibility to children—neither distinguish broadcast from cable, nor explain the relaxed application of the principles of the First Amendment to broadcast.

A. Spectrum Scarcity

In 1943, the Court determined that the "unique characteristic" of broadcast—that "[u]nlike other modes of expression, radio inherently is not available to all"—explained "why, unlike other modes of expression, it is subject to governmental regulation." NBC v. United States, 319 U.S. 190, 226 (1943). Twenty-six years later, the Court spun out the First Amendment implications of this burgeoning scarcity theory. Red Lion Broadcasting Co. v. FCC, 395 U.S. 367, 388–90 (1967). The Court first offered an economic scarcity theory,[10] finding that "[w]here there are substantially more individuals who want to broadcast than there are frequencies to allocate, it is idle to posit an unabridgeable First Amendment right to broadcast comparable to the right of every individual to speak, write, or publish." *Id.* at 388. The Court also offered a technological scarcity theory: recognizing the need to prevent "overcrowd[ing of] the spectrum,"[11] *id.* at 389, the Court held that, "[b]ecause of the scarcity of radio frequencies, the Government is permitted to put restraints on licensees in favor of others whose views should be expressed on this unique medium," *id.* at 390.

In my view, it is no longer responsible for courts to apply a reduced level of First Amendment protection for regulations imposed on broadcast based on an indefensible notion of spectrum scarcity. It is time to revisit this rationale. For years, scholars have argued that the scarcity of the broadcast spectrum is neither an accurate technological description of the spectrum, nor a "unique characteristic" that should make any difference in terms of First Amendment protection. First, in response to the problem of broadcast interference when multiple broadcasters attempt to transmit on the same frequency, critics point out that this problem does not distinguish broadcasting from print and is easily remedied with a system of administrative licensing or private property rights. Another problem alluded to by the Court in *Red Lion* is the claim that the spectrum is inherently limited, in contrast to cable stations or newsprint. Today, however, the nation enjoys a proliferation of broadcast stations, and should the country decide to increase the number of channels, it need only devote more resources toward the development of the electromagnetic spectrum.

---

10. Interestingly, in responding to Government's argument that cable and broadcast are alike in that they both are beset by "market dysfunction," the *TBS* Court stated that "the special physical characteristics of broadcast transmission, not the economic characteristics of the broadcast market, are what underlies our broadcast jurisprudence." TBS v. FCC, 512 U.S. 622, 640 (1994) (citations omitted). Apparently, the Court is now prepared to abandon the *economic* scarcity theory.

11. The Court recently restated this concern: "if two broadcasters were to attempt to transmit over the same frequency in the same locale, they would interfere with one another's signals, so that neither could be heard at all." *TBS*, 512 U.S. at 637, (citing *NBC*, 319 U.S. at 212).

In response to the economic scarcity argument — that there are more would-be broadcasters than spectrum frequencies available — economists argue that all resources are scarce in the sense that people often would like to use more than exists. Especially when the Government gives away a valuable commodity, such as the right to use certain airwaves free of charge, the demand will likely always exceed the supply. And with the development of cable, spectrum-based communications media now have an abundance of alternatives, essentially rendering the economic scarcity argument superfluous.

In short, neither technological nor economic scarcity distinguish broadcast from other media. And while some may argue that spectrum scarcity may justify a system of administrative regulation as opposed to a free market approach to stations, the theory does not justify reduced First Amendment protection.

B. Accessibility to Children and Pervasiveness

The two additional rationales offered by the plurality opinion in *Pacifica*, attempting to distinguish broadcasting from other media, also fail to justify limited First Amendment protection of broadcast. The plurality found that "broadcasting is uniquely accessible to children, even those too young to read." *Pacifica*, 438 U.S. at 749. This characteristic, however, fails to distinguish broadcast from cable; and, notably, the rationale is absent from the Court's *TBS* opinion.

The plurality in *Pacifica* added another rationale which really has two components. The opinion reasoned that "the broadcast media have established a uniquely pervasive presence in the lives of all Americans.... [The] material presented over the airwaves confronts the citizen, not only in public, but also in the privacy of the home." *Id.* at 748. Again, the pervasiveness of its programming hardly distinguishes broadcast from cable. As noted above, cable is pervasive: a majority of television households have cable today, and this percentage has increased every year over the last two decades. The intrusiveness rationale, that the material confronts the citizen in the privacy of his or her home, likewise, does not distinguish broadcast from cable, nor account for the divergent First Amendment treatment of the two media. Finally, in light of *TBS*, in which the Court omitted any discussion of these rationales, the *Pacifica* rationales no longer can be seen to serve as justifications for reduced First Amendment protection afforded to broadcast.

[I]t seems clear now that *Pacifica* is a flawed decision, at least when one considers it in light of enlightened economic theory, technological advancements, and subsequent case law. The critical underpinnings of the decision are no longer present. Thus, there is no reason to uphold a distinction between broadcast and cable media pursuant to a bifurcated First Amendment analysis.

II. Full First Amendment Protection of Broadcast

Because no reasonable basis can be found to distinguish broadcast from cable in terms of the First Amendment protection the two media should receive, I would review section 16(a) and the *Enforcement Order* under the stricter level of scrutiny courts apply to content-based regulations of cable. This means "the most exacting scrutiny" should be applied "to regulations that suppress, disadvantage, or impose differential burdens upon speech because of its content." *TBS*, 512 U.S. at 642.

[Judge Edwards then concluded that the "safe harbor" was not narrowly tailored to serve a compelling governmental interest and was therefore an impermissible content based regulation.]

WALD, Circuit Judge, with whom ROGERS and TATEL, Circuit Judges, join, dissenting:

[P]resumptively, expression that many or even most of us find deeply reprehensible may not be, on that basis alone, proscribed. Thus, whatever our collective interests in a "meritorious polity" and the moral development of the "people [who] govern it," Majority Opinion, *supra*, governmental enforcement of those interests is radically constrained by the First Amendment's guarantee of freedom of expression.

I believe that the "safe harbor" proposed by the government here is unconstitutional even if the Court does not reconsider *Pacifica*.

Because indecent speech is fully within the ambit of First Amendment protection, the permissibility of government regulation of indecency depends crucially on the distinction between *banning* and *channeling* speech. Any time-based ban on the airing of indecency intrudes substantially into the rights of adult viewers and listeners and places the government in the extraordinarily sensitive role of censor.

Because the Commission insists that indecency determinations must be made on a case-by-case basis and depend upon a multi-faceted consideration of the context of allegedly indecent material, broadcasters have next-to-no guidance in making complex judgment calls. Thus, conscientious broadcasters and radio and television hosts seeking to steer clear of indecency face the herculean task of predicting on the basis of a series of hazy case-by-case determinations by the Commission which side of the line their program will fall on.

Because of th[e] potential for significant incursion into the First Amendment rights of adult viewers and listeners during the hours of the day and evening when the ban is in effect, it is particularly important that the channelling "balance" struck by the government preserve a meaningful place on the spectrum for adult rights to hear and view controversial or graphic nonobscene material—that airing of such material not be restricted to a safe harbor that is in reality a ship's graveyard. Thus, I cannot agree with the majority that determining the perimeter of the safe harbor can be relegated to the category of discretionary line-drawing akin to the distance from polls at which electioneering is allowed and so largely shielded from judicial review. God or the Devil (pick your figure of speech) is in the details. Because the safe harbor constitutes the exclusive repository for the substantial First Amendment rights of adults, its boundaries are of "constitutional dimension." Burson v. Freeman, 504 U.S. 191, 210 (1992). For that reason, it cannot be beyond the competence of this court to ensure that the safe harbor ensures *meaningful* as opposed to *pro forma* accommodation of adult rights.

On the basis of the information given us by the Commission and that was before Congress, it is impossible to conclude that the midnight to 6 a.m. safe harbor strikes a constitutionally acceptable balance.[12] Recent Supreme Court cases have made clear that "[w]hen the Government defends a regulation on speech as a means to ... prevent anticipated harms, it must do more than simply posit the existence of the disease sought to be cured. It must demonstrate that the recited harms are real, not merely conjectural, and that the regulation will in fact alleviate these harms in a direct and material way." TBS, 512 U.S. at 664. Yet, in the record before Congress, there is as little evidence regarding the magnitude of psychological or moral harm, if any, to children and teenagers who see and hear indecency as there is that such exposure even occurs inside the current safe harbor. In the six years that the safe harbor has been operating from 8 p.m. to 6 a.m., and the prior

---

12. Although the end result of the majority's decision is to extend the safe harbor from 10 p.m. to 6 a.m., it holds that so long as Congress enacts a uniform rule, the midnight to 6 a.m. safe harbor is constitutionally adequate. Accordingly, I address my discussion to the narrower safe harbor. [Footnote relocated.]

years in which it covered 10 p.m. to 6 a.m., the government has adduced no concrete evidence of real or even potential harm suffered by the exposure of children to indecent material. We have not a scintilla of evidence as to how many allegedly indecent programs have been either aired or seen or heard by children inside or outside the safe harbor. Thus, even if the government were allowed to presume harm from mere exposure to indecency, surely it cannot progressively constrict the safe harbor in the absence of *any* indication that the presumed harm is even occurring under the existing regime.

Even if the government were acting on a *tabula rasa*, rather than on the basis of years of experience with a less restrictive ban, its delineation of the midnight to 6 a.m. safe harbor would be unjustifiable. In the end, the majority admits the government's own interest in children is limited to "shielding minors from being exposed to indecent speech by persons other than a parent." Majority Opinion, *supra*.

The majority is right: the government's primary if not exclusive interest is in "shielding minors from being exposed to indecent speech by persons other than a parent." Given the significant First Amendment rights of adults at stake, moreover, the government has a constitutional responsibility to key its response to the presumed harm from indecency to facilitating parental control, rather than to government censorship *per se*. When most parents are presumably able to supervise their children, adult viewers should have access to the speech to which they are entitled.

Because the government can pursue whatever legitimate interests it has in protecting children by facilitating parental control, I do not believe that it can impose a valid ban during any hours it pleases solely because some children are in the audience. Nor do I believe that we can throw up our hands at the assumed impossibility of parental supervision simply because large numbers of children have television sets in their own room. Either or both of these excuses would justify a 24-hour ban as easily as the current 18-hour ban. Reasoning along these lines totally ignores the adult First Amendment interest that the majority purportedly recognizes and, effectively, gives the government unharnessed power to censor.

[T]he government should be put to the task of demonstrating that the banned hours are based on a showing that these are the times of preponderant children viewing and the times when parents are otherwise absorbed in work in or out of the home. As the initial panel opinion explained, "[t]he Commission[] ... appears to assume that, regardless of the time of day or night, parents cannot effectively supervise their children's television or radio habits. Accordingly, the government has not adduced any evidence suggesting that the effectiveness of parental supervision varies by time of day or night, or that the particular safe harbor from midnight to 6 a.m. was crafted to assist parents at specific times when they especially require the government's help to supervise their children." Action for Children's Television v. FCC, 11 F.3d 170, 178 (D.C. Cir. 1993).

Despite the majority's valiant effort to extract evidence for the government's position from the sparse record before us, the pickings are too slim for constitutional legitimacy. There is no evidence at all of psychological harm from exposure to indecent programs aired inside the current safe harbor. There is no evidence either that parents cannot supervise their children in those safe harbor hours or that "grazing" is leading to any significant viewing of indecency. Finally, the imminence of "V-chip" technology to enable parental control of all violence- and indecency-viewing suggests that a draconian ban from 6 a.m. to midnight is decidedly premature.

In spite of this evidentiary black hole, we have a broadside ban on vaguely defined indecency during all hours when most working people are awake, with a small bow to prior judicial rulings that a complete ban is unconstitutional, but no attempt to fashion an accommodation between the First Amendment and family values. The net effect of the majority's decision is a gratuitous grant of power allowing casual and lightly reviewed administrative decision-making about fundamental liberties. I respectfully dissent.

Notes and Questions

1. The Standard. Under *ACT III*, what is required to show a harm to children that would justify content-based regulation of broadcast? What is required to show that the means chosen by Congress are sufficiently tailored? To put the point a bit differently, what would have to happen in order for Congress to fail to satisfy the requirements of compelling interest or narrow tailoring?

2. Strict Scrutiny? Relatedly, what sort of strict scrutiny did *ACT III* apply? Was it consistent with strict scrutiny applied in other contexts? Was it consistent with *Pacifica*?

3. Empowering Parents, Protecting Children. Note the treatment, in the various opinions, of the goals of empowering parents and of protecting children. Are those goals complementary? In tension with each other? Irrelevant to each other? What sorts of regulation would empowering parents justify? What sorts would protecting children justify?

4. More Guidance. In April 2001, the FCC issued a policy statement that was designed, according to the FCC, to "provide guidance to the broadcast industry" on the Commission's indecency enforcement policies. Industry Guidance on the Commission's Case Law Interpreting 18 U.S.C. § 1464 and Enforcement Policies Regarding Broadcast Indecency, Policy Statement, 16 FCC Rcd. 7999 (2001) (known as the 2001 Indecency Policy Statement). It restated the FCC's existing position on indecency enforcement, but most of its length was devoted to examples of broadcasts that the FCC found either indecent or not indecent. This policy statement, like previous FCC statements about indecency, was immediately lampooned as drawing arbitrary lines; and, indeed, not long after issuing the report, the Commission found a broadcast indecent and then quickly reversed itself. In KBOO Foundation, Notice of Apparent Liability for Forfeiture, 16 FCC Rcd. 10,731 (2001), the FCC— speaking through the chief of its Enforcement Bureau, as is its usual practice—concluded that a broadcast of the song "Your Revolution" by Sarah Jones was indecent, even though its most graphic phrase was "A six foot blow job machine." The FCC's reasoning occupied a paragraph. *See id.* ¶ 8. After an outcry, the FCC—again, through the chief of its Enforcement Bureau—rescinded the order. *See* KBOO Foundation, Memorandum Opinion and Order, 18 FCC Rcd. 2472 (2003). The Commission did not suggest that any new facts had come to light, and instead (again, with reasoning that occupied a mere paragraph) stated that "we now conclude that the broadcast was not indecent because, on balance and in context, the sexual descriptions in the song are not sufficiently graphic to warrant sanction." *Id.* ¶ 9; *see also* Citadel Broadcasting Company, Notice of Apparent Liability for Forfeiture, 16 FCC Rcd. 11,839 (2001) (imposing a fine for the airing of the "radio edit" version of Eminem's song "The Real Slim Shady," even though the radio edit omitted the most offensive language); Citadel Broadcasting Company, Memorandum Opinion and Order, 17 FCC Rcd. 483 (2002) (reversing that fine, despite the absence of any new facts). Reversals and close calls are not new, of course; the point is that the 2001 Indecency Policy Statement did not end them.

More broadly, until 2003, FCC fines for indecency (called "Notices of Apparent Liability") were fairly rare and relatively small. From November 1999 through September 2003, for example, the FCC issued a total of twenty-two Notices of Apparent Liability totaling $265,900, for an average of $12,086 per fine. *See* FCC Enforcement Bureau, Obscene, Profane & Indecent Broadcasts: Notices of Apparent Liability, http://www.fcc.gov/eb/broadcast/NAL.html. Beginning in October 2003, however, the Commission started issuing big fines in some high-profile cases—such as a fine totaling $357,500 against Infinity Broadcasting for a program that encouraged people to have sex in public, the result being reports of public sex in St. Patrick's Cathedral, among other places. Infinity Broadcasting Operations, Inc., Notice of Apparent Liability for Forfeiture, 18 FCC Rcd. 19,954 (2003). In imposing these larger penalties, though, the FCC did not purport to be changing course. The penalties were larger in significant part because the fines were aimed at programs that were aired on multiple stations, and the FCC imposed the same substantive guidelines that it had used in the past and had collected in the 2001 Indecency Policy Statement.

Then along came Bono. The U2 singer put new pressure on the FCC's indecency rules when, upon receiving a Golden Globe Award and thus speaking before a large and diverse broadcast television audience, he said "This is really, really fucking brilliant." Complaints Against Various Broadcast Licensees Regarding Their Airing of the "Golden Globe Awards" Program, Memorandum Opinion and Order, 18 FCC Rcd. 19,859 (2003). The Commission (as usual through its enforcement head) responded in October 2003—the day after it issued the *Infinity* order and the above-mentioned public sex fine—and issued an order finding that, despite the public outcry, Bono's utterance was not indecent. Here is the relevant reasoning, in its entirety:

> 5. "Indecency findings involve at least two fundamental determinations. First, the material alleged to be indecent must fall within the subject matter scope of our indecency definition—that is, the material must describe or depict sexual or excretory organs or activities.... Second, the broadcast must be *patently offensive* as measured by contemporary community standards for the broadcast medium." 2001 Indecency Policy Statement, 16 FCC Rcd. 7999, 8002 ¶¶ 7–8 (2001) (emphasis in original). As a threshold matter, the material aired during the "Golden Globe Awards" program does not describe or depict sexual and excretory activities and organs. The word "fucking" may be crude and offensive, but, in the context presented here, did not describe sexual or excretory organs or activities. Rather, the performer used the word "fucking" as an adjective or expletive to emphasize an exclamation. Indeed, in similar circumstances, we have found that offensive language used as an insult rather than as a description of sexual or excretory activity or organs is not within the scope of the Commission's prohibition of indecent program content.
>
> 6. Moreover, we have previously found that fleeting and isolated remarks of this nature do not warrant Commission action. *See, e.g.*, L.M. Communications of South Carolina, Inc., 7 FCC Rcd. 1595 ([finding that] a fleeting and isolated utterance ("[t]he hell I did, I drove the mother-fucker...") within the context of live and spontaneous programming [was] not actionable). Thus, because the complained-of material does not fall within the scope of the Commission's indecency prohibition, we reject the claims that this program content is indecent, and we need not reach the second element of the indecency analysis.

Golden Globe Awards, 18 FCC Rcd. 19,860–61 ¶¶ 5–6.

The above-quoted order proved somewhat controversial, given that the utterance was on television (as opposed to radio) and on a relatively high-profile program. Indeed, the FCC received 237,215 letters after it issued its ruling. *See* Anne Marie Squeo, A Job for

Solomon: Was Bono's Blurt a Verb or Modifier?, Wall St. Journal, March 11, 2004, at A1. Still, the matter would likely have rested there were it not for the infamous "wardrobe malfunction" in the 2004 Super Bowl halftime show that resulted in part of Janet Jackson's breast being shown on national broadcast television. The reaction was swift and furious. The House and Senate held hearings in which members excoriated the FCC for finding so few utterances actionably indecent, imposing such small penalties, and failing to have ever revoked a license based on broadcast indecency.

For its part, the Commission did not sit still. The FCC—this time acting through its Commissioners, rather than the head of the Enforcement Bureau—reversed the earlier decision forgiving Bono's utterance. After quoting the language from the 2001 Indecency Policy Statement (and quoted in ¶ 5 immediately above) that indecent material "must describe or depict sexual or excretory organs or activities" and "must be *patently offensive* as measured by contemporary community standards for the broadcast medium," the order proceeded as follows.

COMPLAINTS AGAINST VARIOUS BROADCAST LICENSEES REGARDING THEIR AIRING OF THE "GOLDEN GLOBE AWARDS" PROGRAM

Memorandum Opinion and Order, 19 FCC Rcd. 4975 (2004)

7. In making indecency determinations, the Commission has indicated that the "*full context* in which the material appeared is critically important," and has articulated three "principal factors" for its analysis: "(1) the *explicitness or graphic nature* of the description or depiction of sexual or excretory organs or activities; (2) whether the material *dwells on or repeats at length* descriptions of sexual or excretory organs or activities; (3) *whether the material appears to pander or is used to titillate*, or *whether the material appears to have been presented for its shock value*." Indecency Policy Statement, 16 FCC Rcd. 7999 (2001) (emphasis in original). In examining these three factors, we must weigh and balance them to determine whether the broadcast material is patently offensive because "[e]ach indecency case presents its own particular mix of these, and possibly, other factors." Id. In particular cases, one or two of the factors may outweigh the others, either rendering the broadcast material patently offensive and consequently indecent, or, alternatively, removing the broadcast material from the realm of indecency. *Id.*

8. With respect to the first step of the indecency analysis, we disagree with the Bureau and conclude that use of the phrase at issue is within the scope of our indecency definition because it does depict or describe sexual activities. We recognize NBC's argument that the "F-Word" here was used "as an intensifier." Nevertheless, we believe that, given the core meaning of the "F-Word," any use of that word or a variation, in any context, inherently has a sexual connotation, and therefore falls within the first prong of our indecency definition. This conclusion is consistent with the Commission's original *Pacifica* decision, affirmed by the Supreme Court, in which the Commission held that the "F-Word" does depict or describe sexual activities.

9. We now turn to the second step of the analysis—whether the broadcast of the phrase at issue here is patently offensive under contemporary community standards for the broadcast medium and therefore indecent. We conclude that the answer to this question is yes. The "F-Word" is one of the most vulgar, graphic and explicit descriptions of sexual activity in the English language. Its use invariably invokes a coarse sexual image. The use

of the "F-Word" here, on a nationally telecast awards ceremony, was shocking and gratuitous. In this regard, NBC does not claim that there was any political, scientific or other independent value of use of the word here, or any other factors to mitigate its offensiveness. If the Commission were routinely not to take action against isolated and gratuitous uses of such language on broadcasts when children were expected to be in the audience, this would likely lead to more widespread use of the offensive language. Neither Congress nor the courts have ever indicated that broadcasters should be given free rein to air any vulgar language, including isolated and gratuitous instances of vulgar language. The fact that the use of this word may have been unintentional is irrelevant; it still has the same effect of exposing children to indecent language. Our action today furthers our responsibility to safeguard the well-being of the nation's children from the most objectionable, most offensive language.

10. We also note that in this case NBC and other licensees were on notice that an award presenter or recipient might use offensive language during the live broadcast, and it could have taken appropriate steps to ensure that it did not broadcast such language. In this regard, this is not the first case where such language has been used by an award recipient in a live program. For example, we note that, during the broadcast of the 2002 Billboard Awards Ceremony, Cher, in receiving an award, reportedly used the "F-Word." Indeed, Bono himself reportedly used the "F-Word" on the 1994 Grammy Awards broadcast.[13]

11. We note also that technological advances have made it possible as a general matter to prevent the broadcast of a single offending word or action without blocking or disproportionately disrupting the message of the speaker or performer. NBC and other licensees could have easily avoided the indecency violation here by delaying the broadcast for a period of time sufficient for them to effectively bleep the offending word. Indeed, we encourage networks and broadcasters to undertake such technological measures. The ease with which broadcasters today can block even fleeting words in a live broadcast is an element in our decision to act upon a single and gratuitous use of a vulgar expletive.

12. While prior Commission and staff action have indicated that isolated or fleeting broadcasts of the "F-Word" such as that here are not indecent or would not be acted upon, consistent with our decision today we conclude that any such interpretation is no longer good law. In Pacifica Foundation, Inc., 2 FCC Rcd. 2698 ¶ 13 (1987) (subsequent history omitted), for example, the Commission stated as follows: "If a complaint focuses solely on the use of expletives, we believe that ... deliberate and repetitive use in a patently offensive manner is a requisite to a finding of indecency." The staff has since found that the isolated or fleeting use of the "F-Word" is not indecent in situations arguably similar to that here. We now depart from this portion of the Commission's 1987 *Pacifica* decision and any similar cases holding that isolated or fleeting use of the "F-Word" or a variant thereof in situations such as this is not indecent and conclude that such cases are not good law to that extent. We now clarify, as we have made clear with respect to complaints going beyond the use of expletives, that the mere fact that specific words or phrases are not sustained or repeated does not mandate a finding that material that is otherwise patently offensive to the broadcast medium is not indecent.

---

13. [Bono said the following at the end of his speech accepting the Grammy for Best Alternative Music Album in 1994: "I think I'd like to give a message to the young people of America. And that is: We shall continue to abuse our position and fuck up the mainstream. God bless you." *See* https://www.youtube.com/watch?v=PHE8pRTK1Ls. Eds.]

17. We conclude, therefore, that NBC and other licensees that broadcast Bono's use of the "F-Word" during the live broadcast of the Golden Globe Awards violated 18 U.S.C. § 1464. By our action today, broadcasters are on clear notice that, in the future, they will be subject to potential enforcement action for any broadcast of the "F-Word" or a variation thereof in situations such as that here. We also take this opportunity to reiterate our recent admonition (which took place after the behavior at issue here) that serious multiple violations of our indecency rule by broadcasters may well lead to the commencement of license revocation proceedings, and that we may issue forfeitures for each indecent utterance in a particular broadcast. We note that one way broadcasters can easily ensure that they are not subject to enforcement action under our decision today is to adopt and successfully implement a delay/bleeping system for live broadcasts.

Notes and Questions

1. Bigger Fines. As we noted above, beginning in 2003 the Commission started issuing bigger fines—e.g., $3.6 million for CBS broadcasters' airing an episode of "Without a Trace" featuring a teenage orgy, $1.1 million for Fox broadcasters' airing of contestants cavorting with strippers on "Married with America," $550,000 against Viacom for the 2004 Super Bowl halftime show, and $495,000 against Clear Channel for a Howard Stern episode featuring "dialogue between cast members regarding the sexual practices of certain program cast members and a discussion with a guest regarding 'Sphincterine,' a purported personal hygiene product designed for use prior to sexual activity." Clear Channel Broadcasting Licenses, Inc., Notice of Apparent Liability for Forfeiture, 19 FCC Rcd. 6773 ¶ 2 (2004). In June 2006, Congress raised the stakes further by passing legislation raising the Commission's maximum authority to fine broadcast licensees from $32,500 per violation to $325,000 per violation, with a $3 million cap for a multiday continuing violation. See Broadcast Decency Enforcement Act of 2005, Pub. L. No. 109-235, 120 Stat. 491.

2. Broadcasters' Response. Broadcasters recognized that they were operating in a changed environment. Their operational responses to the new indecency landscape included admonishing those on the air against using indecent language, suspending some performers (e.g., Clear Channel suspended Howard Stern from its stations), and putting live broadcasts on short tape delays, so that censors could bleep offending words before they aired. One interesting instance involved a PBS documentary on the Iraq war that contained soldiers using profanity. PBS decided to send member stations an edited satellite feed of the program that cut out profanity used by soldiers, and demanded that any station that chose to air the unedited version of the program sign a legal waiver acknowledging that the normal legal protection offered by PBS would not apply if the unedited version was found to violate federal broadcast standards. See Edward Wyatt, PBS Warns Stations of Risks From Profanity in War Film, N.Y. Times, Feb. 18, 2005, at C2.

3. The "F-Word" and Clarity. After the order excerpted above, it might have seemed that any iteration of the word "fuck" on broadcast television was going to expose the broadcaster to liability. That was the fear of many stations, and in the aftermath of this ruling many refused to air "Saving Private Ryan," which ABC planned to air on Veterans' Day 2004 without bleeping "fuck" or any of the other potentially offensive language ("shit," "asshole," etc.). After the movie aired, the FCC issued an order finding that the language was not indecent in context. The order stated that, "in context, the dialogue, including the complained-of material, is neither gratuitous nor in any way intended or used to pander, titillate or shock," and it concluded as follows:

Thus, in light of the overall context of the film, including the fact that it is designed to show the horrors of war, its presentation to honor American veterans on the national holiday specifically designated for that purpose, the introduction, which articulated the importance of presenting the film in its unedited form, and the clear and repeated warnings provided by ABC, not only in the introduction but also at each commercial break, we find that the complained-of material is not patently offensive as measured by contemporary community standards for the broadcast medium, and, therefore, not indecent.

Complaints Against Various Television Licensees Regarding Their Broadcast on November 11, 2004, of the ABC Television Network's Presentation of the Film "Saving Private Ryan," Memorandum Opinion and Order, 20 FCC Rcd. 4507 ¶ 16 (2005).

4. Once More Unto the Breach. The indecency question about "Saving Private Ryan" was just one of many indecency challenges that had been building up at the Commission. In a single 2006 order the Commission eliminated that backlog, resolving over 300,000 backlogged indecency complaints involving almost 50 programs aired between February 2002 and March 2005. The FCC presented its order as another attempt to provide guidance to broadcasters and the public as to what would run afoul of the indecency standards. Complaints Regarding Various Television Broadcasts Between February 2, 2002 and March 8, 2005, Notices of Apparent Liability and Memorandum Opinion and Order, 21 FCC Rcd. 2664 ¶ 2 (2006). The 2006 order followed the template created by the 2004 order excerpted above, relying on the factors and analysis articulated in that order.

The 2006 order then applied those standards to dozens of different shows that had been the subject of complaints. For instance, the Commission found that iterations of "bullshit" on "NYPD Blue" were indecent: the show did not dwell upon the word, but "bullshit" is "vulgar, graphic and explicit" and its use was "shocking and gratuitous," id. ¶¶ 128–30. But the order also found that "dick" and "dickhead" said on "NYPD Blue" were not patently offensive and thus not indecent. The order stated: "First, we find that the terms 'dick' and 'dickhead,' in this context, while understandably offensive to some viewers, are not sufficiently vulgar, explicit, or graphic descriptions of sexual organs or activities to support a finding of patent offensiveness. Second, while not dispositive, it is relevant that none of the programs dwell on these terms. Third, we find that those words, in context, are not sufficiently shocking to support a finding that they are patently offensive. Although the words are undeniably coarse and vulgar, they do not have the same level of offensiveness as the 'F-Word' or 'S-Word.'" Id. ¶ 127.

The March 2006 order also found indecent the iteration of "fuck" by Cher at the 2002 Billboard Music Awards, and iterations of "shit" and "fucking" by Nicole Richie at the 2003 Billboard Music Awards. Again, it applied the factors it presented in the 2004 order, and found these statements indecent for the same basic reasons that it found Bono's utterance indecent.

Fox brought a challenge to the FCC's indecency fines for Richie and Cher in the Second Circuit. That court rejected the FCC's shift in policy as violating the Administrative Procedure Act's prohibition on arbitrary and capricious policy determinations. Fox presented First Amendment arguments to the Second Circuit, but the court did not rule on those arguments, applying the well-established principle that courts avoid reaching constitutional questions in advance of the necessity of deciding them. After articulating that principle, the court added: "We note, however, that in reviewing these numerous constitutional challenges, which were fully briefed to this court and discussed at length during oral argument, we are skeptical that the Commission can provide a reasoned explanation for its 'fleeting expletive' regime that would pass constitutional muster," and the court then proceeded to cast doubt on the government's First Amendment arguments. Fox Television Stations, Inc. v. FCC, 489 F.3d 444, 462 (2d Cir. 2007).

The Supreme Court granted certiorari and issued the following opinion.

FCC v. Fox Television Stations, Inc.
556 U.S. 502 (2009)

SCALIA, J., announced the judgment of the Court and delivered the opinion of the Court with respect to Parts I, II, III-A through III-D, and IV, in which ROBERTS, C.J., and KENNEDY, THOMAS, and ALITO, JJ., joined, and an opinion with respect to Part III-E, in which ROBERTS, C.J., and THOMAS and ALITO, JJ., joined. THOMAS, J., filed a concurring opinion. KENNEDY, J., filed an opinion concurring in part and concurring in the judgment. STEVENS, J., and GINSBURG, J., filed dissenting opinions. BREYER, J., filed a dissenting opinion, in which STEVENS, SOUTER, and GINSBURG, JJ., joined.

Justice SCALIA delivered the opinion of the Court, except as to Part III-E.

I. Statutory and Regulatory Background

One of the burdens that [broadcast] licensees shoulder is the indecency ban—the statutory proscription against "utter[ing] any obscene, indecent, or profane language by means of radio communication," 18 U.S.C. § 1464—which Congress has instructed the Commission to enforce between the hours of 6 a.m. and 10 p.m.

The Commission first invoked the statutory ban on indecent broadcasts in 1975, declaring a daytime broadcast of George Carlin's "Filthy Words" monologue actionably indecent. Citizen's Complaint Against Pacifica Found. Station WBAI (FM), New York, N.Y., Memorandum Opinion & Order, 56 F.C.C. 2d 94 (1975). At that time, the Commission announced the definition of indecent speech that it uses to this day, prohibiting "language that describes, in terms patently offensive as measured by contemporary community standards for the broadcast medium, sexual or excretory activities or organs, at times of the day when there is a reasonable risk that children may be in the audience." *Id.* at 98.

[In 2001], the Commission emphasized that the "full context" in which particular materials appear is "critically important," but that a few "principal" factors guide the inquiry, such as the "explicitness or graphic nature" of the material, the extent to which the material "dwells on or repeats" the offensive material, and the extent to which the material was presented to "pander," to "titillate," or to "shock." Indus. Guidance On the Comm'ns Case Law Interpreting 18 U.S.C. § 1464 and Enforcement Policies Regarding Broad. Indecency, Policy Statement, 16 FCC Rcd. 7999, 8002 ¶ 9, 8003 ¶ 10 (2001) (emphasis deleted). "No single factor," the Commission said, "generally provides the basis for an indecency finding," but "where sexual or excretory references have been made once or have been passing or fleeting in nature, this characteristic has tended to weigh against a finding of indecency." *Id.* at 8003 ¶ 10, 8008 ¶ 17.

In 2004, the Commission took one step further by declaring for the first time that a nonliteral (expletive) use of the F- and S-Words could be actionably indecent, even when the word is used only once. The first order to this effect dealt with an NBC broadcast of the Golden Globe Awards, in which the performer Bono commented, "This is really, really, f* * *ing brilliant." Complaints Against Various Broad. Licensees Regarding Their Airing of the "Golden Globe Awards" Program, 19 FCC Rcd. 4975, 4976 n.4 (2004)

(*Golden Globes Order*). Although the Commission had received numerous complaints directed at the broadcast, its enforcement bureau had concluded that the material was not indecent because "Bono did not describe, in context, sexual or excretory organs or activities and ... the utterance was fleeting and isolated." *Id.* at 4975–76 ¶ 3. The full Commission reviewed and reversed the staff ruling.

II. The Present Case

This case concerns utterances in two live broadcasts aired by Fox Television Stations, Inc., and its affiliates prior to the Commission's *Golden Globes Order*. The first occurred during the 2002 Billboard Music Awards, when the singer Cher exclaimed, "I've also had critics for the last 40 years saying that I was on my way out every year. Right. So f* * * 'em." Brief for Petitioners 9. The second involved a segment of the 2003 Billboard Music Awards, during the presentation of an award by Nicole Richie and Paris Hilton, principals in a Fox television series called "The Simple Life." Ms. Hilton began their interchange by reminding Ms. Richie to "watch the bad language," but Ms. Richie proceeded to ask the audience, "Why do they even call it 'The Simple Life?' Have you ever tried to get cow s* * * out of a Prada purse? It's not so f* * *ing simple." *Id.* at 9–10. Following each of these broadcasts, the Commission received numerous complaints from parents whose children were exposed to the language.

On March 15, 2006, the Commission released Notices of Apparent Liability for a number of broadcasts that the Commission deemed actionably indecent, including the two described above. Complaints Regarding Various Television Broads. Between Feb. 2, 2002 and Mar. 8, 2005, Notices of Apparent Liability & Memorandum Opinion & Order, 21 FCC Rcd. 2664 (2006). Multiple parties petitioned the Court of Appeals for the Second Circuit for judicial review of the order, asserting a variety of constitutional and statutory challenges. Since the order had declined to impose sanctions, the Commission had not previously given the broadcasters an opportunity to respond to the indecency charges. It therefore requested and obtained from the Court of Appeals a voluntary remand so that the parties could air their objections. The Commission's order on remand upheld the indecency findings for the broadcasts described above. *See* Complaints Regarding Various Television Broads. Between Feb. 2, 2002, and Mar. 8, 2005, Order, 21 FCC Rcd. 13,299 (2006) (Remand Order).

The order first explained that both broadcasts fell comfortably within the subject-matter scope of the Commission's indecency test because the 2003 broadcast involved a literal description of excrement and both broadcasts invoked the "F-Word," which inherently has a sexual connotation. *Id.* at 13,304 ¶ 16, 13,323 ¶ 58. The order next determined that the broadcasts were patently offensive under community standards for the medium. Both broadcasts, it noted, involved entirely gratuitous uses of "one of the most vulgar, graphic, and explicit words for sexual activity in the English language." *Id.* at 13,305 ¶ 17, 13,324 ¶ 59. It found Ms. Richie's use of the "F-Word" and her "explicit description of the handling of excrement" to be "vulgar and shocking," as well as to constitute "pandering," after Ms. Hilton had playfully warned her to "'watch the bad language.'" *Id.* at 13,305 ¶ 17. And it found Cher's statement patently offensive in part because she metaphorically suggested a sexual act as a means of expressing hostility to her critics. *Id.* at 13,324 ¶ 60. The order relied upon the "critically important" context of the utterances, *id.* at 13,304 ¶ 15, noting that they were aired during prime-time awards shows "designed to draw a large nationwide audience that could be expected to include many children interested in seeing their favorite music stars," *id.* at 13,305 ¶ 18, 13,324 ¶ 59. Indeed, approximately 2.5 million minors witnessed each of the broadcasts. *Id.* at 13,306 ¶ 18, 13,326 ¶ 65.

The order asserted that both broadcasts under review would have been actionably indecent under the staff rulings and Commission dicta in effect prior to the *Golden Globes*

Order—the 2003 broadcast because it involved a literal description of excrement, rather than a mere expletive, because it used more than one offensive word, and because it was planned, *id.* at 13,307 ¶ 22; and the 2002 broadcast because Cher used the F-Word not as a mere intensifier, but as a description of the sexual act to express hostility to her critics, *id.* at 13,324 ¶ 60. The order stated, however, that the pre-*Golden Globes* regime of immunity for isolated indecent expletives rested only upon staff rulings and Commission dicta, and that the Commission itself had never held "that the isolated use of an expletive ... was not indecent or could not be indecent," *id.* at 13,307 ¶ 21. In any event, the order made clear, the *Golden Globes Order* eliminated any doubt that fleeting expletives could be actionably indecent, *id.* at 13,308 ¶ 23, 13,325 ¶ 61, and the Commission disavowed the bureau-level decisions and its own dicta that had said otherwise, *id.* at 13,306–13,307 ¶¶ 20–21. Under the new policy, a lack of repetition "weigh[s] against a finding of indecency," *id.* at 13,325 ¶ 61, but is not a safe harbor.

The order explained that the Commission's prior "strict dichotomy between 'expletives' and 'descriptions or depictions of sexual or excretory functions' is artificial and does not make sense in light of the fact that an 'expletive's' power to offend derives from its sexual or excretory meaning." *Id.* at 13,308 ¶ 23. In the Commission's view, "granting an automatic exemption for 'isolated or fleeting' expletives unfairly forces viewers (including children)" to take "'the first blow'" and would allow broadcasters "to air expletives at all hours of a day so long as they did so one at a time." *Id.* at 13,309 ¶ 25. Although the Commission determined that Fox encouraged the offensive language by using suggestive scripting in the 2003 broadcast, and unreasonably failed to take adequate precautions in both broadcasts, *id.* at 13,311–13,314 ¶¶ 31–37, the order again declined to impose any forfeiture or other sanction for either of the broadcasts, *id.* at 13,321 ¶ 53, 13,326 ¶ 66.

Fox returned to the Second Circuit for review of the Remand Order, and various intervenors including CBS, NBC, and ABC joined the action. The Court of Appeals reversed the agency's orders, finding the Commission's reasoning inadequate under the Administrative Procedure Act. Fox Television Stations, Inc. v. FCC, 489 F.3d 444 (2d Cir. 2007). The majority was "skeptical that the Commission [could] provide a reasoned explanation for its 'fleeting expletive' regime that would pass constitutional muster," but it declined to reach the constitutional question. *Id.* at 462. Judge Leval dissented. *Id.* at 467. We granted certiorari, FCC v. Fox Television Stations, Inc., 552 U.S. 1255 (2008).

III. Analysis

A. Governing Principles

The Administrative Procedure Act, 5 U.S.C. § 551 *et seq.*, which sets forth the full extent of judicial authority to review executive agency action for procedural correctness, permits (insofar as relevant here) the setting aside of agency action that is "arbitrary" or "capricious," 5 U.S.C. § 706(2)(A). Under what we have called this "narrow" standard of review, we insist that an agency "examine the relevant data and articulate a satisfactory explanation for its action." Motor Vehicle Mfrs. Assn. of United States, Inc. v. State Farm Mut. Auto. Ins. Co., 463 U.S. 29, 43 (1983). We have made clear, however, that "a court is not to substitute its judgment for that of the agency," *id.*, and should "uphold a decision of less than ideal clarity if the agency's path may reasonably be discerned." Bowman Transp., Inc. v. Arkansas-Best Freight Sys., Inc., 419 U.S. 281, 286 (1974).

B. Application to This Case

Judged under the above described standards, the Commission's new enforcement policy and its order finding the broadcasts actionably indecent were neither arbitrary nor capricious. First, the Commission forthrightly acknowledged that its recent actions have broken new ground, taking account of inconsistent "prior Commission and staff action" and explicitly disavowing them as "no longer good law." *Golden Globes Order*, 19 FCC Rcd. at 4980 ¶ 12. To be sure, the (superfluous) explanation in its Remand Order of why the Cher broadcast would even have violated its earlier policy may not be entirely convincing. But that unnecessary detour is irrelevant. There is no doubt that the Commission knew it was making a change. That is why it declined to assess penalties; and it relied on the *Golden Globes Order* as removing any lingering doubt. Remand Order, 21 FCC Rcd. at 13,308 ¶ 23, 13,325 ¶ 61.

Moreover, the agency's reasons for expanding the scope of its enforcement activity were entirely rational. It was certainly reasonable to determine that it made no sense to distinguish between literal and nonliteral uses of offensive words, requiring repetitive use to render only the latter indecent. As the Commission said with regard to expletive use of the F-Word, "the word's power to insult and offend derives from its sexual meaning." *Id.* at 13,323 ¶ 58. And the Commission's decision to look at the patent offensiveness of even isolated uses of sexual and excretory words fits with the context-based approach we sanctioned in *Pacifica*, 438 U.S. at 750. Even isolated utterances can be made in "pander[ing,] ... vulgar and shocking" manners, Remand Order, 21 FCC Rcd. at 13,305 ¶ 17, and can constitute harmful "first blow[s]" to children, *id.* at 13,309 ¶ 25. It is surely rational (if not inescapable) to believe that a safe harbor for single words would "likely lead to more widespread use of the offensive language." *Golden Globes Order*, 18 FCC Rcd. at 4979 ¶ 9.

The fact that technological advances have made it easier for broadcasters to bleep out offending words further supports the Commission's stepped-up enforcement policy. *Id.* at 4980 ¶ 11. And the agency's decision not to impose any forfeiture or other sanction precludes any argument that it is arbitrarily punishing parties without notice of the potential consequences of their action.

C. *The Court of Appeals' Reasoning*

The Court of Appeals found the Commission's action arbitrary and capricious on three grounds. First, the court criticized the Commission for failing to explain why it had not previously banned fleeting expletives as "harmful 'first blow[s].'" 489 F.3d at 458. In the majority's view, without "evidence that suggests a fleeting expletive is harmful [and] ... serious enough to warrant government regulation," the agency could not regulate more broadly. *Id.* at 461. As explained above, the fact that an agency had a prior stance does not alone prevent it from changing its view or create a higher hurdle for doing so. And it is not the Commission, but Congress that has proscribed "any ... indecent ... language." 18 U.S.C. § 1464.

There are some propositions for which scant empirical evidence can be marshaled, and the harmful effect of broadcast profanity on children is one of them. One cannot demand a multiyear controlled study, in which some children are intentionally exposed to indecent broadcasts (and insulated from all other indecency), and others are shielded from all indecency. It is one thing to set aside agency action under the Administrative Procedure Act because of failure to adduce empirical data that can readily be obtained. It is something else to insist upon obtaining the unobtainable. Here it suffices to know that children mimic the behavior they observe—or at least the behavior that is presented to them as normal and appropriate. Programming replete with one-word indecent expletives will tend to produce children who use (at least) one-word indecent expletives. Congress has made the determination that indecent material is harmful to children, and has left enforcement of the ban to the Commission. If enforcement had to be supported by empirical data, the ban would effectively be a nullity.

The Commission had adduced no quantifiable measure of the harm caused by the language in *Pacifica*, and we nonetheless held that the "government's interest in the 'well-being of its youth'... justified the regulation of otherwise protected expression." 438 U.S. at 749 (quoting Ginsberg v. New York, 390 U.S. 629 (1968)). If the Constitution itself demands of agencies no more scientifically certain criteria to comply with the First Amendment, neither does the Administrative Procedure Act to comply with the requirement of reasoned decisionmaking.

The court's second objection is that fidelity to the agency's "first blow" theory of harm would require a categorical ban on *all* broadcasts of expletives; the Commission's failure to go to this extreme thus undermined the coherence of its rationale. 489 F.3d at 458–59. This objection, however, is not responsive to the Commission's actual policy under review— the decision to include patently offensive fleeting expletives within the definition of indecency. The Commission's prior enforcement practice, unchallenged here, already drew distinctions between the offensiveness of particular words based upon the context in which they appeared. Any complaint about the Commission's failure to ban only some fleeting expletives is better directed at the agency's context-based system generally rather than its inclusion of isolated expletives.

More fundamentally, however, the agency's decision to consider the patent offensiveness of isolated expletives on a case-by-case basis is not arbitrary or capricious. "Even a prime-time recitation of Geoffrey Chaucer's Miller's Tale," we have explained, "would not be likely to command the attention of many children who are both old enough to understand and young enough to be adversely affected." *Pacifica*, 438 U.S. at 750 n.29. The same rationale could support the Commission's finding that a broadcast of the film "Saving Private Ryan" was not indecent—a finding to which the broadcasters point as supposed evidence of the Commission's inconsistency. The frightening suspense and the graphic violence in the movie could well dissuade the most vulnerable from watching and would put parents on notice of potentially objectionable material. *See* Complaints Against Various Television Licensees Regarding Their Broad. on Nov. 11, 2004 of the ABC Television Network's Presentation of the Film "Saving Private Ryan," Memorandum Opinion & Order, 20 FCC Rcd. 4507, 4513 ¶ 15 (2005) (noting that the broadcast was not "intended as family entertainment"). The agency's decision to retain some discretion does not render arbitrary or capricious its regulation of the deliberate and shocking uses of offensive language at the award shows under review—shows that were expected to (and did) draw the attention of millions of children.

Finally, the Court of Appeals found unconvincing the agency's prediction (without any evidence) that a *per se* exemption for fleeting expletives would lead to increased use of expletives one at a time. 489 F.3d at 460. But even in the absence of evidence, the agency's predictive judgment (which merits deference) makes entire sense. To predict that complete immunity for fleeting expletives, ardently desired by broadcasters, will lead to a substantial increase in fleeting expletives seems to us an exercise in logic rather than clairvoyance. The Court of Appeals was perhaps correct that the Commission's prior policy had not yet caused broadcasters to "barrag[e] the airwaves with expletives." *Id.* That may have been because its prior permissive policy had been confirmed (save in dicta) only at the staff level. In any event, as the *Golden Globes Order* demonstrated, it did produce more expletives than the Commission (which has the first call in this matter) deemed in conformity with the statute.

IV. Constitutionality

The Second Circuit did not definitively rule on the constitutionality of the Commission's orders, but respondents nonetheless ask us to decide their validity under the First

Amendment. This Court, however, is one of final review, "not of first view." Cutter v. Wilkinson, 544 U.S. 709, 718 n.7 (2005). It is conceivable that the Commission's orders may cause some broadcasters to avoid certain language that is beyond the Commission's reach under the Constitution. Whether that is so, and, if so, whether it is unconstitutional, will be determined soon enough, perhaps in this very case. Meanwhile, any chilled references to excretory and sexual material "surely lie at the periphery of First Amendment concern." *Pacifica*, 438 U.S. at 743 (plurality opinion of STEVENS, J.). We see no reason to abandon our usual procedures in a rush to judgment without a lower court opinion. We decline to address the constitutional questions at this time.

* * *

The Second Circuit believed that children today "likely hear this language far more often from other sources than they did in the 1970's when the Commission first began sanctioning indecent speech," and that this cuts against more stringent regulation of broadcasts. 489 F.3d at 461. Assuming the premise is true (for this point the Second Circuit did not demand empirical evidence) the conclusion does not necessarily follow. The Commission could reasonably conclude that the pervasiveness of foul language, and the coarsening of public entertainment in other media such as cable, justify more stringent regulation of broadcast programs so as to give conscientious parents a relatively safe haven for their children. In the end, the Second Circuit and the broadcasters quibble with the Commission's policy choices and not with the explanation it has given. We decline to "substitute [our] judgment for that of the agency," *State Farm*, 463 U.S. at 43, and we find the Commission's orders neither arbitrary nor capricious.

Justice THOMAS, concurring.

I join the Court's opinion, which, as a matter of administrative law, correctly upholds the Federal Communications Commission's (FCC) policy with respect to indecent broadcast speech under the Administrative Procedure Act. I write separately, however, to note the questionable viability of the two precedents that support the FCC's assertion of constitutional authority to regulate the programming at issue in this case. *See* Red Lion Broad. Co. v. FCC, 395 U.S. 367 (1969); FCC v. Pacifica Found., 438 U.S. 726 (1978). *Red Lion* and *Pacifica* were unconvincing when they were issued, and the passage of time has only increased doubt regarding their continued validity.

In *Red Lion*, this Court upheld the so-called "fairness doctrine," a Government requirement "that discussion of public issues be presented on broadcast stations, and that each side of those issues must be given fair coverage." 395 U.S. at 369, 400–01. The decision relied heavily on the scarcity of available broadcast frequencies. According to the Court, because broadcast spectrum was so scarce, it "could be regulated and rationalized only by the Government. Without government control, the medium would be of little use because of the cacophony of competing voices, none of which could be clearly and predictably heard." *Id.* at 376. To this end, the Court concluded that the Government should be "permitted to put restraints on licensees in favor of others whose views should be expressed on this unique medium." *Id.* at 390. Applying this principle, the Court held that "[i]t does not violate the First Amendment to treat licensees given the privilege of using scarce radio frequencies as proxies for the entire community, obligated to give suitable time and attention to matters of great public concern." *Id.* at 394.

Red Lion specifically declined to answer whether the First Amendment authorized the Government's "refusal to permit the broadcaster to carry a particular program or to publish his own views... [or] government censorship of a particular program." *Id.* at 396. But then in *Pacifica*, this Court rejected a challenge to the FCC's authority to impose sanctions on the broadcast of indecent material. *See* 438 U.S. at 729–30, 750–51; *id.* at 742 (plurality opinion). Relying on *Red Lion*, the Court noted that "broadcasting ... has received the most limited First Amendment protection." *Id.* at 748. The Court also emphasized the "uniquely pervasive presence" of the broadcast media in Americans' lives and the fact that broadcast programming was "uniquely accessible to children." *Id.* at 748–49.

This deep intrusion into the First Amendment rights of broadcasters, which the Court has justified based only on the nature of the medium, is problematic on two levels. First, instead of looking to first principles to evaluate the constitutional question, the Court relied on a set of transitory facts, *e.g.*, the "scarcity of radio frequencies," *Red Lion*, 395 U.S. at 390, to determine the applicable First Amendment standard. But the original meaning of the Constitution cannot turn on modern necessity: "Constitutional rights are enshrined with the scope they were understood to have when the people adopted them, whether or not future legislatures or (yes) even future judges think that scope too broad." Dist. of Columbia v. Heller, 554 U.S. 570, 634–35 (2008). In breaching this principle, *Red Lion* adopted, and *Pacifica* reaffirmed, a legal rule that lacks any textual basis in the Constitution. Indeed, the logical weakness of *Red Lion* and *Pacifica* has been apparent for some time: "It is certainly true that broadcast frequencies are scarce but it is unclear why that fact justifies content regulation of broadcasting in a way that would be intolerable if applied to the editorial process of the print media." Telecomms. Research & Action Ctr. v. FCC, 801 F.2d 501, 508 (D.C. Cir. 1986) (Bork, J.).

Highlighting the doctrinal incoherence of *Red Lion* and *Pacifica*, the Court has declined to apply the lesser standard of First Amendment scrutiny imposed on broadcast speech to federal regulation of telephone dial-in services, *see* Sable Commc'ns of Cal., Inc. v. FCC, 492 U.S. 115, 127–28 (1989), cable television programming, *see* Turner Broad. Sys., Inc. v. FCC, 512 U.S. 622, 637 (1994), and the Internet, *see* Reno v. Am. Civil Liberties Union, 521 U.S. 844, 867–68 (1997). "There is no justification for this apparent dichotomy in First Amendment jurisprudence. Whatever the merits of *Pacifica* when it was issued[,] ... it makes no sense now." Action for Children's Television v. FCC, 58 F.3d 654, 673 (D.C. Cir. 1995) (Edwards, C.J., dissenting). The justifications relied on by the Court in *Red Lion* and *Pacifica* — "spectrum scarcity, intrusiveness, and accessibility to children — neither distinguish broadcast from cable, nor explain the relaxed application of the principles of the First Amendment to broadcast." *Id.*

Second, even if this Court's disfavored treatment of broadcasters under the First Amendment could have been justified at the time of *Red Lion* and *Pacifica*, dramatic technological advances have eviscerated the factual assumptions underlying those decisions. Broadcast spectrum is significantly less scarce than it was 40 years ago. As NBC notes, the number of over-the-air broadcast stations grew from 7,411 in 1969, when *Red Lion* was issued, to 15,273 by the end of 2004. And the trend should continue with broadcast television's imminent switch from analog to digital transmission, which will allow the FCC to "stack broadcast channels right beside one another along the spectrum, and ultimately utilize significantly less than the 400 MHz of spectrum the analog system absorbs today." Consumer Elecs. Ass'n v. FCC, 347 F.3d 291, 294 (D.C. Cir. 2003).

Moreover, traditional broadcast television and radio are no longer the "uniquely pervasive" media forms they once were. For most consumers, traditional broadcast media programming is now bundled with cable or satellite services. Broadcast and other video programming is also widely available over the Internet. And like radio and television broadcasts, Internet access is now often freely available over the airwaves and can be accessed by portable computer, cell phones, and other wireless devices. The extant facts that drove this Court to subject broadcasters to unique disfavor under the First Amendment simply do not exist today. *See* [2001 Indecency Policy Statement], 16 FCC Rcd. at 8020 (statement of Commissioner Furchtgott-Roth) ("If rules regulating broadcast content were ever a justifiable infringement of speech, it was because of the relative dominance of that medium in the communications marketplace of the past. As the Commission has long recognized, the facts underlying this justification are no longer true" (footnote omitted)).[14]

Justice GINSBURG, dissenting.

I write separately only to note that there is no way to hide the long shadow the First Amendment casts over what the Commission has done. Today's decision does nothing to diminish that shadow.

More than 30 years ago, a sharply divided Court allowed the FCC to sanction a midafternoon radio broadcast of comedian George Carlin's 12-minute "Filthy Words" monologue. Carlin satirized the "original" seven dirty words and repeated them relentlessly in a variety of colloquialisms. The monologue was aired as part of a program on contemporary attitudes toward the use of language. Citizen's Complaint Against Pacifica Found. Station WBAI (FM), Memorandum Opinion & Order, 56 F.C.C. 2d 94, 95 (1975). In rejecting the First Amendment challenge, the Court "emphasize[d] the narrowness of [its] holding." *Pacifica*, 438 U.S. at 750. In this regard, the majority stressed that the Carlin monologue deliberately repeated the dirty words "over and over again." *Id.* at 729.

In contrast, the unscripted fleeting expletives at issue here are neither deliberate nor relentlessly repetitive. Nor does the Commission's policy home in on expressions used to describe sexual or excretory activities or organs. Spontaneous utterances used simply to convey an emotion or intensify a statement fall within the order's compass. *Cf.* Cohen v. Cal., 403 U.S. 15, 26 (1971) ("[W]ords are often chosen as much for their emotive as their cognitive force. We cannot sanction the view that the Constitution, while solicitous of the cognitive content of individual speech, has little or no regard for that emotive function which, practically speaking, may often be the more important element of the overall message sought to be communicated.").

The *Pacifica* decision, however it might fare on reassessment, was tightly cabined, and for good reason. In dissent, Justice Brennan observed that the Government should take care before enjoining the broadcast of words or expressions spoken by many "in our land of cultural pluralism." 438 U.S. at 775. That comment, fitting in the 1970's, is even more potent today. If the reserved constitutional question reaches this Court, we should be mindful that words unpalatable to some may be "commonplace" for others, "the stuff of everyday conversations." 438 U.S. at 776 (Brennan, J., dissenting).

[Concurring opinion of Justice KENNEDY, and dissenting opinions of Justice STEVENS and Justice BREYER, are omitted.]

Notes and Questions

1. First Amendment Shadows. The Court's holding is framed entirely in terms of administrative law—how to apply the Administrative Procedure Act's prohibition on "arbitrary" or "capricious" agency actions when an agency changes a policy judgment. The

---

14. With respect to reliance by FCC v. Pacifica Foundation, 438 U.S. 726 (1978), on the ease with which children could be exposed to indecent television programming, technology has provided innovative solutions to assist adults in screening their children from unsuitable programming—even when that programming appears on broadcast channels. *See* NBC Brief 43–47 (discussing V-chip technology, which allows targeted blocking of television programs based on content).

majority opinion discusses this question at great length, and Justice Breyer's dissent (which your casebook editors deleted for space reasons) does so at even greater length. The majority opinion clearly states that it does not address any First Amendment questions. Are you persuaded by Justice Ginsburg's claim that the First Amendment casts a shadow over the case? If so, what should the Court have done in this case? Acknowledge the shadow (what would that entail)? Rule on the First Amendment issues, despite the fact that the Second Circuit did not rule on them?

2. **First Amendment Tea Leaves.** In light of those shadows, what, if anything, can we glean from the various opinions about the Court's approach to broadcast indecency regulation? Justice Thomas's concurrence is the clearest in this regard. Indeed, it is the clearest statement by a Justice since the dissents in *Pacifica* that the Court should reconsider and (apparently) overrule *Red Lion* and *Pacifica*.[15] Is it useful—or folly—to parse it and the other opinions in an attempt to predict the Court's approach to the First Amendment?

3. **Empirical Evidence.** Does the majority opinion indicate that looking for empirical evidence regarding the impact of indecency is a fool's errand? In this regard, consider Justice Breyer's response on this point, from his dissent:

> The FCC points to no empirical (or other) evidence to demonstrate that it previously understated the importance of avoiding the "first blow." Like the majority, I do not believe that an agency must always conduct full empirical studies of such matters. But the FCC could have referred to, and explained, relevant empirical studies that suggest the contrary. One review of the empirical evidence, for example, reports that "[i]t is doubtful that children under the age of 12 understand sexual language and innuendo; therefore it is unlikely that vulgarities have any negative effect." Barbara K. Kaye & Barry S. Sapolsky, Watch Your Mouth! An Analysis of Profanity Uttered by Children on Prime-Time Television, 7 J. Mass Comm'n & Soc'y 429, 433 (2004) (citing two studies). The Commission need not have accepted this conclusion. But its failure to discuss this or any other such evidence, while providing no empirical evidence at all that favors its position, must weaken the logical force of its conclusion.

FCC v. Fox, 556 U.S. at 564 (Breyer, J., dissenting). What, if any, role should such studies play in considering the First Amendment issues raised by broadcast indecency regulation?

4. **Back Again.** On remand, with the Administrative Procedure Act issues resolved in the FCC's favor, the Second Circuit now confronted the First Amendment issues that it had avoided in its original opinion. In Fox Television Stations, Inc. v. FCC, 613 F.3d 317 (2d Cir. 2010), the court held that the FCC's indecency policy was unconstitutionally vague. The court held that the FCC's flexible standard for determining patent offensiveness provided too little guidance. The opinion emphasized the example from the Commission's 2006 order (noted above) finding "bullshit" but not "dick" or "dickhead" patently offensive as highlighting the lack of notice. The court concluded: "By prohibiting all 'patently offensive' references to sex, sexual organs, and excretion without giving adequate guidance as to what 'patently offensive' means, the FCC effectively chills speech, because broadcasters have no way of knowing what the FCC will find offensive. To place any discussion of these vast topics at the broadcaster's peril has the effect of promoting wide self-censorship

---

15. Justice Stevens, in dissent, was the only Justice to respond to Justice Thomas's concurrence, stating in a footnote: "While Justice Thomas and I disagree about the continued wisdom of *Pacifica*, the changes in technology and the availability of broadcast spectrum he identifies certainly counsel a restrained approach to indecency regulation, not the wildly expansive path the FCC has chosen." *FCC v. Fox*, 556 U.S. at 544 n.5 (Stevens, J., dissenting).

of valuable material which should be completely protected under the First Amendment." *Id.* at 335. The Supreme Court granted certiorari and vacated the Second Circuit's opinion in the opinion below based on a different vagueness problem—an absence of fair notice.

FCC v. Fox Television Stations, Inc.
132 S. Ct. 2307 (2012)

KENNEDY, J., delivered the opinion of the Court, in which ROBERTS, C.J., and SCALIA, THOMAS, BREYER, ALITO, and KAGAN, JJ., joined. GINSBURG, J., filed an opinion concurring in the judgment. SOTOMAYOR, J., took no part in the consideration or decision of the cases.

Justice KENNEDY delivered the opinion of the Court:

[The Court laid out the history presented on pages 762–767 of the casebook, emphasizing that "[e]ven though the incidents at issue in these cases took place before the *Golden Globes Order*, 19 FCC Rcd. 4975 (2004), the Commission applied its new policy regarding fleeting expletives and fleeting nudity. It found the broadcasts by respondents Fox and ABC to be in violation of this standard."]

II

A fundamental principle in our legal system is that laws which regulate persons or entities must give fair notice of conduct that is forbidden or required. This requirement of clarity in regulation is essential to the protections provided by the Due Process Clause of the Fifth Amendment. It requires the invalidation of laws that are impermissibly vague.

Even when speech is not at issue, the void for vagueness doctrine addresses at least two connected but discrete due process concerns: first, that regulated parties should know what is required of them so they may act accordingly; second, precision and guidance are necessary so that those enforcing the law do not act in an arbitrary or discriminatory way. When speech is involved, rigorous adherence to those requirements is necessary to ensure that ambiguity does not chill protected speech.

These concerns are implicated here because, at the outset, the broadcasters claim they did not have, and do not have, sufficient notice of what is proscribed. And leaving aside any concerns about facial invalidity, they contend that the lengthy procedural history set forth above shows that the broadcasters did not have fair notice of what was forbidden. Under the 2001 Indecency Policy Statement, 16 FCC Rcd. 7999 (2001), in force when the broadcasts occurred, a key consideration was "'whether the material dwell[ed] on or repeat[ed] at length'" the offending description or depiction. Fox Television Stations, Inc. v. FCC, 613 F. 3d 317, 322 (2d Cir. 2010). In the 2004 *Golden Globes Order*, issued after the broadcasts, the Commission changed course and held that fleeting expletives could be a statutory violation. In the challenged orders now under review the Commission applied the new principle promulgated in the *Golden Globes Order* and determined fleeting expletives and a brief moment of indecency were actionably indecent. This regulatory history, however, makes it apparent that the Commission policy in place at the time of the broadcasts gave no notice to Fox or ABC that a fleeting expletive or a brief shot of nudity could be actionably indecent; yet Fox and ABC were found to be in violation. The Commission's lack of notice to Fox and ABC that its interpretation had changed so the fleeting moments of indecency contained in their broadcasts were a violation of 18 U.S.C.

§ 1464 as interpreted and enforced by the agency "fail[ed] to provide a person of ordinary intelligence fair notice of what is prohibited." See United States v. Williams, 553 U.S. 285, 304 (2008). This would be true with respect to a regulatory change this abrupt on any subject, but it is surely the case when applied to the regulations in question, regulations that touch upon "sensitive areas of basic First Amendment freedoms," Baggett v. Bullitt, 377 U.S. 360, 372 (1964).

[I]t is true that the Commission declined to impose any forfeiture on Fox, see FCC v. Fox Television Stations, Inc., 556 U.S. 502, 513 (2009), and in its order the Commission claimed that it would not consider the indecent broadcasts either when considering whether to renew stations' licenses or "in any other context," Complaints Regarding Various Television Broads. Between Feb. 2, 2002 and Mar. 8, 2005, Order, 21 FCC Rcd. 13,299, 13,321, 13,326 (2006). This "policy of forbearance," as the Government calls it, does not suffice to make the issue moot. Brief for Petitioners 31. Though the Commission claims it will not consider the prior indecent broadcasts "in any context," it has the statutory power to take into account "any history of prior offenses" when setting the level of a forfeiture penalty. See 47 U.S.C. § 503(b)(2)(E). Just as in the First Amendment context, the due process protection against vague regulations "does not leave [regulated parties] ... at the mercy of *noblesse oblige*." United States v. Stevens, 130 S. Ct. 1577, 1591 (2010).

In addition, when combined with the legal consequence described above, reputational injury provides further reason for granting relief to Fox. As respondent CBS points out, findings of wrongdoing can result in harm to a broadcaster's "reputation with viewers and advertisers." Brief for Respondent CBS Television Network Affiliates Ass'n et al. 17. This observation is hardly surprising given that the challenged orders, which are contained in the permanent Commission record, describe in strongly disapproving terms the indecent material broadcast by Fox, see, e.g., 21 FCC Rcd. at 13,310–13,311, ¶ 30 (noting the "explicit, graphic, vulgar, and shocking nature of Ms. Richie's comments"), and Fox's efforts to protect children from being exposed to it, *see id.* at 13,311, ¶ 33 (finding Fox had failed to exercise "'reasonable judgment, responsibility, and sensitivity to the public's needs and tastes to avoid [a] patently offensive broadcast[]'"). Commission sanctions on broadcasters for indecent material are widely publicized. The challenged orders could have an adverse impact on Fox's reputation that audiences and advertisers alike are entitled to take into account.

With respect to ABC, the Government with good reason does not argue no sanction was imposed. The fine against ABC and its network affiliates for the seven seconds of nudity was nearly $1.24 million. The Government argues instead that ABC had notice that the scene in "NYPD Blue" would be considered indecent in light of a 1960 decision where the Commission declared that the "televising of nudes might well raise a serious question of programming contrary to 18 U.S.C. § 1464." Brief for Petitioners 32 (quoting En banc Programming Inquiry, 44 F.C.C. 2303, 2307 (1960) (internal quotation marks omitted)). This argument does not prevail. An isolated and ambiguous statement from a 1960 Commission decision does not suffice for the fair notice required when the Government intends to impose over a $1 million fine for allegedly impermissible speech. The Commission, furthermore, had released decisions before sanctioning ABC that declined to find isolated and brief moments of nudity actionably indecent. *See, e.g.*, Application of WGBH, 69 F.C.C. 2d 1250, 1251, 1255 (1978) (declining to find broadcasts containing nudity to be indecent and emphasizing the difference between repeated and isolated expletives); WPBN/ WTOM License Subsidiary, Inc., 15 FCC Rcd. 1838, 1840 (2000) (finding full frontal nudity in "Schindler's List" not indecent). This is not to say, of course, that a graphic scene from "Schindler's List" involving nude concentration camp prisoners is the same as the shower scene from "NYPD Blue." It does show, however, that the Government can point to nothing that would have given ABC affirmative notice that its broadcast would be considered actionably indecent. It is likewise not sufficient for the Commission to assert, as it did in its order, that though "the depiction [of nudity] here is not as lengthy or repeated" as in some cases, the shower scene nonetheless "does contain more shots or lengthier depictions of nudity" than in other broadcasts found not indecent. Complaints Against Various Television Licensees Concerning Their February 24, 2003 Broadcast of the Program "NYPD Blue", 23 FCC Rcd. 3147, 3153 (2008). This broad language fails to demonstrate that ABC had fair notice that its broadcast could be found indecent. In fact, a Commission ruling prior to the airing of the "NYPD Blue" episode had deemed 30 seconds of nude buttocks "very brief" and not actionably indecent in the context of the broadcast. *See* Letter from Norman Goldstein to David Molina, FCC File No. 97110028 (May 26, 1999). In light of this record of agency decisions, and the absence of any notice in the 2001 Guidance that seven seconds of nude buttocks would be found indecent, ABC lacked constitutionally sufficient notice prior to being sanctioned.

The Commission failed to give Fox or ABC fair notice prior to the broadcasts in question that fleeting expletives and momentary nudity could be found actionably indecent. Therefore, the Commission's standards as applied to these broadcasts were vague, and the Commission's orders must be set aside.

III

It is necessary to make three observations about the scope of this decision. First, because the Court resolves these cases on fair notice grounds under the Due Process Clause, it need not address the First Amendment implications of the Commission's indecency policy. It is argued that this Court's ruling in FCC v. Pacifica Foundation, 438 U.S. 726 (1978) (and the less rigorous standard of scrutiny it provided for the regulation of broadcasters) should be overruled because the rationale of that case has been overtaken by technological change and the wide availability of multiple other choices for listeners and viewers. The Government for its part maintains that when it licenses a conventional broadcast spectrum, the public may assume that the Government has its own interest in setting certain standards. These arguments need not be addressed here. In light of the Court's holding that the Commission's policy failed to provide fair notice it is unnecessary to reconsider *Pacifica* at this time.

This leads to a second observation. Here, the Court rules that Fox and ABC lacked notice at the time of their broadcasts that the material they were broadcasting could be found actionably indecent under then-existing policies. Given this disposition, it is unnecessary for the Court to address the constitutionality of the current indecency policy as expressed in the *Golden Globes Order* and subsequent adjudications. The Court adheres to its normal practice of declining to decide cases not before it.

Third, this opinion leaves the Commission free to modify its current indecency policy in light of its determination of the public interest and applicable legal requirements. And it leaves the courts free to review the current policy or any modified policy in light of its content and application.

Justice SOTOMAYOR took no part in the consideration or decision of these cases.

Justice GINSBURG, concurring in the judgment.

In my view, the Court's decision in FCC v. Pacifica Foundation, 438 U.S. 726 (1978), was wrong when it issued. Time, technological advances, and the Commission's untenable rulings in the cases now before the Court show why *Pacifica* bears reconsideration. *Cf.* FCC v. Fox Television Stations, Inc., 556 U.S. 502, 532–35 (2009) (THOMAS, J., concurring).

Notes and Questions

1. **Fair Notice.** The year is 2003, and you are advising a broadcaster. Do you think you would advise that the broadcaster was running a serious risk of a big fine if it allowed a performer to say "fuck" or "shit" on the air, particularly if those words seemed gratuitous? If you showed nude buttocks for seven seconds in a scene that could fairly be characterized as titillating? If the answer to either question is yes, does that mean that at least one of these broadcasters in fact had fair notice?

2. **Avoiding *Pacifica*.** The FCC's handling of Cher's and Nicole Richie's language resulted in two Supreme Court oral arguments that addressed *Pacifica* at some length and two Supreme Court opinions that managed to avoid any holding on, or even discussion of, *Pacifica*. What, if anything, should we make of that?

3. **Where To from Here?** The opinion pointedly leaves much undecided. (Indeed, the case was decided on the narrowest of the grounds presented to the Court.) What advice would you give to: (a) a member of Congress who wanted to regulate broadcast indecency as much as the First Amendment allows? (b) an FCC Commissioner who wanted to have some enforceable and meaningful limits on broadcast indecency? (c) a television broadcaster who wanted to air as much indecency as possible without being subject to huge fines?

---

§ 16.A.2. Regulation of Cable Indecency

18 U.S.C. § 1464 prohibits "any obscene, indecent, profane language by means of radio communication," and so does not apply outside the "radio communication" context. 18 U.S.C. § 1468 is the companion statute that specifically applies to "cable television [and] subscription services on television," but it prohibits only obscenity. More broadly, the FCC's longstanding position has been that "subscription-based services do not call into play the issue of indecency," Litigation Recovery Trust, Memorandum Opinion and Order, 17 FCC Rcd. 21,852, 21,856 (2002), and that "[c]onsistent with existing case law, the Commission does not impose regulations regarding indecency on services lacking the indiscriminate access to children that characterizes broadcasting." Harriscope of Chicago, Inc., Memorandum Opinion and Order, 3 FCC Rcd. 757, 760 n.2 (1988). Thus, not only cable and DBS but also digital radio are not subject to bans on indecency.

Congress has, though, enacted legislation aimed at channeling (though not banning) cable indecency. And that legislation has produced the two Supreme Court cases excerpted below. Those cases are the focus of this section, but we begin by noting that, although the issue has not been frequently litigated, no federal court decision has upheld states' or municipalities' attempts to bar indecent programs from cable television. Cruz v. Ferre, 755 F.2d 1415 (11th Cir. 1985), is representative of judicial opinions reviewing local efforts to suppress cable indecency. The case turned on the application of *Pacifica*. The heart of the court's discussion follows.

> Appellants' primary argument on appeal is that authority for the city's regulation is found in *Pacifica*. The district court, after "a careful consideration of

Pacifica," found *Pacifica* to be "inapplicable to the facts herein." The district court contrasted the cable medium with broadcast television. A Cablevision subscriber must make the affirmative decision to bring Cablevision into his home. By using monthly program guides, the Cablevision subscriber may avoid the unpleasant surprises that sometimes occur in broadcast programming. Additionally, the district court noted, the ability to protect children is provided through the use of a free "lockbox" or "parental key" available from Cablevision.

Pacifica, it must be remembered, focused upon broadcasting's "pervasive presence," and the fact that broadcasting "is uniquely accessible to children, even those too young to read." The Court's concern with the pervasiveness of the broadcast media can best be seen in its description of broadcasted material as an "intruder" into the privacy of the home. Cablevision, however, does not "intrude" into the home. The Cablevision subscriber must affirmatively elect to have cable service come into his home. Additionally, the subscriber must make the additional affirmative decision whether to purchase any "extra" programming services, such as HBO. The subscriber must make a monthly decision whether to continue to subscribe to cable, and if dissatisfied with the cable service, he may cancel his subscription. The Supreme Court's reference to "a nuisance rationale" is not applicable to the Cablevision system, where there is no possibility that a non-cable subscriber will be confronted with materials carried only on cable. One of the keys to the very existence of cable television is the fact that cable programming is available only to those who have the cable attached to their television sets.[16]

Probably the more important justification recognized in *Pacifica* for the FCC's authority to regulate the broadcasting of indecent materials was the accessibility of broadcasting to children. This interest, however, is significantly weaker in the context of cable television because parental manageability of cable television greatly exceeds the ability to manage the broadcast media. Again, parents must decide whether to allow Cablevision into the home. Parents decide whether to select supplementary programming services such as HBO. These services publish programming guides which identify programs containing "vulgarity," "nudity," and "violence." Additionally, parents may obtain a "lockbox" or "parental key" device enabling parents to prevent children from gaining access to "objectionable" channels of programming. Cablevision provides these without charge to subscribers.

Does this discussion identify any material difference between cable and conventional broadcasting other than the availability of lockboxes for cable subscribers? Given that the government could require that radio and television sets be engineered so that parents can lock out broadcast channels, did the *Pacifica* Court err in failing to insist on this less intrusive alternative?

§ 16.A.2.a. *Denver Area*

As *Pacifica*, *ACT III*, and *Fox v. FCC* showed, the federal government has long sought to reduce the amount of indecent programming available on broadcast television. The federal government's efforts at regulating cable indecency, by contrast, are both of more

---

16. Appellants seem to want to extend Justice Stevens's "pig in the parlor" analogy. *See* Brief of Appellants at 16 ("it makes no difference whether the pig enters the parlor through the door of broadcast, cable, or amplified speech: government is entitled to keep the pig out of the parlor"). It seems to us, however, that if an individual voluntarily opens his door and allows a pig into his parlor, he is in less of a position to squeal.

recent vintage and of somewhat narrower scope. It was not until the 1992 Cable Act that Congress made any serious effort to regulate cable indecency. And, even then, the regulation of choice was not a complete ban, but instead a statutory provision that allowed cable operators to decide whether or not to prohibit indecent programs on the only channels (apart from those subject to must-carry) that they do not themselves program: the commercial leased access and public, educational, or governmental (PEG) channels. The Supreme Court's splintered response follows.

DENVER AREA EDUCATIONAL TELECOMMUNICATIONS CONSORTIUM, INC. v. FCC
518 U.S. 727 (1996)

BREYER, J., announced the judgment of the Court and delivered the opinion of the Court with respect to Part III, in which STEVENS, O'CONNOR, KENNEDY, SOUTER, and GINSBURG, JJ., joined, an opinion with respect to Parts I, II, and V, in which STEVENS, O'CONNOR and SOUTER, JJ., joined, and an opinion with respect to Parts IV and VI, in which STEVENS and SOUTER, JJ., joined. STEVENS, J., and SOUTER, J., filed concurring opinions. O'CONNOR, J., filed an opinion concurring in part and dissenting in part. KENNEDY, J., filed an opinion concurring in part, concurring in the judgment in part, and dissenting in part, in which GINSBURG, J., joined. THOMAS, J., filed an opinion concurring in the judgment in part and dissenting in part, in which REHNQUIST, C.J., and SCALIA, J., joined.

JUSTICE BREYER announced the judgment of the Court and delivered the opinion of the Court with respect to Part III, an opinion with respect to Parts I, II, and V, in which JUSTICE STEVENS, JUSTICE O'CONNOR, and JUSTICE SOUTER join, and an opinion with respect to Parts IV and VI, in which JUSTICE STEVENS and JUSTICE SOUTER join.

These cases present First Amendment challenges to three statutory provisions that seek to regulate the broadcasting of "patently offensive" sex-related material on cable television. Cable Television Consumer Protection and Competition Act of 1992 (1992 Act or Act), §§ 10(a), 10(b), and 10(c), 47 U.S.C. §§ 532(h), 532(j), and note following § 531. The provisions apply to programs broadcast over cable on what are known as "leased access channels" and "public, educational, or governmental channels." Two of the provisions essentially permit a cable system operator to prohibit the broadcasting of "programming" that the "operator reasonably believes describes or depicts sexual or excretory activities or organs in a patently offensive manner." 1992 Act, § 10(a); *see* § 10(c). The remaining provision requires cable system operators to segregate certain "patently offensive" programming, to place it on a single channel, and to block that channel from viewer access unless the viewer requests access in advance and in writing. 1992 Act, § 10(b).

We conclude that the first provision—that *permits* the operator to decide whether or not to broadcast such programs on *leased* access channels—is consistent with the First Amendment. The second provision, that *requires* leased channel operators to segregate and to block that programming, and the third provision, applicable to public, educational, and governmental channels, violate the First Amendment, for they are not appropriately tailored to achieve the basic, legitimate objective of protecting children from exposure to "patently offensive" material.

I

A "leased channel" is a channel that federal law requires a cable system operator to reserve for commercial lease by unaffiliated third parties. About 10 to 15 percent of a cable system's channels would typically fall into this category. *See* 47 U.S.C. §532(b). "Public, educational, or governmental channels" (which we shall call "public access" channels) are channels that, over the years, local governments have required cable system operators to set aside for public, educational, or governmental purposes as part of the consideration an operator gives in return for permission to install cables under city streets and to use public rights-of-way. *See* §531; *see also* H.R. Rep. No. 98-934, p. 30 (1984) (authorizing local authorities to require creation of public access channels). Between 1984 and 1992, federal law (as had much pre-1984 state law, in respect to public access channels) prohibited cable system operators from exercising *any* editorial control over the content of any program broadcast over either leased or public access channels. *See* 47 U.S.C. §§531(e) (public access), 532(c)(2) (leased access).

In 1992, in an effort to control sexually explicit programming conveyed over access channels, Congress enacted the three provisions before us. The first two provisions relate to leased channels. The first says:

> This subsection shall permit a cable operator to enforce prospectively a written and published policy of prohibiting programming that the cable operator reasonably believes describes or depicts sexual or excretory activities or organs in a patently offensive manner as measured by contemporary community standards.

1992 Act, §10(a)(2), 106 Stat. 1486.

The second provision, applicable only to leased channels, requires cable operators to segregate and to block similar programming if they decide to permit, rather than to prohibit, its broadcast. The provision tells the Federal Communications Commission (FCC or Commission) to promulgate regulations that will (a) require "programmers to inform cable operators if the program[ming] would be indecent as defined by Commission regulations"; (b) require "cable operators to place" such material "on a single channel"; and (c) require "cable operators to block such single channel unless the subscriber requests access to such channel in writing." 1992 Act, §10(b)(1).

The third provision is similar to the first provision, but applies only to public access channels. The relevant statutory section instructs the FCC to promulgate regulations that will

> enable a cable operator of a cable system to prohibit the use, on such system, of any channel capacity of any public, educational, or governmental access facility for any programming which contains obscene material, sexually explicit conduct, or material soliciting or promoting unlawful conduct.

1992 Act, §10(c).

The FCC, carrying out this statutory instruction, promulgated regulations defining "sexually explicit" in language almost identical to that in the statute's leased channel provision, namely as descriptions or depictions of "sexual or excretory activities or organs in a patently offensive manner" as measured by the cable viewing community.

The upshot is, as we said at the beginning, that the federal law before us (the statute as implemented through regulations) now *permits* cable operators either to allow or to forbid the transmission of "patently offensive" sex-related materials over both leased and public access channels, and *requires* those operators, at a minimum, to segregate and to block transmission of that same material on leased channels.

II

We turn initially to the provision that *permits* cable system operators to prohibit "patently offensive" (or "indecent") programming transmitted over leased access channels. 1992 Act, § 10(a). [The Court of Appeals] viewed this statute's "permissive" provisions as not themselves restricting speech, but, rather, as simply reaffirming the authority to pick and choose programming that a private entity, say, a private broadcaster, would have had in the absence of intervention by any federal, or local, governmental entity.

Nonetheless, petitioners point to circumstances that, in their view, make the analogy with private broadcasters inapposite and make this case a special one, warranting a different constitutional result. As a practical matter, they say, cable system operators have considerably more power to "censor" program viewing than do broadcasters, for individual communities typically have only one cable system, linking broadcasters and other program providers with each community's many subscribers. Moreover, concern about system operators' exercise of this considerable power originally led government—local and federal—to insist that operators provide leased and public access channels free of operator editorial control. To permit system operators to supervise programming on leased access channels will create the very private-censorship risk that this anticensorship effort sought to avoid.

Under these circumstances, petitioners conclude, Congress' "permissive" law, *in actuality*, will "abridge" their free speech. And this Court should treat that law as a congressionally imposed, content-based, restriction unredeemed as a properly tailored effort to serve a "compelling interest."

Like petitioners, Justices Kennedy and Thomas would have us decide these cases simply by transferring and applying literally categorical standards this Court has developed in other contexts. For Justice Kennedy, leased access channels are like a common carrier, cablecast is a protected medium, strict scrutiny applies, § 10(a) fails this test, and, therefore, § 10(a) is invalid. For Justice Thomas, the case is simple because the cable operator who owns the system over which access channels are broadcast, like a bookstore owner with respect to what it displays on the shelves, has a predominant First Amendment interest. Both categorical approaches suffer from the same flaws: They import law developed in very different contexts into a new and changing environment, and they lack the flexibility necessary to allow government to respond to very serious practical problems without sacrificing the free exchange of ideas the First Amendment is designed to protect.

The history of this Court's First Amendment jurisprudence, however, is one of continual development, as the Constitution's general command that "Congress shall make no law ... abridging the freedom of speech, or of the press," has been applied to new circumstances requiring different adaptations of prior principles and precedents.

This tradition teaches that the First Amendment embodies an overarching commitment to protect speech from government regulation through close judicial scrutiny, thereby enforcing the Constitution's constraints, but without imposing judicial formulas so rigid that they become a straitjacket that disables government from responding to serious problems. This Court, in different contexts, has consistently held that government may directly regulate speech to address extraordinary problems, where its regulations are appropriately tailored to resolve those problems without imposing an unnecessarily great restriction on speech. Justices Kennedy and Thomas would have us further declare which, among the many applications of the general approach that this Court has developed over the years, we are applying here. But no definitive choice among competing analogies (broadcast, common carrier, bookstore) allows us to declare a rigid single standard, good for now and for all future media and purposes. That is not to say that we reject all the more specific formulations of the standard—they appropriately cover the vast majority of cases involving government regulation of speech. Rather, aware as we are of the changes taking place in the law, the technology, and the industrial structure related to telecommunications, we believe it unwise and unnecessary definitively to pick one analogy or one specific set of words now. We therefore think it premature to answer the broad questions that Justices Kennedy and Thomas raise in their efforts to find a definitive analogy, deciding, for example, the extent to which private property can be designated a public forum; whether public access channels are a public forum; whether the Government's viewpoint neutral decision to limit a public forum is subject to the same scrutiny as a selective exclusion from a pre-existing public forum; whether exclusion from common carriage must for all purposes be treated like exclusion from a public forum; and whether the interests of the owners of communications media always subordinate the interests of all other users of a medium.

Rather than decide these issues, we can decide these cases more narrowly, by closely scrutinizing § 10(a) to assure that it properly addresses an extremely important problem, without imposing, in light of the relevant interests, an unnecessarily great restriction on speech. The importance of the interest at stake here—protecting children from exposure to patently offensive depictions of sex; the accommodation of the interests of programmers in maintaining access channels and of cable operators in editing the contents of their channels; the similarity of the problem and its solution to those at issue in *Pacifica*; and the flexibility inherent in an approach that *permits* private cable operators to make editorial decisions, lead us to conclude that § 10(a) is a sufficiently tailored response to an extraordinarily important problem.

First, the provision before us comes accompanied with an extremely important justification, one that this Court has often found compelling—the need to protect children from exposure to patently offensive sex-related material. Sable Communications of California, Inc. v. FCC, 492 U.S. 115, 126 (1989); Ginsberg v. New York, 390 U.S. 629, 639–40 (1968).

Second, the provision arises in a very particular context—congressional *permission* for cable operators to regulate programming that, but for a previous Act of Congress, would have had no path of access to cable channels free of an operator's control. The First Amendment interests involved are therefore complex, and require a balance between those interests served by the access requirements themselves (increasing the availability of avenues of expression to programmers who otherwise would not have them) and the disadvantage to the First Amendment interests of cable operators and other programmers (those to whom the cable operator would have assigned the channels devoted to access).

Third, the problem Congress addressed here is remarkably similar to the problem addressed by the FCC in *Pacifica*, and the balance Congress struck is commensurate with the balance we approved there. In *Pacifica* this Court considered a governmental ban of a radio broadcast of "indecent" materials, defined in part, like the provisions before us, to include

> language that describes, in terms patently offensive as measured by contemporary community standards for the broadcast medium, sexual or excretory activities and organs, at times of the day when there is a reasonable risk that children may be in the audience.

438 U.S. at 732 (quoting 56 F.C.C.2d 94, 98 (1975)).

The Court found this ban constitutionally permissible primarily because "broadcasting is uniquely accessible to children" and children were likely listeners to the program there at issue—an afternoon radio broadcast. *Id.* at 749–50. In addition, the Court wrote, "the broadcast media have established a uniquely pervasive presence in the lives of all Americans," *id.* at 748, "[p]atently offensive, indecent material ... confronts the citizen, not only in public, but also in the privacy of the home," generally without sufficient prior warning to allow the recipient to avert his or her eyes or ears, *id.*; and "[a]dults who feel the need may purchase tapes and records or go to theaters and nightclubs" to hear similar performances. *Id.* at 750 n.28.

All these factors are present here. Cable television broadcasting, including access channel broadcasting, is as "accessible to children" as over-the-air broadcasting, if not more so. Cable television systems, including access channels, "have established a uniquely pervasive presence in the lives of all Americans." *Pacifica, supra*, at 748. "Patently offensive" material from these stations can "confront[] the citizen" in the "privacy of the home," *Pacifica, supra*, at 748, with little or no prior warning. There is nothing to stop "adults who feel the need" from finding similar programming elsewhere, say, on tape or in theaters.

Fourth, the permissive nature of §10(a) means that it likely restricts speech less than, not more than, the ban at issue in *Pacifica*. [A]lthough the provision does create a risk that a program will not appear, that risk is not the same as the certainty that accompanies a governmental ban. Finally, the provision's permissive nature brings with it a flexibility that allows cable operators, for example, not to ban broadcasts, but, say, to rearrange broadcast times, better to fit the desires of adult audiences while lessening the risks of harm to children. In all these respects, the permissive nature of the approach taken by Congress renders this measure appropriate as a means of achieving the underlying purpose of protecting children.

The existence of this complex balance of interests persuades us that the permissive nature of the provision, coupled with its viewpoint-neutral application, is a constitutionally permissible way to protect children from the type of sexual material that concerned Congress, while accommodating both the First Amendment interests served by the access requirements and those served in restoring to cable operators a degree of the editorial control that Congress removed in 1984.

III

The statute's second provision significantly differs from the first, for it does not simply permit, but rather requires, cable system operators to restrict speech—by segregating and blocking "patently offensive" sex-related material appearing on leased channels (but not on other channels). 1992 Act, §10(b). In particular, this provision and its implementing regulations require cable system operators to place "patently offensive" leased channel programming on a separate channel; to block that channel; to unblock the channel within 30 days of a subscriber's written request for access; and to reblock the channel within 30 days of a subscriber's request for reblocking. Also, leased channel programmers must notify cable operators of an intended "patently offensive" broadcast up to 30 days before its scheduled broadcast date.

These requirements have obvious restrictive effects. The Government argues that, despite these adverse consequences, the "segregate and block" requirements are lawful because they are "the least restrictive means of realizing" a "compelling interest," namely "protecting the physical and psychological well-being of minors." *See* Brief for Federal Respondents at 11 (quoting *Sable*, 492 U.S. at 126).

We agree with the Government that protection of children is a "compelling interest." But we do not agree that the "segregate and block" requirements properly accommodate the speech restrictions they impose and the legitimate objective they seek to attain. Nor need we here determine whether, or the extent to which, *Pacifica* does, or does not, impose some lesser standard of review where indecent speech is at issue, *compare* 438 U.S. at 745–48 (opinion of Stevens, J.) (indecent materials enjoy lesser First Amendment protection), *with id.* at 761–62 (Powell, J., concurring in part and concurring in judgment) (refusing to accept a lesser standard for nonobscene, indecent material). That is because once one examines this governmental restriction, it becomes apparent that, not only is it not a "least restrictive alternative" and is not "narrowly tailored" to meet its legitimate objective, it also seems considerably "more extensive than necessary." That is to say, it fails to satisfy this Court's formulations of the First Amendment's "strictest," as well as its somewhat less "strict," requirements.

Several circumstances lead us to this conclusion. For one thing, the law, as recently amended, uses other means to protect children from similar "patently offensive" material broadcast on *un*leased cable channels, i.e., broadcast over any of a system's numerous ordinary, or public access, channels. The law, as recently amended, requires cable operators to "scramble or ... block" such programming on any (unleased) channel "*primarily dedicated* to sexually-oriented programming." Telecommunications Act of 1996, §505, 110 Stat. 136 (emphasis added). In addition, cable operators must honor a subscriber's request to block any, or all, programs on any channel to which he or she does not wish to subscribe. §504. And manufacturers, in the future, will have to make television sets with a so-called "V-chip"—a device that will be able automatically to identify and block sexually explicit or violent programs. §551.

Although we cannot, and do not, decide whether the new provisions are themselves lawful (a matter not before us), we note that they are significantly less restrictive than the provision here at issue. They do not force the viewer to receive (for days or weeks at a time) all "patently offensive" programming or none; they will not lead the viewer automatically to judge the few by the reputation of the many; and they will not automatically place the occasional viewer's name on a special list. They therefore inevitably lead us to ask why, if they adequately protect children from "patently offensive" material broadcast on ordinary channels, they would not offer adequate protection from similar leased channel broadcasts as well? Alternatively, if these provisions do not adequately protect children from "patently offensive" material broadcast on ordinary channels, how could one justify more severe leased channel restrictions when (given ordinary channel programming) they would yield so little additional protection for children?

The record does not answer these questions. It does not explain why, under the new Act, blocking alone—without written access-requests—adequately protects children from exposure to regular sex-dedicated channels, but cannot adequately protect those children from programming on similarly sex-dedicated channels that are leased. It does not explain why a simple subscriber blocking request system, perhaps a phone-call based system, would adequately protect children from "patently offensive" material broadcast on ordinary non-sex-dedicated channels (i.e., almost all channels) but a far more restrictive segregate/block/written-access system is needed to protect children from similar broadcasts on what (in the absence of the segregation requirement) would be non-sex-dedicated channels that are leased. Nor is there any indication Congress thought the new ordinary channel protections less than adequate.

Consequently, we cannot find that the "segregate and block" restrictions on speech are a narrowly, or reasonably, tailored effort to protect children. Rather, they are overly restrictive, "sacrific[ing]" important First Amendment interests for too "speculative a gain." Columbia Broadcasting System, Inc. v. Democratic National Committee, 412 U.S. 94, 127 (1973). For that reason they are not consistent with the First Amendment.

IV

The statute's third provision, as implemented by FCC regulation, is similar to its first provision, in that it too *permits* a cable operator to prevent transmission of "patently offensive" programming, in this case on public access channels. 1992 Act § 10(c); 47 C.F.R. § 76.702 (1995). But there are four important differences.

The first is the historical background. [C]able operators have traditionally agreed to reserve channel capacity for public, governmental, and educational channels as part of the consideration they give municipalities that award them cable franchises. Significantly, these are channels over which cable operators have not historically exercised editorial control. Unlike § 10(a) therefore, § 10(c) does not restore to cable operators editorial rights that they once had.

The second difference is the institutional background that has developed as a result of the historical difference. When a "leased channel" is made available by the operator to a private lessee, the lessee has total control of programming during the leased time slot. Public access channels, on the other hand, are normally subject to complex supervisory systems of various sorts, often with both public and private elements. *See* § 531(b) (franchising authorities "may require rules and procedures for the use of the [public access] channel capacity"). Municipalities generally provide in their cable franchising agreements for an access channel manager, who is most commonly a nonprofit organization, but may also be the municipality, or, in some instances, the cable system owner. Access channel activity and management are partly financed with public funds — through franchise fees or other payments pursuant to the franchise agreement, or from general municipal funds and are commonly subject to supervision by a local supervisory board.

This system of public, private, and mixed nonprofit elements, through its supervising boards and nonprofit or governmental access managers, can set programming policy and approve or disapprove particular programming services. And this system can police that policy by, for example, requiring indemnification by programmers, certification of compliance with local standards, time segregation, adult content advisories, or even by pre-screening individual programs. Whether these locally accountable bodies prescreen programming, promulgate rules for the use of public access channels, or are merely available to respond when problems arise, the upshot is the same: There is a locally accountable body capable of addressing the problem, should it arise, of patently offensive programming broadcast to children, making it unlikely that many children will in fact be exposed to programming considered patently offensive in that community.

Third, the existence of a system aimed at encouraging and securing programming that the community considers valuable strongly suggests that a "cable operator's veto" is less likely necessary to achieve the statute's basic objective, protecting children, than a similar veto in the context of leased channels.

Finally, our examination of the legislative history and the record before us is consistent with what common sense suggests, namely that the public/nonprofit programming control systems now in place would normally avoid, minimize, or eliminate any child-related problems concerning "patently offensive" programming. The Commission itself did not report *any* examples of "indecent" programs on public access channels. Moreover, comments submitted to the FCC undermine any suggestion that prior to 1992 there were significant problems of indecent programming on public access channels.

The upshot, in respect to the public access channels, is a law that could radically change present programming-related relationships among local community and nonprofit supervising boards and access managers, which relationships are established through municipal law, regulation, and contract. In doing so, it would not significantly restore editorial rights of cable operators, but would greatly increase the risk that certain categories of programming (say, borderline offensive programs) will not appear. At the same time, given present supervisory mechanisms, the need for this particular provision, aimed directly at public access channels, is not obvious. [W]e conclude that the Government cannot sustain its burden of showing that § 10(c) is necessary to protect children or that it is appropriately tailored to secure that end. Consequently, we find that this third provision violates the First Amendment.

VI

For these reasons, the judgment of the Court of Appeals is affirmed insofar as it upheld § 10(a); the judgment of the Court of Appeals is reversed insofar as it upheld § 10(b) and § 10(c).

[Concurring opinions of JUSTICES STEVENS and SOUTER are omitted.]

JUSTICE O'CONNOR, concurring in part and dissenting in part.

I agree that § 10(a) is constitutional and that § 10(b) is unconstitutional, and I join Parts I, II, III, and V, and the judgment in part. I am not persuaded, however, that the asserted "important differences" between §§ 10(a) and 10(c), are sufficient to justify striking down § 10(c). I find the features shared by § 10(a), which covers leased access channels, and § 10(c), which covers public access channels, to be more significant than the differences. For that reason, I would find that § 10(c) also withstands constitutional scrutiny.

Both §§ 10(a) and 10(c) serve an important governmental interest: the well-established compelling interest of protecting children from exposure to indecent material. Furthermore, both provisions are permissive. Neither presents an outright ban on a category of speech, such as we struck down in *Sable Communications of Cal., Inc. v. FCC, supra.*

It is also significant that neither § 10(a) nor § 10(c) is more restrictive than the governmental speech restriction we upheld in FCC v. Pacifica Foundation, 438 U.S. 726 (1978). I agree with Justice Breyer that we should not yet undertake fully to adapt our First Amendment doctrine to the new context we confront here. Because we refrain from doing so, the precedent established by *Pacifica* offers an important guide. Section 10(c), no less than § 10(a), is within the range of acceptability set by *Pacifica*.

I am not persuaded that the difference in the origin of the access channels is sufficient to justify upholding § 10(a) and striking down § 10(c). The interest in protecting children remains the same, whether on a leased access channel or a public access channel, and allowing the cable operator the option of prohibiting the transmission of indecent speech seems a constitutionally permissible means of addressing that interest. Nor is the fact that public access programming may be subject to supervisory systems in addition to the cable operator, sufficient in my mind to render § 10(c) so ill-tailored to its goal as to be unconstitutional.

Given the compelling interest served by § 10(c), its permissive nature, and its fit within our precedent, I would hold § 10(c), like § 10(a), constitutional.

JUSTICE KENNEDY, with whom JUSTICE GINSBURG joins, concurring in part, concurring in the judgment in part, and dissenting in part.

Though I join Part III of the opinion (there for the Court) striking down § 10(b) of the Act, and concur in the judgment that § 10(c) is unconstitutional, with respect I dissent from the remainder.

I

Two provisions of the 1992 Act, §§ 10(a) and (c), authorize the operator of a cable system to exclude certain programming from two different kinds of channels. Section 10(a) concerns leased access channels. Section 10(c) involves public, educational, and governmental access channels (or PEG access channels, as they are known).

Though the two provisions differ in significant respects, they have common flaws. In both instances, Congress singles out one sort of speech for vulnerability to private censorship in a context where content-based discrimination is not otherwise permitted. Sections 10(a) and (c) disadvantage nonobscene, indecent programming, a protected category of expression, Sable Communications of Cal., Inc. v. FCC, 492 U.S. 115, 126 (1989), on the basis of its content. The Constitution in general does not tolerate content-based restriction of, or discrimination against, speech. R. A. V. v. St. Paul, 505 U.S. 377, 382 (1992) ("Content-based regulations are presumptively invalid."). In the realm of speech and expression, the First Amendment envisions the citizen shaping the government, not the reverse; it removes "governmental restraints from the arena of public discussion, putting the decision as to what views shall be voiced largely into the hands of each of us, in the hope that use of such freedom will ultimately produce a more capable citizenry and more perfect polity." Cohen v. California, 403 U.S. 15, 24 (1971).

Sections 10(a) and (c) are unusual. They do not require direct action against speech, but do authorize a cable operator to deny the use of its property to certain forms of speech. As a general matter, a private person may exclude certain speakers from his or her property without violating the First Amendment, and if §§ 10(a) and (c) were no more than affirmations of this principle they might be unremarkable. Access channels, however, are property of the cable operator, dedicated or otherwise reserved for programming of other speakers or the government. A public access channel is a public forum, and laws requiring leased access channels create common-carrier obligations. When the government identifies certain speech on the basis of its content as vulnerable to exclusion from a common carrier or public forum, strict scrutiny applies. These laws cannot survive this exacting review. However compelling Congress' interest in shielding children from indecent programming, the provisions in this case are not drawn with enough care to withstand scrutiny under our precedents.

II

Before engaging the complexities of cable access channels and explaining my reasons for thinking all of § 10 unconstitutional, I start with the most disturbing aspect of the plurality opinion: its evasion of any clear legal standard in deciding these cases.

[T]he creation of standards and adherence to them, even when it means affording protection to speech unpopular or distasteful, is the central achievement of our First Amendment jurisprudence. Standards are the means by which we state in advance how to test a law's validity, rather than letting the height of the bar be determined by the apparent exigencies of the day. They also provide notice and fair warning to those who must predict how the courts will respond to attempts to suppress their speech. Yet formulations like strict scrutiny, used in a number of constitutional settings to ensure that the inequities of the moment are subordinated to commitments made for the long run, mean little if they can be watered down whenever they seem too strong. They mean still less if they can be ignored altogether when considering a case not on all fours with what we have seen before.

The plurality cannot bring itself to apply strict scrutiny, yet realizes it cannot decide these cases without uttering some sort of standard; so it has settled for synonyms. "Close judicial scrutiny," is substituted for strict scrutiny, and "extremely important problem," or "extraordinary problem[]," is substituted for "compelling interest." The admonition that the restriction not be unnecessarily great in light of the interest it serves, is substituted for the usual narrow tailoring requirements. All we know about the substitutes is that they are inferior to their antecedents. We are told the Act must be "appropriately tailored," "sufficiently tailored," or "carefully and appropriately addressed," to the problems at hand—anything, evidently, except narrowly tailored.

These restatements have unfortunate consequences. The first is to make principles intended to protect speech easy to manipulate. The words end up being a legalistic cover for an ad hoc balancing of interests; in this respect the plurality succeeds after all in avoiding the use of a standard. Second, the plurality's exercise in pushing around synonyms for the words of our usual standards will sow confusion in the courts bound by our precedents.

Another troubling aspect of the plurality's approach is its suggestion that Congress has more leeway than usual to enact restrictions on speech where emerging technologies are concerned, because we are unsure what standard should be used to assess them.

III

B

In providing public access channels under their franchise agreements, cable operators are not exercising their own First Amendment rights. They serve as conduits for the speech of others. Section 10(c) thus restores no power of editorial discretion over public access channels that the cable operator once had; the discretion never existed. It vests the cable operator with a power under federal law, defined by reference to the content of speech, to override the franchise agreement and undercut the public forum the agreement creates. By enacting a law in 1992 excluding indecent programming from protection but retaining the prohibition on cable operators' editorial control over all other protected speech, the Federal Government at the same time ratified the public-forum character of public access channels but discriminated against certain speech based on its content.

[I]t seems to me clear that when a local government contracts to use private property for public expressive activity, it creates a public forum. Regulations of speech content in a designated public forum, whether of limited or unlimited character, are "subject to the highest scrutiny" and "survive only if they are narrowly drawn to achieve a compelling state interest." International Soc. for Krishna Consciousness, Inc. v. Lee, 505 U.S. 672, 678 (1992).

C

The constitutionality under Turner Broadcasting System, Inc. v. FCC, 512 U.S. 622 (1994), of requiring a cable operator to set aside leased access channels is not before us. For purposes of this case, we should treat the cable operator's rights in these channels as extinguished, and address the issue these petitioners present: namely, whether the Government can discriminate on the basis of content in affording protection to certain programmers.

Laws removing common-carriage protection from a single form of speech based on its content should be reviewed under the same standard as content-based restrictions on speech in a public forum. Making a cable operator a common carrier does not create a public forum in the sense of taking property from private control and dedicating it to public use; rather, regulations of a common carrier dictate the manner in which private control is exercised. A common-carriage mandate, nonetheless, serves the same function as a public forum. It ensures open, nondiscriminatory access to the means of communication. This purpose is evident in the statute itself and in the committee findings supporting it.

Giving government free rein to exclude speech it dislikes by delimiting public fora (or common-carriage provisions) would have pernicious effects in the modern age. Minds are not changed in streets and parks as they once were. To an increasing degree, the more significant interchanges of ideas and shaping of public consciousness occur in mass and electronic media. The extent of public entitlement to participate in those means of communication may be changed as technologies change; and in expanding those entitlements the Government has no greater right to discriminate on suspect grounds than it does when it effects a ban on speech against the backdrop of the entitlements to which we have been more accustomed. It contravenes the First Amendment to give Government a general license to single out some categories of speech for lesser protection so long as it stops short of viewpoint discrimination.

D

Pacifica teaches that access channels, even if analogous to ordinary public fora from the standpoint of the programmer, must also be considered from the standpoint of the viewer. An access channel is not a forum confined to a discrete public space; it can bring indecent expression into the home of every cable subscriber, where children spend astounding amounts of time watching television. Though in *Cohen* we explained that people in public areas may have to avert their eyes from messages that offend them, 403 U.S. at 21, we further acknowledged that "government may properly act in many situations to prohibit intrusion into the privacy of the home of unwelcome views and ideas which cannot be totally banned from the public dialogue," *id.*

These concerns are weighty and will be relevant to whether the law passes strict scrutiny. They do not justify, however, a blanket rule of lesser protection for indecent speech. Other than the few categories of expression that can be proscribed, we have been reluctant to mark off new categories of speech for diminished constitutional protection. Our hesitancy reflects skepticism about the possibility of courts' drawing principled distinctions to use in judging governmental restrictions on speech and ideas, a concern heightened here by the inextricability of indecency from expression. "[W]e cannot indulge the facile assumption that one can forbid particular words without also running a substantial risk of suppressing ideas in the process." *Id.* at 26. The same is true of forbidding programs indecent in some respect. In artistic or political settings, indecency may have strong communicative content, protesting conventional norms or giving an edge to a work by conveying "otherwise inexpressible emotions," *id.* In scientific programs, the more graphic the depiction (even if to the point of offensiveness), the more accurate and comprehensive the portrayal of the truth may be. Indecency often is inseparable from the ideas and viewpoints conveyed, or separable only with loss of truth or expressive power. Under our traditional First Amendment jurisprudence, factors perhaps justifying some restriction on indecent cable programming may all be taken into account without derogating this category of protected speech as marginal.

IV

At a minimum, the proper standard for reviewing §§ 10(a) and (c) is strict scrutiny. The plurality gives no reason why it should be otherwise. I would hold these enactments unconstitutional because they are not narrowly tailored to serve a compelling interest.

The Government has no compelling interest in restoring a cable operator's First Amendment right of editorial discretion. As to § 10(c), Congress has no interest at all, since under most franchises operators had no rights of editorial discretion over PEG access channels in the first place. As to § 10(a), any governmental interest in restoring operator discretion over indecent programming on leased access channels is too minimal to justify the law. First, the transmission of indecent programming over leased access channels is not forced speech of the operator. *Turner, supra*, at 655–56. Second, the discretion conferred by the law is slight. The operator is not authorized to place programs of its own liking on the leased access channels, nor to remove other speech (racist or violent, for example) that might be offensive to it or to viewers. The operator is just given a veto over the one kind of lawful speech Congress disdains.

Congress does have, however, a compelling interest in protecting children from indecent speech. Sections 10(a) and (c) nonetheless are not narrowly tailored to protect children from indecent programs on access channels. First, to the extent some operators may allow indecent programming, children in localities those operators serve will be left unprotected. [T]he interest in protecting children from indecency only at the caprice of the cable operator is not compelling.

Second, to the extent cable operators prohibit indecent programming on access channels, not only children but adults will be deprived of it. The Government may not "reduce the adult population ... to [viewing] only what is fit for children." Butler v. Michigan, 352 U.S. 380, 383 (1957). A block-and-segregate requirement similar to § 10(b), but without its constitutional infirmity of requiring persons to place themselves on a list to receive programming, protects children with far less intrusion on the liberties of programmers and adult viewers than allowing cable operators to ban indecent programming from access channels altogether.

Sections 10(a) and (c) present a classic case of discrimination against speech based on its content. There are legitimate reasons why the Government might wish to regulate or even restrict the speech at issue here, but §§ 10(a) and 10(c) are not drawn to address those reasons with the precision the First Amendment requires.

VI

In agreement with the plurality's analysis of § 10(b) of the Act, insofar as it applies strict scrutiny, I join Part III of its opinion. Its position there, however, cannot be reconciled with upholding § 10(a). In the plurality's view, § 10(b), which standing alone would guarantee an indecent programmer some access to a cable audience, violates the First Amendment, but § 10(a), which authorizes exclusion of indecent programming from access channels altogether, does not. There is little to commend this logic or result. I dissent from the judgment of the Court insofar as it upholds the constitutionality of § 10(a).

JUSTICE THOMAS, joined by CHIEF JUSTICE REHNQUIST and JUSTICE SCALIA, concurring in the judgment in part and dissenting in part.

I agree with the principal opinion's conclusion that § 10(a) is constitutionally permissible, but I disagree with its conclusion that §§ 10(b) and (c) violate the First Amendment. For many years, we have failed to articulate how and to what extent the First Amendment protects cable operators, programmers, and viewers from state and federal regulation. I think it is time we did so, and I cannot go along with Justice Breyer's assiduous attempts to avoid addressing that issue openly.

I

The Court in *Turner* found that the FCC's must-carry rules implicated the First Amendment rights of both cable operators and cable programmers. The rules interfered with the operators' editorial discretion by forcing them to carry broadcast programming that they might not otherwise carry, and they interfered with the programmers' ability to compete for space on the operators' channels. We implicitly recognized in *Turner* that the programmer's right to compete for channel space is derivative of, and subordinate to, the operator's editorial discretion. Like a free-lance writer seeking a paper in which to publish newspaper editorials, a programmer is protected in searching for an outlet for cable programming, but has no free-standing First Amendment right to have that programming transmitted. *Cf.* Miami Herald Publishing Co. v. Tornillo, 418 U.S. at 256–58. Likewise, the rights of would-be viewers are derivative of the speech rights of operators and programmers. Viewers have a general right to see what a willing operator transmits, but, under *Tornillo* and *Pacific Gas*, they certainly have no right to force an unwilling operator to speak.

By recognizing the general primacy of the cable operator's editorial rights over the rights of programmers and viewers, *Turner* raises serious questions about the merits of petitioners' claims. None of the petitioners in these cases are cable operators; they are all cable viewers or access programmers or their representative organizations. It is not intuitively obvious that the First Amendment protects the interests petitioners assert, and neither petitioners nor the plurality have adequately explained the source or justification of those asserted rights.

In the process of deciding not to decide on a governing standard, Justice Breyer purports to discover in our cases an expansive, general principle permitting government to "directly regulate speech to address extraordinary problems, where its regulations are appropriately tailored to resolve those problems without imposing an unnecessarily great restriction on speech." *Ante*, at 2385. This heretofore unknown standard is facially subjective and openly invites balancing of asserted speech interests to a degree not ordinarily permitted. It is true that the standard I endorse lacks the "flexibility" inherent in the plurality's balancing approach, but that relative rigidity is required by our precedents and is not of my own making.

In any event, even if the plurality's balancing test were an appropriate standard, it could only be applied to protect speech interests that, under the circumstances, are themselves protected by the First Amendment. But, by shifting the focus to the balancing of "complex" interests, Justice Breyer never explains whether (and if so, how) a programmer's ordinarily unprotected interest in affirmative transmission of its programming acquires constitutional significance on leased and public access channels. It is that question, left unanswered by the plurality, to which I now turn.

II

A

As I read [the provisions on leased access and PEG channels], they provide leased and public access programmers with an expansive and federally enforced statutory right to transmit virtually any programming over access channels, limited only by the bounds of decency.

Petitioners must concede that cable access is not a constitutionally required entitlement and that the right they claim to leased and public access has, by definition, been governmentally created at the expense of cable operators' editorial discretion. Just because the Court has apparently accepted, for now, the proposition that the Constitution permits some degree of forced speech in the cable context does not mean that the beneficiaries of a government-imposed forced speech program enjoy additional First Amendment protections beyond those normally afforded to purely private speakers.

The question petitioners pose is whether §§ 10(a) and (c) are improper restrictions on their free speech rights, but *Turner* strongly suggests that the proper question is whether the leased and public access requirements (with §§ 10(a) and (c)) are improper restrictions on the *operators*' free speech rights. In my view, the constitutional presumption properly runs in favor of the operators' editorial discretion, and that discretion may not be burdened without a compelling reason for doing so.

It is one thing to compel an operator to carry leased and public access speech, in apparent violation of *Tornillo*, but it is another thing altogether to say that the First Amendment forbids Congress to give back part of the operators' editorial discretion, which all recognize as fundamentally protected, in favor of a broader access right. It is no answer to say that leased and public access are content neutral and that §§ 10(a) and (c) are not, for that does not change the fundamental fact, which petitioners never address, that it is the operators' journalistic freedom that is infringed, whether the challenged restrictions be content neutral or content based.

Sections 10(a) and (c) do not burden a programmer's right to seek access for its indecent programming on an operator's system. Rather, they merely restore part of the editorial discretion an operator would have absent Government regulation without burdening the programmer's underlying speech rights.

B

That the leased access provisions may be described in common carrier terms does not demonstrate that access programmers have obtained a First Amendment right to transmit programming over leased access channels. Labeling leased access a common carrier scheme has no real First Amendment consequences. It simply does not follow from common carrier status that cable operators may not, with Congress' blessing, decline to carry indecent speech on their leased access channels. Common carriers are private entities and may, consistent with the First Amendment, exercise editorial discretion in the absence of a specific statutory prohibition.

C

Petitioners argue that public access channels are public forums in which they have First Amendment rights to speak and that § 10(c) is invalid because it imposes content-based burdens on those rights.

Cable systems are not public property. Cable systems are privately owned and privately managed, and petitioners point to no case in which we have held that government may designate private property as a public forum. The public forum doctrine is a rule governing claims of "a right of access to public property," Perry Ed. Assn. v. Perry Local Educators' Assn., 460 U.S. 37, 44 (1983), and has never been thought to extend beyond property generally understood to belong to the government.

Government control over its own property or private property in which it has taken a cognizable property interest is consistent with designation of a public forum. But we have never even hinted that regulatory control, and particularly direct regulatory control over a private entity's First Amendment speech rights, could justify creation of a public forum.

[E]ven were I inclined to view public access channels as public property, which I am not, the numerous additional obligations imposed on the cable operator in managing and operating the public access channels convince me that these channels share few, if any, of the basic characteristics of a public forum. For this reason, and the other reasons articulated earlier, I would sustain both § 10(a) and § 10(c).

III

Most sexually oriented programming appears on premium or pay-per-view channels that are naturally blocked from nonpaying customers by market forces, and it is only governmental intervention in the first instance that requires access channels, on which indecent programming may appear, to be made part of the basic cable package. Section 10(b) does nothing more than adjust the nature of government-imposed leased access requirements in order to emulate the market forces that keep indecent programming primarily on premium channels (without permitting the operator to charge subscribers for that programming).

Unlike §§ 10(a) and (c), § 10(b) clearly implicates petitioners' free speech rights. Though § 10(b) by no means bans indecent speech, it clearly places content-based restrictions on the transmission of private speech by requiring cable operators to block and segregate indecent programming that the operator has agreed to carry. Consequently, § 10(b) must be subjected to strict scrutiny and can be upheld only if it furthers a compelling governmental interest by the least restrictive means available. *See Sable*, 492 U.S. at 126. The parties agree that Congress has a "compelling interest in protecting the physical and psychological well-being of minors" and that its interest "extends to shielding minors from the influence of [indecent speech] that is not obscene by adult standards." *Id.* Because § 10(b) is narrowly tailored to achieve that well-established compelling interest, I would uphold it.

The Court strikes down § 10(b) by pointing to alternatives, such as reverse blocking and lockboxes, that it says are less restrictive than segregation and blocking. Though these methods attempt to place in parents' hands the ability to permit their children to watch as little, or as much, indecent programming as the parents think proper, they do not effectively support parents' authority to direct the moral upbringing of their children. The FCC recognized that leased-access programming comes "from a wide variety of independent sources, with no single editor controlling [its] selection and presentation." Implementation of Section 10 of the Cable Consumer Protection and Competition Act of 1992: Indecent Programming and Other Types of Materials on Cable Access Channels, First Report and Order, 8 FCC Rcd. 998, 1000 (1993). Thus, indecent programming on leased access channels is "especially likely to be shown randomly or intermittently between non-indecent programs." *Id.* Rather than being able to simply block out certain channels at certain times, a subscriber armed with only a lockbox must carefully monitor all leased-access programming and constantly reprogram the lockbox to keep out undesired programming. Thus, even assuming that cable subscribers generally have the technical proficiency to properly operate a lockbox, by no means a given, this distinguishing characteristic of leased access channels makes lockboxes and reverse-blocking largely ineffective.

[P]etitioners argue that forcing customers to submit a written request for access will chill dissemination of speech. [H]owever, petitioners' allegations of an official list "of those who wish to watch the 'patently offensive' channel," as the majority puts it, are pure hyperbole. The FCC regulation implementing § 10(b)'s written request requirement, 47 C.F.R. § 76.701(b) (1995), says nothing about the creation of a list, much less an official Government list. It requires only that the cable operator receive written consent. Other statutory provisions make clear that the cable operator may not share that, or any other, information with any other person, including the Government. Section 551 mandates that all personally identifiable information regarding a subscriber be kept strictly confidential and further requires cable operators to destroy any information that is no longer necessary for the purpose for which it was collected. 47 U.S.C. § 551.

Any request for access to blocked programming—by whatever method—ultimately will make the subscriber's identity knowable. But this is hardly the kind of chilling effect that implicates the First Amendment.

The United States has carried its burden of demonstrating that § 10(b) and its implementing regulations are narrowly tailored to satisfy a compelling governmental interest.

Accordingly, I would affirm the judgment of the Court of Appeals in its entirety. I therefore concur in the judgment upholding § 10(a) and respectfully dissent from that portion of the judgment striking down §§ 10(b) and (c).

Notes and Questions

1. Do No Harm. Justice Souter's concurring opinion in *Denver Area* expresses agreement with Justice Breyer's unwillingness to choose a doctrinal category in analyzing the First Amendment issues, and Souter closes by invoking a "rule familiar to every doctor of medicine: 'First, do no harm.'" 518 U.S. at 778. Justice Kennedy, in his partial concurrence and partial dissent, quotes this statement but adds: "The question, though, is whether the harm is in sustaining the law or striking it down." *Id.* at 787. What *is* the "do no harm" position in this case? Is there an answer to that question that does not subsume the entire controversy?

2. Zoning Indecency. *Denver Area*, at least to some extent, expands to cable television *Pacifica*'s toleration of "zoning" broadcast indecency. Does this mean that the Court no longer believes that over-the-air broadcasting is a "*uniquely* pervasive" medium that is also "*uniquely* accessible to children" (emphases added)? If so, then just what is the surviving rationale of *Pacifica*? Note that several members of the Court voted to uphold some provisions of the Act on the grounds that those provisions are no more intrusive than the policies upheld in *Pacifica*.

3. Rules or Standards. Justice Breyer explicitly refuses to pick a rigid standard of scrutiny, and Justices Kennedy and Thomas criticize him for so refusing. This clash invokes the longstanding dispute over whether we should prefer clear rules or fluid standards. One added element in this instance is that everyone expects continued technological change. Both sides, though, suggest that the uncertainty produced by such change supports their position. Who is right? Does the likelihood of continued technological development indicate that courts should lay down clear rules so that people can rely on them in choosing a course of action, or that courts should allow themselves the flexibility to craft new approaches when they seem appropriate?

4. Satisfying the Standard. In Part II of his opinion—joined by three other justices—Justice Breyer describes § 10(a) as "a sufficiently tailored response to an extraordinarily important problem." In what respects is § 10(a) "tailored"? What is the "extraordinarily important problem" the provision cures? Perhaps it is the risk that a sixteen-year-old child will hear an "offensive sex-related" word? If this constitutes an "extraordinarily important problem" confronting the federal government, how many problems might have a similar level of importance? And how should one describe problems that seem even more important (e.g., nuclear war)?

§ 16.A.2.b. *Playboy Entertainment*

The Telecommunications Act of 1996 added three provisions affecting "indecency" on cable. Section 506, codified at 47 U.S.C. § 531(e) and § 532(c)(2), informs cable operators that they can refuse to transmit any PEG or leased access program or portion thereof "which contains obscenity, indecency, or nudity." Is the portion of § 506 applicable to PEG channels constitutional after *Denver Area*? The portion applicable to leased access? What does § 506 add to the powers that cable operators already had under pre-1996 law?

The other two provisions are §§ 504 and 505 of the Telecommunications Act. Both provisions are discussed in the following case, which invalidated § 505, in part because of the less restrictive alternative presented by § 504.

UNITED STATES v. PLAYBOY ENTERTAINMENT GROUP, INC.
529 U.S. 803 (2000)

KENNEDY, J., delivered the opinion of the Court, in which STEVENS, SOUTER, THOMAS, and GINSBURG, JJ., joined. STEVENS, J., and THOMAS, J., filed concurring opinions. SCALIA, J., filed a dissenting opinion. BREYER, J., filed a dissenting opinion, in which REHNQUIST, C.J., and O'CONNOR and SCALIA, JJ., joined.

JUSTICE KENNEDY delivered the opinion of the Court.

This case presents a challenge to § 505 of the Telecommunications Act of 1996 (Act), 47 U.S.C. § 561. Section 505 requires cable television operators who provide channels "primarily dedicated to sexually-oriented programming" either to "fully scramble or otherwise fully block" those channels or to limit their transmission to hours when children are unlikely to be viewing, set by administrative regulation as the time between 10 p.m. and 6 a.m. 47 U.S.C. § 561(a); 47 C.F.R. § 76.227 (1999). Even before enactment of the statute, signal scrambling was already in use. Cable operators used scrambling in the regular course of business, so that only paying customers had access to certain programs. Scrambling could be imprecise, however; and either or both audio and visual portions of the scrambled programs might be heard or seen, a phenomenon known as "signal bleed." The purpose of § 505 is to shield children from hearing or seeing images resulting from signal bleed.

To comply with the statute, the majority of cable operators adopted the second, or "time channeling," approach. The effect of the widespread adoption of time channeling was to eliminate altogether the transmission of the targeted programming outside the safe harbor period in affected cable service areas.

Appellee Playboy Entertainment Group, Inc., challenged the statute as unnecessarily restrictive content-based legislation violative of the First Amendment. After a trial, a three-judge District Court concluded that a regime in which viewers could order signal blocking on a household-by-household basis presented an effective, less restrictive alternative to § 505. 30 F. Supp. 2d 702, 719 (D. Del. 1998). Finding no error in this conclusion, we affirm.

II

Two essential points should be understood concerning the speech at issue here. First, we shall assume that many adults themselves would find the material highly offensive; and when we consider the further circumstance that the material comes unwanted into homes where children might see or hear it against parental wishes or consent, there are legitimate reasons for regulating it. Second, all parties bring the case to us on the premise that Playboy's programming has First Amendment protection. As this case has been litigated, it is not alleged to be obscene; adults have a constitutional right to view it; the Government disclaims any interest in preventing children from seeing or hearing it with the consent of their parents; and Playboy has concomitant rights under the First Amendment to transmit it. These points are undisputed.

The speech in question is defined by its content; and the statute which seeks to restrict it is content based. Section 505 applies only to channels primarily dedicated to "sexually explicit adult programming or other programming that is indecent." The statute is unconcerned with signal bleed from any other channels. The overriding justification for the regulation is concern for the effect of the subject matter on young viewers.

Not only does § 505 single out particular programming content for regulation, it also singles out particular programmers. [T]he statutory disability applies only to channels "primarily dedicated to sexually-oriented programming." 47 U.S.C. § 561(a). Laws designed or intended to suppress or restrict the expression of specific speakers contradict basic First Amendment principles. Section 505 limited Playboy's market as a penalty for its programming choice, though other channels capable of transmitting like material are altogether exempt.

The effect of the federal statute on the protected speech is now apparent. It is evident that the only reasonable way for a substantial number of cable operators to comply with the letter of § 505 is to time channel, which silences the protected speech for two-thirds of the day in every home in a cable service area, regardless of the presence or likely presence of children or of the wishes of the viewers. According to the District Court, "30 to 50% of all adult programming is viewed by households prior to 10 p.m.," when the safe-harbor period begins. 30 F. Supp. 2d at 711. To prohibit this much speech is a significant restriction of communication between speakers and willing adult listeners, communication which enjoys First Amendment protection. It is of no moment that the statute does not impose a complete prohibition. The distinction between laws burdening and laws banning speech is but a matter of degree. The Government's content-based burdens must satisfy the same rigorous scrutiny as its content-based bans.

Since § 505 is a content-based speech restriction, it can stand only if it satisfies strict scrutiny. If a statute regulates speech based on its content, it must be narrowly tailored to promote a compelling Government interest. If a less restrictive alternative would serve the Government's purpose, the legislature must use that alternative. To do otherwise would be to restrict speech without an adequate justification, a course the First Amendment does not permit.

Our precedents teach these principles. Where the designed benefit of a content-based speech restriction is to shield the sensibilities of listeners, the general rule is that the right of expression prevails, even where no less restrictive alternative exists. We are expected to protect our own sensibilities "simply by averting [our] eyes." Cohen v. California, 403 U.S. 15, 21 (1971). Here, of course, we consider images transmitted to some homes where they are not wanted and where parents often are not present to give immediate guidance. Cable television, like broadcast media, presents unique problems, which inform our assessment of the interests at stake, and which may justify restrictions that would be unacceptable in other contexts. *See* Denver Area Educational Telecommunications Consortium, Inc. v. FCC, 518 U.S. 727, 744 (1996) (plurality opinion); *id.* at 804–05 (Kennedy, J., concurring in part, concurring in judgment in part, and dissenting in part); FCC v. Pacifica Foundation, 438 U.S. 726 (1978). No one suggests the Government must be indifferent to unwanted, indecent speech that comes into the home without parental consent. The speech here, all agree, is protected speech; and the question is what standard the Government must meet in order to restrict it. As we consider a content-based regulation, the answer should be clear: The standard is strict scrutiny. This case involves speech alone; and even where speech is indecent and enters the home, the objective of shielding children does not suffice to support a blanket ban if the protection can be accomplished by a less restrictive alternative.

There is, moreover, a key difference between cable television and the broadcasting media, which is the point on which this case turns: Cable systems have the capacity to block unwanted channels on a household-by-household basis. The option to block reduces the likelihood, so concerning to the Court in *Pacifica*, that traditional First Amendment scrutiny would deprive the Government of all authority to address this sort of problem. The corollary, of course, is that targeted blocking enables the Government to support parental authority without affecting the First Amendment interests of speakers and willing listeners—listeners for whom, if the speech is unpopular or indecent, the privacy of their own homes may be the optimal place of receipt. Simply put, targeted blocking is less restrictive than banning, and the Government cannot ban speech if targeted blocking is a feasible and effective means of furthering its compelling interests. This is not to say that the absence of an effective blocking mechanism will in all cases suffice to support a law restricting the speech in question; but if a less restrictive means is available for the Government to achieve its goals, the Government must use it.

III

The District Court concluded that a less restrictive alternative is available: §504 [of the Act], with adequate publicity. [§504 provides that "[u]pon request by a cable service subscriber, a cable operator shall, without charge, fully scramble or otherwise fully block" any channel the subscriber does not wish to receive. 47 U.S.C. §560.] No one disputes that §504, which requires cable operators to block undesired channels at individual households upon request, is narrowly tailored to the Government's goal of supporting parents who want those channels blocked. The question is whether §504 can be effective.

When a plausible, less restrictive alternative is offered to a content-based speech restriction, it is the Government's obligation to prove that the alternative will be ineffective to achieve its goals. The Government has not met that burden here. In support of its position, the Government cites empirical evidence showing that §504, as promulgated and implemented before trial, generated few requests for household-by-household blocking. Between March 1996 and May 1997, while the Government was enjoined from enforcing §505, §504 remained in operation. A survey of cable operators determined that fewer than 0.5% of cable subscribers requested full blocking during that time. The uncomfortable fact is that §504 was the sole blocking regulation in effect for over a year; and the public greeted it with a collective yawn.

The District Court was correct to direct its attention to the import of this tepid response. Placing the burden of proof upon the Government, the District Court examined whether §504 was capable of serving as an effective, less restrictive means of reaching the Government's goals. It concluded that §504, if publicized in an adequate manner, could be.

The District Court employed the proper approach. When the Government restricts speech, the Government bears the burden of proving the constitutionality of its actions. When the Government seeks to restrict speech based on its content, the usual presumption of constitutionality afforded congressional enactments is reversed.

This is for good reason. "[T]he line between speech unconditionally guaranteed and speech which may legitimately be regulated, suppressed, or punished is finely drawn." Speiser v. Randall, 357 U.S. 513, 525 (1958). Error in marking that line exacts an extraordinary cost. It is through speech that our convictions and beliefs are influenced, expressed, and tested. It is through speech that we bring those beliefs to bear on Government and on society. It is through speech that our personalities are formed and expressed. The citizen is entitled to seek out or reject certain ideas or influences without Government interference or control.

When a student first encounters our free speech jurisprudence, he or she might think it is influenced by the philosophy that one idea is as good as any other, and that in art and literature objective standards of style, taste, decorum, beauty, and esthetics are deemed by the Constitution to be inappropriate, indeed unattainable. Quite the opposite is true. The Constitution no more enforces a relativistic philosophy or moral nihilism than it does any other point of view. The Constitution exists precisely so that opinions and judgments, including esthetic and moral judgments about art and literature, can be formed, tested, and expressed. What the Constitution says is that these judgments are for the individual to make, not for the Government to decree, even with the mandate or approval of a majority. Technology expands the capacity to choose; and it denies the potential of this revolution if we assume the Government is best positioned to make these choices for us.

It is rare that a regulation restricting speech because of its content will ever be permissible. Indeed, were we to give the Government the benefit of the doubt when it attempted to restrict speech, we would risk leaving regulations in place that sought to shape our unique personalities or to silence dissenting ideas. When First Amendment compliance is the point to be proved, the risk of nonpersuasion—operative in all trials—must rest with the Government, not with the citizen.

With this burden in mind, the District Court explored three explanations for the lack of individual blocking requests. First, individual blocking might not be an effective alternative, due to technological or other limitations. Second, although an adequately advertised blocking provision might have been effective, § 504 as written did not require sufficient notice to make it so. Third, the actual signal bleed problem might be far less of a concern than the Government at first had supposed.

To sustain its statute, the Government was required to show that the first was the right answer. According to the District Court, however, the first and third possibilities were "equally consistent" with the record before it. As for the second, the record was "not clear" as to whether enough notice had been issued to give § 504 a fighting chance. The case, then, was at best a draw. Unless the District Court's findings are clearly erroneous, the tie goes to free expression.

The District Court began with the problem of signal bleed itself, concluding "the Government has not convinced us that [signal bleed] is a pervasive problem." 30 F. Supp. 2d at 708–09, 718. The District Court's thorough discussion exposes a central weakness in the Government's proof: There is little hard evidence of how widespread or how serious the problem of signal bleed is. Indeed, there is no proof as to how likely any child is to view a discernible explicit image, and no proof of the duration of the bleed or the quality of the pictures or sound. To say that millions of children are subject to a risk of viewing signal bleed is one thing; to avoid articulating the true nature and extent of the risk is quite another. Under § 505, sanctionable signal bleed can include instances as fleeting as an image appearing on a screen for just a few seconds. The First Amendment requires a more careful assessment and characterization of an evil in order to justify a regulation as sweeping as this.

The Government relied at trial on anecdotal evidence to support its regulation, which the District Court summarized as follows:

> The Government has presented evidence of only a handful of isolated incidents over the 16 years since 1982 when Playboy started broadcasting. The Government has not presented any survey-type evidence on the magnitude of the 'problem.'

30 F. Supp. 2d at 709. Spurred by the District Court's express request for more specific evidence of the problem, the Government also presented an expert's spreadsheet estimate that 39 million homes with 29.5 million children had the potential to be exposed to signal bleed. The Government made no attempt to confirm the accuracy of its estimate through surveys or other field tests, however. Accordingly, the District Court discounted the figures and made this finding: "[T]he Government presented no evidence on the number of households actually exposed to signal bleed and thus has not quantified the actual extent of the problem of signal bleed." *Id.* The finding is not clearly erroneous; indeed it is all but required.

Once § 505 went into effect, of course, a significant percentage of cable operators felt it necessary to time channel their sexually explicit programmers. This is an indication that scrambling technology is not yet perfected. That is not to say, however, that scrambling is completely ineffective. Different cable systems use different scrambling systems, which vary in their dependability. "The severity of the problem varies from time to time and place to place, depending on the weather, the quality of the equipment, its installation, and maintenance." *Id.* at 708. At even the good end of the spectrum a system might bleed to an extent sufficient to trigger the time-channeling requirement for a cautious cable operator. (The statute requires the signal to be "*fully* block[ed]." 47 U.S.C. § 561(a) (emphasis added).) A rational cable operator, faced with the possibility of sanctions for intermittent bleeding, could well choose to time channel even if the bleeding is too momentary to pose any concern to most households. To affirm that the Government failed to prove the existence of a problem, while at the same time observing that the statute imposes a severe burden on speech, is consistent with the analysis our cases require. Here, there is no probative evidence in the record which differentiates among the extent of bleed at individual households and no evidence which otherwise quantifies the signal bleed problem.

In addition, market-based solutions such as programmable televisions, VCR's, and mapping systems (which display a blue screen when tuned to a scrambled signal) may eliminate signal bleed at the consumer end of the cable. Playboy made the point at trial that the Government's estimate failed to account for these factors. Without some sort of field survey, it is impossible to know how widespread the problem in fact is, and the only indicator in the record is a handful of complaints. *Cf.* Turner Broadcasting System, Inc. v. FCC, 520 U.S. 180, 187 (1997) (reviewing "'a record of tens of thousands of pages' of evidence" developed through "three years of pre-enactment hearings, ... as well as additional expert submissions, sworn declarations and testimony, and industry documents" in support of complex must-carry provisions).

No support for the restriction can be found in the near barren legislative record relevant to this provision. Section 505 was added to the Act by floor amendment, accompanied by only brief statements, and without committee hearing or debate. One of the measure's sponsors did indicate she considered time channeling to be superior to voluntary blocking, which "put[s] the burden of action on the subscriber, not the cable company." 141 Cong. Rec. 15,587 (1995) (statement of Sen. Feinstein). This sole conclusory statement, however, tells little about the relative efficacy of voluntary blocking versus time channeling, other than offering the unhelpful, self-evident generality that voluntary measures require voluntary action. The Court has declined to rely on similar evidence before. *See* Sable Communications of Cal., Inc. v. FCC, 492 U.S. 115, 129–30 (1989) ("[A]side from conclusory statements during the debates by proponents of the bill, ... the congressional record presented to us contains no evidence as to *how* effective or ineffective the ... regulations were or might prove to be"); Reno v. American Civil Liberties Union, 521 U.S. 844, 858, and n.24, 875–76, n.41 (1997) (same). This is not to suggest that a 10,000 page record must be compiled in every case or that the Government must delay in acting to address a real problem; but the Government must present more than anecdote and supposition. The question is whether an actual problem has been proven in this case. We agree that the Government has failed to establish a pervasive, nationwide problem justifying its nationwide daytime speech ban.

Nor did the District Court err in its second conclusion. The Government also failed to prove §504 with adequate notice would be an ineffective alternative to §505. Once again, the District Court invited the Government to produce its proof. Once again, the Government fell short. There is no evidence that a well-promoted voluntary blocking provision would not be capable at least of informing parents about signal bleed (if they are not yet aware of it) and about their rights to have the bleed blocked (if they consider it a problem and have not yet controlled it themselves).

The Government finds at least two problems with the conclusion of the three-judge District Court. First, the Government takes issue with the District Court's reliance, without proof, on a "hypothetical, enhanced version of Section 504." Brief for United States et al. 32. It was not the District Court's obligation, however, to predict the extent to which an improved notice scheme would improve §504. It was for the Government, presented with a plausible, less restrictive alternative, to prove the alternative to be ineffective, and §505 to be the least restrictive available means.

The Government also contends a publicized §504 will be just as restrictive as §505, on the theory that the cost of installing blocking devices will outstrip the revenues from distributing Playboy's programming and lead to its cancellation. This conclusion rests on the assumption that a sufficient percentage of households, informed of the potential for signal bleed, would consider it enough of a problem to order blocking devices—an assumption for which there is no support in the record. It should be noted, furthermore, that Playboy is willing to incur the costs of an effective §504. One might infer that Playboy believes an advertised §504 will be ineffective for its object, or one might infer the company believes the signal bleed problem is not widespread. In the absence of proof, it is not for the Court to assume the former.

It is no response that voluntary blocking requires a consumer to take action, or may be inconvenient, or may not go perfectly every time. A court should not assume a plausible, less restrictive alternative would be ineffective; and a court should not presume parents, given full information, will fail to act. If unresponsive operators are a concern, moreover, a notice statute could give cable operators ample incentive, through fines or other penalties for noncompliance, to respond to blocking requests in prompt and efficient fashion.

Having adduced no evidence in the District Court showing that an adequately advertised §504 would not be effective to aid desirous parents in keeping signal bleed out of their own households, the Government can now cite nothing in the record to support the point. The Government instead takes quite a different approach. After only an offhand suggestion that the success of a well-communicated §504 is "highly unlikely," the Government sets the point aside, arguing instead that society's independent interests will be unserved if parents fail to act on that information. Brief for United States et al. 33 ("Even an enhanced version of Section 504 would succeed in blocking signal bleed only if, and after, parents affirmatively decided to avail themselves of the means offered them to do so. There would certainly be parents—perhaps a large number of parents—who out of inertia, indifference, or distraction, simply would take no action to block signal bleed, even if fully informed of the problem and even if offered a relatively easy solution.").

Even upon the assumption that the Government has an interest in substituting itself for informed and empowered parents, its interest is not sufficiently compelling to justify this widespread restriction on speech. The Government's argument stems from the idea that parents do not know their children are viewing the material on a scale or frequency to cause concern, or if so, that parents do not want to take affirmative steps to block it and their decisions are to be superseded. The assumptions have not been established; and in any event the assumptions apply only in a regime where the option of blocking has not been explained. The whole point of a publicized §504 would be to advise parents that indecent material may be shown and to afford them an opportunity to block it at all times, even when they are not at home and even after 10 p.m. Time channeling does not offer this assistance. The regulatory alternative of a publicized §504, which has the real possibility of promoting more open disclosure and the choice of an effective blocking system, would provide parents the information needed to engage in active supervision. The Government has not shown that this alternative, a regime of added communication and support, would be insufficient to secure its objective, or that any overriding harm justifies its intervention.

There can be little doubt, of course, that under a voluntary blocking regime, even with adequate notice, some children will be exposed to signal bleed; and we need not discount the possibility that a graphic image could have a negative impact on a young child. It must be remembered, however, that children will be exposed to signal bleed under time channeling as well. Time channeling, unlike blocking, does not eliminate signal bleed around the clock. Just as adolescents may be unsupervised outside of their own households, it is hardly unknown for them to be unsupervised in front of the television set after 10 p.m. The record is silent as to the comparative effectiveness of the two alternatives.

Basic speech principles are at stake in this case. When the purpose and design of a statute is to regulate speech by reason of its content, special consideration or latitude is not accorded to the Government merely because the law can somehow be described as a burden rather than outright suppression. We cannot be influenced, moreover, by the perception that the regulation in question is not a major one because the speech is not very important. The history of the law of free expression is one of vindication in cases involving speech that many citizens may find shabby, offensive, or even ugly. It follows that all content-based restrictions on speech must give us more than a moment's pause. If television broadcasts can expose children to the real risk of harmful exposure to indecent materials, even in their own home and without parental consent, there is a problem the Government can address. It must do so, however, in a way consistent with First Amendment principles. Here the Government has not met the burden the First Amendment imposes.

[Concurring opinions of JUSTICES STEVENS and THOMAS, and dissenting opinion of JUSTICE SCALIA, are omitted.]

JUSTICE BREYER, with whom CHIEF JUSTICE REHNQUIST, JUSTICE O'CONNOR, and JUSTICE SCALIA join, dissenting.

I

At the outset, I would describe the statutory scheme somewhat differently than does the majority. I would emphasize three background points. First, the statutory scheme reflects more than a congressional effort to control incomplete scrambling. Previously, federal law had left cable operators free to decide whether, when, and how to transmit adult channels. Most channel operators on their own had decided not to send adult channels into a subscriber's home except on request. But the operators then implemented that decision with inexpensive technology. Through signal "bleeding," the scrambling technology (either inadvertently or by way of enticement) allowed nonsubscribers to see and hear what was going on. That is why Congress decided to act.

The statute is carefully tailored to respect viewer preferences. It regulates transmissions by creating two "default rules" applicable unless the subscriber decides otherwise. Taken together, [§§ 504 and 505] create a scheme that permits subscribers to choose to see what they want. But each law creates a different "default" assumption about silent subscribers. Section 504 assumes a silent subscriber wants to see the ordinary (non-adult) channels that the cable operator includes in the paid-for bundle sent into the home. Section 505 assumes that a silent subscriber does not want to receive adult channels. Consequently, a subscriber wishing to view an adult channel must "opt in," and specifically request that channel. *See* § 505. A subscriber wishing not to view any other channel (sent into the home) must "opt out." *See* § 504.

The scheme addresses signal bleed but only indirectly. From the statute's perspective signal "bleeding"—i.e., a failure to fully "rearrange the content of the signal ... so that the programming cannot be viewed or heard in an understandable manner," § 505(c)— amounts to transmission into a home. Hence "bleeding" violates the statute whenever a clear transmission of an unrequested adult channel would violate the statute.

Second, the majority's characterization of this statutory scheme as "prohibit[ing] ... speech" is an exaggeration. Rather, the statute places a *burden* on adult channel speech by requiring the relevant cable operator either to use better scrambling technology, or, if that technology is too expensive, to broadcast only between 10 p.m. and 6 a.m. Laws that burden speech, say, by making speech less profitable, may create serious First Amendment issues, but they are not the equivalent of an absolute ban on speech itself. The difference—between imposing a burden and enacting a ban—can matter even when strict First Amendment rules are at issue.

Third, this case concerns only the regulation of commercial actors who broadcast "virtually 100% sexually explicit" material. 30 F. Supp. 2d at 707. The channels do not broadcast more than trivial amounts of more serious material such as birth control information, artistic images, or the visual equivalents of classical or serious literature. This case therefore does not present the kind of narrow tailoring concerns seen in other cases.

With this background in mind, the reader will better understand my basic disagreement with each of the Court's two conclusions.

II

The majority first concludes that the Government failed to prove the seriousness of the problem—receipt of adult channels by children whose parents did not request their broadcast. This claim is flat-out wrong. For one thing, the parties concede that basic RF scrambling does not scramble the audio portion of the program. For another, Playboy itself conducted a survey of cable operators who were asked: "Is your system in full compliance with Section 505 (no discernible audio or video bleed)?" To this question, 75% of cable operators answered "no." Further, the Government's expert took the number of homes subscribing to Playboy or Spice, multiplied by the fraction of cable households with children and the average number of children per household, and found 29 million children are potentially exposed to audio and video bleed from adult programming. Even discounting by 25% for systems that might be considered in full compliance, this left 22 million children in homes with faulty scrambling systems. And, of course, the record contains additional anecdotal evidence and the concerns expressed by elected officials, probative of a larger problem.

If signal bleed is not a significant empirical problem, then why, in light of the cost of its cure, must so many cable operators switch to night time hours? There is no realistic answer to this question. I do not think it realistic to imagine that signal bleed occurs just enough to make cable operators skittish, without also significantly exposing children to these images.

If, as the majority suggests, the signal bleed problem is not significant, then there is also no significant burden on speech created by § 505. The majority cannot have this evidence both ways. And if, given this logical difficulty and the quantity of empirical evidence, the majority still believes that the Government has not proved its case, then it imposes a burden upon the Government beyond that suggested in any other First Amendment case of which I am aware.

III

The majority's second claim—that the Government failed to demonstrate the absence of a "less restrictive alternative"—presents a closer question. The specific question is whether § 504's "opt-out" amounts to a "less restrictive," but *similarly* practical and *effective*, way to accomplish § 505's child-protecting objective. As *Reno* tells us, a "less restrictive alternative[]" must be "at least as effective in achieving the legitimate purpose that the statute was enacted to serve." 521 U.S. at 874.

The words I have just emphasized, "similarly" and "effective," are critical. In an appropriate case they ask a judge not to apply First Amendment rules mechanically, but to decide whether, in light of the benefits and potential alternatives, the statute works speech-related harm (here to adult speech) out of proportion to the benefits that the statute seeks to provide (here, child protection).

These words imply a degree of leeway, however small, for the legislature when it chooses among possible alternatives in light of predicted comparative effects. Without some such empirical leeway, the undoubted ability of lawyers and judges to imagine *some* kind of slightly less drastic or restrictive an approach would make it impossible to write laws that deal with the harm that called the statute into being. As Justice Blackmun pointed out, a "judge would be unimaginative indeed if he could not come up with something a little less 'drastic' or a little less 'restrictive' in almost any situation, and thereby enable himself to vote to strike legislation down." Illinois Bd. of Elections v. Socialist Workers Party, 440 U.S. 173, 188–89 (1979) (concurring opinion). Used without a sense of the practical choices that face legislatures, "the test merely announces an inevitable [negative] result, and the test is no test at all." *Id.* at 188.

Unlike the majority, I believe the record makes clear that § 504's opt-out is not a similarly effective alternative. Section 504 (opt-out) and § 505 (opt-in) work differently in order to achieve very different legislative objectives. Section 504 gives parents the power to tell cable operators to keep any channel out of their home. Section 505 does more. Unless parents explicitly consent, it inhibits the transmission of adult cable channels to children whose parents may be unaware of what they are watching, whose parents cannot easily supervise television viewing habits, whose parents do not know of their § 504 "opt-out" rights, or whose parents are simply unavailable at critical times. In this respect, § 505 serves the same interests as the laws that deny children access to adult cabarets or X-rated movies. These laws, and § 505, all act in the absence of direct parental supervision.

This legislative objective is perfectly legitimate. Where over 28 million school age children have both parents or their only parent in the work force, where at least 5 million children are left alone at home without supervision each week, and where children may spend afternoons and evenings watching television outside of the home with friends, § 505 offers independent protection for a large number of families. I could not disagree more when the majority implies that the Government's independent interest in offering such protection—preventing, say, an 8-year-old child from watching virulent pornography without parental consent—might not be "compelling." No previous case in which the protection of children was at issue has suggested any such thing. Indeed, they all say precisely the opposite. *See Reno*, 521 U.S. at 865 (State has an "independent interest in the well-being of its youth"); *Denver Area*, 518 U.S. at 743. They make clear that Government has a compelling interest in helping parents by preventing minors from accessing sexually explicit materials in the absence of parental supervision.

By definition, § 504 does *nothing at all* to further the compelling interest I have just described. How then is it a similarly effective § 505 alternative?

The record, moreover, sets forth empirical evidence showing that the two laws are not equivalent with respect to the Government's objectives. As the majority observes, during the 14 months the Government was enjoined from enforcing § 505, "fewer than 0.5% of cable subscribers requested full blocking" under § 504. *Ante*, at 11. The majority describes this public reaction as "a collective yawn," *id*., adding that the Government failed to prove that the "yawn" reflected anything other than the lack of a serious signal bleed problem or a lack of notice which better information about § 504 might cure. The record excludes the first possibility—at least in respect to exposure, as discussed above. And I doubt that the public, though it may well consider the viewing habits of *adults* a matter of personal choice, would "yawn" when the exposure in question concerns young children, the absence of parental consent, and the sexually explicit material here at issue.

Neither is the record neutral in respect to the curative power of better notice. Section 504's opt-out right works only when parents (1) become aware of their § 504 rights, (2) discover that their children are watching sexually-explicit signal "bleed," (3) reach their cable operator and ask that it block the sending of its signal to their home, (4) await installation of an individual blocking device, and, perhaps (5) (where the block fails or the channel number changes) make a new request. Better notice of § 504 rights does little to help parents discover their children's viewing habits (step two). And it does nothing at all in respect to steps three through five. Yet the record contains considerable evidence that those problems matter, i.e., evidence of endlessly delayed phone call responses, faulty installations, blocking failures, and other mishaps, leaving those steps as significant § 504 obstacles.

Further, the District Court's actual plan for "better notice"—the only plan that makes concrete the majority's "better notice" requirement—is fraught with difficulties. The District Court ordered Playboy to insist that cable operators place notice of § 504 in "inserts in monthly billing statements, barker channels ... and on-air advertising." 30 F. Supp. 2d at 719. But how can one say that placing one more insert in a monthly billing statement stuffed with others, or calling additional attention to adult channels through a "notice" on "barker" channels, will make more than a small difference? More importantly, why would doing so not interfere to some extent with the cable operators' own freedom to decide what to broadcast?

Even if better notice did adequately inform viewers of their § 504 rights, exercise of those rights by more than 6% of the subscriber base would itself raise Playboy's costs to the point that Playboy would be forced off the air entirely—a consequence that would not seem to further anyone's interest in free speech. Section 504 is not a similarly effective alternative to § 505 (in respect to the Government's interest in protecting children), unless more than a minimal number of viewers actually use it; yet the economic evidence shows that if more than 6% do so, Playboy's programming would be totally eliminated.

Of course, it is logically *possible* that "better notice" will bring about near perfect parental knowledge (of what children watch and § 504 opt-out rights), that cable operators will respond rapidly to blocking requests, and that still 94% of all informed parents will decide not to have adult channels blocked for free. But the *probability* that this remote *possibility* will occur is neither a "draw" nor a "tie." *Ante*, at 14. And that fact is sufficient for the Government to have met its burden of proof.

IV

Section 505 raises the cost of adult channel broadcasting. In doing so, it restricts, but does not ban, adult speech. Adults may continue to watch adult channels, though less conveniently, by watching at night, recording programs with a VCR, or by subscribing to digital cable with better blocking systems. The Government's justification for imposing this restriction — limiting the access of children to channels that broadcast virtually 100% "sexually explicit" material — is "compelling." The record shows no similarly effective, less restrictive alternative. Consequently § 505's restriction, viewed in light of the proposed alternative, is proportionate to need. That is to say, it restricts speech no more than necessary to further that compelling need. Taken together, these considerations lead to the conclusion that § 505 is lawful.

I repeat that my disagreement with the majority lies in the fact that, in my view, the Government has satisfied its burden of proof. In particular, it has proved both the existence of a serious problem and the comparative ineffectiveness of § 504 in resolving that problem. This disagreement is not about allocation of First Amendment burdens of proof, basic First Amendment principle, nor the importance of that Amendment to our scheme of Government. First Amendment standards are rigorous. They safeguard speech. But they also permit Congress to enact a law that increases the costs associated with certain speech, where doing so serves a compelling interest that cannot be served through the adoption of a less restrictive, similarly effective alternative. Those standards at their strictest make it difficult for the Government to prevail. But they do not make it impossible for the Government to prevail.

The majority here, however, has applied those standards without making a realistic assessment of the alternatives. It thereby threatens to leave Congress without power to help the millions of parents who do not want to expose their children to commercial pornography — but will remain ill served by the Court's chosen remedy. Worse still, the logic of the majority's "505/504" comparison (but not its holding that the problem has not been established) would seem to apply whether "bleeding" or totally unscrambled transmission is at issue. If so, the public would have to depend solely upon the voluntary conduct of cable channel operators to avert considerably greater harm.

Case law does not mandate the Court's result. To the contrary, as I have pointed out, our prior cases recognize that, where the protection of children is at issue, the First Amendment poses a barrier that properly is high, but not insurmountable. It is difficult to reconcile today's decision with our foundational cases that have upheld similar laws, such as *Pacifica*. It is not difficult to distinguish our cases striking down such laws — either because they applied far more broadly than the narrow regulation of adult channels here, *see, e.g., Reno*, imposed a total ban on a form of adult speech, *see, e.g., Sable*, or because a less restrictive, similarly effective alternative was otherwise available, *see, e.g., Denver Area*, 518 U.S. at 753–60.

Congress has taken seriously the importance of maintaining adult access to the sexually explicit channels here at issue. It has tailored the restrictions to minimize their impact upon adults while offering parents help in keeping unwanted transmissions from their children. By finding "adequate alternatives" where there are none, the Court reduces Congress' protective power to the vanishing point. That is not what the First Amendment demands.

Notes and Questions

1. *Pacifica.* Is Justice Breyer correct that the majority opinion is in tension with *Pacifica*? If so, what does that mean for *Pacifica*?

2. **What's the Disagreement?** What, precisely, is the disagreement between the majority and the dissent? Justice Breyer contends that "[t]his disagreement is not about allocation of First Amendment burdens of proof, basic First Amendment principle, nor the importance of that Amendment to our scheme of Government." What does he believe is the basis of the disagreement, then?

3. **A Severe Burden on Speech?** Does it make sense "to affirm" (as the majority did) "that the Government failed to prove the existence of a problem, while at the same time observing that the statute imposes a severe burden on speech"? What are the implications of a negative answer to that question?

4. **Protecting Children.** In this case, the government relies not only on its interest in empowering parents, but also on its interest in protecting children. Section 504 gives concerned parents the opportunity to block the signal from any channel they do not want to receive. But, as the government pointed out, that may not protect the children of parents who "out of inertia, indifference, or distraction" fail to avail themselves of this option. If the Court accepted such an interest as sufficient, could the Court have later deemed any limitations on indecency impermissible? That is, can you imagine any indecency restriction not responsive to the goal of protecting children from inattentive parents? Relatedly, does the Court's rejection of the government's argument regarding inattentive parents mean that, if a filter is available, no regulation limiting indecency will be constitutional?

5. *ACT III* **and Parental Control.** The issue of empowering parents versus protecting children also arose in *ACT III*. Are there any differences between the way *Playboy* and *ACT III* handle the interest in protecting children? Does *Playboy* suggest that the court in *ACT III* erred, and, if so, how?

6. **Revising the Law.** If Congress wanted to enact a new § 505 that would pass muster under *Playboy*, what sort of factual support would it need to amass? Is satisfying that standard a realistic possibility? Is the *Playboy* standard consistent with the standard imposed on Congress by *ACT III*? With *Turner II*? How might these cases be harmonized?

§ 16.A.3. Regulation of Indecency via Telephone

In the 1980s, Congress had become concerned about children's ability to use services that offer sexual content, and Congress addressed that concern with legislation prohibiting indecent or obscene communications over the telephone network. Litigation followed (of course), producing the following opinion.

Sable Communications of California, Inc. v. FCC
492 U.S. 115 (1989)

WHITE, J., delivered the opinion for a unanimous Court with respect to Parts I, II, and IV, and the opinion of the Court with respect to Part III, in which REHNQUIST, C.J., and BLACKMUN, O'CONNOR, SCALIA, and KENNEDY, JJ., joined. SCALIA, J., filed a concurring opinion. BRENNAN, J., filed an opinion concurring in part and dissenting in part, in which MARSHALL and STEVENS, JJ., joined.

JUSTICE WHITE delivered the opinion of the Court.

The issue before us is the constitutionality of § 223(b) of the Communications Act of 1934. 47 U.S.C. § 223(b). The statute, as amended in 1988, imposes an outright ban on indecent as well as obscene interstate commercial telephone messages. The District Court upheld the prohibition against obscene interstate telephone communications for commercial purposes, but enjoined the enforcement of the statute insofar as it applied to indecent messages. We affirm the District Court in both respects.

I

In 1983, Sable Communications, Inc., a Los Angeles-based affiliate of Carlin Communications, Inc., began offering sexually oriented prerecorded telephone messages (popularly known as "dial-a-porn") through the Pacific Bell telephone network.[17] Sable arranged with Pacific Bell to use special telephone lines, designed to handle large volumes of calls simultaneously. Those who called the adult message number were charged a special fee. The fee was collected by Pacific Bell and divided between the phone company and the message provider.

In 1988, Sable brought suit in District Court seeking declaratory and injunctive relief against enforcement of the recently amended § 223(b). The 1988 amendments to the statute imposed a blanket prohibition on indecent as well as obscene interstate commercial telephone messages. [The FCC appealed the District Court's decision striking down the prohibition on indecent messages, and Sable appealed the decision upholding the ban on obscene messages.]

II

Congress made its first effort explicitly to address "dial-a-porn" when it added subsection 223(b) to the 1934 Communications Act. The relevant provision of the Act made it a crime to use telephone facilities to make "obscene or indecent" interstate telephone communications "for commercial purposes to any person under eighteen years of age or to any other person without that person's consent." The statute required the FCC to promulgate regulations laying out the means by which dial-a-porn sponsors could screen out underage callers.

The FCC initially promulgated regulations that would have established a defense to message providers operating only between the hours of 9:00 p.m. and 8:00 a.m. Eastern Time ("time channeling") and to providers requiring payment by credit card ("screening") before transmission of the dial-a-porn message. In Carlin Communications, Inc. v. FCC, 749 F.2d 113 (2d Cir. 1984) (*Carlin I*), the Court of Appeals for the Second Circuit set aside the time channeling regulations and remanded to the FCC to examine other alternatives, concluding that the operating hours requirement was "both overinclusive and underinclusive" because it denied "access to adults between certain hours, but not to youths who can easily pick up a private or public telephone and call dial-a-porn during the remaining hours." The Court of Appeals did not reach the constitutionality of the underlying legislation.

In 1985, the FCC promulgated new regulations which continued to permit credit card payment as a defense to prosecution. Instead of time restrictions, however, the Com-

---

17. Dial-a-porn is big business. The dial-a-porn service in New York City alone received six to seven million calls a month for the six-month period ending in April of 1985. Carlin Communications, Inc. v. FCC, 787 F.2d 846, 848 (2d Cir. 1986). [Footnote relocated.]

mission added a defense based on use of access codes (user identification codes). Thus, it would be a defense to prosecution if the defendant, before transmission of the message, restricted customer access by requiring either payment by credit card or authorization by access or identification code. The regulations required each dial-a-porn vendor to develop an identification code database and implementation scheme. Callers would be required to provide an access number for identification (or a credit card) before receiving the message. The access code would be received through the mail after the message provider reviewed the application and concluded through a written age ascertainment procedure that the applicant was at least eighteen years of age. The FCC rejected a proposal for "exchange blocking" which would block or screen telephone numbers at the customer's premises or at the telephone company offices. In Carlin Communications, Inc. v. FCC, 787 F.2d 846 (2d Cir. 1986) (*Carlin II*), the Court of Appeals set aside the new regulations because of the FCC's failure adequately to consider customer premises blocking. Again, the constitutionality of the underlying legislation was not addressed.

The FCC then promulgated a third set of regulations, which again rejected customer-premises blocking but added to the prior defenses of credit card payment and access-code use a third defense: message scrambling. Under this system, providers would scramble the message, which would then be unintelligible without the use of a descrambler, the sale of which would be limited to adults. On January 15, 1988, in Carlin Communications, Inc. v. FCC, 837 F.2d 546 (2d Cir.) (*Carlin III*), *cert. denied* 488 U.S. 924 (1988), the Court of Appeals for the Second Circuit held that the new regulations, which made access codes, along with credit card payments and scrambled messages, defenses to prosecution for dial-a-porn providers, were supported by the evidence, had been properly arrived at, and were a "feasible and effective way to serve" the "compelling state interest" in protecting minors; but the Court directed the FCC to reopen proceedings if a less restrictive technology became available. The Court of Appeals, however, this time reaching the constitutionality of the statute, invalidated § 223(b) insofar as it sought to apply to nonobscene speech.

Thereafter, in April 1988, Congress amended § 223(b) of the Communications Act to prohibit indecent as well as obscene interstate commercial telephone communications directed to any person regardless of age. The amended statute, which took effect on July 1, 1988, also eliminated the requirement that the FCC promulgate regulations for restricting access to minors since a total ban was imposed on dial-a-porn, making it illegal for adults, as well as children, to have access to the sexually explicit messages, Pub. L. No. 100-297, 102 Stat. 424 (1988). It was this version of the statute that was in effect when Sable commenced this action.

III

[T]he District Court upheld § 223(b)'s prohibition of obscene telephone messages as constitutional. We agree with that judgment. We have repeatedly held that the protection of the First Amendment does not extend to obscene speech.

Sable argues that the legislation creates an impermissible national standard of obscenity, and that it places message senders in a "double bind" by compelling them to tailor all their messages to the least tolerant community.

Section 223(b) no more establishes a "national standard" of obscenity than do federal statutes prohibiting the mailing of obscene materials, 18 U.S.C. § 1461, *see* Hamling v. United States, 418 U.S. 87 (1974), or the broadcasting of obscene messages, 18 U.S.C. § 1464. Furthermore, Sable is free to tailor its messages, on a selective basis, if it so chooses, to the communities it chooses to serve. Whether Sable chooses to hire operators to determine the source of the calls or engages with the telephone company to arrange for the screening and blocking of out-of-area calls or finds another means for providing messages compatible with community standards is a decision for the message provider to make.

IV

[T]he District Court concluded that while the government has a legitimate interest in protecting children from exposure to indecent dial-a-porn messages, §223(b) was not sufficiently narrowly drawn to serve that purpose and thus violated the First Amendment. We agree.

Sexual expression which is indecent but not obscene is protected by the First Amendment; and the federal parties do not submit that the sale of such materials to adults could be criminalized solely because they are indecent. The Government may, however, regulate the content of constitutionally protected speech in order to promote a compelling interest if it chooses the least restrictive means to further the articulated interest. We have recognized that there is a compelling interest in protecting the physical and psychological well-being of minors. This interest extends to shielding minors from the influence of literature that is not obscene by adult standards. Ginsberg v. New York, 390 U.S. 629, 639–40 (1968); New York v. Ferber, 458 U.S. 747, 756–57 (1982). The Government may serve this legitimate interest, but to withstand constitutional scrutiny, "it must do so by narrowly drawn regulations designed to serve those interests without unnecessarily interfering with First Amendment freedoms." Schaumburg v. Citizens for a Better Environment, 444 U.S. 620, 637 (1980). It is not enough to show that the government's ends are compelling; the means must be carefully tailored to achieve those ends.

In Butler v. Michigan, 352 U.S. 380 (1957), a unanimous Court reversed a conviction under a statute which made it an offense to make available to the general public materials found to have a potentially harmful influence on minors. The Court found the law to be insufficiently tailored since it denied adults their free speech rights by allowing them to read only what was acceptable for children. As Justice Frankfurter said in that case, "Surely this is to burn the house to roast the pig." Id. at 383. In our judgment, this case, like *Butler*, presents us with "legislation not reasonably restricted to the evil with which it is said to deal." Id.

In attempting to justify the complete ban and criminalization of the indecent commercial telephone communications with adults as well as minors, the government relies on FCC v. Pacifica Foundation, 438 U.S. 726 (1978), a case in which the Court considered whether the FCC has the power to regulate a radio broadcast that is indecent but not obscene. In an emphatically narrow holding, the *Pacifica* Court concluded that special treatment of indecent broadcasting was justified.

Pacifica is readily distinguishable from this case, most obviously because it did not involve a total ban on broadcasting indecent material. The FCC rule was not "intended to place an absolute prohibition on the broadcast of this type of language, but rather sought to channel it to times of day when children most likely would not be exposed to it." Id. at 733. The issue of a total ban was not before the Court.

The *Pacifica* opinion also relied on the "unique" attributes of broadcasting, noting that broadcasting is "uniquely pervasive," can intrude on the privacy of the home without prior warning as to program content, and is "uniquely accessible to children, even those too young to read." Id. at 748–49. The private commercial telephone communications at issue here are substantially different from the public radio broadcast at issue in *Pacifica*. In contrast to public displays, unsolicited mailings and other means of expression which the recipient has no meaningful opportunity to avoid, the dial-it medium requires the listener to take affirmative steps to receive the communication. There is no "captive audience" problem here; callers will generally not be unwilling listeners. The context of dial-in services, where a caller seeks and is willing to pay for the communication, is manifestly different from a situation in which a listener does not want the received message. Placing a telephone call is not the same as turning on a radio and being taken by surprise by an indecent message. Unlike an unexpected outburst on a radio broadcast, the message received by one who places a call to a dial-a-porn service is not so invasive or surprising that it prevents an unwilling listener from avoiding exposure to it.

The federal parties nevertheless argue that the total ban on indecent commercial telephone communications is justified because nothing less could prevent children from gaining access to such messages. We find the argument quite unpersuasive. The FCC, after lengthy proceedings, determined that its credit card, access code, and scrambling rules were a satisfactory solution to the problem of keeping indecent dial-a-porn messages out of the reach of minors. The Court of Appeals, after careful consideration, agreed that these rules represented a "feasible and effective" way to serve the Government's compelling interest in protecting children.

The federal parties now insist that the rules would not be effective enough—that enterprising youngsters could and would evade the rules and gain access to communications from which they should be shielded. But aside from conclusory statements during the debates by proponents of the bill, the congressional record presented to us contains no evidence as to *how* effective or ineffective the FCC's most recent regulations were or might prove to be.

For all we know from this record, the FCC's technological approach to restricting dial-a-porn messages to adults who seek them would be extremely effective, and only a few of the most enterprising and disobedient young people will manage to secure access to such messages. If this is the case, it seems to us that §223(b) is not a narrowly tailored effort to serve the compelling interest of preventing minors from being exposed to indecent telephone messages.

Because the statute's denial of adult access to telephone messages which are indecent but not obscene far exceeds that which is necessary to limit the access of minors to such messages, we hold that the ban does not survive constitutional scrutiny.

JUSTICE SCALIA, concurring.

I join the Court's opinion because I think it correct that a wholesale prohibition upon adult access to indecent speech cannot be adopted merely because the FCC's alternate proposal could be circumvented by as few children as the evidence suggests. But where a reasonable person draws the line in this balancing process—that is, how few children render the risk unacceptable—depends in part upon what mere "indecency" (as opposed to "obscenity") includes. The more narrow the understanding of what is "obscene," and hence the more pornographic what is embraced within the residual category of "indecency," the more reasonable it becomes to insist upon greater assurance of insulation from minors. So while the Court is unanimous on the reasoning of Part IV, I am not sure it is unanimous on the assumptions underlying that reasoning. I do not believe, for example, that any sort of sexual activity portrayed or enacted over the phone lines would fall outside of the obscenity portion of the statute that we uphold, and within the indecency portion that we strike down, so long as it appeals only to "normal, healthy sexual desires" as opposed to "shameful or morbid" ones. Brockett v. Spokane Arcades, Inc., 472 U.S. 491, 498 (1985).

Finally, I note that while we hold the Constitution prevents Congress from banning indecent speech in this fashion, we do not hold that the Constitution requires public utilities to carry it.

JUSTICE BRENNAN, with whom JUSTICE MARSHALL and JUSTICE STEVENS join, concurring in part and dissenting in part.

I agree that a statute imposing criminal penalties for making any indecent telephonic communication for a commercial purpose is patently unconstitutional.

In my view, however, §223(b)(1)(A)'s parallel criminal prohibition with regard to obscene commercial communications likewise violates the First Amendment. [T]he exaction of criminal penalties for the distribution of obscene materials to consenting adults is constitutionally intolerable. The very evidence the Court adduces to show that denying adults access to all indecent commercial messages "far exceeds that which is necessary to limit the access of minors to such messages," also demonstrates that forbidding the transmission of all obscene messages is unduly heavy-handed. Hence, the federal parties cannot plausibly claim that its legitimate interest in protecting children warrants this draconian restriction on the First Amendment rights of adults who seek to hear the messages that Sable and others provide.

Notes and Questions

1. Consenting Adults. Precisely what is wrong with Justice Brennan's view in *Sable* that it is unconstitutional to penalize the distribution over telephone wires of obscene materials to consenting adults? Will the *Sable* decision allow the government to control other messages that might be sent over telephone lines simply because the government disagrees with the form or content of those messages?

2. Common Carriage and Indecency. In his concurrence, Justice Scalia states that the Constitution does not "require[] public utilities to carry [indecent speech]." Usually, the common carriage principle demands that carriers allow all traffic on their network without regard to what type of traffic it is. On what authority does Justice Scalia suggest that an exception to general common carrier principles is warranted in the case of indecent speech? Does that suggestion comport with *Denver Area*?

3. Yet Another Congressional Response. Less than six months after the Supreme Court issued its opinion in *Sable*, Congress passed legislation (labeled "Restoration and Correction of Dial-a-Porn Sanctions") that amended §223 in order to bring it into conformity with the Court's opinion. See Pub. L. No. 101-166, Title V, §521(1) (1989). The 1989 amendments to §223, and the FCC's response to those amendments, are discussed in the following order.

REGULATIONS CONCERNING INDECENT COMMUNICATIONS BY TELEPHONE

Report and Order, 5 FCC Rcd. 4926 (1990)

I. INTRODUCTION

1. Section 223 of the Communications Act of 1934, as amended [in November 1989 in response to the Supreme Court's decision in *Sable*], imposes penalties on those who knowingly make obscene communications by telephone for commercial purposes and on those who knowingly make available indecent communications by telephone for commercial purposes to persons under 18 years of age or to adults without their consent. The section establishes that it is a defense to prosecution for the defendant to restrict access

to the prohibited indecent communications to persons eighteen years of age or older by complying with such procedures as the Commission may prescribe by regulation. The statute also requires telephone companies, to the extent technically feasible, to prohibit access to indecent communications from the telephone of a subscriber who has not previously requested access in writing.[18]

2. In this decision we adopt final rules which provide that in order to establish a defense to prosecution under section 223 of the Act, adult information service providers are required to utilize credit card authorization, access codes, or scrambling in order to limit access to consenting adults over the age of eighteen. Finally, we codify that a common carrier shall not provide access to a communication specified in section 223(b) from the telephone of any subscriber who has not previously requested in writing the carrier to provide access to such communication.

III. DISCUSSION

A. Constitutionality

14. [W]e note that the government may regulate indecent speech in order to promote a compelling interest if the means are narrowly tailored to achieve those ends. Providers Coalition and Fleishman argue that dial-a-porn providers should also have a defense if they operate in areas served by telephone companies that permit customers to block access to adult messages.[19]

16. [B]locking alone—reverse or voluntary—is insufficient to satisfy Congress' objective of protecting children. Without the additional restrictions on access put in place by dial-a-porn providers (scrambling, access codes, credit cards), children will still be able to gain access to indecent communications. Blocking, as a technical matter, will not prevent children from accessing dial-a-porn messages in another area code. Moreover, even if a child's home telephone is blocked, the child may still be able to receive indecent communications from a payphone, or a telephone in a home or other location where the blocking option has not been exercised.

18. The First Amendment does not preclude Congress from imposing a burden on message providers. *See Sable.* Regulations need not be so weak that they are completely useless. It was reasonable for Congress to conclude that its reverse blocking scheme would be considerably more effective than a voluntary scheme in preventing children from accessing indecent material. A voluntary blocking scheme would be far less effective in protecting children from exposure to indecent material because it is likely that most parents would not realize the need for blocking until their children had already obtained access to indecent messages. Nor would neighbors or relatives where children are only occasional visitors recognize the need to, nor act to, have access blocked. It is reasonable, therefore, to implement a reverse blocking scheme that brings the potential problem to

---

18. The statute imposes this obligation to block only if "the carrier collects from subscribers an identifiable charge for [the] communication that the carrier remits, in whole or in part, to the provider of such communication." Section 223(c)(1), 47 U.S.C. § 223(c)(1).

19. We use the term "blocking" to include both "voluntary blocking" and "reverse blocking." By "voluntary blocking" we mean the telephone company will, at the central office, prevent calls from going through to specified exchanges or numbers if the customer has requested this blocking service. By "reverse blocking," we mean the telephone company will, at the central office, prevent calls from going through to specified exchanges or numbers unless the customer has requested access. Subsection (c) of the statute requires telephone companies to institute reverse blocking where technically feasible if they provide billing and collection services to indecent message providers.

the attention of parents before the damage to children has occurred, rather than waiting until the damage has been done. *See generally FCC v. Pacifica*, 438 U.S. at 748–49.

22. This approach may cause message providers to incur additional costs, and perhaps to raise their prices, but the Supreme Court has said that raising the cost of providing a service is not unconstitutional. *Sable*, 492 U.S. at 125.

B. *Defenses to Prosecution*

27. *Credit Cards, Access Codes, and Scrambling.* No single defense is intended as the sole means by which all information providers must operate in order to avoid prosecution. We find that the use of credit card validation, scrambling or access codes before transmission places a minimal burden on the information provider and consenting adult while helping to assure that access by minors is restricted. Nevertheless, we believe Congress could reasonably conclude that each of these is far from foolproof and can be counteracted by less than the "most enterprising and disobedient young [person]," *see Sable*, 492 U.S. at 130. Accordingly, it is necessary to impose reverse blocking, where technically feasible, to achieve Congress's compelling interest in protecting children.

51. Several commenters argue that restrictions on indecent communications will have an adverse impact on the fight against AIDS by restricting open discussion of related issues by telephone. The proposed regulatory scheme does not restrict communications which are clinical discussions of AIDS or any other topic. Legitimate scientific or social endeavors such as community hotlines generally fall outside the definition of obscenity or indecency. In addition, we note that the statute encompasses only those indecent or obscene communications which are produced for commercial purposes.

Notes and Questions

1. Comparisons. What are the key features of the reasoning in *Sable*, and how might these materials bear on the government's ability to regulate indecent broadcast programming, cable programming, or material on the Internet?

(a) *Broadcasting.* What is the difference between indecency via broadcast and indecency via telephone? Apparently, broadcast indecency is "uniquely pervasive" and "uniquely accessible." But on what relevant distinctions is the Court relying? What is the factual basis for those distinctions? If *Pacifica* survives *Sable* because the former dealt with the "unique" broadcast medium, does this mean that cellular telephone services, which employ over-the-air transmissions that anyone with the proper tuner can intercept, are subject to *Pacifica*'s rules?

Is the key point that the FCC must use carefully tailored means to regulate indecent broadcasting so that only children are excluded from access to it? If narrowly tailored means are necessary, does this mean that, when regulating broadcast indecency, the Commission must (1) adopt local standards, rather than a single national standard, of indecency (because stations broadcast only to local areas); (2) set aside a "safe harbor" for those times when adults far outnumber children in the audience; or (3) carefully define "child" as someone susceptible to harm from the particular broadcast at issue? Why does the narrow-tailoring requirement not mean that government must abandon broadcast program censorship in favor of regulating radio and television set manufacturing so that parents can lock out selected channels?

(b) *Cable.* Does *Sable*, in the manner in which it distinguishes *Pacifica*, undercut or reinforce the view that indecency regulation of cable is unconstitutional? Conversely, if the

FCC is persuasive in arguing that voluntary blocking by telephone subscribers is insufficient to protect children from indecent phone messages (¶¶ 16–22), why does it not follow that the government may also protect children from indecent cable programming regardless of subscribers' ability to voluntarily block that programming (for example, by not subscribing or by purchasing a lockbox that prevents unauthorized people from accessing certain channels)?

(c) *Internet.* Should opponents of Internet indecency regulation be encouraged by the statement that "the message received by one who places a call to a dial-a-porn service is not so invasive or surprising that it prevents an unwilling listener from avoiding exposure to it"? Should the government be encouraged by the lower courts' willingness to uphold the post-*Sable* statute and the Supreme Court's apparent disinterest in disturbing those holdings?

2. Subsequent Litigation. Litigants challenged both the federal dial-a-porn statute (i.e., § 223, as amended in 1989) and the 1990 FCC Report and Order excerpted above as inconsistent with the First Amendment. The Ninth Circuit rejected this challenge in Information Providers' Coalition for Defense of the First Amendment v. FCC, 928 F.2d 866 (1991), and the Second Circuit upheld the statute against a First Amendment challenge in Dial Information Services Corp. of New York v. Thornburgh, 938 F.2d 1535 (1991). There was a petition for certiorari only in the latter case, and the Supreme Court denied it. 502 U.S. 1072 (1992).

---

§ 16.A.4. Regulation of Internet Indecency

There are myriad laws that affect Internet content. Almost every category of law that applies to offline activity can apply as well to online activity. In many cases, the law is one of general application and questions arise regarding exactly how it will apply to the online world. For instance, a number of lawsuits have involved questions over the online contacts sufficient to establish personal jurisdiction. *See, e.g.,* Cybersell, Inc. v. Cybersell, Inc., 130 F.3d 414 (9th Cir. 1997). In a few situations, Congress has enacted statutes with the Internet specifically in mind.[20] An example is the Twenty-First Century Communications and Video Accessibility Act, Pub. L. No. 111-260, 124 Stat. 2751 (2010), which directs the FCC to ensure access for people with disabilities to communications technologies including the Internet. And copyright has been a significant regulatory focus. Notably, Congress passed the Digital Millennium Copyright Act, 17 U.S.C. §§ 1201–1332, which creates protections against the circumvention of technological measures designed to protect copyrighted works. More generally, content providers very much want Internet service providers (ISPs), such as cable and telephone companies, to assist them in monitoring peer-to-peer file sharing and to terminate the accounts of customers engaged in copyright infringement. In some other countries, ISPs must take such measures. In the United States, cooperation has been limited, but a group of ISPs jointly agreed to provide education and warnings to their consumers about behavior that appears to violate copyright law.

Congress and the FCC have generally shied away from direct regulation of Internet content, however.[21] That is, the government by and large has not promulgated regula-

---

20. States have also passed legislation regulating aspects of online activity, but those statutes face the hurdle posed by the negative implications of the Commerce Clause of the Constitution (often called the "dormant commerce clause"). *See, e.g.,* ACLU v. Johnson, 194 F.3d 1149 (10th Cir. 1999).

21. Copyright laws affect content (although the Supreme Court has ruled copyright regulation does not trigger rigorous First Amendment scrutiny, see Eldred v. Reno, 537 U.S. 186, 218–221 (2003)), but they do not involve the government favoring or disfavoring specific content.

tions aimed specifically at the content traveling via the Internet. There is one major exception, however: Congress has attempted to limit the availability of content it disfavors—specifically, indecency.

A few years after the *Sable* litigation and Congress's response to it, Congress became concerned about the ability of children to gain access to sexual material via the Internet. Congress returned to the provision regulating telephone smut (47 U.S.C. §223) and amended it so that it regulated sexual material delivered not only via telephone but also via the Internet. The new legislation, known as the Communications Decency Act, was challenged immediately, resulting in the opinion below.

Reno v. ACLU
521 U.S. 844 (1997)

STEVENS, J., delivered the opinion of the Court, in which SCALIA, KENNEDY, SOUTER, THOMAS, GINSBURG, and BREYER, JJ., joined. O'CONNOR, J., filed an opinion concurring in the judgment in part and dissenting in part, in which REHNQUIST, C.J., joined.

JUSTICE STEVENS delivered the opinion of the Court.

At issue is the constitutionality of two statutory provisions enacted to protect minors from "indecent" and "patently offensive" communications on the Internet. Notwithstanding the legitimacy and importance of the congressional goal of protecting children from harmful materials, we agree with the three-judge District Court that the statute abridges "the freedom of speech" protected by the First Amendment.

I
Sexually Explicit Material

Sexually explicit material on the Internet includes text, pictures, and chat and extends from the modestly titillating to the hardest-core. These files are created, named, and posted in the same manner as material that is not sexually explicit, and may be accessed either deliberately or unintentionally during the course of an imprecise search. Once a provider posts its content on the Internet, it cannot prevent that content from entering any community.

Though [sexually explicit] material is widely available, users seldom encounter such content accidentally. A document's title or a description of the document will usually appear before the document itself, and in many cases the user will receive detailed information about a site's content before he or she need take the step to access the document. Almost all sexually explicit images are preceded by warnings as to the content. For that reason, the odds are slim that a user would enter a sexually explicit site by accident. Unlike communications received by radio or television, the receipt of information on the Internet requires a series of affirmative steps more deliberate and directed than merely turning a dial. A child requires some sophistication and some ability to read to retrieve material and thereby to use the Internet unattended.

Systems have been developed to help parents control the material that may be available on a home computer with Internet access. A system may either limit a computer's access to an approved list of sources that have been identified as containing no adult material, it may block designated inappropriate sites, or it may attempt to block messages containing identifiable objectionable features. Although parental control software currently can screen for certain suggestive words or for known sexually explicit sites, it cannot now screen for sexually explicit images. Nevertheless, the evidence indicates that a reasonably effective method by which parents can prevent their children from accessing sexually explicit and other material which parents may believe is inappropriate for their children will soon be available.

II

The Telecommunications Act of 1996, Pub. L. No. 104-104, 110 Stat. 56, was an unusually important legislative enactment. As stated on the first of its 103 pages, its primary purpose was to reduce regulation and encourage "the rapid deployment of new telecommunications technologies." The major components of the statute have nothing to do with the Internet; they were designed to promote competition in the local telephone service market, the multichannel video market, and the market for over-the-air broadcasting. The Act includes seven Titles, six of which are the product of extensive committee hearings and the subject of discussion in Reports prepared by Committees of the Senate and the House of Representatives. By contrast, Title V—known as the "Communications Decency Act of 1996" (CDA)—contains provisions that were either added in executive committee after the hearings were concluded or as amendments offered during floor debate on the legislation. An amendment offered in the Senate was the source of the two statutory provisions challenged in this case. They are informally described as the "indecent transmission" provision and the "patently offensive display" provision.[22]

The first, 47 U.S.C. § 223(a) (Supp. 1997), prohibits the knowing transmission of obscene or indecent messages to any recipient under 18 years of age. It provides in pertinent part:

"(a) Whoever—

"(1) in interstate or foreign communications—

* * *

"(B) by means of a telecommunications device knowingly—

"(i) makes, creates, or solicits, and

"(ii) initiates the transmission of,

"any comment, request, suggestion, proposal, image, or other communication which is obscene or indecent, knowing that the recipient of the communication is under 18 years of age, regardless of whether the maker of such communication placed the call or initiated the communication;

* * *

"(2) knowingly permits any telecommunications facility under his control to be used for any activity prohibited by paragraph (1) with the intent that it be used for such activity,

"shall be fined under Title 18, or imprisoned not more than two years, or both."

The second provision, § 223(d), prohibits the knowing sending or displaying of patently offensive messages in a manner that is available to a person under 18 years of age. It provides:

"(d) Whoever—

---

22. Although the Government and the dissent break § 223(d)(1) into two separate "patently offensive" and "display" provisions, we follow the convention of both parties below, as well as the District Court's order and opinion, in describing § 223(d)(1) as one provision.

"(1) in interstate or foreign communications knowingly—

"(A) uses an interactive computer service to send to a specific person or persons under 18 years of age, or

"(B) uses any interactive computer service to display in a manner available to a person under 18 years of age,

"any comment, request, suggestion, proposal, image, or other communication that, in context, depicts or describes, in terms patently offensive as measured by contemporary community standards, sexual or excretory activities or organs, regardless of whether the user of such service placed the call or initiated the communication; or

"(2) knowingly permits any telecommunications facility under such person's control to be used for an activity prohibited by paragraph (1) with the intent that it be used for such activity,

"shall be fined under Title 18, or imprisoned not more than two years, or both."

The breadth of these prohibitions is qualified by two affirmative defenses. One covers those who take "good faith, reasonable, effective, and appropriate actions" to restrict access by minors to the prohibited communications. § 223(e)(5)(A). The other covers those who restrict access to covered material by requiring certain designated forms of age proof, such as a verified credit card or an adult identification number or code. § 223(e)(5)(B).

IV

In arguing for reversal, the Government contends that the CDA is plainly constitutional under Ginsberg v. New York, 390 U.S. 629 (1968) [and] FCC v. Pacifica Foundation, 438 U.S. 726 (1978). A close look at these cases, however, raises—rather than relieves—doubts concerning the constitutionality of the CDA.

In *Ginsberg*, we upheld the constitutionality of a New York statute that prohibited selling to minors under 17 years of age material that was considered obscene as to them even if not obscene as to adults. We relied not only on the State's independent interest in the well-being of its youth, but also on our consistent recognition of the principle that "the parents' claim to authority in their own household to direct the rearing of their children is basic in the structure of our society." 390 U.S. at 639.

In four important respects, the statute upheld in *Ginsberg* was narrower than the CDA. First, we noted in *Ginsberg* that "the prohibition against sales to minors does not bar parents who so desire from purchasing the magazines for their children." *Id.* at 639. Under the CDA, by contrast, neither the parents' consent—nor even their participation—in the communication would avoid the application of the statute. Second, the New York statute applied only to commercial transactions, *id.* at 647, whereas the CDA contains no such limitation. Third, the New York statute cabined its definition of material that is harmful to minors with the requirement that it be "utterly without redeeming social importance for minors." *Id.* at 646. The CDA fails to provide us with any definition of the term "indecent" as used in § 223(a)(1) and, importantly, omits any requirement that the "patently offensive" material covered by § 223(d) lack serious literary, artistic, political, or scientific value. Fourth, the New York statute defined a minor as a person under the age of 17, whereas the CDA, in applying to all those under 18 years, includes an additional year of those nearest majority.

In *Pacifica*, we upheld a declaratory order of the Federal Communications Commission, holding that the broadcast of a recording of a 12-minute monologue entitled "Filthy

Words" that had previously been delivered to a live audience "could have been the subject of administrative sanctions." 438 U.S. at 730.

As with the New York statute at issue in *Ginsberg*, there are significant differences between the order upheld in *Pacifica* and the CDA. First, the order in *Pacifica*, issued by an agency that had been regulating radio stations for decades, targeted a specific broadcast that represented a rather dramatic departure from traditional program content in order to designate when—rather than whether—it would be permissible to air such a program in that particular medium. The CDA's broad categorical prohibitions are not limited to particular times and are not dependent on any evaluation by an agency familiar with the unique characteristics of the Internet. Second, unlike the CDA, the Commission's declaratory order was not punitive; we expressly refused to decide whether the indecent broadcast "would justify a criminal prosecution." *Id.* at 750. Finally, the Commission's order applied to a medium which as a matter of history had "received the most limited First Amendment protection," *id.* at 748, in large part because warnings could not adequately protect the listener from unexpected program content. The Internet, however, has no comparable history. Moreover, the District Court found that the risk of encountering indecent material by accident is remote because a series of affirmative steps is required to access specific material.

These precedents, then, surely do not require us to uphold the CDA and are fully consistent with the application of the most stringent review of its provisions.

V

[S]ome of our cases have recognized special justifications for regulation of the broadcast media that are not applicable to other speakers, *see* Red Lion Broadcasting Co. v. FCC, 395 U.S. 367 (1969); FCC v. Pacifica Foundation, 438 U.S. 726 (1978). In these cases, the Court relied on the history of extensive government regulation of the broadcast medium; the scarcity of available frequencies at its inception; and its "invasive" nature.

Those factors are not present in cyberspace. Neither before nor after the enactment of the CDA have the vast democratic fora of the Internet been subject to the type of government supervision and regulation that has attended the broadcast industry. Moreover, the Internet is not as "invasive" as radio or television. The District Court specifically found that "communications over the Internet do not 'invade' an individual's home or appear on one's computer screen unbidden. Users seldom encounter content 'by accident.'" 929 F. Supp. at 844 (finding 88). It also found that "almost all sexually explicit images are preceded by warnings as to the content," and cited testimony that "'odds are slim' that a user would come across a sexually explicit sight by accident." *Id.*

We distinguished *Pacifica* in *Sable*, 492 U.S. at 128, on just this basis. We explained that "the dial-it medium requires the listener to take affirmative steps to receive the communication." *Id.* at 127–28. "Placing a telephone call," we continued, "is not the same as turning on a radio and being taken by surprise by an indecent message." *Id.* at 128.

Finally, unlike the conditions that prevailed when Congress first authorized regulation of the broadcast spectrum, the Internet can hardly be considered a "scarce" expressive commodity. It provides relatively unlimited, low-cost capacity for communication of all kinds. This dynamic, multifaceted category of communication includes not only traditional print and news services, but also audio, video, and still images, as well as interactive, real-time dialogue. Through the use of chat rooms, any person with a phone line can become a town crier with a voice that resonates farther than it could from any soapbox. Through the use of Web pages, mail exploders, and newsgroups, the same individual can become a pamphleteer. As the District Court found, "the content on the Internet is as diverse as human thought." 929 F. Supp. at 842 (finding 74). We agree with its conclusion that our cases provide no basis for qualifying the level of First Amendment scrutiny that should be applied to this medium.

VII

We are persuaded that the CDA lacks the precision that the First Amendment requires when a statute regulates the content of speech. In order to deny minors access to potentially harmful speech, the CDA effectively suppresses a large amount of speech that adults have a constitutional right to receive and to address to one another. That burden on adult speech is unacceptable if less restrictive alternatives would be at least as effective in achieving the legitimate purpose that the statute was enacted to serve.

The District Court was correct to conclude that the CDA effectively resembles the ban on "dial-a-porn" invalidated in *Sable*. In *Sable*, this Court rejected the argument that we should defer to the congressional judgment that nothing less than a total ban would be effective in preventing enterprising youngsters from gaining access to indecent communications.

In arguing that the CDA does not so diminish adult communication, the Government relies on the incorrect factual premise that prohibiting a transmission whenever it is known that one of its recipients is a minor would not interfere with adult-to-adult communication. The findings of the District Court make clear that this premise is untenable.

The District Court found that at the time of trial existing technology did not include any effective method for a sender to prevent minors from obtaining access to its communications on the Internet without also denying access to adults. By contrast, the District Court found that "despite its limitations, currently available *user-based* software suggests that a reasonably effective method by which *parents* can prevent their children from accessing sexually explicit and other material which *parents* may believe is inappropriate for their children will soon be widely available." *Id.* at 842 (finding 73) (emphases added).

The breadth of the CDA's coverage is wholly unprecedented. Unlike the regulations upheld in *Ginsberg* and *Pacifica*, the scope of the CDA is not limited to commercial speech or commercial entities. Its open-ended prohibitions embrace all nonprofit entities and individuals posting indecent messages or displaying them on their own computers in the presence of minors. The general, undefined terms "indecent" and "patently offensive" cover large amounts of nonpornographic material with serious educational or other value. Moreover, the "community standards" criterion as applied to the Internet means that any communication available to a nationwide audience will be judged by the standards of the community most likely to be offended by the message.

The breadth of this content-based restriction of speech imposes an especially heavy burden on the Government to explain why a less restrictive provision would not be as effective as the CDA. It has not done so. The arguments in this Court have referred to possible alternatives such as requiring that indecent material be "tagged" in a way that facilitates parental control of material coming into their homes, making exceptions for messages with artistic or educational value, providing some tolerance for parental choice, and regulating some portions of the Internet—such as commercial web sites—differently than others, such as chat rooms. Particularly in the light of the absence of any detailed findings by the Congress, or even hearings addressing the special problems of the CDA, we are persuaded that the CDA is not narrowly tailored if that requirement has any meaning at all.

XI

In this Court, though not in the District Court, the Government asserts that—in addition to its interest in protecting children—its "equally significant" interest in fostering the growth of the Internet provides an independent basis for upholding the constitutionality of the CDA. Brief for Appellants 19. The Government apparently assumes that the unregulated availability of "indecent" and "patently offensive" material on the Internet is driving countless citizens away from the medium because of the risk of exposing themselves or their children to harmful material.

We find this argument singularly unpersuasive. The dramatic expansion of this new marketplace of ideas contradicts the factual basis of this contention. The record demonstrates that the growth of the Internet has been and continues to be phenomenal. As a matter of constitutional tradition, in the absence of evidence to the contrary, we presume that governmental regulation of the content of speech is more likely to interfere with the free exchange of ideas than to encourage it. The interest in encouraging freedom of expression in a democratic society outweighs any theoretical but unproven benefit of censorship.

For the foregoing reasons, the judgment of the District Court is affirmed.

[Concurring and dissenting opinion of JUSTICE O'CONNOR is omitted.]

Notes and Questions

1. Dial-a-Porn. In light of *Reno*, are the FCC's dial-a-porn regulations unconstitutional? Do they impose an excessive burden on adult access to protected speech relative to the harm to minors that is avoided by imposing that burden? Is this the test that emerges from *Reno*?

2. Pacifica. After *Reno*, what is left of the rationale articulated in *Pacifica*? Is the point that *Pacifica* protects children "too young to read" who might be harmed by hearing or learning a dirty word over the radio, but who are unable to access Internet indecency? If this is the case, what are we to make of *ACT III*, which affirmed Commission regulations of indecent broadcasting that, among other things, (1) define as a "child" anyone under eighteen, and (2) do not require that the Commission have evidence that children are in the listening or viewing audience before the agency can conclude that programming on a certain station is indecent?

Is *Pacifica* now explicable only by the post hoc justification for it offered in *Reno*—the history of extensive government regulation of broadcast? Does the Court's reliance on the absence of existing Internet regulation mean that Congress's choice was to regulate the Internet at its inception or else? In other words, by waiting for the Internet to develop, did Congress forego its chance to regulate at all? Is that an appropriate message to send to Congress? Does it create the right incentives?

3. The Child Online Protection Act. Is it possible to draft a statute that would pass constitutional muster but nonetheless restrict indecency on the Internet? Congress, in an apparent attempt at doing so, responded to *Reno v. ACLU* by enacting the Child Online Protection Act, Pub. L. No. 105-277, 112 Stat. 2681 (1998) (COPA). Like the Communications Decency Act, COPA criminalizes certain disfavored online speech, and like the CDA it has affirmative defenses for those who restrict minors' access to covered material via credit card authorization, adult identification numbers, or other reasonable measures. COPA, however, is narrower than the CDA in several ways, including: (a) COPA's restrictions apply only to communications on the World Wide Web; content distributed through other Internet-based services (such as email) is not covered; (b) whereas the CDA applied to commercial and noncommercial speakers alike, COPA applies only to communications made "for commercial purposes"; and (c) COPA applies only to "material that is harmful to minors," a term of art that is arguably narrower than "indecent" or "patently offensive" speech.

Shortly after COPA was enacted, the ACLU challenged its constitutionality, and a U.S. District Court granted the ACLU's motion for a preliminary injunction. The Third Circuit affirmed the injunction, finding that COPA was likely overbroad because its definition of "harmful to minors" relied on "contemporary community standards." *See* 47 U.S.C. § 231(e)(6); ACLU v. Reno [*Reno II*], 31 F. Supp. 2d 473 (E.D. Pa. 1999), *aff'd* 217 F.3d 162 (3d Cir. 2000).

The Supreme Court granted certiorari in that case and, in 2002, a splintered Court reversed. Ashcroft v. ACLU (*Ashcroft I*), 535 U.S. 564 (2002). There was no majority for a rationale, but a majority of the Court did agree on the conclusion:

> We hold only that COPA's reliance on community standards to identify "material that is harmful to minors" does not *by itself* render the statute substantially overbroad for purposes of the First Amendment. We do not express any view as to whether COPA suffers from substantial overbreadth for other reasons, whether the statute is unconstitutionally vague, or whether the District Court correctly concluded that the statute likely will not survive strict scrutiny analysis once adjudication of the case is completed below. While respondents urge us to resolve these questions at this time, prudence dictates allowing the Court of Appeals to first examine these difficult issues.
>
> Petitioner does not ask us to vacate the preliminary injunction entered by the District Court, and in any event, we could not do so without addressing matters yet to be considered by the Court of Appeals. As a result, the Government remains enjoined from enforcing COPA absent further action by the Court of Appeals or the District Court.

Id. at 585–86.

So the case was remanded for consideration of the many arguments that the challengers to the statute actually put forward, as opposed to the community standards argument that the Third Circuit had seized on. In the meantime, the injunction remained in effect. On remand, the Third Circuit turned to the questions left open by *Ashcroft I*. Once again it affirmed the district court's grant of a preliminary injunction against the enforcement of COPA, albeit on different grounds—indeed, on multiple grounds. The Third Circuit concluded as follows:

> In sum, the District Court did not abuse its discretion in granting the plaintiffs a preliminary injunction on the grounds that COPA, in failing to satisfy strict scrutiny, had no probability of success on the merits. COPA is clearly a content-based restriction on speech. Although it does purport to serve a compelling governmental interest, it is not narrowly tailored, and thus fails strict scrutiny. COPA also fails strict scrutiny because it does not use the least restrictive means to achieve its ends. The breadth of the "harmful to minors" and "commercial purpose" text of COPA, especially in light of applying community standards to a global medium and the burdens on speech created by the statute's affirmative defenses, as well as the fact that Congress could have, but failed to, employ the least restrictive means to accomplish its legitimate goal, persuade us that the District Court did not abuse its discretion in preliminarily enjoining the enforcement of COPA....
>
> Our analysis of whether COPA is overbroad is akin to the portion of the strict scrutiny analysis we have conducted in which we concluded that COPA is not narrowly tailored. We conclude that the statute is substantially overbroad in that it places significant burdens on Web publishers' communication of speech that

is constitutionally protected as to adults and adults' ability to access such speech. In so doing, COPA encroaches upon a significant amount of protected speech beyond that which the Government may target constitutionally in preventing children's exposure to material that is obscene for minors.

ACLU v. Ashcroft, 322 F.3d 240, 265–66, 266–67 (3d Cir. 2003). The Supreme Court then granted certiorari. On the last day of its 2003 Term, it affirmed and remanded in the opinion excerpted below.

ASHCROFT v. ACLU [*ASHCROFT II*]
542 U.S. 656 (2004)

KENNEDY, J., delivered the opinion of the Court, in which STEVENS, SOUTER, THOMAS, and GINSBURG, JJ., joined. STEVENS, J., filed a concurring opinion, in which GINSBURG, J., joined. SCALIA, J., filed a dissenting opinion. BREYER, J., filed a dissenting opinion, in which REHNQUIST, C.J., and O'CONNOR, J., joined.

JUSTICE KENNEDY delivered the opinion of the Court.

I

In response to the Court's decision in *Reno v. ACLU*, Congress passed the Child Online Protection Act (COPA). COPA imposes criminal penalties of a $50,000 fine and six months in prison for the knowing posting, for "commercial purposes," of World Wide Web content that is "harmful to minors." § 231(a)(1). Material that is "harmful to minors" is defined as:

> any communication, picture, image, graphic image file, article, recording, writing, or other matter of any kind that is obscene or that—
>
> (A) the average person, applying contemporary community standards, would find, taking the material as a whole and with respect to minors, is designed to appeal to, or is designed to pander to, the prurient interest;
>
> (B) depicts, describes, or represents, in a manner patently offensive with respect to minors, an actual or simulated sexual act or sexual contact, an actual or simulated normal or perverted sexual act, or a lewd exhibition of the genitals or post-pubescent female breast; and
>
> (C) taken as a whole, lacks serious literary, artistic, political, or scientific value for minors.

§ 231(e)(6).

"Minors" are defined as "any person under 17 years of age." § 231(e)(7). A person acts for "commercial purposes only if such person is engaged in the business of making such communications." "Engaged in the business," in turn,

> "means that the person who makes a communication, or offers to make a communication, by means of the World Wide Web, that includes any material that is harmful to minors, devotes time, attention, or labor to such activities, as a regular course of such person's trade or business, with the objective of earning a profit as a result of such activities (although it is not necessary that the person make a profit or that the making or offering to make such communications be the person's sole or principal business or source of income)."

§ 231(e)(2).

While the statute labels all speech that falls within these definitions as criminal speech, it also provides an affirmative defense to those who employ specified means to prevent minors from gaining access to the prohibited materials on their Web site. A person may escape conviction under the statute by demonstrating that he

> has restricted access by minors to material that is harmful to minors—
>
> (A) by requiring use of a credit card, debit account, adult access code, or adult personal identification number[,]
>
> (B) by accepting a digital certificate that verifies age, or
>
> (C) by any other reasonable measures that are feasible under available technology.

§ 231(c)(1).

Since the passage of COPA, Congress has enacted additional laws regulating the Internet in an attempt to protect minors. For example, it has enacted a prohibition on misleading Internet domain names, 18 U.S.C. § 2252B, in order to prevent Web site owners from disguising pornographic Web sites in a way likely to cause uninterested persons to visit them. It has also passed a statute creating a "Dot Kids" second-level Internet domain, the content of which is restricted to that which is fit for minors under the age of 13. 47 U.S.C. § 941.

II

A

"This Court, like other appellate courts, has always applied the abuse of discretion standard on the review of a preliminary injunction." Walters v. National Ass'n of Radiation Survivors, 473 U.S. 305, 336 (1985) (O'CONNOR, J., concurring). If the underlying constitutional question is close, therefore, we should uphold the injunction and remand for trial on the merits. Applying this mode of inquiry, we agree with the Court of Appeals that the District Court did not abuse its discretion in entering the preliminary injunction.

The District Court, in deciding to grant the preliminary injunction, concentrated primarily on the argument that there are plausible, less restrictive alternatives to COPA. A statute that "effectively suppresses a large amount of speech that adults have a constitutional right to receive and to address to one another ... is unacceptable if less restrictive alternatives would be at least as effective in achieving the legitimate purpose that the statute was enacted to serve." *Reno*, 521 U.S. at 874. When plaintiffs challenge a content-based speech restriction, the burden is on the Government to prove that the proposed alternatives will not be as effective as the challenged statute. *Id.* at 874.

In considering this question, a court assumes that certain protected speech may be regulated, and then asks what is the least restrictive alternative that can be used to achieve that goal. The purpose of the test is not to consider whether the challenged restriction has some effect in achieving Congress' goal, regardless of the restriction it imposes. The purpose of the test is to ensure that speech is restricted no further than necessary to achieve the goal, for it is important to assure that legitimate speech is not chilled or punished. For that reason, the test does not begin with the status quo of existing regulations, then ask whether the challenged restriction has some additional ability to achieve Congress' legitimate interest. Any restriction on speech could be justified under that analysis. Instead, the court should ask whether the challenged regulation is the least restrictive means among available, effective alternatives.

[O]n this record there are a number of plausible, less restrictive alternatives to the statute. The primary alternative considered by the District Court was blocking and filtering software. Blocking and filtering software is an alternative that is less restrictive than COPA, and, in addition, likely more effective as a means of restricting children's access to materials harmful to them.

Filters are less restrictive than COPA. They impose selective restrictions on speech at the receiving end, not universal restrictions at the source. Under a filtering regime, adults without children may gain access to speech they have a right to see without having to identify themselves or provide their credit card information. Even adults with children may obtain access to the same speech on the same terms simply by turning off the filter on their home computers. Above all, promoting the use of filters does not condemn as criminal any category of speech, and so the potential chilling effect is eliminated, or at least much diminished. All of these things are true, moreover, regardless of how broadly or narrowly the definitions in COPA are construed.

Filters also may well be more effective than COPA. First, a filter can prevent minors from seeing all pornography, not just pornography posted to the Web from America. The District Court noted in its factfindings that one witness estimated that 40% of harmful-to-minors content comes from overseas. COPA does not prevent minors from having access to those foreign harmful materials. That alone makes it possible that filtering software might be more effective in serving Congress' goals. Effectiveness is likely to diminish even further if COPA is upheld, because the providers of the materials that would be covered by the statute simply can move their operations overseas. It is not an answer to say that COPA reaches some amount of materials that are harmful to minors; the question is whether it would reach more of them than less restrictive alternatives. In addition, the District Court found that verification systems may be subject to evasion and circumvention, for example by minors who have their own credit cards. Finally, filters also may be more effective because they can be applied to all forms of Internet communication, including e-mail, not just communications available via the World Wide Web.

That filtering software may well be more effective than COPA is confirmed by the findings of the Commission on Child Online Protection, a blue-ribbon commission created by Congress in COPA itself. It unambiguously found that filters are more effective than age-verification requirements. *See* Commission on Child Online Protection, Report to Congress, at 19–21, 23–25, 27 (Oct. 20, 2000).

Filtering software, of course, is not a perfect solution to the problem of children gaining access to harmful-to-minors materials. It may block some materials that are not harmful to minors and fail to catch some that are. Whatever the deficiencies of filters, however, the Government failed to introduce specific evidence proving that existing technologies are less effective than the restrictions in COPA. The District Court made a specific factfinding that "[n]o evidence was presented to the Court as to the percentage of time that blocking and filtering technology is over- or underinclusive." ACLU v. Reno, 31 F. Supp. 2d at 492 (E.D. Pa. 1999). In the absence of a showing as to the relative effectiveness of COPA and the alternatives proposed by respondents, it was not an abuse of discretion for the District Court to grant the preliminary injunction. The Government's burden is not merely to show that a proposed less restrictive alternative has some flaws; its burden is to show that it is less effective. *Reno*, 521 U.S. at 874. It is not enough for the Government to show that COPA has some effect. Nor do respondents bear a burden to introduce, or offer to introduce, evidence that their proposed alternatives are more effective. The Government has the burden to show they are less so. The Government having failed to carry its burden, it was not an abuse of discretion for the District Court to grant the preliminary injunction.

One argument to the contrary is worth mentioning—the argument that filtering software is not an available alternative because Congress may not require it to be used. That argument carries little weight, because Congress undoubtedly may act to encourage the use of filters. We have held that Congress can give strong incentives to schools and libraries to use them. United States v. American Library Ass'n., Inc, 539 U.S. 194 (2003). It could also take steps to promote their development by industry, and their use by parents. It is incorrect, for that reason, to say that filters are part of the current regulatory status quo. The need for parental cooperation does not automatically disqualify a proposed less restrictive alternative. United States v. Playboy Entertainment Group, Inc., 529 U.S. 803, 824 (2000) ("A court should not assume a plausible, less restrictive alternative would be ineffective; and a court should not presume parents, given full information, will fail to act.").

The closest precedent on the general point is our decision in *Playboy Entertainment Group*. The reasoning of *Playboy Entertainment Group*, and the holdings and force of our precedents require us to affirm the preliminary injunction. To do otherwise would be to do less than the First Amendment commands.

B

There are also important practical reasons to let the injunction stand pending a full trial on the merits. First, the potential harms from reversing the injunction outweigh those of leaving it in place by mistake.

Second, there are substantial factual disputes remaining in the case. As mentioned above, there is a serious gap in the evidence as to the effectiveness of filtering software.

Third, and on a related point, the factual record does not reflect current technological reality—a serious flaw in any case involving the Internet. The technology of the Internet evolves at a rapid pace. Yet the factfindings of the District Court were entered in February 1999, over five years ago. Since then, certain facts about the Internet are known to have changed. *Compare, e.g.*, 31 F. Supp. 2d at 481 (36.7 million Internet hosts as of July 1998) *with* Internet Systems Consortium, Internet Domain Survey, Jan. 2004, http://www.isc.org/index.pl?/ops/ds (as visited June 22, 2004) (233.1 million hosts as of Jan. 2004). It is reasonable to assume that other technological developments important to the First Amendment analysis have also occurred during that time. More and better filtering alternatives may exist than when the District Court entered its findings. Indeed, we know that after the District Court entered its factfindings, a congressionally appointed commission issued a report that found that filters are more effective than verification screens. *See supra*.

By affirming the preliminary injunction and remanding for trial, we allow the parties to update and supplement the factual record to reflect current technological realities. Remand will also permit the District Court to take account of a changed legal landscape. Since the District Court made its factfindings, Congress has passed at least two further statutes that might qualify as less restrictive alternatives to COPA—a prohibition on misleading domain names, and a statute creating a minors-safe "Dot Kids" domain. *See supra*. Remanding for trial will allow the District Court to take into account those additional potential alternatives.

On this record, the Government has not shown that the less restrictive alternatives proposed by respondents should be disregarded. Those alternatives, indeed, may be more effective than the provisions of COPA. The District Court did not abuse its discretion when it entered the preliminary injunction. The judgment of the Court of Appeals is affirmed, and the case is remanded for proceedings consistent with this opinion.

[Concurring opinion of JUSTICE STEVENS and dissenting opinion of JUSTICE SCALIA are omitted.]

JUSTICE BREYER, with whom THE CHIEF JUSTICE and JUSTICE O'CONNOR join, dissenting.

Like the Court, I would subject the Act to "the most exacting scrutiny," Turner Broadcasting System, Inc. v. FCC, 512 U.S. 622, 642 (1994), requiring the Government to show that any restriction of nonobscene expression is "narrowly drawn" to further a "compelling interest" and that the restriction amounts to the "least restrictive means" available to further that interest, Sable Communications of Cal., Inc. v. FCC, 492 U.S. 115, 126 (1989). *See also* Denver Area Ed. Telecommunications Consortium, Inc. v. FCC, 518 U.S. 727, 755–56 (1996).

Nonetheless, my examination of (1) the burdens the Act imposes on protected expression, (2) the Act's ability to further a compelling interest, and (3) the proposed "less restrictive alternatives" convinces me that the Court is wrong. I cannot accept its conclusion that Congress could have accomplished its statutory objective—protecting children from commercial pornography on the Internet—in other, less restrictive ways.

I

[T]he Act, properly interpreted, imposes a burden on protected speech that is no more than modest.

A

The Act's definitions limit the material it regulates to material that does not enjoy First Amendment protection, namely legally obscene material, and very little more. [T]he Act's definitions limit the statute's scope to commercial pornography. It affects unprotected obscene material. Given the inevitable uncertainty about how to characterize close-to-obscene material, it could apply to (or chill the production of) a limited class of borderline material that courts might ultimately find is protected.

B

The Act does not censor the material it covers. Rather, it requires providers of the "harmful to minors" material to restrict minors' access to it by verifying age. They can do so by inserting screens that verify age using a credit card, adult personal identification number, or other similar technology. *See* § 231(c)(1). In this way, the Act requires creation of an Internet screen that minors, but not adults, will find difficult to bypass.

II

I turn next to the question of "compelling interest," that of protecting minors from exposure to commercial pornography. No one denies that such an interest is "compelling." *See Denver Area*, 518 U.S. at 743 (interest in protecting minors is "compelling"); *Sable Communications*, 492 U.S. at 126 (same). Rather, the question here is whether the Act, given its restrictions on adult access, significantly advances that interest. In other words, is the game worth the candle?

The majority argues that it is not, because of the existence of "blocking and filtering software." *Ante*. The majority refers to the presence of that software as a "less restrictive alternative." But that is a misnomer—a misnomer that may lead the reader to believe that all we need do is look to see if the blocking and filtering software is less restrictive; and to believe that, because in one sense it is (one can turn off the software), that is the end of the constitutional matter.

But such reasoning has no place here. Conceptually speaking, the presence of filtering software is not an *alternative* legislative approach to the problem of protecting children from exposure to commercial pornography. Rather, it is part of the status quo, i.e., the backdrop against which Congress enacted the present statute. It is always true, by definition, that the status quo is less restrictive than a new regulatory law. It is always less restrictive to do *nothing* than to do *something*. But "doing nothing" does not address the problem Congress sought to address — namely that, despite the availability of filtering software, children were still being exposed to harmful material on the Internet.

Thus, the relevant constitutional question is not the question the Court asks: Would it be less restrictive to do nothing? Of course it would be. Rather, the relevant question posits a comparison of (a) a status quo that includes filtering software with (b) a change in that status quo that adds to it an age-verification screen requirement. Given the existence of filtering software, does the problem Congress identified remain significant? Does the Act help to address it? These are questions about the relation of the Act to the compelling interest. Does the Act, compared to the status quo, significantly advance the ball? (An affirmative answer to these questions will not justify "[a]ny restriction on speech," as the Court claims, for a final answer in respect to constitutionality must take account of burdens and alternatives as well.)

The answers to these intermediate questions are clear: Filtering software, as presently available, does not solve the "child protection" problem. It suffers from four serious inadequacies that prompted Congress to pass legislation instead of relying on its voluntary use. First, its filtering is faulty, allowing some pornographic material to pass through without hindrance. Just last year, in *American Library Ass'n*, Justice Stevens described "fundamental defects in the filtering software that is now available or that will be available in the foreseeable future." 539 U.S. at 221 (dissenting opinion). He pointed to the problem of underblocking: "Because the software relies on key words or phrases to block undesirable sites, it does not have the capacity to exclude a precisely defined category of images." *Id.* That is to say, in the absence of words, the software alone cannot distinguish between the most obscene pictorial image and the Venus de Milo. No Member of this Court disagreed.

Second, filtering software costs money. Not every family has the $40 or so necessary to install it. By way of contrast, age screening costs less.

Third, filtering software depends upon parents willing to decide where their children will surf the Web and able to enforce that decision. As to millions of American families, that is not a reasonable possibility. More than 28 million school age children have both parents or their sole parent in the work force, at least 5 million children are left alone at home without supervision each week, and many of those children will spend afternoons and evenings with friends who may well have access to computers and more lenient parents.

Fourth, software blocking lacks precision, with the result that those who wish to use it to screen out pornography find that it blocks a great deal of material that is valuable. As Justice Stevens pointed out, "the software's reliance on words to identify undesirable sites necessarily results in the blocking of thousands of pages that contain content that is completely innocuous for both adults and minors, and that no rational person could conclude matches the filtering companies' category definitions, such as pornography or sex." *Id.* at 222 (internal quotation marks and citations omitted).

Nothing in the District Court record suggests the contrary.

In sum, a "filtering software status quo" means filtering that underblocks, imposes a cost upon each family that uses it, fails to screen outside the home, and lacks precision.

Thus, Congress could reasonably conclude that a system that relies entirely upon the use of such software is not an effective system. And a law that adds to that system an age-verification screen requirement significantly increases the system's efficacy. That is to say, at a modest additional cost to those adults who wish to obtain access to a screened program, that law will bring about better, more precise blocking, both inside and outside the home.

The Court's response—that 40% of all pornographic material may be of foreign origin—is beside the point. Even assuming (I believe unrealistically) that *all* foreign originators will refuse to use screening, the Act would make a difference in respect to 60% of the Internet's commercial pornography. I cannot call that difference insignificant.

The upshot is that Congress could reasonably conclude that, despite the current availability of filtering software, a child protection problem exists. It also could conclude that a precisely targeted regulatory statute, adding an age-verification requirement for a narrow range of material, would more effectively shield children from commercial pornography.

IV

My conclusion is that the Act, as properly interpreted, risks imposition of minor burdens on some protected material—burdens that adults wishing to view the material may overcome at modest cost. At the same time, it significantly helps to achieve a compelling congressional goal, protecting children from exposure to commercial pornography. There is no serious, practically available "less restrictive" way similarly to further this compelling interest. Hence the Act is constitutional.

Notes and Questions

1. Battle Lines. What is the nature of the disagreement between the majority and Justice Breyer's dissent? Do they interpret the law differently, or is their dispute mainly over the underlying facts? Does the majority agree with Justice Breyer that COPA regulates "legally obscene material, and very little more"? Is the dispute between the majority and Justice Breyer mainly over the effectiveness of filtering?

2. Why Remand? In Part II-B, the Court emphasizes that "the factual record does not reflect current technological reality." The Court acknowledges that some delay is inevitable, but says that the delay in this case was particularly long because of the many trips to appellate courts. (Whose fault is that?) But should the Court remand yet again? Or should the Court have updated the record and determined the degree to which filtering is an effective alternative to COPA? Is that the appropriate role for an appellate court?

3. How Should Congress Respond? If you were a supporter of COPA and you feared that it would eventually be struck down, what legislative strategy would you pursue? If COPA is unconstitutional, what legislative options are open to Congress if it wants to restrict the dissemination of Internet indecency? If the answer is that Congress cannot place any restrictions on indecency, is that an indictment of the Court and/or the First Amendment? A tribute to them?

4. *Playboy* **Redux.** The lineup in *Ashcroft II* was quite unusual for this Supreme Court, but it did appear in one other case—*United States v. Playboy Entertainment Group*—and the majority in *Ashcroft II* found that *Playboy* was the closest precedent on point. Does this suggest that the Court is moving toward a cross-media negative response to restrictions on speech so long as filters are available? Won't filters always be available, in every medium?

5. The Final Chapter on COPA. The Supreme Court's opinion in *Ashcroft II* upheld the injunction and remanded the case for yet further proceedings. The district court then invalidated COPA as violating the First Amendment. The United States appealed to the Third Circuit, which issued the opinion excerpted below.

ACLU v. Mukasey
534 F.3d 181 (3d Cir. 2008)

Opinion for the court filed by Circuit Judge GREENBERG, in which Circuit Judges AMBRO and CHAGARES concur.

GREENBERG, Circuit Judge:

[The court recited the history of the COPA litigation.] After a bench trial, the District Court on March 22, 2007, issued extensive findings of fact, determined that plaintiffs have standing to maintain this action, and concluded that:

> COPA facially violates the First and Fifth Amendment rights of the plaintiffs because: (1) COPA is not narrowly tailored to the compelling interest of Congress; (2) defendant has failed to meet his burden of showing that COPA is the least restrictive and most effective alternative in achieving the compelling interest; and (3) COPA is impermissibly vague and overbroad.

ACLU v. Gonzales, 478 F. Supp. 2d 775, 821 (E.D. Pa. 2007) (*Gonzales*).

IV. DISCUSSION

B. Strict Scrutiny

First, the Government challenges the District Court's decision that COPA is unconstitutional because it does not survive strict scrutiny, the standard that we apply in this case inasmuch as COPA is a content-based restriction on speech. To survive strict scrutiny analysis, a statute must: (1) serve a compelling governmental interest; (2) be narrowly tailored to achieve that interest; and (3) be the least restrictive means of advancing that interest.

1. Compelling Interest

Congress enacted COPA to protect minors from exposure to sexually explicit material on the Web. The Supreme Court has held that "there is a compelling interest in protecting the physical and psychological well-being of minors," Sable Communications of California, Inc. v. FCC, 492 U.S. 115, 126 (1989), and the parties agree that the Government has a compelling interest to protect minors from exposure to harmful material on the Web. Inasmuch as we agree with them on that point, we turn to the question of whether COPA is narrowly tailored to effectuate its purpose.

2. Narrowly Tailored

In its decision made after the trial on the merits now on appeal before us, the District Court concluded that COPA is not narrowly tailored because it is overinclusive. First, the court determined that COPA is impermissibly overinclusive because it "prohibits much more speech than is necessary to further Congress' compelling interest. For example, the definitions of 'commercial purposes' and 'engaged in the business' apply to an inordinate amount of Internet speech and certainly cover more than just commercial pornographers...." *Gonzales*, 478 F. Supp. 2d at 810 (citations omitted). The court also concluded that COPA is overinclusive because it "applies to speech that is obscene as to all minors from newborns to age sixteen, and not just to speech that is obscene as to older minors...." *Id.*

The Government contends that COPA is narrowly tailored because it applies only to commercial pornographers and only to material that is harmful to "older" minors. But we addressed and rejected the Government's arguments in ACLU v. Ashcroft, 322 F.3d 240 (3d Cir. 2003) (*ACLU II*), when we found there is nothing in the text of COPA to limit its application solely to "commercial pornographers" or to limit the phrase "material that is harmful to minors" to include material that only is harmful to "older" minors. *See id.* at 253–57. Our prior decision is binding on these issues on this appeal.

The District Court also found that COPA's affirmative defenses "do not aid in narrowly tailoring COPA to Congress' compelling interest." *Gonzales*, 478 F. Supp. 2d at 813. Specifically, the court found that:

> there is no evidence of age verification services or products available on the market to owners of Web sites that actually reliably establish or verify the age of Internet users. Nor is there evidence of such services or products that can effectively prevent access to Web pages by a minor.

Id. at 800. The court found that "[t]he rules of payment card associations in this country prohibit Web sites from claiming that use of a payment card is an effective method of verifying age, and prohibit Web site owners from using credit or debit cards to verify age," and that "a significant number of minors have access to [payment cards]." *Id.* at 801. The court also reviewed data verification services, which are "non-payment card-based services that attempt to verify the age or identity of an individual Internet user," and found that they are unreliable because they "cannot determine whether the person entering information into the Web site is the person to whom the information pertains." *Id.* at 802. The court further found that the minimum information required by a data verification services company "can easily be circumvented by children who generally know the first and last name, street address and zip codes of their parents or another adult." *Id.*

The court later explained, "[t]he affirmative defenses cannot cure COPA's failure to be narrowly tailored because they are effectively unavailable. Credit cards, debit accounts, adult access codes, and adult personal identification numbers do not in fact verify age. As a result, their use does not, in good faith, 'restrict [] access' by minors." *Id.* at 811 (second alteration in original) (quoting 47 U.S.C. § 231(c)(1)(A)).

The court also concluded that COPA's affirmative defenses "raise unique First Amendment issues" that make the statute unconstitutional. *Id.* at 813. The court found that due to the fees associated with the use of the procedures enumerated in all of the affirmative defenses and verification services, "Web sites ... which desire to provide free distribution of their information, will be prevented from doing so." *Id.* at 804. The court also found that:

> [f]or a plethora of reasons including privacy and financial concerns ... and the fact that so much Web content is available for free, many Web users already refuse to register, provide credit card information, or provide real personal information to Web sites if they have any alternative. Because requiring age verification would lead to a significant loss of users, content providers would have to either self-censor, risk prosecution, or shoulder the large financial burden of age verification.

Id. at 805. Based on these findings, the court concluded that:

> [t]he affirmative defenses also raise their own First Amendment concerns. For example, the utilization of those devices to trigger COPA's affirmative defenses

will deter listeners, many of whom will be unwilling to reveal personal and financial information in order to access content and, thus, will chill speech. Similarly, the affirmative defenses also impermissibly burden Web site operators with demonstrating that their speech is lawful. Under the COPA regime, Web site operators are unable to defend themselves until after they are prosecuted. Moreover, the affirmative defenses place substantial economic burdens on the exercise of protected speech because all of them involve significant cost and the loss of Web site visitors, especially to those plaintiffs who provide their content for free.

Id. at 812–13 (citations and quotations omitted).

The Government argues that the District Court erred in rejecting the limiting effect of COPA's affirmative defenses. It contends that "[t]he possibility that some minors may have access to credit cards merely demonstrates that no system of age verification is foolproof. It does not call into question the availability of credit card screening as an affirmative defense that tailors COPA more narrowly." Appellant's Br. at 37. The Government also argues that "the court ignored testimony that minors do *not* have access to traditional payment cards under their own control but simply have access to cards supervised by adults." Id.

But the District Court found that even if there is parental supervision of payment card use, the supervision does not prevent access to harmful material by minors because parents "may not be able to identify transactions on sexually explicit Web sites because the adult nature of such transactions is often not readily identifiable...." *Gonzales*, 478 F. Supp. 2d at 802. In any event, we conclude that the District Court correctly found that the affirmative defenses are "effectively unavailable" because they do not actually verify age.

We conclude that the District Court correctly found that implementation of COPA's affirmative defenses by a Web publisher so as to avoid prosecution would involve high costs and also would deter users from visiting implicated Web sites. It is clear that these burdens would chill protected speech and thus that the affirmative defenses fail a strict scrutiny analysis.

The Government contends that nevertheless these burdens "are no different in kind or degree from the burdens imposed by state laws regulating the sale and commercial display of 'harmful to minors' materials.... [T]he effect of the statute is simply to requir[e] the commercial pornographer to put sexually explicit images behind the counter." Appellant's Br. at 43 (citations and certain internal quotation marks omitted) (second alteration in original).

We rejected this argument in *ACLU II*. Blinder racks do not require adults to pay for speech that otherwise would be accessible for free, they do not require adults to relinquish their anonymity to access protected speech, and they do not create a potentially permanent electronic record. Blinder racks simply do not involve the privacy and security concerns that COPA's affirmative defenses raise, and so the Government's attempted analogy is ill-fitting.

In sum, after considering our previous conclusions in *ACLU II* and our analyses of the issues *ACLU II* has not resolved, we are quite certain that notwithstanding Congress's laudable purpose in enacting COPA, the Government has not met its burden of showing that it is narrowly tailored so as to survive a strict scrutiny analysis and thereby permit us to hold it to be constitutional.

3. Least Restrictive Alternative

In addition to failing the strict scrutiny test because it is not narrowly tailored, COPA does not employ the least restrictive alternative to advance the Government's compelling interest in its purpose, the third prong of the three-prong strict scrutiny test.

The District Court found that "[f]ilters are widely available and easy to obtain," and that "[f]iltering programs are fairly easy to install, configure, and use and require only minimal effort by the end user to configure and update." *Gonzales*, 478 F. Supp. 2d at 793. The court found that "[i]nstalling and setting up a filter will usually take a typical computer user no more than ten or fifteen minutes. The installation and set-up process is not technically complex and does not require any special training or knowledge." *Id.* at 794. The court then considered the evidence regarding the effectiveness of filters. It found that:

> [f]iltering products have improved over time and are now more effective than ever before. This is because, as with all software, the filtering companies have addressed problems with the earlier versions of the products in an attempt to make their products better. Another reason the effectiveness of filtering products has improved is that many products now provide multiple layers of filtering. Whereas many filters once only relied on black lists or white lists, many of today's products utilize black lists, white lists, and real-time, dynamic filtering to catch any inappropriate sites that have not previously been classified by the product. There is a high level of competition in the field of Internet content filtering. That factor, along with the development of new technologies, has also caused the products to improve over time.

Id. at 794–95 (citations omitted).

The District Court then found that:

> [o]ne of the features of filtering programs that adds to their effectiveness is that they have built-in mechanisms to prevent children from bypassing or circumventing the filters, including password protection and other devices to prevent children from uninstalling the product or changing the settings. Some products even have a tamper detection feature, by which they can detect when someone is trying to uninstall or disable the product, and then cut off Internet access altogether until it has been properly reconfigured. Filtering companies actively take steps to make sure that children are not able to come up with ways to circumvent their filters. Filtering companies monitor the Web to identify any methods for circumventing filters, and when such methods are found, the filtering companies respond by putting in extra protections in an attempt to make sure that those methods do not succeed with their products.

Id. at 795 (citations omitted). The court also found that "[i]t is difficult for children to circumvent filters because of the technical ability and expertise necessary to do so...." *Id.* Finally, the court found that "filters generally block about 95% of sexually explicit material." *Id.*

After describing filtering technology, the District Court concluded that the Government "failed to successfully defend against the plaintiffs' assertion that filter software and the Government's promotion and support thereof is a less restrictive alternative to COPA." *Id.* at 813. The court reasoned that "unlike COPA there are no fines or prison sentences associated with filters which would chill speech. Also unlike COPA, ... filters are fully customizable and may be set for different ages and for different categories of speech or may be disabled altogether for adult use. As a result, filters are less restrictive than COPA." *Id.* (citations omitted).

The District Court also concluded that the Government "failed to show that filters are not at least as effective as COPA at protecting minors from harmful material on the Web." *Id.* at 814. The court determined that COPA will not reach sexually explicit materials on the Web that originate from foreign sources, its affirmative defenses are not effective, and it is unlikely that COPA will be enforced widely.

The court concluded that "[e]ven [the government's] own study shows that all but the worst performing filters are far more effective than COPA would be at protecting children from sexually explicit material on the Web...." *Id.*

We agree with the District Court's conclusion that filters and the Government's promotion of filters are more effective than COPA.

As the District Court pointed out, filters can be used to block foreign Web sites, which COPA does not regulate.

Given the vast quantity of speech that COPA does not cover but that filters do cover, it is apparent that filters are more effective in advancing Congress's interest, as it made plain it is in COPA. Moreover, filters are more flexible than COPA because parents can tailor them to their own values and needs and to the age and maturity of their children and thus use an appropriate flexible approach differing from COPA's "one size fits all" approach. Finally, the evidence makes clear that, although not flawless, with proper use filters are highly effective in preventing minors from accessing sexually explicit material on the Web.

In addition to being more effective, it is clear that filters are less restrictive than COPA. [T]he Supreme Court [so stated in *Ashcroft II*]. Although the Supreme Court made this statement after reviewing the record from the hearing on the preliminary injunction, the evidence produced at the trial on the merits confirms the Court's initial impression. Unlike COPA, filters permit adults to determine if and when they want to use them and do not subject speakers to criminal or civil penalties.

During oral argument, the Government contended that the First Amendment does not prohibit Congress from adopting a "belt-and-suspenders" approach to addressing the compelling government interest of protecting minors from accessing harmful material on the Web, with filters acting as the "belt" and COPA as the "suspenders." But as counsel for plaintiffs correctly pointed out, under the First Amendment, if the belt works at least as effectively as the suspenders, then the Government cannot prosecute people for not wearing suspenders.

C. Vagueness and Overbreadth

2. Overbreadth

In *ACLU II* [w]e found that COPA's definition of "material harmful to minors" "impermissibly places at risk a wide spectrum of speech that is constitutionally protected" because it "calls for evaluation of 'any material' on the Web in *isolation*." 322 F.3d at 267. Thus, we explained:

> an isolated item located somewhere on a Web site that meets the 'harmful to minors' definition can subject the publisher of the site to liability under COPA, even though the entire Web page (or Web site) that provides the context for the item would be constitutionally protected for adults (and indeed, may be protected as to minors).

Id. We also found that COPA's definition of "minors" renders the statute overinclusive because it "broadens the reach of 'material that is harmful to minors' under the statute to encompass a vast array of speech that is clearly protected for adults—and indeed, may not be obscene as to older minors...." *Id.* at 268. We next found that COPA's definition of "commercial purposes" rendered the statute overbroad for the same reasons that it failed strict scrutiny. *Id.* at 269.

We also found that "COPA's application of 'community standards' exacerbates these constitutional problems in that it further widens the spectrum of protected speech that

COPA affects." *Id.* at 270. We stated that "COPA essentially requires that every Web publisher subject to the statute abide by the most restrictive and conservative state's community standards in order to avoid criminal liability." *Id.* (quoting ACLU v. Reno, 217 F.3d 162, 166 (3d Cir. 2000)). Finally, we found that there was no available narrowing construction that would make COPA constitutional. *Id.* at 270–71. These conclusions bind us here.

The Government claims that COPA is not overbroad, but it is clear that our prior decision in *ACLU II* binds us on this issue. It is apparent that COPA, like the Communications Decency Act before it, "effectively suppresses a large amount of speech that adults have a constitutional right to receive and to address to one another," Reno v. ACLU, 521 U.S. 844, 874 (1997), and thus is overbroad. For this reason, COPA violates the First Amendment.

Notes and Questions

1. Surprise? What, if anything, was a surprise in this opinion, given all that came before it? Does this outcome vindicate the majority in *Ashcroft II*? The dissent?

2. The Third Appellate Opinion Is the Charm. The United States requested that the Supreme Court review the Third Circuit's opinion. In January 2009, the Supreme Court denied certiorari, leaving the opinion excerpted above as the last word on COPA. So, at the beginning of the Obama Administration, we finally had resolution of a case that began in the middle of President Clinton's second term. What, if anything, should this decade-long litigation process tell us about the ability of courts to respond to the fast-changing world of the Internet?

3. What Now? If you were a supporter of COPA, what would you do now? Would you push for new legislation? But what, exactly, should that legislation provide? Would you instead pursue other avenues to protect children from indecent online material? What avenues would those be, and how much confidence would you have in their efficacy?

4. Libraries, Filtering, and Federal Assistance. While the federal government has lost in its efforts under COPA, it has found other ways to encourage the use of Internet filters. As *Ashcroft II* notes, in 2003 a fractured Supreme Court upheld the Children's Internet Protection Act (CIPA), 114 Stat. 2763A-335 (2000), against a facial First Amendment challenge. CIPA places conditions on the E-rate program that allows libraries to buy Internet access at a discount (see the materials on universal service in Chapter Thirteen). Specifically, CIPA provides that a library may not receive federal assistance for Internet access unless it has "a policy of Internet safety for minors that includes the operation of a technology protection measure ... that protects against access" by all persons to visual depictions that constitute "obscen[ity]" or "child pornography," and that protects against access by minors to visual depictions that are "harmful to minors." 20 U.S.C. §§ 9134(f)(1)(A)(i) and (B)(i); 47 U.S.C. §§ 254(h)(6)(B)(i) and (C)(i). Public libraries, library associations, library patrons, and Web site publishers brought a facial constitutional challenge to CIPA, and a three-judge district court held that it unconstitutionally induced libraries to violate the First Amendment. American Library Ass'n, Inc. v. United States, 201 F. Supp. 2d 401 (E.D. Pa. 2002).

The Supreme Court reversed, although no opinion commanded a majority of the Court. United States v. American Library Ass'n, Inc., 539 U.S. 194 (2003). The opinions did not focus on the Internet as a special category, nor did they purport to alter the approach to Internet indecency laid out in *Reno v. ACLU*. Rather, the analysis centered on the status of libraries. Indeed, Chief Justice Rehnquist's plurality opinion relied on its finding that libraries were not a public forum. The opinion also emphasized that libraries had the same authority over Internet access that they had over their print collections:

> A library's need to exercise judgment in making collection decisions depends on its traditional role in identifying suitable and worthwhile material; it is no less entitled to play that role when it collects material from the Internet than when it collects material from any other source. Most libraries already exclude pornography from their print collections because they deem it inappropriate for inclusion. We do not subject these decisions to heightened scrutiny; it would make little sense to treat libraries' judgments to block online pornography any differently, when these judgments are made for just the same reason.

American Library Ass'n, 539 U.S. at 208.

There was some discussion of an issue specific to the Internet — the significance of the district court's finding that the use of the filters would result in the blocking of "content that is completely innocuous for both adults and minors, and that no rational person could conclude matches the filtering companies' category definitions, such as 'pornography' or 'sex.'" *Id.* at 208–09 (quoting *American Library Ass'n*, 201 F. Supp. 2d at 449). Justice Stevens emphasized such "overblocking" in his dissent, and argued that CIPA did not clearly provide adults with a ready means of avoiding those filters. The other Justices did not dispute the existence of overblocking, but instead argued that adults could easily have sites unblocked, or filters removed, at their request, and that this allowed the statute to pass muster as against a facial challenge. Indeed, Justices Kennedy and Breyer (who concurred only in the judgment, providing the fifth and sixth votes to reverse) relied on these points. *See American Library Ass'n*, 539 U.S. at 219 (Breyer, J., concurring) (emphasizing that this was a facial challenge, and that, "As the plurality points out, the Act allows libraries to permit any adult patron access to an 'overblocked' Web site; the adult patron need only ask a librarian to unblock the specific Web site or, alternatively, ask the librarian, 'Please disable the entire filter.'"); *id.* at 215 (Kennedy, J., concurring) (noting the same points and adding that, "If some libraries do not have the capacity to unblock specific Web sites or to disable the filter or if it is shown that an adult user's election to view constitutionally protected Internet material is burdened in some other substantial way, that would be the subject for an as-applied challenge, not the facial challenge made in this case.").

5. Canning Spam. State and federal authorities have turned their attention to another sort of filtering, this time filtering not of the Internet but of the email inbox. In 2003, Congress passed the CAN-SPAM Act, Pub. L. No. 108-187, 117 Stat. 2699 (codified at 15 U.S.C. §§ 7701–7713). It requires that commercial email contain opt-out provisions — including clear and conspicuous notice that the recipient may decline to receive future emails from the sender, and a valid email address for the sender — and it prohibits emailers from sending unsolicited email to those who have opted out. CAN-SPAM also prohibits false or misleading transmission information and deceptive subject headings.

A number of anti-spam groups criticize the CAN-SPAM Act for not going far enough, and for preempting state laws that would have been more restrictive. California, for example, had passed legislation prohibiting any person or entity from initiating or advertising in an unsolicited commercial email advertisement to or from California, which effectively imposes an opt-in regime. Cal. Bus. & Prof. Code § 17,529.2. Such a regime likely would have prohibited many more communications than does the federal act, but the CAN-SPAM Act preempted it before it could take effect.

Other critics of the CAN-SPAM Act, meanwhile, allege that it goes too far — in particular that it violates First Amendment rights. Does email filtering raise different issues than Internet filtering? Can the government ban unsolicited email once a recipient has opted out, or can the government ban only (say) unsolicited commercial messages or only unsolicited messages that contain materials indecent for children? Are there technical differences between Internet browsing and email access that should have implications for the legal analysis?

Meanwhile, it is not clear that the CAN-SPAM Act is having any effect on the most aggressive spammers. Many have proved willing and able to flout the law. What is the legal and policy significance of the difficulties of enforcing any limits on spam? If the government can be only partially successful in blocking spam, and only partially successful in blocking indecency, should the legal status of each sort of blocking be the same? And what should that legal status be?

6. Do-Not-Call Lists. The previous note explores your intuitions when it comes to filtering email inboxes; do you have different intuitions when it comes to filtering telephone calls? In June 2003, the Federal Trade Commission, along with the FCC, put in place a program designed to minimize the disruption caused by unsolicited commercial telephone calls. The program has several components, the most important being the creation of a national Do Not Call Registry. The registry is in essence a list of telephone numbers that commercial telemarketers cannot legally call. A consumer can choose to put his or her number on the list and in that way opt out of unwanted commercial telephone calls. Not all types of unsolicited calls are covered; calls immune from the registry include "calls from organizations with which you have established a business relationship"; "calls for which you have given prior written consent"; "calls which are not commercial or do not include unsolicited advertisements"; and "calls by or on behalf of tax-exempt non-profit organizations." National Do Not Call Registry, available at http://www.fcc.gov/cgb/donotcall/. In part because of these exemptions, the Tenth Circuit Court of Appeals upheld the constitutionality of the Do Not Call List in the face of a First Amendment challenge. *See* Mainstream Mktg. v. FTC, 358 F.3d 1228 (10th Cir. 2004).

In addition to the registry, the FCC has promulgated other rules designed to limit telephone intrusions. Among those rules are requirements that telemarketers identify themselves to caller ID systems; requirements that telemarketers transfer 97% of all answered calls to a live sales agent within two seconds of the recipient's greeting, thereby reducing the percentage of calls where a telemarketer hangs up on an answered call or puts such a call on hold; requirements that telemarketers do not call before 8 am or after 9 pm; and requirements that anyone making a telephone solicitation identify him/herself, the name of the entity on whose behalf the call is made, and contact information for that entity. For more information on the Do Not Call registry and related reforms, see Rules and Regulations Implementing the Telephone Consumer Protection Act of 1991, Report and Order, 18 FCC Rcd. 14,014 (2003).

---

§ 16.B. Violent Programming

While there is almost no evidence supporting the proposition that exposure to indecent materials harms children,[23] there is considerable evidence linking the viewing of vio-

---

23. Indeed, as Justice Breyer notes in his dissent in *Fox v. FCC* (quoted in number 3, on page 776), researchers have found that the few studies on the effect of exposure to indecent material have shown no effect or harm to children under the age of eighteen. *See, e.g.*, Judith Becker & Robert M. Stein, Is Sexual Erotica Associated with Sexual Deviance in Adolescent Males?, 14 Int'l J.L. & Psychiatry 85

lent images to subsequent aggressive behavior.[24] Correlation is of course not causation (much of the data can be explained by the hypothesis that people with violent tendencies both watch violent television and commit violent acts); and it is admittedly difficult to define, let alone regulate, the sorts of violent images that are most likely to be associated with aggressive behavior. But given that the evidence here is stronger than it is for indecency, it is perhaps surprising that the government has consistently gone to great lengths to limit indecency, but has addressed violence only more recently, much more modestly, and with a focus on broadcasting. Until 1996 there was no legislation related to violent programming, and even that 1996 measure did not directly regulate violence.

Specifically, under §551 of the Telecommunications Act of 1996,[25] entitled "Parental Choice in Television Programming," unless distributors of video programming established "voluntary rules for rating video programming that contains sexual, violent, or other indecent material" and, further, agreed "voluntarily to broadcast signals that contain ratings of such programming," the FCC was to create an advisory committee, develop such a regime, and impose it upon broadcasters through regulation. §551(e) (codified as a note to 47 U.S.C. §303). The provision also requires that television manufacturers include in all new television sets (13-inch diagonal or greater) a feature — colloquially known as a "V-chip" — that enables viewers to block the display of programs based on their ratings. §551(c) (codified at 47 U.S.C. §303(x)). Details of this requirement, including its phase-in period, were handled by the FCC. Section 551 thus does not directly limit (much less ban) violence on television, but rather creates a mechanism for rating television programming.

Note that this mechanism is not limited to violence. Rather, it is a tool to allow viewers to block categories of programming they find objectionable. So it might be more accurate to refer to the feature as an "unwanted programming chip." But it is known as a V-chip for a reason: as the statutory language quoted above reveals, in this legislation Congress focused not only on its usual target (indecency) but also specifically on violence. So although a rating system could include many kinds of programming viewers might find objectionable, the core focus was "sexual, violent, or other indecent material." §551(e).

Once §551 was enacted, the broadcast industry, of course, was not about to permit a group picked by the FCC to rate its programs, so the industry "voluntarily" came up with a ratings system on its own. In 1996 industry groups proposed and implemented a system that rates programs by viewer age but not by content. There was no problem

---

(1991); Milton Diamond & Ayako Uchiyama, Pornography, Rape, and Sex Crimes in Japan, 22 Int'l J.L. and Psychiatry 1, 15–19 (1999); Edward Donnerstein et al., On the Regulation of Broadcast Indecency to Protect Children, 36 J. Broad. & Elec. Media 111, 115 (1992); see also Jeremy Harris Lipschultz, Conceptual Problems of Broadcast Indecency Policy and Application, 14 Comm. & L. 3 (June 1992). Note that neither the majority in Fox v. FCC, the majority in ACT III, nor the government in either case disputed this point; the courts in both cases found that such evidence was not necessary.

24. See, e.g., Paul Boxer et al., The Role of Violent Media Preference in Cumulative Developmental Risk for Violence and General Aggression, 38 J. of Youth and Adolescence 417 (2009); Brad J. Bushman & L. Rowell Huesmann, Short-term and Long-term Effects of Violent Media on Aggression in Children and Adults, 160 Archives of Pediatrics & Adolescent Medicine 348 (2006); Harry T. Edwards & Mitchell N. Berman, Regulating Violence on Television, 89 Nw. U. L. Rev. 1487, 1536–51 (1995); Thomas G. Krattenmaker & Lucas A. Powe, Jr., Regulating Broadcast Programming 120–34 (1994). But see, e.g., Christopher J. Ferguson & John Kilburn, The Public Health Risks of Media Violence: A Meta-Analytic Review, 154 J. of Pediatrics 759 (2009).

25. Pub. L. No. 104-104, 110 Stat. 56, 139–42 (1996) (codified as amended in scattered sections of 47 U.S.C.). The text appears in the Statutory Appendix to this book at section 303.

with this system technologically, but it failed politically: a number of groups complained that the age-based ratings provided too little information about why the program might be inappropriate. Members of Congress and the White House pressured the broadcast industry to "voluntarily" add information on content to its ratings system, and in 1997 the industry did just that. In 1998, the FCC adopted an order finding these modified ratings (the "TV Parental Guidelines") acceptable and mandating that television receivers include a blocking system that incorporates them. Implementation of Section 551 of the Telecommunications Act of 1996: Video Programming Ratings, Report and Order, 13 FCC Rcd. 8232 (1998). These TV Parental Guidelines apply to all television programming except for news, sports, and unedited MPAA (Motion Picture Association of America) rated movies on premium cable channels. The age-based categories are: TV-Y (appropriate for all children); TV-Y7 (designed for children age seven and older); TV-G (suitable for general audiences); TV-PG (may be unsuitable for younger children); TV-14 ("contains some material that many parents would find unsuitable for children under 14 years of age"); and TV-MA (designed for mature viewers). *Id.* ¶ 7. The following content labels are coupled with the age-based ratings as appropriate: FV (for fantasy violence); S (for sexual situations); V (for violence); L (for coarse language); and D (for suggestive dialogue).

Some broadcasters complained that the ratings would be lead to consumer boycotts of advertisers who buy spots on programs with disfavored ratings. Other broadcasters feared that the ratings system was just a first step toward banning programs that do not receive "acceptable" ratings. But all the major broadcast (and most of the cable) networks ultimately agreed to adopt the ratings in their programs.

Most cable and DBS channels put ratings on their programming in the same way that broadcasters do, and the FCC has required that cable and satellite operators include that information in their transmissions. *See* Implementation of the Satellite Home Viewer Improvement Act of 1999: Broadcast Signal Carriage Issues & Retransmission Consent Issues, Report and Order, 16 FCC Rcd. 1918 ¶ 103 (2000). Beyond that, cable operators must block any channel that a subscriber does not wish to receive. 47 U.S.C. § 560. This provision is discussed at greater length in *Playboy Entertainment Group*, above.

Notes and Questions

1. Alternate Rating Systems. The FCC required that television receivers be equipped with a blocking system that responds to the TV Parental Guidelines. Some commenters proposed to the FCC that it require television receivers to be accessible to alternative rating systems so that groups unsatisfied with the TV Parental Guidelines could devise their own ratings. The FCC rejected that proposal, based on its reading of the V-chip provision and its concern about the costs and complications (for manufacturers and consumers) of mandating such a system in every television. The FCC added that "[a]lthough we are not mandating that TV receiver manufacturers provide for alternative rating systems, we encourage manufacturers to design TV receivers to provide for additional rating systems to the extent practical." Technical Requirements to Enable Blocking of Video Programming Based on Program Ratings, Report and Order, 13 FCC Rcd. 11,248 ¶ 11 (1998). What is the point of adding that sentence? Who is the intended audience for it?

2. Market Deference. One of the arguments frequently made against additional ratings systems is that the marketplace can determine whether there is a need or demand for TV receivers that can accommodate supplemental rating systems. *See, e.g., id.* ¶ 9. Indeed, the Commission explicitly stated that, in its view, "manufacturers will be driven by the marketplace to meet any consumer demands to accommodate additional rating systems." *Id.* ¶ 11. If that argument is persuasive, why doesn't it also apply to (and therefore undercut) the rationale behind mandating a rating system and the V-chip in the first place?

3. Mandatory Rating and the First Amendment. One advantage of a statute encouraging voluntary ratings systems is that the networks that adopt such systems will have little basis for a First Amendment challenge (since the system is not imposed on them). Some have suggested adapting the indecency regulations to violent programming—i.e., restricting violence during hours that children are more likely to be watching television and allowing it at other hours. Such direct regulation would, of course, be subject to First Amendment challenge. Would the constitutional analysis be different for violent, as opposed to indecent, programs? If so, how?

4. Use of the V-chip. Creating a rating system, and requiring the embedding of a chip that can block programs based on the user's input, does not mean that the rating system will actually be used. Use depends on (a) parents' desire to use it; (b) their ability to use it; and (c) their children's inability (or lack of desire) to circumvent it or find another source for the forbidden content.[26] The evidence suggests that the usage rates of the V-chip have been less than overwhelming. As the FCC noted in a 2009 report, studies suggest that less than half of parents who purchased a television set with a V-chip were aware that they had a V-chip, and that few parents used the V-chip. Implementation of the Child Safe Viewing Act; Examination of Parental Control Technologies for Video or Audio Programming, Report, 24 FCC Rcd. 11,413 ¶¶ 15–17 (2009). The Annenberg Center conducted an in-depth study of some randomly selected households to determine whether the V-chip was being used and, if so, how. They gave televisions equipped with V-chips to 110 families, 58 of whom received detailed instructions about it (the remainder received more cursory instruction), and found that only 33 families out of the 110 ever programmed it, and only 9 used it one year later. These families reported that the ratings and the use of the V-chip were confusing, and also that they felt that they did not need the V-chip to supervise their children's viewing. Amy Jordan & Emory Woodward, Parents' Use of the V-chip to Supervise Children's Television Use, The Annenberg Public Policy Center, *available at* http://www.annenbergpublicpolicycenter.org/Downloads/Media_and_Developing_Child/Childrens_Programming/20030402_Children_and_TV_Roundtable/20030402_ParentsVchip_report.pdf.

5. FCC Action? Congressional frustration with violence on television and congressional dissatisfaction with the public's response to the V-chip led many members of Congress to push the FCC to consider regulation of televised violence. The FCC responded by issuing a notice of inquiry in 2004 and a report in 2007. The 2007 report is excerpted below.

---

26. On this last point, it bears noting that several studies have demonstrated that television parental advisory warnings for violent shows have a "forbidden fruit" appeal to children. *See, e.g.*, Brad J. Bushman & Angela D. Stack, Forbidden Fruit Versus Tainted Fruit: Effects of Warnings Labels on Attraction to Television Violence, 2 J. Experimental Psychol.: Applied 207, 208 (1996).

Violent Television Programming and Its Impact on Children
Report, 22 FCC Rcd. 7929 (2007)

I. INTRODUCTION

1. Television is an integral part of the lives of American families. An average American household has the television set turned on 8 hours and 11 minutes daily, and children watch on average between two and four hours of television every day. Depending on their age, one to two thirds of children have televisions in their bedrooms. By the time most children begin the first grade, they will have spent the equivalent of three school years in front of the television set.

2. Violent content in television programming has been a matter of private and governmental concern and discussion almost from the beginning of television broadcasting. A broad range of television programming aired today contains such content, including, for example, cartoons, dramatic series, professional sports such as boxing, news coverage, and nature programs. The public is concerned about the amount of violent television programming available to children, with many urging action to restrict such content.

3. It is within this context that the Commission received a request from thirty-nine members of the U.S. House of Representatives asking us to undertake an inquiry on television violence. In response, the Commission issued a Notice of Inquiry (NOI) in this proceeding, Violent Television Programming and its Impact on Children, 19 FCC Rcd. 14,394 (2004), seeking public input on a variety of matters tied to the issue of violent television content. The Commission has received hundreds of filings from interested parties and individuals.

4. The House members asked the Commission to solicit comment on three essential issues:

- What are the negative effects on children caused by the cumulative viewing of excessively violent programming?

- What are the constitutional limits on the government's ability to restrict the broadcast of excessively violent programming when children are likely to be a significant or substantial part of the viewing audience? In particular, could television violence regulations, including possible time channeling requirements, be narrowly tailored to the governmental interests they are intended to serve?

- Is it in the public interest for the government to adopt a definition of "excessively violent programming that is harmful to children," and could the government formulate and implement such a definition in a constitutional manner?

5. *Summary.* In the NOI, the Commission sought comment on the relationship between media violence and aggression in children. In this Report, we find that there is deep concern among many American parents and health professionals regarding harm from viewing violence in media. We also agree with the views of the Surgeon General that there is strong evidence that exposure to violence in the media can increase aggressive behavior in children, at least in the short term. In the NOI, the Commission sought comment on proposals aimed at regulating violent television content, such as a "safe harbor" period similar to the one in place for indecent broadcast content. In this Report, we recognize that violent content is a protected form of speech under the First Amendment, but note that the government interests at stake, such as protecting children from excessively violent television programming, are similar to those which have been found to justify other con-

tent-based regulations. In the NOI, the Commission asked questions concerning the adequacy of current program blocking technology and the effectiveness of the TV ratings system in helping parents control access to violent programming. In this Report, we find that although the V-chip and TV ratings system appear useful in the abstract, they are not effective at protecting children from violent content for a number of reasons. In particular, we find that the TV ratings system has certain weaknesses that prevent parents from screening out much programming that they find objectionable. In the NOI, the Commission asked how the government might define "violence" for regulatory purposes. In this Report, we recognize the difficulties associated with drafting a concise and legally sustainable definition of violence for regulatory purposes, but we suggest an approach that Congress may want to consider in crafting a definition. Finally, we note our conclusion that, given the findings in this report, action should be taken to address violent programming and suggest that Congress could implement a time-channeling solution that would more effectively protect children from violent programming and/or mandate other forms of consumer choice that would better support parents' efforts to safeguard their children from exposure to violent programming.

II. THE EFFECTS OF VIEWING VIOLENT TELEVISION PROGRAMMING ON CHILDREN

6. We agree with the views of the Surgeon General and find that, on balance, research provides strong evidence that exposure to violence in the media can increase aggressive behavior in children, at least in the short term. Over the course of several decades, considerable research has been undertaken to examine television's impact on children's learning and behavior. Three types of studies are generally described in the literature: (1) field experiments in which subjects are shown video programming and their short-term post-viewing behavior is monitored by researchers; (2) cross-sectional studies involving samples of individuals whose conduct is correlated with the amount and type of their television viewing; and (3) longitudinal studies that survey the same group of individuals at different times over many years to determine the effects of television viewing on subsequent behavior. Through these studies, scholars have attempted to establish a cause-and-effect relationship between viewing violent content and subsequent aggression in children.

7. The researchers have focused on three possible harmful effects: (1) increased anti-social behavior, including imitations of aggression or negative interactions with others, (2) increased desensitization to violence, and (3) increased fear of becoming a victim of violence. Researchers have theorized that children's viewing of violent television programming may affect later behavior in three ways: (1) through observing schemas about a hostile world, (2) through scripts for social problem solving that focus on aggression, and (3) through normative beliefs that aggression is acceptable. Alternatively, exposure to violent programming may desensitize the child's innate negative emotional response to violence, thus making aggressive acts easier to commit or tolerate. While the Commission sought evidence relating to such research, very little new information on the issue was submitted into the record of this proceeding.

8. Some studies find evidence of a cause-and-effect relationship between viewing televised violence by children and aggression or other changes in the behavior of the children on both a short-term and a longer-term basis. For example, Craig Anderson, a professor and former chair of the Psychology Department at Iowa State University who has conducted and published numerous "media harms" studies, asserts that research on violent television, films, video games, and music reveals "unequivocal evidence" that media violence increases the likelihood of aggressive and violent behavior in both immediate and long-term contexts.

9. Joanne Cantor, a professor at the University of Wisconsin–Madison, concurs and states that her research has found that children show higher levels of hostility after exposure to media violence—ranging from being in a "nasty mood" to an increased tendency to interpret a neutral comment or action as an attack.

10. The Notice of Inquiry in this proceeding referenced two recent significant efforts to summarize the state of the evidence regarding the effects of televised violence on children. A review of the scientific research, which appears as part of the Federal Trade Commission's report on Marketing Violent Entertainment to Children, summarized the research as follows:

> A majority of the investigations into the impact of media violence on children find that there is a high *correlation* between exposure to media violence and aggressive and at times violent behavior. In addition, a number of research efforts report that exposure to media violence is correlated with increased acceptance of violent behavior in others, as well as an exaggerated perception of the amount of violence in society. Regarding *causation*, however, the studies appear to be less conclusive. Most researchers and investigators agree that exposure to media violence alone does not cause a child to commit a violent act, and that it is not the sole, or even necessarily the most important, factor contributing to youth aggression, anti-social attitudes, and violence. Although a consensus among researchers exists regarding the empirical relationships, significant differences remain over the interpretation of these associations and their implications for public policy.

Federal Trade Commission, Marketing Violent Entertainment to Children (2000), Appendix A (footnotes omitted). Others agree that while studies show a correlation, a clear causal link has not been conclusively proven. More recently, researchers at Boston Children's Hospital report that violent shows might teach and encourage aggressive behavior in children, which in turn isolates them from their peers. Like the FTC Report, the study shows a correlation, but does not prove causation.

16. Others argue, however, that children are not necessarily harmed by exposure to television violence or that the research on the topic is flawed or inconclusive. The Media Coalition, a group of trade associations representing book and magazine publishers, along with movie, recording and video manufacturers and retailers, disputes that research supports the conclusion that violence in the media causes actual violence. In support of this view, they contend that the existing research is inconclusive and that there is no correlation between media violence and actual crime statistics. The Media Associations, a group consisting of advertising, broadcast, and television production entities, have examined the studies on media violence and assert that the literature does not support either the claim of a causal relationship between media violence and aggression or the proposition that exposure to violent media leads to desensitization. The Media Associations assert that research findings often are mischaracterized, and, in some cases, reach conclusions that are the opposite of what has been reported. To support their claims, the Media Associations note that Jonathan Freedman, a professor at the University of Toronto and critic of the media violence cause-and-effect theory, conducted a comprehensive review of all of the available research on this topic and concluded that "evidence does not support the hypothesis that exposure to film or television violence causes children or adults to be aggressive."

20. Given the totality of the record before us, we agree with the view of the Surgeon General that: "a diverse body of research provides strong evidence that exposure to violence in the media can increase children's aggressive behavior in the short term." Youth Vi-

olence: A Report of the Surgeon General, Appendix 4-B (2001). At the same time, we do recognize that "many questions remain regarding the short- and long-term effects of media violence, especially on violent behavior." We note that a significant number of health professionals, parents and members of the general public are concerned about television violence and its effects on children.

III. LAW AND POLICY ADDRESSING THE DISTRIBUTION OF VIOLENT TELEVISION PROGRAMMING

21. Members of Congress asked the Commission to address the government's authority, consistent with the First Amendment, to restrict the broadcast or other distribution of excessively violent programming and what measures to constrain or regulate such programming are most likely to be sustained in court. Accordingly, we discuss below regulatory alternatives for protecting children from violent television content. We begin, however, with a brief overview of the relevant constitutional framework.

22. Violent speech and depictions of violence have been found by the courts to be protected by the First Amendment. However, "each medium of expression presents special First Amendment problems," with broadcasting historically receiving "the most limited First Amendment protection." FCC v. Pacifica Found., 438 U.S. 726, 744 (1978). Thus, even when broadcast speech "lies at the heart of First Amendment protection," the government may regulate it so long as its interest in doing so is "substantial" and the restriction is "narrowly tailored" to further that interest. FCC v. League of Women Voters, 468 U.S. 364, 380–81 (1984). While a restriction on the content of protected speech will generally be upheld only if it satisfies strict scrutiny, meaning that the restriction must further a compelling government interest and be the least restrictive means to further that interest, this exacting standard does not apply to the regulation of broadcast speech.

23. In the realm of indecency, the U.S. Supreme Court has identified two principal reasons for the reduced First Amendment protection afforded to broadcasting: first, its "uniquely pervasive presence in the lives of all Americans;" and second, its accessibility to children, coupled with the government's interests in the well-being of children and in supporting parental supervision of children. *Pacifica*, 438 U.S. at 748–50. In light of these characteristics, the Court, in *Pacifica*, upheld the Commission's authority to regulate the broadcast of indecent material. Relying on *Pacifica*, the U.S. Court of Appeals for the District of Columbia Circuit later concluded in Action for Children's Television v. FCC, 58 F.3d 654 (1995) (*ACT III*) that the "channeling" of indecent content to the hours between 10:00 p.m. and 6:00 a.m. would not unduly burden First Amendment rights. It held that such regulation would promote the government's "compelling interest in supporting parental supervision of what children see and hear on the public airwaves." It also noted that it is "evident beyond the need for elaboration" that the government's "interest in safeguarding the physical and psychological well-being of a minor is compelling." In addition, in light of relevant U.S. Supreme Court precedent, the D.C. Circuit refused in *ACT III* to insist on scientific evidence that indecent content harms children, concluding that the government's interest in the well-being of minors is not "limited to protecting them from clinically measurable injury."

24. *Time Channeling*. As stated above, members of Congress asked the Commission to address possible measures to protect children from excessively violent television content. We begin by discussing time channeling restrictions that would restrict such programming to hours when children are less likely to be in the viewing audience. We note that commenters disagreed about the constitutionality of such requirements. Pappas Telecasting argued that they would be likely to pass constitutional muster because the government interests are

substantially the same as those at stake in regulating broadcast indecency. Other commenters maintain that such requirements would be unconstitutional and unworkable.

25. After carefully evaluating these comments and relevant precedent, we find that Congress could impose time channeling restrictions on excessively violent television programming in a constitutional manner. Just as the government has a compelling interest in protecting children from sexually explicit programming, a strong argument can be made, for the reasons discussed in Section II above, that the government also has a compelling interest in protecting children from violent programming and supporting parental supervision of minors' viewing of violent programming. We also believe that, if properly defined, excessively violent programming, like indecent programming, occupies a relatively low position in the hierarchy of First Amendment values because it is of "'slight social value as a step to truth.'" *Pacifica*, 438 U.S. at 746, quoting Chaplinsky v. New Hampshire, 315 U.S. 568, 572 (1942). Such programming is entitled to reduced First Amendment protection because of its pervasiveness and accessibility to children pursuant to the U.S. Supreme Court's reasoning in *Pacifica*.

26. To be sure, the government, when imposing time channeling, would have to show that such regulation is a narrowly tailored means of vindicating its interests in promoting parental supervision and protecting children. In this regard, however, we note that while the alternative measures discussed below—viewer-initiated blocking and mandatory ratings—would impose lesser burdens on protected speech, we are skeptical that they will fully serve the government's interests in promoting parental supervision and protecting the well-being of minors. In addition to these measures, as discussed below, another way of providing consumers greater control—and therefore greater ability to avoid violent programming—could be to require video channels to be offered on an "a la carte" basis. As the D.C. Circuit has noted in the context of indecency: "It is fanciful to believe that the vast majority of parents who wish to shield their children from indecent material can effectively do so without meaningful restrictions on the airing of broadcast indecency." *ACT III*, 58 F.3d at 663. To cite just some of the relevant data, 81 percent of children ages two through seven sometimes watch television without adult supervision, and 91 percent of children ages four through six have turned on the television by themselves. In addition, as discussed below, the studies and surveys conducted to date tend to show that blocking technologies and the associated TV ratings system are of limited effectiveness in supporting parental supervision of minors' viewing habits.

28. *Viewer-Initiated Blocking* and *Mandatory Ratings*. Besides time channeling, another possible means of protecting children from violent television content is to strengthen mechanisms that enable viewer-initiated blocking of such content. In 1996, Congress amended Title III of the Communications Act to require the incorporation of blocking technology into television sets. As of January 1, 2000, all television sets manufactured in the United States or shipped in interstate commerce with a picture screen of thirteen inches or larger must be equipped with a "V-chip" system that can be programmed to block violent, sexual, or other programming that parents do not wish their children to view. However, out of a total universe of 280 million sets in U.S. households, only about 119 million sets in use today, or less than half, are equipped with V-chips.

29. Based on the studies and surveys conducted to date, we believe that the evidence clearly points to one conclusion: the V-chip is of limited effectiveness in protecting children from violent television content. In order for V-chip technology to block a specific category of television programming, such as violent content, it must be activated. However, many parents do not even know if the television sets in their households incorporate this technology and, of those who do, many do not use it. In 2004, the Kaiser Family Foundation

conducted a telephone survey of 1,001 parents of children ages 2–17. The results showed: (1) only 15 percent of all parents have used the V-chip; (2) 26 percent of all parents have not bought a new television set since January 2000 (when the V-chip was first required in *all* sets); (3) 39 percent of parents have bought a new television set since January 2000, but do not think it includes a V-chip; and (4) 20 percent of parents know they have a V-chip, but have not used it. According to a 2003 study, parents' low level of V-chip use is explained in part by parents' unawareness of the device and the "multi-step and often confusing process" necessary to use it. Amy Jordan & Emory Woodward, Parents' Use of the V-chip to Supervise Children's Television Use 3, The Annenberg Public Policy Center. Only 27 percent of parents in the study group could figure out how to program the V-chip, and many parents "who might otherwise have used the V-chip were frustrated by an inability to get it to work properly." A March 2007 Zogby poll indicates, among other things, that 88 percent of respondents did not use a V-chip or cable box parental controls in the previous week, leading the Parents Television Council to call the television industry's V-chip education campaign "a failure." PTC Declares the Industry's V-chip Education Campaign a Failure, *available at* http://www.parentstv.org/PTC/news/release/2007/0315.asp.

30. In addition to mandating inclusion of V-chip technology in television sets, the Act provides cable subscribers with some ways to block unwanted programming. These provisions of the Act, however, do not benefit households receiving their television programming via over-the-air broadcasting or satellite. Further, similar to the V-chip, to take advantage of these measures a cable subscriber first must be aware of and then affirmatively request that such measures be employed. Finally, to receive these protections, a cable subscriber must take several steps and incur some costs.

32. We believe that further action to enable viewer-initiated blocking of violent television content would serve the government's interests in protecting the well-being of children and facilitating parental supervision and would be reasonably likely to be upheld as constitutional. As indicated above, however, reliance on blocking technology alone would probably not fulfill the government's interest in protecting the well-being of children. Blocking technology does not ensure that children are prevented from viewing violent programming unless it is activated, and courts have recognized the practical limits of parental supervision.

33. In addition, any successful viewer-initiated blocking regime with respect to violent programming would depend upon the adoption and successful implementation of an effective ratings system. Currently, to facilitate operation of the V-chip and other blocking mechanisms, broadcast, cable, and satellite television providers, on a voluntary basis, rate programming using the industry-devised TV ratings system guidelines and encode programs accordingly. Most television programming, except for news and sports programming, carries an age-based TV rating set by program networks and producers, and most include content-based ratings as well.

34. Studies and surveys demonstrate, however, that the voluntary TV ratings system is of limited effectiveness in protecting children from violent television content. In the 2004 Kaiser survey discussed above, 50 percent of all parents surveyed stated that they have used the TV ratings. But about 4 in 10 parents (39 percent) stated that most programs are not rated accurately, and many parents did not fully understand what the various ratings categories mean. For example, only 24 percent of parents of young children (two to six years old) could name any of the ratings that would apply to programming appropriate for children that age. Only 12 percent of parents knew that the rating FV ("fantasy violence") is related to violent content, while 8 percent thought it meant "family viewing." One in five (20 percent) parents said that they had never heard of the TV rat-

ings system, an increase from 14 percent in 2000 and 2001. A more recent survey indicates that only 8 percent of respondents could correctly identify the categories.

37. To address these issues, Congress could seek to establish a mandatory ratings system that would address the shortcomings of the current system set forth above. Such a system could be defended on the grounds that it merely requires the disclosure of truthful information about a potentially harmful product (violent television programming), thereby advancing the compelling government interests without significantly burdening First Amendment rights. It could also be defended as a necessary predicate for the operation of a successful system of viewer-initiated blocking. As stated above, however, although mandatory television ratings would impose lesser burdens on protected speech, we believe the evidence demonstrates that they would not fully serve the government's interest in the well-being of minors given the limits of parental supervision recognized by the D.C. Circuit in *ACT III*. Experience also leads us to question whether such a ratings system would ever be sufficiently accurate given the myriad of practical difficulties that would accompany any comprehensive effort to ensure the accuracy of ratings. Moreover, such a requirement may have an unintended practical consequence. There is some evidence that TV ratings may actually serve to attract certain underage viewers to programming that is violent or is otherwise labeled as not intended for a child audience.

IV. DEFINING VIOLENT OR EXCESSIVELY OR GRATUITOUSLY VIOLENT PROGRAMMING

38. Members of Congress asked the Commission to address whether it would be in the public interest to adopt a definition of "excessively violent programming harmful to children" and to consider the constitutional limitations on the government's ability to formulate and implement such a definition. While developing a definition would be challenging, we believe that Congress could do so.

39. Several considerations are relevant to the adoption of a definition, including the regulatory function of the definition. A definition used for TV ratings purposes might be based on different criteria than a definition used for identifying video programming that must not be shown or must be channeled to a later hour. For example, the definition used in a mandatory ratings regime intended to facilitate parental control might take into account a depiction's potential for harm without requiring a finding of a likelihood of harm. Ratings and blocking regulations might require multiple definitions for different kinds of violent programming to which parents might want to restrict their children's access. Another variable is what type and degree of violent content the research demonstrates, with a reasonable probability, is harmful to children.

40. In addition, any definition would have to be sufficiently clear to provide fair notice to regulated entities. NAB and other commenters principally argue that violent programming cannot be sufficiently defined to give affected parties the requisite notice to be able to predictably comply with any such regulation.

41. Judicial decisions and scholarly articles discussing violence almost invariably make this definitional point by referencing classic works of literature of undisputed merit that involve graphic violence. For example, in a case involving violent video games, Judge Posner opined that even the sponsors of the regulation would no doubt concede that restrictions would not be warranted:

> if the question were whether to forbid children to read without the presence of an adult "The Odyssey," with its graphic descriptions of Odysseus's grinding out the eye of Polyphemus with a heated, sharpened stake, killing the suitors, and hanging the treacherous maidservants; or "The Divine Comedy" with its graphic

descriptions of the tortures of the damned; or "War and Peace" with its graphic descriptions of execution by firing squad, death in childbirth, and death from war wounds.

American Amusement Machine Ass'n v. Kendrick, 244 F.3d 572, 576 (7th Cir. 2001). The UCLA Center for Communications Policy notes in its 1997 TV Violence Report:

> For centuries, violence has been an important element of storytelling, and violent themes have been found in the Bible, "The Iliad" and "The Odyssey," fairy tales, theater, literature, film and, of course, television. Descriptions of violence in the Bible have been important for teaching lessons and establishing a moral code. Lessons of the evils of jealousy and revenge are learned from the story of Cain and Abel. Early fairy tales were filled with violence and gruesomeness designed to frighten children into behaving and to teach them right from wrong.

1997 UCLA Television Violence Monitoring Report at 8.

42. Several commenters advocate adopting specific definitions. Those that do chose pre-existing definitions in the literature or selected regulatory proxies as a model. For example, Pappas Telecasting suggests that the Commission essentially adopt the definition used by the National TV Violence Study, which defined violence as "any overt depiction of a credible threat of physical force or the actual use of such force intended to physically harm an animate being or group of beings." Morality in Media (MIM) suggests enhancing the existing indecency definition by including references to violence. According to MIM, indecent speech should be defined as content that, in context, describes or depicts: "(1) sexual or excretory activities or organs or (2) outrageously offensive or outrageously disgusting violence or (3) severed or mutilated human bodies or body parts, in terms patently offensive as measured by contemporary community standards for the broadcast medium." MIM Comments at 3. MIM defines violence as: "intense, rough or injurious use of physical force or treatment either recklessly or with an apparent intent to harm."

44. We believe that developing an appropriate definition of excessively violent programming would be possible, but such language needs to be narrowly tailored and in conformance with judicial precedent. Any definition would need to be clear enough to provide fair warning of the conduct required. A definition sufficient to give notice of upcoming violent programming content to parents and potential viewers could make use of, or be a refinement of, existing voluntary rating system definitions or could make use of definitions used in the research community when studying the consequences of violent programming. For more restrictive time channeling rules, a definition based on the scientific literature discussed above, which recognizes the factors most important to determining the likely impact of violence on the child audience, could be developed. For example, such a definition might cover depictions of physical force against an animate being that, in context, are patently offensive. In determining whether such depictions are patently offensive, the Government could consider among other factors the presence of weapons, whether the violence is extensive or graphic, and whether the violence is realistic.

V. CONCLUSIONS AND RECOMMENDATIONS

45. In response to the specific questions posed, we draw the following conclusions. First, with respect to the evidence of harm to children from viewing violent television content, there is strong evidence that exposure to violence in the media can increase aggressive behavior in children, at least in the short term.

46. Second, although there are constitutional barriers to directly limiting or time channeling the distribution of violent television programming, the Supreme Court's *Pacifica*

decision and other decisions relating to restrictions on the broadcast of indecent content provide possible parallels for regulating violent television content. Third, while there are legal, evidentiary, analytical, and social science obstacles that need to be overcome in defining harmful violence, Congress likely has the ability and authority to craft a sustainable definition.

49. In sum, Congress could implement a time channeling solution, as discussed above, and/or mandate some other form of consumer choice in obtaining video programming, such as the provision by MVPDs of video channels provided on family tiers or on an a la carte basis (e.g., channel blocking and reimbursement).

Notes and Questions

1. Definitional Questions. A definition of violent programming would be crucial for any direct regulation of violence, and a court would parse that definition very closely. Do any of the definitions mentioned in the report strike you as appropriate and likely to withstand judicial scrutiny? Should the definition consider whether the violence is designed to pander, as with indecency? Whether it is gratuitous? Whether it glorifies violence? And how would that standard be applied? Consider which of the definitions would apply to cartoons that make violence seem harmless and fun, or hand-to-hand combat (would it matter whether such combat was shown on a "bona fide news interview" show?), or boxing matches. Does the difficulty of crafting a definition cast doubt on the enterprise of regulating violence, or is it par for the course (or both)?

2. The Significance of the Data on V-chip Use. This report notes what we mentioned above — that studies have found that parental use of the V-chip has been limited. What do these data on the use of the V-chip tell us? That it is not an effective alternative to regulatory limits on inappropriate television? That it has not been sufficiently publicized? (Whose fault would that be?) That in reality parents are far less interested in limiting the programs that their children watch than politicians imagine them to be? (Note that similar questions arose in United States v. Playboy Entertainment Group, Inc., 529 U.S. 803 (2000).) What do these answers suggest, in terms of the desirability and constitutionality of further regulation designed to limit unwanted programming?

3. Passing the Buck. This report does not contain any new regulations. What does it do? In a separate statement, Commissioner Jonathan Adelstein suggests that the FCC "passe[d] the buck" by failing to adopt or recommend any specific regulatory program. Should the FCC have been more specific in adopting a particular recommendation? What would you recommend?

4. "If It Bleeds, It Leads." In his separate statement, Commissioner Adelstein characterizes America as "hooked on violence" and notes that lists of "the top ten highest rated broadcast programs consistently have programs with violent content leading the pack." Can violence be eradicated from or limited in TV programming? What about news programming? Is any regulatory program aimed at limiting TV violence bound to be overbroad in its application?

5. Correlation, Causation, and Strict Scrutiny. In Brown v. Entertainment Merchants Ass'n, 131 S. Ct. 2729 (2011), the Supreme Court invalidated a California law restricting the sale or rental of violent video games to minors. The Court held that video games qualify for First Amendment protection and, because the regulation was content-based, applied strict scrutiny. California contended that studies on exposure to violence gave rise to a compelling government interest (as strict scrutiny requires), but the Court rejected that argument:

> The State's evidence is not compelling. California relies primarily on the research of Dr. Craig Anderson and a few other research psychologists whose studies purport to show a connection between exposure to violent video games and harmful effects on children. These studies have been rejected by every court to consider them, and with good reason: They do not prove that violent video games *cause* minors to *act* aggressively (which would at least be a beginning). Instead, "[n]early all of the research is based on correlation, not evidence of causation, and most of the studies suffer from significant, admitted flaws in methodology." Video Software Dealers Assn. v. Schwarzenegger, 556 F.3d 950, 964 (9th Cir. 2009). They show at best some correlation between exposure to violent entertainment and minuscule real-world effects, such as children's feeling more aggressive or making louder noises in the few minutes after playing a violent game than after playing a nonviolent game.
>
> Even taking for granted Dr. Anderson's conclusions that violent video games produce some effect on children's feelings of aggression, those effects are both small and indistinguishable from effects produced by other media. In his testimony in a similar lawsuit, Dr. Anderson admitted that the "effect sizes" of children's exposure to violent video games are "about the same" as that produced by their exposure to violence on television. App. 1263. And he admits that the *same* effects have been found when children watch cartoons starring Bugs Bunny or the Road Runner, *id.*, at 1304, or when they play video games like *Sonic the Hedgehog* that are rated "E" (appropriate for all ages), *id.*, at 1270, or even when they "vie[w] a picture of a gun," *id.*, at 1315–1316.

131 S. Ct. at 2739. This discussion focuses on violent video games, so it does not foreclose the possibility that the Court would find a compelling interest in restricting children's access to violent television programming. But the studies on the effects of video games on children generally found stronger correlations with antisocial behavior than have studies of effects of violent television on children. Indeed, many of the studies emphasize that violent video games do more harm than violent television does, as Justice Breyer noted in his summary of the studies in his dissent in *Brown v. Entertainment Merchants Ass'n*. And it is not clear how easily a researcher could design a rigorous study that would overcome the Court's objections above. This highlights the high hurdle that restrictions on violent television would face if ordinary First Amendment scrutiny applies to broadcasting and the government thus must demonstrate a compelling interest.

6. Turning the TV Off. Is the "off" option a sufficient safeguard? What about other media— the Internet, video games, or even content on cell phones? Are regulatory programs aimed at protecting children likely to be necessary in those contexts too?

Epilogue

EPILOGUE

Chapter Seventeen

Why an FCC?

Introduction

We began this book with broad considerations about regulatory policy and the FCC, and in succeeding chapters we looked more closely at specific areas of telecommunications regulation. Now that we have examined this array of FCC actions, we can return to a broader perspective, asking fundamental questions about both the FCC and the jumble of highly specialized statutes and regulations we call "telecommunications law." Specifically, as you read the excerpts that follow, ask yourself three questions: What should be the role of the FCC in the future? Will there ever come a time when the FCC should be abolished—or, indeed, might that time already be upon us? And (relatedly) will there ever come a time when we should eliminate "telecommunications law" and instead allow statutes and regulations of a more general nature to govern, and how can we identify such a time?

The first question—the appropriate role for the FCC—is a question we have seen time and again throughout this book. In virtually every chapter we have tried to weigh the potential capabilities and limitations of the FCC against those of the market. We have thought hard about the limitations of both approaches. After all, it would be foolhardy to define the agency's appropriate role by comparing the strengths of an idealized regulator with the strengths of an idealized market. Perfect regulation, like perfect competition, is difficult to find in the real world. Thus, we have attempted to focus on what we can realistically expect from any given level of FCC involvement and, similarly, what we can realistically expect from imperfect market interactions.

We start this chapter with that same balancing question, but this time with the entire agency on the line. Drawing on all the materials we have considered thus far, let us assess regulators and markets in light of their actual capabilities. How do they stack up against each other? Or, perhaps more fairly, what should be the balance between the two in determining telecommunications outcomes?

We begin with a vision for the FCC that the Commission articulated years ago.

A NEW FEDERAL COMMUNICATIONS COMMISSION FOR THE 21ST CENTURY

Report presented by FCC Chairman William Kennard to the House Subcommittee on Telecommunications, Trade, and Consumer Protection (hearing on Reauthorization of the FCC), March 17, 1999, *available at* http://transition.fcc.gov/Reports/fcc21.html

II. The 21st Century: A New Role for the FCC

A. The Transition Period

As history has shown, markets that have been highly monopolistic do not naturally become competitive. Strong incumbents still retain significant power in their traditional markets and have significant financial incentives to delay the arrival of competition. Strong and enforceable rules are needed initially so that new entrants have a chance to compete. At the same time, historical subsidy mechanisms for telecommunications services must be reformed to eliminate arbitrage opportunities by both incumbents and new entrants.

The technologies needed for the telecommunications marketplace of the future are still evolving, and developing them fully requires significant time and investment. Moreover, there is no guarantee that market forces will dictate that these new technologies will be universally deployed. The massive fixed-cost investments required in some industries will mean that new technologies initially will be targeted primarily at businesses and higher-income households. Even as deployment expands, the economics of these new networks may favor heavy users over lighter users, and in some areas of the country deployment may lag behind.

At the same time, consumer preferences will not change overnight. The expansion of communications choices is already leading to greater consumer confusion. Especially in a world of robust competition, consumers will need clear and accurate information about their choices, guarantees of basic privacy, and swift action if any company cheats rather than competes for their business.

In sum, although the long-term future of the telecommunications marketplace looks bright, the length and difficulty of the transition to that future is far from certain. To achieve the goal of fully competitive communications markets in five years, we must continue to work to ensure that all consumers have a choice of local telephone carriers and broadband service providers, and that companies are effectively deterred from unscrupulous behavior. We must also continue to promote competition between different media, promote the transition to digital technology, and continue to ensure that all Americans have a wide and robust variety of entertainment and information sources.

B. The FCC's Role During the Transition to Competition

During the transition to fully competitive communications markets, the FCC, working in conjunction with the states, Congress, other federal agencies, industry, and consumer groups, has six critical goals, all derived from the Communications Act and other applicable statutes:

<u>Promote Competition</u>: Goal number one is to promote competition throughout the communications industry, particularly in the area of local telephony. The benefits of competition are well documented in many communications sectors—long distance, wireless, customer-premises equipment, and information services. The benefits of local telephone competition are accruing at this time to large and small companies, but not, for the most part, to residential consumers. We must work to ensure that all communications markets are open, so that all consumers can enjoy the benefits of competition.

To meet this goal, we must continue our efforts to clarify the provisions of the Telecom Act relating to interconnection and unbundled network elements, work with the Bell Operating Companies (BOCs), their competitors, states and consumer groups on meeting the requirements of the statute related to BOC entry into the long distance market, reform access charges, and, as required by Sections 214 and 310(d) of the Communications Act and section 7 of the Clayton Act, continue to review mergers of telecommunications companies that raise significant public interest issues related to competition and consumers.

In the mass media area, we must continue the pro-competitive deployment of new technologies, such as digital television and direct broadcast satellites, and the maintenance of robust competition in the marketplace of ideas. To meet these goals, we must continue rapid deployment of new technologies and services and regular oversight of the structure of local markets to ensure multiple voices, all the while updating our rules to keep pace with the ever-changing mass media marketplace.

Deregulate: Our second goal is to deregulate as competition develops. Consumers ultimately pay the cost of unnecessary regulation, and we are committed to aggressively eliminating unnecessarily regulatory burdens or delays. We want to eliminate reporting and accounting requirements that no longer are necessary to serve the public interest. Also, where competition is thriving, we intend to increase flexibility in the pricing of access services. We have already deregulated the domestic, long distance market as a result of increased competition, and we stand ready to do so for other communications markets as competition develops. We have also streamlined our rules and privatized some of the functions involved in the certification of telephones and other equipment. We are currently streamlining and automating our processes to issue licenses faster, resolve complaints quicker, and be more responsive to competitors and consumers in the marketplace.

Protect Consumers: Our third goal is to empower consumers with the information they need to make wise choices in a robust and competitive marketplace, and to protect them from unscrupulous competitors. Consumer bills must be truthful, clear, and understandable. We will have "zero tolerance" for perpetrators of consumer fraud. Further, we will remain vigilant in protecting consumer privacy. We will also continue to carry out our statutory mandates aimed at protecting the welfare of children, such as the laws governing obscene and indecent programming.

Bring Communications Services and Technology to Every American: Our fourth goal is to ensure that all Americans—no matter where they live, what they look like, what their age, or what special needs they have—should have access to new technologies created by the communications revolution. Toward this end, we must complete universal service reform to ensure that communications services in high-cost areas of the nation are both available and affordable. We must also ensure that our support mechanisms and other tools to achieve universal service are compatible and consistent with competition. We must evaluate—and if necessary, improve—our support mechanisms for low income consumers, and in particular Native Americans, whose telephone penetration rates are some of the lowest in the country. We must make certain that the support mechanisms for schools, libraries, and rural health care providers operate efficiently and effectively. We must make sure that the 54 million Americans with disabilities have access to communications networks, new technologies and services, and news and entertainment programming.

Foster Innovation: Our fifth goal is to foster innovation. We will promote the development and deployment of high-speed Internet connections to all Americans. That means clearing regulatory hurdles so that innovation—and new markets—can flourish. We must continue to promote the compatibility of digital video technologies with existing equipment and services. Further, we will continue to encourage the more efficient use of the radio spectrum so that new and expanding uses can be accommodated within this limited resource. More generally, we will continue to promote competitive alternatives in all communications markets.

Advance Competitive Goals Worldwide: Our sixth goal is to advance global competition in communications markets. The pro-competitive regulatory framework Congress set forth in the Telecom Act is being emulated around the world through the World Trade Organization Agreement. We will continue to assist other nations in establishing conditions for deregulation, competition, and increased private investment in their communications infrastructure so that they can share in the promise of the Information Age and become our trading partners. We must continue to intensify competition at home and create growth opportunities for U.S. companies abroad. We will continue to promote fair spectrum use by all countries.

C. *The FCC's Core Functions in a Competitive Environment*

As we accomplish our transition goals, we set the stage for a competitive environment in which communications markets look and function like other competitive industries. At that point, the FCC must refocus our efforts on those functions that are appropriate for an age of competition and convergence. In particular, we must refocus our efforts from managing monopolies to addressing issues that will not be solved by normal market forces. In a competitive environment, the FCC's core functions would focus on:

Universal Service, Consumer Protection and Information. The FCC will continue to have a critical responsibility, as dictated by our governing statutes, to support and promote universal service and other public interest policies. The shared aspirations and values of the American people are not entirely met by market forces. Equal access to opportunity as well as to the public sphere are quintessential American values upon which the communications sector will have an increasingly large impact. We will be expected to continue to monitor the competitive landscape on behalf of the public interest and implement important policies such as universal service in ways compatible with competition.

In addition, as communications markets become more competitive and take on attributes of other competitive markets, the need for increased information to consumers and strong consumer protection will increase. We must work to ensure that Americans are provided with clear information so that they can make sense of new technologies and services and choose the ones best for them. We must also continue to monitor the marketplace for illegal or questionable market practices.

Enforcement and Promotion of Pro-Competition Communications Goals Domestically and Worldwide. As markets become more competitive, the focus of industry regulation will shift from protecting buyers of monopoly services to resolving disputes among competitors, whether over interconnection terms and conditions, program access, equipment compatibility, or technical interference. In the fast-paced world of competition, we must be able to respond swiftly and effectively to such disputes to ensure that companies do not take advantage of other companies or consumers.

The FCC is a model for other countries of a transparent and independent government body establishing and enforcing fair, pro-competitive rules. This model is critical for continuing to foster fair competition domestically as well as to open markets in other countries, to the benefit of U.S. consumers and firms and consumers and firms worldwide. There always will be government-to-government relations and the need to coordinate among nations as communications systems become increasingly global. As other nations continue to move from government-owned monopolies to competitive, privately-owned communications firms, they will increasingly look to the FCC's experience for guidance.

Spectrum Management. The need for setting ground rules for how people use the radio spectrum will not disappear. We need to make sure adequate spectrum exists to accommodate the rapid growth in existing services as well as new applications of this national and international resource. Even with new technologies such as software-defined radios and ultra-wideband microwave transmission, concerns about interference will continue (and perhaps grow) and the need for defining licensees and other users' rights will continue to be a critical function of the government. We will thus continue to conduct auctions of available spectrum to speed introduction of new services. In order to protect the safety of life and property, we must also continue to consider public safety needs as new spectrum-consuming technologies and techniques are deployed.

Notes and Questions

1. Transitions. The FCC says that the time (1999) is one of transition, and it refers to "the goal of fully competitive communications markets in five years." It seems safe to say that no one thinks that the transition period actually ended in 2004. Whose fault is that?

How will we be able to determine when the transition envisioned by this report is complete? And what exactly will the post-transition, fully competitive period look like? What role does the FCC envision for itself in that post-transition period? Are you persuaded that it will have the role it envisions? That it should?

2. Market Imperfections. The FCC says that "[t]he shared aspirations and values of the American people are not entirely met by market forces." It may be that market forces do not meet these aspirations, but the question is whether FCC involvement improves matters. As to that comparative issue, what does the FCC tell us?

3. And FCC Imperfections, Too. Is the FCC "a model for other countries of a transparent and independent government body establishing and enforcing fair, pro-competitive rules"? Or is that an ideal that it rarely meets? If the latter, what does that indicate about the advisability of letting the FCC play the role that it defines for itself in this report? The next two excerpts take up this issue—and take on the FCC.

ABOLISH THE FCC AND LET COMMON LAW RULE THE TELECOSM

Peter Huber, LAW AND DISORDER IN CYBERSPACE 3–9 (1997)

Until 1996 the telecosm was governed by laws written half a century ago. The rules for the telephone industry dated back to 1887. They had been written at a time when land, air, water, and energy all seemed abundant, while the telecosm seemed small and crowded, a place of scarcity, cartel, and monopoly, one that required strict rationing and tight, central control.

In the last decade, however, glass and silicon have amplified beyond all prior recognition our power to communicate. Engineers double the capacity of the wires and the radios about every two years, again and again and again. New technology has replaced scarcity with abundance and cartels with competition.

The electronic web of connection that is now being woven amongst us all is a catalyst for change more powerful than Gutenberg's press or Goebbels's radio. Every constraint of the old order is crumbling. The limitless, anarchic possibilities of the telecosm contrast sharply with the limits to growth we now encounter at every turn in the physical world.

In early 1996 Congress passed the most important piece of economic legislation of the twentieth century. The Telecommunications Act of 1996 runs some one hundred pages. The Act's ostensible purpose is to open markets to competition and deregulate them. It may eventually have that effect. The process of deregulating, however, seems to require more regulation than ever. The FCC no longer aspires to immortality through its work. Like Woody Allen, it aspires to immortality through not dying.

It is time for fundamental change. It is time for the Federal Communications Commission to go.

The Future and the Past

The telecosm—the universe of communications and computers—is expanding faster than any other technocosm has ever expanded before. It is the telephone unleashed, the personal computer connected, and the television brought down to human scale at last. Its capacity to carry information has expanded a millionfold in the last decade or two. It will expand another millionfold in our lifetime—or perhaps a billionfold. No one really knows. The only certainty is that the change will be enormous.

This change is characterized by a paradox: It is both fragmentation and convergence.

The old integrated, centralized media are being broken apart. Terminals—dumb endpoints to the network—are giving way to "seminals"—nodes of equal rank that can process, switch, store, and retrieve information with a power that was once lodged exclusively in the massive switches and mainframe computers housed in fortified basements. This is the fragmentation.

At the same time the functions of these nodes are coming together. In digital systems a bit is a bit, whether it represents a hiccup in a voice conversation, a digit in a stock quote, or a pixel of light in a rerun of "I Love Lucy." This is the convergence.

Then there is the law. Until 1996 most of telephony was viewed as a "natural monopoly." The high cost of fixed plant, the steadily declining average cost of service, and the need for all customers to interconnect with one another made monopoly seem inevitable. The broadcast industry was viewed as a natural oligopoly. It depended on inherently "scarce" airwaves, and was therefore populated by a small, government-appointed elite.

The FCC and comparable state-level commissions were established in the 1920s and 1930s to ration the scarcity and police the monopoly. The administrative structures, their statutory mandates, and the whole logic of commission control reflected the political attitudes of the New Deal. Markets didn't work; government did. Competition was wasteful; central planning was efficient. A fateful choice was made: Marketplace and common law were rejected. Central planning and the commission were embraced.

The common law evolves from the bottom up. Private action comes first. Rules follow, when private conflicts arise and are brought to court. Commission law was to be top-down. A government corps of managers, lawyers, economists, and technicians would settle in at the FCC first. Private action would follow later, when authorized. Common law is created by the accretion of small rulings in discrete, crystallized controversies. Commission law would be published in elaborate statutes and ten-thousand-page rule books; while these were being written, the world would wait. Common law centers on contract and property, legal concepts that are themselves creations of the common law. Commission law would center on public edicts, licenses, and permits. Common law is developed and enforced largely by private litigants. Commission law would come to court only at the end of the process, when public prosecutors filed suits against private miscreants.

Common law would have suited the American ethic of governance far better, particularly in matters so directly related to free speech. But between 1927 and 1934, when the FCC was erected, the winds of history were blowing in the opposite direction. National socialism, right-wing or left, seemed more efficient, the only workable approach to modern industrialism. Around the globe, people in power persuaded themselves that the technical complexities of broadcasting, and the natural-monopoly economics of telephony, had to be managed through centralized control. The night of totalitarian government, always said to be descending on America, came to earth only in Europe. But America was darkened by some of the same shadows. One was the FCC.

Once in place, the FCC grew and grew. Today it has 2,200 full-time employees and a $200 million budget—more offices, more employees, and more money than at any other time in its history. As competition increases, monopolies fade, and the supposed scarcity of spectrum is engineered into vast abundance, the Commission just gets bigger. An institution created to ration scarcity now thrives by brokering plenty. It is an "Alice-in-Wonderland" sort of world, in which the less reason the Queen has to exist at all, the more corpulent and powerful she becomes.

For the next several years at least, the FCC will have the most important mission in Washington. Wireline and wireless telephony, broadcasting, cable, and significant aspects of network computing together generate some $200 billion in revenues a year. For better or worse, the FCC will profoundly influence how they all develop. And in so doing it will exert a pivotal influence over the entire infrastructure of the information age and thus the economy, culture, and society of the twenty-first century.

The faster that power is dissipated, the better it will be for America.

Deconstructing the Telecosm

The beginning of the end was cable television. Cable demonstrated that spectrum could be bottled, and made abundant. Cable refused to be merely "broadcaster" or merely "carrier." It threatened all the old regulatory paradigms. It was just too capacious and flexible for regulators, even with the relatively primitive technology it used at that time. Now cable is moving into telephony. Meanwhile, by boosting the capacities of their wires, phone companies are poised to move into video. They already carry most of the Internet traffic, which is television in slow motion.

Wireless services are changing even faster. Once dedicated largely to feeding the idiot box, wireless is now the flourishing center of cellular telephony, direct broadcast satellite, wireless cable, and personal communications services. Spectrum is gradually being privatized and dezoned. The new owners are using their wireless bandwidth to provide whatever services they like, to whichever customers they choose.

The fundamentals of deregulation are now clear. The concepts are simple. They can be implemented quickly.

First, throw open the markets. For wireless, this means privatizing the critical asset—spectrum—by giving it away or (better still) selling it. For wires, it means letting anyone deploy new metal and glass alongside the old. Contrary to what Congress assumed for half a century, no commission is needed to protect against "wasteful duplication," "ruinous competition," or "inefficient deployment of resources." Markets take care of that.

Second, dezone the bandwidth. On wire or wireless, a bit is a bit. No government office should zone some bandwidth for pictures, some for voice, some for data. The market can work this out far better than any central planner.

Won't new robber barons then buy up all the wires, corner the spectrum, jack up prices, ruin service, and impoverish consumers? With the entire industry in ferment, with engineers doubling the capacity of every medium every few years, and with the telecosm expanding at big-bang rates, these fears are utterly implausible. But in any event, the traditional antitrust laws will remain in place. For all practical purposes, antitrust law is common law. It addresses specific problems in courts, not commissions. It is decentralized, adaptable, and resilient. Sclerotic commissions just get in the way. Indeed, for decades the FCC has legitimized telecom practices that antitrust courts would never have tolerated in its absence.

Ironically, the Commission can justify much of its current frenetic activity by blaming its predecessors. If the airwaves hadn't been nationalized in 1927, they wouldn't have to be sold off today. If the FCC hadn't spent half a century protecting telephone monopolies, it wouldn't have to dismantle them now. If the Commission hadn't spent so long separating carriage from broadcast, broadcast from cable, and cable from carriage, it wouldn't have to be desegregating those media today. If it hadn't worked so diligently to outlaw competitive entry back then, it wouldn't have to labor so hard to promote it now.

I-broke-it-then-so-I'll-fix-it-now has a certain logic to it, even if the confession of past breaking is always much less emphatic than the promise of future fix. But the fixing somehow always seems to take as long, or longer, than the breaking. And while the Commission plans and plans for perfect competition, competition itself waits uselessly in the wings.

The telecosm would be vastly more competitive today if Congress had just stayed out of session in 1927, in 1934, in 1984, and again in 1992—if Congress had never created the Federal Radio Commission, never folded it into the FCC, never extended the Commission's jurisdiction to cable, and never expanded the Commission's powers over cable further still. The 1996 legislation guarantees that the Commission will grow in size and influence for the rest of this decade while it uproots the anticompetitive vineyard planted and cultivated by its predecessors.

But the uprooting should be done quickly. Five years is time enough; ten would be too long. And then? Then the Commission should shut its doors, once and for all, and never darken American liberty again.

Common Law for the Telecosm

Who, then, will maintain order in all these areas when the Commission is gone? Private actors and private litigants, common-law courts, and the market. It is the Commission that must go, not the rule of law.

We still need laws to defend the property rights of people who lay wires and build transmitters, to enforce contracts and carriage agreements, to defend the freedom to speak and to listen, and to protect copyright and privacy. Anarchy works no better in virtuality than in actuality. The question is not whether there will be rules of law, but where they will come from.

Commissions proclaim the "public interest, convenience, and necessity." They issue general edicts. They publish rules in a massive Code of Federal Regulations. Common law, by contrast, evolves out of rulings handed down by many different judges in many different courtrooms. The good rules gain acceptance by the community at large, as people conform their conduct to rulings that make practical sense. In this kind of jurisprudence, constitutions and codes provide, at most, a broad, general mandate to develop the law by adjudication. They operate like the Bill of Rights or the Sherman Act.

Commission law has been tried. Not just in the telecosm but in command-and-control economies around the globe. Like Communism, commission law has failed. It is rigid, slow, and—despite all the earnest expertise of bureaucrats—ignorant. Market forces, mediated by common law, elicit information faster and more reliably. Markets constantly probe new technology, try out new forms of supply, and assess demand with a determination, precision, and persistence that no commission can ever match. Property-centered, contract-centered, common-law markets allow people to get on with life first and litigate later, if they have to. Most of the time they don't. Rules evolve spontaneously in the marketplace and are mostly accepted by common consent. Common-law courts just keep things tidy at the edges.

The one strength of commission law is that it reduces uncertainty all around. But only because the market must wait for the commission to invent a whole framework of law up front. That often takes years, and the framework is always rigid and inadequate. In a universe where technology transforms itself every few months, where supply and demand grow apace, where new trillion-dollar economies can emerge from thin air in a decade or so—in such a universe, uncertainty is a sign of health and vigor. In a place like that, nothing except common law can keep up. The law must build itself the old-fashioned way, through action in the market first and reaction in the courts thereafter.

If that suggestion seems outlandish, it is only because the FCC has been around so long that people can no longer imagine life without it. Once Henry the Eighth's licensing of printing presses had become routine, it would have seemed equally outlandish to suggest that such an unfamiliar, complicated, and important technology might be left to open markets and common-law courts. When it was created in 1887, the Interstate Commerce Commission seemed essential to proper management of railroads. But when it was abolished in early 1996, hardly anyone even noticed. We never did create a Federal Computer Commission. The computer industry has nonetheless developed interconnection rules and open systems, set reasonable prices, and delivered more hardware and more service to more people faster than any other industry in history.

Now, in the 1990s, with the telecosm growing explosively all around us, with the cacophony of free markets already drowning out the reedy proclamations of a senescent Commission, the only outlandish proposal is that we should keep it.

It is time to finish the job. The Commission must go.

Notes and Questions

1. Huber or the FCC? Relative to the FCC, does Huber have greater faith in markets, less faith in the Commission, or both? Consider the materials we have covered in this book. As between the FCC and Huber, whose faith is more justified?

2. A Difference of Timing? Are Huber's proposals consistent with the FCC's vision for itself once the transition period is over? Put differently, is the difference between the FCC's position and Huber's position that one sees telecommunications as in the middle of a transition and the other sees that transition as complete?

3. The Commission's Record. In evaluating the choice between common law courts and a federal telecommunications agency, is the Commission's historical record relevant? One could, after all, ignore the history of the FCC and focus instead on the realistic ability of the FCC, or some new replacement agency, to perform in desirable ways. Would that approach make more sense? Does one's choice here change the ultimate answer about the extent to which regulation by a federal telecommunications agency is desirable?

4. Common Law Courts. Does Huber overestimate the ability of common law courts to keep order in the telecommunications realm? What about the need to coordinate activities in different states, or among different kinds of technologies? Does Huber reject these as unworthy goals, or does he believe that they are worthy but that common law courts can handle them? Consider in this regard the following statement from the conclusion of Huber's book: "Nothing grander than common law is even practical anymore. The telecosm is too large, too heterogeneous, too turbulent, too creatively chaotic to be governed wholesale, from the top down." *Id.* at 206. Is he right, or is a "top down" approach necessary in the interconnected world of telecommunications? Are there ways to implement a common law approach that allow for coordination across state lines and among different technologies and activities? Would that be less bureaucratic than regulation by the FCC? Would it be preferable?

5. Abolish Other Administrative Agencies? Do you think Huber would also be in favor of abolishing other administrative agencies and shifting their duties to common law courts? Is that because common law courts have done such a good job in other areas, like tort law, where they dominate?

6. And Abolish Telecommunications Law, Too. Huber is not merely suggesting that the FCC should be abolished. He is also challenging the notion that there should be laws specifically aimed at telecommunications. He wants to replace the regime of telecommunications law with generally applicable laws that would be adapted as needed by common law courts. Many of these would involve traditional common law causes of action like contract and property claims. Notably, he also wants to rely on antitrust law (which, he argues, is for all practical purposes common law). This takes us back to the many regulations we have seen that are aimed at telecommunications firms with market power. Huber would do away with all these regulations and revert to generic antitrust enforcement. To put the question from his perspective: Given that we rely on antitrust to address market power in almost every other industry, why can't we rely on it in the telecommunications context as well? What makes telecommunications so special that ordinary antitrust principles would not suffice?

It's Time to Demolish the FCC

Lawrence Lessig, Newsweek, December 22, 2008 (updated March 13, 2010),
available at http://www.newsweek.com/lessig-its-time-demolish-fcc-83409

Economic growth requires innovation. Trouble is, Washington is practically designed to resist it. Built into the DNA of the most important agencies created to protect innovation, is an almost irresistible urge to protect the most powerful instead.

The FCC is a perfect example. Born in the 1930s, at a time when the utmost importance was put on stability, the agency has become the focal point for almost every important innovation in technology. It is the presumptive protector of the Internet, and the continued regulator of radio, TV and satellite communications. In the next decades, it could well become the default regulator for every new communications technology, including, and especially, fantastic new ways to use wireless technologies, which today carry television, radio, Internet, and cellular phone signals through the air, and which may soon provide high-speed Internet access on-the-go, something that Google cofounder Larry Page calls "Wi-Fi on steroids."

If history is our guide, these new technologies are at risk, and with them, everything they make possible. With so much in its reach, the FCC has become the target of enormous campaigns for influence. Its commissioners are meant to be "expert" and "independent," but they've never really been expert, and are now openly embracing the political role they play. Commissioners issue press releases touting their own personal policies. And lobbyists spend years getting close to members of this junior varsity Congress. Think about the storm around former FCC Chairman Michael Powell's decision to relax media ownership rules, giving a green light to the concentration of newspapers and television stations into fewer and fewer hands. This is policy by committee, influenced by money and power, and with no one, not even the President, responsible for its failures.

The solution here is not tinkering. You can't fix DNA. You have to bury it. President Obama should get Congress to shut down the FCC and similar vestigial regulators, which put stability and special interests above the public good. In their place, Congress should create something we could call the Innovation Environment Protection Agency (iEPA), charged with a simple founding mission: "minimal intervention to maximize innovation." The iEPA's core purpose would be to protect innovation from its two historical enemies—excessive government favors, and excessive private monopoly power.

Since the birth of the Republic, the U.S. government has been in the business of handing out "exclusive rights" (a.k.a., monopolies) in order to "promote progress" or enable new markets of communication. Patents and copyrights accomplish the first goal; giving away slices of the airwaves serves the second. No one doubts that these monopolies are sometimes necessary to stimulate innovation. Hollywood could not survive without a copyright system; privately funded drug development won't happen without patents. But if history has taught us anything, it is that special interests—the Disneys and Pfizers of the world—have become very good at clambering for more and more monopoly rights. Copyrights last almost a century now, and patents regulate "anything under the sun that is made by man," as the Supreme Court has put it. This is the story of endless bloat, with each round of new monopolies met with a gluttonous demand for more.

The problem is that the government has never given a thought to when these monopolies help, and when they're merely handouts to companies with high-powered lobbyists. The iEPA's first task would thus be to reverse the unrestrained growth of these monopolies. For example, much of the wireless spectrum has been auctioned off to telecom monopolies, on the assumption that only by granting a monopoly could companies be encouraged to undertake the expensive task of building a network of cell towers or broadcasting stations. The iEPA would test this assumption, and essentially ask the question: do these monopolies do more harm than good? With a strong agency head, and a staff absolutely barred from industry ties, the iEPA could avoid the culture of favoritism that's come to define the FCC. And if it became credible in its monopoly-checking role, the agency could eventually apply this expertise to the area of patents and copyrights, guiding Congress's policymaking in these special-interest hornet nests.

The iEPA's second task should be to assure that the nation's basic communications infrastructure spectrum—the wires, cables and cellular towers that serve as the highways of the information economy—remain open to new innovation, no matter who owns them. For example, "network neutrality" rules, when done right, aim simply to keep companies like Comcast and Verizon from skewing the rules in favor of or against certain types of content and services that run over their networks. The investors behind the next Skype or Amazon need to be sure that their hard work won't be thwarted by an arbitrary decision on the part of one of the gatekeepers of the Net. Such regulation need not, in my view, go as far as some Democrats have demanded. It need not put extreme limits on what the Verizons of the world can do with their network—they did, after all, build it in the first place—but no doubt a minimal set of rules is necessary to make sure that the Net continues to be a crucial platform for economic growth.

Beyond these two tasks, what's most needed from the iEPA is benign neglect. Certainly, it should keep competition information flowing smoothly and limit destructive regulation at the state level, and it might encourage the government to spend more on public communications infrastructure, for example in the rural areas which private companies often ignore. But beyond these limited tasks, whole phone-books worth of regulation could simply be erased. And with it, we would remove many of the levers that lobbyists use to win favors to protect today's monopolists.

America's economic future depends upon restarting an engine of innovation and technological growth. A first step is to remove the government from the mix as much as possible. This is the biggest problem with communication innovation around the world, as too many nations who should know better continue to preference legacy communication monopolies. It is a growing problem in our own country as well, as corporate America has come to believe that investments in influencing Washington pay more than investments in building a better mousetrap. That will only change when regulation is crafted as narrowly as possible. Only then can regulators serve the public good, instead of private protection. We need to kill a philosophy of regulation born with the 20th century, if we're to make possible a world of innovation in the 21st.

Notes and Questions

1. Public Choice Theory from Left and Right. As Lessig puts it, "if history has taught us anything, it is that special interests—the Disneys and Pfizers of the world—have become very good at clambering for more and more monopoly rights." The case of copyright term extension is one that Lessig has highlighted elsewhere as an example of public choice pressures. What is notable about Lessig's invocation of public choice theory is that it underscores the coalescence of liberal and conservative thinking about the use of government power to protect private interests against the public interest. This coalescence of thought was one of the spurs for a number of important deregulatory efforts in the 1970s and 1980s.

2. Leadership and Culture. Lessig does not recommend reliance on common law courts. Rather, his view is that abolishing the FCC and reconstituting a different body—an iEPA—can ensure that the new agency operates differently than its predecessor. Do you agree? What constitutive choices can be made in structuring a new agency that can influence its effectiveness?

3. Alternatives. Note that reductions in FCC authority less radical than complete abolition are possible. We could limit the FCC to a few functions that we are confident it will do better than either another regulator (e.g., common law courts or the Department of Justice) or the market. What would those functions be?

(a) One candidate would be coordinating spectrum assignment and mediating interference claims. Because spectrum does not respect state boundaries, and because of the complexities of potential interference problems, we might prefer that a regulator with expertise, continuity, and a national purview manage the use of the spectrum. Even if we do not want the government owning or controlling the spectrum, we might want the FCC to play the role of policeman and protect private owners' rights to it.

(b) Relatedly, we might want to have a federal entity with the power to negotiate on behalf of the United States with other countries—regarding, for example, which frequencies, and which orbital slots, each country will use.

(c) A third obvious candidate would be a federal entity (or a series of state entities) that would play some role in ensuring that local exchange carriers with entrenched monopoly power provide reasonably priced, technologically sophisticated, and nondiscriminatory access to other providers of allied or competing telecommunications services. These interconnection issues have loomed large in the history of telephony, and many might fear that incumbent LECs would discriminate against other providers unless a regulatory entity watched them carefully.

Option (c) does not suggest that there is anything special about telecommunications, as it is really just an application of traditional antitrust principles to the regulation of telecommunications. Thus, it is not necessarily inconsistent with Huber's approach, and in any event could be accomplished by ordinary antitrust enforcement (which is usually undertaken by the Department of Justice or the Federal Trade Commission). By contrast, options (a) and (b) do rely on special properties of the spectrum—that it both crosses boundaries and is subject to fairly subtle and complex forms of interference. But if we stopped at the spectrum management suggested in the first two options, we would radically reduce the role of telecommunications law and the FCC.

Are there other important functions for which we need laws aimed specifically at telecommunications? Think, for example, about universal service. The Huber excerpt and the three proposals listed above do not provide for a system whereby some users subsidize others. But recall our discussion in Chapter Thirteen about the relative desirability of a program to provide cheap telephone service as compared to a program to provide, say, cheap clothing. The question is whether something about telecommunications justifies subsidizing it specifically, rather than subsidizing other purchases or, more simply, providing the same amount of money in cash to be used for whatever the recipient thinks is needed.

The discussion above also leaves out perhaps the most obvious special feature of telecommunications—the "communications" part. Telecommunications systems are an important means of transmitting ideas and values. This raises a host of policy questions about the significance we might attribute to that power. It also raises (as many of the materials in this book demonstrate) complicated First Amendment issues. And, importantly, conflicting values as well as conflicting visions of the First Amendment may lead different people to draw different conclusions from the communicative power of various media.

The inquiry does not end, of course, with the assertion that telecommunications has certain unique attributes or communicative power. We must still consider what regulatory response is appropriate to those attributes and that power. If, for example, we reject the contention of former FCC chairman Mark Fowler that a television is merely "a toaster with pictures"[1] and instead assert that a television is unlike other appliances in important ways, we still must identify those distinguishing features and then craft the regulatory scheme that most appropriately takes them into account.

---

1. Caroline E. Mayer, FCC Chief's Fears: Fowler Sees Threat in Regulation, Wash. Post, Feb. 6, 1983, at K1.

Statutory Appendix

COMMUNICATIONS ACT OF 1934, AS AMENDED
47 U.S.C. §§ 151 et seq.
[Edited for Clarity]

TITLE I — GENERAL PROVISIONS

SEC. 1. [47 U.S.C. § 151]
PURPOSES OF CHAPTER

For the purpose of regulating interstate and foreign commerce in communication by wire and radio so as to make available, so far as possible, to all the people of the United States, without discrimination on the basis of race, color, religion, national origin, or sex, a rapid, efficient, Nation-wide, and world-wide wire and radio communication service with adequate facilities at reasonable charges, for the purpose of the national defense, for the purpose of promoting safety of life and property through the use of wire and radio communications, and for the purpose of securing a more effective execution of this policy by centralizing authority heretofore granted by law to several agencies and by granting additional authority with respect to interstate and foreign commerce in wire and radio communication, there is created commission to be known as the "Federal Communications Commission," which shall be constituted as hereinafter provided, and which shall execute and enforce the provisions of this chapter.

SEC. 2. [47 U.S.C. § 152]
APPLICATION OF CHAPTER

(a) The provisions of this Act shall apply to all interstate and foreign communication by wire or radio and all interstate and foreign transmission of energy by radio, which originates and/or is received within the United States, ... and to the licensing and regulating of all radio stations.... The provisions of this Act shall apply with respect to cable service.

(b) Except as provided in sections 223 through 227 of this title, inclusive, and section 332 of this title, and subject to the provisions of section 301 of this title and subchapter V-A of this chapter, nothing in this chapter shall be construed to apply or to give the Commission jurisdiction with respect to (1) charges, classifications, practices, services, facilities, or regulations for or in connection with intrastate communication service by wire or radio of any carrier....

SEC. 3. [47 U.S.C. § 153]
DEFINITIONS

(1) ADVANCED COMMUNICATIONS SERVICES. The term "advanced communications services" means—

(A) interconnected VoIP service;

(B) non-interconnected VoIP service;

(C) electronic messaging service; and

(D) interoperable video conferencing service.

(14) CONSUMER GENERATED MEDIA. The term "consumer generated media" means content created and made available by consumers to online websites and services on the Internet, including video, audio, and multimedia content.

(16) CUSTOMER PREMISES EQUIPMENT. The term "customer premises equipment" means equipment employed on the premises of a person (other than a carrier) to originate, route, or terminate telecommunications.

(17) DIALING PARITY. The term "dialing parity" means that a person that is not an affiliate of a local exchange carrier is able to provide telecommunications services in such a manner that customers have the ability to route automatically, without the use of any access code, their telecommunications to the telecommunications services provider of the customer's designation from among 2 or more telecommunications services providers (including such local exchange carrier).

(19) ELECTRONIC MESSAGING SERVICE. The term "electronic messaging service" means a service that provides real-time or near real-time non-voice messages in text form between individuals over communications networks.

(20) EXCHANGE ACCESS. The term "exchange access" means the offering of access to telephone exchange services or facilities for the purpose of the origination or termination of telephone toll services.

(24) INFORMATION SERVICE. The term "information service" means the offering of a capability for generating, acquiring, storing, transforming, processing, retrieving, utilizing, or making available information via telecommunications, and includes electronic publishing, but does not include any use of any such capability for the management, control, or operation of a telecommunications system or the management of a telecommunications service.

(25) INTERCONNECTED VOIP SERVICE. The term "interconnected VoIP service" has the meaning given such term under section 9.3 of title 47, Code of Federal Regulations, as such section may be amended from time to time.

(32) LOCAL EXCHANGE CARRIER. The term "local exchange carrier" means any person that is engaged in the provision of telephone exchange service or exchange access. Such term does not include a person insofar as such person is engaged in the provision of a commercial mobile service under section 332(c), except to the extent that the Commission finds that such service should be included in the definition of such term.

(35) NETWORK ELEMENT. The term "network element" means a facility or equipment used in the provision of a telecommunications service. Such term also includes features, functions, and capabilities that are provided by means of such facility or equipment, including subscriber numbers, databases, signaling systems, and information sufficient for billing and collection or used in the transmission, routing, or other provision of a telecommunications service.

(36) NON-INTERCONNECTED VOIP SERVICE. The term "non-interconnected VoIP service"—

(A) means a service that—

(i) enables real-time voice communications that originate from or terminate to the user's location using Internet protocol or any successor protocol; and

(ii) requires Internet protocol compatible customer premises equipment; and

(B) does not include any service that is an interconnected VoIP service.

(37) NUMBER PORTABILITY. The term "number portability" means the ability of users of telecommunications services to retain, at the same location, existing telecommunications numbers without impairment of quality, reliability, or convenience when switching from one telecommunications carrier to another.

(50) TELECOMMUNICATIONS. The term "telecommunications" means the transmission, between or among points specified by the user, of information of the user's choosing, without change in the form or content of the information as sent and received.

(51) TELECOMMUNICATIONS CARRIER. The term "telecommunications carrier" means any provider of telecommunications services, except that such term does not include aggregators of telecommunications services (as defined in section 226 of this title). A telecommunications carrier shall be treated as a common carrier under this chapter only to the extent that it is engaged in providing telecommunications services, except that the Commission shall determine whether the provision of fixed and mobile satellite service shall be treated as common carriage.

(52) TELECOMMUNICATIONS EQUIPMENT. The term "telecommunications equipment" means equipment, other than customer premises equipment, used by a carrier to provide telecommunications services, and includes software integral to such equipment (including upgrades).

(53) TELECOMMUNICATIONS SERVICE. The term "telecommunications service" means the offering of telecommunications for a fee directly to the public, or to such classes of users as to be effectively available directly to the public, regardless of the facilities used.

SEC. 4. [47 U.S.C. § 154]
PROVISIONS RELATING TO THE COMMISSION

(a) NUMBER OF COMMISSIONERS; APPOINTMENT. The Commission shall be composed of five Commissioners appointed by the President, by and with the advice and consent of the Senate, one of whom the President shall designate as chairman.

(c) TERMS OF OFFICE; VACANCIES. Commissioners shall be appointed for terms of five years ... except that any person chosen to fill a vacancy shall be appointed only for the unexpired term of the Commissioner whom he succeeds.

(i) DUTIES AND POWERS. The Commission may perform any and all acts, make such rules and regulations, and issue such orders, not inconsistent with this Act, as may be necessary in the execution of its functions.

SEC. 7. [47 U.S.C. § 157]
NEW TECHNOLOGIES AND SERVICES

(a) It shall be the policy of the United States to encourage the provision of new technologies and services to the public. Any person or party (other than the Commission) who opposes a new technology or service proposed to be permitted under this Act shall have the burden to demonstrate that such proposal is inconsistent with the public interest.

(b) The Commission shall determine whether any new technology or service proposed in a petition or application is in the public interest within one year after such petition or application is filed. If the Commission initiates its own proceeding for a new technology or service, such proceeding shall be completed within 12 months after it is initiated.

SEC. 10. [47 U.S.C. § 160]
COMPETITION IN PROVISION OF TELECOMMUNICATIONS SERVICE

(a) REGULATORY FLEXIBILITY. Notwithstanding section 332(c)(1)(A) of this Act, the Commission shall forbear from applying any regulation or any provision of this Act to a telecommunications carrier or telecommunications service, or class of telecommunications carriers or telecommunications services, in any or some of its or their geographic markets, if the Commission determines that—

(1) enforcement of such regulation or provision is not necessary to ensure that the charges, practices, classifications, or regulations by, for, or in connection with that telecommunications carrier or telecommunications service are just and reasonable and are not unjustly or unreasonably discriminatory;

(2) enforcement of such regulation or provision is not necessary for the protection of consumers; and

(3) forbearance from applying such provision or regulation is consistent with the public interest.

(b) COMPETITIVE EFFECT TO BE WEIGHED. If the Commission determines that forbearance will promote competition among providers of telecommunications services, that determination may be the basis for a Commission finding that forbearance is in the public interest.

(c) PETITION FOR FORBEARANCE. Any telecommunications carrier, or class of telecommunications carriers, may submit a petition to the Commission requesting that the Commission exercise the authority granted under this section with respect to that carrier or those carriers, or any service offered by that carrier or carriers. Any such petition shall be deemed granted if the Commission does not deny the petition for failure to meet the requirements for forbearance under subsection (a) of this section within one year after the Commission receives it, unless the one-year period is extended by the Commission. The Commission may extend the initial one-year period by an additional 90 days if the Commission finds that an extension is necessary to meet the requirements of subsection (a) of this section. The Commission may grant or deny a petition in whole or in part and shall explain its decision in writing.

(d) LIMITATION. Except as provided in section 251(f) of this title, the Commission may not forbear from applying the requirements of section 251(c) or 271 of this title under subsection (a) of this section until it determines that those requirements have been fully implemented.

(e) STATE ENFORCEMENT AFTER COMMISSION FORBEARANCE. A State commission may not continue to apply or enforce any provision of this Act that the Commission has determined to forbear from applying under subsection (a).

SEC. 11. [47 U.S.C. § 161]
REGULATORY REFORM

(a) BIENNIAL REVIEW OF REGULATIONS. In every even-numbered year (beginning with 1998), the Commission—

(1) shall review all regulations issued under this Act in effect at the time of the review that apply to the operations or activities of any provider of telecommunications service; and

(2) shall determine whether any such regulation is no longer necessary in the public interest as the result of meaningful economic competition between providers of such service.

(b) EFFECT OF DETERMINATION. The Commission shall repeal or modify any regulation it determines to be no longer necessary in the public interest.

TITLE II — COMMON CARRIERS

PART I — COMMON CARRIER REGULATION

SEC. 201. [47 U.S.C. § 201]
SERVICE AND CHARGES

(a) It shall be the duty of every common carrier engaged in interstate or foreign communication by wire or radio to furnish such communication service upon reasonable request therefor; and ... to establish physical connections with other carriers....

(b) All charges, practices, classifications, and regulations for and in connection with such communication service, shall be just and reasonable, and any such charge, practice, classification, or regulation that is unjust or unreasonable is declared to be unlawful....

SEC. 202. [47 U.S.C. § 202]
DISCRIMINATION AND PREFERENCES

(a) It shall be unlawful for any common carrier to make any unjust or unreasonable discrimination in charges, practices, classifications, regulations, facilities, or services for or in connection with like communication service, directly or indirectly, by any means or device, or to make or give any undue or unreasonable preference or advantage to any particular person, class of persons, or locality, or to subject any particular person, class of persons, or locality to any undue or unreasonable prejudice or disadvantage.

SEC. 203. [47 U.S.C. § 203]
SCHEDULES OF CHARGES

(a) Every common carrier ... shall ... file with the Commission and print and keep open for public inspection schedules showing all charges for itself and its connecting carriers for interstate and foreign wire or radio communication ... and showing the classifications, practices, and regulations affecting such charges. [E]ach such schedule shall give notice of its effective date.

SEC. 205. [47 U.S.C. § 205]
COMMISSION AUTHORIZED TO PRESCRIBE JUST AND REASONABLE CHARGES

(a) Whenever, after full opportunity for hearing, ... the Commission shall be of opinion that any charge ... or practice of any carrier or carriers is or will be in violation of any of the provisions of this Act, the Commission is authorized and empowered to determine and prescribe what will be the just and reasonable charge ... to be thereafter observed, and what ... practice is or will be just, fair, and reasonable....

SEC. 214. [47 U.S.C. § 214]
EXTENSION OF LINES

(a) EXCEPTIONS. No carrier shall undertake the construction of a new line or of an extension of any line, or shall acquire or operate any line, or extension thereof ... until there shall first have been obtained from the Commission a certificate that the present or future public convenience and necessity require or will require ... such additional or extended line....

(e) PROVISION OF UNIVERSAL SERVICE

(1) ELIGIBLE TELECOMMUNICATIONS CARRIERS. A common carrier designated as an eligible telecommunications carrier under paragraph (2), (3), or (6) shall be eligible to receive universal service support in accordance with section 254 of this title and shall, throughout the service area for which the designation is received—

(A) offer the services that are supported by Federal universal service support mechanisms under section 254(c) of this title, either using its own facilities or a combination of its own facilities and resale of another carrier's services (including the services offered by another eligible telecommunications carrier); and

(B) advertise the availability of such services and the charges therefor using media of general distribution.

(2) DESIGNATION OF ELIGIBLE TELECOMMUNICATIONS CARRIERS. A State commission shall upon its own motion or upon request designate a common carrier that meets the requirements of paragraph (1) as an eligible telecommunications carrier for a service area designated by the State commission. Upon request and consistent with the public interest, convenience, and necessity, the State commission may, in the case of an area served by a rural telephone company, and shall, in the case of all other areas, designate more than one common carrier as an eligible telecommunications carrier for a service area designated by the State commission, so long as each additional requesting carrier meets the requirements of paragraph (1) Before designating an additional eligible telecommunications carrier for an area served by a rural telephone company, the State commission shall find that the designation is in the public interest.

SEC. 220. [47 U.S.C. § 220]
ACCOUNTS, RECORDS, AND MEMORANDA

(a) FORMS

(1) The Commission may, in its discretion, prescribe the forms of any and all accounts, records, and memoranda to be kept by carriers subject to this chapter, including the accounts, records, and memoranda of the movement of traffic, as well as of the receipts and expenditures of moneys.

(2) The Commission shall, by rule, prescribe a uniform system of accounts for use by telephone companies. Such uniform system shall require that each common carrier shall maintain a system of accounting methods, procedures, and techniques (including accounts and supporting records and memoranda) which shall ensure a proper allocation of all costs to and among telecommunications services, facilities, and products (and to and among classes of such services, facilities, and products) which are developed, manufactured, or offered by such common carrier.

(b) DEPRECIATION CHARGES. The Commission may prescribe, for such carriers as it determines to be appropriate, the classes of property for which depreciation charges may be properly included under operating expenses, and the percentages of depreciation which shall be charged with respect to each of such classes of property, classifying the carriers as it may deem proper for this purpose. The Commission may, when it deems necessary, modify the classes and percentages so prescribed. Such carriers shall not, after the Commission has prescribed the classes of property for which depreciation charges may be included, charge to operating expenses any depreciation charges on classes of property other than those prescribed by the Commission, or after the Commission has prescribed percentages of depreciation, charge with respect to any class of property a percentage of depreciation other than that prescribed therefor by the Commission. No such carrier shall in any case include in any form under its operating or other expenses any depreciation or other charge or expenditure included elsewhere as a depreciation charge or otherwise under its operating or other expenses.

(c) ACCESS TO INFORMATION; BURDEN OF PROOF; USE OF INDEPENDENT AUDITORS. The Commission shall at all times have access to and the right of inspection and examination of all accounts, records, and memoranda, including all documents, papers, and correspondence now or hereafter existing, and kept or required to be kept by such carriers, and the provisions of this section respecting the preservation and destruction of books, papers, and documents shall apply thereto. The burden of proof to justify every accounting entry questioned by the Commission shall be on the person making, authorizing, or requiring such entry and the Commission may suspend a charge or credit pending submission of proof by such person....

SEC. 223. [47 U.S.C. § 223]
OBSCENE OR HARASSING TELEPHONE CALLS

(a) PROHIBITED ACTS GENERALLY. Whoever—

(1) in interstate or foreign communications—

(A) by means of a telecommunications device knowingly—

(i) makes, creates, or solicits, and

(ii) initiates the transmission of, any comment, request, suggestion, proposal, image, or other communication which is obscene or child pornography, with intent to annoy, abuse, threaten, or harass another person;

(B) by means of a telecommunications device knowingly—

(i) makes, creates, or solicits, and

(ii) initiates the transmission of, any comment, request, suggestion, proposal, image, or other communication which is obscene or child pornography, knowing that the recipient of the communication is under 18 years of age, regardless of whether the maker of such communication placed the call or initiated the communication;

(C) makes a telephone call or utilizes a telecommunications device, whether or not conversation or communication ensues, without disclosing his identity and with intent to annoy, abuse, threaten, or harass any person at the called number or who receives the communications;

(D) makes or causes the telephone of another repeatedly or continuously to ring, with intent to harass any person at the called number; or

(E) makes repeated telephone calls or repeatedly initiates communication with a telecommunications device, during which conversation or communication ensues, solely to harass any person at the called number or who receives the communication; or

(2) knowingly permits any telecommunications facility under his control to be used for any activity prohibited by paragraph (1) with the intent that it be used for such activity, shall be fined under title 18, United States Code, or imprisoned not more than two years, or both; and

(b) PROHIBITED ACTS FOR COMMERCIAL PURPOSES; DEFENSE TO PROSECUTION

(1) Whoever knowingly—

(A) within the United States, by means of telephone, makes (directly or by recording device) any obscene communication for commercial purposes to any person, regardless of whether the maker of such communication placed the call; or

(B) permits any telephone facility under such person's control to be used for an activity prohibited by subparagraph (A) shall be fined in accordance with title 18, United States Code, or imprisoned not more than two years, or both.

(2) Whoever knowingly—

(A) within the United States, by means of telephone, makes (directly or by recording device) any indecent communication for commercial purposes which is available to any person under 18 years of age or to any other person without that person's consent, regardless of whether the maker of such communication placed the call; or

(B) permits any telephone facility under such person's control to be used for an activity prohibited by subparagraph (A), shall be fined not more than $ 50,000 or imprisoned not more than six months, or both.

(3) It is a defense to prosecution under paragraph (2) of this subsection that the defendant restrict access to the prohibited communication to persons 18 years of age or older in accordance with subsection (c) of this section and with such procedures as the Commission may prescribe by regulation.

(d) SENDING OR DISPLAYING OFFENSIVE MATERIAL TO PERSONS UNDER 18. Whoever—

(1) in interstate or foreign communications knowingly—

(A) uses an interactive computer service to send to a specific person or persons under 18 years of age, or

(B) uses any interactive computer service to display in a manner available to a person under 18 years of age, any comment, request, suggestion, proposal, image, or other communication that is obscene or child pornography; or

(2) knowingly permits any telecommunications facility under such person's control to be used for an activity prohibited by paragraph (1) with the intent that it be used for such activity, shall be fined under title 18, United States Code, or imprisoned not more than two years, or both.

(e) DEFENSES. In addition to any other defenses available by law:

(1) No person shall be held to have violated subsection (a) or (d) solely for providing access or connection to or from a facility, system, or network not under that person's control, including transmission, downloading, intermediate storage, access software, or other related capabilities that are incidental to providing such access or connection that does not include the creation of the content of the communication.

(2) The defenses provided by paragraph (1) of this subsection shall not be applicable to a person who is a conspirator with an entity actively involved in the creation or knowing distribution of communications that violate this section, or who knowingly advertises the availability of such communications.

(3) The defenses provided in paragraph (1) of this subsection shall not be applicable to a person who provides access or connection to a facility, system, or network engaged in the violation of this section that is owned or controlled by such person.

(4) No employer shall be held liable under this section for the actions of an employee or agent unless the employee's or agent's conduct is within the scope of his or her employment or agency and the employer (A) having knowledge of such conduct, authorizes or ratifies such conduct, or (B) recklessly disregards such conduct.

(5) It is a defense to a prosecution under subsection (a)(1)(B) or (d), or under subsection (a)(2) with respect to the use of a facility for an activity under subsection (a)(1)(B) that a person—

(A) has taken, in good faith, reasonable, effective, and appropriate actions under the circumstances to restrict or prevent access by minors to a communication specified in such subsections, which may involve any appropriate measures to restrict minors from such communications, including any method which is feasible under available technology; or

(B) has restricted access to such communication by requiring use of a verified credit card, debit account, adult access code, or adult personal identification number.

(6) The Commission may describe measures which are reasonable, effective, and appropriate to restrict access to prohibited communications under subsection (d). Nothing in this section authorizes the Commission to enforce, or is intended to provide the Commission with the authority to approve, sanction, or permit, the use of such measures. The Commission shall have no enforcement authority over the failure to utilize such measures. The Commission shall not endorse specific products relating to such measures. The use of such measures shall be admitted as evidence of good faith efforts for purposes of paragraph (5) in any action arising under subsection (d). Nothing in this section shall be construed to treat interactive computer services as common carriers or telecommunications carriers.

SEC. 224. [47 U.S.C. § 224]
POLE ATTACHMENTS

(a) DEFINITIONS

(1) The term "utility" means any person who is a local exchange carrier or an electric, gas, water, steam, or other public utility, and who owns or controls poles, ducts, conduits, or rights-of-way used, in whole or in part, for any wire communications.

(e) REGULATIONS GOVERNING CHANGE

(1) The Commission shall, no later than 2 years after the date of enactment of the Telecommunications Act of 1996, prescribe regulations in accordance with this subsection to govern the charges for pole attachments used by telecommunications carriers to provide telecommunications services, when the parties fail to resolve a dispute over such charges. Such regulations shall ensure that a utility charges just, reasonable, and nondiscriminatory rates for pole attachments.

(f) NONDISCRIMINATORY ACCESS

(1) A utility shall provide a cable television system or any telecommunications carrier with nondiscriminatory access to any pole, duct, conduit, or right-of-way owned or controlled by it.

(2) Notwithstanding paragraph (1), a utility providing electric service may deny a cable television system or any telecommunications carrier access to its poles, ducts, conduits, or rights-of-way, on a non-discriminatory basis where there is insufficient capacity and for reasons of safety, reliability and generally applicable engineering purposes.

SEC. 227. [47 U.S.C. § 227]
RESTRICTIONS ON THE USE OF TELEPHONE EQUIPMENT

(b) RESTRICTIONS ON THE USE OF AUTOMATED TELEPHONE EQUIPMENT.

(1) PROHIBITIONS. It shall be unlawful for any person within the United States—

(B) to initiate any telephone call to any residential telephone line using an artificial or prerecorded voice to deliver a message without the prior express consent of the called party, unless the call is initiated for emergency purposes or is exempted by rule or order by the Commission ...

(C) to use any telephone facsimile machine, computer, or other device to send, to a telephone facsimile machine, an unsolicited advertisement unless [exceptions omitted]; or

(D) to use an automatic telephone dialing system in such a way that two or more telephone lines of a multi-line business are engaged simultaneously.

SEC. 230. [47 U.S.C. § 230]
PROTECTION FOR PRIVATE BLOCKING AND SCREENING OF OFFENSIVE MATERIAL

(a) FINDINGS. The Congress finds the following:

(1) The rapidly developing array of Internet and other interactive computer services available to individual Americans represent an extraordinary advance in the availability of educational and informational resources to our citizens.

(2) These services offer users a great degree of control over the information that they receive, as well as the potential for even greater control in the future as technology develops.

(3) The Internet and other interactive computer services offer a forum for a true diversity of political discourse, unique opportunities for cultural development, and myriad avenues for intellectual activity.

(4) The Internet and other interactive computer services have flourished, to the benefit of all Americans, with a minimum of government regulation.

(5) Increasingly Americans are relying on interactive media for a variety of political, educational, cultural, and entertainment services.

(b) POLICY. It is the policy of the United States—

(1) to promote the continued development of the Internet and other interactive computer services and other interactive media;

(2) to preserve the vibrant and competitive free market that presently exists for the Internet and other interactive computer services, unfettered by Federal or State regulation;

(3) to encourage the development of technologies which maximize user control over what information is received by individuals, families, and schools who use the Internet and other interactive computer services;

(4) to remove disincentives for the development and utilization of blocking and filtering technologies that empower parents to restrict their children's access to objectionable or inappropriate online material; and

(5) to ensure vigorous enforcement of Federal criminal laws to deter and punish trafficking in obscenity, stalking, and harassment by means of computer.

(c) PROTECTION FOR "GOOD SAMARITAN" BLOCKING AND SCREENING OF OFFENSIVE MATERIAL.

(1) TREATMENT OF PUBLISHER OR SPEAKER. No provider or user of an interactive computer service shall be treated as the publisher or speaker of any information provided by another information content provider.

(2) CIVIL LIABILITY. No provider or user of an interactive computer service shall be held liable on account of—

(A) any action voluntarily taken in good faith to restrict access to or availability of material that the provider or user considers to be obscene, lewd, lascivious, filthy, excessively violent, harassing, or otherwise objectionable, whether or not such material is constitutionally protected; or

(B) any action taken to enable or make available to information content providers or others the technical means to restrict access to material described in paragraph (1).

(d) OBLIGATIONS OF INTERACTIVE COMPUTER SERVICE. A provider of interactive computer service shall, at the time of entering an agreement with a customer for the provision of interactive computer service and in a manner deemed appropriate by the provider, notify such customer that parental control protections (such as computer hardware, software, or filtering services) are commercially available that may assist the customer in limiting access to material that is harmful to minors. Such notice shall identify, or provide the customer with access to information identifying, current providers of such protections.

PART II — DEVELOPMENT OF COMPETITIVE MARKETS

SEC. 251. [47 U.S.C. § 251]
INTERCONNECTION

(a) GENERAL DUTY OF TELECOMMUNICATIONS CARRIERS. Each telecommunications carrier has the duty—

(1) to interconnect directly or indirectly with the facilities and equipment of other telecommunications carriers; and

(2) not to install network features, functions, or capabilities that do not comply with the guidelines and standards established pursuant to section 255 or 256.

(b) OBLIGATIONS OF ALL LOCAL EXCHANGE CARRIERS. Each local exchange carrier has the following duties:

(1) RESALE. The duty not to prohibit, and not to impose unreasonable or discriminatory conditions or limitations on, the resale of its telecommunications services.

(2) NUMBER PORTABILITY. The duty to provide, to the extent technically feasible, number portability in accordance with requirements prescribed by the Commission.

(3) DIALING PARITY. The duty to provide dialing parity to competing providers of telephone exchange service and telephone toll service, and the duty to permit all such providers to have nondiscriminatory access to telephone numbers, operator services, directory assistance, and directory listing, with no unreasonable dialing delays.

(4) ACCESS TO RIGHTS-OF-WAY. The duty to afford access to the poles, ducts, conduits, and rights-of-way of such carrier to competing providers of telecommunications services on rates, terms, and conditions that are consistent with section 224.

(5) RECIPROCAL COMPENSATION. The duty to establish reciprocal compensation arrangements for the transport and termination of telecommunications.

(c) ADDITIONAL OBLIGATIONS OF INCUMBENT LOCAL EXCHANGE CARRIERS. In addition to the duties contained in subsection (b), each incumbent local exchange carrier has the following duties:

(1) DUTY TO NEGOTIATE. The duty to negotiate in good faith in accordance with section 252 the particular terms and conditions of agreements to fulfill the duties described paragraphs (1) through (5) of subsection (b) and this subsection. The requesting telecommunications carrier also has the duty to negotiate in good faith the terms and conditions of such agreements.

(2) INTERCONNECTION. The duty to provide, for the facilities and equipment of any requesting telecommunications carrier, interconnection with the local exchange carrier's network—

(A) for the transmission and routing of telephone exchange service and exchange access;

(B) at any technically feasible point within the carrier's network;

(C) that is at least equal in quality to that provided by the local exchange carrier to itself or to any subsidiary, affiliate, or any other party to which the carrier provides interconnection; and

(D) on rates, terms, and conditions that are just, reasonable, and nondiscriminatory.

(3) UNBUNDLED ACCESS. The duty to provide, to any requesting telecommunications carrier for the provision of a telecommunications service, nondiscriminatory access to network elements on an unbundled basis at any technically feasible point on rates, terms, and conditions that are just, reasonable, and nondiscriminatory. An incumbent local exchange carrier shall provide such unbundled network elements in a manner that allows requesting carriers to combine such elements in order to provide such telecommunications service.

(4) RESALE. The duty—

(A) to offer for resale at wholesale rates any telecommunications service that the carrier provides at retail to subscribers who are not telecommunications carriers; and

(B) not to prohibit, and not to impose unreasonable or discriminatory conditions or limitations on, the resale of such telecommunications service, except that a State commission may, consistent with regulations prescribed by the Commission under this section, prohibit a reseller that obtains at wholesale rates a telecommunications service that is available at retail only to a category of subscribers from offering such service to a different category of subscribers.

(5) NOTICE OF CHANGES. The duty to provide reasonable public notice of changes in the information necessary for the transmission and routing of services using that local exchange carrier's facilities or networks, as well as of any other changes that would affect the interoperability of those facilities and networks.

(6) COLLOCATION. The duty to provide, on rates, terms, and conditions that are just, reasonable, and nondiscriminatory, for physical collocation of equipment necessary for interconnection or access to unbundled network elements at the premises of the local exchange carrier, except that the carrier may provide for virtual collocation if the local exchange carrier demonstrates to the State commission that physical collocation is not practical for technical reasons or because of space limitations.

(d) IMPLEMENTATION

(2) ACCESS STANDARDS. In determining what network elements should be made available for purposes of subsection (c)(3) of this section, the Commission shall consider, at a minimum, whether—

(A) access to such network elements as are proprietary in nature is necessary; and

(B) the failure to provide access to such network elements would impair the ability of the telecommunications carrier seeking access to provide the services that it seeks to offer.

(e) NUMBERING ADMINISTRATION—

(1) COMMISSION AUTHORITY AND JURISDICTION. The Commission shall create or designate one or more impartial entities to administer telecommunications numbering and to make such numbers available on an equitable basis.

(g) CONTINUED ENFORCEMENT OF EXCHANGE ACCESS AND INTERCONNECTION REQUIREMENTS. On and after the date of enactment of the Telecommunications Act of 1996, each local exchange carrier, to the extent that it provides wireline services, shall provide exchange access, information access, and exchange services for such access to interexchange carriers and information service providers in accordance with the same equal access and nondiscriminatory interconnection restrictions and obligations (including receipt of compensation) that apply to such carrier on the date immediately preceding the date of enactment of the Telecommunications Act of 1996 under any court order, consent decree, or regulation, order, or policy of the Commission, until such restrictions and obligations are explicitly superseded by regulations prescribed by the Commission after such date of enactment.

(h) DEFINITION OF INCUMBENT LOCAL EXCHANGE CARRIER.

(1) DEFINITION. For purposes of this section, the term "incumbent local exchange carrier" means, with respect to an area, the local exchange carrier that—

(A) on the date of enactment of the Telecommunications Act of 1996, provided telephone exchange service in such area.

SEC. 252. [47 U.S.C. § 252]
PROCEDURES FOR NEGOTIATION, ARBITRATION, AND APPROVAL OF AGREEMENTS

(a) AGREEMENTS ARRIVED AT THROUGH NEGOTIATION.

(1) VOLUNTARY NEGOTIATIONS. Upon receiving a request for interconnection, services, or network elements pursuant to section 251, an incumbent local exchange carrier may negotiate and enter into a binding agreement with the requesting telecommunications carrier or carriers without regard to the standards set forth in subsections (b) and (c) of section 251. The agreement shall include a detailed schedule of itemized charges for interconnection and each service or network element included in the agreement. The agreement ... shall be submitted to the State commission under subsection (e) of this section.

(2) MEDIATION. Any party negotiating an agreement under this section may, at any point in the negotiation, ask a State commission to participate in the negotiation and to mediate any differences arising in the course of the negotiation.

(b) AGREEMENTS ARRIVED AT THROUGH COMPULSORY ARBITRATION.

(1) ARBITRATION. During the period from the 135th to the 160th day (inclusive) after the date on which an incumbent local exchange carrier receives a request for ne-

gotiation under this section, the carrier or any other party to the negotiation may petition a State commission to arbitrate any open issues.

(4) ACTION BY STATE COMMISSION.

(C) The State commission shall resolve each issue set forth in the petition and the response, if any, by imposing appropriate conditions as required to implement subsection (c) upon the parties to the agreement, and shall conclude the resolution of any unresolved issues not later than 9 months after the date on which the local exchange carrier received the request under this section.

(c) STANDARDS FOR ARBITRATION. In resolving by arbitration under subsection (b) any open issues and imposing conditions upon the parties to the agreement, a State commission shall—

(1) ensure that such resolution and conditions meet the requirements of section 251, including the regulations prescribed by the Commission pursuant to section 251;

(2) establish any rates for interconnection, services, or network elements according to subsection (d); and

(3) provide a schedule for implementation of the terms and conditions by the parties to the agreement.

(d) PRICING STANDARDS.

(1) INTERCONNECTION AND NETWORK ELEMENT CHARGES. Determinations by a State commission of the just and reasonable rate for the interconnection of facilities and equipment for purposes of subsection (c)(2) of section 251, and the just and reasonable rate for network elements for purposes of subsection (c)(3) of such section—

(A) shall be—

(i) based on the cost (determined without reference to a rate-of-return or other rate-based proceeding) of providing the interconnection or network element (whichever is applicable), and

(ii) nondiscriminatory, and

(B) may include a reasonable profit.

(2) Charges for transport and termination of traffic

(A) IN GENERAL. For the purposes of compliance by an incumbent local exchange carrier with section 251 (b)(5) of this title, a State commission shall not consider the terms and conditions for reciprocal compensation to be just and reasonable unless—

(i) such terms and conditions provide for the mutual and reciprocal recovery by each carrier of costs associated with the transport and termination on each carrier's network facilities of calls that originate on the network facilities of the other carrier; and

(ii) such terms and conditions determine such costs on the basis of a reasonable approximation of the additional costs of terminating such calls.

(B) RULES OF CONSTRUCTION. This paragraph shall not be construed—

(i) to preclude arrangements that afford the mutual recovery of costs through the offsetting of reciprocal obligations, including arrangements that waive mutual recovery (such as bill-and-keep arrangements); or

(ii) to authorize the Commission or any State commission to engage in any rate regulation proceeding to establish with particularity the additional costs of transporting or terminating calls, or to require carriers to maintain records with respect to the additional costs of such calls.

(3) WHOLESALE PRICES FOR TELECOMMUNICATIONS SERVICES. For the purposes of section 251(c)(4), a State commission shall determine wholesale rates on the basis of retail rates charged to subscribers for the telecommunications service requested, excluding the portion thereof attributable to any marketing, billing, collection, and other costs that will be avoided by the local exchange carrier.

(e) APPROVAL BY STATE COMMISSION.

(1) APPROVAL REQUIRED. Any interconnection agreement adopted by negotiation or arbitration shall be submitted for approval to the State commission. A State commission to which an agreement is submitted shall approve or reject the agreement, with written findings as to any deficiencies.

(2) GROUNDS FOR REJECTION. The State commission may only reject—

(A) an agreement (or any portion thereof) adopted by negotiation under subsection (a) if it finds that—

(i) the agreement (or portion thereof) discriminates against a telecommunications carrier not a party to the agreement; or

(ii) the implementation of such agreement or portion is not consistent with the public interest, convenience, and necessity; or

(B) an agreement (or any portion thereof) adopted by arbitration under subsection (b) if it finds that the agreement does not meet the requirements of section 251, including the regulations prescribed by the Commission pursuant to section 251, or the standards set forth in subsection (d) of this section.

(5) COMMISSION TO ACT IF STATE WILL NOT ACT. If a State commission fails to act to carry out its responsibility under this section in any proceeding or other matter under this section, then the Commission shall issue an order preempting the State commission's jurisdiction of that proceeding or matter within 90 days after being notified (or taking notice) of such failure, and shall assume the responsibility of the State commission under this section with respect to the proceeding or matter and act for the State commission.

(f) STATEMENTS OF GENERALLY AVAILABLE TERMS.

(1) IN GENERAL. A Bell operating company may prepare and file with a State commission a statement of the terms and conditions that such company generally offers within that State to comply with the requirements of section 251 and the regulations thereunder and the standards applicable under this section.

(2) STATE COMMISSION REVIEW. A State commission may not approve such statement unless such statement complies with subsection (d) of this section and section 251 and the regulations thereunder. Except as provided in section 253, nothing in this section shall prohibit a State commission from establishing or enforcing other requirements of State law in its review of such statement, including requiring compliance with intrastate telecommunications service quality standards or requirements.

(h) FILING REQUIRED. A State commission shall make a copy of each agreement approved under subsection (e) and each statement approved under subsection (f) available for public inspection and copying within 10 days after the agreement or statement is approved.

(i) AVAILABILITY TO OTHER TELECOMMUNICATIONS CARRIERS. A local exchange carrier shall make available any interconnection, service, or network element provided under an agreement approved under this section to which it is a party to any other requesting telecommunications carrier upon the same terms and conditions as those provided in the agreement.

(j) DEFINITION OF INCUMBENT LOCAL EXCHANGE CARRIER. For purposes of this section, the term "incumbent local exchange carrier" has the meaning provided in section 251(h).

SEC. 253. [47 U.S.C. § 253]
REMOVAL OF BARRIERS TO ENTRY

(a) IN GENERAL. No State or local statute or regulation, or other State or local legal requirement, may prohibit or have the effect of prohibiting the ability of any entity to provide any interstate or intrastate telecommunications service.

(b) STATE REGULATORY AUTHORITY. Nothing in this section shall affect the ability of a State to impose, on a competitively neutral basis and consistent with section 254, requirements necessary to preserve and advance universal service, protect the public safety and welfare, ensure the continued quality of telecommunications services, and safeguard the rights of consumers.

(c) STATE AND LOCAL GOVERNMENT AUTHORITY. Nothing in this section affects the authority of a State or local government to manage the public rights-of-way or to require fair and reasonable compensation from telecommunications providers, on a competitively neutral and nondiscriminatory basis, for use of public rights-of-way on a nondiscriminatory basis.

(d) PREEMPTION. If, after notice and an opportunity for public comment, the Commission determines that a State or local government has permitted or imposed any statute, regulation, or legal requirement that violates subsection (a) or (b), the Commission shall preempt the enforcement of such statute, regulation, or legal requirement to the extent necessary to correct such violation or inconsistency.

SEC. 254. [47 U.S.C. § 254]
UNIVERSAL SERVICE

(a) PROCEDURES TO REVIEW UNIVERSAL SERVICE REQUIREMENTS.

(1) FEDERAL-STATE JOINT BOARD ON UNIVERSAL SERVICE. Within one month after the date of enactment of the Telecommunications Act of 1996, the Commission shall institute and refer to a Federal-State Joint Board under section 410(c) a proceeding to recommend changes to any of its regulations in order to implement sections 214(e) and this section, including the definition of the services that are supported by Federal universal service support mechanisms and a specific timetable for completion of such recommendations.

(2) COMMISSION ACTION. The Commission shall initiate a single proceeding to implement the recommendations from the Joint Board required by paragraph (1). The rules established by such proceeding shall include a definition of the services that are supported by Federal universal service support mechanisms and a specific timetable for implementation.

(b) UNIVERSAL SERVICE PRINCIPLES. The Joint Board and the Commission shall base policies for the preservation and advancement of universal service on the following principles:

(1) QUALITY AND RATES. Quality services should be available at just, reasonable, and affordable rates.

(2) ACCESS TO ADVANCED SERVICES. Access to advanced telecommunications and information services should be provided in all regions of the Nation.

(3) ACCESS IN RURAL AND HIGH COST AREAS. Consumers in all regions of the Nation, including low-income consumers and those in rural, insular, and high cost areas, should have access to telecommunications and information services, including interexchange services and advanced telecommunications and information services, that are reasonably comparable to those services provided in urban areas and that are available at rates that are reasonably comparable to rates charged for similar services in urban areas.

(4) EQUITABLE AND NONDISCRIMINATORY CONTRIBUTIONS. All providers of telecommunications services should make an equitable and nondiscriminatory contribution to the preservation and advancement of universal service.

(5) SPECIFIC AND PREDICTABLE SUPPORT MECHANISMS. There should be specific, predictable and sufficient Federal and State mechanisms to preserve and advance universal service.

(6) ACCESS TO ADVANCED TELECOMMUNICATIONS SERVICES FOR SCHOOLS, HEALTH CARE, AND LIBRARIES. Elementary and secondary schools and classrooms, health care providers, and libraries should have access to advanced telecommunications services as described in subsection (h).

(7) ADDITIONAL PRINCIPLES. Such other principles as the Joint Board and the Commission determine are necessary and appropriate for the protection of the public interest, convenience, and necessity and are consistent with this Act.

(c) DEFINITION.

(1) IN GENERAL. Universal service is an evolving level of telecommunications services that the Commission shall establish periodically under this section, taking into account advances in telecommunications and information technologies and services. The Joint Board in recommending, and the Commission in establishing, the definition of the services that are supported by Federal universal service support mechanisms shall consider the extent to which such telecommunications services —

(A) are essential to education, public health, or public safety;

(B) have, through the operation of market choices by customers, been subscribed to by a substantial majority of residential customers;

(C) are being deployed in public telecommunications networks by telecommunications carriers; and

(D) are consistent with the public interest, convenience, and necessity.

(3) SPECIAL SERVICES. In addition to the services included in the definition of universal service under paragraph (1), the Commission may designate additional services for such support mechanisms for schools, libraries, and health care providers for the purposes of subsection (h).

(d) TELECOMMUNICATIONS CARRIER CONTRIBUTION. Every telecommunications carrier that provides interstate telecommunications services shall contribute, on an equitable and nondiscriminatory basis, to the specific, predictable, and sufficient mechanisms established by the Commission to preserve and advance universal service. The

Commission may exempt a carrier or class of carriers from this requirement if the carrier's telecommunications activities are limited to such an extent that the level of such carrier's contribution to the preservation and advancement of universal service would be de minimis. Any other provider of interstate telecommunications may be required to contribute to the preservation and advancement of universal service if the public interest so requires.

(e) UNIVERSAL SERVICE SUPPORT. After the date on which Commission regulations implementing this section take effect, only an eligible telecommunications carrier designated under section 214(e) shall be eligible to receive specific Federal universal service support. A carrier that receives such support shall use that support only for the provision, maintenance, and upgrading of facilities and services for which the support is intended.

(f) STATE AUTHORITY. A State may adopt regulations not inconsistent with the Commission's rules to preserve and advance universal service. Every telecommunications carrier that provides intrastate telecommunications services shall contribute, on an equitable and nondiscriminatory basis, in a manner determined by the State to the preservation and advancement of universal service in that State.

(g) INTEREXCHANGE AND INTERSTATE SERVICES. The Commission shall adopt rules to require that the communications services to subscribers in rural and high cost areas shall be no higher than the rates charged by each such provider to its subscribers in urban areas Such rules shall also require that a provider of interstate interexchange telecommunications services shall provide such services to its subscribers in each State at rates no higher than the rates charged to its subscribers in any other State

(h) TELECOMMUNICATIONS SERVICES FOR CERTAIN PROVIDERS.

(1) IN GENERAL.

(B) EDUCATIONAL PROVIDERS AND LIBRARIES. All telecommunications carriers serving a geographic area shall, upon a bona fide request for any of its services that are within the definition of universal service under subsection (c)(3), provide such services to elementary schools, secondary schools, and libraries for educational purposes at rates less than the amounts charged for similar services to other parties. The discount shall be an amount that the Commission, with respect to interstate services, and the States, with respect to intrastate services, determine is appropriate and necessary to ensure affordable access to and use of such services by such entities.

(2) ADVANCED SERVICES. The Commission shall establish competitively neutral rules—

(A) to enhance, to the extent technically feasible and economically reasonable, access to advanced telecommunications and information services for all public and nonprofit elementary and secondary school classrooms, health care providers, and libraries; and

(B) to define the circumstances under which a telecommunications carrier may be required to connect its network to such public institutional telecommunications users.

(3) TERMS AND CONDITIONS. Telecommunications services and network capacity provided to a public institutional telecommunications user under this subsection may not be sold, resold, or otherwise transferred by such user in consideration for money or any other thing of value.

(i) CONSUMER PROTECTION. The Commission and the States should ensure that universal service is available at rates that are just, reasonable, and affordable.

SEC. 255. [47 U.S.C. § 255]
ACCESS BY PERSONS WITH DISABILITIES

(b) MANUFACTURING. A manufacturer of telecommunications equipment or customer premises equipment shall ensure that the equipment is designed, developed, and fabricated to be accessible to and usable by individuals with disabilities, if readily achievable.

(c) TELECOMMUNICATIONS SERVICES. A provider of telecommunications service shall ensure that the service is accessible to and usable by individuals with disabilities, if readily achievable.

(d) COMPATIBILITY. Whenever the requirements of subsections (b) and (c) are not readily achievable, such a manufacturer or provider shall ensure that the equipment or service is compatible with existing peripheral devices or specialized customer premises equipment commonly used by individuals with disabilities to achieve access, if readily achievable.

SEC. 257. [47 U.S.C. § 257]
MARKET ENTRY BARRIERS PROCEEDING

(a) ELIMINATION OF BARRIERS. Within 15 months after the date of enactment of the Telecommunications Act of 1996, the Commission shall complete a proceeding for the purpose of identifying and eliminating, by regulations pursuant to its authority under this Act (other than this section), market entry barriers for entrepreneurs and other small businesses in the provision and ownership of telecommunications services and information services, or in the provision of parts or services to providers of telecommunications services and information services.

(b) NATIONAL POLICY. In carrying out subsection (a), the Commission shall seek to promote the policies and purposes of this Act favoring diversity of media voices, vigorous economic competition, technological advancement, and promotion of the public interest, convenience, and necessity.

(c) PERIODIC REVIEW. Every 3 years following the completion of the proceeding required by subsection (a), the Commission shall review and report to Congress on—

(1) any regulations prescribed to eliminate barriers within its jurisdiction that are identified under subsection (a) and that can be prescribed consistent with the public interest, convenience, and necessity; and

(2) the statutory barriers identified under subsection (a) that the Commission recommends be eliminated, consistent with the public interest, convenience, and necessity.

SEC. 259. [47 U.S.C. § 259]
INFRASTRUCTURE SHARING

(a) REGULATIONS REQUIRED. The Commission shall prescribe regulations that require incumbent local exchange carriers (as defined in section 251(h)) to make available to any qualifying carrier such public switched network infrastructure, technology, information, and telecommunications facilities and functions as may be requested by such qualifying carrier for the purpose of enabling such qualifying carrier to provide telecommunications services, or to provide access to information services, in the service area in which such qualifying carrier has requested and obtained designation as an eligible telecommunications carrier.

(b) TERMS AND CONDITIONS OF REGULATIONS. The regulations prescribed by the Commission pursuant to this section shall—

(1) not require a local exchange carrier to which this section applies to take any action that is economically unreasonable or that is contrary to the public interest;

(2) permit, but shall not require, the joint ownership or operation of public switched network infrastructure and services by or among such local exchange carrier and a qualifying carrier;

(3) ensure that such local exchange carrier will not be treated by the Commission or any State as a common carrier for hire or as offering common carrier services with respect to any infrastructure, technology, information, facilities, or functions made available to a qualifying carrier in accordance with regulations issued pursuant to this section;

(4) ensure that such local exchange carrier makes such infrastructure, technology, information, facilities, or functions available to a qualifying carrier on just and reasonable terms and conditions that permit such qualifying carrier to fully benefit from the economies of scale and scope of such local exchange carrier, as determined in accordance with guidelines prescribed by the Commission in regulations issued pursuant to this section;

(5) establish conditions that promote cooperation between local exchange carriers to which this section applies and qualifying carriers;

(6) not require a local exchange carrier to which this section applies to engage in any infrastructure sharing agreement for any services or access which are to be provided or offered to consumers by the qualifying carrier in such local exchange carrier's telephone exchange area; and

(7) require that such local exchange carrier file with the Commission or State for public inspection, any tariffs, contracts, or other arrangements showing the rates, terms, and conditions under which such carrier is making available public switched network infrastructure and functions under this section.

(c) INFORMATION CONCERNING DEPLOYMENT OF NEW SERVICES AND EQUIPMENT. A local exchange carrier to which this section applies that has entered into an infrastructure sharing agreement under this section shall provide to each party to such agreement timely information on the planned deployment of telecommunications services and equipment, including any software or upgrades of software integral to the use or operation of such telecommunications equipment.

(d) DEFINITION. For purposes of this section, the term "qualifying carrier" means a telecommunications carrier that—

(1) lacks economies of scale or scope, as determined in accordance with regulations prescribed by the Commission pursuant to this section; and

(2) offers telephone exchange service, exchange access, and any other service that is included in universal service, to all consumers without preference throughout the service area for which such carrier has been designated as an eligible telecommunications carrier.

PART III—SPECIAL PROVISIONS CONCERNING BELL OPERATING COMPANIES

SEC. 271. [47 U.S.C. § 271]
BELL OPERATING COMPANY ENTRY INTO INTERLATA [Local Access and Transport Area] SERVICES

(a) GENERAL LIMITATION. Neither a Bell operating company, nor any affiliate of a Bell operating company, may provide interLATA services except as provided in this section.

(b) INTERLATA SERVICES TO WHICH THIS SECTION APPLIES.

(1) IN-REGION SERVICES. A Bell operating company, or any affiliate of that Bell operating company, may provide interLATA services originating in any of its in-region States (as defined in subsection (i)) if the Commission approves the application of such company for such State under subsection (d)(3).

(2) OUT-OF-REGION SERVICES. A Bell operating company, or any affiliate of that Bell operating company, may provide interLATA services originating outside its in-region States after the date of enactment of the Telecommunications Act of 1996, subject to subsection (j).

(4) TERMINATION. Nothing in this section prohibits a Bell operating company or any of its affiliates from providing termination for interLATA services, subject to subsection (j).

(c) REQUIREMENTS FOR PROVIDING CERTAIN IN-REGION INTERLATA SERVICES.

(1) AGREEMENT OR STATEMENT. A Bell operating company meets the requirements of this paragraph if it meets the requirements of subparagraph (A) or subparagraph (B) of this paragraph for each State for which the authorization is sought.

(A) PRESENCE OF A FACILITIES-BASED COMPETITOR. A Bell operating company meets the requirements of this subparagraph if it has entered into one or more binding agreements that have been approved under section 252 specifying the terms and conditions under which the Bell operating company is providing access and interconnection to its network facilities for the network facilities of one or more unaffiliated competing providers of telephone exchange service to residential and business subscribers.

(B) FAILURE TO REQUEST ACCESS. A Bell operating company meets the requirements of this subparagraph if, after 10 months after the date of enactment of the Telecommunications Act of 1996, no such provider has requested the access and interconnection described in subparagraph (A) ... and a statement of the terms and conditions that the company generally offers to provide such access and interconnection has been approved or permitted to take effect by the State commission under section 252(f).

(2) SPECIFIC INTERCONNECTION REQUIREMENTS.

(A) AGREEMENT REQUIRED. A Bell operating company meets the requirements of this paragraph if, within the State for which the authorization is sought—

(i) (I) such company is providing access and interconnection pursuant to one or more agreements described in paragraph (1)(A), or

(II) such company is generally offering access and interconnection pursuant to a statement described in paragraph (1)(B), and

(ii) such access and interconnection meets the requirements of subparagraph (B) of this paragraph.

(B) COMPETITIVE CHECKLIST. Access or interconnection provided or generally offered by a Bell operating company to other telecommunications carriers meets the requirements of this subparagraph if such access and interconnection includes each of the following:

(i) Interconnection in accordance with the requirements of sections 251(c)(2) and 252(d)(1).

(ii) Nondiscriminatory access to network elements in accordance with the requirements of sections 251(c)(3) and 252(d)(1).

(iii) Nondiscriminatory access to the poles, ducts, conduits, and rights-of-way owned or controlled by the Bell operating company at just and reasonable rates in accordance with the requirements of section 224.

(iv) Local loop transmission from the central office to the customer's premises, unbundled from local switching or other services.

(v) Local transport from the trunk side of a wireline local exchange carrier switch unbundled from switching or other services.

(vi) Local switching unbundled from transport, local loop transmission, or other services.

(vii) Nondiscriminatory access to—

(I) 911 and E911 services;

(II) directory assistance services to allow the other carrier's customers to obtain telephone numbers; and

(III) operator call completion services.

(viii) White pages directory listings for customers of the other carrier's telephone exchange service.

(ix) Until the date by which telecommunications numbering administration guidelines, plan, or rules are established, nondiscriminatory access to telephone numbers for assignment to the other carrier's telephone exchange service customers. After that date, compliance with such guidelines, plan, or rules.

(x) Nondiscriminatory access to databases and associated signaling necessary for call routing and completion.

(xi) Until the date by which the Commission issues regulations pursuant to section 251 to require number portability, interim telecommunications number portability through remote call forwarding, direct inward dialing trunks, or other comparable arrangements, with as little impairment of functioning, quality, reliability, and convenience as possible. After that date, full compliance with such regulations.

(xii) Nondiscriminatory access to such services or information as are necessary to allow the requesting carrier to implement local dialing parity in accordance with the requirements of section 251(b)(3).

(xiii) Reciprocal compensation arrangements in accordance with the requirements of section 252(d)(2).

(xiv) Telecommunications services are available for resale in accordance with the requirements of sections 251(c)(4) and 252(d)(3).

(d) ADMINISTRATIVE PROVISIONS.

(1) APPLICATION TO COMMISSION. On and after the date of enactment of the Telecommunications Act of 1996, a Bell operating company or its affiliate may apply to the Commission for authorization to provide interLATA services originating in any in-region State. The application shall identify each State for which the authorization is sought.

(2) CONSULTATION.

(A) CONSULTATION WITH THE ATTORNEY GENERAL. Before making any determination under this subsection, the Commission shall consult with the Attorney General. The Attorney General shall provide to the Commission an evaluation of the application using any standard the Attorney General considers appropriate The Commission shall give substantial weight to the Attorney General's evaluation, but such evaluation shall not have any preclusive effect on any Commission decision under paragraph (3)

(B) CONSULTATION WITH STATE COMMISSIONS. Before making any determination under this subsection, the Commission shall consult with the State commission of any State that is the subject of the application in order to verify the compliance of the Bell operating company with the requirements of subsection (c).

(3) DETERMINATION. Not later than 90 days after receiving an application under paragraph (1), the Commission shall issue a written determination approving or denying the authorization requested in the application for each State. The Commission shall not approve the authorization requested in an application submitted under paragraph (1) unless it finds that—

(A) the petitioning Bell operating company has met the requirements of subsection (c)(1) and—

(i) with respect to access and interconnection provided pursuant to subsection (c)(1)(A), has fully implemented the competitive checklist in subsection (c)(2)(B); or

(ii) with respect to access and interconnection generally offered pursuant to a statement under subsection (c)(1)(B), such statement offers all of the items included in the competitive checklist in subsection (c)(2)(B);

(B) the requested authorization will be carried out in accordance with the requirements of section 272; and

(C) the requested authorization is consistent with the public interest, convenience, and necessity.

(4) LIMITATION ON COMMISSION—The Commission may not, by rule or otherwise, limit or extend the terms used in the competitive checklist set forth in subsection (c)(2)(B).

SEC. 272. [47 U.S.C. § 272]
SEPARATE AFFILIATE; SAFEGUARDS

(a) SEPARATE AFFILIATE REQUIRED FOR COMPETITIVE ACTIVITIES.

(1) IN GENERAL. A Bell operating company (including any affiliate) which is a local exchange carrier that is subject to the requirements of section 251(c) may not provide any service described in paragraph (2) unless it provides that service through one or more affiliates that—

(A) are separate from any operating company entity that is subject to the requirements of section 251(c); and

(B) meet the requirements of subsection (b).

(2) SERVICES FOR WHICH A SEPARATE AFFILIATE IS REQUIRED. The services for which a separate affiliate is required by paragraph (1) are:

(A) Manufacturing activities (as defined in section 273(h)).

(B) Origination of interLATA telecommunications services, other than—

(ii) out-of-region services described in section 271(b)(2); or

(C) InterLATA information services, other than electronic publishing (as defined in section 274(h)) and alarm monitoring services (as defined in section 275(e)).

(b) STRUCTURAL AND TRANSACTIONAL REQUIREMENTS. The separate affiliate required by this section—

(1) shall operate independently from the Bell operating company;

(2) shall maintain books, records, and accounts in the manner prescribed by the Commission which shall be separate from the books, records, and accounts maintained by the Bell operating company of which it is an affiliate;

(3) shall have separate officers, directors, and employees from the Bell operating company of which it is an affiliate;

(4) may not obtain credit under any arrangement that would permit a creditor, upon default, to have recourse to the assets of the Bell operating company; and

(5) shall conduct all transactions with the Bell operating company of which it is an affiliate on an arm's length basis with any such transactions reduced to writing and available for public inspection.

(c) NONDISCRIMINATION SAFEGUARDS. In its dealings with its affiliate described in subsection (a), a Bell operating company—

(1) may not discriminate between that company or affiliate and any other entity in the provision or procurement of goods, services, facilities, and information, or in the establishment of standards; and

(2) shall account for all transactions with an affiliate described in subsection (a) in accordance with accounting principles designated or approved by the Commission.

(d) BIENNIAL AUDIT.

(1) GENERAL REQUIREMENT. A company required to operate a separate affiliate under this section shall obtain and pay for a joint Federal/State audit every 2 years conducted by an independent auditor to determine whether such company has complied with this section and the regulations promulgated under this section.

(e) FULFILLMENT OF CERTAIN REQUESTS. A Bell operating company and an affiliate that is subject to the requirements of section 251(c)—

(1) shall fulfill any requests from an unaffiliated entity for telephone exchange service and exchange access within a period no longer than the period in which it provides such telephone exchange service and exchange access to itself or to its affiliates;

(2) shall not provide any facilities, services, or information concerning its provision of exchange access to the affiliate described in subsection (a) unless such facilities, services, or information are made available to other providers of interLATA services in that market on the same terms and conditions;

(3) shall charge the affiliate described in subsection (a), or impute to itself (if using the access for its provision of its own services), an amount for access to its telephone exchange service and exchange access that is no less than the amount charged to any unaffiliated interexchange carriers for such service; and

(4) may provide any interLATA or intraLATA facilities or services to its interLATA affiliate if such services or facilities are made available to all carriers at the same rates and on the same terms and conditions, and so long as the costs are appropriately allocated.

(f) SUNSET.

(1) MANUFACTURING AND LONG DISTANCE. The provisions of this section (other than subsection (e)) shall cease to apply with respect to the manufacturing activities or the interLATA telecommunications services of a Bell operating company 3 years after the date such Bell operating company or any Bell operating company affiliate is authorized to provide interLATA telecommunications services under section 271(d), unless the Commission extends such 3-year period by rule or order.

(2) INTERLATA INFORMATION SERVICES. The provisions of this section (other than subsection (e)) shall cease to apply with respect to the interLATA information services of a Bell operating company 4 years after the date of enactment of the Telecommunications Act of 1996, unless the Commission extends such 4-year period by rule or order.

SEC. 273. [47 U.S.C. § 273]
MANUFACTURING BY BELL OPERATING COMPANIES

(a) AUTHORIZATION. A Bell operating company may manufacture and provide telecommunications equipment, and manufacture customer premises equipment, if the Commission authorizes that Bell operating company or any Bell operating company affiliate to provide interLATA services under section 271(d), subject to the requirements of this section and the regulations prescribed thereunder.

(c) INFORMATION REQUIREMENTS.

(1) INFORMATION ON PROTOCOLS AND TECHNICAL REQUIREMENTS. Each Bell operating company shall, in accordance with regulations prescribed by the Commission, maintain and file with the Commission full and complete information with respect to the protocols and technical requirements for connection with and use of its telephone exchange service facilities.

(4) PLANNING INFORMATION. Each Bell operating company shall provide, to interconnecting carriers providing telephone exchange service, timely information on the planned deployment of telecommunications equipment.

(d) MANUFACTURING LIMITATIONS FOR STANDARD-SETTING ORGANIZATIONS.

(3) MANUFACTURING SAFEGUARDS.

(A) [A]ny entity which certifies telecommunications equipment or customer premises equipment manufactured by an unaffiliated entity shall only manufacture a particular class of telecommunications equipment or customer premises equipment for which it is undertaking or has undertaken, during the previous 18 months, certification activity for such class of equipment through a separate affiliate

(C) Such entity that certifies such equipment shall—

(i) not discriminate in favor of its manufacturing affiliate in the establishment of standards, generic requirements, or product certification;

(ii) not disclose to the manufacturing affiliate any proprietary information that has been received at any time from an unaffiliated manufacturer, unless authorized in writing by the owner of the information; and

(iii) not permit any employee engaged in product certification for telecommunications equipment or customer premises equipment to engage jointly in sales or marketing of any such equipment with the affiliated manufacturer.

(6) SUNSET. The requirements of paragraphs (3) and (4) shall terminate for the particular relevant activity when the Commission determines that there are alternative sources of industry-wide standards, industry-wide generic requirements, or product certification for a particular class of telecommunications equipment or customer premises equipment available in the United States. Alternative sources shall be deemed to exist when such sources provide commercially viable alternatives that are providing such services to customers.

(8) DEFINITIONS. For purposes of this subsection:

(B) The term "generic requirement" means a description of acceptable product attributes for use by local exchange carriers in establishing product specifications for the purchase of telecommunications equipment, customer premises equipment, and software integral thereto.

(C) The term "industry-wide" means activities funded by or performed on behalf of local exchange carriers for use in providing wireline telephone exchange service whose combined total of deployed access lines in the United States constitutes at least 30 percent of all access lines deployed by telecommunications carriers in the United States as of the date of enactment of the Telecommunications Act of 1996.

(D) The term "certification" means any technical process whereby a party determines whether a product, for use by more than one local exchange carrier, conforms with the specified requirements pertaining to such product.

(E) The term "accredited standards development organization" means an entity composed of industry members which has been accredited by an institution vested with the responsibility for standards accreditation by the industry.

(e) BELL OPERATING COMPANY EQUIPMENT PROCUREMENT AND SALES.

(1) NONDISCRIMINATION STANDARDS FOR MANUFACTURING. In the procurement or awarding of supply contracts for telecommunications equipment, a Bell operating company, or any entity acting on its behalf, for the duration of the requirement for a separate subsidiary including manufacturing under this Act—

(A) shall consider such equipment, produced or supplied by unrelated persons; and

(B) may not discriminate in favor of equipment produced or supplied by an affiliate or related person.

(2) PROCUREMENT STANDARDS. Each Bell operating company or any entity acting on its behalf shall make procurement decisions and award all supply contracts for equipment, services, and software on the basis of an objective assessment of price, quality, delivery, and other commercial factors.

(3) NETWORK PLANNING AND DESIGN. A Bell operating company shall, to the extent consistent with the antitrust laws, engage in joint network planning and design with local exchange carriers operating in the same area of interest.

(4) SALES RESTRICTIONS. Neither a Bell operating company engaged in manufacturing nor a manufacturing affiliate of such a company shall restrict sales to any

local exchange carrier of telecommunications equipment, including software integral to the operation of such equipment and related upgrades.

SEC. 274. [47 U.S.C. § 274]
ELECTRONIC PUBLISHING BY BELL OPERATING COMPANIES

(a) LIMITATIONS. No Bell operating company or any affiliate may engage in the provision of electronic publishing that is disseminated by means of such Bell operating company's or any of its affiliates' basic telephone service, except that nothing in this section shall prohibit a separated affiliate or electronic publishing joint venture operated in accordance with this section from engaging in the provision of electronic publishing.

(b) SEPARATED AFFILIATE OR ELECTRONIC PUBLISHING JOINT VENTURE REQUIREMENTS. A separated affiliate or electronic publishing joint venture shall be operated independently from the Bell operating company. Such separated affiliate or joint venture and the Bell operating company with which it is affiliated shall—

(1) maintain separate books, records, and accounts and prepare separate financial statements;

(3) carry out transactions

(A) in a manner consistent with such independence,

(B) pursuant to written contracts or tariffs that are filed with the Commission and made publicly available, and

(C) in a manner that is auditable in accordance with generally accepted auditing standards;

(6) not use for the marketing of any product or service of the separated affiliate or joint venture, the name, trademarks, or service marks of an existing Bell operating company except for names, trademarks, or service marks that are owned by the entity that owns or controls the Bell operating company;

(c) JOINT MARKETING.

(1) IN GENERAL. Except as provided in paragraph (2)—

(A) a Bell operating company shall not carry out any promotion, marketing, sales, or advertising for or in conjunction with a separated affiliate; and

(B) a Bell operating company shall not carry out any promotion, marketing, sales, or advertising for or in conjunction with an affiliate that is related to the provision of electronic publishing.

(2) PERMISSIBLE JOINT ACTIVITIES.

(A) JOINT TELEMARKETING. A Bell operating company may provide inbound telemarketing or referral services related to the provision of electronic publishing for a separated affiliate, electronic publishing joint venture, affiliate, or unaffiliated electronic publisher: Provided, That if such services are provided to a separated affiliate, electronic publishing joint venture, or affiliate, such services shall be made available to all electronic publishers on request, on nondiscriminatory terms.

(B) TEAMING ARRANGEMENTS. A Bell operating company may engage in nondiscriminatory teaming or business arrangements to engage in electronic publishing with any separated affiliate or with any other electronic publisher if

(i) the Bell operating company only provides facilities, services, and basic telephone service information as authorized by this section, and

(ii) the Bell operating company does not own such teaming or business arrangement.

(C) ELECTRONIC PUBLISHING JOINT VENTURES. A Bell operating company or affiliate may participate on a nonexclusive basis in electronic publishing joint ventures with entities that are not a Bell operating company, affiliate, or separated affiliate to provide electronic publishing services, if the Bell operating company or affiliate has not more than a 50 percent direct or indirect equity interest (or the equivalent thereof) or the right to more than 50 percent of the gross revenues under a revenue sharing or royalty agreement in any electronic publishing joint venture.

(d) BELL OPERATING COMPANY REQUIREMENT. A Bell operating company under common ownership or control with a separated affiliate or electronic publishing joint venture shall provide network access and interconnections for basic telephone service to electronic publishers at just and reasonable rates that are tariffed (so long as rates for such services are subject to regulation) and that are not higher on a per-unit basis than those charged for such services to any other electronic publisher or any separated affiliate engaged in electronic publishing.

(g) EFFECTIVE DATES.

(1) TRANSITION. Any electronic publishing service being offered to the public by a Bell operating company or affiliate on the date of enactment of the Telecommunications Act of 1996 shall have one year from such date of enactment to comply with the requirements of this section.

(2) SUNSET. The provisions of this section shall not apply to conduct occurring after 4 years after the date of enactment of the Telecommunications Act of 1996.

(h) DEFINITION OF ELECTRONIC PUBLISHING.

(1) IN GENERAL. The term "electronic publishing" means the dissemination, provision, publication, or sale to an unaffiliated entity or person, of any one or more of the following: news (including sports); entertainment (other than interactive games); business, financial, legal, consumer, or credit materials; editorials, columns, or features; advertising; photos or images; archival or research material; legal notices or public records; scientific, educational, instructional, technical, professional, trade, or other literary materials; or other like or similar information.

(2) EXCEPTIONS. The term "electronic publishing" shall not include the following services:

(A) Information access, as that term is defined by the AT&T Consent Decree.

(B) The transmission of information as a common carrier.

(C) The transmission of information as part of a gateway to an information service that does not involve the generation or alteration of the content of information, including data transmission, address translation, protocol conversion, billing management, introductory information content, and navigational systems that enable users to access electronic publishing services, which do not affect the presentation of such electronic publishing services to users.

(D) Voice storage and retrieval services, including voice messaging and electronic mail services.

(E) Data processing or transaction processing services that do not involve the generation or alteration of the content of information.

(I) The provision of directory assistance that provides names, addresses, and telephone numbers and does not include advertising.

(J) Caller identification services.

(M) Any other network service of a type that is like or similar to these network services and that does not involve the generation or alteration of the content of information.

(O) Video programming or full motion video entertainment on demand.

SEC. 275. [47 U.S.C. § 275]
ALARM MONITORING SERVICES

(a) DELAYED ENTRY INTO ALARM MONITORING.

(1) PROHIBITION. No Bell operating company or affiliate thereof shall engage in the provision of alarm monitoring services before the date which is 5 years after the date of enactment of the Telecommunications Act of 1996.

(b) NONDISCRIMINATION. An incumbent local exchange carrier (as defined in section 251(h)) engaged in the provision of alarm monitoring services shall—

(1) provide nonaffiliated entities, upon reasonable request, with the network services it provides to its own alarm monitoring operations, on nondiscriminatory terms and conditions; and

(2) not subsidize its alarm monitoring services either directly or indirectly from telephone exchange service operations.

TITLE III—PROVISIONS RELATING TO RADIO

PART I—GENERAL PROVISIONS

SEC. 301. [47 U.S.C. § 301]
LICENSE FOR RADIO COMMUNICATION OR TRANSMISSION OF ENERGY

It is the purpose of this Act, among other things, to maintain the control of the United States over all the channels of radio transmission; and to provide for the use of such channels, but not the ownership thereof, by persons for limited periods of time, under licenses granted by Federal authority, and no such license shall be construed to create any right, beyond the terms, conditions, and periods of the license. No person shall use or operate any apparatus for the transmission of energy or communications or signals by radio ... except under and in accordance with this Act and with a license in that behalf granted under the provisions of this Act.

SEC. 303. [47 U.S.C. § 303]
GENERAL POWERS OF COMMISSION

Except as otherwise provided in this Act, the Commission from time to time, as public convenience, interest, or necessity requires, shall—

(a) Classify radio stations;

(b) Prescribe the nature of the service to be rendered by each class of licensed stations and each station within any class;

(c) Assign bands of frequencies to the various classes of stations, and assign frequencies for each individual station and determine the power which each station shall use and the time during which it may operate;

(f) Make such regulations not inconsistent with law as it may deem necessary to prevent interference between stations and to carry out the provisions of this Act....

(g) Study new uses for radio, provide for experimental uses of frequencies, and generally encourage the larger and more effective use of radio in the public interest;

(i) Have authority to make special regulations applicable to radio stations engaged in chain broadcasting;

(r) Make such rules and regulations and prescribe such restrictions and conditions, not inconsistent with law, as may be necessary to carry out the provisions of this Act, or any international radio or wire communications treaty or convention....

(x) Require, in the case of an apparatus designed to receive television signals that are shipped in interstate commerce or manufactured in the United States and that have a picture screen 13 inches or greater in size (measured diagonally), that such apparatus be equipped with a feature designed to enable viewers to block display of all programs with a common rating, except as otherwise permitted by regulations pursuant to section 330(c)(4).

SEC. 304. [47 U.S.C. § 304]
WAIVER BY LICENSEE

No station license shall be granted by the Commission until the applicant therefor shall have waived any claim to the use of any particular frequency or of the electromagnetic spectrum as against the regulatory power of the United States because of the previous use of the same, whether by license or otherwise.

SEC. 307. [47 U.S.C. § 307]
ALLOCATION OF FACILITIES; TERM OF LICENSES

(a) The Commission, if public convenience, interest, or necessity will be served thereby, subject to the limitations of this Act, shall grant to any applicant therefor, a station license provided for by this Act.

(b) The Commission shall make such distribution of licenses, frequencies, hours of operation, and of power among the several States and communities as to provide a fair, efficient, and equitable distribution of radio service to each of the same

(c) TERMS OF LICENSES.

(1) INITIAL AND RENEWAL LICENSES. Each license granted for the operation of a broadcasting station shall be for a term of not to exceed 8 years. Upon application therefor, a renewal of such license may be granted from time to time for a term of not to exceed 8 years from the date of expiration of the preceding license, if the Commission finds that public interest, convenience, and necessity would be served thereby.

SEC. 308. [47 U.S.C. § 308]
REQUIREMENTS FOR LICENSE

(b) CONDITIONS. All applications for station licenses, or modifications or renewals thereof, shall set forth such facts as the Commission by regulation may prescribe as to the citizenship, character, and financial, technical, and other qualifications of the applicant to operate the station; the ownership and location of the proposed station and of the stations, if any, with which it is proposed to communicate; the frequencies and the power desired to be used; the hours of the day or other periods of time during which it is proposed to operate the station; the purposes for which the station is to be used; and such other information as it may require. The Commission, at any time after the filing of such original application and during the term of any such license, may require from an applicant or licensee further written statements of fact to enable it to determine whether such original application should be granted or denied or such license revoked. Such application and/or such statement of fact shall be signed by the applicant and/or licensee in any manner or form, including by electronic means, as the Commission may prescribe by regulation.

(d) SUMMARY OF COMPLAINTS [ON VIOLENT PROGRAMMING]. Each applicant for the renewal of a commercial or noncommercial television license shall attach as an exhibit to the application a summary of written comments and suggestions received from the public and maintained by the licensee (in accordance with Commission regulations) that comment on the applicant's programming, if any, and that are characterized by the commentor as constituting violent programming.

SEC. 309. [47 U.S.C. § 309]
APPLICATION FOR LICENSE

(a) CONSIDERATIONS IN GRANTING APPLICATION. Subject to the provisions of this section, the Commission shall determine, in the case of each application filed with it to which section 308 of this title applies, whether the public interest, convenience, and necessity will be served by the granting of such application, and, if the Commission, upon examination of such application and upon consideration of such other matters as the Commission may officially notice, shall find that public interest, convenience, and necessity would be served by the granting thereof, it shall grant such application.

(d) PETITION TO DENY APPLICATION; TIME; CONTENTS; REPLY; FINDINGS

(1) Any party in interest may file with the Commission a petition to deny any application....

(e) HEARINGS; INTERVENTION; EVIDENCE; BURDEN OF PROOF. If, in the case of any application ... a substantial and material question of fact is presented ... [the Commission] shall formally designate the application for hearing. Any hearing subsequently held upon such application shall be a full hearing in which the applicant and all other parties in interest shall be permitted to participate....

(j) USE OF COMPETITIVE BIDDING

(1) General authority. If, consistent with the obligations described in paragraph (6)(E), mutually exclusive applications are accepted for any initial license or construction permit, then, except as provided in paragraph (2), the Commission shall grant the license or permit to a qualified applicant through a system of competitive bidding that meets the requirements of this subsection.

(2) Exemptions. The competitive bidding authority granted by this subsection shall not apply to licenses or construction permits issued by the Commission—

(A) for public safety radio services, including private internal radio services used by State and local governments and non-government entities and including emergency road services provided by not-for-profit organizations, that—

(i) are used to protect the safety of life, health, or property; and

(ii) are not made commercially available to the public;

(B) for initial licenses or construction permits for digital television service given to existing terrestrial broadcast licensees to replace their analog television service licenses; or

(C) for stations described in section 397(6) of this title.

(3) DESIGN OF SYSTEMS OF COMPETITIVE BIDDING. For each class of licenses or permits that the Commission grants through the use of a competitive bid-

ding system, the Commission shall, by regulation, establish a competitive bidding methodology. The Commission shall seek to design and test multiple alternative methodologies under appropriate circumstances. The Commission shall, directly or by contract, provide for the design and conduct (for purposes of testing) of competitive bidding using a contingent combinatorial bidding system that permits prospective bidders to bid on combinations or groups of licenses in a single bid and to enter multiple alternative bids within a single bidding round. In identifying classes of licenses and permits to be issued by competitive bidding, in specifying eligibility and other characteristics of such licenses and permits, and in designing the methodologies for use under this subsection, the Commission shall include safeguards to protect the public interest in the use of the spectrum and shall seek to promote the purposes specified in section 151 of this title and the following objectives:

(A) the development and rapid deployment of new technologies, products, and services for the benefit of the public, including those residing in rural areas, without administrative or judicial delays;

(B) promoting economic opportunity and competition and ensuring that new and innovative technologies are readily accessible to the American people by avoiding excessive concentration of licenses and by disseminating licenses among a wide variety of applicants, including small businesses, rural telephone companies, and businesses owned by members of minority groups and women;

(C) recovery for the public of a portion of the value of the public spectrum resource made available for commercial use and avoidance of unjust enrichment through the methods employed to award uses of that resource;

(D) efficient and intensive use of the electromagnetic spectrum;

(E) ensure that, in the scheduling of any competitive bidding under this subsection, an adequate period is allowed-

(i) before issuance of bidding rules, to permit notice and comment on proposed auction procedures; and

(ii) after issuance of bidding rules, to ensure that interested parties have a sufficient time to develop business plans, assess market conditions, and evaluate the availability of equipment for the relevant services; and

(F) for any auction of eligible frequencies described in section 923(g)(2) of this title, the recovery of 110 percent of estimated relocation or sharing costs as provided to the Commission pursuant to section 923(g)(4) of this title.

(4) CONTENTS OF REGULATIONS. In prescribing regulations pursuant to paragraph (3), the Commission shall—

(A) consider alternative payment schedules and methods of calculation, including lump sums or guaranteed installment payments, with or without royalty payments, or other schedules or methods that promote the objectives described in paragraph (3)(B), and combinations of such schedules and methods;

(B) include performance requirements, such as appropriate deadlines and penalties for performance failures, to ensure prompt delivery of service to rural areas, to prevent stockpiling or warehousing of spectrum by licensees or permittees, and to promote investment in and rapid deployment of new technologies and services;

(C) consistent with the public interest, convenience, and necessity, the purposes of this chapter, and the characteristics of the proposed service, prescribe area designations and bandwidth assignments that promote (i) an equitable distribution of licenses and services among geographic areas, (ii) economic opportunity for a wide variety of applicants, including small businesses, rural telephone companies, and businesses owned by members of minority groups and women, and (iii) investment in and rapid deployment of new technologies and services;

(D) ensure that small businesses, rural telephone companies, and businesses owned by members of minority groups and women are given the opportunity to participate in the provision of spectrum-based services, and, for such purposes, consider the use of tax certificates, bidding preferences, and other procedures;

(E) require such transfer disclosures and antitrafficking restrictions and payment schedules as may be necessary to prevent unjust enrichment as a result of the methods employed to issue licenses and permits; and

(F) prescribe methods by which a reasonable reserve price will be required, or a minimum bid will be established, to obtain any license or permit being assigned pursuant to the competitive bidding, unless the Commission determines that such a reserve price or minimum bid is not in the public interest.

(5) BIDDER AND LICENSEE QUALIFICATION. No person shall be permitted to participate in a system of competitive bidding pursuant to this subsection unless such bidder submits such information and assurances as the Commission may require to demonstrate that such bidder's application is acceptable for filing. No license shall be granted to an applicant selected pursuant to this subsection unless the Commission determines that the applicant is qualified pursuant to subsection (a) of this section and sections 308(b) and 310 of this title. Consistent with the objectives described in paragraph (3), the Commission shall, by regulation, prescribe expedited procedures consistent with the procedures authorized by subsection (i)(2) of this section for the resolution of any substantial and material issues of fact concerning qualifications.

(7) CONSIDERATION OF REVENUES IN PUBLIC INTEREST DETERMINATIONS

(A) CONSIDERATION PROHIBITED. In making a decision pursuant to section 303(c) of this title to assign a band of frequencies to a use for which licenses or permits will be issued pursuant to this subsection, and in prescribing regulations pursuant to paragraph (4)(C) of this subsection, the Commission may not base a finding of public interest, convenience, and necessity on the expectation of Federal revenues from the use of a system of competitive bidding under this subsection.

(B) CONSIDERATION LIMITED. In prescribing regulations pursuant to paragraph (4)(A) of this subsection, the Commission may not base a finding of public interest, convenience, and necessity solely or predominantly on the expectation of Federal revenues from the use of a system of competitive bidding under this subsection.

(C) CONSIDERATION OF DEMAND FOR SPECTRUM NOT AFFECTED. Nothing in this paragraph shall be construed to prevent the Commission from continuing to consider consumer demand for spectrum-based services.

(8) TREATMENT OF REVENUES

(G) INCENTIVE AUCTIONS

(i) In general. Notwithstanding subparagraph (A) and except as provided in subparagraph (B), the Commission may encourage a licensee to relinquish voluntarily some or all of its licensed spectrum usage rights in order to permit the assignment of new initial licenses subject to flexible-use service rules by sharing with such licensee a portion, based on the value of the relinquished rights as determined in the reverse auction required by clause (ii)(I), of the proceeds (including deposits and upfront payments from successful bidders) from the use of a competitive bidding system under this subsection.

(ii) Limitations. The Commission may not enter into an agreement for a licensee to relinquish spectrum usage rights in exchange for a share of auction proceeds under clause (i) unless—

(I) the Commission conducts a reverse auction to determine the amount of compensation that licensees would accept in return for voluntarily relinquishing spectrum usage rights; and

(II) at least two competing licensees participate in the reverse auction.

(11) TERMINATION. The authority of the Commission to grant a license or permit under this subsection shall expire September 30, 2022.

(14) AUCTION OF RECAPTURED BROADCAST TELEVISION SPECTRUM

(A) LIMITATIONS ON TERMS OF TERRESTRIAL TELEVISION BROADCAST LICENSES. A full-power television broadcast license that authorizes analog television service may not be renewed to authorize such service for a period that extends beyond June 12, 2009.

(B) SPECTRUM REVERSION AND RESALE

(i) The Commission shall—

(I) ensure that, as licenses for analog television service expire pursuant to subparagraph (A), each licensee shall cease using electromagnetic spectrum assigned to such service according to the Commission's direction; and

(II) reclaim and organize the electromagnetic spectrum in a manner consistent with the objectives described in paragraph (3) of this subsection.

(ii) Licensees for new services occupying spectrum reclaimed pursuant to clause (i) shall be assigned in accordance with this subsection.

(C) CERTAIN LIMITATIONS ON QUALIFIED BIDDERS PROHIBITED. In prescribing any regulations relating to the qualification of bidders for spectrum reclaimed pursuant to subparagraph (B)(i), the Commission, for any license that may be used for any digital television service where the grade A contour of the station is projected to encompass the entirety of a city with a population in excess of 400,000 (as determined using the 1990 decennial census), shall not—

(i) preclude any party from being a qualified bidder for such spectrum on the basis of—

(I) the Commission's duopoly rule (47 C.F.R. 73.3555(b)); or

(II) the Commission's newspaper cross-ownership rule (47 C.F.R. 73.3555(d)); or

(ii) apply either such rule to preclude such a party that is a winning bidder in a competitive bidding for such spectrum from using such spectrum for digital television service.

(17) CERTAIN CONDITIONS ON AUCTION PARTICIPATION PROHIBITED

(A) IN GENERAL. Notwithstanding any other provision of law, the Commission may not prevent a person from participating in a system of competitive bidding under this subsection if such person—

(i) complies with all the auction procedures and other requirements to protect the auction process established by the Commission; and

(ii) either—

(I) meets the technical, financial, character, and citizenship qualifications that the Commission may require under section 303(*l*)(1), 308(b), or 310 of this title to hold a license; or

(II) would meet such license qualifications by means approved by the Commission prior to the grant of the license.

(B) CLARIFICATION OF AUTHORITY. Nothing in subparagraph (A) affects any authority the Commission has to adopt and enforce rules of general applicability, including rules concerning spectrum aggregation that promote competition.

(k) BROADCAST STATION RENEWAL PROCEDURES.

(1) STANDARDS FOR RENEWAL. If the licensee of a broadcast station submits an application to the Commission for renewal of such license, the Commission shall grant the application if it finds, with respect to that station, during the preceding term of its license—

(A) the station has served the public interest, convenience, and necessity;

(B) there have been no serious violations by the licensee of this Act or the rules and regulations of the Commission; and

(C) there have been no other violations by the licensee of this Act or the rules and regulations of the Commission which, taken together, would constitute a pattern of abuse.

(2) CONSEQUENCE OF FAILURE TO MEET STANDARD. If any licensee of a broadcast station fails to meet the requirements of this subsection, the Commission may deny the application for renewal ... or grant such application on terms and conditions as are appropriate, including renewal for a term less than the maximum otherwise permitted.

(4) COMPETITOR CONSIDERATION PROHIBITED. In making the determinations specified in paragraph (1) or (2), the Commission shall not consider whether the public interest, convenience, and necessity might be served by the grant of a license to a person other than the renewal applicant.

(*l*) APPLICABILITY OF COMPETITIVE BIDDING TO PENDING COMPARATIVE LICENSING CASES. With respect to competing applications for initial licenses or construction permits for commercial radio or television stations that were filed with the Commission before July 1, 1997, the Commission shall—

(1) have the authority to conduct a competitive bidding proceeding pursuant to subsection (j) of this section to assign such license or permit;

(2) treat the persons filing such applications as the only persons eligible to be qualified bidders for purposes of such proceeding; and

(3) waive any provisions of its regulations necessary to permit such persons to enter an agreement to procure the removal of a conflict between their applications during the 180-day period beginning on August 5, 1997.

SEC. 310. [47 U.S.C. § 310]
LIMITATION ON HOLDING AND TRANSFER OF LICENSES

(b) No broadcast or common carrier ... license shall be granted to or held by—

(1) any alien or the representative of any alien;

(d) No construction permit or station license ... shall be transferred ... to any person except upon application to the Commission and upon finding by the Commission that the public interest, convenience, and necessity will be served thereby.... but in acting thereon the Commission may not consider whether the public interest, convenience, and necessity might be served by the transfer, assignment, or disposal of the permit or license to a person other than the proposed transferee or assignee

SEC. 311. [47 U.S.C. § 311]
SPECIAL REQUIREMENTS WITH RESPECT TO CERTAIN APPLICATIONS IN THE BROADCASTING SERVICE

(c) AGREEMENT BETWEEN TWO OR MORE APPLICANTS; APPROVAL OF COMMISSION; PENDENCY OF APPLICATION

(1) If there are pending before the Commission two or more applications for a permit for construction of a broadcasting station, only one of which can be granted, it shall be unlawful, without approval of the Commission, for the applicants or any of them to effectuate an agreement whereby one or more of such applicants withdraws his or their application or applications.

(3) The Commission shall approve the agreement only if it determines that

(A) the agreement is consistent with the public interest, convenience, or necessity; and

(B) no party to the agreement filed its application for the purpose of reaching or carrying out such agreement.

(d) LICENSE FOR OPERATION OF STATION; AGREEMENT TO WITHDRAW APPLICATION; APPROVAL OF COMMISSION

(1) If there are pending before the Commission an application for the renewal of a license granted for the operation of a broadcasting station and one or more applications for a construction permit relating to such station, only one of which can be granted, it shall be unlawful, without approval of the Commission, for the applicants or any of them to effectuate an agreement whereby one or more of such applicants withdraws his or their application or applications in exchange for the payment of money, or the transfer of assets or any other thing of value by the remaining applicant or applicants.

(3) The Commission shall approve the agreement only if it determines that

(A) the agreement is consistent with the public interest, convenience, or necessity; and

(B) no party to the agreement filed its application for the purpose of reaching or carrying out such agreement.

SEC. 312. [47 U.S.C. § 312]
ADMINISTRATIVE SANCTIONS

(a) The Commission may revoke any station license or construction permit

(2) because of conditions coming to the attention of the Commission which would warrant it in refusing to grant a license or permit on an original application;

(3) for willful or repeated failure to operate substantially as set forth in the license; [or]

(7) for willful or repeated failure to allow reasonable access to or to permit purchase of reasonable amounts of time for the use of a broadcasting station by a legally qualified candidate for Federal elective office on behalf of his candidacy.

SEC. 315. [47 U.S.C. § 315]
CANDIDATES FOR PUBLIC OFFICE

(a) EQUAL OPPORTUNITIES REQUIREMENT; CENSORSHIP PROHIBITION; ALLOWANCE OF STATION USE; NEWS APPEARANCES EXCEPTION; PUBLIC INTEREST; PUBLIC ISSUES DISCUSSION OPPORTUNITIES. If any licensee shall permit any person who is a legally qualified candidate for any public office to use a broadcasting station, he shall afford equal opportunities to all other such candidates for that office in the use of such broadcasting station: Provided, That such licensee shall have no power of censorship over the material broadcast under the provisions of this section. No obligation is hereby imposed under this subsection upon any licensee to allow the use of its station by any such candidate. Appearance by a legally qualified candidate on any—

(1) bona fide newscast,

(2) bona fide news interview,

(3) bona fide news documentary (if the appearance of the candidate is incidental to the presentation of the subject or subjects covered by the news documentary), or

(4) on-the-spot coverage of bona fide news events (including but not limited to political conventions and activities incidental thereto),

shall not be deemed to be use of a broadcasting station within the meaning of this subsection. Nothing in the foregoing sentence shall be construed as relieving broadcasters, in connection with the presentation of newscasts, news interviews, news documentaries, and on-the-spot coverage of news events, from the obligation imposed upon them under this Act to operate in the public interest and to afford reasonable opportunity for the discussion of conflicting views on issues of public importance.

(b) CHARGES

(1) IN GENERAL. The charges made for the use of any broadcasting station by any person who is a legally qualified candidate for any public office in connection with his campaign for nomination for election, or election, to such office shall not exceed—

(A) subject to paragraph (2), during the forty-five days preceding the date of a primary or primary runoff election and during the sixty days preceding the date of a general or special election in which such person is a candidate, the lowest unit charge of the station for the same class and amount of time for the same period; and

(B) at any other time, the charges made for comparable use of such station by other users thereof.

(2) CONTENT OF BROADCASTS

(A) IN GENERAL. In the case of a candidate for Federal office, such candidate shall not be entitled to receive the rate under paragraph (1)(A) for the use of any broadcasting station unless the candidate provides written certification to the broadcast station that the candidate (and any authorized committee of the candidate) shall not make any direct reference to another candidate for the same office, in any broadcast using the rights and conditions of access under this chapter, unless such reference meets the requirements of subparagraph (C) or (D).

(B) LIMITATION ON CHARGES. If a candidate for Federal office (or any authorized committee of such candidate) makes a reference described in subparagraph (A) in any broadcast that does not meet the requirements of subparagraph

(C) or (D), such candidate shall not be entitled to receive the rate under paragraph (1)(A) for such broadcast or any other broadcast during any portion of the 45-day and 60-day periods described in paragraph (1)(A), that occur on or after the date of such broadcast, for election to such office.

(C) TELEVISION BROADCASTS. A candidate meets the requirements of this subparagraph if, in the case of a television broadcast, at the end of such broadcast there appears simultaneously, for a period no less than 4 seconds—

(i) a clearly identifiable photographic or similar image of the candidate; and

(ii) a clearly readable printed statement, identifying the candidate and stating that the candidate has approved the broadcast and that the candidate's authorized committee paid for the broadcast.

(D) RADIO BROADCASTS. A candidate meets the requirements of this subparagraph if, in the case of a radio broadcast, the broadcast includes a personal audio statement by the candidate that identifies the candidate, the office the candidate is seeking, and indicates that the candidate has approved the broadcast.

(c) DEFINITIONS. For purposes of this section—

(1) the term "broadcasting station" includes a community antenna television system; and

(2) the terms "licensee" and "station licensee" when used with respect to a community antenna television system mean the operator of such system.

(e) POLITICAL RECORD

(1) IN GENERAL. A licensee shall maintain, and make available for public inspection, a complete record of a request to purchase broadcast time that—

(A) is made by or on behalf of a legally qualified candidate for public office; or

(B) communicates a message relating to any political matter of national importance, including—

(i) a legally qualified candidate;

(ii) any election to Federal office; or

(iii) a national legislative issue of public importance.

(2) CONTENTS OF RECORD. A record maintained under paragraph (1) shall contain information regarding—

(A) whether the request to purchase broadcast time is accepted or rejected by the licensee;

(B) the rate charged for the broadcast time;

(C) the date and time on which the communication is aired;

(D) the class of time that is purchased;

(E) the name of the candidate to which the communication refers and the office to which the candidate is seeking election, the election to which the communication refers, or the issue to which the communication refers (as applicable);

(F) in the case of a request made by, or on behalf of, a candidate, the name of the candidate, the authorized committee of the candidate, and the treasurer of such committee; and

(G) in the case of any other request, the name of the person purchasing the time, the name, address, and phone number of a contact person for such person, and a list of the chief executive officers or members of the executive committee or of the board of directors of such person.

SEC. 319. [47 U.S.C. § 319]
CONSTRUCTION PERMITS

(a) No license shall be issued under the authority of this Act for the operation of any station unless a permit for its construction has been granted by the Commission.

SEC. 325. [47 U.S.C. § 325]
FALSE DISTRESS SIGNALS; REBROADCASTING; STUDIOS OF FOREIGN STATIONS

(a) No person within the jurisdiction of the United States shall knowingly utter or transmit, or cause to be uttered or transmitted, any false or fraudulent signal of distress, or communication relating thereto, nor shall any broadcasting station rebroadcast the program or any part thereof of another broadcasting station without the express authority of the originating station.

(b) CONSENT TO RETRANSMISSION OF BROADCASTING STATION SIGNALS

(1) No cable system or other multichannel video programming distributor shall retransmit the signal of a broadcasting station, or any part thereof, except

(A) with the express authority of the originating station;

(B) under section 534 of this title, in the case of a station electing, in accordance with this subsection, to assert the right to carriage under such section; or

(C) under section 338 of this title, in the case of a station electing, in accordance with this subsection, to assert the right to carriage under such section.

(2) This subsection shall not apply—

(A) to retransmission of the signal of a noncommercial television broadcast station;

(B) to retransmission of the signal of a television broadcast station outside the station's local market by a satellite carrier directly to its subscribers, if—

(i) such station was a superstation on May 1, 1991;

(ii) as of July 1, 1998, such station was retransmitted by a satellite carrier under the statutory license of section 119 of Title 17; and

(iii) the satellite carrier complies with any network nonduplication, syndicated exclusivity, and sports blackout rules adopted by the Commission under section 339(b) of this title;

(C) until December 31, 2014, to retransmission of the signals of network stations directly to a home satellite antenna, if the subscriber receiving the signal—

(i) is located in an area outside the local market of such stations; and

(ii) resides in an unserved household;

(D) to retransmission by a cable operator or other multichannel video provider, other than a satellite carrier, of the signal of a television broadcast station outside the station's local market if such signal was obtained from a satellite carrier and—

(i) the originating station was a superstation on May 1, 1991; and

(ii) as of July 1, 1998, such station was retransmitted by a satellite carrier under the statutory license of section 119 of Title 17; or

(E) during the 6-month period beginning on November 29, 1999, to the retransmission of the signal of a television broadcast station within the station's local market by a satellite carrier directly to its subscribers under the statutory license of section 122 of Title 17.

For purposes of this paragraph, the terms "satellite carrier" and "superstation" have the meanings given those terms, respectively, in section 119(d) of Title 17, as in effect on October 5, 1992, the term "unserved household" has the meaning given that term under section 119(d) of such title, and the term "local market" has the meaning given that term in section 122(j) of such title.

(3) (A) Within 45 days after October 5, 1992, the Commission shall commence a rulemaking proceeding to establish regulations to govern the exercise by television broadcast stations of the right to grant retransmission consent under this subsection and of the right to signal carriage under section 534 of this title, and such other regulations as are necessary to administer the limitations contained in paragraph (2). The Commission shall consider in such proceeding the impact that the grant of retransmission consent by television stations may have on the rates for the basic service tier and shall ensure that the regulations prescribed under this subsection do not conflict with the Commission's obligation under section 543(b)(1) of this title to ensure that the rates for the basic service tier are reasonable. Such rulemaking proceeding shall be completed within 180 days after October 5, 1992.

(B) The regulations required by subparagraph (A) shall require that television stations, within one year after October 5, 1992, and every three years thereafter, make an election between the right to grant retransmission consent under this subsection and the right to signal carriage under section 534 of this title. If there is more than one cable system which services the same geographic area, a station's election shall apply to all such cable systems.

(C) The Commission shall commence a rulemaking proceeding to revise the regulations governing the exercise by television broadcast stations of the right to grant retransmission consent under this subsection, and such other regulations as are necessary to administer the limitations contained in paragraph (2). Such regulations shall—

(i) establish election time periods that correspond with those regulations adopted under subparagraph (B) of this paragraph;

(ii) until January 1, 2015, prohibit a television broadcast station that provides retransmission consent from engaging in exclusive contracts for carriage or failing to negotiate in good faith, and it shall not be a failure to negotiate in good faith if the television broadcast station enters into retransmission consent agreements containing different terms and conditions, including price terms, with different multichannel video programming distributors if such different terms and conditions are based on competitive marketplace considerations; and

(iii) until January 1, 2015, prohibit a multichannel video programming distributor from failing to negotiate in good faith for retransmission consent under this section, and it shall not be a failure to negotiate in good faith if the distributor enters into retransmission consent agreements containing different terms and conditions, including price terms, with different broadcast stations if such different terms and conditions are based on competitive marketplace considerations.

(4) If an originating television station elects under paragraph (3)(B) to exercise its right to grant retransmission consent under this subsection with respect to a cable system, the provisions of section 534 of this title shall not apply to the carriage of the signal of such station by such cable system. If an originating television station elects under paragraph (3)(C) to exercise its right to grant retransmission consent under this subsection with respect to a satellite carrier, section 338 of this title shall not apply to the carriage of the signal of such station by such satellite carrier.

(5) The exercise by a television broadcast station of the right to grant retransmission consent under this subsection shall not interfere with or supersede the rights under section 338, 534, or 535 of this title of any station electing to assert the right to signal carriage under that section.

(6) Nothing in this section shall be construed as modifying the compulsory copyright license established in section 111 of Title 17 or as affecting existing or future video programming licensing agreements between broadcasting stations and video programmers.

(7) For purposes of this subsection, the term—

(A) "network station" has the meaning given such term under section 119(d) of Title 17; and

(B) "television broadcast station" means an over-the-air commercial or non-commercial television broadcast station licensed by the Commission under subpart E of part 73 of title 47, Code of Federal Regulations, except that such term does not include a low-power or translator television station.

(c) BROADCAST TO FOREIGN COUNTRIES FOR REBROADCAST TO UNITED STATES; PERMIT. No person shall be permitted to locate, use, or maintain a radio broadcast studio or other place or apparatus from which or whereby sound waves are converted into electrical energy, or mechanical or physical reproduction of sound waves produced, and caused to be transmitted or delivered to a radio station in a foreign country for the purpose of being broadcast from any radio station there having a power output of sufficient intensity and/or being so located geographically that its emissions may be received consistently in the United States, without first obtaining a permit from the Commission upon proper application therefor.

(e) ENFORCEMENT PROCEEDINGS AGAINST SATELLITE CARRIERS CONCERNING RETRANSMISSIONS OF TELEVISION BROADCAST STATIONS IN THE RESPECTIVE LOCAL MARKETS OF SUCH CARRIERS

(8) RELIEF. If the Commission determines that a satellite carrier has retransmitted the television broadcast station to at least one person in the local market of such station and has failed to meet its burden of proving one of the defenses under paragraph (4) with respect to such retransmission, the Commission shall be required to—

(A) make a finding that the satellite carrier violated subsection (b)(1) with respect to that station; and

(B) issue an order, within 45 days after the filing of the complaint, containing—

(i) a cease-and-desist order directing the satellite carrier immediately to stop making any further retransmissions of the television broadcast station to any person within the local market of such station until such time as the Commission determines that the satellite carrier is in compliance with subsection (b)(1) of this section with respect to such station;

(ii) if the satellite carrier is found to have violated subsection (b)(1) of this section with respect to more than two television broadcast stations, a cease-and-desist order directing the satellite carrier to stop making any further retransmission of any television broadcast station to any person within the local market of such station, until such time as the Commission, after giving notice to the station, that the satellite carrier is in compliance with subsection (b)(1) of this section with respect to such stations; and

(iii) an award to the complainant of that complainant's costs and reasonable attorney's fees.

SEC. 326. [47 U.S.C. § 326]
CENSORSHIP; INDECENT LANGUAGE

Nothing in this chapter shall be understood or construed to give the Commission the power of censorship over the radio communications or signals transmitted by any radio station, and no regulation or condition shall be promulgated or fixed by the Commission which shall interfere with the right of free speech by means of radio communication.

SEC. 333. [47 U.S.C. § 333]
WILLFUL OR MALICIOUS INTERFERENCE

No person shall willfully or maliciously interfere with or cause interference to any radio communications of any station licensed or authorized by or under this Act or operated by the United States Government.

SEC. 335. [47 U.S.C. § 335]
DIRECT BROADCAST SATELLITE SERVICE OBLIGATIONS

(a) PROCEEDING REQUIRED TO REVIEW DBS RESPONSIBILITIES. The Commission shall ... impose, on providers of direct broadcast satellite service, public interest or other requirements for providing video programming. Any regulations prescribed pursuant to such rulemaking shall, at a minimum, apply the access to broadcast time requirement of section 312(a)(7) of this title and the use of facilities requirements of section 315 of this title to providers of direct broadcast satellite service providing video programming. Such proceeding also shall examine the opportunities that the establishment of direct broadcast satellite service provides for the principle of localism under this chapter, and the methods by which such principle may be served through technological and other developments in, or regulation of, such service.

(b) CARRIAGE OBLIGATIONS FOR NONCOMMERCIAL, EDUCATIONAL, STATE PUBLIC AFFAIRS, AND INFORMATIONAL PROGRAMMING.

(1) CHANNEL CAPACITY REQUIRED.

(A) IN GENERAL.... the Commission shall require, as a condition of any provision, initial authorization, or authorization renewal for a provider of direct broadcast satellite service providing video programming, that the provider of such service reserve a portion of its channel capacity, equal to not less than 4 percent nor more than 7 percent, exclusively for noncommercial programming of an educational or informational nature.

(2) USE OF UNUSED CHANNEL CAPACITY. A provider of such service may utilize for any purpose any unused channel capacity required to be reserved under this subsection pending the actual use of such channel capacity for noncommercial programming of an educational or informational nature.

(3) PRICES, TERMS, AND CONDITIONS; EDITORIAL CONTROL. A provider of direct broadcast satellite service shall meet the requirements of this subsection by making channel capacity available to national educational programming suppliers, upon reasonable prices, terms, and conditions, as determined by the Commission. The provider of direct broadcast satellite service shall not exercise any editorial control over any video programming provided pursuant to this subsection.

SEC. 336. [47 U.S.C. § 336]
BROADCAST SPECTRUM FLEXIBILITY

(a) COMMISSION ACTION. If the Commission determines to issue additional licenses for advanced television services, the Commission—

(1) should limit the initial eligibility for such licenses to persons that, as of the date of such issuance, are licensed to operate a television broadcast station or hold a permit to construct such a station (or both); and

(2) shall adopt regulations that allow the holders of such licenses to offer such ancillary or supplementary services on designated frequencies as may be consistent with the public interest, convenience, and necessity.

(c) RECOVERY OF LICENSE. If the Commission grants a license for advanced television services to a person that, as of the date of such issuance, is licensed to operate a television broadcast station or holds a permit to construct such a station (or both), the Commission shall, as a condition of such license, require that either the additional license or the original license held by the licensee be surrendered to the Commission for reallocation or reassignment (or both) pursuant to Commission regulation.

(d) PUBLIC INTEREST REQUIREMENT. Nothing in this section shall be construed as relieving a television broadcasting station from its obligation to serve the public interest, convenience, and necessity. In the Commission's review of any application for renewal of a broadcast license for a television station that provides ancillary or supplementary services, the television licensee shall establish that all of its program services on the existing or advanced television spectrum are in the public interest.

(e) FEES.

(1) SERVICES TO WHICH FEES APPLY. If the regulations prescribed pursuant to subsection (a) permit a licensee to offer ancillary or supplementary services on a designated frequency—

(A) for which the payment of a subscription fee is required in order to receive such services, or

(B) for which the licensee directly or indirectly receives compensation from a third party in return for transmitting material furnished by such third party (other than commercial advertisements used to support broadcasting for which a subscription fee is not required), the Commission shall establish a program to assess and collect from the licensee for such designated frequency an annual fee or other schedule or method of payment that promotes the objectives described in subparagraphs (A) and (B) of paragraph (2).

(2) COLLECTION OF FEES. The program required by paragraph (1) shall—

(A) be designed (i) to recover for the public a portion of the value of the public spectrum resource made available for such commercial use, and (ii) to avoid unjust enrichment through the method employed to permit such uses of that resource;

(B) recover for the public an amount that, to the extent feasible, equals but does not exceed (over the term of the license) the amount that would have been recovered had such services been licensed pursuant to the provisions of section 309(j) of this title and the Commission's regulations thereunder; and

(C) be adjusted by the Commission from time to time in order to continue to comply with the requirements of this paragraph.

(f) EVALUATION. Within 10 years after the date the Commission first issues additional licenses for advanced television services, the Commission shall conduct an evaluation of the advanced television services program. Such evaluation shall include—

(1) an assessment of the willingness of consumers to purchase the television receivers necessary to receive broadcasts of advanced television services;

(2) an assessment of alternative uses, including public safety use, of the frequencies used for such broadcasts; and

(3) the extent to which the Commission has been or will be able to reduce the amount of spectrum assigned to licensees.

SEC. 338. [47 U.S.C. § 338]
CARRIAGE OF LOCAL TELEVISION SIGNALS BY SATELLITE CARRIERS

(a) CARRIAGE OBLIGATIONS

(1) IN GENERAL. Each satellite carrier providing, under section 122 of Title 17, secondary transmissions to subscribers located within the local market of a television broadcast station of a primary transmission made by that station shall carry upon request the signals of all television broadcast stations located within that local market, subject to section 325(b) of this title.

(2) REMEDIES FOR FAILURE TO CARRY. In addition to the remedies available to television broadcast stations under section 501(f) of Title 17, the Commission may use the Commission's authority under this chapter to assure compliance with the obligations of this subsection, but in no instance shall a Commission enforcement proceeding be required as a predicate to the pursuit of a remedy available under such section 501(f).

(3) LOW POWER STATION CARRIAGE OPTIONAL. No low power television station whose signals are provided under section 119(a)(14) of Title 17 shall be entitled to insist on carriage under this section, regardless of whether the satellite carrier provides secondary transmissions of the primary transmissions of other stations in the same local market pursuant to section 122 of such title nor shall any such carriage be considered in connection with the requirements of subsection (c) of this section.

(4) CARRIAGE OF SIGNALS OF LOCAL STATIONS IN CERTAIN MARKETS. A satellite carrier that offers multichannel video programming distribution service in the United States to more than 5,000,000 subscribers shall (A) within 1 year after December 8, 2004, retransmit the signals originating as analog signals of each television broadcast station located in any local market within a State that is not part of the contiguous United States, and (B) within 30 months after December 8, 2004, retransmit the signals originating as digital signals of each such station. The retransmissions of such stations shall be made available to substantially all of the satellite carrier's subscribers in each station's local market, and the retransmissions of the stations in at least one market in the State shall be made available to substantially all of the satel-

lite carrier's subscribers in areas of the State that are not within a designated market area. The cost to subscribers of such retransmissions shall not exceed the cost of retransmissions of local television stations in other States. Within 1 year after December 8, 2004, the Commission shall promulgate regulations concerning elections by television stations in such State between mandatory carriage pursuant to this section and retransmission consent pursuant to section 325(b) of this title, which shall take into account the schedule on which local television stations are made available to viewers in such State.

(5) NONDISCRIMINATION IN CARRIAGE OF HIGH DEFINITION SIGNALS OF NONCOMMERCIAL EDUCATIONAL TELEVISION STATIONS

(A) EXISTING CARRIAGE OF HIGH DEFINITION SIGNALS. If, before the date of enactment of the Satellite Television Extension and Localism Act of 2010, an eligible satellite carrier is providing, under section 122 of Title 17, any secondary transmissions in high definition format to subscribers located within the local market of a television broadcast station of a primary transmission made by that station, then such satellite carrier shall carry the signals in high-definition format of qualified noncommercial educational television stations located within that local market in accordance with the following schedule:

(i) By December 31, 2010, in at least 50 percent of the markets in which such satellite carrier provides such secondary transmissions in high definition format.

(ii) By December 31, 2011, in every market in which such satellite carrier provides such secondary transmissions in high definition format.

(B) NEW INITIATION OF SERVICE. If, on or after the date of enactment of the Satellite Television Extension and Localism Act of 2010, an eligible satellite carrier initiates the provision, under section 122 of Title 17, of any secondary transmissions in high definition format to subscribers located within the local market of a television broadcast station of a primary transmission made by that station, then such satellite carrier shall carry the signals in high-definition format of all qualified noncommercial educational television stations located within that local market.

SEC. 339. [47 U.S.C. § 339]

(a) PROVISIONS RELATING TO CARRIAGE OF DISTANT SIGNALS

(1) CARRIAGE PERMITTED

(A) IN GENERAL. Subject to section 119 of Title 17, any satellite carrier shall be permitted to provide the signals of no more than two network stations in a single day for each television network to any household not located within the local markets of those network stations.

(B) ADDITIONAL SERVICE. In addition to signals provided under subparagraph (A), any satellite carrier may also provide service under the statutory license of section 122 of Title 17, to the local market within which such household is located. The service provided under section 122 of such title may be in addition to the two signals provided under section 119 of such title.

(2) REPLACEMENT OF DISTANT SIGNALS WITH LOCAL SIGNALS. Notwithstanding any other provision of paragraph (1), the following rules shall apply after December 8, 2004:

(A) RULES FOR GRANDFATHERED SUBSCRIBERS

(i) For those receiving distant signals. In the case of a subscriber of a satellite carrier who is eligible to receive the signal of a network station solely by reason of section 119(e) of Title 17 (in this subparagraph referred to as a "distant signal"), and who, as of October 1, 2009, is receiving the distant signal of that network station, the following shall apply:

(I) In a case in which the satellite carrier makes available to the subscriber the signal of a local network station affiliated with the same television network pursuant to section 338 of this title, the carrier may only provide the secondary transmissions of the distant signal of a station affiliated with the same network to that subscriber—

(aa) if, within 60 days after receiving the notice of the satellite carrier under section 338(h)(1) of this title, the subscriber elects to retain the distant signal; but

(bb) only until such time as the subscriber elects to receive such local signal.

(II) Notwithstanding subclause (I), the carrier may not retransmit the distant signal to any subscriber who is eligible to receive the signal of a network station solely by reason of section 119(e) of Title 17, unless such carrier, within 60 days after December 8, 2004, submits to that television network the list and statement required by subparagraph (F)(i).

(ii) For those not receiving distant signals. In the case of any subscriber of a satellite carrier who is eligible to receive the distant signal of a network station solely by reason of section 119(e) of Title 17 and who did not receive a distant signal of a station affiliated with the same network on October 1, 2009, the carrier may not provide the secondary transmissions of the distant signal of a station affiliated with the same network to that subscriber.

SEC. 397. [47 U.S.C. § 397]
DEFINITIONS

(6) The terms "noncommercial educational broadcast station" and "public broadcast station" mean a television or radio broadcast station which—

(A) under the rules and regulations of the Commission in effect on November 2, 1978, is eligible to be licensed by the Commission as a noncommercial educational radio or television broadcast station and which is owned and operated by a public agency or nonprofit private foundation, corporation, or association; or

(B) is owned and operated by a municipality and which transmits only noncommercial programs for education purposes.

TITLE IV—PROCEDURAL AND ADMINISTRATIVE PROVISIONS

SEC. 401. [47 U.S.C. § 401]
JURISDICTION TO ENFORCE ACT AND ORDERS OF THE COMMISSION

(a) The district courts of the United States shall have jurisdiction, upon application of the Attorney General of the United States at the request of the Commission, alleging a failure to comply with or a violation of any of the provisions of this Act by any person, to issue a writ or writs of mandamus commanding such person to comply with the provisions of this Act.

SEC. 402. [47 U.S.C. § 402]
PROCEEDINGS TO ENJOIN, SET ASIDE, ANNUL, OR SUSPEND ORDERS OF THE COMMISSION

(a) Any proceeding to enjoin, set aside, annul, or suspend any order of the Commission under this Act (except those appealable under subsection (b) of this section) shall be brought [in the circuit court of appeal where the filing party has its residence or principal office or in the D.C. Circuit].

(b) Appeals may be taken from decisions and orders of the Commission to the United States Court of Appeals for the District of Columbia in [licensing cases or proceedings in which a cease and desist order was issued].

TITLE V — PENAL PROVISIONS — FORFEITURES

SEC. 501. [47 U.S.C. § 501]
GENERAL PENALTY

Any person who willfully and knowingly does or causes or suffers to be done any act, matter, or thing, in this Act prohibited or declared to be unlawful, or who willfully and knowingly omits or fails to do any act, matter, or thing in this Act required to be done, or willfully and knowingly causes or suffers such omission or failure, shall upon conviction thereof, be punished for such offense, for which no penalty (other than a forfeiture) is provided in this Act, by a fine of not more than $10,000 or by imprisonment for a term not exceeding one year, or both; except that any person, having been once convicted of an offense punishable under this section, who is subsequently convicted of violating any provision of this Act punishable under this section, shall be punished by a fine of not more than $10,000 or by imprisonment for a term not exceeding two years, or both.

SEC. 502. [47 U.S.C. § 502]
VIOLATION OF RULES, REGULATIONS, AND SO FORTH

Any person who willfully and knowingly violates any rule, regulation, restriction, or condition made or imposed by the Commission under authority of this Act ... shall, in addition to any other penalties provided by law, be punished, upon conviction thereof, by a fine of not more than $500 for each and every day during which such offense occurs.

SEC. 503. [47 U.S.C. § 503]
FORFEITURES

(b) Activities constituting violations authorizing imposition of forfeiture penalty; amount of penalty; procedures applicable; persons subject to penalty; liability exemption period

(1) Any person who is determined by the Commission, in accordance with paragraph (3) or (4) of this subsection, to have—

(A) willfully or repeatedly failed to comply substantially with the terms and conditions of any license, permit, certificate, or other instrument or authorization issued by the Commission;

(B) willfully or repeatedly failed to comply with any of the provisions of this Act or of any rule, regulation, or order issued by the Commission under this Act ...;

shall be liable to the United States for a forfeiture penalty. A forfeiture penalty under this subsection shall be in addition to any other penalty provided for by this Act....

(2) (A) If the violator is (i) a broadcast station licensee or permittee, (ii) a cable television operator, or (iii) an applicant for any broadcast or cable television operator license, permit, certificate, or other instrument or authorization issued by the Commission, the amount of any forfeiture penalty determined under this section shall not exceed $25,000 for each violation or each day of a continuing violation, except that the amount assessed for any continuing violation shall not exceed a total of $250,000 for any single act or failure to act described in paragraph (1) of this subsection.

(B) If the violator is a common carrier subject to the provisions of this chapter or an applicant for any common carrier license, permit, certificate, or other instrument of authorization issued by the Commission, the amount of any forfeiture penalty determined under this subsection shall not exceed $100,000 for each violation or each day of a continuing violation, except that the amount assessed for any continuing violation shall not exceed a total of $1,000,000 for any single act or failure to act described in paragraph (1) of this subsection.

(C) Notwithstanding subparagraph (A), if the violator is

(i) (I) a broadcast station licensee or permittee; or

(II) an applicant for any broadcast license, permit, certificate, or other instrument or authorization issued by the Commission; and

(ii) determined by the Commission under paragraph (1) to have broadcast obscene, indecent, or profane language, the amount of any forfeiture penalty determined under this subsection shall not exceed $325,000 for each violation or each day of a continuing violation, except that the amount assessed for any continuing violation shall not exceed a total of $3,000,000 for any single act or failure to act.

(D) In any case not covered in subparagraph (A), (B), or (C), the amount of any forfeiture penalty determined under this subsection shall not exceed $10,000 for each violation or each day of a continuing violation, except that the amount assessed for any continuing violation shall not exceed a total of $75,000 for any single act or failure to act described in paragraph (1) of this subsection.

TITLE VI — CABLE COMMUNICATIONS

PART I — GENERAL PROVISIONS

SEC. 601. [47 U.S.C. § 521]
PURPOSES

The purposes of this title are to—

(1) establish a national policy concerning cable communications;

(2) establish franchise procedures and standards which encourage the growth and development of cable systems and which assure that cable systems are responsive to the needs and interests of the local community;

(3) establish guidelines for the exercise of Federal, State, and local authority with respect to the regulation of cable systems;

(4) assure that cable communications provide and are encouraged to provide the widest possible diversity of information sources and services to the public;

(5) establish an orderly process for franchise renewal which protects cable operators against unfair denials of renewal where the operator's past performance and proposal for future performance meet the standards established by this title; and

(6) promote competition in cable communications and minimize unnecessary regulation that would impose an undue economic burden on cable systems.

(a) APPLICABILITY OF AMENDMENTS TO FUTURE CONDUCT.

(1) AT&T CONSENT DECREE. Any conduct or activity that was, before the date of enactment of this Act, subject to any restriction or obligation imposed by the AT&T Consent Decree shall, on and after such date, be subject to the restrictions and obligations imposed by the Communications Act of 1934 as amended by this Act and shall not be subject to the restrictions and the obligations imposed by such Consent Decree.

SEC. 602. [47 U.S.C. § 522]
DEFINITIONS

For purposes of this title—

(1) the term "activated channels" means those channels engineered at the headend of a cable system for the provision of services generally available to residential subscribers of the cable system ...;

(3) the term "basic cable service" means any service tier which includes the retransmission of local television broadcast signals;

(6) the term "cable service" means—

(A) the one-way transmission to subscribers of (i) video programming, or (ii) other programming service;

(7) the term "cable system" means a facility, consisting of a set of closed transmission paths and associated signal generation, reception, and control equipment that is designed to provide cable service which includes video programming and which is provided to multiple subscribers within a community ...;

(11) the term "grade B contour" means the field strength of a television broadcast station computed in accordance with regulations promulgated by the Commission;

(13) the term "multichannel video programming distributor" means a person such as, but not limited to, a cable operator, a multichannel multipoint distribution service, a direct broadcast satellite service, or a television receive-only satellite program distributor, who makes available for purchase, by subscribers or customers, multiple channels of video programming;

(14) the term "other programming service" means information that a cable operator makes available to all subscribers generally;

(17) the term "service tier" means a category of cable service or other services provided by a cable operator and for which a separate rate is charged by the cable operator;

(20) the term "video programming" means programming provided by, or generally considered comparable to programming provided by, a television broadcast station.

PART II — USE OF CABLE CHANNELS AND CABLE OWNERSHIP RESTRICTIONS

SEC. 611. [47 U.S.C. § 531]
CABLE CHANNELS FOR PUBLIC, EDUCATIONAL, OR GOVERNMENTAL USE

(a) A franchising authority may establish requirements in a franchise with respect to the designation or use of channel capacity for public, educational, or governmental use only to the extent provided in this section.

(b) A franchising authority may in its request for proposals require as part of a franchise, and may require as part of a cable operator's proposal for a franchise renewal, subject to section 626 [47 U.S.C. § 546], that channel capacity be designated for public, educational, or governmental use, and channel capacity on institutional networks be designated for educational or governmental use, and may require rules and procedures for the use of the channel capacity designated pursuant to this section.

(c) A franchising authority may enforce any requirement in any franchise regarding the providing or use of such channel capacity. Such enforcement authority includes the authority to enforce any provisions of the franchise for services, facilities, or equipment proposed by the cable operator which relate to public, educational, or governmental use of channel capacity, whether or not required by the franchising authority pursuant to subsection (b).

(d) In the case of any franchise under which channel capacity is designated under subsection (b), the franchising authority shall prescribe—

(1) rules and procedures under which the cable operator is permitted to use such channel capacity for the provision of other services if such channel capacity is not being used for the purposes designated, and

(2) rules and procedures under which such permitted use shall cease.

(e) Subject to section 624(d) [47 U.S.C. § 544(d)], a cable operator shall not exercise any editorial control over any public, educational, or governmental use of channel capacity provided pursuant to this section, except a cable operator may refuse to transmit any public access program or portion of a public access program which contains obscenity, indecency, or nudity.

(f) For purposes of this section, the term "institutional network" means a communication network which is constructed or operated by the cable operator and which is generally available only to subscribers who are not residential subscribers.

SEC. 612. [47 U.S.C. § 532]
CABLE CHANNELS FOR COMMERCIAL USE

(a) The purpose of this section is to promote competition in the delivery of diverse sources of video programming and to assure that the widest possible diversity of information sources are made available to the public from cable systems in a manner consistent with growth and development of cable systems.

(b) (1) A cable operator shall designate channel capacity for commercial use by persons unaffiliated with the operator in accordance with the following requirements:

(A) An operator of any cable system with 36 or more (but not more than 54) activated channels shall designate 10 percent of such channels which are not otherwise required for use (or the use of which is not prohibited) by Federal law or regulation.

(B) An operator of any cable system with 55 or more (but not more than 100) activated channels shall designate 15 percent of such channels which are not otherwise required for use (or the use of which is not prohibited) by Federal law or regulation.

(C) An operator of any cable system with more than 100 activated channels shall designate 15 percent of all such channels.

(D) An operator of any cable system with fewer than 36 activated channels shall not be required to designate channel capacity for commercial use by persons unaffiliated with the operator.

(c) (1) If a person unaffiliated with the cable operator seeks to use channel capacity designated pursuant to subsection (b) for commercial use, the cable operator shall establish, consistent with the purpose of this section and with rules prescribed by the Commission ... the price, terms, and conditions of such use which are at least sufficient to assure that such use will not adversely affect the operation, financial condition, or market development of the cable system.

(2) A cable operator shall not exercise any editorial control over any video programming provided pursuant to this section, or in any other way consider the content of such programming, except that a cable operator may refuse to transmit any leased access program or portion of a leased access program which contains obscenity, indecency, or nudity and consider such content to the minimum extent necessary to establish a reasonable price for the commercial use of designated channel capacity by an unaffiliated person.

(4) (A) The Commission shall have the authority to—

(i) determine the maximum reasonable rates that a cable operator may establish pursuant to paragraph (1) for commercial use of designated channel capacity, including the rate charged for the billing of rates to subscribers and for the collection of revenue from subscribers by the cable operator for such use;

(f) In any action brought under this section in any Federal district court or before the Commission, there shall be a presumption that the price, terms, and conditions for use of channel capacity designated pursuant to subsection (b) are reasonable and in good faith unless shown by clear and convincing evidence to the contrary.

(h) Any cable service offered pursuant to this section shall not be provided, or shall be provided subject to conditions, if such cable service in the judgment of the franchising authority or the cable operator is obscene, or is in conflict with community standards in that it is lewd, lascivious, filthy, or indecent or is otherwise unprotected by the Constitution of the United States. This subsection shall permit a cable operator to enforce prospectively a written and published policy of prohibiting programming that the cable operator reasonably believes describes or depicts sexual or excretory activities or organs in a patently offensive manner as measured by contemporary community standards.

(i) (1) Notwithstanding the provisions of subsections (b) and (c), a cable operator required by this section to designate channel capacity for commercial use may use any such channel capacity for the provision of programming from a qualified minority programming source or from any qualified educational programming source, whether or not such source is affiliated with the cable operator. The channel capacity used to provide programming from a qualified minority programming source or from any qualified educational programming source pursuant to this subsection may not exceed 33 percent of the channel capacity designated pursuant to this section....

(j) (1) The Commission shall promulgate regulations designed to limit the access of children to indecent programming, as defined by Commission regulations, and which cable operators have not voluntarily prohibited under subsection (h) by—

(A) requiring cable operators to place on a single channel all indecent programs, as identified by program providers, intended for carriage on channels designated for commercial use under this section;

(B) requiring cable operators to block such single channel unless the subscriber requests access to such channel in writing; and

(C) requiring programmers to inform cable operators if the program would be indecent as defined by Commission regulations.

SEC. 613. [47 U.S.C. § 533]
OWNERSHIP RESTRICTIONS

(a) (2) It shall be unlawful for a cable operator to hold a license for multichannel multipoint distribution service ... in any portion of the franchise area served by that cable operator's cable system....

(c) The Commission may prescribe rules with respect to the ownership or control of cable systems by persons who own or control other media of mass communications which serve the same community served by a cable system.

(f) (1) In order to enhance effective competition, the Commission shall ... conduct a proceeding—

(A) to prescribe rules and regulations establishing reasonable limits on the number of cable subscribers a person is authorized to reach through cable systems owned by such person ...;

(B) to prescribe rules and regulations establishing reasonable limits on the number of channels on a cable system that can be occupied by a video programmer in which a cable operator has an attributable interest; and

(C) to consider the necessity and appropriateness of imposing limitations on the degree to which multichannel video programming distributors may engage in the creation or production of video programming.

(2) In prescribing rules and regulations under paragraph (1), the Commission shall, among other public interest objectives—

(A) ensure that no cable operator or group of cable operators can unfairly impede, either because of the size of any individual operator or because of joint actions by a group of operators of sufficient size, the flow of video programming from the video programmer to the consumer;

(B) ensure that cable operators affiliated with video programmers do not favor such programmers in determining carriage on their cable systems or do not unreasonably restrict the flow of the video programming of such programmers to other video distributors;

(D) account for any efficiencies and other benefits that might be gained through increased ownership or control; [and]

(G) not impose limitations which would impair the development of diverse and high quality video programming.

SEC. 614. [47 U.S.C. § 534]
CARRIAGE OF LOCAL COMMERCIAL TELEVISION SIGNALS

(a) CARRIAGE OBLIGATIONS. Each cable operator shall carry, on the cable system of that operator, the signals of local commercial television stations and qualified low power stations as provided by this section. Carriage of additional broadcast television signals on such system shall be at the discretion of such operator, subject to section 325(b) of this title.

(b) SIGNALS REQUIRED

(1) IN GENERAL

(A) A cable operator of a cable system with 12 or fewer usable activated channels shall carry the signals of at least three local commercial television stations, except that if such a system has 300 or fewer subscribers, it shall not be subject to any requirements under this section so long as such system does not delete from carriage by that system any signal of a broadcast television station.

(B) A cable operator of a cable system with more than 12 usable activated channels shall carry the signals of local commercial television stations, up to one-third of the aggregate number of usable activated channels of such system.

(2) SELECTION OF SIGNALS. Whenever the number of local commercial television stations exceeds the maximum number of signals a cable system is required to carry under paragraph (1), the cable operator shall have discretion in selecting which such stations shall be carried on its cable system, except that—

(A) under no circumstances shall a cable operator carry a qualified low power station in lieu of a local commercial television station; and

(B) if the cable operator elects to carry an affiliate of a broadcast network (as such term is defined by the Commission by regulation), such cable operator shall carry the affiliate of such broadcast network whose city of license reference point, as defined in section 76.53 of title 47, Code of Federal Regulations (in effect on January 1, 1991), or any successor regulation thereto, is closest to the principal headend of the cable system.

(3) CONTENT TO BE CARRIED

(A) A cable operator shall carry in its entirety, on the cable system of that operator, the primary video, accompanying audio, and line 21 closed caption transmission of each of the local commercial television stations carried on the cable system and, to the extent technically feasible, program-related material carried in the vertical blanking interval or on subcarriers. Retransmission of other material in the vertical blanking internal or other nonprogram-related material (including teletext and other subscription and advertiser-supported information services) shall be at the discretion of the cable operator. Where appropriate and feasible, operators may delete signal enhancements, such as ghost-canceling, from the broadcast signal and employ such enhancements at the system headend or headends.

(B) The cable operator shall carry the entirety of the program schedule of any television station carried on the cable system unless carriage of specific programming is prohibited, and other programming authorized to be substituted, under section 76.67 or subpart F of part 76 of title 47, Code of Federal Regulations (as in effect on January 1, 1991), or any successor regulations thereto.

(4) SIGNAL QUALITY

(A) NONDEGRADATION; TECHNICAL SPECIFICATIONS. The signals of local commercial television stations that a cable operator carries shall be carried without material degradation. The Commission shall adopt carriage standards to ensure that, to the extent technically feasible, the quality of signal processing and carriage provided by a cable system for the carriage of local commercial television stations will be no less than that provided by the system for carriage of any other type of signal.

(B) ADVANCED TELEVISION. At such time as the Commission prescribes modifications of the standards for television broadcast signals, the Commission shall initiate a proceeding to establish any changes in the signal carriage requirements of cable television systems necessary to ensure cable carriage of such broadcast signals of local commercial television stations which have been changed to conform with such modified standards.

(5) DUPLICATION NOT REQUIRED. Notwithstanding paragraph (1), a cable operator shall not be required to carry the signal of any local commercial television station that substantially duplicates the signal of another local commercial television station which is carried on its cable system, or to carry the signals of more than one local commercial television station affiliated with a particular broadcast network (as such term is defined by regulation). If a cable operator elects to carry on its cable system a signal which substantially duplicates the signal of another local commercial television station carried on the cable system, or to carry on its system the signals of more than one local commercial television station affiliated with a particular broadcast network, all such signals shall be counted toward the number of signals the operator is required to carry under paragraph (1).

(6) CHANNEL POSITIONING. Each signal carried in fulfillment of the carriage obligations of a cable operator under this section shall be carried on the cable system channel number on which the local commercial television station is broadcast over the air, or on the channel on which it was carried on July 19, 1985, or on the channel on which it was carried on January 1, 1992, at the election of the station, or on such other channel number as is mutually agreed upon by the station and the cable operator. Any dispute regarding the positioning of a local commercial television station shall be resolved by the Commission.

(7) SIGNAL AVAILABILITY. Signals carried in fulfillment of the requirements of this section shall be provided to every subscriber of a cable system. Such signals shall be viewable via cable on all television receivers of a subscriber which are connected to a cable system by a cable operator or for which a cable operator provides a connection. If a cable operator authorizes subscribers to install additional receiver connections, but does not provide the subscriber with such connections, or with the equipment and materials for such connections, the operator shall notify such subscribers of all broadcast stations carried on the cable system which cannot be viewed via cable without a converter box and shall offer to sell or lease such a converter box to such subscribers at rates in accordance with section 543(b)(3) of this title.

(10) COMPENSATION FOR CARRIAGE. A cable operator shall not accept or request monetary payment or other valuable consideration in exchange either for carriage of local commercial television stations in fulfillment of the requirements of this section or for the channel positioning rights provided to such stations under this section....

SEC. 615. [47 U.S.C. § 535]
CARRIAGE OF NONCOMMERCIAL TELEVISION STATIONS

(a) CARRIAGE OBLIGATIONS. In addition to the carriage requirements set forth in section 534 of this title, each cable operator of a cable system shall carry the signals of qualified noncommercial educational television stations in accordance with the provisions of this section.

(b) REQUIREMENTS TO CARRY QUALIFIED STATIONS

(1) GENERAL REQUIREMENT TO CARRY EACH QUALIFIED STATION. Subject to paragraphs (2) and (3) and subsection (e) of this section, each cable operator shall carry, on the cable system of that cable operator, any qualified local noncommercial educational television station requesting carriage.

(2) SYSTEMS WITH 12 OR FEWER CHANNELS

(A) Notwithstanding paragraph (1), a cable operator of a cable system with 12 or fewer usable activated channels shall be required to carry the signal of one qualified local noncommercial educational television station; except that a cable operator of such a system shall comply with subsection (c) of this section and may, in its discretion, carry the signals of other qualified noncommercial educational television stations.

(B) In the case of a cable system described in subparagraph (A) which operates beyond the presence of any qualified local noncommercial educational television station—

(i) the cable operator shall import and carry on that system the signal of one qualified noncommercial educational television station;

(ii) the selection for carriage of such a signal shall be at the election of the cable operator; and

(iii) in order to satisfy the requirements for carriage specified in this subsection, the cable operator of the system shall not be required to remove any other programming service actually provided to subscribers on March 29, 1990; except that such cable operator shall use the first channel available to satisfy the requirements of this subparagraph.

(3) SYSTEMS WITH 13 TO 36 CHANNELS

(A) Subject to subsection (c) of this section, a cable operator of a cable system with 13 to 36 usable activated channels—

(i) shall carry the signal of at least one qualified local noncommercial educational television station but shall not be required to carry the signals of more than three such stations, and

(ii) may, in its discretion, carry additional such stations.

(B) In the case of a cable system described in this paragraph which operates beyond the presence of any qualified local noncommercial educational television station, the cable operator shall import and carry on that system the signal of at least one qualified noncommercial educational television station to comply with subparagraph (A)(i).

(C) The cable operator of a cable system described in this paragraph which carries the signal of a qualified local noncommercial educational station affiliated with a State public television network shall not be required to carry the signal of any additional qualified local noncommercial educational television stations affiliated with the same network if the programming of such additional stations is substantially duplicated by the programming of the qualified local noncommercial educational television station receiving carriage.

(D) A cable operator of a system described in this paragraph which increases the usable activated channel capacity of the system to more than 36 channels on or after March 29, 1990, shall, in accordance with the other provisions of this section, carry the signal of each qualified local noncommercial educational television station requesting carriage, subject to subsection (e) of this section.

(e) SYSTEMS WITH MORE THAN 36 CHANNELS

A cable operator of a cable system with a capacity of more than 36 usable activated channels which is required to carry the signals of three qualified local noncommercial educational television stations shall not be required to carry the signals of additional such stations the programming of which substantially duplicates the programming broadcast by another qualified local noncommercial educational television station requesting carriage. Substantial duplication shall be defined by the Commission in a manner that promotes access to distinctive noncommercial educational television services.

PART III — FRANCHISING AND REGULATION

SEC. 621. [47 U.S.C. § 541]
GENERAL FRANCHISE REQUIREMENTS

(a) (1) A franchising authority may award ... one or more franchises within its jurisdiction; except that a franchising authority may not grant an exclusive franchise and may not unreasonably refuse to award an additional competitive franchise....

(2) Any franchise shall be construed to authorize the construction of a cable system over public rights-of-way, and through easements, which is within the area to be served by the cable system and which have been dedicated for compatible uses....

(3) In awarding a franchise or franchises, a franchising authority shall assure that access to cable service is not denied to any group of potential residential cable subscribers because of the income of the residents of the local area in which such group resides.

(4) In awarding a franchise, the franchising authority—

(A) shall allow the applicant's cable system a reasonable period of time to become capable of providing cable service to all households in the franchise area;

(B) may require adequate assurance that the cable operator will provide adequate public, educational, and governmental access channel capacity, facilities, or financial support; and

(C) may require adequate assurance that the cable operator has the financial, technical, or legal qualifications to provide cable service.

(b) (1) [A] cable operator may not provide cable service without a franchise.

(c) Any cable system shall not be subject to regulation as a common carrier or utility by reason of providing any cable service.

SEC. 622. [47 U.S.C. § 542]
FRANCHISE FEES

(a) Subject to the limitation of subsection (b), any cable operator may be required under the terms of any franchise to pay a franchise fee.

(b) For any twelve-month period, the franchise fees paid by a cable operator with respect to any cable system shall not exceed 5 percent of such cable operator's gross revenues derived in such period from the operation of the cable system....

SEC. 623. [47 U.S.C. § 543]
REGULATION OF RATES

(a) (1) No Federal agency or State may regulate the rates for the provision of cable service except to the extent provided under this section and section 612 [47 U.S.C. § 532].

(2) If the Commission finds that a cable system is subject to effective competition, the rates for the provision of cable service by such system shall not be subject to reg-

ulation by the Commission or by a State or franchising authority under this section. If the Commission finds that a cable system is not subject to effective competition—

(A) the rates for the provision of basic cable service shall be subject to regulation by a franchising authority ... and

(B) the rates for cable programming services shall be subject to regulation by the Commission under subsection (c).

(b) (1) The Commission shall, by regulation, ensure that the rates for the basic service tier are reasonable. Such regulations shall be designed to achieve the goal of protecting subscribers of any cable system that is not subject to effective competition from rates for the basic service tier that exceed the rates that would be charged for the basic service tier if such cable system were subject to effective competition.

(2) The Commission shall prescribe, and periodically thereafter revise, regulations to carry out its obligations under paragraph (1). In prescribing such regulations, the Commission—

(A) shall seek to reduce the administrative burdens on subscribers, cable operators, franchising authorities, and the Commission;

(B) may adopt formulas or other mechanisms and procedures in complying with the requirements of subparagraph (A); and

(C) shall take into account the following factors:

(i) the rates for cable systems, if any, that are subject to effective competition;

(ii) the direct costs (if any) of obtaining, transmitting, and otherwise providing signals carried on the basic service tier, including signals and services carried on the basic service tier pursuant to paragraph (7)(B), and changes in such costs;

(iii) only such portion of the joint and common costs (if any) of obtaining, transmitting, and otherwise providing such signals as is determined, in accordance with regulations prescribed by the Commission, to be reasonably and properly allocable to the basic service tier, and changes in such costs;

(iv) the revenues (if any) received by a cable operator from advertising from programming that is carried as part of the basic service tier or from other consideration obtained in connection with the basic service tier;

(v) the reasonably and properly allocable portion of any amount assessed as a franchise fee, tax, or charge of any kind imposed by any State or local authority on the transactions between cable operators and cable subscribers or any other fee, tax, or assessment of general applicability imposed by a governmental entity applied against cable operators or cable subscribers;

(vi) any amount required, in accordance with paragraph (4), to satisfy franchise requirements to support public, educational, or governmental channels or the use of such channels or any other services required under the franchise; and

(vii) a reasonable profit, as defined by the Commission consistent with the Commission's obligations to subscribers under paragraph (1).

(7) (A) Each cable operator of a cable system shall provide its subscribers a separately available basic service tier to which subscription is required for access to any other tier of service. Such basic service tier shall, at a minimum, consist of the following:

(i) All signals carried in fulfillment of the requirements of sections 614 and 615 [47 U.S.C. §§ 534 and 535].

(ii) Any public, educational, and governmental access programming required by the franchise of the cable system to be provided to subscribers.

(iii) Any signal of any television broadcast station that is provided by the cable operator to any subscriber, except a signal which is secondarily transmitted by a satellite carrier beyond the local service area of such station.

(B) A cable operator may add additional video programming signals or services to the basic service tier. Any such additional signals or services provided on the basic service tier shall be provided to subscribers at rates determined under the regulations prescribed by the Commission under this subsection.

(8) (A) A cable operator may not require the subscription to any tier other than the basic service tier required by paragraph (7) as a condition of access to video programming offered on a per channel or per program basis. A cable operator may not discriminate between subscribers to the basic service tier and other subscribers with regard to the rates charged for video programming offered on a per channel or per program basis.

(c) (1) The Commission shall, by regulation, establish the following:

(A) criteria prescribed in accordance with paragraph (2) for identifying, in individual cases, rates for cable programming services that are unreasonable;

(B) fair and expeditious procedures for the receipt, consideration, and resolution of complaints from any subscriber, franchising authority, or other relevant State or local government entity alleging that a rate for cable programming services charged by a cable operator violates the criteria prescribed under subparagraph (A)....

(2) In establishing the criteria for determining in individual cases whether rates for cable programming services are unreasonable under paragraph (1)(A), the Commission shall consider, among other factors—

(A) the rates for similarly situated cable systems offering comparable cable programming services ...;

(B) the rates for cable systems, if any, that are subject to effective competition;

(C) the history of the rates for cable programming services of the system, including the relationship of such rates to changes in general consumer prices;

(D) the rates, as a whole, for all the cable programming, cable equipment, and cable services provided by the system, other than programming provided on a per channel or per program basis;

(E) capital and operating costs of the cable system, including the quality and costs of the customer service provided by the cable system; and

(F) the revenues (if any) received by a cable operator from advertising from programming that is carried as part of the service for which a rate is being established....

(4) SUNSET OF UPPER TIER RATE REGULATION. This subsection shall not apply to cable programming services provided after March 31, 1999.

(*l*) As used in this section—

(1) The term "effective competition" means that—

(A) fewer than 30 percent of the households in the franchise area subscribe to the cable service of a cable system;

(B) the franchise area is—

(i) served by at least two unaffiliated multichannel video programming distributors each of which offers comparable video programming to at least 50 percent of the households in the franchise area; and

(ii) the number of households subscribing to programming services offered by multichannel video programming distributors other than the largest multichannel video programming distributor exceeds 15 percent of the households in the franchise area; or

(C) a multichannel video programming distributor operated by the franchising authority for that franchise area offers video programming to at least 50 percent of the households in that franchise area.

(D) a local exchange carrier or its affiliate (or any multichannel video programming distributor using the facilities of such carrier or its affiliate) offers video programming services directly to subscribers by any means (other than direct-to-home satellite services) in the franchise area of an unaffiliated cable operator which is providing cable service in that franchise area, but only if the video programming services so offered in that area are comparable to the video programming services provided by the unaffiliated cable operator in that area.

(2) The term "cable programming service" means any video programming provided over a cable system, regardless of service tier, including installation or rental of equipment used for the receipt of such video programming, other than (A) video programming carried on the basic service tier, and (B) video programming offered on a per channel or per program basis.

SEC. 624. [47 U.S.C. § 544]
REGULATION OF SERVICES, FACILITIES, AND EQUIPMENT

(a) Any franchising authority may not regulate the services, facilities, and equipment provided by a cable operator except to the extent consistent with this title.

(b) In the case of any franchise granted after the effective date of this title, the franchising authority, to the extent related to the establishment or operation of a cable system—

(1) in its request for proposals for a franchise (including requests for renewal proposals, subject to section 626 [47 U.S.C. § 546]), may establish requirements for facilities and equipment, but may not, except as provided in subsection (h), establish requirements for video programming or other information services; and

(2) subject to section 625 [47 U.S.C. § 545], may enforce any requirements contained within the franchise—

(A) for facilities and equipment; and

(B) for broad categories of video programming or other services.

(d) (1) Nothing in this title shall be construed as prohibiting a franchising authority and a cable operator from specifying ... that certain cable services shall not be provided or shall be provided subject to conditions, if such cable services are obscene or are otherwise unprotected by the Constitution of the United States.

(2) (A) In order to restrict the viewing of programming which is obscene or indecent, upon the request of a subscriber, a cable operator shall provide (by sale or lease) a device by which the subscriber can prohibit viewing of a particular cable service during periods selected by that subscriber.

SEC. 626. [47 U.S.C. § 546]
RENEWAL

(a) (1) A franchising authority may, on its own initiative during the 6-month period which begins with the 36th month before the franchise expiration, commence a proceeding which affords the public in the franchise area appropriate notice and participation for the purpose of (A) identifying the future cable-related community needs and interests, and (B) reviewing the performance of the cable operator under the franchise during the then current franchise term....

(b) (1) Upon completion of a proceeding under subsection (a), a cable operator seeking renewal of a franchise may, on its own initiative or at the request of a franchising authority, submit a proposal for renewal.

(c) (1) Upon submittal by a cable operator of a proposal to the franchising authority for the renewal of a franchise pursuant to subsection (b), the franchising authority shall provide prompt public notice of such proposal and, during the 4-month period which begins on the date of the submission of the cable operator's proposal pursuant to subsection (b), renew the franchise or, issue a preliminary assessment that the franchise should not be renewed and, at the request of the operator or on its own initiative, commence an administrative proceeding....

(2) To consider whether—

(A) the cable operator has substantially complied with the material terms of the existing franchise and with applicable law;

(B) the quality of the operator's service, including signal quality, response to consumer complaints, and billing practices, but without regard to the mix or quality of cable services or other services provided over the system, has been reasonable in light of community needs;

(C) the operator has the financial, legal, and technical ability to provide the services, facilities, and equipment as set forth in the operator's proposal; and

(D) the operator's proposal is reasonable to meet the future cable-related community needs and interests, taking into account the cost of meeting such needs and interests.

(d) Any denial of a proposal for renewal that has been submitted in compliance with subsection (b) shall be based on one or more adverse findings made with respect to the factors described in subparagraphs (A) through (D) of subsection (c)(1), pursuant to the record of the proceeding under subsection (c).

(e) (1) Any cable operator whose proposal for renewal has been denied by a final decision of a franchising authority made pursuant to this section, or has been adversely affected by a failure of the franchising authority to act in accordance with the procedural requirements of this section, may appeal such final decision or failure....

SEC. 628. [47 U.S.C. § 548]
DEVELOPMENT OF COMPETITION AND DIVERSITY IN VIDEO PROGRAMMING DISTRIBUTION

(a) PURPOSE. The purpose of this section is to promote the public interest, convenience, and necessity by increasing competition and diversity in the multichannel video programming market, to increase the availability of satellite cable programming and satellite broadcast programming to persons in rural and other areas not currently able to receive such programming, and to spur the development of communications technologies.

(b) PROHIBITION. It shall be unlawful for a cable operator, a satellite cable programming vendor in which a cable operator has an attributable interest, or a satellite broadcast programming vendor to engage in unfair methods of competition or unfair or deceptive acts or practices, the purpose or effect of which is to hinder significantly or to prevent any multichannel video programming distributor from providing satellite cable programming or satellite broadcast programming to subscribers or consumers.

(c) REGULATIONS REQUIRED.

(2) MINIMUM CONTENTS OF REGULATIONS. The regulations to be promulgated under this section shall—

(A) establish effective safeguards to prevent a cable operator which has an attributable interest in a satellite cable programming vendor or a satellite broadcast programming vendor from unduly or improperly influencing the decision of such vendor to sell, or the prices, terms, and conditions of sale of, satellite cable programming or satellite broadcast programming to any unaffiliated multichannel video programming distributor;

(B) prohibit discrimination by a satellite cable programming vendor in which a cable operator has an attributable interest or by a satellite broadcast programming vendor in the prices, terms, and conditions of sale or delivery of satellite cable programming or satellite broadcast programming among or between cable systems, cable operators, or other multichannel video programming distributors, or their agents or buying groups; except that such a satellite cable programming vendor in which a cable operator has an attributable interest or such a satellite broadcast programming vendor shall not be prohibited from—

(i) imposing reasonable requirements for creditworthiness, offering of service, and financial stability and standards regarding character and technical quality;

(ii) establishing different prices, terms, and conditions to take into account actual and reasonable differences in the cost of creation, sale, delivery, or transmission of satellite cable programming or satellite broadcast programming;

(iii) establishing different prices, terms, and conditions which take into account economies of scale, cost savings, or other direct and legitimate economic benefits reasonably attributable to the number of subscribers served by the distributor; or

(iv) entering into an exclusive contract that is permitted under subparagraph (D);

(C) prohibit practices, understandings, arrangements, and activities, including exclusive contracts for satellite cable programming or satellite broadcast programming between a cable operator and a satellite cable programming vendor or satellite broadcast programming vendor, that prevent a multichannel video programming distributor from obtaining such programming from any satellite cable programming vendor in which a cable operator has an attributable interest or any satellite broadcast programming vendor in which a cable operator has an attributable interest for distribution to persons in areas not served by a cable operator as of the date of enactment of this section; and

(D) with respect to distribution to persons in areas served by a cable operator, prohibit exclusive contracts for satellite cable programming or satellite broadcast programming between a cable operator and a satellite cable programming vendor in which a cable operator has an attributable interest or a satellite broadcast programming vendor in which a cable operator has an attributable interest, unless the Commission determines (in accordance with paragraph (4)) that such contract is in the public interest.

(4) PUBLIC INTEREST DETERMINATIONS ON EXCLUSIVE CONTRACTS. In determining whether an exclusive contract is in the public interest for purposes of paragraph (2)(D), the Commission shall consider each of the following factors with respect to the effect of such contract on the distribution of video programming in areas that are served by a cable operator:

(A) the effect of such exclusive contract on the development of competition in local and national multichannel video programming distribution markets;

(B) the effect of such exclusive contract on competition from multichannel video programming distribution technologies other than cable;

(C) the effect of such exclusive contract on the attraction of capital investment in the production and distribution of new satellite cable programming;

(D) the effect of such exclusive contract on diversity of programming in the multichannel video programming distribution market; and

(E) the duration of the exclusive contract.

(d) ADJUDICATORY PROCEEDING. Any multichannel video programming distributor aggrieved by conduct that it alleges constitutes a violation of subsection (b), or the regulations of the Commission under subsection (c), may commence an adjudicatory proceeding at the Commission.

(e) REMEDIES FOR VIOLATIONS.

(1) REMEDIES AUTHORIZED. Upon completion of such adjudicatory proceeding, the Commission shall have the power to order appropriate remedies, including, if necessary, the power to establish prices, terms, and conditions of sale of programming to the aggrieved multichannel video programming distributor.

PART IV — MISCELLANEOUS PROVISIONS

SEC. 631. [47 U.S.C. § 551]
PROTECTION OF SUBSCRIBER PRIVACY

(a) (1) At the time of entering into an agreement to provide any cable service or other service to a subscriber and at least once a year thereafter, a cable operator shall provide notice in the form of a separate, written statement to such subscriber which clearly and conspicuously informs the subscriber of—

(A) the nature of personally identifiable information collected or to be collected with respect to the subscriber and the nature of the use of such information;

(B) the nature, frequency, and purpose of any disclosure which may be made of such information, including an identification of the types of persons to whom the disclosure may be made;

(C) the period during which such information will be maintained by the cable operator;

(D) the times and place at which the subscriber may have access to such information in accordance with subsection (d); and

(E) the limitations provided by this section with respect to the collection and disclosure of information by a cable operator and the right of the subscriber under subsections (f) and (h) to enforce such limitations.

(b) (1) Except as provided in paragraph (2), a cable operator shall not use the cable system to collect personally identifiable information concerning any subscriber without the prior written or electronic consent of the subscriber concerned.

(2) A cable operator may use the cable system to collect such information in order to—

    (A) obtain information necessary to render a cable service or other service provided by the cable operator to the subscriber; or

    (B) detect unauthorized reception of cable communications.

(c) (1) Except as provided in paragraph (2), a cable operator shall not disclose personally identifiable information concerning any subscriber without the prior written or electronic consent of the subscriber concerned and shall take such actions as are necessary to prevent unauthorized access to such information by a person other than the subscriber or cable operator.

(2) A cable operator may disclose such information if the disclosure is—

    (A) necessary to render, or conduct a legitimate business activity related to, a cable service or other service provided by the cable operator to the subscriber;

    (B) subject to subsection (h), made pursuant to a court order authorizing such disclosure, if the subscriber is notified of such order by the person to whom the order is directed; or

    (C) a disclosure of the names and addresses of subscribers to any cable service or other service, if—

        (i) the cable operator has provided the subscriber the opportunity to prohibit or limit such disclosure, and

        (ii) the disclosure does not reveal, directly or indirectly, the—

            (I) extent of any viewing or other use by the subscriber of a cable service or other service provided by the cable operator, or

            (II) the nature of any transaction made by the subscriber over the cable system of the cable operator.

(d) A cable subscriber shall be provided access to all personally identifiable information regarding that subscriber which is collected and maintained by a cable operator.

(h) A governmental entity may obtain personally identifiable information concerning a cable subscriber pursuant to a court order only if, in the court proceeding relevant to such court order—

    (1) such entity offers clear and convincing evidence that the subject of the information is reasonably suspected of engaging in criminal activity and that the information sought would be material evidence in the case; and

    (2) the subject of the information is afforded the opportunity to appear and contest such entity's claim.

SEC. 632. [47 U.S.C. § 552]
CONSUMER PROTECTION AND CUSTOMER SERVICE

(a) A franchising authority may establish and enforce—

    (1) customer service requirements of the cable operator; and

    (2) construction schedules and other construction-related requirements, including construction-related performance requirements, of the cable operator.

(b) The Commission shall ... establish standards by which cable operators may fulfill their customer service requirements. Such standards shall include, at a minimum, requirements governing—

(1) cable system office hours and telephone availability;

(2) installations, outages, and service calls; and

(3) communications between the cable operator and the subscriber (including standards governing bills and refunds).

SEC. 633. [47 U.S.C. § 553]
UNAUTHORIZED RECEPTION OF CABLE SERVICE

(a) (1) No person shall intercept or receive or assist in intercepting or receiving any communications service offered over a cable system, unless specifically authorized to do so by a cable operator or as may otherwise be specifically authorized by law.

(2) For the purpose of this section, the term "assist in intercepting or receiving" shall include the manufacture or distribution of equipment intended by the manufacturer or distributor (as the case may be) for unauthorized reception of any communications service offered over a cable system in violation of subparagraph (1).

SEC. 634. [47 U.S.C. § 554]
EQUAL EMPLOYMENT OPPORTUNITY

(a) This section shall apply to any corporation, partnership, association, joint-stock company, or trust engaged primarily in the management or operation of any cable system.

(b) Equal opportunity in employment shall be afforded by each entity specified in subsection (a), and no person shall be discriminated against in employment by such entity because of race, color, religion, national origin, age, or sex.

(e) (2) The Commission shall, periodically, but not less frequently than every five years, investigate the employment practices of each entity described in subsection (a), in the aggregate, as well as in individual job categories, and determine whether such entity is in compliance with the requirements of subsections (b), (c), and (d), including whether such entity's employment practices deny or abridge women and minorities equal employment opportunities.

(f) (1) If the Commission finds after notice and hearing that the entity involved has willfully or repeatedly without good cause failed to comply with the requirements of this section, such failure shall constitute a substantial failure to comply with this title.

(2) Any person who is determined by the Commission, through an investigation pursuant to subsection (e) or otherwise, to have failed to meet or failed to make best efforts to meet the requirements of this section, or rules under this section, shall be liable to the United States for a forfeiture penalty of $500 for each violation....

SEC. 638. [47 U.S.C. § 558]
CRIMINAL AND CIVIL LIABILITY

Nothing in this title shall be deemed to affect the criminal or civil liability of cable programmers or cable operators pursuant to the Federal, State, or local law of libel, slander, obscenity, incitement, invasions of privacy, false or misleading advertising, or other similar laws, except that cable operators shall not incur any such liability for any program carried on any channel designated for public, educational, governmental use or on any other channel obtained under section 612 [47 U.S.C. § 532] or under similar arrangements unless the program involves obscene material.

SEC. 639. [47 U.S.C. § 559]
OBSCENE PROGRAMMING

Whoever transmits over any cable system any matter which is obscene or otherwise unprotected by the Constitution of the United States shall be fined not more than $10,000 or imprisoned not more than 2 years, or both.

SEC. 640. [47 U.S.C. § 560]
SCRAMBLING OF CABLE CHANNELS FOR NONSUBSCRIBERS

(a) SUBSCRIBER REQUEST. Upon request by a cable service subscriber, a cable operator shall, without charge, fully scramble or otherwise fully block the audio and video programming of each channel carrying such programming so that one not a subscriber does not receive it.

SEC. 641. [47 U.S.C. § 561]
SCRAMBLING OF SEXUALLY EXPLICIT ADULT VIDEO SERVICE PROGRAMMING

(a) REQUIREMENT. In providing sexually explicit adult programming or other programming that is indecent on any channel of its service primarily dedicated to sexually-oriented programming, a multichannel video programming distributor shall fully scramble or otherwise fully block the video and audio portion of such channel so that one not a subscriber to such channel or programming does not receive it.

(b) IMPLEMENTATION. Until a multichannel video programming distributor complies with the requirement set forth in subsection (a), the distributor shall limit the access of children to the programming referred to in that subsection by not providing such programming during the hours of the day (as determined by the Commission) when a significant number of children are likely to view it.

PART V — VIDEO PROGRAMMING SERVICES
PROVIDED BY TELEPHONE COMPANIES

SEC. 651. [47 U.S.C. § 571]
REGULATORY TREATMENT OF VIDEO PROGRAMMING SERVICES

(a) LIMITATIONS ON CABLE REGULATION.

(1) RADIO-BASED SYSTEMS. To the extent that a common carrier (or any other person) is providing video programming to subscribers using radio communication, such carrier (or other person) shall be subject to the requirements of title III and section 652 [47 U.S.C. § 572], but shall not otherwise be subject to the requirements of this title.

(2) COMMON CARRIAGE OF VIDEO TRAFFIC. To the extent that a common carrier is providing transmission of video programming on a common carrier basis, such carrier shall be subject to the requirements of title II and section 652 [47 U.S.C. § 572], but shall not otherwise be subject to the requirements of this title.

(3) CABLE SYSTEMS AND OPEN VIDEO SYSTEMS. To the extent that a common carrier is providing video programming to its subscribers in any manner other than that described in paragraphs (1) and (2) —

(A) such carrier shall be subject to the requirements of this title, unless such programming is provided by means of an open video system for which the Commission has approved a certification under section 653 [47 U.S.C. § 573]; or

(B) if such programming is provided by means of an open video system for which the Commission has approved a certification under section 653 [47 U.S.C. § 573], such carrier shall be subject to the requirements of this part, but shall be subject to parts I through IV of this title only as provided in 653(c) [47 U.S.C. § 573(c)].

(b) LIMITATIONS ON INTERCONNECTION OBLIGATIONS. A local exchange carrier that provides cable service through an open video system or a cable system shall not be required, pursuant to title II of this Act, to make capacity available on a nondiscriminatory basis to any other person for the provision of cable service directly to subscribers.

SEC. 652. [47 U.S.C. § 572]
PROHIBITION ON BUY OUTS

(a) ACQUISITIONS BY CARRIERS. No local exchange carrier ... may acquire more than a 10 percent financial interest, or any management interest, in any cable operator providing cable service within the local exchange carrier's telephone service area.

(b) ACQUISITIONS BY CABLE OPERATORS. No cable operator ... may acquire more than a 10 percent financial interest, or any management interest, in any local exchange carrier providing telephone exchange service within such cable operator's franchise area.

(c) JOINT VENTURES. A local exchange carrier and a cable operator whose telephone service area and cable franchise area, respectively, are in the same market may not enter into any joint venture or partnership to provide video programming directly to subscribers or to provide telecommunications services within such market.

(d) EXCEPTIONS. [Several sub-sub-sections provide exemptions for certain rural systems, for certain competitive cable systems, and for certain small cable systems. The FCC is also granted limited authority to waive the requirements of (a), (b), and (c).]

SEC. 653. [47 U.S.C. § 573]
ESTABLISHMENT OF OPEN VIDEO SYSTEMS

(a) OPEN VIDEO SYSTEMS.

(1) CERTIFICATES OF COMPLIANCE. A local exchange carrier may provide cable service to its cable service subscribers in its telephone service area through an open video system that complies with this section. To the extent permitted by such regulations as the Commission may prescribe consistent with the public interest, convenience, and necessity, an operator of a cable system or any other person may provide video programming through an open video system that complies with this section.

(b) COMMISSION ACTIONS.

(1) REGULATIONS REQUIRED. The Commission shall prescribe regulations that—

(A) except as required pursuant to section 611, 614, or 615 [47 U.S.C. §§ 531, 534, or 535], prohibit an operator of an open video system from discriminating among video programming providers with regard to carriage on its open video system, and ensure that the rates, terms, and conditions for such carriage are just and reasonable, and are not unjustly or unreasonably discriminatory;

(B) if demand exceeds the channel capacity of the open video system, prohibit an operator of an open video system and its affiliates from selecting the video programming services for carriage on more than one-third of the activated channel capacity on such system, but nothing in this subparagraph shall be construed to limit the number of channels that the carrier and its affiliates may offer to provide directly to subscribers;

(D) extend to the distribution of video programming over open video systems the Commission's regulations concerning sports exclusivity, network nonduplication, and syndicated exclusivity; and

(E) (i) prohibit an operator of an open video system from unreasonably discriminating in favor of the operator or its affiliates with regard to material or information (including advertising) provided by the operator to subscribers for the purposes of selecting programming on the open video system, or in the way such material or information is presented to subscribers; [and]

(iv) prohibit an operator of an open video system from omitting television broadcast stations or other unaffiliated video programming services carried on such system from any navigational device, guide, or menu.

(c) REDUCED REGULATORY BURDENS FOR OPEN VIDEO SYSTEMS.

(1) IN GENERAL. Any provision that applies to a cable operator under—

(A) sections 613 (other than subsection (a) thereof), 616, 623(f), 628, 631, and 634 [47 U.S.C. §§ 533 (other than subsection (a) thereof), 536, 543(f), 551, and 554] of this title, shall apply,

(B) sections 611, 614, and 615 [47 U.S.C. §§ 531, 534, and 535] of this title, and section 325 of title III, shall apply in accordance with the regulations prescribed under paragraph (2), and

(C) sections 612 and 617 [47 U.S.C. §§ 532 and 537], and parts III and IV (other than sections 623(f), 628, 631 and 634 [47 U.S.C. §§ 543(f), 551, and 554]) of this title, shall not apply, to any operator of an open video system for which the Commission has approved a certification under this section.

(2) (B) FEES. An operator of an open video system under this part may be subject to the payment of fees on the gross revenues of the operator for the provision of cable service imposed by a local franchising authority or other governmental entity, in lieu of the franchise fees permitted under section 622 [47 U.S.C. § 542]. The rate at which such fees are imposed shall not exceed the rate at which franchise fees are imposed on any cable operator transmitting video programming in the franchise area.

(4) TREATMENT AS CABLE OPERATOR. Nothing in this Act precludes a video programming provider making use of an open video system from being treated as an operator of a cable system for purposes of section 111 of title 17, United States Code.

TITLE VII—MISCELLANEOUS PROVISIONS

SEC. 705. [47 U.S.C. § 605]
UNAUTHORIZED PUBLICATION OF COMMUNICATIONS

(a) Except as authorized by chapter 119, title 18, United States Code, no person receiving, assisting in receiving, transmitting, or assisting in transmitting, any interstate or foreign communication by wire or radio shall divulge or publish the existence, contents, substance, purport, effect, or meaning thereof, except through authorized channels of transmission or reception, (1) to any person other than the addressee, his agent, or attorney, (2) to a person employed or authorized to forward such communication to its destination, (3) to proper accounting or distributing officers of the various communicating centers over which the communication may be passed, (4) to the master of a ship under whom he is serving, (5) in response to subpoena issued by a court of competent jurisdiction, or (6) on demand of other lawful authority. No person not being authorized by the sender shall intercept any radio communication and divulge or publish the existence, contents, substance, purport, effect, or meaning of such intercepted communication to any person. No person not being entitled thereto shall receive or assist in receiving any interstate or foreign communication by radio and use such communication (or any information therein contained) for his own benefit or for the benefit of another not entitled thereto. No person having received any intercepted radio communication or having become acquainted with the contents, substance, purport, effect, or meaning of such communication (or any part thereof) knowing that such communication was intercepted, shall divulge or publish the existence, contents, substance, purport, effect, or meaning of such communication (or any part thereof) or use such communication (or any information therein contained) for his own benefit or for the benefit of another not entitled thereto. This section shall not apply to the receiving, divulging, publishing, or utilizing the contents of any radio communication which is transmitted by any station for the use of the general public, which relates to ships in distress, or which is transmitted by an amateur radio station operator or by a citizens band radio operator.

(b) The provisions of subsection (a) shall not apply to the interception or receipt by any individual, or the assisting (including the manufacture or sale) of such interception or receipt, of any satellite cable programming for private viewing if—

(1) the programming involved is not encrypted; and

(2) (A) a marketing system is not established under which—

(i) an agent or agents have been lawfully designated for the purpose of authorizing private viewing by individuals, and

(ii) such authorization is available to the individual involved from the appropriate agent or agents; or

(B) a marketing system described in subparagraph (A) is established and the individuals receiving such programming has obtained authorization for private viewing under that system.

SEC. 1302 [47 U.S.C. § 1302]
ADVANCED TELECOMMUNICATIONS INCENTIVES

(a) IN GENERAL. The Commission and each State commission with regulatory jurisdiction over telecommunications services shall encourage the deployment on a reasonable and timely basis of advanced telecommunications capability to all Americans (including, in particular, elementary and secondary schools and classrooms) by utilizing, in a manner consistent with the public interest, convenience, and necessity, price cap regulation, regulatory forbearance, measures that promote competition in the local telecommunications market, or other regulating methods that remove barriers to infrastructure investment.

(b) INQUIRY. The Commission shall, within 30 months after February 8, 1996, and annually thereafter, initiate a notice of inquiry concerning the availability of advanced telecommunications capability to all Americans (including, in particular, elementary and secondary schools and classrooms) and shall complete the inquiry within 180 days after its initiation. In the inquiry, the Commission shall determine whether advanced telecommunications capability is being deployed to all Americans in a reasonable and timely fashion. If the Commission's determination is negative, it shall take immediate action to accelerate deployment of such capability by removing barriers to infrastructure investment and by promoting competition in the telecommunications market.

(c) DEMOGRAPHIC INFORMATION FOR UNSERVED AREAS. As part of the inquiry required by subsection (b), the Commission shall compile a list of geographical areas that are not served by any provider of advanced telecommunications capability (as defined by subsection (d)(1)) and to the extent that data from the Census Bureau is available, determine, for each such unserved area—

(1) the population;

(2) the population density; and

(3) the average per capita income.

(d) DEFINITIONS. For purposes of this subsection:

(1) ADVANCED TELECOMMUNICATIONS CAPABILITY. The term "advanced telecommunications capability" is defined, without regard to any transmission media or technology, as high-speed, switched, broadband telecommunications capability that enables users to originate and receive high-quality voice, data, graphics, and video telecommunications using any technology.

SEC. 1452 [47 U.S.C. § 1452]
SPECIAL REQUIREMENTS FOR INCENTIVE AUCTION OF BROADCAST TV SPECTRUM

(a) REVERSE AUCTION TO IDENTIFY INCENTIVE AMOUNT

(1) IN GENERAL. The Commission shall conduct a reverse auction to determine the amount of compensation that each broadcast television licensee would accept in return for voluntarily relinquishing some or all of its broadcast television spectrum usage rights in order to make spectrum available for assignment through a system of competitive bidding under subparagraph (G) of section 309(j)(8) of this title.

(2) ELIGIBLE RELINQUISHMENTS. A relinquishment of usage rights for purposes of paragraph (1) shall include the following:

(A) Relinquishing all usage rights with respect to a particular television channel without receiving in return any usage rights with respect to another television channel.

(B) Relinquishing all usage rights with respect to an ultra high frequency television channel in return for receiving usage rights with respect to a very high frequency television channel.

(C) Relinquishing usage rights in order to share a television channel with another licensee.

(3) CONFIDENTIALITY. The Commission shall take all reasonable steps necessary to protect the confidentiality of Commission-held data of a licensee participating in the reverse auction under paragraph (1), including withholding the identity of such licensee until the reassignments and reallocations (if any) under subsection (b)(1)(B) become effective, as described in subsection (f)(2).

(4) PROTECTION OF CARRIAGE RIGHTS OF LICENSEES SHARING A CHANNEL. A broadcast television station that voluntarily relinquishes spectrum usage rights under this subsection in order to share a television channel and that possessed carriage rights under section 338, 534, or 535 of this title on November 30, 2010, shall have, at its shared location, the carriage rights under such section that would apply to such station at such location if it were not sharing a channel.

(b) REORGANIZATION OF BROADCAST TV SPECTRUM

(1) IN GENERAL. For purposes of making available spectrum to carry out the forward auction under subsection (c)(1), the Commission—

(A) shall evaluate the broadcast television spectrum (including spectrum made available through the reverse auction under subsection (a)(1)); and

(B) may, subject to international coordination along the border with Mexico and Canada—

(i) make such reassignments of television channels as the Commission considers appropriate; and

(ii) reallocate such portions of such spectrum as the Commission determines are available for reallocation.

(2) FACTORS FOR CONSIDERATION. In making any reassignments or reallocations under paragraph (1)(B), the Commission shall make all reasonable efforts to preserve, as of February 22, 2012, the coverage area and population served of each broadcast television licensee, as determined using the methodology described in OET Bulletin 69 of the Office of Engineering and Technology of the Commission.

(3) NO INVOLUNTARY RELOCATION FROM UHF TO VHF. In making any reassignments under paragraph (1)(B)(i), the Commission may not involuntarily reassign a broadcast television licensee—

(A) from an ultra high frequency television channel to a very high frequency television channel; or

(B) from a television channel between the frequencies from 174 megahertz to 216 megahertz to a television channel between the frequencies from 54 megahertz to 88 megahertz.

(4) PAYMENT OF RELOCATION COSTS

(A) IN GENERAL. Except as provided in subparagraph (B), from amounts made available under subsection (d)(2), the Commission shall reimburse costs reasonably incurred by—

(i) a broadcast television licensee that was reassigned under paragraph (1)(B)(i) from one ultra high frequency television channel to a different ultra high frequency television channel, from one very high frequency television channel to a different very high frequency television channel, or, in accordance with subsection (g)(1)(B), from a very high frequency television channel to an ultra high frequency television channel, in order for the licensee to relocate its television service from one channel to the other;

(ii) a multichannel video programming distributor in order to continue to carry the signal of a broadcast television licensee that—

(I) is described in clause (i);

(II) voluntarily relinquishes spectrum usage rights under subsection (a) with respect to an ultra high frequency television channel in return for receiving usage rights with respect to a very high frequency television channel; or

(III) voluntarily relinquishes spectrum usage rights under subsection (a) to share a television channel with another licensee; or

(iii) a channel 37 incumbent user, in order to relocate to other suitable spectrum, provided that all such users can be relocated and that the total relocation costs of such users do not exceed $300,000,000. For the purpose of this section, the spectrum made available through relocation of channel 37 incumbent users shall be deemed as spectrum reclaimed through a reverse auction under subsection (a).

(B) REGULATORY RELIEF. In lieu of reimbursement for relocation costs under subparagraph (A), a broadcast television licensee may accept, and the Commission may grant as it considers appropriate, a waiver of the service rules of the Commission to permit the licensee, subject to interference protections, to make flexible use of the spectrum assigned to the licensee to provide services other than broadcast television services. Such waiver shall only remain in effect while the licensee provides at least 1 broadcast television program stream on such spectrum at no charge to the public.

(C) LIMITATION. The Commission may not make reimbursements under subparagraph (A) for lost revenues.

(D) DEADLINE. The Commission shall make all reimbursements required by subparagraph (A) not later than the date that is 3 years after the completion of the forward auction under subsection (c)(1).

(5) LOW-POWER TELEVISION USAGE RIGHTS. Nothing in this subsection shall be construed to alter the spectrum usage rights of low-power television stations.

(c) FORWARD AUCTION

(1) AUCTION REQUIRED. The Commission shall conduct a forward auction in which—

(A) the Commission assigns licenses for the use of the spectrum that the Commission reallocates under subsection (b)(1)(B)(ii); and

(B) the amount of the proceeds that the Commission shares under clause (i) of section 309(j)(8)(G) of this title with each licensee whose bid the Commission accepts in the reverse auction under subsection (a)(1) is not less than the amount of such bid.

(2) MINIMUM PROCEEDS.

(A) IN GENERAL. If the amount of the proceeds from the forward auction under paragraph (1) is not greater than the sum described in subparagraph (B), no licenses shall be assigned through such forward auction, no reassignments or reallocations under subsection (b)(1)(B) shall become effective, and the Commission may not revoke any spectrum usage rights by reason of a bid that the Commission accepts in the reverse auction under subsection (a)(1).

(B) SUM DESCRIBED. The sum described in this subparagraph is the sum of—

(i) the total amount of compensation that the Commission must pay successful bidders in the reverse auction under subsection (a)(1);

(ii) the costs of conducting such forward auction that the salaries and expenses account of the Commission is required to retain under section 309(j)(8)(B) of this title; and

(iii) the estimated costs for which the Commission is required to make reimbursements under subsection (b)(4)(A).

(C) ADMINISTRATIVE COSTS. The amount of the proceeds from the forward auction under paragraph (1) that the salaries and expenses account of the Commission is required to retain under section 309(j)(8)(B) of this title shall be sufficient to cover the costs incurred by the Commission in conducting the reverse auction under subsection (a)(1), conducting the evaluation of the broadcast television spectrum under subparagraph (A) of subsection (b)(1), and making any reassignments or reallocations under subparagraph (B) of such subsection, in addition to the costs incurred by the Commission in conducting such forward auction.

(3) FACTOR FOR CONSIDERATION. In conducting the forward auction under paragraph (1), the Commission shall consider assigning licenses that cover geographic areas of a variety of different sizes.

(d) TV BROADCASTER RELOCATION FUND

(1) ESTABLISHMENT. There is established in the Treasury of the United States a fund to be known as the TV Broadcaster Relocation Fund.

(2) PAYMENT OF RELOCATION COSTS. Any amounts borrowed under paragraph (3)(A) and any amounts in the TV Broadcaster Relocation Fund that are not necessary for reimbursement of the general fund of the Treasury for such borrowed amounts shall be available to the Commission to make the payments required by subsection (b)(4)(A).

(3) BORROWING AUTHORITY

(A) IN GENERAL. Beginning on the date when any reassignments or reallocations under subsection (b)(1)(B) become effective, as provided in subsection (f)(2), and ending when $1,000,000,000 has been deposited in the TV Broadcaster Relocation Fund, the Commission may borrow from the Treasury of the United States an amount not to exceed $1,000,000,000 to use toward the payments required by subsection (b)(4)(A).

(B) REIMBURSEMENT. The Commission shall reimburse the general fund of the Treasury, without interest, for any amounts borrowed under subparagraph (A) as funds are deposited into the TV Broadcaster Relocation Fund.

(4) TRANSFER OF UNUSED FUNDS. If any amounts remain in the TV Broadcaster Relocation Fund after the date that is 3 years after the completion of the forward auction under subsection (c)(1), the Secretary of the Treasury shall—

(A) prior to the end of fiscal year 2022, transfer such amounts to the Public Safety Trust Fund established by section 1457(a)(1) of this title; and

(B) after the end of fiscal year 2022, transfer such amounts to the general fund of the Treasury, where such amounts shall be dedicated for the sole purpose of deficit reduction.

(e) NUMERICAL LIMITATION ON AUCTIONS AND REORGANIZATION. The Commission may not complete more than one reverse auction under subsection (a)(1) or more than one reorganization of the broadcast television spectrum under subsection (b).

(f) TIMING

(1) CONTEMPORANEOUS AUCTIONS AND REORGANIZATION PERMITTED

The Commission may conduct the reverse auction under subsection (a)(1), any reassignments or reallocations under subsection (b)(1)(B), and the forward auction under subsection (c)(1) on a contemporaneous basis.

(2) EFFECTIVENESS OF REASSIGNMENTS AND REALLOCATIONS

Notwithstanding paragraph (1), no reassignments or reallocations under subsection (b)(1)(B) shall become effective until the completion of the reverse auction under subsection (a)(1) and the forward auction under subsection (c)(1), and, to the extent practicable, all such reassignments and reallocations shall become effective simultaneously.

(3) DEADLINE

The Commission may not conduct the reverse auction under subsection (a)(1) or the forward auction under subsection (c)(1) after the end of fiscal year 2022.

(4) LIMIT ON DISCRETION REGARDING AUCTION TIMING

Section 309(j)(15)(A) of this title shall not apply in the case of an auction conducted under this section.

(g) LIMITATION ON REORGANIZATION AUTHORITY

(1) IN GENERAL. During the period described in paragraph (2), the Commission may not—

(A) involuntarily modify the spectrum usage rights of a broadcast television licensee or reassign such a licensee to another television channel except—

(i) in accordance with this section; or

(ii) in the case of a violation by such licensee of the terms of its license or a specific provision of a statute administered by the Commission, or a regulation of the Commission promulgated under any such provision; or

(B) reassign a broadcast television licensee from a very high frequency television channel to an ultra high frequency television channel, unless—

(i) such a reassignment will not decrease the total amount of ultra high frequency spectrum made available for reallocation under this section; or

(ii) a request from such licensee for the reassignment was pending at the Commission on May 31, 2011.

(2) PERIOD DESCRIBED. The period described in this paragraph is the period beginning on February 22, 2012, and ending on the earliest of—

(A) the first date when the reverse auction under subsection (a)(1), the reassignments and reallocations (if any) under subsection (b)(1)(B), and the forward auction under subsection (c)(1) have been completed;

(B) the date of a determination by the Commission that the amount of the proceeds from the forward auction under subsection (c)(1) is not greater than the sum described in subsection (c)(2)(B); or

(C) September 30, 2022.

(h) PROTEST RIGHT INAPPLICABLE. The right of a licensee to protest a proposed order of modification of its license under section 316 of this title shall not apply in the case of a modification made under this section.

(i) COMMISSION AUTHORITY. Nothing in subsection (b) shall be construed to—

(1) expand or contract the authority of the Commission, except as otherwise expressly provided; or

(2) prevent the implementation of the Commission's "White Spaces" Second Report and Order and Memorandum Opinion and Order (FCC 08-260, adopted November 4, 2008) in the spectrum that remains allocated for broadcast television use after the reorganization required by such subsection.

SEC. 1453 [47 U.S.C. § 1453]
UNLICENSED USE IN THE 5 GHz BAND

(a) MODIFICATION OF COMMISSION REGULATIONS TO ALLOW CERTAIN UNLICENSED USE

(1) IN GENERAL. Subject to paragraph (2), not later than 1 year after February 22, 2012, the Commission shall begin a proceeding to modify part 15 of title 47, Code

of Federal Regulations, to allow unlicensed U-NII devices to operate in the 5350–5470 MHz band.

(2) REQUIRED DETERMINATIONS. The Commission may make the modification described in paragraph (1) only if the Commission, in consultation with the Assistant Secretary, determines that—

(A) licensed users will be protected by technical solutions, including use of existing, modified, or new spectrum-sharing technologies and solutions, such as dynamic frequency selection; and

(B) the primary mission of Federal spectrum users in the 5350–5470 MHz band will not be compromised by the introduction of unlicensed devices.

SEC. 1454 [47 U.S.C. § 1454]
GUARD BANDS AND UNLICENSED USE

(a) IN GENERAL. Nothing in subparagraph (G) of section 309(j)(8) of this title or in section 1452 of this title shall be construed to prevent the Commission from using relinquished or other spectrum to implement band plans with guard bands.

(b) SIZE OF GUARD BANDS. Such guard bands shall be no larger than is technically reasonable to prevent harmful interference between licensed services outside the guard bands.

(c) UNLICENSED USE IN GUARD BANDS. The Commission may permit the use of such guard bands for unlicensed use.

(d) DATABASE. Unlicensed use shall rely on a database or subsequent methodology as determined by the Commission.

(e) PROTECTIONS AGAINST HARMFUL INTERFERENCE. The Commission may not permit any use of a guard band that the Commission determines would cause harmful interference to licensed services.

Conceptual Index and Telecommunications Glossary

1934 Act • An abbreviation for the Communications Act of 1934, the principal statute governing telecommunications regulation in the United States. Most other telecommunications statutes are actually just amendments to this Act. The Act is codified at 47 U.S.C. and is discussed throughout this text.

1992 Cable Act • An abbreviation for the Cable Television Consumer Protection and Competition Act of 1992, a significant piece of legislation that amended the Communications Act of 1934 and also the Copyright Act of 1976. The 1992 Cable Act established many of the current rules governing cable service provision; it is discussed primarily in Chapters Two, Eight, Nine, and Ten (pp. 405–68).

1996 Act • An abbreviation for the Telecommunications Act of 1996. This statute amended the Communications Act of 1934 and, among other things, established most of the rules under which the telephone industry is today regulated. The 1996 Act is analyzed extensively in Chapter Seven, although provisions of the Act are discussed pervasively throughout the book.

Access Charges • Charges that are paid by IXCs to LECs to compensate LECs for their costs of originating and terminating interexchange calls. These charges have to date overcompensated LECs for those costs and in that way forced IXCs to contribute to LEC universal service obligations. This system is discussed in Chapter Thirteen (pp. 549–61). *See also* Intercarrier Compensation, Reciprocal Compensation.

Advanced Services • A term used by both Congress and the FCC to refer to a wide range of technologies and services capable of delivering large quantities of data at high speeds. Examples include digital subscriber line (DSL) service and cable modem technology. Advanced services are considered in Chapter Fourteen (pp. 628–53).

Amplitude Modulation (AM) • A method of modulating information on a radio wave by varying the strength (voltage) of some agreed-upon baseline signal. To take a simple example: the baseline strength might be 2 volts, and all parties might understand that every time the signal increases to 5 volts the sender intends to tell the receiver that a customer has entered the building. AM modulation is one of two common methods of encoding typically used for radio transmission. Modulation and modulation technologies are introduced in Chapter Three (pp. 45–47). *See also* FM, Carrier Wave.

Analog • A signaling method that uses continuous changes in the amplitude or frequency of a carrier wave to convey information. Analog signal transmission is discussed in Chapter Three (pp. 42–47). *See also* Carrier Wave, Digital.

Ancillary Jurisdiction • This doctrine provides the FCC with authority to regulate services "ancillary" to those services within its specifically authorized jurisdiction. This doctrine, which is relevant to the FCC's effort to regulate broadband communication, is discussed in Chapter Fourteen (pp. 588–95, 628–32).

AT&T • An acronym for the American Telephone and Telegraph Company. The acronym is sometimes used to refer to the firm that ran most of the nation's telephone system prior to 1982 (which in this text we refer to as "Bell"); but, in this text it is used to refer to the subsidiary of Bell that provided long distance service after the breakup of the Bell System. Note that, in 2006, SBC merged with AT&T and took the AT&T name; so now, once again, AT&T refers to a company that provides local telephone service, long distance service, and also advanced services like DSL and video programming. The breakup of Bell is discussed in Chapter Six (pp. 203–16).

Baby Bell • One of several terms for the LECs that were once part of the Bell System. The phrase sometimes refers to a single LEC, but it is more often used to refer to the Regional Holding Companies of which the LECs were a part. Baby Bells are particularly discussed in Chapter Six (pp. 212–13). *See also* LEC, RBOC, RHC.

Band Plan • A set of decisions regarding how radio spectrum will be used. The band plan for a given block of spectrum typically establishes (1) which services can be offered, (2) how the block will be divided both across and within geographical areas, and (3) the rules for actually assigning licenses to use that spectrum to specific parties. Chapter Three discusses the concept of the band plan and its role in spectrum management.

Bandwidth • The transmission capacity of a communications medium. Bandwidth is explained in Chapter Three (pp. 43–44).

Bell • The telecommunications firm built on Alexander Graham Bell's initial telephone patents. In this text, the word is used exclusively to refer to that company as it existed before divestiture. Bell is particularly discussed in Chapter Six.

Bell Operating Company (BOC) • One of several terms for the LECs that were once part of the Bell System. The creation of the BOCs under the MFJ is discussed in Chapter Six. *See also* Baby Bell, LEC, RHC.

Bill-and-Keep • An arrangement between two LECs where each agrees to terminate, at no charge, traffic that originates on the other's network. Each LEC *bills* its own customers and *keeps* those payments instead of sharing them with the other LEC. The concept is discussed as part of Chapter Seven's introduction to interconnection obligations and reciprocal compensation; it comes up again in Chapter Twelve's discussion of Internet backbone interconnection arrangements. *See also* Intercarrier Compensation, Reciprocal Compensation.

Bit • A contraction of the term "binary digit" which refers to the smallest unit of information that a computer processes. A bit has a value of either zero or one. Digital information is transmitted as a string of bits. The concept is discussed in Chapter Three (p. 47). *See also* Digital.

Bottleneck • The point in a system or production process at which the traffic of competing providers must flow over facilities owned by a single provider. Bottlenecks raise concerns for competition policy because of the potential for the firm controlling the bottleneck to discriminate against competitors in access to the facility and thereby to exercise monopoly power over the good or service at issue. The concept is illustrated in, among other contexts, discussions of content access found in Chapters Nine and Ten.

Broadband • Broadband is a descriptive term for evolving technologies that provide consumers with access to high-speed services. At present, the FCC defines broadband as the capability to provide 4 megabits per second (Mbps) for downstream Internet traffic and 1 megabit per second for upstream Internet traffic. Broadband is discussed in Chapters Twelve and Thirteen. *See also* Advanced Services.

Broadband Plan • In 2009, the Congress required the FCC to develop a plan for how the agency and other parts of the government would approach broadband communications. This Broadband Plan, issued in March 2010, covered a number of topics and is discussed in Chapters Four, Thirteen, and Fourteen.

Carrier Wave • In situations where a radio wave or signal on a wire is being modified for the purposes of providing information on the wave, the "carrier wave" is the baseline, unmodified wave against which the modified waves are to be compared. A carrier wave is discussed in Chapter Three (pp. 44–47).

Cellular Telephony • Wireless telephone technology that divides the service area into small geographic "cells" each of which contains its own transmitter and receiver. As a caller moves from cell to cell, her call is handed off from the equipment in one cell to the equipment in the next, allowing the first cell to handle other callers' signals. In this way, callers moving around the same general area can use the same frequencies without interfering with one another. We consider cellular telephony throughout the text, but we discuss the basic technology in Chapter Three (pp. 47–49), consider some spectrum allocation issues related to cellular telephony in Chapter Five (pp. 164–84), and look at interconnection obligations between wireline and cellular systems in Chapter Seven (pp. 262–66). *See also* CMRS, PCS.

Central Office • The primary place where a LEC houses its switches and other equipment for the routing and processing of telephone calls. The central office is discussed in Chapter Six (p. 193). *See also* Switch.

Circuit Switching • A circuit-switched network is one in which the path for a particular communication is kept open from the time the communication is initiated until the time transmission is complete. The primary example is the telephone system, in which each voice call has a unique channel that is kept open for that call, even during pauses at which time nothing is traveling along the voice path. In this way communications are not interrupted and flow smoothly from end-to-end as they are transmitted. *Compare* Packet Switching.

Command and Control Regulation • The basic term for regulatory approaches that dictate how private actors can operate. In the case of spectrum regulation, this mode of regulation has predominated since the enactment of the Radio Act of 1927; more recently, however, criticisms of this approach have led to regulatory reforms in this area. Chapter Two introduces this concept (pp. 25–26).

Commercial Mobile Radio Service (CMRS) • The generic term for commercially available wireless services like cellular telephony, paging, and digital PCS. *See also* Cellular Telephony, PCS.

Common Carrier • A firm that sells its services to the general public and serves all comers for a set fee. A telephone carrier, for example, serves anyone who wishes to subscribe and does so on non-discriminatory terms. By definition, a provider of "telecommunications services" is subject to common carrier obligations unless the FCC lifts those obligations as a result of a forbearance determination. For further discussion of the implications of common carrier obligations and its role in the net neutrality debate see Chapters One (pp. 11–12) and Fourteen (pp. 633–53).

Comparative Hearing • The means by which the FCC for many years decided which among competing applicants would receive licenses to use the radio spectrum. This mechanism, as used to assign broadcast licenses, is discussed and evaluated in Chapter Five (pp. 140–64). *See also* Spectrum Auction.

Competitive Local Exchange Carrier (CLEC) • Firms that provide local telephone service in competition with the incumbent local exchange carrier (ILEC) in a given area. An introduction to CLECs is found in Chapter Seven (pp. 224–25).

Computer Inquiries • The name given to the series of decisions, culminating in the *Computer III* decision, which set forth the rules governing the access of "information service providers" to "telecommunications services." Notably, the *Computer III* rules—explained in Chapter Six—historically required incumbent providers to make available telecommunications capability to information service providers at non-discriminatory terms and conditions. As we explain in Chapter Six, the Commission has begun to lift many of these rules as to broadband services such as DSL and cable modem offerings.

Convergence • Convergence occurs when a single infrastructure—a single network—is capable of carrying many services. It is used in contrast to the manner in which the PSTN was designed for and largely carried voice traffic, spectrum carried radio and then television, and cable systems only carried linear video. A general purpose data network—such as those underlying the Internet—can carry any digital service (and most services can be digitized). The concept and the consequences for communications regulation are discussed most explicitly in Chapter One. *See also* Analog, Digital.

Cost-of-Service Regulation • *See* Rate-of-Return Regulation.

Cream Skimming • When a carrier seeks to serve only highly profitable customers, or to provide only highly profitable services, the strategy is called "cream skimming" or "cherry picking." Incumbent telephone firms have used the term to describe the strategies of new entrants into the telephone market, arguing that such strategies interfere with the incumbents' abilities to meet their universal service obligations. Cream skimming is examined most closely in Chapter Six (pp. 201, 206).

Cross-Ownership Rules • Rules that restrict ownership across different communications services in an effort to foster competition. For example, FCC regulations restrict the number of TV stations a firm can own in a given locality. Discussion of the Rules is found in Chapter Ten. *See also* Multiple-Ownership Rules.

Customer Premises Equipment (CPE) • Products like ordinary telephones, fax machines, modems, computers, answering machines, and even private branch exchange (PBX) equipment that connect to the telephone network at a customer's home or business are discussed in Chapter Six (pp. 198–201). *See also* PBX.

Department of Justice (DOJ) • The Department of Justice is the cabinet department entrusted with law enforcement. Relevant to this text, the DOJ enforces the antitrust laws, including being one agency that reviews large mergers prior to their closing. The DOJ is discussed generally in Chapter Two; its work in antitrust and merger review is discussed in Chapter Eleven. *See also* Federal Communications Commission; Federal Trade Commission.

Digital • A signal consisting of binary code (a stream of ones and zeroes) to represent voice, video or data is discussed in Chapter Three (p. 47).

Direct Broadcast Satellite (DBS) • High-powered satellite transmission of signals intended for direct reception by the public. The signals are transmitted to small dishes (usually the size of a large pizza) mounted on homes or other buildings. The term DBS refers most often to satellite-based multichannel video services to which consumers can subscribe and which are competitors to conventional cable television service. Regulatory issues related to DBS are considered in Chapters Eight and Nine.

Digital Subscriber Line (DSL) • A high-speed data service provided over conventional telephone networks. DSL refers to the technology that allows telephone carriers to attach certain electronics to the telephone line that can transform the copper loop that already provides voice service into a conduit for high-speed data traffic. With most DSL technologies today, a high-speed signal is sent from the end-user's terminal over the local copper loop until it reaches a Digital Subscriber Line Access Multiplexer (DSLAM), usually located in the carrier's central office. Regulatory issues related to DSL and other advanced services are considered in Chapter Fourteen. *See also* Advanced Services.

Divestiture • From the verb "divest" which means to separate or take away, this term refers to the breakup of the Bell System that came as a result of the Department of Justice's 1974 antitrust prosecution. Divestiture is considered extensively in Chapter Six.

Economy of Scale • An economy of scale is said to exist whenever the average cost of producing one unit of a good decreases over some range of increasing production (where the production of additional units has lower average cost). The concept is important to telecommunications regulation because it can lead to natural monopoly conditions in the relevant market and is discussed further in Chapter One (pp. 6–8). *See also* Economy of Scope, Natural Monopoly.

Economy of Scope • An economy of scope is said to exist whenever a single firm can produce a given quantity of two or more goods more cheaply than could separate firms. Bell argued that economies of scope existed in the provision of local and long distance telephone service and, thus, that it was desirable to have a single national telephone company. The concept is discussed in Chapter Six (pp. 210–12). *See also* Economy of Scale, Natural Monopoly.

End-to-End • A design principle that calls for all Internet traffic to be delivered to and processed at the ends of the network. Under this form of open architecture, no application developed for the Internet would be subject to blocking, filtering, or alteration by a network provider. This principle is discussed in Chapter Fourteen (pp. 628–53). *See also* Network Neutrality, Open Access.

Facilities-Based Competition • Under the 1996 Act, this phrase refers to competition from CLECs that build all or most of their own infrastructure. This form of local telephone competition is discussed alongside other forms—such as entry via resale, and entry via unbundled network elements—in Chapter Seven.

Federal Communications Commission (FCC) • The federal agency in charge of telecommunications regulation, created by the 1934 Act. The FCC is also referred to as the Commission, and its actions are the core subjects of this text. The Commission's early history, structure and basic powers are considered in depth in Chapter Two. *See also* FRC.

Federal Radio Commission (FRC) • The predecessor agency to the FCC, created by the Radio Act of 1927 and abolished by the 1934 Act. The history of the FRC is discussed in Chapter Two (pp. 20–21).

Federal Trade Commission (FTC) • The FTC is an independent agency whose organic statute gives it authority (among other powers) to address "unfair methods of competition." It may enforce the antitrust law and is one agency that reviews large mergers before they close. The FTC is discussed generally in Chapter Two; antitrust and merger enforcement are discussed in Chapter Eleven. *See also* Department of Justice, Federal Communications Commission.

Financial Interest and Syndication Rules (Finsyn Rules) • The now-repealed finsyn rules prohibited the major TV networks from exercising certain types of control over already-broadcast television content. The concern motivating these rules was that the major networks could use this control to deny independent stations access to high-quality syndicated reruns. The finsyn rules are discussed in Chapter Ten (pp. 371–79).

Frequency Modulation (FM) • A method of modulating information on a radio wave by varying the frequency of some agreed-upon baseline signal. To take a simple example: the baseline signal might reach its peak once every two seconds, and all parties might understand that every time the signal frequency drops below this level a customer has entered the building. FM modulation is one of two common methods of modulation typically used for radio transmission. Frequency modulation is discussed in Chapter Three (pp. 45–47). *See also* AM, Carrier Wave.

Incumbent Local Exchange Carrier (ILEC) • The established provider of local telephone service in a given area, which until the 1996 Act usually had a monopoly franchise. The regulation of ILECs, and the obligations put upon them under the 1996 Act, are discussed primarily in Chapter Seven.

Information Services • The name given, under the 1996 Act, to services that use "telecommunications" to deliver a service—ranging from "Dial-A-Joke" to Lexis-Nexis to Internet Service—to the public. Information services, formerly called "enhanced services," are not subject to traditional common carriage regulation. These services are also exempt from access charges (*i.e.*, they are treated as local and not long distance calls). This regulatory category is discussed in connection with the FCC's decision to classify DSL and cable modem services as information services in Chapter Fourteen (pp. 595–614). *See also* Telecommunications Services.

Intercarrier Compensation • The compensation due from the telecommunications carrier whose customer has initiated a call to another carrier for that latter's handling of the call. In the case of long-distance carriers, intercarrier compensation might be owed to a LEC for origination access and to another LEC for terminating access. One LEC might owe another LEC if its customer calls a customer of the other LEC. Intercarrier compensation is a more general term that encompasses both access charges (IXC/LEC) and reciprocal compensation (LEC/LEC). The FCC's move to a "bill-and-keep" regime for intercarrier compensation, under which no carrier pays another for handling a call, is discussed in Chapter Thirteen. *See also* Bill-and-Keep, Access Charges, Reciprocal Compensation.

Interexchange Carrier (IXC) • An IXC is a long distance telephone company. The term comes from the fact that long distance carriers transport calls across the boundaries that separate one local exchange area from another. IXCs are introduced in Chapter Six (pp. 193–94). *See also* Local Exchange Carrier, Local Access, Transport Area.

InterLATA Telephone Service • Long-distance service that involves the transport of calls across LATA boundaries; this is another term for interexchange service, introduced by the MFJ. InterLATA service is discussed in Chapter Six (p. 213). *See also* Local Access and Transport Area.

Internet • The Internet is a decentralized network of computer networks. The basic technology and structure of the Internet is discussed in Chapter Twelve (pp. 529–37); relevant regulations are introduced throughout Chapters Twelve and Fourteen.

Internet Backbone • Long-haul fiber optic networks that transport traffic among ISPs, content providers, online service companies, and other Internet customers. Each backbone provider essentially creates a network over which customers and content providers can communicate. The technology of the Internet backbone is discussed in Chapter

Twelve (pp. 533–34); its regulation, of lack thereof, is discussed in later in Chapter Fourteen.

Internet Service Provider (ISP) • ISPs provide customers with access to the Internet. An ISP is a firm that, at a minimum, receives and translates Internet-bound data. The ISP takes data in whatever form it arrives and translates it into a form consistent with the TCP/IP protocol of the Internet. Regulatory issues related to ISPs are considered in Chapters Twelve and Fourteen.

IntraLATA Telephone Service • Telephone service within a LATA. Much intraLATA service is just local exchange service, but some calls between distant points within a LATA have an additional toll charge. The concept of a LATA was introduced by the MFJ. IntraLATA service is discussed in Chapter Six (p. 213). *See also* Local Access, Transport Area.

Last Mile • The segment of a telecommunications network that connects directly to a customer's premises. The term often refers to the twisted pair of copper wires that connects a customer to a LEC's switch and over which a telephone call begins and ends its journey and is discussed in Chapter Six (pp. 193–94). Many people believe the "last mile" to be a bottleneck, although that belief is today less strongly held than it once was. *See also* Natural Monopoly.

Local Access and Transport Area (LATA) • Geographic service areas created by the MFJ to define the boundaries between local and long distance calls. The MFJ authorized the divested Bell Operating Companies to transport calls within each LATA, but strictly prohibited them from carrying telephone calls across any LATA boundaries. LATAs were generally drawn to center around a metropolitan area or to incorporate a region comprising a community of common interest. LATAs are introduced in Chapter Six (p. 213). *See also* InterLATA Telephone Service, IntraLATA Telephone Service.

Local Exchange • A geographical area in which customers receive service from a common central office or set of central offices. Sometimes an exchange is served by a single central office switch, in which case the switch itself is referred to as the "exchange." Local exchanges are explained in Chapter Six (pp. 193–95). *See also* LEC, ILEC, CLEC.

Local Exchange Carrier (LEC) • A provider of local telephone services. The term includes the BOCs, independent telephone companies, and also the CLECs that have entered the market since the effective date of the 1996 Act. Local exchange carriers are discussed in Chapters Six and Seven.

Loop • The part of a local exchange network connecting the customer to the carrier's switch; in essence, the loop is the customer's telephone line. (It was called a "loop" because, in telephony, there are actually two wires connected—one for sound in each direction.") Sometimes an entire local exchange network is referred to as "the local loop" for a given area. *See* Last Mile, Natural Monopoly. The local loop is discussed in Chapter Six (pp. 193–94).

Market Failure • The concept of market failure captures situations where private markets fail to produce a socially optimal mix of resources. This situation takes place when, for example, a monopolist controls a market and can withhold supply to raise its profits. The concept is discussed in Chapter One (pp. 6–10).

Modification of Final Judgment or Modified Final Judgment (MFJ) • The 1982 consent decree between Bell and the Department of Justice, which took effect on January 1, 1984, and broke up the Bell System into AT&T long distance and seven independent Regional Bell Operating Companies (RBOCs) that would provide local exchange service. The MFJ also imposed line of business restrictions on the local Bell operating companies. "Modification" here refers to the fact that the decree technically "modified" the 1956 consent decree entered against Bell's Western Electric manufacturing subsidiary. The MFJ is considered extensively in Chapter Six (pp. 203–16).

Multichannel Video Programming Distributor (MVPD) • An entity engaged in the business of selling multiple channels of video programming to paying subscribers. Such entities include, but are not limited to, cable operators, multichannel multipoint distribution services (MMDS, often called "wireless cable"), and direct broadcast satellite (DBS) services. MVPDs and relevant regulatory issues are considered in Chapters Eight and Nine .

Multiple Ownership Rules • Rules that restrict ownership within the same service or closely connected services, designed to foster competition. These rules can apply nationally or locally, and they can set caps by stipulating a maximum number of licenses/franchises, a maximum percentage of the relevant audience, or both. So, for example, the "local television ownership rules" limit the number of broadcast licenses that a single entity can hold in a given market; and the "national television ownership rules" limit the percentage of the national audience that a single broadcaster can reach through stations it owns or controls. These rules are discussed in Chapter Ten.

Must-Carry Obligation • A 1992 Cable Act term referring to the statutory requirement that cable systems carry the signals of a certain number of commercial and noncommercial television broadcast stations that are "local" to the area served by the cable system. In the Satellite Home Viewer Improvement Act (SHVIA), a form of must-carry obligations was imposed on DBS providers. The must-carry obligations, and the First Amendment challenges to them, are discussed in Chapter Nine (pp. 331–58).

Natural Monopoly • A natural monopoly is said to exist in any market where the costs of production are such that it is less expensive for demand to be met by one firm than it would be for that same demand to be met by more than one firm. For example, this occurs when, over a sufficiently large range of output, the addition of each new customer lowers the average cost of serving every other customer. The concept and its implications are explained in Chapters One and Seven (pp. 6–10, 218–20).

Network Effect or Network Externality • A condition that causes the value a given consumer places on an item to increase as the number of other consumers of that product increases. There is a network effect or network externality at work in the telephone industry because, the more subscribers, the more people to call, and hence the more each subscriber values his or her own telephone subscription. The concept of network effects and its implications are discussed in Chapter One (pp. 8–10).

Network Neutrality or Net Neutrality • This phrase refers to a proposed regulatory regime under which the owners of Internet infrastructure would be constrained in their ability to charge different prices to different content or service providers, for example, based on quality of service differences. Absolute network neutrality would require that all bits on the network be treated exactly the same. The network neutrality debate is considered in Chapter Fourteen (pp. 614–53).

Network Nonduplication • Network nonduplication rules are companion rules to the syndicated exclusivity rules. They enable a local broadcaster to prevent a cable system from exhibiting that part of an imported distant broadcaster's signal that contains network programming for which the local broadcaster has obtained exclusive broadcast rights in that local area. The local broadcaster must acquire exclusive rights by contract with the network. Network nonduplication rules were later expanded to apply against retransmission by DBS providers as well. These rules are discussed in Chapter Nine (pp. 318–20). *See also* Syndicated Exclusivity.

Norm Entrepreneurship • Government agencies can act as "norm entrepreneurs" by developing norms and promoting them through their use of the "bully pulpit." FCC Chairman Michael Powell's call for Internet freedom—an earlier form of network neutrality—constituted one such effort. Norm entrepreneurs are discussed in Chapter Two (pp. 29–30).

Notice of Inquiry (NOI) • The Commission releases an NOI for the purpose of gathering information about a broad subject or as a means of generating ideas on a specific issue. The Commission may issue an NOI *sua sponte*, or in response to an outside request. An NOI need not occur in order for a rulemaking to commence; that is, a rulemaking can begin with or without an NOI. NOIs are explained in Chapter Two (p. 26). *See also* NPRM, R&O.

Notice of Proposed Rulemaking (NPRM) • A rulemaking proceeding ordinarily begins with a Notice of Proposed Rulemaking. An NPRM contains a discussion of the issues to be addressed and proposed regulations in response to those issues. Readers are invited to comment on both the issues and the proposed rules. After reviewing comments on the NPRM, the FCC might choose to issue a further Notice of Proposed Rulemaking— thereby providing an opportunity for the public to comment further on a related or specific proposal—or the Commission might go ahead and release a final order (usually in the form of a Report and Order) that adopts some variant of the proposed rule, alters an existing rule, or decides not to take any action. This vocabulary is further introduced in Chapter Two (pp. 26–27); NPRMs themselves are excerpted throughout the text. *See also* NOI, R&O.

Open Access • The term used for the concept of mandating that broadband providers, in particular cable modem services, be required to carry multiple ISPs. As discussed in Chapter Fourteen (pp. 595–614), the FCC does not today require open access. *See also* Network Neutrality.

Open Platform • The term used for applying requirements to certain blocks of spectrum offered in the 700 MHz auction that the carrier purchasing that spectrum agree that consumers may bring their own devices and that device features will not be locked down or locked out. This is discussed in Chapter Fourteen.

Over the Top Video • Over the top video describes a video service provided and accessible over any Internet network, frequently offered by parties entirely independent of the network operators. Over the top video is discussed in Chapter Fourteen. *See also* Convergence.

Packet Switching • In packet-switched networks, messages between network users are divided into units, commonly referred to as packets, frames, or cells. These individual units are then routed from one network user to another user that has a specific destination IP address. Unlike circuit switching, however, the path between network users is not kept open for any particular communication. This allows for more efficient use of the telecommunications infrastructure, but it also introduces the possibility of delays, often undetectable, in the movement of packets from end-to-end. The switches that route packets are called "packet switches," and the function of routing individual data packets based on information contained in the packets is "packet switching." Packet switching is explained in Chapter Twelve (pp. 532–33). *See also* Circuit Switching.

Personal Communications Service (PCS) • A wireless communications service similar to cellular telephony, but transmitted at lower power and generally using digital rather than analog signals. The FCC licensed PCS providers in the mid-1990s to compete with the two cellular providers originally licensed in each geographic market. The history and division of spectrum allocation to PCS is discussed in Chapter Four (pp. 79–90). *See also* Cellular Telephony, CMRS.

Plain Old Telephone Service (POTS) • Basic, traditional telephone service without any enhanced features like call-waiting, caller-ID, integrated voice messaging, Internet service, and so on. POTS, which is sometimes also referred to as basic dial tone service, is defined in Chapter Six (p. 193).

Price Cap Regulation • A method of rate regulation that has largely replaced rate of return regulation for telecommunications carriers. Price cap regulation limits the prices firms can charge rather than limiting the returns a firm can earn. The theory behind price caps is that they give regulated firms incentives to reduce costs and become more efficient because, for at least some period of time before regulators readjust the caps, firms can thereby increase their profits. Price caps are discussed in Chapter Seven (p. 220). *See also* Rate of Return Regulation.

Program Access Rules • The requirement that cable networks affiliated with cable distributors be offered, at non-discriminatory terms, to rival distributors. These rules are discussed in Chapter Ten (pp. 418–46).

Public Good • A term used to describe a product or service for which demand is "non-rivalrous" and from which consumers cannot be excluded. National defense is a classic example: one person's benefit from national defense does not preclude any fellow citizen's benefit from national defense, nor can anyone be excluded from the benefits it provides. The concept and economics of public goods is explained in Chapter One (p. 10). Traditional broadcast television and radio programming are public goods and that fact, which is discussed in Chapter Eight (pp. 271–77), has important implications for the treatment of video programming.

Public Interest Standard • The standard that the Communications Act directs the FCC to apply in a variety of settings, ranging from licensing broadcasters to authorizing service operations by telecommunications carriers. The phrase—"public interest, convenience, and necessity"—appears throughout the 1934 Act. This standard is discussed in Chapters Three and Fifteen (pp. 50–68, 675–737).

Public Switched Telephone Network (PSTN) • Usually refers to the incumbent local exchange network that offers service to all customers in its operating area. Connections over a PSTN are mentioned in Chapter Seven (pp. 235–66). Connections not over a PSTN are discussed in Chapters Twelve and Fourteen (pp. 531–37, 654–72).

Public Trustee • This term is often attached to holders of broadcast licenses. It refers to their obligation to operate their stations in a manner that serves the interests of the viewing public. The term incorporates the idea that holders of scarce licenses have received a special benefit—use of the government's precious spectrum—in return for which they must serve the public's, and not just their own private, objectives. Prominent public trustee obligations are surveyed in Chapter Fifteen.

Public Utilities Commission (PUC) • A state regulatory authority that oversees the intrastate aspects of telephone (and usually other utility) services. Sometimes called a "public service commission" or another similar term. PUCs are often forced to share jurisdiction and authority with the FCC. PUCs and rate regulation are explained in Chapters Six and Seven (pp. 196–98, 217–22).

Ramsey Pricing • Ramsey pricing is a method of setting prices applicable in many situations, including situations where a single firm or entity must recover fixed costs and can do so by manipulating prices on more than one good. Ramsey pricing suggests that the most efficient way to recover those fixed costs is to set price levels for the goods such that, when comparing the goods, the good for which consumers are less sensitive to price is priced such that there is a greater difference between price and marginal cost than there is for the good for which consumers are more sensitive to price. We introduce this pricing strategy in Chapter Thirteen (pp. 547–49).

Rate of Return Regulation • A form of regulation under which firms are permitted to charge prices that both cover their total costs of providing a service and, in addition, pay a "reasonable" rate of return on their capital investments in providing the service. This form of regulation, which was for decades the primary means of regulating telephone rates, requires the regulator to determine the regulated firm's costs and then to decide what rate of return is reasonable for the firm to earn. Rate of return regulation is explained and discussed in Chapter Seven (pp. 218–20). *See also* Price Cap Regulation.

Reciprocal Compensation • Payment by one local exchange carrier to another for the additional, or marginal, costs of terminating calls that originated on the paying carrier's network. Reciprocal compensation is the general rule established by the Telecommunications Act of 1996 for interconnection among competing local exchange carriers. This regime is discussed in Chapter Thirteen.

Regional Bell Operating Company (RBOC) • Term for each of the seven regional local exchange carriers created by the MFJ. An RBOC (or RHC) was a holding company generally consisting of several LECs. Thus, for example, Pacific Telesis (now part of SBC) was an RBOC that in turn consisted of several subsidiaries, such as Nevada Bell and Pacific Bell. Pacific Bell, in turn, owned and operated local telephone companies throughout California. The word "regional" distinguishes these firms from the Bell Operating Companies of which they are comprised. RBOCs and the MFJ are explained in Chapter Six (pp. 204–16). *See also* Baby Bell, Bell Operating Company.

Regulation by Raised Eyebrow • A form of implicit regulation where an agency—here, the FCC—does not use the rulemaking process to announce its policies but, instead, indicates its desires less formally and then threatens to enforce those desires through the exercise of its discretion. One prominent example in this text: for many years, the Commission used its discretion in license renewal to encourage broadcast licensees to air diverse and also educational fare. We introduce the concept of regulation by raised eyebrow in Chapter Two (p. 30) and further discuss examples in Chapter Five (pp. 126–35).

Regulatory Capture • Phrase used to describe situations where a regulatory agency falls under the influence of a powerful interest group. The paradigmatic case of capture arises when an agency does the bidding of the very parties it was originally designed to regulate and therefore stops regulating in the public's interest and starts, instead, regulating for the benefit of the regulated parties. This is not an uncommon allegation, especially because regulators necessarily work closely with the parties they regulate, for example gathering information from them, and thus at least some form of a relationship is bound to form. Moreover, regulators and regulatees in some sense rely on one another for their survival: should the industry disappear or become fully competitive, the regulators might find themselves without work; should the regulators become too strict, the regulatees might find themselves losing considerable profits and freedoms. All this intuitively could cloud a regulator's judgment. Regulatory capture is defined in Chapter Fifteen (p. 692).

Regulatory Parity • The idea that competing or similar services and technologies should face equivalent or similar regulatory regimes. This idea is discussed in Chapter Eight (pp. 277–85).

Report and Order (R&O) • The title of the document that the FCC customarily uses to take final action on a proposed rule. After considering comments to a Notice of Proposed Rulemaking (or further Notice of Proposed Rulemaking), the FCC issues a Report and

Order. The R&O might establish new rules, amend existing rules, or announce a decision not to make any changes. We introduce this and related vocabulary in Chapter Two (pp. 26–28). *See also* NOI, NPRM.

Resale • One of the means by which Congress and the FCC have attempted to introduce competition into the local telecommunications market. A key example is the 1996 Act's mandate that ILECs make their services available at wholesale rates to new entrants such that those new entrants can, in turn, resell those services directly to consumers. This mode of entry and its regulation is discussed in Chapter Seven.

Retransmission Consent • A requirement of the 1992 Act that cable operators receive consent from the relevant broadcaster before retransmitting that broadcaster's signal to cable subscribers. A broadcaster has a choice between demanding carriage under the 1992 Act's must-carry provisions or demanding that a cable operator obtain its consent for carriage. Similar obligations are also imposed on DBS providers. This regime is discussed in Chapter Nine (pp. 321–31).

Satellite Home Viewer Act of 1988 (SHVA) • An Act that, among other things, granted satellite carriers a statutory license to retransmit network television programming to "unserved households" even without copyright permission from the relevant copyright holders. The Act has since been significantly mooted by the Satellite Home Viewer Improvement Act of 1999 (SHVIA); both Acts are discussed throughout Chapter Nine.

Satellite Home Viewer Improvement Act of 1999 (SHVIA) • An Act that established for DBS a regime of rules and licenses similar to that which governs retransmission of broadcast signals over cable television. For example, the Act establishes a retransmission consent requirement, must-carry obligations, and statutory licenses under which DBS providers can, in certain circumstances, retransmit copyrighted content without the relevant copyright holder's permission. This Act is discussed in Chapter Nine.

Separations • The regulatory division of facilities or costs between interstate and intrastate telecommunications services, usually for the purpose of drawing the line between state and federal regulatory jurisdiction. This division is explored in the context of access charge reform in Chapters Six and Thirteen (pp. 196–98, 549–51).

Spectrum • The electromagnetic radio frequencies used in the transmission of television and other signals carrying video, sound, and data through the air. One of the Commission's major tasks is spectrum management. We introduce the concept of spectrum in Chapter Three (pp. 42–50); however, spectrum is considered extensively in Part One. *See also* Band Plan, Comparative Hearings.

Spectrum Auction • Spectrum auctions, distinguished from comparative hearings, are the allocation of spectrum licenses to parties with the highest bid in structured auctions. Auctions have been used to allocate much of the mobile and broadband spectrum and are discussed in Chapter Five. *See also* Comparative Hearings.

Standard Setting • The development of standards can emerge through a number of forms, including regulatory oversight. The concept is introduced in Chapter Two (pp. 30–31).

Subscriber Line Charge (SLC) • The federally mandated flat charge that LECs pass along to customers. The SLC was first instituted as part of the access charge regime the FCC put in place in response to the MFJ, as discussed in Chapter Thirteen (pp. 550–51).

Switch • The critical piece of telephone network equipment that routes calls among telephone subscribers. A switch is what enables a telephone network to operate efficiently: every customer need not have a line to every other customer, but instead need only have a single line to the switch, which then will connect a call from any customer's line to any other customer's line. The use of switches in the telephone network is demonstrated in Chapter Six (pp. 193).

Syndicated Exclusivity • Syndicated exclusivity ("syndex") rules are companion regulations to the network nonduplication rules. Syndex rules enable a local broadcaster to prevent a cable system from exhibiting that part of an imported distant broadcaster's signal that contains programs (or episodes from a television series) for which the local broadcaster has obtained exclusive broadcast rights in that local area from the copyright holder. These rules, discussed in Chapter Nine (pp. 318–20), were later applied against DBS providers as well. *See also* Network Nonduplication.

Syndication • The process of licensing television programming for rebroadcast after the program's primary network run has ended. Syndication is explained in Chapter Ten (pp. 371–72). *See* Finsyn, Syndicated Exclusivity.

Tariff • The document filed by a telecommunications provider (usually filed with the FCC or a PUC) describing a particular service and the terms, including price, under which that service will be offered. A "tariffed service" is one for which a service provider is required to file a tariff and, thus, one that is regulated by either state or federal authorities. Tariffs in general are introduced in Chapter One (p. 12). Tariffed service is discussed in Chapter Seven (pp. 218–20).

Taxation by Regulation • Phrase that refers to any situation where the government imposes a financial burden on a regulated party not directly, but instead by requiring a particular unprofitable behavior. The phrase is designed to remind policymakers to consider the explicit alternative: actually taxing the regulated party in that same amount and then using the money to further the policy goal at issue. There are myriad examples of taxation by regulation in this text. One such example is found in Chapter Fifteen (pp. 715–37).

TCP/IP • A set of protocols that controls (1) the division of information into packets, (2) the addressing and identification of those packets, and (3) the transfer of those packets from host to host, on the Internet. TCP/IP, and Internet technology more generally, is discussed in Chapter Twelve (pp. 531–37).

Telecommunications Services • This regulatory category governs all services provided under Title II of the 1934 Act and subjects such services (unless otherwise deregulated through a forbearance process) to common carrier regulation. Notably, Internet broadband access, as discussed in Chapter Fourteen (pp. 595–614), is treated as an "information service" and not classified as a "telecommunications service" even though it does use a component of "telecommunications."

Total Element Long-Run Incremental Cost (TELRIC) • The rule that the FCC adopted in 1996 for determining the price at which an ILEC must sell unbundled network elements to CLECs. TELRIC is explained and discussed in Chapter Seven (pp. 253–62).

Ultra High Frequency (UHF) • A phrase that refers to television stations occupying frequencies above the 30 to 300 MHz bands used by VHF stations. Channels 60 to 69, for example, broadcast over the 700 MHz frequencies. UHF signals are weaker than VHF signals and can deliver a high-quality television picture only over a comparatively smaller geographic range. Broadcast stations thus for a long time preferred VHF licenses over UHF licenses, although because cable can retransmit VHF and UHF equally well, the "UHF handicap" is less important in modern times.

Unbundled Network Element (UNE) • A part ("element") of a telephone network, such as a switch or customer loop, that the 1996 Act requires ILECs to lease to CLECs at cost-based rates. The UNE regime is discussed in Chapter Seven. *See also* TELRIC, Resale.

Universal Service • Historically, a set of policies designed to keep rates for local telephone service affordable and reasonably homogenous for subscribers. At times, the phrase refers more broadly to any subsidy or program designed to assist low-income or otherwise disadvantaged telecommunications consumers access services, including now broadband services. This concept is discussed in Chapter Thirteen.

Unlicensed Spectrum • Spectrum that is authorized for use without a license under the FCC's Part 15 Rules, which require merely that certain power limits are respected. The authorization of the use of spectrum without a license allowed a number of technologies, including cordless phones and Wi-Fi to develop. Another term for unlicensed spectrum is "commons" spectrum. The concept of unlicensed spectrum is discussed in Chapter Four (pp. 97–117). *See also* White Spaces.

V-Chip • Device in a television that allows viewers to screen out unwanted television broadcasts. (The "V" stands for "violence.") The chip detects a description signal embedded in the broadcast and blocks programs that meet criteria selected by the viewer. It is not widely used even though it is today widely available. V-chips are discussed in Chapter Sixteen (pp. 839–52).

Very High Frequency (VHF) • A phrase that refers to the part of the radio spectrum from 30 to 300 MHz. These bands are used to broadcast (among other things) television channels 2 through 13. *See also* UHF.

Voice over Internet Protocol (VoIP) • VoIP is a digitized voice service carried over an Internet network or networks. It is a converged service, in the sense that it works on any digital network, including modern cable television networks and spectrum services. The regulatory challenges presented by VoIP are discussed in Chapter Fourteen. *See also* Convergence.

Western Electric • The equipment manufacturing subsidiary of Bell before divestiture in 1984. Western Electric's history is described in Chapter Six (pp. 202–216).

White Spaces • This term describes the unused parts of the wireless spectrum. It is specifically used to describe the bands of unused spectrum dedicated to over the air TV broadcasting. The FCC appropriated this term in an order enabling the unlicensed use of white spaces in the TV bands. The concept is discussed in Chapter Four (pp. 97–106). *See also* Unlicensed Spectrum.